Sociology

Eighth Edition

ANTHONY GIDDENS
AND PHILIP W. SUTTON

SOCIOLOGY

8TH EDITION

polity

First edition published in 1989 by Polity Press
This eighth edition first published in 2017 by Polity Press

Polity Press
65 Bridge Street
Cambridge CB2 1UR, UK

Polity Press
350 Main Street
Malden, MA 02148, USA

ISBN-13: 978-0-7456-9667-6
ISBN-13: 978-0-7456-9668-3 (pb)

A catalogue record for this book is available from the British Library.

Typeset in 9.5 on 12.5pt Utopia Std by
Servis Filmsetting Ltd, Stockport, Cheshire
Printed and bound in Italy by Rotolito Lombarda

For further information on Polity, visit our website:
politybooks.com

Contents

Preface to the Eighth Edition

Almost thirty years ago now, in 1989, the first edition of *Sociology* was published. Many readers of this eighth edition were not even born then, but it was a period of world-historical change. The post-1945 Cold War was ending, the Berlin Wall came down, Germany was reunited, and the former Soviet-bloc countries of Eastern Europe became independent. For younger generations, the post-Cold War era is normal, but many other facets of daily life today, such as the Internet, the worldwide web and email had yet to make an impact in 1989. Similarly, the ubiquitous mobile phone, social media, digital television and all the other technological necessities we take for granted today were only in their infancy. Like sociology itself, the social world is much changed since that first edition, and yet some things remain the same. This book, despite its expansion and increasing weight, is still produced in satisfying hardcopy format.

Consecutive editions have mapped the myriad changes we have witnessed in societies and sociologists' attempts to understand them. This eighth edition is no different, though it has been carefully revised to take account of recent global developments and new ideas in sociology. Endless innovations in digital media, the long-term problem of climate change, a global financial crisis, the 'Arab Spring' and its aftermath, the rapid economic growth of China, India and Brazil, and the disruptive impact of global terrorism are all shaping the human world in new ways. This new edition examines all of these issues and is comprehensively revised and up to date.

Students sometimes find sociological ideas and evidence difficult to handle. In part, that is because sociology demands a concerted attempt to set aside our personal beliefs and opinions when analysing research findings and theories. In this sense, 'thinking sociologically' involves a profound intellectual and emotional challenge which can be unsettling. Little wonder that most people who study sociology are changed by the experience. The discipline offers a different perspective on the world from that which most people have when they start out. Sociology helps us look beyond the immediate context of our lives and brings us to a deeper understanding of the causes and consequences of our own and other people's actions. We hope you are both challenged and enlightened by reading and engaging with the book.

Acknowledgements

Researching, writing and producing this book is always a major undertaking, which involves a creative collective, not just two authors. First, thanks must go to all of the chapter reviewers, whose guidance and constructive comments on drafts have, once again, proved to be invaluable in helping us to keep the book at the forefront of sociological research and theorizing. Thanks also to the many lecturers and student readers of the seventh edition, whose experiences of actually working with the book enabled us to strengthen the links between contemporary research and undergraduate teaching. As ever, the Polity staff made the production process relatively painless, and a special mention must go to Neil de Cort, Sarah Dobson and Breffni O'Connor, who all helped to lighten the load. We are also grateful to Caroline Richmond, who never lets us get away with sloppiness or inconsistency, and the book is all the better for it. Our commissioning editor, Jonathan Skerrett, once again managed to remain sane during the process, and we thank him for his diligence, judgement and many suggestions for improvement. Finally, we thank Pat Sutton for more or less everything and Alena Ledeneva for her constant help and encouragement.

AG & PWS

Introduction

However fixed and solid they may appear on the surface, human societies are always in the process of change. When we began to write this eighth edition of *Sociology*, the UK was an important member of the European Union. By the end, a UK-wide referendum had produced a majority vote to leave the EU, with all of the political, economic, social and cultural consequences that follow. For instance, in Scotland, a majority voted to stay inside the EU, and the Scottish government began planning for a second referendum within three years on whether Scotland should leave the UK. It is feasible that, before our ninth edition, the union of the UK will have broken up and the process of EU expansion will have gone into reverse. Institutions in the human world, such as the UK, the EU and nation-states, are always open to change and major transformation.

As the academic discipline which studies and tries to make sense of societies and social life, sociology cannot stand still or rest on its laurels. If it did it would quickly become irrelevant and would certainly fail to provide adequate and realistic accounts of and explanations for social life. This basic fact helps to explain why, from the outside at least, sociology's constantly changing theories often appear quite unfathomable. Because the task of sociology is to understand and explain the ever-changing social world, we cannot afford to cling to comfortable, yet increasingly outdated theories and explanations. We must be prepared to test these against new realities and, if found wanting, to jettison them and devise new theories and explanations that are adequate to the task.

This eighth edition of *Sociology* introduces the latest theories and ideas alongside older 'classical' ones, enabling readers to see how sociology has developed in parallel with the societies of which it is a part. One of our main aims is to inspire a new generation of sociologists by presenting some of the most exciting research across a wide range of subject areas, from crime, inequality and education to sexuality, cyberbullying and global terrorism. But there is not much abstract or mere conceptual discussion in the book. Instead, we have tried to illustrate ideas, concepts and theories using concrete examples taken mainly from sociological studies, though we also make use of material from other sources (such as newspaper reports) where these stimulate discussion.

The writing style is as straightforward and direct as we can make it and, by creating a quite seamless narrative throughout each chapter, we hope the book is 'a good read'. The chapters follow a sequence designed to help readers achieve a progressive mastery of the different fields of sociology, but the book can also be used flexibly and is easily adapted to the needs of teachers. Chapters can be ignored or studied in a different order, as each one is written as an autonomous piece, with substantial cross-referencing to help readers see the connections across the varied subjects.

Sociology has a central place within the social sciences and a key role in modern intellectual culture. Like all scientific disciplines, sociology has its own technical language which is absolutely necessary if sociologists are to make their arguments with clarity. However, we try hard to avoid the 'jargon' that finds its way into social science, which we know most newcomers to the discipline (and many professional sociologists!) find impenetrable and unnecessary. Findings drawn from the cutting edge of the discipline are presented alongside contemporary events, issues and data, and we endeavour to cover these in an even-handed, though not indiscriminate, way. Underpinning the whole enterprise is our shared vision that a general sociological approach continues to be the best way of setting our personal life experience into a broader social context so we are able to make sense of the intimate connections between the individual and society.

Central themes

The book consists of twenty-two chapters, each of which deals with a specific subject such as crime, ethnicity, social class, work or the environment. There are some recurring themes across the whole book, three of which reflect key issues shaping contemporary sociology.

One central theme is social change, but particularly globalization. Sociology emerged in the wake of the major transformations wrought by the Industrial Revolution of the eighteenth and early nineteenth centuries, which changed the human world forever. But social change did not stop in the nineteenth century. Indeed, many sociologists argue that, since the 1970s, the pace of social change has actually speeded up and, with it, the key organizing structures of social class, the traditional family and manufacturing industry have lost their previously strong hold over individual lives. Part of the reason is that we now live in an increasingly global human world with a global economic system, the mass movement of people around the world and the internationalization of politics. Processes of globalization also connect the countries of the relatively wealthy developed world more closely to those of the relatively poor developing world. The book covers globalization in all of its varied manifestations, from the international politics of climate change to viral pandemics, organized crime and global inequality. Rapidly developing globalization is perhaps the clearest demonstration of the necessity for sociologists to stay close to major social changes in the real world.

A second theme is the digital revolution in communications, which has not just facilitated globalization but is transforming almost every aspect of the way we live, work and enjoy our leisure time. Younger generations are today growing up with a range of technological devices and new opportunities for communication that seemed like pure science fiction fantasy to their parents and grandparents. Thanks to the Internet, instantaneous contact can be made between people many thousands of miles apart by email and social media on smartphones and tablets. Continuing developments in microprocessing have made the personal computer so powerful that it dwarfs the amount of computing power available to the world's largest corporations just thirty years ago. The advancement of robotics is also gathering pace and, though we are used to seeing robots at work in industrial factories, the next stage will see driverless cars on the roads and robots in the home. Yet it is the integration of the Internet, supercomputing and robotics which makes digitization genuinely revolutionary, enabling work tasks – many of them the preserve of the middle classes – to be performed without human beings, with serious consequences for future employment levels. We may be in the early stages of this revolution, but the book covers many aspects of it as it spreads across the whole of social life.

A third theme takes us right back to the origins of sociology – social inequality. The book has discrete chapters covering gender and sexuality, 'race' and ethnicity, ageing, social class and disability, and each looks at sociological research in that particular field. Yet sociologists increasingly recognize that important social inequalities are interrelated, producing a complex set of individual life experiences. For example, a young, working-class, white woman may have a very different life experience to an older, middle-class, black woman, which makes it difficult to discuss the common experience of 'women' in general. Hence, today there are many more studies of the complex diversity of individual life experiences. Exploring the ways in which social inequalities intersect is a continuous theme throughout the book. We also explore inequalities between countries and look at the evidence suggesting that, in many aspects, these are decreasing in the twenty-first century.

Key elements of our approach

Our approach to sociology in this book is shaped by three main concerns. First, we seek to connect the small-scale or micro level of social encounters and interactions with the large-scale, macro level of societies and their institutions. Individual interactions in micro-level contexts can impact on the larger world of social institutions, but the latter also influence our daily lives in very profound ways. This two-way interchange is at the heart of many social processes, and it is our view that comprehensive sociological analysis requires situations and events to be understood at both the micro and macro levels.

Second, the book adopts a comparative-historical standpoint. Sociology cannot be limited to understanding a single society but must investigate the relationships between a range of societies and the varied ways in which they influence each other's development. The globalization of social life has made this an urgent necessity, and the book introduces a wide variety of source material drawn from around the world. In particular, many of the chapters cover both the developed and developing countries, which makes for some intriguing comparisons. In our view, comparative historical sociology is essential if we are to understand today's global social life.

Finally, we try to connect the social with the personal. Sociological thinking is a vital source of self-understanding, helping to situate our personal experiences in a broader social setting. But our self-understanding can in turn be focused back on an improved understanding of the social world at large. Studying sociology should be a liberating experience that enlarges our imaginations, opens up new perspectives on the sources of personal behaviour, and creates an awareness of cultural settings that are very different from our own. This aspect of our approach is the starting point for developing a sociological way of thinking, or what sociologists themselves call a sociological imagination.

Interactive features

The eighth edition continues with the interactive features designed to engage readers actively with the text. These include *Classic studies* boxes, introducing readers to some of sociology's most influential pieces of work. It is important to be aware that 'classic' is not merely another word for 'old'. Sociology makes progress through the constant testing of ideas and methods in the thousands of research projects, journal articles and books that constitute academic sociology. This means that the majority of research studies do not achieve the status of 'classics', but this doesn't mean they are not valuable – far from it. But, sometimes, significant new discoveries are made, a novel research method is devised or a new theory exerts a special influence on the future direction of the discipline. In such cases these examples may come to be recognized by professional sociologists as 'classics'. In this sense, a 'classic' can be any age, and our selections in the book reflect this. Of course, not everyone will agree with all of our choices, but we have tested them on numerous anonymous reviewers, lecturers and readers and have been reassured that they are not randomly chosen or the result of our own preferences. Hopefully, these examples will help students to appreciate the possibilities opened up by thinking sociologically.

We have also retained all of the other interactive elements for this new edition. We have kept the *Thinking critically* boxes, which mark 'stopping off' points where the reader can reflect on what they have been reading and think through the significance of what they have learned. We strongly recommend that readers work through these boxes to get the most from the book. *Global society* boxes encourage students to think globally about even the most apparently local or domestic issues. Boxes labelled *Using your sociological imagination* often contain unusual or arresting material designed to illustrate or expand on themes found in the chapter, and the *Glossary* continues to expand as sociologists devise new concepts. All *Glossary* terms are highlighted in bold in the text for easy reference.

The 'sociological workshops' at the end of each chapter have proved useful for teaching and learning, and these have also been retained and revised. The *Chapter review* asks questions based on that chapter's material, and it is a good idea to work through these immediately after reading the chapter, though they are also designed to form the basis for revision at a later date. *Research in practice* follows, which concentrates on sociological research methods and their application in real-world studies. Here, we point readers to a piece of contemporary research, usually in a journal article, and ask them to track it down, read it and make notes as they do so. A series of questions then allows readers to think about the different types of research and methods, what they are used for and how successful their application has been. Many lecturers tell us that this approach helps them to convey how essential an understanding of research methods is for the practice of 'doing' sociology.

Next, we shift the focus from methods to theories with *Thinking it through*. For most of these activities, we have chosen a theoretical paper, an online discussion or a newspaper article which raises issues of theory and explanation. Part of the activity is simply to make sure readers understand the concepts used and the meaning of the paper. A fair number of students tell us they find 'theory' difficult to grasp, mainly because it seems abstract and distant from their own lives. We have therefore selected theoretical pieces which bear directly on real events to bridge the apparent divide between theory and daily life.

Society in the arts takes us outside academic social science and into the arts and humanities. In this section we suggest films, TV programmes or plays, novels, artworks or sculptures, music and exhibitions. All of our recommendations are closely linked to the chapter material, and we ask readers to consider how these add to their knowledge of society. For example, it has been suggested that most people's understanding of nineteenth-century industrialization as a time of huge factories, chimneys belching out pollutants and grimy expanding cities is not taken from social scientific evidence, but from the novels of Charles Dickens and other novelists and writers. How is *contemporary* social life and the emerging digital revolution represented in the arts? Do the arts just tell us something different about the world that social sciences never could? We encourage readers to consider such questions carefully as they work through the exercises in this section.

Finally, the *Further readings* have again been updated and are annotated, so readers can make a more informed choice about what they choose to read. Similarly, the *Internet links* have been checked and updated, so readers can explore some of the mass of material now available online. In addition, the book is designed to be used in conjunction with the extensive material on its own website: **www.politybooks.com/giddens**. Both lecturers and students will find a wealth of resources to aid further research and support teaching and learning.

CHAPTER 1

What is Sociology?

Contents

The digital revolution in communications is transforming everyday life, enabling communication and information sharing almost anywhere. Although commuters today may be no more 'antisocial' than in the past, there is a world of difference between the immediacy and interactive potential of contemporary mobile devices and older, more passive media forms such as newspapers.

The world we live in today can feel liberating and exciting but, at the same time, confusing and worrying. Global communication and friendships across national boundaries are in many ways easier to sustain than in previous times, yet we also see violent crime, international terrorism, emerging wars and persistent economic and social inequality. The modern world presents us with many opportunities and possibilities, but it is also fraught with high-consequence risks, most notably the damaging impact of our high-consumption lifestyles on the quality of the natural environment. Most people within the relatively rich countries are materially better off than ever before, but in other parts of the world many millions live in situations of poverty where children die for the lack of fundamental things such as food, safe water supplies and basic healthcare. How can this be, when humanity as a whole has the capability to control its own destiny that would have been unimaginable to previous generations?

How did this world come about? Why are the conditions of life today so different from those of the past? Why is the human world riven with such gross inequalities? Where are today's societies heading in the future? If you have ever asked yourself such large questions, then consider yourself a novice sociologist. These and many more are among the prime concerns of sociology, a field of study that has a fundamental role to play in modern life.

Sociology can be simply defined as the scientific study of human life, social groups, whole societies and the human world as such. It can be a dazzling and compelling enterprise, as its subject matter is our own behaviour as social beings in relationships with many other people. The scope of sociology is extremely wide, ranging from the analysis of passing encounters between individuals on the street to the investigation of crime, international relations and global forms of terrorism.

Most of us see the world in terms of the familiar features of our own lives – our families, friendships and working lives, for example. But sociology insists that we take a broader view in order to understand why we act in the ways we do. It teaches us that much of what we regard as natural, inevitable, good and true may not be so, and that things we take for granted are actually shaped by historical events and social processes. Understanding the subtle yet complex and profound ways in which our individual lives reflect the contexts of our social experience is basic to the sociologist's outlook.

What to expect from this chapter

This chapter is the first of a block of three. Taken together, these provide a broad introduction to sociology: what it is, where it came from, how it developed over time, how sociologists go about their work and what kinds of explanations they use. As the opening to the whole book, this chapter provides a brief introduction to what sociology is, how and why

it came into existence and what it is used for. Chapter 2 then covers how sociologists actually 'do' sociology. It describes the questions they ask, the wide range of research methods they use to answer those questions and how they assess their findings. It also tackles the thorny issue of whether sociology is a science at all.

Chapter 3 looks at sociological theories. Theories are an essential part of all academic subjects because they allow us to provide explanations rather than simply listing a series of facts. For example, we might find that the proportion of married women in the UK who are in work today is higher than in the 1950s. The bare statistics are certainly useful, but they are crying out for an explanation – *why* are more married women working today than in the past? – and that is what good theories provide. They try to tell us why something has happened or changed and in that way they broaden our knowledge. In chapter 3 you will find some important modern sociological theories such as feminism, functionalism, structuration theory, figurational studies, postmodernism and more. You should not be put off by these apparently difficult terms. They are really just a shorthand way of describing the different ways that sociologists interpret and understand the social world.

In the rest of this chapter we first discuss sociology as *a way of thinking* about the world or as a different way of seeing which, once you have mastered it, becomes very difficult to avoid. In short, once a sociologist, always a sociologist! World events, personal relationships, family life, international politics and much more: you will see all of these in a different light once you have developed a sociological way of seeing and thinking.

Second, we introduce the ideas of some of the very earliest sociological thinkers of the nineteenth and early twentieth centuries – those who essentially founded modern sociology as an academic discipline. We connect these thinkers to the times they lived through in order to illustrate the new social problems they tried to solve and how they went about it. We then discuss some of the approaches to sociology that came afterwards. However, this is not a comprehensive list, and you will need to read chapter 3 on 'Theories and Perspectives' for the more recent theories.

Third, we look at some of the uses of sociology. Many students are attracted to sociology because they have a desire to help others and see the subject as a way into a suitable 'people-centred' career. For example, sociology graduates find careers in the caring professions, social work, teaching or the criminal justice system. Others use their research skills and knowledge to good effect in management, market research, local and national government administration or research consultancy. Still others (after more study) become professional sociologists working in universities and colleges. Studying sociology can be the first step on the path to a rewarding and satisfying career. However, others study sociology simply because they want to understand better the world we live in. This is sociology as a kind of personal enlightenment, which may or may not lead down a particular career path.

Some sociologists use their training and skills to try to improve the world by intervening to change an existing situation. This is 'applied sociology', and much of the research on social problems such as homelessness, poverty, unemployment, drug addiction, self-harm, and so on, is applied research. Based on their findings, applied researchers may try out possible solutions or make recommendations for changes to government policies or service provision.

Finally, the chapter ends with recent ideas of the need for sociologists to engage with the general public and the media if sociology is to have a greater impact on society. We are used to seeing psychologists, historians and political scientists as experts on television news and documentaries, but rarely do we see sociologists. This section discusses why this is so and what sociologists can do about it. However, we begin by outlining what it means to 'think sociologically' – a basic prerequisite to the practice of 'doing sociology'.

The sociological imagination

Learning to think sociologically means cultivating our imagination. Studying sociology is not just a routine process of acquiring knowledge from books like this one. A sociologist has to be able to break free from the immediacy of their personal circumstances to see things in a wider social context. Doing sociological work depends on developing what the American sociologist C. Wright Mills (1970), in a famous phrase, called a sociological imagination.

The sociological imagination demands that we should 'think ourselves away' from the familiar routines of our daily lives in order to look at them from a new point of view. The best way to illustrate this is with something many millions of people do every day without a second thought, the simple act of drinking a cup of coffee. What could we possibly find to say, from a sociological point of view, about such a commonplace and uninteresting act?

First, coffee is not just a refreshing drink but it has symbolic value as part of our day-to-day social activities. Often the rituals associated with coffee drinking are more important than consuming the drink itself. The morning cup of coffee is often the centrepiece of a personal routine and an essential first step to starting the day. Morning coffee can then be followed later in the day by coffee with others – the basis of a group, not just an individual ritual. Two people who arrange to meet for coffee are probably more interested in socializing and chatting than drinking coffee. In all societies, drinking and eating provide occasions for social interaction, and these offer a rich subject matter for sociological study.

Second, coffee contains caffeine, a drug which has a stimulating effect on the brain, and many people drink coffee for the 'extra lift' it provides. Long days at the office or late nights studying sociology – some students do this, we are told – are made more tolerable by regular coffee breaks. Coffee is a habit-forming substance, but coffee addicts are not regarded as 'drug users'. This is because, like alcohol,

5

Meeting friends for coffee is part of a social ritual which also situates people within their broader social context.

coffee is a socially acceptable drug, whereas cocaine and heroin, for example, are not. Yet some societies tolerate the consumption of cocaine but frown on both coffee and alcohol. Sociologists are interested in why these differences exist and how they came about.

Third, when we drink a cup of coffee we are unwittingly caught up in a complex set of social and economic relationships that stretch right across the planet. Coffee links people in the wealthiest and the most impoverished parts of the world. It is consumed mainly in the relatively rich countries but grown primarily in relatively poor ones. Coffee is one of the most valuable commodities in international trade, providing many countries with their largest source of foreign exchange. The production, transportation and distribution of coffee require continuous transactions between people thousands of miles away from the coffee drinker. Studying such global connections is an important task for sociologists.

Fourth, sipping coffee is not 'natural' but presumes a long process of social, political and economic development. Along with other familiar items of Western diets – like tea, bananas, potatoes and white sugar – coffee became widely consumed only from the late 1800s, though it was fashionable among social elites before then. The drink originated in the Middle East, but its mass consumption dates from the period of Western colonial expansion more than 200 years ago. Virtually all the coffee we drink today comes from areas such as South America and Africa that were colonized by Europeans. The drink is not a 'natural' part of the Western diet, however normal buying and consuming coffee appears to people today.

Finally, coffee has been 'branded' and politicized within current debates about globalization, international fair trade, human rights and environmental damage. The decisions consumers make about what kind of coffee to drink and where to buy it are political as well as lifestyle choices. Some people drink only organic coffee, decaffeinated coffee or coffee that is 'fairly traded' through schemes that

Coffee is more than a pleasant drink for these workers, whose livelihoods depend on the coffee plant.

pay the full market price to small producers in developing countries. Others patronize 'independent' coffee houses rather than 'corporate' chains such as Starbucks and Costa.

When we begin to develop a sociological imagination, our morning coffee becomes a thing of great fascination which we approach with a new understanding. Indeed, as we will see throughout the book, the best sociological studies always tell us something we did not know before or make us see the familiar routines and patterns of life in new ways.

> ### THINKING CRITICALLY
>
> Sociology deepens our understanding of routine activities such as coffee drinking, but it has been argued that sociological research findings could also lead to changes in behaviour. In what ways might a wider understanding of the 'sociology of coffee' lead individuals to alter their own behaviour?

Studying people and societies

It is often said that sociology is simply the 'science of society'. But what then is 'society'? When sociologists speak of a society, they generally mean a group of people living in a bounded territory who share common cultural features such as language, values and basic norms of behaviour. Hence we can discuss, say, French society, Danish society or Argentinian society. However, 'society' also includes institutions – such as particular types of government, education systems and family types – and the relatively stable relationships between them. The enduring patterns formed by relationships among people, groups and institutions form the basic social structure of a society. When we start thinking about social life through the concepts of society, institutions and social structures, we are beginning to use a sociological imagination and to 'think sociologically'.

Adopting a sociological imagination allows us to see that events that affect the individual person actually reflect larger social issues. Divorce, for instance, may be emotionally traumatic for someone who goes through it – what Mills calls a 'personal trouble'. But the level of divorce is also a significant 'public issue' that has an impact on pension provisions, welfare benefit systems and housing need. Similarly, losing a job and being unable to find another one quickly may be a personal tragedy for the individual. However, it is far more than a matter of private despair when millions of people find themselves in the same situation; it is a public issue expressing broad economic and social trends.

Try to apply a sociological imagination to your own life. It is not necessary to think only of troubling events. Consider why you are turning the pages of this book at all – why did you decide to study sociology? You could be a reluctant sociology student (surely not?) taking a course to fulfil the degree requirement for a career in law, teaching, journalism or management. Or you might just be enthusiastic to understand better the world you live in. Whatever your motivation, you are likely to have a good deal in common, without necessarily knowing it, with other sociology students. This is because your private decision also reflects your position within the wider society.

Do any of the following characteristics apply to you? Are you young? White? From a professional or white-collar background? Have you done, or do you still do, some part-time work to boost your income? Do you want to find a good job when you finish your education but are not especially dedicated to studying? More than three-quarters of readers will answer 'yes' to all of these questions. That is because university students are not typical of the population as a whole but tend to be drawn from more privileged social groups, and their attitudes generally reflect those held by friends and acquaintances. The social backgrounds from which we come have a great deal to do with the kind of lifestyle choices we make.

On the other hand, none of the characteristics above may apply to you. You might come from a minority ethnic group, from a working-class family or from a background of relative poverty. You may be in mid-life or older. All the same, we can make some tentative assumptions about you. You are likely to have had to struggle to get where you are; you probably had to overcome hostile reactions from friends and others who thought you were quite mad to give up a decent job, take on a large debt or risk failing, and you may well be combining higher education study with full-time parenthood. For sociologists, there is no such thing as the 'isolated individual' who makes choices without any reference to other people.

While we are all influenced by social context, our behaviour is never determined entirely by that context. Sociology investigates the connections between what society makes of us and what we make of society and ourselves. Our activities both structure – or give shape to – the social world around us and, at the same time, are structured by that world. The social contexts of our lives are not a mass of completely random events and actions; they are structured, or patterned, in distinct ways. There are certain regularities in the ways we behave and in the relationships we have with one another.

Although the idea of a 'structure' reminds us of a building, social structures are not really like physical structures, which, once built, exist independently of our actions. Human societies are always in the process of structuration (Giddens 1984). That is, they are reconstructed at every moment by the very 'building blocks' that compose them – human beings like us. Consider again the case of coffee. A cup of coffee does not drop into your hands. You *choose* to go to a particular coffee shop, you *choose* whether to drink a latte, a cappuccino or an espresso. As you make those decisions, along with millions of other people, you also help to shape the world market for coffee, and that affects the lives of coffee producers in distant countries whom you will never meet.

In recent decades, the malleable character of social structures has been dramatically demonstrated. The communist regimes of Eastern Europe, including the former Soviet Union, collapsed rapidly in the late 1980s and 1990s as ordinary people took to the streets to protest at the lack of freedom and economic development. No one foresaw that the apparently solid and unyielding social structures of communism would wilt as people simply withdrew their legitimacy from the regimes and their leaders. In 2011, countries of the Middle East and North Africa saw numerous uprisings against authoritarian governments in the region as people expressed their dissatisfaction and called for change. In Libya, the 42-year regime of Colonel Muammar Gaddafi was ended and, in Egypt, President Hosni Mubarak was forced from office after protesters took over Tahrir Square in the capital city, Cairo. Such revolutionary events show us that social structures are always 'in process' and are never set in stone, however solid or 'natural' they may feel.

> Recent political developments, including those noted here, are further discussed in chapter 21, 'Politics, Government and Social Movements', and chapter 22, 'Nations, War and Terrorism'.

The development of sociological thinking

When they begin studying sociology, many students are puzzled by the diversity of theories they encounter. Sociology has never been a discipline where a single body of ideas is accepted as valid by everyone, though some theories have been more widely accepted than others. Sociologists often disagree about how to study human behaviour and how research findings should be interpreted. This is quite normal and is an aspect of all scientific subjects. However, unlike physics or chemistry, sociology involves studying ourselves, and this can severely challenge our long-held views and attitudes. Sociology can be very unsettling and disturbing. Nonetheless, we have to make every effort to set aside our emotional and political commitments, at least while we are in the process of 'doing sociology'. If we do not,

then there is a risk that we will be misled and our findings will not be valid.

Theories and theoretical perspectives

It is a fact that I bought a cup of coffee this morning, that it cost a certain amount of money and that the coffee beans used to make it were grown in Central America. But in sociology we also want to know *why* things happen, and that means we have to construct theories which explain the bare facts. For instance, we know that many millions of people now use the Internet and social networking sites to stay in touch with friends or maintain an online diary. But this is a very recent development which begs some questions. Why did Internet use spread so rapidly? Why did online social media come about and why do so many people get involved with them? Why are younger people more likely to use social media than older people? What impact is social media having on earlier forms of communication? To address questions such as these, we need to collect and assemble the evidence and engage in theorizing.

Theorizing means constructing abstract interpretations of events using a series of logically related statements that explain a wide variety of empirical or 'factual' situations. A theory about social media, for example, would be concerned with identifying how communications technology has developed over time and what were the prerequisites for their success. In the best sociology, factual research and explanatory theories are closely related. We can only develop valid theoretical explanations if we are able to test them by means of empirical research; sociological theories are not mere speculation. Contrary to popular belief, the facts do *not* speak for themselves; they need to be interpreted, and interpretation takes place within a set of underlying theoretical assumptions. Many sociologists work primarily on factual research projects, but, unless they are guided by some knowledge of theory, their work is unlikely to *explain* satisfactorily the complexity they find. This is

9

In this painting by Brueghel, a chaotic range of often bizarre activities can be seen which collectively make little sense. However, the title – *Netherlandish Proverbs* – provides the key to interpreting the painting. There are more than a hundred proverbs illustrated here that were common in the sixteenth century. For example, at the bottom left someone is 'banging their head against a brick wall', on which sits a man who is 'armed to the teeth'. The evidence collected by sociologists can appear similarly unintelligible unless it is set within the context of a general theory which guides our interpretation of the facts.

true even of research carried out with strictly practical objectives.

Many people see themselves as essentially practical and 'down to earth' and are suspicious of theorists and theories which seem far removed from their everyday life. Yet all apparently practical decisions make some theoretical assumptions. The manager of a business, for example, may have no regard for 'theory'. Nonetheless, she might also believe that her employees are motivated by monetary rewards and that the promise of these leads them to work hard. This is a simple underlying theoretical interpretation of human behaviour, which the manager takes for granted without realizing or acknowledging it. An alternative view is that most people work in order to make a decent life for their families

and monetary reward is merely a means to that less individualistic end. Once we begin to look for satisfactory interpretations of human actions we have to become interested in competing theories.

Without some kind of theoretical approach, we do not even know what to look for when beginning a study or when interpreting results at the end of the research process. But the interpretation of factual evidence is not the only reason for theorizing. Theoretical thinking must also tackle general problems of how social life can and should be studied in the first place. Should sociological methods be modelled on the natural sciences? How can we conceptualize human consciousness, social action and social institutions? How can sociologists avoid introducing personal bias into their research? Should they even try? There are no easy answers to such questions, which have been answered in different ways since the emergence of sociology in the nineteenth century.

Founders of sociology

Human beings have long been curious about the sources of their own behaviour, but for thousands of years attempts to understand people relied on ways of thinking passed down from generation to generation. Before the rise of modern sciences, 'folkways' – traditional knowledge and practices passed down though generations – held sway in most communities, and these persisted well into the twentieth century. One example is people's understanding of their health or illness. Older people, with a good knowledge of a community's folkways, provided advice on how to prevent illness and cure diseases. Reflecting on his American childhood in Lawrence County, Kentucky, Cratis Williams gives us a flavour of the Appalachian culture of the time (Williams 2003: 397–8):

> A plaque of lead suspended on a string around a child's neck warded off colds and kept witches away while the child was sleeping. Children plagued by nightmares could wear these lead charms to assure themselves of sweet sleep and pleasant dreams, for nightmares were caused by witches and evil creatures that could not operate in the presence of lead. Adults given to snoring and nightmares sought relief by smelling a dirty sock as they went to sleep.

In today's modern societies, very few people advocate such measures or hold similar beliefs. Instead, a more scientific approach to health and illness means that children are vaccinated against previously common diseases and taught that nightmares are normal and generally harmless. Pharmacies do not routinely sell smelly socks to cure snoring either. The origins of systematic studies of social life lie in a series of sweeping changes ushered in by the French Revolution of 1789 and the mid-eighteenth-century Industrial Revolution in Europe. These events shattered older, traditional ways of life, and the founders of sociology looked to understand how such radical changes had come about. But, in doing so, they also developed more systematic, scientific ways of looking at the social and natural worlds, which challenged conventional religious beliefs.

> The process of industrialization is discussed in chapter 4, 'Globalization and Social Change', and chapter 6, 'Cities and Urban Life'. Some of the damaging consequences of industrialization are outlined in chapter 5, 'The Environment'.

Auguste Comte

No single individual can found a whole field of study, and there were many contributors to early sociological thinking. However, particular prominence is usually given to Auguste Comte (1798–1857), who invented the word 'sociology' around 1840. Comte had originally used the term 'social physics' to describe the new subject, but some of his intellectual rivals at the time were also using that term. To distinguish his own approach from theirs he coined the term 'sociology' – the systematic study of the social world.

Comte's thinking reflected the turbulent events of his age. He looked to create a science of society that would discover the 'laws' of the social world, just as natural science had discovered laws in the natural world. Although he recognized that each scientific discipline has its own subject matter, Comte thought that a similar logic and scientific method could be applied to them all. Uncovering the laws that govern human societies could help us to shape our destiny and improve the welfare of all humanity.

Comte wanted sociology to become a 'positive science' that would use the same rigorous methods as astronomy, physics and chemistry. Positivism is a doctrine which says that science should be concerned only with observable entities that are known directly to experience. On the basis of careful observation, laws can then be inferred that explain the relationships between those observed phenomena. By understanding the causal relationships between events, scientists can then predict how future events will occur. A positivist approach in sociology aims to produce knowledge about society based on evidence drawn from observation, comparison and experimentation.

Comte argued that human efforts to understand the world have passed through three broad stages: the theological, the metaphysical and the positive. In the theological stage, thinking was guided by religious ideas and a belief that society was an expression of God's will. In the metaphysical stage, society came to be seen in natural rather than supernatural terms, with events being explained by reference to natural laws. The positive stage, ushered in by the discoveries of Copernicus, Galileo and Newton, encouraged the application of scientific methods. Comte regarded sociology as the last of the sciences to develop, but he argued that it was also the most significant and complex.

In the latter part of his career, Comte was keenly aware of the state of the society in which he lived and was concerned with the inequalities produced by industrialization and the threat they posed to social cohesion. The long-term solution, in his view, was the production of moral consensus through a new 'religion of humanity' to hold society together despite the new patterns of inequality. Although Comte's vision was never realized, his contribution in founding a science of society was important to the later professionalization of sociology as an academic discipline.

Emile Durkheim

The ideas of another French sociologist, Emile Durkheim (1858–1917), had a more lasting impact on sociology than those of Comte. Durkheim saw sociology as a new science that turned traditional philosophical questions into sociological ones which demanded real-world – empirical – research studies. He argued that we must study social life with the same objectivity as scientists study the natural world, which he summed up in his famous injunction to 'study social facts as things'. By this he meant that social institutions have a hard, objective reality that enables them to be analysed as rigorously as objects in the natural world.

But what is a social fact? Durkheim explains that social facts are all those institutions and rules of action which constrain or channel human behaviour. For the individual, social facts can feel rather like an external force, though most of the time they are simply taken for granted as 'natural' or 'normal' parts of life. For instance, the monetary system is a social fact we rarely think about. We are paid in money, we borrow money from banks to buy a car or a house, and if we have not been good at managing money we will be considered a high risk and may not be allowed to borrow. But the monetary system was already in place before we were born and, as we are forced to use it if we want to take part in our society, we are subject to its rules. In that sense, the system constrains or shapes our actions. This is typical of all social facts; they exist independently of the individual and shape their choices and actions.

In his analysis of suicide rates, Durkheim used the concept of social facts to explain why some countries have higher suicide rates than others (see the 'Classic study', p. 13). Suicide seems to be a purely individual act, the outcome of extreme unhappiness or perhaps deep depression. Yet Durkheim showed that social facts such as religion, marriage, divorce and social class all exert an influence on suicide rates. And, as there are regular patterns across different countries, these patterns must be explained in a sociological not a psychological way.

Durkheim was preoccupied with the changes transforming society in his own lifetime and was particularly interested in social and moral solidarity – what it is that binds society together. Solidarity is maintained when individuals are integrated into social groups and regulated by a set of shared values and customs. In *The Division of Labour in Society*, Durkheim (1984 [1893]) argued that the advent

Classic Studies 1.1 Emile Durkheim's study of suicide

The research problem

One of the more unsettling aspects of our lives is the phenomenon of suicide, which often leaves those left behind with more questions than answers. Why do some people decide to take their own lives? Where do the pressures they experience actually come from? One of the early sociological classics which explores the relationship between the individual and society is Emile Durkheim's analysis of suicide rates, *Suicide: A Study in Sociology* (Durkheim 1952 [1897]). Even though people see themselves as individuals exercising free will and choice, Durkheim's study showed that even a highly personal act such as suicide is influenced by what happens in the social world.

Research had been conducted on suicide before Durkheim's study, but he was the first to insist on a sociological explanation. Previous writers had acknowledged the influence of 'racial type', climate or mental disorder to explain an individual's likelihood of committing suicide. But Durkheim argued that the suicide rate – the percentage of suicides per 100,000 of the population – was a social fact that could only be explained by other social facts and that suicide rates vary widely across the world's societies (see figure 1.1).

By examining official statistics in France, Durkheim found that certain social groups were more likely to commit suicide than others. He discovered that more men committed suicide than women, more Protestants than Catholics, the wealthy more than the poor, and single people more than those who were married. The question was, why?

Durkheim's explanation

These findings led Durkheim to conclude that there are social forces *external to the individual* which influence suicide rates. He related his explanation to the idea of social solidarity and to two types of bonds within society – social integration and social regulation. Durkheim argued that people who were strongly integrated into social groups, and whose desires and aspirations were regulated by social norms, were less likely to commit suicide. From this he

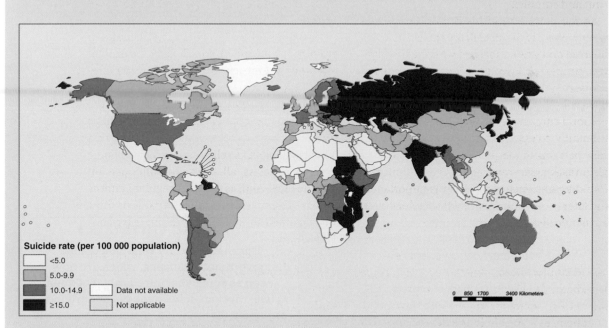

Suicide rate (per 100 000 population)
- <5.0
- 5.0-9.9
- 10.0-14.9
- ≥15.0
- Data not available
- Not applicable

0   850   1700   3400 Kilometers

Figure 1.1 Age-standardized suicide rates by country and region, 2012

Source: WHO (2014b).

deduced four types of suicide, in accordance with the relative presence or absence of integration and regulation.

1 *Egoistic suicides* are marked by low integration and occur when an individual becomes isolated or when their ties to a social group are weakened or broken. For example, the low rates of suicide among Catholics could be explained by their strong community, while the personal and moral freedom of Protestants meant that they 'stand alone' before God. Marriage protects against suicide by integrating the individual into a stable social relationship, while single people remain more isolated.

2 *Anomic suicide* is caused by a lack of social regulation. By this, Durkheim referred to the condition of *anomie*, when people are rendered 'normless' as a result of rapid change or economic instability. The loss of a fixed point of reference for norms and desires – such as in times of economic upheaval or in personal troubles such as divorce – can upset the balance between people's circumstances and their desires such that they no longer know how to carry on.

3 *Altruistic suicide* occurs when an individual is 'over-integrated' – social bonds are too strong – and comes to value the group more than him- or herself. In such a case, suicide becomes a sacrifice for the 'greater good'. Japanese kamikaze pilots or Islamist 'suicide bombers' are examples. Durkheim saw these as more common in traditional societies where mechanical solidarity prevails.

4 The final type is *fatalistic suicide*. Although Durkheim saw this as of little contemporary relevance, it occurs when an individual is over-regulated by society. The oppression of the individual in dictatorial regimes can result in feelings of powerlessness and hopelessness.

Suicide rates vary across societies but are also quite stable *within* particular societies over time. Durkheim took this as evidence that there are consistent social forces that influence suicide rates, and therefore we can see that general social patterns can be detected even within individual actions.

Critical points

Since its publication, many objections have been raised to Durkheim's study of suicide, particularly in relation to his uncritical use of official statistics, his dismissal of non-social influences and his insistence in classifying all types of suicide together. Some critics have shown that it is vitally important to understand the social process involved in collecting data on suicides, as coroners' definitions and criteria influence the number of deaths that are recorded as 'suicides' in the first place. Because of this, suicide statistics may be highly variable across societies, as Durkheim suggests, but this is not necessarily because of differences in suicidal behaviour; rather, it is due to divergent practices adopted by coroners in recording 'unexplained deaths'.

Contemporary significance

The arguments of his critics are legitimate, yet Durkheim's study remains a sociological classic. It helped to establish sociology as a discipline with its own subject – the study of social facts – and his fundamental argument retains much of its force: that to grasp fully even the apparently most personal act of suicide demands a sociological explanation rather than simply one rooted in the exploration of personal motivation. Durkheim's identification of suicide *rates* as a subject for study is today widely accepted, and the study is also important for its demonstration that social phenomena are amenable to systematic, scientific analysis using a rigorous methodology.

THINKING CRITICALLY

Durkheim's study relied on official government statistics, which are now seen as somewhat unreliable. But does this criticism undermine his underlying argument that 'suicide' is not an exclusively personal act and therefore it requires a sociological rather than individualistic psychological explanation?

of the industrial age also led to a new type of solidarity.

According to Durkheim, older cultures with a low division of labour (specialized roles such as work occupations) are characterized by mechanical solidarity. Most people are involved in similar occupations and bound together by common experiences and shared beliefs. But the development of modern industry and the enlargement of cities produced an expanding division of labour which broke down mechanical forms of solidarity. With the increasing specialization of tasks and roles, a new type of organic solidarity was created. As the division of labour expands, people become increasingly dependent upon one another, because each person needs goods and services that those in other occupations supply. Like the human 'organic' body, each part or organ depends on all the others if the whole society or body is to function properly.

Nonetheless, Durkheim thought that social change in the modern world was so rapid and intense that major difficulties could arise. As societies change, so do lifestyles, morals, beliefs and accepted patterns of behaviour. But, when change is rapid and continuous, the old values lose their grip on people without any new ones becoming established. Durkheim called such an unsettling condition anomie – deep feelings of aimlessness, dread and despair, as many people are left perceiving that their lives lack meaning and structure without clear guidelines for action. The big question is whether people can ever get used to continuous rapid change as the 'normal' condition of living in conditions of modernity.

Karl Marx

The ideas of Karl Marx (1818–83) contrast sharply with those of Comte and Durkheim, though he too sought to explain the changes associated with the Industrial Revolution. When he was a young man, Marx's political activities brought him into conflict with the German authorities, and after a brief stay in France he settled permanently in exile in Britain, where he saw the growth of factories and industrial production as well as growing inequality. His interest in the European labour movement and socialist ideas were reflected in his writings, and much of his work concentrated on political and economic issues. Yet, since he connected economic problems to social institutions, his work was rich in sociological insights.

Although he wrote about the broad sweep of human history, Marx's primary focus was on the development of capitalism: a system of production that contrasts radically with all previous economies. Marx identified two main elements of capitalism. The first is capital – that is, any asset, including money, machines or even factories, that can be used or invested to make future assets. The accumulation of capital goes hand in hand with the second element, wage-labour. Wage-labour refers to the pool of workers who do not own any means of production themselves but must find employment provided by the owners of capital.

Marx argued that those who own capital – capitalists – form a ruling class, while the mass of the population make up a class of waged workers – the working class. As industrialization spread, large numbers of peasants, who used to support themselves by working the land, moved to the expanding cities and helped to form an urban industrial working class, which Marx also called the proletariat. For Marx, this means that capitalism is a class system in which relations between the two main classes are characterized by an underlying conflict. Although owners of capital and workers are dependent on each other – capitalists need labour, workers need wages – this dependency is unbalanced. Workers have little or no control over their labour, and employers are able to generate profit by appropriating the products of the workers' labour – paying them less than their labour is worth.

Marx saw conflicts between classes as the motivation for historical development; as he put it, they are the 'motor of history'. Marx and Engels (2008 [1848]) wrote at the beginning of *The Communist Manifesto*, 'The history of all hitherto existing society is the history of class struggles.' According to Marx, there have been a series of historical stages, beginning with

So-called Occupy protests around the world target 'greedy' forms of capitalism in which vast wealth accumulates among a tiny percentage of the population while 'the 99 per cent' majority struggle to make a living. Twenty-first-century anti-capitalist movements continue to take their inspiration from the analyses of Marx and Engels, though they rarely advocate communism as their preferred alternative.

'primitive communist' societies of hunters and gatherers and passing through ancient slave-owning systems and feudal systems with land-owners and peasant farmers. The emergence of a new commercial or capitalist class displaced the landed nobility, and, just as capitalists had overthrown the feudal order, so too would the capitalists be overthrown by the proletariat.

Marx theorized that a workers' revolution would bring about a new society in which there would be no large-scale division between owners and workers. He called this historical stage communism. This does not mean that all inequalities would magically disappear, but society would no longer be split into a small class that monopolizes economic and political power and a mass of people who benefit little from their labour. The economic system would be under communal ownership and a more humane, egalitarian society would slowly emerge.

Marx's ideas had a far-reaching effect on the twentieth century. Until only a generation ago, more than a third of the Earth's population lived in societies whose governments derived inspiration from Marx's ideas. However, since the revolutionary wave that began in Poland in 1989 and swept aside communist regimes across Eastern Europe, ending with the collapse of communism in the Soviet Union itself in 1991, Marx's ideas have lost ground. Even in China, where a communist party still holds political power, capitalist economic development has taken a firm hold. In spite of the spread of capitalism around the world, the working-class revolution that Marx looked forward to seems further away today than it did in Marx's own time.

Max Weber

Like Marx, Max Weber (1864–1920) was not just a sociologist; his interests ranged across many areas. He was born in Germany, where he spent most of his academic career, and his work covered economics, law, philosophy and comparative history as well as sociology. He was also concerned with the development of capitalism and how modern societies differed from earlier types. In a series of studies, Weber set out some of the basic characteristics of modern industrial societies and identified key issues that remain central to sociology today.

Weber recognized class conflict but saw it as less significant than Marx did. In Weber's view, economic factors *are* important, but ideas and values can also bring about social change. His celebrated and much discussed work *The Protestant Ethic and the Spirit of Capitalism* (1992 [1904–5]) proposed that religious values – especially those associated with Puritanism – were of fundamental importance in creating a capitalistic outlook. Unlike the other early sociologists, Weber argued that sociologists should study social action – the subjectively meaningful actions of people that are oriented towards others. It is the job of sociology to understand the meanings behind all of those individual actions.

An important element in Weber's sociological perspective is the ideal type. Ideal types are models that are created to alert us to some social phenomenon and to help us to make sense of it. These hypothetical constructions can be very useful in pointing researchers towards a subject. For example, we could construct a simple ideal-typical 'terrorist group', based on the most striking aspects that have been observed in the cases of the IRA in Northern Ireland, ETA in Spain, the Red Brigades in Italy and the global networks of al-Qaeda. We might note that all these groups operate outside mainstream politics; they use violence against the state and they often target civilians to demonstrate their power. We can then use this ideal type to analyse other real-world instances of political violence.

Of course, in reality there are many differences between our four groups. The Red Brigades were communist, the IRA was an Irish nationalist group, ETA is a Basque separatist organization and al-Qaeda is a global Islamist network. Nonetheless, using our ideal type we can accommodate these differences while also recognizing that they share enough features to be described collectively as 'terrorist groups'. It is important to note that, by 'ideal' type, Weber did not mean that the conception was perfect or desirable. Ideal types are 'pure' or 'one-sided' forms of real social phenomena. But constructing an ideal type of terrorism (or anything else) from common aspects of many observed cases is more effective and useful than using one real terrorist group as a template for others.

Weber saw the emergence of modern society as accompanied by important shifts in patterns of social action. People were moving away from traditional beliefs grounded in superstition, religion, custom and longstanding habit. Instead, they engaged increasingly in rational, instrumental calculation that took into account efficiency and the future consequences of the action. In industrial society, there was little room for sentiment or doing things just because they had 'always been done that way'. The emergence of science, modern technology and bureaucracies was described by Weber as rationalization – the organization of social life according to principles of efficiency and on the basis of technical knowledge. If religion and longstanding customs previously guided people's attitudes and values, modern society was marked by the rationalization of politics, religion, economic activity and even music.

Weber had major concerns about the outcome of the rationalization process. He feared that the spread of bureaucracy, which is the most efficient form of administration, would stifle creativity and imprison

Some of the major trade and economic transactions today take place on the stock market in highly rationalized format, with barely any personal interactions between global traders. This is in stark contrast to the personalized bartering and market stall negotiations which continue in many local communities.

individuals in a 'steel-hard cage' from which there would be little chance of escape. This bureaucratic domination, although based on rational principles, could crush the human spirit by over-regulating every aspect of life. For Weber, the seemingly progressive agenda of the eighteenth-century Age of Enlightenment, of scientific progress, rising wealth and increasing happiness, also brought with it a dark side with new dangers.

Three theoretical traditions

As we have seen, the classical founders of sociology – Durkheim, Marx and Weber –
adopted different approaches to their studies. Durkheim emphasized the coercive strength of social forces in generating shared values and consensus. Marx also saw social structures as powerful, but argued that conflict and inequality were endemic in all societies. On the other hand, Max Weber focused attention on the meaningful character of social life and the social actions of individuals. These basic differences have persisted throughout the history of sociology, developing into three broad sociological traditions: functionalism (Durkheim), conflict theory (Marx) and social action or 'interactionist' approaches (Weber).

The three traditions are introduced briefly

1.1   Neglected founders of sociology?

Although Comte, Durkheim, Marx and Weber are, without doubt, foundational figures in sociology, there were some in the same period and others from earlier times whose contributions should also be taken into account. Sociology, like many academic fields, has not always lived up to its ideal of acknowledging the importance of every thinker whose work has intrinsic merit. Very few women or members of minority ethnic groups had the opportunity to become professional sociologists during the 'classical' period of the late nineteenth and early twentieth century. In addition, the few who *were* given the opportunity to do sociological research of lasting importance have frequently been neglected. Important scholars such as Harriet Martineau and the Muslim scholar Ibn Khaldun have attracted the attention of sociologists in recent years.

Harriet Martineau (1802–76)

Harriet Martineau has been called the 'first woman sociologist', but, like Marx and Weber, she cannot be thought of simply as a sociologist. She was born and educated in England and was the author of more than fifty books as well as numerous essays. Martineau is now credited with introducing sociology to Britain through her translation of Comte's founding treatise, *Positive Philosophy* (see Rossi 1973). In addition, she conducted a first-hand, systematic study of American society during her extensive travels throughout the United States in the 1830s, the subject of her book *Society in America* (Martineau 1962 [1837]). Martineau is significant to sociologists today for several reasons.

First, she argued that, when one studies a society, one must focus on all its aspects, including key political, religious and social institutions. Second, she insisted that an analysis of a society must include an understanding of women's lives, something that only became commonplace in mainstream sociology with feminist interventions in the 1970s. Third, she was the first to turn a sociological eye on previously ignored issues, among them

marriage, children, domestic and religious life, and race relations. As she once wrote: 'The nursery, the boudoir, and the kitchen are all excellent schools in which to learn the morals and manners of a people' (1962 [1837]). Finally, she argued that sociologists should do more than just observe; they should also act in ways to benefit a society. As a result, Martineau was an active proponent of both women's rights and the emancipation of slaves.

Ibn Khaldun (1332–1406)

The Muslim scholar Ibn Khaldun was born in what is today Tunisia and is famous for his historical, sociological and political-economic studies. He wrote many books, the most widely known of which is a six-volume work, the *Muqaddimah* ('Introduction'), completed in 1378. This is viewed by some scholars today as essentially an early foundational work of sociology (see Alatas 2006). The *Muqaddimah* criticized existing historical approaches and methods as dealing only with description, claiming instead the discovery of a new 'science of social organization' or 'science of society', capable of getting at the underlying meaning of events.

Ibn Khaldun devised a theory of social conflict based on understanding the central characteristics of the 'nomadic' and 'sedentary' societies of his time. Central to this theory was the concept of 'group feeling' or solidarity (*asabiyyah*). Groups and societies with a strong group feeling were able to dominate and control those with weaker forms of internal solidarity. Ibn Khaldun developed these ideas in an attempt to explain the rise and decline of Maghribian and Arab states, and in this sense he may be seen as studying the process of state-formation – itself a main concern of modern, Western historical sociology. Nomadic Bedouin tribes tended towards a very strong group feeling, which enabled them to overrun and dominate the weaker sedentary town-dwellers and establish new dynasties. However, the Bedouin then became settled into more urbanized lifestyles and their previously strong group feeling and military force diminished, thus leaving them open to attack from external enemies once again. This completed a long cycle in the rise and decline of states. Although Western historians and sociologists of the late nineteenth and early twentieth century referred to Ibn Khaldun's work, only in very recent years has it again come to be seen as potentially significant.

THINKING CRITICALLY

Why do you think Harriet Martineau's sociological ideas on marriage, children and the domestic life of women were largely ignored in her own time? How might we account for the renewed interest in Ibn Khaldun's fourteenth-century ideas in the twenty-first century?

---

below, but you will encounter arguments and ideas that draw upon them throughout the book. After a while you should be able to identify which tradition any particular research study you come across is closest to.

We look in detail at more recently developed theoretical approaches, such as feminism, postmodernism and figurational studies, in chapter 3, 'Theories and Perspectives'.

Functionalism

Functionalism holds that society is a complex system whose various parts work together to produce stability and that sociology should investigate their relationships. For example, we can analyse the religious beliefs and customs of a society by showing how they relate to other institutions because the different parts of a society always develop in close relation to one another. Functionalists, including Comte and Durkheim, have often used an organic analogy, comparing the operation of society to a living organism. They argue that the parts of society work together, just as the various parts of the human body do, for the benefit of society as a whole. To study a bodily organ such as the heart, we need to show how it relates to other parts of the body. By pumping blood around the body, the heart plays a vital role in the continuation of the life of the organism. Similarly, analysing the function of a social institution such as the education system means showing the part it plays in the smooth running of a society.

Functionalism emphasizes the importance of moral consensus in maintaining order and stability. Moral consensus exists when most people in a society share the same values. Functionalists regard order and balance as the normal state of society, and this social equilibrium is grounded in the moral consensus among society's members. For instance, Durkheim argued that religious beliefs reaffirm people's adherence to core social values, thereby contributing to the maintenance of social cohesion.

Until the 1960s, functionalism was probably the leading theoretical tradition in sociology, particularly in the United States. Talcott Parsons (1902–79) and Robert K. Merton (1910–2003) were two of its most prominent exponents. Merton's version of functionalism has been particularly influential. He distinguished between manifest and latent functions. Manifest functions are those known to, and intended by, the participants in a specific type of social activity. Latent functions are consequences of that activity of which the participants are unaware. For instance, Merton examined the rain dance performed by the Hopi tribe of Arizona and New Mexico. The Hopi believe that this ceremony will bring the rain they need for their crops (a manifest function). But the rain dance, Merton argued, also has the effect of promoting group cohesion of Hopi society (its latent function). A major part of sociological explanations, according to Merton, consists in uncovering the latent functions of intentional social activities and institutions.

Merton also distinguished between

Sport is part of the school curriculum ostensibly to encourage healthy living. However, from a functionalist perspective, sport is also an important part of socialization, teaching children both competitiveness and how to work as part of a team.

functions and dysfunctions. To look for the dysfunctional aspects of social behaviour means focusing on features of social life that challenge the existing order of things. For example, it is mistaken to suppose that religion is always functional and that it only contributes to social cohesion. When religious groups disagree with one another the result can be major social conflict, causing widespread social disruption. Thus, wars have often been fought between religious communities – as can be seen in the struggles between Protestants and Catholics in Europe or between Sunni and Shia Muslims in the Middle East.

Since the late 1970s the popularity of functionalism has waned as its limitations have become apparent. Though it is not true of Merton, many functionalist thinkers focused on stability and social order, minimizing social divisions and inequalities based on factors such as class, ethnicity and gender. Functionalism also placed too little emphasis on the role that creative social action can play within society. Many critics argued that functional analysis attributes to societies social qualities that they do not have. For instance, many functionalists often wrote as though whole societies have 'needs' and 'purposes', even though these concepts make sense only when applied to individual human beings. Just as significantly, in the 1960s and 1970s there emerged a wave of so-called new social movements – involving, among others, students, environmentalists and peace movements – which functional analysis seemed particularly ill-equipped to understand and explain.

Conflict theories

Like functionalists, sociologists using conflict theories emphasize the importance of social structures, and they advance a comprehensive 'model' to explain how society works. However, conflict theorists reject functionalism's emphasis on consensus. Instead, they highlight the importance of divisions in society and, in doing so, concentrate on issues of power, inequality and competitive struggle. They tend to see society as composed of distinct groups, each pursuing its own interests, which means the potential for conflict is always present. Conflict theorists examine the tensions between dominant and disadvantaged groups, looking to understand how relationships of control are established and maintained.

Both Marx and later Marxist approaches have been highly influential in conflict theory, though it is important to note that by no means

21

all conflict theories are Marxist. Feminism, for example, is a form of conflict theory which concentrates on gender inequality – the unequal situation between men and women that exists in most societies. For some feminist theorists, gender inequality is more significant than class-based inequality and has a much longer history. Male domination of society continues even today, though women's political activism has made an impact in many areas of life, bringing about a measure of equality (Abbott et al. 2005).

As a conflict perspective in sociology, feminism draws attention to issues that sociologists previously ignored. In particular, feminist research and theorizing looks at the micro level as well as the macro world of large social structures. For example, feminists have studied unequal gender relations in domestic situations and other 'private' spheres of life (such as sexual relations), a controversial move in the 1960s and 1970s (Rahman and Jackson 2010). Feminists have also carried out research into the use of gender stereotypes and language in interactions, pointing out and challenging many taken-for-granted 'malestream' assumptions (favouring men over women) built into the structure of how we describe and think about the world. We can see this in numerous everyday words and expressions, such as chairman, mankind (to discuss humanity as such) and man-made. This is a simple illustration of the myriad ways in which women's subordinate position in society is reflected in the unacknowledged male domination of language itself.

Of course feminists do not ignore the macro level either. Feminist studies have shown that gender inequality is embedded within modern social structures such as legal systems, education and schooling, government and politics, and many more. Similarly, in order to demonstrate the extent and scope of gender inequality, feminist work has made use of official statistics and examined patterns of change over long time periods. Feminist theorizing has continually developed into new areas and types of theory, and these are covered in more detail later in the book.

The conflict tradition in sociology has benefited from feminist research and theorizing. In particular, combining macro- and micro-level studies has shown that evidence of structured inequality can be found in the private sphere of social life every bit as much as in its large social structures. The 1970s slogan 'the personal is political' adequately summarizes why conflict sociology cannot ignore the personal aspects of our everyday lives (Jackson and Jones 1998).

> Feminist research and theorizing can be found throughout the various chapters of the book, but there are significant discussions of feminist theory and its development in chapter 3, 'Theories and Perspectives', and chapter 15, 'Gender and Sexuality'.

Symbolic interactionism

Weber's social action approach inspired many 'interactionist' forms of sociology. One of the most influential has been symbolic interactionism, which also owes much to the American social philosopher George Herbert Mead (1863–1931). Symbolic interactionism springs from a concern with language and meaning. Mead argues that language allows us to become self-conscious beings – aware of our own individuality and able to see ourselves 'as others see us'. The key element in this process is the symbol. A symbol is something that stands for something else. For example, words that refer to objects are symbols which represent what we mean. The word 'spoon' is a symbol we use to describe the utensil that we use to consume soup. Non-verbal gestures and forms of communication are also symbols. Waving at someone or making a rude gesture both have symbolic value.

Symbolic interactionism directs our attention to the details of interpersonal interaction and how that detail is used to make sense of what others say and do. Sociologists influenced by symbolic interactionism often focus on face-to-face interactions in the context of everyday life. They stress the role interactions

In many service industries, workers' skills extend to the management of the public display of their emotions.

play in creating society and its institutions. Max Weber was an important indirect influence on this theoretical approach because, although he acknowledged the existence of social structures, he held that these were created through the actions of individuals.

While the symbolic interactionist perspective has yielded many insights into the nature of our actions in the course of day-to-day social life, it has been criticized for ignoring the larger issues of power and social structure and how these serve to constrain individual action. However, one very good example of interactionism that does take into account such issues is Arlie Hochschild's (1983) *The Managed Heart: Commercialization of Human Feeling*. Hochschild observed training sessions and carried out interviews at Delta Airlines' Stewardess Training Centre in Atlanta, USA. She watched flight attendants being trained to

manage their feelings as well as learning other skills. Hochschild recalled the comments of one instructor, a pilot. 'Now girls, I want you to go out there and really smile', he instructed. 'Your smile is your biggest asset. I want you to go out there and use it. Smile. Really smile. Really lay it on.'

Hochschild's research found that, as Western economies have become increasingly based on the delivery of services, the emotional style of the work we do needs to be understood. Her study of 'customer service' training might be familiar to anyone who has worked in fast food restaurants, shops or bars. Hochschild calls this training a form of 'emotional labour' – labour that requires the management of feelings in order to create a publicly observable and acceptable facial and bodily display. According to Hochschild, companies providing services increasingly lay claim not only to workers' physical activity but also to their presentation of emotions.

This research considered an aspect of life that most people took for granted and showed that sociology could deepen our understanding of it. Hochschild found that service workers – like physical labourers – often feel a sense of distance or alienation from the particular aspect of themselves that is given up in work. The physical labourer's arm, for example, might come to feel like a piece of machinery and only incidentally a part of the person moving it. Likewise, service workers often told Hochschild that their smiles were *on* them but not *of* them. In other words, they felt distanced from their own emotions. Hochschild's book is an influential application of symbolic interactionism, and many other scholars have built on her ideas to expand the interactionist tradition.

Traditions and theories

Functionalism, conflict theory and symbolic interactionism are theoretical traditions – broad, overall orientations to the subject matter of sociology. However, we can make a distinction between these broad *traditions* and the particular *theories* which develop from them. Theories are more narrowly focused and are attempts to explain particular social conditions, events or social changes. For example, feminism is part of the conflict tradition, as feminists see a basic conflict in society between the interests of men and women. But feminist sociologists have also devised numerous narrower theories to explain specific aspects of gender relations (patterned relationships between men and women), such as why more married women are entering paid work, why women are still seen as responsible for childcare, or why young men now do less well in education than young women. Many theories of this kind have been developed in the different areas of life that sociologists study.

The fact that sociology is not dominated by a single theoretical tradition might seem to be a sign of weakness, but this is not the case. The jostling of rival traditions and theories

is an expression of the vitality of the sociological enterprise. In studying human beings – ourselves – theoretical diversity rescues us from dogma and stagnation. Human behaviour is many-sided, and it is unlikely that a single theoretical perspective could cover all of its aspects. Diversity in theoretical thinking provides a rich source of ideas which stimulate the creative capacities that are so essential to progress in social scientific work.

Levels of analysis: microsociology and macrosociology

One important distinction between different theoretical perspectives involves the level of analysis at which each is directed. The study of everyday behaviour in situations of face-to-face interaction is usually called microsociology, while macrosociology is the analysis of large-scale social structures and long-term processes of change. At first glance, it might seem that microanalysis and macroanalysis are entirely distinct from each other, but in fact the two are closely connected (Knorr-Cetina and Cicourel 1981; Giddens 1984).

Macroanalysis is essential if we are to understand the institutional backdrop of daily life. The ways in which people live their everyday lives are influenced by social institutions, as is obvious when we consider the impact on our lives of the education system, the political framework and the system of laws by which we live. Similarly, while we may choose to send an acquaintance an email message, we can also choose to fly thousands of miles to spend the weekend with a friend. Neither of these communications would be possible without the amazingly complex global infrastructure of our world and the many people, organizations and institutions required to build and operate them.

Microanalysis is in turn necessary for illuminating the details of such broad institutional patterns. Face-to-face interaction is clearly the main basis of all forms of social organization, no matter how large the scale. Suppose we are studying a business corporation. We can understand its activities by looking at face-to-face behaviour – the interaction of directors in the boardroom, workers in the various offices, or workers on the factory floor. We may not build up a complete picture of the whole corporation this way, but we could certainly make a significant contribution to understanding how the organization works 'on the ground'.

Of course, people do not live their lives as isolated individuals, nor are their lives completely determined by large social structures. Sociology tells us that everyday life is lived in families, social groups, communities and neighbourhoods. At this level – the meso (or 'middle') level of society – it is possible to see the influence and effects of both micro- and macro-level phenomena. Many sociological studies of local communities deal with the macrosociological impact of huge social changes, such as economic restructuring, but they also explore the ways in which individuals, groups and social movements cope with such changes and turn them to their advantage.

For example, when in the mid-1980s the British government decided to reduce the role of coal in its energy policy, this was disastrous for traditional mining communities, as people's livelihoods were threatened by mine closures and unemployment. However, many former miners retrained with local companies to find work in other industries (Waddington et al. 2001). Similarly, the 2008 financial crisis led to rising unemployment and falling living standards, but this also forced some people to learn new skills or start their own small businesses. Individuals are not simply at the mercy of large-scale social and economic changes but adapt creatively to them. Studying the community level of social life provides a window through which to observe the interaction of micro and macro levels of society. Much applied research (research with a practical aim) in sociology takes place at this *meso* level of social reality.

In later chapters, we will see further examples of how interaction in micro contexts affects larger social processes, and how macro systems in turn influence more confined settings of social life. However, there remains one fundamental issue to be tackled in this chapter: what exactly is sociology for?

What is sociology for?

Sociology has several practical implications for our lives, as C. Wright Mills emphasized when developing his idea of the sociological imagination. First, sociology gives us an awareness of cultural differences that allows us to see the social world from many perspectives. Quite often, if we properly understand how others live, we also acquire a better understanding of what their problems are. Practical policies that are not based on an informed awareness of the ways of life of people they affect have little chance of success. For example, a white English social worker operating in a predominantly Latin American community in South London will not gain the confidence of its members without being sensitive to the different experiences of ethnic groups in the UK.

Second, sociological research provides practical help in assessing the results of policy initiatives. A programme of practical reform may simply fail to achieve what its designers sought or may produce unintended consequences of an unfortunate kind. In the years following the Second World War, large public housing blocks were built in city centres in many countries. These aimed to provide high standards of accommodation for low-income groups from slum areas. However, research later showed that many people who had moved from their previous dwellings to large apartment blocks felt isolated and unhappy. High-rise apartment blocks often became dilapidated and provided breeding grounds for crime.

Third, many sociologists concern themselves directly with practical matters as professionals. People trained in sociology are to be found as industrial consultants, researchers in 'think tanks', urban planners, social workers and personnel managers, as well as in many other careers. An understanding of society and social relations can also be useful for future careers in law and criminal justice, journalism, business and the health professions.

Fourth, and in some ways most importantly, sociology can provide us all with self-enlightenment or increased self-understanding. The more we know about why we act as we do and about the overall workings of our society, the more likely we are to be able to influence our own future. Sociology does not just assist powerful groups or governments. The knowledge sociologists produce is made available to everyone and is often used by voluntary agencies, charities and social movements to bolster their case for change. However, sociological research findings, in themselves, are 'neutral'. That is, they can tell us what society is like, how it 'works' and how it changes over time, but they cannot advise on whether it *should* be that way. That is the proper subject of competing political and moral debates involving everyone.

Public and professional sociology

In recent years, some sociologists have argued that sociology has not engaged enough with the public and has concentrated too much on internal professional debates. In 2004, in his presidential address to the annual meeting of the American Sociological Association, Michael Burawoy argued for a new 'public sociology' that would forge relationships with audiences beyond the narrow confines of universities. He maintains that the professionalization of sociology in the twentieth century has been beneficial, but it also led to sociologists talking more to each other than to the public 'out there' (Burawoy 2005).

Burawoy says there are four types of sociology: professional sociology, public sociology, policy sociology and critical sociology. *Professional sociology* is the conventional, university-based, scientific sociology which generates large research programmes and bodies of knowledge and provides academic careers. *Policy sociology* includes all those studies which pursue goals defined by clients, such as funding bodies and government departments looking to tackle social problems.

Critical sociology is 'the conscience of professional sociology', pointing out the assumptions of research projects and professional sociology (Burawoy 2005: 9). Feminist theory is one example of this strand, drawing attention to the lacunae in and unstated biases of scientific sociology. *Public sociology* is the fourth type and is rooted in dialogue. That is, public sociology speaks with social groups such as trade unions, social movements, faith groups and organizations in civil society in a genuine conversation about the future direction of society. In this sense, the suggestion is that a more politically engaged sociology is necessary, though this is not something that all sociologists would support.

For Burawoy and others, public sociology still depends on professional sociology, but the two exist in a relationship of 'antagonistic interdependence'. Scientific sociology produces research methods, empirical evidence and theories which are necessary for public sociology's engagement with non-academic audiences. But, unlike professional sociology, the public version opens up a dialogue with those audiences, allowing the discipline itself to be partly shaped by the concerns of non-sociologists.

Critics point out that this is a very stark dividing line. In practice, much of today's professional sociology already tries hard to engage with participants and outside audiences. There is also much more overlap between the four types described (Calhoun 2005; Ericson 2005). Many feminist studies, for instance, are not simply critiques of scientific sociology but are empirical themselves, using research methods and questionnaires and contributing to professional sociology. Critics also argue that there is a danger that the discipline will become subordinated to the political motives of social movements and activist groups. If the image and reputation of professional sociology is tainted, then it may, paradoxically, have serious consequences for public support for the discipline. And if public sociology really is dependent on the hard-won scientific credibility of professional sociology, it too could suffer.

Nonetheless, in spite of such criticisms, the basic argument that professional sociology has not done enough to engage with public concerns has been quite widely welcomed. The lack of a public presence for sociology is seen as damaging to the public awareness of sociological theories and evidence, which leaves a gap to be filled by other disciplines such as political science, history or psychology. Professional associations, such as the British Sociological Association, have taken steps to encourage their members to develop more of a media presence as an initial move towards raising the profile of sociology in society, and we can probably expect this trend to continue.

Conclusion

In this chapter, we have seen that sociology has developed as a discipline in which we set aside our personal view of the world in order to look more carefully at the influences that shape our lives and those of others. Sociology emerged as a distinct intellectual endeavour with the development of modern societies, and the study of such societies remains a central concern. However, in an increasingly interconnected global world, sociologists must take a similarly global view of their subject matter if they are properly to understand and explain it. During the founding period of sociology,

society's central problems included social class conflict, wealth distribution, the alleviation of poverty and the question of where the process of modernization was headed.

In the contemporary period, though most of these issues remain, it can be argued that sociology's central problems are shifting. Today, societies are grappling with other issues, such as rapid globalization, international terrorism, environmental damage, global risks with potentially high consequences, multiculturalism and gender inequality, to name just a few. This means that sociologists have to question whether the theories designed to grasp the problems of an earlier period have any purchase on the problems of today. If not, then they will need to design new theories that are able to perceive what Karl Mannheim once called 'the secret of these new times'. The ongoing debate about the status and continuing relevance of the classical sociological theories occurs throughout this book.

Sociology is not just an abstract intellectual field, but has practical implications for people's lives. Learning to become a sociologist should not be a dull or tedious endeavour. The best way to make sure it does not become so is to approach the subject in an imaginative way and to relate sociological ideas and findings to situations in your own life. In that way, you should learn important things about yourself, societies and the wider human world.

Chapter review

1 If asked to explain to a friend what sociology is, how would you briefly define the subject? What is distinctive about 'the sociological imagination'?

2 Explain how sociology came into being as an academic subject, outlining the major social, economic and political shifts that early sociologists sought to understand.

3 List the main contributions made to the founding of sociology by Auguste Comte, Karl Marx, Emile Durkheim and Max Weber. What assumptions about the social world are shared by all four and in what ways do their perspectives diverge?

4 Theoretical disputes are difficult to resolve even in the natural sciences, but why should they be peculiarly problematic in sociology?

5 Outline the three central theoretical traditions in sociological theory. Is it fair to suggest that sociology needs all three if it is to be successful, or does one tradition

have a better grasp of social reality than the others? What social issues have risen to prominence in the latter part of the twentieth century onwards which none of the three approaches have adequately incorporated?

6   Microsociology is the study of everyday behaviour in face-to-face encounters. Macrosociology analyses large-scale social systems and whole societies. Using the example of social class, briefly explain how micro and macro levels are connected in the real world. What is meant by the meso level of social life?

7   What are the practical implications and applications of sociological research? List the ways in which sociology can make a valuable contribution to improving social life.

8   If sociologists have not done enough to engage with the wider public in the past, how can they do so in the future? Should sociologists just get on with their research and let others decide how their findings should be used, or is it necessary for them to engage in political debates?

Research in practice

Since Michael Burawoy's address to the American Sociological Association in 2004, the issue of public sociology has received much attention. One way of bringing sociology to a wider set of audiences is to take sociological findings to those audiences via the mass media. But, even when sociological research does make its way into the media, how is it used, presented and interpreted?

Read Annaliza Gaber's (2005) 'Media Coverage of Sociology', *Sociological Research Online*, 10(3): www.socresonline.org.uk/10/3/gaber.html, and answer the following questions.

1   Who commissioned this research and why?
2   How was the research carried out?
3   What were the key findings of the study?
4   'Sociological communication in these [mass media] and other public arenas may sometimes be impossible' (Ericson 2005: 365). On balance, does the paper provide evidence in support of this statement or is it is unduly pessimistic?

Thinking it through

Sociology is said to have arisen with industrialization, the French Revolution and the beginning of European modernity. The early sociologists tried to understand and solve the many social problems associated with rapid urban development and a new industrial civilization. However, they could not have been expected to forecast the Internet, the worldwide web, smartphones and online social networking.

Can the theories and concepts that served sociology well during the industrial twentieth century still be effective in today's digital world? Suggest ways in which the ideas of sociology's founders could help us to understand the popularity among citizens, businesses and voluntary bodies of social networking services such as Twitter, Facebook and Instagram. Should we consider cyberspace as merely an extension of the 'real' social world or as somehow distinct from it?

Society in the arts

Read the following statement carefully.

> . . . to speak of art and social theory as equal partners is to say that art represents a source of existential social knowledge that is of its own worth and is not inferior to the knowledge of social science. It is to say that there are certain things that art can tell us about society that social science cannot tell us . . . Novels, plays, films, paintings and drawings tell us different things about social life from the things a piece of social scientific research can tell us about social life, and to the extent that they tell us these different things, they tell us *more things*. (Harrington 2004: 3)

Consider a novel, play, film, painting or other work of art you have recently read, seen or heard. What does this work tell us about social life that is a) *different from* what sociology tells us and b) *more than* sociological knowledge? Can the knowledge provided by the work be compared to social scientific findings or are they simply incommensurable?

Further reading

For anyone new to sociology, Evan Willis's (2011) *The Sociological Quest: An Introduction to the Study of Social Life* (5th edn, Crow's Nest, NSW: Allen & Unwin) is a lively book and a good place to start. Following this, Zygmunt Bauman and Tim May's (2001) *Thinking Sociologically* (Oxford: Blackwell) is a guide to developing and using your sociological imagination with many everyday examples. Something a little more advanced is Richard Jenkins's (2002) *Foundations of Sociology: Towards a Better Understanding of the Human World* (Basingstoke: Palgrave Macmillan), which contains a central argument about the role of sociology and sociologists in an age of globalization.

One other useful resource is a good sociology dictionary, and there are several possibilities. John Scott's (2014) *A Dictionary of Sociology* (Oxford: Oxford University Press) and Bryan S. Turner's (2006) *The Cambridge Dictionary of Sociology* (Cambridge: Cambridge University Press) are reliable and comprehensive. For a guide to some of the key concepts used in sociological work, see our own book, Giddens and Sutton's (2017) *Essential Concepts in Sociology* (2nd edn, Cambridge: Polity).

For a collection of readings covering the range of sociology, see the accompanying *Sociology: Introductory Readings* (3rd edn, Cambridge: Polity, 2010).

Internet links

Additional information and support for this book at Polity:
www.politybooks.com/giddens

29

@ **SocioSite – the Social Science Information System, based at the University of Amsterdam:**
www.sociosite.net

@ **The International Sociological Association – represents sociologists around the world:**
www.isa-sociology.org

The European Sociological Association – aims to facilitate research into European issues:
www.europeansociology.org

@ **The British Sociological Association – some helpful information on graduate careers from the BSA:**
www.britsoc.co.uk/what-is-sociology/sociologist-careers.aspx

@ **Public Sociology – Michael Burawoy's version of public sociology and some of his critics:**
http://burawoy.berkeley.edu/PS.Webpage/ps.mainpage.htm

CHAPTER 2

Asking and Answering Sociological Questions

Contents

· ·

What are public toilets for?

In the early evening, the public toilets in a park in St Louis, Missouri, become busy. One man walks in dressed in a grey suit; another has on a baseball cap, trainers, shorts and a T-shirt; a third is wearing a mechanic's uniform from the garage where he works. None of these men is visiting the toilets to use them for the purposes for which they were built. Instead, they are there for spontaneous sexual encounters. Many men – married and unmarried, those with straight identities and those whose identify themselves as gay – seek sex with people they do not know. They are hoping to experience sexual excitement, but without any emotional involvement or commitment.

The search for anonymous, instant sex between men is known all over the world. However, until the late 1960s spontaneous same-sex activity in public places was rarely studied as a form of human inter-action. In the USA, the gay community called the toilets where these activities occurred 'tearooms'; in the UK, the same activity was known as 'cottaging'. The American sociologist Laud Humphreys (1970) conducted research into the use of 'tearooms' and wrote about the impact on participants. *Tearoom Trade* caused widespread controversy at the time, and the issues raised can still be difficult for some.

Humphreys' study was carried out before the emergence of HIV/AIDS in the 1980s, but the activities he witnessed are seen today as carrying more risks. In modern China, for instance, men who have sex with men (MSM) seek out similar experiences in saunas, public parks, clubs and public toilets in a society that has long viewed homosexuality as 'sick, abnormal or perverted'. Many of these encounters take place without regard for safe sex practices, such as using condoms. One reason lies in mainstream Chinese culture, where the concept of '*rouyu*' – a desire for direct physical contact – is widely used to mean 'making love'. For those men seeking out spontaneous, uncommitted sex with other men, condoms may be seen to interfere with achieving *rouyu*. As one research participant told researchers, 'No matter how thin a condom is, there is still a layer of something, and it [sex] is not between fleshes' (Li et al. 2010: 1481).

Humphreys' methodology was criticized as unethical because his fieldwork was conducted covertly, without the consent of the men he studied. The research was undertaken at a time when there was a heavy stigma associated with gay and lesbian identities and when police were vigilant in enforcing the laws against same-sex activity. Humphreys showed that many men who otherwise live 'normal' lives also found ways – and places – to engage in sexual behaviour that would not harm their careers or family lives. He spent an extended period of time researching public toilets, showing that one way to understand social processes is to participate in and observe them at very close quarters. He also conducted survey interviews that enabled him to gather more information than he could have obtained through simple observation.

Both projects opened a window on an aspect of social life that many people did not know existed or just did not understand.

Humphreys' work was conducted and reported with the necessary scientific detachment, but at the same time his selection of the research problem was influenced by his emotional involvement in society. He argued that acceptance of homosexuality would help men to provide one another with self-esteem and mutual support. The research by Li et al. was reported in similarly detached fashion, though their project was prompted by a desire to understand why many MSM shun the use of condoms despite the known risks of HIV infection. What is shown by these two studies, over four decades apart, is that sociologists always strive for relative *detachment* from their subjects, yet at the same time, as members of society, they are emotionally and politically *involved*, looking for solutions to social problems of the day. Achieving a productive balance between involvement and detachment is crucial to all good sociology (Elias 1987b).

We look further into these issues in this chapter. First, we looking at some of the ethical dilemmas that face sociologists engaged in empirical research with people. We then outline some important answers to the question of what, exactly, 'science' is, before exploring the nature of sociology as a distinct discipline. From here we move on to examine the stages involved in sociological research and briefly summarize the most widely used research methods and their applications. The chapter concludes with a discussion on the uses of sociology in society. As we shall see, there are some significant differences between the ideal of scientific work and real-world studies that have to overcome practical obstacles and problems. A good way of thinking about sociological research, we suggest, is to see it, like all scientific research, as the art of the possible.

Human subjects, ethical issues

All research concerned with human beings potentially poses ethical dilemmas. A key question asked by funding bodies today is whether the research 'poses risks to the subjects that are greater than the risks they face in their everyday lives'. If it does, the research may not go ahead, especially where vulnerable social groups – such as children – are involved. Similarly, ethical issues are more prominent today than in the past, and researchers are no longer seen as the only knowledgeable experts while participants are deemed mere 'subjects'. Increasingly, the subjects are themselves involved in the research process and may help to formulate questions, comment on the researcher's interpretation and receive a copy of the final research report.

As in many other relationships in social life (such as doctors and patients or university professors and students), 'lay people' no longer automatically defer to 'experts' in the way they might have done just one generation ago. This broader social process is also transforming research practice. Indeed, funding bodies now routinely ask research teams to anticipate the ethical issues they may confront, suggest how they will deal with these, whether deception will be used, what measures are in place to protect participants from risk, and how findings will be fed back at the end of the study. Clearly, research practice is always embedded within a social and historical context which partly determines what can and cannot legitimately be studied.

In carrying out his research, Humphreys did not reveal his identity as a sociologist, and men who came into the tearoom assumed he was there for the same reasons they were. Although he did not tell any direct lies, he did not reveal the real reason for his presence. Was his behaviour ethical? This specific aspect of the research did not put any of the men *directly* at risk, and perhaps it could therefore by justified. What really made Humphreys' project notable was that he took down the vehicle licence plates of the men in the tearooms, obtained their home addresses from a friend who worked at the Department of Motor Vehicles, and then visited their

homes in the guise of conducting a survey unrelated to the tearoom. How ethical was this element of the study? Could it ever be justified? Even though he did not reveal to the men's families anything about the tearooms, the information he gathered *could* have been damaging. The same-sex activity he observed was illegal at the time, and police officers could have demanded the release of information concerning the men's identities. It is also possible that a less skilled investigator could have slipped up when interviewing the families, or that Humphreys' notes could have been seen by others.

The methodology of Li et al. (2010) in Guangzhou, China, shows just how much research ethics and governance have changed since the 1970s. This research team conducted semi-structured interviews to find out about participants' biographies. Like Humphreys, they also used participant observation in various venues, including four public toilets, and one team member joined a volunteer outreach group in order to build relationships with the target communities. A sample was then recruited from these social networks. However, unlike Humphreys, the researchers openly engaged with the participants about the project and its aims: 'After briefing about the objectives of the study, informed consent was obtained from the participants, who were assured of confidentiality, the use of pseudonyms, and safe storage of the data' (ibid.: 1482).

Considering the number of things that could go wrong in the research process, researchers today do not consider Humphreys' methods to be legitimate. Funding bodies such as the European Science Foundation or the UK's Economic and Social Research Council (ESRC), as well as universities, have much stricter ethical guidelines than in the past. It is unlikely that covert research involving the deception of subjects would be officially sanctioned today. Yet Humphreys was one of the first sociologists to study this aspect of social life, and his account was a humane treatment of the subject going well beyond the existing stock of knowledge.

> **THINKING CRITICALLY**
>
> Humphreys later said that, were he to undertake the study again, he would not trace number-plates or go to people's homes. But how else could information on the men's lives and backgrounds be obtained legitimately? For instance, do you think the subjects would be prepared to be interviewed? Are there any other ways of gathering the data?

Science and sociological research

Tearoom Trade is a good example of the kind of questions that sociologists ask. In looking at the surprising activities that occur in public toilets, Humphreys explored how society works in ways that are different from the official or public versions. He also found that something we take to be obvious – a public toilet – is actually *socially constructed*, depending on how people use it. Social constructionism is a perspective which begins from the premise that social reality is – to varying degrees – the product of interactions between individuals and groups, not something that we should take as 'natural' (see chapter 8, 'Social Interaction and Daily Life', and chapter 5, 'The Environment'). In this case, what most people believed to be a public building with an obvious function was, for a particular group, *primarily* a venue for the pursuit of sexual activity.

The issues that concern sociologists, both in their theorizing and in their research, are often similar to those that worry other people. After all, sociologists are members of society too. Good research should help us to understand social life better and, quite often, to view it in new ways. Research can take us by surprise, both in the questions it asks and in the findings it reports, and in this way sociology frequently runs counter to our 'common-sense' beliefs. What are the circumstances in which ethnic or sexual minorities live? Why does large-scale poverty still exist alongside the immense personal wealth of a small minority? What effects will the widespread and increasing reliance on the Internet have on all our lives? Sociologists try to provide answers to these and many other questions. Their findings are by no means final, as society is always in a process of change. Nevertheless, it is the aim of sociological theorizing and research to break away from speculation and to base our understanding on evidence. Good sociology makes its research questions as precise as possible and seeks to gather factual evidence before reaching general conclusions. To achieve these aims, we must select the most useful research methods to use for a given study and know how best to analyse the results.

Sociologists often ask empirical or factual questions. For example, what kinds of occupation and domestic arrangement are most common among men who use the tearooms? What proportion of tearoom participants do the police arrest? Even factual questions of this kind can be difficult to answer. There are no official statistics on 'tearooms', as these do not exist in official or government documents. Similarly, official crime statistics have been found to be of dubious value in revealing the real level of criminal activity in society. Researchers who study crime say that police-recorded crime figures are just the visible tip of a much larger 'iceberg' of crime and that only about half of all serious crimes are reported to the police. Some criminal activities may not be seen by their victims as 'crimes' at all (see chapter 20, 'Crime and Deviance', for a discussion of crime statistics).

Factual information about one national society will not tell us whether we are dealing with an unusual case or a more general set of social influences. Hence, sociologists often ask comparative questions, relating findings from one society to another social context or using contrasting examples drawn from different societies across the world. There are significant differences, for example, between the social and legal systems of Turkey, Italy and South Africa. A typical

Law enforcement exists in all countries, but comparative empirical studies of police forces are needed to reveal their similarities and differences.

comparative question might be: how much do patterns of criminal behaviour and law enforcement vary between these three countries? Answering this question might lead us to others, such as how did systems of law enforcement develop over time and how similar or different are the penal regimes in these countries?

In sociology, we need to compare not only existing societies but also the present and past to gain a better understanding of social development. In this case we ask historical or developmental questions: how did we get from there to here? To understand the nature of the modern world, we have to look at previous forms of society and processes of social change. Thus we can investigate how the first prisons originated and what they are like today, tracing key periods or phases of change in this development. Doing so provides us with a good part of an explanation.

Sociological research does not consist of just collecting facts, however important and interesting they may be. It is a truism in sociology that 'the facts don't speak for themselves'; they always need to be interpreted. This means we must learn how to ask theoretical questions concerned with *why* things happen the way they do. Some sociologists work primarily on empirical questions, but, unless their research is guided by some knowledge of theory, their findings are unlikely to be particularly illuminating (see table 2.1). At the same time, sociologists do not pursue theoretical knowledge for its own sake, as this runs the risk of falling into pure speculation far removed from the evidence. Reliable sociological knowledge can therefore be seen as essentially theoretical-empirical in character. The combination of empirical research alongside theorizing is a key defining characteristic of all scientific disciplines, and sociology is no exception.

Table 2.1 The sociologist's line of questioning		
Factual question	What happened?	It is reported that some men in the UK use Internet chatrooms to find male sexual partners.
Comparative question	Did this happen everywhere?	Is this a widespread phenomenon, or is it occurring only in Britain? Is the behaviour restricted to gay men?
Developmental question	Has this happened over time?	What methods have men used in the past to meet other men for sex? Are they essentially similar to or different from the use of chatrooms?
Theoretical question	What underlies this phenomenon?	Why are men now using chatrooms rather than older methods? What factors should we look at that might explain this changing behaviour?

What is 'science' anyway?

As we saw in chapter 1, in the early nineteenth century, Auguste Comte described sociology as an emerging science that should adopt the successful methods of the natural sciences such as physics and chemistry. Durkheim, Marx and other founders also saw sociology as a scientific subject, but today many sociologists are not so sure. Can and should social life be studied in a scientific way? Are Laud Humphreys' observations on the tearooms really scientific? And what is 'science' anyway? Surprisingly, perhaps, there is no simple or agreed answer to that last question. The best way to understand why is to take a whistle-stop tour of some key arguments from studies in the philosophy and history of science. This will help us to understand better the academic status of sociology.

Comte argued that the positive stage of human knowledge produced reliable, valid knowledge that would, ultimately, enable progressive interventions into nature and society. Science is superior to all previous routes to knowledge and a prerequisite for development in the modern world. For Comte, science is also an essentially unitary endeavour. That is, all scientific subjects use a similar method, which means that the social and natural sciences are not fundamentally different. Science begins with observation and the collection of data, then proceeds to look for patterns within the observed facts, before moving on to develop general theories which provide explanations of the evidence. This 'ground-up' process of research is known as induction. However, Comte's argument is rooted in a rather idealized picture of science that is not based on the actual practice of scientists. From the early twentieth century, this inductive description of science began to be overturned.

Positivism and the philosophy of science

In 1920s Austria, an influential group of philosophers, known as the Vienna Circle, set out important modifications to Comte's positivist position. In particular, they tried to clarify what counts as 'science' and why the statements scientists make about the world can be accepted as 'true'. They focused on logic and deductive reasoning rather than simple induction, and their approach was described as logical positivism. This recognized that scientists do not go around collecting data and later try to explain what they find (inductive method). Rather, they *begin* by formulating hypotheses – clearly framed questions or statements about some aspect of reality – and then set out to collect empirical evidence that will verify these (hypothetico-deductive method).

To be scientifically valid, they argued, scientific statements and theories always have to be tested against evidence. This is unlike other forms of 'knowledge'. For example, it is just not possible to say that any particular moral standpoint on poverty or an aesthetic judgement about what is beautiful is 'true', however much we debate these subjects. Statements in these fields do not uncover truths about the world and are therefore scientifically meaningless.

Logical positivists adopt a correspondence theory of truth which accepts statements as true only where they 'correspond' exactly with what exists in the real world. Hence the key to valid knowledge is empirical verification, and it is the job of scientists constantly to seek out evidence which supports their statements. Logical positivism was highly influential in defining what constitutes a scientific approach to knowledge. But by the late 1930s its central principle of verification was under attack.

Sir Karl Popper (1902–44), a former member of the Vienna Circle, provided the most systematic critique of logical positivism. Popper argued that verification is not a powerful principle, as almost any theory, however unrealistic, can find *some* evidence that supports its arguments and verification can never definitively settle theoretical disputes. A much stronger principle is disconfirmation. Broad theories should lead to hypotheses which are, in principle at least, capable of being falsified. Scientists then actively seek out cases that disconfirm or falsify their own hypotheses. In this way, one disconfirming case can tell us much more about the world than thousands of instances of verification ever could (Delanty 1997: 31–2). For instance, we may hypothesize that 'all swans are white' and set out to verify this statement. Yet, however many white swans we observe, the hypothesis can never be proved true because non-white swans *might* still exist. But we need to find only a single black swan in order conclusively to falsify our hypothesis and find a simple truth about the world – not all swans are white.

Popper suggests that the best hypotheses are not cautious ones but 'bold conjectures' which offer the potential for significant knowledge gains. Yet most scientific knowledge is never accepted as universally 'true', as it is always open (potentially) to being falsified. In fifty years' time all black swans may have died out, making our accepted truth about swans (they're not all white) incorrect. All we can say is that the currently accepted scientific theories and explanations are the best we have because they have not been conclusively falsified – yet. This might seem a weak description of science, unlike common-sense notions of scientific

Sir Karl Popper (1902–44) criticized social scientific theories such as Marxism and Freudian psychoanalysis, which offer no criteria for falsification. For Popper, all such theories are essentially unscientific. No amount of verification can make for a solid scientific theory – for instance, no matter how many white swans a researcher might find, it does not rule out the possibility of the existence of a black swan.

laws as being universally true. The essentially 'open' character of scientific knowledge and the necessary open-mindedness of scientists are both crucial to Popper's vision of science. But, in the 1960s and 1970s, both were called into question by the detailed work of historians of science.

Lessons from the history of science

Probably the most important critique of Popper's model of science as an open enterprise remains Thomas Kuhn's (1962) *The Structure of Scientific Revolutions*. Kuhn was less interested in what philosophers thought science *should* be like and more concerned with what we can learn from the real history and development of science and its theories. He argued that the history of natural sciences shows that scientists tend to work within the overall assumptions of a particular theoretical framework which he terms a paradigm, such as Newtonian mechanics in physics, which led scientists accurately to calculate planetary orbits and much more throughout the eighteenth and nineteenth centuries. Scientists become committed to expanding 'their' paradigm and practise a problem-solving form of 'normal science', which expands the evidence base of the paradigm and teaches its assumptions to new scientists without ever seriously challenging it. Normal science accounts for the bulk of all scientific work.

Over time, anomalous findings occur that do not 'fit' into the existing paradigm. In the case of Newtonian mechanics, a crucial failure was the paradigm's inability to explain the movement of light. Yet, rather than these leading to challenges to the existing paradigm, scientists may query the data or the experiments that produced them. In short, while Popper expected scientists to work in an open-minded way, Kuhn found that, in practice, they resolutely defended their paradigms, dismissing contrary evidence and shaking off quite legitimate challenges (Benton and Craib 2001: 58–61). Why would they do this? The answer is a sociological one. Science is not an isolated enterprise but takes place within communities of scholars with a shared interest in defending the paradigms within which they have built careers and reputations and earned a high status.

However, Kuhn argues that, in some periods, younger scientists, less bound into and committed to a specific paradigm, may work on emerging anomalies and, in order to account for them, are led to devise new theories and build alternative paradigms. In the early twentieth century, a revolutionary new theory was developed – Einstein's theory of relativity – which had a satisfactory explanation for the motion of light. The new theory became the centre of a new paradigm, which enabled 'normal science' to proceed again (Weinberg 1998). Kuhn calls this move a period of 'revolutionary science', when there is a real possibility of a paradigm shift. But this process is not the kind of cumulative scientific progress Popper had in mind. Kuhn is at pains to point out that, even where a new paradigm develops, this does not occur because the old one was conclusively falsified. Old and new paradigms are usually incommensurate; they just cannot be compared. Instead, as more and more scientists become attracted to the new paradigm, the old one simply withers away for lack of interest. On this account, real scientific practice diverges radically from all the pure methodologies proposed by philosophers.

An even more radical position was taken by Paul Feyerabend, who was interested in how significant scientific discoveries were achieved. The philosophy of science suggests that these ought to be the outcome of strict adherence to proper scientific methods and years of painstaking research. However, Feyerabend argues this is not the case. In fact, the episodes he describes most often came about by chance or when scientists deviated from established scientific practice, or even by laypeople making discoveries outside the scientific community altogether. In the appropriately titled book *Against Method* (1975), he concludes that, contrary to all philosophical notions of science as both a method and a form of logic, history shows us that there is only one proven methodological principle: 'anything goes'. Scientific discoveries have been made in all sorts of ways, and forcing researchers to stick within one set of rules stunts progress rather than encouraging it. Thus Feyerabend declares himself to be an 'epistemological anarchist' in relation to scientific method.

Scientific sociology?

What do the debates on the nature of science tell us about the status of sociology? First, science cannot be defined by any one method or a fixed set of methodological rules. In

"I'm a social scientist, Michael. That means I can't explain electricity or anything like that, but if you ever want to know about people I'm the man."

practice, scientists adopt a variety of methods in their pursuit of knowledge. As Ray Pawson argues (2013: xi):

> If science was merely a matter of routine and compunction, of compliance and rule following, it would be pre-programmed – done already or awaiting completion in the pipeline. In reality, scientific research undergoes constant change as fresh discoveries are made and new fields open up. Accordingly, methodological rules cannot be carved in stone . . . Each time the researcher dreams up a project, responds to a tender, enters the field, draws conclusions, makes observations and pens a paper, that individual will seed minute modifications to the methodological rules.

Pawson's argument applies to both natural and social sciences, though he does not accept Feyerabend's anarchistic conclusion. Methodological rules *are* always in a process of development, but they are not irrelevant altogether.

Second, although there is no single scientific method or single methodological principle (which have been sought by philosophers), science does involve certain key elements, including theoretical thinking and the logical assessment of arguments, systematic empirical investigation, rigorous analysis of data, and a commitment to publish research findings to develop a body of cumulative knowledge. This means that the social disciplines, sociology and psychology among them, must be considered scientific because both quantitative and qualitative research involves all of these elements.

However, third, we should not expect sociologists to adopt exactly the same methods of investigation as the natural sciences. This is because people, social groups and societies are, in significant ways, very different from the other animals and events in the physical world. In particular, humans are self-aware beings who confer meaning and purpose on what they do. We cannot even *describe* social life accurately unless we first grasp the meanings that people apply to their actions. For instance, to describe a death as a 'suicide' means knowing what the person in question was intending when they died. If a person steps in front of a car and is killed, objective observation may suggest suicide, but this can only be established if we know that their action was not accidental. Intention and meaning are crucial explanatory features of human action, which sociologists cannot ignore if their accounts are to be valid.

Fourth, in acknowledging this significant difference between the social and natural sciences, it may appear that sociologists are at a distinct disadvantage. Trying to 'get inside the mind' of an individual is notoriously problematic and seems like an added complication for researchers. Yet there may be a major benefit too. Sociologists are able to ask questions directly of those they study – other human beings – and get responses they and other researchers understand. Biologists, for instance, have no such direct communication with the animals whose behaviour they try to interpret. The opportunity to converse with research participants who can confirm or criticize the researcher's interpretation means that sociological findings are, potentially, more *reliable* (different researchers would arrive at the same results) and *valid* (the research actually measures what it is supposed to) than many in the natural sciences.

At the same time, studying human beings brings problems that do not trouble natural scientists. People who are aware that their activities are being scrutinized may alter their usual behaviour and opinions, thus invalidating the researcher's conclusions. Participants may consciously or unconsciously manage the presentation of their self and even try to 'assist' the researcher by providing the responses they think are being sought. Sociologists must be aware of these problems and devise strategies to counter them. Scientists studying the behaviour of chemicals or frogs do not have to deal with this additional problem.

To conclude, we can agree with philosophers of science that there are criteria which distinguish scientific work from other types of inquiry, though these criteria are not fixed but change over time alongside ongoing research programmes and studies. We can also agree with historians that science takes place within communities and broad theoretical frameworks or paradigms. As chapter 3 shows, sociology has moved forward through competitive struggles between rival perspectives and, over time, the number of perspectives and theoretical syntheses has increased. Yet, in spite of this variety and competition, and against the anarchist position taken by Feyerabend, there remains a logic to the process of research that is common across the majority of sociological studies, and these are outlined in the next section.

> **THINKING CRITICALLY**
>
> Look back at Laud Humphreys' study. Does this fulfil the criteria of 'science' referred to above? If you used his methods to carry out a similar study today, would you be likely to get the same or different results? What does this mean for the study's status?

The research process

Carrying out research in sociology involves a number of steps, leading from identifying a research problem and devising a methodology right through to publishing the findings and responding to criticisms from colleagues (see figure 2.1). However, all research begins with the desire to know or understand better some aspect of the social world.

Defining the problem

All research starts from a problem or question about social life. This is sometimes an area of factual ignorance: we may simply wish to improve our knowledge about certain institutions, social processes or cultures. A researcher might set out to answer questions such as 'What proportion of the population today holds strong religious beliefs?' or 'How far does the economic position of women still lag behind that of men?' Such questions are necessary and useful.

However, the best sociological research begins with problems that are also puzzles. A puzzle is not just a lack of information but a *gap in our understanding*. Much of the skill in producing worthwhile sociological research consists in correctly identifying puzzles. Rather than simply answering the question 'What is going on here?', puzzle-solving research tries to contribute to our understanding of *why* events happen as they do. Thus we might ask: 'What accounts for the decline in the proportions of the population voting in elections in recent years?' 'Why are women poorly represented in high-status jobs?' These questions are not simple factual questions but require us to go a stage further to provide *explanations* for the evidence we find.

It is important to remember that no piece of research stands alone. Research problems arise as part of ongoing work, and one research project may easily lead to another because it raises issues the researcher had not previously considered. A sociologist may also discover puzzles by reading the work of other researchers in books and professional journals or by being aware of specific trends in society.

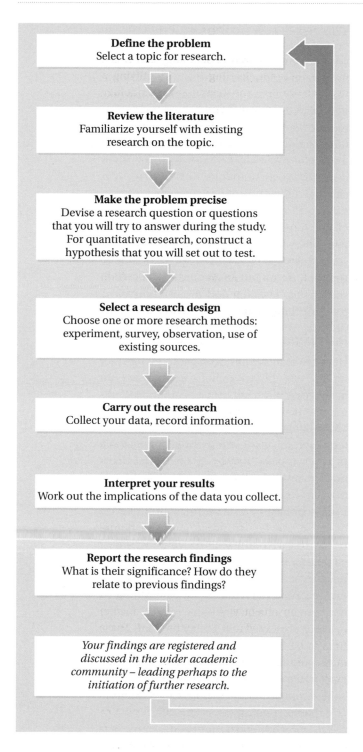

Define the problem
Select a topic for research.

Review the literature
Familiarize yourself with existing research on the topic.

Make the problem precise
Devise a research question or questions that you will try to answer during the study. For quantitative research, construct a hypothesis that you will set out to test.

Select a research design
Choose one or more research methods: experiment, survey, observation, use of existing sources.

Carry out the research
Collect your data, record information.

Interpret your results
Work out the implications of the data you collect.

Report the research findings
What is their significance? How do they relate to previous findings?

Your findings are registered and discussed in the wider academic community – leading perhaps to the initiation of further research.

Figure 2.1 Steps in the research process

Reviewing existing evidence

Once the problem is identified, the next step is usually to review the available evidence in a particular field, which means conducting a review of the existing literature. It could be that previous research has already satisfactorily answered our question and there is no need to repeat the process. But, if not, the sociologist will need to sift through whatever related research does exist to see how useful it is for their purpose. Have previous researchers spotted the same puzzle? How have they tried to resolve it? What aspects of the problem have their studies left unanalysed? Drawing upon others' ideas helps the sociologist to clarify the issues that might be raised and the methods that might be used in their own research. Reviewing the literature is an essential step that helps to avoid unnecessary duplication and repetition, and it can also point up where gaps in our knowledge still exist.

Making the problem precise

A third stage involves working out a clear formulation of the research problem. If relevant literature already exists, the researcher might return from the library with a good idea of how the problem should be approached. Hunches about the nature of the problem can sometimes be turned into research questions, which, though rooted in an educated guess about what is going on, clearly state this in precise language. If the study is to be effective, research questions must be formulated in such a way that the empirical material gathered will provide evidence that either supports or challenges them. Studies involving the collection and analysis of numerical data, such as social surveys, tend to favour statistical testing as a method of verifying or falsifying clearly stated hypotheses, while qualitative research will often be exploratory in character and allow research questions to emerge during the research process itself.

Working out a design

The researcher must then decide just how the research materials are to be collected. A range of different research methods exists, and which one is chosen depends on the overall objective of the study, as well as on which aspects of behaviour are to be analysed. For some purposes, a social survey (in which questionnaires are normally used) might be suitable, especially where we need to gather a large quantity of data. In other circumstances, if we want to study small social groups in great detail, interviews or an observational study might be more appropriate. We shall learn more about these and other research methods later in this chapter.

Conducting the research

At the point of proceeding with the research, unforeseen practical difficulties can crop up, and very often do. For example, it might prove impossible to contact some of those to whom questionnaires are to be sent or those people the researcher wishes to interview. A business firm or school may be unwilling to let the researcher carry out the work they had planned due to concerns about sensitive information being leaked. Difficulties such as this could result in bias, as the researcher may be able to gain access only to a partial sample, which subsequently leads to a false overall result. For example, if the researcher is studying how business corporations have complied with equal opportunities programmes for disabled people, companies that have not complied may not want to be studied, but omitting them will result in a systematic bias in the study's findings.

Bias can enter the research process in other ways too. For example, if a study is based on surveys of participants' views, the researcher may, even unwittingly, push the discussion in a particular direction, such as asking leading questions that follow their own particular viewpoint (as the Doonesbury cartoon on p. 47 shows). Alternatively, interviewees may evade a question that they just do not want to answer. The use of questionnaires with fixed wording can help to reduce interview bias, but it will not eliminate it entirely. Another source of bias occurs when *potential* participants in a survey, such as a distributed voluntary questionnaire, decide that they do not want to take part. This is known as *non-response bias*, and, as a general rule, the higher the proportion of non-responses in the sample, the more likely it is that the survey of those who *do* take part will be skewed. Even if every attempt is made to reduce bias in surveys, the observations that sociologists make in carrying out a piece of research are likely to reflect their own cultural assumptions. This *observer bias* can be difficult and perhaps even impossible to eliminate, as sociologists – believe it or not – are human beings and members of particular societies even before they become sociologists! Later in this chapter we look at some of the other pitfalls and difficulties of sociological research and discuss how these can be avoided.

Interpreting and reporting the findings

Once the material has been gathered together for analysis, the researcher's troubles are not over – they may be only just beginning! Working out the implications of the data collected and relating these back to the research problem are rarely easy. While it may be possible to reach a clear answer to the initial questions, many investigations are, in the end, less than fully conclusive. The research findings, usually published in a report, journal article or book, provide an account of the nature of the research and seek to justify whatever conclusions are drawn. This is a final stage only in terms of the individual research project. Most reports also indicate questions that remain unanswered and suggest further research that might profitably be done in the future. All individual investigations are part of the continuing process of research which takes place within the international sociological community. Other scholars have built on Humphreys' findings.

The preceding sequence of steps is a simplified version of what happens in actual research projects (see figure 2.1). In real-world research, these stages rarely succeed each other so neatly and there is almost always a certain amount of 'muddling through'. The difference is a bit like that between following

2.1 Reading and interpreting tables

Table 2.2 Internet users in the European Union, selected countries, 2000–2015

	Population (2015 est.)	Internet users, latest data	Penetration (% population)	User growth (%, 2000–10)	Users % of EU
Bulgaria	7,202,198	**4,083,950**	56.7	689.5	1.0
Czech Republic	10,538,275	**8,400,059**	79.7	568.1	2.1
Denmark	5,659,715	**5,432,760**	96.0	143.6	1.3
Finland	5,471,753	**5,117,600**	93.5	132.5	1.3
France	66,132,169	**55,429,382**	83.8	425.0	13.8
Germany	81,174,000	**71,727,551**	88.4	171.3	17.8
Greece	10,812,467	**6,834,560**	63.2	397.1	1.7
Italy	60,795,612	**37,668,891**	62.0	127.5	9.3
Latvia	1,986,096	**1,628,854**	82.0	902.3	0.4
Netherlands	16,900,726	**16,143,879**	95.5	281.3	4.0
Poland	38,005,614	**25,666,238**	67.5	701.8	6.4
Portugal	10,374,822	**7,015,519**	67.6	106.8	1.7
Romania	19,861,408	**11,178,477**	56.3	873.3	2.8
Slovakia	5,421,349	**4,507,849**	83.1	525.2	1.1
Sweden	9,747,355	**9,216,226**	94.6	107.5	2.3
United Kingdom	64,767,115	**59,333,154**	91.6	234.0	14.7
European Union	**507,970,816**	**402,937,674**	**79.3**	**257.8**	**100.0**

Notes: (1) The European Union Internet Statistics were updated to 30 November 2015. (2) Population is based mainly on data from Eurostats. (3) The Internet usage numbers come from various sources, mainly from data published by Nielsen Online, ITU, GfK, local agencies and other trustworthy sources.
Source: www.internetworldstats.com/stats9.htm. Copyright © 2015, Miniwatts Marketing Group. All rights reserved.

You will often come across tables when reading sociological literature and research studies. They can appear quite complex but are actually easy to decipher if you follow the basic steps listed below. With practice, reading them will become automatic. Do not succumb to the temptation to skip over tables; they contain information in concentrated form which can be read more quickly than would be possible if expressed in words. In becoming skilled in the interpretation of tables, you will be able to check how far the evidence used justifies the conclusions drawn by a researcher, and in this way you will be developing a critical approach to your reading.

1 Read the title in full. Tables frequently have long titles, which represent an attempt by the researcher to state accurately the nature of the information conveyed. The title of table 2.2 gives first the *subject* of the data, second the fact that the table provides a *date* and material for *comparison*, and third the fact that data are given for a *limited number* of countries.

2 Look for explanatory comments, or notes, about the data. Notes may say *how* the material was collected or *why* it is displayed in a particular way. Many of the tables used throughout this book contain explanatory notes. If the data have not been gathered by the researcher but are based on findings

originally reported elsewhere, a *source* will be included. The source sometimes gives you some insight into how *reliable* the information is likely to be, as well as showing where to find the *original data*. In table 2.2, the notes make clear that the data have been collated from several different sources.

3 Read the headings along the top and left-hand side of the table. (Sometimes tables are arranged with 'headings' at the foot rather than the top.) These tell you *what type of information* is contained in each row and column. In reading the table, keep in mind each set of headings as you scan the figures. In our example, the headings on the left give the countries involved, while those at the top refer to the national comparative figures in numbers and percentages.

4 Identify the units used. The figures in the body of the table may represent cases, percentages, averages or other measures. Sometimes it may be helpful to convert the figures to a form more useful to you: if percentages are not provided, for example, it may be worth calculating them for yourself.

5 Consider the conclusions that might be reached from the information in the table. Most tables are discussed by the author, and what he or she has to say should of course be borne in mind. But you should also ask *what further issues or questions could be suggested* by the data.

Some interesting trends can be seen from the figures in our table. First, the level of Internet penetration – Internet users as a percentage of the national population – varies widely across the countries of the European Union. Not much more than half of the Romanian (56.3%) and Bulgarian (56.7%) population were Internet users compared with more than 95% in Denmark and the Netherlands. Second, Internet use in the EU has increased dramatically in just one decade (2000–10), by 257.8%. Third, In the same period, many Eastern European countries, such as Latvia, the Czech Republic, Poland and Slovakia, have seen Internet usage grow by well above the EU average. In the case of Latvia, the increase has been over 900% in ten years. We might assume this is because these countries began the decade from a very low base, which has grown as they have become integrated within the structures of the European Community and start to 'catch up' to the average level. Clearly, more research will be needed to validate our assumptions, which is just one example of the way research tends to lead to more research as our knowledge of society and social development grows.

> **THINKING CRITICALLY**
>
> What research questions might arise from table 2.2? For example, did you find anything surprising? How could we find out *why* Italy and Portugal have been overtaken by the Czech Republic, Latvia, Poland and Slovakia in Internet penetration? Construct a research question that might lead to an explanation for this trend.

a recipe in a cookbook and the actual process of cooking a meal. People who are experienced cooks often do not work from recipes at all, yet their food may be better than that cooked by those who do. As Feyerabend saw, following a rigid set of stages can be unduly restrictive, and many outstanding pieces of sociological research have not followed this strict sequence. However, most of the steps discussed above would be in there somewhere.

Understanding cause and effect

One of the main problems to be tackled in research methods is the analysis of cause and effect, especially in quantitative research which is based on statistical testing. A causal relationship between two events or situations is an association in which one event or situation produces another. If the handbrake is released in a car that is parked on a hill, the car will roll down the incline, gathering speed

DOONESBURY

by Garry Trudeau

progressively as it does so. Taking the brake off was the immediate cause of this event, and the reasons for this can readily be understood by reference to the physical principles involved. Like natural science, sociology depends on the assumption that all events have causes. Social life is *not* a random array of occurrences happening without rhyme or reason. One of the main tasks of sociological research – in combination with theoretical thinking – is to identify causes and effects.

Causation and correlation

Causation cannot be directly inferred from correlation. Correlation means the existence of a regular relationship between two sets of occurrences or variables. A variable is any dimension along which individuals or groups vary. Age, gender, ethnicity, income and social-class position are among the many variables that sociologists study. It might seem, when two variables are found to be closely correlated, as though one must be the cause of the other. However, this is very often not the case. Many correlations exist without any corresponding causal relationship between the variables involved. For example, over the period since the Second World War, a strong correlation can be found between the decline in pipe-smoking and the decrease in the number of people who regularly go to the cinema. Clearly one change does not cause the other, and we would find it difficult to discover even a remote causal connection between them. There are other instances in which it is not quite so obvious that an observed correlation does not imply a causal relationship. Such correlations are traps for the unwary and easily lead to questionable or false conclusions.

In his classic work of 1897, *Suicide* (discussed in chapter 1), Emile Durkheim found a correlation between rates of suicide and the seasons of the year: levels of suicide increased progressively from January to around June or July and then declined over the remainder of the year. It might be supposed that this demonstrates that temperature or climatic change is *causally related* to the propensity of individuals to commit suicide. We might perhaps surmise that, as temperatures increase, people become more impulsive and hot-headed, leading to higher suicide rates. However, the causal relationship here has nothing to do *directly* with temperature or climate at all. In spring and summer, most people engage in a more intensive social life than they do in the winter months. Those who are isolated or unhappy tend to experience an intensification of these feelings as the activity level of other people around them rises. Hence they are likely to experience acute suicidal tendencies more in the spring and summer than they do in autumn and winter, when the pace of social activity slackens. This is another example of the meaningful character of human life which sociologists must understand. We always have to be on our guard, both in assessing whether

47

correlation involves causation and in deciding in which direction causal relations run.

Causal mechanisms

Working out the causal connections involved in identified correlations is often a difficult process. For instance, there is a strong correlation in modern societies between level of educational achievement and occupational success. The better the grades an individual gets in school, the better paid the job they are likely to get when they leave. What explains this correlation? Research tends to show that it is not school experience itself; levels of educational attainment are influenced much more by the type of home from which the person comes. Children from better-off homes, whose parents take a strong interest in their learning, where books are abundant and a place to study exists, are more likely to do well than those coming from poorer homes where these aspects are lacking. The causal mechanisms here are the attitudes of parents towards their children, together with the facilities for learning that the home provides.

Causal connections in sociology should not be understood in too mechanical a way. The attitudes people have and their subjective reasons for acting as they do are causal factors in relationships between variables in social life, and qualitative research is required if we are to gain the kind of in-depth understanding of how individuals interpret their world. Max Weber was quite clear that all sociological work must eventually be explicable at this individual and interactional level, which is where the meaningfulness of social life is produced.

 A discussion of some recent 'critical realist' approaches which focus on establishing causal mechanisms in social life can be found in chapter 5, 'The Environment'.

Controls

In quantitative research, assessing the cause or causes that explain a correlation usually involves distinguishing independent from dependent variables. An independent variable is one that produces an effect on another variable. The variable affected is called the dependent variable. In the example above, academic achievement is the independent variable and occupational income the dependent variable. The distinction refers to the direction of the causal relation. However, the same factor may be an independent variable in one study and a dependent variable in another. It depends on what causal processes are being analysed. If we were looking at the effects of differences in occupational income on people's lifestyles, then occupational income would be the independent variable rather than the dependent one.

To find out whether a correlation between variables is a causal connection, we can use controls, which means we hold some variables constant in order to look at the effects of others. By doing this, we are able to judge between explanations of observed correlations, separating causal from non-causal relationships. Researchers studying child development claim there is a causal connection between maternal deprivation in infancy – where an infant is separated from the mother for a long period, such as during a long hospital stay – and serious personality problems in adulthood. We could test this by trying to control, or 'screen out', other possible influences that might explain the proposed causal connection.

For example, is *maternal* deprivation the crucial factor in child development or could it be deprivation from a care-giver, regardless of who that may be? To investigate this, we would compare cases where children were deprived of regular care from anyone with other cases in which children were separated from their mothers *but* still received care from someone else. If the first group developed severe personality difficulties but the second group did not, we would suspect that regular care from *someone* is what matters, regardless of whether that person is the mother. In fact, children do seem to prosper as long as they have a loving, stable relationship with someone caring for them, though that does not necessarily have to be the biological mother.

Identifying causes

A good example of how difficult it is to be sure of the causal relations involved in a correlation is given by the long history of studies of smoking and lung cancer. Research has consistently demonstrated a strong correlation between these two. Smokers are more likely to contract lung cancer than non-smokers and very heavy smokers are more likely to do so than light

Sociologists may be interested in why some young Muslims in the UK, but not others, wear headscarves. However, it can be difficult to establish a causal relationship between the different factors involved.

smokers. The correlation can also be expressed the other way around. A high proportion of those who have lung cancer are smokers or have smoked for long periods in the past. There have been so many studies confirming these correlations that today it is generally accepted that a causal link is involved, but the *exact* causal mechanism is thus far largely unknown.

However much correlational work is done on any issue, there always remains some doubt about the possible causal relationship. Other interpretations of the correlation are at least theoretically possible. It has been proposed, for instance, that people who are predisposed to lung cancer are also predisposed to smoke. On this view, it is not smoking *per se* that causes lung cancer but, rather, some in-built biological disposition to both smoking and cancer. Identifying causal relationships is normally guided by previous research into the subject at hand. If we do not have some reasonable idea beforehand of the causal mechanisms involved in a correlation, we would probably find it very difficult to discover what the real causal connections are. In short, we would not know what to test *for*.

Sociological research methods

A common distinction is often made in sociology between quantitative and qualitative research methods and traditions. The former are associated with functionalism and positivism, the latter with interactionism and the search for meanings and understanding. As the term suggests, quantitative methods try to *measure* social phenomena and will use mathematical models and, often, statistical analysis to explain them. Qualitative methods attempt to gather detailed, rich data, allowing for an in-depth understanding of individual actions within the context of social life. As a rough-and-ready guide to a diverse range of sociological research methods, this distinction is a useful starting point. Many sociologists do tend to specialize or even favour one tradition

over the other. However, there is a danger that the two traditions will be seen as opposing 'camps' with entirely different approaches to research. This would not be very productive, nor does it adequately describe the situation that exists.

In fact, many research projects use mixed methods – both quantitative and qualitative – in order to gain a more comprehensive and rounded understanding and explanation of the subject being studied. The findings from separate quantitative and qualitative studies can also be combined. For example, some feminist sociologists favour qualitative methods, which, they argue, allow the authentic voices of women to be heard in ways that quantitative studies just cannot match. This latter point is undoubtedly correct. But without quantitative studies it would not have been possible to measure the full extent of gender inequality in society or to set those individual women's voices into a wider societal context. Sociologists have to be prepared to use the most appropriate methods for the specific questions they want to answer.

Next, we look at some of the various research methods sociologists commonly employ in their work (see table 2.3).

Ethnography

The approach of both Laud Humphreys and Li and his colleagues in China were forms of ethnography, a type of fieldwork, or first-hand study of people, using participant observation and/or interviews as the main research methods. Here, the investigator hangs out, works or lives with a group, organization or community and sometimes plays a direct part in their activities. Where it is successful, ethnography provides information on the behaviour of people in groups, organizations and communities as well as on how those people understand their own behaviour. Once we see how things look from inside a given group, we are likely to gain a better understanding not only of that group but also of social processes that transcend the

Table 2.3   Four widely used methods in sociological research

Research method	Strengths	Limitations
Fieldwork	Usually generates richer and more in-depth information than other methods.	Only successful with smaller groups or communities.
	Ethnography can provide a better understanding of social processes.	Findings might apply only to the groups studied. Not easy to generalize on the basis of a single fieldwork study.
Surveys	Make possible the efficient collection of data on large numbers of people.	The material gathered may be superficial; where a questionnaire is highly standardized, important differences between respondents' viewpoints may be glossed over.
	Allow for precise comparisons to be made between the answers of respondents.	Responses may be what people profess to believe rather than what they actually believe.
Experiments	The influence of specific variables can be controlled by the investigator.	Many aspects of social life cannot be brought into the laboratory.
	Are usually easier for subsequent researchers to repeat.	The responses of those studied may be affected by their experimental situation.
Documentary research	Can provide source of in-depth materials as well as data on large numbers, depending on the type of documents studied.	The researcher is dependent on the sources that exist, which may be partial.
	Is often essential when a study is either wholly historical or has a defined historical dimension.	The sources may be difficult to interpret in terms of how far they represent real tendencies, as in the case of some official statistics.

situation under study. Ethnography is one of a number of qualitative research methods used in sociology that aim to gain an in-depth knowledge and understanding of relatively small-scale social phenomena.

In the traditional works of ethnography, accounts were presented without much information about the researchers themselves being included, as it was thought that an ethnographer could present objective pictures of the societies they studied. More recently, though, ethnographers have increasingly tended to talk about themselves and the nature of their connection to the people under study. Sometimes this reflexivity might be a matter of trying to consider how one's own ethnicity, class or gender has influenced or affected the work, or how the power differences between

In fieldwork, sociologists have to get close to the communities they are studying, but not so close that they lose their outsider's relatively detached eye.

observer and observed have distorted the dialogue between them.

Ethnographic studies also have other major limitations. Only fairly small groups or communities can be studied, and much depends on the skill of the individual researcher in gaining the confidence of the individuals involved. Without this skill, the research is unlikely to get off the ground at all. The reverse is also possible. A researcher could begin to identify so closely with the group that he or she becomes too much of an 'insider' and loses the perspective of an outside observer. When so much

rests on the skills of a single individual the study becomes hard to replicate, and thus its reliability may be called into question.

Surveys

Interpreting field studies usually involves problems of generalization. Since only a small number of people are under study, we cannot be sure that what is found in one context will apply in another, or even that two researchers would come to the same conclusions when studying the same group. This is usually less of a problem in large-scale survey research. In a survey, questionnaires are either sent out or administered directly in interviews to a selected group of people – sometimes as many as several thousand. Sociologists refer to this group of people, whatever its size, as a population. While ethnographic work is well suited to in-depth studies of small slices of social life, survey research tends to produce information that is less detailed but can usually be applied over a broader area. Surveys are the most widely used type of quantitative research method, allowing social phenomena to be measured and then analysed using mathematical models and statistical techniques.

Many government bodies and private polling agencies make extensive use of surveys to gain knowledge of people's attitudes or voting intentions. These may be conducted through face-to-face interviews, telephone calls, postal questionnaires or, increasingly, online. Whichever method is adopted, the great advantage of surveys is that they allow researchers to collect large amounts of comparable data, which can be manipulated, usually using computer software, to find out whether there are any significant correlations between variables. Creating an accurate picture of the shape, size and diversity of a society's population would be quite impossible without such social survey research.

The questionnaire – standardized, open-ended or semi-structured?

Three types of questionnaire are used in surveys. Some contain a standardized, or fixed-choice, set of questions, to which only a given range of responses is possible – for instance, '*Yes/No/Don't know*' or '*Very likely/Likely/Unlikely/Very unlikely*'. Standardized questionnaires have the advantage that responses are easy to count and compare, since only a small number of categories are involved. On the other hand, because they do not allow for subtleties of opinion or verbal expression, the information they yield is likely to be restricted in scope and can sometimes be misleading.

Other questionnaires are open-ended, giving respondents more opportunity to express their views in their own words rather than limiting them to fixed-choice responses. Open-ended questionnaires typically provide more detailed information than standardized ones, and the researcher can follow up initial answers to probe more deeply into what the respondent thinks and feels. On the other hand, the lack of standardization means that responses are likely to be more difficult to compare statistically, and this limits attempts to draw general conclusions from the study.

A very popular and widely used compromise between these two alternatives is the semi-structured interview questionnaire, which presents *some* standardized questions – the data from which may be analysed statistically – but also includes interview prompts for more in-depth answers and sometimes allows interviewees to stray from the schedule when necessary. Semi-structured interview schedules tend to pursue relevant broad research themes rather than highly specific, researcher-defined questions.

Questionnaire items are normally listed so that a team of interviewers can ask the questions and record responses in the same predetermined order, and all the items must be readily understandable to interviewers and interviewees alike. In the large national surveys undertaken regularly by government agencies and private research organizations, interviews are carried out more or less simultaneously across the whole country. Those who conduct the interviews and those who analyse the results could not do their work effectively if they constantly had to check with each other about ambiguities in the questions or answers.

Questionnaires should also take into consideration the characteristics of respondents. Will they see the point the researcher has in mind in asking a particular question? Have they enough information to answer usefully? Will they answer at all? The terms and concepts used in a questionnaire might be unfamiliar to the respondents. For instance, the question 'What is your marital status?' might baffle some people, and it would be more appropriate to ask, 'Are you single, married, separated, or divorced?' Most surveys are preceded by pilot studies in which just a few people complete a questionnaire in order to pick up just such ambiguities and iron out problems that may not be anticipated by the investigator before the main survey is carried out.

Sociologists also make use of focus groups, previously the preserve of marketing agencies and opinion pollsters. Focus groups are essentially 'group interviews' in which a particular group of individuals – usually between four and ten people – are gathered together to discuss a subject and exchange views. The researcher acts as moderator but also asks specific questions relating to the research study in order to direct the discussion. Focus groups can increase the size of a sample quite easily and, because of their interactive nature, any possible misunderstandings can be clarified, thereby increasing the validity of a study. However, critics point out that the researcher in a focus group is more participant than detached observer and may well influence the responses. There is therefore a danger that participants will perform according to the researcher's expectations.

Sampling

Often sociologists are interested in the characteristics of large numbers of individuals – for example, the political attitudes of the British population as a whole. It would be impossible to study all 62 million or so people directly, so in such situations researchers engage in sampling – concentrating on a small proportion – a sample – of this overall population. One can usually be confident that the results from a population sample, as long as it is properly chosen, can be generalized to the total population. Studies of only 2,000 to 3,000 voters, for instance, can give a very accurate indication of the attitudes and voting intentions of the entire population. But, to achieve such accuracy, a sample must be representative – that is, the group of individuals studied must be typical of the population as a whole. Representative sampling is more complex than it may appear, and statisticians have developed rules for working out the correct size and nature of samples.

A particularly important procedure used to ensure that a sample is representative is random sampling, in which a sample is chosen so that every member of the population has the same probability of being included. The most sophisticated way of obtaining a random sample is to give each member of the population a number and then use a computer to generate a random list from which the sample is derived – for instance, by picking every tenth number.

There are other types of sampling used by sociologists. In some types of research, it may be necessary to use convenience sampling. This means taking your sample from wherever you can! Because convenience sampling is less systematic and rigorous than other types, the results it generates have to be treated with caution. Nonetheless, in applied research, or in studies of hard-to-reach social groups who may be reluctant to come forward – for example, substance users or people who self-harm – it may be the only practical way of gathering an adequate sample. Without convenience sampling, the voices of some social groups may just not get heard. Similarly, snowball sampling, in which existing participants are used to recruit other participants via their own network of contacts and friends, is a tried and tested method of gaining access to a larger sample than would otherwise be the case.

Advantages and disadvantages of surveys

Surveys are widely used in sociological research for several reasons. Responses to questionnaires can be more easily quantified and analysed than material generated by most other research methods; large numbers of people can be studied; and, given sufficient funds, researchers can employ an agency specializing in survey work to collect the responses. The scientific method is the model for this kind of research, as surveys give researchers a statistical measure of what they are studying.

Many sociologists today, however, are critical of the survey method. They argue that an *appearance* of precision can be lent to findings whose accuracy may be dubious, given the relatively shallow nature of most survey responses. Levels of non-response are sometimes high, especially when questionnaires are sent and returned through the mail. It is not uncommon for studies to be published based on results derived from little over half of those in a sample, although normally an effort is made to recontact non-respondents or to substitute other people. Little is known about those who choose not to respond to surveys or refuse to be interviewed, but survey research is often experienced as intrusive and time-consuming.

Experiments

An experiment can be defined as an attempt to test a hypothesis under highly controlled conditions established by the investigator. Experiments are commonplace in the natural sciences and psychology, as they offer major advantages over other research procedures. In an experimental situation the researcher directly controls the circumstances under study. Psychologists examining individual behaviour use laboratory-based experimentation extensively. However, in comparison with these disciplines, the scope for experimentation in sociology is quite severely restricted. Most sociological studies, even those of individual actions, look to investigate the relationship between micro- and macrosocial phenomena. To remove individuals from their social context for the purposes of experimentation would make little, if any, sense.

Sometimes, sociologists may want to explore group dynamics – the way individuals behave when in groups – and experiments may then be possible. However, only small groups of individuals can be brought into a laboratory setting, and in such experiments people know that they are being studied and may not behave normally. Such changes in the behaviour of research subjects are referred to as the 'Hawthorne effect'. In the 1930s, researchers conducting a work productivity study at the Western Electric Company's Hawthorne plant near Chicago found to their surprise that worker productivity continued to rise regardless of which experimental conditions they imposed (levels of lighting, break patterns, work team size, and so forth). The workers were conscious of being under scrutiny and accelerated their normal work pace as a result. Nevertheless, as 'Classic studies 2.1' shows, we can still learn important things about social life from small-scale experiments in social psychology.

Biographical research

In contrast to experiments, biographical research belongs purely to sociology and the other social sciences and has no place in the natural sciences. Biographical research has become much more popular and widely used in sociology over recent decades and includes oral histories, narratives, autobiographies, biographies and life histories (Bryman 2015). These methods are used to explore how individuals experience social life and periods of social change and how they interpret their relationships with others in the context of a changing world. In this way, biographical methods allow new voices to enter sociological research, and life histories are one good example.

Life histories consist of biographical material assembled about particular individuals – usually as recalled by the individuals themselves. Life histories have been successfully employed in sociological studies of major importance. One celebrated early study was *The Polish Peasant in Europe and America*, by W. I. Thomas and Florian Znaniecki, the five volumes of which were first published between 1918 and 1920 (Thomas and Znaniecki 1966). Thomas and Znaniecki were able to provide a more sensitive and subtle account of the experience of migration than would have been possible without the interviews, letters and newspaper articles they collected. Biographical research aims to give us a feel for how life is experienced – something that can never be achieved by large surveys and statistical testing. Other methods do not usually yield as much information about the development of beliefs and attitudes over time. Life-historical studies rarely rely wholly on people's memories, however. Normally, sources such as letters, contemporary reports and newspaper descriptions are used to expand on and check the validity of the information that individuals provide.

Sociologists' views differ on the value of biographical methods. Some feel they are too unreliable and subjective to provide useful information, but others believe they offer sources of insight that few other research methods can match. Indeed, some sociologists have begun to offer reflections on their own lives within their research studies as a way of offering insights into the origins and development of their own theoretical assumptions (see, for example, Mouzelis 1995).

Comparative and historical research

The research methods described so far are generally applied in a comparative context. Comparative research is of central importance in sociology, because making comparisons allows us to clarify what is going on in a particular area of social life. Take the rate of divorce in many developed societies as an example. In the early 1960s there were fewer than 30,000 divorces per year in England and Wales, and by 2003 this figure had risen to 153,000. However, since 2003 the annual number of divorces has steadily fallen, to 121,779 in 2008, which was the lowest number since 1975. The *divorce rate* also fell by 5.1

Classic Studies 2.1 | The social psychology of prison life

The research problem

Most people have not experienced life in prison and find it hard to imagine how they would cope 'inside'. How would you fare? What kind of prison officer would you be – a disciplinarian maybe? Or perhaps you would adopt a more humanitarian approach to your prisoners? In 1971, a research team led by Philip Zimbardo decided to try and find out what impact the prison environment would have on 'ordinary people'.

In a study funded by the US Navy, Zimbardo set out to test the 'dispositional hypothesis', which dominated within the armed forces. This hypothesis suggested that constant conflicts between prisoners and guards were a result of the conflicting individual characters of the guards and inmates – their personal dispositions. Zimbardo thought this might be wrong and set up an experimental prison to find out.

Zimbardo's explanation

Zimbardo's research team set up an imitation jail at Stanford University, advertised for male volunteers to participate in a study of prison life, and selected twenty-four mainly middle-class students who did not know one another before the experiment. Each participant was then randomly assigned as either a guard or a prisoner. Following a standard induction process, which involved being stripped, de-loused and photographed naked, prisoners stayed in jail for twenty-four hours a day, but the guards worked shifts and went home in between times. Standardized uniforms were used for both roles. The aim was to see how playing these different roles would lead to changes in attitude and behaviour. What followed shocked the investigators.

Students who played the part of guards quickly assumed an authoritarian manner, displaying real hostility towards prisoners, ordering them around, verbally abusing and bullying them. The prisoners, by contrast, showed a mixture of apathy and rebelliousness – a response often noted among inmates in studies of real prisons. These effects were so marked

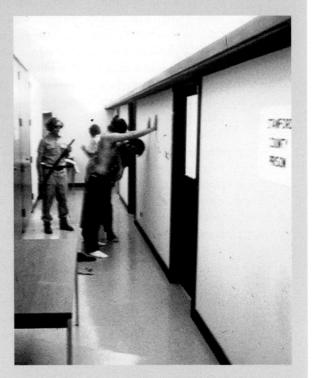

Reactions to the mock prison regime in the Stanford prison experiment led one inmate to stage a hunger strike to be allowed out.

and the level of tension so high that the fourteen-day experiment had to be called off after just six days because of the distress exhibited by participants. Even before this, five 'prisoners' were released because of extreme anxiety and emotional problems. However, many 'guards' were unhappy that the study had ended prematurely, suggesting they enjoyed the power the experiment afforded them.

On the basis of the findings, Zimbardo concluded that the dispositional hypothesis could not account for the participants' reactions. Instead, he proposed an alternative 'situational' explanation: behaviour in prisons is influenced by the prison situation itself, not by the individual characteristics of those involved. In particular, the expectations attached to the roles being played tended to shape people's behaviour. Some of the guards' behaviour had deteriorated – they treated prisoners badly, regularly handing out punishments and appearing to take pleasure in the distress of the prisoners. Zimbardo suggested this was due to the power relationships the jail had established. Their control over prisoners' lives very quickly became a source of enjoyment for the guards. On the other hand, following a short period of rebelliousness, prisoners exhibited a 'learned helplessness' and dependency. The study tells us something important about why social relationships often deteriorate within prisons and, by implication, in other 'total institutions' (Goffman 1968 [1961]). This has little to do with individual personalities and much more to do with the social structure of the prison environment and the social roles within it.

Critical points

Critics argue that there were real ethical problems with this study. Participants were not given full information about the purpose of the research, and it is questionable whether they could really have given 'informed consent'. Should the study even have been allowed to go ahead? The sample selected was clearly not representative of the population as a whole, as all were students and all were male. Generalizing about the effects of 'prison life' is therefore very difficult based on such a small and unrepresentative sample. A final criticism is that the constructed nature of the situation may invalidate the findings for generalizing to real-world prison regimes. For example, participants knew their imprisonment would last only fourteen days, and they were paid $15 a day for their participation. Well-established problems of prisons, such as racism and involuntary homosexuality, were also absent. Critics say that the experiment is therefore not a meaningful comparison with real prison life.

Contemporary significance

In spite of the somewhat artificial situation – it was an experiment, after all – Zimbardo's findings have been widely referred to since the 1970s. For example, Zygmunt Bauman's (1989) *Modernity and the Holocaust* draws on this study to help explain the behaviour of inmates and guards in Nazi-run concentration camps during the Second World War. In recent years the issue of mistreatment and bullying of older and disabled people in care-home settings in England has been exposed in a series of scandals, resulting in dismissals and the prosecution of staff members. Cases such as these show that the general thesis emerging from Zimbardo's research – that institutional settings can shape social relations and behaviour – remains a powerful one.

THINKING CRITICALLY

Can an experimental situation really reproduce the authentic experience of prison life? Which aspects of the prison experience could an experiment *never* replicate? Thinking more critically, should social scientists be allowed to 'experiment' on human beings at all? If not, does that mean there are things we will just never know about?

---

per cent in 2008, to 11.2 divorcing persons per 1,000 married population (ONS 2010b). Do these changes reflect specific features of British society? We can find out by comparing divorce rates in the UK with those of other countries. Comparison with figures for other Western societies reveals that the overall trends are similar. A majority of Western countries experienced steadily climbing divorce rates over the later part of the twentieth century, which appears to have peaked early in the twenty-first century before stabilizing or falling back in recent years. What we may conclude is that the statistics for England and Wales illustrate one part of a more general trend or pattern within modern Western societies.

A historical perspective is often essential in sociological research, as we frequently need a *time perspective* to make sense of the material we collect about a particular problem. Sociologists commonly want to investigate past events directly. Some periods of history can be studied in a direct way while there are still survivors around – such as studies of the Holocaust in Europe during the Second World War. Research in oral history means interviewing people about events they were part of or witnessed at some earlier point in their lives. This kind of direct testimony can be gained at the most only for some sixty or seventy years back in time.

For historical research on an earlier period, sociologists use documentary research from written records, often contained in the special collections of libraries or archives. The range of useful documents is extensive, taking in personal sources such as diaries, official sources such as policy documents, records of births and deaths, and tax records, and documents from private bodies such as businesses and voluntary organizations, as well as magazines and newspapers. Depending on the research question, historical documents such as these can all constitute primary sources just as much as the data recorded in interviews with war survivors. However, historical sociologists also make much use of secondary sources: accounts of historical events written by people after the event. Most documentary studies utilize both primary and secondary sources. However, sociologists face the same issues as historians when they make use of such sources. How authentic are the documents? Is the information within them reliable? Do they represent only a partial viewpoint? Documentary research requires a patient, systematic approach to sources and their interpretation.

An interesting example of the use of historical documents is Anthony Ashworth's study of trench warfare during the First World War (Ashworth 1980). Ashworth drew on diverse documentary sources: official histories of the war, official publications of the time, notes and records kept by soldiers, and personal accounts of war experiences. He was then able to develop a rich and detailed description of life in the trenches. He discovered that most soldiers formed their own ideas about how often they intended to engage in combat and often ignored the rules and commands of their officers.

Ashworth's research concentrated on a relatively short time period – 1914 to 1918 – but there have been many studies that have investigated social change over much longer periods, making use of comparative research in that historical context. One modern classic of comparative historical sociology is Theda Skocpol's (1979) analysis of social revolutions, which is discussed in 'Classic studies 2.2'.

Visual sociology

Although anthropology has long made use of visual sources of information such as photographs and film footage, sociology has tended to be a subject focused on written texts (Harper 2010). That is not to say that sociologists do not produce their own visual materials. Representations of numerical and statistical information are turned into easy-to-read pie charts and tables, while ethnographic research is often presented with photographs included. However, these visual elements are almost always ancillary to the main text, which is the more significant part of the articles and books through which the sociologist's arguments are made (Chaplin 1994).

In very recent years a few research studies have made use of some of the new digital technologies and devices, such as iPads and smartphones, to document areas of social life that are hard to gain access to. For example, Bancroft and his colleagues (2014) recruited female students into their project aimed at exploring young women's drinking culture in Edinburgh, Scotland. The students effectively became participant-researchers using smartphone cameras to document their own pleasure-seeking activities in the night-time economy. We can probably expect this kind of approach to become more commonplace in certain types of research project in the future.

Some sociologists have become increasingly interested in a 'visual sociology', in which photographs, film, television programmes, video, and so on, are objects of study in their own right. Hence, family photograph albums can be treated as key resources in understanding the passage of generations, and the history

Classic Studies 2.2 Theda Skocpol's comparison of social revolutions

The research problem

As all students of sociology and history are taught, the French Revolution of 1789 transformed France forever. But why did it happen then? Was it just a historical accident or was it inevitable? The early twentieth-century revolutions in China and Russia not only turned those countries into communist societies, they also significantly shaped the direction of the modern world itself. Again, why then? The American sociologist Theda Skocpol (1947–) set out to uncover the similarities and differences across these revolutionary periods. Her ambitious task was to produce a general theory of the origins and nature of revolution grounded in detailed empirical studies. The result was *States and Social Revolutions* (1979), now one of the classic studies of long-term social transformation.

Skocpol's explanation

Skocpol looked at the processes of revolution in three different historical contexts: the 1789 French Revolution (1786–1800); the 1917 revolutions in Russia (1917–21) and the revolutionary period in China (1911–49). Given the essentially historical questions she asked, her main method was the use and careful interpretation of a range of primary and secondary documentary sources. Although there are many differences between the three cases, Skocpol argues that their underlying structural causes are in fact similar. She rejects the Marxist idea that revolutions are the intentional product of mass, class-based movements with deep grievances. Instead, she argues that revolutions are not made, they come. That is, social revolutions are largely the result of the unintended consequences of intentional human actions. Before the Russian Revolution, for instance, various political groups were trying to overthrow the existing regime, but none of these – including the Bolsheviks, who eventually came to power – anticipated the revolution that occurred. A series of clashes and confrontations gave rise to a process of social transformation

Social unrest does not necessarily lead to revolution. What will be the outcome of the protests against Chinese rule in Tibet?

much deeper and more radical than anyone had foreseen.

Skocpol's explanation is that all three revolutions occurred in predominantly agrarian societies and were made possible only when the existing state structures (administrative and military) were breaking down as they came under intense competitive pressure from other states. In this context, it was peasant revolts and mass mobilizations that brought about social revolutions in France, China and Russia. Thus Skocpol argued against the widespread notion that peasants were *not* a 'revolutionary class'. Some similarities with other revolutions in Vietnam, Cuba, Mexico and Yugoslavia can also be seen. Skocpol's causal explanation focuses on state structures; as these began to break down, a power vacuum was created and states lost their legitimacy, enabling revolutionary forces to take power.

Skocpol's research makes use of the 'logic of scientific experiment' for comparative studies outlined by John Stuart Mill in the mid-nineteenth century. She adopts Mill's 'method of similarity', taking three similar events (revolutions) in very different national contexts. This allows her to look for key similarities across the three cases which can be identified as *independent variables* and thus help to explain the causes of political revolutions.

Critical points

Some of Skocpol's critics have raised questions about the structural argument of her thesis. This, they say, leaves little room for active agency on the part of people. *How* did peasant groups revolt? Did leaders not play a part in the revolutions? Could things have turned out differently if individual actors and groups had chosen alternative courses of action? Are individuals so powerless to influence change in the face of structural pressures?

A further criticism is of Skocpol's notion of 'cause' in this context. Some have argued that what her argument amounts to is really a set of sophisticated generalizations in relation to the cases she studied. And, although such generalizations work quite well for these specific cases, this is not the same thing as a general causal theory of social revolutions. Does the thesis hold for, say, the Iranian Revolution of 1979, the 'Velvet Revolution' in (former) Czechoslovakia in 1989, or the uprisings in the Middle East and North Africa during the so-called Arab Spring which spread from Tunisia in 2010? So, critics say, despite setting out to discover the underlying causes and nature of social revolutions, in the end, Skocpol's study showed that each revolution has to be studied in its own right.

Contemporary significance

Skocpol's study has become a modern classic for two reasons. First, it developed a powerful causal explanation of revolutionary change which emphasized the underlying social structural conditions of revolution. Such a strong central thesis was, nevertheless, underpinned by very detailed analysis of primary and secondary documentary sources. Hence, Skocpol successfully demonstrated that comparative-historical sociology could combine the study of large-scale, long-term social change with the empirical investigation of historical events 'on the ground'. In essence, she brought together the macro- and microsociological aspects into one theoretical framework. Second, Skocpol made a very significant contribution to our understanding of revolutions. She showed that there are enough similarities across different revolutions to warrant pursuing general theories of social change. In this way, her thesis helped to bridge the gap between mainstream historical studies and the sociology of revolutions.

of film or art can tell us something of the social norms, dress codes and manners of earlier times. But the process of production through which visual materials come into being also forms a field of study, and we can ask some familiar questions about them. Who produced them? For what reason? How were they produced? What has been included and what omitted? Studying the production of visual materials forms one part of the broader field of the production of culture, through which we gain a better understanding of how different societies represent their ways of life to their members.

The Internet as a tool and method

The emergence of the Internet as a communications technology and the worldwide web as an online information store presents new opportunities and challenges for sociologists. One opportunity not to be missed is simply gaining access to an unrivalled range of information from right across the globe with just a few clicks of a button. The Internet has become an invaluable research tool. We can gain access to articles, books, research reports, government documents, parliamentary debates (live or in document form), historical documents, archives and lots, lots more. In this way, the Internet is capable of speeding up academic exchanges and spreading local research across the international scholarly community.

There is a constant danger, though, that this startling accessibility of information may be mistaken for accuracy of information. Students (and researchers) have to be constantly critical of their sources and ask the same questions they would of all other sources. Who produced it? How was it produced? How credible is the source? Does the source have any direct interest in the information that might lead to bias? Many lecturers today are engaged in teaching students the skills required to be able to make effective use of online sources (Ó Dochartaigh 2009). The Internet's popularity is partly due to the ease of publication offered by the worldwide web, but the lack of peer review on many non-academic websites means that a fair amount of online material is not suitable for student use. Learning how to assess such material will be much more important in the future.

However, the Internet can also become part of research methodologies (Hewson et al. 2002). The huge number of online 'virtual' communities offers the possibility for researchers to tap into these to carry out research in much the same way that they would in 'real-world' social groups and communities. Chatrooms, forums and very specific interest groups that organize online may even present the best or only way into a particular subject. For instance, sociologists have found that many people who perceive eating disorders as a lifestyle choice, rather than a medical problem, are not prepared to come forward for interview in the conventional way but may be far more accessible in the relatively anonymous, virtual world of the Internet and worldwide web. Researchers can also make use of email, Skype, online questionnaires and webcam interviews as part of their research projects. Indeed, what these examples show is that sociologists need to think creatively about the process of research if they are properly to understand how the Internet is leading to significant changes in the way people actually live their social lives today.

Sociology in the real world

All research methods have their advantages and limitations. Hence, today it is commonplace to find sociologists combining several methods in a single piece of research, using each to supplement and check on the others. This process is known as triangulation. Advocates of triangulation argue that it produces more reliable, valid and comprehensive knowledge than a single research method. However, Norman Denzin (1970) actually distinguished four types of triangulation. *Data triangulation* occurs when data are collected at different times and perhaps uses different sampling strategies within the same research project. *Investigator triangulation* is where a team of researchers, rather than a single researcher, carries out the fieldwork. *Theoretical triangulation* is more controversial, as it involves using several theoretical approaches when interpreting the data. Finally, *methodological triangulation* is the adoption of more than one research method in a study.

We can see the value of combining methods – and, more generally, the problems and pitfalls of real sociological research – by looking once again at Laud Humphreys' *Tearoom Trade*. One of the questions that Humphreys wanted to answer was 'What kind of men came to the tearooms?' It was very hard for him to find this out because all he could really do was observe. The norm of silence made it difficult to ask questions or even to talk. It would have been very odd if he asked personal questions of those seeking anonymous sex! As we have seen, Humphreys noted car number-plates of those involved, giving the numbers to a friend at the Department of Motor Vehicles, who secured the owners' addresses. Some months later, he persuaded a work colleague at Washington University in St Louis, who was conducting a door-to-door survey of sexual habits, to add the names and addresses of his own tearoom sample. Disguised as an investigator, Humphreys interviewed the men in their homes to learn more about their backgrounds and lives, interviewing wives and family members too. Leaving aside the unconventional and ethically dubious tactics he employed, Humphreys engaged in methodological triangulation. He tried to overcome the limitations of participant observation by joining a social survey, and by combining the results he was able to produce a richer, more detailed and powerful piece of research. Mixing methods has become very common today for precisely this reason.

> **THINKING CRITICALLY**
>
> What potential problems can you foresee with each type of triangulation? What happens if your survey and ethnography produce radically different results – how do you assess their respective value? Does one method inevitably have to be subordinate to the other?

The influence of sociology

Because sociologists often study things that most people have some personal experience of, it is possible to believe that sociological knowledge is not dissimilar to that of 'ordinary people'. Is sociology merely a restatement, in abstract jargon, of things we already know? Very rarely is this the case. Because sociological findings must be rooted in evidence, they are never just personal opinion or mere speculation. In fact, good sociology sharpens our understanding of things that seem obvious (Berger 1963) or it completely transforms our common-sense perspective. In either event, sociology is neither tedious nor a restatement of the obvious. Sociological research has allowed us to see aspects of society about which we had no previous knowledge, and research findings often challenge our personal beliefs and prejudices about social groups, individuals and institutions.

Similarly, sociologists may begin with a problem that many people are already aware of. Is crime getting worse? Why are boys underachieving in secondary school? Is terrorism today any different from that of the past? But, in addressing such questions, sociologists are never content with anecdotal evidence, newspaper reports or television news reports. They always seek to use research methods to collect evidence, which they then analyse and interpret using theoretical ideas to generate a deeper understanding of the phenomena under study. In this way sociology often challenges the 'obvious' or simple answers and sets our local knowledge within a much wider frame of reference, most recently the global level of social interactions.

Sociological research is rarely of interest only to the intellectual community of sociologists. A fair amount of research funding comes from government sources and is directly linked to social issues and problems. Many studies of crime and deviance, for example, target specific offences or types of offender with a view to gaining better knowledge, so that the problems associated with crime can be tackled more effectively. Sociologists also work with voluntary agencies, public bodies and businesses, bringing their research skills to bear on matters of their interest. Much of this work is applied social research, which does not simply endeavour to produce better knowledge but also seeks to inform interventions aimed at improving society. Those undertaking a study of the effects on children of parental alcohol use, for instance, may be interested in whether a particular treatment programme has any effect on reducing alcohol abuse.

The results of sociological research are also disseminated throughout society. Sociology, it must be emphasized, is not just the *study* of societies; it is a significant element *in the continuing life* of societies. Consider the transformations taking place in relation to marriage, sexuality and the family (discussed in chapters 9, 10 and 15). Most people have some knowledge of these changes as a result of the filtering down into society of sociological research findings. Our thinking and

behaviour are thus affected by sociological knowledge in complex and often subtle ways. However, as our behaviour changes, so does society – the very subject of sociological investigation. A way of describing this two-way phenomenon, using our technical language, is to say that sociology stands in a 'reflexive relation' to the human beings whose behaviour it studies. Reflexivity, as we shall see in chapter 3, describes the interchange between sociology and social life. We should not be surprised that sociological findings often correlate closely with common sense. But this is not because sociology tells us what we know already. Rather, sociological research helps to shape our common-sense knowledge of society in the first place, even though we may not immediately realize it.

Chapter review

1 Explain what is meant by factual research, comparative research, developmental research and theoretical research. Give examples of research questions that would lead you to select each of the different types.

2 Explain the difference between verification and falsification. Why does Popper believe the latter is a more powerful principle for science?

3 'Sociology is a scientific discipline.' Does the philosophy and history of science support or contradict this statement?

4 What is the difference between a correlation and a cause? Provide an example of one spurious and one genuine causal relationship.

5 List as many sociological research methods as you can think of and note which are primarily quantitative and which are qualitative. Taking each in turn, what are the main benefits and limitations of the methods you have listed?

6 Devise a research strategy involving at least TWO research methods to investigate the following subjects, explaining what ethical and practical problems you foresee and how you would handle them:
   a) domestic violence within female same-sex relationships
   b) the extent of self-harming behaviour among schoolchildren aged eleven to sixteen
   c) the coping strategies adopted by 'lifers' in male prisons.
   Are any of these subjects effectively 'off-limits' to sociological research? Why?

7 Look again at table 2.2 above. Track down the sources used to construct this table. How credible are these sources? Do any of the organizations involved have a direct interest in the subject of the research that would give you cause for concern about the accuracy of the data?

Research in practice

Most sociology graduates will remember the classic research studies. But sociology lives through its research studies, the majority of which are published in academic journals. Journal articles (called 'papers') are part of the ongoing process of data collection and theory building which deepens and changes our knowledge of the topic at hand.

Some sociologists have sought to narrow the gap between researchers and those being researched by involving participants in the *conduct* of their projects. In this way an extra level of reflexivity is possible and findings may be more valid, particularly when trying to tap into experiences that researchers otherwise find difficult to access.

Read the following article on alcohol drinking and the night time economy: Bancroft, A., Zimpfer, M. J., Murray, O., and Karels, M. (2014) 'Working at Pleasure in Young Women's Alcohol Consumption: A Participatory Visual Ethnography', *Sociological Research Online*, 19(3): 20, www.socresonline.org.uk/19/3/20.html. Now try these questions:

1 What research question(s) guide this study?
2 What do the authors mean by 'participatory ethnography'?
3 Which other methods are used in the research?
4 Is the chosen sample representative of the group(s) the researchers want to understand? What criticisms can be made of the sample selection?
5 The study made extensive use of digital technology and mobile devices. What were the pros and cons of this? Is there evidence of selective presentation of images and video clips by the participants? How could this problem be overcome?
6 The researchers 'wrote up and controlled the final output'. Does this undermine the initial aim of the participatory research strategy or is it simply inevitable?
7 What do we learn about young women and their 'intoxication culture' from this paper? Can the findings be generalized to the wider female population?

Thinking it through

As we have seen, research begins from a problem or question and a research project involves several consecutive stages. Have a go at designing your own project. Refer back to figure 2.1, then follow the first four stages of the process which involve planning and designing a study.

- Choose a topic that interests you but raises questions that you want to answer. Narrow down the subject to a definite research question.
- Identify some key words in relation to the subject and carry out a search of the relevant literature using those words. Note down the references of the ten closest matches to your question.
- Consult the first three of these to help construct a hypothesis for your project. What do you actually want to find out?
- Now think about exactly *how* you would carry out the research. Which method or methods are most likely to provide the answers you are looking for? Do you need to quantify your results? Would a qualitative method be more effective? Could you use more than one method?
- Finally, what obstacles do you foresee when the research gets under way and how might you head them off?

Society in the arts

1   Watch Davis Guggenheim's film *An Inconvenient Truth* (2006), a documentary film about climate change. The film follows the former US vice-president and presidential candidate Al Gore around the world as he presents scientific evidence demonstrating human-induced global warming. During the course of the film, Gore is seen countering objections from climate change sceptics. Is this kind of campaigning film inevitably biased, or are the voices of sceptics given a fair hearing? How might films such as this be more persuasive than scientific papers? What can film, novels and plays add to our understanding that academic writing cannot match?

2   Interviews are conducted not just by sociologists but also by journalists, market researchers and others, and all interviewers find practical ways of eliciting the information they seek. The investigative journalist Louis Theroux likes to use *unstructured interviews* to draw out information from his subjects.

Watch Theroux's technique in *Louis Theroux: Behind Bars* (2008), directed by Stuart Cabb, as he interviews guards and inmates at San Quentin State Prison in San Francisco, California: https://archive.org/details/BehindBarsInSanQuentin-LouisTheroux. Does the unstructured interview method work in this context? Is Theroux able to gather information from inmates and guards which helps illuminate the relationship between them? Is there any evidence that inmates were 'playing to the camera', giving responses that make good TV rather than telling the truth? What obstacles might you face – practical, political and institutional – if you wanted to interview inmates in your own national prison system?

3   *The Insider* (1999), directed by Michael Mann, is a film based on a real-life event. A former executive of a large tobacco company in the USA gave an interview to a TV news show, saying that not only did other chief executives know that tobacco was harmful, they also sought to enhance cigarettes to make them even more addictive. The story covers attempts to silence the truth, including CBS News succumbing to pressure not to show the interview. As you watch, consider the use made of scientific research and of scientists themselves. Could you conceive of a situation in which you would falsify or amend your findings to avoid damaging your employer's business? Can scientists work for private corporations and still maintain their professional commitment to scientific norms?

Further reading

There are many books on research methods pitched at introductory level students. This selection is just the tip of a large iceberg of literature, and it is important to dip into several sources to see which one you find most accessible.

Novice researchers need a text that is both informative and practical, so something like Judith Bell (with Stephen Walters) (2014) *Doing Your Research Project: A Guide for First-Time Researchers* (6th edn, Maidenhead: Open University Press) is a very good place to begin. Similarly, Keith F. Punch's (2014) *Introduction to Social Research: Quantitative and Qualitative Approaches* (3rd edn, London: Sage) does exactly what it says. Gary D. Bouma and Rod Ling's (2005) *The Research Process* (5th edn, Oxford: Oxford University Press) is also an excellent introduction.

For something a little more detailed and comprehensive, try Alan Bryman's (2015) *Social Research Methods* (5th edn, Oxford: Oxford University Press), which is widely adopted by lecturers for their research methods courses. Tim May's (2011) *Social Research: Issues, Methods and Process* (4th edn, Maidenhead: Open University Press) is also a reliable guide.

For an introduction to statistics and SPSS, Andy Field's (2013) *Discovering Statistics Using IBM SPSS Statistics* (4th edn, London: Sage) is very accessible for beginners as well as those with more experience. One other worthwhile book is Darrell Huff's (1991) *How to Lie with Statistics* (London: Penguin), which is apparently 'the best-selling statistics book ever written' (see J. M. Steele (2005), 'Darrell Huff and Fifty Years of How to Lie with Statistics', *Statistical Science*, 20(3): 205–9). This is probably because of its irreverent tone. It is, however, an excellent guide to the misuse of statistical information in society and carries a serious message.

A good dictionary is usually a good investment, so Victor Jupp's (2006) *The Sage Dictionary of Social Research Methods* (London: Sage) is well worth consulting on specific topics.

For a collection of readings on research methods and different methodological approaches, see the accompanying *Sociology: Introductory Readings* (3rd edn, Cambridge: Polity, 2010).

Internet links

@

Additional information and support for this book at Polity:
www.politybooks.com/giddens

Research methods at Manchester – exactly what it says, a useful resource for social science methods at the University of Manchester, UK:
www.methods.manchester.ac.uk

@

The UK Office for National Statistics, which includes lots of survey research, but other types as well:
www.ons.gov.uk

@

The UK Data Archive – a large collection of digital data on a variety of subjects:
www.data-archive.ac.uk

@

CESSDA – Council of European Social Science Data Archives – houses many social science data archives from across Europe covering many different types of research:
http://cessda.net

Ipsos MORI – a merged company (Ipsos UK and MORI) focusing on market research and social research:
www.ipsos-mori.com

CHAPTER 3

Theories and Perspectives

Contents

The theory of man-made global warming has been the subject of acrimonious debate and theoretical disagreement.

O ver the last twenty-five years a fierce debate has developed over the issue of global climate change. The main arguments focus on the evidence on shrinking glacial ice, average global surface temperature, rises in sea levels and other symptoms of global warming. Other disputes concern research methods: how should global temperatures be measured and how satisfactory are the assumptions underlying computer models of climate change? However, the most acrimonious exchanges are essentially theoretical conflicts between the overwhelming majority of scientists, who say the evidence strongly supports their theory of anthropogenic (human-forced) global warming, and the minority, most of whom draw on the same evidence but reject the anthropogenic thesis. This dispute shows that the available evidence, however diverse and extensive it may be, very rarely 'speaks for itself' but has to be interpreted within a theoretical framework.

> See chapter 5, 'The Environment', for a lengthy discussion of the sociology of climate change.

In chapter 1 we saw that, just as in the natural sciences, sociologists need to devise abstract interpretations – theories – to explain the evidence they collect in their research studies. They also need to adopt a theoretical approach at the outset of their studies if they are to formulate appropriate questions that focus their research effort. Yet sociological theorizing does not take place in an isolated academic ivory tower. This is clear from the questions posed by the discipline's founders, which were closely tied to major social and political issues of the day. For example, Marx sought to explain the dynamics of the capitalist economy, the causes of poverty and growing social inequality. Durkheim's studies investigated the character of industrial society and the process of secularization, while Weber sought to explain the emergence of capitalism and the consequences of bureaucratic organizations for the individual. But are these still the central issues today?

Many sociologists think that the central problems in society are shifting. What are the social and political consequences of globalization? How, why and with what consequences are gender relations being transformed? What is the future for multicultural societies? Indeed, what is the future for human populations across the world in the light of climate change and global environmental problems? In order to address these matters, sociologists have been forced to re-evaluate the classical theories and, where these are found wanting, to develop novel theories of their own. We will look at some of the latter in the chapter.

For newcomers to sociology, a historical perspective is vital. Not only does it help readers to understand how the discipline emerged and changed into its present shape, but it also encourages us all to avoid trying to reinvent the (theoretical) wheel when there is no need to do so. Critics of sociological theorizing – more than a few from within the discipline itself – complain that too many 'new' theories are really just 'old' theories dressed up in a new language. An appreciation of the development of sociological theory over time sensitizes us to this criticism.

Things are made more complex because some theories are described as 'sociological theories', others as 'social theories'. Is this just splitting hairs? In blunt terms, sociological theories adopt scientific methods and aim to explain empirical research findings while guarding against normative or political bias. Social theories do not necessarily originate from within the discipline of sociology and often contain normative critiques of current social and political arrangements. Bear this division in mind as you read through the chapter. However, as we will see, the basic distinction is not hard and fast as some scholars move between the two basic types, devising sociological theories to understand and explain aspects of social life but also criticizing what they see as pernicious inequalities and injustice. You might also reflect on which theories you find attractive and what role your own background and life experience plays in your choice.

Coming to terms with the array of theories and perspectives in sociology is challenging. It would be much easier if sociology had one central theory around which all sociologists could work, and for a time in the 1950s and 1960s the structural functionalist approach of Talcott Parsons did come close to that. However, as societies have become more culturally diverse, so the present period is marked by a diversity of theoretical approaches and perspectives. This makes the task of evaluating competing theories more difficult than once it was. Yet theoretical pluralism also brings vitality to sociological theory, arguably deepening our overall understanding of social life. And, while sociology today includes numerous 'middle-range' theories that try

1750	European Enlightenment philosophers (1750–1800)
1800	Auguste Comte (1798–1857) Harriet Martineau (1802–76)
1850	Karl Marx (1818–83) Herbert Spencer (1820–1903)
1900	Emile Durkheim (1858–1917)
	Max Weber (1864–1920)
	Georg Simmel (1858–1918) Edmund Husserl (1859–1938)
1930	George H. Mead (1863–1931) Alfred Schutz (1899–1959)
	Chicago School (1920s) Antonio Gramsci (1891–1937)
1940	Talcott Parsons (1902–79)
	Frankfurt School (1923–1960s)
	Simone de Beauvoir (1908–86)
1950	Robert Merton (1910–2003)
1960	Erving Goffman (1922–82)
	Betty Friedan (1921–2006)
	Howard Becker (1928–)
	Harold Garfinkel (1917–2011) Norbert Elias (1897–1990)
1970	Jürgen Habermas (1929–)
	Michel Foucault (1926–84)
1980	Pierre Bourdieu (1930–2002) Immanuel Wallerstein (1930–)
	Jean Baudrillard (1929–2007)
1990	Anthony Giddens (1938–) Ulrich Beck (1944–2015) Judith Butler (1956–)
	Vandana Shiva (1952–) Zygmunt Bauman (1925–2017)
2000 onwards	Manuel Castells (1942–) Slavoj Žižek (1949–)

Key:

Selected theorists associated with or inspired by the different sociological perspectives are identified thus:

☐ Philosophical thinkers
☐ Functionalism
☐ Marxism
☐ Interactionism
☐ Feminism
☐ Postmodernism/poststructuralism
☐ Theoretical syntheses

Figure 3.1 Chronology of major sociological theorists and schools, 1750 to the present

to explain a very specific aspect of social life (Merton 1957), there is also room for grand theories that try to explain social structures or the long-term development of modern societies (Skinner 1990).

This chapter rounds off a block of three at the start of the book which provides a firm foundation for students approaching sociology. In chapter 1 we explored what sociology adds to the sum total of scientific knowledge. Chapter 2 presented some of the main research methods and techniques used by sociologists – their 'tools of the trade', as it were. And in this chapter we provide a fairly brief account of the history and development of sociological theorizing since the nineteenth century. Of course, we cannot cover all of the important theorists in this short chapter, so, for example, Pierre Bourdieu and Manuel Castells are not discussed here. Their work is found in later chapters where it has been especially influential: Bourdieu's ideas are covered in detail in chapter 19, 'Education', while those of Castells can be found in chapter 7, 'Work and the Economy', and 8, 'Social Interaction and Daily Life'.

Our presentation is generally chronological, but not slavishly so. When we introduce Marx, inevitably the discussion stretches from the mid-nineteenth century to Marxisms in the early and late twentieth century. The outline of feminist theories covers a similarly long time period. Our judgement is that this method produces a more coherent narrative, allowing readers to see more easily how and why theoretical perspectives developed in the ways they did.

In the next two sections we trace the emergence of sociological theory and the establishment of sociology through the work of the 'classical founders' and the traditions of inquiry they began. We then explore two recurring theoretical dilemmas around which major theoretical debates turn, before ending the chapter with a look at the way that rapid and wide-ranging social changes since the 1970s have forced sociologists to devise new theoretical perspectives. Figure 3.1 provides a simple chronological chart which illustrates the emergence and development of theories and perspectives through certain influential theorists and schools of thought. The place of individuals in the sequence is determined roughly by the date of their major publication(s) and the place of schools by their date of formation. This is of course merely a selection and is not meant to be exhaustive. The figure provides some signposts both for this chapter and for the book as a whole.

THINKING CRITICALLY

Based on the perspectives in figure 3.1, do you see any patterns in the chronology? Which perspectives appear to have lost or gained ground, for example?

Towards sociology

A sociological perspective was made possible by two revolutionary transformations. First, the Industrial Revolution of the late eighteenth and the nineteenth century radically transformed material conditions of life and ways of making a living, initially bringing with it many new social problems such as urban overcrowding, poor sanitation, disease and industrial pollution. Social reformers sought ways to mitigate and solve these problems, which led them to carry out research and gather evidence on their extent and nature to reinforce the case for change.

Second, the French Revolution of 1789 marked the symbolic endpoint of the old European agrarian regimes and absolute monarchies as republican ideals of freedom, liberty and citizenship rights came to the fore. This revolution is often seen as, in part, the outcome of mid-eighteenth-century European Enlightenment ideas, which challenged tradition and religious authorities, promoting philosophical and scientific notions of reason, rationality and critical thinking as the keys to progress in human affairs. Enlightenment philosophers saw the advancement of reliable knowledge in the natural sciences, particularly astronomy, physics and chemistry, as showing the way forward. The English physicist Sir Isaac Newton (1643–1727) was singled out as an exemplary scientist whose ideas of Natural Law and scientific method appealed to Enlightenment scholars. They argued that, in principle, it should be possible to discover similar laws (using similar methods) in social and political life as well. This idea is the basis of positivist philosophy in the sciences.

Positivism and social evolution

Auguste Comte (1798–1857) saw the science of society – which he termed 'sociology' – as essentially similar to the natural sciences. His positivist approach was based on the principle of direct observation, with theoretical statements aimed at establishing causal, law-like generalizations. The task of sociology, according to Comte, was to gain reliable knowledge of the social world in order to make predictions about it and, on the basis of those predictions, to intervene and shape it in progressive ways. Comte's positivist philosophy was clearly inspired by the achievements of the natural sciences, which were producing reliable knowledge that could find useful practical applications.

More than 150 years after Comte's death, anyone who watched (probably on television) NASA's space shuttles taking off, spending weeks orbiting the Earth and landing in the manner of commercial aeroplanes has witnessed the predictive power of science in action. Thinking about the different types of reliable knowledge required to achieve such a feat of science and engineering illustrates why the natural sciences are held in high regard today.

But could such reliable, predictive knowledge ever be achieved in relation to societies and human behaviour? Most sociologists today think it cannot, and few would use the term 'positivist' to describe their work. Most sociologists reject Comtean positivism because they view the idea of shaping and controlling people and societies as either impossible or potentially dangerous – or, indeed, both. Self-conscious human beings cannot be studied in the same way as, say, frogs, because they are capable of acting in ways that confound our predictions about them. Even if Comte was right and humans *could* be scientifically studied, their behaviour forecast and interventions made to direct society in positive directions, who would intervene and who decides what constitutes a 'positive direction'? Scientists? Politicians? Religious authorities? Would central direction of this kind be compatible with democratic politics?

> See chapter 1, 'What is Sociology?', for a longer discussion of Comte's ideas.

Today there is widespread scepticism of Comte's version of sociology as a predictive science, but it is important to remember his formative role in establishing the case for a science of society. Comte's ideas were extremely influential at the time and his theory of the development of the sciences was an inspiration to others. Comte saw the dominant forms of human knowledge passing through three stages: the theological (or religious), the metaphysical (or philosophical) and, finally, the positive (or scientific). The history of the sciences demonstrated this gradual movement and, as social life was the last area to move into the positive stage, sociology was destined to be the final scientific discipline.

The English philosopher and sociologist Herbert Spencer (1820–1903) drew on Comte's ideas and was among the first to argue that, as the world of nature was subject to biological evolution, so societies were subject to social evolution. This took the form of *structural differentiation*, through which simple societies develop into more complex forms with an increasingly diverse array of social institutions, and *functional adaptation*, as societies accommodate themselves to the external environment. Spencer argued that the industrial societies of the nineteenth century were essentially exhibiting social evolution, emerging out of the more static and hierarchical societies that preceded them. Spencer also thought that the 'survival of the fittest' applied in social as well as biological evolution and was against state intervention to support the vulnerable or disadvantaged (M. W. Taylor 1992).

Although Spencer's theory of social evolution was generally well received, the twentieth century saw his ideas, along with other evolutionary theories, fall into decline, and few sociology courses today make more than passing reference to them. This stands in stark contrast to another of the grand 'evolutionary' theorists of the nineteenth century, Karl Marx, whose influence on sociology, politics and world history is difficult to overestimate.

Karl Marx: the capitalist revolution

Marx's basic ideas on class conflict and social change were introduced in chapter 1, and

73

at this point you may want to refresh your knowledge of these. Marx and his colleague, Friedrich Engels, never considered themselves professional sociologists. However, they did seek a scientific understanding of society and, from this, an explanation of long-term social change. Marx viewed his social scientific work as marking a break with speculative philosophy and all philosophical forms of thought, arguing that 'the philosophers have only interpreted the world in various ways, the point however is to change it' (Marx and Engels 1970 [1846]: 123). His interest in and commitment to the European industrial working class was closely linked to his studies of capitalism and its workings.

Marx's theoretical approach: historical materialism

Marx's work is important for sociology in a number of ways, but we will focus on just one aspect in this chapter: the analysis of capitalism, which is part of his broader theory of class conflict as the driving force in history. This 'grand theory' formed the basis of many later research studies and theoretical developments in sociology and the social sciences. Marxist theory was also reinterpreted and used by numerous political movements and governments in the twentieth century, including the communist regimes of the former Soviet Union, Eastern Europe, Cuba, Vietnam and China. Clearly, Marxism is much more than just an academic sociological theory.

Marx's theoretical perspective is sometimes referred to as historical materialism; more accurately, perhaps, it is a materialist conception of history. This means that Marx is opposed to idealism, a philosophical doctrine which says that the historical development of societies is driven by abstract ideas or ideals, such as freedom and democracy. Instead, Marx argues that the dominant ideas and ideals of an age are reflections of the dominant way of life, specifically of a society's mode of production. For example, in an age when absolute monarchs reigned, it is not surprising that the dominant ideas suggested that kings and queens had a 'divine right [from God] to rule',

while in our own age of free-market capitalism the dominant ideas are those of sovereign individuals who make 'free' choices. Marx argues that the dominant ideas of an age are those which support the ruling groups. His 'historical materialism' is interested primarily in how people collectively produce a life together. How do they produce food, shelter and other material goods, and what kind of division of labour exists which enables them to do so?

> ### THINKING CRITICALLY
>
> Is Marx right, and do the dominant ideas of the age always reflect ruling class interests? How might the concept of universal human rights be useful for capitalists? Or is the human rights discourse best seen as opposed to certain aspects of capitalist development?

Successive modes of production: a successful grand theory?

Marx argued that the historical development of human societies is structured, not random or chaotic. In the ancient past, small-scale human groups existed with no developed system of property-ownership. Instead, all the resources acquired were communally owned and no class divisions were present. Marx called this a form of *primitive communism*. As the group produced more, this mode of production was effectively outgrown and a new one emerged, this time with some private property-ownership (including slavery), as in ancient Greece and Rome.

From here, societies based on settled agriculture and feudal property relations developed. The medieval system of European *feudalism* was based on a class division between landowners and landless peasants and tenant farmers, who were forced to work for landowners in order to survive. But the feudal mode of production also reached its productive limitations and gave way to the *capitalist society* with which we are now familiar. The early capitalists

Marx argued that, as workers were brought together in large numbers, class-consciousness would develop.

began to invest in workshops and manufacturing in the sixteenth century, and by the time of the French Revolution in 1789 they were numerous and powerful enough to become a revolutionary force in history.

Under capitalism, class antagonisms were greatly simplified as society 'split into two great camps' – the property-owners (capitalists or the *bourgeoisie*) and the workers (or proletariat). The capitalist revolution broke the bounds of traditional feudal production, demanding tighter discipline and long working hours so capitalists could extract a profit from using workers' labour power. In fact, Marx and Engels (2008 [1848]: 13–14) produce a glowing account of capitalism as a revolutionary transformation of society. In its first 100 years it had 'created more massive and more colossal productive forces than have all preceding generations together'. But this was achieved by the ruthless exploitation of workers and, consequently, inevitable and endemic alienation among the workforce.

Marx expected capitalism itself, just like feudalism, to give way to another mode of production – communism – brought about by disaffected workers who develop class-consciousness – an awareness of their exploited position. Under communism, private property would be abolished and genuinely communal social relations established. Unlike primitive communism, though, modern communism would retain all the benefits of the highly productive industrial system bequeathed by capitalism. This would produce an advanced, humane and sophisticated form of communal life, capable of delivering on the communist principle 'from each, according to his [*sic*] ability, to each, according to his need' (Marx 1938 [1875]: 10).

Evaluation

For Marx, a theory of industrialism *per se* makes no sense. Industrial development required industrialists, who were also capitalist entrepreneurs. To understand the industrial system also means understanding that the new capitalistic social relationships favour a few and disadvantage the majority. In addition, Marx's perspective provides a useful reminder that factories, workshops and offices, along with computers, robots and the Internet, do not materialize from thin air. They are the products of a system of antagonistic social relations, rooted in conflict, not consensus.

Marx's perspective shows that grand theorizing can be useful. The concept of a 'mode of production' is helpful as it allows us to place the welter of historical facts into a general framework, which makes them easier to understand. Many social scientists have operated with this framework, expanding, refining or criticizing it since Marx's death, and many continue to do so today. Though Marx's theory may be flawed, most sociologists would agree that discovering those flaws has been immensely fruitful for the discipline as a whole.

However, Marx's work also illustrates the main problem with grand theories: the difficulty of subjecting them to empirical testing. What would we have to find in order conclusively to prove a theory wrong? Does the fact that a communist revolution has not happened in the industrialized countries more than 160 years after the publication of *The Communist Manifesto* (1848) show that the theory's central prediction was misguided? Later Marxists sought to explain exactly why a communist revolution did not occur and, in doing so, modified Marx's ideas. 'Classic studies 3.1' looks at one especially influential group – the Frankfurt School – whose theories have influenced the development of conflict sociology.

Classic Studies 3.1 **Neo-Marxism: the Frankfurt School of critical theory**

In the mid-nineteenth century, Marx forecast that a working-class revolution was at hand; but it did not materialize in his lifetime. Then, in 1917, the Russian Revolution amid the turmoil of the First World War seemed to indicate that, at last, Marx's forecast was on the verge of being proved right. But communism did not spread into the industrialized Western countries. Instead, the 1930s saw the rise of fascism in Italy and Nazism in Germany, both of which were aggressively anti-communist movements. These developments presented Marxists with a dilemma: was Marx's theory still adequate for understanding the development of capitalism? If it was, then an orthodox form of Marxism would remain valuable. But, if not, then new forms of Marxist theorizing (called neo-Marxism) would be needed.

Marxist thought, in fact, developed in several directions over the twentieth century, particularly among 'Western Marxists', who rejected the Soviet version of communism (Kolakowski 2005). One group within Western Marxism has been especially influential – the Frankfurt School of critical theory. It was originally based at the Institute for Social Research in Frankfurt under the directorship of Max Horkheimer, but many critical theorists were forced out of Germany when the National Socialists expelled around one-third of the university's staff, resulting in their relocation to Europe and America. The Nazis systematically undermined universities and removed or forced out many Jewish intellectuals.

Drawing on the ideas of Marx and Freud and the philosophy of Immanuel Kant, the Frankfurt School produced a series of important studies of capitalism, fascism, mass culture and the emerging consumer society in the USA. For example, Theodor Adorno (1976 [1950]) and his colleagues analysed the emergence and popularity of fascism as, in part, a consequence of the rise of an authoritarian personality type, susceptible to the attractions of a strong leader. Herbert Marcuse's *One-Dimensional Man* (1964) distinguished between 'real' human needs and the many 'false' needs produced by the consumer form of industrial capitalism, with its seductive advertising, which suppressed

The rise of fascism in Europe forced Western Marxists to rethink Marx's ideas.

people's ability to think critically and instead produced a one-dimensional and uncritical form of thinking.

In studies such as these, we can see the Frankfurt thinkers attempting to come to terms with a very different form of capitalism from that which Marx had investigated. At the same time, the optimistic Marxist vision of a working-class revolution began to fade, as the obstacles to revolution seemed to mount in the consumer-capitalist societies.

The most recent critical theorist to exert an influence in sociology is the German social philosopher Jürgen Habermas. Among other things, Habermas devised a theory of 'communicative action' based on the deceptively simple notion that, when people make statements to each other ('speech acts'), they expect to be understood. But much of the time,

he argues, asymmetrical power relations work systematically to distort such communication, giving rise to fundamental misunderstanding and a lack of genuine debate. However, the solution is not to abandon modern ways of rational thinking, as some postmodern thinkers would have it, but to deepen modernity by defending and extending democracy and eliminating the huge inequalities of power and status that prevent proper communication. Habermas continues to work in the tradition of neo-Marxist critical theory.

After the ending of the Soviet Union's communist regime in 1991, Marx's ideas, and Marxist theories generally, lost ground in sociology. Some even talked of a crisis in Marxist thought as a result of the demise of actually existing socialism and communism (Gamble 1999). However, the 2008 credit crisis and subsequent economic recession have reminded scholars that capitalism is an economic system that thrives on periodic booms and slumps. Though the Marxist theory of revolution may seem unsatisfactory, a broadly Marxist analysis of capitalist economies still plays a part in debates about social change. For instance, the Slovenian philosopher Slavoj Žižek (2011, 2012), though critical of some of Marx's ideas, which he melds with other theories, still argues that communism is the only genuine alternative to capitalism. Even in the twenty-first century, it seems, scholars continue to engage in debates with Marx.

> **THINKING CRITICALLY**
>
> Why has the communist revolution, forecast by Marx, not materialized? List all the factors that have prevented the working class from revolting against capitalism. Can we say that the theory has been definitively falsified?

Establishing sociology

Comte, Spencer, Marx and other early theorists laid some of the foundations for sociology's development. But there was no academic discipline in the period through which they lived, and the subject had no institutional presence within universities. If sociology was to become part of Comte's 'hierarchy of the sciences', then it needed to carve out a place alongside the natural sciences in the academy, where a sociological training could be offered to students. In short, sociology needed to become respectable, and Emile Durkheim's work in France went a long way towards achieving this aim. However, it took much longer for sociology to become established within universities across Europe and elsewhere.

Emile Durkheim: the social level of reality

Durkheim is a pivotal figure in the development of academic sociology. Like Marx, he moved decisively away from philosophy, which he saw as too far removed from the real issues of the day, and towards social science, which was able to clarify the main moral questions facing French society. After working at the University of Bordeaux as the first professor of social science, Durkheim transferred to the Sorbonne in Paris and became the first ever professor of 'the science of education and sociology' (Coser 1977). Sociology was gaining a foothold in the academic establishment.

Durkheim also influenced the nature of the discipline itself. He saw that the study of specifically *social* phenomena was needed whenever research into people's behaviour went beyond individual interactions. Social institutions and social forms – such as social movements, organizations or the family – outlive the particular individuals who inhabit them and therefore they must have a reality of their own. This reality cannot adequately be understood by individualistic psychology or abstract philosophy but demands a genuinely sociological explanation. In Durkheim's terms, what we call 'the social' or social life is a level of reality *in its own right* that cannot be reduced to individual actions or thought of as a simple aggregate of individual minds.

This explains why Durkheim focused on group phenomena and social facts such as suicide rates, social solidarity and religion. People experienced social facts as 'things' external to the individual, rather like tables, bridges or buildings. The latter are all human creations, but their existence has to be taken into account and cannot be wished away. Similarly, social facts have a 'thing-like' existence which individuals must accept and take into account in their actions.

This thing-like reality of social facts means that, in Durkheim's view, the psychology of individuals was not the proper subject for sociology, which concerns itself with collective phenomena. For example, in *The Division of Labour in Society* (1893), Durkheim outlined his distinction between the *mechanical* forms of solidarity found in less complex societies and the *organic* form that characterizes large-scale, modern, industrial ones. Mechanical solidarity exists when individualism is minimized and the individual is subsumed within the collectivity. By contrast, organic solidarity is generated by the extensive division of labour within industrial societies, which tends to produce differences rather than similarities, but cohesion is achieved via economic interdependence.

Durkheim therefore rejected the idea – common at the time and since – that industrialism inevitably destroys social solidarity and threatens the fabric of society. In fact, said Durkheim, *stronger* bonds of mutual interdependence are created under organic forms of solidarity, which have the potential to create a better balance between individual differences and collective purpose. Here we can see how Durkheim's scientific sociological analysis is closely tied to a moral and social problem of the day – how can industrial societies hold together in an age of increasing individualism?

Evaluation

As we saw in chapter 1, Durkheim's approach to sociology is known as functionalism – the study of society and the way its institutions connect together and change. And, though it has been very influential in sociology in the past, today functionalism is in retreat. There are several reasons why.

First, many have argued that functionalism is good at explaining consensus – why societies hold together – but less effective in explaining conflict and radical social change. Others argue that Durkheimian functionalism prioritizes societies' constraints on people and does not allow enough room for the creative actions of individuals. Finally, functional analysis tends to impute 'purposes' and 'needs' to society itself. For example, we might say that the function of the education system is to train young people for the *needs* of a modern society. This seems to suggest that societies have 'needs' in

the same way that people do. But is this really an adequate form of explanation? Modern economies may well require certain skills, but is the present education system the only or even the best way to provide them? What we really want to know is how, exactly, did the education system develop into its present form and could things have been different? Functionalism does not prioritize such questions.

> **THINKING CRITICALLY**
>
> Durkheim rejected the idea that sociologists should study individual psychology. But can we ever understand social life if we ignore the intentions of individuals? How did Durkheim answer this criticism?

Twentieth-century structural functionalism

In the 1940s, 1950s and 1960s, a version of functionalist theory known as structural functionalism became the central paradigm of sociology, though it was never totally dominant. It is hard for students today, who see sociology as a discipline that is *inevitably* pluralistic, argumentative and theoretically diverse, to appreciate just how different *doing* sociology was at that time. Sociology and structural functionalism were often seen as one and the same thing (Davis 1949). Two American sociologists stand out during this period: Robert Merton and his mentor, Talcott Parsons.

Parsons combined the ideas of Durkheim, Weber and Vilfredo Pareto into his own brand of structural functionalism, which began from the so-called problem of social order (Lee and Newby 1983). This asks how society can hold together when all the individuals within it are self-interested and pursue their own wants and needs, often at the expense of others. Philosophers such as Thomas Hobbes (1588–1679) answered this by saying that the emergence of the modern state, with all of its policing and military powers, was the crucial factor. The state protects individuals from one another and from external enemies, and, in return, citizens accept the state's legitimate right to exercise power over them. In essence, an informal contract exists between the state and each individual.

Parsons rejected this solution. He recognized that conformity to social rules was not produced simply through the *negative* fear of punishment; instead, people conformed in *positive* ways, even teaching others the moral rules of society. Such a positive commitment to an orderly society showed, says Parsons, that social rules are not just an external force acting on individuals but have become *internalized* during the process of socialization. Society exists not only 'out there' but 'in here' as well.

Having established the primacy of a sociological understanding of social order, Parsons turned his attention to the social system itself. He devised a model which identified the needs of the social system, known as the AGIL paradigm (Parsons and Smelser 1956). If a social system (or society) is to continue, there are four basic functions it must perform. First, it must be capable of adapting to its environment, gathering enough resources to do so. Second, it must set out and put in place goals to be attained and the mechanisms for their achievement. Third, the system must be integrated and the various sub-systems must be effectively coordinated. Finally, the social system must have ways of preserving and transmitting its values and culture to new generations.

In less abstract terms, Parsons saw the *economic* sub-system performing an *adaptive* function, the *political* sub-system as setting society's *goals* and the means of attaining them, the *community* sub-system ('societal community') as doing *integrative* work, and the *educational* sub-system (and other socializing agencies) as transmitting *culture and values* – the latency function (see figure 3.2). Structural functionalism was a theory which gave priority to the overall system and its 'needs', but it was always vulnerable to the charge that it overemphasized consensus and agreement. The task of solving this problems passed to Robert Merton, who pursued a more critical version of functionalism.

Merton saw that many sociological studies focused on either the macro level of society or the micro level of social interaction, but failed to 'fill in the gaps' between macro and micro. To rectify this, he argued for middle-range theories of the meso level in particular areas or on specific subjects. An excellent example is his study of working-class criminality and deviance. Why was there so much acquisitive crime among the working classes? Merton's explanation was that, in an American society which promotes the cultural goal of material success but offers very few legitimate opportunities for lower social-class groups, working-class criminality represented an adaptation to the circumstances in which many young people found themselves. The fact that they aimed to achieve the material success the system promoted meant they were not evil or incapable of reform. Rather, it was the structure of society that needed to change. This thesis shows that Merton tried to develop functionalism in new directions, and, in doing so, he moved closer to conflict theory.

Merton also distinguished between manifest and latent functions: the former are observable consequences of action, the latter are those that remain unspoken. In studying latent functions, Merton argued, we can learn much more about the way that societies work. For example, we might observe a rain dance among tribal people, the manifest function of which appears to be to bring about rain. But, empirically, the rain dance often fails and yet continues to be practised – why? Merton argues that this is because its latent function is to build and sustain group solidarity, which is a continuing requirement. Similarly, Merton argued that institutions contained certain dysfunctional elements which create tensions, and the existence of these allowed him to discuss the potential for conflict within society in ways that Parsons could not.

> See chapter 20, 'Crime and Deviance', for a more detailed discussion and critique of Merton's ideas.

The social system

ADAPTATION FUNCTION	GOAL ATTAINMENT FUNCTION
Economic sub-system	Political sub-system
A	G
LATENCY FUNCTION	INTEGRATIVE FUNCTION
Education/socialization sub-system	Community sub-system
L	I

Figure 3.2   Parsons's AGIL scheme

The rain dance may appear doomed to fail, but are there any rituals which perform similar functions in modern societies?

What became of structural functionalism? Following the death of Parsons in 1979, Jeffrey Alexander (1985) sought to revisit and revive the approach, aiming to tackle its theoretical flaws. But, by 1997, even Alexander was forced to concede that the 'internal contradictions' of his 'new' or neofunctionalism meant that it was finished. Instead, he argued for a reconstruction of sociological theory beyond functionalist assumptions (Alexander 1997). Parsonian structural functionalism is, to all intents and purposes, for the time being at least, defunct within mainstream sociology.

> ### THINKING CRITICALLY
>
> What conclusions should we draw from the rise and fall of structural functionalism? Could sociology ever dispense with the basic concept of 'function' in understanding social institutions?

Parsons's ideas became so influential because they spoke to the developed societies about their post-1945 situation of gradually rising affluence and political consensus. But they lost ground in the late 1960s and the 1970s as conflicts began to mount, with new peace and anti-nuclear movements, protests against American involvement in Vietnam, and radical student movements emerging in Europe and North America. At that point, conflict theories were reinvigorated, as they seemed more relevant to understanding and accounting for the new situation. As we will see later in the chapter, understanding globalization, multiculturalism, shifting gender relations, risk and environmental degradation have similarly led to another new round of theorizing.

Max Weber: capitalism and religion

A founding figure in sociology whose ideas stand behind many actor-centred approaches is Max Weber. His most famous work, *The Protestant Ethic and the Spirit of Capitalism*

(1992 [1904–5]), tackled a fundamental problem: why did capitalism originate in the West? For around thirteen centuries after the fall of ancient Rome, other civilizations were more prominent than those in the West. In fact, Europe was a rather insignificant part of the world, while China, India and the Ottoman Empire in the Near East were all major powers. China in particular was a long way ahead of the West in its level of technological and economic development. So how did Europe's economies become so dynamic?

Weber reasoned that the key is to show what makes modern capitalism different from earlier types of economic activity. The desire to accumulate wealth can be found in many historical civilizations, and people have valued wealth for the comfort, security, power and enjoyment it can bring. Contrary to popular belief, capitalist economies are not simply a natural outgrowth of the desire for personal wealth. Something different must be at work.

Religion in the heart of capitalism?

Weber argued that, in the economic development of the West, the key difference is an attitude towards the accumulation of wealth that is found nowhere else in history. He called this attitude the 'spirit of capitalism' – a motivating set of beliefs and values held by the first capitalist merchants and industrialists. Yet, quite unlike wealthy people elsewhere, these industrialists did not spend their accumulated riches on luxurious, materialistic lifestyles. On the contrary, many of them were frugal and self-denying, living soberly without the trappings of affluence we are used to seeing today. This very unusual combination of characteristics was vital to the rapid economic development of the West. The early capitalists reinvested their wealth to promote further expansion of the enterprises they owned, and this continual reinvestment of profits produced a cycle of investment, production, profit and reinvestment that enabled businesses to grow and capitalism to expand quickly.

The controversial part of Weber's theory is that the 'spirit of capitalism' actually had its origins in religion. The essential motivating force was provided by the impact of Protestantism and one variety in particular: Puritanism. The early capitalists were mostly Puritans and many subscribed to Calvinism. Calvinists believed that human beings are God's instruments on Earth, required by the Almighty to work in a vocation – an occupation for the greater glory of God. They also believed in predestination, according to which only certain individuals are among the 'elect' and will enter heaven in the afterlife. In Calvin's original doctrine, nothing a person does on Earth can alter whether they are one of the elect; this is predetermined by God. However, this belief was difficult to live with and produced much anxiety among followers, leading to a constant search for 'signs' of election to quell salvation anxiety.

People's success when working in a vocation, indicated by their increasing prosperity, came to be seen as a sign that they were part of the elect few. Thus, a motivation towards profitability was generated as an unintended consequence of religious adherence, producing a paradoxical outcome. Puritans believed luxury to be evil, so their drive to accumulate wealth was combined with severe and unadorned personal lifestyles. This means the early capitalists were not self-conscious revolutionaries and did not set out to produce a capitalist revolution. Today, the idea of working in a calling has faded, and successful entrepreneurs have stupendous quantities of material goods and live luxurious lifestyles. In a famous passage, Weber (1992 [1904–5]: 182) says:

> The Puritan wanted to work in a calling; we are forced to do so . . . Since asceticism undertook to remodel the world and to work out its ideals in the world, material goods have gained an increasingly and finally an inexorable power over the lives of men as at no previous period in history. . . . The idea of duty in one's calling prowls about in our lives like the ghost of dead religious beliefs.

Evaluation

Weber's theory has been criticized from many angles. Some have argued that the outlook he called 'the spirit of capitalism' can be seen in early Italian merchant cities of the twelfth century, long before Calvinism. Others claim that the idea of 'working in a vocation', which Weber associated with Protestantism, already existed within Catholic beliefs. Yet the essentials of Weber's account are accepted by many and the thesis he advanced remains bold and illuminating. If Weber's thesis is valid, then modern economic and social development has been decisively influenced by something that seems at first sight utterly distant from it – a set of religious ideals.

Weber's theory also meets important criteria for theoretical thinking in sociology. First, it suggests an interpretation that breaks with common sense and develops a fresh perspective on an issue. Most scholars before Weber gave little thought to possible links between religious ideas and the origins of capitalism. Second, the theory makes sense of something that is otherwise puzzling: why would individuals want to live frugally while making great efforts to accumulate wealth? Third, the theory sheds light on circumstances beyond those it was created to explain. Weber tried to grasp the origins of modern capitalism, but it seems reasonable to suppose that parallel values could be part of societies which became capitalist much later. Finally, a good theory is not just valid but also fruitful in generating new ideas and stimulating further research. Weber's theory has been highly successful in all these respects, providing the springboard for a large amount of research and theoretical analysis. Weber's approach to sociology was also an important stimulus to many later theories which place human actors at the centre of their analyses, and we look at some of these in the next section.

THINKING CRITICALLY

Weber's theory of the origins of capitalism goes beyond Merton's idea of a 'middle-range theory'. What, if anything, does this theory add to our understanding of contemporary consumer-based capitalist societies?

Symbolic interactionism, phenomenology and ethnomethodology

In this section we briefly outline some important perspectives which place human actors and social interaction at the centre of their analysis. A significant exponent of this perspective is Georg Simmel (1858–1918), often described as the 'first sociologist of modernity' on account of his work on the experience of modern city life (discussed in chapter 6, 'Cities and Urban Life'). Simmel saw sociology as a discipline that was concerned primarily with the different forms of social interactions or 'sociation' (Frisby 2002). His broadly interactionist ideas influenced the work of many of his peers and later sociologists. This section looks at some key ideas from symbolic interactionism, phenomenology and ethnomethodology. Although there are impor-tant differences between them, as a group they stand in contrast to structural theories in sociology.

George Herbert Mead (1863–1931) is cred-ited with laying the foundations for an approach to sociology called *symbolic inter-actionism*. This is a general label covering all those approaches that investigate social inter-actions with a focus on language and symbols at their core. Interactionists often reject the very idea that social structures exist objec-tively, and in their work they do not focus on them. Herbert Blumer (who coined the term symbolic interactionism) argued that all talk of social structures or social systems is unjusti-fied, as only individuals and their interactions can really be said to 'exist' at all.

Symbolic interactionism focuses on micro-level interactions and the ways in which meanings are constructed and transmitted. George Herbert Mead (1934) argued that

Meeting people is a normal occurrence in our lives, but interactionists study the rituals and unsaid assumptions that are in play during such an everyday phenomenon.

the individual person is in fact a social self, produced during interaction processes rather than being biologically given. His theory traces the emergence and development of the self through a series of stages in childhood, and his ideas of the social self underpin much interactionist research (see chapter 1 for a detailed discussion of Mead's ideas). Recognizing that humans use symbols in communication is a basic premise of the approach.

A symbol is something that refers to or stands for something else, so words, gestures or objects can all be used to convey meaning during interactions. However, the same symbol can convey different meanings, even in the same setting. A wedding ring, for instance, may be interpreted by one person as a sign of love and commitment but by their spouse as signifying a loss of freedom. The symbolic character of human communication marks it out as different from most animal behaviour, which involves responses to objective stimuli. Human interactions are not simply automatic behavioural responses but involve symbols in the creation of meaning. This is why sociologists reject biologically based theories of human action.

The centre of symbolic interactionism for some thirty years until 1950 was the University of Chicago's Department of Sociology (known as the Chicago School), though by no means all Chicago sociologists were interactionists. The department was also home to the 'ecological' approach of Louis Wirth, Robert E. Park and Ernest Burgess (see chapter 6, 'Cities and Urban Life', for a discussion of this approach). Nonetheless, having an institutional base was an important factor in popularizing the approach.

Arguably, the most successful symbolic interactionist is Erving Goffman (1922–82). Goffman's studies of mental 'asylums', processes of stigmatization, and the ways in which people present their selves in social encounters have become sociological classics, as much for their methodology and observational style as for their findings. In developing his 'dramaturgical analysis', which works with the metaphor of the theatre, Goffman has had

a wide influence on sociology students across the world.

 See chapter 8, 'Social Interaction and Daily Life', for a discussion of Goffman's perspective.

Phenomenology is an actor-centred perspective which deals with the ways in which social life is actually experienced. Literally, phenomenology is the systematic study of phenomena – things as they appear in our experience. Its roots in sociology lie in the philosophical work of the German philosopher Edmund Husserl, though in sociological research the Austrian-born philosopher and sociologist Alfred Schutz (1899–1959) has been more important. Schutz concentrated on people's experience of everyday life and the ways in which this comes to be 'taken for granted' as part of the lifeworld – the world as routinely experienced and lived as 'natural'. Schutz refers to this routine acceptance of the world as adopting a 'natural attitude'. For him, the task of phenomenological sociology is to understand better how this happens and what its consequences are.

Schutz was interested in *typifications* – the ways in which experienced phenomena are classified according to previous experience. Typification is commonplace. When we meet someone we perhaps think, 'Oh, so she's *that* kind of person', or 'He seems an honest type'. Typification helps to order our world and make it more predictable and therefore 'safe'. But if this becomes stereotypification it can also be dangerous – the illegitimate generalization about people based simply on their membership of a certain social group. Examples of stereotyping are racism, sexism and negative attitudes towards disabled people.

Individuals also tend to make the assumption that everyone thinks in much the same way as they do and that they can safely forget about problems of interpersonal communication. Once assumptions of this kind become internalized, they are sedimented below the surface of conscious existence, forming

85

the basis of the natural attitude. In this way, people experience important aspects of the social world, such as language and culture, as objective and external to themselves, and 'society' (as Durkheim suggested) is taken as a thing-like entity, separate from the individual. Phenomenology has not had the same impact on sociology as some of the other perspectives, though it did give rise to ethnomethodology.

Ethnomethodology – the systematic study of the methods used by 'natives' (members of a particular society) to construct their social worlds – is a third interactionist perspective. Its roots can be traced back to phenomenological philosophy, but it rose to prominence only in the 1960s with the research studies of Harold Garfinkel (1917–2011) and Aaron Cicourel (1928–). Ethnomethodologists were highly critical of mainstream sociology, particularly Parsonian structural functionalism, which Garfinkel thought treated people as if they were 'cultural dopes' – passive recipients of society's socializing agents – rather than creative actors in their own right. Garfinkel also took issue with Durkheim's famous statement that sociologists should 'treat social facts as things'. For Garfinkel, this should be the starting point for inquiry, not assumed in advance of it. Ethnomethodology seeks to uncover just how social facts are created by society's members and come to have that thing-like quality.

> Ethnomethodology is discussed more widely in chapter 8, 'Social Interaction and Daily Life'.

In contrast to many other actor-oriented perspectives, the work of Max Weber explores both individual actions and social structures. Although he was certainly interested in social interactions and the micro level of social life, his work on world religions, economic sociology and legal systems was historically informed, strongly comparative and concerned with the overall development and direction of societies. This is in contrast to the interactionist tradition as it developed after Weber, which became focused much more on the micro level of social life. The divide between micro and structural (or 'macro') approaches is one of sociology's longstanding theoretical dilemmas.

Enduring theoretical dilemmas

Since the time of the classical sociologists, it has become commonplace to argue that their work, and that of sociology in general, has bequeathed some theoretical dilemmas – matters of recurring controversy and dispute. These dilemmas concern general approaches that pose questions about how we *can* or *should* 'do' sociology, and two of them have proved remarkably persistent.

One of the enduring problems concerns the relative weight we should afford to social structure and human agency. How far are individuals creative actors who actively control the conditions of their lives? Is most of what we do the result of general social forces outside individual control? This issue became known as 'the problem of structure and agency'. It is a 'problem' because sociologists are divided on where their focus should be. Action-oriented approaches, for example, stress the active, creative side of human behaviour, while functionalism and some variants of Marxism emphasize the constraining nature of social structures on individuals.

A second dilemma concerns consensus and conflict. Some theories see the inherent order and harmony of human societies as their most enduring aspect. On this view, continuity and consensus are the most striking characteristics of societies, however much those societies change over time. Others see the pervasiveness of conflict as part of the basic fabric of social life rather than just an unusual or transitory aspect. Societies, they argue, are riven with social divisions, tensions and struggles, and it is wishful thinking to believe that people live amicably most of the time. We will explore these two dilemmas in turn.

Social structure and human agency

Durkheim argued that society has primacy over the individual person as it is far more than the sum of individual acts; it has a 'firmness' or 'solidity' comparable to structures in the material environment. Think of a person in a room with several doors. The structure of the room constrains the range of possible activities. The siting of the walls and the doors, for example, defines the routes of exit and entry. Social structure sets similar limits to what we can do, and in this sense it is 'external' to the individual. Durkheim (1982 [1895]: 50) expresses the point this way:

> When I perform my duties as a brother, a husband or a citizen and carry out the commitments I have entered into, I fulfil obligations which are defined in law and custom and which are external to myself and my actions. . . . Similarly, the believer has discovered from birth, ready fashioned, the beliefs and practices of his religious life; if they existed before he did, it follows that they exist outside him. The systems of signs that I employ to express my thoughts, the monetary system I use to pay my debts, the credit instruments I utilize in my commercial relationships, the practices I follow in my profession, etc. – all function independently of the use I make of them.

Although this structural perspective has many adherents, it has also met with sharp criticism. What is 'society' if it is not the composite of many individual actions? If we study a social group we do not see a collective entity or 'thing', only many individuals interacting with one another in various ways. In the same way, what we call 'society' is only an aggregate of individuals behaving in regular ways in relation to one another. According to interactionists, human beings have reasons for what they do and they inhabit a social world constructed by meanings. Social phenomena are *not* like 'things' but depend on the symbolic meanings we invest in them, which means we are not at the mercy of an external 'society' but are instead its creators.

Yet the differences between structure and agency perspectives can be exaggerated, and we can easily see connections between them. Social structures do precede and constrain the individual. For example, I did not invent the monetary system I use, nor do I have a choice about whether I want to use it if I wish to have the goods and services money can buy. On the other hand, it is mistaken to suppose that society is 'external' in the same way as the physical world. The physical world would still exist if no human beings were alive, but the monetary system would not. Moreover, 'social facts' do not entirely *determine* our actions. I could choose to live without using money, even if it proved very difficult to eke out an existence. As human beings, we can make choices and do not simply respond passively to events.

Beyond structure and agency?

The divide between structural and agency perspectives is seen as unproductive by many sociologists, and several attempts have been made to bring them together in one theoretical perspective. In this sub-section we look briefly at just two of the more successful attempts in the contrasting approaches of Norbert Elias and Anthony Giddens.

Norbert Elias and figurational sociology

The German sociologist Norbert Elias (1897–1990) saw the structure–agency dilemma as a hangover from earlier philosophical ways of thinking and an obstacle to be overcome. Sociology inherited this 'problem' from philosophy, which also left a series of other dualisms, such as mind–body, individual–society and micro–macro. Sociological theorists tended to defer to the expertise of philosophers in matters of logic and assessing the validity of knowledge claims. But, for Elias, sociology is a distinct theoretical-empirical science that produces a more empirically adequate knowledge, and therefore sociologists do not need philosophers to adjudicate for them (Kilminster 2007).

The structure–agency dilemma is unhelpful and inaccurate (as are all other such dualisms). For example, the distinction between

An antiques and vintage market demonstrates structure and agency in economic exchanges. Buyers are constrained to pay using an established currency (structure), but the final prices can be bartered (agency) rather than being based on a fixed value.

individual and society implies that each has a 'thing-like' existence and that the individual is distinct from society. But discussing social life using these terms is highly misleading because 'they encourage the impression that society is made up of structures external to oneself, the individual, and the individual is at one and the same time surrounded by society yet cut off from it by some invisible barrier' (Elias 1978: 15).

Elias argues that sociology studies *people* (in the plural), who are always in networks or relations of interdependence. Elias calls these interdependent networks figurations, and the approach he pioneered is known as figurational studies or, sometimes, process

sociology (Mennell 1998). This theoretical move is deceptively simple. But, if we *start* from social figurations, then radical conclusions follow. The individual person is not an autonomous, 'closed' being entombed within a physical body, coming into contact with others only during interactions, a little like snooker balls colliding. Elias argues that human beings are 'open people', whose individual identities and 'selves' are socially produced in networks of social relations – they are social selves (Burkitt 2008).

On the other hand, the 'thing' that is routinely called 'society' is not a thing at all but is, in reality, a long-term social process of ever-changing figurations (Van Krieken 1998: 5–6).

A long-term perspective is necessary, in Elias's view, because it is only by tracing the development of social life in the past that we can arrive at a realistic understanding of the present and of ourselves. Elias insists that a figurational perspective, which focuses attention on this continual social process, is a clear advance over theories which discuss 'society' as a static thing-like entity.

For example, in *The Civilizing Process* (2000 [1939]), Elias traces the development of 'civilized' codes of manners, such as etiquette at the dinner table, from the European Middle Ages onwards. These codes first developed in the royal courts, where people were expected to control their behaviour and emotions, but subsequently spread to other social classes through a process of status competition. Hence, the rather strange habits and customs of people in previous times are not just historical curiosities unrelated to modern life. In fact, we can never understand why the standards we accept as 'natural' exist unless we appreciate how they developed over very long periods of time.

> See 'Classic Studies 22.1' in chapter 22, 'Nations, War and Terrorism', for a discussion of Elias's 'civilizing process' theory, which shows how he handles social structures and individual actions.

Elias's figurational perspective does not try to 'bridge' the structure–agency dilemma in sociology. Rather, it effectively dissolves the 'problem' altogether. There is no need for sociologists to focus exclusively on the micro level of small-scale interactions or the macro level of social structures and institutions. Understanding the shifting figurations formed by interdependent people means we have to be concerned with every aspect of human life, from individual personalities to the large figurations represented by the concepts of nation-state or the city.

However, one problem with Elias's approach is that the concept of figuration is hardly novel. Many sociological studies have used the ideas of networks, configurations or interdependent relations (Fletcher 1997: 60). Does Elias claim too much for his central concept? In his defence, perhaps it is not the concept of figuration which is important but the uses to which it is put. A second issue is that Elias tends to see 'society' as largely the unintended outcome of many intentional actions. Yet this may not give enough weight to the influence of very powerful actors such as states, social movements or multinational corporations in shaping society in their interests (Van Krieken 1998). Nevertheless, figurational sociology has developed into a thriving research tradition with its own journal, which has produced some fascinating studies.

Anthony Giddens and structuration theory

An alternative way forward which looks to bridge the gap between 'structure' and 'action' was developed by Anthony Giddens. Unlike Elias, Giddens (1984: vii) does not reject philosophy, arguing that sociology must be 'alive' to philosophical problems: 'The social sciences are lost if they are not directly related to philosophical problems by those who practise them.' Debates in philosophy can contribute to our understanding of social life and should not be ignored. However, Giddens also adopts a central focus on the structuring activity of individual actions which bears some similarity to Elias's interest in social processes.

Giddens's approach begins from the recognition that people actively make and remake social structure during the course of their everyday activities. For instance, the fact that I use the monetary system contributes in a minor, yet essential way to the very existence of that system. If everyone, or even a majority of people, at some point decided not to use money, the 'thing-like' monetary system would collapse. A useful concept for analysing such processes of the active making and remaking of social structure is structuration (Giddens 1984). Structuration theory holds that 'structure' and 'action' are necessarily related to each other and are not opposites. Societies, communities and groups have 'structure' only insofar as people behave in regular and fairly predictable ways. On the other hand, 'action' is only possible because each individual possesses an enormous amount of socially structured knowledge which pre-exists them as individuals.

Take the example of language. To exist at all, language must be structured – that is, it must have properties which every speaker must observe. What someone says in any given context would not make sense unless it followed certain grammatical rules. Yet the structural qualities of language exist only insofar as individual language users actually follow those rules in practice. We can say that language, as with other social institutions, is constantly in the process of structuration.

Interactionists are quite right to suggest that human agents are highly knowledgeable actors. Social life demands that we follow complex sets of conventions, such as the rituals strangers observe when passing by or meeting in the street. On the other hand, as we apply that knowledge to our own actions, we give force and content to those rules and conventions on which we draw. Structuration always presumes this 'duality of structure' in which all social action presumes the existence of structure. But, at the same time, structure presumes action because it depends on regularities of human behaviour.

This resolution to the structure–agency problem has its critics. One issue is the relative weight afforded to structure and agency in particular settings. Despite the laudable attempt to bridge the divide, Giddens's structuration theory does seem to put heavy emphasis on the structuring power of actors in shaping social life. Even though social structures, such as language, are seen as effective, structuration theory still views human agency as capable of changing and reshaping them, however powerful or long established they may be. But the extent to which this is true in reality cannot be decided in advance of empirical research into concrete cases.

Margaret Archer (1995, 2003) is sympathetic to structuration theory but sees Giddens's

Digital technology, such as IM and SMS messaging, has led to people inventing language rules and methods (e.g., emojis) for these new contexts – a small example of how the structure and rules of language are changed by its speakers.

theoretical discussion as overly descriptive. It is not enough simply to note that structure and agency are co-constitutive – one implies the other. Sociological explanations need to establish whether structure or agency is the *cause* of social phenomena in particular cases. The continuous interplay of structure and agency that Giddens rightly identifies has a definite chronological sequence: existing social structure → individual actions → modified social structure, and so on. In tracing this continuous sequence in specific studies, it should be possible to discover whether structure or agency is more effective.

It seems unlikely that the structure–agency problem will ever be resolved to the satisfaction of all sociologists, especially as various perspectives and theories lie closer to one side or the other of the dilemma. It is also the case that sociologists tend to lean towards structure or agency perspectives depending on their own social backgrounds and life experiences. However, the two approaches discussed above show that there is a growing desire to take some of the heat out of this longstanding problem.

> ### THINKING CRITICALLY
>
> How satisfactory are the concepts of figuration and structuration in helping us to resolve the structure–agency problem? Does figurational sociology really bypass the need to bridge the divide between structure and agency? According to structuration theory, what exactly are social structures?

Consensus versus conflict

The second enduring dilemma is that of consensus versus conflict. For Durkheim, society is a set of interdependent institutions. For all functionalist thinkers, in fact, society is treated as an integrated whole, composed of structures which mesh closely with one another. This is very much in accord with Durkheim's focus on the constraining, 'external' character of 'social facts'. However, the analogy here is not with the walls of a building but with the physiology of the human body.

The body consists of various specialized parts, such as the brain, heart, lungs, liver, and so on, each of which contributes to sustaining the continuing life of the whole organism. These necessarily work in harmony with one another; if they do not, the life of the organism is under threat. Similarly, for a society to have a continuing existence over time, its specialized institutions, such as the political system, religion, the family and the educational system, must all work in harmony with one another. This is a consensus perspective, which focuses on how societies hold together.

Those who focus mainly on conflict have a very different outlook. Their guiding assumptions can be seen in Marx's theory of class conflict. According to Marx, societies are divided into classes with unequal resources and, since marked inequalities exist, there are divisions of interest that are 'built into' the social system. These conflicts at some point break out into active social change. Since Marx, others have identified gender and ethnic divisions or political differences as sources of

conflict. For conflict theorists, society inevitably contains divisions and tensions regardless of which social groups are stronger than others.

As with the case of structure and action, it is unlikely that this theoretical dispute can be resolved fully. Yet, once more, the differences between consensus and conflict standpoints may not be as wide as it appears. All societies probably have some loose, general agreement on values, and all certainly involve conflict. As a general rule, sociologists always have to examine the connections between consensus and conflict within societies. The values held by different groups and the goals that their members pursue often reflect a mixture of common and opposed interests. For instance, even in Marx's theory of class conflict, the different classes share some common interests. Capitalists depend on a labour force to work in their businesses, just as workers depend on capitalists to provide wages. Open conflict is not continuous, as what both sides have in common tends to override their differences. For this reason, Max Weber argued that the future of the working classes lay in wringing concessions from capitalism, not in trying to overthrow it.

A useful concept for analysing the interrelation of conflict and consensus is ideology – ideas, values and beliefs which help secure the position of more powerful groups at the expense of less powerful ones. Power, ideology and conflict are always closely connected. Ideological dominance can often create the appearance of consensus, as the internalization of ideological notions leads people to accept gross inequalities of opportunity, status and condition.

Those who hold power may depend mainly on the influence of ideology to retain their dominance but are usually able to use force when necessary. For instance, in feudal times, aristocratic rule was supported by the idea that a minority of people were 'born to govern', but aristocratic rulers often resorted to violence against those who dared to oppose their power. In recent times, the so-called Arab Spring of 2010–12 saw the apparently stable societies of the Middle East and North Africa riven with protests and demonstrations which expressed pent-up frustrations and underlying conflicts of interest. In Libya, Bahrain and Syria, when appeals to national pride and shared solidarity had failed, the governing regimes turned to military force to try to put down the protests. The example shows that neither consensus nor conflict are 'natural'; both are outcomes of social processes.

The transformation of societies – and sociology

For much of its history, sociology was dominated by the so-called Marx–Weber debate on the character and future of capitalist societies. For both Marx and Weber, the emergence of capitalism was a fateful development which shaped the direction of societies around the world, though they differed on where it might lead. Marx saw capitalism as more dynamic than any preceding type of economic system. Capitalists compete to sell their goods to consumers, and, in order to survive in a competitive market, firms have to produce their wares as cheaply and efficiently as possible. This leads to constant technological innovation as companies strive to gain an edge over their rivals. Capitalist firms also seek out new markets for goods, cheap raw materials and cheaper sources of labour. For Marx, capitalism is a restlessly expanding system spreading to all parts of the globe.

USING YOUR SOCIOLOGICAL IMAGINATION

3.1 Marx and Weber – the shaping of the modern world

Broadly Marxist ideas	Broadly Weberian ideas
1 The main dynamic of modern development is the expansion of capitalistic economic mechanisms.	1 The main dynamic of modern development is the rationalization of production.
2 Modern societies are riven with class inequalities, which are basic to their very nature.	2 Class is one type of inequality among many – such as inequalities between men and women – in modern societies.
3 Major divisions of power, such as those affecting the differential position of men and women, derive ultimately from economic inequalities.	3 Power in the economic system is separable from other sources. For instance, male–female inequalities cannot be explained in economic terms.
4 Modern societies (capitalist societies) are a transitional type – we may expect them to become radically reorganized in the future. Socialism will eventually replace capitalism.	4 Rationalization is bound to progress further in the future, in all spheres of social life. All modern societies are dependent on the same basic modes of social and economic organization.
5 The spread of Western influence across the world is mainly a result of the expansionist tendencies of capitalist enterprise.	5 The global impact of the West comes from its command over industrial resources, together with superior military power.

THINKING CRITICALLY

Taking each contrast in turn, assess which of the two theories has stood the test of time better. Is it possible to reach an overall conclusion about which theoretical perspective provides the most accurate account of the direction of social change over the twentieth century?

Marx's explanation of capitalist expansion is a powerful one, but not all scholars agree that capitalism is the most significant force shaping the modern world, and most are sceptical of the thesis that socialism or communism are likely future modes of production. With the passage of time and no sign of working-class revolution, Marx's theoretical perspective has been called into question.

Max Weber is one of Marx's most perceptive critics, and his work has been described as involving a lifelong struggle with 'the ghost of Marx' – the intellectual legacy Marx left behind. Weber agreed that economic factors played a crucial role in social change, but *non-economic* factors, such as ideas and ideologies, also played their part. For example, Weber argued (as did Marx) that material interests are the main driving force in history, but for Weber these interests are channelled in particular directions by ideas, which act rather like the 'switchmen' who direct powerful trains at railway junctions. Weber's understanding of modern societies and their direction of travel contrasts sharply with that of Marx.

According to Weber, capitalism is just one of several major factors shaping social development, and in some ways the impact of science and bureaucracy has been more influential. Science has shaped modern technology and would continue to do so in any future socialist society, while bureaucracy remains the most efficient way of organizing large numbers of people effectively. Bureaucracies inevitably

Global Society 3.1 Rationalization as McDonaldization?

Anyone who has eaten at a McDonald's restaurant abroad as well as at home will have noticed many similarities. The interior decorations may vary, the language spoken will differ, but the layout, the procedure for ordering, staff uniforms, and 'service with a smile' are essentially similar. Compared with many other restaurants, one of the obvious differences at McDonald's is just how efficient the whole process is. Staff members work on specialized, straightforward jobs: one makes the fries, another flips the burgers, a third puts the burger in a bun and adds the salad. Much of the process is also automated – milkshakes at the press of a button, deep fryers that work at set temperatures, and tills with buttons for each item so staff do not even have to learn food prices.

But why should sociologists be interested in fast food? George Ritzer (1983, 1993, 1998) argues that McDonald's provides a vivid metaphor of recent economic and cultural transformations. What we are witnessing, he says, is the 'McDonaldization' of society: the process by which the basic principles of fast-food restaurants come to dominate other areas of society. Using the four guiding principles of McDonald's restaurants – *efficiency, calculability, uniformity* and *control through automation* – Ritzer argues that modern societies are becoming ever more 'rationalized' and that McDonald's is simply the best exemplar of the process. 'McDonaldization', he notes, is catchier than 'Burger Kingization' or 'Starbuckization'.

Like Weber, Ritzer claims that the long-term process of **rationalization** can, paradoxically, generate irrational outcomes. Weber saw that bureaucracies take on a life of their own, spreading through social life with harmful as well as positive consequences. Similarly, Ritzer argues that the apparently rational process of McDonaldization spawns a series of irrationalities – damage to our health, from a 'high calorie, fat, cholesterol, salt, and sugar content' diet, and to the environment, with all the packaging that is thrown away after each meal. Most of all, McDonaldization is 'dehumanizing'. People file forward in queues as if on a conveyor belt, while staff repeat the same tasks over and over again, like robots.

Ritzer's thesis has been very influential in sociology, though in recent years McDonald's has been forced to change its practices to compete in the global economy, tailoring its 'product' to fit the local cultures in particular markets around the world – an excellent example of **glocalization** in practice.

expand with modern life, becoming a key source of rationalization – the organization of social and economic life according to principles of efficiency on the basis of technical knowledge. Weber also suggests, against Marx, that capitalism actually provides a counterbalancing source of creativity to the stultifying 'dead hand' of bureaucratic domination.

Which interpretation of social change is correct? Perhaps today this is not the most pressing question for sociologists. For sociology to be successful, its theories and perspectives must be capable of illuminating the central aspects of societies and social life. While the classical theories of Marx, Durkheim and Weber and their later incarnations certainly did so in relation to industrialization, capitalism and bureaucratic expansion, they may not be the best guides to shifting gender relations, multicultural societies, globalization, manufactured risks or environmental problems. Do we need new theories that move beyond the classics, perhaps taking sociology in different directions?

This question of the continuing relevance of the classics underlies the rest of the chapter, as we look at some recent theories and perspectives that are reshaping the discipline. First we discuss important criticisms of sociology itself from the standpoint of feminism and postcolonialism. These perspectives point out sociological theory's neglect of the experience of women and of colonial domination. Then we move on to some recent perspectives which suggest that contemporary societies have changed in ways that earlier theories did not foresee. The issue this raises is whether the classics have any life left in them in an age of risk, globalization and postmodernism.

Feminism and malestream sociology

The accepted founders of sociology were all men (as we saw in chapter 1), and they paid scant regard to the differential experience of men and women or to gender relations. Where they did, their ideas tended to be descriptive and theoretically unsatisfactory. For exam-

ple, differences between women and men are discussed occasionally in Durkheim's writings, but not in a consistently sociological manner (Rahman and Jackson 2010: 56). Durkheim (1952 [1897]) suggested that, while men are 'almost entirely' products of society, women are 'to a far greater extent' products of nature, leading to differing bases for identities, tastes and inclinations. Sociologists today do not accept this stereotypical conclusion, which illegitimately essentializes female identities.

Marx and Engels's ideas are substantially at odds with those of Durkheim. For them, differences in power and status between men and women mainly reflect other divisions, especially class divisions. According to Marx, in the earliest forms of human society (primitive communism) neither gender nor class divisions were present. The power of men over women came about only as class divisions appeared. Women then came to be seen as a type of 'private property', owned by men through the institution of marriage. The only way for women to be freed from their situation of bondage would be when capitalism is overthrown and class divisions are eliminated.

Again, though, few sociologists today would accept this analysis. Class is not the only factor shaping social divisions which affect relations between men and women; among others are ethnicity and cultural background. For instance, it might be argued that women in some minority ethnic groups have more in common with men in that group than they do with women in the ethnic majority. In recent years, sociologists have become much more interested in intersectionality – the ways in which divisions of class, gender and ethnicity combine or 'intersect' to produce complex forms of social inequality (Brewer 1993; P. H. Collins 2000). Intersectionality does not mean the end of class analysis, but it does point to the need for more research which crosses conventional theoretical boundaries.

Since it left very little to build on in relating issues of gender to more established forms of theoretical thinking, the classical legacy bequeathed a difficult problem to sociologists.

How should 'gender' as a general category be brought within existing sociological theories? The issues involved here are important and bear directly on the challenge that feminist scholars have laid down. There is no real dispute that a great deal of sociology in the past has either ignored women or operated with an inadequate understanding of gender relations. Yet bringing the study of women into sociology is not the same as dealing with issues of gender, because gender concerns relations between women *and* men. For example, research into gender has explored changing forms of masculinity as well as femininities, and, with the emergence of queer theory, the instability of the concept of gender itself has been exposed.

The next section presents a fairly brief outline of the impact of feminist theorizing on sociology, but an extended discussion of gender can be found in chapter 15, 'Gender and Sexuality'. Taken together, these sections provide an introduction to the significance of gender in society and for sociology.

Feminist theories

The campaigning activity of women's movements in the 1960s and 1970s led to many legislative changes aimed at tackling the unequal position of women in society. Once feminist scholars became part of the academy within universities, feminist theories challenged male-dominated or malestream sociology. The latter involved a perceived male bias in sociological theorizing that drew general conclusions from the experience of men – research methods that were not designed to capture women's experience, and sociology's subject matter itself, which focused on the (male-dominated) public sphere, ignoring the perceived female-oriented private sphere of households and families. One feminist slogan of the time was 'the personal is political', and, as such, matters previously considered private became legitimate subjects for sociology.

Some feminist sociologists also called for a comprehensive reconstruction of the entire discipline, including the central problems that form its core, emphasizing the centrality of gender for any satisfactory analysis of the social world. In short,

> The feminist challenge to malestream sociology is one that requires a radical rethink of the content and methodology of the whole enterprise; one that recognises the need, not simply to see society from the standpoint of women as well as from the standpoint of men, but to see the world as fundamentally gendered. (Abbott et al. 2005: 3)

How far sociology has moved in this direction remains a matter of debate. Some have argued that sociological theory continues in 'a pre-feminist mode' (Acker 1989: 65), while others see the promise of feminism to transform the discipline as a 'still-missing revolution' in sociology (Alway 1995). However, it is also the case that there are many disagreements between feminist perspectives on just how issues of gender should or can be theorized.

'Feminist theory' is a term covering an increasing range of positions, with six or seven different perspectives currently identified. These range from early theories of liberal, socialist/Marxist and radical feminism, through dual-systems and critical feminism, to postmodern/poststructuralist, black and postcolonial feminism. Most of these perspectives are discussed in more detail in chapter 15, 'Gender and Sexuality'.

The diversity of feminist theories makes it impossible to speak of a single or unified 'feminist theory of society', but we can say they all agree that knowledge is related to questions of sex and gender and that women face oppression in patriarchal societies. However, theoretical explanations of women's position differ, sometimes quite markedly. For example, while radical feminists see patriarchy as the main source of oppression, dual-systems theorists argue that both patriarchy and capitalism combine to reproduce male dominance. Black feminism both insists that race, racism and ethnicity need to be part of feminist theorizing and criticizes earlier theories for assuming that all women have essentially similar interests despite their radically divergent living conditions.

Because men and women have different experiences and view the world from different perspectives, they do not construct their understandings of the world in identical ways. Feminists often argue that malestream sociological theory has denied or ignored the 'gendered' nature of knowledge, producing supposedly universal conclusions from the specific experience of (usually white) men. As men conventionally occupy the main positions of power and authority in most societies, they have an investment in maintaining their privileged position. Under such conditions, gendered knowledge becomes a vital force in perpetuating established social arrangements and legitimating continued male domination.

Some feminist scholars influenced by poststructuralist or postmodern thinking (discussed below), including Donna Haraway

(1989, 1991), Hélène Cixous (1976) and Judith Butler (1990, 1997, 2004), have argued that it is a mistake to suppose that either 'men' or 'women' are even distinct groups with interests or characteristics. According to Butler (2004), gender itself is not a fixed category or an essence, but something fluid that is exhibited through what people *do* rather than what they *are*. If, as Butler (1990) argues, gender is something that is 'done' or performed, then it is also something that can be 'undone' when it is used by one group to exert power over another (see chapter 8, 'Social Interaction and Daily Life').

Is there, in fact, *any* essential gendered being at all, or is 'gender' in a constant process of social construction with no fixed biological foundations? Such foundational questions illustrate how far feminist thinking has travelled, though some see these matters as of

Black feminism – both within academia and in social activism, such as the Southall Black Sisters shown here – challenges the idea that 'women' share similar experiences and have the same interests.

secondary importance to tackling inequality and improving the material conditions of life for women, particularly in developing countries (Shiva 1993). Rahman and Jackson (2010: 81) argue that

> We live today within a global context characterized by extremely stark and worsening inequalities – and it is often women who are most disadvantaged by the intersections between global and local exploitation . . . Differences among women are not merely 'cultural'; the most significant of them are founded upon real, material inequalities deriving from institutionalized racism, the heritage of centuries of slavery, colonialism and imperialism and local and global divisions of labour.

Feminist theory has developed markedly since the 1970s, and some of the themes pursued today are quite different from the material feminism that emerged within 'second-wave' feminist movements. However, what these differing perspectives show is that feminist thinking has not stood still but continues to develop and expand into new areas.

 Feminist movements are discussed further in chapter 21, 'Politics, Government and Social Movements'.

THINKING CRITICALLY

Would you describe yourself as a 'feminist'? If so, why? If not, why not? What issues do you think feminism should focus on if it is to remain relevant to younger generations?

Postcolonial sociology?

Conventional sociology and sociological theory is charged by feminist scholars with neglecting the core issue of gender. A similar charge could have been made about the neglect of disability, sexuality and ethnicity. To some extent the discipline was found guilty, though this is much less so today. Over recent years, questions have also been raised about yet another 'missing revolution' in sociology, that of postcolonialism (Bhambra 2007).

Postcolonial theories are quite diverse, but their central concern is to explore the ways in which the legacy of European colonialism remains active in both societies and academic disciplines, long after former colonies have achieved independence. Postcolonial studies try not only to expose this continuing legacy but also to transform the core concepts and theories which failed to take account of colonial and postcolonial relations. For example, standard accounts of the origins of sociology (including that in chapter 1, 'What is Sociology?') list the Industrial and French revolutions as formative for sociology but give no weight to the significance of colonialism and imperialism in shaping modern societies. Similarly, postcolonial critics argue that, because sociology emerged as an integral part of European modernity, the sociological gaze was and still is a Eurocentric one, limited to the analysis of 'modern' societies and failing to incorporate the experience of the colonized societies. Sociology, they say, is badly in need of 'decolonization'.

In a parallel way, sociological theory focused on explaining the emergence of modernity and analysing its radical difference from previous societies. This is evident in the work of Marx on Western capitalism, Durkheim on mechanical and organic solidarity, and Weber's thesis of Protestantism and the origins of capitalism. But, in doing so, early sociologists effectively characterized non-European societies as 'pre-modern' or in some way 'traditional'. From the late nineteenth century, this created a disciplinary division of labour, with sociology focusing on modern, industrial societies and anthropology dealing with the non-European and non-modern world (Boatcă and Costa 2010). Anthropology was forced to acknowledge the impact of colonial regimes and, later, the postcolonial situation, but sociology sidestepped any systematic engagement with colonialism, imperialism and postcolonial relations between states.

Many postcolonial accounts seek to enable previously marginalized people and viewpoints – the subalterns – to participate on equal terms to reshape disciplines such as sociology. The problem was starkly illustrated in an early postcolonial work, Edward Said's (1978) *Orientalism*, which criticized Western academic studies of 'the Orient' or 'the East'. Said took issue with Orientalists, scholars in the so-called Area Studies tradition of the late nineteenth and early twentieth century, who analysed the Middle East, Africa and Asia. Their discussions of the Orient relied on a sharp contrast with the Occident ('the West'), where the Orient was seen as the exotic 'Other' to the 'normal' and superior Occident. To put this another way, academics in the West produced what were perceived to be authoritative accounts of the East, but without any input from indigenous people or scholars.

Said argued that Oriental Studies operated with the assumption that Eastern societies, as a group, shared some essential similarities which enabled them to be discussed collectively, while at the same time they were very different from Western cultures. This contrast was then used to 'explain' the failure of the Orient to modernize. Following Foucault's ideas on the power of discourses in society, Said saw academic Orientalism as one aspect of a society-wide discourse of Western superiority, which supported the political and economic colonial regimes on the ground. Far from being an objective, politically neutral and scholarly activity, Orientalism was one way in which the West exerted its authority over the countries of the East.

You may think that contemporary sociology has moved far beyond the early Eurocentrism, as globalization has forced sociologists to take a much broader view and to study developing countries as well as the industrialized ones. However, postcolonial theorists argue that even recent sociological theories remain stuck in the old ways of thinking. For example, many globalization theories see the process as involving capitalism and industrialism spreading outwards from the West into 'the rest' of the world, taking with them fundamental features of Western culture. Seen this way, sociological theorizing is then able to continue

with 'business as usual', without revising its core concepts and theories. You will have to reach your own conclusions as to how far this conclusion is accurate.

Recent feminist and postcolonial critiques demand a rethinking of the very foundations of sociology. However, not everyone agrees that this is either possible or necessary. First, the fact that this textbook and others cover gender relations, feminist theories, disability, sexualities and ethnicity alongside global inequalities, nations and nationalism, war, and much more, shows that sociology has not been immune to social trends, new theories and changing attitudes. Indeed, sociology is a discipline that *has* to change and 'move with the times' if it is to be relevant in the rapidly changing social world. Whether it moves far enough for those committed to a particular perspective is a rather different question.

Second, internal debates within feminist theory and postcolonialism mean that their critiques of sociology have also changed over time. As McLennan (2010: 119) argues, 'it is important to be realistic, and to resist any overbearing moralism; all thought systems are inevitably ethnocentric in focus, style and available expertise. Moreover, what it even *means* to "decolonize" or to "postcolonialize" sociology is far from crystal clear.' What we should expect is that sociology will continue to adapt to the many and varied challenges it faces and, in so doing, will develop theories accordingly.

Poststructuralism and postmodernity

Michel Foucault (1926–84), Jacques Derrida (1976, 1978) and Julia Kristeva (1984, 1977) are the most influential figures in an intellectual movement known as poststructuralism. However, Foucault's ideas have had the most influence on sociology and the social sciences. In his writings on crime, the body, madness and sexuality, Foucault analysed the emergence of modern institutions, such as prisons, hospitals and schools, that have played an increasing role in monitoring and controlling the population. He wanted to show that there was a darker side to Enlightenment ideals of individual liberty – one concerned with discipline and surveillance. Foucault advanced important ideas about the relationship between power, ideology and discourse in modern organizational systems.

The study of power is of fundamental importance in sociology, and Foucault continued some of the lines of thought pioneered in classical sociology. The role of discourse is central to his thinking, and he used the term to refer to ways of talking or thinking about particular subjects that are united by common assumptions. Foucault demonstrated, for example, the dramatic way in which discourses of madness changed from medieval times through to the present day. In the Middle Ages the insane were generally regarded as harmless, and some believed that they may even have possessed a special 'gift' of perception. In modern societies, however, 'madness' has been shaped by a scientific, medicalized discourse which emphasizes illness and treatment. This discourse is supported and perpetuated by a highly developed and influential network of doctors, medical experts, hospitals, professional associations and medical journals.

> Foucault's work is discussed in more detail in chapter 11, 'Health, Illness and Disability'.

According to Foucault, power works through discourse to shape public attitudes. Expert discourses established by those with power or authority can often be countered only by competing expert discourses. In this way, discourses can be used as powerful tools to restrict alternative ways of thinking or speaking and knowledge becomes a force of control. A prominent theme throughout Foucault's writings is the way power and knowledge are linked to technologies of surveillance, enforcement and discipline. In sociology, this perspective has expanded the way sociologists think about power relations in many areas of the discipline.

Since the mid-1980s, advocates of postmodernism claim that the classic social thinkers took their inspiration from the idea that history has a shape – it 'goes somewhere' and is progressive. But this idea has now collapsed and there are no longer any 'metanarratives' – overall conceptions of history or society – that make any sense (Lyotard 1984). The postmodern world is not destined, as Marx hoped, to be a harmonious socialist one. Similarly, the idea that science would lead inexorably to social progress is much less plausible in an age of nuclear weaponry and global warming. Democracy has spread around the world, but in many developed political systems voters are apathetic and politicians reviled. In short, for many postmodern theorists, the grand project of modernity has run into the sand.

For Jean Baudrillard (1929–2007), the postmodern age is a world where people respond to media images rather than to real persons or places. Thus when Diana, princess of Wales, died in 1997, there was an enormous outpouring of grief all over the world. But were people mourning a real person? Princess Diana existed for most people only through the mass media, and her death was presented like an event in a soap opera rather than an event in real life. Separating out reality from representation has become impossible when all that exists is 'hyperreality' – the mixing of the two.

> See chapter 18, 'The Media', for a discussion of Baudrillard and hyperreality.

Zygmunt Bauman (1992) offers a helpful distinction between two ways of thinking about the postmodern. Do we need a sociology of postmodernity or a postmodern sociology? The first view accepts that the social world has moved rapidly in a postmodern direction. The enormous growth and spread of the mass media, new information technologies, the more fluid movement of people across the world and the development of multicultural societies – all of these mean that we no longer live in a modern world but in a postmodern

ZDF spezial Aber dass man die Möglichkeit hat,
Das Interview mit
Bundespräsident Wulff auch darüber ein Gespräch zu führen.

Postmodern theory is exemplified by Baudrillard's ideas on the domination of social life by the mass media, particularly television.

one. However, on this view there is no compelling reason to think that sociology cannot describe, understand and explain the emerging postmodern world.

The second view suggests that the type of sociology which successfully analysed the modern world of capitalism, industrialization and nation-states is no longer capable of dealing with the de-centred, pluralistic, media-saturated, globalizing postmodern world, and new theories and concepts will have to be devised. In short, we need a *postmodern sociology* for a postmodern world. It remains unclear what such a sociology would look like.

Bauman accepts that the modern project originating in the European Enlightenment of rationally shaping society no longer makes

sense, at least not in the way thought possible by Comte, Marx or other classical theorists. However, since the turn of the century he has also moved away from the term 'postmodern' – which he says has become corrupted through too diverse usage – and now describes our age as one of 'liquid modernity', reflecting the fact that it is in constant flux and uncertainty *in spite of* all attempts to impose (a modern) order and stability onto it (Bauman 2000, 2007).

Of course, many sociologists reject the thesis that we are entering a postmodern age altogether. One staunch critic of postmodern theory is Jürgen Habermas (1983), who sees modernity as 'an incomplete project'. Instead of consigning it to the dustbin of history, we should be extending it, pushing for *more* democracy, *more* freedom and *more* rational policies. Postmodernists, Habermas argues, are essentially pessimists and defeatists.

Whichever view you think more plausible, it is the case that postmodern analyses have lost ground to the theory of globalization, which has become the dominant theoretical framework for understanding the direction of social change in the twenty-first century.

THINKING CRITICALLY

List all the social changes which might support the theory of postmodernity. Do these add up to the kind of fundamental social transformation identified by postmodernists, or is there an alternative way of describing them?

Reflexivity, risk and cosmopolitanism

The theory of globalization is discussed extensively in chapter 4, and we will not anticipate that discussion here. Instead, we look at three significant contemporary theories which assume that globalization *is* transforming human societies. These are chosen as representative of sociologists who reject the postmodern idea of the death of modernity.

Anthony Giddens on social reflexivity

In his own writings, Giddens has developed a theoretical perspective on the changes happening in the present-day world (Giddens 2002, 2009). We live today in what he calls a 'runaway world' marked by new risks and uncertainties of the sort outlined by Ulrich Beck (1999). Living in an information age also means an increase in social reflexivity. Social reflexivity refers to the fact that we have constantly to think about, or reflect upon, the circumstances in which we live our lives.

When societies were shaped by custom and tradition, people could follow established ways of doing things in a more unreflective fashion.

Today, many aspects of life that for earlier generations were simply taken for granted become matters of open decision-making. For example, for hundreds of years people had no effective ways of limiting the size of their families. With modern forms of contraception, and other forms of technological involvement in reproduction, parents can not only choose how many children they have but even decide what sex those children will be. These new possibilities, of course, are fraught with new ethical dilemmas.

However, the idea of the runaway world does not imply that we have *inevitably* lost control of our own future. In a global age, nations certainly lose some of the power they used to have. For example, the 2008 credit crunch and ensuing recession clearly demonstrated that individual governments have much less influence over their national economies than once they had. But, as many governments acted collaboratively to formulate strategy and provide funds to assist the worst-hit countries, the crisis also showed that nations can work together to reassert their influence over the runaway world.

Voluntary groups and social movements outside the framework of formal politics can also have an important role, but they will not supplant orthodox democratic politics. Democracy is still crucial, because these groups make divergent claims and have different interests – those who actively campaign for more tolerance of abortion and those who believe entirely the opposite, for instance. Democratic governments must assess and react to these varying claims and concerns.

Sociology as a discipline is not unaffected by these social changes, and sociologists are becoming more reflexive about their own research practice and its effects on participants. The divide between academic 'experts' and unknowledgeable 'lay people' seems far less rigid today. Those who participate in interviews, focus groups, questionnaires, and so on, are increasingly included in other aspects of the research process – advising on appropriate questions, identifying ethical issues, and reading and commenting on draft research reports. This deeper involvement can enhance the validity of research findings, as sociologists can check their interpretations with participants before arriving at firm conclusions. On present trends it is likely that reflexivity will continue to spread to more areas of social life.

Ulrich Beck – risk in the second modernity

The German sociologist Ulrich Beck (1944–2015) also rejects postmodernism. Rather than living in a world 'beyond the modern', we are moving into a phase of what he calls 'the second modernity'. The second modernity refers to the fact that modern institutions are becoming global, while everyday life is breaking free from the hold of tradition and custom. The old industrial society is disappearing and is being replaced by a 'risk society'.

Beck is not arguing that the contemporary world is more risky than that of previous ages. Rather, it is the nature of the risks we must face that is changing. Risk now derives less from natural dangers or hazards than from our own social development and by the development of science and technology. For example, global warming represents possibly the most serious environmental issue today. Yet the scientific consensus is that this is not a simple natural disaster but the product of excessive greenhouse gases from industrial pollution and modern transportation emissions over the past 250 years. Popular science writers have dubbed such problems the 'revenges of nature'.

The advance of science and technology creates new risk situations that are very different from those of previous ages. Science and technology obviously provide us with many benefits. Yet they create risks that are hard to measure. Thus no one quite knows what the risks involved in the development of new technologies, such as gene therapy or nanotechnology, might be. Supporters of genetically modified crops, for example, claim that at best they give us the possibility of ending malnutrition in the world's poorest countries and providing cheap food for everyone. Sceptics claim that they could have dangerous, unintended health consequences.

Beck's ideas on risk are discussed in more detail in chapter 5, 'The Environment'.

According to Beck, an important aspect of the risk society is that its hazards are not restricted spatially, temporally or socially. Today's risks affect all countries and all social classes; they have global, not merely personal, consequences. The self-defined 'Islamic' terror attacks on New York and Washington in 2001, Bali in 2002, Casablanca and Madrid in 2004, London in 2005, and many more, changed the extent to which people thought of their communities as being at risk from extreme violence. The fear of terrorism created inertia in economies around the world, particularly in the months after September 2001, as businesses became reluctant to risk large-scale investment. Terrorist attacks also changed the assessment that states made over the balance between the freedom of its citizens and their security, with many curtailing civil liberties to increase surveillance of potential terrorist threats.

Many decisions taken at the level of everyday life also become infused with risk. Risk and gender relations are actually closely linked, as many uncertainties have entered the relationships between the sexes (see chapter 10, 'Families and Intimate Relationships'). A generation ago, in the developed societies, marriage was a fairly straightforward process of life transition – people moved from being unmarried to being married, and this was assumed to be a fairly permanent situation. Today, many people live together without getting married and divorce rates are relatively high. Anyone contemplating a relationship with another person must take these facts into account and must calculate the risk, setting the likelihood of happiness and security against an uncertain backdrop.

Cosmopolitanism

In recent years, Beck's thinking followed that of others (Vertovec and Cohen 2002; Benhabib 2006) into a theory of cosmopolitanism

In March 2011, a magnitude 9.0 earthquake off the coast of Japan caused a tsunami which crashed into the Fukushima Daiichi nuclear power plant, resulting in three nuclear meltdowns and the release of radioactive material. While earthquakes and tsunamis have always been a risk on the east coast of Japan, our development of nuclear power plants made this a much more serious disaster.

(Beck 2006; Beck and Grande 2007). Beck's version begins from a critique of 'nation-state-based' thinking – that is, sociological theories which take national societies as the main unit of analysis. Beck (2006: 18) argues that this 'national outlook' 'fails to grasp that political, economic and cultural action and their (intended and unintended) consequences know no borders'. In our age of globalization, where national borders are becoming more permeable and individual states are less powerful, social reality is being transformed in a thoroughly cosmopolitan direction. The process of 'cosmopolitanization' is occurring even behind the backs of sociologists who continue to think in terms of national societies and international relationships. If allowed to develop without direction, cosmopolitanization presents as many threats as opportunities, particularly for those who are exploited by multinational corporations traversing the globe seeking cheaper labour and maximal profits.

Beck argues that the narrow viewpoint of the nation-state becomes an impediment when it comes to dealing with new risks, such as global warming. And, when it comes to fighting international terrorism, we must ask what we are fighting *for*. Beck suggests this must be a cosmopolitan system based on the acknowledgement and acceptance of cultural diversity. Cosmopolitan states do not fight only against terrorism but also against the *causes* of terrorism in the world. To Beck, cosmopolitanism provides the most positive way to deal with global problems, which appear insoluble at the level of the individual state but are manageable through cooperation. New forms of activism are also appearing, and we see the emergence of a field of 'sub-politics'. This refers to the activities of groups and agencies operating outside the formal mechanisms of democratic politics, such as ecological, consumer or human rights groups.

Beck concedes that thinking in universal or cosmopolitan terms is not really new. Previously, the idea of citizenship beyond the nation-state was the preserve of well-travelled and well-connected social elites who *voluntarily* chose to see themselves as 'Europeans', for example, or as 'citizens of the world'. But cosmopolitanism now has much stronger roots in global processes and is potentially more effective. Beck argues that it is not enough for sociologists simply to analyse the emerging cosmopolitan world society; they should also be involved in shaping it in positive directions if the problems associated with globalization are to be tackled.

> ### THINKING CRITICALLY
>
> What are the implications of environmental risks for the developing countries? Are environmental risks likely to be more evenly distributed globally than, say, poverty or malnutrition?

Conclusion: sociological theory in development

This chapter has provided a whistle-stop tour of the history of sociological theorizing, illustrated with fairly brief discussions of some influential theories, trends and critiques.

The ideas of the classical thinkers – Marx, Durkheim and Weber – were formed during times of great social, political and economic change, which their perspectives sought to understand. Arguably, we are living through a period of global transformation that is just as profound and yet is much more widely felt across more regions of the world. The need to refresh and update our theoretical perspectives seems increasingly necessary if sociology is to explain the developments that are transforming societies today.

Yet this conclusion does not mean we should abandon the older theoretical perspectives altogether. Sociological theory cannot be successful if it develops only through internal debate. It has to give us insights into the key issues of the day and must be empirically adequate as well as internally coherent. What is likely to be more productive is to bring the older perspectives into contact with the new, in order to test and compare their effectiveness. The history of sociological theory shows that successful perspectives are always in the process of development rather than remaining static. For example, neo-Marxist theories today remain close enough to Marx's original ideas to be recognizable, but they have also been modified, amended and renewed along the way by the force of changing circumstances. The same process has happened in relation to Durkheimian and Weberian ideas.

At the same time, the diversity of modern sociological theory has led to more combinations of theories that cross the divide between the classical and the contemporary. Indeed, it might be argued that such theoretical syntheses offer the best hope of preserving the best of the classical traditions while updating them to deal with significant social changes. As the final section above has shown, the best contemporary theories retain the ability to illuminate the emerging issues of our time.

Chapter review

1 What were the main attractions of positivism for the early sociologists?
2 Outline Marx's 'materialist conception of history'. Explain how Marx used this in his account of the emergence of capitalism.
3 Durkheim said that we should 'treat social facts as things'. What does this statement mean? In what ways did the later functionalist theorists differ from Durkheim's?
4 In Max Weber's 'Protestant ethic' thesis, what is the role of religion in the origins of capitalism? Can this account be combined with that of Marx or are they competing theories?

5 What is symbolic about 'symbolic interactionism'? What do you see as the main differences between phenomenology and ethnomethodology?
6 How did Norbert Elias attempt to resolve the 'problem' of structure and agency via the concept of 'figurations'? Using the example of money, explain how Giddens's idea of the 'duality of structure' might bridge the divide between structure and agency.
7 Feminist theories and research changed sociology forever. But is there such a thing as 'feminist sociology' or are these two basically opposed? On what basis do some feminist theorists argue that sociology has failed fully to embrace the concept of gender?

8 Does the prefix 'post-' in postcolonial, postmodern and poststructuralist theories imply criticism of existing perspectives without putting anything new in their place? How convinced are you by the postmodern idea that the age of modernity is over?
9 What does Ulrich Beck mean by a 'risk society'? How are risks today different from those faced by people in the past?
10 Are the classical theories of Durkheim, Marx and Weber still good guides to the contemporary globalizing world? Which aspects of social life today do they help us to understand?

Research in practice

As we have seen, sociology is said to have emerged from the social, economic and political consequences of industrialization and the aftermath of the French Revolution. However, the subsequent history and development of sociology was littered with theoretical disagreements and the creation of new perspectives. How can we make sense of this history? Read Richard Kilminster's article and answer the questions that follow. Kilminster, R. (2014) 'The Dawn of Detachment: Norbert Elias and Sociology's Two Tracks', *History of the Human Sciences*, 27(3): 96–115.

1 Describe the 'two tracks' which Kilminster discusses in the paper, bringing out their main differences.
2 What is meant by 'involvement' and 'detachment' in relation to sociological theories?
3 Outline the argument that sociology emerged out of philosophical thought but ultimately separated from it. Is sociology really a 'post-philosophical' discipline?
4 If, as the author suggests, Elias's theory is a 'synthesis', what are its constituent theoretical elements?

5   Is sociology likely to remain a theoretically pluralistic discipline or would its scientific progress be better served via Kilminster's 'Eliasian' alternative?

Thinking it through

It is conventional to distinguish between classical and contemporary sociological or social theory. But this way of discussing theories pits one set against the other and has no place for those that fall between the classical and the contemporary. Perhaps a better way of thinking through the movement of sociological theory since Marx is to see it as a continuous process of development.

Using this idea and figure 3.1 above as starting points, do your own research on the key ideas of three of the individual theorists listed between 1960 and 2000. Is it possible to find *both* classical *and* contemporary themes within their arguments? What or who would you say were the main theoretical influences on your three theorists? How have they taken sociological theorizing beyond the ideas of the classics?

Society in the arts

A good many movies and novels trade on conspiracy theories – theories that emphasize the role of clever, resourceful and/or powerful groups in shaping events and social life to their own ends. *The Adjustment Bureau* (2011), directed by George Nolfi, is a recent example. Watch the film, taking notes on how it deals with the following themes:

- issues of social structure and human agency
- Weberian ideas of bureaucratic domination
- modernity, rationality and postmodern ideas
- gender stereotypes.

If there is a central *sociological* message within this film, what would you say it is?

Further reading

Books on social and sociological theory are among the most numerous of any subject in sociology, and it is a good idea to dip into several to get a feel for which presentation suits your needs. For a well-written introduction to the theories discussed in this chapter, try Pip Jones and Liz Bradbury's (2017) *Introducing Social Theory* (3rd edn, Cambridge: Polity). A somewhat different approach is taken by Steven Miles (2001) in *Social Theory in the Real World* (London: Sage), which shows how theory can help us to understand the everyday world.

From here, a comprehensive text is Michelle Dillon's (2014) *Introduction to Sociological Theory: Theorists, Concepts and their Applicability to the Twenty-First Century* (2nd edn, Chichester: Wiley-Blackwell). George Ritzer's (2011) *Sociological Theory* (8th edn, Maidenhead: McGraw-Hill) is also an excellent book by a renowned expert.

For the classical theories, Kenneth Morrison's (2006) *Marx, Durkheim, Weber: Formations of Modern Social Thought* (London: Sage) is reliable and into its second edition, while George Ritzer and Douglas J. Goodman's (2010) *Classical Sociological Theory* (4th edn, New York: McGraw-Hill) covers a wider range of theorists. For contemporary theorists, Anthony Elliott's (2014) *Contemporary Social Theory: An Introduction* (2nd edn, London: Routledge) is well written and comprehensive.

Remember that at some point it will be necessary to consult the ideas of the theorists in this chapter in their original texts. Ultimately this is the only way to form your own assessment of their relative merits and for that reason is strongly recommended.

For a collection of original readings on sociological theories, see the accompanying *Sociology: Introductory Readings* (3rd edn, Cambridge: Polity, 2010).

Internet links

Additional information and support for this book at Polity:
www.politybooks.com/giddens

The Dead Sociologists' Society – very good resources on the classical and early theorists:
http://media.pfeiffer.edu/lridener/dss/deadsoc.html

The Feminist Theory Website – feminist theories and perspectives from academics based at Virginia Tech University:
www.cddc.vt.edu/feminism/enin.html

The Institute for Social Research – Frankfurt Critical Theory today [in German]:
www.ifs.uni-frankfurt.de/forschung

Phenomenology Online – phenomenologists and ethnomethodologists:
www.phenomenologyonline.com

A series of websites devoted to the work of some contemporary theorists:
Jean Baudrillard: http://englishscholar.com/baudrillard.htm
Judith Butler: www.theory.org.uk/ctr-butl.htm
Norbert Elias: www.norberteliasfoundation.nl
Michel Foucault: http://foucault.info
Erving Goffman: http://people.brandeis.edu/~teuber/goffmanbio.html

CHAPTER 4

Globalization and Social Change

Contents

Supporters of Iran at the 2014 football World Cup in Brazil.

The first football World Cup was held in Uruguay in 1930. Thirteen national teams took part and Uruguay were the inaugural winners. In 2014 the World Cup finals were held in Brazil with thirty-two participating teams, and Germany became champions. However, the qualifying stages for the 2014 event involved 208 national teams drawn from every continent on Earth. Around 3.4 million fans attended the sixty-four games in Brazil and hundreds of millions watched the final on television, making the World Cup the most watched global sporting event, beating the Olympic Games. In a very simple way, the increasing scale and scope of the football World Cup illustrates the growing connection between and interdependence of the global human population, a multifaceted process described by sociologists as globalization.

Yet international sporting events do not just illustrate the process of globalization, they also contribute to that process. The globalization of sport involves athletes drawn from across the world, an increasingly global television audience, advertisers attracted from many countries and the shaping of consumer demand for sporting products and spin-offs such as sports clothing, books, videos and much more (Sage 2002: 226–7). In this way individual sports and games such as tennis, golf and snooker, as well as team sports including football, rugby and basketball, have become not simply cultural phenomena but also economic businesses, involving the production of sport as a spectacle, together with the manufacture of sporting goods and their consumption in global markets. The commercial and cultural success of American basketball in recent years is an excellent example, nicely summarized by Maguire (1999: 14):

> Citizens of countries spread across the globe regularly tune in by satellite broadcasts to National Basketball Association (NBA) games. In these games perform the best male players drawn from North America and Europe. The players use equipment – balls, shoes, uniform, etc. – that is designed in a range of European and North American locations, financed in the USA and assembled in the Pacific Rim. This equipment is then sold on to a mass market across the globe. This equipment, basketball boots for example, is made out of raw materials from 'developing countries', the molecular structure of which was researched and patented, in the case of Nike, in Washington State (USA) and fabricated in Taiwan. Several other transnational corporations are also involved in the production and consumption phases of this global cultural product. The product is itself provided by a global media sport production complex and is viewed on a television that was itself manufactured as part of a global telecommunications network.

In the twentieth century, Association Football was enormously successful and is widely seen as 'the global game'. Football spread across the world, and the by the end of the century the English Premier League (EPL) emerged as the most commercially successful national league. However, in the twenty-first century, American basketball has grown rapidly to challenge football's status as the principal global sport. In particular, the US National Basketball Association has successfully promoted the game in China, and twice as many Chinese people in urban areas now play basketball than play football (Borger 2008). In terms of the sheer number of active players globally, basketball has more participants.

However, sport is only one sphere of life that is being transformed by an increasingly global connectedness. Later in the chapter we will explore the claim that both the speed and the intensity of globalization have increased radically over just the last forty years or so. Before that we need to set the current globalization debate into a much longer time frame, and there follows a sketch of human development over the very long term. This is necessary in order to understand better how the development of modern industrial-capitalist societies set the human world on its present global trajectory.

A disappearing world

Today we are accustomed to societies of tens of millions of people living in densely populated urban areas. But this is historically unusual. For most of human history, populations were smaller and less dense, and it is only quite recently that societies have existed in which the *majority* of their population are urban dwellers. To understand the forms of society that existed before modern industrialism, we have to draw on the historical dimension of our sociological imagination.

The explorers, traders and missionaries sent out during Europe's 'great age of discovery' met with many different peoples and cultures. European explorers came across small-scale, nomadic, hunter-gatherer groups of just twenty or thirty people who were constantly travelling and who survived by eating wild animals and plants. In parts of Southern and Northern America and East Asia were larger, fairly settled communities based on agriculture and farming. In China and elsewhere they found well-developed empires with cities, classes, palaces and, significantly, armed forces (Harris 1978).

This variety of human groups and societies can actually be organized into three main categories: *hunters and gatherers*, larger *agrarian* or *pastoral societies* (involving agriculture or the tending of domesticated animals) and *traditional states and civilizations*. As table 4.1 shows, successive societal types tended to increase the size of the global human population.

Early societies

For all but a tiny part of their existence on Earth, human beings have lived in hunting and gathering societies. Hunters and gatherers gain their livelihood from hunting, fishing and gathering edible plants from the wild. These cultures continue to exist in a few arid parts of Africa and the jungles of Brazil and New Guinea. However, most hunting and gathering cultures have been destroyed or absorbed by the spread of Western culture (the culture of Europe, the United States and Australasia), and those that remain are unlikely to stay intact for much longer. By 1970, fewer than a quarter of a million people in the world were hunter-gatherers – about 0.001 per cent of the world's human population at that time (see figure 4.1).

Table 4.1	Types of pre-modern human society	
Type	Period of existence	Characteristics
Hunting and gathering societies	50,000 BCE to the present. Now on the verge of complete disappearance.	Small numbers gaining a livelihood from hunting, fishing and gathering edible plants. Few inequalities. Differences of rank limited by age and gender.
Agrarian societies	12,000 BCE to the present. Most are now part of larger political entities, thus losing their distinct identity.	Based on small rural communities without towns or cities. Livelihood through agriculture, often supplemented by hunting and gathering. Stronger inequalities than hunters and gatherers. Ruled by chiefs.
Pastoral societies	12,000 BCE to the present. Today mostly part of larger states; traditional ways of life are being undermined.	Size ranges from a few hundred people to many thousands. Dependent on tending domesticated animals for subsistence. Marked by distinct inequalities. Ruled by chiefs or warrior kings.
Traditional societies or civilizations	6000 BCE to the nineteenth century. All traditional civilizations have now disappeared.	Very large in size, some numbering several millions of people. Some cities exist, in which trade and manufacture are concentrated. Based largely on agriculture. Major inequalities exist among different classes. Distinct government apparatus headed by a king or emperor.

Several hundred people of the Hadza tribe continue to live as hunter-gatherers, the last of their kind in East Africa. Survival International estimates that the Hadza have lost about half of their land over the last fifty years.

There is little inequality within most hunting and gathering groups as they do not accumulate material wealth beyond that required for basic needs. Their main preoccupations are normally religious values, ceremonies and ritual activities. The material goods required are limited to weapons for hunting, tools for digging and building, traps and cooking utensils. Thus there are no marked differences of wealth and possessions and, hence, no clear division of rich and poor. Differences of position or rank tend to be limited to age and sex; men are almost always hunters, while women gather wild crops, cook and bring up the children. This gendered division of labour is significant as men tend to dominate public and ceremonial positions.

The founder of psychoanalysis, Sigmund Freud (1856–1939), once described hunter-gatherers, such as traditional Australian Aborigines, as 'the most backward and miserable of savages', who had no 'proper' religion or housing (cited in Barnard 2004: 1). But hunter-gatherers are not 'primitive' people whose ways of life no longer have relevance for today's societies. Studying these cultures allows us to see more clearly that modern institutions are not 'natural' features of all societies. We should not idealize hunter-gatherer ways of life, but the absence of war, few major inequalities of wealth and power, and the emphasis on cooperation rather than competition do challenge Freud's negative assessment.

World population: 10 million
Percentage of hunters and gatherers: 100

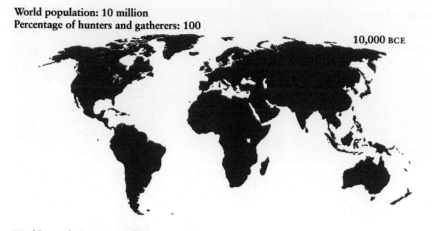

10,000 BCE

World population: 350 million
Percentage of hunters and gatherers: 1.0

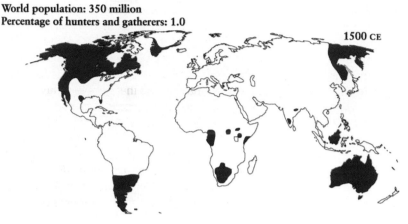

1500 CE

World population: 6 billion
Percentage of hunters and gatherers: 0.001

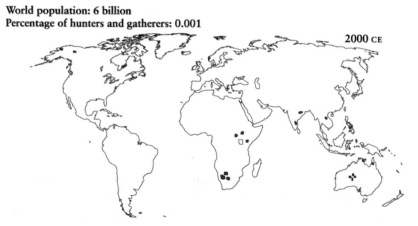

2000 CE

Figure 4.1 The decline of hunting and gathering societies

Source: Lee and De Vore (1968).

Global Society 4.1 | Humans and the domestication of fire

Over the course of human history, human beings gradually learned how to exert more control over the natural environment and were able to pass on this useful knowledge to geographically distant groups and to their own younger generations. In *Fire and Civilization* (1992), the Dutch sociologist Johan Goudsblom (1932–) argues that an especially significant development was the discovery of fire and the invention of techniques for making, managing and keeping it under control.

Human groups that learned how to make and use fire gained dominance over those that did not. Eventually all human societies were able to make and use fire, which enabled them to dominate other animal species. Goudsblom's developmental history of fire shows something of the way that societies try to manipulate and manage the natural environment to their own advantage. In the process, though, there is also pressure on societies to change their own social organization.

From small domestic fires used for keeping warm and cooking food, all the way to modern central heating systems and large power plants, the gradual expansion of fire-making has necessitated more complex forms of social organization. When early humans learned how to make and manage small fires, they had to organize themselves to keep fires going, to monitor them and, at the same time, to stay safe. Much later, with the introduction of domesticated fires into private homes, societies needed specialists in fire control – fire brigades and fire-prevention advisers. With the advent of large power-generating stations, it has become important to protect these, militarily if necessary, from potential attack. Today, more people are more dependent on the easy availability and control of fire than ever before.

Goudsblom notes one further consequence of the domestication of fire: the changing psychology of individuals. To be able to use fire, people had to overcome their previous fear of it, perhaps born of seeing naturally occurring bush fires, lightning strikes or volcanoes. This was not an easy task. It meant controlling their fears and emotions long enough to be able to take advantage of the possible benefits of fire use. Such emotional control slowly came to be experienced as 'natural', so that people today hardly ever think about how long it has taken for humans to arrive at such high levels of emotional control over their feelings and deep-seated fears.

Even today, fires still cause harm, destroying forests, homes, families and businesses. Fire is always threatening to escape the control of human societies, however firmly established that control might seem. The sociological lesson we can take from this study is that the relationship between human societies and the natural environment is an unavoidable two-way process: human societies try to exert control over the natural environment, but, as they do so, the natural environment also imposes certain constraints and requirements on them.

Pastoral and agrarian societies

Around 20,000 BCE – the peak of the last Ice Age – some hunting and gathering groups began to raise domesticated animals and cultivate fixed plots of land as their means of livelihood. By 5000 BCE many groups and societies across the world lived by farming (Mithen 2003). Pastoral societies are those that rely mainly on domesticated livestock, while agrarian societies are those that grow crops (practise agriculture), though many societies have had mixed pastoral and agrarian economies.

Depending on the environment in which they live, pastoralists rear and herd animals such as cattle, sheep, goats, camels and horses. Many pastoral societies still exist in the modern world, concentrated especially in parts of Africa, the Middle East and Central Asia. These societies are usually found in regions with dense grasslands, deserts or mountains. Such regions are not amenable to fruitful agriculture but may support various kinds of livestock. Pastoral societies usually migrate between different areas according

Pastoral societies still exist in many regions of the world, such as the 'Tuareg' or Imuhagh people of the North African Sahara, who are nomadic pastoralists.

to seasonal changes. Given their nomadic lifestyle, people in pastoral societies do not normally accumulate many material possessions, although their way of life is more complex in material terms than that of hunters and gatherers.

At some point, some hunting and gathering groups began to sow their own crops. This practice first developed as what is usually called 'horticulture', where small areas were cultivated using simple hoes and digging instruments. Like pastoralism, horticulture provided for a more secure food supply than was possible by hunting and gathering and could therefore support larger communities. Since they were more settled, people could then develop larger stocks of material possessions than either hunting and gathering or pastoral communities. As table 4.2 shows, only a small minority of people in the industrialized countries today still work on the land. However, agriculture remains the primary source of employment for numerous developing countries, many of them in Africa.

Traditional civilizations

From about 6000 BCE onwards, archaeologists have found evidence of much larger societies than existed previously (see figure 4.2). These societies were based on the development of cities and had pronounced inequalities of wealth and power associated with the rule of kings or emperors. Because they used writing, science and art flourished, and they are often called *civilizations*.

The earliest large civilizations developed in the Middle East, usually in fertile river areas. The Chinese Empire originated around 2000 BCE, when powerful states were also

Table 4.2 Agricultural employment (percentage of workforce), selected countries, up to 2015

Country	Percentage of workers in agriculture
Burundi	93.6
Rwanda	90
Niger	90
Ethiopia	85
Tanzania	80
The impact of industrialization	
Australia	3.6
Japan	2.9
Canada	2.0
Germany	1.6
United Kingdom	1.3

Note: Figures based on the most recent national estimates available.

Source: Adapted from CIA World Factbook online (2015).

founded in what are now India and Pakistan and a number of large civilizations existed in Mexico and Latin America, such as the Aztecs of Mexico, the Mayas of the Yucatan peninsula and the Incas of Peru. Most traditional civilizations were also *empires* – that is, they expanded through the conquest and incorporation of other peoples (Kautsky 1982). This was true, for instance, of traditional China and Rome. At its peak, in the first century CE, the Roman Empire stretched from Britain in North-West Europe to beyond the Middle East. The Chinese Empire, which lasted more than 2,000 years up to the threshold of the twentieth century, covered most of the region of eastern Asia now occupied by China.

The emergence of large-scale civilizations and empires shows that the very long-term process of human expansion or 'globalization' has involved invasion, war and violent conquest every bit as much as cooperation and mutual exchange between societies. Nevertheless, by the dawn of the modern era, humans had already settled right across the globe, though the world population was still

relatively small. However, this was about to change in a radical way.

Population growth and demographic trends

Human beings have existed on Earth for less than half a million years or so. Agriculture, the necessary basis of fixed settlements, is even more recent, being just 12,000 years old. Large-scale human civilizations date back no more than 6,000 years. If we think of the entire span of human existence as a 24-hour day, agriculture came into existence at 11.56 p.m. – four minutes to midnight – and civilizations at 11.57 p.m. Over this very long time scale, human beings gradually spread into most parts of the planet as relationships between different groups became more regular, often riven with conflicts (Mennell 1996).

The development of modern societies began only at 11.59 and 30 seconds and yet, in the last 30 seconds of the human day, there has been more rapid social and environmental change than in all the ages leading up to it. As we will see in this chapter, the period

4.1 Isolation in a globalizing world?

The following is taken from a BBC News item from 2008.

Isolated tribe spotted in Brazil

One of South America's few remaining uncontacted indigenous tribes has been spotted and photographed on the border between Brazil and Peru. The Brazilian government says it took the images to prove the tribe exists and help protect its land. The pictures, taken from an aeroplane, show red-painted tribe members brandishing bows and arrows.

More than half the world's 100 uncontacted tribes live in Brazil or Peru, Survival International says. Stephen Corry, the director of the group – which supports tribal people around the world – said such tribes would 'soon be made extinct' if their land was not protected.

'Monumental crime'

Survival International says that although this particular group is increasing in number, others in the area are at risk from illegal logging.

The photos were taken during several flights over one of the most remote parts of the Amazon rainforest in Brazil's Acre region. They show tribe members outside thatched huts, surrounded by the dense jungle, pointing bows and arrows up at the camera.

'We did the overflight to show their houses, to show they are there, to show they exist', the group quoted Jose Carlos dos Reis Meirelles Junior, an official in the Brazilian government's Indian affairs department, as saying. 'This is very important because there are some who doubt their existence.' He described the threats to such tribes and their land as 'a monumental crime against the natural world' and 'further testimony to the complete irrationality with which we, the "civilised" ones, treat the world.'

Disease is also a risk, as members of tribal groups that have been contacted in the past have died of illnesses that they have no defence against, ranging from chicken pox to the common cold.

Source: BBC (2008b).

THINKING CRITICALLY

When this story was reported, many people believed it to be a hoax. But Survival, an organization that campaigns for tribal people's rights, blamed inaccurate reporting, saying, 'you might have thought that the fact that the Indians are living in a government reserve set aside for isolated Indian groups would tend to indicate that they weren't exactly "unknown" . . . anthropologists, Survival, other NGOs and the Brazilian government have known that there are many isolated tribes living in that region for decades.'

Did you think this story was a hoax? Is it correct to say that this tribe and others in the region do live an 'independent existence' isolated from the rest of the world?

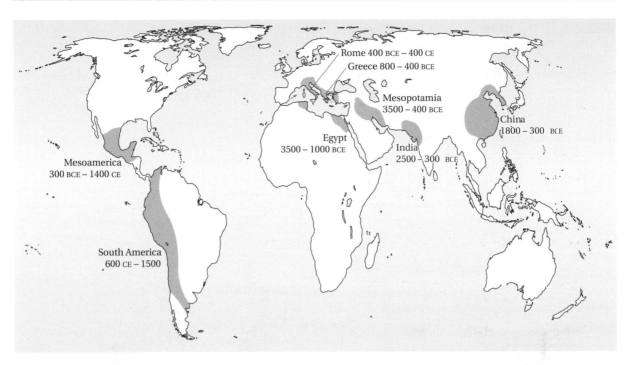

Figure 4.2 Civilizations in the ancient world

sociologists call modernity brought about a more *rapid* globalization of social life, connecting large-scale societies together in a variety of ways, from systematic trade and long-range economic exchanges, international political agreements and global tourism to electronic communications technology and fluid mass migration. In all these ways, people have become more interconnected, interdependent and geographically mobile than ever before (Sheller and Urry 2004; Urry 2007).

> The emerging research agenda on 'mobilities' in sociology is discussed in chapter 16, 'Race, Ethnicity and Migration'.

The sheer pace of change in the modern era is evident in rates of human population growth. The Italian demographer Massimo Livi-Bacci (2012) studied the global population and its long-term growth. From an estimated 6 *million* people in 10,000 BCE, the global population rose to more than 6 *billion* by 2000 (see table 4.3), and by the end of

2011 it topped 7 billion. However, the pace of population growth has been very uneven, accelerating from around 1750, the start of the industrial period. Perhaps the most striking demographic aspect here is the shrinking 'doubling time' of the global population. Even in 1750, the time it took for the population to double in size was quite slow, taking more than 1,000 years. By 1950 this was down to 118 years, and in 2000 it was a mere forty years. The United Nations Department of Economic and Social Affairs (UN 2011) forecasts that there will be more than 10 billion people on the planet by 2100.

If that figure seems unsustainable, we have to remember that in the nineteenth century the idea that 7 billion people could survive on Earth was quite literally unthinkable, and yet it has happened. The UN also points out that the global population growth rate is actually declining, and it expects the population to stabilize at just over 10 billion people after 2100. Whether such unprecedentedly high levels can be sustained depends not simply on the carrying capacity of the natural environ-

Table 4.3 Population, total births and life expectancy (10,000 BCE – 2000 CE)

Demographic index	10,000 BCE*	0	1750	1950	2000
Population (millions)	6	252	771	2,529	6,115
Annual growth (%)	0.008	0.037	0.064	0.594	1.766
Doubling time (years)	8,369	1,854	1,083	116	40
Births (billions)	9.29	33.6	22.64	10.42	5.97
Life expectancy	20	22	27	35	56

Notes: For births and life expectancy, the data refer to interval between the date at the head of the column and that of the preceding column (for the first column the interval runs from the hypothetical origin of the human species to 10,000 BCE).
*Many historians now use BCE (Before the Common Era) and CE (Common Era) rather than BC and AD.

Source: Adapted from Livi-Bacci (2012: 25).

ment but also on economic and technological development, social organization and political agreements.

> Chapter 5, 'The Environment', looks more closely at the impact of such rapid human expansion on the natural environment and other species.

Livi-Bacci's work shows us the dramatic step-change in the pace of population growth, global change and interdependence since the 1950s. In the rest of this chapter we look at the spread of key aspects of modernity before examining the various meanings of the concept of globalization. Many social scientists see the contemporary globalizing phase as *the* most significant development that will shape humanity's future.

> Chapter 14, 'Global inequality', looks in more detail at some of the key evidence and theories from the discipline of demography.

The transformation of societies

What happened to transform types of society that had existed for the majority of human history? A large part of the answer is industrialization – a concept discussed in detail in chapter 6, 'Cities and Urban Life'. Industrialization refers to the emergence of machine production, based on the widespread use of inanimate power resources such as steam and electricity to replace humans and animals wherever possible. The industrial societies (often called 'modern' or 'developed' societies) are very different from all previous types of social order, and their spread has had genuinely revolutionary consequences.

Modernity and industrial technology

In even the most advanced of traditional civilizations, the relatively low level of technological development permitted only a small minority to escape agricultural work. Modern technology has transformed the way of life enjoyed by a very large proportion of the human population. As the economic historian David Landes (2003: 5) observes:

> Modern technology produces not only more, faster; it turns out objects that could not have been produced under any circumstances by the craft methods of yesterday. The best Indian hand-spinner could not turn out yarn so fine and regular as that of the [spinning] mule; all the forges in eighteenth century Christendom could not have produced steel sheets so large, smooth and homogeneous as

those of a modern strip mill. Most important, modern technology has created things that could scarcely have been conceived in the pre-industrial era: the camera, the motor car, the airplane, the whole array of electronic devices from the radio to the high-speed computer, the nuclear power plant, and so on almost ad infinitum.

Even so, the continuing existence of gross global inequalities means that this technological development is not equally shared across the world's societies.

The modes of life and social institutions characteristic of the modern world are radically different from those of even the recent past, and over a period of less than three centuries – a sliver of time in human history – people have shifted away from ways of life that endured for many thousands of years. For example, a large majority of the employed population now work in factories, offices, shops and services rather than agriculture, while the largest cities are denser and greater in size than any urban settlements found in traditional civilizations.

The role of cities in the new global order is discussed in chapter 6, 'Cities and Urban Life'.

In traditional civilizations, the political authorities (monarchs and emperors) had little direct influence on the customs and habits of most of their subjects, who lived in fairly self-contained local villages. With industrialization, transportation and communication became much more rapid, making for a more integrated 'national' community. The industrial societies were the first nation-states to come into existence. Nation-states are political communities, divided from each other by clearly delimited borders rather than the vague frontier areas that separated traditional states. National governments have extensive powers over many aspects of citizens' lives, framing laws that apply to all those within their borders. Virtually all societies in the world today are nation-states of this kind.

Industrial technology has by no means been limited to peaceful economic development. From the earliest phases, production has been put to military use, radically altering how societies wage war, creating weaponry and military organizations far more advanced than in earlier cultures. Together, superior economic strength, political cohesion and military superiority account for the seemingly irresistible spread of 'Western' ways of life across the world over the last 250 years. Once again we have to acknowledge that globalization is a process that has often been characterized by wars, violence and conquest.

Issues of war and violence are taken up in chapter 22, 'Nations, War and Terrorism'.

THINKING CRITICALLY

Karl Marx forecast that the industrialized countries showed to the non-industrialized ones a picture of their own future. Which three aspects of modern, industrialized countries would you pick out as the most significant that make them radically different from earlier societies?

Classifying societies

From the seventeenth to the early twentieth century, Western countries used their overwhelming military strength and technology to establish colonies in areas previously occupied by traditional societies. The policy and practice of colonialism shaped the map of the world until former colonies were able to break free and become independent countries in their own right. In some regions, such as North America, Australia and New Zealand, which were thinly populated by hunting and gathering groups, European colonists became the majority population. In other areas, including much of Asia, Africa and South America, local populations remained in the majority.

The legacy of colonialism and the postcolonialist critique of sociology are discussed in chapter 3, 'Theories and Perspectives'.

Societies of the first type, among them the USA, became thoroughly industrialized and today have high levels of gross domestic product (GDP) per capita – they are referred to as developed countries. Those of the second type are less industrialized, have lower levels of GDP per capita and, because they are in a process of economic improvement, are referred to as developing countries. These include China, India, most of the African countries and most of those in South America. Seen globally, the majority of these countries lie in the southern hemisphere, and you may see them described collectively as 'the South' in comparison to the wealthier 'North'. This, however, is a rough and ready generalization because, as southern countries industrialize and develop further, such a simple division of the world becomes less accurate. The World Bank reclassifies developing countries as 'developed' once they attain a high level of GDP per capita.

Classification schemes are always contentious, as they are likely, or may be perceived, to contain value judgements. For example, developing countries used to be referred to collectively as the 'Third World'. The Third World was part of a model which placed the industrialized countries in the First World and the communist countries of the Soviet Union (USSR) and Eastern Europe in the Second World. But it is hard to avoid the implication that the First World is somehow superior to the Second and the latter is superior to the Third. In short, this scheme was produced by scholars from the First World who, during the Cold War period, saw their societies as the norm towards which all others should strive. The collapse of Eastern European communism after 1989 and the rapid industrialization of some 'Third World' countries made this model less empirically adequate, and few sociologists use this scheme today.

On the other hand, some now contrast the majority world with the minority world. This scheme compares the population of developing countries (the global majority) with that of developed countries (the global minority). But, again, although this is an attempt to reverse the previous bias, the majority–minority contrast contains an implicit normative bias in favour of developing countries. Given the difficulties involved in all of these classification schemes, we will use 'developed' and 'developing' countries, as this at least has the benefit of drawing attention to ongoing processes of change and development in all countries of the world. In our view, though it is imperfect, this is an improvement on static classification schemes.

> **THINKING CRITICALLY**
>
> Is it possible to avoid bias in devising a classification scheme for types of society? Avoiding terms such as 'majority', 'First World' and 'developing countries', have a go at devising a politically neutral scheme based on the brief discussion above.

There is an introduction to classification schemes in chapter 14, 'Global Inequality', which you may wish to refer to at this point.

The developing world

Many developing countries today are in areas of Asia, Africa and South America that faced colonial domination and colonial rule. A few colonized areas gained independence quite early, such as Haiti, which became the first autonomous black republic in 1804. The Spanish colonies in South America gained their freedom in 1810, while Brazil broke away from Portuguese rule in 1822. However, most colonized countries became independent states after 1945, often following bloody anti-colonial struggles against Western powers. In India, a range of other Asian countries, including Burma, Malaysia and Singapore, and those in Africa such as Kenya, Nigeria, Zaire, Tanzania and Algeria, nationalist movements and popular uprisings were needed to challenge Western colonial powers.

However, though they may include many people who live traditional lifestyles, developing countries today are, in fact, very different from earlier traditional societies. Their political systems tend to be modelled on those first established in the West – that is to say, they are nation-states. And, while most of the population still live in rural areas, many of these societies are experiencing a rapid process of urbanization.

The growth of cities in the developing world is discussed in chapter 6, 'Cities and Urban Life'.

Similarly, agriculture remains the main economic activity of many developing countries, but crops are produced for sale in world markets rather than for local consumption. What we can see is that developing countries are by no means 'primitive' societies that have simply 'lagged behind'. Western colonialism systematically 'underdeveloped' these countries in order to plunder their resources, which, in turn, helped to generate rapid economic development in the West. Colonial regimes undermined the earlier, more traditional economic and social systems, leaving former colonies severely disadvantaged on independence.

Global poverty is discussed briefly in chapter 13, 'Poverty, Social Exclusion and Welfare', and in much more detail in chapter 14, 'Global Inequality'.

Newly industrializing countries

While the majority of developing countries are not as economically developed as those in the developed world, some have embarked successfully on a process of rapid industrialization.

These are referred to as *newly industrializing countries* (NICs), or newly industrializing economies (NIEs), and include Brazil, Mexico and the four so-called Asian tigers (or dragons) of Hong Kong, South Korea, Singapore and Taiwan. The rates of economic growth of the NICs in East Asia are several times those of the Western industrial economies. No developing country figured among the top thirty exporters in the world in 1968, but twenty-five years later South Korea was in the top fifteen.

The East Asian NICs have shown sustained levels of economic prosperity and are investing abroad as well as promoting growth at home. South Korea's shipbuilding and electronics industries are among the world's leaders, Singapore is becoming the major financial and commercial centre of South-East Asia, and Taiwan is an important presence in the manufacturing and electronics industries. These developments have directly affected countries such as the USA, whose share of global steel production, for example, has dropped significantly. Some economists argue that the reclassification of some previously poor countries, and especially the rapid development of Brazil, Russia, India and China (the 'BRIC' countries), may even signal an emergent shift in the pattern of global power in favour of the developing world (O'Neill 2013). However, it is probably too early to draw this conclusion with much confidence.

Nonetheless, the NICs have achieved something truly remarkable, transforming their economies over just three or four decades, moving from the status of 'developing' to 'developed' countries. And, even though the 2008 financial crisis and recession did lead to some economic contraction, the NICs have weathered recession and recovered more quickly than most of the longer-established developed economies. Singapore and Taiwan, for example, saw remarkable rises in GDP of 14.5 per cent and 10 per cent, respectively, in 2010 (CIA 2012). What the NICs demonstrate is that sustained economic and social development is possible, though we cannot expect all developing countries to follow the same path. The very different starting points and situations of developing countries mean that the NIC experience is unlikely to be repeated across Africa, where economic growth tends to be more gradual.

The NICs are discussed in more detail in chapter 14, 'Global Inequality'.

How societies change

Sociology's founders all saw the modern world as, in crucial ways, a radically different place than it had been in the recent past. Yet social change is difficult to define because, in a sense, society is changing or 'in process' all of the time. Sociologists try to decide when there has been fundamental social change leading to a new form or structure of society and then look for explanations of what brought such change about. Identifying major shifts means showing how far there has been change in the *underlying structure* of an institution, society or situation over a period of time. In the case of human societies, we have to assess to what degree there is a modification of *basic institutions* during a specific period. All accounts of social change must also show what remains stable, as a baseline against which to measure change. Auguste Comte described this as the study of social *dynamics* (processes of change) and social *statics* (stable institutional patterns).

In the rapidly moving world of today there are still continuities with the distant past. Major religions such as Christianity and Islam retain their ties with ideas and practices initiated in ancient times. Yet most institutions in modern societies change much more rapidly than the institutions of earlier civilizations, and we can identify the main elements that consistently influence patterns of social change as *economic* development, *sociocultural* change and *political* organization.

Economic development

Many human societies and groups thrive and generate wealth in even the most inhospitable regions of the world. On the other hand, some survive quite well without exploiting the natural resources at their disposal. For example, Alaskans have been able to develop oil and mineral resources to produce economic development, while hunting and gathering cultures have frequently lived in fertile regions without ever becoming pastoralists or farmers.

Physical environments may enable or constrain the kind of economic development that is possible. The indigenous people of Australia have never stopped being hunters and gatherers, since the continent contained hardly any indigenous plants suitable for regular cultivation or animals that could be domesticated for pastoral production. Similarly, the world's early civilizations originated in areas with rich agricultural land such as river deltas. The ease of communication across land and the availability of sea routes are also important: societies cut off from others by mountain ranges, impassable jungles or deserts often remain relatively unchanged over long periods of time.

However, the physical environment is not just a constraint but also forms the basis for economic activity and development, as raw materials are turned into useful or saleable things. The primary economic influence during the period of modernity has been the emergence of capitalist economic relations. Capitalism differs in a fundamental way from previous production systems, because it involves the *constant* expansion of production and the accumulation of wealth without limits. In traditional systems, levels of production were fairly stable, as they were geared to habitual, customary needs. But capitalism promotes the constant revision of production technology, a process into which science is increasingly drawn. The rate of technological innovation in modern industry is vastly greater than in any previous type of economy, and raw materials have been used in production processes in quantities undreamed of in earlier times.

Consider information communications technology (ICT). Over recent decades, the power of computers has increased many thousand times over. A large computer in the 1960s was constructed with thousands of hand-made connectors, but an equivalent device today is much smaller (often hand-held) and needs just a few elements in an integrated circuit. The impact of science and technology on how we live may be driven largely by economic factors, but it also stretches beyond the economic sphere. Science and technology both influence and are influenced by cultural and political factors. Scientific and technological development helped create modern forms of communication such as radio, television and the Internet, and these electronic forms have changed the way politics is conducted and partly shapes how we all think and feel about the world.

Socio-cultural change

Socio-cultural change includes, as a minimum, the impact of religion and beliefs, communications and leadership on social life. Religion may be a conservative or an innovative force, emphasizing the continuity of traditional values and behaviour or actively promoting change. As Max Weber showed, religious convictions have played a significant mobilizing role in the pressure to transform societies. Weber's 'Protestant ethic thesis' is the best-known example, but in recent times the Catholic Church, seen by many as essentially conservative, played a key role in supporting the Solidarity movement in Poland, which overthrew the communist regime. Similarly, many activists who took part in the 'Arab Spring' of 2010–12 saw their actions as part of an attempt to reclaim Islam for their countries from corrupt political leaders and authoritarian regimes.

Communication systems have played an important and enduring role in changing the underlying character of societies. The invention of writing, for instance, allowed record-keeping and made possible an increasing control of material resources and the development of large-scale organizations. Writing altered people's perception of the relationship between past, present and future. Societies that keep written records know themselves to have a history,

and understanding that history can create a sense of the overall development of a society. With the advent of the Internet, communication has become much faster and distance is no longer a significant obstacle. In addition, it has generated a more effective perception of a global society – a cosmopolitan outlook – made concrete in events such as Live Aid, fundraising campaigns in the rich countries on behalf of aid for people in need in Africa, and recent global movements against capitalism.

Leadership is a further socio-cultural element of social change, which Weber explored through the concept of charisma. Individual

Mahatma Gandhi fits Weber's concept of a charismatic leader. His leadership of the national independence movement helped to free India from British rule.

charismatic leaders have played important roles in world history. Religious leaders such as Jesus or Muhammad, political and military leaders such as Julius Caesar, or innovators in science and philosophy such as Isaac Newton have all influenced how societies change. An individual leader capable of pursuing dynamic policies, generating a popular following or radically altering existing modes of thought can help overturn an established order.

> Weber's conception of leadership is discussed in chapter 17, 'Religion'.

However, individuals can reach positions of leadership and become effective only if favourable social conditions exist. Adolf Hitler rose to power in Germany in the 1930s, for instance, partly as a result of the tensions and crises that beset the country at that time, which made his apparently simple solutions much more attractive. Similarly, Mahatma Gandhi, the famous pacifist leader in India during the period leading to independence in 1947, was an effective figurehead because the 1939–45 war and other events had unsettled the British colonial institutions in India, creating a political opportunity for change.

THINKING CRITICALLY

A fair amount of sociological research is dedicated to studying social structures and their impact on individuals. Is it really possible for a single charismatic individual to change a society? Give some reasons as to why we should be cautious of such a claim.

In modern times, the development of science and the secularization of social life have been very influential agents of change, contributing to the critical and innovative character of the modern outlook. People no longer accept customs or habits just because they have the age-old authority of tradition and are more likely to be persuaded by

rational, scientific answers. In addition to *how* we think, the *content* of ideas has also changed. Ideals of self-betterment, individual freedom, equality and democratic participation are part and parcel of modern life. These ideals may have developed initially in the West, but they have become genuinely universal in their application, promoting social and political change in most regions of the world.

Political organization

A third element in fundamental social change is political organization. In most types of society, the existence of distinct political agencies such as chiefs, lords, kings and governments is highly significant in shaping society's course of development. Political systems are not, as Marx argued, merely the direct expression of underlying economic organization; different types of political order may exist in societies with very similar economic systems. For instance, some industrial capitalist societies have had authoritarian political systems (Nazi Germany and South Africa under apartheid), while others are based on democratic participation (the USA, Britain or Sweden).

The political and military struggle between nations has driven social change in modern times. Political change in traditional civilizations was confined to small groups of elites, such as members of aristocratic families who replaced each other as rulers, but, for the majority, life went on virtually unchanged. This is not true of modern political systems, in which the activities of political leaders and government officials constantly affect the lives of the population. Both externally and internally, political decision-making promotes and directs social change far more effectively. Governments play a major role in stimulating, and sometimes retarding, economic growth and in all industrial societies there is a high level of state intervention in the economy. Even in apparently 'free-market' economies, trade unions help to regulate market forces and governments set the legislative framework within which companies operate.

Marx studied political economy in the nineteenth century. Although its meaning has changed since then, political economy generally refers to the study of all the ways in which political institutions and economic systems influence one another. It is often important, for the purposes of analysis, to separate the economic, the political and the socio-cultural aspects of social change, but we should remember that phenomena in the social world are complex amalgams of these different spheres. Nowhere is this more significant than in trying to grasp the multifaceted process of globalization, which is transforming social life and challenging the longstanding autonomy of individual nation-states.

Globalization

The concept of globalization has become common currency in political, business and media debates over recent years. Yet, just thirty-five years ago, it was a relatively unknown concept. For some, globalization refers to a set of processes which involve the increasing multidirectional flows of things, people and information across the planet (Ritzer 2009). However, although this definition highlights the increasing fluidity or liquidity of the contemporary world, many scholars also see globalization as the fact of individuals, companies, groups and nations becoming ever more *interdependent* as part of a single global community. As we saw in the introduction to this chapter, globalization in the latter sense has been occurring over a very long period of human history and is certainly not restricted to the contemporary situation (Nederveen Pieterse 2004; Hopper 2007). Göran Therborn (2011: 2) makes this point well:

Segments of humanity have been in global, or at least transcontinental, transoceanic, contact for a long time. There were trading links between ancient Rome and India about 2,000 years ago, and between India and China. The foray of Alexander of Macedonia into Central Asia 2,300 years ago is evident from the Greek-looking Buddha statues in the British Museum. What is new is the mass of contact, and the contact of masses, mass travel and mass self-communication.

Global Society 4.2 | **Globalization in the eighth edition**

There is hardly a sociological topic that has *not* been influenced by the emerging global frame of reference. It is *not* possible to cover every impact of globalization in this single chapter, but a quick reference guide to global issues and globalization will help to direct readers to relevant chapters:

chapter 1 – introduction to globalization in sociology and illustrative example of coffee

chapter 5 – the global risk society; global environmental issues (including global warming)

chapter 6 – global cities and their governance

chapter 7 – globalization, the workplace and employment trends

chapter 9 – global life expectancy and issues of ageing societies across the world

chapter 10 – families in global context

chapter 11 – globalization and disability; HIV/AIDS in a global context

chapter 12 – the impact of globalization on stratification systems

chapter 14 – inequalities and unequal life chances across the world

chapter 15 – globalization and the gender order; the global sex industry

chapter 16 – the nascent global 'age of migration'

chapter 17 – religious beliefs and responses to globalization

chapter 18 – global mass media; information technology and globalization

chapter 19 – education in a global context; globalization and e-universities

chapter 20 – globalization, organized crime and cybercrime

chapter 21 – the global spread of democracy; globalization and social movements

chapter 22 – global terrorist networks, world wars, old and new wars.

Classic Studies 4.1 Immanuel Wallerstein on the modern world-system

The research problem

Many students come to sociology looking for answers to big questions. Why are some countries rich and others desperately poor? How have some previously poor countries managed to become relatively wealthy, while others have not? Such questions of global inequality and economic development underpin the work of the American historical sociologist Immanuel Wallerstein (1930–). In addressing these issues, Wallerstein sought to take forward Marxist theories of social change for a global age. In 1976 he helped to found the Fernand Braudel Center for the Study of Economies, Historical Systems and Civilizations at Binghamton University, New York, which has become a focus for his own world-system research.

Wallerstein's explanation

Before the 1970s, social scientists tended to discuss the world's societies in terms of First, Second and Third worlds, based on their levels of capitalist enterprise, industrialization and urbanization. The solution to Third World 'underdevelopment' was therefore thought to be more capitalism, more industry and more urbanization. Wallerstein rejected this dominant way of categorizing societies, arguing instead that there is one world economy and all the societies within it are connected by capitalist economic relationships. He described this complex intertwining of economies as the 'modern world-system', which was a pioneer of today's globalization theories. His main arguments about how the world-system emerged were outlined in a three-volume work, *The Modern World-System* (1974, 1980, 1989), which set out his macrosociological perspective.

The origins of the modern world-system lie in sixteenth- and seventeenth-century Europe, where colonialism enabled countries such as Britain, Holland and France to exploit the resources of the countries they colonized. This allowed them to accumulate capital, which was ploughed back into their economy, driving forward production and development. This global division of labour created a group of rich countries but impoverished many others, thus stunting their development. Wallerstein argues that the process produced a world-system made up of a *core*, a *periphery* and a *semi-periphery* (see figure 4.3). And although it is clearly possible for individual countries to move 'up' into the core or to drop 'down' into the semi-periphery and periphery, the basic structure of the modern world-system remains constant.

Wallerstein's theory tries to explain why developing countries have found it so difficult to improve their position, but it also extends Marx's class-based conflict theory to a global level.

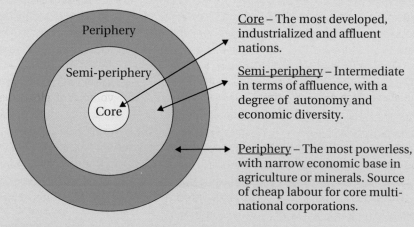

Core – The most developed, industrialized and affluent nations.

Semi-periphery – Intermediate in terms of affluence, with a degree of autonomy and economic diversity.

Periphery – The most powerless, with narrow economic base in agriculture or minerals. Source of cheap labour for core multi-national corporations.

Figure 4.3 The modern world-system

In global terms, the world's periphery becomes 'the working class', while the core forms the exploitative 'capitalist class'. In Marxist theory, this means any future socialist revolution is now likely to occur in the developing countries rather than in the wealthy core, as originally forecast by Marx. This is one reason why Wallerstein's ideas have been well received by political activists in the anti-capitalist and anti-globalization movements.

> See chapter 21, 'Politics, Government and Social Movements', for more on anti-globalization and anti-capitalist movements.

Critical points

With its origins in the work of Marx and Marxism, world-systems theory has faced some similar criticisms. First, the theory tends to emphasize the economic dimension of social life and underplays the role of culture in explanations of social change. It has been argued, for example, that one reason why Australia and New Zealand were able to move out of the periphery more easily than others was due to their close ties with British industrialization, which enabled an industrial culture to take root more quickly.

Second, the theory underplays the role of ethnicity, which is seen merely as a defensive reaction against the globalizing forces of the world-system. Therefore, major differences of religion and language are not considered to be particularly significant. Finally, it has been argued that Wallerstein uses his world-systems perspective to explain current events but is never prepared to consider that such events may falsify the theory or that alternative theories may provide a better explanation.

Contemporary significance

Wallerstein's work has been important in alerting sociologists to the interconnected character of the capitalist world economy and its globalizing effects. He therefore has to be given credit for early recognition of the significance of globalization processes, even though his emphasis on economic activity is widely seen as limiting. Wallerstein's approach has attracted many scholars, and, with an institutional base in the Fernand Braudel Center and an academic journal devoted to its extension – the *Journal of World-Systems Research* (since 1995) – world-systems analysis is now an established research tradition.

> **THINKING CRITICALLY**
>
> Look back at the section on newly industrializing countries. What evidence do these provide for Wallerstein's theoretical model? Are there historical examples of countries within the 'core' slipping into the semi-periphery or even the periphery? Why did the 2008 global recession not lead to a raft of countries being forced out of the core?

As Therborn suggests, contemporary sociological debates are focused much more on the sheer pace and intensity of globalization over the past forty years or so. It is this central idea of an intensification of the globalization process which marks our period out as different, and this forms the basis for our discussion below.

The process of globalization is often portrayed as an economic phenomenon. Much is made of the role of transnational corporations, whose operations stretch across national borders, influencing global production processes and the international division of labour. Others point to the electronic integration of global financial markets and the enormous volume of global capital flows, along with the unprecedented scope of world trade, involving a much broader range of goods and services than ever before. As we will see, contemporary globalization is better viewed as the coming together of political, social, cultural and economic factors.

Elements of globalization

The process of globalization is closely linked to the development of information and communication technology, which has intensified the speed and scope of interactions between people around the world. Think of our opening example of the 2014 football World Cup. Because of satellite technology, global television links, submarine communication cables, fast broadband Internet connections and widening computer access, games could potentially be seen *live* by billions of people right across the world. The example shows how globalization is becoming embedded within the everyday routines of more people in more regions of the world, creating genuinely global shared experiences – one prerequisite for a global society.

Information technology

The explosion in global communications has been facilitated by a number of important technological advances in the world's communications infrastructure. Since the Second World War, there has been a profound transformation in the scope and intensity of telecommunication flows. Traditional telephonic communication, which depended on analogue signals sent through wires and cables with the help of mechanical crossbar switching, has been replaced by integrated systems in which vast amounts of information are compressed and transferred digitally. Cable technology has become more efficient and less expensive, and the development of fibre-optic cables has dramatically expanded the number of channels that can be carried.

The earliest transatlantic cables, laid in the 1950s, were capable of carrying fewer than 100 telephone channels, but by 1992 a single

Most superfast broadband is delivered not by satellite but via the much older method of transoceanic cables, laid on or under the seabed. The 14,000 kilometre West Africa system of fibre-optic cables offers reliable and potentially cheaper Internet access to millions of new users.

transoceanic cable could carry some 80,000 channels. In 2001, a transatlantic submarine fibre-optic cable was laid that is capable of carrying the equivalent of a staggering 9.7 million telephone channels (Atlantic Cable 2010). Today, such cables carry not just telephony but Internet traffic, video and many other types of data. The spread of communications satellites, beginning in the 1960s, has also been significant in expanding international communications. Today, a network of more than 200 satellites is in orbit facilitating the transfer of information around the globe, though the bulk of communication continues to be via submarine cables, which remain more reliable.

In countries with highly developed telecommunications infrastructures, homes and offices now have multiple links to the outside world, including landline and mobile phones, digital, satellite and cable television, electronic mail and the Internet. The Internet has emerged as the fastest-growing communications tool ever developed. In mid-1998, around 140 million people worldwide were using the Internet. By the end of 2000 this had risen to over 360 million, and at the end of 2015 a colossal 3.4 billion people across the world were Internet users, over 46 per cent of the global human population (table 4.4).

These technologies facilitate the compression of time and space (Harvey 1989). Two individuals located on opposite sides of the planet – in Tokyo and London, for example – can not only hold a conversation in real time but also send documents, audio, images, video and much more. Widespread use of the Internet and smartphones is deepening and accelerating processes of globalization as more people are interconnected, including those in places previously isolated or poorly served by traditional communications. The telecommunications infrastructure is not evenly developed around the world, but a growing number of countries can access global communications networks, and, as table 4.4 shows, the fastest growth in Internet access is currently in Africa, Asia, the Middle East, Latin America and the Caribbean.

Information flows

If the spread of information technology has expanded the possibilities for cultural contact among people around the globe, it has also facilitated the flow of information about people and events. Every day, news and information is brought into people's homes, linking them directly and continuously to the outside world. Some of the most gripping

Table 4.4 The global spread of Internet usage, 2015

World regions	Population (2015 estimates)	Internet users 30 Nov 2015	Penetration (% population)	Growth (%) 2000–2015
Africa	1,158,355,663	330,965,359	28.6	7,231.3
Asia	4,032,466,882	1,622,084,293	40.2	1,319.1
Europe	821,555,904	604,147,280	73.5	474.9
Middle East	236,137,235	123,172,132	52.2	3,649.8
North America	357,178,284	313,867,363	87.9	190.4
Latin America/ Caribbean	617,049,712	344,824,199	55.9	1,808.4
Oceania/Australia	37,158,563	27,200,530	73.2	256.9
World total	**7,259,902,243**	**3,366,261,156**	**46.4**	**832.5**

Source: Adapted from www.internetworldstats.com/stats.htm (2016). Copyright © 2001– 2016, Miniwatts Marketing Group. All rights reserved worldwide.

events of recent times – the fall of the Berlin Wall in 1989, pro-democracy protests and the crackdown in China's Tiananmen Square (also in 1989), terrorist attacks on America in 2001, the US-led invasion of Iraq in 2003, and the occupation of Egypt's Tahrir Square in 2011 as the 'Arab Spring' developed – have unfolded before a truly global audience. The interactive character of the Internet and social media has also led to citizens helping to produce the news by reporting 'direct from the scene' of world events.

The shift to a global outlook has two significant dimensions. First, people increasingly perceive that their responsibility does not stop at national borders. Disasters and injustices facing people around the world are no longer misfortunes that cannot be tackled but legitimate grounds for action and intervention. A growing assumption has arisen that 'the international community' has an obligation to act in crisis situations to protect the human rights of individuals. In the case of natural disasters, interventions take the form of humanitarian relief and technical assistance. There have also been stronger calls in recent years for intervention and peacekeeping forces in civil wars and ethnic conflicts, though such mobilizations are politically problematic compared to those for natural disasters.

Second, a global outlook seems to be undermining many people's sense of national (or nation-state) identity. Local cultural identities are experiencing powerful revivals at a time when the traditional hold of the nation-state is undergoing profound transformation. In Europe, for example, inhabitants of Scotland and the Basque region of Spain may be more likely to identify as Scottish or Basque – or simply as Europeans – rather than as British or Spanish. The referendum on Scottish independence in September 2014 was lost, but 45 per cent of the population voted 'Yes', while an unofficial vote in Catalonia in November returned an overwhelming majority of 80 per cent voting for independence from Spain. Nation-state identification seems to be waning as globalization loosens people's orientation to the states in which they live.

The interweaving of cultures and economies

For some socialist and Marxist sociologists, although culture and politics play a part in global trends, these are underpinned by capitalist economic globalization and the continuing pursuit of profits. Martell (2016: 4), for example, argues that 'it is difficult to see many areas of globalization where lying behind them are not also underlying economic structures that affect the equality or power relations with which globalization is produced or received, or economic incentive to do with making money.' This viewpoint accepts the multidimensional character of globalization but rejects the notion that cultural, political and economic factors should be given equal weight. Analysing material interests and the way these are pursued remains the key to understanding globalization in this neo-Marxist perspective.

Of course, others disagree. Those adopting a broadly culturalist position argue that globalization does depend on the continuing integration of the world economy, but that this is achieved in various cultural, not purely economic ways. For example, tourism is a huge 'industry' around the world. In Britain it is the third highest export-earning sector, worth some £90 billion of business and supporting around 1.36 million jobs (DCMS 2011). Conversely, UK citizens make more than 50 million visits abroad every year (Urry 2002: 6). The desire to travel and experience new sights and cultures is not a purely material interest but is influenced by the shifting cultural tastes of the 'tourist gaze' (Urry and Larsen 2011). This thesis is outlined in 'Global society 4.3'.

Waters (2001) argues that the realm of culture is crucial for globalization because it is through cultural forms that economic and political development are freed from the material constraints of geography. The *weightless economy* is one in which products have their base in information, such as computer software, media and entertainment products – computer games, films, music and Internet-based services (Quah 1999). This new

Global Society 4.3 International tourist interactions

Have you ever had a face-to-face conversation with someone from another country or connected to an overseas website? Have you ever travelled to another continent on business or for a holiday? If you answered 'yes' then you have experienced one of the consequences of globalization. Globalization has changed both the frequency and the character of interactions between people of different nations. The historical sociologist Charles Tilly defines globalization in terms of these changes. According to Tilly (1995: 1–2), 'globalization means an increase in the geographic range of locally consequential social interactions.' In other words, a greater proportion of our interactions come to involve, directly or indirectly, people from other countries.

Globalization has greatly expanded the possibilities for international travel, both by encouraging an interest in other countries and by facilitating the movement of tourists across borders. High levels of international tourism translate into an increase in the number of face-to-face interactions between people of different countries. John Urry (2002; Urry and Larsen 2011) argues that the 'tourist gaze' – the expectations on the part of tourists of what they will experience while travelling abroad – shapes many of these interactions.

Urry compares the tourist gaze to Foucault's conception of the medical gaze (see chapter 11, 'Health, Illness and Disability'). He argues that the tourist gaze is just as socially organized by professional experts, just as systematic in its application and just as detached as the medical gaze, but this time in its search for 'exotic' experiences. These are experiences that violate everyday expectations about how social interaction and interaction with the physical environment are supposed to proceed.

Britons travelling in the USA, for example, may delight in the fact that Americans drive on the right-hand side of the road. At the same time,

such behaviour is disconcerting. UK rules of the road are so ingrained that Britons experience their systematic violation as strange, weird and exotic. Imagine how disappointed you would be if you were to travel to a different country only to find that it was just like the city or town in which you grew up.

Yet, apart from those seeking out extreme experiences, most tourists do not want their experiences to be *too* exotic. A popular destination for young travellers in Paris, for example, is a McDonald's restaurant. Some go to see if there is any truth to the line from Quentin Tarantino's movie *Pulp Fiction* that, because the French use the metric system, McDonald's 'quarter pounder with cheese' hamburgers are called 'Royales with cheese' (it is true). Britons travelling abroad often cannot resist eating and drinking in comfortable British- and Irish-style pubs. The contradictory demands for the exotic and the familiar are at the heart of the tourist gaze.

The tourist gaze may put strains on face-to-face interactions between tourists and locals. Locals who are part of the tourist industry may appreciate the economic benefits, but others may resent tourists for their demanding attitudes and the overdevelopment that occurs in popular destinations. As with most aspects of globalization, the overall impact of these intercultural encounters has both positive and negative consequences.

> ### THINKING CRITICALLY
>
> Do you consider the impact of your foreign holidays on the *society* and *people* you visit? How do your *travel plans* and the *infrastructure* required for tourists damage the country's *ecosystems*? Do the cultural benefits of global tourism outweigh any environmental damage caused?

economic context has been described as the 'knowledge society', 'the information age' or, more simply, 'the new economy'. The emergence of the knowledge society is linked to the development of a broad base of technologically literate consumers who integrate advances in computing, entertainment and

Coca-Cola is a transnational company which sells its products all over the world. This image shows Diet Coke on sale in Jordan in the Middle East.

telecommunications into their everyday lives. Perhaps the best example is computer gamers, who await the latest games and updates with eager anticipation and, of course, are prepared to pay for them.

This 'electronic economy' underpins the broader economic globalization. Banks, corporations, fund managers and individual investors are able to shift funds internationally with just a click. The ability to move electronic money instantaneously carries with it greater risks. Transfers of vast amounts of capital can destabilize economies, triggering international financial crises. As the global economy becomes more tightly integrated, a financial collapse in one part of the world can have an enormous effect on distant economies.

The operation of the global economy reflects changes that have occurred in the information age. Many aspects of the economy now operate through networks that cross national

boundaries rather than stopping at them (Castells 1996). In order to be competitive, businesses and corporations have restructured to become more flexible and networked rather than hierarchical, as in older bureaucratic organizations. Production practices and organizational patterns have become more flexible, partnering arrangements with other firms are more commonplace, and participation in worldwide distribution networks is essential for doing business in rapidly moving global markets.

Transnational corporations

Among the many economic factors driving globalization, the role of transnational corporations is especially important, despite their relatively small number. Transnational corporations are companies that produce goods or market services across several countries. These may be relatively small firms, with one or two factories outside their home country, or gigantic international ventures whose operations criss-cross the globe. Some of the biggest transnational corporations are companies known all around the world and include Coca-Cola, General Motors, Unilever, Nestlé and Mitsubishi. Even when transnational corporations have a national base they remain oriented towards global markets and profit-making.

Transnational corporations became increasingly significant after 1945. Expansion in the initial postwar years came from firms based in the United States, but by the 1970s European and Japanese firms increasingly invested abroad. In the late 1980s and the 1990s, transnational corporations expanded dramatically with the establishment of three powerful regional markets: Europe (the Single European Market), Asia-Pacific (the Osaka Declaration guaranteed free and open trade by 2010) and North America (the North American Free Trade Agreement). Since the early 1990s countries in other areas of the world have also liberalized restrictions on foreign investment, and by the turn of the twenty-first century there were few economies in the world beyond the reach of transnational corporations. In

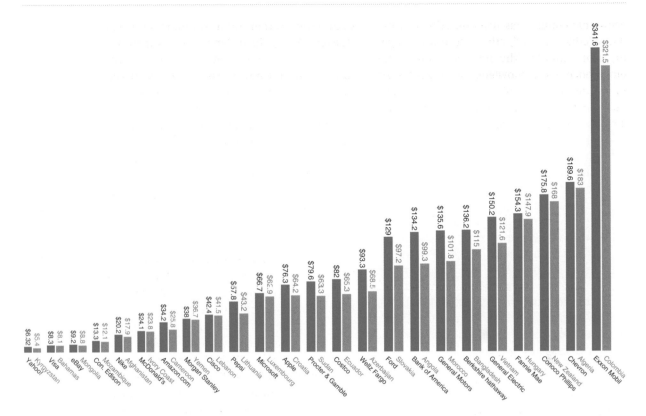

Figure 4.4 Top 25 US companies by sales compared with GDP of selected countries (in $US billion)

Source: Foreign Policy (2014).

very recent years, transnational corporations have expanded their operations into developing countries and Eastern Europe, with China providing the next major challenge and opportunity.

Transnational corporations lie at the heart of economic globalization, accounting for two-thirds of all world trade. They are instrumental in the diffusion of new technologies around the globe and are major actors in financial markets (Held et al. 1999). Some 500 transnational corporations had annual sales of more than $10 billion in 2001, while only seventy-five *countries* could boast gross domestic products of at least that amount. In other words, the world's leading transnational corporations are, in some respects, larger than many of the world's countries (see figure 4.4). In fact, the combined sales of the world's largest 500 transnational corporations totalled

$14.1 trillion – nearly half of the value of goods and services produced by the entire world.

The argument that manufacturing industry is becoming increasingly globalized is often expressed in terms of global commodity chains – worldwide networks of labour and production processes yielding a finished product. Such networks consist of production

> **THINKING CRITICALLY**
>
> Does the economic strength of transnational corporations mean they hold more power than national governments? How have nation-states organized themselves to regulate the activities of transnationals? Which of the sociological theories in chapter 1 best explains the rise of transnational corporations?

4.2 'Barbie' and the development of global commodity chains

One illustration of the global commodity chain is the manufacture of the Barbie doll, the most profitable toy in history. The forty-something teenage doll once sold at a rate of two per second, bringing the Mattel Corporation, based in Los Angeles, USA, well over $1 billion in annual revenues. Although the doll sells mainly in the United States, Europe and Japan, Barbie can be found in 140 countries around the world – a truly global citizen (Tempest 1996). Barbie is global not only in sales but in terms of her birthplace as well. She was never made in the United States. The first doll was made in Japan in 1959, when that country was still recovering from the Second World War and wages were low. As wages rose in Japan, Barbie moved to other low-wage countries in Asia. Her multiple origins today tell us a great deal about the operation of global commodity chains.

Barbie is designed in the United States, where her marketing and advertising strategies are devised and where most of the profits are made. But the only physical aspect of the doll that is 'made in the USA' is the cardboard packaging, along with some of the paints and oils used in decoration.

Barbie's body and wardrobe span the globe in their origins:

1 Barbie begins life in Saudi Arabia, where oil is extracted and refined into the ethylene used to create the plastic body.
2 Taiwan's state-owned oil importer, the Chinese Petroleum Corporation, buys the ethylene and sells it to Taiwan's Formosa Plastic Corporation, the world's largest producer of polyvinyl chloride (PVC) plastics, which are used in toys. Formosa Plastics converts the ethylene into PVC pellets that are shaped to make Barbie's body.
3 The pellets are then shipped to one of the four Asian factories that make Barbie – two in southern China, one in Indonesia and one in Malaysia. The plastic mould injection machines that shape the doll's body, which

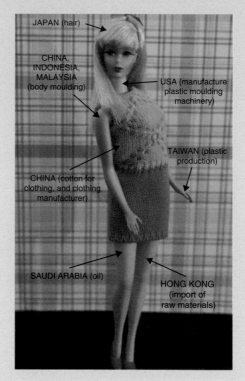

'Barbie' is a global product.

are the most expensive part, are made in the USA and shipped to the factories.
4 Once Barbie's body is moulded, she gets her nylon hair from Japan. Her cotton dresses are made in China, with Chinese cotton – the only raw material actually to come from the country where most of the dolls are made.
5 Hong Kong plays a key role in the manufacturing process of Chinese Barbies. Nearly all the material used in her manufacture is shipped into Hong Kong – one of the world's largest ports – and then trucked to the factories in China. The finished Barbies leave by the same route. Some 23,000 trucks make the daily trip between Hong Kong and southern China's toy factories.

But where is Barbie actually from? The box containing the 'My First Tea Party' Barbie is labelled 'Made in China', but, as we have seen, few of the materials that go into making her originate in that country. Most of the money from sales goes to pay for machinery and equipment, transoceanic shipping and domestic trucking, advertising and merchandising, retail floor space – and, of course, the profits of retailers. What Barbie production and consumption shows us is the effectiveness of globalization in connecting the world's economies. However, it also demonstrates the unevenness of globalization, which enables some countries to benefit at the expense of others. We cannot assume that global commodity chains will inevitably promote development across the chain of societies involved.

As for Barbie, sales have slumped in recent years as children choose other types of toy.

Barbie sales were down 6 per cent in 2013. But, if you immediately thought she was losing out to computer games and smartphones, think again. In 2014, the most popular toy was the low-tech, high-creativity rainbow loom band (Peterson 2014).

THINKING CRITICALLY

Is global Barbie an example of the positive potential of globalization to provide work and a wage to those outside the rich, developed world? Or is the situation more complex than this assessment suggests? Explain which social groups, organizations and societies stand to benefit most from the operation of global commodity chains.

---

activities that form a tightly interlocked 'chain', from raw materials to the final consumer (Gereffi 1995; Appelbaum and Christerson 1997). China, for instance, has moved from the position of low- to middle-income country because of its role as an exporter of manufactured goods. Yet the most profitable activities in the commodity chain – engineering, design and advertising – remain mainly in high-income countries, while the least profitable aspects, such as factory production, occur in low-income ones, thus reproducing rather than challenging global inequality.

Political globalization

Contemporary globalization is linked to political developments, and there are several aspects to this – first, the collapse of communism in a series of dramatic revolutions in Eastern Europe from 1989, culminating in the dissolution of the Soviet Union itself in 1991. Since then, countries in the former Soviet bloc – including Russia, Ukraine, Poland, Hungary, the Czech Republic, the Baltic states, the states of the Caucasus and Central Asia, and elsewhere – have moved towards Western-style political and economic systems. The collapse of communism hastened the

process of globalization, though the collapse was itself partly its product. The centrally planned communist economies and the ideological and cultural control of communist parties were ultimately unable to survive in the emerging era of global media and the electronically integrated world economy.

A second political development is the growth of international and regional mechanisms of government which bring nation-states together and move international relations closer to forms of global governance. The United Nations and the European Union are the two most prominent examples of international organizations which bring nation-states into common political forums. The United Nations achieves this through the association of individual nation-states, but the EU has pioneered forms of transnational governance in which a degree of national sovereignty is relinquished by member states. Governments of individual EU states are bound by directives, regulations and court judgements from common EU bodies, but they also reap the economic, social and political benefits from their participation.

International governmental organizations (IGOs) and international non-governmental organizations (INGOs) are also important forms of an increasingly global politics. IGOs are bodies established by participating governments and given responsibility for regulating or overseeing a particular domain of activity that is transnational in scope. The International Telegraph Union, founded in 1865, was the first, but since that time a great number of similar bodies have been created, regulating issues from civil aviation to broadcasting and the disposal of hazardous waste. They include the United Nations (UN), the International Monetary Fund (IMF) and the North Atlantic Treaty Organization (NATO).

INGOs differ from IGOs in that they are not affiliated with government institutions. They are independent and work alongside governmental bodies in making policy decisions and addressing international issues. Some of the best-known – such as Greenpeace, Médecins Sans Frontières (Doctors Without Borders), the Red Cross and Amnesty International – are involved in environmental protection and humanitarian efforts. But the activities of thousands of lesser-known groups also link together countries and communities. What we can see emerging from the increasing range of transnational political bodies is essentially a political globalization, where the central issues are no longer ones of national interest but international and global matters.

Debating globalization

Globalization has become a hotly debated topic. Most scholars accept that there are important changes occurring, but the extent to which it is valid to bundle these together as 'globalization' is contested. One influential account is that of David Held and his colleagues (Held et al. 1999), who divided the arguments into three broad schools: hyperglobalizers, sceptics and transformationalists. These three tendencies are summarized in table 4.5. The authors cited for each school are selected because their work contains some of the key arguments that define that school's approach.

Hyperglobalizers

Hyperglobalizers see globalization as a very real, ongoing process with wide-ranging consequences. Globalization is producing a new global order, swept along by powerful flows of cross-border trade and production. The Japanese writer Kenichi Ohmae (1990, 1995) sees globalization leading to a 'borderless world' in which market forces are more powerful than national governments. A large part of this argument rests on the idea that nation-states are losing the power to control their own destiny. Individual countries no longer oversee their economies because of the vast growth in world trade, while governments are increasingly unable to exercise authority over cross-border volatile financial markets, investment decisions, increasing migration, environmental dangers or terrorist networks. Citizens also recognize that politicians have limited ability to address these problems and, as a result, lose faith in existing systems of national governance.

The hyperglobalization argument suggests that national governments are caught in a pincer movement, being challenged from above (by regional and international institutions, such as the European Union and World Trade Organization) and from below (by international protest movements, global terrorism and citizens' initiatives). Taken together, these shifts signal the dawning of an age in which a global consciousness develops and the influence of national governments declines (Albrow 1997).

Sceptics

Some argue that the 'reality' of globalization is overstated and most theories of globalization amount to a lot of talk about something that is really quite longstanding. For example, current levels of economic interdependence are not unprecedented. Nineteenth-century statistics on world trade and investment lead some to argue that contemporary globalization differs from the past only in the intensity of interactions between nation-states. If so, then it may be more accurate to talk of

Table 4.5 Conceptualizing globalization: three tendencies

	Hyperglobalizers (Ohmae 1990, 1995; Albrow 1997)	Sceptics (Boyer and Drache 1996; Hirst 1997; Hirst and Thompson 1999)	Transformationalists (Sassen 1991; Rosenau 1997)
What's new?	A global age	Trading blocs, weaker geo-governance than in earlier periods	Historically unprecedented levels of global interconnectedness
Dominant features?	Global capitalism, global governance, global civil society	World less interdependent than in the 1890s	'Thick' (intensive and extensive) globalization
Power of national governments?	Declining or eroding	Reinforced or enhanced	Reconstituted, restructured
Driving forces of globalization?	Capitalism and technology	Governments and markets	Combined forces of modernity
Pattern of stratification?	Erosion of old hierarchies	Increased marginalization of South	New architecture of world order
Dominant motif?	McDonald's, Madonna, etc.	National interest	Transformation of political community
Conceptualization of globalization?	A reordering of the framework of human action	Internationalization and regionalization	Reordering of interregional relations and action at a distance
Historical trajectory?	Global civilization	Regional blocs/clash of civilizations	Indeterminate: global integration and fragmentation
Summary argument	The end of the nation-state	Internationalization depends on government acquiescence and support	Globalization transforming government power and world politics

Source: Adapted from Held et al. (1999: 10).

'internationalization' rather than globalization. This preserves the idea that nation-states have been and are likely to continue as the central political actors. National governments remain key players because they are involved in regulating and coordinating economic activity, and some are driving through trade agreements and policies of economic liberalization.

Sceptics agree that there may be more contact between countries than in previous eras, but there is currently insufficient integration to constitute a truly globalized economy. This is because the bulk of trade occurs within just three regional groups – Europe, Asia-Pacific and North America – rather than in a genuinely global context. The countries of the European Union, for example, trade predominantly among themselves, and the same is true of the other regional groups, thereby invalidating the concept of a single global economy (Hirst 1997). Whether the latter will become a reality in the long run is not yet clear.

As a result, many sceptics focus on processes of *regionalization* within the world economy – such as the emergence of financial and trading blocs. The growth of regionalization is evidence that the world economy has become *less* rather than more integrated (Boyer and Drache 1996; Hirst and Thompson 1999). Compared with the patterns of trade that prevailed a century ago, the world economy is actually less global in its geographical scope and more concentrated in intense pockets of activity. In this sense, hyperglobalizers are misreading the historical evidence.

Transformationalists

Transformationalists take a position somewhere between those of sceptics and hyperglobalizers, contending that globalization is breaking down established boundaries between the internal and the external, the international and the domestic. Yet many older patterns remain, and national governments retain a good deal of their power and influence. Rather than losing sovereignty, nation-states are restructuring and pooling sovereignty in response to new forms of economic and social organization that are non-territorial, including corporations, social movements and international bodies. The transformationalist argument is that we no longer live in a state-centric world, but states are adopting a more active and outward-looking stance towards governance under complex conditions of global interdependence (Rosenau 1997).

It may also be wrong to see globalization as inevitable, something that is happening to ordinary people and is beyond their control. In fact, it is a quite dynamic and open process that is subject to influence and change. Thus, globalization proceeds in a contradictory fashion, encompassing tendencies that operate in opposition to one another. There is a two-way flow of images, information and influences from the global to the local and vice versa. Global migration, international tourism, mass media and telecommunications contribute to the diffusion of widely varying cultural influences. The world's vibrant 'global cities', such as London, New York and Tokyo, are thoroughly multicultural, with ethnic groups and cultures intersecting, sharing and living side by side (Sassen 1991). Globalization is a decentred and reflexive process characterized by links and cultural flows that work in a multi-directional way. Because it is the product of these numerous intertwined global networks, it should not be seen as driven from the USA, 'the West' or any single part of the world (Held et al. 1999).

Evaluating the evidence

The transformationalist view fits the present evidence quite well, though in the future we cannot rule out that globalizing processes may become more systematic and effective. Many sceptics underestimate just how much the world is moving in a global direction as world finance markets are increasingly organized on a global level, the Internet facilitates regular long-distance relationships, and tourism and cross-cultural communications transform people's everyday experience. On the other hand, the hyperglobalizers' portrayal of a steady movement towards a global economy cannot be inferred only from present trends; these may well alter direction, as the recent global financial crisis illustrated.

The 2008 global financial crisis brought home some of the risks inherent in an emerging 'borderless economy'. In the European Union, huge economic bailouts of the Republic of Ireland, Cyprus, Greece and Portugal led to renewed questioning of the single currency and the logic of 'ever closer union'. It is possible to envisage a situation in which the centripetal tendency towards closer integration may go into reverse as national governments make the political decision to protect their own economies. Similarly, in many European countries there has been a backlash against increasing migration into Europe and the principle of 'freedom of movement' within the EU. One consequence is the rise of nationalist and anti-immigration parties based on restricting or stopping inward migration or, in the case of the United Kingdom Independence Party (UKIP), leaving the European Union altogether. In 2016, concerns and fears about large-scale immigration from EU countries into the UK were a key factor in the UK voting to leave the EU, as many people sought additional controls over the level and type of inward migration. In effect, these parties actively seek to prevent the borderless world forecast by hyberglobalizers from ever coming into being.

> The 2008 financial crisis and recovery plans are discussed in detail in Chapter 7, 'Work and the Economy'.

However, not all political and social movements oppose globalization *per se*. During the 1990s, social movements developed across the world that were highly critical of the capitalist free-market version of globalization but did not reject closer global connectedness. Rather, these movements promote an alternative vision of what globalization could look like if ecological sustainability, human rights and community governance were at its heart. As a result, the varied elements – including the World Economic Forum – are known collectively as alter-globalization movements rather than being simply anti-globalization.

> Anti- and alter-globalization movements are discussed in chapter 21, 'Politics, Government and Social Movements'.

In this debate, all three positions focus primarily on the *contemporary* process of rapid globalization and its consequences for the future. However, as we have noted, it is possible to set globalization processes into a much longer historical time frame. On this view, the extended development of human societies is leading *towards* more global patterns of interdependent relations, but this was not and still is not inevitable (Hopper 2007). Historically, globalization is the product of conflict, wars and invasions just as much as cooperation and mutual help, which means that reversals of global trends such as national economic protectionism are always possible. Conflicts *have* made a major contribution to globalization, but they also have the potential to send it into reverse.

> Chapter 22, 'Nations, War and Terrorism', contains an extended discussion of war and conflict.

The consequences of globalization

The main focus of sociology has historically been the study of the industrialized societies, with all other societies being the province of anthropology. However, as our awareness of globalization grows, this academic division of labour has become less tenable. The developed and developing societies have long been interconnected, as the history of colonial expansion and empire-building demonstrates. Those living in the developed world depend on raw materials and manufactured products from developing countries, while the continued progress of the economies of developing countries depends on trade with developed ones. Globalization means the minority and majority 'worlds' are increasingly forming parts of one global human world.

As a result, the cultural map of the world also changes: networks of people span national borders and even continents, providing cultural connections between their birthplaces and adoptive countries (Appadurai 1986). Although there are between 5,000 and 6,000 languages spoken on the planet, around 98 per cent of these are used by just 10 per cent of the global population. A mere dozen languages have come to dominate the global language system, with more than 100 million speakers each: Arabic, Chinese, English, French, German, Hindi, Japanese, Malay, Portuguese, Russian, Spanish and Swahili. And just one language – English – has become 'hypercentral', as first choice for most second-language speakers. It is these 'bilinguals' who bind together the whole global language system that exists today (de Swaan 2001).

It is increasingly impossible for any society to exist apart from the rest of the human world, and there are few, if any, places left on Earth that are so remote as to escape radio, television, mobile phones, computers, air travel and the masses of tourists they bring. A generation ago, there were still small tribal groups whose way of life was completely untouched, but today most of these use machetes and other tools made in China and other manufacturing centres, wear T-shirts and shorts manufactured in garment factories in the Dominican Republic or Guatemala, and take medicines manufactured in Germany or Switzerland to combat diseases contracted through contact with outsiders. These same people are able to broadcast their own stories to others around the globe through the Internet and television, which also bring British and American culture into homes throughout the world while adapting cultural products from the Netherlands (*Big Brother*) or the UK (*Pop Idol*). Does this process produce a uniform culture too?

Globalization or glocalization?

Many have argued that the rapid growth of the Internet around the world will hasten the spread of a global culture resembling the powerful nations of Europe and North America. Belief in the values of equality between men and women, the right to speak freely, democratic participation in government and the pursuit of pleasure through consumption are readily diffused throughout the world over the Internet. Moreover, Internet technology itself seems to foster such values: global communication, seemingly unlimited and uncensored information, and instant gratification are all characteristics of the worldwide web.

However, it may be premature to conclude that globalization will sweep aside traditional cultures. There is evidence that global forces may even be strengthening traditional values. To capture this balancing of the

Rooftop satellite dishes in Marrakech, Morocco, with Ben Salah mosque in the background. Digital technology has enabled companies, advertisers and cultural producers to market their wares in every part of the world. However, this does not necessarily mean that local cultures, beliefs and practices are weakened.

consequences of globalization, the British sociologist Roland Robertson (1992) coined the term glocalization – a mixture of *globalization* and *localization*. Local communities are often active rather than passive in modifying and shaping global processes. Similarly, transnational companies tailor their products and services to take account of local conditions 'on the ground'. If this is so, then we may find that globalization does not lead inevitably to a

---

Global Society 4.4 | **Reggae – a global musical style?**

When those knowledgeable about popular music listen to a song, they can often pick out the stylistic influences that helped shape it. Each musical style, after all, represents a unique way of combining rhythm, melody, harmony and lyrics. And, while it does not take a genius to notice the differences between rock, rap or folk, for example, musicians often combine a number of styles in composing songs. Different musical styles tend to emerge from different social groups, and studying how these combine and fuse is a good way to chart the cultural contact between social groups.

Some sociologists turned their attention to reggae music because it exemplifies the process whereby contacts between social groups result in the creation of new musical forms. Reggae's roots can be traced to West Africa. In the seventeenth century, large numbers of West Africans were enslaved by British colonists and brought by ship to work in the sugar-cane fields of the West Indies. Although the British attempted to prevent slaves from playing traditional African music for fear it would serve as a rallying cry to revolt, the slaves managed to keep alive the tradition of African drumming, sometimes by integrating it with European musical styles imposed by slave-owners. In Jamaica, the drumming of one group of slaves, the Burru, was openly tolerated by slave-owners because it helped meter the pace of their work. Slavery was finally abolished in Jamaica in 1834, but the tradition of Burru drumming continued, even as many Burru men migrated from rural areas to the slums of Kingston.

It was in these slums that a new religious cult began to emerge – one that would prove crucial to the development of reggae. In 1930, Haile Selassie was crowned emperor of Ethiopia. While opponents of European colonialism throughout the world cheered Selassie's ascension to the throne, some in the West Indies came to believe that he was a god, sent to Earth to lead the oppressed of Africa to freedom. One of Selassie's names was 'Prince Ras Tafari', and the West Indians who worshipped him called themselves 'Rastafarians'. The Rastafarian cult soon merged with the Burru, and Rastafarian music combined Burru styles of drumming with biblical themes of oppression and liberation. In the 1950s, West Indian musicians began mixing Rastafarian rhythms and lyrics with elements of American jazz and black rhythm and blues. These combinations eventually developed into 'ska' music and then, in the late 1960s, into reggae, with its relatively slow beat, its emphasis on bass and its stories of urban deprivation and of the power of collective social consciousness. Many reggae artists, such as Bob Marley, became commercial successes, and by the 1970s people the world over were listening to reggae music. In the 1980s and 1990s, reggae was fused with hip-hop (or rap) to produce new sounds (Hebdige 1997), heard in the work of the groups such as the Wu-Tang Clan, Shaggy or Sean Paul.

The history of reggae is thus the history of contact between different social groups and of the meanings – political, spiritual and personal – those groups expressed through their music. Globalization has increased the intensity of these contacts. It is now possible for a young musician in Scandinavia, for example, to grow up listening to music produced by men and women in the basements of Notting Hill in London and to be deeply influenced as well by, say, a mariachi performance broadcast live via satellite from Mexico City. If the number of contacts between groups is an important determinant of the pace of musical evolution, we can forecast that there will be a profusion of new styles in the coming years as the process of globalization develops.

uniform, global (Western) culture but, instead, allows for diversity and multidirectional flows of cultural products across the world's societies.

Consider the Middle Eastern country of Kuwait, a traditional Islamic culture that has recently experienced strong American and European influences. Kuwait is an oil-rich country on the Persian Gulf and has one of the highest average per capita incomes in the world. The government provides free public education through to university level, resulting in high rates of literacy and education for both men and women. Kuwaiti television frequently carries American football, although broadcasts are regularly interrupted for the traditional Muslim calls to prayer. Around 57 per cent of Kuwait's people are under the age of twenty-five, and, like their counterparts in Europe and North America, many surf the Internet for new ideas, information and consumer products.

Although Kuwait is in many respects a 'modern' country, traditional gender norms that treat men and women differently remain strong. Women are generally expected to wear traditional clothing that leaves only the face and hands visible and are forbidden to leave home at night or to be seen in public at any time with a man who is not a spouse or relative. The Internet is increasingly popular, and the majority of Kuwaiti Internet users, around 67 per cent, are young people. Interview data suggest that the main attraction of the Internet is that it enables young people to cross strictly enforced gender lines. Deborah Wheeler's (2006) interviews with male and female Kuwaiti students studying in the UK and the USA found that most reported communicating with the opposite sex as the most common use of the Internet in a country which segregates men and women, even in Internet cafes.

One female student, Sabiha, reported that 'The main reason [the] Internet is so popular with the Kuwaiti youth is because it's the most effective way for boys and girls to communicate with each other' (Wheeler 2006: 148). Another interviewee, Buthayna, said that 'Girls especially cannot form relationships with boys, even as friends in many families in Kuwait, so the Internet is a "safe" place I guess for them to do so. And the fact that the two sides don't know each other, they feel safer to voice their concerns, ideas, without having their reputations ruined or without it affecting their social life' (ibid.: 146). Other women reported that some well-known chatrooms had themselves gained a 'bad reputation' for explicit conversation, and just using them now risked girls and young women attracting the label of 'not being a decent girl'.

Wheeler's work shows in microcosm the way in which the global and the local interact through the contemporary medium of the Internet. Internet use clearly does offer new opportunities for global communication, information exchange, research and much more, and in this sense it is a force for globalization. However, the way it is used is still shaped in part by national context and local cultural norms. Young Kuwaiti women (and men) have made use of the Internet to circumvent some of the social rules and taboos of their society, but local gender norms are reasserted through social interactions and word of mouth, which stigmatize certain chatrooms and the girls who use them.

Kuwaiti culture, which is hundreds of years old, is not likely to be easily transformed by simple exposure to different beliefs and values on the Internet. The fact that young people participate in potentially global chatrooms does not mean that Kuwaiti culture will adopt the sexual attitudes or gender relations of the West. The culture that eventually emerges from this process of glocalization is likely to be recognizably Kuwaiti.

> **THINKING CRITICALLY**
>
> Think of examples where Western products, brands or culture have changed non-Western cultures. List some examples where these have been significantly altered at the local level. Does such localization mean that indigenous cultures can withstand the forces of globalization?

Intensified individualism

Although globalization is often associated with macro changes in world markets, production and trade, and telecommunications, the effects of globalization are also felt in the private realm. Globalization is not something that is simply 'out there', it is also 'in here', affecting people's intimate and personal lives in diverse ways. Inevitably, personal lives have been altered as globalizing forces enter local contexts, homes and communities through impersonal sources – such as the media and popular culture – and through personal contact with people from other countries.

Today people have much more opportunity to shape their own lives than in the past, when the main influences were tradition and custom. Social class, gender, ethnicity and even religious affiliation could close off certain life avenues or open up others. Being born the eldest son of a tailor, for example, would probably ensure a young man would learn his father's craft and practise it throughout his lifetime. Tradition held that a woman's natural place was in the home, with her life and identity defined largely by those of her husband or father. Personal identities were formed within the context of the community into which people were born, and the values, lifestyles and ethics of the community provided a relatively fixed guide for life.

Under conditions of globalization, people are faced with a new *individualism*, in which

---

Classic Studies 4.2 | **Anthony Giddens: riding the juggernaut of modernity**

The research problem

What impact is globalization likely to have on people's everyday lives? How will globalization change the modern world that we all increasingly inhabit? In a series of books, articles and lectures since the early 1990s, Anthony Giddens has tried to explore the characteristics of the emerging global form of modernity and its consequences for everyday life (1991a, 1991b, 1993, 2001). In particular, he has been interested in the decline of tradition, our increasing risk awareness and the changing nature of trust in relationships.

Giddens's explanation

In *The Consequences of Modernity* (1991b), Giddens outlined his view that the global spread of modernity tends to produce a 'runaway world' in which, it appears, no one and no government is in overall control. While Marx used the image of a monster to describe capitalist modernity, Giddens (ibid.: 139) likens it to riding on board a large truck:

> I suggest we should substitute that of the juggernaut – a runaway engine of enormous power, which, collectively as human beings, we can drive to some extent but which also threatens to rush out of our control and which could rend itself asunder. The juggernaut crushes those who resist it, and while it sometimes seems to have a steady path, there are times when it veers away erratically in directions we cannot foresee. The ride is by no means unpleasant or unrewarding; it can often be exhilarating and charged with hopeful anticipation. But, as long as the institutions of modernity endure, we shall never be able to control completely either the path or the pace of the journey.

The globalizing form of modernity is marked by new uncertainties, risks and changes to people's trust in others and social institutions. In a world of rapid change, traditional forms of trust are dissolved. Our trust in other people used to be based in local communities, but in globalized societies our lives are influenced by people we never meet or know, who may live on the far side of the world from us. Such impersonal relationships mean we are pushed to 'trust' or have confidence in 'abstract systems', such as food production and environmental regulation agencies or international banking systems. In this way, trust and risk are closely bound together. Trust in authorities is necessary if we are to confront the risks around us and react to them in an effective way. However, *this* type of trust is not habitually given but is the subject of reflection and revision.

When societies were more reliant on knowledge gained from custom and tradition, people could follow established ways of doing things without much reflection. For modern people, aspects of life that earlier generations were able to take for granted become matters of open decision-making, producing what Giddens calls 'reflexivity' – the continuous reflection on our everyday actions and the re-formation of these in the light of new knowledge. For example, whether to marry (or divorce) is a very personal decision, which may take account of the advice of family and friends. But official statistics and sociological research on marriage and divorce also filter into social life, becoming widely known and shared, thus becoming part of an individual's decision-making.

For Giddens, these characteristic features point to the conclusion that global modernity is a form of social life that is discontinuous with previous ones. In many ways, the globalization of modernity marks not the end of modern societies or a movement beyond them (as in *post*modernism – see chapter 3) but a new stage of 'late' or 'high' modernity which takes the tendencies embedded within modern life into a more far-reaching global phase.

Critical points

Giddens's critics argue that perhaps he exaggerates the discontinuity between modernity and previous societies and that tradition and habit continue to structure people's everyday activities. The modern period is not so unique, they say, and modern people are not so different from those who went before. Others think that his account of globalizing modernity underplays the central sociological question of power – in particular that of transnational corporations to promote a form of globalization that privileges their needs at the expense of the world's poor. The concept of 'modernity' essentially masks the power of capitalist corporations.

Some critics also argue that Giddens sees reflexivity in almost wholly positive terms, reflecting the opening up of social life to more choice. However, such reflexivity could also be leading to heightened levels of 'anomie', as described by Durkheim, and, in that sense, reflexivity may be more of a problem to be solved than a welcome development to be promoted.

Contemporary significance

Because theories of globalization are relatively recent and Giddens continues to develop his theories of modern life, these constitute very much a 'work in progress'. The ideas he has developed have been taken in fruitful directions by other sociologists, and, in that sense, he has provided a theoretical framework and some conceptual tools for younger generations to take forward. As is evident from the contribution of the critics of his work on modernity, reflexivity and trust relationships, this has provoked much sociological debate. No doubt it will continue to do so in the future and readers will come to their own assessment of it.

they actively construct their own identities. The social codes that previously guided people's choices and activities have significantly loosened. That eldest son of a tailor could now choose numerous paths to construct his future, and women are no longer restricted to the domestic realm. Girls do better than boys in most school subjects, women make up a majority of students in higher education, and more women work in the formal economy, often in jobs with attractive career paths. The social norms that guided an older generation's gendered expectations are no longer appropriate for the lives their children lead, as new norms are still emerging.

Globalization is pushing people to live in more open, reflexive ways, and this means that they constantly respond and adjust to their changing environment. Even the small choices we make in our daily lives – what we wear, how we spend our leisure time, and how we take care of our health and our bodies – are part of the ongoing process of creating and re-creating our self-identities. A simple conclusion is to say that people in many countries today have lost a clear sense of belonging and gained more freedom of choice. Whether this constitutes progress, though, is part of continuing debates on the pros and cons of globalization.

Conclusion: governing a global society?

As globalization progresses, existing political structures and models seem inadequate for a world full of challenges that transcend national borders. In particular, national governments cannot individually control oil and energy prices or the spread of disease pandemics, tackle global warming and organized crime, or regulate volatile financial markets. There is no global government or world parliament, and no one votes in a global election. And yet,

> . . . on any given day, mail is delivered across borders; people travel from one country to another via a variety of transport modes; goods and services are freighted across land, air, sea and cyberspace; and a whole range of other cross-border activities takes place in the reasonable expectation of safety and security for the people, groups, firms and governments involved . . . This immediately raises a puzzle: How is the world governed even in the absence of a world government to produce norms, codes of conduct, and regulatory, surveillance, and compliance instruments? (Weiss and Thakur 2010: 1)

The question is apposite, but on reflection we can see that it conflates *government* with *governance*. While government is a set of institutions with executive power over a given territory, governance is rather less tangible. Precisely because there is no world government or any prospect of one, some scholars have called instead for more effective global governance as a way of addressing global issues. The first book title on the subject was published in 1993, but since then there have been well over 500 academic books on global governance (Harman and Williams 2013: 2).

In 1995, in the wake of the demise of the Soviet Union and the end of the Cold War, a UN report, *Our Global Neighbourhood*, looked at emerging challenges for humanity and

ways of dealing with them. The report argued that governance at the global level could no longer be restricted to relations and agreements between national governments but must also include NGOs, citizens' movements, multinational companies, academia and the mass media. Its version of global governance suggested a 'broad, dynamic, complex process of interactive decision-making that is constantly evolving and responding to changing circumstances' (UN Commission on Global Governance 2005 [1995]: 27). The involvement of so many diverse participants also means that global governance must be more inclusive, participatory and democratic than international relations have been in the past and that a shared, global, civic ethic also needs to be developed.

Global governance is a concept that aims to capture all those rules and norms, policies, institutions and practices through which global humanity orders its collective affairs. In this sense we already have some global governance in the form of international law, the UN Security Council, the International Atomic Energy Agency, multilateral treaties, and norms of conflict and conflict resolution alongside institutions such as the United Nations, the International Monetary Fund and the World Bank. Some scholars suggest that global governance is merely a different discourse – a new way of talking about existing institutional arrangements. However, much of this architecture remains *international* rather than truly global, as it was designed in an age of competing nation-states, assumed the state was the primary actor, and relied on powerful states to enforce the rules. Global issues and problems are outgrowing this state-centred international system.

There is a discussion of global governance in chapter 21, 'Politics, Government and Social Movements'.

The case for global governance appears a sound one, but it may be far from easy to achieve. Nation-states and large corporations compete with one another, while citizens' affiliation to 'their' nations is as much an emotional matter as a logical or rational one. Moving beyond nation-state-based thinking may be implied in theories of globalization, but it could also be that globalization generates a context which produces intensified competition rather than cooperation. Some activists are also suspicious of the very idea of global governance, which they fear may be just a dangerous but acceptable term for an emergent and possibly tyrannical 'world government' by elites (Sinclair 2012: 6).

It may seem optimistic, even unrealistic, to speak of global ethics or governance beyond the nation-state, but perhaps these goals are not quite as fanciful as at first they sound. The creation of new rules and norms and more effective regulatory institutions is certainly not misplaced when global interdependence and the rapid pace of change link all of us together more than ever before. Indeed, as the global issues of terrorism, environmental damage, climate change, transnational criminal networks, human trafficking and global financial crises show, better global governance is becoming a necessity. As Thomas Weiss (2013: 3) argues, perhaps the main motivation for seeking new ways of strengthening global governance is not for the latter to 'take mankind to heaven, but to save mankind from hell'.

Chapter review

1 Describe the main differences between hunting and gathering societies, pastoral societies and agrarian societies.

2 In what ways did cities in traditional states and civilizations differ from modern cities?

3 'Industrialization transformed human societies forever.' Provide some examples which illustrate how it did so.

4 How did colonial expansion and domination hold back the economic progress of developing countries?

5 Outline Wallerstein's world-systems theory and evaluate its ability to account for the experience of newly industrializing countries (NICs).

6 Provide some examples from the chapter which illustrate the significance of *economic*, *socio-cultural* and *political* factors in the production of social change. Is any one factor more important or causal than the others?

7 Give two brief definitions of *globalization*. Using a specific example, explain how the concept of *glocalization* differs from globalization.

8 List some of the factors contributing to contemporary globalization. Are these factors primarily economic, socio-cultural or political in character?

9 Outline the main arguments of hyperglobalizers, sceptics and transformationalists. Is globalization a falsifiable theory? What evidence would be conclusive in this regard?

10 List what you consider to be the main consequences of globalization. Are these primarily positive or negative for the developing countries? Do people in the developed countries stand to benefit most from globalization?

11 What is the difference between global government and global governance? Is a form of global governance really necessary? Are there international problems which demand a global governance structure?

Research in practice

How is globalization affecting national media cultures? Is it likely that we will see increasingly similar television output or will national cultures reassert themselves? One small area where this might be tested is the advent of so-called reality TV shows, whose formats are often sold across numerous countries. When this happens there may be cultural barriers that prompt producers to modify the format to fit their national context. Read the following empirical study and answer the questions: Van Keulen, J., and Krijnen, T. (2014) 'The Limitations of Localization: A Cross-cultural Comparative Study of *Farmer Wants a Wife*', *International Journal of Cultural Studies*, 17(3): 277–92.

1 What is the question guiding this research?
2 How did the researchers select their cases?
3 What criteria were used to conduct the national comparisons?
4 Is this British TV format culturally specific or has it translated across national boundaries?
5 What conclusions do the authors draw about globalization, localization and the preservation of cultural diversity in television?

Thinking it through

If globalization is a reality, then academic research cannot be immune from its impact. For example, we might expect that social science publications in the first half of the twentieth century would be dominated by European and North American scholars, but, by the start of the twenty-first century, research from all around the world would be making an equal impact.

Read this article: Mosbah-Natanson, S., and Gingras, Y. (2014) 'The Globalization of Social Sciences? Evidence from a Quantitative Analysis of 30 Years of Production, Collaboration and Citations in the Social Sciences (1980–2009)', *Current Sociology*, 62(5): 626–46. Rehearse the paper's main arguments suggesting that Europe and North America remain the dominant forces in the production of social scientific journal articles. Why have other regions not made the kind of breakthrough we might have expected? What evidence do the authors produce to show that researchers in 'peripheral' regions continue to show deference to those from the 'centre'? How successful do you think the use of a 'centre–periphery' model is in the context of this study? What, if anything, do we learn about globalization from this paper?

Society in the arts

1 A former prime minister of Canada, Kim Campbell, once said that 'images of America are so pervasive in this global village that it is almost as if, instead of the world immigrating to America, America has emigrated to the world, allowing people to aspire to be Americans even in distant countries.' This assessment suggests an emerging uniformity of cultural products rooted in Western, specifically American, values and lifestyles.

To what extent does the evidence from popular culture, including pop music, television programming and films, support or contradict this view? Make a list of the television programmes, novels and films *you* have watched in the last month as well as your own music collections. What proportion of this material is *produced* in the USA and/or *contains content* that is primarily about life in the USA? What impact do you think daily exposure to this material has had on your own values, thinking and political outlook? What evidence is there that images and content in the 'global village' are more pluralistic than Campbell suggests?

2 Theories of globalization which suggest we are moving towards a more uniform global culture have been criticized by cultural sociologists who devised the alternative concept of glocalization. However, there is evidence of both tendencies at work in any given situation, making our observations appear somewhat contradictory but no less accurate. The way these contradictory trends are managed in everyday life can sometimes be seen more easily in works of fiction than in social science research.

Watch the film *The Cup* (*Phörpa*, 1999), directed by Khyentse Norbu, which includes aspects of both global- and glocalization. As you watch, make a list of the evidence for both tendencies. For example, what global and local products and commodities are shown and how are these viewed and consumed or used? What impact has globalization had on the lives and beliefs of the Buddhist monks, the villagers and the two novice monks? Is there a central message about globalization in this film? If so, what is it? Do some research into the making of the film. Where and how was it made and was it a global commercial success? Does the story of the film's production tell a different story about globalization from that in the film itself?

Further reading

The subject matter of this chapter is so wide-ranging that a single book will not cover it. But there are two formats you should find useful. First are those that cover global human history and the development of societies. Noel Cowen's (2001) *Global History: A Short Overview* (Cambridge: Polity) is a well-written, concise, yet comprehensive account which assumes no specialist knowledge. Bruce Mazlish's (2006) *The New Global History* (London: Routledge) traces global history and globalization processes over the long term, linking historical and sociological approaches.

Second are those books that deal with current theories and debates on globalization. Picking out two short introductions, you could try George Ritzer and Paul Dean's (2015) *Globalization: A Basic Text* (2nd edn, Oxford: Wiley-Blackwell), which covers global governance and other key aspects of the main debates. Paul Hirst, Grahame Thompson and Simon Bromley's (2009) *Globalization in Question* (3rd edn, Cambridge: Polity) provides an essential critique of globalization theories and is well worth your attention.

Specific reviews of globalization theory and evidence can then be had in Luke Martell's (2016) *Sociology of Globalization* (2nd edn, Cambridge: Polity), Paul Hopper's (2007) *Understanding Cultural Globalization* (Cambridge: Polity) and Timothy J. Sinclair's (2012) simply titled *Global Governance* (Cambridge: Polity). Collectively these three cover the economic, cultural and political aspects.

A good dictionary of world history is always useful for key dates and events, so something suitably large and reliable, such as Bruce Lenman and Hilary Marsden's (2005) *Chambers Dictionary of World History* (new edn, London: Harrap) or *A Dictionary of World History* (2006) (2nd edn, Oxford: Oxford University Press) would fit the bill.

Internet links

@ **Additional information and support for this book at Polity:**
www.politybooks.com/giddens

@ *TimeMaps* **information on hunter-gatherers – covers hunter-gatherers, agrarian societies and early civilizations:**
www.timemaps.com/hunter-gatherer

@ **BBC World Service on globalization – some basic information on aspects of 'global society':**
www.bbc.co.uk/worldservice/programmes/globalisation

The 1999 Reith Lectures – Anthony Giddens on 'The runaway world':
http://news.bbc.co.uk/hi/english/static/events/reith_99

@ **International Forum on Globalization – an alliance of activists, scholars and researchers interested in globalization processes:**
http://ifg.org

@ **Centre for Research on Globalization – Canadian-based 'think site' with lots of comment by researchers and academics:**
www.globalresearch.ca

Global Policy Forum – monitors policy-making at the United Nations:
www.globalpolicy.org/globalization.html

@ **LSE Global Governance – London School of Economics Research Centre:**
www.lse.ac.uk/globalGovernance/HomePage.aspx

CHAPTER 5

The Environment

Contents

Greenpeace activists protest outside Volkswagen's plant in Wolfsburg, Germany – No More Lies!

Private cars have in the past generally run on petrol, with diesel fuel being reserved for commercial vehicles and public transport. Over recent years this has changed, as many manufacturers have invested heavily in 'clean diesel' cars, said to be less polluting than previous versions. In particular, claims have been made that their emission of nitrogen oxide pollutants and carbon dioxide are low enough to pass the strictest emissions testing regimes. Volkswagen made a determined attempt to sell their clean diesel cars into the American market, where they successfully passed the US government's stringent tests. But, in September 2015, the company found itself at the centre of a major scandal.

The US Environmental Protection Agency (EPA) (which raised concerns in 2014) reported that Volkswagen cars had higher emissions levels out 'on the road' than was evident from the laboratory tests on which their claims were made. Even worse, the EPA found software embedded within the vehicles that was capable of falsifying emissions testing. The cars had been factory fitted with a 'defeat device', which recognized the signs associated with emissions testing – a stationary vehicle, static steering, air pressure level, and so on – and put the car into an alternative mode which temporarily lowered emissions. When the EPA tested cars out on the road, it found that they actually emitted up to forty times more nitrogen oxide pollutants than US regulations allowed. Volkswagen admitted trying to cheat the testing regime and acknowledged that some 11 million of their diesel cars had the device fitted, about 8 million of them in Europe.

The consequences for Volkswagen have been senior resignations, a falling share price, a drop in sales, and reputational damage for the VW brand. More seriously, the company seems to have viewed emissions testing as merely an obstacle to commercial success rather than as part of the necessary regulation for improving air quality for all, particularly those living and working in cities and densely populated urban areas. Nitrogen oxides from car exhausts produce ozone and very fine particulate matter which can have a detrimental impact on human health. The British government suggests that airborne nitrogen oxides lead to the premature deaths of some 23,500 citizens every year, and the European Environment Agency estimates around 430,000 people across Europe died from the same causes in 2012 (*New Scientist* 2015). Air pollution is a serious health issue, and motor vehicles are a major contributor.

The Volkswagen scandal alerts us to the tensions that exist between corporations' constant pursuit of new markets and profits and environmental regulatory regimes seeking to reduce pollution and protect human health. The private motor car is also a potent symbol of personal freedom, mobility and consumerism for many millions of people. Most of us are extremely reluctant to give up our family cars, 4 × 4s, SUVs and sports cars on purely environmental grounds, despite a growing body of evidence demonstrating the negative aspects of private car-ownership. Cities built around vehicle movements rather than cycling or walking, thousands of deaths due to low-level pollution in urban areas, and residential streets blighted by mass vehicle ownership – despite all this, the private car remains deeply enmeshed in our daily lives (Mattioli 2014). Yet, as we shall see later in the chapter, there are now reasons to believe that the 'age of the car' may be – slowly – drawing to a close.

> See chapter 20, 'Crime and Deviance', for a discussion of corporate criminality and social harm.

In this chapter we look at shifting ideas of nature and environment, and what constitutes an 'environmental issue', before outlining sociological approaches to the study of these topics. From here we discuss some important environmental issues, including pollution, resource depletion, genetic modification and global warming. Sociological theories of consumerism and the risk society, together with proposals aimed at dealing with environmental dilemmas such as sustainable development and ecological modernization, are then debated. The chapter ends with an investigation into how justice and citizenship may be extended to take in natural environments, and we look ahead to the future of society–environment relations.

Nature, environment and society

Nature and environment

Environmental issues always involve nature in some way, but 'nature' is not a simple word with a single meaning. In fact, dictionary definitions usually describe some twelve distinct meanings of the word. Raymond Williams (1987) says that nature is one of the most complex and difficult words in the English language because its dominant meaning has changed over time along with the development of societies.

'Nature' can mean something that is *essential* to a person or a thing. Why do some birds build their nests at the same time every year, for instance? We may be told that this is instinctive behaviour and an essential part of the 'nature' of these birds. In fourteenth-century Europe, however, a new dominant meaning began to emerge. Nature came to be seen instead as a *series of forces* that directed the world and ultimately explained why things happen. For example, even today many people consult astrological charts, looking for their birth-date-based 'star sign' and the life guidance it can offer. When they do this, they implicitly draw on this same idea of 'natural forces' – in this case, the movement of stars and planets – directing human affairs.

By the nineteenth century, the dominant meaning of 'nature' had changed again. This time it was seen as the whole *material world of things* rather than as a series of forces. The natural world was a world full of *natural things*: animals, fields, mountains, and much more. For instance, there was a trend towards looking at 'scenery' as landscapes and pictorials, with nature literally framed for our appreciation and enjoyment. Similarly, eighteenth- and nineteenth-century naturalists collected and classified natural 'things', creating plant and animal taxonomies that are still in use today.

From the seventeenth century onwards, wealthy groups in Britain began to take pleasure in landscape scenes such as this one, which also became the focus of the 'tourist gaze' (Urry 2002).

Two major and related causes of this latest change in meaning were industrialization, which shifted people away from working the land, and urbanization, which led to larger human settlements and new living environments largely divorced from natural things (Thomas 1984). Nature was seen as an obstacle that society had to tame and master in order to make progress, as the popular ideas of nature 'in the raw' or nature 'red in tooth and claw' suggest. Humans can fly (in planes), cross oceans (in ships) and even orbit the planet (in spacecraft). Catton and Dunlap (1978) argued that the technological advances of the industrial age produced an ideology of 'human exemptionalism' – the widely accepted idea that, unlike all other animals, the human species was practically exempt from natural laws.

Yet, for a minority of people, nature was not in need of taming. Instead, industrial society was the problem, polluting and wasting nature to feed new urban lifestyles. Wild nature needed protection, not domestication. Nevertheless, for both the tamers and the protectors, society and nature were seen as *separate things*. Nature was that which society was not, and vice versa. This meaning remains the dominant one today, though more people would probably now agree with the nature protectors than did so in earlier periods.

Since the 1950s, use of the word 'nature' started to give way to another term: the environment. Dictionary definitions of 'environment' suggest that it is the external conditions or surroundings of people, especially those in which they live or work. David Harvey (1993) notes that this definition can apply to a number of situations. For example, we have a working environment, a business environment and an urban environment. However, most people today would probably expect this chapter to discuss pollution, climate change, animal welfare, and so on, indicating that *the* environment has taken on a widespread and special meaning. *The* environment is assumed to mean all of those non-human, natural surroundings within which human beings exist – sometimes called the 'natural environment' – and in its widest sense this is simply planet Earth as a whole. We will use this as our working definition throughout this chapter.

> ### Thinking critically
> How satisfactory is our working definition above of 'the environment'? Are human beings part of nature? If they are, explain why cities and urban areas are often seen as artificial.

Sociology and the environment

Just before 3 p.m. (Japanese Standard Time) on 11 March 2011, the most powerful earthquake ever to affect Japan, with a magnitude of 9.0, occurred off the eastern coast of the country. The quake produced tsunami waves of up to 40 metres high which rolled inexorably towards the Tōhoku region. Travelling up to 10 kilometres inland, the tsunami swept all before it; buildings, vehicles, power lines and people were all caught up in the emerging disaster. Police statistics show that at least 15,000 people were killed, more than 9,000 were missing and another 5,000 were injured. Cooling systems failed at the coastal Fukushima nuclear reactor site, and a state of emergency was declared as food products, tap water and soil samples were all reported to be contaminated with radioactive matter. The Japanese government announced that it would be reviewing its energy policy, particularly Japan's reliance on nuclear power, to ensure the country's future energy security.

Earthquakes such as this one are by no means uncommon. Christchurch, New Zealand (2011), Haiti (2010), Muzzafarabad, Kashmir (2005), and Aceh, Indonesia (2004), are all twenty-first-century quakes which collectively killed over half a million people and made millions more homeless. Earthquakes and the tsunamis they often generate are reminders that the natural environment is not simply an inert, passive backdrop to the dramas played out in social and political life. It is an active force, which plays a significant role in shaping societies. But surely understanding natural forces and processes is the job of physicists and earth scientists. What role is there for sociologists in understanding and explaining environmental issues?

First, sociology can help us to understand how environmental problems are distributed. Although global warming – the increase in average surface temperature across the globe – affects everyone on the planet, it will do so in different ways. Flooding affects people in both rich and poor countries, but it kills many more people in low-lying, poor countries, such as Bangladesh, where housing and emergency infrastructure are less able to cope with severe weather than in Europe, where expensive flood defence projects have been put in place. In richer countries, such as the USA, issues raised by global warming are likely to concern indirect effects, such as rising levels of immigration as people try to enter the country from areas more directly affected.

Second, sociologists can provide an account of how patterns of human behaviour create pressure on the natural environment (Cylke 1993). Although the 2011 Japanese tsunami was not the direct result of human action, many of the environmental challenges discussed in this chapter – such as pollution from diesel vehicles – are. The levels of pollution already produced by industrialized countries would be greatly intensified if repeated in the world's developing nations. If the impoverished regions of the world are to catch up with the richer ones, then citizens of the rich world have to revise their expectations about continuous economic growth. Sociological theories of capitalist expansion, globalization or rationalization can help us to understand how human societies are transforming the environment.

Third, sociology can help us to evaluate policies and proposals aimed at providing solutions to environmental problems. For example, before the earthquake and tsunami in Japan, many governments in the developed world had begun re-evaluating the option of nuclear power. Anti-nuclear campaigns in the 1980s were successful in raising concerns about the safety of underground disposal for radioactive nuclear waste, and governments eventually turned away from the nuclear industry. However, today's uncertainties about oil and gas supplies in national energy security plans and the need to reduce carbon emissions to tackle global warming have brought the nuclear power option back into contention. Given the negligible carbon emissions produced by nuclear reactors, concern with safety now has to be weighed against the environmental benefits of nuclear power. Analysing how different groups put together their claims and counter-claims about environmental problems deepens our understanding of the issues involved – an essential prerequisite for informed public debate.

Similarly, some environmental activists and 'green' writers argue that people in the rich countries must turn away from capitalist consumerism and return to simpler ways of living close to the land if global ecological disaster is to be avoided (Devall 1990; Cowie and Heathcott 2003; Elgin 2010). They maintain that rescuing the global environment will mean radical social as well as technological changes. Yet, given the enormous global inequalities that currently exist, there is little chance that poorer countries will sacrifice their economic growth because of environmental problems created by the rich countries. Some governments in developing countries have argued that, in relation to global warming, there is no parallel between the 'luxury emissions' of the developed world and their own 'survival emissions'. Sociological accounts of international relations and global inequality can clarify some of the underlying causes of the environmental problems we face today.

Sociology's founders – Marx, Durkheim and Weber – paid little attention to what we now call 'environmental issues'. The relationship between human societies and the natural environment was not their central theoretical concern. Instead, they focused on social inequality, poverty and its alleviation, and assessing the direction of industrial development. This situation became problematic once sociologists began to explore the issues identified by environmental campaigners in the 1970s. Could the classical theories provide any insights into human–environment relations? Some sociologists *have* returned to classical sociology, reinterpreting the classics in the light of environmental issues (Dickens 2004; Dunlap et al. 2002; Murphy 1997). However, most have not. Rather, the majority of sociological studies of the environment have developed through a long-running dispute between social constructionist and critical realist approaches over just *how* environmental issues should be studied.

Theorizing the social and the natural

Social constructionism is an approach to studying social problems, including environmental issues. Social constructionists have investigated how some environmental issues come to be seen as significant and in need of urgent action, while others are considered as less important or are largely ignored (Braun and Castree 1998; Hannigan 2006, 2014). Much depends on how the issue is framed *as a problem* demanding a policy response from government. Are the environmental problems considered most important today really the ones which are the most serious and in need of urgent action?

> For more on social constructionism, see chapter 3, 'Theories and Perspectives', and chapter 8, 'Social Interaction and Daily Life'.

Constructionists ask a series of important questions. What is the *history of the problem* and how has it developed? *Who* is making the claim that it is a problem and do they have any vested interest and stand to benefit from doing so? *What do they say* about it and does the evidence support this? *How* do they say it? Do they use scientific, emotional, political or moral arguments? Who *opposes* the claim and on what grounds? Do opponents stand to lose if the claim is successful and could that, rather than the evidence, explain their opposition?

Such questions give sociologists a clearly defined role in the study of environmental issues which no other discipline performs. They also add something new to our understanding of this area.

Social constructionists remind us that all environmental problems are, in part, socially created or 'constructed' by groups of people. Nature never 'speaks for itself', but people do speak on its behalf. This process of construction can be examined, understood and explained. And, in doing so, the public should be in a better position to assess whether an environmental problem really is as serious as the claims-makers say it is.

For some sociologists, though, constructionism is problematic, as it tends to be 'agnostic' about the central problem at issue (Irwin 2001). For example, a constructionist study of the loss of biodiversity and species extinctions would tell us a lot about how this problem came to be seen as important, what arguments were made about it and who opposed the claim. But social constructionism does not offer a direct answer to the central scientific question – is the biodiversity really becoming a serious problem? For environmental activists and those committed to solving environmental problems, this is not helpful. Constructionism tells us a lot about people and social interactions but almost nothing about society–environment relations.

An alternative approach, known as 'environmental realism' (Bell 2004) or critical realism, approaches environmental issues in a scientific way, bringing together evidence from across the social and natural sciences to understand why environmental problems occur. Critical realism aims to get beneath the surface of the visible evidence to uncover the underlying 'causal mechanisms' of events and problems (Benton 1994; Dickens 1996, 2004; Martell 1994). In contrast to the agnosticism of social constructionists, critical realists are prepared to accept and debate knowledge and evidence from the natural and environmental sciences in their own analyses. 'Using your sociological imagination 5.1', on BSE in the UK, illustrates some key points of this approach.

Most environmental problems are socially created. For example, consumerism generates a huge amount of waste, which has conventionally been dumped in landfill sites.

Realist approaches require the findings from a range of academic disciplines: biology, zoology, history, sociology, political science and more. Only in this way can we properly explain how and why BSE and vCJD posed such a problem in the 1980s and 1990s. Like constructionists, realists would agree that cows are social as well as natural creatures. Arguing a constructionist case, Alan Irwin says: 'The modern cow is the product of generations of human-controlled cattle-breeding, feeding and housing' (2001: 80). But, unlike constructionists, realists search for *causal mechanisms* and are prepared to explore and debate the natural science of environmental issues in ways that social constructionists do not. Critical realism takes into account the *objective reality* of natural objects and environments, and this means rethinking our sociological theories and concepts with this in mind.

From this brief sketch of these two approaches, we can say that social constructionism leads in the direction of a *sociology of the environment* that explores environmental issues from a conventional sociological standpoint, using concepts and theories from within the discipline. By contrast, critical realism leads towards an *environmental sociology*, which demands the revision of existing sociological approaches to take account of the complex intertwining of society and environment (Sutton 2007). However, as we will see in the chapter, many research studies in this field tend to veer between these two polarized alternatives.

5.1 'Mad cow disease' in the UK

In 1996, British government ministers admitted the possibility that at least ten recent human deaths had been caused by a new variant of Creutzfeldt–Jakob Disease (vCJD) in humans, which may have developed through people eating beef infected with Bovine Spongiform Encephalopathy (BSE) during the 1980s. This was a huge shock. Millions of people had eaten beef in this period and, at least theoretically, could develop the disease. How had this happened?

BSE is a fatal neurodegenerative disease of cattle whose symptoms – loss of coordination, nervousness, loss of memory and aggression (hence 'mad' cows) – are similar to those of Creutzfeldt–Jakob Disease (CJD) in human beings. From the experience of sheep farming, it was thought that BSE could not cross the species barrier into the human population. CJD is a recognized but very rare disease in human beings but is unrelated to BSE. The UK BSE inquiry (1998–2000) identified the cause of BSE in cattle as a gene mutation in a single cow (named Cow 133). But the most widely accepted explanation for the *spread* of BSE is that cattle were being fed BSE-infected offal (Macnaghten and Urry 1998: 253–65). The inquiry report said that the problem was 'the recycling of animal protein in ruminant feed'. The report also noted that the link between BSE and the human vCJD 'was now clearly established'. As of 2 November 2015, the National Creutzfeldt–Jakob Disease Surveillance Unit in Edinburgh reported that 177 people had died from vCJD. Meat-rendering practices were changed and new rules brought in to prevent a recurrence, but public confidence in science,

politics, regulatory bodies and the meat industry were thoroughly shaken by the events.

On the face of it, this seems like an episode of a naturally occurring disease in animals, unrelated to social processes. However, the transmission and spread of BSE was the product of decisions taken within the animal feed production system. The previous assumption that BSE would not cross the species barrier was shown to be wrong. BSE-infected beef *did* lead to vCJD in humans. Treating cattle as commercial products and denying their herbivorous nature by feeding them dead cattle produced an unexpected outcome that no one had forecast.

A critical realist approach would suggest that, to understand this event properly, we need to know what kind of creatures cows are: what are their natural capacities? We also need to understand human beings to know why the disease had such devastating effects on people. What happens when infected foodstuffs find their way into the human body? We also need to know how the food production system operates and what political and economic decisions were made that allowed dead animals to be fed to others. And we need culturally specific knowledge – just why do so many people eat so much beef in the UK?

THINKING CRITICALLY

How would social constructionists investigate the BSE epidemic and its consequences, as outlined above? What would this approach focus on exploring?

What are environmental issues?

There are many different environmental issues confronting the contemporary world. Some are local or regional in character while others are global in scale and impact. However, what they all share and what makes them specifically environmental issues is that they involve *both* social relationships and interactions *and* non-human, natural phenomena. In this sense, they are *hybrid* issues of society and

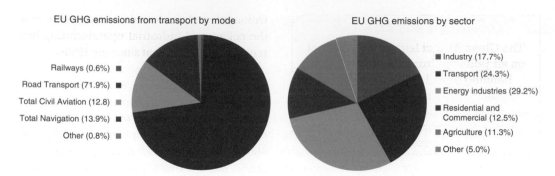

Figure 5.1 EU28 greenhouse gas emission (ghg) by mode of transport and sector, 2012

Source: European Commission (2015)

environment (Irwin 2001: 26). Keep this point in mind when you read the rest of this section, which covers a range of environmental issues and problems.

Pollution and waste

Air pollution

It is possible to make a distinction between two types of air pollution: 'outdoor pollution', produced mainly by industrial pollutants and automobile emissions, and 'indoor pollution', which is caused by burning fuels in the home for heating and cooking. Traditionally, air pollution has been seen as a problem that afflicts mainly the industrialized countries as a result of mass production and large numbers of motorized vehicles. However, in recent years attention has been drawn to the dangers of 'indoor pollution' in the developing world, where many of the fuels used, such as wood and dung, are not as clean-burning as modern fuels such as kerosene and propane.

Until the middle of the twentieth century, air pollution in many countries was caused primarily by the widespread burning of coal – a fossil fuel – which emits sulphur dioxide and thick black smoke into the atmosphere. In many Eastern European countries and in the developing world, the practice remains widespread today. In Britain, coal was used extensively to heat homes and to power industry, but in 1956 the Clean Air Act was passed to try to regulate smoke pollution and smog.

Smokeless fuels, such as kerosene, propane and natural gas, were promoted as alternatives and are now more widely used.

Since the 1960s the main source of air pollution has been the growing number of motorized vehicles. In the twenty-eight countries of the European Union, transport is responsible for almost one-quarter of greenhouse gases, and 72 per cent of these come from road transport (European Commission 2015a; see figure 5.1). Road transport emissions are particularly harmful because they enter the environment at a much lower level than emissions from tall industrial chimneys. As a result, cities have long been among the most polluted environments for pedestrians and workers.

Cars, which account for some 80 per cent of travel in Europe, have a particularly harmful impact on the environment. A single occupancy car journey can produce more carbon per passenger, per kilometre travelled, than fully loaded short- or long-haul flights (Beggs 2009: 77–8). For this reason, attempts to reduce air pollution have focused on the use of low-emission travel alternatives such as passenger trains, high-occupancy buses and the sharing of car journeys. Since 2008, greenhouse gases from road vehicles in the EU and elsewhere have started to fall due to high oil prices and the increasing efficiency of private cars (European Commission 2015a). Yet, as the Volkswagen emissions scandal shows, stricter pollution targets do not, in themselves, guarantee reductions in real-world vehicle emissions.

Air pollution is linked to a number of health problems, including respiratory difficulties, cancers and lung disease. Outdoor pollution is now growing rapidly in the developing countries as they undergo rapid industrialization and the number of vehicles on the roads grows. In many developing countries, leaded petrol is still in use, though it has been phased out in much of the developed world. Levels of air pollution were also high in many parts of Eastern Europe and the (former) Soviet Union, though economic restructuring and the collapse of industrial manufacturing has reduced this somewhat since the 1990s.

Water pollution

Throughout history, people have depended on water to fulfil a host of needs – drinking, cooking, washing, irrigating crops, fishing and many other pursuits. Although water is one of the most valuable and essential natural resources, for many years, waste products – both human and manufactured – were dumped directly into rivers and oceans with barely a second thought. For instance, in the summer of 1858, the River Thames in London emitted a stench so foul it brought the city to a standstill, forcing politicians to act. Only in the past sixty years or so have concerted efforts been made in many countries to protect the quality of water, to conserve fish stocks and the wildlife that depend on it, and to ensure

Even in lush rainforests where water is abundant, urban settlements, factories and intensive farming practices can make access to clean water difficult.

access to clean water for the global human population. Regardless of these efforts, water pollution remains a serious problem in many parts of the world.

Water pollution can be understood as contamination of the water supply by toxic chemicals and minerals, pesticides or untreated sewage, and it poses the greatest threat to people in the developing world. Sanitation systems are underdeveloped in many of the world's poorest countries, and human waste products are often emptied directly into streams, rivers and lakes. The high levels of bacteria that result from untreated sewage lead to a variety of water-borne diseases, such as diarrhoea, dysentery and hepatitis. Some 2 billion cases of diarrhoea are caused annually by contaminated water and around 5 million people die each year from diarrhoeal diseases.

Much progress has been made in the last twenty-five years to improve access to safe drinking water. During the 1990s, nearly 1 billion people gained access to safe water and the same number to sanitation, though ensuring safe water supplies remains a problem, particularly in some parts of Africa, where people drink from unprotected wells and springs along with surface water (figure 5.2). The problem may worsen as water supplies in some developing countries are privatized, raising the cost for customers, while the effects of global warming also produce more regular droughts (see 'Global Society 5.1', p. 169).

One of the 'Millennium Development Goals' set by the United Nations in 2000 was to 'reduce by half the proportion of people without access to safe drinking water' by 2015. This target was met well ahead of schedule in 2010. By 2015, 91 per cent of the world population had access to improved drinking water sources, and 2.6 billion people had gained such access since 1990. However, in the same year, the Caucasus region, Central Asia, Northern Africa, Oceania and sub-Saharan Africa missed their MDG targets, and some 663 million people – mainly in rural areas – still did not have access to improved sources of safe water (UNICEF/WHO 2015: 4). Many of the least developed countries store around 4 per cent of their annual renewable water flow compared with the 70 to 90 per cent stored in developed countries (UNESCO 2009a).

Progress on sanitation has been much slower. The MDG target was for 77 per cent of the global population to be using improved facilities by 2015, but only 68 per cent did so. This represents around 700 million people fewer than the target. Some 2.4 billion people did not have access to improved sanitation; of these, seven out of ten lived in rural areas, as did nine out of ten of those still practising open defecation (UNICEF/WHO 2015: 5). Clearly the MDG targets have proved to be an effective tool for encouraging and measuring progress on the provision of safe water and effective sanitation, but there remains much to be done, especially in the rural areas of developing countries.

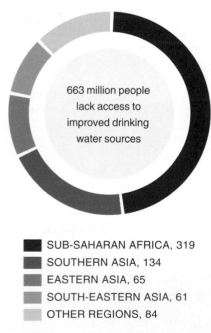

■ SUB-SAHARAN AFRICA, 319
■ SOUTHERN ASIA, 134
■ EASTERN ASIA, 65
■ SOUTH-EASTERN ASIA, 61
□ OTHER REGIONS, 84

Figure 5.2 Population without access to improved water sources, 2015 (millions)

Source: UNICEF/WHO (2015: 7).

Solid waste

Next time you visit a supermarket, toy store or fast-food restaurant, pay attention to the amount of packaging that accompanies the products you see. There are few things you can buy without packaging and, though there are clear benefits, in terms of displaying goods attractively and guaranteeing the safety of products, there are enormous drawbacks too.

Waste generation is closely tied to the relative prosperity of countries. Poland, Hungary and Slovenia, for example – countries that have only recently started to emulate the model of Western capitalism and consumer culture – generate less than half the waste per capita of the USA, Denmark and Australia. However, the more established high-consumption societies now manage their waste more effectively. As figure 5.3 shows, countries such as Germany, Norway and Ireland are steadily reducing the proportion of waste that ends up in landfill. The European Union aims to become a 'recycling society', and there is a move to recycle or compost waste (50 per cent of all municipal waste in the European economic area by 2020) as well as to reduce the amount of packaging used for

Figure 5.3 Proportion of municipal waste going to landfill, by European economic area country, 2001 and 2010

Source: European Environment Agency (2013: 21).

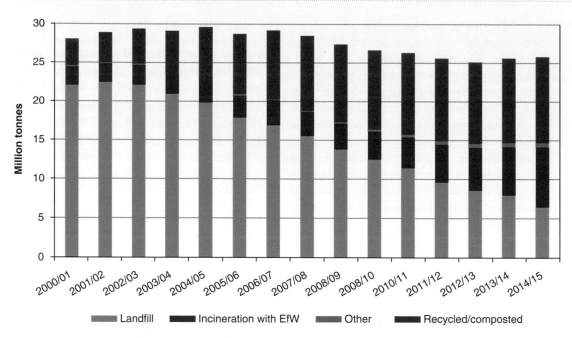

Figure 5.4 Municipal waste management methods in England, 2000/1 to 2014/15 (millions of tonnes)

Note: EfW (Energy from Waste) refers to electricity being generated from the heat of incinerating waste materials.
Source: Defra (2016: 26).

products at the point of production (European Environment Agency 2013).

The industrialized societies have been called 'throw-away societies' because the volume of items discarded as a matter of course is so large. In most countries of the industrialized world, waste collection services are almost universal, but it is increasingly difficult to dispose of the enormous amounts of waste. Landfill sites are becoming full, and many urban areas have run out of disposal room. In Scotland, for example, around 90 per cent of household waste was still going to landfill sites in 2006, and the Scottish Environment Protection Agency reported that household waste was growing at 2 per cent per annum. The international trade in waste has led to the export of recycling to China, where waste is often sorted by hand in poorly regulated working environments that produce environmental degradation.

The UK government set a target of recycling 40 per cent of municipal waste by 2005, but by 2010 it was still falling narrowly short of this target, at 39.7 per cent. In recent years, the amount of household waste has started to increase, though more is recycled year on year (Defra 2016). Figure 5.4 shows the trend away from landfill in England in favour of alternative methods of disposal. Although the amount of household waste recycled may still seem low in comparison with the overall amount produced, a large proportion of what is thrown away cannot be easily reprocessed or reused. Many plastics employed in food packaging simply become unusable waste and have to be buried in refuse tips, where they may remain for centuries. Recycling is becoming a huge industry around the world, but there is still a long way to go to transform the world's 'throw-away societies'.

In the developing world, the biggest problem with domestic waste is the *lack* of refuse collection services. It has been estimated that 20 to 50 per cent of domestic waste in the

Increasing numbers of local councils have extended their provision for recycling as part of refuse collections, and many people have built recycling into their everyday routines.

developing world goes uncollected. Poorly managed waste systems mean that refuse piles up in the streets, contributing to the spread of disease. Over time it is very likely that the developing world will have to deal with problems of waste disposal that are even more acute than those in industrialized countries. This is because, as societies become richer, there is a gradual shift from organic waste, such as food remains, to plastic and synthetic materials, such as packaging, which take much longer to decompose.

Resource depletion

Human societies depend on many resources from the natural world – for example, water, wood, fish, animals and plant life. These elements are often termed 'renewable resources' because, in a healthy ecosystem, they replace themselves automatically with the passing of time. Yet, if the consumption of renewable resources gets out of balance or is too extreme, there is a danger that they will be depleted altogether. Some evidence suggests that this may be occurring, and the deterioration of renewable resources is of great concern to many environmentalists.

Water insecurity

You may not think of water as a depletable resource – after all, it constantly replenishes itself through rainfall. If you live in Europe or North America, for most of the time you probably do not give much thought to your water supply at all. The rapid growth of the market for bottled water is seen by some as illustrative of the state of global inequality, with many consumers in the developed world choosing to buy water when they could get it for free – literally 'on tap'. Yet, for people in many parts of developing countries, access to a reliable water supply is a chronic problem.

In some densely populated regions, the demand for water cannot be met by available resources. In the arid climates of North Africa and the Middle East, for example, the pressure on water supply is acute and shortages are commonplace. This trend is likely to intensify as much of the projected world population growth over the next thirty years will be in areas that are already experiencing water shortages. The infrastructure of urban areas will struggle to accommodate the water and sanitation needs of this population, but the consequences of global warming, as we shall see later, may be even more serious.

Forecasts of a future water crisis tend to focus on the developing countries, but it is important to understand why this is so. In terms of the availability of water and the stressors on its availability, one recent study

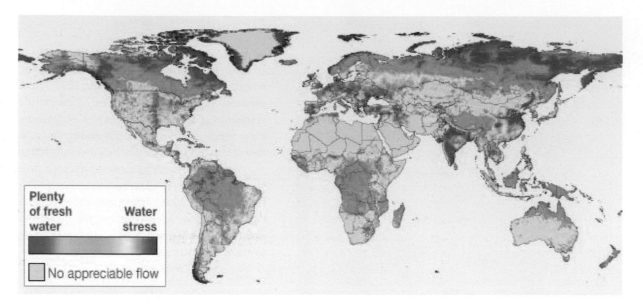

Plenty
of fresh   Water
water   stress

No appreciable flow

Figure 5.5   'Natural' water security, the global picture

Source: BBC News, 29 September 2010: www.bbc.co.uk/news/science-environment-11435522.

suggests that, at first glance, Western Europe and North America appear to face a less secure water supply than most of Africa (Vörösmarty et al. 2010; see also figure 5.5). However, when we take into account the way that water is managed, the picture changes dramatically. As the developed countries spend large sums of money on water infrastructure and technology such as dams, altering watercourses, and constructing canals and pipelines, water insecurity becomes much less of an issue (figure 5.6). Conversely, in much of Africa, where the same kind of expensive investment has not been and is not yet possible, water insecurity looks set to become a very serious matter.

On the other hand, expensive water infrastructure projects aimed at achieving water security have also damaged the environment, potentially producing deleterious consequences in the future (Palmer 2010). Even if developing countries were to use similar 'concrete and steel' projects to enhance their water security, this may be at the cost of damaging the environment and reducing biodiversity. An alternative would be to adopt a water management approach that protects flood plains and wetlands and safeguards watersheds, working with natural processes rather than trying to change them.

The need to put in place measures to safeguard water supplies is made even more urgent today because 'global warming' also has a potential impact on the depletion of water. As temperatures rise, more water will be needed for drinking and irrigation. Yet it is also likely that groundwater may not replenish itself as rapidly as before and that rates of evaporation may increase. Changes in climate patterns which are forecast to accompany global warming are likely to affect existing patterns of precipitation, altering access to water supplies and making planning for water management much more difficult.

Food shortages and GM crops

Some 900 million people around the globe experience hunger every day, lacking access to sufficient nutrients, while increasing soil degradation threatens to undermine

Global Society 5.1 The privatization of water

Richard Wachman's article was published in 2007.

The midday sun beats down on a phalanx of riot police facing thousands of jeering demonstrators, angry at proposals to put up their water bills by more than a third. Moments later a uniformed officer astride a horse shouts an order and the police charge down the street to embark on a club-wielding melee that leaves dozens of bloodied protesters with broken limbs.

A film clip from the latest offering from Hollywood? Unfortunately not. It's a description of a real-life event in Cochabamba, Bolivia's third largest city, where a subsidiary of Bechtel, the US engineering giant, took over the municipal water utility and increased bills to a level that the poorest could not afford.

Welcome to a new world, where war and civil strife loom in the wake of chronic water shortages caused by rising population, drought (exacerbated by global warming) and increased demand from the newly affluent middle classes in the emerging economies of Asia and Latin America. At a City briefing by an international bank last week, a senior executive said: 'Today everyone is talking about global warming, but my prediction is that in two years water will move to the top of the geopolitical agenda.'

The question for countries as far apart as China and Argentina is whether to unleash market forces by allowing access to private European and American multinationals that have the technological know-how to help bring water to the masses – but at a price that many may be unable, or unwilling, to pay [. . .]

A report out today from accountancy giant Deloitte & Touche says humans seem to have a peculiar talent for making previously abundant resources scarce: 'This is especially the case with water', it observes. According to the firm's findings, more than 1 billion people will lack access to clean water by next year. Paul Lee, research director at Deloitte, and one of the

authors of the report, says: 'Demand for water is expected to be driven by economic growth and population increases. India's demand for water is expected to exceed supply by 2020.'

The World Wildlife Fund has forecast that in the Himalayas, the retreat of glaciers could reduce summer water flows by up to two-thirds. In the Ganges area, this would cause a water shortage for 500 million people. Lee says: 'The lack of the most important form of liquid in the world is therefore a fundamental issue and one that the technology sector can play a major role in addressing.'

[. . .]

But the crux of the problem remains: according to a report from Credit Suisse, annual world water use has risen sixfold during the past century, more than double the rate of population growth. By 2025, almost two-thirds of the global population will live in countries where water will be a scarce commodity. And that could lead to conflict, as United Nations secretary-general Ban Ki-moon warned last week.

Asia looks vulnerable, with China planning to syphon off Tibet's water supply to make up for shortages in the parched north. Elsewhere, the Israel–Palestine conflict is at least partly about securing supplies from the River Jordan; similarly, water is a major feature of the strife in Sudan that has left Darfur devastated. When it comes to this most basic of commodities, the stakes could hardly be higher.

Source: Wachman (2007).

THINKING CRITICALLY

If privatizing water supplies leads to a higher cost, this should stop people from wasting water and therefore, indirectly, to water conservation. Why might privatization have very different consequences in developed and developing countries?

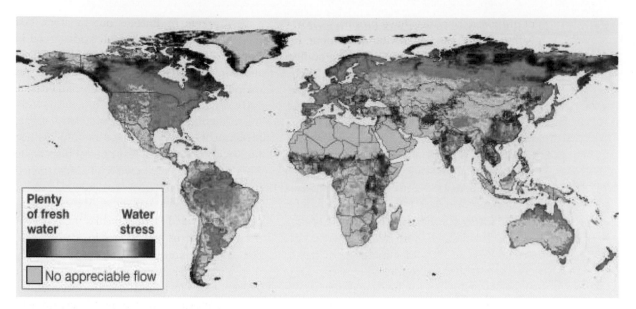

Figure 5.6   'Managed' water security, the global picture

Source: BBC News, 29 September 2010: www.bbc.co.uk/news/science-environment-11435522.

economic development in much of Africa. The process of global warming may increase desertification and lead to poor harvests, which has led to fears that food shortages may become more widespread. In some of the world's most densely populated areas, people are highly dependent on staple food crops – such as rice – stocks of which are dwindling. Many worry that present farming techniques will not be able to produce rice yields sufficient to support the growing population. As with many environmental challenges, the threat of famine is not evenly distributed. The industrialized countries have extensive surpluses of grain, but it is in the poorer countries that shortfalls are likely to become a chronic problem.

A recent UK report, based on two years of research into the future of food supplies and farming, argued strongly that the present global food system is not sustainable and cannot end the problem of hunger (Foresight 2011). As the global population grows from 7 billion to over 8 billion by 2030 and 9 billion by 2050, competition for water, land and energy will intensify and global warming will increase the pressure on food production systems.

The combination of these factors, the report suggests, constitutes a major threat which demands urgent action – piecemeal changes will not solve the problem, nor will attempts to achieve national food self-sufficiency. The report argues for a coordinated policy approach and action on four fronts: more food needs to be produced sustainably, demand for resource-intensive foods must be contained, waste in all areas of the food system should be minimized, and political and economic governance of the food system needs to be improved (ibid.: 12–13).

The Foresight report also argues that no policy options or technologies should be closed off in the quest for a sustainable food system, and some scientists and politicians see one key to averting a future food crisis may be advances in biotechnology. By manipulating the genetic composition of basic crops, it is possible to boost a plant's rate of photosynthesis to produce bigger yields. This process is known as genetic modification, and plants that are produced this way are called genetically modified organisms (GMOs). Genetic modification can be carried out for a variety of purposes. Scientists have produced GMOs with higher than normal vitamin content, for example, while other genetically modified crops are resistant to commonly used agricultural herbicides that can be used to kill the weeds around them, as well as insects and fungal and viral pests. Food products that are made from, or contain traces of, GMOs are known as GM foods, and GM crops are sometimes called 'transgenic' crops.

GM crops are different from anything that has existed before, because they involve transplanting genes between different organisms. This is a much more radical intervention in nature than the older methods of crossbreeding. GMOs are produced by techniques of gene splicing that can be used to transplant genes between animals as well as plants. For instance, in recent experiments, human genes have been introduced into farm animals, such as pigs, with a view eventually to providing replacement parts for human transplants. Human genes have even been spliced into plants, although the GM crops that have been marketed so far do not involve this kind of radical bioengineering.

Scientists claim that a GM strain of 'super-rice' could boost rice yields by as much as 35 per cent. Another strain, called 'golden rice' – which contains added amounts of vitamin A – could reduce vitamin A deficiency in more than 120 million children worldwide. You might think that such advances in biotechnology would be welcomed enthusiastically, but, in fact, genetic modification has become one of the most controversial issues of our age. For many people, it highlights the fine line that exists between the benefits of technology and scientific innovation and the risks of environmental destruction.

The GM food controversy

The intense debate on GM foods began in the mid-1990s, when the first shipment of GM soya beans from the USA arrived in Europe before EU labelling rules had been put in place (Horlick-Jones et al. 2009: 4). Greenpeace and Friends of the Earth campaigned strongly against GM, and pressure built on supermarkets in Europe not to stock GM food. Concern was especially widespread in Europe (Toke 2004). In Britain, hostility to the commercial growing of GM crops was stimulated by the findings of Dr Arpad Pusztai, an internationally renowned geneticist working in a government laboratory in Aberdeen, Scotland. Pusztai had tested potatoes which had a gene for a particular natural insecticide inserted – a protein known as lectin, extracted from a certain type of flower. The results indicated that rats which ate the GM potatoes experienced significant damage to their immune systems and reduced organ growth. His findings were criticized by other scientists, and he was dismissed from his post after speaking on television about his concerns.

The American company Monsanto was the leader in developing GM technology. Monsanto bought seed companies, sold off its chemical division and devoted much of its energy to bringing the new crops to market. Its chief executive, Robert Shapiro, launched a huge advertising campaign in America promoting the benefits of GM crops to farmers and consumers. Monsanto's campaign claimed that GM crops could help feed the world's poor and reduce the use of chemical pollutants, especially the chemicals used in pesticides and herbicides. It is claimed that biotechnology will allow us to grow better-quality crops with higher yields, while at the same time sustaining and protecting the environment. However, since GM crops are essentially novel, no one can be certain about what their effects will be once they are introduced into the environment, and many consumer groups became concerned about the potential risks involved.

Numerous TV and radio debates, chat shows and phone-ins were organized to discuss the issue. Many members of the British public registered their opposition to GM crops. A typical 2003 survey showed that 59 per cent of the UK population strongly agreed that genetically modified foods should be banned (ONS 2005). Campaigners engaged in 'direct actions', pulling GM crops out of the ground at official trial sites across the country.

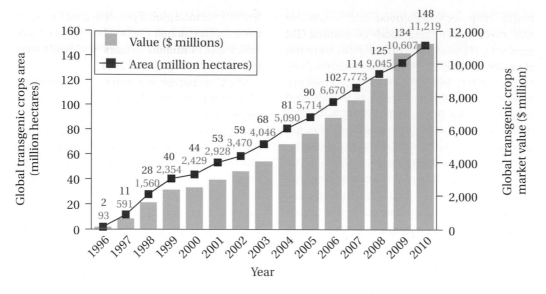

Figure 5.7 Global transgenic crops by area and market value (US$), 1996–2010

Source: Peng (2011: 302).

Similar responses occurred in a range of other European countries. In the UK, seven out of the eight major supermarket chains changed their policy on GM foods. Five imposed a complete ban on GM ingredients in their own-brand products, which is still in place, and all of them insisted on better labelling. Two large companies, Unilever and Nestlé, announced they would withdraw their acceptance of genetically modified foodstuffs. Some farmers in the USA who had been engaged in the large-scale cultivation of GM crops changed back to conventional crop production.

The protests of environmentalists and consumer groups had a major impact on the fate of Monsanto, causing a serious decline in its share value. Matsuura (2004) argues that, in the early days, the biotechnology industry made two mistakes: first it tried to ignore public concerns, then it attempted to address them through purely rational arguments. GM is also an emotional issue. Robert Shapiro appeared on television to admit that his company had made major mistakes and 'irritated and antagonized more people than we have persuaded'. It was an extraordinary turnaround, and Monsanto was forced to drop

one of its most controversial plans – the idea of using a gene called 'the terminator'. This gene would have ensured that seeds which Monsanto sold to farmers would be sterile after one generation. The farmers would have had to order seeds each year from the company. Critics claimed Monsanto was trying to lure farmers into a form of 'bioslavery', and the issue highlights again the inequalities of power between companies looking to take advantage of globalization and those at the sharp end.

GM crops continue to generate controversy in Europe and large parts of Africa. For example, in Africa, GM food aid ran into trouble. In 2002, Zambia refused to accept American food-aid donations of corn and soya because much of it was genetically modified and reduced the genetic diversity which was essential for long-term sustainable agriculture. Zambia's president, Levy Mwanawasa, called the imports 'poison'. By 2004 Zambia had been joined by Zimbabwe, Malawi, Mozambique, Lesotho and Angola in refusing genetically modified food aid.

The European Union refused patents of new GM crops between 1998 and 2004, but, in the latter year, imports of a further GM maize crop were approved and a scheme was introduced to label foods containing GM products. However, the EU's actions were too slow for the big GM producers, particularly in the United States. They filed a complaint with the World Trade Organization (WTO) in 2003 against the EU's failure to authorize the commercialization of GM crops, claiming that the European position had no scientific basis and broke free-trade laws. In 2006 the WTO ruled that a series of European countries, including Austria, Germany, Greece, France and Luxembourg, *had* broken international trade rules by imposing bans on the marketing and growing of GM foods (Horlick-Jones et al. 2009: 4). Yet it is hard to imagine that European consumers, who have consistently refused to buy GM foods, will suddenly drop their opposition based purely on this ruling.

The issue of GM crops highlights the point that environmental issues always involve complex combinations of the natural and the social, and it is not realistic to expect them to be easily separated. In May 2000, the British government admitted that thousands of acres of conventional oilseed rape planted by farmers had been 'contaminated' as GM crops pollinated those nearby. German research published just weeks later claimed that a gene commonly used to modify oilseed rape had jumped the species barrier into bees. Such findings have been taken by environmental activists as supportive of their advocacy of a precautionary principle. This proposes that, where there is sufficient doubt about the possible risks of new technologies, it is up to producers to prove they will not cause harm before they are approved for use. Critics argue that this principle would stifle innovation and is historically naïve, as many unproven technologies have actually had major benefits that would have been lost.

Despite the concerns of environmentalists, the amount of land given over to growing GM crops has continued to increase, particularly in the developing world, where the environmental movement is not as strongly established and laws restricting the growth of GM crops are generally less strict (figure 5.7). However,

in 2010 the total global planting area for transgenic crops reached 1 billion hectares globally, and some 13 million farmers worldwide were growing GM crops (Peng 2011).

The GM controversy is an excellent example of a 'manufactured risk' – that is, an apparently 'natural' issue which actually arises from human intervention. We will discuss ideas of risk in relation to the environment later in the chapter, looking specifically at the important work of Ulrich Beck. However, in the next section we move on to explore what has become *the* most widely debated and potentially serious environmental issue of the twenty-first century: global warming.

> **THINKING CRITICALLY**
>
> How realistic is the 'precautionary principle' – that we should always err on the side of caution with untested new technologies? What real-world examples of unproven technologies are there which call this principle into question?

Global warming

Based on average surface global temperatures, 2015 was the warmest year on record, followed by 2014, 2010 and 2005. Nine of the ten warmest years recorded since reliable records began in the late nineteenth century have occurred since 2000 (the exception was 1998). Although the planet, on average, has warmed by just 0.85°C since 1880, scientists forecast that trend will continue, and even apparently small rises can alter climate systems across the world (IPCC 2015: 2). The effects of very hot weather can be catastrophic. The Earth Policy Institute, an environmental think tank, estimated that a heat wave in 2003 killed almost 40,000 people in Europe. France suffered the most, as 14,802 people died from causes attributable to the high temperatures, with older people being particularly affected (Bhattacharya 2003).

The environmental issue of global warming – a form of climate change – is the clearest example of a genuinely *global environmental*

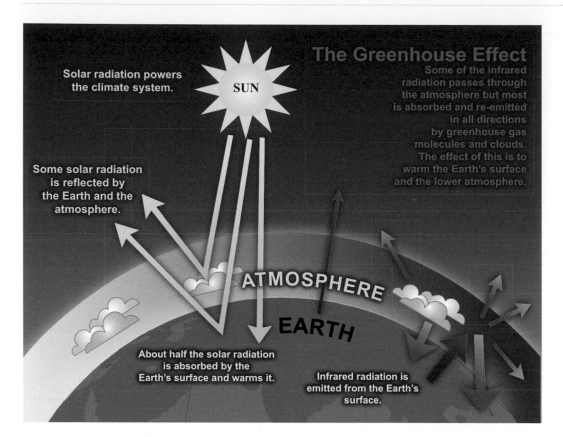

Figure 5.8   The greenhouse effect

Source: IPCC (2015): https://www.ipcc.unibe.ch/publications/wg1-ar4/faq/wg1_faq-1.3.html.

problem. Its effects will have an impact on every society on the planet, albeit to varying degrees. To understand it, we have to see 'the environment' in its widest sense – the Earth as a whole – as the atmosphere shrouds the entire planet rather than one region. The problem of global warming cannot be understood without modern science, and sociologists need to engage with debates on the science of climate change if they want to say anything useful about the matter.

What is global warming?

Global warming is regarded by many people as the most serious environmental challenge of our time. If scientific forecasts are correct, then it has the potential to alter irreversibly the functioning of the Earth's climate, producing a series of devastating environmental consequences which will be felt worldwide. Global warming

refers to the gradual rise in the Earth's average surface temperature resulting from changes in the chemical composition of the atmosphere. The current scientific consensus is that this is caused in large measure by humans, because the gases that have built up and altered the Earth's atmosphere are ones that are produced in large quantities by industrial processes.

Global warming is closely related to the concept of the greenhouse effect – the build-up of heat-trapping gases within the Earth's atmosphere. The principle is a simple one. Energy from the sun passes through the atmosphere and heats the Earth's surface. Although most of the solar radiation is absorbed directly, some of it is reflected back. The greenhouse gases act as a barrier to this outgoing energy, trapping heat within the atmosphere much like the glass panels of a greenhouse (see figure 5.8). This natural greenhouse effect is what keeps the Earth at a reasonably comfortable surface temperature – about 15.5°C. If it were not for the role of greenhouse gases in retaining heat, the Earth would be a much colder place, with an average temperature of –17°C.

When concentrations of atmospheric greenhouse gases rise, the greenhouse effect is intensified and much warmer temperatures are produced. Since the start of industrialization, the concentration of greenhouse gases has risen significantly. Concentrations of carbon dioxide (the main greenhouse gas) have increased by around 40 per cent since 1750 – the onset of modern industrialization; methane has increased by 150 per cent and nitrous oxide by 20 per cent (IPCC 2015: 44) (see 'Global society 5.2').

Most climate scientists agree that the large increase in carbon dioxide in the atmosphere can be attributed to the burning of fossil fuels as well as other human activities, such as industrial production, large-scale agriculture, deforestation, mining and landfill, and vehicle emissions. The overall impact on the climate of industrial processes such as these is referred to as anthropogenic (human-created) climate change. Clearly the Industrial Revolution of the eighteenth and nineteenth centuries and the spread of industrialization around the globe have produced major, world-historical changes.

The Fifth Assessment of the Intergovernmental Panel on Climate Change (IPCC 2015) reports that, on the basis of analyses comparing actual observations with a model forecast based only on natural climate changes and a second model based on natural changes *plus* anthropogenic climate change, it is *extremely likely* that the increase in observed temperatures since the mid-twentieth century is due to human activity. This is a much stronger conclusion than that arrived at in the Third and Fourth Assessment Reports of 2001 and 2007 respectively. Figure 5.9 shows the observed upward trend in surface temperatures between 1910 and 2010 compared to the IPCC models.

Global Society 5.2 Guide to greenhouse gases

Some greenhouse gases, such as carbon dioxide, occur naturally and are emitted to the atmosphere through natural processes and human activities. Others (e.g., fluorinated gases) are created and emitted solely through human activities. The principal greenhouse gases that enter the atmosphere because of human activities are:

• *Carbon dioxide (CO$_2$)*: Carbon dioxide enters the atmosphere through the burning of fossil fuels (oil, natural gas, and coal), solid waste, trees and wood products, and as a result of other chemical reactions (e.g., manufacture of cement). It is also removed from the atmosphere (or 'sequestered') when it is absorbed by plants as part of the biological carbon cycle.
• *Methane (CH$_4$)*: Methane is emitted during the production and transport of coal, natural gas and oil. Methane emissions also result from livestock and other agricultural practices and by the decay of organic waste in municipal solid waste landfills.
• *Nitrous oxide (N$_2$O)*: Nitrous oxide is emitted during agricultural and industrial activities, as well as during combustion of fossil fuels and solid waste.
• *Fluorinated gases*: Hydrofluorocarbons, perfluorocarbons and sulfur hexafluoride are synthetic, powerful greenhouse gases that are emitted from a variety of industrial processes. Fluorinated gases are sometimes used as substitutes for ozone-depleting substances (i.e., CFCs, HCFCs and halons). These gases are typically emitted in smaller quantities but, because they are potent greenhouse gases, are sometimes referred to as High Global Warming Potential gases ('High GWP gases').

Source: US Environmental Protection Agency: www.epa.gov/climatechange/emissions/index.html#ggo.

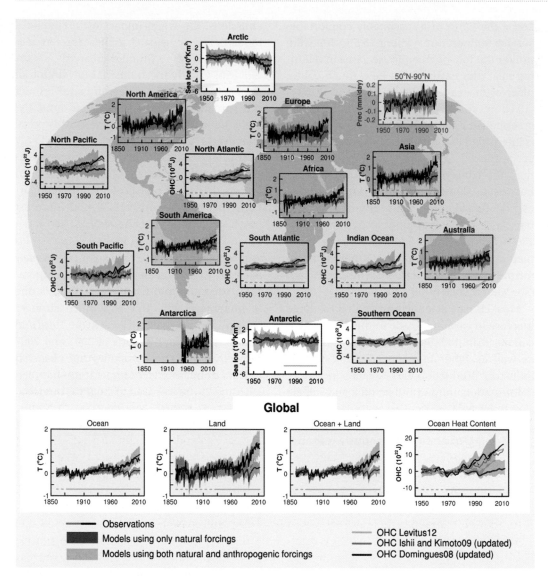

Figure 5.9 Global and regional temperature changes: observed, natural forcing, and natural plus anthropogenic forcing

Note: All time-series are decadal averages plotted at the centre of the decade.
Source: IPCC (2015: 49).

The potential consequences of global warming

The consequences of global warming are likely to be unevenly experienced, with devastating outcomes for some regions and countries but not for all. The IPCC's Fourth Assessment Report (2007: 50–2) suggested a range of social impacts, some of the more significant of which are listed by region below.

Low-lying areas are more susceptible to flooding as a result of global climate change, though the effects on the lives of people in these regions will vary. The picture on the left shows emergency supplies of food and medicines being delivered to a community in Bangladesh. On the right, RSPCA officers in England rescue stranded pets.

1 By 2020, some 75 to 250 million people across Africa will experience greater stress on water supplies, and agricultural yields may fall by as much as 50 per cent, severely compromising access to adequate levels of food and increasing levels of undernourishment. The IPCC also forecast an increase in arid land by 2080 of between 5 and 8 per cent in Africa, while a rise in sea levels would affect the low-lying coastal areas with large populations.

2 In Central, East, South and South-East Asia, availability of freshwater is forecast to be reduced by 2050, leading to increasing problems with water security. Coastal areas are likely to be subject to flooding, both from rivers and from the sea. Sickness and deaths from diarrhoeal diseases will rise as global warming changes the hydrological cycle, making floods and drought more common.

3 In Latin America, eastern Amazonia is likely to see tropical forests becoming savannah as soils dry out, and semi-arid vegetation will be lost. Food security will be reduced as the productivity of crops and livestock declines, resulting in more people at risk of undernourishment and chronic hunger. Shifting rainfall patterns will lead to uncertain water supplies for drinking water and agriculture.

4 In Australia and New Zealand the forecast is for a loss of biodiversity in some important sites, including the Great Barrier Reef. Water insecurity will increase in southern and eastern Australia and parts of New Zealand. Agricultural production will decline in much of southern and eastern Australia and eastern New Zealand because of increasing droughts and fires.

5 In Europe, more frequent coastal flooding and coastal erosion are expected due to sea level rises and more severe storms. Southern Europe will see more drought and higher temperatures that will reduce the availability of water and crop productivity, and higher temperatures will worsen health problems arising from heat waves.

6 North America will experience more intense and frequent heat waves in cities that already have problems, bringing increasing health problems. Warming in the western mountains is likely to cause more flooding in winter and reduced flows in the summer months.

7 Rising sea levels are likely to present major challenges for many small island communities in the Pacific and Caribbean. Storm surges will be higher and erosion exacerbated, threatening communities

and infrastructure. By the mid-twenty-first century, water resources are likely to be reduced to the point that they will not be sufficient to meet demand during times of low rainfall.

The IPCC's Fifth Assessment (2015) argued that the worst effects of global warming could be averted if average temperatures can be limited to a maximum of 2°C higher than those in 1750. However, this would require a much more focused and determined, wide-ranging and global programme of mitigation to reduce the emissions of greenhouse gases alongside adaptive measures. In particular, the IPCC (ibid.: 20) suggests that global emissions of CO_2 (and other greenhouse gases) would have to be reduced to 'near zero' over the next few decades. With current technological means and political realities in relation to energy generation, this goal appears positively utopian. Indeed, the IPCC also notes that

> Surface temperature is projected to rise over the 21st century under all assessed emissions scenarios. It is *very likely* that heatwaves will occur more often and last longer, and that extreme precipitation events will become more intense and frequent in many regions. The ocean will continue to warm and acidify, and global mean sea level to rise. (Ibid.: 10)

The negative consequences of such changes will be distributed unevenly, with already disadvantaged people and communities around the world bearing the brunt of environmental change. As we will see later, this is one reason why campaigners argue for 'sustainable development', which foregrounds the issue of global inequality and its reduction as the way to tackle emissions reductions.

Questioning the science of climate change

Since its creation in 1988, the IPCC has made it increasingly clear in its reports that global warming is partly the result of anthropogenic causes such as industrial pollution, vehicle emissions, deforestation and the burning of fossil fuels, all of which release greenhouse gases into the atmosphere. However, although the evidence base is large, diverse and consistent in showing that global warming is a reality, there are several contentious debates surrounding the thesis and its implications which bring the consensus view into conflict with a range of 'climate change sceptics'.

The IPCC (2015: 2) says that 'Warming of the climate is unequivocal, and since the 1950s, many of the observed changes are unprecedented over decades to millenia.' Yet some question the evidence that global warming is actually occurring at all. For example, Lord (Nigel) Lawson (2009: 1), a former energy secretary and chancellor in the British government, maintains that global warming is 'the latest scare' in a series that includes overpopulation and total resource depletion. Lawson argues that there was a 'mild warming' in the last quarter of the twentieth century, but this has been followed by a 'lull' in the twenty-first century when warming has apparently 'stopped'. The sceptical charge here is that climate scientists fail to deal adequately with contrary evidence and either ignore it or cherry-pick their evidence. However, in 2011, the government's chief scientific adviser, Sir John Beddington, engaged in an exchange of letters with Lord Lawson, arguing that his book showed little grasp of climate science, that short-term temperature trends are not meaningful in the context of long-term global warming, and that the scientific evidence from multiple sources clearly showed that 'the risks are real' (Boffey 2011).

Second, some sceptics argue that there is good evidence that global warming *is* real but deny any anthropogenic cause. For this strand of criticism, global warming is an entirely natural phenomenon, probably related to the fluctuating activity of the sun. They also claim that CO_2 is not a significant greenhouse gas. As solar activity fluctuates, so does the Earth's climate, and it is this which explains the current warming trend. The majority scientific view is that, although solar activity does affect surface temperature, there is no evidence of a positive trend in solar activity since the 1960s that could have produced the present global warming. CO_2 is certainly not the *only* greenhouse gas, but it does remain in the atmosphere for many decades and even centuries, which leads to a steady accumulation over time from industrial activity. It is this, say the majority, which mainly accounts for global warming.

Recent evidence also shows that some sceptical research and websites are funded by multinational fossil fuel companies. For example, in 2011, a Greenpeace investigation into a leading sceptical climate astrophysicist, Dr Willie Soon, at the Harvard–Smithsonian Center for Astrophysics revealed that he had received more than US$1 million over the previous ten years from major energy companies, including ExxonMobil, the American Petroleum Institute and Koch Industries (Vidal 2011). Soon has been a leading academic making the case that global warming is the product of 'solar variation' and is unrelated to human activity. He claims that his scientific research remains independent regardless of who provides the funding. Similarly, the Charles Koch Foundation (Koch Industries is a large US energy company) has been a major funder of groups and individuals which promote sceptical views on global warming. The links between wealthy multinational oil, gas and coal corporations and global warming sceptics have effectively enabled a minority viewpoint to gain disproportionate visibility and influence in the mass media.

Third, even if we accept that global warming *is* real and *is* partly explained by anthropogenic impact, some argue that the predicted consequences are highly speculative at best and grossly exaggerated at worst. Computer modelling of the kind used by the IPCC is notoriously unreliable, especially when extrapolating current trends far into the future, and suggestions of a 6°C rise by 2100 amount to scaremongering. Politically, economically and socially, our efforts would be better directed at tackling other more urgent social problems, such as poverty in developing countries, rather than wasting valuable resources on an uncertain 'problem' (Lomborg 2001).

Although some forecasts at the extreme end of climate science do suggest an increase of 6°C is possible by 2100, this assumes no change in the policies of governments aimed at reducing carbon emissions, which is surely unlikely. However, we have to bear in mind that there are many uncertainties in climate forecasting, including cloud feedback, changing ice-sheet flows in Antarctica and Greenland, land-use change, technological developments, the impact of aerosols, the extent of behavioural changes and a lack of data in some regions, which hinder accurate modelling. The IPCC (2015) reports that greenhouse gas emissions have actually risen globally between 1970 and 2010, especially from 2000 to 2010, despite an increasing number of governments adopting mitigation policies. Hence, it is not possible to rule out completely the much more radical and devastating effects of global warming.

Nevertheless, the history of environmental politics in the twentieth century is littered with failed predictions of global disaster and catastrophic human collapse. It therefore makes sense for social scientists to work with the best available scientific research, which is currently found in the ongoing IPCC research programme.

The IPCC's best estimate is a warming of 0.2°C per decade for the next two decades, which would produce only a 2 degree warming by 2100 (IPCC 2007: 45). It is also correct that computer modelling can conflict with real-world evidence, but climate models are complex and built from evidence gathered from many sources around the world. The Fourth Assessment Report noted that, since 1990, IPCC forecast values have averaged 0.15 to 0.3°C increase per decade, which compares favourably with the observed increase between 1990 and 2005 of 0.2°C per decade. Such evidence suggests that the IPCC modelling is, in fact, quite realistic.

The 'ClimateGate' affair, discussed in 'Using your sociological imagination 5.2', has been a salutary experience, not just for climate scientists, but for the academic community as a whole. In an increasingly global academic environment which operates within societies

5.2 'ClimateGate' – just a storm in an email?

Climate change science was called into question in 2009, when the Climatic Research Unit at the University of East Anglia in the UK had its email system hacked and around 1,000 emails, including exchanges between members of the unit and colleagues around the world, were published on the worldwide web – an affair now known as 'ClimateGate'.

In some of these emails, the director, Professor Phil Jones, referred to performing 'a trick' with climate data and talked of 'hiding the decline' in temperature for one data series. He also admitted refusing repeated requests to share data with critics and asking a colleague to delete all emails relating to the IPCC's Fourth Assessment. Jones later argued that the email comments were taken out of context; the 'trick' was simply finding a creative way of joining two datasets, while 'hiding the decline' meant correcting a false impression in one dataset by making a composite set that also included instrumental data (BBC 2010).

Sceptics see this episode as supportive of their case that many climate scientists, whose careers and reputations have become intertwined with proving anthropogenic global warming, are prepared to sacrifice key scientific principles of openness and peer review in order to protect themselves and their 'unproven' thesis. Then, in 2010, after criticism from glaciologists, the vice-chair of the IPCC admitted that a claim in the 2007 report that Himalayan glaciers 'could disappear by 2035' was wrong. Mistakes such as this, say sceptics, raise the issue of how many other IPCC predictions are incorrect, calling into question the existence of global warming.

'ClimateGate' was the subject of three independent inquiries: a parliamentary inquiry, a university inquiry into eleven key scientific papers, and a university-commissioned inquiry led by a senior civil servant, Sir Muir Russell, into the hacked and leaked email exchanges. All three found no evidence of scientific malpractice, falsification of data or attempts to subvert the peer review process. However, the Russell Review (Russell 2010: 10–11) did criticize the unit for being unhelpful and defensive when requests for data were made under the Freedom of Information (FoI) Act. It also criticized the university and the unit for failing to appreciate the statutory requirements of the FoI Act and the potential damage that could be caused to climate science research and the university itself by withholding data. A separate review of the IPCC's main forecasts, commissioned by the Dutch government in 2010, found no errors that might call into question the finding that anthropogenic climate change was occurring.

> ### THINKING CRITICALLY
> If the evidence of global warming is compelling, why would this unit be wary of giving out information and withhold some of its data? What impact might hacking of this kind have on the practice of climate science?

where easy access to the Internet and ideals of freedom of information combine to create expectations of complete open access to information and data, science seems still to be catching up. It is certainly not unusual for groups of scientists to guard jealously their raw data in order to protect their own knowledge claims, and, although it is common to speak of a 'scientific community', it is important to remember that scientific work, like all other spheres of social life, is also highly competitive. For the foreseeable future at least, it is likely that an uneasy tension between established scientific practice and the emerging culture of open access to information will continue.

Responding to global warming

The industrial countries currently produce far more greenhouse gases than the developing world, though China has now overtaken the

USA and emits more carbon dioxide than any other single country. However, emissions from the developing world are increasing precipitately, particularly in countries that are undergoing rapid industrialization, and are expected to be roughly equal to those of industrialized countries sometime around 2035. When we take population size into account and look at emissions per capita, then China and India currently produce lower levels than the USA, Europe, the Russian Federation and Japan, which shows why some developing countries see their own 'survival' emissions as far less damaging than the 'luxury' emissions of the already rich countries.

However, there is also a disjunction between the widespread acceptance of global warming and people being prepared to change their routine behaviour to help tackle it. Giddens (2011: 2) calls this (unsurprisingly) 'the Giddens Paradox'. This paradox states that, as people experience no clearly tangible effects of the dangers of unchecked global warming in their everyday lives, they will not change their environmentally damaging actions. Car dependency is a clear example of this. Yet, if they wait until global warming clearly interferes with their lives, it will be too late to do anything about it. Before that happens, ways have to be found to 'embed a concern with climate change into people's everyday lives, while recognizing the formidable problems involved in doing so' (Giddens 2009: 12).

Without the positive involvement of the critical mass of individual citizens, it seems unlikely that government policies alone will succeed. But, clearly, a coordinated global approach to cutting greenhouse gas emissions is made more difficult in the context of uneven economic development at the national level, which produces as much disagreement as agreement on how to tackle the problem.

The United Nations Framework Convention on Climate Change was created in 1997 in Kyoto, Japan, where agreement was reached to cut emissions significantly by 2012 in order to stabilize and eventually reduce greenhouse gas levels in the atmosphere. Targets ranged from an average 8 per cent cut for most of Europe to a maximum 10 per cent increase for Iceland and an 8 per cent increase for Australia. The USA originally committed itself to a 7 per cent cut, but has never ratified the protocol. By 2010, the industrialized countries looked on course to meet their targets. However, many scientists see the targets as too modest when it takes more than a century for carbon dioxide to be removed from the atmosphere through natural processes. In recent years, several of the largest producers of greenhouse gases have successfully cut emissions, including the UK, Germany, China and Russia – although Russia's cuts can be explained largely by the decline in its economy.

The Kyoto Protocol took 1990 greenhouse emission levels as its starting point. But this was seen by many in the developing world as favouring the industrialized countries, as it fails to take into account the latter's 'historical responsibility' for the problem of global warming and, hence, avoids attributing blame. It is also unclear exactly when developing countries will be asked to reduce their emissions, or by how much. Will it allow for the inevitably higher emissions levels as their economic development catches up with the industrialized world? If it does not, then it may be seen as unfair and unworkable (Najam et al. 2003).

A successor to Kyoto was formally approved by the G8+5 countries (the G8 countries plus China, India, Brazil, Mexico and South Africa) in the so-called Washington Declaration of 2007. This would see the introduction of a global 'cap and trade' system (involving all countries) in which emissions caps will be introduced alongside a trading system (focused on carbon trading) that forces polluters to pay. The system works by rewarding those countries that reduce emissions (and sell credits) and penalizing those which do not (and are forced to pay for carbon credits). However, the overall effect of the cap and trade system is to push all countries towards lowering their emissions.

Following acrimonious disagreements and failure to secure a binding agreement at the Copenhagen talks in 2009, the 2010 Cancun meeting was, at last, widely seen as marking progress: 190 countries agreed to bring the voluntary targets set out in Copenhagen into the process, to accept the goal of limiting temperature rises to less than 2°C (but strive for 1.5°C) and to set up a green climate fund as part of a US$100 billion commitment to help developing countries to move their economies forward in non-polluting ways. The overall agreement is legally binding, but specific aspects such as pledges by individual nation-states to reduce emissions are not (Goldenberg et al. 2015). Nonetheless, after years of disagreements and acrimony, the Paris agreement in 2015, involving 196 countries, was widely hailed as an important step forward in tackling global warming.

As with other manufactured risks, no one can be certain what the effects of global warming will be. Would a 'high' emissions scenario truly result in widespread natural disasters? Will stabilizing the level of carbon dioxide emissions protect most people from the negative effects of climate change? Is it possible that global warming has already triggered a series of further climatic disturbances? We cannot answer these questions with any certainty, but international scientific collaboration and political processes do seem to offer the most viable ways of dealing with the problem. In addition, the underlying anthropogenic causes of global warming require an understanding not just of the basic environmental science but also of social processes. This means that there is a clear role for sociological theories which connect human societies and practices to the natural environment, and it is to these that we now turn.

> ### THINKING CRITICALLY
>
> 'People in the developed world are responsible for causing global warming and they should accept a lower standard of living to rapidly reduce greenhouse gas emissions.' What arguments would you make to persuade people in the rich world to accept a lower material standard of living? Would they be likely to accept them?

Consumerism, risk and paths to a sustainable future

Natural scientists have been at the forefront of debates on environmental issues. As the examples above of pollution, resource depletion, genetic modification and global warming show, environmental issues are different from most sociological subjects, because they involve getting to grips with *natural scientific* research and evidence. However, the hybrid character of environmental issues means that natural scientists can never have a monopoly on them. Our brief introduction to the problem of global warming is the most striking example of this.

The IPCC scientists acknowledge that twentieth-century global warming was largely the product of human activities – industrialization, urbanization and globalization processes, for example – and the experts in these areas are sociologists and other *social* scientists such as political scientists, human geographers and all of those studying development and international relations (Urry 2011). If environmental problems are to be successfully comprehended, then social and natural scientists will have to try to understand each other rather better than they have done so far. This must surely be a positive challenge for the whole academic community.

The rest of this section will explore some of the main sociological theories linking social development with environmental damage, along with some of the major approaches to solving global environmental problems.

Consumerism and environmental damage

One important issue relating to the environment and economic development is that of consumption patterns. Consumption refers to the goods, services, energy and resources that are used by people. It is a phenomenon with both positive and negative dimensions. On the one hand, rising levels of consumption around the world mean that people are living under better conditions than in the past. Consumption is linked to economic development – as living standards rise, people are able to afford more food, clothing, personal items, leisure time, holidays and cars. On the other hand, mass consumption has negative impacts too. Consumption patterns can damage the environmental resource base and exacerbate patterns of inequality.

Trends in world consumption over the course of the twentieth century are startling. In 1900, world consumption levels were just over $1.5 trillion, but by the end of the century private and public consumption expenditures amounted to around $24 trillion – twice the level of 1975 and six times that of 1950 (UNDP 1998). In developed countries, consumption per head has been growing at a rate of 2.3 per cent annually; in East Asia growth has been even faster – 6.1 per cent annually. By contrast, the average African household consumes 20 per cent less today than it did thirty years ago. There is widespread concern that the consumption explosion has passed by the poorest fifth of the world's population.

It has been argued that industrial capitalism sets societies on a 'treadmill of production' leading to environmental damage, using up natural resources at a rapid rate and generating high levels of pollution and waste (Schnaiberg 1980). However, in the twentieth century it was modern consumerism which kept that treadmill running faster in this direction (Bell 2011). Consumption is something that human beings have to engage in to survive, but modern consumption is very different from earlier forms.

Mass production must be accompanied by large-scale consumption. The products of industry have to be bought and consumed, though producing and consuming may well be carried out in geographically distant locations. Products are made wherever it is cheapest to do so and consumed wherever the best price can be gained. In the past sixty years or so, this has led to industrial production moving to developing countries. The rapid transformation of the newly industrializing countries (NICs) such as Hong Kong, South Korea, Singapore and Taiwan in the 1970s and recent industrial development in India, China and Malaysia testify to this, which is part of the globalization process.

Sociologists have argued that consumerism is also a way of thinking, a mentality or even an ideology (Corrigan 1997; Campbell 1992). We can understand this aspect if we ask why people continually consume and want to consume. Perhaps it is simply because consumer goods have 'use-value' for people, helping to save them time and effort. But luxury items fit this explanation less well. They show another side to modern consumerism – its role in the social status competition within society (see chapter 8, 'Social Interaction and Daily Life'). Differentiated mass consumption allows for complex, fine-grained distinctions to be made according to the styles and fashions of the day. People may be prepared to pay a premium for the latest fashions because these products allow them to say something about themselves, to communicate their status or aspirations in a highly visible way. Even products with a clear use-value, such as clothes, are also fashionable items that are discarded and replaced before their 'use-value' has expired. Large amounts of such fashion-fuelled waste increase pressure on the environment.

Over time, consumer products become embedded into the routines of everyday life and are taken for granted. When this happens, it becomes difficult to think there is an alternative. A small example is the ubiquitous and free plastic shopping bag which litters streets and causes injury and death to many seabirds and marine animals. Rather than reuse plastic bags, people tend to throw them away. In 2015 the UK government introduced a compulsory 5p charge for plastic bags, which led to rising sales and the use of stronger, renewable shopping bags – a simple example of targeted, pro-environment behaviour modification.

Perhaps the best example of environmentally damaging consumer products is the private motor vehicle, particularly the car (Lucas et al. 2011). Many households have one, two, or more cars, and people use them even for short trips to the shops or to visit friends and relatives who live close by. But large-scale car-ownership and use generates large amounts of pollution and waste in both production and consumption. Why has it proved so difficult to reduce our use of the car?

One survey of attitudes to car-ownership found a range of consumer types among visitors to National Trust properties in the north-west of England (Anable 2005). The largest group consisted of *Malcontented Motorists*. They are unhappy with many aspects of their car use but feel that public transport has too many constraints to be a genuine alternative, so they do not switch. Second are *Complacent Car Addicts*, who accept that there are alternatives to using the car but do not feel any pressing moral imperative to change. Third are *Aspiring Environmentalists*. This group has already reduced their usage but feel the car has advantages that force them not to give it up altogether. Fourth are *Die-hard Drivers*, who feel they have a right to drive, enjoy driving and have negative feelings towards other modes of transportation, such as buses and trains. Fifth, *Car-less Crusaders* have given up their cars for environmental reasons and see alternative modes of travel in a positive light. Last are the *Reluctant Riders*, who use public transport but would prefer to use a car; however, for a variety of reasons, such as health problems, they cannot do this, but will accept lifts from others.

This study shows that blanket appeals to an emerging environmental awareness are likely to fail. Instead, 'the segmentation approach illustrates that policy interventions need to be responsive to the different motivations and constraints of the sub-groups' (Anable 2005: 77). However, some sociologists argue that, seen in the long term, the 'century of the car' may be coming to an end anyway, as oil supplies appear to have peaked, the mitigation of global warming is leading to a push for new, 'low-carbon' technologies, and rising population levels make mass individual car-ownership less likely (Dennis and Urry 2009).

Of course, 'the car' remains an important symbol of the transition to independent living and adulthood as well as embodying modern

As oil supplies are said to have peaked, will the private motor car have any place in the low-carbon societies of the future?

ideals of freedom and liberation. But Dennis and Urry argue that the twentieth-century 'car system' of mass individual ownership of petrol-fuelled vehicles driving around extensive road networks may not survive in its present form. What will replace it, though, has yet to take any firm outline.

Another aspect of modern consumerism is its pleasurable aspect. But *why* is it pleasurable? Some have argued that the pleasure of consumerism lies not in the *use* of products but in the *anticipation* of purchasing them. Colin Campbell (1992) argues that this is *the most* pleasurable part of the process – the wanting, the longing after, the seeking out and desiring

THINKING CRITICALLY

Looking at the typology of car users above, think of an appropriate environmental policy aimed at each consumer type to generate pro-environmental behaviour in that group. Are there any general policies that might have the desired effect on all the groups?

of products, not the use of them. It is a 'romantic ethic' of consumption based on desire and longing. Marketing of products and services draws on this anticipatory consumerism in seductive ways to create and intensify people's desires. That is why we keep going back for more and are never truly satisfied.

From an environmental perspective, the 'romantic ethic' of consumerism is disastrous. We constantly demand new products and more of them. That means more production, so the cycle of mass production and mass consumption continues to churn out pollution and wastes natural resources. At the input side of production, natural resources are used up in enormous quantities, and, at the output end in consumption, people throw away useful things not because they are *use-less*, but because they are no longer in fashion or fail to represent their status aspirations.

The sociology of consumption shows us that the combination of industrialization, capitalism and consumerism has transformed society–environment relations. Many environmentalists and more than a few social and natural scientists have concluded that continuous economic growth cannot carry on indefinitely. The resulting pollution might have been ecologically insignificant if it had been restricted to a small part of the global human population. However, when industrialization spreads across the planet, when a majority of people live in huge cities, and when capitalist companies become multinational and consumerism seduces people in all countries, then the natural environment's capacity for recovery and resilience becomes severely weakened.

Although the rich are the world's main consumers, the environmental damage that is caused by growing consumption has the heaviest impact on the poor. As we saw in our discussion of global warming, the wealthy are in a better position to enjoy the many benefits of consumption without having to deal with its negative effects. At the local level, affluent groups can usually afford to move away from problem areas, leaving the poor to bear the costs. Chemical plants, power stations, major roads, railways and airports are often sited close to low-income areas, and on a global level we can see a similar process at work: soil degradation, deforestation, water shortages, lead emissions and air pollution are all increasingly concentrated within the developing world. What is needed is a perspective which connects the developed and developing countries in a single project. Sustainable development was created to do just that.

Limits to growth and sustainable development

A central motivating idea for environmental campaigners has been that of 'sustainability' – ensuring that human activity does not compromise the ecology of planet Earth. In *The Ecologist*, a UK campaigning magazine, Edward Goldsmith and his colleagues set out the charge against industrial expansion in their *A Blueprint for Survival* (1972: 15): 'The principal defect of the industrial way of life with its ethos of expansion is that it is not sustainable . . . we can be certain . . . that sooner or later it will end.' Such doom-laden forecasts used to be described as 'catastrophist' and were restricted to the wilder fringes of the environmental movement. However, the idea now has a wider currency among the general public and policy-makers, for which the scientific predictions of global warming are largely responsible. Anyone who recycles their plastic, paper and glass, conserves water or tries to use their car less is probably aware that they too are trying to put into practice the idea of sustainability.

One important influence on the rise of environmental movements and public concern about environmental problems can be traced back to a famous report first published in the early 1970s, which set out the case that economic growth could not continue indefinitely. The report and its findings are discussed in 'Classic studies 5.1'.

Sustainable development

Rather than simply calling for economic growth to be reined in, more recent developments turn on the concept of sustainable development. This was first introduced in a report commissioned by the United Nations, *Our Common Future* (WCED 1987). This is

---

Classic Studies 5.1 | **Modelling the limits to economic growth**

The research problem

Global human population has grown enormously since industrialization took hold, and the resulting pressure on the environment has led to soil degradation, deforestation and pollution. Are there any limits to this pattern of development? Will food supplies keep up with increasing demand or will the world see mass famine? How many people can the planet support without ruining the environment? These hugely significant questions were asked of a group of scientists by a global think tank, the Club of Rome, almost forty years ago. The resulting book was published as *The Limits to Growth* (Meadows et al. 1972).

Meadows and colleagues' explanation

The *Limits* study used modern computer-modelling techniques to make forecasts about the consequences of continued economic growth, population growth, pollution and the depletion of natural resources. Their computer model – *World3* – showed what would happen if the trends that were established between 1900 and 1970 were to continue to the year 2100. The computer projections were then altered to generate a variety of possible consequences, depending on different rates of growth of the factors considered. The researchers found that, each time they altered one variable, there would eventually be an environmental crisis. If the world's societies failed to change, then growth would end anyway sometime before 2100, through the depletion of resources, food shortages or industrial collapse.

The research team used computer modelling to explore five global trends (Meadows et al. 1972: 21):

- accelerating industrialization across the world
- rapid population growth
- widespread malnutrition in some regions
- depletion of non-renewable resources
- a deteriorating natural environment.

The programme was then run to test twelve alternative scenarios, each one manipulated to resolve some of the identified problems. This allowed the researchers to ask questions about which combinations of population levels, industrial output and natural resources would be sustainable. The conclusion they drew in 1972 was that there *was* still time to put off the emerging environmental crisis. But, if nothing was done – and even if the amount of available resources in the model were doubled, pollution were reduced to pre-1970s levels and new technologies were introduced – economic growth would still grind to a halt before 2100. Some campaigners saw this as vindicating the radical environmental argument that industrial societies were just not sustainable over the long term.

Critical points

Many economists, politicians and industrialists roundly condemned the report, arguing that it was unbalanced, irresponsible and, when its predictions failed to materialize, just plain wrong. The modelling was largely devoid of political and social variables and was therefore just a partial account of reality. The researchers later accepted that some of the criticisms were justified. The method used focused on *physical* limits and assumed existing rates of economic growth and technological innovation, but this did not take account of the capacity of human beings to respond to environmental challenges.

For example, market forces could be made to work to limit the over-exploitation of resources. If a mineral such as magnesium starts to become scarce, its price will rise. As its price rises it will be used less, and producers might even find alternatives should costs rise too steeply. *Limits* was seen by many as yet another overly pessimistic, catastrophist tract that engaged in unreliable 'futurology' – predicting the future from current trends.

Contemporary significance

Whatever its limitations, the original report made a significant impact on public debate and environmental activism. It made many more people aware of the damaging consequences of industrial development and technology, as well as warning about the perils of allowing pollution to increase. The report was an important catalyst for the modern environmental movement (for a wider discussion, see chapter 21, 'Politics, Government and Social Movements'). Twenty years later, the team published *Beyond the Limits* (1992), an even more pessimistic report, castigating the world's politicians for wasting the time, arguing that ecological 'overshoot' was *already* occurring. Then, in 2004, their *30-Year Update* was released, arguing that, although some progress had been made in environmental awareness and technological development, the evidence of global warming, declining fish stocks, and much more, showed a world 'overshooting' its natural limits. This conclusion was also that of the UN Millennium Ecosystem Assessment Board of 2005, which is tellingly titled *Living Beyond our Means*. The basic conclusion from the original *Limits* report and its updates continues to resonate.

also known as the Brundtland Report, after the chair of the organizing committee, Gro Harlem Brundtland, then prime minister of Norway. The report's authors argued that use of the Earth's resources by the present generation was unsustainable.

The Brundtland Commission regarded sustainable development as 'development which meets the needs of the present generation, without compromising the ability of future generations to meet their own needs' (WCED 1987) – a pithy definition, but one which carries enormous significance. Sustainable development means that economic growth should be carried on in such a way as to recycle physical resources rather than deplete them and to keep levels of pollution to a minimum. However, the definition is open to criticism. How many generations should be considered – five, ten, or more? How can we know what are the 'needs' of the present generation? How can we compare human needs in developing countries with those in the relatively rich countries? These questions are still being debated, though the concept of sustainable development – however problematic – continues to motivate many individuals and voluntary groups.

Following the publication of *Our Common Future*, 'sustainable development' came to be widely used by both environmentalists and governments. It was employed at the UN Earth Summit in Rio de Janeiro in 1992 and has subsequently appeared in other meetings organized by the UN, such as the World Summit on Sustainable Development in Johannesburg in 2002. Sustainable development is also one of the Millennium Development Goals (MDGs), which were agreed by 191 states aiming to reduce poverty in the coming decades. Among other relevant MDGs are the integration of the principles of sustainable development into national policies and programmes, reversal of the loss of environmental resources, reduction by half of the proportion of people without sustainable access to safe drinking water, and achieving a significant improvement in the lives of at least 100 million slum-dwellers – all by 2020.

> For more on the Millennium Development Goals, see chapter 14, 'Global Inequality'.

Critics see the concept of sustainable development as too vague, neglecting the specific needs of poorer countries. It has been argued that the idea of sustainable development tends to focus attention only on the needs of richer countries; it does not consider how high levels of consumption in the more affluent countries are satisfied at the expense of people in developing countries. For instance, demands on Indonesia to conserve its rainforests could be seen as unfair, because Indonesia has a greater need than the industrialized countries for the revenue it must forgo.

Linking the concept of ecological sustainability to that of economic development appears contradictory at first sight. This is particularly pertinent where sustainability and development clash – for example, when considering new roads or retail sites, it is often the case that the prospect of new jobs and economic prosperity means sustainability takes second place, especially in times of economic recession. This is even more pronounced for governments in developing countries, which are badly in need of more economic activity. In recent years, ideas of environmental justice and ecological citizenship have come to the fore (as we see below) partly as a result of the severe problems associated with the concept and practice of sustainable development.

It is easy to be sceptical about the future prospects for sustainable development. Its aim of finding ways of balancing human activity with sustaining natural ecosystems may appear impossibly utopian. Nonetheless, sustainable development looks to create common ground among nation-states and connects the world development movement with the environmental movement in a way that no other project has yet managed to do. It gives radical environmentalists the opportunity to push for full implementation of its widest goals, but, at the same time, moderate campaigners can be involved locally and have an impact. This inclusivity can be seen as a weakness, but it is also a strength of the sustainable development project.

> ### THINKING CRITICALLY
> Sustainable development is 'development which meets the needs of the present generation, without compromising the ability of future generations to meet their own needs'. How could we find out what the *needs* of future generations will be? Can sustainable development policies be devised from this definition?

Living in the global 'risk society'

Humans have always had to face risks of one kind or another, but today's risks are qualitatively different from those that came in earlier times. Until quite recently, human societies were threatened by external risk – dangers such as drought, earthquakes, famines and storms that spring from the natural world and are unrelated to the actions of humans. The Japanese earthquake discussed at the outset of this chapter shows that external risks of this kind will continue, as planet Earth is characterized by many natural processes. However, we are also increasingly confronted by various types of manufactured risk that are created by the impact of our own knowledge and technology on the natural world.

Debates on genetically modified foods and global warming have presented individuals with new choices and challenges in their everyday lives. Because there are no definitive answers as to the consequences of such risks, each individual is forced to make decisions about which risks they are prepared to take. Should we use food and raw materials if their production or consumption has a negative impact on our health and the natural environment? Even seemingly simple decisions about what to eat are made in the context of conflicting information and opinions about the product's relative merits and drawbacks.

Ulrich Beck (1992, 1999, 2009) wrote extensively about risk and globalization. As technological change progresses more rapidly, producing new forms of risk, we must constantly respond and adjust to the changes.

Risks today involve a series of interrelated changes in contemporary social life: shifting employment patterns, heightened job insecurity, the declining influence of tradition and custom on self-identity, the erosion of traditional family patterns and the democratization of personal relationships. Because personal futures are much less fixed than in the past, decisions of all kinds present risks for individuals. Getting married, for example, is a more risky course today than it was when marriage was a lifelong commitment. Decisions about educational qualifications and career paths can also feel risky: it is difficult to predict what skills will be valuable in an economy that changes as rapidly as ours. 'Classic studies 5.2' explores Beck's arguments, specifically in relation to environmental risks.

Ecological modernization

For environmentalists, both capitalist and communist forms of modernization have signally failed. They have delivered wealth and

---

Classic Studies 5.2 | **Ulrich Beck and the global risk society**

The research problem

This chapter has explored some of the environmental consequences of industrial production and high levels of consumption. Taking a long-term view, we can see that the spread of industrialization produces more widespread and potentially serious side effects in the form of environmental risks. But is modern life really more risky, or are we just more 'risk aware'? Are we worrying unnecessarily about environmental problems? The German sociologist Ulrich Beck (1944–2015) has been the foremost sociological theorist of risk, which he understood as much more significant than sociologists previously thought.

Beck's explanation

Throughout the nineteenth and twentieth centuries, the politics of modern societies was dominated by a major conflict of interest between workers and employers – in Marx's terms, between the non-owning working class and the property-owning capitalist class. The conflict centred on issues of wealth distribution as trade unions and labour parties sought a more equal distribution of the socially produced wealth. Such struggles still continue, of course. But Ulrich Beck (1992, 2002, 2009) argues that this distributional conflict is losing its significance as environmental risks rise to prominence. He says that more people are beginning to realize that their fight for a share of the 'wealth cake' is futile if the cake itself is being poisoned as a result of pollution and environmental damage (Beck 2002: 128). Beck argues that:

> the knowledge is spreading that the sources of wealth are 'polluted' by growing 'hazardous side effects'. This is not at all new, but it has remained unnoticed for a long time in the efforts to overcome poverty. . . . To put it differently, in the risk society the unknown and unintended consequences come to be a dominant force in history and society. (1992: 20-1)

Industrial societies are slowly dissolving as environmental problems build up; this is an unintended consequence of the rush for economic growth and material prosperity. Beck (1999) argues that we are, in effect, moving into a 'world risk society' – a new type of society in which risk consciousness and risk avoidance are becoming central features – because environmental pollution does not respect national boundaries. No matter where industrial production or consumption takes place, its consequences can be felt in very distant locations. The relatively rich countries are not immune from industrial pollution and global environmental damage. We will remain dependent on science and high technology, though, because it is only through these that industrial processes can be safely and effectively managed.

Beck wants to show us that the environmental issue is moving from the margins of political concern towards the centre. Most of the risks we face are the products of human activity; they are not like the purely natural disasters of film and television. This means that the environment becomes an issue for political debate and decision-making, and we can see the creation of environmental organizations and Green political parties in the 1970s as the first step towards inclusion of environmental issues into mainstream politics.

Critical points

One of the main criticisms of Beck's overall thesis is that there is not (yet) enough evidence to support his theory of the transition to a 'risk society', even though there is today more awareness of environmental risks (Hajer 1996). Similarly, the idea that older forms of class-based politics are losing out to a new politics of risk seems premature. In most countries, Green political parties have not broken through the conventional party system, and globally the issue of wealth creation and distribution still tends to dominate over environmental protection whenever these objectives clash. Finally, it has been argued that the thesis fails to take account of cultural variability in definitions of risk (Douglas 1994; Scott 2000). What is defined as 'risk' in some societies may not be so defined in others, in the same way that what is defined as pollution in wealthy industrial societies is often seen as a sign of healthy economic development in poorer developing countries.

Contemporary significance

The concept of risk holds a special place in current sociological debates on environmental issues and the direction of social change. Beck's risk thesis is useful, because it provides part of an explanation for why environmental movement concerns have found such a receptive audience. Once people become sensitized to risks, the arguments of environmentalists begin to make more sense. Beck's *Risk Society* has taken sociological thinking on modernity and its possible futures in a new and highly original direction, making us rethink the sociological tradition, and for this reason it has rightly become a modern classic of social theory.

THINKING CRITICALLY

How aware are you of risks in your everyday life? Do you engage in any 'risk-taking activities' and, if so, why do you do it? Is risk always a negative part of modern life or can you think of any positive aspects?

---

material success, but at the price of massive environmental damage. In recent years, groups of academic social scientists in Western Europe have tried to develop a theoretical perspective called ecological modernization, which accepts that 'business as usual' is no longer possible but also rejects radical environmentalist solutions involving deindustrialization. Instead they focus on technological innovation and the use of market mechanisms to bring about positive outcomes, transforming production methods and reducing pollution at its source.

Ecological modernizers see huge potential in the leading European industries to reduce the use of natural resources *without* this affecting economic growth. This is an unusual position, but it does have a certain logic. Rather than simply rejecting economic growth, they argue that an *ecological form* of growth is theoretically possible. An example is the introduction of catalytic converters and emission controls on motor vehicles, which has been delivered within a short period of time and shows that advanced technologies can make a big difference to greenhouse gas emissions. If environmental protection really can be achieved this way, especially in renewable energy generation and transport, then we can continue to enjoy our high-technology lifestyles.

Ecological modernizers also argue that, if consumers demand environmentally sound production methods and products, market mechanisms will be forced to try and deliver them. Opposition to GM food in Europe

Global Society 5.3 | Solar power: ecological modernization in practice?

A key plank of the ecological modernization perspective is that non-polluting technologies, such as renewable energy projects, can make a big impact on greenhouse gas emissions. Renewable technologies can also be made available to developing countries to help them avoid the high-polluting forms of industrialization which have caused so much environmental degradation.

One widely reported recent example is the massive solar power plant (actually four linked sites) being constructed in Ouarzazate, Morocco, which could supply the energy needs of 1 million people. This is crucial to the country's ambitious target of generating over 40 per cent of its electricity from renewables by 2020 – a huge change given its previously heavy reliance on imported fossil fuels such as coal and gas. The technologically innovative aspect of the plant is not just its size – the many rows of solar mirrors cover an area as large as thirty-five football pitches or the size of the capital city, Rabat – but also its attempt to store the energy generated from the sun using salt.

The plant generates heat that melts the salt, which is then able to store the heat, which generates enough steam to power turbines overnight. Morocco's hot, desert climate is a necessary environment for such a scheme. The solar mirrors are more expensive to produce than conventional photovoltaic panels, but the big advantage is that they continue generating power even after sundown. The storage system promises to hold energy for up to eight hours, meaning that a continuous solar energy supply should be possible.

When the plant is completed, the hope is that enough energy will be generated to allow Morocco to export some of it to Europe. The project is a public–private partnership and will cost around $9 billion, much of which is from the World Bank and other private and public financial institutions. But, if it fulfils its promises, the Noor Ouarzazate complex may be one of the most striking and successful practical examples of ecological modernization yet seen.

Sources: World Bank (2015); Harrabin (2015); Neslen (2015).

(discussed above) is a good example of this idea in practice. Supermarkets have not stocked or pushed the supply of GM foods, because large numbers of consumers have made it clear that they will stay on the shelves.

The theory of ecological modernization sees that five social and institutional structures need to be ecologically transformed:

1 *science and technology*: to work towards the invention and delivery of sustainable technologies
2 *markets and economic agents*: to introduce incentives for environmentally benign outcomes
3 *nation-states*: to shape market conditions which allow this to happen

Rather than abandoning the modernization process, which some radical Green activists insist is necessary for sustainability, an ecological form of modernization may be possible, based on renewable energy and environmentally benign technologies.

4 *social movements*: to put pressure on business and the state to continue moving in an ecological direction

5 *ecological ideologies*: to assist in persuading more people to get involved in the ecological modernization of society (Mol and Sonnenfeld 2000).

Science and technology have a particularly crucial role in developing preventative solutions, building in ecological considerations at the design stage. This will transform currently polluting production systems.

Since the mid-1990s, three new areas of debate have entered the ecological modernization perspective. First, research began to expand to the developing countries, significantly challenging the Eurocentrism of the original perspective. Second, once ecological modernizers started to think beyond the West, the theory of globalization became more relevant, and recent research seeks to link globalization with ecological modernization (Mol 2001). Third, ecological modernization has started to take account of the sociology of consumption and theories of consumer societies. These studies look at how consumers can play a part in the ecological modernization of society and how domestic technologies can be improved to reduce energy consumption, save scarce resources (such as water) and contribute to waste reduction through recycling.

The possibilities offered by ecological modernization can be illustrated by reference to the waste disposal industry, which gets rid of the waste products that industries and consumers generate every day. Until recently, most of this waste was simply processed and buried in landfill sites. Today, the whole industry is being transformed. Technological developments make it much cheaper to produce newsprint from recycled paper than from wood pulp. Hence there are good economic reasons, as well as environmental ones, to use and reuse paper instead of endlessly cutting down trees. Not just individual companies, but whole industries are actively pursuing the goal of 'zero waste' – the complete recycling of all waste products for future industrial use. Toyota and Honda have already reached a level of 85 per cent recyclability for the car parts they use. In this context, waste is no longer just the harmful dumping of materials but a resource for industry and, to some extent, a means of driving further innovation.

Significantly, some of the major contributions to recycling, and therefore to sustainable development, have come from areas with a heavy concentration of information technology industries, such as California's Silicon Valley. Some economic modernizers suggest that information technology, unlike many older forms of industrial production, is environmentally clean and, the more it plays a part in industrial production, the greater the likelihood that harmful environmental effects will be reduced. However, such optimism may be misguided. IT systems, the Internet and cloud computing are energy intensive, demanding huge data-storage facilities. They have been seen as a new form of 'heavy industry' rather than as part of some 'weightless economy' and, as such, do not provide a simple solution to problems of economic development (Strand 2008).

> The issue of energy-intensive information technology is discussed in chapter 6, 'Cities and Urban Life'. Cloud computing and related matters can be found in chapter 18, 'The Media'.

Unlike other perspectives, ecological modernization is concerned less with global inequality and more with how businesses, individuals and non-state actors can all play a part in transforming society. This makes it different from sustainable development, which begins from the premise that reducing global inequality is a prerequisite for environmental protection. Ecological modernizers also argue that, if the capitalist economic system can be made to work for environmental protection, capitalism will continue; but, if not, something different will necessarily emerge, because the ecological modernization of global society is already well under way.

Critics have seen ecological modernization as overly reliant on technological fixes and relatively ignorant of cultural, social and political conflicts. It is probably correct to say that ecological modernization is imbued with technological optimism rather than having a fully worked-out theory of how to get to a sustainable society. But the myriad real-world examples it produces, of practical technologies and suggestions for change, could collectively make a big difference, especially if ways can be found to make them financially viable in developing countries. However, these will also need to be introduced alongside the kind of international agreements that characterized the Kyoto Protocol, which could then ensure the spread of best practice and knowledge of what works.

Even the strongest advocates of ecological modernization accept that rescuing the global environment will require changes in the levels of inequality that currently exist. The average person in the developed world consumes natural resources at ten times the rate of the

> **THINKING CRITICALLY**
>
> Look again at the five social and institutional structures that constitute an ecologically modernist approach to environmental problems. List them in order of current progress – which structure has been transformed the most and which the least? What obstacles are harder to overcome in transforming social structures in environmentally sensitive directions?

average individual in less developed countries. Poverty is itself a prime contributor to practices that lead to environmental damage in poor countries, and people living in conditions of economic hardship have no choice but to make maximum use of the local resources available to them. What will be needed, then, are 'just sustainabilities' (Agyeman et al. 2003; Smith and Pangsapa 2008). Achieving ecological sustainability demands that concerted international efforts are made to tackle global inequalities as a necessary condition for environmental protection.

Environmental justice and ecological citizenship

If ecological modernization perhaps leans too heavily on technological fixes, one way of balancing this is by promoting the active involvement of all social groups and classes in the project of achieving sustainable societies. For example, environmental and social goals should be built into modernization projects at the outset and to involve communities in decision-making. In affordable housing projects within urban areas, it is important to avoid building on landfill sites in order not to put potentially vulnerable residents at risk from such historic hazards. Similarly, as those taking up affordable housing are likely to be those least able to afford post-build energy conservation measures (such as solar heating and insulation), the latter need to be incorporated during construction.

Environmental justice is a term that originated in the USA with the formation of grass-roots networks of activists in working-class communities (Szasz 1994; Bell 2004: ch. 1; Visgilio and Whitelaw 2003). Many of these were African-American neighbourhoods, and the selection of these areas for dumping hazardous waste and siting incinerators was seen by activists as a type of 'environmental racism' (Bullard 1993). Environmental justice campaigns can be seen as an extension of civil rights discourse into the arena of environmental issues, focusing on the way that many environmental problems 'bear down disproportionately on the poor' (Agyeman et al. 2003: 1).

One touchstone campaign was that of Lois Gibbs in Niagara Falls, New York, in 1978, in seeking to relocate the Love Canal community, which she discovered had been built on a 20,000-ton toxic chemical dump. The community campaign was ultimately successful when 900 working-class families were relocated away from the leaking dump in 1980 (Gibbs 2002). Linking environmental quality to social class inequalities shows that environmentalism is not just a middle-class concern but can be related to working-class interests and takes account of social inequalities and real-world 'risk positions'. In the USA, toxic waste sites have tended to be situated in black and Hispanic communities, where citizens' action groups are relatively less powerful, but Gibbs's campaign showed that they are not powerless.

Environmental justice groups can be very significant. Their emergence has the potential to broaden the support base of environmental politics to currently under-represented groups within the wider environmental movement. For instance, Friends of the Earth International (among others), recognizing the need to tackle social problems if pressures on the natural environment are to be relieved (Rootes 2005), has expanded its agenda. Environmental justice takes us into the urban and inner-city areas, where most of the waste products of modern life wind up, and this opens environmental politics to people who may not have thought about their problems as being at all 'environmental'.

Perhaps the most significant consequence of environmental justice groups is that they offer the possibility of linking environmental politics in the rich countries with that in the relatively poorer ones. An important example was the protest against the impact of the multinational oil company Shell on the environment of the indigenous Ogoni people in Nigeria. The campaign of the Movement for the Survival of the Ogoni People (formed in 1990) and the international support it garnered is just one example of the potentially unifying concept of environmental justice. Attempts by the Nigerian government to put down the resistance movement involved torture, ransacking of villages and, in 1995, the execution of nine members of the movement's leadership, including the writer Ken Saro-Wiwa, in the face of international protest (Watts 1997).

Such events reinforce the argument that the relatively powerless are made to bear the brunt of environmental pollution. Environmental justice campaigns demonstrate the potential to link social inequalities and poverty to environmental issues, promising to make environmentalism more than just a nature-defence movement. Recently the concept of a 'social licence' has been used to describe the dynamic relations between companies and communities (Soyka 2012: ch. 4). For instance, communities and citizens' groups may informally 'grant' an ongoing social licence to a company seeking to begin mining operations, promising new jobs and economic development. But that approval or 'licence' may be withdrawn if unnecessary environmental damage is caused, perceptions change and business operations are deemed illegitimate. Awareness of the need for a social licence to operate can empower local communities, as it has to be earned and sustained by companies if they are to benefit from citizens' approval (Syn 2014).

One final development worthy of note is the emergence of a type of citizenship linked to the defence of the natural environment. In recent years, some sociologists and political scientists have argued that a new form of citizenship is emerging, something Mark J. Smith (1998) has called ecological citizenship and Dobson and Bell (2006) refer to as environmental citizenship.

The concept of citizenship is not new and can be divided into different types. *Civil citizenship* emerged with modern property-ownership, which imposed certain mutual obligations on people to respect each other's rights to property. *Political citizenship* emerged later, during which voting rights expanded, working-class groups and women were brought into the suffrage, and rights of association (as in trade unions) and free speech developed. The third stage, *social citizenship*, saw rights to welfare and responsibilities for collective provision of social benefits. What Smith and others see is a fourth stage developing, in which ecological citizenship rights and responsibilities form the centrepiece.

>> See chapter 13, 'Poverty, Social Exclusion and Welfare', for more on citizenship.

Ecological citizenship involves new obligations: to non-human animals, to future generations of human beings and to maintaining the integrity of the natural environment (Sandilands 1999). Obligations to animals means reconsidering human uses of animals that infringe their right to lead a natural life and express their natures. Hence, vivisection, hunting, farming methods, breeding and even pet-keeping would all need to be reassessed. Ecological citizenship's obligation to future generations of people means working towards sustainability over a long time period. If economic development plans threaten the ability of future generations to provide for their own needs, then other forms will need to be designed and planned. Political and economic planning must become future-oriented and take a long-term view rather than adopting a short-term, free-market or laissez-faire approach. Finally, all human activity should be considered with reference to its effects on the natural environment, and a *precautionary principle* should be adopted that puts the onus on developers to justify their actions in ecological terms.

In essence, then, ecological citizenship introduces a new demand for people to take account of their 'ecological footprint' – the impact of human activity on the natural environment. Clearly, ecological citizenship demands some fundamental changes to modern societies. Perhaps the most radical change would be to people themselves, as ecological citizenship requires a transformed human experience of nature and the self as tightly bound together. In the same way that people had to start to perceive themselves as citizens with rights in order for political citizenship to take hold, so ecological citizenship is unlikely to develop fully unless people's identities also include the experience of having an 'ecological self'.

Conclusion

Today, unlike the classical sociologists, we see more clearly the dark side of modern industry, technology and science, and we know their applications and consequences are by no means wholly beneficial. We cannot 'unlearn' this knowledge. Scientific and technological developments have created a world that contains high-consequence risks that make possible huge gains and losses. Especially in the developed world, the population is wealthier than ever before, yet the world as a whole is riven with gross inequalities and ecological dilemmas.

What ecological modernization and sustainable development show us is that turning our backs on science and technology is not possible with a global population of over 7 billion people. Advanced technologies and scientific research will be absolutely necessary if global environmental problems are to be effectively tackled and inequalities reduced. For example, finding ways of generating energy from solar, wind and other renewable sources to replace polluting fossil fuels may be one key to a genuinely 'sustainable' and 'ecological' form of development.

The sociological imagination offers a profound awareness of the human authorship or 'social creation' of social institutions, which helps us avoid being resigned to an attitude of despair in the face of such global problems. Instead, it shows that there exists at least the possibility of exerting more control over the destiny of humanity to an extent that was simply unimaginable to previous generations. However, as the 'Giddens Paradox' and protracted international climate change negotiations show, fulfilling this promise will be neither easy nor free of conflicts.

Chapter review

1 On what basis might it be argued that 'the natural environment' must include human beings and societies?

2 With evidence from the chapter, explain what is meant by 'the social construction of environmental problems'. Why is 'agnosticism' a virtue in the study of environmental problems?

3 Explain how critical or environmental realism differs in its approach to social constructionism. Are these two really so far apart? What similarities do they exhibit?

4 Most environmental issues involve manufactured risks, as they have been generated by human activity. Give four examples of a 'manufactured risk'.

5 How can we explain the enthusiastic adoption of GM foods in North America and their rejection in Europe?

6 List the evidence in support of the anthropogenic global warming thesis and the counter-arguments of sceptics. Is it possible to arrive at a firm conclusion as to who is right?

7 'International agreement will be necessary if global warming is to be effectively tackled.' What are the main obstacles in the way of such an agreement?

8 What is the 'treadmill of production and consumption' and what are its main environmental consequences for a) developed countries and b) developing countries?

9 With examples, outline what is meant by 'sustainable development'. Why do critics see the concept as an oxymoron?

10 What are the main differences between Ulrich Beck's risk society thesis and ideas from ecological modernization? Are they essentially at odds or could they be compatible?

11 Explain what is meant by 'environmental justice' and 'ecological citizenship'. How can these concepts be linked to the international politics of climate change?

Research in practice

The modern culture of car-ownership (some say dependency) is blamed for numerous social and environmental problems. But there is still much to understand about why it is so hard for people to give up their private motor vehicles. Why are we so wedded to our individual cars? Read the article below, which provides some insights into this problem, and then answer the questions that follow: Shove, E., Watson, M., and Spurling, N. (2015) 'Conceptualizing Connections: Energy Demand, Infrastructures and Social Practices', *European Journal of Social Theory*, 18(3): 274–87.

1 What kind of study is this?

2 'Car dependence' is not based at the level of the individual. Why do the authors take this position?

3 List the four shared characteristics of infrastructures identified by the authors.

4 What role do professionals such as planners and designers play in creating car dependency?

5 Provide some examples of social practices which show how car dependence can be better understood by asking 'what driving is for'.

Thinking it through

Environmental issues are said to be 'hybrids' of nature and society, and it would seem obvious that interdisciplinary approaches, bringing together the natural and social sciences, should offer a way forward. But why have such collaborations not routinely happened? Why do the social and natural sciences tend to go their separate ways? How are their research methods different? Do the social and natural sciences enjoy a similar or different status in society at large? Write a short essay exploring these questions and conclude with your own view of whether more interdisciplinarity is likely in future studies of environmental issues.

Society in the arts

Global warming is an issue that lends itself to dramatization. However, even in fiction, it is hard to avoid taking sides between the scientific consensus and sceptics on the anthropogenic causation of climate change. Read one or both of these novels and answer the questions below.

- Michael Crichton (2005) *State of Fear* (New York: HarperCollins)
- Marcel Theroux (2009) *Far North* (London: Faber & Faber).

Which side, if any, is the story on? How does the novel make its case – primarily through characterization, story or context? How is the other side of the argument represented, if at all? Does the author make use of real-world scientific findings and/or academic work? In fictional works of this kind, would it matter if scientific findings are misrepresented in order to make for a more dramatic read? Is this kind of fiction a help or a hindrance to the wider public understanding of global warming debates?

Further reading

A good place to start is with Philip W. Sutton's (2007) *The Environment: A Sociological Introduction* (Cambridge: Polity), which is a genuinely introductory-level text. Michael M. Bell and Loka Ashwood's (2015) *An Invitation to Environmental Sociology* (5th edn, New York: Sage) is up to date and has lots of helpful examples to illustrate key environmental dilemmas.

For something more theoretical, John Hannigan's (2014) excellent *Environmental Sociology: A Social Constructionist Perspective* (3rd edn, London: Routledge) includes some very effective case studies. Peter Dickens's (2004) *Social Theory and the Environment: Changing Nature, Changing Ourselves* (Cambridge: Polity) adopts a critical realist position and explains this with great clarity. *Sociological Theory and the Environment: Classical Foundations, Contemporary Insights* (2002), edited by Riley E. Dunlap, Frederick H. Buttel, Peter Dickens and August Gijswijt (Oxford: Rowman & Littlefield), is also a fine collection.

On sustainable development, Susan Baker's (2015) *Sustainable Development* (2nd edn, London: Routledge) is a very good introduction. On the risk society, Ulrich Beck's (2009) *World at Risk* (Cambridge: Polity) is quite accessible. For ecological modernization, *The Ecological Modernisation Reader: Environmental Reform in Theory and Practice* (2009), edited by Arthur P. J. Mol, David A. Sonnenfeld and Gert Spaargaren (London: Routledge), offers exactly what it says.

For environmental justice and ecological citizenship, try Benito Cao's (2015) *Environment and Citizenship* (London: Routledge), a genuinely introductory text. Then, Mark J. Smith and Piya Pangsapa's (2008) *Environment and Citizenship: Integrating Justice, Responsibility and Civic Engagement* (London: Zed Books) is a stimulating read.

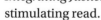

For a collection of original readings on natural and urban environments, see the accompanying *Sociology: Introductory Readings* (3rd edn, Cambridge: Polity, 2010).

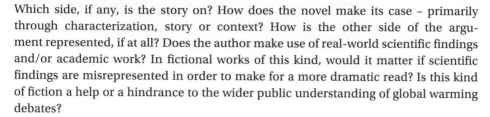

Internet links

@ **Additional information and support for this book at Polity:**
www.politybooks.com/giddens

@ **Environmental Organization Web Directory – US-based repository with lots of useful resources:**
www.webdirectory.com

@ **European Environment Agency – a good resource base with some interesting surveys and other research:**
www.eea.europa.eu

@ **Intergovernmental Panel on Climate Change – read the Fifth Assessment Report here:**
www.ipcc.ch/report/ar5

@ **Friends of the Earth International – campaigning environmental organization:**
www.foei.org

@ **Greenpeace International – campaigning environmental organization:**
www.greenpeace.org/international/en

@ **OECD – environment site with lots of data from OECD countries:**
www.oecd.org/environment

@ **United Nations Development Programme – link to Human Development Reports and the UN Millennium Goals:**
www.undp.org

CHAPTER 6

Cities and Urban Life

Contents

....

Eighteenth-century Paris was a place of extremes of wealth and poverty, but it was also seen as the epitome of modernity.

In the late eighteenth century, many who travelled to the city of Paris recorded their shock on actually encountering it. The size of the city was truly amazing, with 810 streets, 23,019 houses and a population thought to be somewhere between 500,000 and 1 million people. Some thought it a wondrous and beautiful place, while others wrote that it must be the worst kind of hell to be a poor person living there. Whatever their overall assessment, they all agreed that Paris looked and felt like a different world.

The average traveller was overwhelmed – many of them recorded these first impressions – by the din, the confusion of traffic, animals, cries, the crowds of people, the labyrinth of streets winding interminably in every direction. In provincial cities, even during Carnival, there was nothing to compare with this. (Garrioch 2004: 1)

Over the last 250 years, what Kingsley Davis (1965) called the 'urbanization of the human population' has continued apace. More than half of the world's people now live in cities and urban areas. Indeed, by twenty-first-century standards, eighteenth-century Paris was not especially large – equivalent in size to Turin, Dublin or Edmonton today, all of which have populations of around 1 million people. In stark contrast are London and New York, two of the world's 'global cities' that have been described as highly integrated 'command centres' for the world economy and whose influence extends far beyond national borders (Sassen 2001). Huge transnational corporations and a profusion of financial, technological and consulting services have their headquarters in global cities.

London has a population of over 8.5 million people, speaking more than 300 languages between them, and a resident workforce of around 4.5 million. It also has an unrivalled cultural and artistic heritage, confirming its place as a vibrant and dynamic capital where almost 30 million tourists stay for one night or more each year. London also has a large proportion of young people aged twenty to twenty-four, who move there to find work, education and culture and perhaps to escape the perceived conformity and provincialism of rural life.

New York houses Wall Street, since 1945 one of the world's primary economic centres and a major hub for international diplomacy, being home to the United Nations headquarters. It has more than 8 million inhabitants and is the most densely populated city in the USA. New York has seen the development of some major popular musical trends, such as jazz in the 1940s and punk rock in the 1970s. The Bronx area was the birthplace of rap music

and hip-hop in the 1970s and 1980s. The city is also extremely culturally diverse, with more than one-third of the population born outside the USA.

The Globalization and World Cities Research Centre (GaWC) categorizes cities according to their global connectivity, placing London and New York as unrivalled in their level of integration in the global economy. Just below these two, but still with high levels of integration and connectivity, are cities such as Hong Kong, Singapore, Shanghai, Sydney and Dubai (GaWC 2012). Shanghai, for example, has experienced the fastest economic growth of any city, averaging 12 per cent per annum since the early 1990s (apart from during the 2008–9 global recession). Around fifty-five multinationals created headquarters in the city and more than 4,000 high-rise buildings were constructed, both in the first decade of the twenty-first century, changing the look and feel of Shanghai's urban environment (Chen 2009: xv–xx). The city population had risen to 24 million by 2013 and is forecast to more than double, to around 50 million people, by 2050 (World Population Review 2015). Shanghai may be well on the way to joining London and New York as a key command centre for the global economy.

Large cities and urban areas provide unrivalled work opportunities and cultural experiences, and yet, at the same time, many people actually find them lonely and unfriendly places. Why should this be so? A distinctive characteristic of contemporary urban living is the frequency of interactions between strangers. If you live in a town or city, think about the number of times you interact everyday with people you do not know: a bus driver, shop workers, students and people with whom you exchange 'pleasantries' in the street. These fleeting, relatively impersonal interactions make contemporary city life very different from other areas today or during earlier times. Even within the same neighbourhood or block of flats, it is unlikely that people will know most of their neighbours. Marshall Berman (1983) sees this kind of urban experience as definitive of the period sociologists call 'modernity' (see chapter 1).

> Social interaction is discussed in detail in chapter 8, 'Social Interaction and Daily Life'.

In this chapter, we begin with a brief history of the development of city types from the ancient world to the industrialized cities of today. From here, we outline some key sociological theories of cities and urban culture which aim to help us understand better how people experience the modern city and what forces are shaping its future. We move on to look at differences between cities in the developed and developing countries and what an environmentally sustainable city might look like. The chapter ends with a discussion of the changing forms of city governance in the twenty-first century. It is worth noting at the outset that researchers studying cities and urban life are just as likely to be working in human geography as in sociology, and the chapter includes theories and evidence from both disciplines.

Cities – ancient and modern

Although there were great cities in the ancient world, such as Athens and Rome in Europe, city life today is very different from that experienced in previous ages. Early urban sociologists discussed the development of the modern city, which they saw was changing how humans felt and thought about the world and the ways in which they interacted. Here, we look at the development of the city, from its beginnings in the ancient world to the most recent trends in urban development.

A typical cityscape of the modern megalopolis – a desolate concrete jungle or the very pinnacle of human achievement?

Cities in the ancient world

The world's first cities appeared around 3500 BCE, in the river valleys of the Nile in Egypt, the Tigris and Euphrates in what is now Iraq, and the Indus in what is today Pakistan. Cities in ancient societies were very small by modern standards. Babylon, for example, one of the largest ancient Near Eastern cities, extended over an area of only 3.2 square miles and at its height, around 2000 BCE, probably numbered no more that 15,000 to 20,000 people. Rome under Emperor Augustus in the first century BCE was easily the largest premodern city outside China, with some 300,000 inhabitants – the size of quite a 'small' modern city today.

Most cities of the ancient world shared some common features, such as high walls that served as military defence and emphasized the separation of the urban community from those outside. The central area was usually occupied by a religious temple, a royal palace, government and commercial buildings, and a public square. This ceremonial, commercial and political centre was sometimes enclosed within a second, inner wall and was usually too small to hold more than a minority of the citizens. Although it usually contained a market, the centre was different from business districts today because the main buildings were nearly always religious and political (Sjoberg 1960, 1963; Cox 1964; Wheatley 1971).

The dwellings of the ruling elite tended to be concentrated near the centre. Less privileged groups lived towards the perimeter outside the city walls, moving inside only when the city came under attack. Different ethnic and religious communities were often allocated separate neighbourhoods, where their members both lived and worked. Sometimes these neighbourhoods were also surrounded by walls. Communications among city-dwellers were erratic. Lacking any form of printing press, public officials had to shout to deliver pronouncements, in the manner of ceremonial 'town criers' today. 'Streets' were usually strips of as yet undeveloped land. A few ancient civilizations boasted sophisticated road systems linking cities, but these were mainly for military purposes, with general transportation being slow and restricted. Merchants and soldiers were the only people who regularly travelled long distances.

While cities were the main centres for science, the arts and cosmopolitan culture, their influence over the rest of the country was always weak. No more than a tiny proportion of the population lived in them, and the division between cities and countryside was quite pronounced. By far the majority of people lived in small rural communities and rarely encountered more than the occasional state official or merchant from the towns and cities.

Industrialization and urbanization

The contrast between the largest modern cities and those of chronologically earlier civilizations is extraordinary. The most populous cities in the industrialized countries number well over 20 million inhabitants – Tokyo being the largest, with some 37 million people living in the city and its suburbs (World Atlas 2016). A conurbation – a cluster of cities and towns forming a continuous network – often includes even larger numbers. The largest form of urban life today is represented by the megalopolis, or the 'city of cities'. This term was originally coined in ancient Greece to refer to a city-state that was planned to be the envy of all civilizations, but in current usage is applied to areas such as the north-eastern seaboard of the United States, a conurbation covering some 450 miles from north of Boston to below Washington, DC, where around 40 million people live at a density of more than 700 persons per square mile.

Britain was the first society to undergo industrialization, a process that began in the mid-eighteenth century. The process of industrialization generated increasing urbanization – the movement of the population from rural areas into towns and cities. In 1800, fewer than 20 per cent of the British population lived in towns or cities of more than 10,000 inhabitants. By 1900, the proportion had risen to 74 per cent. The capital city, London, was home to about 1.1 million people in 1800; by the beginning of the twentieth century, it had a population of more than 7 million. London was then by far the largest city ever seen – a vast manufacturing, commercial and financial centre at the heart of a still expanding British Empire. The urbanization of most other European countries and the United States took place somewhat later – but, once under way, tended to accelerate faster.

Urbanization is now a global process, into which the developing countries are

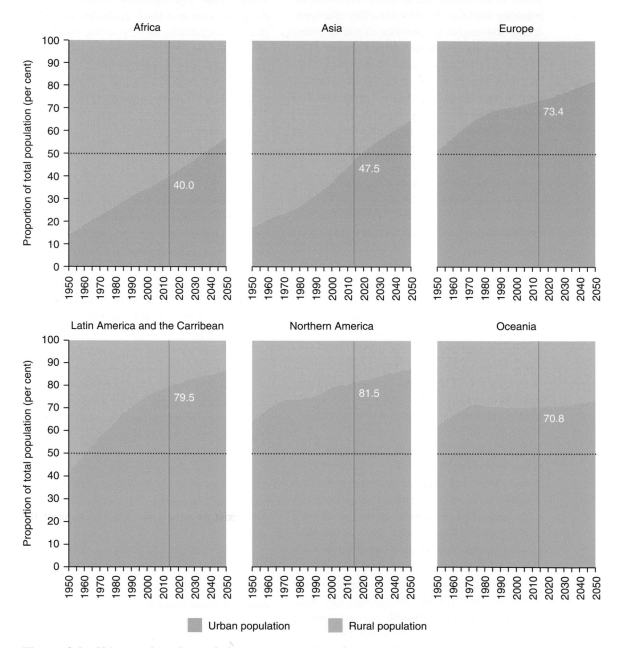

Figure 6.1 Urban and rural population as a proportion of the total, by major areas, 1950–2050 (projected)

Source: UN ESA (2014: 8).

increasingly drawn. In 1950, only 30 per cent of the world's population were urban-dwellers; by 2000, this had reached 47 per cent – 2.9 billion people – and by 2030 it is forecast to reach 60 per cent – some 5 billion people. In 2007, the number of people living in urban areas overtook the number of people in rural areas for the first time (UN 2010). Most urbanization is now taking place in the developing world. The urban population of the less developed regions is expected to rise from 2 billion in 2000 to 4 billion in 2030. As figure 6.1 shows, urbanization in Africa, Asia, Latin America and the Caribbean is rapidly increasing (a steeper line), while the rate of urban population growth within developed regions of Europe and Oceania has slowed over the same period. Nonetheless, a majority of the populations of Africa and Asia today still live in rural areas.

Development of the modern city

What is a city? No generally agreed definition exists, but most urban sociologists and human geographers would include at least the following features of modern, industrial cities: large populations, dense settlements, occupational specialization and permanent markets, and the predominance of an impersonal, rational orientation among residents (Abrahamson 2014: 5–6). In short, a specific mix of demographic, economic, social and psychological features come together in creating 'the city', though, as we shall see, the modern city has no walls, and these features spread outwards into 'suburban' and rural areas too. Indeed, in the USA, metropolitan regions often cover up to 100 miles beyond the city centre, connected by roads, rail networks and communications infrastructure. This has led some scholars to suggest that the language of the 'city' and the 'suburbs' no longer captures the everyday reality of metropolitan life (Gottdiener et al. 2015: 2). However, the world's cities and urban areas are diverse, and many regions are much smaller than in the American case.

Only at the turn of the twentieth century did statisticians and social commentators begin to distinguish between the town and the city.

Cities with large populations were usually more cosmopolitan than smaller centres, and the expansion of cities depended on migration, which was often international. The emigration of very large numbers of Europeans from poor farming backgrounds to the United States is one clear example. Peasants and villagers migrated to towns because of the lack of opportunities in rural areas and the apparent advantages and attractions of cities, such as more work, better wages and a range of goods and services. Cities were also becoming concentrated centres of financial and industrial power, and some entrepreneurs created new towns and urban areas almost from scratch.

As cities grew, many were horrified to see that inequalities and poverty also intensified. The extent of urban poverty and the vast differences between city neighbourhoods were motivating factors for early sociological analyses of urban life. The development of modern cities has had an enormous impact not only on habits and modes of behaviour but also on patterns of thought and feeling. From the time when large urban agglomerations first formed in the eighteenth century, views about the effects of cities on social life have been polarized. For many, cities represent 'civilized virtue' and are the wellspring of dynamism and cultural creativity. They maximize opportunities for economic and cultural development and provide the means for living a comfortable and satisfying existence. But, for others, the city is a smoking inferno thronged with aggressive and mutually distrustful crowds, riddled with crime, violence, corruption and poverty. It is of course, perfectly possible for both views to coexist as partial characterizations of the realities of city living.

>> See chapter 5, 'The Environment', for a discussion of environmental issues.

Global cities

The role of cities in the global order has attracted a great deal of attention from sociologists (Marcuse and van Kempen 2000;

Massey 2007). Globalization is often thought of in terms of a duality between the national level and the global, yet it is the largest cities of the world that comprise the main circuits through which globalization occurs (Sassen 1998). The functioning of the global economy is dependent on a set of central locations with developed informational infrastructures and a 'hyperconcentration' of facilities. It is in such points that the 'work' of globalization is performed and directed. As business, production, advertising and marketing assume a global scale, there is an enormous amount of organizational activity which maintains and develops these networks.

Sassen uses the concept of the global city to describe urban centres that are home to the headquarters of large, transnational corporations and a superabundance of financial, technological and consulting services. In *The Global City* (1991), she studied New York, London and Tokyo. The contemporary development of the world economy, she argued, has created a novel strategic role for such major cities which have long been centres of international trade, but now they have four new traits.

1 They have developed into 'command posts' – centres of direction and policy-making – for the global economy.
2 They are the key locations for financial and specialized service firms, which have become more important in influencing economic development than manufacturing industries.
3 They are the sites of production and innovation in the newly expanded industries.
4 They are markets in which the 'products' of financial and service industries are bought, sold or otherwise disposed of.

Since Sassen's account, New York and London have come to be seen as the preeminent command centres compared with other key cities such as Tokyo, Singapore, Beijing and Paris. Clearly, cities have very different histories, yet we can trace comparable changes in their recent development. Within the contemporary, highly dispersed world economy, cities provide for the central control of crucial operations. Global cities are much more than places of coordination and are also contexts of production. What is important is the production, not of material goods, but of specialized services required by business organizations for administering offices and factories scattered across the world and of financial innovations and markets. Services and financial goods are the 'things' made by global cities.

The downtown areas of global cities provide concentrated sites within which whole clusters of 'producers' can work in close interaction with one another, often involving personal contact. In the global city, local firms mingle with national and multinational organizations, including a multiplicity of foreign companies. Thus 350 foreign banks and 2,500 other foreign financial corporations have offices in New York City; one out of every four bank employees there works for a foreign bank. Global cities compete with one another, but they also constitute an interdependent system, relatively separate from the nations in which they are located.

Other researchers have noted that, as globalization progresses, more and more cities are joining the ranks of 'global cities'. Castells (1996: ch. 6) describes the creation of a tiered hierarchy of world cities – with places such as Hong Kong, Singapore, Chicago, Frankfurt, Los Angeles, Milan, Zurich and Osaka serving as major centres for business and financial services. Beneath these, a new set of 'regional centres' is developing as key nodes within the global economy. Another group of cities, including Madrid, São Paulo, Moscow, Seoul, Jakarta and Buenos Aires, are becoming important hubs for activity within 'emerging markets'.

Theorizing urbanism

Cities, then, are relatively large forms of human settlement within which a wide range of activities are performed, enabling them to become centres of power in relation to outlying areas

Global Society 6.1 Designing and building a global city

At the end of the 1960s the town of Dubai sat in a relatively undeveloped region of the Persian Gulf that was still a home to nomadic groups and fishing communities. In 1971 it became part of the United Arab Emirates, and a plan was devised that would utterly transform the town and region. With billions of dollars from oil export profits and Western banks, Dubai's leaders brought together architects, planners and other professionals from the developed countries with the specific intention of creating a global city based on finance, commerce and the cultural industries.

Large numbers of professionals moved to Dubai from the USA, the UK, Australia and Japan, as well as from countries across the world, and a huge building programme was set in train. This produced a typical modern city centre of office blocks and skyscrapers (including the world's tallest, Burj Khalifa) and a 1,000 berth marina, one of the largest in the world. First-class leisure and tourist attractions were added to the mix, among them an indoor snow park (not easy in a hot desert climate!), palm-shaped islands, shopping centres, golf courses, entertainment complexes and a zoo.

There is little doubt that the plan was successful in its own terms. However, an important consequence of the way it was devised and implemented is that, despite the region being ostensibly Muslim, culturally, the Western influence on Dubai is particularly strong. English is the second language and is commonly spoken, supermarkets stock products familiar to expatriate communities, and many other aspects of daily life are

Dubai's Palm Island illustrates the city's plan to become a major global tourist destination.

recognizably Western. Abrahamson (2014: 205) notes that 'Dubai's financial analysts, corporate managers, engineers, and architects live in a variety of familiar-to-Westerners types of housing in gated communities (with names such as Emirates Hills) and suburban-style developments, villas, and apartments . . . Their leisure time is spent in malls and on beaches and golf courses. The rhythm of life is that of the generic global city.'

> **THINKING CRITICALLY**
>
> Look back to chapter 4, 'Globalization and Social Change', and its discussion of glocalization. Do your own research and find out more about life in Dubai. Does this city illustrate the powerful process of globalization or is it best characterized as glocalization in practice? Provide some examples to support your conclusion.

and smaller settlements. This fits London, New York and Shanghai pretty well, though it is less applicable to smaller cities which lack the power resources of larger centres. If urbanization refers to the process which brings large cities into being, then urbanism refers to the lifestyles and personality types that characterizes modern cities.

It is important to note that the contrast between urban and rural areas is neither clearcut nor fixed, as the human settlement process is dynamic and characterized by constant movements of people. Some scholars see cities as 'spatially open' to such movement, making the city as 'a thing' something of an anachronism (Amin and Thrift 2002). Indeed, long before current theories of 'mobilities' (Urry 2007), Buckminster Fuller (1978) thought that 'unsettlement' would be a more accurate description of the mobile character of modern life.

> The concept of mobilities is discussed in chapter 16, 'Race, Ethnicity and Migration'.

Community and the urban personality

We will encounter differing ways of defining and thinking about cities in this chapter, but a useful way of evaluating urban theories is to assess the way they handle the 'four C's of urban experience': culture (the built environment, belief systems, cultural production),

consumption (of public and private goods and services), conflict (over resources and development plans) and community (the social life and make-up of populations) (Parker 2003: 4–5). As we will see, most urban theories focus on one of these aspects in order to throw light on the others, and, though our discussion is not framed by the four C's, readers should consider which theories deal most satisfactorily with these aspects.

The German sociologist Ferdinand Tönnies (1855–1936) was particularly concerned with the effects of urbanization on social bonds and community solidarity. Tönnies charted, with some regret, the gradual loss of what he called *Gemeinschaft* – community bonds – which he characterized as traditional close-knit ties, personal and often lifelong relationships between neighbours and friends, and a sense of duty and commitment (Tönnies 2001 [1887]).

Gesellschaft, or 'associational' bonds, were rapidly impinging on community relations. *Gesellschaft* bonds were impersonal, relatively short-lived, transitory and instrumental in character. And while all societies contain social bonds of both types, with industrialization and urbanization the balance was shifting decisively away from *Gemeinschaft*. In this society, relationships tend to be specific to a particular setting and purpose and take into account only a part of the whole person. When we are travelling by bus into work, our interaction with the driver is limited to a brief impersonal exchange at the door as we pay, and our use for him will be limited to his ability to get

Classic Studies 6.1 The metropolis and mental life

The research problem

Many people in the nineteenth century saw that urbanization fundamentally changed societies, but what effects would this have on individuals? Would it alter their attitudes and behaviour? And what exactly is it about city living that produces such changes? One of Tönnies's German contemporaries, Georg Simmel (1858–1918), provided a theoretical account of how the city shapes its inhabitants' 'mental life'. Simmel's 'The Metropolis and Mental Life' (1950 [1903]), Tönnies remarked, had managed to capture 'the flavour of the metropolis'.

Simmel's explanation

Simmel's study would today be described as a piece of interpretative sociology that seeks to understand and convey something about how people *experience* the city. City life, says Simmel, bombards the mind with images and impressions, sensations and activity. This is 'a deep contrast with the slower, more habitual, more smoothly flowing rhythm' of the small town or village. But it is just not possible to respond to all of these stimuli, so how do people deal with the sensual bombardment?

Simmel argues that people protect themselves from the city's assault on their senses by becoming quite blasé and disinterested, adopting a 'seen-it-all-before' attitude. They 'tune out' much of the urban buzz that surrounds them, becoming highly selective and focusing on whatever they need to do. The result of this blasé attitude is that, although all city-dwellers are part of the 'metropolitan crush', they distance themselves from one another emotionally as well as physically. Typically, the myriad fleeting contacts with others result in an 'urban reserve' in interactions, which can be perceived as emotionless and rather cold, leading to widespread feelings of impersonality and even isolation. But Simmel points out that city people are not *by nature* uncaring or indifferent to others. Rather, they are forced to adopt such modes of behaviour in order to preserve their individual selves in the face of pressures from the densely populated urban environment.

Simmel notes that the sheer pace of urban life partly explains the typical urban personality. But he also says that the city is 'the seat of the money economy'. Many cities – such as London, Hong Kong and Seoul – are large, capitalistic financial centres that demand punctuality, rational exchange and an instrumental approach to business. This encourages relentless matter-of-fact dealings between people and offers little room for emotional connection, resulting in 'calculating minds' capable of weighing the benefits and costs of involvement in relationships. Like the work of Tönnies, Simmel's study points to some of the emerging problems of life in the modern, urbanized world.

Critical points

Critics of Simmel's study have raised a number of objections. His arguments seem to be based on personal observation and insights rather than on any formal or replicable research method, and thus his findings can be seen as somewhat speculative. Also, despite Simmel's insistence that he set out merely to understand urban life and not to damn it, the overall tone of the study has been seen as negative, revealing a normative bias against the capitalist city. It is true that his work focuses on ways in which individuals can resist being 'levelled down and worn out by a socio-technological mechanism'. In this sense, critics say, Simmel plays down the liberating experience of many people who move to cities to experience its greater freedoms and room for individual expression.

Finally, the study may be guilty of overgeneralizing from a specific type of large city to all cities. After all, only a minority of cities are financial centres, and those that are not may well be less alienating and isolating than Simmel allows for. Can we really say that *all* urbanites have the same experience?

Contemporary significance

Simmel's account of life in the modern metropolis provides a sociological explanation of some key characteristics of contemporary urbanism. His theoretical study shows how the quality of social interactions is shaped by pressures arising from the wider social environment. An important consequence of this is his view that the city 'is not a spatial entity with social consequences, but a sociological entity that is formed spatially'. This has proved a very productive starting point for later urban studies.

Simmel's influence can also be felt in modern social theory. He argued that 'The deepest problems of modern life derive from the claim of the individual to preserve the autonomy and individuality of his existence in the face of overwhelming social forces' (Simmel 1950 [1903]: 409). There is more than an echo of this perspective in the more recent work of Ulrich Beck, Zygmunt Bauman and other contemporary theorists of modern individualism.

> **THINKING CRITICALLY**
>
> List the freedoms, opportunities and experiences that city inhabitants enjoy which are not available to those living in small towns and villages. Which aspects of Simmel's analysis do you recognize as still relevant for understanding today's cities and urban regions?

us to our destination. This kind of instrumental exchange between strangers has become more commonplace and now passes without comment as 'normal'. Indeed, even Tönnies recognized that, in spite of his concerns, rapid urbanization was leading inexorably to the dominance of *Gesellschaft* bonds.

The early theorists of the city had a deep and enduring influence on urban sociology. Robert Park, for example, a key member of the Chicago School of Sociology, studied under Simmel in Germany at the turn of the twentieth century, and it is to this school that we now turn.

The Chicago School

A number of sociologists associated with the University of Chicago from the 1920s to the 1940s, including Robert Park, Ernest Burgess and Louis Wirth, developed ideas that were for many years the basis of theory and research in urban sociology. Two concepts developed by the Chicago School are worthy of special attention. One is the 'ecological approach' in urban analysis; the other is the characterization of urbanism as 'a way of life', developed by Wirth (Wirth 1938; Park 1952).

Urban ecology

Ecology is a physical science which studies the adaptation of plant and animal organisms to their environment, and it is this sense of ecology that is used in the context of environmental issues and problems (see chapter 5, 'The Environment'). In the natural world, organisms tend to be distributed in systematic ways so that, over time, a balance or equilibrium between different species is achieved. The Chicago School of Sociology argued that the siting of major urban settlements and the distribution of different types of neighbourhood and social groups within them could be understood in terms of similar principles. Cities do not grow up at random but develop in response to advantageous features of the environment. For example, large urban areas in modern societies have developed along the shores of rivers, on fertile plains or at the intersection of trading routes or railways.

However, cities are also internally divided. 'Once set up', in Park's words, 'a city is, it seems, a great sorting mechanism which . . . infallibly selects out of the population as a whole the individuals best suited to live in a particular region or a particular milieu' (1952: 79). Thus, through processes of competition, invasion and succession – all concepts taken from biological ecology – cities become ordered into different zones or areas. Different neighbourhoods develop through the adjustments made by inhabitants as they struggle to gain their livelihoods. A city can be pictured as a map of areas with distinct and contrasting social characteristics.

In the initial stages of growth, industries congregate at sites suitable for the raw materials they need and close to supply lines. Populations cluster around these, amenities follow, and land values and property taxes rise, making it difficult for families to carry on living in the central neighbourhood, except in cramped conditions or decaying housing where rents are still low. The centre becomes dominated by businesses and entertainment, with the more affluent residents moving out to newly forming suburbs.

Cities tend to form in concentric rings, broken up into segments. In the centre are the inner-city areas, a mixture of big business prosperity and decaying private houses. Beyond these are longer-established neighbourhoods, housing workers employed in stable manual occupations. Further out still are the suburbs in which higher-income groups tend to live. Processes of 'invasion' and 'succession' occur within the segments of the concentric rings. Thus, as property decays in a central area, the pre-existing population moves out, precipitating a wholesale flight to neighbourhoods elsewhere in the city or out to the suburbs.

The urban ecology approach was extended in the work of a series of later researchers. Rather than concentrating on competition for scarce resources, Hawley (1950, 1968) emphasized the *interdependence* of different city areas. *Differentiation* – the specialization of groups and occupational roles – is the main way in which human beings adapt to their environment. Groups on which many others depend will take dominant roles, often reflected in their central geographical position. Business groups, for example, such as large banks or insurance companies, provide key services for many community members and are usually to be found in the central areas. But the zones

The Lozells area of Birmingham in the UK saw an eruption of violence in 2005 between the ethnic communities who make up the majority of its population. Was this the result of ethnic groups leading lives in increasingly segregated communities?

which develop in urban areas, Hawley points out, arise from relationships both of space and of time. Business dominance, for example, is expressed not only in patterns of land-use but also in the rhythm of activities in daily life, such as the 'rush hour'. The ordering in time of people's daily lives reflects the hierarchy of neighbourhoods in the city.

The ecological approach has been as important for the empirical research it promoted as for its theoretical perspective. However, legitimate criticisms can be made of it. Its biological analogy has been seen as intimating an unfounded link between human and animal societies. The ecological perspective also underemphasizes the importance of conscious design and planning in city organization, regarding urban development as a more 'natural' process. Also, the models of spatial organization developed by Park, Burgess and their colleagues were drawn from their American experience and cannot readily be generalized beyond this. Many European cities, as well as those in developing countries and elsewhere, just do not conform to the urban ecology model.

Classic Studies 6.2 Urbanism as a way of life

The research problem

We know from Simmel that the urban environment tends to create particular personality types and that there is a broad pattern to the development of cities. But how do cities relate to and interact with the rest of society? Does urbanism exert any influence outside city boundaries? Louis Wirth (1897–1952) explored the idea that urbanism was, in fact, a whole way of life, not an experience limited to the city.

Wirth's explanation

While other members of the Chicago School focused on understanding the shape of the city – how it came to be internally divided – Wirth was concerned more with urbanism as a distinct way of life. Urbanism, he argued, could not be reduced to or understood simply by measuring the size of urban populations. Instead, it has to be grasped as a form of social existence. Wirth (1938: 342) observed that:

> The influences which cities exert on the social life of man are greater than the ratio of the urban population would indicate; for the city is not only increasingly the dwelling-place and the workshop of modern man, but it is the initiating and controlling centre of economic, political and cultural life that has drawn the most remote communities of the world into its orbit and woven diverse areas, peoples and activities into a cosmos.

In cities, large numbers of people live in close proximity, without knowing one another personally. This is in fundamental contrast to the situation in small villages and towns. Many contacts between city-dwellers are, as Tönnies suggested, fleeting and partial; they are means to other ends rather than being satisfying relationships in themselves. Wirth calls these 'secondary contacts', compared to the 'primary contacts' of familial and strong community relationships. For example, interactions with salespeople in shops, cashiers in banks or ticket collectors on trains are passing encounters, entered into not for their own sake, as in communal relations, but merely as means to other ends.

Since those who live in urban areas tend to be highly mobile, moving around to find work and to enjoy leisure and travel, the bonds between them are relatively weak. People are involved in many different activities and situations each day, and the 'pace of life' in cities is much faster than in rural areas. Competition prevails over cooperation and social relationships appear flimsy and brittle. Of course, the Chicago School's ecological approach found that the density of social life in cities leads to the formation of neighbourhoods with distinct characteristics, some of which may preserve the characteristics of small communities. In immigrant areas, for example, traditional connections between families are found, with most people knowing most others on a personal basis. Similarly, Young and Willmott's (1957) *Family and Kinship in East London* found strong connections among working-class families in the city.

However, although Wirth accepted this, he argued that, the more these areas became absorbed into the wider patterns of city life, the less would community characteristics survive. The urban way of life weakens bonds of kinship and erodes families and communities and older bases of social solidarity are rendered ineffective. Wirth was not blind to the benefits of urbanism. He saw that modern cities were centres of freedom, toleration and progress, but he also argued that urbanism spread beyond city boundaries, as is shown by the process of suburbanization, with all of its necessary transport systems and infrastructure. In that sense, modern societies themselves are necessarily shaped by the forces of urbanism.

Critical points

Critics have pointed out the limitations of Wirth's ideas. Like the ecological perspective, Wirth's thesis is rooted in the experience of American cities and should not be seen as a general theory of city life. Urbanism is not the same at all times and in all places. Ancient cities were quite different from modern ones, and cities in developing countries today are quite different from those in the developed ones.

Wirth has also been criticized for exaggerating the extent of impersonality in modern cities. Communities involving close friendship or kinship links are more persistent than he thought. Hughes (cited in Kasarda and Janowitz 1974: 338) notes that 'Louis used to say all those things about how the city is impersonal – while living with a whole clan of kin and friends on a very personal basis.' Similarly, Herbert Gans (1962) argued that 'urban villagers' – such as Italian-Americans living in inner-city Boston – were quite commonly found in even the largest cities. Wirth's picture of modern cities needs to be expanded by acknowledging that city life can lead to the *building* of communities rather than *always* destroying them.

Contemporary significance

Wirth's ideas have deservedly enjoyed wide currency. The impersonality of many day-to-day contacts in modern cities is undeniable, and to some degree this is true of contemporary social life more generally. His theory is also important for its recognition that urbanism is not just one part of society but actually expresses and influences the character of the wider social system. Given the expanding process of urbanization in many developing countries and the fact that a majority of people in the developed world already live in urban areas, Wirth's ideas will continue to be a reference point for sociologists looking to understand urbanism as a way of life.

Fischer (1984) argued that urbanism promotes diverse subcultures rather than submerging everyone within an anonymous mass. Those who live in cities are able to collaborate with others of similar backgrounds or interests to develop local connections and can voluntarily join distinctive religious, ethnic, political and other subcultural groups. A small town or village does not allow for the development of such cultural diversity.

A large city may well be a 'world of strangers', but it also helps to create new personal relationships. This is not paradoxical. We must separate the public sphere of encounters with strangers from the more private world of family, friends and work colleagues. It may be difficult to 'meet people' when first moving to a large city. But people settling in a small, established rural community may find the friendliness of the inhabitants to be a matter of public politeness while it may take years to become properly 'accepted'. This is not so in the city. As Krupat (1985: 36) notes:

the overwhelming evidence is that because of the diversity of strangers – each one is a potential friend – and the wide range of lifestyles and interests in the city, people do move from the outside in. And once they are on the inside of one group or network, the possibilities for expanding their connections multiply greatly. As a result, the evidence indicates that the positive opportunities in the city often seem to outweigh the constraining forces, allowing people to develop and maintain satisfying relationships.

Modern cities do frequently involve impersonal, anonymous social relationships, but they are also sources of diversity and voluntary friendships.

City spaces, surveillance and urban inequality

More recent theories have stressed that urban development is not an autonomous or wholly endogenous process but one that has to be analysed in relation to major patterns of political and economic change. Two leading scholars of urban analysis, David Harvey (1982, 1985, 2006) and Manuel Castells (1983, 1991, 1997), are both influenced by the ideas of Karl Marx. Harvey argues that urbanism is one aspect of the created environment brought about by the spread of industrial capitalism. In older societies, city and countryside were clearly differentiated, but, in the modern world, industrial development blurs the distinction between city and countryside. Farming and agricultural production become mechanized and run according to considerations of price and profit, which reduces the differences between urban and rural life.

Modern urbanism, Harvey points out, continually *restructures* space. The process is determined by where large firms choose to place their factories, research and development centres, and so on, as well as by the controls asserted by governments over land use and industrial production and the activities of private investors, buying and selling property and land. Business firms constantly weigh the relative advantages of new locations against existing ones, and, as production becomes cheaper in one area than another or as firms move from one product to another, offices and factories will be closed down in one place and opened up elsewhere. Thus, when there are considerable profits to be made, there may be a spate of office blocks built in the centre of large cities but, once the central area is 'redeveloped', investors look for speculative building elsewhere. Hence, what is profitable in one period will not necessarily be so in another, depending on shifts in the prevailing financial climate.

Similarly, the decisions of private home-buyers are strongly influenced by how far, and where, business interests buy land, as well as by interest rates and taxes set by local and central government. After the Second World War, for instance, there was a vast expansion of suburban development in major cities in the USA, partly the result of ethnic discrimination and the decisions of white Americans to move away from inner-city areas. However, this was made possible, Harvey argues, only because of government decisions to give tax concessions to home-buyers and construction firms and the setting up of special credit arrangements by financial organizations. These provided the basis for the building and buying of new homes on city peripheries and at the same time promoted demand for industrial products such as the motor car.

Harvey (2006) has also applied his theory of uneven spatial development to global inequalities between the relatively rich countries of the northern hemisphere and the relatively poor developing countries in the South. The turn towards neo-liberal political ideas, especially in the USA and the UK from the 1970s and 1980s, has laid bare the myth that developing countries just need to 'catch up with the West'. As capitalist profits were invested in city-centre housing, office blocks and other urban projects in developed countries such as Britain and Spain, the property-driven boom also led to rapid urbanization in China, Mexico and elsewhere.

Ciudad Nezahualcóyotl is a municipality in the Mexico City Metropolitan Area. The land was sold to private owners in the twentieth century and a sprawling conurbation was built with inadequate public services. It has now become a notorious slum, while in 2009 Mexico City itself was named the eighth richest city in the world.

Yet the overall result has been not a 'catching-up' by developing countries but the restoration of power to class elites, leaving immense wealth in the hands of relatively few people. Harvey (2008: 32) notes that 'Fourteen billionaires have emerged in Mexico since then [the 1980s], and in 2006 that country boasted the richest man on earth, Carlos Slim, at the same time as the incomes of the poor had either stagnated or diminished.' The result is increasingly divided cities with heightened surveillance, gated communities to protect the wealthy and the privatization of public spaces.

Of course, many cities in the developed world are also divided into rich and poor areas, with intensified surveillance systems and wealthy, gated communities. And, while there are some clear differences between cities in the developed and developing countries, there is increasing convergence in the use of surveillance to identify and remove threats to security (such as drugs, criminals and terrorists) that lie hidden within the urban environment. For example, many cities in both the northern and the southern hemisphere make use of computerized CCTV systems, identity checkpoints and biometric surveillance to defend financial districts, shopping arcades, airports and gated communities (see Mike Davis's ideas in 'Using your sociological imagination 6.1').

One reason why cities everywhere are becoming places of heightened surveillance is suggested by Stephen Graham (2011), who argues that techniques and technologies

6.1 Social inequalities in 'cities of quartz'

Within global cities, a geography of 'centrality and marginality' is taking shape. Alongside very visible affluence, there is also acute poverty. Yet though these two worlds exist side by side, the contact between them can be surprisingly minimal. As Davis (1990, 2006) noted in his studies of Los Angeles, there has been a 'conscious hardening' of the city's surface against the poor – hence the metaphor of rock-hard 'quartz'. Accessible public spaces have been replaced by walled compounds, neighbourhoods are guarded by electronic surveillance, rich residents hire private police to keep street gangs at bay, and 'corporate citadels' have been created. In Davis's words (1990: 232):

> To reduce contact with untouchables, urban redevelopment has converted once vital pedestrian streets into traffic sewers and transformed public parks into temporary receptacles for the homeless and wretched. The American city . . . is being systematically turned inside out – or, rather, outside in. The valorized spaces of the new megastructures and super-malls are concentrated in the center, street frontage is denuded, public activity is sorted into strictly functional compartments, and circulation is internalized in corridors under the gaze of private police.

According to Davis, life is made as 'unliveable' as possible for the poorest and most marginalized residents of Los Angeles. Benches at bus stops are barrel-shaped to prevent people from sleeping on them, the number of public toilets is fewer than in any other North American city, and sprinkler systems have been installed in parks to deter the homeless from living there. Police and city planners have attempted to contain the homeless population within certain regions of the city, but, in periodically sweeping through and confiscating makeshift shelters, they have effectively created a population of 'urban bedouins'.

Abrahamson (2014: 116) notes that around 100,000 people in Los Angeles county sleep rough in doorways, sidewalks or shelters every night, many of them in outlying suburbs rather than in the city centre, where they are not welcome. He argues that, as the police continually move them on or arrest them for loitering, begging and other minor misdemeanours, homelessness in the city of Los Angeles has effectively been criminalized.

See chapter 20, 'Crime and Deviance', for a discussion of situational crime prevention and other recent crime-prevention techniques.

THINKING CRITICALLY

Which aspects of Davis's description are familiar from cities that you know? If poor people are excluded from large parts of cities, where are they likely to live in the future? What could governments do to tackle these forms of urban social exclusion?

which were designed for war zones have crossed over into civilian applications in urban environments. Twenty-first-century terrorist attacks in New York, London, Madrid, Mumbai, Brussels and Paris suggest that urban environments have become key sites for groups waging war against states by targeting urban populations. In response, governments have adopted military-style surveillance techniques of monitoring and targeting suspected terrorists and other threats to urban security, including extensive use of satellite communications, offender risk profiling and the monitoring of postal systems, Internet use, financial transactions and transportation systems (Mills and Huber 2002). Similarly, the language of a 'war against drugs', the 'war against crime' or the 'war against terror' shows that military metaphors have become an accepted part of public policy debates.

 Terrorism is discussed in chapter 22, 'Nations, War and Terrorism'.

Graham argues that, collectively, these developments constitute a 'new military urbanism' – a type of urbanism that diverges from earlier forms. Cities are being steadily transformed from places of creativity, free movement and cosmopolitan diversity into highly securitized zones:

> The new military urbanism feeds on experiments with styles of targeting, and technology in colonial war-zones, such as Gaza or Baghdad, or security operations at international sports events or political summits. These operations act as testing grounds for technology and techniques to be sold on through the world's burgeoning homeland security markets. (2011: xvi)

In this environment, non-violent demonstrations, urban social movements and the dissenting voices of the past find their activities continuously monitored or curtailed in the interests of maintaining order and security.

The operation of the global economy also generates new dynamics of inequality that are clearly visible within the city. The juxtaposition of a central business district and impoverished inner-city areas is interrelated. The 'growth sectors' of the new economy – financial services, marketing, high technology – reap greater profits than any found in traditional economic sectors. As the salaries and bonuses of the very affluent continue to climb, the wages of those employed to clean and guard their offices are falling. This process echoes the analysis of David Harvey, who argues that the city is not just a place or location for social relations but is itself the *product* of struggles and conflicts among social groups. Sassen (2001) contends that we are witnessing the 'valorization' of work located at the forefront of the global economy and

the 'devalorization' of work which takes place behind the scenes.

Deprivation and social exclusion are discussed in chapter 13, 'Poverty, Social Exclusion and Welfare', and inequalities in chapter 14, 'Global Inequality'.

Disparities in profit-making capabilities are expected in market economies, but their magnitude has many negative effects on the social world, from housing to the labour market. Those who work in finance and global services receive high salaries, and the areas where they live become gentrified. At the same time, manufacturing jobs are lost and the process of gentrification creates a huge supply of low-wage, insecure employment – in restaurants, shops, hotels and boutiques. Affordable housing is scarce in gentrified areas and, while central business districts receive massive influxes of investment in property, development and telecommunications, the marginalized areas are left with few resources.

Social movements and collective consumption

Like Harvey, Manuel Castells stresses that the spatial form of society is closely linked to the overall mechanisms of its development. To understand cities, we have to grasp the processes whereby spatial forms are created and transformed. The layout and architectural features of cities and neighbourhoods express struggles and conflicts between different groups in society. In other words, urban environments represent symbolic and spatial manifestations of broader social forces (Tonkiss 2006). For example, skyscrapers may be built because they are expected to provide profit, but the giant buildings also 'symbolise the power of money over the city through technology and self-confidence and are the cathedrals of the period of rising corporate capitalism' (Castells 1983: 103).

In contrast to the Chicago sociologists, Castells sees the city not only as a distinct location – the urban area – but also as an integral part of processes of collective consumption, which in turn form an inherent aspect of industrial capitalism. Schools, transport services and leisure amenities are ways in which people collectively 'consume' the products of modern industry. The taxation system influences who is able to buy or rent where, and who builds where. Large corporations, banks and insurance companies, which provide capital for building projects, have a great deal of power over these processes. But government agencies also directly affect many aspects of city life by building roads and public housing, planning green belts on which new development cannot encroach, and so on. The physical shape of cities is thus a product of both market forces and the power of government.

The character of the created environment is not just the result of the activities of wealthy and powerful people. Castells stresses the importance of the struggles of less privileged groups to alter their own living conditions. Urban problems stimulate a range of social movements – concerned with improving housing conditions, protesting against air pollution, defending parks and green belts, and combating building development that changes the nature of an area. Castells studied the gay rights movement in San Francisco, which succeeded in restructuring neighbourhoods around its own cultural values – allowing many gay organizations, clubs and bars to flourish – and gaining a prominent position in local politics.

Castells (1991) maintains not only that cities have been shaped by the restructuring of capitalism since the 1970s but that a new 'informational mode of development' has emerged, based on the introduction of new technology and its uneven distribution across societies. What information technology offers is more flexibility for organizations to achieve their goals, as it enables them to be partially freed from specific places and territories. The combination of the informational mode of development and capitalist restructuring allows corporations to sidestep some of the established, place-based control mechanisms.

Global flows of information, capital and marketing messages can bypass the regulatory systems of territorial city and local governments and nation-states. Castells (1991: 349) puts this succinctly: 'People live in places, power rules through flows.' However, he argues that networks of local governments and organized citizens' groups should look to form their own strategic alliances with the aim of avoiding the kind of 'tribal' divisions which allow the powerful to 'divide and rule'. Only by acting collectively can citizens hope to exert an influence over the future shape of the urban landscape.

Evaluation

The work of Harvey and Castells has been widely debated and has been important in redirecting urban analysis. In contrast to the urban ecology approach, it highlights not the 'natural' or internal spatial processes within cities but how the created environment reflects social and economic systems of power. This marks a significant shift of emphasis. In some ways, the theories of Harvey and Castells and those of the Chicago School usefully complement each other and may be combined to give a more comprehensive picture of urban processes such as regeneration.

Regeneration of the physical environment tends to move according to discontinuous investment cycles rather than being a continuous process. For example, between 1980 and 2000, urban development witnessed a boom, followed by a slump and then another round of significant investment (Fainstein 2001). In the early 1980s, many large cities experienced a development boom promoted by investment from private property developers, public officials and financial institutions, though these were not identical in character. For example, although in both the UK and the USA the strategy was for some form of public–private partnership, in London redevelopment was essentially state-led, while in New York it was private-sector involvement that led the process.

However, economic recession in the early 1990s brought the boom to an end, with some major projects failing. London's Canary Wharf development was bankrupt by 1993, while New York's Time Square project had stalled a year later. But, by the end of the decade, booming real-estate markets in the developed world stimulated a new cycle of building investment (Fainstein 2001). Urban space, land and buildings are bought and sold, just like other goods, and the city is shaped by the way that various groups want to use the property they buy and sell. However, as Fainstein shows, urban development is enabled or constrained by global economic forces too. For instance, wealthy parts of London, such as Knightsbridge and Belgravia, have seen the growth of 'buy to leave' as international investors buy mainly new-build properties, with the intention of leaving them empty, to be sold on later at a profit. Low interest rates and a booming housing market have created new opportunites for this kind of property speculation, which some see as creating 'ghost towns of the super-rich' (Norwood 2016).

Many tensions and conflicts arise in different localities as a result of regeneration planning, and these are key factors which structure neighbourhoods. For instance, large financial and business firms continually try to intensify land use in specific areas. The more they can do so, the more there are opportunities for land speculation and the profitable construction of new buildings, but there is little concern with the social and physical effects of their activities, which may mean attractive older residences being destroyed to make room for large office blocks.

Development processes fostered by large property development companies are often challenged by local businesses or residents. People come together in neighbourhood groups in order to defend their interests by campaigning for the extension of zoning restrictions or seeking to defend green spaces. The uncertain outcome of these conflicts shows that the urban ecology approach, rooted in struggles over scarce resources and processes of invasion and succession, still has a role to play in understanding urban restructuring.

Urban trends and the sustainable city

Before modern times, cities were self-contained entities that stood apart from the predominantly rural areas in which they were located. Travel was a specialized affair for merchants, soldiers and others who needed to cross distances with any regularity, but communication between cities was limited. The twenty-first-century picture could hardly be more different. Globalization has had a profound effect, making cities more interdependent and encouraging the proliferation of horizontal links between them across national borders.

Some people predict that globalization and new communications technology might lead to the demise of cities as we know them. This is because many older functions of cities can now be carried out in cyberspace rather than in dense and congested urban areas. Financial markets are electronic, e-commerce reduces the need for producers and consumers to rely on city centres, and 'e-commuting' permits a growing number of employees to work from home rather than in city offices. Yet, thus far, rather than undermining cities, globalization is transforming them into vital hubs within the global economy. Urban centres have become crucial in coordinating information flows, managing business activities and innovating new services and technologies.

Urban trends in the developed world

Cities and urban areas today are in some ways very different environments from those of the early twentieth century, and we now turn to some of the more significant processes of change. In this section, we consider some of the main patterns in Western urban development in the postwar era, using Britain and the United States as examples. Attention will focus on the rise of suburban areas, the decline of inner-city areas, and strategies aimed at urban renewal.

Suburbanization

In the USA, the process of suburbanization – the growth of areas on the edge of cities – reached its peak in the 1950s and 1960s, when city centres had a 10 per cent growth rate and that of the suburban areas was 48 per cent. Most of the early movement to the suburbs involved white families. The enforcement of racial mixing in schools can be seen as a major factor in the decision of many whites to move out of inner-city areas. Relocating to the suburbs was an attractive option for families who wished to put their children in all-white schools. Even today, many American suburbs remain dominated by white families.

However, the white domination of suburbia in the USA is being eroded as more members of minority ethnic groups move there. Data from the 2000 US Census showed that minority ethnic groups made up 27 per cent of suburban populations, up from 19 per cent in 1990. Like the people who began the exodus to suburbia in the 1950s, members of minority ethnic groups who move to the suburbs are mostly middle-class professionals in search of better housing, schools and amenities. The chairman of the Chicago Housing Authority argued that movement into the suburbs in the 1990s was, in fact, more about escaping from poor areas with a range of social problems, from poor schools to street crime, than because of racial prejudice (De Witt 1994).

In the UK, many of the suburbs around London grew up between the two world wars and were clustered around new roads and links by underground trains that brought commuters into the centre. Some converts to city life looked with disdain on the large expanses of suburbia, with their semi-detached villas and well-tended gardens blanketing the fringes of English cities. Others, such as the poet John Betjeman (1906–84), celebrated the modest eccentricity of the architecture of the suburbs and their possibilities for combining the employment opportunities of the city with another mode of life connected by owner-occupation, car-ownership and conventional family life.

In Britain, the migration of the residential population from central city areas to outlying suburbs and dormitory towns (towns outside the city boundaries occupied by people who work in the city) in the 1970s and early 1980s saw the population of Greater London drop by about half a million. In the industrial towns of the North, the rapid loss of manufacturing industry during this period also reduced the population of inner-city areas. At the same time, many smaller cities and towns grew quickly, including Cambridge, Ipswich, Norwich, Oxford and Leicester. The 'flight to the suburbs' has had dramatic implications for the health and vitality of both British and American urban centres, though this population decline has been reversed over recent years, and many large city populations have been growing again, partly because of inward migration.

Inner-city decay

Inner-city decay has marked all large cities since the 1980s as a direct consequence of the growth of the suburbs. The movement of high-income groups away from city centres meant a loss of local tax revenues. Since those that remain or replace them include many poorer social groups, there is little scope for covering the lost income. This situation is worsened by the fact that the building stock in city centres becomes run-down and crime rates and unemployment rise. More must therefore be spent on welfare services, schools, the upkeep of buildings, and police and fire services. A cycle of deterioration develops in which the more suburbia expands, the greater become the problems of city centres.

One reason for the decay in Britain's inner cities is the financial crises that affected many of these areas. From the late 1970s onwards, central government put pressure on local authorities to limit their budgets and cut local services, even in those areas most subject to decay. This led to intense conflict between government and many of the councils that ran distressed inner-city areas when they could not meet their set budgets. A number of city councils had less revenue and were compelled

6.2 'Engendering' the city

Writing from a feminist perspective, several authors have examined how the city reflects the unequal gender relations in society and have looked at ways to overcome this. Jo Beall (1998) noted that, if social relations – in this case between men and women – are underpinned by power, cities demonstrate the correlation between power and space in terms of what gets built, where it is built, how it is built and for whom. Beall writes: 'Cities are literally concrete manifestations of ideas on how society was, is and how it should be.'

The growth of the city in the nineteenth century is associated with gender separation. Public life and space was dominated by men, who were free to travel through the city as they wanted. Women were not expected to be seen in most public places; those who did venture into such areas were likely to be regarded as prostitutes or 'street walkers'. As the process of suburbanization began, the gender separation grew even more obvious. While the male head of the family commuted into the city on a daily basis, the women (wives) were expected to remain at home to care for the family. Transport links were built for travel between the suburbs and the city centre, but little thought was given by male designers to transportation within the suburbs, as a result of which it was more difficult for women to leave home (Greed 1994).

Elizabeth Wilson (2002) has argued that the development of the city was not all bad for women. She suggests that some feminist arguments reduce the role of women in the city to that of passive victims. But, in fact, the development of the city offered opportunities that previous forms of life could not provide. With the emergence of female white-collar work in the city and, later, the expansion of service industries, women increasingly entered the workforce and earned their own incomes. Thus the city offered women an escape from unpaid labour at home and new opportunities that did not exist elsewhere.

THINKING CRITICALLY

Is Wilson right – have cities become much more 'female-friendly' over time? Look for examples – such as 'mother and child' car-parking spaces – which might provide evidence of this. What do you conclude about how far gender relations and roles have changed?

to cut back on what were regarded as essential services. Since the credit crisis of 2008 and its aftermath, councils have again found themselves struggling to maintain key services, and the situation seems unlikely to change in the near future.

As the financial crisis of 2008 demonstrates, inner-city decay is related to changes in the global economy. Newly industrialized countries such as Singapore, Taiwan or Mexico often provide much cheaper labour costs than places such as the UK, thus making them attractive locations for manufacturing. In response, some industrialized nations such as Japan and (West) Germany shifted their economies to the kinds of activity that require a high level of capital investment and a highly skilled, well-educated workforce.

In an important UK study, *Inside the Inner City*, Paul Harrison (1983) examined the impact of global changes on Hackney, one of London's poorest boroughs. The number of manufacturing jobs there dropped from 45,500 in 1973 to 27,400 in 1981 – a fall of 40 per cent. Until the mid-1970s, Hackney's male unemployment rate was roughly level with the national average, but by 1981 it had risen to 17.1 per cent (50 per cent above the average). As the number of people out of work increased, so too did the number living in poverty. Harrison (1983: 23–4) summarizes the effects of such a concentration of disadvantaged people:

Local government poor in resources and sometimes in the quality of staffing; a poor health service, since doctors cannot find a decent accommodation or much in the way of private practice; a low level of educational attainment due primarily to poor home backgrounds and the low average ability in schools; and, finally, high levels of crime, vandalism and family breakdown, and, wherever communities of divergent cultures live together, conflicts based on religion or race.

Sometimes these multiple disadvantages overlap to such an extent that they burst forth in the form of urban conflict and unrest. In an era of globalization, population movements and rapid change, large cities have become concentrated and intensified expressions of social problems in society as a whole. Simmering tensions rise to the surface, sometimes violently in the form of riots, looting and destruction of property.

For example, in 2005, around 5,000 people in Sydney, Australia, took part in disturbances, known as the Cronulla Riots, following reports of intimidatory behaviour by 'outsiders', said to be Middle Eastern youths, and the involvement of right-wing groups within the crowds of protesters. Ethnic tensions fuelled by decaying infrastructure and housing led to unrest in French cities in late 2005, and in Britain neighbourhood disturbances occurred in Brixton, South London, in 1981, 1985 and 1995; in Ely, Cardiff, in 1991; in Oldham, Burnley, and Lidget Green, Bradford, in 2001; and in Birmingham in 2005.

Following the unrest in Bradford in 2001, the British government commissioned a report, which found a deep polarization between ethnic communities. It also argued that many aspects of people's everyday lives compounded this, including separate educational arrangements, voluntary bodies, employment patterns, places of worship and language (Cantle 2001). What this report and others show is that many 'riots', which are commonly seen as random acts of violence and destruction, arise from serious underlying social and economic problems that just need the trigger of a local event to spark protests. Attempts to tackle these underlying causes have become part of urban renewal programmes.

Global economic restructuring led to the deterioration of many inner-city areas in the 1970s and 1980s. The 2008 financial crisis and rapid growth of online shopping have contributed further to the economic decay of such areas, with boarded-up shops again becoming a common sight.

In August 2011, London was again the scene of major unrest which spread to other major English cities. A peaceful protest concerning the fatal shooting of a local man by police was the prelude to later attacks on the police, arson, and looting of shops, which continued over five consecutive nights and involved between 13,000 and 15,000 people. Five people died during the riots, more than 4,000 were arrested around the country, and some 1,700 were charged with criminal offences. Just over half of those appearing in court were between ten and twenty years old.

A government-commissioned report, *5 days in August* (Riots Panel 2011), interviewed residents and victims of the rioting and analysed the available data. It found that, although the fatal shooting in Tottenham was the trigger, no single cause explained the rioting. However, it did point to a strong link between social deprivation and the riots. For example, some 70 per cent of people arrested and brought before the courts lived in the most deprived areas of the country, and residents reported a widespread feeling that some young people 'had no hope and nothing to lose'. In some areas, relations between police and the public were very poor, and many complaints were noted about the 'inappropriate conduct' of police 'stop and search' procedures, particularly from black and Asian men (ibid.: 12; Lewis and Newburn 2012). Concern about the collapse of morals and values was also reported, with many interviewees citing the size of bankers' bonuses, the scandal over MPs' expenses, consumerism and a lack of personal responsibility as underlying causes of the riots.

Clearly, in spite of the many urban regeneration projects undertaken since the early 1980s, the multiple social problems of several deprived inner-city areas continue to blight the lives of many citizens and remain a serious problem for governments and policy-makers.

> See chapter 16, 'Race, Ethnicity and Migration', for a more detailed discussion of multiculturalism and ethnic relations. Problems arising from inner-city decay are also covered in chapter 12, 'Stratification and Social Class', and chapter 13, 'Poverty, Social Exclusion and Welfare'.

Urban renewal

What kind of approach should local, regional and national governments take in addressing the complex problems of inner cities? How can the rapid expansion of outlying suburban areas be checked to prevent the erosion of green areas and countryside? A successful urban renewal policy is particularly challenging because it demands simultaneous action on multiple fronts.

In many developed countries, a range of national schemes have been introduced to try to revive the fortunes of the inner cities. In 1988, the UK Conservative government's 'Action for Cities' programme encouraged private investment and free-market forces to generate urban renewal. However, the response from business was weaker than anticipated, and, because of the seeming intractability of inner-city problems, the tendency has frequently been for programmes to be dropped when quick results do not materialize. Research studies have found that providing incentives for private enterprise to drive urban renewal is largely ineffective. So many oppressive circumstances come together in the inner city that reversing processes of decay is exceedingly difficult and takes long periods of sustained effort. *The Scarman Report* (Scarman 1982) into the 1981 riots in Brixton, London, noted the lack of a coordinated approach to inner-city problems, and without major public expenditure the prospects for radical improvement are slender (MacGregor and Pimlott 1991).

The 1997 Labour government launched two main regeneration funds: the New Deal for Communities and the Neighbourhood Renewal Fund. There was also finance from the National Lottery funding action zones in health, employment and education and Housing Corporation money for new social housing. The New Deal for Communities (NDC) was Labour's flagship regeneration scheme for England. It was launched in 1998 and completed in 2010 after involving thirty-nine deprived neighbourhoods with around 9,900 people each and 6,900 projects. The whole scheme spent £1.71 billion of public money and £730 million from public, private and voluntary-sector sources, making it 'one of the most intensive and innovative area-based initiatives (ABIs) ever introduced in England' (Batty et al. 2010: 5). The ten-year goal was to close the gap between these areas and the rest of the country by focusing on three *place-related* outcomes – crime, community and housing – along with three *people-related* ones – education, health and worklessness. But did it succeed?

The final evaluation report suggests that, in some areas, it did. Residents reported they felt more positive about their neighbourhoods and were generally satisfied that the NDC partnerships had improved their areas. There were also improvements on a majority of indicators, including low-level crime, urban dereliction, the condition of housing and mental health. However, the report notes little change in levels of worklessness, educational attainment, fear of becoming a victim of crime, or feeling that people could influence decision-making processes.

The programme sought to put in place post-NDC funding to continue the improvements. However, the 2008 financial crisis, ensuing economic recession, and government public spending cuts called this into question. The report's authors noted that 'It is not the best of times to be thinking of sustaining "post regeneration programme" activity' (Batty et al. 2010: 34). In many other cities, residential and retail projects were severely affected by the global 'credit crunch' of 2008, as major financial institutions tightened their lending criteria and withdrew funding. Restrictions on bank lending, alongside government austerity measures, led to a loss of confidence and many stalled developments.

Clearly, questions remain about the effectiveness of regeneration schemes. How can top-down government programmes gain the backing and involvement of local people that is usually crucial to their success? Can public money really stimulate local economies and create jobs, and how can regeneration schemes prevent displacing problems from one area to another (Weaver 2001)? The experience of NDCs in England shows that, after ten years of activity and investment, the relevant neighbourhoods remained 'deprived areas', and solving the multiple problems of such urban regions will take much longer.

Gentrification and 'urban recycling'

Urban recycling – the refurbishing or replacement of old buildings and new uses for previously developed land – has become common in large cities. Occasionally this has been attempted as part of planning programmes, but more often it is the result of gentrification – the transformation of a working-class or vacant area of the central city into residential and/or commercial use by the middle classes (Lees et al. 2008: xv).

In the USA, Elijah Anderson (1990) analysed the impact of gentrification in his book *Streetwise: Race, Class, and Change in an*

Gentrification can lead to economic revitalization, but it can just as effectively result in segregation and the exclusion of poorer residents.

Urban Community. While the renovation of a neighbourhood generally increases its value, it rarely improves the living standards of its current low-income residents, who are usually forced to move out. In the Philadelphia neighbourhood that Anderson studied, many black residences were condemned, forcing more than 1,000 people to leave. Although they were told that their property would be used to build low-cost housing and that they would be given the first opportunity to buy, instead large businesses and a high school now stand there.

The poor residents who stayed received some benefits in the form of improved schools and police protection, but the resulting increase in taxes and rents finally forced them to leave for more affordable neighbourhoods, often in areas of greater social exclusion. Black residents interviewed by Anderson expressed resentment at the influx of 'yuppies', whom they held responsible for the changes that drove poorer people out. The white newcomers had arrived in the city in search of cheap 'antique' housing, closer access to their city-based jobs, and a trendy urban lifestyle. They professed to be 'open-minded' about racial and ethnic differences, but in reality little fraternizing took place between the new and old residents unless they were of the same social class. While some middle-class blacks lived in the area, most who could afford to do so left for the suburbs, fearing that they would otherwise receive from whites the same treatment that was reserved for the black underclass. Over time, the neighbourhood was gradually transformed into a white middle-class enclave.

One reason behind gentrification is demographic. Young professional people are choosing to marry and start families later in life, and as a result more housing is needed for individuals and couples rather than for families. Because young people are having families later and their careers often demand long hours in inner-city office buildings, life in suburbia is more of an inconvenience than an asset (Urban Task Force 1999). Affluent couples are able to afford expensive housing in refurbished inner-city areas and may prefer to build lifestyles around the high-quality cultural,

culinary and entertainment options available. Older couples whose children have left home may be tempted back into inner-city areas for similar reasons.

In London, Docklands was seen as a notable example of 'urban recycling'. The Docklands area in East London occupies 8.5 square miles of territory adjoining the Thames that lost its economic function when docks closed and industries declined. It is close to the financial district of the City of London but also adjoins poor, working-class areas. Many living in or close to Docklands favoured redevelopment by means of community projects that would protect the interests of poorer residents. But, with the setting up of the Docklands Development Corporation in 1981, the region became a central part of the Conservative government's strategy of encouraging private enterprise to drive 'regeneration'. This terminology is instructive. Several researchers point out that numerous governments avoid using 'gentrification' for such projects. For example, in the USA in the 1970s, the term 'homesteading' was adopted, while in the UK and elsewhere, 'renaissance', 'revitalization' or 'renewal' have been preferred, to 'disguise' the negative connotations associated with gentrification (Lees et al. 2008: xxi).

An empirical study of gentrification in London, based on some 450 interviews with residents, including the Docklands area, found that inner London has become a 'middle-class city', even though the middle classes remain in a minority (Butler with Robson 2003). The relaxation of planning constraints and regulations has led to Docklands being covered in modern buildings, often adventurous in design. Warehouses have been converted into luxury flats, and new blocks have been constructed alongside them. Yet amid all the glitter there are still dilapidated buildings and empty stretches of wasteland. This research discovered that the middle-class residents of Docklands were certainly 'in the city' but were never 'of the city'. That is, in Docklands and the other London boroughs in the study, gentrified areas were not integrated into the wider, urban social context. And, in spite of the many differences between the UK and the USA, this finding suggests that gentrification processes may be leading to some broadly similar social consequences.

For example, although London as a whole is one of the most multi-ethnic cities in the world, in its gentrified zones the middle classes 'huddle together into essentially white settlements in the inner city. Their children, for the most part, like their parents, have friends just like themselves. Not a great surprise but perhaps a worrying sign for the future' (Butler with Robson 2003: 2). Little wonder, then, that people living in some of the poorest housing stock in the UK feel they have not benefited from all the physical reconstruction that has gone on around them in recent decades.

It seems that modern cities are far from the 'humane city' described by Richard Sennett (1993). He argues that large, impersonal buildings in cities turn people inwards, away from one another. But cities can also turn people outwards, bringing them into contact with a variety of cultures. For example, many older Italian city centres mix diversity with an elegance of design. Cities, Sennett says, do not have to be soulless and impersonal.

Urbanization in the developing world

The world's urban population is forecast to reach almost 5 billion people by 2030, and the United Nations estimates that almost 4 billion of these will be residents of cities in the developing world. The number of cities of all types continues to grow, but the number of people living in the very largest cities has tripled since 1990 and constitutes around 12 per cent of the global urban population. As Figure 6.2 shows, the UN forecasts that this pattern will continue into the future. Most megacities are in the developing countries of the global South. China currently has six megacities and Latin America, four. India will have seven megacities by 2030 and Africa is forecast to have six, including Cairo, Kinshasa, Dar es Salaam and Luanda.

Castells (1996) refers to megacities as one of the main features of third millennium urbanization. These are defined not by their size alone but also by their role as connection points between enormous human populations and the global economy. Megacities are intensely concentrated pockets of activity through which politics, media, communications, finances and production flow. According to Castells, they function as magnets for the countries or regions in which they are located. Besides serving as nodes in the global economy, megacities become 'depositories of all these segments of the population who fight to survive' (ibid.: 434). For example, Mumbai in India is a burgeoning employment and financial centre and home to the extraordinarily popular Bollywood film industry. It is a thriving and expanding city with exactly the kind of magnetic attraction that Castells talks of (see 'Global society 6.2').

One of the largest urban settlements in history is currently being formed in Asia, in an area of 50,000 square kilometres reaching from Hong Kong to mainland China, the Pearl River Delta and Macao. Although the region has no formal name or administrative structure, by 1995 it had already encompassed a population of 50 million people. According to Castells, it is poised to become one of the most significant industrial, business and cultural centres of the century.

Castells points to several interrelated factors that explain the emergence of this enormous conurbation. First, China is undergoing an economic transformation and Hong Kong is one of the most important 'nodal points' linking China into the global economy. Second, between the mid-1980s and mid-1990s, industrialists initiated a dramatic process of industrialization within the Pearl River Delta, and by the mid-1990s more than 6 million people were employed in 20,000 factories and 10,000 firms. Finally, Hong Kong's role as a global business and financial centre has grown and its economic base is shifting away from manufacturing towards services. The result has been an 'unprecedented urban explosion' (Castells 1996).

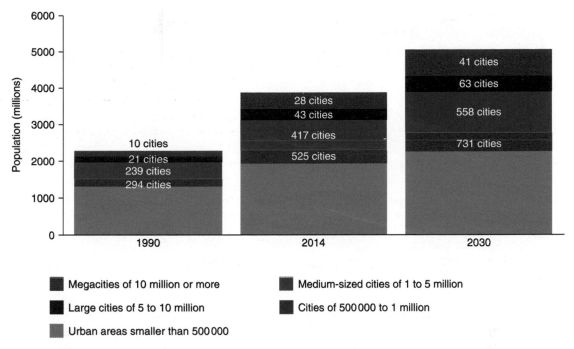

Figure 6.2 Global urban population by city size, 1990, 2014 and 2030 (projected)

Source: UN ESA (2014): 13.

Global Society 6.2 **Mumbai – a megacity in the developing world**

India gained independence from British colonial rule in 1947, at a time when the country was relatively poor and underdeveloped. Since independence, the country has changed quite dramatically and nowhere is this change seen more than in Mumbai, a megacity of some 12 million people in an urban area with more than 21 million inhabitants. Like other cities across the world, Mumbai is a place of stark contrasts between rich and poor. The discussion below is adapted from a 2007 BBC News article written for the sixtieth anniversary of independence.

Not enough

In Mumbai, India's financial capital, symbols of India's economic success are all around – from flashy billboards advertising the latest perfumes to trendy young women dressed in the latest Tommy jeans. The India of today is vibrant, confident and ambitious – and not afraid to show it.

Take Rishi Rajani for example. The 30-something garment tycoon based in Mumbai and Denmark is a self-confessed workaholic who also loves the good life. His latest acquisition is a black Porsche sports car, which he drives through the streets of Mumbai. In the money capital of India, flaunting your wealth is now fashionable. Mr Rajani has always dreamed of owning the mean machine, and now his dream is a reality thanks to the success of the economy and his business.

'I work hard, you know, for my money', he says. 'And I need a reward. This is my reward. But it's not enough. My next goal? A yacht. That's when I'll know I've really made it. I'm already working towards it.'

Fast city

This is the stuff dreams are made of. Fast life, fast city – money in Mumbai cannot be spent or made quickly enough. And it is this dream that leads millions of migrants to the city every single

Extremes of wealth and poverty exist side by side in many cities of the developing world.

day. They come here in packs, having heard legendary tales of Mumbai's streets being paved with gold. Travelling thousands of miles by train, they leave behind their families, their friends and their desperate lives. Many end up in one of the city's numerous slums and struggling to survive by doing odd jobs on the street. The city they came to conquer, ends up engulfing them.

Demolition job

Saunji Kesarwadi is a potter by profession who lives in a 10 × 10 foot flat in Dharavi, Asia's biggest slum. In this box, he works and supports a family of six who live in the attic. Barely eking out an existence, he fears being thrown out of his home to make way for development.

'We hear the builders are coming', Mr Kesarwadi says as his two little girls look on. 'But no one has told us anything. They say they'll give us a flat if we sell them this land – but how can all of us leave? This is where my

work, my life is. It may not be much but it's all I have.' But while life in the big city often falls short of expectations, thanks to the growth in the country's economy there are new opportunities in some villages.

Rural choice

Some 300 kilometres away from India's technology capital, Bangalore, lies Bellary – an industrial town born out of a sleepy village. When you first arrive, all you can see is dusty farmland for miles around. But behind the quiet exterior, there is a dramatic change afoot.

Bellary is home to one of India's first rural outsourcing centres, run by Indian steel maker JSW Steel Limited. The organisation has started two small operations on its Bellary campus, hiring young women from nearby villages to work in their rural processing centres. Here the girls spend their shifts punching in details of American patients' dental records, typing in a language many of them have only recently learned, using a machine many had never seen or heard of before.

Twenty-year-old Savithri Amma has a basic high school diploma. She earns about $80 (£40) a month doing this work – the same as one of her peers might earn working as a house-help in Mumbai. For that money she has to turn up to work every weekday by 7 a.m. – picked up from her village by a JSW bus at 5 a.m. and taken home when her shift ends at 3 p.m. 'At first, when I started this job, my parents were sceptical', she says shyly. 'Girls here used never to go out – but now we can because our position in life has improved financially and socially thanks to our work here. My father makes a little more than I do every month. I'm proud to contribute to the family finances.'

Growth promise

In Ms Amma's village, she is looked upon as a role model for many of her peers. The daily evening prayers at the village temple are a time for her to reflect on her day's work, and give thanks to the ancient Hindu gods for her good fortune. She has much to be thankful for. Ms Amma is one of the lucky ones, she is someone who did not have to leave home to battle the millions in urban India to survive. Growth in India's economy has to make its way off the streets of Mumbai and Delhi and into all of India's villages. Only when it does will it truly be here to stay – and the promise of independence will be met.

Source: Vaswani (2007).

THINKING CRITICALLY
Are there similarities between Mumbai and, say, Los Angeles, London, Tokyo or New York? What are the main differences? Will India's position within the global capitalist economy prevent Mumbai from 'closing the wealth gap'?

Why is the rate of urban growth in the world's lesser-developed regions so much higher than elsewhere? Rates of population growth are higher in developing countries, and urban growth is fuelled by high fertility rates among people already living in cities. Second, there is widespread internal migration from rural areas into urban ones, as in the case of the developing Hong Kong–Guangdong megacity. People are drawn to cities in the developing world either because their systems of rural production have disintegrated or because urban areas offer better job opportunities. Rural poverty prompts many to try city life, and, though they may intend to migrate only for a relatively short time, most find themselves forced to stay, having lost their position in the previous communities.

See chapter 5, 'The Environment', for a discussion of the ecological consequences of population growth.

Challenges of urbanization in the developing world

As a growing number of unskilled and agricultural workers migrate to urban centres, the formal economy struggles to absorb the influx into the workforce. In most cities in the developing world, it is the informal economy which enables those who cannot find formal work to survive. From casual work in manufacturing and construction to small-scale trading activities, the unregulated informal sector offers opportunities to poor or unskilled workers. However, the informal economy is also untaxed, unregulated and less productive than the formal economy, and many developing countries lose much-needed tax revenues.

The OECD (Organization for Economic Cooperation and Development) estimates that a billion new jobs will be needed by 2025 to sustain the expected population growth in cities in the developing world. It is unlikely that all of these jobs will be created within the formal economy, and some development analysts argue that attention should be paid to formalizing or regulating the large informal economy, where much of the 'excess' workforce is likely to cluster in the future.

The rapidly expanding urban areas of developing countries also differ dramatically from cities in the developed world. Although cities everywhere face environmental problems, those in developing countries are confronted by particularly severe risks. Pollution, housing shortages, inadequate sanitation and unsafe water supplies are chronic problems. Cities such as Kolkata and São Paulo are highly congested, and the rate of internal migration is too high for the provision of permanent housing. Migrants crowd into shanty dwellings in squatters' zones, which mushroom around the edges of cities. This congestion and over-development in city centres leads to serious environmental problems such as the loss of 'green spaces' and pollution from vehicles and industrial areas.

In many urban areas of the developing world, poverty is very widespread and existing social services cannot meet the demands for healthcare, family planning advice, education and training. The larger proportion of young people in developing countries in comparison with the industrialized countries also creates social problems. A youthful population needs support and education, but many developing countries lack the resources to provide universal education. When their families are poor, many children must work full time and others have to scratch a living as street children, begging for whatever they can. When street children mature, most become unemployed, homeless or both, again highlighting the different kinds of economic difficulties that urbanization creates for developing countries.

In considering the scope of the challenges facing urban areas in developing countries, it can be difficult to see prospects for change and development. Conditions of life in many of the world's largest cities seem likely to decline even further in the years to come. But the picture is not entirely negative. Although birth rates remain high in many countries, they are likely to fall in the future as urbanization

proceeds. This in turn will feed into a gradual decrease in the rate of urbanization itself.

> Population growth is discussed in chapter 4, 'Globalization and Social Change', chapter 14, 'Global Inequality', and chapter 5, 'The Environment'.

Globalization is presenting important opportunities for urban areas in developing countries. With economic integration, cities around the world are able to enter international markets, to promote themselves as locations for investment and development, and to create economic links across the borders of nation-states. Globalization presents one of the most dynamic openings for growing urban centres to become major forces in economic development and innovation. Indeed, as we have seen, many cities in the developing world are already joining the ranks of the world's 'global cities'.

Urban infrastructure and the sustainable city

In the twenty-first century, urban studies have seen a growing 'infrastructural turn', in which numerous studies have drawn attention to the enormously complex, varied and extensive infrastructural networks on which cities depend for the supply of services such as water and energy, transportation and urban waste management and disposal. This shift of focus connects the material reality of the city with social relations through the varied ways in which urban residents actually experience the urban environment. There are large differences across types of city, especially between the industrial cities of the developed world and cities in most developing countries.

In many developing countries, where the urban infrastructure can be unreliable at best, the vulnerability of all those invisible networks of pipes, cables, generating plants and workers to disruption are in the foreground of city life. However, in the industrialized countries, precisely because these systems tend to be hidden and more reliable, people normally live without giving much thought to what enables them to enjoy the modern city. As Graham (2010: 2) argues,

> the very nature of urbanization means that every aspect of people's lives tends to become more dependent on the infrastructural circuits of the city to sustain individual and collective health, security, economic opportunity, social well-being, and biological life. Moreover, because they rely on the continuous agency of infrastructure to eat, wash, heat, cook, light, work, travel, communicate, and remove dangerous or poisonous wastes from their living place, urbanites often have few or no real alternatives when the complex infrastructures that sometimes manage to achieve this are removed or disrupted.

Disasters such as earthquakes and floods, or more prosaic disruptions such as the clogging of sewage pipes by an excess of fat from restaurants and households or urgent transport repairs, serve to bring the urban infrastructure out of its normal invisibility.

Many urban sociologists connect studies of the construction and maintenance of the urban material infrastructure to social and political inequalities (Graham and McFarlane 2015). For example, some social groups are excluded from certain infrastructural features, while others enjoy privileged access. In 2009, many informal settlements in Mumbai saw intensified police raids aimed at destroying their water connections after a disappointing monsoon season, thus protecting water supplies for middle-class communities in the wealthier parts of the city (Graham et al. 2015). Hence, the form of urban infrastructure is not a simple, neutral matter of administration and city planning but is always bound up with political struggles and social inequalities that often lead to the kinds of urban social movements identified by Harvey and Castells.

While sociologists have done much to identify the dynamics of urban development and the social problems associated with cities, until recently they were not particularly interested in the impact of cities on the natural environment. Yet, for many within the environmental movement, cities demonstrate in an acute way exactly what is wrong with modern societies. Edward Goldsmith (1988) argued that industrialization has given rise to a 'surrogate world' (Harvey's 'created environment') of material goods, buildings and technological devices which can only be built from 'the real world' of the global biosphere. Resources extracted from the natural world are transformed into roads, housing and commodities, but, in the process, topsoils are covered in asphalt, forests are destroyed to make room for factories and housing estates, and the generation and disposal of waste pollutes the environment.

Even the apparently benign technology of the Internet turns out to be completely dependent on polluting energy industries. The global expansion of the Internet makes the worldwide web an increasingly heavy user of electricity. To function at all, the Internet depends on fossil fuel extraction, refinement, transportation and use just as much as any other technological device. Internet users typing into Google to search the web are probably aware of neither the vast 'server farms' the company has built to handle their requests nor the energy demands these make. Some estimates suggest that Google alone owns up to 1 million servers, while its Dalles plant in Oregon, USA, may demand some 103 megawatts of electricity – similar to the power demand of 82,000 homes (Strand 2008). Strand concludes that, in fact, 'The Internet is a new heavy industry, an energy glutton that is only becoming hungrier.'

For many environmentalists, the modern city is akin to a huge beast, devouring energy, water and oxygen while giving out large quantities of noxious gases, sewage and other pollutants that have to go somewhere, usually into landfill, the atmosphere or waterways and oceans. The American ecologist Eugene Odum (1989: 17) described the city as 'a parasite . . . since it makes no food, cleans no air, and cleans very little water to a point where it could be reused.' This may have been tolerable with very few 'beasts' or 'parasites', but continued urbanization means there are now hundreds of cities, many more than the planet can cope with over the long term. Goldsmith's solution is a simple one: deindustrialization and the decentralization of cities. But, given the sheer size of the global human population, is this a realistic prospect?

It seems unlikely, for several reasons. First, large-scale movement of people into the countryside would probably mean more environmental damage, not less, as human populations and their attendant pollution spread into new areas, swallowing up more land in the process (Lewis 1994). Second, the infrastructure of cities may actually be less damaging to the natural environment than small communities in rural areas. For example, public transport in cities tends to be less polluting per head of population than individual car use in rural areas. A denser city population actually makes public transport more efficient and less polluting (Banister 1992). In this sense, environmental sustainability and enhanced city resilience to potential crises, such as energy disruption or natural disasters, may be seen as complementary (Pearson et al. 2014). The more compact character of cities also enables more widespread use of environmentally benign transport forms such as bicycles – and even plain old walking. Conversely, many rural dwellers insist their private cars are real necessities. Finally, the myriad collective housing projects and high-rise developments of modern cities are more capable of accommodating the large human population than housing types typical of the suburbs.

Towards the sustainable city

Rather than giving up on cities altogether, as some radical environmentalists have argued, there is a growing interest in modifying and transforming them into eco-cities, 'smart cities', or simply sustainable cities. A sustainable city is one that aims to minimize its inputs of energy and resources and to reduce its outputs of pollutants and waste products. The concept offers the enticing prospect of maintaining the freedoms, opportunities and

cultural diversity of city living while protecting the natural world from increasing damage, and thus contributing to the wider project of sustainable development (Haughton and Hunter 2003; Jenks and Jones 2009).

 See chapter 5, 'The Environment', for more on sustainable development.

Urban sustainability requires changing from *linear* to *circular* flows of materials and goods. Simple examples are recycling waste, rather than dumping it into landfill or incinerating it, and recycling domestic 'grey' (used) water by using it to flush toilets or water garden plants. In this way a circular process is created which becomes less ecologically damaging and more sustainable (Mega 2010). This logic can be embedded within businesses and local authorities, which can use eco-audits to build in eco-efficiency and design to all their activities.

Micro power generation at household and community levels, using renewable technologies such as solar cells and wind turbines, reduces CO_2 emissions and airborne pollutants, while shifting public and private transport towards electric hybrids or biofuels improves the quality of the urban environment. Intensifying the use of 'brownfield' (previously used) land to preserve the surrounding countryside, redesigning city space to create a pedestrian-friendly infrastructure, and introducing more bikeways and 'light' transit routes to encourage alternatives to the private car are all elements of the sustainable city project (Jenks and Jones 2009: 3).

Sustainable urban development also demands active, environmentally knowledgeable and committed citizens who are prepared to change their routine, habitual everyday actions to improve the quality of city life. Advocates of sustainability argue that decentralizing decision-making to the local level is a crucial way of increasing citizen participation and involvement in the project of reducing the city's ecological footprint.

However, cities across the world are not uniform but very diverse in scale, population

Global Society 6.3 Designing a sustainable city

China is experiencing rapid and large-scale urbanization – and the resulting local and global urban environmental challenges are unprecedented. . . . At the local level, many urban areas are creating 'eco-city' developments, which aim to introduce new standards, technologies, and low-carbon lifestyles. More than one hundred eco-city initiatives have been launched in recent years in China.

The new World Bank Report, called *Sino-Singapore Tianjin Eco-City: A Case Study of an Emerging Eco-City in China*, reviews one such initiative. 'Addressing the environmental sustainability of cities is a critical development challenge facing China right now – not only locally but also in terms of Chinese cities' global carbon footprint. Given the recent prominence of various "eco-city" initiatives, we wanted to analyse one such case in greater detail to extract some practical lessons learned which may be relevant for others,' says Axel Baeumler, World Bank's Senior Infrastructure Economist and leader of the study.

The Sino-Singapore Tianjin Eco-City envisages an 'economically sustainable, socially harmonious, environmentally friendly and resource-conserving' city which will become a 'model eco and low carbon city replicable by other cities in China'. The Tianjin Eco-City is a new development area being designed for 350,000 residents on the perimeter of the Binhai New Area. The 'Sino-Singapore' part of the name refers to the project's design and financing partners.

One notable feature of the Tianjin Eco-City is that it sets explicit sustainability targets by 2020, including (i) limiting carbon emissions per unit of GDP; (ii) ensuring that all buildings are Green Buildings; (iii) having a share of Green Trips (i.e., walking, cycling, or the use of public transport) that exceeds 90 per cent; and (iv) receiving at least 50 percent of its water

from non-conventional sources. If achieved, these ambitious targets would indeed point to greater environmental sustainability. However, the report finds that many implementation challenges need to be addressed in such projects, including:

- ensuring that land use plans and corresponding detailed urban designs are conducive to supporting Green Trips;
- incentivizing green building construction at efficiency standards that are higher than those prevailing at the provincial or national level;
- complementing technological solutions with adequate economic incentives to direct new urban development towards sustainability; and
- ensuring that these new urban developments will remain affordable and socially inclusive.

Funding for the study was provided by the Australian Agency for International Development (AusAID). This report complements the recently approved Sino-Singapore Tianjin Eco-City Project supported by a grant from the Global Environmental Facility (GEF). The World Bank has been a partner in China's urban development since 1985. It has provided over $9.8 billion for more than 86 investment projects in many cities and conducted research on many aspects of the urbanization process.

Source: World Bank 2011b.

THINKING CRITICALLY

In 2010, China overtook the USA as the world's largest energy consumer. It also has sixteen of the world's twenty most polluted cities. Which elements of the Tianjin project could be rolled out across other cities? Why would critics have described China's eco-city experiments as 'ideological'?

size, the state of their industrial development and, therefore, in the types of challenges they face moving towards sustainability. In the developed world, the main problems are consumption-oriented ones such as how to deal with waste and issues of traffic congestion and pollution, but, in many former communist countries of Eastern Europe, pollution from industrial production remains the most pressing problem at hand. China has some of the most polluted cities in the world, while most developing countries have cross-cutting problems of industrial pollution, poorly maintained basic infrastructure, increasing traffic problems and a lack of service provision (Haughton and Hunter 2003: 7–8). Sustainable initiatives need to be sensitive to this diversity and uneven development.

Like the concept of sustainable development itself, ideas of sustainable cities are ambitious, even utopian. Yet it is possible to envisage the *process of change* itself as an 'active utopia' (Bauman 1976), motivating people to become involved even though there may be no real endpoint to the process. And, though there are serious obstacles to be overcome, cities and urban areas and therefore the experience of modernity itself, may well look and feel very different in the future.

Governing the city

Although globalization aggravates the challenges facing cities around the world, it also makes room for cities and local governments to play a revitalized political role. Cities have become more important as nation-states are increasingly unable to manage global trends. Ecological risks and volatile financial markets operate at levels above that of the nation-state, and individual countries – even the most powerful – are too 'small' to counter such forces. Yet nation-states also remain too 'large' to address adequately the diverse needs found within cosmopolitan urban areas. Where the nation-state is unable to act effectively, local and city governments may be more suited to the task.

A great many organizations, institutions and groups cross paths within cities. Domestic and international businesses, potential investors, government bodies, civic associations, professional groups, trade unions and others meet and form links in urban areas. These links can lead to collective and joint actions in which cities act as social agents in political, economic, cultural and media spheres.

Cities as active agents for change

Examples of cities as economic actors in their own right have been increasing in recent years. In Europe, beginning in the 1970s recession, cities banded together to promote investment and generate new forms of employment. The Eurocities movement, which now encompasses over 130 of Europe's largest cities, was formed in 1989 (with just six) to work with and influence EU policy. Asian cities such as Seoul, Singapore and Bangkok have also been effective economic actors, acknowledging the importance of speed of information about international markets and the need for flexible productive and commercial structures.

Some cities construct medium- and long-term strategic plans to address the complex challenges before them. Under such plans, local government authorities, civic groups and private economic agents work together to refurbish the urban infrastructure, organize a world-class event or shift the employment base away from industrial enterprises to knowledge-based ones. Birmingham, Amsterdam, Lyons, Lisbon, Glasgow and Barcelona are examples of European cities that have carried out successful urban renewal projects with the help of strategic plans.

The case of Barcelona is particularly noteworthy. Launched in 1988, the Barcelona 2000 Economic and Social Strategic Plan brought together public and private organizations under a shared vision and action plan for transforming the city. The Barcelona municipal government and ten additional bodies (including the chamber of commerce, the university, the city port authority and trade unions) have been overseeing the implementation of the plan's three main objectives: to connect Barcelona with a network of European cities by improving the communication and transport infrastructure, to improve the quality of life of the city's inhabitants, and to make the industrial and service sector more competitive while promoting promising new economic sectors.

One of the cornerstones of the Barcelona 2000 plan took place in 1992, when the city hosted the Olympic Games. Staging the Olympics allowed Barcelona to 'internationalize' itself, as its assets and vision were on display for the whole world to see. In the case of Barcelona, organizing a world-class event was crucial on two fronts: it enhanced the profile of the city in the eyes of the world and it generated additional enthusiasm within the city for completing the urban transformation (Borja and Castells 1997). Sport, it seems, can now play an important part in urban regeneration (Taylor et al. 1996). London used its staging of the 2012 Olympic Games to promote an explicit and ambitious urban regeneration (see 'Using your sociological imagination 6.3').

The role of city mayors

As cities assume a new importance, the role of city mayors is also changing. Major world cities are becoming relatively independent actors, and their elected mayors are able to provide a personalized leadership that can be crucial in raising a city's international profile. The London-based organization City Mayors works to raise the profile of mayors internationally and, since 2004, has awarded

6.3   Global sport as urban renewal? The 2012 London Olympic Games

The article abridged below appeared in *The Independent* on 16 July 2013.

The Olympics brought more than £9bn of investment to east London, much of which went into transport. Stratford is now second only to King's Cross as the most connected part of London. As well as two Underground lines, a high-speed 'javelin' train to King's Cross and the Docklands Light Railway, it may soon be a stop-off for the Eurostar to Paris.

'A lot of major developments and improvements have been moving eastwards in the capital for decades now', Dennis Hone, chief executive of the London Legacy Development Corporation told The Independent. 'I'm in my 50s and I remember the East End when if you lived on the Isle of Dogs you had to get two buses to get to Stratford to shop. Now it's transformed.'

The second of the five legacy pledges made in Britain's pitch for the Games was that it would 'transform the heart of east London'. At the Olympic Park site – now rebranded the Queen Elizabeth Olympic Park – there is tangible evidence of change.

The athletes' village, once draped with national flags and buzzing with people hoping to catch Usain Bolt or Mo Farah in the dinner queue, has been relaunched as a housing estate called the East Village. In September,

its first non-athletes will move into their new apartments, which have had kitchens added and walls knocked through. Promisingly, almost half of these 2,818 new homes will be affordable. This is just the start of a much-needed boost to housing in the region. Olympic parkland – as well as some of the surrounding area – will eventually become five new neighbourhoods housing 8,000 people, with about 40 per cent in affordable homes.

But Anne Power at the London School of Economics, who is examining the legacy of the Games, has warned against assuming this housing will be within the reach of most people. She wrote last summer: 'The "affordable rents" for the 2,800 new homes that will be converted from the athlete's village will be unaffordable to Newham's poorest households. As one-third of all children in the borough live in workless households, their families will almost certainly be excluded.' This is particularly problematic following reforms to the way the Government subsidises housing. It now classes 'affordable' housing as being at 80 per cent of the market rent – an increase of 10 per cent from the rate under Labour. In London, this means many families are priced out.

[. . .] Beyond the building and transport developments around the park itself, however,

The East Village at Stratford was a key part of the regeneration strategy for the 2012 Olympic Games.

questions remain about whether a more substantial transformation has taken place in the area. Rushanara Ali, MP for Bethnal Green and Bow, in the Olympic borough of Tower Hamlets, said: 'The impact of the infrastructure investment has been really fantastic . . . But – and there's a big but – in my borough unemployment actually went up during the Olympics.'

Ali argues that the Games did not deliver on the promise to improve unemployment levels, which would have helped lift many of these still-deprived boroughs out of poverty. She said: 'During the construction of the Olympics, very few jobs were created for local people. There are still high levels of unemployment in the borough and it was a missed opportunity to train people up for work. Tower Hamlets got very little out of the Olympics.'

It will probably be a decade – or more – before we can say with any certainty whether the Games improved east London's employment prospects. But the money spent on transport and housing is already providing the beginnings of a legacy that is 'more than just talk'.

Source: The Independent (2013).

> ### THINKING CRITICALLY
> Can sporting events really lead to lasting urban regeneration? How have the 2012 Games benefited property developers, local residents and the deprived communities of East London? What infrastructural elements have been left behind for residents after the Olympics?

the title of 'World Mayor' based on the outcome of an online poll. In 2010, the title was won by Marcelo Ebrard, mayor of Mexico City, with city mayors from Caracas in Venezuela, New Plymouth in New Zealand and Ulm in Germany in the top ten places, showing the global spread of the mayoral role.

In some prominent cases in which cities have transformed their image, the role of the mayor has been decisive. The mayors of Lisbon and Barcelona were driving forces behind efforts to elevate their cities to the ranks of the world's major urban centres. Likewise, mayors in smaller places can play a crucial role in making the city known internationally and in attracting new economic investment.

In the United States, mayors have become a powerful economic and political force. As gun-related violence soared in American cities, more than twenty mayors abandoned reliance on federal attempts to pass gun control legislation and filed lawsuits against the gun manufacturers on behalf of their constituents. The former New York mayor Rudolph Giuliani generated controversy and division by implementing tough 'law-and-order' policies aimed at lowering crime rates. New York's violent crime rate did fall dramatically during the 1990s, and strict 'quality of life' policies aimed at the homeless population transformed the face of its busy streets. However, crime rates had been falling for some years before Giuliani took office and may be related as much to the improving economic situation at that time as the mayor's law-and-order policies. Giuliani's leadership in the aftermath of the terrorist attacks on 11 September 2001 led to his being named *Time* magazine's 'Person of the Year' for 2001.

In many places around the world, mayors are enjoying increased influence as spokespeople for their cities and regions. City mayors are often able to shape the policy agenda for areas that lie outside the city limits by entering into agreements with communities in the general metropolitan area. These types of partnership can be drawn on in attracting foreign investment, for example, or in bidding to play host to world-class events.

Cities and global forces

Borja and Castells (1997) argue that there are three main realms in which local authorities can act effectively to manage global forces. First, cities can contribute to economic productivity and competitiveness by managing the local 'habitat' – the conditions and facilities that form the social base for economic productivity. Competitiveness depends on a qualified workforce, and this requires a strong educational system, good public transport, adequate and affordable housing, capable law enforcement, effective emergency services and vibrant cultural resources.

Second, cities play an important role in ensuring socio-cultural integration within diverse multi-ethnic populations. Global cities bring together individuals from many countries, varying religious and linguistic backgrounds, and different socio-economic levels. If the intense pluralism found within cosmopolitan cities is not countered by forces of integration, then fragmentation and intolerance can result. However, in cases where the effectiveness of the nation-state in promoting social cohesion is compromised, the voluntary associations and governance structures within cities can be positive forces for social integration.

Third, cities are important venues for political representation and management. Local authorities have two advantages over the nation-state: they generally enjoy greater legitimacy with those they represent and they have more flexibility and room for manoeuvre. Many citizens feel that national politics no longer represents their interests and concerns. In cases where the nation-state is too distant to represent specific cultural or regional interests, city and local authorities are more accessible forums for political activity.

Cooperation between cities is not restricted to the regional level. There is a growing acknowledgement that cities can and should play a significant role in addressing international political, economic and social issues. Informal and formal networks of cities are emerging as globalizing forces draw disparate parts of the world more closely together. The

Shanghai is China's financial and economic hub, yet innovative use of city spaces can ameliorate the impact on traditional cultural practices. Here, people are practising tai chi right in the heart of the city.

problems facing the world's largest cities are not isolated ones; they are embedded in the larger context of a global economy, international migration, new trade patterns and the power of information technology.

We have noted elsewhere that the complexities of our changing world are demanding new forms of democratic international governance. Networks of cities should figure prominently among these new mechanisms. One such structure already exists – a World Assembly of Cities and Local Authorities is convened in parallel to the UN's Habitat Conference. Bodies such as the World Assembly promise to allow the gradual integration of city organizations into structures presently composed of national governments. As the world's urban population continues to grow, city governments will be necessary and vital partners in bringing about political and economic reform.

Chapter review

1   Outline the process through which the global human population has become urbanized and explain how and why this developed.
2   How does urbanization in developing countries differ from the early processes that took place in European countries?

3   Define what is meant by global cities. What are their key features and functions?

4   Outline the central elements of the Chicago School's ecological approach to urban studies. Which concepts derived from natural ecology does this approach make use of?

5   How does the city influence the behaviour of its inhabitants? Explain Simmel's key concepts in this area.

6   Provide an outline of Louis Wirth's thesis of 'urbanism as a way of life'. What is meant by 'secondary contacts' and why are they significant?

7   How does David Harvey connect processes of urban restructuring to broad socio-economic changes? How does Harvey's approach differ from that of the Chicago School?

8   How are inner-city decay and suburbanization closely tied together? Is it inevitable that suburban growth contributes to problems in city centres?

9   Define 'urban recycling' and 'gentrification' and give some examples of how they operate.

10 Give some examples of initiatives which may help to bring about a sustainable city. Are sustainable cities a realistic prospect in developing countries?

11 Why are city governments becoming political and economic agents? Why might cities be better placed than nation-states to deal with some of the problems of globalization?

Research in practice

Many studies of cities and urban areas have discussed the problems of such growing population centres, and we have reported on some of these in this chapter: increased surveillance and militarization, terrorist threats, vulnerable infrastructure and chronic conflicts, to name just a few. However, perhaps this perspective misses some of the mundane, routine work that goes on within cities, recognition of which may alter our evaluation of the city's prospects. Read the following article with this in mind: Hall, T., and Smith, R. J. (2015) 'Care and Repair and the Politics of Urban Kindness', *Sociology*, 49(1): 3–18.

- What does Thrift mean by 'urban repair'? Give some examples of urban repair work.
- The authors are critical of Thrift's analysis. Why?
- What do the authors mean by a 'sociology of hope'? What would this entail?
- Using the paper's examples of street cleaners and outreach workers, explain what is meant by 'urban kindness'.
- Given the structural issues underlying many urban problems identified by David Harvey and Manuel Castells, could the measures proposed by Hall and Smith really be enough to produce a 'good city'?

Thinking it through

Georg Simmel said that 'The deepest problems of modern life derive from the claim of the individual to preserve the autonomy and individuality of his existence in the face of overwhelming social forces, of historical heritage, of external culture, and of the technique of life.' Read 'The Metropolis and Mental Life' (1903) in full; it is available online or in various edited collections.

This analysis is a real classic and is now almost 115 years old! But how do its main claims about city life and individuality fare in the twenty-first century? Address this question in relation to *the blasé attitude, urban reserve, the money economy* and the *matter-of-fact, calculative personality type*. What conclusions should we draw about the differences between cities at the start of the twentieth century and those in the twenty-first century?

Society in the arts

 1 It has been argued that the image many people have of nineteenth-century industrial cities is based on fictional accounts such as Charles Dickens's (1854) *Hard Times*, set in 'Coketown', a northern mill town akin at that time to Manchester. But might this also be true of contemporary fiction? Compare any of the following novels with the empirical evidence in this chapter on *urban inequality, inner-city decay, gentrification* and *urban restructuring/recycling*.

- Lauren Weisberger (2003) *The Devil Wears Prada* (London: HarperCollins) – *New York*
- Ian Rankin (2004) *Fleshmarket Close* (London: Orion) – *Edinburgh*

- James Ellroy (2005) *White Jazz* (London: Arrow) – *Los Angeles*
- Vikram Chandra (2007) *Sacred Games: A Novel* (London: Faber & Faber) – *Mumbai*

 How similar and different are the fictional representations from the sociological research findings? What political and policy implications are there if fiction has a wider public resonance than empirical research?

2 Many fictional representations of rural, village life tend to see this as idyllic, healthy and authentic as a place to live, and television programmes, both fictional and factual (such as *Escape to the Country*), follow the same pattern. Given that the majority of people now live in cities and urban areas, why has the rural village idyll persisted over such a long period? Is it suggestive of the fact that urban life does not make for a satisfying existence? Was Tönnies right about the problems associated with a shifting balance of *Gemeinschaft* and *Gesellschaft* bonds in the modern world? How else would you account for the apparent longing for rural lifestyles? Or can you find alternatives which present city living as the ideal? How widespread are these representations?

Further reading

 To get an overview of the field of urban sociology, David Parker's (2010) *Cities and Everyday Life* (London: Routledge) is an excellent place to begin. Mark Abrahamson's (2014) *Urban Sociology: A Global Introduction* (New York: Cambridge University Press) is also excellent, with many case studies as illustrations of key issues. For a critical overview and assessment of urban theories, see Alan Harding and Talja Blokland's (2014) *Urban Theory: A Critical Introduction to Power, Cities and Urbanism in the 21st Century* (London: Sage).

 On cities, Doreen Massey's (2007) *World City* (Cambridge: Polity) takes London as a case study of the global city, while the UN ESA's (2014) *World Urbanization*

Prospects: The 2014 Revision, Highlights (New York: UN ESA) provides lots of comparative information on cities across the world. It is also available online: http://esa.un.org/unpd/wup/Highlights/WUP2014-Highlights.pdf.

It may be rather old now, but Marshall Berman's (1983) *All That is Solid Melts into Air: The Experience of Modernity* (London: Verso) remains an inspiring book on the *experience* of modern urbanism and is well worth the effort. For ideas on the sustainable city and how it might be brought into being, see *Resilient Sustainable Cities: A Future*, edited by Leonie J. Pearson, Peter W. Newton and Peter Roberts (2014) (New York: Routledge).

Debates on cities and the restructuring of space are well handled in Fran Tonkiss's (2006) *Space, the City and Social Theory: Social Relations and Urban Forms* (Cambridge: Polity), which offers a valuable account of social theories of the city. Finally, Jan Lin and Christopher Mele's (2012) *The Urban Sociology Reader* (2nd edn, Abingdon: Routledge) is an edited collection of classic and contemporary pieces which is a very useful resource.

For a collection of original readings on urban environments, see the accompanying *Sociology: Introductory Readings* (3rd edn, Cambridge: Polity, 2010).

Internet links

@ **Additional information and support for this book at Polity:**
www.politybooks.com/giddens

@ **Centre for Urban History, based at the University of Leicester, UK:**
www.le.ac.uk/urbanhist

@ **H-Urban – a discussion forum for urban history and urban studies:**
www.h-net.org/~urban

@ **Globalization and World Cities Network, based at Loughborough University, UK – tracks the growth and integration of cities in the world economy:**
www.lboro.ac.uk/gawc

@ **City Mayors – a useful resource on mayors across the world:**
www.citymayors.com

@ **Virtual Cities Resource Centre – looks at urban form as represented on the worldwideweb:**
www.casa.ucl.ac.uk/planning/virtualcities.html

@ **A US site on sustainable architecture, building and culture:**
www.sustainableabc.com

CHAPTER 7

Work and the Economy

Contents

In June and July 2015, people in Greece queued to use ATMs as banks closed their doors to avoid running out of money. Withdrawals were restricted to €60 per day.

In late June and early July 2015, banks in Greece shut their doors and imposed a withdrawal limit of just €60 per account. ATMs were inundated with people trying to get their money out, and many soon ran out of cash. This was the most visible symbol of the economic trouble the country was in. Greece's national debt stood at €323 billion, its Gross Domestic Product (GDP) fell by a full one-quarter in just the five years after 2010, Greece's debt to GDP ratio was 177 per cent, and unemployment reached a staggering 26 per cent – 60 per cent among young people between the age of fifteen and twenty-five. But it wasn't always like this.

Greece was a prosperous and prospering country in the twenty-first century. It joined the euro in 2001, enjoyed an enviable average economic growth rate of 4 per cent per annum between 2000 and 2008, and hosted the successful 2004 Olympic Games (Karyotis and Gerodimos 2015: 2). So what went wrong? The short answer is that, like many other countries in Europe and around the world, Greece's internal, national problems were severely compounded by a global financial crash in 2008, which originated in the USA but spread widely and rapidly. The crisis led to economic recession, business collapses, rising unemployment and, in many countries, a new austerity politics aimed at reducing high and unsustainable levels of national debt. In practice this meant pay freezes, reduced hours, redundancies and an uncertain future.

Crisis in the global economy

Economists traced the origins of the US banking crisis to risky lending practices, especially on home loans. As part of their growth strategy, many American banks provided a large number of loans to home-buyers with poor credit histories – a practice known as 'sub-prime lending'. These loans were then rolled into portfolios including other assets and bonds and sold to investors around the world. But, between 2004 and 2006, US interest rates rose from 1 per cent to over 5 per cent, and default rates on sub-prime mortgages rose to record levels. People just could not afford their rising monthly repayments. Global investors suffered huge losses as a result, the US housing market slumped as banks became wary of lending to each other, and the availability of credit dried up.

Because the financial system is global, the US crisis spread quickly around the world. Investment banks in Europe, China, Australia and elsewhere all suffered losses, and the credit crunch – a severe shortage of credit or money – pushed the global economy towards recession. In Britain, Iceland and France, major banks were effectively taken into government ownership – nationalized – to prevent them from collapsing. National governments and the European Central Bank intervened, making more money available to banks, hoping this would encourage them to start lending again. But the strategy did not work, and the result was a global economic recession.

The crash had particularly dramatic consequences for countries with high levels of indebtedness, such as Ireland, Portugal, Spain and, of course, Greece. With shrinking or static economic growth and no access to additional funding, they struggled to cover existing debt repayments and looked for international help in the form of EU/IMF 'bailout funds'. This was provided only alongside guarantees of a new fiscal discipline and austerity policies, which gave donors confidence that recipients were actively trying to reduce their national debts.

> See chapter 21, 'Politics, Government and Social Movements', for more on the eurozone crisis as highlighting problems of global governance.

In Greece, national debt levels rose to 115 per cent of GDP, raising fears that the country might default. In 2010 the Greek government introduced an 'austerity package' of spending cuts and tax rises, triggering mass protests and strikes. In the worsening situation, the European Central Bank (ECB), the European Commission (EC) and the International Monetary Fund (IMF) provided Greece with a bailout of €110 billion. In return a tough austerity package was agreed, including cuts in public spending, wage cuts, large tax rises, pension reform and privatization. Mass protests followed, but these measures were not enough. A second bailout of €130 was granted in 2011, and private investors agreed to lower interest rates and accept some debt write-off.

When the government missed a payment to the IMF of €1.5 billion on 30 June 2015, the possibility of Greece having to leave the euro and even the EU was very real. By now a radical left-wing party – Syriza – was in government promising to oppose the creditors' austerity measures. A referendum was held on whether to accept even harsher conditions attached to a third bailout of some €86 billion, which brought a decisive 'no' vote of 61 per cent. But, despite this, Greece's situation and prospects were so dire that even Syriza ignored the result and accepted radical measures to tackle the debt issue, involving radical changes to pensions, banking, labour markets and taxation along with a broad programme of privatization of assets (Plummer 2015). Seven years after the credit crunch, EU leaders were still heavily embroiled in attempts to hold the union together.

Economic recession – defined as a fall in Gross Domestic Product in two consecutive quarters – is nothing new. Periodic downturns in the long history of capitalist development have turned into recessions, and the recent one has similarities with the 'great crash' of 1929. The turn towards neo-liberal economics in the 1970s and 1980s in the USA and the UK, the deregulation of financial markets, the promotion of economic individualism and high levels of personal indebtedness generated a culture of risky finance and indulgent consumerism (Bone 2009). But the 2008 crisis also owed much to globalization, which facilitates the rapid movement of money and debt around the world, creating a more tightly interconnected global economic system.

Clearly the first economic recession of the twenty-first century has had a major impact on many aspects of social life. Large numbers of people have lost their jobs as a result of business failures or government cuts to public spending. Public spending cuts and 'austerity politics' have created a climate in which the public sector is widely represented in the media and by some politicians as a drain on the wealth-generating private sector. The prospect of tensions, conflicts and widening inequality are increased. It is also unclear whether younger generations will be able to 'do better' than their parents – a basic assumption that has long underpinned the economic ambition of 'modernity'.

Today these issues form part of the field of economic sociology, and the next section briefly traces the fall and rise of this field. This leads us into a discussion of economic organizations and transnational corporations, which have become ever more powerful. We then look at theories of a broad shift from 'Fordist' to 'post-Fordist' principles in the sphere of economic production and consumption, particularly the increasing flexibility demanded from modern workers. From here, the chapter moves on to the area of work, asking what we mean by 'work', before looking at the changing character of working lives as the developed societies have shifted towards service-based employment. In the final section, we examine growing job insecurity, unemployment and the link between work and the development of personal character.

Economic sociology

Sociology's founders – Karl Marx, Emile Durkheim and Max Weber – sought to understand and explain the origins and development of industrial capitalist societies. That this involved studying economic phenomena is clear from just the titles of some of their key works: Marx's (1867) three volumes of *Capital*, Durkheim's (1893) *The Division of Labour in Society*, and Max Weber's (1925) posthumous *Economy and Society*. Georg Simmel's (1907) *The Philosophy of Money* and Alexis de Tocqueville's (1835–40) *Democracy in America* also touched on economic phenomena in a broader social context, but, unlike the three main founders, their work did not lead to distinct sociological traditions.

Marx's main interest was in understanding capitalism as a dynamic, but exploitative and destructive economic system. In particular, he saw capitalism as founded on grossly unequal, structured social relations and on the ownership of private property. Durkheim traced the way that industrial capitalism continually expanded the division of labour, leading to increasing specialization. But he saw that economic specialization also performed an integrative function for society.

In Weber's work, the focus is on what constitutes specifically economic forms of action and organization, but the concept of 'interest' is also central to his approach. Actions that are determined simply by self-interest, such as those observed in markets, are 'instrumentally rational' and rely on every individual behaving in a similar way (Smelser and Swedberg 2005: 9). This is typical of economically rational action. Weber also discussed the religious origins of the capitalist outlook in early forms of Protestantism, noting that, over time, religious ideas were eroded, leaving a secular economic system centred on profit-seeking. However, the idea of a 'calling' still exists in ideas of duty, accountability and integrity within the ethical codes adopted by professions such as lawyers, doctors and engineers.

> Weber's Protestant ethic thesis is discussed in more detail in chapter 3, 'Theories and Perspectives'.

The classical sociologists differentiated their ideas from pure economics by showing how 'the economy' is part of society as a whole. Economic sociology differs from mainstream or 'orthodox' economics in various ways, but the central difference is that 'the analytic starting point of economics is the individual; the analytic starting points of economic sociology are typically groups, institutions and society' (Smelser and Swedberg 2005: 4). Orthodox economics embodies some key assumptions: individuals act according to their own interests, economic actions are based on maximizing utility, and the latter therefore constitutes economically 'rational' action. In economic sociology, individuals are always embedded within a social context and the interests of individual actors are formed in relations with other people.

Despite the focus of much classical sociology on economic issues, and with some notable exceptions, for most of the twentieth century, sociology separated economic matters from social relations and concentrated on the latter.

Only in the 1980s did a number of influential works reinvigorate economic sociology after half a century of relative neglect (White 1981; Burt 1982; Granovetter 1985). Mark Granovetter (1985) produced a stringent critique of mainstream economic theory, arguing that economic action cannot be reduced to rational, individual calculations of profit or interest maximization but must be seen as embedded within social networks involving social divisions, power relations, organizations, culture and politics. This concept of social embeddedness is central to the new economic sociology, as it enables sociologists to 'reformulate economic issues in sociological terms' (Hass 2007: 8).

Granovetter also argued against the notion that economic markets are 'natural' and operate more or less autonomously. Instead, he insisted that markets are social phenomena that are influenced by social relations and status competition. Again, as with the actions of individuals, markets, along with business organizations and other economic phenomena, are always embedded within society and are not outside of social structures (Portes 2007: 17). Looking at the development of these organizations allows us to see how broad social changes affect economic agents but also how those agents impact on millions of people's working lives. We can get a clearer sense of this by briefly tracing the emergence and development of capitalist businesses from the small, family-based companies of the nineteenth century to the enormous transnational corporations of today whose organization spans the globe.

Economic organizations

There have been three general stages in the development of business corporations, although each overlaps with the others and all coexist today. The first, characteristic of the nineteenth and early twentieth century, was family capitalism. Large firms were run either by individual entrepreneurs or by generations of the same family, such as Sainsbury in the UK or Rockefeller in the USA. Most of these family firms have become public companies whose shares are traded on the open market and where (with some exceptions) managerial control is the norm. Among small firms, family capitalism continues, for instance, with shops that remain in the same family for two or more generations.

In the large corporate sector, family capitalism was succeeded by managerial capitalism. As managers became more influential, entrepreneurial families were gradually displaced. Managerial capitalism left an indelible imprint on modern life. The large corporation drives patterns of consumption and the experience of employment in large factories and corporate bureaucracies. Sociologists have also identified welfare capitalism as a specific form. Beginning at the end of the nineteenth century, larger firms began to provide services to their employees, including childcare, recreational facilities, profit-sharing plans, paid holidays, unemployment insurance and life insurance. These companies were often of a paternalistic bent – for example, sponsoring home visits for the 'moral education' of employees. Viewed in less benevolent terms, an objective of welfare capitalism was to avoid unionization and maintain control over the workforce.

Many scholars now see the contours of a new phase in the evolution of the corporation, as managerial capitalism has given way to institutional capitalism. This refers to the emergence of a consolidated network of business leadership based on the practice of corporations holding shares in other firms. One of the main reasons for the spread of institutional capitalism is the shifting pattern of investment. Rather than investing directly by buying shares in a business, individuals now invest in money-market, trust, insurance and pension funds that are controlled by large financial organizations, which in turn invest the resulting grouped savings in industrial corporations. In effect, interlocking boards of directors exercise control over much of the corporate landscape. This reverses the process of increasing managerial control, since the managers' shareholdings are dwarfed by large blocks of shares owned by corporations.

There are many thousands of small and medium-sized enterprises (SMEs) where the entrepreneur – the boss who owns and runs the firm – is still common, but, since the early twentieth century, capitalist economies have increasingly been dominated by large business corporations. In 1912 the market value of the 100 largest publicly quoted companies was US$280 billion, but in 2010 this had reached US$11.8 trillion. There are many more large corporations in the world today, and, by 2009, 'large multinational corporations were responsible for approximately one-third of international trade as products flowed between subsidiaries located in different countries, but all integrated into global production and sales networks' (Michie 2012: 33). In theory, large corporations are the property of their shareholders, who have the right to make all-important decisions. Yet, as share-ownership is dispersed, the day-to-day control has passed into the hands of managers, so ownership of corporations is thus separated from control of them. Whether they are run by owners or managers, the power of the major corporations is extensive.

Transnational corporations

Most large corporations now operate in a global economic context. When they establish branches in two or several countries, they are referred to as multinational or transnational corporations (TNCs). 'Transnational' is the preferred term, indicating that they operate across many national boundaries. The very largest transnationals are gigantic, with wealth outstripping that of entire countries.

About half of the 100 largest economic units in the world today are nation-states, but the other half are transnational corporations. Six industries dominated the activities of TNCs over the twentieth century: motor vehicles, pharmaceuticals, telecommunications, utilities, petroleum and electrical/electronic equipment. These account for 60 per cent of TNC activity worldwide. In 2004, 85 per cent of the top 100 TNCs still had their main headquarters in Europe, Japan and the USA, though five of the top 100 originated in developing countries, including China, Malaysia, Singapore and South Korea – the largest ever number (UNCTAD 2007: 3–4).

Of the top 200 companies in the year 2000, US corporations dominated, with eighty-two slots (41 per cent of the total); Japanese firms came second, with forty-one (Anderson and Cavanagh 2000). The proportion of American companies in the top 200 has fallen significantly since 1960, when just five Japanese corporations were included in the list. Around three-quarters of all foreign direct investment is between the industrialized countries, though the involvement of transnationals in developing countries is also extensive, with Brazil, Mexico and India showing the highest levels of foreign investment. The most rapid rate of increase in corporate investment by far has been in the Asian newly industrializing countries (NICs) of Singapore, Taiwan, Hong Kong, South Korea and Malaysia.

The reach of transnationals would not have been possible without advances in transport and communications. Air travel now allows people to move around the world at a speed that would have seemed inconceivable even sixty years ago. The development of superfreighters – extremely large ocean-going vessels – together with containers that can be shifted directly from one type of carrier onto another, makes possible the easy transport of bulk materials. Communications technology now permits more or less instantaneous contact from one part of the world to another, and the larger transnationals have their own satellite-based systems. The Mitsubishi Corporation, for instance, has a massive network, across which 5 million words are transmitted to and from its Tokyo headquarters every day.

Types of transnational corporation

Transnational corporations are of key importance in the international division of labour – the specialization in producing goods for the world market that divides regions into zones of industrial or agricultural production or high- or low-skilled labour (McMichael 1996).

Just as national economies have become dominated by a limited number of very large companies, so too has the world economy.

Perlmutter (1972) divided transnational corporations into three types. In the ethnocentric transnational, company policy is set and put into practice from a headquarters in the country of origin. Companies and plants that the parent corporation owns around the world are cultural extensions of the originating company and its practices are standardized across the globe. A second type is the polycentric transnational, where overseas subsidiaries are managed by local firms in each country. The headquarters in the country or countries of origin of the main company establish broad guidelines within which local companies manage their own affairs. Finally, there are geocentric transnationals, which are international in their management structure, with managerial systems integrated on a global basis.

Transnational corporations are the first organizations to be able to plan on a truly *global* scale. A few companies with developed global networks are able to shape the commercial activities of diverse nations. There are major differences between the large corporation of the twenty-first century and its counterpart from the mid-twentieth century. The former US labour secretary Robert Reich (1991) saw that major shifts were taking place in America's business corporations. Many corporations were no longer 'American': they did not invest in factories, machines and laboratories, nor did they employ masses of workers. Instead, the American corporation was a kind of front or façade, hiding a range of decentralized groupings which contracted with similar groups in different parts of the world. In short, the large corporation is less and less a big business and more an 'enterprise web' – a central organization that links smaller firms together. IBM, which used to be one of the more self-sufficient of large corporations, in the 1980s and early 1990s joined with dozens of US-based companies and more than eighty foreign-based firms to share strategic planning and cope with production problems.

Advertising for Pepsi and Coca-Cola in the city of Tripoli in the north of Lebanon.

Some corporations remain strongly bureaucratic, centred in the country in which they first became established, but most are no longer clearly located anywhere. The old transnational corporation had a national headquarters from where its overseas production plants and subsidiaries were controlled. Now, groups situated in any region of the world are able, via telecommunications and computers, to work systematically with others. Nations still try to influence flows of information, resources and money across their borders, but modern communications technologies make this increasingly difficult, if not impossible. Given the size and power of transnational corporations, what responsibilities should business organizations have in relation to the wider society?

Corporate social responsibility

Although issues of business responsibility have been part of academic debates since the 1950s, only since the 1990s have companies shown a sustained interest in the way that businesses can become, or be seen to become, socially responsible (European Commission 2001). The idea of 'corporate social responsibility' is open to varying interpretations, but is generally meant to indicate that companies go beyond strict legal obligations and compliance with health and safety rules in order to fulfil the wider social and environmental ambitions of the public, including, for example, a commitment to environmental sustainability.

> The issue of sustainable development is discussed in detail in Chapter 5, 'The Environment'.

A simple working definition is that corporate social responsibility (CSR) means 'the ways in which a business seeks to align its values and behaviour with those of its various stakeholders' (Mallin 2009: 1). Given that the latter may include government, suppliers, customers, employees and campaigning interest groups, this is not an easy task, as their diverse values and behaviour may be in conflict. It is also important to note that CSR does not simply equate to philanthropy. Rather, it is part of the attempt to create a sustainable business model over the longer term by improving relationships with key stakeholders. In this sense, incorporating CSR may become essential to corporate practice rather than being a voluntary addition.

The CSR movement may appear either strange or strangely irrelevant given the string of cases of corporate *irresponsibility* of recent decades. For example, the 1992 Bhopal disaster at a Union Carbide plant in India killed and injured many thousands of people, but ten years afterwards there had still been no compensation at all paid to the victims. In 2002, the collapse of Enron and its accountants, Arthur Andersen, in a staggering case of corporate fraud and cover-up shocked the financial world (Crowther and Rayman-Bacchus 2004: 1). Then, in 2008, the credit crunch and financial crisis that dragged the global economy into recession in 2009 was sparked by irresponsible mortgage lending by major banks and financial institutions.

Such cases suggest that there is a long way to go before the CSR agenda is seen as sincere by the public, whose trust in authorities of all kinds has diminished since the 1960s. In addition, the emergence of anti-globalization and anti-capitalist movements around the world, alongside widespread concerns about the unethical practices of business and banks and the 'Occupy' protest camps in New York, London and elsewhere, demonstrate a widening gap between large corporations and the individual. They also show that, in an age of rapid global communications, people are increasingly prepared to take to the streets with their concerns rather than grumbling in private.

In this situation, CSR offers one way of reconnecting business organizations with the changing societies in which they are embedded. However, it seems unlikely that oil companies, the fast food business or arms manufacturers will ever be perceived by their critics as 'socially responsible' while continuing with their primary business. Clearly there are limitations to what we should expect from attempts to incorporate social responsibility into corporate best practice.

> **THINKING CRITICALLY**
>
> Google agreed to abide by Chinese law and filter 'contentious' content found via the search engine. UBS Bank used shareholders' money to cut its carbon emissions when it was under no legal obligation to do so. Heineken provides HIV/AIDS treatments to its employees, knowing that this will not produce any financial returns to the company (Schwartz 2011: 16). Which of these behaviours do you consider to be examples of CSR? Explain the reasons for your answers.

Taylorism and Fordism

Since the 1970s there have been some major shifts in manufacturing industries, away from uniform mass production and towards more flexible systems which allow differentiated niche markets to flourish. Exploring this broad pattern illustrates the central point of economic sociology, that economic actors of all kinds are deeply embedded in the wider system of social relations and institutions.

Adam Smith, one of the founders of modern economics, identified advantages that the division of labour provides in terms of increasing productivity. Smith's (1991 [1776]) *The Wealth of Nations* opens with a description of the division of labour in a pin factory. A person working alone could perhaps make twenty pins per day. By breaking down that worker's task into a number of simple operations, ten workers carrying out specialized tasks could collectively produce 48,000 pins per day. The rate of production per worker, in other words, is increased from twenty to 4,800 pins, each specialist operator producing 240 times more than when working alone.

253

More than a century later, these ideas became formalized in the work of Frederick Winslow Taylor (1865–1915), an American management consultant. Taylor's approach, known as 'scientific management', involved the detailed study of industrial processes, breaking them down into simple operations that could be precisely timed and organized. Taylorism was a system of production designed to maximize industrial output which also had a widespread impact on the organization of production and workplace politics. In particular, Taylor's time-and-motion studies wrested control over knowledge of the production process from workers, placing it in the hands of management, thus eroding the basis on which craft workers maintained their autonomy (Braverman 1974). Taylorism has been widely associated with the deskilling and degradation of labour.

Taylorist principles were adopted by the industrialist Henry Ford (1863–1947). He designed his first car factory at Highland Park, Michigan, in 1908 to manufacture only one product – the Model T Ford – using specialized tools and machinery designed for speed, precision and simplicity of operation. One of Ford's significant innovations was the moving

Fordist production methods brought huge numbers of workers together in enormous factories, which facilitated the growth of strong trade unionism.

assembly line, said to have been inspired by Chicago slaughterhouses where animals were disassembled section by section on a moving line. Each worker on Ford's assembly line was assigned a specialized task, such as fitting the left-side door handles, as car bodies moved along the line. By 1929, when production of the Model T ceased, more than 15 million cars had been produced in this way.

Ford was among the first to realize that mass production requires mass consumption in mass markets. He reasoned that, if standardized commodities – such as cars – were to be produced on a large scale, there had to be enough consumers able to buy them. In 1914, Ford took the unprecedented step of raising wages to US$5 for an eight-hour day – a very generous amount at the time. It was aimed at ensuring that a working-class lifestyle could include owning a Ford car. As Harvey (1989: 126) remarks: 'The purpose of the five-dollar, eight-hour day was only in part to secure worker compliance with the discipline required to work the highly productive assembly-line system. It was coincidentally meant to provide workers with sufficient income to consume the mass-produced products the corporations were about to turn out in ever vaster quantities.' Ford also enlisted the services of a small army of social workers, who were sent into the homes of employees to educate them in the habits of consumption.

In economic sociology, Fordism refers to the historical period from the early twentieth century to the early 1970s, which was characterized by mass production, relative stability in labour relations and a high degree of unionization. Under Fordism, firms made long-term commitments to workers and wages were linked to productivity. Collective bargaining agreements – formal agreements between firms and unions on working conditions and wages – ensured both that workers accepted automated regimes and that there was sufficient demand for mass-produced commodities. But by the 1970s the Fordist system was breaking down.

The reasons for the demise of Fordism are complex. It was based on supplying goods to domestic markets but, as multinational corporations spread and international markets became more important, the domestic-oriented Fordist system was effectively outgrown. Multinationals also bought new competition. What was then West Germany, plus Japan (and, later, the NICs of South-East Asia), broke the intimate link between domestic production and consumption. Imported goods became more popular to domestic consumers and the 'cosy' Fordist arrangements were breached (Tonkiss 2006: 93–4).

It had looked as though Fordism was the likely future of industrial production everywhere, but this proved not to be the case. Fordist principles can be applied successfully only in those industries that produce standardized products for large markets. To set up mechanized production lines is enormously expensive, and once the system is established it is quite rigid. To alter a product, substantial reinvestment is needed. Firms in countries where labour is expensive find it difficult to compete with those where wages are cheaper. This was one factor which led to the rise of the Japanese car industry (though Japanese wage levels today are no longer low) and, subsequently, that of South Korea.

Fordism and Taylorism are also low-trust systems in which jobs are set by management and geared to machines. Those who carry out work tasks are closely supervised and have very little autonomy. In order to maintain discipline and high-quality production standards, employees are continuously monitored through surveillance systems and scientific management. Such constant supervision tends to produce the opposite of its intended result, as the commitment and morale of workers is eroded. In workplaces with many low-trust positions, the level of employee dissatisfaction and absenteeism is high and industrial conflict is common. A high-trust system, by contrast, is one in which workers are permitted, within overall guidelines, to control the pace and even the content, of their work. Such systems have become more common today, transforming the way we think about workplace organization and the execution of work tasks.

255

Post-Fordist trends

Since the mid-1970s, flexible practices have been widely adopted in product development, production techniques, management style, the working environment, employee involvement and marketing. Group production, problem-solving teams, multi-tasking and niche marketing are just some of the strategies that companies have adopted to take advantage of an increasingly global economy. The concept of post-Fordism was devised to capture this overall radical departure from Fordist principles (Amin 1994; Beynon and Nichols 2006). The concept was popularized by Michael Piore and Charles Sabel (1984) to describe the era after Fordism in which flexibility and innovation are maximized to meet new demands for diverse, customized products.

Post-Fordism includes the set of overlapping changes occurring in design, manufacturing and distribution, though some argue that these have to be related to changes in the wider society. Flexibility and opposition to uniformity can also be seen in areas as diverse as party politics, welfare programmes, consumer demand and lifestyle choices. Hence, post-Fordism is used to discuss a narrow set of changes in production processes but also the much broader shift to a more diverse, individualized social order. We shall consider these trends before looking at some criticisms of the general post-Fordist thesis. Connecting the world of economic production to politics, policy and changing lifestyles in this way is of course fundamental to the new economic sociology.

Group production, flexibility and global production

One significant change is the spread of flexible production and computer-aided design (CAD) and manufacture (CAM). The Fordist system was very successful in creating mass products for mass consumption, but it was unable to produce small orders, let alone goods tailored to an individual customer. This problem is symbolized in Henry Ford's famous quip about the first mass-produced car: 'People can have the Model T in any colour – so long as it's black.' Computer-aided designs coupled with computer-based technology altered this situation in a radical way, enabling 'mass customization' of products (Davis 1988). For example, 5,000 shirts might be produced each day using an assembly line, but it is now possible to customize every one of those shirts just as quickly and at no greater expense.

Internet data are used to gain information about individual consumer demand, which is then turned into products made to their precise specifications. Some proponents argue that mass customization is a new Industrial Revolution, as momentous as the introduction of mass production at the start of the twentieth century. Sceptics are less convinced, pointing out that mass customization creates the illusion of choice, but, in reality, options available to Internet customers are no greater than those offered by a typical mail-order catalogue (J. Collins 2000).

Dell Computers has taken mass customization a long way. Its customers must go online, as Dell does not have retail outlets. From there, people can select the precise mix of features they desire. On receipt of an order, the computer is custom built and then shipped. In effect, Dell has turned traditional ways of doing business upside down: firms used to build a product first, then worry about how to sell it. Today, mass customizers like Dell sell first and build second. This shift has had important consequences. The need to hold large stocks of parts – a major cost for manufacturers – has been dramatically reduced as 'just-in-time' methods, where components are delivered only as required (just in time), have been introduced. In addition, an increasing share of production is outsourced, and the rapid transfer of information between manufacturer and supplier made possible by the Internet is now vital.

Changes in manufacturing include not just *how* products are made but also *where*. For most of the twentieth century, giant companies such as Ford and General Motors employed tens of thousands of factory workers, making everything from individual components to the

Even when production has become customized, such as in the electronics industry, elements of the production line can still exist.

final cars, which were then sold in the manufacturers' own showrooms. The post-Fordist turn has seen another type of production become important in which giant retailers such as Amazon, not manufacturers, are in control. In the early twenty-first century, Amazon began setting up its own spaces inside the warehouses of suppliers – a strategy termed 'under-their-tents' (IMS 2013). Essentially an extension of the just-in-time principle, this move allows Amazon to reduce its own stock and warehouse building costs and to take, process and deliver orders from their 'host' company's product range much faster than the competition. Instead of moving consumer packaged goods (CPG) all around the country, they can now simply be moved across the floor of the same warehouse.

Bonacich and Appelbaum (2000) found that, in clothing manufacture, most 'manufacturers' actually employ no garment workers at all. Instead, they use thousands of factories around the world to make the clothing, which they then sell in department stores and retail outlets. The manufacturers do not own factories and are not responsible for working conditions. Around two-thirds of all clothing sold in America is made in factories outside the USA, including China, Taiwan and the Philippines, where workers are paid a fraction of the American average wage. Retailers and manufacturers scour the globe for the lowest wage costs, and much of the clothing bought by people in the developed countries today is likely to have been manufactured in sweatshops by young workers who are paid mere pennies for making clothing or sportswear that sells for tens or hundreds of pounds per item.

Group production – collaborative groups of workers – has been used in conjunction with automation as a way of reorganizing work. The central idea is to increase employees' motivation by letting groups collaborate rather than requiring individuals to perform a single repetitive task. However, some studies have identified a number of negative consequences. Although direct managerial authority is less apparent in a team process, constant supervision by other team workers represents a new form of mutual surveillance. Laurie Graham (1995) worked for six months on the production line at the Japanese-owned Subaru-Isuzu car plant in Indiana. She found that peer pressure from other workers to achieve higher productivity was relentless.

One co-worker told her that, after initially being enthusiastic about group production, peer supervision was just a new means of management trying to 'work people to death'. Graham also found that Subaru-Isuzu used the group-production concept to resist trade unions. If management and workers were perceived as being on the same team, there should be no conflict: a good 'team player' does not complain. Demands for higher pay or a lessening of responsibility were seen as a lack of cooperativeness and commitment. So, while group production can provide workers with opportunities for less monotonous work, systems of power and control continue to characterize the workplace.

Criticisms of post-Fordism

While acknowledging that the world of work and economic life has undergone significant changes, the label 'post-Fordist' as an overall characterization of these is rejected by some scholars. One recurring criticism is that Fordist practices have not been abandoned wholesale. What we have seen, say critics, is the integration of some new approaches into existing Fordist techniques – a new or 'neo-Fordism' rather than post-Fordism (Wood 1989). Others see both Fordism and post-Fordism as overgeneralizations which mask the fact that economic production has always been characterized by a diversity of techniques across different industries (Pollert 1988).

Nonetheless, there is little doubt that, whatever name we give them, the shifting methods of production outlined above are part and parcel of the increasing globalization of economic life. Post-Fordist trends have reshaped the experience of work as the previously predictable, stable world has given way to a more flexible, less secure working environment, which, as we will see later in the chapter, has had consequences right across society, from trade union organization to the introduction of automation and digital technology. Before we explore these, we need to take a step back to look at what we mean by 'work'.

The changing nature of work

What is work?

We can initially define work, whether paid or unpaid, as the carrying out of tasks requiring the expenditure of mental and physical effort, which has as its objective the production of goods and services that cater to human needs. An occupation, or job, is work that is done in exchange for a regular wage or salary. In all cultures, work is the basis of the economy, and the economic system consists of institutions that provide for the production and distribution of goods and services.

We often think of work as equivalent to having a paid job, as is implied by being 'out of work', but this is, in fact, an oversimplified view. Unpaid labour, such as housework or repairing your own car, looms large in many people's lives and makes an enormous contribution to society. Voluntary work, for charities or other organizations, is also a type of work that has an important social role, filling the gaps left by commercial service providers and enhancing people's quality of life. Indeed, Budd (2011) discusses ten different ways of thinking about work, though there may be even more than that. 'Work' has many meanings in social life. For example, for some, work is 'a curse' – something necessary but unpleasant; for others, it is a central source of satisfaction and fulfilment. Work can also be part of our identity and a route to personal freedom.

However we think about work, sociologically we must start with the recognition that, above all else, 'work' is a social relationship and, as such, has to be placed within its social context if we are to fully understand it (Strangleman 2015: 137). Many types of work just do not conform to orthodox categories of 'paid employment'. Work carried out in the informal economy, for example, is not recorded in any direct way in official employment statistics.

The term informal economy refers to transactions outside the sphere of regular employment, involving sometimes the exchange of cash for services provided but often the direct exchange of goods or services. Many forms of sex work, for example, take place within the informal sector of the economy and do not conform to standard norms of paid employment. However, someone who mends your leaking pipe and is paid in cash without a receipt is also working 'informally', while others exchange stolen goods with friends or associates in return for other favours. The informal economy includes not only 'hidden' cash transactions but many forms of self-provisioning, which people carry on inside and outside the home. Do-it-yourself activities, domestic machinery and household tools, for instance, provide goods and services which would otherwise have to be purchased (Gershuny and Miles 1983).

THINKING CRITICALLY

What type of paid work do you do or what type of career are you aiming for? Is your choice of work or career influenced more by its status in the wider society or its intrinsic satisfaction?

If we take a *global* view of the experience of work, there are large differences between the developed and developing countries. One major difference is that agriculture remains the main source of employment in much of the developing world but is a tiny source of employment in the industrialized countries. Clearly, the lived experience of paid work is very different in the rural settings of developing countries and in the office environments that are typical of the developed world. Similarly, while a series of employment laws in developed countries have protected the working hours, health, safety and rights of workers over many years, 'sweatshops' operate in the less tightly regulated environments of developing countries (Louie 2001).

See chapter 14, 'Global Inequality', for more on child labour.

Employment patterns are also very different across the world. In most developed countries, the informal economy is relatively small in comparison with the formal paid sector, though recent migrant workers often earn their livings in the former. But the pattern is reversed in developing countries, where the informal economy thrives on the cheap labour and enforced flexibility of workers. In many developing countries, people's main experience of work is in the informal sector, which is often seen as the norm (see 'Global society 7.1'). Though such informal work is crucial for individuals, government spending plans are constrained by the loss of tax revenues and, some argue, economic development is made more difficult. Again, it is not just the experience of work but what work means for people that is potentially very different in different regions of the world.

Issues associated with migrant working and relations between migrant workers and host communities are covered in chapter 16, 'Race, Ethnicity and Migration'.

Having a paid job is important, particularly in the developed world, but the category of 'work' stretches much more widely to include unpaid labour such as housework. Housework, which has traditionally been carried out mainly by women, is usually unpaid, even

Global Society 7.1 Nigeria's reliance on an informal economy

The informal economy and entrepreneurial development

According to World Bank estimates, between 25% and 40% of GDP in developing Asian and African countries comes from the informal sector. In Nigeria, Africa's largest country, the figure might be close to 65% of GNP according to independent research. Truth is it's well nigh impossible to quantify the exact size of Nigeria's informal economy or its contribution to national indicators because relevant data for the country is wanting. It is often left to local newspaper reports to provide an occasional, much-needed glimpse into the actual state of Nigerian affairs.

In September 2008, the prominent Vanguard newspaper published an interview with a senior labour department bureaucrat who admitted that 90% of new jobs in the country were being accounted for by the informal sector. Quoting an unnamed survey, the official went on to add that the sector was also responsible for 80% of all non-agricultural employment and 60% of urban jobs. The figures are credible in source, but for a country now intent on revamping its economy for accelerated growth, they are incredible in import.

The informal economy is described as the sum total of economic activity that happens outside state regulation, which is neither taxed nor represented in a country's GDP. It includes a range of goods and services – from handicrafts and street traders to farm labour and money lending – that, by tradition or necessity, operate outside formal regulation and are oftentimes marked by a lack of social benefits. In the case of Nigeria, it accounts for a considerable chunk of the formal economy.

[. . .]

Informal street trading is a very common practice across Nigeria and in many other developing countries.

The informal sector in Nigeria is a mammoth, heterogeneous operation that continues outside the purview of official regulation and monitoring. It transcends a wide variety of unorganised and often unobserved small-scale activities that have traditionally sustained the country's urban and rural poor.

[. . .]

For Nigeria, tapping into the informal economy requires more than just policy directives; it calls for an emphatic mind-shift in official and popular perception on the validity and inherent economic worth of activities that have colloquially been docketed, not for lack of better idiom, as 'black market' enterprises.

[. . .]

The informal economy has withstood the worst circumstances of historic and institutional neglect in Nigeria, and continues to flourish in the best traditions of entrepreneurial spirit despite tremendous local and international pressures. The country's long-term macroeconomic performance is critically tied to its management of this sector, which can eventually prove much more valuable than its rich reserves of oil.

Source: From Osalor (2011).

though it is often very hard and exhausting work. It is worth exploring housework in more detail through Ann Oakley's classic studies of housework (see 'Classic studies 7.1').

One of the main questions of interest to sociologists is how the growing involvement of women in the labour market has affected the domestic division of labour. If the quantity of domestic work has not diminished but fewer women are now full-time housewives, it follows that the domestic affairs of households must be arranged rather differently today.

The social organization of work

Work in the developed societies is characterized by a highly complex division of labour, with an enormous number of different occupations in which people are able to specialize. Before industrialization, non-agricultural work entailed the mastery of a craft, and craft skills were learned through a lengthy apprenticeship. Craft workers normally carried out all aspects of the production process, from beginning to end. For example, a metalworker making a plough would forge the iron, shape it and assemble the implement.

With the rise of industrial production, most traditional craftwork disappeared, to be replaced by specialized skills that form part of larger production processes. Industrialization also saw a shift in the main location of work.

With the growth of workshops and factories enabling the use of large pieces of machinery operating on electricity and coal, work and home life became increasingly separated. Factories became the focal points of industrial development, and the mass production of goods began to eclipse small-scale artisanship based in the home, exemplified in the Fordist system discussed above.

The contrast in the division of labour between industrialized and other types of society is extraordinary. Even in the largest pre-industrial societies, there were no more than twenty or thirty major craft trades, together with specialized roles such as merchant, soldier and priest. In modern societies there are literally thousands of distinct occupations. For example, the UK Census lists over 20,000 distinct jobs in the British economy. This situation implies a much tighter economic interdependence than in earlier times, as people depend on an immense number of other workers stretching right across the world for products and services. With few exceptions, the vast majority of people in modern societies do not produce the food they eat, the houses they live in or the material goods they consume.

Early sociologists were interested in the consequences of such an extensive division of labour. Karl Marx argued that modern industry would reduce work to a series of dull,

Classic Studies 7.1 Ann Oakley on housework and the housewife role

The research problem

Before the 1970s, sociological studies of work focused almost exclusively on paid employment in the public sphere. But this ignored the domestic sphere and simply assumed that what happened within families was a private matter. Such ingrained assumptions were thoroughly shaken by second-wave feminism, which challenged the idea that personal life was not a sociological issue. But how had such assumptions become so widespread in the first place? What is the relationship between paid work and domestic tasks and why has the latter been seen as an exclusively female preserve? Ann Oakley explored these issues in two related books published in 1974, *The Sociology of Housework and Housewife*.

Oakley's explanation

Oakley (1974b) argued that housework, in its current form in the West, came into existence with the separation of the home from the workplace. With industrialization, 'work' took place away from the home and family and 'home' became a place of consumption and leisure. Domestic work then became largely invisible as 'real work' was increasingly defined as that which receives a direct wage. Housework was then seen as the 'natural' domain of women, while the realm of 'real work' outside the home was reserved for men.

Before the inventions and facilities provided by industrialization, work in the household was hard and exacting. The weekly wash, for example, was a heavy and demanding task. The introduction of hot and cold running water into homes eliminated many time-consuming tasks; previously, water had to be carried to the home and heated there, as it still is in much of the developing world. The piping of electricity and gas made coal and wood stoves obsolete, and chores such as the regular chopping of wood, the carrying of coal and constant cleaning of the stove were largely eliminated.

Yet, Oakley argues, the average amount of time spent on domestic work by women has not declined markedly with labour-saving equipment. The amount of time spent on housework by British women not in paid employment remained quite constant as homes had to be cleaned more thoroughly than before. Household appliances eliminated some heavier chores, but new tasks were created in their place. Time spent on childcare, stocking up the home with purchases and meal preparation all increased. This unpaid domestic labour is of enormous significance to the economy. For instance, it has been estimated that housework accounts for between 25 and 40 per cent of the wealth created in the industrialized countries. One UK study of time use estimated that, if housework were paid, it would be worth £700 billion to the economy (ONS 2002a). Oakley argued that such unacknowledged and unrewarded domestic work props up the rest of the economy, providing free services on which many of those in paid work depend.

Women's full-time occupation with domestic tasks can also be very isolating, alienating and lacking in intrinsic satisfaction. Housewives in Oakley's study (1974a) found domestic tasks monotonous and had difficulty escaping the self-imposed psychological pressure to meet standards which they established for their work. Because housework is not paid and brings no direct monetary reward, women gain satisfaction and psychological rewards from meeting standards of cleanliness and order, which feel like externally imposed rules. Unlike male workers, though, women cannot leave their 'workplace' at the end of the day.

Although some of the women interviewed said they were 'their own boss' at home, Oakley argued this was illusory. While men work fixed hours and avoid additional domestic duties, women's extra domestic duties, such as caring for sick children, partners or older relatives, means that their working hours are increased. Hence, men tend to divide work and leisure quite sharply and see extra duties as impinging on their protected leisure time, but for women this makes little sense, as they do not experience such a clear division. Paid work brings an income, which in turn creates an unequal power relationship, making housewives dependent on male partners for economic survival.

Critical points

Some critics took issue with Oakley's argument that patriarchy rather than social class was the most significant factor in explaining the gendered division of household labour. This neglected important differences between working- and middle-class households in relation to decision-making and sharing of resources. Recent social change has also raised the question of whether working women really do carry a greater 'double burden' than men in having to combine paid work with housework.

The amount of housework done by men has been increasing, if slowly. If we measure the *total* amount of work (paid and domestic) carried out by men and women, then a real movement towards more equality seems to be taking place, though society's adaptation to more working women has lagged behind. Sullivan's (2000) study of UK time-budget data found that, since the late 1950s, women's share of domestic duties had fallen by about one-fifth across all social class groups, and the more women worked in paid employment, the lower was their time-commitment to domestic tasks. Perhaps Oakley was too pessimistic about the prospects for change in household gender relations?

Contemporary significance

Ann Oakley's work was immensely influential in the 1970s and 1980s when feminist studies were opening up the sociological study of gender and household relations. And, despite the legitimate points made by more recent critics, her ideas remain important. Even the work of Gershuny, Sullivan and others concede that women still continue do more housework than men. This supports Oakley's contention that Western societies have deeply embedded attitudes and assumptions about women's 'proper place' within the domestic sphere.

More recently, Crompton et al. (2005) found that, as global economic pressures increase competition and push firms to demand more commitment from their (mostly male) workers, the process of equalization noted by Sullivan (2000) and others has 'stalled'. Attitudes towards the domestic division of labour *were* becoming less traditional, but the real *practices* within households had actually reverted to a more traditional pattern.

Clearly there is more comparative research to be done on the impact of global economic change on the household division of labour, but what Ann Oakley's research did in the 1970s was to convince sociologists that understanding societies and social change must involve an analysis of relations within domestic situations every bit as much as those in the public sphere of work and paid employment.

> **THINKING CRITICALLY**
>
> What is your own experience of the gendered domestic labour in relation to parents, aunts and uncles, and grandparents? Which aspects have seen most change – housework, childcare, paying bills, looking after ill relatives, and so on? Which aspects have been most resistant to change and why?

uninteresting tasks. According to Marx, the capitalist division of labour alienates human beings from their own labour, a key aspect of their sense of self. For Marx, alienation refers to the loss of control over the production process, often leading to feelings of indifference or hostility to work and the overall framework of industrial production. Industrial workers have little control over their work, how it is performed and for how long. Thus, work appears as something alien to them, an intrinsically unsatisfying aspect of life that must be carried out in order to survive.

Durkheim held a more optimistic outlook about the division of labour, though he also acknowledged its potentially harmful effects. According to Durkheim, the specialization of roles would strengthen social solidarity through the multidirectional relationships of production and consumption. Durkheim saw this arrangement as a highly functional one, although he was aware that solidarity could

You may find it useful to look at the overview of Durkheim and Marx's ideas in chapter 1, 'What is Sociology?'

be disrupted if economic change occurred too rapidly.

Of course, the occupational structure of the industrialized countries has changed substantially since the end of the nineteenth century. At the start of the twentieth century the labour market was dominated by 'blue-collar' manufacturing work, but over time the balance has shifted towards white-collar positions in the service sector. The decline of manufacturing jobs in developed economies was especially rapid from the mid-1970s, and table 7.1 shows the concomitant rise of the service sector in the UK since 1981.

In 1900, more than three-quarters of the employed population of the UK were in manual (blue-collar) work. Around 28 per cent of these were skilled workers, 35 per cent semi-skilled and 10 per cent unskilled. White-collar and professional jobs were relatively few in number. But, by the middle of the century, manual workers made up less than two-thirds of the working population. Between 1981 and 2006, manufacturing jobs were reduced from 31 per cent to just 17 per cent (for men) and from 18 per cent to 6 per cent (for women) (see table 7.1).

There is considerable debate over why this major shift occurred, but there are several reasons. One is the continual introduction of labour-saving machinery, culminating in the spread of information technology over the last thirty-five years. Most technological advances replace human labour with machines, even in farming and agriculture, which reduces the size of the workforce. Second, as we saw above, globalization has led to manufacturing processes moving to the developing countries,

Table 7.1 UK employee jobs by gender and industry, 1981–2006 (percentages)

	Men				Women			
	1981	1991	2001	2006	1981	1991	2001	2006
Distribution, hotels and restaurants	16	19	22	22	26	26	26	26
Banking, finance and insurance	11	16	20	21	12	16	19	19
Manufacturing	31	25	21	17	18	12	8	6
Public administration, education and health	13	14	14	15	34	36	36	39
Transport and communication	10	10	9	9	2	2	3	3
Construction	9	8	8	8	2	2	1	2
Agriculture and fishing	2	2	1	1	1	1	1	1
Energy and water	4	3	1	1	1	1	–	–
Other services[a]	3	4	5	5	5	5	5	5
All employee jobs (=100%) (millions)	13.1	12.0	13.1	13.5	10.2	11.8	12.9	13.3

Note: [a] Community, social and personal services including sanitation, dry cleaning, personal care, and recreational, cultural and sporting activities.

Source: ONS (2007b: 48).

where costs are lower. The older industries in developed societies have experienced major cutbacks because of their inability to compete with cheaper production in other parts of the world. Third, the development of welfare states after 1945 generated large bureaucracies associated with healthcare and the administration of welfare and public services, which created many new service-sector jobs.

As consumerism became a more significant part of life, many service-sector jobs were also created in advertising and the creative industries which underpin and sustain consumer demand. In the 1960s, some sociologists were already theorizing the emergence of a post-industrial society, which meant fewer huge factories with large workforces. A consequence of the shift to services was therefore a less favourable environment for workers' collective identities and collective action and for trade unionism (Touraine 1971; Inglehart 1997).

> For more on global production systems, see chapter 4, 'Globalization and Social Change'.

Trade unionism in decline?

As the proportion of people working in blue-collar jobs in industrial countries has progressively fallen, one major consequence has been a reduction in the membership of trade unions. In the early development of modern industry, workers had no political rights and little influence over their conditions of work. Unions developed as a means of redressing this imbalance of power between workers and employers. Through collective organization workers' influence was considerably increased, but it should be remembered that trade unions were primarily 'defensive' organizations, providing the means whereby workers could counter the overwhelming power of employers.

The post-1945 period witnessed a dramatic reversal in the position of unions in the advanced industrial societies. The period from 1950 to 1980 was a time of steady growth in union density and, by the late 1970s and early 1980s, over 50 per cent of the British workforce was unionized. High union density was common in Western countries for several reasons. First, strong working-class political parties created favourable conditions for labour organization. Second, bargaining between companies and trade unions was coordinated at the national level rather than in decentralized fashion at the local level. Third, unions rather than the state directly administered unemployment insurance, ensuring that workers who lost their jobs did not leave the labour movement. Countries in which some combination of these factors was present (but not all three) had lower rates of union density, between two-fifths to two-thirds of the working population.

From a peak in the 1970s, union membership began to decline. Traditionally, manufacturing has been a stronghold for labour, whereas jobs in services are more resistant to unionization. Hence, the decline of the older manufacturing industries and the rise of the service sector could be expected to lead to a decline in trade union members. However, Bruce Western (1997) argues that this explanation cannot account for the experience of the 1970s, which was generally a good time for unions (though not in the USA) but also saw a structural shift from manufacturing to services. Similarly, a significant share of growth in service-sector employment has occurred in social services – typically public-sector, unionized jobs. Western argued that the decline in unionization may be more significant within manufacturing than across different sectors.

Several explanations are consistent with the fall in union density within as well as between industries. First, the recession in world economic activity, associated with high levels of unemployment, particularly during the 1980s, weakened the bargaining position of organized labour. Second, the increasing intensity of international competition, particularly from Far Eastern countries, where wages are lower than in the West, also weakened unions' bargaining power. Third, the rise to power of right-wing governments, such as the British Conservatives in 1979, saw an aggressive assault on trade unions, which were perceived as too powerful.

In the UK, unions came out second-best in several major disputes, notably the strike by the National Union of Mineworkers in 1984–5, which lasted a whole year. Yet this is not a typical example of a strike today. In 2014, the National Union of Teachers (NUT), Unison's health workers and three other unions voted in favour of strike action following the government's planned two-year pay freeze. The aim was to bring the government into negotiations to resolve the dispute over the pay of teachers, midwives, nurses, porters, cooks, medical secretaries, healthcare assistants and other

groups of workers. In 2015–16, the government attempted to introduce a new contract for junior doctors in the NHS in England to fulfil a manifesto promise of a 24/7 NHS service. Following the breakdown of talks in late 2015, the British Medical Association (BMA) began the process of moving towards a series of short strikes by junior doctors.

Disputes such as these in the public-service sector are more representative of the way that strike action is used today. Mass walkouts, 'wildcat' strikes (those that are not authorized by union leaders) and private-sector manufacturing disputes are far less common than in the 1970s and 1980s. Part of the reason is, of course, that more people now work in services rather than in manufacturing. It is also the

---

USING YOUR SOCIOLOGICAL IMAGINATION

7.1 Industrial conflict and strikes

There have long been conflicts between workers and those in authority over them. Riots against conscription and high taxes and food riots at periods of harvest failure were common in urban areas of Europe in the eighteenth century and continued in some areas well into the nineteenth century. Traditional forms of confrontation were not just sporadic, irrational outbursts of violence: the threat or use of violence had the effect of limiting the price of grain and other essential foodstuffs (Rudé 1964; Booth 1977). Industrial conflict between workers and employers at first tended to follow these older patterns, but, today, we are more familiar with organized bargaining between workers and management.

Strikes

A strike is a temporary stoppage of work by a group of employees in order to express a grievance or enforce a demand (Hyman 1984). All the components of this definition are important in separating strikes from other forms of opposition and conflict. A strike is temporary, since workers intend to return to the same job with the same employer. Where workers quit altogether, the term 'strike' is

not appropriate. As a stoppage of work, a strike is distinguishable from an overtime ban or 'slowdown'. A group of workers has to be involved, because a strike involves *collective action*, not the response of one individual worker. That those involved are employees serves to separate strikes from protests such as may be conducted by tenants or students. Finally, a strike involves seeking to make known a grievance or to press a demand.

The strike is essentially a mechanism of power: a weapon of people who are relatively powerless in the workplace and whose lives are affected by managerial decisions over which they have little or no control. It is usually a weapon of 'last resort' because workers on strike either receive no income or depend on union funds, which are limited.

> ### THINKING CRITICALLY
> Why should strikes be less common in post-Fordist times among 'white-collar' occupational groups? What are the implications of the transformation of work for the Marxist theory of social class revolution?

case that governments have brought in stricter laws governing industrial action. But the most important change is the general economic climate of historically high unemployment levels, more part-time, flexible and zero-hours contracts, and an increasing divide between full-time, relatively secure jobs and insecure, poorly paid work. Perhaps the best example of the consequences of this divide is that, during and after the 2008 financial crisis, unions worked collaboratively with employers to negotiate reductions in hours and pay for their members rather than seeing companies make a proportion of their staff redundant. This kind of pragmatism is characteristic of trade unionism across the private sector today.

The power of unions tends to become weaker during periods when unemployment is relatively high because members are fearful for their jobs and are less likely to support industrial action. The trend towards flexible production has further weakened trade unionism. Still, since the 1980s there have been many mergers of unions as they try to maintain their strength and influence, and they have worked hard to stabilize their position in a very difficult climate. Given the relatively weak status of workers in relation to employers, the collective strength afforded by trade unions is unlikely to disappear altogether.

The feminization of work

Until the latter part of the twentieth century, paid work in the developed countries was predominantly the sphere of men, who needed a 'breadwinner's wage' to support the whole family. This situation has changed radically, as more and more women have moved into the labour force in what has been described as the gradual 'feminization' of work (Caraway 2007). This multifaceted process is a major historical shift that not only transformed the experience of paid work but is also transforming gender relations in every area of society. This is why it demands special attention.

Most new jobs today are created in offices, retail and service centres such as supermarkets,

call centres, airports, financial services and more. Many of these vacancies have been filled by women. In addition, there has been a shift towards less hierarchical management practices as part of the move away from the male-dominated world of industry (McDowell 2004). Globally, the overwhelming majority of workers are now employed in services (developed countries) or agriculture (developing countries), with less than one-quarter in manufacturing. In 2002, for the first time, a higher percentage of the global workforce was employed in services compared with either agriculture or industry (figure 7.1). It seems likely that the trend towards service employment will continue.

In most regions of the world, women make up at least half of the workforce (see figure 7.2), though the types of employment in which they are engaged differs widely. For example, in the European Union, Central and Eastern Europe, the Commonwealth of Independent States and Latin America, as well as in the Middle East and North Africa, women are employed predominantly in the service sector. In sub-Saharan Africa, where more than 60 per cent of the workforce is female, women work largely in agriculture. The ILO (2007a) reports that women also make up a larger share of agricultural employment than men in East Asia, South Asia, sub-Saharan Africa, the Middle East and North Africa.

The *nature* of women's employment is also different from that of men. Reports from the UK suggest that three-quarters of the working female population are engaged in part-time, low-paid work – such as clerical, cleaning, cashiering and catering – and this pattern is repeated across the developed economies (Women and Equality Unit 2004). In the following sections, we look at the origins and implications of the feminization of work.

Women and the workplace: a historical view

For the vast majority of the population in pre-industrial societies, productive activity and the activities of the household were not separate. Production was carried on either in

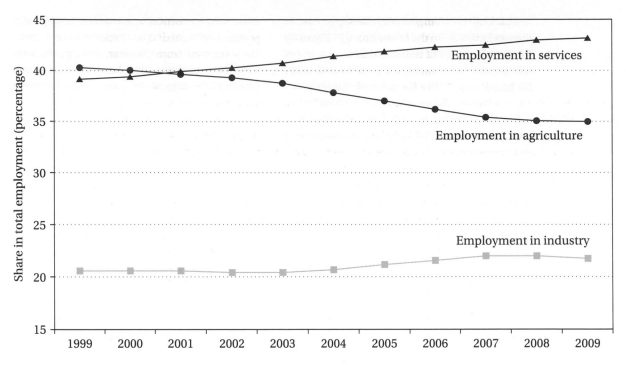

Figure 7.1 Global employment by sector (share of total), 1999–2009

Source: ILO (2011a: 20).

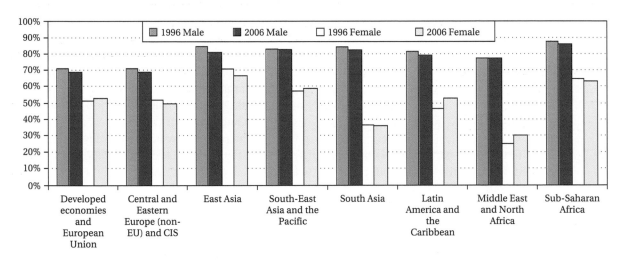

Figure 7.2 The global workforce by gender and region, 1996 and 2006

Source: ILO (2007a).

the home or nearby, and all members of the family participated in work on the land or in handicrafts. Women often had considerable influence within the household as a result of their importance in economic processes, even if they were excluded from the male-dominated realms of politics and warfare. Wives of craftsmen and farmers often kept business accounts and widows quite commonly owned and managed businesses.

Much of this changed with the separation of the workplace from the home brought about by the development of industrial factories. Work was done at the machine's pace by individuals hired specifically for the task, so employers gradually began to contract individual workers rather than families. An increasing division was established between home and workplace and the idea of separate spheres – public and private – became entrenched. Men, by merit of their employment outside the home, spent more time in the public realm and became involved in local affairs, politics and the market. Women came to be associated with 'domestic' values and were responsible for childcare, maintaining the home and preparing food for the family. The idea that 'a woman's place is in the home' had different implications for women at varying levels in society. Affluent women enjoyed the services of maids, nurses and domestic servants. The burdens were harshest for poorer women, who had to cope with the household chores as well as engaging in work to supplement their husbands' income.

Women's participation in the paid labour force rose more or less continuously over the twentieth century. One major influence was the labour shortage during the First World War, when women carried out many jobs previously regarded as exclusively for men. On returning from the war, men again took over most of those jobs, but the myth of the supposedly 'natural', pre-established pattern had been broken. In the years since 1945, the gendered division of labour has changed dramatically.

The UK employment rate for women – the proportion of those of working age in employment – rose between 1971 and 2009 from 53 per cent to 67 per cent. By contrast, the employment rate for men fell from 92 per cent to 76 per cent. Thus the gap between men's and women's employment rates narrowed significantly, but they have still not equalized (see figure 7.3). This narrowing of the gender gap looks likely to continue, though much of the increase in women's economic activity has been the result of a growth in relatively lower-paid, part-time work.

There are several reasons why the gender gap in economic activity rates has been narrowing. As the average age at first childbirth has increased, many women take on paid work before having children and return to work afterwards. Smaller families means the length of time women spend at home caring for young children has been reduced.

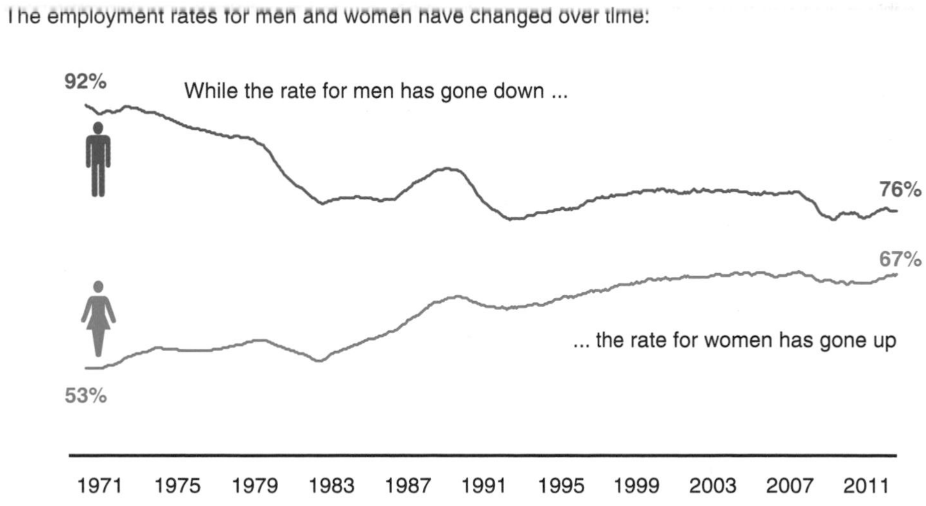

The employment rates for men and women have changed over time:

Figure 7.3 UK employment rates for men and women, 1971–2013

Source: ONS (2013b: 3).

Financial reasons are crucial in explaining why more women have entered the labour market. Economic pressures on the household, including higher male unemployment, have led more women to seek paid work. Many households find that two incomes are required to sustain their desired lifestyle and the dual-income family has become commonplace. Additionally, recent efforts to reform welfare policies, both in Britain and the United States, have sought to encourage women into the workforce as part of strategies to reduce welfare and public spending after the 2008 financial crash.

Finally, it is important to note that many women have chosen to enter the labour market (as well as higher education) out of a desire for personal fulfilment and in response to the drive for equality of the women's movement of the 1960s and 1970s. Having gained legal equality with men, many women have seized on new opportunities to realize these rights in their own lives. As we have already noted, work remains central to contemporary societies, and employment is almost always a prerequisite for living an independent life. But how do women fare when they do enter the workforce?

Gender inequality at work

The rise of feminist scholarship in the 1970s led to the analysis of gender relations in all the main institutions of society. Feminist sociologists not only focused on the gender imbalance within economic organizations but also explored the ways in which modern organizations developed in a specifically gendered way.

Feminist researchers point to two main ways in which gender is embedded in the very structure of economic organizations. First, these organizations are characterized by occupational gender segregation. As women began to enter the labour market in greater numbers, they tended to be segregated into *categories of occupations* that were low paying, involved routine work and did not provide opportunities for promotion. Second, the idea of a career was, in fact, a male one in which women played supporting roles. In the

workplace women performed routine tasks – as clerks, typists, secretaries and office managers – thereby freeing up men to advance their careers. In the domestic sphere, women also supported the male career by caring for the home, the children and the man's day-to-day well-being.

As a result of these two tendencies, modern corporations have developed as male-dominated preserves in which women are excluded from power, denied opportunities and victimized on the basis of their gender through sexual harassment and discrimination. Women workers have traditionally been concentrated in poorly paid, routine occupations, and many of these jobs are gendered – that is, they are commonly seen as 'women's work'. Secretarial and caring jobs (such as nursing, social work and childcare) are overwhelmingly held by women and are generally regarded as 'feminine' occupations. Gendered occupational segregation refers to the fact that men and women are concentrated in *different types* of jobs, based on prevailing understandings of what is appropriate 'male' and 'female' work.

Occupational segregation has both vertical and horizontal components. Vertical segregation refers to the tendency for women to be concentrated in jobs with little authority and room for advancement (at the bottom), while men occupy more powerful and influential positions (at the top). For example, in Scotland, women make up 89 per cent of the health and social sector, but just 19 per cent of NHS heads and chief executives are women (EHRC 2010b). Horizontal segregation refers to the tendency for men and women to occupy different categories of job. Women dominate in domestic and routine clerical positions, while men are clustered in semi-skilled and skilled manual positions. In Britain, the Equality and Human Rights Commission's *Triennial Review* (EHRC 2010a) found that women made up 83 per cent of all those working in personal services, 77 per cent of those in administrative and secretarial posts, and 65 per cent of sales positions. Conversely, they took just 6 per cent of engineering

Occupations dominated by women tend to be the lowest paid.

posts, 13 per cent of ICT jobs, and 14 per cent of positions as architects, planners and surveyors (also see 'Using your sociological imagination 7.2').

Women are also found disproportionately in the public rather than the private sector, making them more vulnerable to the cuts in public-sector employment that followed the 2008–9 recession. In 2010, 40 per cent of working women were employed in public services compared with just 15 per cent of men. The *Triennial Review* concluded that, overall, gender was more significant than social class in accounting for young people's career expectations and aspirations. Boys expected to work in engineering, computing, construction, architecture and skilled trades such as mechanics, while girls' expectations were for jobs in teaching, hairdressing, beauty therapy, childcare, nursing and midwifery. Clearly, gendered horizontal segregation is

proving to be extremely resistant to fundamental change.

The average pay of employed women in Britain, as elsewhere, is well below that of men, although the difference has narrowed somewhat over the last forty years. This general tendency towards closing the 'gender wage gap' is a significant step in the move towards equality. In 2014 the gender pay gap – the difference between men's and women's median earnings as a percentage of men's median earnings – was still 19 per cent for all employees (full- and part-time), 11 per cent for full-time employees in the public sector and 17.5 per cent in the private sector (ONS 2014f: 10–16). Much of this gap can be accounted for by interruptions to employment as women perform caring roles. Occupational segregation by gender is one of the main factors in the persistence of a wage gap between men and women, as

7.2 'The five deadly Cs'

Jobs traditionally done by women are poorly paid and undervalued. Low-paid jobs dominated by women are found in each of the five 'Cs' – cleaning, catering, caring, cashiering and clerical work. It is the concentration of women in these roles that contributes particularly to their poor reward. Sometimes women are doing jobs they love, but almost certainly they are low paid. Historically described as working for 'pin money', they could also be described as 'labourers of love' doing tasks 'naturally' associated with women, because of what is regarded as their 'innate' attributes rather than their skills. As a result, this undervaluation of women's work is often not taken seriously, so women in these roles have been largely overlooked by policy-makers.

THINKING CRITICALLY

What factors account for the dominance of men in higher-paid occupations? Is there anything 'natural' about this? Can you think of any professions which were male-dominated in the past but where positions are now mainly occupied by women? What impact has feminization had on this profession?

women are over-represented in the more poorly paid job sectors.

Several related processes have affected these trends. One is that more women are moving into higher-paid professional positions. Young women with good qualifications are now just as likely as their male counterparts to get well paid work. Girls regularly outperform boys at school, and in many university subjects women outnumber men. Their improved educational qualifications seem to lead inexorably towards more women finding their way into the professions, looking for a long career and promotion to the higher levels. Yet this progress at the top of the occupational structure is offset by the enormous increase in the number of women in low-paid, part-time jobs within the rapidly expanding service sector.

The introduction of a UK national minimum wage (NMW) in 1999 also helped to narrow the pay gap, since many women are concentrated in occupations such as hairdressing and waitressing, which previously paid below the minimum wage level. It was estimated that nearly 2 million people enjoyed a pay rise of approximately 30 per cent after the minimum wage was introduced. In 2015 the newly elected Conservative government announced that a new 'National Living Wage' (NLW) would be introduced in April 2016 at a rate some 10.8 per cent higher than the 2015 NMW – the largest annual rise since the NMW was introduced. Yet rebranding the NMW as a 'living wage' is controversial, as critics point out that the rate takes no account of in-work benefits or the requirements of different family types. D'Arcy and Kelly (2015) argue that '. . . it is a misnomer to label it a 'Living Wage'. The government's proposed NLW is in fact a minimum wage "premium" for those aged 25 and over . . .'. The benefits of the minimum wage do not negate the fact that a large proportion of women are in jobs which pay at or slightly above the minimum, and there are still many men and women who are employed (illegally) to work for less – earnings on which it is exceedingly difficult to live, especially with dependent children.

Taken over a lifetime, the gendered wage gap produces striking differences in overall earnings. One UK study found that a midskilled woman would experience a 'female forfeit' of more than £240,000 over her lifetime.

For more on women in poverty in the UK, see chapter 13, 'Poverty, Social Exclusion and Welfare'.

The female forfeit refers to how much less a woman will earn over her lifetime than a man with similar qualifications, even if she has no children (Rake 2000). Being on the wrong side of the gender pay gap has serious consequences for people's quality of life and long-term life chances.

Changes in the domestic division of labour

A consequence of more women entering paid work is that traditional family patterns are being renegotiated. The 'male breadwinner' model has become the exception rather than the rule and, in terms of both housework and financial decision-making, women's traditional domestic roles are undergoing significant change as the number of dual-earner households grows. In some households there has been a move towards more egalitarian relationships, though women continue to shoulder the main responsibility for housework.

Although more women are entering the workforce, they still shoulder the main responsibility for housework, which they juggle with paid employment, working the so-called second shift at home.

A UK survey at the start of the twenty-first century found that women still spent nearly three hours a day on average on housework (excluding shopping and childcare), compared with the 1 hour 40 minutes spent by men (ONS 2003). Once shopping and childcare are included, the difference becomes even wider. Men are contributing more to domestic tasks than in the past, although some suggest that the process is one of 'lagged adaptation' (Gershuny 1994). This means the renegotiation of domestic tasks is proceeding more slowly than women's entry into the labour market. Married women employed outside the home do less domestic work than those who are not in employment, although they almost always continue to take responsibility for care of the home. The pattern of their activities is rather different. They do more housework in the early evenings and for longer hours at weekends than do those who are full-time housewives. Findings such as these bear out the conclusion of Crompton and her colleagues (2005) that the process of equalization in sharing household tasks has, in fact, stalled.

Vogler and Pahl (1994) examined a different aspect of the domestic division of labour – that of household 'financial management' systems. Their study sought to understand whether women's access to money

This issue is examined in more detail in chapter 10, 'Families and Intimate Relationships'.

and control over spending decisions had become more egalitarian with the increase in women's employment. Through interviews with couples in six different British communities, they found the distribution of financial resources, on the whole, to be more equal than in the past, though it remained linked with social class.

In lower-income families, women were often responsible for day-to-day management of household finances, but they were not necessarily in charge of strategic decisions about budgeting and spending. In these cases,

Vogler and Pahl noted a tendency for women to protect their husbands' access to spending money while depriving themselves of the same right. In other words, there appeared to be a disjunction between women's everyday control over finances and their own access to money. Among higher-income couples, 'pooled' finances tended to be managed jointly and there was a greater degree of equality in accessing money and making spending decisions. The more a woman contributes to the household financially, the greater the level of control she exercises over financial decisions.

We may conclude that women are now an accepted part of the workforce in most developed countries, and this change continues to reshape gender relations. However, women still make up the bulk of the part-time workforce, with its attendant low pay and job insecurity. There is also gendered vertical segregation which appears much harder to change. Similarly, changes in the domestic division of labour seem to be progressing at a glacial pace, and men are not embracing the sharing of domestic tasks enthusiastically. Nevertheless, compared with the position in the 1950s, the changes outlined above still amount to a significant shift in gender relations.

Automation, the knowledge economy and 'skill'

The relationship between technology and work has long been of interest to sociologists. How is our experience of work affected by the type of technology that is involved? The current digital revolution has attracted renewed interest in this question in relation to integration of the Internet, computerization and robotics.

The majority of the robots used in industry today are found in vehicle manufacture and electronics industries producing televisions, computers, CD/DVD players, tablets, smartphones and lots more. A robot is an automatic device that can perform functions ordinarily done by human workers. The term 'robot' comes from the Czech word *robota*, or 'serf', popularized about fifty years ago by the playwright Karel Čapek. The usefulness of robots has been relatively limited so far but, as the technology rapidly develops, costs fall and we approach a 'tipping point', it is clear that robotics, automated production and computerization will spread. Consider the following examples.

Software 'bots' use an algorithm which automatically creates an article when an earthquake is detected, removing the need for journalists. BBC news has already adopted robotic cameras in its studio that eliminate the need for human camera operators. The online retailer Amazon announced that it is experimenting with a new delivery system – Amazon Prime Air – which would deliver products to customers using unmanned drones. Google has developed automated 'self-driving' (mainly electric) cars which are able to negotiate their way through traffic, and several states in the USA have legislated to allow self-driving vehicles to operate on their roads. The boss of the taxi firm Uber Technologies, Travis Kalanick, says that it is his ultimate aim to replace human drivers with driverless vehicles in the not too distant future. 'Bob', an 'autonomous android' or robot security guard, moves around the offices of G4S Technologies in Gloucestershire, UK, scanning for unusual events and reporting directly to the authorities. Armed forces routinely use drones, mine sweepers, bomb disposal droids and remote-controlled machines to reduce troop numbers and protect their soldiers (Crossley 2014; Zolfagharifard 2014). As these examples show, computerization, automation and robotics have the potential radically to eliminate large swathes of existing human employment roles.

For example, Frey and Osborne (2013) suggested that up to 47 per cent of jobs in the USA might be at risk from increasing automation and robotics in the next twenty years. In particular they argue that 'most workers in transportation and logistics occupations, together with the bulk of office and administrative support workers, and labour in production occupations, are at risk' (ibid.: 44). They also find that many service jobs are susceptible to computerization. On the other hand, high-skill and relatively high-wage jobs are the least susceptible to computerization. For instance, legal assistants and 'paralegals' may well find their work being taken over by computers, but lawyers are in low-risk positions. Some see such forecasts as scaremongering, but the social impact of automation has been the subject of much heated debate since at least the 1960s.

In an influential book, *Alienation and Freedom* (1964), Robert Blauner examined the experience of workers in four different industries with varying levels of technology. Using the ideas of Durkheim and Marx, Blauner operationalized the concept of alienation, measuring the extent to which workers in each industry experienced powerlessness, meaninglessness, isolation and self-estrangement. He concluded that workers on assembly lines were the most disaffected, with levels of alienation somewhat lower in workplaces using automation. In other words, Blauner argued that the introduction of automation was responsible for reversing the otherwise steady trend towards increasing worker alienation. Automation helped to integrate the workforce and gave employees a sense of control over their work that had been lacking previously. However, as shown by 'Classic studies 7.2', by no means all sociologists agreed with Blauner's assessment.

The American sociologist Richard Sennett (1998) studied people who worked in a bakery that had been bought by a large food conglomerate and automated with the introduction of high-tech machinery. Computerized baking radically altered the way that bread was made. Instead of using their hands to mix the ingredients and knead the dough and their noses and eyes to judge when the bread was baked, the workers now had no physical contact with the materials or finished loaves. In fact, the entire process was controlled and monitored by computer. Computers decided the temperature and the baking time of the ovens.

Bakery workers were then hired because they were skilled with computers, not because they knew how to bake bread. Ironically, they used very few of their computer skills either.

The production process involved little more than pushing buttons. In fact, when at one point the computerized machinery broke down, the entire production process was halted because none of the bakery's 'skilled' workers were trained or empowered to repair the fault. Automation had diminished their autonomy. The introduction of computerized technology in workplaces has led to a general increase in all workers' skills but also to a bifurcated workforce, composed of a small group of highly skilled professionals with a great degree of autonomy and a larger group of clerical, service and production workers with little or no control or freedom.

The skills debate is a complex one, because, as feminist researchers have argued, what constitutes a 'skill' is socially constructed and subject to change (Steinberg 1990). As such, conventional understandings of 'skilled' work tend to reflect the status of the typical incumbent of the job rather than the objective difficulty of the task. The history of occupations is littered with examples of jobs in which the same task was assigned a different skill level (and even renamed) once women entered the field (Reskin and Roos 1990). For example, in the twentieth-century clothing industry in Britain, both men and women worked as machinists, but male machinists were classed as 'skilled' workers and women as 'semi-skilled' workers. These classifications seem to be based not on levels of objective skill or types of training but on the gender of the person performing the task. The same, of course, holds for other low-status workers, such as minority ethnic groups.

Studies that have examined skill in terms of the substantive complexity of tasks tend to support the 'upskilling' position, whereas those that examine skill in terms of autonomy and/or control exercised by workers argue that automation leads to deskilling (Zuboff 1988; Vallas and Beck 1996). Skill levels are also related to geographical location and local employment conditions. For instance, in developed countries, call- (or 'contact'-) centre work is generally seen as a relatively low-skill, mundane form of employment, and

Classic Studies 7.2 Harry Braverman on the degradation of work in capitalist economies

The research problem

Can technological innovations positively influence workers' experience of the labour process? Why are some technologies more widely adopted than others in the production process? Blauner's optimistic conclusions about the impact of automation were rejected by the American Marxist writer Harry Braverman in his famous book *Labor and Monopoly Capital* (1974). In this he set out a very different evaluation of automation and Fordist methods of production and management, which he saw as part of a general deskilling of the workforce.

Braverman's explanation

Braverman did not come to the study of capitalist production as a sociologist. He had been (among other things) an apprentice coppersmith, pipe-fitter, sheet-metal worker and office worker, and in his teenage years became a socialist. Hence, he approached the problem of technology, automation and human skills having experienced at first-hand some of the effects of technological change. This highly involved and committed perspective comes through clearly in Braverman's account.

Braverman argued that, far from improving their lot, automation, combined with Taylorist management methods, actually intensified workers' estrangement from the production process and 'deskilled' the labour force. By imposing Taylorist organizational techniques and breaking up the labour process into specialized tasks, managers were able to exert more control over the workforce. In both industrial settings and modern offices, the introduction of new technology contributed to the overall degradation of work by limiting the need for creative human input. Instead, all that was required was an unthinking, unreflective body capable of endlessly carrying out the same unskilled task.

Braverman rejected the idea that technologies were somehow 'neutral' or inevitable. Instead, he argued, they are developed and introduced to serve the needs of capitalists. Similarly, he did not see any point in blaming machines or technologies themselves for worker alienation.

The problem lay in social class divisions which determined how such machinery was used. In particular, Braverman argued that, since the late nineteenth century, an era of 'monopoly capitalism' had developed. As smaller firms were swallowed up or put out of business by larger corporations, the new monopolistic businesses were able to afford a whole tier of technicians, scientists and managers whose task was to find better, more effective ways of controlling workers – scientific management or Taylorism is one example.

Some industrial sociologists had seen technological development and automated processes leading to the need for a better educated, better trained and more involved workforce. Yet Braverman disagreed. In fact, he argued that exactly the reverse was true. While 'average skill levels' may well be higher than in previous times, as with all averages, this conceals the fact that most workers have actually been deskilled. As he caustically put it, 'to then say that the "average" skill has been raised is to adopt the logic of the statistician who, with one foot in the fire and the other in ice water, will tell you that, "on the average", he is perfectly comfortable' (1974: 424).

Paradoxically, the more that scientific knowledge becomes embedded in the labour process, the less the workers need to know and the less they understand about the machinery and the process itself. Instead, an increasing divide emerges as the control by managers of workers intensifies. Braverman saw monopoly capitalism as a stronger form of capitalism that would be much more difficult to overthrow.

Critical points

Several objections have been raised to Braverman's thesis. First, he overstates the spread of Taylorism, assuming that it will become the dominant form of management, but it never did become widely implemented, which leaves Braverman arguing against a 'straw man'. Second, some feminists have contended that the thesis is really focused on male workers and fails to explain the particular nature of women's oppression. Others suggest that he does not provide an adequate account of changing family structures and their impact on working life. Finally, it may be argued that Braverman's thesis of deskilling tends to romanticize earlier, especially craft-based, forms of production, which are then contrasted with modern mass manufacture. Such a view could be said to be ahistorical – not properly taking into account historical development.

Contemporary significance

Braverman's thesis had a major impact. It challenged the dominant functionalist perspectives within industrial sociology and influenced many later sociologists working in this field. The book was also a popular success, having sold some 125,000 copies by the year 2000. However, Braverman's main aim was arguably to contribute to the renewal of Marxist theory itself, which he thought had failed to adapt to the radically different form of capitalism of the twentieth century. And though some Marxists have criticized his thesis as too pessimistic, failing to leave enough room for workers to resist, it can be argued that the decreasing number of workers joining trade unions, along with the widespread introduction of information technology today, shows that his central argument retains much of its force.

many sociologists criticize the pay levels, tight surveillance and conditions of work, seeing call centres as the office equivalent of assembly-line production (Moran 2005). However, in several cities in India, where contact centres have grown very rapidly, the work is viewed as relatively highly skilled, well paid and an attractive option for graduates. Recent research finds that many Indian call-centre workers share similar values and lifestyles with the Western middle classes, representing part of the vanguard of an emerging global middle class (Murphy 2011).

>> **Economic growth and development are discussed in chapter 13, 'Poverty, Social Exclusion and Welfare'.**

The knowledge economy

Some observers have suggested that what is occurring today is a phase of development beyond the industrial era altogether. A variety of terms have been coined to describe this new social order, such as the post-industrial society, the information age and the new economy. The term that has come into most common usage, however, is the knowledge economy. A precise definition of the knowledge economy is difficult to formulate, but in general terms it refers to an economy in which much of the workforce is involved not in the physical production or distribution of material goods but in their design, development, technology, marketing, sale and servicing. As Leadbeater (1999: vii) observed:

> Most of us [knowledge workers] make our money from thin air: we produce nothing that can be weighed, touched or easily measured. Our output is not stockpiled at harbours, stored in warehouses or shipped in railway cars. Most of us earn our livings providing service, judgement, information and analysis, whether in a telephone call centre, a lawyer's office, a government department or a scientific laboratory. We are all in the thin-air business.

Knowledge-based industries include high technology, education and training, research and development, and the financial and investment sectors. Among OECD countries, knowledge-based industries accounted for more than half of all business output in the mid-1990s. In 2006, the Work Foundation produced a report for the EU which found that over 40 per cent of European Union workers were employed in the knowledge-based industries, with Sweden, Denmark, the UK and Finland leading the way (see table 7.2). Education and health services constituted the largest group, with recreational and cultural

Global Society 7.2 | Upskilling and deskilling in the world of contact centres

City centre offices often function as a brand statement, flaunting the status and prestige of the company with their high-rise towers, mirror-glass walls and imposing atria for important visitors. Call centres, though, are largely unnoticed features of the peri-urban landscape. They are typically found in anonymous warehouses or sheds in out-of-town office parks surrounded by parking lots and security barriers, without even a logo outside identifying the company. The technology of the call centre allows for flexibility over location, so they can be built in areas where land and labour are cheap, such as the north east, Merseyside and the 'Celtic fringe' in the UK, or the Midwest in America. British and American companies are also increasingly locating their call centres to parts of the English-speaking developing world, such as the West Indies, Malaysia, and, especially, India.

[. . .]

The multimedia stage production *Alladeen* . . . toured the world from 2003–2005. . . . *Alladeen* is set principally in Bangalore, the call centre destination of choice for many Western companies because of its particular reputation for IT expertise. *Alladeen* follows a group of call centre workers as they go through their training. They learn to watch out for 'mother-tongue interference', the unconscious lapsing into their own accents, and attend 'culture-sensitization' modules, where they are taught the rules of American football and the names of sitcom characters, so they can identify more readily with their callers. . . . In the opening scene, for example, a group of sari-clad Indian women adopt the personae of *Friends* characters: 'This is Phoebe. How can I help you today?' Later on, when a caller says he is from Chicago, the Bangalore worker cries cheerily: 'My kind of town!'

[. . .]

Is Blauner right? Do these workers experience less alienation than those working on mass production lines in industrial factories?

As its title suggests, *Alladeen* sees its characters as modern-day Aladdins, searching vainly for personal transformation and wish-fulfilment in a technology that only entraps them in their mundane lives. For young, Indian graduates, working in a call centre is a 'good' job with relatively high status. The characters in *Alladeen* suffer the double-bind of the *Angestellten* [employee], caught between these frustratingly abstract pretensions to professionalism and the depressingly concrete nature of their actual working conditions. *Alladeen* explores the hidden politics of the call centre by juxtaposing visibility and invisibility. A big screen hanging above the stage relays computer graphics, documentary footage of a real Banglaore call centre, snatches of Bollywood movies and Hollywood versions of Aladdin films.

While it explores the theatrical possibilities of technology in this way, though, *Alladeen* makes some of the scenes that take place in the call centre invisible to the audience – which, of course, is exactly what Indian call centre workers are to Western callers.

Source: Moran (2005: 32–5).

THINKING CRITICALLY

Call-centre workers in India tend to be young, single and relatively well paid. Are they becoming more skilled or de-skilled? To what extent does your evaluation depend on the national, social context? Are call-centre workers in the developed countries upskilling?

Table 7.2 **Employment in knowledge-based industries, EU15 countries, 2005 (percentages)**

	Manufacturing	Services	Total
Sweden	6.5	47.8	54.3
Denmark	6.3	42.8	49.1
UK	5.6	42.4	48.0
Finland	6.8	40.5	47.3
Netherlands	3.3	41.9	45.2
Belgium	6.5	38.3	44.8
Germany	10.4	33.4	43.8
France	6.3	36.3	42.6
Ireland	6.0	33.9	39.9
Austria	6.5	31.0	37.5
Italy	7.4	29.8	37.2
Spain	4.7	27.0	31.7
Greece	2.1	24.5	26.6
Portugal	3.3	22.7	26.0

Source: Brinkley and Lee (2007: 6).

services next; together these sectors employed almost 20 per cent of European Union workers. Market-based sectors, including financial services, business and communication services, accounted for a further 15 per cent.

Investment in the knowledge economy – in the form of public education, spending on software development, and research and development – comprises a significant part of many countries' budgets. However, following the 2008 credit crisis and subsequent austerity packages it seems likely that levels of investment in the knowledge sectors will fall, at least in the short term. Admittedly, the knowledge economy remains a difficult phenomenon to investigate. It is easier to measure the value of physical things than 'weightless' ideas, research and knowledge. Yet it is undeniable that the generation and application of knowledge has become increasingly central to the contemporary global economy.

Multi-skilling and portfolio working

One of the arguments of post-Fordist theorists is that new forms of work allow employees to increase the breadth of their skills by engaging in a variety of tasks rather than performing one specific task. The move towards 'multi-skilling' has implications for employers. If at one time employment decisions were made on the basis of education and qualifications, now employers look for individuals who are adaptable and can learn new skills quickly. Thus, expert knowledge of a particular software application might not be as valuable as the ability to pick up ideas easily.

Specializations are often assets but, if employees have difficulty in applying narrow skills creatively in new contexts, they may not be sought after in a flexible, innovative workplace. In both skilled and unskilled occupational sectors, 'personal skills' are increasingly valued. The ability to collaborate and to work independently, to take the initiative, and to adopt creative approaches in the face of challenges are among the best skills an individual can bring to a job (Meadows 1996). Rather than employing narrow specialists, many companies would prefer to hire capable non-specialists who are able to develop new skills on the job. As technology and market demands change, companies retrain their own employees instead of bringing in expensive consultants or replacing existing staff. Investing in a core of people who may become valuable lifelong workers is seen as a strategic way to keep up with rapidly changing times.

For example, homeworking allows valued employees to perform some or all of their responsibilities from home, via phone and the Internet. In jobs that do not require regular contact with clients or co-workers, such as computer-based graphic design work, proof-reading or copy-writing for publishing, employees find that working from home allows them to balance non-work responsibilities and perform more productively. The phenomenon of 'wired workers' has grown in recent years as digital technology creates new opportunities for changing the way we work.

Melissa Gregg (2011) argues that, for professionals, the advent of wireless mobile technological devices, such as smartphones, tablets and laptops, seems to offer more freedom alongside liberation from the fixed office environment. But one consequence is that work is shifted out of fixed buildings and into every other area of public and private life, including the home. As a result, there is a temptation for people to work longer hours as the boundary between work and leisure is eroded, and for work to become the centre of people's daily lives at the expense of family or other dimensions of social life (Felstead et al. 2005). Homeworking does allow for different ways of working, but it is by no means a simple 'escape' from the pressures of conventional work.

In light of the impact of the global economy and the demand for a 'flexible' labour force, some sociologists argue that more people in the future will become portfolio workers. They will have a 'skills portfolio' – a number of different job skills and credentials – which they will use to move between different kinds of job during the course of their working lives. Only a relatively small proportion of them will have continuous 'careers'. Indeed the idea of a 'job for life' is a thing of the past as people develop 'boundaryless careers'. This does not necessarily mean a state of anarchy, though. People garner 'career capital' and social networks as they move around, and they experiment with skills, developing a greater sense of self-confidence, and effectively 'make sense' of their working life as they enact it (Watson 2008: 256–7).

Among young people, especially consultants and specialists in information technology,

Global Society 7.3 'Offshoring' and its discontents

The changing occupational structure today has to be viewed in a global perspective, as the production and delivery of many services now involve people working collectively across several national boundaries. In general, this is the result of firms in the developed world moving certain jobs to the developing world, where the work can be done more cheaply, thus maintaining or improving profitability. India – which has many English speakers – has become a centre for banking transactions and contact centres; China is a major producer of toys, clothing and consumer goods; and Taiwan produces many of the electronic components needed in the information age. This process has been called 'offshoring' (sometimes 'outsourcing') and, although it is by no means a recent development, there is much debate today on its future and consequences, particularly for the industrialized countries.

Systematic studies of offshoring are not numerous, but two views have emerged. On one view, offshoring is simply another extension of international trade – it is just that there are now more things to trade and more places in which to trade. There is nothing special to be concerned about. On the second view, offshoring could in future be a major world-historical force that transforms the global economy and may be particularly worrying for the developed countries. A leading exponent of the second view is the American economist Alan S. Blinder (2006), who explains exactly why governments in the developed world should be planning for a different future.

Blinder argues that manufacturing workers and firms in the relatively rich countries are used to competing with workers and firms in developing countries, but well-educated service-sector workers are not. Yet, in future, these service-sector workers will, Blinder forecasts, face the biggest challenge. A major divide is now emerging, which Blinder describes as that between those types of work that are 'easily deliverable down an electronic wire (or via wireless connections) without a loss of quality and those that are not'. For example, it is impossible to see German or

American taxi drivers or airline pilots losing out to offshoring, but it is possible to envisage those employed in typing services, security analysis, radiology services, accountancy, higher education, research and development, computer programming, banking services, and many, many more, doing so.

Blinder notes that the big change here is that jobs requiring high levels of education are no longer 'safe', so the oft-repeated government mantra that developing a highly educated workforce is the key to the economy of the future could be mistaken. What may be required is to invest in those 'personal services' that have to be delivered face to face and thus can escape offshoring (so far). All other 'impersonal services' that can be delivered electronically are fair game. Because of this, Blinder suggests that the main challenge to developed countries today is not China, which specializes in manufacturing, but India, which is better placed to take advantage of the movement of services offshore. As the following article demonstrates, though, China is already aware of this and is taking steps to be able to compete in the future.

Blinder admits that his thesis is a form of speculation or 'futurology' and that much more research and evidence of current patterns is required, but the process he describes is clearly already under way. Given the present period of rapid globalization, it seems that offshoring is here to stay. The short BBC News article below looks at offshoring in the financial sector.

Offshore boost for finance sector

The shifting of UK financial services jobs to developing countries such as India and China has saved the sector about £1.5 billion a year, a study suggests. Accountants Deloitte said the number of financial jobs going overseas over the past four years had increased 18-fold. More than 75 per cent of major financial institutions have operations overseas, compared with fewer than 10 per cent in 2001. But the trade union Unite said an effective case for offshoring had not been made, and pointed to growing staff turnover. It says that many companies are having to retrain an entire workforce over the course of a year and that wages are rising.

China vs India

Offshoring has spread across nearly all business functions, with significant growth around transaction processing, finance and human resources. India has kept the top spot for firms looking to move processes overseas, with about two-thirds of global offshored staff employed there. But it is in danger of losing its crown to China, with one-third of financial institutions now having back-office – mainly IT – processes there. Some 200 million Chinese people are currently learning English, providing a potential pool of skilled workers that may compete with India in coming years.

'Complexities'

Chris Gentle, associated partner for financial services at Deloitte and author of the study, said: 'Financial institutions need to re-engineer business processes, or risk simply transferring offshore the legacy inefficiencies of older,

onshore processes.' The typical financial services firm now has 6 per cent of its staff outside the host country, with the proportion having doubled in the past year.

However David Fleming, national officer at Unite, said the human and social costs of moving jobs 'have been absolutely huge, and customer dissatisfaction is widespread'. He added: 'Unite still believes that organizations are overlooking the complexities of offshoring and are still failing to make a sound business case for exporting work overseas.'

Source: BBC (2007f).

THINKING CRITICALLY

Blinder notes that the Industrial Revolution did not end agriculture – 'we still eat' – but it did transform it. Similarly, the Information Revolution has not ended industry – we still use machines, but with fewer human workers. What types of paid work will people in the developed societies actually do to earn a living in the future?

---

there is a tendency towards portfolio work. On some estimates, young graduates can expect to work in eleven different jobs using three different skill bases over the course of their working lives. Yet this remains the exception rather than the rule. One reason is that managers recognize a high degree of turnover among workers can be costly and bad for morale. King et al. (2005) found that employment agencies looking for IT workers tend to prefer 'known' candidates for permanent jobs, viewing those with mobile 'portfolio' career profiles with suspicion.

Nonetheless, many thousands of workers may be forced to develop and diversify their skills in order to sustain employment in very difficult labour market conditions. The shift towards portfolio working may be positive for some. Workers will not be stuck in the same job and can plan their work–life balance in more creative ways (Handy 1994). Others hold that 'flexibility' in practice means that companies

can hire and fire more readily, undermining any sense of job security for workers.

The social significance of work

While new ways of working present exciting opportunities for many people, they can also produce deep ambivalence on the part of others, who feel that they are caught up in a runaway world (Giddens 2002). As we have seen in this chapter, labour markets have undergone profound change with the shift away from manufacturing to service-oriented employment and the incorporation of information technology. Rapid change can be destabilizing, and many workers across different types of occupation now experience heightened insecurity.

Job insecurity has become an important topic in the sociology of work. Many commentators argue that over the last thirty-five years there has been a steady increase in job insecurity that has reached unprecedented levels in the developed countries. The drive for efficiency and profit means that those with few skills – or the 'wrong' skills – find themselves in insecure, marginal jobs that are vulnerable to shifts in global markets. Despite the benefits of flexibility, some argue that we are witnessing a shift in the very meaning of 'work'.

For most adults, work occupies a larger part of our lives than any other activity. We often associate the notion of work with drudgery, but this is far from the whole story. How would you feel if you thought you would never get a job? Being gainfully employed is important for maintaining our self-esteem and, even where working conditions are relatively unpleasant and the tasks dull, work still provides a structure for the cycle of daily activities. Several characteristics of work are important.

1 *Money* A wage is the main resource on which people depend to meet their needs. Without an income, day-to-day life is almost inconceiveable.
2 *Activity level* Work provides a basis for the acquisition and exercise of skills. Even where work is routine, it offers a structured environment in which a person's energies may be absorbed.
3 *Variety* Work provides access to new contexts. In the working environment people may enjoy doing something different from home chores.
4 *Temporal structure* For people in regular employment, the day is usually organized around the rhythms of work. Those who are out of work frequently complain of boredom and apathy.
5 *Social contacts* The work environment provides friendships and opportunities to participate in shared activities. Separated from work settings, a person's circle of friends and acquaintances is likely to dwindle.
6 *Personal identity* Work is usually valued for the sense of stable social identity it offers. Self-esteem is often bound up with the

economic contribution people make to the maintenance of their household.

Against the backdrop of this formidable list, it is not difficult to see why being without work may undermine an individual's confidence in their own value as a person.

The rise in job insecurity

Job insecurity refers to the situation in which workers lack the assurance that their job will be a stable one they can rely on over a period of time. Security of work means individuals can pay their rent or get a mortgage to buy a home, take a holiday, buy consumer goods and generally make life plans. But without relatively secure employment, many of the basic expectations of modern life may seem out of reach. The rise in flexible working, temporary and short-term contracts, zero-hours working and part-time work have all been seen as contributing to increasing job insecurity, which has been rising since the mid-1960s (Burchell et al. 1999).

For many workers, job insecurity is much more than a fear of redundancy. It also encompasses anxieties about the transformation of work itself and the effects of that transformation on health and personal life. Workers may see their chances of promotion decreasing at the same time that their workloads are increasing. This combination leads them to experience 'losing control' over important aspects of the job. Rather than adjusting to insecure conditions, workers remain anxious and under constant stress, and this often transfers into the home environment.

Job insecurity can have a severe impact on home life and family relationships. For instance, research in Spain found that Spanish men over thirty years of age who experience high job insecurity are less likely to get married (Golsh 2003). And, though the traditional stereotype of the male breadwinner may be less widespread today, many men still experience job insecurity as a threat to their self-identity. As one British survey respondent remarked, 'The man is the breadwinner. This is

7.3 Beyond work – a path to paradise?

Persistent unemployment, job insecurity, downsizing, portfolio careers, part-time work, flexible employment patterns, job sharing: it seems that, more than ever, people are working in non-standard ways. Perhaps it is time to rethink the nature of work and in particular the dominant position it has in people's lives.

Because we associate 'work' with 'paid employment', it is sometimes difficult to see what alternatives might be possible. The French sociologist and social critic André Gorz (1923–2007) argued that, in the future, paid work will play a less important part in people's lives. Gorz based his view on a critical assessment of Marx's writings. Marx argued that the working class would lead a revolution that would bring about a more humane type of society, in which work would be central to life satisfaction. Although writing as a socialist, Gorz rejected this view. Rather than the working class growing and leading a successful revolution, it is actually shrinking. Blue-collar workers have become a declining minority of the labour force.

It no longer makes sense to suppose that workers can take over the enterprises of which they are a part, let alone seize state power. There is no real hope of transforming the nature of paid work, because it is organized according to technical considerations that are unavoidable if an economy is to be efficient. 'The point now', as Gorz put it, 'is to free oneself from work' (1982: 67). This is particularly necessary where work is organized along Taylorist lines or is otherwise oppressive and dull.

Investment in new technology traditionally led to more full-time jobs, but investment in information technology now leads to fewer jobs, as it allows fewer workers to produce

Investment in information technology is just as likely to lead to job losses as it is to new 'high-skill' jobs. What happened to the workers?

the same or more products. The result is likely to be a rejection of the 'productivist' outlook of Western society, with its emphasis on wealth, economic growth and material goods. A diversity of lifestyles, followed outside the sphere of permanent, paid work, will be pursued by a majority of the population in the future. Gorz (1985) approvingly cited the French trade union centre (CFDT): 'Less work for everyone means work for all . . . and a better life.'

According to Gorz, we are moving towards a 'dual society'. In one sector, production and political administration will be organized to maximize efficiency. The other sector will be a sphere in which individuals occupy themselves with a variety of non-work pursuits offering enjoyment and personal fulfilment. Perhaps more and more individuals will engage in life planning, by which they arrange to work in different ways at different stages of their lives.

How valid is this argument? That there are major changes in the nature and organization of work in the industrialized countries is beyond dispute. Yet, thus far at least, progress in the direction of freedom from work has been slight, and there has been a rise, not a fall, in the number of people actively interested in securing paid employment. Paid work remains, for most, the key to generating the material resources necessary to sustain a varied life.

> **THINKING CRITICALLY**
>
> Gorz (1985) argued that the declining significance of work means we can spend less time in paid work, leaving more time to engage in creative activities. Outline and discuss the main obstacles to his utopian vision presented by capitalist economics.

how you're brought up anyway. If the man hasn't got a job it's not just the job insecurity, he feels less of a man, doesn't he?' (Charles and James 2003: 527). Job insecurity may also have similar effects to unemployment, though this body of work is not yet conclusive (Council of Europe 2005).

On the other hand, some people question whether job insecurity really is getting worse, suggesting that job tenure may, in fact, be rising (Doogan 2009). Grint and Nixon (2015) argue that since the 1970s there has been an overall reduction in average job tenure, but this has not been dramatic. Estimates suggest that job tenure was around ten years in the 1970s and 9.5 years in 2000. Indeed, length of tenure for women has actually been increasing, though this may reflect recent changes in the previously male-dominated job market. Around 80 per cent of British workers had full-time employment and between one-quarter and one-third had been with the same employer for over ten years. While such statistics may suggest job insecurity is not the norm, perceptions of rising insecurity may still tell us something of workers' experience and

concerns about economic change and shifting labour markets.

Unemployment

In the developed economies, unemployment reached a peak during the economic depression of the early 1930s, with some countries experiencing 20 per cent of the labour force out of work. The ideas of the economist John Maynard Keynes (1883–1946) strongly influenced public policies in Europe and the United States in the postwar period. Keynes argued that unemployment results from a lack of sufficient purchasing power to buy goods, so that production is not stimulated and fewer workers are needed. However, governments can intervene to increase the level of demand for goods and services, leading to the creation of new jobs. With such state management of economic life, many came to believe that high rates of unemployment were consigned to the past.

During the 1970s and 1980s, unemployment rates proved more difficult to control and Keynesianism was largely abandoned.

From less than 2 per cent unemployment in the 1950s and 1960s, unemployment in Britain rose as high as 12 per cent in the early 1980s before falling back by the end of the decade. From the mid- to late 1990s, unemployment in Britain once again began to decline, and by 2005 it stood at just under 5 per cent. However, rates of employment have not returned to post-1945 levels and relatively high unemployment has become normalized. In May to July 2011, UK unemployment stood at 7.9 per cent, around 2.51 million people, around 1 million of whom were young people aged sixteen to twenty-four (ONS 2011d), though this fell steadily to around 6 per cent by the end of 2014 (ONS 2014e).

Globally, unemployment rates are also historically high – they were at around 6.3 per cent or some 200 million in 2006 – though we also have to bear in mind that much informal work, particularly in developing countries, falls outside official statistics. It is probably the case that many people who are 'officially' unemployed are, in reality, employed or working in some capacity. Young people aged fifteen to twenty-four made up 44 per cent of the unemployed population and a persistent gender gap exists: just 48.9 per cent of women over the age of fifteen were working compared with 74 per cent of men. Unemployment rates differ widely too, with East Asia averaging 3.6 per cent, sub-Saharan Africa 9.8 per cent, and the Middle East and North Africa highest, at 12.2 per cent (Europaworld 2007). Regional statistics also mask very different national economic situations. In Southern Africa at the same period, for instance, unemployment rates ranged from around 80 per cent in Zimbabwe to 50 per cent in Zambia, and from 21 per cent in Mozambique to just 5.3 per cent in Namibia (CIA 2007).

Interpreting official unemployment statistics is not straightforward (see figure 7.4). Unemployment is also not easy to define. It means 'being out of work', but 'work' here means 'paid work' and 'work in a recognized occupation'. People who are properly registered as unemployed may engage in many forms of productive activity, such as domestic work, painting the house or tending the garden. Many people are in part-time paid work or in paid jobs only sporadically, while students and retired people are 'economically inactive' and therefore not counted as 'unemployed'.

General unemployment statistics are also complicated by the fact that they encompass two different 'types' of unemployment. *Frictional unemployment*, sometimes called 'temporary unemployment', refers to the natural, short-term entry and exit of individuals into and out of the labour market across the life course. *Structural unemployment*, by contrast, describes joblessness which results from large shifts in the economy rather than circumstances affecting particular individuals. The decline of heavy industries in the 1970s and 1980s, for example, contributed to higher levels of structural unemployment in many industrialized economies.

Trends in unemployment

Variations in the distribution of government-defined unemployment within Britain are well documented. Unemployment is generally higher for men than for women. For example, at the end of 2010 there were 1.43 million unemployed men compared with just over 1 million women. In 2007, the UK's Office for National Statistics reported that unemployed men were almost twice as likely as women to have previously been in work, while women registering as unemployed were ten times more likely than men to have been at home caring for children or the household (ONS 2007: 42). Clearly, despite recent trends towards increasing numbers of women moving into paid work, traditional gender roles persist in many regions and among some social groups.

On average, minority ethnic groups have higher unemployment rates than whites and much higher rates of long-term unemployment (see figure 7.5). However, these general trends hide much diversity. Unemployment among the white population stood at less than 5 per cent in 2004. For Indians, the rate was only slightly higher than this, at around 7 per

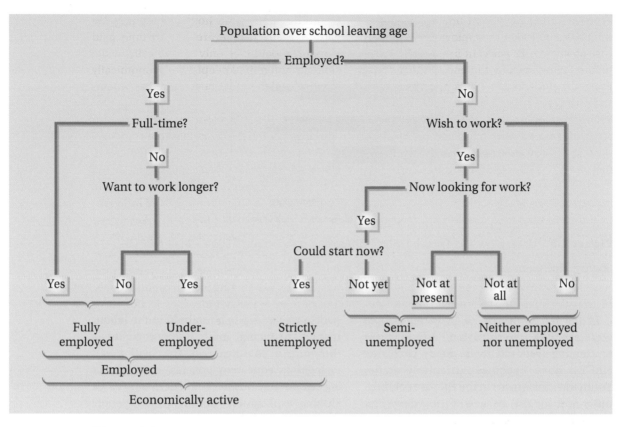

Figure 7.4 A taxonomy of possible employment, unemployment and non-employment states

Source: Sinclair (1987: 2).

cent – one of the factors which lead some to suggest that the British Indian population has nearly attained socio-economic parity with the white population.

For all other minority ethnic groups, unemployment rates were between two and three times higher than those for white men. In 2004, the unemployment rate among Pakistani women was the highest in the UK, at 20 per cent, five times that of white British and white Irish women. Among men, black Caribbean, black African, Bangladeshi and mixed ethnic groups had the highest rates, at between 13 and 14 per cent, almost three times higher than the 5 per cent unemployment of white British and white Irish men (ONS 2004a). The relevance of the concept of intersectionality is illustrated in such blunt unemployment statistics. In particular, the compounding of patterns of disadvantage produced by intersecting forms of inequality, such as gender and ethnicity, is evident here.

Young people are especially affected by unemployment. Globally, youth unemployment is consistently around 12 to 13 per cent, while, in Europe, average unemployment rates for young people increased by 60 per cent between the 2008 financial crisis and 2012 (ILO 2012). In 2012 the countries worst affected by the crisis, Greece and Spain, recorded youth unemployment rates of more than 50 per cent. For young people, prolonged periods of early unemployment can have effects that last into the future, including lower wages, health problems and financial difficulties for families. For societies, the failure to integrate young people into the economy risks a loss of tax revenues, social stability and economic growth (Vogel 2015).

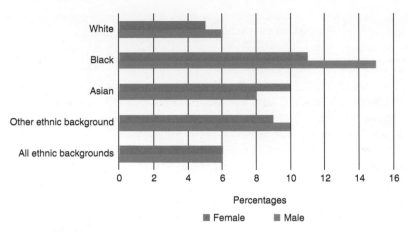

Figure 7.5 Unemployment rates by ethnic group and gender, April 2014 – March 2015

Source: McGuinness (2015).

In the UK, concerns about young people who are not in education, employment or training (referred to in policy circles as NEETs) have become particularly acute. Youth unemployment in the UK rose continuously over the first decade of the twenty-first century (figure 7.6). Figures from the Department for Education (DfE 2015) showed that, in January 2015, the unemployment rate for young people aged sixteen to twenty-four was 12.3 per cent (738,000 people), more than twice as high as the overall unemployment rate. Unemployment is an even bigger problem for young black people: in 2010, almost half (48 per cent) were unemployed. Around one-quarter of all young unemployed people are also long-term unemployed, which means they have been out of work for one year or more (Cavanagh 2011).

Why should unemployment affect so many young people? Vogel (2015: 4–6) argues that this is a multifaceted problem. In the developed economies there are rising numbers of younger workers with good qualifications, but qualifications that are non-vocational. This has resulted in a skills deficit for many industries and a mismatch between labour supply and demand in relation to young workers. In addition, there is the continuing growth of part-time, short-term and zero-hours contracts which particularly affect young people trying to gain a foothold in the labour market. Reducing youth unemployment is therefore a complex task that will mean changes to education policies, employment legislation and business practices as well as shifting expectations among young people themselves.

Social class and unemployment rates are also correlated. According to the ESRC cohort study for young people born in 1970, those whose fathers were from social classes I or II experienced the lowest rates of unemployment. Those whose fathers were from social class V, or who were raised by lone mothers, had the highest rates of unemployment, among them a high proportion who had never been in work at all. Unemployment rates are further linked to educational qualifications: the higher the level of qualification, the lower the unemployment rate (Begum 2004).

The experience of unemployment can be devastating to those accustomed to having secure work and an income. Studies of the emotional effects of unemployment have noted that people who are without work often pass through a series of stages as they adjust to their new status. While the experience is of course an individual one, the newly unemployed often experience a sense of shock, followed by optimism about new

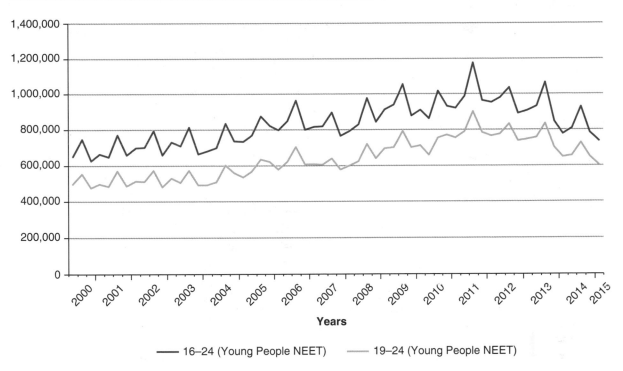

- 16–24 (Young People NEET)   - 19–24 (Young People NEET)

Figure 7.6 Number of young people not in education, employment or training, UK, 2000–2015

Source: DfE (2015).

opportunities. When that optimism is not rewarded, as is often the case, individuals can slip into periods of depression and deep pessimism about themselves and their prospects. If the period of unemployment stretches on, the process of adjustment is eventually completed, with people resigning themselves to the realities of their situation (Ashton 1986).

Recently, Guy Standing (2011) suggests that a new class grouping is emerging – a 'class in the making' – which he calls the precariat. This group consists of those who are unable to gain access to the labour markets which offer secure employment and decent wages. It includes older people, unskilled workers, young people with few qualifications, and all of those who regularly move into and out or work. Standing sees the growing precariat participating in protests and demonstrations against austerity in Greece and Spain and in the Middle East, arguing that their fitful involvement in paid work and resulting insecure lives may lead them towards populist and fascist parties that blame their situation on immigrants or 'big' government. The issue for government and policy-makers is how to tackle the debilitating work and life insecurity of the precariat in a global economy that is increasingly reliant on flexible working practices.

> **THINKING CRITICALLY**
>
> What social and psychological effects might unemployment have on the traditional 'breadwinners' – men – and on the traditional 'housewives' – women? Given that more women are now in paid work, is high unemployment potentially a more disruptive social problem today than in the past?

Conclusion: flexibility and the 'corrosion of character'

In 1970, as part of his study of blue-collar workers in Boston, USA, Richard Sennett drew up a profile of Enrico, an Italian immigrant who spent his working years as a janitor in a downtown office building. Although Enrico did not enjoy the poor conditions and meagre pay, his job provided him with a sense of self-respect and an 'honest' way to provide for his wife and children. He cleaned toilets and mopped floors day in and day out for fifteen years before being able to afford a house in a suburb of the city.

Although it was not glamorous, his work was secure, his job was protected by a union, and Enrico and his wife could confidently plan their future and that of their children. Enrico knew well in advance exactly when he would retire and how much money he would have at his disposal. As Sennett says, Enrico's work 'had one single and durable purpose, the service of his family'. Although Enrico was proud of his honest hard work, he did not want the same future for his children. It was important to him that he create the conditions for his children to be upwardly mobile.

Fifteen years later, in a chance meeting with Enrico's son Rico, Sennett found that the children *did* become more mobile. Rico finished his first degree in engineering before going on to business school in New York. In the fourteen years following his graduation he built up a highly lucrative career. Rico and his wife, Jeanette, had moved four times during their marriage in order to advance their respective careers. In taking risks and being open to change, Rico and Jeanette had adapted to the turbulent times and become affluent as a result. Yet, despite their success, the story is not an entirely happy one.

Rico and his wife worried that they were close to 'losing control of their lives'. As a consultant, Rico felt a lack of control over time and his work: contracts were vague and always changing, he had no fixed role, and his fate depended largely on the fortunes and pitfalls of networking. Jeanette similarly felt that she had only a tenuous hold on her job. She managed a team of accountants who were geographically divided: some worked at home, some at the office and some thousands of miles away in a different branch of the company. In managing this 'flexible' team, Jeanette could not rely on face-to-face interactions and personal knowledge of an individual's work. Instead, she managed from afar, using email and phone calls.

In moving around the country, Rico and Jeanette's meaningful friendships fell by the wayside; new neighbours and communities knew nothing about their pasts, where they came from or who they were as people. At home, Rico and Jeanette found that their work lives interfered with their ability to fulfil their goals as parents. Hours were long and they worried that they neglected their children. More troublesome than juggling time and schedules, however, was the concern that they were setting a disorienting example. While trying to teach their children the value of hard work, commitment and long-term goals, they feared that their own lives told a different story. Rico and Jeanette are examples of the short-term, flexible approach to work increasingly common today. Their work histories are characterized by constant movement, temporary commitments and short-term investments in what they are doing. The couple realized that 'the qualities of good work are not the qualities of good character'.

To Sennett, the experience of this family illustrates some of the consequences of flexibility at work for the personal lives and character of individuals. Sennett (1998) argues that the growing emphasis on flexible behaviour and working styles can produce successful results but inevitably leads to confusion and harm. This is because the expectations placed on workers today directly contradict many of the core features of strong character: loyalty, the pursuit of long-term goals, commitment, trust and purpose.

Work and life insecurity appear to be inevitable in the era of post-Fordist flexibility. Loyalty has become a liability rather than an asset. When life becomes a series of discrete jobs rather than a coherent career, long-term goals are eroded, social bonds fail to develop and trust is fleeting. People can no longer judge which risks will pay off in the end, and the old 'rules' for promotion, dismissal and reward no longer seem to apply. The central challenge for adults today is how to pursue their long-term life goals in a society that increasingly emphasizes the short term.

Chapter review

1 What is an economic recession? How did globalization influence the 2008 financial crisis?

2 In what ways does economic sociology differ from mainstream or orthodox economics?

3 With examples, outline the successive forms of capitalism since industrialization.

4 How does the organization and operation of transnational companies today differ from previous international companies? Is corporate social responsibility genuine or merely a public relations exercise for transnationals?

5 Describe the main aspects of Taylorism, Fordism and post-Fordism. Explain how 'flexibility' has become a key part of production and consumption today.

6 Provide some meanings of 'work'? How did paid employment become separated from domestic labour?

7 Trade union membership has been declining since the 1970s. Give some reasons for the decline.

8 What is the feminization of work? Using evidence from the chapter, explain why this does not mean that gender equality has been achieved.

9 What is a 'knowledge economy'? On balance, has this produced upskilling and greater autonomy or – as Gorz suggests – does information technology simply deskill the workforce?

10 Which social groups are most and least likely to be unemployed in the developed countries? What are the personal and social consequences of unemployment for men and women?

11 How might it be argued that the modern economy creates increasing job insecurity? Why should insecurity be problematic for individuals?

Research in practice

Of countries that received EU/IMF bailouts during the 2008–12 financial crisis, the Republic of Ireland was widely praised as the first to pay back its debt. But what impact did austerity measures have on everyday life and was the burden equitably shared across society? Read the following article, which focuses on intergenerational issues, then answer the questions: Carney, G. M., Scharf, T., Timonen, V., and Conlon, C. (2014) 'Blessed are the Young for They Shall Inherit the National Debt: Solidarity Between Generations in the Irish Crisis', *Critical Social Policy*, 34(3): 312–32.

1 Describe the research methods used in this study. What is 'constructivist grounded theory'?

2 How did families respond to government austerity measures? How did people adjust to the cuts to or removal of certain welfare benefits?

3   Outline the impact of austerity on different socio-economic groups.

4   What is the authors' conclusion about the role of families in helping people to cope with austerity? What do they suggest was the political import of this family assistance?

Thinking it through

The ideas of André Gorz on the radical impact of information technology on production and working lives were discussed above. Here is Wassily Levontief's parable of the declining significance of work (cited approvingly in Gorz 1985):

> Adam and Eve enjoyed, before they were expelled from Paradise, a high standard of living without working. After their expulsion they and their successors were condemned to eke out a miserable existence, working from dawn to dusk. The history of technological progress over the past 200 years is essentially the story of the human species working its way slowly back into Paradise. What would happen, however, if we suddenly found ourselves in it? With all goods and services provided without work, no one would be gainfully employed. Being unemployed means receiving no wages. As a result until appropriate new income policies were formulated to fit the changed technological conditions everyone would starve in Paradise.

Read 'Using your sociological imagination 7.3' on Gorz again (p. 284). Among your own circle of family, friends and acquaintances, have any of them downsized or moved to part-time work and lower pay in order to enjoy more freedom to do other things? What obstacles lie in the way if everyone wanted to do this? Suggest some ways in which these could be overcome.

Society in the arts

The participation of women in the workforce has changed significantly since the 1960s. Watch two or more episodes of the TV drama series *Mad Men* (2007–15), created by Matthew Weiner. This series begins in the early 1960s and looks at the working and private lives of employees in an American advertising agency. Concentrate on how the programmes represent:

- the roles women adopt in the workplace
- relationships between men and women, both at work and outside
- evidence of changes in both of the above.

Does the statistical evidence in this chapter show the fictional portrayal in *Mad Men* to be broadly accurate or wide of the mark?

Further reading

For an introduction to economic sociology, its history and current concerns, try Jeffrey K. Hass's (2007) *Economic Sociology: An Introduction* (London: Routledge), which is a very good guide to this field. Fran Tonkiss's (2006) *Contemporary Economic Sociology: Globalization, Production, Inequality* (London:

Routledge) is an application of economic sociology to recent globalization processes.

One of the most widely used and referenced textbooks on the sociology of work is Keith Grint and Darren Nixon's (2015) excellent *The Sociology of Work: An Introduction* (4th edn, Cambridge: Polity). Michael Noon, Paul Blyton and Kevin Morrell's (2013) *The Realities of Work: Experiencing Work and Employment in Contemporary Society* (4th edn, Basingstoke: Palgrave Macmillan) looks at the experience of work from the viewpoint of employees. Stephen Edgell's (2012) *The Sociology of Work: Continuity and Change in Paid and Unpaid Work* (2nd edn, London: Sage) does exactly what it should – tries to make sociological sense of paid and unpaid work.

 Finally, two comprehensive reference works are the edited volumes by Neil J. Smelser and Richard Swedberg (2005) *The Handbook of Economic Sociology* (2nd edn, Princeton, NJ: Princeton University Press) and Stephen Ackroyd, Rosemary Batt, Paul Thompson and Pamela S. Tolbert (2006) *The Oxford Handbook of Work and Organization* (Oxford: Oxford University Press).

Internet links

Additional information and support for this book at Polity:
www.politybooks.com/giddens

Center for the Study of Economy and Society – research centre at Cornell University, USA:
www.economyandsociety.org

Economic Sociology – site run by Copenhagen-based Brooke Harrington that 'examines the social underpinnings of money and markets'. Search the archives for material:
http://thesocietypages.org/economicsociology/about

The International Labour Organization – campaigns for decent work for all. Many useful resources here:
www.ilo.org

The Work Foundation, UK – Lancaster University-based organization engaged in 'high quality applied research':
www.theworkfoundation.com

Economic Sociology and Political Economy – Facebook page of this group for the latest news, books and articles in this field:
www.facebook.com/EconSociology

European Commission – Employment, Social Affairs and Inclusion pages with many helpful resources and statistics on work:
http://ec.europa.eu/employment_social/index_en.html

CHAPTER 8

Social Interaction and Daily Life

Contents

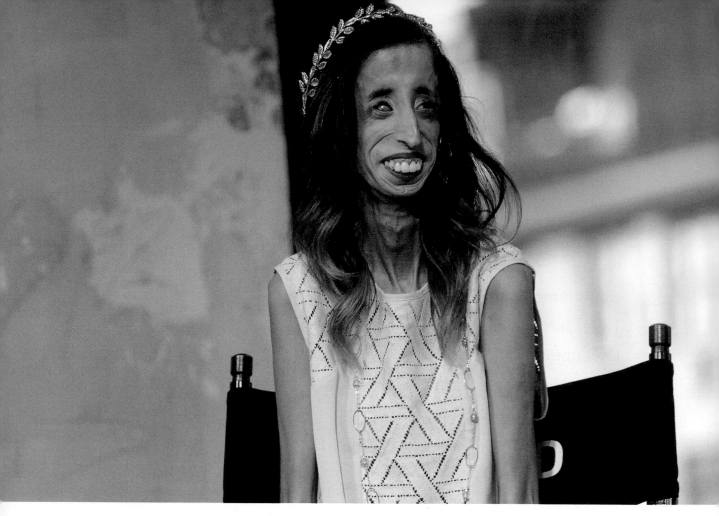

Lizzie Velásquez was picked on in childhood for her appearance, but was shocked by the vicious comments posted with a video clip of her on YouTube.

Most of us have personal experience of bullying, as victims or as bystanders to the bullying of others or, of course, as bullies ourselves. Contrary to the bulk of media reports, bullying affects not just children but many adults too. Being a target can have severe psychological consequences for the individual long after the bullying has ended, leaving the victim with an enduring sense of shame and deep-seated feelings of guilt that they somehow allowed it to happen or even contributed to their own abuse. Some cases of suicide have also been linked to persistent bullying.

Martocci (2015: xi–xii) describes the continuing impact of being bullied while studying for her doctorate: '[Yet] even now, as I sit in front of my computer and contemplate sharing this story I shudder, I feel a faint inner quaking. I imagine *her* reading the words and reviving her campaigns of subversion. I can *feel* the exaggerated eye roll that curdled my confidence, the one that preceded a contemptuous "*Ohhhh pleeeeeeassse*" . . . .' Martocci reflects that being bullied was not only a physical experience but one which changed her own self-concept, the very essence of how she perceived herself. She asks, 'What could have caused me to view accomplishments as inconsequential and self-image as fraudulent? How did I come to believe that the angry, insecure woman I was reduced to was my true self, unmasked at last?'

The beginning of a sociological answer comes in the discomfiting realization that the individual's self is not a 'thing', like a 'pearl' sitting within the 'shell' of the human body. Rather, the self is, in part, a social creation that is built from a whole series of relationships and interactions with others. That is why the type and quality of the interactions we have with others have the potential to change our perception of who we 'really' are – our true self, as it were. Bullying, however else we may legitimately wish to characterize it, is a particular type of social interaction between individuals which involves the attempt to exercise power over others.

> Sociological theories of self formation and development can be found in chapter 9, 'The Life Course' and chapter 3, 'Theories and Perspectives'.

In recent years, a related type of bullying via digital media has caused much concern, widely discussed as cyberbullying. Cyberbullying can be an extension of physical bullying, but in many cases it is wholly indirect, via the Internet, text and instant messaging, or email. Peter K. Smith and his colleagues (2008: 376) define cyberbullying as 'an aggressive, intentional act carried out by a group or individual, using electronic forms of contact, repeatedly and over time against a victim who cannot easily defend

him or herself'. Those involved in the interaction may never actually meet face to face. Like traditional bullying, the cyber form makes use of mundane social acts such as gossip, stigmatizing, stereotyping, ostracizing and shaming. Yet, unlike traditional forms, comments on gaming sites or Internet forums have a much wider reach. John Halligan (2012: vii), whose thirteen-year-old son Ryan took his own life as a result of being bullied, points out that 'It's one thing to be bullied and humiliated in front of a few kids. It's one thing to feel rejection and have your heart crushed by a girl. But it must be a totally different experience, compared to a generation ago, to have these hurts and humiliation witnessed by a far larger, online adolescent audience.'

Lizzie Velásquez (above) was picked on in school and received negative comments about her appearance, which actually results from two rare conditions that cause multiple impairments and an inability to gain weight. However, at the age of seventeen she accidentally came upon a short video clip of herself on YouTube entitled 'The World's Ugliest Woman'. Below it, she says, sat thousands of derogatory and very hurtful posts, such as 'Kill it with fire' and 'Why would her parents keep her?'. Velásquez felt bullied and alone: 'I cried for many nights – as a teenager I thought my life was over. I couldn't bring myself to talk to anybody about it, I didn't tell any of my friends, I was just so shocked that it had happened' (cited in Hawkins 2015). With the support of her parents and friends, she managed to take control of the situation and developed her own online presence into something of an anti-bullying online community; by 2015 she had over 240,000 followers.

The experience of Lizzie Velásquez shows that Internet bullies and so-called trolls (who set out to disrupt forums or provoke emotional responses) are able to depersonalize their targets and thus avoid much of the emotional reality of face-to-face encounters. Without ever having met her or knowing anything about her life, many people were prepared to add abusive comments to the video clip. Cyberbullying has attracted political and academic interest, but, as we will see later in this chapter, the digital age in which we live continually produces novel forms of interaction which sociologists must get to grips with.

Next, we set out some key concepts and ideas which sociologists have used to study the micro level of social interactions. We begin with some 'hidden' aspects of human communication, such as unacknowledged body language and gestures, before moving on to look at the unwritten 'rules' of interaction and what happens when we break those rules. From here we are able to set our encounters within shifting social contexts, and in the final sections we explore some of the emerging rules and norms of behaviour in online environments. The chapter ends with the question of whether people will still privilege face-to-face contact over cyber communication once daily life is saturated with digital devices and online environments.

The drama of daily life

When passers-by glance at one another quickly and then look away again, they demonstrate what Erving Goffman (1967, 1971) calls civil inattention. This is not the same as simply ignoring another person. Each individual indicates recognition of other people's presence but avoids any gesture that might be taken as too intrusive, which might be perceived as hostile. In a sense, civil inattention is the opposite of bullying. While the latter is action focused and targeted on a specific individual, the former represents a studious yet, with practice, more or less unconscious form of *avoidance* of direct contact.

Civil inattention is something we may all recognize, but why should sociologists concern themselves with such apparently trivial aspects of life? Passing someone on the street or exchanging a few words with a friend seem minor and uninteresting things we do countless times every day. Yet, just because we do not have to think about our everyday routines does not mean they fall outside

sociological analysis. In fact, Alfred Schutz (1899–1959) saw them as the starting point for phenomenology – the study of how people arrive at that taken-for-granted attitude and how it is reproduced in interactions (see chapter 3 for a discussion of Schutz and phenomenology).

Conventionally, interaction is taken to be face-to-face meetings or 'the reciprocal influence of individuals upon one another's actions when in one another's immediate physical presence' (Goffman 1980 [1959]: 26). With the advent of online environments such as chatrooms, blogs and social media and their routine adoption into our lives, a broader definition that takes in these new forms (which we will discuss later) seems appropriate. Alex Dennis and his colleagues (2013: 1) suggest that social interaction can be defined as 'the actions and responses of people to each other's activities'. The study of apparently insignificant forms of social interaction is of major importance in sociology and is one of the discipline's most absorbing subjects. There are three main reasons for this.

First, our day-to-day routines and constant interaction with others give structure and form to what we do. We can learn a great deal about ourselves as social beings and about the nature of social life from studying them. Our lives are organized around the repetition of similar patterns of behaviour from day to day, week to week, month to month, and year to year. Think of what you did yesterday and the day before that. If they were both weekdays, it is likely that you got up at about the same time each day. If you are a student, you may have gone to a class in the early morning, making the journey from home to campus that you do almost every weekday. Of course, the everyday routines we follow are not identical, and our patterns of activity at weekends usually contrast with those on weekdays. If we make a major change in our life, such as leaving college to take a job, alterations in daily routines are necessary, but we establish a new and fairly regular set of habits all over again.

Second, the study of daily life reveals how humans act creatively to shape their social reality. Although our behaviour is guided by social roles, norms and shared expectations, individuals perceive reality differently according to their background, interests and motivations. Because individuals are capable of creative action, they continuously shape reality through the decisions and actions they take. In other words, social reality is not a fixed or static 'thing' but is created through human interaction. This idea of the 'social construction of reality' lies at the heart of the symbolic interactionist perspective and was introduced briefly in chapter 1 (see also chapter 5, 'The Environment').

Third, studying social interaction sheds light on larger social institutions. All social institutions depend on the patterns of social interaction that we engage in daily. Consider again the case of two strangers passing in the street. The event may seem to have little direct relevance to large-scale, structured and more permanent forms of social organization. But when we take into account many, many such interactions, this is no longer so. In the contemporary world, most people live in towns and cities and constantly interact with people they do not know personally. Civil inattention is one among many mechanisms that gives city life, with its bustling crowds and fleeting, impersonal contacts, the vibrant character it has. City life is effectively reproduced via the myriad interactions of both inhabitants and visitors.

As you read on, bear in mind that the study of micro-level, everyday practices of social interaction are not separate from the large-scale, macro issues explored in other chapters of the book. Some of the best sociological work connects micro and macro phenomena to give us a more rounded picture of the social world.

> Theories of the impact of social structures on the everyday 'lifeworld' can be found in chapter 3, 'Theories and Perspectives'.

Non-verbal communication

Social interaction involves numerous forms of non-verbal communication – the exchange of information and meaning through facial expressions, gestures and movements of the body. Non-verbal communication is sometimes referred to as 'body language', but this can be misleading, because people characteristically use non-verbal cues to eliminate or expand on what is said with words.

The human face, gestures and emotions

One major aspect of non-verbal communication is the facial expression of emotions. When we compare the human face with other species, it does seem remarkably flexible and capable of manipulation. The German sociologist Norbert Elias (1897–1990) argued that studying the face shows how human beings, like all other species, have naturally evolved over a long period of time, but also how this biological basis has been overlain with cultural features in the process of *social development*.

Compare the human face with that of our closest evolutionary relatives, the apes. The ape face is furry and quite rigid in structure, permitting a limited amount of movement. The human face, in contrast, is naked and very flexible, capable of contorting into a wide variety of postures. In some parts of the world, 'gurning' competitions are even held to see who can pull the strangest facial expressions, and some of these appear *very* strange indeed. Without this evolved physiological malleability, human communication, as we know it, would be impossible. Therefore, Elias (1987a) sees the development of the human face as closely linked to the evolutionary 'survival value' of effective communication systems. While apes do make extensive use of 'whole body' communication, humans can communicate a varied range of emotions on just the 'signalling board' of the face. For Elias, facial communication demonstrates that, in human

Paul Ekman's photographs of the facial expressions of a tribesman from a remote community in New Guinea tested the idea that basic modes of emotional expression are the same among all people. Look carefully at each facial expression. Which of the six emotions used by Ekman above do you think is being conveyed in each one? Check by looking at the 'Thinking critically' box overleaf.

beings, the biological and the social are inextricably intertwined.

The American psychologist Paul Ekman and his colleagues developed a Facial Action Coding System (FACS) for describing movements of the facial muscles that give rise to particular expressions. They devised a system to inject some precision into an area notoriously open to inconsistent and contradictory interpretations. This is because there has been little agreement about how emotions should be identified and classified. Charles Darwin, the originator of evolutionary theory, claimed that there are basic modes of emotional expression across the human species. Although this claim is disputed, Ekman's research, covering people from widely different cultural backgrounds, provides some evidence in support of it. Ekman and Friesen (1978) carried out a study of an isolated community in New Guinea whose members had previously had virtually no contact with outsiders. When they were shown pictures of facial expressions expressing six emotions (happiness, sadness, anger, disgust, fear, surprise), the New Guineans were able to identify which emotions were being expressed.

According to Ekman, the results of his own and similar studies support the view that the facial expression of emotion and its interpretation are innate in human beings. However, he acknowledges that the evidence does not conclusively demonstrate this, as it may be that widely shared cultural learning experiences are involved. Nonetheless, other types of research support his conclusion. The human ethologist Irenäus Eibl-Eibesfeldt (1973) studied six children who were born deaf and blind to see how far their facial expressions were similar in particular emotional situations to those of sighted, hearing individuals. He found that the children smiled when engaged in obviously pleasurable activities, raised their eyebrows in surprise when sniffing an object with an unaccustomed smell and frowned when repeatedly offered an object they disliked. Using the FACS, Ekman and Friesen identified a number of discrete facial muscle actions in newborn infants that are also found in adult expressions of emotion. For instance, infants seem to produce facial expressions similar to the adult expression of disgust (pursing the lips and frowning) in response to sour tastes.

Although the facial expression of emotion seems to be innate, individual and cultural factors influence the exact form that facial movements take and the contexts in which they are deemed appropriate. Exactly *how* people smile, for example, the precise movement of the lips and other facial muscles, and how fleeting the smile is all vary between cultures.

By contrast, there are no gestures or bodily postures that have been shown to characterize all, or even most, cultures. In some societies, people nod when they mean 'no', while in others a nod means 'yes'. Gestures that Europeans and Americans tend to use a great deal, such as finger pointing, seem not to exist in other cultures (Bull 1983). Similarly, a straightened forefinger placed at the centre of the cheek and rotated is used in parts of Italy as a gesture of praise, but seems unknown elsewhere. Like facial expressions, gestures and bodily posture are continually used to fill out our utterances as well as conveying meanings when nothing is actually spoken. All three can be used to joke or to show irony or scepticism.

The non-verbal impressions we convey often inadvertently indicate that what we say is not quite what we mean. Blushing is perhaps the most obvious example of how physical indicators can contradict our stated meanings. But there are more subtle signs that can be picked up by other people. A trained eye can often detect deceit by studying non-verbal cues. Sweating, fidgeting, staring or shifting eyes, and facial expressions held for a long time (genuine facial expressions tend

to evaporate after four or five seconds) could indicate that a person is acting deceptively. Thus, we use the facial expressions and bodily gestures of other people to add to what they communicate verbally and to check how far they are sincere in what they say and whether they can be trusted.

Gender and the body

Marcel Mauss (1973) was among the first to argue that gestures and bodily movements are not simply natural but are linked to social context. People learn how to use their bodies in walking, digging, eating, and much more, and these 'techniques of the body' are transmitted across generations. But is there a gender dimension to everyday social interactions? Because interactions are shaped by the larger social context, it is not really surprising that both verbal and non-verbal communication may be perceived and expressed differently by men and women. There are also social class and ethnic dimensions to embodied interactions.

The political philosopher Iris Marion Young (1949–2006) explored gendered bodily experience in a famous article, 'Throwing Like a Girl' (1980, 2005). Young argued that the distinctive 'half-hearted' movements made by women – such as throwing a ball or stone – are not biologically determined but the product of discourses and practices which encourage girls and young women from an early age to experience their bodies as 'objects for others'. Such bodily training, she suggested, embodies an 'inhibited intentionality', reflecting feminine norms of restricted bodily comportment and movement. In short, male-dominated societies produce a majority of women who are essentially 'physically handicapped'. In contrast, men learn to experience their bodies as active and forceful 'objects for themselves', which is reflected in their more aggressive bodily movements, particularly noticeable in sports. For young boys, therefore, to be accused of 'throwing like a girl' is a dreadful insult and an attack on their identity as a male.

> ## THINKING CRITICALLY
>
> From left to right, Ekman's instructions were to show how your face would look
> 1 if your friend had come and you were *happy*
> 2 if your child had died and you were *sad*
> 3 if you were *angry* and about to fight
> 4 if you saw a dead pig that had been lying there a long time: *disgust*.
> Look at the faces again – is it easier to see the emotions being expressed when you know the context? Have you ever misunderstood how someone is feeling, and, if so, why did their facial expression not give away their emotional state?

On public transport, the open posture often adopted by men (sometimes called 'manspreading') is a routine expression of power, compared to the inward-directed position of women. In 2014 it was reported that the Istanbul Feminist Collective in Turkey ran a 'close your legs' campaign against the typical male posture on trains; the hashtag 'don't occupy my space' trended on Twitter.

These dynamics are evident even in routine social interactions. Take as an example one of the most common non-verbal expressions: eye contact. Individuals use eye contact in a wide variety of ways, often to catch someone's attention or to begin a social interaction. In male-dominated societies, a man who stares at a woman can be seen as acting in a 'natural' or 'innocent' way; however, the woman is not expected to stare back but to look away to evade the male gaze. On the other hand, a woman who stares at a man is often regarded as behaving in a suggestive or inappropriate leading manner. Taken individually, such cases may seem inconsequential, but, when viewed collectively, they help to reinforce patterns of gender inequality (Jeffreys 2015: 22; Burgoon et al. 1996).

There are other gender differences in non-verbal communication. Men tend to sit in more relaxed ways than women, leaning back with their legs apart, whereas women tend to have a more closed body position, sitting upright, with their hands in their lap and legs crossed. Women tend to stand closer to the person they are talking to than men, while men make physical contact with women during conversation far more often than the other way around. Women are generally expected to view this situation as normal. Other studies have shown that women show their emotions more explicitly through facial expressions and seek and break eye contact more often than men.

Sociologists argue that these seemingly inconsequential, micro-level interactions reinforce wider macro-level social inequalities. Men control more space when standing and sitting than women because they tend to stand further away from the person they are talking to and 'sprawl' when sitting. They also demonstrate control through more frequent physical contact. Women tend to seek approval through eye contact and facial expressions, but, when men make eye contact, a woman is more likely than another man to look away. In all these ways, non-verbal forms of communication provide subtle cues, which demonstrate men's power over women in the wider society (Young 1990).

In *Gender Trouble* (1990), Judith Butler argued that expressions of gendered identities illustrate that gender is mainly 'performative'. What does she mean by this? Butler says that many feminists have rejected the idea that gender is biologically or naturally fixed. But, in doing so, they separated gender (culture) from sex (biology), arguing that gendered norms of behaviour were built upon biologically determined male and female bodies. Butler rejects this position, arguing instead that there are *no* biologically determined identities lying beneath the cultural expressions of gender.

Gender identities are established precisely *through* their continuous performance. Hence, there is no essential, natural or biological basis to gender even though the belief that there is remains very widespread and, in a variety of ways, shapes people's behaviour. Butler's position is that gender identity is not a question of *who you are*, but of *what you do*, and it therefore follows that gender identities are much more fluid and unstable than previously thought. This does not mean that people have an entirely free choice of gender identity, as performances involve regularized and repetitively produced gender norms that are enforced by prohibitions, ostracism and other forms of censure (Butler 1993). However, if Butler is right, then there may be more scope for people to make active choices on how they perform gender and thus to resist the dominant or hegemonic forms of gendered identity.

> See chapter 15, 'Gender and Sexuality', for Raewyn Connell's wider theory of hegemony in relation to gender and identity.

Embodiment and identities

The gendering of bodily experience and movement described above complements theories of gender identity, which are discussed in detail in chapter 9, 'The Life Course'. As that chapter shows, people *learn* gender roles and gendered behaviour from a very early age in interactions with significant others such as family members. What we can add to this from sociological work on bodily experience and non-verbal communication is that a person's gender identity is also expressed through experience of their own and other people's bodies and bodily movements. Thus gender identity is both socially created and 'embodied'. In fact, the general concept of identity has become central to many areas of sociology over recent years. But what is an identity?

Richard Jenkins (2008: 5) says that identity is 'the human capacity – rooted in language – to know "who's who" (and hence "what's what"). This involves knowing who we are, knowing who others are, them knowing who we are, us knowing who they think we are, and so on.' It follows that all human identities are 'social identities', because they are formed in the continuing processes of interaction in social life. Identities are made, not given. Nevertheless, there are three aspects of identities: they are partly individual or personal; they are partly collective or social; and they are always 'embodied'. As Jenkins (1996: 47) puts it:

> Selves without bodies don't make much sense in human terms. Even ghosts or spirits, if we recognise them as human, once had bodies; even the disembodied world of cyberspace depends, in the not so final resort, on bodies in front of computer screens. We reach out with our selves and others reach out to us.

A good example of the close linkage between social identity and embodiment is in Goffman's study of 'stigma'. He shows how some disabled people, for example, can be stigmatized on the basis of observable physical impairments, which he calls 'discredited stigma', as such persons experience a loss of control over the presentation of self and the management of individual identity. On the other hand, some impairments that are not readily observable (such as epilepsy) can be more easily hidden from public view and therefore may allow the individual more control over the management of their identity.

8.1   Gender and interaction in public spaces

As we saw in chapter 1, microsociology, the study of small-scale face-to-face interactions, and macrosociology, the study of social structures and institutions, are inextricably connected (Knorr-Cetina and Cicourel 1981; Giddens 1984). Here, we look at an example of how an event that may seem to be a prime example of microsociology – a woman walking down the street who is verbally harassed by a group of men – is linked to macrosociological phenomena.

In *Passing By: Gender and Public Harassment* (1995), Carol Brooks Gardner found that, in various settings – most notably, the edge of construction sites – unwanted interactions instigated by men are frequently experienced by women as abusive. Although the sexual harassment of a single woman can be analysed by looking at just one interaction, it is not fruitful to restrict it in this way. This type of harassment is typical of street talk involving men and women who are strangers, and such interactions cannot be understood without looking into the wider backdrop of gender hierarchy in society. Gardner linked the harassment of women by men to the larger system of gender inequality, represented by male privilege in public spaces, women's physical vulnerability and the omnipresent threat of rape.

The Everyday Sexism Project in the UK is a website (also now a book by Laura Bates (2014)) created specifically to allow people to record their experiences of routine or mundane sexism at work, in the street, while shopping, and so on. For instance, an anonymous poster – a lawyer – recorded that, after successfully defending a haulage company in court, the director of the company turned to her and said, 'Good girl'. Others report persistent and routine catcalls and sexual comments, such as 'I'd have some of that', made by men both on foot and from vehicles as they walk to work.

The term 'sexual harassment' is historically recent, originating in feminist movements of the 1970s. In many countries, legislation on gender equality has now been enacted, and policies outlawing sexual harassment in the workplace have been put in place. However, these changes triggered a backlash in the media, which portrayed them as typical of an unnecessary 'sexual correctness' harking back to Victorian sexual standards (Zippel 2006: 8). Clearly, individual instances of verbal harassment must be related to shifting public norms and legal standards if they are to be properly understood. Understanding the link between micro and macro levels also shows that it is not enough to try to teach people good manners. To tackle the problem of sexual harassment also demands challenging gender inequality.

"So far, so good. Now let's hear your wolf-whistling."

> **THINKING CRITICALLY**
>
> If gender relations are becoming more equal, why does sexism persist? What body postures, movements and non-verbal signs have you noticed which suggest a movement towards gender *equality*? Is your own behaviour noticeably different from that of your parents and grandparents?

For this reason, Goffman calls this type of impairment a potentially 'discrediting stigma'.

Identities are also multi-layered, consisting of several sources, but a simple distinction can be made between *primary* and *secondary* identities, which are connected to the processes of primary and secondary socialization respectively. Primary identities are those that are formed in early life and include gender, race/ethnicity and perhaps also disability. Secondary identities build on these and would include those associated with social roles and achieved statuses such as occupational roles and social status positions. Social identities are quite complex and fluid, changing as people gain new roles or leave behind old ones.

An important consequence of the discussion so far is that identities mark out *similarities* and *differences* in social interaction. Individual or personal identity makes one *feel* quite unique and different from other people, especially in individualized modern societies, and is perceived by others as such. Our personal names are one illustration of this individual difference. In many societies today, parents increasingly seek out unusual names for their offspring to mark them out as different from the crowd, rather than choosing names that are linked to family or are commonly used. For many people today, naming offspring is much more a matter of parental choice than an expression of wider family ties.

In contrast, collective identities display similarity. To identify yourself, and be identified as part of an ethnic group, as working class, an environmentalist or a professional sociologist can be a source of group solidarity,

---

THINKING CRITICALLY

Think of an occasion when your identity has been challenged – perhaps you were asked to provide an ID card or other form of identification. How did you react and how did you 'prove' you were who you claimed to be? What conclusions would you draw about what society considers crucial in establishing identities?

---

pride or perhaps even shame. But, whatever the perception we may have of our own social identity, Goffman's point holds: that individual and social identities are tightly bound together within the embodied self (Burkitt 1999).

Face, body and speech in interaction

Let us summarize what we have learned so far. Everyday interaction depends on subtle relationships between what we convey with our faces and bodies and what we express in words. We use the facial expressions and bodily gestures of other people to expand on what they communicate verbally and to check if they are sincere. But, as we shall see, we also organize our activities in the contexts of social life to achieve the same ends.

Encounters

In many social situations, we engage in unfocused interaction with others. Unfocused interaction takes place whenever people exhibit mutual awareness of one another's presence. This is normally the case where large numbers of people assemble together, as on busy streets, in theatres or at parties. When people are in the presence of others they continually communicate non-verbally through their posture and facial and physical gestures.

Focused interaction occurs when individuals attend directly to what others say or do. Social interaction often involves both focused and unfocused exchanges. An instance of focused interaction is called an encounter, and much of our day-to-day life consists of encounters with other people – family, friends, colleagues – frequently occurring against the background of unfocused interaction with others who happen to be present on the scene. Small talk, seminar discussions, games and routine face-to-face contacts with ticket attendants, waiters and shop assistants are all examples of encounters.

Like conversations, encounters always need 'openings', which indicate that civil inattention is being discarded. When strangers meet and begin to talk, the moment of ceasing civil inattention is always risky, since misunderstandings can easily occur about the nature of the encounter being established (Goffman 1971). Hence, the making of eye contact may at first be ambiguous and tentative. The person looking to make eye contact can then act as though they had made no direct move if the overture is not accepted. In focused interaction, each person communicates as much by facial expression and gestures as by the words exchanged. Goffman distinguishes between the expressions individuals 'give' and those they 'give off'. The first are the words and facial expressions people use to produce certain impressions on others. The second are the clues that others may spot while checking their sincerity or truthfulness. For instance, a restaurant-owner listens with a polite smile to the statements that customers *give* about how much they enjoyed their meals. At the same time, she is noting the signals the customers *give off* – how pleased they seemed while eating the food, whether a lot was left over, and the tone of voice used to express satisfaction.

Waiters and other service-sector workers are often told to smile and be polite in their interactions with customers. In a famous study of the airline industry, Arlie Hochschild (1989) describes this as a form of 'emotional labour' (see chapter 1).

Impression management

Interactionists such as Goffman often use concepts from the theatre in their studies. The concept of social role, for example, originated in a theatrical setting, from the 'rolled-up' scripts used by actors in ancient times. In sociology, roles are socially defined expectations that a person in a given status or social position follows. For example, to be a teacher is to hold a specific position; the teacher's role consists of acting in specified ways towards her pupils, parents and other teachers. Goffman argues that social life is played out a little like actors perform on a stage, or, more accurately,

on many stages, because how we act depends on the roles we are playing in particular situations and times.

People are sensitive to how they are seen by others and use many forms of impression management to shape the way others react to them. Although this may be done in calculated ways, usually it is without conscious attention. For instance, Don attends a business meeting wearing a suit and tie and is on his best behaviour, but later, when relaxing with friends at a football match, he changes to jeans and a sweatshirt and shares bawdy jokes with them. This is impression management.

As we saw above, the social roles we adopt are dependent on our social status, and a person's social status often differs with the social context. As a 'student', you have a certain status and are expected to act in a certain ways in seminar rooms and lecture theatres. But, as a 'son' or 'daughter', you also have a different status from 'student', and expectations differ accordingly. Likewise, as a 'friend', you have yet another different position in the social order and another set of role expectations to meet. Clearly, people have many statuses at the same time, and this group of statuses is referred to as a status set.

Sociologists also distinguish between an ascribed status and an achieved status. An ascribed status is one you are 'assigned' on biological grounds, such as 'race', sex and age. Thus, your ascribed statuses could be 'white', 'female' and 'teenager'. An achieved status is one that is earned through an individual's own effort. Your achieved statuses could be 'graduate', 'athlete' and 'employee', for instance. And while we may like to believe that our achieved statuses are more important, the rest of society may not agree. In any society, some statuses have priority over all others and generally determine a person's overall position. Sociologists refer to this as a master status (Hughes 1945; Becker 1963). The most common master statuses are based on gender and ethnicity, and sociologists have shown that these are among the first things people notice about one another (Omi and Winant 1994).

8.2 Street encounters

Have you ever crossed to the other side of the street because you felt threatened by someone's demeanour? Elijah Anderson (1990) carried out research into this phenomenon in two adjacent urban neighbourhoods in the United States. He found that studying everyday life can shed light on how social order is created by the individual building blocks of many micro-level interactions. Anderson was particularly interested in understanding interactions where at least one party was viewed as threatening. He showed that the ways many black and white people interact with one another on the streets owed much to established racial stereotypes, which were linked to the economic structure of society. Once again, we see sociological work connecting micro interactions with the larger macro structures of society.

Anderson began by recalling Erving Goffman's description of how social roles and statuses come into existence in particular contexts or locations. Goffman (1980 [1959]: 13) wrote that, 'When an individual enters the presence of others, they commonly seek to acquire information about him or bring into play information already possessed. . . . Information about the individual helps to define the situation, enabling others to know in advance what he will expect of them and they may expect of him.'

But what types of behavioural cues and signs make up the vocabulary of public interaction that produces such expectations? Anderson found that factors such as skin colour, age, clothing and jewellery are all taken as identifying markers. Similarly, how fast people move and the type of movements they make then build on these to create more coherent assumptions. But the time of day and who might be expected at that time may explain and therefore 'neutralize' worries about strangers. However, where strangers are not evaluated

as 'safe', the alternative image of 'predator' may take over, and people act accordingly to avoid potential problems.

Anderson showed that those most likely to pass inspection do not fall into common stereotypes of the 'dangerous person'. Children and women come into this group, followed by white men, though more slowly. Black women come next, followed by black men and, finally, black male teenagers. By demonstrating that interactional tensions are linked to social status such as race, class and gender, this research shows that full understanding requires a grasp of macro- and micro-level processes. People are 'streetwise' when they develop skills such as 'the art of avoidance' to deal with fears of violence and crime.

This study shows how useful microsociology can be in highlighting how the broad institutional patterns in society operate in social life. It also adds a very important empirical dimension to large-scale structural theories of social inequalities, helping to ground them in people's everyday experiences.

> **THINKING CRITICALLY**
>
> In some societies today, young people who wear 'hoodies' (a type of jacket with a large hood) have been perceived as 'threatening' by older people. How might Anderson's study help us to understand these interactions and what do they tell us about the macrosociological relationships between younger and older generations?

Complementary roles: staging intimate examinations

Goffman's dramaturgical approach can be usefully applied to situations where social 'actors' collaborate to accomplish specific outcomes. A good example of this is James Henslin and Mae Biggs's (1997 [1971]) study of the potentially embarrassing and delicate encounter between a female patient visiting a male gynaecologist. Men and women in the West are socialized to view the genitals as the most private part of the body, and seeing, but particularly touching, the genitals of another person is usually associated only with intimate sexual encounters. Some women are so worried at the prospect of a pelvic examination that they refuse to visit the doctor even when they suspect there is a strong medical reason to do so.

Henslin and Biggs analysed 12,000 to 14,000 examinations, collected by Biggs, who had trained as an obstetric nurse. In order for the interaction between patient and doctor to run smoothly, a 'dramaturgical desexualization' has to take place in which the patient moves from 'person to pelvic'. That is, for the doctor to perform the highly specialized role and the patient to be comfortable and at ease during

the examination, the patient's personality is effectively screened out via a series of 'scenes', leaving just 'a body'.

Adopting the dramaturgical metaphor, the pelvic examination moves through several discrete scenes during which the parts played by the actors change as the episode unfolds. In the prologue, the person enters the waiting room preparing to assume the role of patient. When called to the consulting room she adopts the 'patient' role and the first scene opens. The doctor assumes a business-like, professional manner and treats the patient as a proper and competent person, maintaining eye contact and listening politely to what she has to say. If he decides an examination is called for, he tells her so and leaves the room – scene one closes.

The female nurse enters; she is an important stagehand for the main scene, soothing any worries the patient might have, acting as both confidante – knowing some of the 'things women have to put up with' – and collaborator in what is to follow. Crucially, the nurse helps to transform the woman from a person to a 'non-person' or body part. The nurse not only supervises the patient's undressing but also takes over aspects that normally the patient would control. She takes the patient's clothes,

Classic Studies 8.1   Erving Goffman – 'all the world's (a bit like) a stage'

The research problem

Very often we watch people in public situations who seem to be 'performing' or 'playing to the crowd'. If we are honest, we would probably admit that we also treat the world a little like a stage at times, putting on a show for the benefit of other people. But why do we do this? And, when we do, is it really *us* – our 'real selves' – doing the performing? If 'all the world's a stage', what happens *behind the scenes* of public performances? Erving Goffman (1922–82) studied this issue in several publications and research studies, producing the most detailed accounts of people's 'performances' and backstage behaviour.

Goffman's explanation

Much of social life, Goffman suggests, can be divided into front regions and back regions. Front regions are social occasions or encounters in which individuals act out formal roles; they are essentially 'on-stage performances'. *Teamwork* is often involved in creating front-region performances. Politicians in the same party may put on a convincing show of unity and friendship for television cameras, even though, privately, they detest each other. A wife and husband may take care to conceal their arguments from their children, preserving a front of harmony, only to fight bitterly once the children are safely in bed.

The back regions are where people assemble 'props' and prepare themselves for interaction in more formal settings. Back regions resemble the backstage of a theatre or the off-camera activities of filmmaking. When they are safely behind the scenes, people can relax and give vent to feelings and behaviour they keep in check when on stage. Back regions permit 'profanity, open sexual remarks, elaborate griping . . . rough informal dress, "sloppy" sitting and standing posture, use of dialect or substandard speech, mumbling and shouting, playful aggressiveness and "kidding," inconsiderateness for the other in minor but potentially symbolic acts, minor self-involvement such as humming, whistling, chewing, nibbling, belching and flatulence' (Goffman 1980 [1959]:

129). Thus, a waitress may be efficient and courteous to a fault when serving customers but become loud and aggressive behind the swing doors of the kitchen.

Spencer Cahill's research team discovered what Goffman called 'performance teams', which retreated into public toilets to conceal embarrassment when their collective performance went wrong. Cahill et al. (1985) describe a conversation between three young women in the toilets of a student centre on a university campus:

> A: That was sooo embarrassing! I can't believe that just happened [general laughter].
> B: He must think we are the biggest bunch of losers.
> A: I can't believe I just screamed loud enough for everyone to hear.
> C: It really wasn't all that loud. I'm sure he didn't hear you.
> B: ——, we didn't see him right away, and I did try to tell you but you were so busy talking that I . . .
> A: I can't believe that just happened. I feel like such an asshole.
> B: Don't worry 'bout it. At least he knows who you are now. Are you ready?

Defensive strategies buy teams the time to gather themselves before going out to face the 'audience' again. Goffman argued that performance teams routinely use back regions for this purpose and also discuss and rehearse the performance backstage before it actually takes place.

Goffman's approach is usually described as 'dramaturgical' – based on an analogy with the theatre. However, we have to bear in mind that this is an analogy. Goffman is *not* suggesting that the social world really *is* a stage, but that, using the dramaturgical analogy, we can study certain aspects of it and learn more about why people behave in the ways they do.

Critical points

Critics of Goffman's approach make some similar points to those levelled at other microsociologies, namely that they do not have

Not a sight you would expect to see outside hospitals today! Smoking can lead to disciplinary action for nurses, as health authorities try to maintain a tight distinction between the front and back regions of healthcare professionals' lives. Nonetheless, a significant number of nurses are smokers (McKenna et al. 2001).

a theory of society and, despite acknowledging inequalities of class, gender and ethnicity in their accounts, that they cannot explain how they developed or why they persist. The dramaturgical analogy can also be questioned. This may be a good model for studies of organizations and 'total institutions' but may not be so useful elsewhere. Similarly, Goffman's theatrical analogy works best in modern Western societies which have developed a clearer division between the public and the private realms of life (front and back regions). But in other societies this division is either less pronounced or just does not exist in the same form, hence Goffman's perspective may not have quite the same purchase on life within these societies.

Contemporary significance

Goffman's work has had a profound influence on sociology as a discipline as well as on numerous scholars, who have been inspired to become professional sociologists after reading his work. He is widely acknowledged to have made some of the most thoughtful and stimulating contributions to the discipline. Many sociologists today continue to refer to his original works for examples of how to carry out microsociology, and the concepts he developed (stigma, master status, front and back region, and so on), have become part of the very fabric of sociology in a variety of fields. His work is discussed in chapter 9, 'The Life Course', chapter 11, 'Health, Illness and Disability', and chapter 20, 'Crime and Deviance'.

THINKING CRITICALLY

Agree to do a supermarket shop for a friend or family member. While performing this activity, note the overt or written rules and the unwritten assumptions that are in place. In what ways do the interactions you engage in serve to reproduce social inequalities of class, gender, ethnicity and disability? How easy or difficult would it be to break the rules and challenge such inequalities?

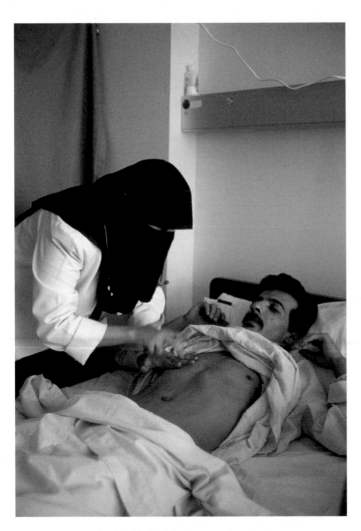

In Saudi Arabia, interaction between men and women is highly regulated, and intimate contact in public is forbidden. However, in a medical setting, other social rules take precedence, although these are still carefully managed.

folds them and makes sure the underwear is out of sight when the doctor returns, as most women feel this is a private matter. The nurse then guides the patient to the examining table and covers most of her body with a sheet before the physician returns.

The central scene now opens with the nurse and doctor taking part. The presence of the nurse helps ensure that the interaction between doctor and patient is free of sexual overtones and also provides a legal witness should the physician be charged with unprofessional conduct. The examination proceeds as though the personality of the patient were absent; the drape sheet separates the genital area from the rest of the body and does not allow her to watch the examination. Apart from specific medical queries, the doctor ignores her, sitting out of her line of vision. The patient collaborates in becoming a temporary non-person, not initiating conversation and keeping movement to a minimum.

In the interval between this and the final scene, the nurse again plays the role of stagehand, helping the patient to become a full person once more. After the doctor has left the room, the two may again engage in conversation, the patient expressing relief that the examination is over. Having dressed and regroomed herself, the patient is ready to enter the concluding scene. The doctor re-enters the room and discusses the results, treating the patient as a complete and responsible person. In resuming his polite, professional manner, he conveys that his reactions to her have not been altered by intimate contact with her body. The epilogue is played out when she leaves the surgery, taking up her identity in the outside world. The patient, doctor and nurse have collaborated in such a way as to manage the interaction and the impression each participant forms of the other.

> See chapter 11, 'Health, Illness and Disability', for a discussion of functionalist ideas on doctor–patient relations and the 'sick role'.

Desexualizing the body in public places

Intimate medical examinations are just one example of difficult social situations involving the human body. Sociological studies have recently explored the 'negotiated order' of the public swimming pool and the creation of a 'hot-tub culture', both of which present issues of the presentation of the body. In the context of public swimming pools and hot tubs, people 'present' their near naked bodies in close proximity to others, creating the risk of encounters being perceived as sexual. Hence, these interaction sites are constructed or organized as desexualized arenas, while rules and rituals have evolved which guide acceptable performances (Scott 2009, 2010). For example, swimmers try to avoid eye contact and strive to respect the varied 'disciplinary regimes' adopted by other people. It is also important that individual swimmers are aware of the social rules of acceptable personal space and do not routinely breach them by encroaching on the space of others.

Over the last two decades the hot tub has become popular in many developed countries, either alongside or as a replacement for the public swimming pool. Many hotels and private homes also have an indoor or outdoor hot tub, and tubs are now an accepted part of community life. The hot tub, though, is a smaller social site than the large public swimming pool and the rules and 'aquatic rituals' that govern interactions can be stricter. In a study of outdoor hot tub use in Iceland, Jónsson (2010: 247) notes that 'minimal touching' is key:

You do not greet each other with a handshake; a nod is sufficient; hot tub conversations are general and impersonal, even between regular visitors . . . Personal questions are not allowed. In some cases pool-goers have frequented the tubs over several years without uttering a single word. Discussions with foreigners rarely surpass the 'How-do-you-like-Iceland' barrier.

There are likely to be variations in hot-tub rituals across cultures. Where tubs have been installed in private homes and become part of 'normal' family life, public conversational and physical norms may not apply.

What both examples illustrate is the way that exposed human bodies pose problems of sexual propriety in public encounters that are dealt with by social rules, rituals and performances. Central to these interaction rituals is the maintenance of the correct personal space, or what some have referred to as the 'bubble', surrounding an individual.

Personal space

There are cultural differences in the definition of personal space. In Western culture, people usually maintain a distance of at least 3 feet when engaged in focused interaction with others; when positioned side by side, they may stand more closely together. In the Middle East, people often stand closer to one another than is thought acceptable in the West. Westerners visiting that part of the world are likely to find themselves disconcerted by this unexpected physical proximity.

Edward T. Hall (1969, 1973), who worked extensively on non-verbal communication, distinguishes four zones of personal space. *Intimate distance*, of up to 1.5 feet, is reserved for very few social contacts. Only those involved in relationships in which regular bodily touching is permitted, such as lovers or parents and children, operate within this zone of private space. *Personal distance*, from 1.5 to 4 feet, is the normal spacing for encounters with friends and close acquaintances. Some intimacy of contact is permitted, but this tends to be strictly limited. *Social distance*, from 4 to 12 feet, is the zone usually maintained in formal settings such as interviews. The fourth zone is that of *public distance*, beyond 12 feet, preserved by those who are performing to an audience.

In ordinary interaction, the most fraught zones are those of intimate and personal distance. If these zones are invaded, people try to recapture their space. We may stare at the intruder, as if to say, 'Move away!', or elbow him aside. When people are forced into proximity closer than they deem desirable, they might create a kind of physical boundary; a reader at a crowded library desk might physically demarcate a private space by stacking books around its edges.

Gender issues also play a role here. Men have traditionally enjoyed greater freedom than women in the use of space, including movement into the personal space of women who may not be intimates or even close acquaintances. A man who guides a woman by the arm when they walk together, or who places a hand on her lower back when showing her through a door, may be doing so as a gesture of friendly care or politeness. The reverse phenomenon, however – a woman entering a man's personal space – is often construed as flirtation. New laws and standards regarding sexual harassment in many Western countries seek to protect people's personal space – men, women and, increasingly, children – from unwanted touching or contact by others.

The rules of social interaction

Although we routinely use non-verbal cues in our own behaviour and in making sense of the behaviour of others, interactions mostly involve talk – casual verbal exchange – carried on in conversation with others. Sociologists, especially symbolic interactionists, have always accepted that language is fundamental to social life. In the late 1960s, however, an approach was devised that is specifically concerned with how people use language in the ordinary contexts of daily life.

Harold Garfinkel, whose work is discussed in 'Classic studies 8.2', coined the term 'ethnomethodology'. Ethnomethodology is the study of 'ethno-methods' – the folk or lay methods people use to *make sense* of what others do, and particularly of what they say. We all apply these methods, normally without paying conscious attention to them. Often we can make sense of what is said in conversation only if we know the social context, which does not appear in the words themselves.

See if you can understand what is going on in this simple conversation (Heritage 1984: 237):

A: I have a fourteen-year-old son.
B: Well, that's all right.
A: I also have a dog.
B: Oh, I'm sorry.

What if you were told that this is a conversation between a prospective tenant and a landlord? The conversation then becomes sensible: some landlords accept children but do not permit tenants to keep pets. Yet, if we do not know the social context, the responses of individual B seem to bear no relation to the statements of A. *Part* of the sense is in the words, and *part* is in the way in which meaning emerges from the social context.

Shared understandings

The most inconsequential forms of everyday talk assume complicated, shared knowledge. Similarly, meaning does not belong to the individual but is produced in the interaction process. Meanings are entirely capable of being communicated to others and are widely shared (Dennis et al. 2013: 15). In fact, small talk is very complex, as words used in ordinary talk do not always have precise meanings, and we 'fix' what we want to say through the unstated assumptions that underlie it. If Maria asks Tom: 'What did you do yesterday?', there is no obvious answer suggested by the words in the question. A day is a long time. It would be logical for Tom to answer: 'Well, at 7.16, I woke up. At 7.18, I got out of bed, went to the bathroom and started to brush my teeth. At 7.19, I

Classic Studies 8.2 | Harold Garfinkel's ethnomethodological experiments

The research problem

Misunderstandings are commonplace in social life. Sometimes they go unresolved, but they can also provoke irritation and frustration. Anyone who has been told, 'Listen when I'm talking to you', will be aware of how quickly apparently trivial misunderstandings can escalate into anger and aggression. But why do people get so upset when the minor conventions of talk are not followed? The founder of ethnomethodology, Harold Garfinkel (1917–2011), investigated this issue with some of his students.

Garfinkel's explanation

For a smooth-running everyday existence, people must be able to take for granted certain aspects of their lives. These 'background expectancies' include the organization of ordinary conversations, such as knowing when and when not to speak, what we can assume without formally stating it, and so on. Garfinkel (1963) explored unspoken assumptions with student volunteers who set out to 'breach' the conventions of daily life. The students were asked to engage a friend or relative in conversation and to insist that casual remarks or general comments be actively pursued to make their meaning much more precise. So, if someone said, 'Have a nice day', the student responded, 'Nice in what sense, exactly?'. Part of one of these exchanges (cited in Heritage 1984: 80) ran as follows (E is the student volunteer, S is their husband, and they are watching television):

> S: All these old movies have the same kind of old iron bedstead in them.
> E: What do you mean? Do you mean all old movies or some of them, or just the ones you've seen?
> S: What's the matter with you? You know what I mean.
> E: I wish you would be more specific.
> S: You know what I mean! Drop dead!

Why would a friend get upset so quickly? Garfinkel's answer is that the stability and meaningfulness of daily life depends on the sharing of unstated assumptions about what is said and why. If we were not able to take these for granted, meaningful communication would be almost impossible. Any question or contribution to a conversation would have to be followed by a massive 'search procedure' of the sort Garfinkel's students were told to initiate, and interaction would break down. What seem at first sight to be unimportant conventions of talk, therefore, turn out to be fundamental to the very fabric of social life, which is why their breach is so serious.

In daily life, people sometimes deliberately feign ignorance of unstated knowledge. This may be done to rebuff others, poke fun at them, cause embarrassment or call attention to a double meaning. Consider, for example, this all too typical exchange between parent (P) and teenager (T):

> P: Where are you going?
> T: Out.
> P: What are you going to do?
> T: Nothing.

The responses of the teenager are the opposite of those of the student volunteers above. Rather than pursuing enquiries where this is not normally done, the teenager provides no appropriate answers at all – essentially saying, 'Mind your own business!'

The first question might elicit a different response from another person in another context:

> A: Where are you going?
> B: I'm going quietly round the bend.

B deliberately misreads A's question in order ironically to convey worry or frustration. Comedy and jokes thrive on such deliberate misunderstandings of the unstated assumptions involved in talk. There is nothing threatening about this as long as the parties concerned recognize that the intent is to provoke laughter.

By delving into the everyday world which we all inhabit, Garfinkel shows that the normal, smooth-running social order that other sociologists simply take for granted is in fact a social process of interaction, which has to be continually reproduced over the course of every day. Social order is hard work! However, in his 'breaching experiments', Garfinkel was also able to demonstrate just how robust the fabric of daily life is. The students were able to explain and apologize to their friends and families once the experiment was over, but what might have happened had they carried on in such pedantic and uncooperative ways? Would they have been referred to a doctor or sent to a psychiatrist as suffering from mental illness? Social reality may be socially constructed, but it is a construction that is impossible to ignore.

Critical points

Given that ethnomethodology set out to criticize mainstream sociology and is usually seen as an alternative to sociology, it is unsurprising that it has been subject to much criticism. We can only note the most important points. First, ethnomethodology seeks to understand the world from the viewpoint of 'ordinary actors'. While this may bring about useful insights, critics argue that it leaves ethnomethodological findings open to the charge of subjectivism – they apply only to the particular subjects being studied. Second, the focus on micro-level order and disorder leaves ethnomethodology remarkably detached from the key structural determinants affecting people's life chances,

such as gender, race/ethnicity and social class. Ethnomethodology's aversion to social structural analysis and general theories of society seems to leave its studies cast adrift from crucial questions about power and the structuring of social life. Finally, ethnomethodology does not look for the causes of social phenomena but seeks to describe how they are experienced and made sense of. Again, many sociologists see this lack of causal explanation to be a major problem, which essentially rules out the idea that the study of social life could ever be 'scientific'.

Contemporary significance

Ethnomethodology is an important approach to the study of daily life and social interaction which is usually seen along with other microsociologies, such as phenomenology and symbolic interactionism. Sociologists who are interested in large-scale social structures, power relations, the international system of nation-states and long-term socio-historical change will always find ethnomethodology disappointing. But, taken on its own terms, this approach has produced much insightful work on the operation of daily life and how the people who constitute and reproduce it actually make sense of their world. It remains an influential perspective among scholars and students of daily life.

turned on the shower . . . ' We understand the response the question calls for only by knowing Maria, what sort of activities she and Tom consider relevant, and what Tom usually does on a particular day of the week, among many other things.

Interactional vandalism

We have seen that conversations are one of the main ways in which our daily lives are maintained in a stable and coherent manner. We feel most comfortable when the tacit conventions of small talk are adhered to; when they are breached, we can feel threatened, confused and insecure. In most everyday talk, conversants are carefully attuned to the cues given by others – such as changes in intonation, slight pauses or gestures – in order to facilitate smooth conversation. By being mutually aware, conversants 'cooperate' in opening and closing interactions and in taking turns to speak. Interactions in which one party is conversationally 'uncooperative', however, can give rise to tensions.

Garfinkel's students intentionally created tense situations by undermining conversational rules as part of their sociological experiments. But what about real-world situations in which people 'make trouble' through conversational practices? One American study investigated verbal interchanges between pedestrians and street people in New York City to understand why passers-by find such interactions problematic. The researchers used conversation analysis to compare a selection of street interchanges with samples of everyday talk. Conversation analysis is a methodology that examines all facets of a conversation for meaning – from the smallest filler words (such as 'er', 'um' and 'ah') to the precise timing of interchanges, including pauses, interruptions and overlaps.

The study looked at interactions between black men – many of whom were homeless, alcoholic or drug addicts – and white women who passed by on the street. The men tried to initiate conversations with passing women by calling out or paying them compliments or asking them questions. But something 'goes wrong' in these putative conversations, because the women rarely responded as they would in normal interactions. The text below is an attempt by 'Mudrick', a black man in his late fifties, to engage women in conversation (Duneier and Molotch 1999: 1273–4):

[Mudrick] begins this interaction as a white woman (who looks about twenty-five years old) approaches at a steady pace:

1 MUDRICK: I love you baby.
She crosses her arms and quickens her walk, ignoring the comment.
2 MUDRICK: Marry me.
Next, it is two white women, also probably in their mid-twenties:
3 MUDRICK: Hi girls, you all look very nice today. You have some money? Buy some books.
They ignore him. Next, it is a young black woman:
4 MUDRICK: Hey pretty. Hey pretty.
She keeps walking without acknowledging him.
5 MUDRICK: 'Scuse me. 'Scuse me. I know you hear me.
Then he addresses a white woman in her thirties:
6 MUDRICK: I'm watching you. You look nice, you know.
She ignores him.

Negotiating smooth 'openings' and 'closings' to conversations is a fundamental requirement for urban civility, but when women resisted the men's attempts at opening

conversations, the men ignored them and persisted. Similarly, if the men succeeded in opening a conversation, they often refused to respond to cues from the women to close it, as happens here:

1 MUDRICK: Hey pretty.
2 WOMAN: Hi how you doin'.
3 MUDRICK: You alright?
4 MUDRICK: You look very nice you know. I like how you have your hair pinned.
5 MUDRICK: You married?
6 WOMAN: Yeah.
7 MUDRICK: Huh?
8 WOMAN: Yeah.
9 MUDRICK: Where the rings at?
10 WOMAN: I have it home.
11 MUDRICK: Y'have it home?
12 WOMAN: Yeah.
13 MUDRICK: Can I get your name?
14 MUDRICK: My name is Mudrick, what's yours?
She does not answer and walks on.
(Duneier and Molotch 1999: 1274)

In this instance, Mudrick made nine out of the fourteen utterances in the interaction to initiate the conversation and elicit further responses from the woman. From the transcript it is evident that the woman is not interested in talking, but, when conversation analysis is applied to the tape recording, her reluctance becomes even clearer. She delays all her responses and, when she does respond, Mudrick replies immediately, his comments sometimes overlapping hers. Timing in conversations is a precise indicator; delaying a response by just a fraction of a second is adequate to signal a desire to change the course of a conversation. By ignoring the tacit rules, Mudrick was 'technically rude'. In return, the woman was also 'technically rude' in ignoring his repeated attempts to engage her in talk, and it is this aspect that made the interactions problematic for passers-by. When standard cues for opening and closing conversations are not adhered to, people can feel profoundly insecure.

The term interactional vandalism describes cases like these, in which a subordinate person breaks the tacit rules of interaction that are of value to the more powerful (Duneier and Molotch 1999). The men on the street often conformed to norms of speech in their interactions with one another, local shopkeepers, the police, relatives and acquaintances. But, when they chose to, they subverted the conventions, leaving passers-by disoriented and unable to articulate what had happened.

This study of interactional vandalism is another example of the link between micro-level interactions and forces operating at the macro level. To the black men on the street, the white women who ignored them were distant and bereft of sympathy, and hence legitimate 'targets'. The women, meanwhile, often took the men's behaviour as proof that they were indeed dangerous and best avoided. Interactional vandalism is closely tied in with over-arching class, gender and racial structures. The fear and anxiety generated in such interactions help to constitute the outside statuses and forces that, in turn, influence the interactions themselves.

Response cries

Some kinds of utterance are not really 'talk' but muttered exclamations, or what Goffman (1981) calls response cries. For instance, when Marsha exclaims, 'Oops!', after knocking over a glass of water, 'Oops!' seems to be an uninteresting reflex response to a mishap, rather like blinking your eye when a person moves a hand sharply towards your face. But the fact that people do not usually make the exclamation when they are alone shows it is not just a reflex. 'Oops!' is a response cry normally directed towards other people. The exclamation demonstrates to others that the lapse is minor and momentary, not something that should cast doubt on Marsha's command of her actions.

The strength of the tacit rules of interaction in public is so strong that even very innocent slip-ups from the rules respecting personal space can be surprisingly embarrassing.

'Oops!' is used for minor failures rather than for major accidents or calamities, which also demonstrates that it is part of our controlled management of the details of social life. Moreover, the exclamation may be used by someone observing Marsha, rather than Marsha herself. 'Oops!' is normally a curt sound, but the 'oo' may be prolonged in some situations. Someone might extend the sound to cover a critical moment when performing a task. A parent may utter an extended 'Oops!' or 'Oopsadaisy!' when playfully tossing a child in the air. The sound covers that brief phase when the child might feel a loss of control, reassuring them and at the same time developing their understanding of response cries.

This may all sound contrived and exaggerated. Surely we do not pay as much attention to what we say as this example suggests? Of course we do not, at least not on a conscious level. The point is that we all take for granted this immensely complicated, continuous control of our appearance and actions. In interactions we are never just 'present'. Others expect, as we expect of them, that we will display what Goffman calls 'controlled alertness' – a demonstration to others that we are competent in the routines of daily life.

Interaction in time and space

The section above has introduced some important aspects of the many implicit rules and norms which pervade our routine, everyday interactions. However, all our actions are distributed in time and space and all interaction is situated, occurring in a particular place and time. For example, Kim (2012) used participant observation to study the behaviour of people riding Greyhound buses and spending time in bus terminals over a two-year period. In particular, she sought to explain why and how people avoid interacting with others in these places.

The longer Greyhound journeys can last anywhere between eight and seventy-two hours, and passengers tend to be strangers to each other. Interactions do occur, but these are brief as, for most, strangers are suspect, and time is best spent looking after belong-ings and trying to put off others from taking the adjoining seat. Travellers adopt all sorts of behaviour to appear busy or uninterested – using mobile phones, checking bags, exploring the contents of wallets, staring out of windows, and sleeping or pretending to sleep. Kim calls this intentional avoidance of interaction, 'non-social transient behaviour'. While civil inattention acknowledges and respects the presence of others, non-social transient behaviour aims at 'invisibility' and does not respect or acknowledge the presence of others. Nonetheless, the actors are still engaged in giving a performance, one which effectively says to others, 'Leave me alone' or 'I don't want to be bothered'.

Kim argues that these performances occur primarily in enclosed spaces where people are forced to spend long periods of time together. However, they also take place in other non-social transient spaces perceived as potentially dangerous, such as nightclubs, pop concerts, sports venues and high-crime areas. One reason why people adopt non-social transient behaviour on long bus journeys is to protect themselves from possible thefts and physical attack. It is uncommon, for instance, for passengers to ask others to 'keep an eye on' their bags, as fellow passengers are also potentially suspect. A second reason is the expectation of delays and subsequent aggravation. Delays themselves do not routinely lead to complaints but, rather, to intensified disengagement and silence. Finally, passengers experience physical and psychological exhaustion on such long trips, and the rule is to keep conversations to a minimum and not to bother others unnecessarily. Kim's (2012: 9) central argument is that, in non-social transient spaces, there exists a set of norms and behavioural rules which new commuters learn in order to 'become non-social'.

The Internet is another good example of how closely forms of social life are bound up with the control of space and time, making it possible for us, in any corner of the world, to interact with people we never see or meet. Such technological change 'rearranges' space – we can interact with anyone without moving from

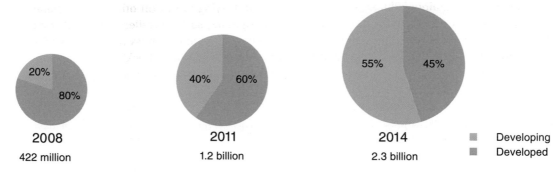

Figure 8.1 Mobile cellular subscriptions by level of development, 2000, 2005, 2014

Source: ITU (2014).

our chair. It also alters our experience of time, because communication is almost immediate. Until the advent of the Internet, most communication across space required a long duration of time. If a letter was sent abroad, there was a time gap while the letter was carried by ship, train, truck or plane to its destination. People still write letters by hand, of course, but instantaneous communication has become basic to the social world, and we look at this developing environment next.

The emergent rules of online interaction

The rapid growth of information communications technology (ICT) use is startling and no longer restricted to the developed world. Globally, mobile cellular phone subscriptions reached 6.9 billion in 2014, with 78 per cent of these being in developing countries (figure 8.1). From a relatively low base, the 'penetration rate' (number of phone connections compared to size of population) in Africa reached 21 per cent in early 2007, with more than 200 million cellular connections. Over the decade 2001–11, cellular phone subscriptions in developing countries rose from fewer than ten per 100 inhabitants to eighty per 100, rapidly catching up with the wealthier nations. By the end of 2014 the global penetration rate for mobile phones was 96 per cent, close to saturation point (ITU 2014). What will be the

impact of these technologies on the social life of societies?

Interaction and communication at a distance

ICT devices are spreading rapidly and have increasingly been integrated into people's everyday routines, both at home and at work (Kraut et al. 2006). This is the conclusion from a 2007 MTV Networks/Nickelodeon survey of 18,000 young people aged eight to twenty-four across sixteen countries, including China, Japan, the UK, the USA, Canada and Mexico. The survey found that 'Young people don't see "tech" as a separate entity – it's an organic part of their lives. … Talking to them about the role of technology in their lifestyle would be like talking to kids in the 1980s about the role the park swing or the telephone played in their social lives – it's invisible' (Reuters 2007).

But how do people communicate and interact with each other using smartphones, the Internet, email and social media sites? Chambers (2006) investigated the thesis that the fairly stable and fixed ties of family, neighbourly relations and community were giving way to more voluntaristic and fluid ties (Putnam 2000). She concluded that new patterns of association and social bonds are emerging based around ideals of 'friendship', many of which are sustained through ICT networks. She also argues that other forms are forged through new social identities among previously marginalized groups, such as those within 'queer communities', resulting in safe spaces for the exploration of 'self'. Yet the new ICTs also bring with them potentially new problems, such as the cyberbullying with which we began this chapter.

Chambers notes that, in spite of the positive aspects of social media, they may not provide an adequate basis for ensuring relationships of care and caring, most of which do need regular face-to-face contact and long-term commitment. Many schools and parents are also concerned about social networking and smartphones in relation to fears about online grooming and the abuse of children by adults. Such fears are not entirely unfounded. One social networking site, MySpace, admitted in 2007 that it had found more than 29,000 registered sex offenders among its 180 million members worldwide (Johnson 2007). Although this is a very small proportion of the overall membership, it is clear that the fast-changing and relatively anonymous online environment presents new problems which could not have been foreseen.

> Friendship and relationships are discussed in more detail in chapter 10, 'Families and Intimate Relationships'.

Many of today's affiliations are created through the Internet or other forms of mobile communication. How will these trends affect the quality of social relationships? For almost all of human history, people interacted face to face with others who were close at hand. And though letters, the telegraph and telephone have all been around for some time, the Internet enables 'interaction at a distance' in much more transformative ways. For instance, Skype enables (almost) real-time 'face-to-face' interactions between people who may be thousands of miles apart. The digital revolution could provide a renewed sense of sociality and personal intimacy for some, but it could also spell isolation and social distance for others. What seems clear is that people are already fitting digital media into their everyday

routines alongside existing face-to-face relationships.

Cybermanners or 'netiquette'

As we saw above, online communication and interactions present both dangers and opportunities, and sociological studies are starting to explore the contours of cyberspace. Some have suggested that, rather than seeing online life as a distinct realm of human experience, it may be more accurate to view it as an extension of the physical social world. On social media sites such as Bebo, LiveJournal and Facebook, for instance, most people tend to interact mainly with friends, relations and people they already know from face-to-face contact (Holmes 2011). Other Facebook 'friends' or 'followers' on Twitter are likely to be kept at a distance. As Baym (2015: 6–7) argues, we should not see 'cyberspace' as an inauthentic realm set apart from the authentic 'real world' of face-to-face or body-to-body interaction, because 'what happens online may be newer, but is no less real'.

With the advent of the 'second generation' of more interactive online services – often referred to as 'Web 2.0' – more people can share information and actually contribute to web-based content. One prominent and widely used example of this is the online encyclopaedia Wikipedia, which allows users to add content, to debate the veracity of entries with others, and effectively to become co-authors. The worldwide web can also be viewed on many more mobile internet devices, including mobile phones, laptop computers and tablets, thus integrating the Internet into more aspects of daily life (Beer and Burrows 2007; see chapter 18, 'The Media'). There is a blurring of the boundary between the private and the public as, for instance, people 'tweet' about their everyday activities and movements and include private details such as their location, gender, relationship status, and so on, in their social media profiles. Online communication has led to the emergence of norms and rules governing interactions and exchanges – often described as netiquette – and there are now many sources of information on how

Global Society 8.1 | The normalization of social media

In the USA, the Pew Research Center's 'Internet and American Life Project' has carried out more than 100 studies looking at the attitudes and behaviour of adults and teenagers in relation to the Internet. Using data from 2009, the project found that 93 per cent of American teenagers (aged twelve to seventeen) went online compared with 74 per cent of adults. However, Internet use among the youngest adults (eighteen to twenty-nine) was comparable to that of teenagers, at 93 per cent. Facilitating the increasing numbers of teens using the Internet is the shift to broadband at home (76 per cent of homes) and the advent of smartphones with Internet accessibility.

Some 73 per cent of American teenagers also use social media, with fourteen- to seventeen-year-olds the most avid users; more than four in five say they use such sites (82 per cent). Perhaps surprisingly, teenagers from lower-income families are more likely to use social media than those from wealthier middle-class backgrounds. In 2006, the Pew project found that teenage girls were more likely to use social media than boys, but by 2009 this had equalized. Adults, on the other hand, were much less likely to be social networkers, at just 47 per cent.

As social networking has become normalized, adults increasingly have profiles on multiple sites, and, as figure 8.2 shows, despite renewed competition, Facebook was easily the most widely used social media site among American online adults in 2014. However, there are also gender differences. Women are more likely to have a profile on Facebook, while men are more likely to be on LinkedIn, and 42 per cent of women online used Pinterest compared to just 13 per cent of men.

For teenagers, 37 per cent used social media to send messages to their friends every day, a fall from 42 per cent in 2008. Smaller numbers were using social media for sending bulletins and group messages. However, 86 per cent sent posted comment to a friend's page or wall and 83 per cent added comments to a friend's picture; 58 per cent of teenagers also sent texts or IMs using social media. Just over one-third (37 per cent) also said they had joined groups on networking sites. Twitter was less popular among teenagers: only 8 per cent of US teenagers used the site in 2009 compared with 19 per cent of adults.

The emergence and rapid growth of social media such as Facebook and Twitter may be interpreted as evidence that friendship is being reinvented for the digital age. Just as adults take the landline phone and TV for granted, so young people, who have never known a world without the Internet, view cyberspace, texting and social media as part of daily life.

% of online adults who use the following social media websites, by year

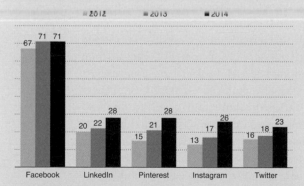

Figure 8.2 US online adults' social media use, 2012–14

Source: Duggan et al. (2015): 2.

THINKING CRITICALLY

Track down the latest Pew survey online – the reports are available free of charge. Take notes of the evidence covering social media use. On balance, what conclusion do you draw from the data about the forging and maintenance of social media friendships?

Online communication is evolving its own forms of manners, or netiquette, derived from the suggestions of users.

people *should* behave in their online communications (Chiles 2013).

Advice on how to communicate using email in the 1990s was an early form of netiquette. Users were told to ensure that their emails should not be insulting or unnecessarily critical of others and that they should avoid using email for trivial or irrelevant information. Further, they should assume the emails of others were honestly written, and that all emails were permanent records. Emails should begin with something like, 'Hi John', and end with 'best wishes' as an appropriate level of informality for the medium, and to use some small talk but not too much (Strawbridge 2006: 9–15). However, with the rapid growth of social media, netiquette rules have changed very rapidly.

Etiquette guides to interaction on social media advise that, although these are similar to 'real-life' interactions, it is important to appreciate that anyone can become a 'friend'. Some guides suggest 'friending' only those people one already knows, while others argue that it is good to accept strangers, who can then be dropped or 'defriended' later if necessary. One etiquette guide to Facebook (Weinberg 2008) advises: 'don't add users as "friends" without proper introductions, be honest about your real identity and don't publicize a private conversation on a "wall" (publicly open) post.' The same guide reminds us to 'Think about the consequences of your engagement on any social site . . . Consider how your comments would be perceived before you actually post them, and think about logic above emotion at all times.'

Given the nature of web-based services, especially social media, which are open to changes driven by users, online manners codes are likely to continue developing along with the technology. At present, netiquette appears to be based largely on attempts to translate existing norms of behaviour and codes of manners into a format which is appropriate online, rather than creating an entirely novel system. For example, a survey of netiquette advice by Holmes (2011) found that, as in 'the real world', social status differences between employee and employer or teachers and students were seen as problematic and potentially embarrassing. Similarly, social divisions of class and ethnicity were seen as needing careful handling.

If online etiquette is a variant of social etiquette, then mainstream sociological theories and concepts may still be useful. For instance, the concept of 'role conflict' helps to makes sense of this situation as users attempt to manage their different roles in relation to the different 'faces' they present to others. This becomes increasingly difficult on social media, where information is potentially open to all of these various audiences at the same time. How many workers would be comfortable to find that their boss was a Facebook 'friend' or Twitter 'follower', for example? Keeping separate the various roles an individual plays and the faces they present seems to be becoming more complex. This conclusion is consistent with the view that the Internet is an extension of the social world, not a clean break from it. This is evident from a brief look at how 'trust' is built and managed online.

Building trust online

Today many of our everyday transactions, such as buying groceries, making a bank deposit or paying a utility bill, bring us into *indirect contact* with strangers. Anyone who has phoned a bank and been put through to an anonymous call centre thousands of miles away has experienced this phenomenon. Now that email, text messaging, instant messaging, online communities, chatrooms and social media have become widely integrated into everyday life, there is a growing interest in understanding their impact and the

norms of online conduct that are emerging (Baym 2015).

There has long been a polarization in debates on the possibilities and dangers of the Internet. For sceptics, Internet communication, often referred to as computer mediated communication (CMC), generates new problems that are just not found in face-to-face social interactions. As Katz et al. (2001: 407) put it: 'To type is not to be human, to be in cyberspace is not to be real; all is pretence and alienation, a poor substitute for the real thing.' In particular, proponents of this view argue that CMC technology is unable to prevent users from hiding behind false identities, which allow trickery, fraud, bullying, manipulation, emotional swindles and the sexual grooming of children. The result is the gradual erosion of mutual trust, not only in online environments but spreading into the wider society too. Indirect, online communication is seen to encourage isolation, substituting superficial online contacts for authentic and long-lasting friendship (Stoll 1995).

On the other hand, Internet enthusiasts argue that online interaction has some advantages over conventional forms. Physical co-presence may enable the display of a wider range of emotions and subtle changes of meaning, but it also conveys information about the speaker's age, gender, ethnicity and social position that may be used to stigmatize and discriminate. Electronic communication masks most or all of these identifying markers, ensuring that attention focuses strictly on the content of the message. This can be a great advantage for minority ethnic groups, women and other traditionally disadvantaged groups whose opinions have been devalued in public situations (Locke and Pascoe 2000).

Optimists argue that Internet users also tend to communicate with others via conventional means, such as phone or face to face, more than do non-users. Hence, far from increasing social isolation and destroying trust, email, blogging, chatrooms and social media present new opportunities for communication and friendship building. Electronic interactions can be experienced as liberating

---

Global Society 8.2 **The creation and maintenance of 'e-trust'**

Public debate on Internet security has tended to focus on issues of online banking fraud, the use of false identities, and the problems associated with children using chatrooms that may be monitored by predatory paedophiles. Such worries make people fearful and erode trust in the online environment. In successful social interactions of all kinds, trust is a key component. According to Cook and her colleagues (2009: 1), 'Trust facilitates social interaction. When it exists, it strengthens cooperation, provides the basis for risk-taking, and grants latitude to the parties involved. When it does not exist, various mechanisms are required to protect against exploitation.' This is particularly evident in transactions between people who are not co-present. Such indirect and geographically distant transactions are potentially problematic because none of the usual gestures, body language or non-verbal cues are in play, which deprives both parties of crucial elements by which each can satisfy themselves as to the sincerity of the other party.

The largest and most well-established Internet auction house is eBay. In 2006, it was estimated that some 165,000 Americans alone were making a living primarily from selling on the site (Epley et al. 2006). Launched in 1995, eBay quickly attracted more than 100 million people around the world, even though it can offer no guarantees for any goods sold. Buyers and sellers take on all the risks. Yet though we might expect this arrangement to be open to large-scale fraud and deceit, in fact the default rate for transactions on eBay is remarkably small.

One reason for this is eBay's 'reputation management system', which effectively replaces face-to-face interactional cues (Kollock 1999; Resnick et al. 2006). The eBay system asks buyers and sellers to rate each other – positive, negative or neutral, though short comments can also be added. Online reputation management systems have been described as the cyber equivalent of 'gossip' in social life, as people's views of one another are both encouraged and widely shared. But, unlike gossip, which tends to be localized and restricted within community boundaries, online systems potentially involve millions of people across the world, and the impact of gaining a bad reputation can be serious for both traders and buyers (Lev-On 2009).

Over time, reputations are established which means eBay users are able to compare and contrast traders in order to minimize the risks they take online. In sum, e-trust in the online eBay auction house, and others which use similar systems, is produced through a form of community self-policing. However, from a trader's perspective, the feedback system also offers an online version of impression management and self-presentation.

> **THINKING CRITICALLY**
>
> How might the wider use of personal webcams increase the trust we have in Internet communications of different kinds? What can we learn about online risks and trust from the eBay feedback system?

and empowering, since people can create online identities and speak more freely than they would elsewhere (Katz et al. 2001).

Conclusion: proximity and distance in human interactions

Despite the rise in indirect communication, it seems that humans still value direct contact.

People in business, for instance, continue to attend meetings, sometimes flying halfway around the world to do so, when it would be cheaper and more efficient to use conference calls, Skype or video links. Family members could arrange 'virtual' reunions or holiday gatherings using electronic real-time communications, but would they really match the warmth and intimacy of face-to-face celebrations?

Boden and Molotch (1994) studied what they call the compulsion to proximity: the need of individuals to meet with one another in situations of co-presence. People prefer this, they suggest, because co-presence supplies much richer information about others' sincerity than any form of electronic communication. Only by being in the presence of people do we feel able to learn what is 'really' going on. Jamieson (2013: 20) cautions against believing that web-based activity will replace face-to-face relations. She argues that the Internet has enabled the existing commercial sex industry – including prostitution and pornography – to expand, noting that 'there are no signs of digitally mediated forms of engagement with sex threatening to reshape or replace "skin on skin" sexual relationships.' Similarly, Urry (2003) argues that, in spite of young people today having grown up with the Internet and digital technology as part of their daily lives, even this generation continues to seek out physical co-presence in global protest sites, holiday experiences, volunteer camps and large, open-air rock music concerts.

Yet, perhaps this conclusion is premature given the relatively recent creation of online environments, which are still developing. The Internet has yet to reach its full potential for

Living a 'second life' through an online avatar offers people the opportunity to develop an alternative self to their embodied version. However, conventional social norms and rituals often transfer seamlessly into virtual worlds.

interaction across time and space, but one glimpse into the future is *Second Life*, a 3D virtual world with more than 7 million 'residents'. On *Second Life* people can register and create their own virtual body or 'avatar' through which they then live out a 'second life' online. For example, they can form relationships and even get 'married' in this environment. One aspect of this virtual world is that users can play their own music, perform their own gigs, stage concerts or attend those held by others. Some see this as a good way of 'breaking' new musical acts, which find it very difficult to get noticed in conventional ways.

Comparing virtual worlds and their events with those in the 'real world', it is likely that the former will always be seen as pale imitations, lacking the physical reality, smells and sounds of real-world rock concerts, for example. But it is not too fanciful to imagine that, as virtual worlds expand and more people have a significant online life, there may be distinct advantages to virtual environments. Beer and Geesin (2009: 124) argue that, in future:

> The draw may not be the physicality of the experience of the gig but of attending events as the imagined avatar rocking-out with fellow avatars – moshing, pogoing or foot-tapping. It may be that rather than a compulsion to proximity these events instead reveal an opportunity to attend live musical happenings without the risks and discomforts of 'being there' at a live musical event – the crushing and pushing, the flailing hands, elbows and feet, the smell, crowd surfers, the unwanted physical contact, the unwelcome advances, the damp, the dirt, and, especially, the heat.

Whether the existing microsociological concepts and theories that have proved so fruitful in analysing face-to-face interactions will be capable of understanding the interactions between real humans and their avatar communities in online, virtual worlds is an intriguing research prospect for sociologists.

Chapter review

1 'The study of micro-level interactions is the province of psychology, not sociology.' Explain why studies of the micro level are, in fact, vital to an understanding of the wider society.

2 Give some examples of body language which bring out its gendered character.

3 What is ethnomethodology? Provide some examples of ethnomethodological 'experiments'. Is ethnomethodology a form of microsociology or something else entirely?

4 To what extent does the social context of everyday conversations contribute to the meaning of speech? Provide some examples from the chapter which support your answer.

5 Explain what is meant by a 'dramaturgical analogy', referring to Goffman's key concepts such as the stage, props, front and back regions, and 'performance'.

6 What are social networks and why do people want to become part of them?

7 'Friendship and community are dying out in the digital age.' Provide some counter-examples to this assertion.

8 What is cyberbullying and how does it differ from traditional bullying? How might cyberbullying be tackled by authorities?

9 List some of the rules and norms of netiquette as they apply to social media and mobile phone exchanges.

10 What are the main consequences of a lack of co-presence for developing trust in online environments? What methods do people use when engaged in impression management online?

Research in practice

Carrying out ethnographic fieldwork in situations that are difficult to access demands that researchers remain keenly aware of their self-presentation and impression management. In a sense, researchers must act out a series of roles in order to garner rich information from the groups under study. Yet, to the researcher, such tactics can seem like subterfuge, and they may feel guilty about their actions. How can they deal with the emotional aspects of fieldwork? Read the following article, which tackles the issue, and then address the questions: Benz, T. (2014) 'Flanking Gestures: Gender and Emotion in Fieldwork', *Sociological Research Online*, 19(2): 15, www.socresonline.org.uk/19/2/15.html.

1 What type of research did the author carry out and what was the target population?
2 Why was gender, rather than age, class or ethnicity, the major status barrier with this study population? What is 'status misalignment'?
3 Describe the specifically emotional problems faced by the author during the course of this project.
4 What is a 'flanking gesture'? Give some examples used by the author to help her to deal with the emotional demands of the research.
5 Which of the emotional problems and issues identified within the paper did her tactics leave unresolved? Do these simply have to be accepted as the price of doing this kind of fieldwork?

Thinking it through

Many interactionist accounts of social life appear particularly persuasive because they are understandable within people's own life experience. For example, Goffman's work on impression management and the presentation of self strikes a chord precisely because we are able to recognize these in our own behaviour. Yet a large amount of sociological research has focused on examining *macrosocial* structures, such as class, ethnicity and gender, socio-historical change and the impact of 'social forces', on the individual.

Work through this chapter from the start up to the heading 'The emergent rules of online interaction' (p. 319), noting wherever macrosocial phenomena and social structures are implied, assumed or referred to in the discussion. Do interactionist sociologies fail satisfactorily to explain the emergence and persistence of structured social divisions? How have other sociological perspectives accounted for social class, ethnic and gender divisions? How fair is the criticism that interactionism is good at *describing* aspects of social life but is not capable of properly *explaining* it?

Society in the arts

The spread of online environments, especially social media, has opened up new possibilities for communication and friendship but also for bullying and a range of other aggressive behaviours. *Cyberbully* (2015, directed by Ben Chanan) is a British docudrama produced by Channel 4 which draws on a number of real-life episodes of online bullying and its consequences. Read an interview with the actor playing Casey, Maisie

Williams, here: www.channel4.com/info/press/news/interview-with-maisie-williams-star-of-cyber-bully. Then watch the programme and address the questions below.

1 List all of the websites, social media and digital devices which appear in the drama. How are each of these used by the hacker for bullying Casey?

2 What role is played by gossip, stigma, ostracizing and stereotyping?

3 How has Casey, unwittingly, provided the hacker with the means to attack her?

4 As the story moves on, Casey finds herself implicated in the bullying of others. She tells the hacker that her online behaviour is 'normal' for teenagers today. What

would you say is (are) the key message(s) about cyberbullying in this drama?

Further reading

For an introductory text covering all of the theories and issues in this chapter, Susie Scott's (2009) *Making Sense of Everyday Life* (Cambridge: Polity) is excellent, as is Brian Roberts's (2006) *Micro Social Theory* (Basingstoke: Palgrave Macmillan). Both are well written and reliable introductions to the development of the microsociological tradition. Particular perspectives can be pursued further in *Encountering the Everyday: An Introduction to the Sociologies of the Unnoticed* (2008), edited by Michael Hviid Jacobsen (Basingstoke: Palgrave Macmillan).

For something specific on the work of Garfinkel and others, you could try David Francis and Stephen Hester's (2004) *An Invitation to Ethnomethodology: Language, Society and Interaction* (London: Sage). Or, if Goffman's ideas are more to your taste, there is no one better than Goffman himself, so see his *The Presentation of Self in Everyday Life* (Harmondsworth: Penguin 1990 [1959]), which is a brilliant example of interactionist sociology. Phil Manning's (1992) *Erving Goffman and Modern Sociology* (Cambridge: Polity) or Greg Smith's (2006) *Erving Goffman* (London: Routledge) are well worth the effort.

For a comprehensive introduction to online communication and interaction, see Nancy K. Baym's (2015) *Personal Connections in the Digital Age* (2nd edn, Cambridge: Polity) or Crispin Thurlow, Laura Lengel and Alice Tomic's (2004) *Computer Mediated Communication: An Introduction to Social Interaction Online* (London: Sage), which is a hands-on guide to CMC.

For a collection of original readings on interaction and communication, see the accompanying *Sociology: Introductory Readings* (3rd edn, Cambridge: Polity, 2010).

Internet links

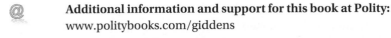

Additional information and support for this book at Polity:
www.politybooks.com/giddens

Society for the Study of Symbolic Interaction – exactly what it says, with journal and resources:
https://sites.google.com/site/sssinteraction

@ **The Everyday Sexism Project – a site dedicated to cataloguing real-world experiences of sexism:**
http://everydaysexism.com

@ **Ethno/CA News – ethnomethodology and conversation analysis on Twitter:**
https://twitter.com/EMCA_News

@ **Website with information on the life and work of Erving Goffman:**
http://people.brandeis.edu/~teuber/goffmanbio.html

@ **Howard Becker's website, which covers his own work and some helpful links too:**
http://howardsbecker.com

@ **Exploring Nonverbal Communication – an introduction to NVC with self-test of reading examples:**
http://nonverbal.ucsc.edu

CHAPTER 9

The Life Course

Contents

How do you reflect on the course of your life? Which events do you remember as being the most important? And how is the course of your life connected to other people such as family, friends and work colleagues? People's interpretation of their life often changes as they grow older, especially as they learn more about the events and relationships that shaped them. Consider the brief 'life story' in 'Global society 9.1'.

| Global Society 9.1 | Events and relationships of a life story |

David Sanchez is now in his fifties. He has a Hispanic name but is a member of the Navajo tribe. He spent most of his life in New Mexico but went to Los Angeles to visit his son Marco, aged twenty-nine, and his grandchildren. While visiting, he was hospitalized for a diabetic coma, perhaps the vestiges of his alcoholism between the ages of twenty and forty-three. During recent visits, David recognized how much his alcohol abuse had hurt his son. After Mrs Sanchez divorced David, he became unreliable and did not provide regular child support.

David was raised by his maternal grandmother after his father was killed in a car accident when David was seven. His mother had been very ill since his birth and could not take care of him. Just as David became attached to his grandmother, the Bureau of Indian Affairs (BIA) moved him to a boarding school, where he was beaten and bullied. Like most Indian children, David suffered in silence. He joined the Marines at eighteen, but his grandmother could not understand why he took part in the 'white man's war.' During his alcohol treatment, he often relived the bombings and killings in Vietnam. Like many veterans, he ended up on the streets, homeless. It was only during Indian medicine retreats that he began to recover.

His father's funeral had been painful, but David experienced his grandmother's funeral in a more spiritual way and now sees this as a turning point in his life. At the funeral, David's great-uncle, a medicine man, asked him to come and live with him. He wanted to teach David age-old cures that would enable him to help others and, though David is still learning, in his work with alcoholics he finds he has a special connection to Vietnam veterans.

Source: Abridged and adapted from Hutchinson (2007: 4–5).

One way of understanding David's story is to see it as *a path or journey*, but one with many twists and downward turns and, eventually, a positive outcome, though of course it is far from finished. We can also understand it as a series of *discrete events*, such as the death of the young boy's father, moving into a boarding school, joining the Marines, getting divorced and going to live with his great-uncle. This 'event history' suggests another possibility – looking at David's life in terms of his constantly *changing relationships* with other people. His parents were key formative influences in early childhood, but David later became very close to his grandmother and great-uncle, while it was only in his fifties that he really became close to his son and grandchildren. All of these methods help us to grasp how and why 'David' has become the person he is today.

David's life story has also been strongly influenced by *the society* of which he is a part and the operation of its social institutions. In the USA when David was a child, boarding school rather than the extended family was considered the best place to bring up adolescents in his position. Joining the military was also considered a normal path for young working-class men, and David just happened to be part of a generation which experienced action in the USA–Vietnam conflict. His problems with alcohol abuse are not uncommon, and he benefited from a healthcare system which was available at a crucial time. However, the life course is also shaped by the wider society in a more profound way through processes of learning and socialization, which have a major impact on how individuals develop.

For sociologists, socialization is the process whereby the helpless human infant gradually becomes a self-aware, knowledgeable person, skilled in the ways of the culture into which he or she was born. Socialization of the young allows for the more general phenomenon of social reproduction – the process through which societies achieve structural continuity over time. All societies have characteristics that endure over long stretches of time, even though their existing members die and new ones are born. Societies have many distinctive social and cultural aspects that have persisted for generations – not least the different languages spoken by their members.

As we will see later, socialization connects the different generations to one another. Although the process of cultural learning is much more intense in infancy and early childhood than later, learning and adjustment go on throughout a person's life, as David's case clearly illustrates. However, socialization is not a deterministic process, and even small children are active participants rather than passive recipients. The interactions between children and adults and among peer groups not only reproduce social structures but also have the potential to change them.

First, we shall examine the main theoretical interpretations put forward by different writers on how and why children develop as they do, including theories that explain the development of gender identities. We then move on to discuss the life course and some of its key stages, before looking at the ageing or 'greying' of the global population and its consequences. We end the chapter with a discussion of some of the most important sociological issues around death, dying and bereavement.

The social self and socialization

Theories of child development

One of the more distinctive features of human beings, compared to other animals, is that humans are *self-aware*. But from where does this awareness originate? During the first months of life, the infant possesses little or no understanding of the difference between human beings and material objects in the environment and has no awareness of their 'self'. Indeed, children do not begin to use concepts such as 'I', 'me', 'you' or 'they' until around the age of two or later. Only gradually do they then come to understand that other people have distinct identities, consciousness and needs that are separate from their own.

The problem of the emergence of the self is much debated and is viewed rather differently in contrasting theoretical perspectives. To some extent, this is because the most prominent theories about child development emphasize different aspects of socialization.

Jean Piaget and the stages of cognitive development

Jean Piaget (1896–1980) worked on many aspects of child development, but his best-known writings concern cognition – the ways in which children learn to think about themselves and their environment. Piaget placed great emphasis on the child's active capability to make sense of the world. Children do not passively soak up information but select and interpret what they see. Piaget (1951, 1957) described several successive stages of cognitive development during which children learn the skills to think about themselves and their environment.

Piaget called the first stage, from birth to about the age of two, the sensorimotor stage. Infants learn mainly by touching objects, manipulating them and physically exploring their environment. Until the age of about four months, infants cannot differentiate themselves from their environment. For example, a child will not realize that their own movements cause the sides of the cot to rattle. They gradually learn to distinguish people from objects, coming to see that both have an existence independent of their immediate perception. The main accomplishment of this stage is that children understand their environment to have distinct and stable properties.

The pre-operational stage follows, lasting from around the ages of two to seven years. Here, children acquire a mastery of language and are able to use words to represent objects and images in a symbolic fashion. A four-year-old might use a sweeping hand, for example, to represent the concept 'aeroplane'. This stage is 'pre-operational' because children are not yet able to use their developing mental capabilities systematically. Children in this stage are also egocentric, interpreting the world exclusively in terms of their own position. Holding a

Classic Studies 9.1 | George Herbert Mead on the social self

The research problem

It has often been said that human beings are the only creatures who know that they exist and that eventually they will die. Sociologically, this means that human individuals are *self-aware*. With a moment's reflection, we may all accept that this is so. But how do humans gain that self-awareness? Is it innate or learned? Is it a research problem for psychology rather than sociology? The American sociologist and philosopher George Herbert Mead (1863–1931) insisted that the self is a social self which requires a sociological perspective if we are to understand how the self emerges and develops.

Mead's explanation

Since Mead's ideas formed the main basis of a general tradition of theoretical thinking – symbolic interactionism – they have had a very broad impact in sociology. Symbolic interactionism emphasizes that interaction between human beings takes place through symbols and the interpretation of meanings (see chapters 1 and 3). But, in addition, Mead's work provides an account of the main phases of child development, paying particular attention to the emergence of a sense of self.

According to Mead, infants and young children first of all develop as *social* beings by imitating the actions of those around them – for example, through play, where young children often imitate what adults do. A child will make mud pies, having seen an adult cooking, or dig with a spoon, having observed someone gardening. Children's play evolves from simple imitation to more complicated games in which a child of four or five years old will act out an adult role. Mead called this step 'taking the role of the other' – learning what it is like to be in the shoes of another person. It is only at this stage that children begin to acquire a developed sense of self. Children achieve an understanding of themselves as separate agents – as a 'me' – by seeing themselves through the eyes of others.

We achieve self-awareness, according to Mead, when we learn to distinguish the 'me' from the 'I'. The 'I' is the unsocialized infant, a bundle of spontaneous wants and desires.

Children's play is also serious, part of developing a social self.

The 'me', as Mead used the term, is the social self. Individuals develop self-consciousness by coming to see themselves as others see them, which allows for an 'internal conversation' between the individual's 'I' and the social 'me'. According to Mead's theory, this internal conversation is what we call 'thinking'.

A further stage of child development occurs when the child is about eight or nine years old. This is when children tend to take part in more organized games rather than in unsystematic play. It is in this period that they begin to understand the overall values and *morality* according to which social life is conducted. To learn organized games, children must understand the rules of play and notions of fairness and equal participation. At this stage they learn to grasp what Mead termed the generalized other – the general values and moral rules of the culture in which they are developing.

Critical points

Mead's theory of the social self has been criticized on several grounds. First, some argue that it effectively eliminates all biological influences on the development of the self, when it is clear from biology and neuroscience that there *is* such a biological basis. However, this criticism appears not to recognize that Mead's notion of the 'I' represents the 'unsocialized infant'. Second, Mead's theory seems to rely on the 'I' and the 'me' working cooperatively to ensure the smooth functioning of the self. But this downplays the internal tensions and conflicts that people experience deeply, and which Freud and Chodorow's theories seem better able to explain (see below). Mead also has little to say about the effects of unbalanced power relationships on children's development. Finally, and again unlike Freud, Mead's explanation has no room for the unconscious mind as a motive force in human behaviour and consequently lacks the concept of 'repression', which has proved essential to psychoanalytic practice.

Contemporary significance

Mead's work was very important for the development of sociology. His was the first genuinely sociological theory of self formation and development, which insisted that, if we are properly to understand ourselves, we must begin not with a mythical isolated individual but with the social process of human interactions. In this way he showed that the self is not an innate part of our biology, nor does it emerge simply with the developing human brain. What Mead demonstrated is that the study of the individual's self cannot be divorced from the study of society – and that requires a sociological perspective.

Although Freud's approach to the human psyche perhaps overshadowed Mead's during the twentieth century, at least in relation to the treatment of mental disorders, symbolic interactionism continues to produce insightful findings from a perspective rooted in Mead's sociological ideas. And, in this sense, Mead still has much to offer new generations of sociological researchers.

book upright, a child may ask about a picture in it, not realizing that the person opposite can only see the back of the book. They also have no general understanding of categories that adults take for granted, such as the concepts causality, speed, weight or number.

A third period, the concrete operational stage, lasts from the ages of around seven to eleven years, when children master abstract, logical notions and are able to handle ideas such as causality without much difficulty. A child will now recognize the false reasoning involved in the idea that a wide container holds less water than a thin, narrow one, even though the water levels are different. They become capable of carrying out the mathematical operations of multiplying, dividing and subtracting and are much less egocentric.

The years from eleven to fifteen cover what Piaget called the formal operational stage. During adolescence, the developing child is able to grasp abstract and hypothetical ideas. When faced with a problem, children at this stage are able to review all the possible ways of solving it and go through them in order to reach a solution. They also understand 'trick questions'. According to Piaget, the first three stages of development are universal; but not all adults reach the fourth, formal operational stage. The development of formal operational thought depends in part on schooling. Adults of limited educational attainment will continue to think in more concrete terms and remain more egocentric.

The Russian psychologist Lev Vygotsky (1986 [1934]) provided a useful critique of Piaget's ideas. He argued that the processes of learning which Piaget describes are actually dependent on social structures and interactions. Vygotsky saw that the opportunities for learning available to children from various social groups differed considerably and that this strongly influenced their ability to learn from their engagements with the outside world. In short, learning and cognitive development are not immune from the social structures within which they are embedded. Just as these structures constrain some groups and enable others to become wealthy, so they also constrain and enable children's cognitive development.

THINKING CRITICALLY

How does socialization differ from common-sense ideas of 'brainwashing'? With reference to Mead and Piaget's idea, what impact might a *lack* of early socialization have on the formation of the human infant's self-awareness?

Agencies of socialization

Sociologists often speak of socialization as occurring in two broad phases involving a number of different agencies. Agencies of socialization are groups or social contexts in which significant socialization occurs. Primary socialization occurs in infancy and childhood and is the most intense period of cultural learning. It is the time when children learn language and the basic behavioural patterns that form the foundation for later learning. The family is the main agent of socialization during this phase. Secondary socialization takes place later in childhood and into maturity. Schools, peer groups, organizations, the media and, eventually, the workplace become socializing forces for individuals. Social interactions in these contexts help people learn the values, norms and beliefs that make up the patterns of their culture.

In developed societies, most primary socialization occurs within a small-scale family context and children spend their early years within the domestic unit. In many other cultures, by contrast, aunts, uncles and grandparents are often part of a single household and serve as caretakers, even for very young infants. Yet even within modern societies there are many variations in family structures. Some children are brought up in single-parent households or same-sex households, and others are cared for by two 'mothering' and 'fathering' agents in their divorced parents and step-parents.

> We look at issues concerning families in more detail in chapter 10, 'Families and Intimate Relationships'.

Another important early socializing agency is the school, which educates children and prepares them for work and future life course stages. Peer groups, often formed in school, consist of children of a similar age. In some cultures, particularly small-scale societies, peer groups are formalized as age-grades (normally confined to males). Specific ceremonies or rites mark the transition of males from one age-grade to another, and those within a particular age-grade generally maintain close and friendly connections throughout life. A typical set of age-grades consists of childhood, junior warriorhood, senior warriorhood, junior elderhood and senior elderhood. Men move through these grades not as individuals but as whole groups.

The family's importance in socialization is obvious, but it is less clear just how significant peer groups are. Yet, even without formal age-grades in contemporary societies, children over the age of four or five usually spend a great deal of time in the company of friends of the same age. Given the increasing number of dual-earner households, peer relationships formed in schools are likely to become more important than in previous decades (Corsaro 2005; Harris 1998).

> We discuss socialization within education systems in chapter 19, 'Education'.

9.1 Playing with gender

In her book *Gender Play* (1993), Barrie Thorne looked at socialization by observing how children interact in the playground. As others had before her, she wanted to understand how children come to know what it means to be 'male' or 'female'. Rather than seeing them as passively learning the meaning of gender from their parents and teachers, she looked at the way in which children actively create and re-create the *meaning* of gender in interactions with each other.

Thorne spent two years observing fourth and fifth graders at two schools, in Michigan and California, sitting in the classroom with them and observing their activities outside the classroom. She watched games such as 'chase and kiss' – known by names such as 'kiss-catch' in the UK – so as to learn how children construct and experience gender meanings in the classroom and in the playground. She found that peer groups have a great influence on gender socialization, particularly as children talk about their changing bodies – a subject of great fascination.

The social context created by these children determined whether a child's bodily change was experienced with embarrassment or worn with pride. Thorne noted that, if the most popular girls started menstruating or wearing bras, the other girls began to want these

In school playgrounds, girls tend to play with other girls and boys with other boys. Why should this be so?

changes as well. However, the opposite was also the case: when popular girls didn't wear bras or had not started menstruating, then others saw these as much less desirable.

Thorne's research is a powerful reminder that children are social actors who help to shape their social world and influence their own socialization. Still, the impact of societal and cultural influences is tremendous, since the activities that children pursue and the values they hold are also partly determined by influences such as their families and the mass media.

THINKING CRITICALLY

Reflect on your own experience of primary and secondary schooling. How important to you were the views and behaviour of peers, especially those you admired? What did you learn from interacting within peer groups about what 'maleness' and 'femaleness' involved?

While research into peer relations shows that children are active agents in the socialization process, much of the early research on media influence on children assumed the opposite – that children are passive and undiscriminating in reaction to what they see and hear. Yet the child's response to television, for instance, still involves interpreting or 'reading' the content of programmes. Today researchers have arrived at a more balanced understanding of the influence of the mass media in socialization processes and now consider television, for example, as one important agency of socialization alongside several others. Chapter 18, 'The Media', contains an extended discussion of television.

Individuals are not just passive subjects of socialization. It is important to appreciate that socialization takes place through processes of *inter-action* within which individuals (including very young children) are actively engaged (Stanley and Wise 2002). For example, it is not unusual for children to oppose, reject or reinterpret the information, norms and values they are taught or see in mass media and for peer groups to form subcultures, or even counter-cultures, in opposition to mainstream culture. Agencies of socialization provide sites or structures for socialization processes, but they do not determine their outcome (see the section covering the 'new' sociology of childhood later in this chapter). Similarly, socialization should not be seen entirely as an imposition or restraint on the individual; the process also enables people to learn and to develop the cultural skills that are essential for leading a good life in their society.

Learning gender

Many studies have been carried out on the degree to which gender differences and the learning of gender roles are the result of gender socialization. Gender learning by infants is almost certainly unconscious. Before a child can accurately label themselves as a boy or a girl, they receive a range of pre-verbal cues. For instance, men and women tend to handle infants differently. The cosmetics used by women contain scents different from those the baby might learn to associate with men. Systematic differences in dress, hairstyle, and so on, provide visual cues for the infant in the learning process.

Zammuner (1986) studied the toy preferences of children aged between seven and ten in Italy and the Netherlands. She analysed children's attitudes towards a variety of toys – stereotypically masculine and feminine toys, as well as those thought not to be gender-typed. Both the children and their parents were asked to assess which toys were suitable for boys and which for girls. There was close agreement between the adults and the children.

On average, the Italian children chose gender-differentiated toys to play with more often than the Dutch children – a finding that conformed to expectations, since Italian culture tends to hold a more traditional view of gender divisions. As in other studies, girls from both societies chose gender-neutral or boys' toys to play with far more than boys chose girls' toys. Clearly, early gender socialization is very powerful and challenges to it can be upsetting. Once gender is 'assigned', it is expected that individuals will act like 'females' and 'males'. It is in the practices of everyday life that these expectations are fulfilled, reproduced and challenged (Bourdieu 1990; Lorber 1994).

USING YOUR SOCIOLOGICAL IMAGINATION

9.2 Gender roles in children's fiction

More than thirty years ago, Weitzman and her colleagues (1972) carried out an analysis of gender roles in some of the most widely used pre-school children's books and found clear differences in gender roles. Males played a much larger part in the stories and pictures, outnumbering females by a ratio of 11 to 1. When animals with gender identities were included, the ratio was 95 to 1. The activities of males and females also differed. The males engaged in adventurous pursuits and outdoor activities that demanded independence and strength. Where girls did appear, they were portrayed as passive and confined mostly to indoor activities. Girls cooked and cleaned for the males or awaited their return. Much the same was true of the adult men and women represented in the storybooks. Women who were not wives and mothers were imaginary creatures such as witches or fairy godmothers. By contrast, the men were depicted as fighters, policemen, judges, kings, and so on. Research studies in the twenty-first century suggest that such gendered stereotypes remain remarkably persistent today (Hamilton et al. 2006).

Although traditional stories may have changed somewhat, the underlying messages within children's literature remain essentially the same (Davies 1991; Parke and Clarke-Stewart 2010: 347–50). Fairy-tales, for example, embody traditional attitudes towards gender and the aims and ambitions girls and boys are expected to have. 'Some day my prince will come', in versions of fairy-tales from several centuries ago, implied that a girl from a poor family might dream of wealth and fortune. Today its meaning has become more closely tied to the ideals of romantic love. Studies of television programmes and films designed for children show that most still conform to the findings about children's books. Studies of the most frequently watched cartoons also show that most of the leading figures are male and that males dominate the active pursuits.

However, there are some exceptions to this repetitively gendered pattern. The 2001 film *Shrek* (and its sequels) told a fairly conventional story of princes, princesses and ogres, while also subverting conventional fairy-tale gender and character roles. The film's marketing tagline was 'The greatest fairy-tale never told' – 'The Prince isn't charming. The Princess isn't sleeping. The sidekick isn't helping. The ogre is the hero. Fairy-tales will never be the same again.'

Shrek (the ugly ogre) is actually the hero of the film, while Fiona (the beautiful princess) is an independent woman with martial arts skills who turns into an ogress at night. The 'happy ending' arrives when Shrek kisses Fiona, she turns permanently into an ogress and they get married, thus reversing the traditional story of the ogre turning into a handsome young prince, reflecting Western ideals of beauty and bodily perfection. Such representations remain a small minority of total output at present.

THINKING CRITICALLY

Next time you go shopping, watch a film or TV soap, or talk to older and younger relatives, note how often conventional gender assumptions occur. Note down anything that might challenge conventional gendered assumptions. Is it possible to discern any generational differences?

Sigmund Freud's theory

Perhaps the most influential – and controversial – theory of the emergence of gender identity is that of the founder of psychoanalysis, Sigmund Freud (1856–1939). According to Freud (1995 [1933]), the learning of gender differences in infants and young children is centred on the possession or absence of the penis. 'I have a penis' is equivalent to 'I am a boy', while 'I am a girl' is equivalent to 'I lack a penis'. Freud is careful to say that it is not just the anatomical distinctions that matter here; the possession or absence of the penis is symbolic of masculinity and femininity.

At around the age of four or five, a boy feels threatened by the discipline and autonomy his father demands of him, fantasizing that the father wishes to remove his penis. Mainly on an unconscious level, the boy recognizes the father as a rival for the affections of his mother. In repressing erotic feelings towards the mother and accepting the father as a superior being, the boy identifies with the father and becomes aware of his male identity. Girls, on the other hand, are said to suffer from 'penis envy' because they do not possess the visible organ that distinguishes boys. The mother becomes devalued in the girl's eyes, because she is also seen to lack a penis. When the girl identifies with the mother, she takes over the submissive attitude involved in the recognition of being 'second best'.

Once this phase is over, the child has learned to repress his or her erotic feelings. The period from about the age of five to puberty, according to Freud, is one of latency – sexual activities tend to be suspended until the biological changes involved in puberty reactivate erotic desires in a direct way. The latency period, covering the early and middle years of school, is the time at which same-gender peer groups are most important in the child's life.

Major criticisms have been made of Freud's ideas, particularly by feminists (Mitchell 1975; Coward 1984). First, Freud seems to identify gender identity too closely with genital awareness, but other more subtle factors are now thought to be involved. Second, the theory seems to depend on the notion that the penis is superior to the vagina, which is represented as just a lack of the male organ. But why should the female genitals not be considered superior to those of the male? Third, Freud treats the father as the primary disciplining agent, whereas in many cultures the mother plays the more significant part in the imposition of discipline. Fourth, Freud argues that gender learning is concentrated at the age of four or five years of age, but later authors have emphasized the importance of much earlier learning, beginning in infancy.

Carol Gilligan's theory

Carol Gilligan (1982) further developed Chodorow's analysis (see 'Classic studies 9.2'). Her work concentrates on the images that adult women and men have of themselves and their attainments. Women do define themselves in terms of personal relationships and judge their achievements by reference to their ability to care for others. But the qualities developed in these tasks are frequently devalued by men, who see their own emphasis on individual achievement as the only form of 'success'. Concern with relationships on the part of women appears to them as a weakness rather than as the strength that in fact it is.

Gilligan carried out intensive interviews with about 200 American women and men of varying ages and social backgrounds. She asked all the interviewees a range of questions concerning their moral outlook and conceptions of self. Consistent differences emerged between the views of the women and the men. For instance, the interviewees were asked: 'What does it mean to say something is morally right or wrong?' The men tended to respond to this question by mentioning abstract ideals of duty, justice and individual freedom, while the women persistently raised the theme of helping others (Gilligan 1982).

The women were more tentative in their moral judgements than the men, seeing possible contradictions between following a strict moral code and avoiding harming others. Gilligan suggests that this outlook reflects the traditional situation of women, anchored in

Classic Studies 9.2   Nancy Chodorow on attachment and separation

The research problem

You may think or have been told that men find it difficult to express their emotions and, instead, tend to 'bottle it up' or 'keep a stiff upper lip'. Conversely, women are apparently more likely to express how they are feeling. But why should this be so? Are women really just naturally better than men at forming close emotional relationships? Such common-sense assumptions formed the basis of Nancy Chodorow's (1978) work on gender identity. Like many others, Chodorow made use of Freud's approach in studying gender development but modified it in major respects to account for important gender differences.

Chodorow's explanation

Chodorow (1978, 1988) argues that learning to feel male or female derives from the infant's attachment to parents from an early age. She places much more emphasis than Freud on the importance of the mother. Children tend to become emotionally involved with the mother, since she is easily the most dominant influence in their early lives. This attachment has at some point to be broken in order for the child to achieve a separate sense of self – the child is required to become less closely dependent.

Chodorow argues that the breaking process occurs in a different way for boys and girls. Girls remain closer to the mother – able, for example, to go on hugging and kissing her and imitating what she does. Because there is no sharp break from the mother, the girl, and later the adult woman, develops a sense of self that is more continuous with other people. Her identity is more likely to be merged with or dependent on another's: first her mother, later a man. In Chodorow's view, this tends to produce characteristics of sensitivity and emotional compassion in women.

Boys gain a sense of self via a more radical rejection of their original closeness to the mother, forging their understanding of masculinity from what is not feminine. They learn not to be 'sissies' or 'mummy's boys'. As a result, boys are relatively unskilled in relating closely to others; they develop more

analytical ways of looking at the world. They take a more active view of their lives, emphasizing achievement, but they have repressed their ability to understand their own feelings and those of others.

To some extent, Chodorow reverses Freud's emphasis. Masculinity, rather than femininity, is defined by a loss, the forfeiting of continued close attachment to the mother. Male identity is formed through separation; thus, men later in life unconsciously feel that their identity is endangered if they become involved in close emotional relationships with others. Women, on the other hand, feel that the absence of a close relation to another person threatens their self-esteem. These patterns are passed on from generation to generation because of the primary role women play in the early socialization of children. Women express and define themselves mainly in terms of relationships. Men have repressed these needs and adopt a more manipulative stance towards the world.

Critical points

Chodorow's work has met with various criticisms. Janet Sayers (1986), for example, suggested that Chodorow does not explain the struggle of women, particularly in current times, to become autonomous, independent beings. Women (and men), she points out, are more contradictory in their psychological make-up than this theory suggests. Femininity may conceal feelings of aggressiveness or assertiveness which are revealed only obliquely or in certain contexts (Brennan 1988). Chodorow has also been criticized for her narrow conception of the family, one based on a white, middle-class model. What happens, for example, in one-parent households or, as in many Chicano communities, families where children are cared for by more than one adult (Segura and Pierce 1993)? Finally, Rich (1980) argued that Chodorow's theory was 'heteronormative', suggesting that lesbian relationships were inferior to heterosexual ones as lesbians had not adequately resolved their desire for their mothers. This idea finds little support among theorists of gender and sexuality today.

caring relationships, more than it does the 'outward-looking' attitudes of men. Women have in the past deferred to the judgements of men, while being aware that they have qualities that most men lack. Their views of themselves are based on successfully fulfilling the needs of others rather than on pride in individual achievement.

The life course

The various transitions through which individuals pass during their lives seem at first to be biologically fixed. This common-sense view of the human life span is widely accepted in society and suggests that there exists a universal and uniform set of stages through which all people pass. For example, everyone who lives to old age has been an infant, a child, a youth, an adult and an old person, and everyone dies eventually. A similar concept is the life cycle, which also explores individual, biological stages, but this concept also carries a sense of life itself, being a continuous circle or 'cycle' of birth, life and death that repeats in every generation. In disciplines such as psychology, medicine and demography, the focus has conventionally been on the human life span and life cycle (Green 2015: 98).

However, historically and sociologically, these concepts are overly simplistic. The apparently natural biological stages are just one aspect of the human life course, which is a social and psychological as well as a biological phenomenon (Vincent 2003; Hunt 2016; Green 2016). The concept of the life course reflects the sociological and historical evidence that there is considerable variation in the stages of life both in different societies and over time in the same society. This means that the individual life course is not universally experienced but is subject to processes of social construction (Chatterjee et al. 2001). Stages of the life course are influenced by cultural norms and the material circumstances of people's lives in given types of society. For example, in modern Western societies, death is usually thought of in relation to elderly people, because most people live into old age. In many societies of the past, however, more people died younger than survived to old age, and death carried a different meaning and set of expectations.

Social divisions of class, gender and ethnicity also influence the way that the life course is experienced, and the intertwining of these major social divisions – known as intersectionality – produces complex patterns of experience. In nineteenth-century Britain, children of the upper classes routinely attended boarding schools and continued their education over an extended period. However, for children from working-class families, the expectation was of work, not education, and it was not unusual for thirteen-year-old boys to work in coal-mining and other industries, while many girls of the same age went into domestic service. Clearly, the notion of a set of *universal* and age-related stages making up the human life course is not borne out by the historical evidence.

 The concept of intersectionality is discussed in detail in chapter 3, 'Theories and Perspectives', Chapter 12, 'Stratification and Social Class', and also chapters 15, 'Gender and Sexuality', and 16, 'Race, Ethnicity and Migration'.

The individual life course is not only structured by major social divisions of class, gender and ethnicity but is also historically situated. One way of thinking about this aspect is to consider the concepts of birth cohorts and generations. Birth cohorts (cohorts for short) are groups of people who are born 'within a few years of each other who share some common experiences, such as going to school or experiencing a war together' (Green 2015: 101). Sociologists argue that cohort experiences have common cultural and political reference points, such as specific governments, conflicts and musical trends, that give shape to the life course. However, a cohort is not usually a cohesive social group.

The Hungarian-born sociologist Karl Mannheim (1893–1947) made a strong claim regarding the influence of particular generations on life course experience. Generations (sometimes called social generations) are groups of people born in the same series of years who, unlike cohorts, share a worldview or common frame of reference (Alwin et al. 2006: 49). Mannheim (1972 [1928]: 105) said that 'Individuals who belong to the same generation . . . are endowed . . . with a common location in the historical dimension of the social process.' His claim is that generational location can be as influential as social-class position in shaping people's attitudes and beliefs.

Generations tend to experience the world, and their place in it, rather differently. Hence we can speak of a 'generation gap', a 'boomerang generation' and 'generation X' to describe the historical location of different generations and their values. For instance, those born between the mid-1980s and the late 1990s have been variously described as 'generation Y', the 'digital generation' and the 'IPOD generation' – Insecure, Pressured, Overtaxed and Debt-ridden – facing job insecurity while

The hippie youth culture of the 1960s and 1970s was an important generational influence on identities in the USA and other developed societies. Its effects and legacy continue to influence later generations.

being entirely at ease with high technology and consumer culture and leaning towards individualistic, neo-liberal politics (Green 2015: 102). The assumption behind all such descriptions is that the generation of people in question is somehow different from that which came before.

Sociologists and historians have identified the different attitudes and experiences of the 'baby-boom' generation (Gillon 2004) and the 'Beat' generation (Charters 2001), to name but two. Baby-boomers are those born in the aftermath of the Second World War, roughly between 1946 and 1964, when many countries experienced large increases in birth rates, arguably a consequence of postwar economic growth, prosperity and peace. Baby-boomers had many new experiences: television in the home, a new youth culture, rising income levels and more liberal attitudes to sex and morality. The experiences of baby-boomers were significantly different from those of their parents, and, with the creation of 'youth' as a stage of life, so too was their experience of the life course. Indeed, Mannheim's argument suggests that this generation actually transformed society itself. This dual aspect of giving shape to the life course and producing social change is why Mannheim sees generations as akin to social classes in their potential impact on individual identities and social life.

Green (2015) argues that the early childhood experiences of people today may be increasingly diverse as the trend towards late childbearing continues, and this may cause problems for those studying generations. Some first-time parents may be in their twenties, while others are in their forties or fifties, and we therefore cannot assume that the parents of children are part of the same generation, passing on the same experiences and values. Although it is true that the study of generations has tended to be rather generalized and lacking precision, it has also produced some very useful socio-historical insights.

The next section looks at some key life course stages, particularly as they have changed over time in the developed countries. This is not exhaustive – we do not spend much time on 'mid-life' (those aged approximately forty to sixty-five), for instance – and should be pursued through the further reading section at the end of the chapter. Childhood, youth and old age have been the main stages covered in sociological research, and the section reflects this. Yet it is important to remember that the bulk of sociology in all of its specialist fields generally takes adult life very much for granted as its main focus without directly engaging with the life course perspective. This basic assumption is also a 'common-sense' one, that childhood and youth are preparatory stages leading to 'normal' adult life, while old age occurs after our period of 'useful' working life. The emergence of a life course perspective has highlighted such assumptions, opening them up for critical scrutiny.

Childhood

Until recently, sociologists tended to discuss children and childhood in the context of primary socialization within the family. This often gave the impression that childhood is a transitory stage leading towards the more sociologically significant period of adulthood. Yet the idea of childhood as 'mere transition' ignores the *social structural* position of children within societies. That is, children can be conceptualized as a distinct social group in the same way as social classes or ethnic groups. Children tend to experience life through their own culture, with its unique symbols and rituals, and they also have a similar status to some other minority groups, which has often led to them being exploited as a cheap source of labour (James et al. 1998).

> **THINKING CRITICALLY**
>
> What important social, political and economic events occurred during your childhood and teenage years? How did you respond to these and to what extent have they shaped your attitudes, voting preferences and values? Reflect on whether you 'freely chose' these.

Since the early 1990s, a new paradigm – often called the new sociology of childhood – has demonstrated that what we call childhood is in large measure a social construction that is not universal (Corsaro 2005). The experience of childhood and its meaning for society are diverse in different historical periods and geographical regions in the same time period. The new paradigm also signalled a shift away from functionalist and other theories which saw children as merely 'becoming' members of society. Instead, children are considered as active participants or 'beings' in their own right, who interpret and construct their own lives, cultures and relationships (Prout and James 1990; Prout 2005). The theoretical move from studying processes of 'becoming' to the actions of 'beings' has been highly significant (Jenks 2005; Thomas 2009).

For instance, placing the active child at the centre of sociological analysis leads to new questions and alternative research strategies. Ethnographies, diaries and other qualitative methods are particularly effective research tools in this field as they allow children's voices to be heard and their reasoning and interpretations to be brought into the open. The study of children's post-divorce experience by Smart et al. (2001) exemplifies this approach, enabling divorce to be viewed from the standpoint of the children involved. Sociologists working with the new paradigm might ask what family or divorce *means* to the children involved or how they are related to children's lives (O'Brien et al. 1996; Seung Lam and Pollard 2006). Looking at family life or schooling from the standpoint of the child opens up new avenues for sociologists, producing a more comprehensive understanding of childhood.

However, the new paradigm has itself been challenged. Some argue that the strong focus on children as 'active beings' falls into an old trap of assuming that there are 'sovereign individuals' who are autonomous and free from their inevitable relations with others. This conception is rooted in the similar notion of a stable *adulthood*. But the latter has recently come under close scrutiny as 'jobs for life' have diminished, along with permanent, lifelong relationships, in the more fluid or 'liquid modernity' characterizing the contemporary world (Bauman 2000). As a result, Nick Lee (2001) argues that *both* childhood *and* adulthood should be seen as 'in process' or in a continuous state of becoming. Even so, Prout (2005: 66) maintains that 'Both adults and children can be seen in these terms as becomings without compromising the need to respect their status as beings or persons.' That the new sociology of childhood has produced some fascinating insights is not in doubt, but it does seem likely that future research will try to balance 'being' and 'becoming' in the study of childhood.

Constructing childhoods

To most people living in contemporary societies, childhood is a clear and distinct stage of life. Children are distinct from babies or toddlers, and childhood intervenes between infancy and teenage years. Yet the concept of 'childhood', like so many other aspects of life today, has come into being over the past two or three centuries. In many other societies, young people move directly from a lengthy infancy into working roles within the community. The French historian Philippe Ariès (1965) argued that 'childhood', as a separate phase of development, did not exist in medieval Europe. In the paintings of the period, children are portrayed as small adults with mature faces and the same style of dress as their elders. Children took part in the same work and play activities as adults, rather than in the childhood games we now take for granted.

In the early twentieth century, children were set to work at what now seems a very early age, and there are countries in the world today in which young children are engaged in full-time work, often in physically demanding circumstances (such as coal-mines and agriculture). The idea that children have distinctive rights and that the use of child labour is 'obviously' morally repugnant is really a quite recent development. The United Nations Convention on the Rights of the Child (UNCRC) came into force in 1990, setting out the basic rights of all children across the world; by 2009, it had been ratified by 194 countries (excluding the USA and Somalia). The UNCRC defines a child as anyone under the age of eighteen, except where nation-states already have an earlier definition.

This attempt to universalize the rights of children and definitions of childhood in very different social and economic contexts is a bold one that raises some important issues. Is the UN definition culturally sensitive to different societies or does it impose Western ideas on the rest of the world? Can the governments of the developing world really put in place the same safeguards for protecting children's rights that already largely exist in the developed societies? And, if they do, will it impede economic development and effectively restrict the income-generating capacity of the poorest families? For example, in many developing countries, 'street children' earn money for poor families by selling goods; if states penalize such practices as 'deviant', how will poor families survive? These are very difficult questions which are currently being worked out in policy and practice across the world.

> The issue of child labour is discussed in chapter 14, 'Global Inequality'.

It seems that, as a result of changes currently under way in modern societies, the separate character of childhood is diminishing once more, bringing adult–child relations towards crisis point. The uncertainties associated with globalization processes and the kind of rapid social changes we explored in chapter 4 are leading to new social constructions of childhood. Prout (2005: 7) suggests that 'These new representations construct children as more active, knowledgeable and socially participative than older discourses allowed. They are more difficult to manage, less biddable and hence are more troublesome and troubling.' It seems that relationships between adults and children are in a period of flux and major disturbance.

Other observers have suggested that children now grow up so fast that the previously solid boundary between adults and children is rapidly diminishing, leading to the 'disappearance' of childhood in developed societies (Postman 1995; Buckingham 2000). They point out that even small children may watch the same television programmes as adults, thereby becoming more familiar with the adult world than preceding generations. Children are becoming consumers at an earlier age, availing themselves of adult products such as TV programmes, mobile phones and advertising.

In addition, there is a widespread concern that children are facing pressure to develop sexualized lifestyles before they are ready to do so. A UK government-commissioned report, *Letting Children Be Children* (Bailey 2011), surveyed a sample of parents, children, businesses and other organizations for their views on the commercialization and sexualization of childhood. Many parents thought that we live in a commercial, sexualized culture that is not appropriate for their children. This culture includes sexualized imagery in magazines, pop videos and television programmes and on many websites.

However, parents in the survey said their biggest concern was 'sexualized and gender-stereotyped clothing, services and products' and a 'prurient press' (Bailey 2011: 9). They also perceived themselves as quite powerless to change the culture or to make an impact on businesses and thought that there was insufficient regulation in the new media such as the Internet and smartphones. All of this suggests that the protected period of childhood, which characterized the developed countries for most of the twentieth century, is being seriously eroded today.

THINKING CRITICALLY

How different was your childhood from that of your parents and grandparents? List the main differences in relation to parenting, discipline, schooling and attitudes to authority. Was your childhood objectively 'better' or just different?

Teenage and youth culture

The idea of the 'teenager', so familiar to us today, also did not exist until relatively recently. The biological changes involved in puberty (the point at which a person becomes capable of adult sexual activity and reproduction) are universal, though in many cultures these do not produce the degree of turmoil and uncertainty found in modern societies. In cultures that foster age-grades, for example, with distinct ceremonials that signal a person's transition to adulthood, the process of psychosexual development generally seems easier to negotiate. In Western societies, children reach a point at which they are expected to act as children no longer, but in other cultures, where children are already working alongside adults, the transition beyond childhood may be much less stark and definitive.

In contemporary developed societies, teenagers are betwixt and between: they often try to follow adult ways, but they are treated in law as children. They may wish to go to work, but they are constrained to stay in school. Thus teenagers live between childhood and adulthood, growing up in a society subject to continuous change, which shifts the apparently fixed boundaries between life stages.

Linked to the idea of the teenager is that of youth culture, a general way of life associated with young people. In many other societies, past and present, the concept of youth culture in this sense does not exist, and children move towards adulthood much earlier without the intermediate stage of 'youth'. Sociologists first reported on youth culture in the 1950s

In the developed societies, young teenagers hover between childhood and adult behaviour.

and 1960s, when older teenagers moving into employment began to benefit from postwar affluence, using their earnings to buy fashionable clothes, pop records and other products in the emerging consumer markets (Savage 2007). A 'culture of youth' began to coalesce that looked different from the mainstream, and that constructed new meaningful worlds out of which sprang the spectacular youth subcultures of teddy boys, mods, rockers and skinheads and, later, hippies, punks, rastas, goths, and many more.

With hindsight, sociologists probably gave disproportionate attention to the small but highly visible subcultures – which tended to be male-dominated – and not enough time to understanding the majority of young people and the ways in which they make sense of their own lives. For instance, McRobbie and Garber (1975) identified a widespread and more concealed 'culture of the bedroom' among girls, which enabled groups of friends to participate in the culture of youth, but which had been largely ignored in the rush to analyse 'deviant' (male) subcultures in the public sphere.

Miles (2000) suggests that the concepts of youth culture and subcultures have misled us into seeing all young people as essentially similar, involved in counter-cultural and deviant activity or experiencing unique disadvantages. But, clearly, the mainstream of young people did not – and still do not – fit this description. Instead, Miles (2000: 2) proposes the concept of *youth lifestyles*, which suggests a diversity of experience within mainstream youth and focuses on the question 'How . . . do young people interact with and negotiate the social worlds in which they construct their everyday lives?' Such a perspective reminds us of both the common, shared experiences of youth in a rapidly changing world and the different responses young people adopt towards it.

> Deviant youth subcultures are discussed in chapter 20, 'Crime and Deviance'.

Young adulthood

The bulk of sociological research has been and still is concerned with the lives of adults. As a result the concept of 'adulthood' has, until recently, remained relatively unquestioned and 'there is yet no convincing sociology of adulthood' (Pilcher et al. 2003). For example, the study of doctor–patient relationships simply assumed mature adult doctors and patients, with little or no regard for the different experiences of children or young adults. Throughout the 1980s and 1990s, sociologists began to theorize a new phase within the life course in developed societies which we can call young adulthood (Goldscheider and Waite 1991). The systematic study of this stage is not yet as fully developed as that of childhood or later life. It also implies that a 'middle' or perhaps a 'mature' adulthood exists, before people move into their 'old age' (Green 2016: 124). Young adulthood is said to characterize people from around eighteen to the mid-thirties, who live quite independent lives but have not yet married or had children and, as a consequence, are still experimenting with relationships and lifestyles.

However, this stage is not experienced in the same way by men and women, all social classes or different ethnic groups. It is particularly among the more affluent groups that people in their early to mid-twenties are taking the time to travel and explore sexual, political and religious affiliations (Heath and Cleaver 2003). Indeed, the importance of this postponement of the responsibilities of full adulthood is likely to increase, given the extended period of education many people in the developed world now undergo.

In recent years, sociologists have studied the problems faced by young adults in a time of austerity politics, rising housing costs, high levels of personal indebtedness and job insecurity. Many young adults today remain dependent on the material and financial support of parents and other family members into their late twenties and beyond. Some have characterized this as the 'boomerang generation' (Newman 2012), because many young adults are trying to move on and live independent lives but find themselves unable to do so without the continuing support of family members. Heath and Calvert (2013) found that such intergenerational support ranges widely from small cash loans and gifts to cover bills and expenses all the way up to large mortgage deposits and the provision of accommodation within the family home. This extended period of dependency is often experienced by young adults as compromising their autonomy and independence.

This particular stage of life is likely to become much less gendered, as more young women now go on to university, forge careers and become independent instead of settling into traditional family life at an early age. We can expect scholars studying the life course to carry out more research on young adulthood over the next decade.

Mature adulthood

Most young adults in the developed world today can look forward to a life stretching into an old age of seventy years and beyond. But, in pre-industrial times, few could anticipate such a future with much confidence – and nor do young adults in the poorer parts of the developing world today. Death through sickness or injury was much more frequent among all age groups than it is today, and women in particular were at risk because of the high rates of mortality in childbirth. On the other hand, some of the strains that mature adults – roughly people in their late thirties to around sixty-five years old – experience today were less pronounced in previous times. People usually maintained a closer connection with their parents and other kin than the more mobile populations of the twenty-first century, and the routines of work they followed were much the same as those of previous generations.

Today there are major uncertainties in work, personal relationships and marriage, family life and many other social contexts. Individuals increasingly have to 'make' their own lives, much more so than in the past. Among many social groups, the creation of

sexual and marital ties now depends mainly on individual initiative and selection rather than being fixed by parents, though this is not the case in all cultures. While individual choice can be experienced as the freedom to decide, the responsibility to *have to* choose also imposes its own pressures. Some have theorized the emergence of a 'new middle age' in adulthood, in which those approaching old age engage in active consumerism and are concerned with youthfulness and personal reinvention as they grow older (Featherstone and Hepworth 1989).

Keeping a forward-looking outlook in mature adulthood has taken on a particular importance. Most people no longer expect to be doing the same thing throughout life. Adults who have worked in one career may find the level they have reached in mature adulthood unsatisfying and that further opportunities are blocked. Women who have spent early adulthood raising a family may feel they have little social value once children have left home. The phenomenon of the 'mid-life crisis' is very real for many mature adults today. A person may feel they have thrown away the opportunities that life had to offer or that they will never attain goals cherished since childhood. Yet growing older need not lead to resignation or bleak despair. For some, a release from childhood dreams can actually be liberating.

Later life

Among early cultures, elders usually had a major – often final – say over matters of importance to the community. Within families, the authority of both men and women tended to increase with age. But, in developed societies, 'retirement' from work may bring the opposite as older people lack authority within both the family and wider community. Having retired from the labour force, they may be materially poorer and be perceived to have little to offer young people by way of advice. Some sociologists have suggested that older people can be cast adrift by the rapid pace of technological and social change, which means they can even become 'strangers in time' (Mead 1978). For example, those born before the Second World War tend to hold a different set of values and norms of behaviour to those born in the late 1960s, when quite radical shifts in gender relations and attitudes towards sex and sexuality developed (Dowd 1986).

In the next section, we look at the sociological issues surrounding ageing in more detail than we did with earlier life course stages. The study of later life and ageing – social gerontology – is very well established, with a significant body of research and evidence, and this is reflected in the rest of this chapter. It is also the case that the consequences of an ageing world population have been at the centre of important social, political and economic debates since the mid-1970s, and these claims will also be considered.

Ageing

Fauja Singh, from Ilford, East London, took up running again in 2000 after a 53-year break. He ran the 2000 London Marathon at the age of eighty-nine in 6 hours and 54 minutes and soon began to run marathons all over the world, raising money for charities (Askwith 2003). He realized a long-held ambition in 2011 when, at the age of 100, he finished the Toronto Waterfront Marathon in 8 hours 25 minutes. Despite holding a passport and receiving a letter from the Queen congratulating him on his 100th birthday, he does not feature in the Guinness World Records. Mr Singh does not have an official birth certificate from 1911, as record-keeping in rural India at that time was not systematic. However, some athletics organizations do accept passports as proof of age and have recognized his achievements.

Fauja Singh is a notable illustration of the fact that people, especially in the richer countries, are on average leading longer, healthier and more productive lives than ever before. For example, when she became monarch in 1952, Queen Elizabeth II sent 273 birthday telegrams to congratulate British centenar-

ians on their 100th birthdays. By the end of the twentieth century she was much busier, sending out more than 3,000 per year (Cayton 2000).

Recent forecasts by the government's Office for National Statistics, based on current demographic trends, suggest that by 2066 there will be more than 500,000 centenarians in the UK. Babies born in 2011 were eight

> **THINKING CRITICALLY**
>
> List the elements of the ageing process that advertisements focus on to sell 'anti-ageing' products. Are these biological, psychological or social aspects? Why do so many people try to delay the *biological* ageing process?

times more likely to live to 100 than those born in 1931. Girls born in 2011 have a 1 in 3 chance of living to 100 years, while for boys this is 1 in 4 (*The Guardian* 2011). Growing old can be a fulfilling and rewarding experience, but it can also be a time of physical distress and social isolation. For most people, the experience of ageing lies somewhere in between these extremes.

The greying of human societies

Human societies all over the world are ageing, but they are not doing so evenly. One example is the startling national differences in average life expectancy (see figure 9.1). Taking two extremes, in 2012, life expectancy at birth in Afghanistan was 49.72 years (48.45 for men, 51.05 for women), but in Monaco it was 89.68 years (85.74 for men and 93.77 for women) (CIA 2012). Such grossly unequal life chances illustrate the very different ageing experiences of people across the world.

They also point to the various meanings attached to the idea of the life course. In the developed world, being forty years of age means people are entering 'mid-life' or 'mature adulthood', but, in some developing

Fauja Singh ran marathons from the age of eighty-nine and completed the Toronto Waterfront Marathon in 2011 at the age of 100; he retired from competitive running in 2013.

countries, reaching the age of forty is effectively to be in 'later life'. Such wide disparities in average life expectancy also shape experiences of death, dying and bereavement. Although most of this section will focus on debates and evidence from the relatively wealthy developed countries, we have to bear in mind that the situation in the developing world is very different, and the 'ageing experience' differs accordingly.

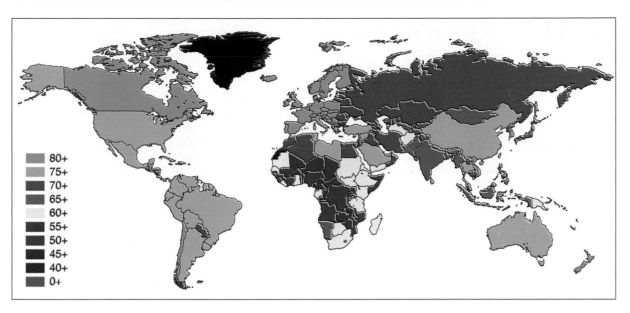

Figure 9.1 Global life expectancy at birth, 2015

Source: WHO (2016a).

> The situation in developing countries is discussed extensively in chapter 14, 'Global Inequality'.

The proportion of the global population aged over sixty years of age was just 8 per cent in 1950 and had risen to 11 per cent by 2009. However, this proportion is forecast to double rapidly by 2050, to 22 per cent. The fastest growth of the sixty-five and older age group will take place in the industrialized nations of the world, where families have fewer children and people live longer than in poorer countries. But, after the middle of this century, the developing nations will follow suit, as they experience their own 'elder explosion' (UNFPA 2011: 33–4).

The populations of most of the world's societies are ageing as the result of a decline in both birth and death rates, although the populations of developing countries continue to have shorter life spans because of economic disadvantage, poverty, malnutrition and disease (see chapter 14, 'Global Inequality'). The world's average life expectancy at birth grew from around 48 years in 1950, to 65.3 years in 1990 and 71.5 years in 2013 (Reuters 2015). Over the period 1950 to 2010, average life expectancy rose by twenty-six years in the developing countries compared with just eleven years in the developed world (UNFPA 2011). The narrowing gap between richer and poorer nations shows that the gross global inequality of life expectancy is not inevitable. A notable exception is seen in the countries of sub-Saharan Africa, where life expectancy has actually reduced since the mid-1980s, mainly because of the enormous and continuing impact of HIV/AIDS.

The ageing of the global population has enormous implications for social policy. More than 150 nations currently provide public assistance for people who are elderly or disabled, or, following their death, for their survivors. Older people are likely to require costly healthcare services, and the rapid growth in numbers strains the medical systems of many nations. Sociologists and gerontologists refer to the changing age structure as the greying of the population (Peterson 1999). 'Greying' is the result of two long-term trends in industrial societies: the tendency of families to have

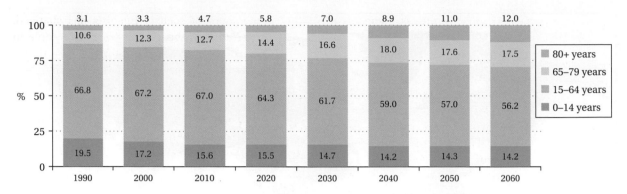

Figure 9.2   Population structure by major age groups, EU-27, 1990–2060 (projected)

Source: Eurostat (2011).

fewer children (discussed in chapter 10, 'Families and Intimate Relationships') and the fact that people are living longer.

As figure 9.2 illustrates in relation to the European Union, such a long-term shift in the age structure of the developed societies is well under way. By the year 2060, almost one-third of Europe's population will be over the age of sixty-five and more than one-fifth will be over the age of eighty, while the current working-age population (those aged fifteen to sixty-four) will decline by about 10 per cent, to 56 per cent of Europe's total population. The definition of 'working age' is also shifting as people continue working well beyond sixty-four. Amid the welter of commentary suggesting that an ageing population will bring difficult problems for governments and policy-makers, it is important to bear in mind the remarkable human success story that such figures demonstrate.

How do people age?

Ageing can be sociologically defined as the combination of biological, psychological and social processes that affect people as they grow older (Abeles and Riley 1987; Atchley 2000). These processes suggest the metaphor of three different, although interrelated, developmental 'clocks': first, a biological one, which refers to the physical body; second, a psychological one, which refers to the mind

and mental capabilities; and, third, a social one, which refers to cultural norms, values and role expectations having to do with age. There is enormous variation in all three. Our ideas about the meaning of age are rapidly changing, both because research is dispelling many myths about ageing and because advances in nutrition and health have enabled many people to live longer, healthier lives than ever before.

In examining the nature of ageing we will draw on studies of social gerontology, a discipline concerned with the study of the social aspects of ageing. This is not easy because, as people grow older, society itself changes, along with the very meaning of being 'old' (Riley et al. 1988). For people born into the developed societies in the mid-twentieth century, secondary education was regarded as adequate for most of the available jobs and the majority of people did not expect to live too long after their fifties – and then with a variety of health problems. Today, many of those same people find themselves in their seventies and eighties, relatively healthy and able to live very active lives.

Biological ageing

There are some well-established biological effects of ageing, although the exact chronological point at which they occur varies greatly depending on genetics and lifestyle. In general, for men and women alike, biological ageing typically means some or all of the following:

- declining vision, as the eye lens loses its elasticity
- hearing loss, first of higher-pitched tones
- wrinkles, as the skin's underlying structure becomes more brittle (skin lotions and surgical face-lifts only delay this)
- a decline of muscle mass and accompanying accumulation of fat, especially around the middle
- a fall in cardiovascular efficiency, as less oxygen can be inhaled and utilized during exercise.

These normal processes of ageing cannot be avoided, but they can be partly compensated for and offset by good health, proper diet and nutrition, and a reasonable amount of exercise (John 1988). For many, the physical changes of ageing do not significantly prevent them from leading active, independent lives well into their eighties. Some scientists have even argued that, with a healthy lifestyle and advances in medicine, more people will live relatively illness-free lives until they reach their biological maximum, experiencing only a brief period of sickness before death (Fries 1980).

There is some debate about when, or even if, people are genetically programmed to die (Kirkwood 2001). About ninety to 100 years seems to be the upper end of the genetically determined age distribution for most human beings, although some have argued that it may be as high as 120 (Rusting 1992; Treas 1995). The world's officially recorded 'oldest man', Walter Breuning, died of natural causes in Montana, USA, in April 2011 at 114 years of age. He told reporters that his longevity was down to eating just two meals a day, working for as long as he could and always embracing change. The world's oldest verified person was a French woman, Jeanne Calment, who died in 1997, aged 122. Others have claimed to be even older, but their ages cannot be reliably verified (BBC News 2011).

Traditionally, older people in the West were seen as knowledgeable, wise and useful members of society, but this has changed. Even though the majority of older people in the developed societies suffer no significant physical impairment and remain physically active, damaging stereotypes about the 'weak and frail elderly' persist (Victor 2005). These stereotypes have more to do with social meanings of ageing in Western cultures, which are increasingly preoccupied with youthfulness and fears of growing old and dying.

Psychological ageing

The psychological effects of ageing are less well established than the physical effects, although research into the psychology of ageing continues to expand (Diehl and Dark-Freudeman 2006). Even though memory, learning, intelligence, skills and motivation to learn are widely assumed to decline with age, research into the psychology of ageing suggests a much more complicated process (Birren and Schaie 2001).

Memory and learning ability, for example, do not decline significantly until very late in life for most people, although the speed with which one recalls or analyses information may slow down, giving the false impression of mental impairment. For most older people whose lives are stimulating and rich, such mental abilities as motivation to learn, clarity of thought and problem-solving capacity do not appear to decline significantly until very late in life (Baltes and Schaie 1977; Schaie 1979; Atchley 2000).

Recent research has focused on the extent to which memory loss relates to other variables, such as health, personality and social structures. Scientists and psychologists argue that intellectual decline is not uncommon but also not inevitable. They are working on ways to identify older people at risk so that medical intervention may allow longer maintenance of higher levels of intellectual function (Schaie 1996). Even Alzheimer's disease, the progressive deterioration of brain cells which is the primary cause of dementia in later life, is relatively uncommon in non-institutionalized persons under seventy-five, though it may afflict as many as half of all people over eighty-five. Recent research, particularly in the controversial area of stem cells, has created the hope that the treatment of Alzheimer's disease may one day be possible.

Social ageing

Social age consists of the norms, values and roles that are culturally associated with a particular chronological age. Ideas about social age differ from one society to another and tend to change over time as well. Societies such as Japan and China have traditionally revered older people, regarding them as a source of historical memories and wisdom. But in the UK and the USA, older people are more likely to be seen as non-productive, dependent and out of step with the times, both because they are less likely to have the high-tech skills valued by young people and because of the cultural obsession with youthfulness.

Role expectations are extremely important sources of personal identity. Some of the roles associated with ageing are generally positive: lord and lady, senior adviser, doting grandparent, religious elder, wise spiritual teacher. But others may be damaging, leading to lowered self-esteem and isolation. Highly stigmatizing stereotypical roles for older people exist: 'grumpy old', 'silly old', 'boring old' and 'dirty old' man or woman, for example (Kirkwood 2001). In fact older people do not simply passively play out socially assigned social roles; they actively shape and redefine them (Riley et al. 1988). A striking example of this is the emergence of older people's campaign groups and movements such as the Gray Panthers in the USA, which was created to fight for older people's rights.

> **THINKING CRITICALLY**
>
> Older people today are often seen as lucky, with good pensions, retired at sixty-five or earlier and owning their own homes. Is this a new stereotype or are younger generations really likely to have a more difficult old age than previously?

Growing old: competing explanations

Sociologists and social gerontologists have offered a number of theories regarding the nature of ageing. Some of the earliest theories emphasized individual adaptation to changing social roles as a person grows older. Later theories focused on how social structures shape the lives of older people and on the concept of the life course. The most recent theories have been more multifaceted, concentrating on the ways in which older people actively create their lives within specific institutional contexts.

First-generation theories: functionalism

The earliest theories of ageing reflected the functionalist approach that was dominant in sociology during the 1950s and 1960s. They emphasized how individuals adjusted to changing social roles as they aged and how those roles were useful to society, assuming that ageing brings with it physical and psychological decline (Hendricks 1992). Parsons argued that societies need to find roles for older people consistent with their advanced age and expressed concern that the USA, in particular, with its emphasis on youth, had failed to provide adequate roles that took advantage of the wisdom and maturity of older citizens. Traditional roles (such as work) have to be abandoned, and new forms of productive activity (such as volunteer service) need to be identified.

Parsons's ideas anticipated those of disengagement theory, which suggests that it is functional for society to remove people from their traditional roles when they grow older, freeing up space for new generations (Cumming and Henry 1961; Estes et al. 1992). According to this perspective, given the increasing frailty, illness and dependency of older people, allowing them to occupy traditional roles which they are no longer capable of adequately performing becomes dysfunctional for society as a whole.

Disengagement is deemed functional for the larger society because it opens up roles that were formerly filled by older people to younger ones, who will carry them out with fresh energy and new skills. Disengagement is also assumed to be functional for older people, as it enables them to take on less taxing roles consistent with advancing age and declining health. A number of older studies reported that a large majority feel good about retiring, which they claim raises morale and increases happiness (Palmore 1985; Howard et al. 1986). However, recent policy changes to raise the state pension age from sixty-five years to sixty-seven, sixty-eight or later will impact on functionalist ideas of disengagement. Rather than looking forward to retirement as purely a period of increased leisure and more time with the family, many retirees may now expect a 'partial retirement', which includes some paid work in the formal economy (Rix 2008: 130). This means that older people may well stay 'engaged' until very late in life.

One problem with disengagement theory is that it takes for granted the prevailing stereotype that later life necessarily involves frailty, illness and dependence. Critics of functionalism argue that it emphasizes the need for older people to adapt to existing conditions, but they do not question whether the circumstances faced by older people are fair or just. Similarly, many older people now live active, healthy lives and are able to continue in their adult roles for much longer than the present default retirement age. In reaction to functionalism, another group of theorists emerged out of the conflict tradition of sociology (Hendricks 1992).

Second-generation theories: age stratification and life course theory

From the mid-1970s, a new range of theories was introduced into gerontology (Estes et al. 2003). Two of the most important contributions were *age stratification theory* and the *life course model*. Age stratification theory looks at the role and influence of social structures, such as state policy, on the process of individual ageing and the wider stratification of older people in society. One important aspect of age stratification theory is the concept of *structural lag* (Riley et al. 1994). This provides an account of how structures do not keep pace with changes in the population and in individuals' lives. For example, in many European countries, when the retirement age was set at sixty-five soon after the Second World War, life expectancy and quality of life for older people was considerably lower than it is today. Only recently, partly as a consequence of economic recession, have governments considered raising the compulsory retirement age or scrapping it altogether.

The life course perspective also moved beyond looking at ageing in terms of individual adjustment. This perspective views ageing as one phase of a whole lifetime shaped by the historical, social, economic and environmental factors that occurred at earlier ages. Thus the life course model views ageing as a process that continues from birth to death, which contrasts with earlier theories focusing solely on the elderly as a distinctive group. Life course theory bridges micro- and macrosociology in examining the relationships between psychological states, social structures and social processes (Elder 1974).

Third-generation theories: political economy theory

One of the most important strands in the study of ageing in recent years has been the *political economy perspective* pioneered by Carroll Estes (Estes et al. 2003). Political economy theory provides an account of the role of the state and capitalism as contributing to systems of domination and the marginalization of older people.

Political economy theory focuses on the role of economic and political systems in shaping and reproducing the prevailing power arrangements and inequalities in society. Social policy – in income, health or social security, for example – is understood as the result of social struggles, conflicts and the dominant power relations of the time. Policy affecting older people reflects the stratification of society by gender, race and class. Hence, the phenomena of ageing and old age are directly related to the larger society in which they are situated and cannot be considered in isolation from other social forces (Minkler and Estes

1991). Understanding old age – and, of course, all other life course stages – therefore requires that we grasp the concept of intersectionality – the way that major social divisions overlap or intersect to produce complex patterns of inequality and advantage.

> Intersectionality is discussed in several chapters, notably chapter 3, 'Theories and Perspectives', chapter 15, 'Gender and Sexuality', and chapter 16, 'Race, Ethnicity and Migration'.

Aspects of ageing

Although ageing is a process which presents new possibilities, it is also accompanied by a set of unfamiliar challenges. As people age, they face a combination of physical, emotional and material problems that can be difficult to negotiate. One significant challenge is retirement. For most people, work does not just pay the bills, it also contributes to our sense of personal identity. Retirement does not lead only to a loss of income but possibly also to a loss of status, and many people find it difficult to adjust. The death of a spouse is another significant transition, which can represent the loss of a partner of many years who has been the main source of companionship and support.

Older people are rich, poor, and everything in between; they belong to all ethnic groups; they live alone and in families of various sorts; they vary in their political values and preferences; and they are gay and lesbian as well as heterosexual. Furthermore, they are diverse with respect to health, which can influence their ability to maintain their autonomy and overall well-being. Today, 'later life' covers a wide and increasing age span.

Contrary to the contemporary stereotype of the well-heeled, active pensioner, the so-called fourth age can, in reality, be a time of poverty, ill health and social isolation.

A distinction is often drawn between the third and fourth ages of life in modern societies. The third age covers the years from fifty to seventy-four, when people continue to lead active independent lives, increasingly free from day-to-day parenting responsibilities and the labour market. Many in this group have the time and money to remain active consumers. By contrast, the so-called fourth age refers to the later years of life when people's independence and ability to care for themselves become more seriously challenged. This section looks at the effects of inequality, gender and ethnicity on the experience of ageing.

Inequality and older people

Although the over sixty-fives constitute a diverse group of people, in general terms older people in most developed societies have been more materially disadvantaged than other segments of the population. For instance, in 2007, about one in six (17 per cent) retired persons in the twenty-seven countries of the European Union was at risk of poverty, compared with 8 per cent of those in employment. The highest risk of poverty for the over sixty-fives was found in the Baltic states, the UK and Cyprus. Only in Poland was the median disposable income of this age group quite similar or just below that of the under sixty-fives (Eurostat 2010: 321–2).

However, since the 2008 financial crash, older people's relative position in the EU has improved. By 2013, those over sixty-five were less at risk of poverty and social exclusion than either the overall EU population or children and young people in twenty of the twenty-eight EU countries (table 9.1). It seems that the brunt of the economic recession and austerity measures fell on vulnerable groups in already precarious jobs and employment sectors, while, for most older people, state pension provision and other measures tended to protect older people from the worst effects (Eurostat 2015). There are some differences however. In Bulgaria, over 57 per cent of over-65s were at risk, while older people also remained most at risk in Estonia, Croatia, Slovenia and Finland.

Subjective feelings about standard of living are not based solely on material factors or statistics but also draw on relevant reference groups. Comparisons with memories of earlier life may still be broadly positive in material terms but not necessarily in moral or social ones. However, older people also compare their position with the materially better standard of living they enjoyed before retirement, and may compare themselves with the average living conditions in society as a whole or of other retirees. Thus there is no common subjective experience of inequality among older people (Vincent 1999).

The inequalities of class, race and gender are often exacerbated when a person stops work, so the added inequality of later life means that older women, minorities and manual workers are poorer than peer equivalents in middle age. The ability to build up a private occupational or personal pension during working life is one of the key determinants of income inequality among the elderly. Consequently, it is older men who were previously employed as professionals or managers who tend to have the highest gross weekly income in later life.

> We look at poverty among older people in more detail in chapter 13, 'Poverty, Social Exclusion and Welfare'.

The feminization of later life

Across all the world's societies, women generally live longer than men. Because of this, widowhood is the norm for older women. In the UK in 2004, for example, almost half of women over the age of sixty-five, and four-fifths of women aged eighty-five and over, were widowed. By contrast, more than three-quarters of men aged between sixty-five and sixty-nine were married, a proportion which had fallen to 60 per cent for those in their early eighties (ONS 2004b). In Britain in mid-2008, there were more than twice as many women aged eighty-five or over (914,000) as men (422,000) (ONS 2010a: 3). This numerical predominance of women has

Table 9.1 People at risk of poverty or social exclusion by age group, EU-28, 2013

	Total	Children (0–17)	Adults (18–64)	Elderly (65 years and over)
EU-28 [1]	24.5	27.6	25.3	18.3
Euro area [1]	23.0	25.0	24.3	16.5
Belgium	20.8	21.9	20.8	19.5
Bulgaria	48.0	51.5	44.3	57.6
Czech Republic	14.6	16.4	45.2	10.4
Denmark	18.9	15.5	22.3	11.4
Germany	20.3	19.4	22.0	16.0
Estonia	23.5	22.3	22.7	28.0
Ireland [2]	30.0	33.1	31.7	14.7
Greece	35.7	38.1	39.1	23.1
Spain	27.3	32.6	29.2	14.5
France	18.1	21.3	19.2	10.4
Croatia	29.9	29.3	29.6	31.9
Italy	28.4	31.9	29.4	31.7
Cyprus	27.8	27.7	28.2	26.1
Latvia	35.1	38.4	34.0	36.1
Lithuania	30.8	35.4	29.3	22.6
Luxembourg	19.0	26.0	19.0	7.0
Hungary	33.5	43.0	34.5	19.0
Malta	24.0	32.0	22.5	20.8
Netherlands	15.9	17.0	18.0	6.1
Austria	18.8	22.9	18.3	16.2
Poland	25.8	29.8	26.1	19.7
Portugal	27.4	31.6	28.5	20.3
Romania	40.4	48.5	39.4	35.0
Slovenia	20.4	17.5	20.6	23.0
Slovakia	19.8	25.5	19.4	13.6
Finland	16.0	13.0	16.7	16.8
Sweden	16.4	16.2	16.5	16.5
United Kingdom	24.8	32.6	24.1	18.1
Iceland	13.0	16.6	13.4	4.2
Norway	14.1	13.4	15.6	9.6
Switzerland	16.4	17.3	12.8	29.6

Notes: [1] Estimated data.

[2] 2013 data not available; 2012 data instead.

Source: Eurostat (2015a).

been described as the 'feminization of later life' (see figure 9.3).

The main reason for the shifting proportion of women is because so many young men died during the First World War (1914–18). The women of this generation began to reach retirement age in 1961, which produced a sharp rise in the sex ratio imbalance among older people. Although there was a larger proportion of women than men in the over sixty-five age group in Europe over the latter half of the twentieth century, this has declined somewhat, and that decline is forecast to continue. Projections to 2050 suggest a levelling off of the gender imbalance (or 'sex ratio') for the sixty-five to seventy-nine age range, with feminization shifting into the rapidly growing eighty-plus age group. One reason for this is the more rapid fall in mortality of men over the age of sixty-five during the second half of the twentieth century. Figure 9.4 uses 'age pyramids' to depict the moving pattern of the sex ratio across the European population from 1950 to 2050.

'Feminization' is not without its problems, however. Older women are more likely than their male contemporaries to be poor. In most countries, women are far less likely to have the same pension entitlements as men because of the gender gap in pay and the loss of lifetime earnings associated with caring for children and relatives. In 2007–8, for example, 42 per cent of single, older women in the UK had only the state pension compared with 31 per cent of single men. More than half of single male pensioners (54 per cent) had some form of occupational pension on top of their state pension, but just 27 per cent of single female pensioners had any income at all from a private pension (ONS 2010a: 118).

With increasing age, women suffer more than men from disability. This means that they

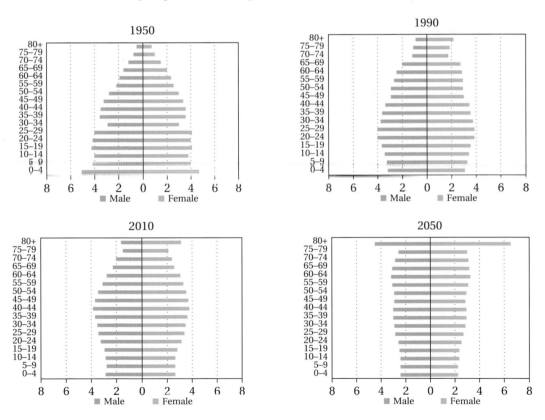

Figure 9.3 European age pyramids, 1950, 1990, 2010 and 2050 (projected)

Source: Adapted from Eurostat (2010: 167).

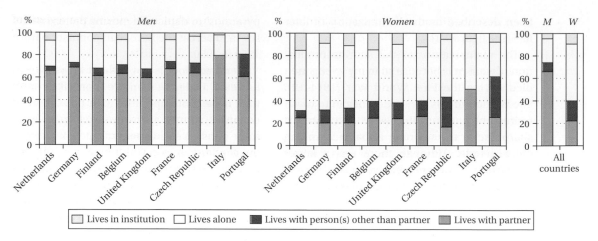

Figure 9.4 Living arrangements of people aged over seventy-five in nine European countries, by gender, 2000

Source: Delbès et al. (2006).

require more assistance and support simply to carry out everyday tasks and personal care routines, such as bathing and getting in and out of bed. The living situations of older men and women also have a gender dimension. One study of a selection of European countries found that women tend to grow old alone, while men grow old with a partner (Delbès et al. 2006; see figure 9.4). In addition, older women were twice as likely as men to live in an institution. The authors suggest that perhaps men find it more difficult to deal with their partners' health problems than do women. There are also some differences between Northern and Southern Europe. For instance, 56 per cent of Finnish women and 59 per cent of German women live alone after the age of seventy-five, compared with just 30 per cent of Portuguese women.

There are some cultural and policy differences that may explain such findings. Southern European countries tend to see 'multigenerational co-residence' as the preferred option for keeping older relatives at home, whereas North European states have better-developed welfare services, which perform some of the same functions but can lead to individuals living alone. It is clear, then, that there are specific gendered patterns of care among the older population.

Age and ethnicity

The income of older people from ethnic minorities tends to be lower than that of their white counterparts, and reliance on means-tested benefits is greater (Berthoud 1998). Older people from ethnic minorities are also disadvantaged in other measures of wealth, such as car-ownership and housing tenure, though certain groups, such as Indians and Chinese, have rates of home-ownership that are comparable to that of white populations. For example, in general, Pakistanis and Bangladeshis in the UK have high rates of poverty compared with other groups, and this pattern is continued into later life.

Ginn and Arber (2000) examined ethnic and gender differences in the income of individuals among the older population in the UK. They found that older Asian women tend to be particularly disadvantaged. Retired ethnic minorities are often unable to supplement their state pension with an occupational or private one. In 2007, almost three-quarters of the white population were in receipt of an occupational pension compared with fewer than half of the Asian/Asian British and black/black British populations (DWP 2007).

The lack of a private pension reflects shorter employment records in Britain for the largely migrant older ethnic population, discrimination in the labour market, the limited availability and type of jobs found in the areas where minorities have settled, and sometimes a lack of fluency in English. For older women in some specific minority groups, economic disadvantage may also result from cultural norms acting as a barrier to employment earlier in life. Such patterns of structured disadvantage can be found among many other ethnic minority populations in Europe and internationally.

The politics of ageing

'The global ageing crisis'?

The significant shift in age distribution within populations presents specific challenges for all developed countries. One way of understanding why is to consider the dependency ratio – the relationship between the number of *children* and *retired people* (considered 'dependent'), on the one hand, and the number of *people of working age*, on the other. However, the 'old-age dependency ratio' can also be distinguished from the 'young-age ratio', and it is the former we are concerned with here. The old-age dependency ratio refers to the ratio between the number of retired people and those adults of working age and is usually expressed as a percentage.

As birth and fertility rates declined in Europe and other developed countries, fewer young people meant that young-age dependency ratios almost halved, from 41 per cent in 1960 to 23 per cent by 2005. But, over the same period, as people increasingly live longer, the old-age dependency ratio rose from 14 to 23 per cent. By contrast, in Africa the total dependency ratio (young- and old-age dependency) rose as high as 80 per cent in 2005, mainly because of the very high proportion of young people in the population (Eurostat 2010: 152–3). Old-age dependency ratios remain relatively high – above 15 per cent – in Europe, North America and Oceania, but relatively low – below 10 per cent – in Asia, Africa and Latin America and the Caribbean. In addition there is much variation at the national level, both within and between the regions of the world.

Changes in the dependency ratio have several causes. Modern agriculture, improved sanitation systems, better epidemic control and medicines have all contributed to a decline in mortality throughout the world. In most societies today, especially in the developed world, fewer children die in infancy and more adults survive into later life. As the proportion of older people continues to grow, the demands on social services and health systems increase, and the growth in life expectancy means that pensions will need to be paid for more years than they are at present.

However, the working population funds the programmes that support the older population and, as the old-age dependency ratio increases (see figure 9.5), some argue that greater strain will be placed on resources. In the light of such projections, some scholars and politicians reasoned that the state pension age (SPA) should be raised. In the wake of the 2008 financial crisis and 2009 recession, these arguments gained credence, and the need to cut public spending, including the state pension bill, became more urgent. As a result, many governments announced plans to raise the SPA. In the UK, between 2010 and 2020, it will rise from sixty to sixty-five for women, thus reaching parity with that for men. The SPA will then rise in stages until between 2044 and 2046, when it will reach sixty-eight for both men and women. Clearly, redefining 'working age' and 'pensionable age' in this way will impact on dependency ratios (ONS 2010c: 17).

> See chapters 7, 'Work and the Economy', 13, 'Poverty, Social Exclusion and Welfare', and 21, 'Politics, Government and Social Movements', for more discussion of the 2008 crisis and its impact on government policies.

Figure 9.5 divides the pensionable age dependency ratio into age bands to show the effects of an ageing population and changes

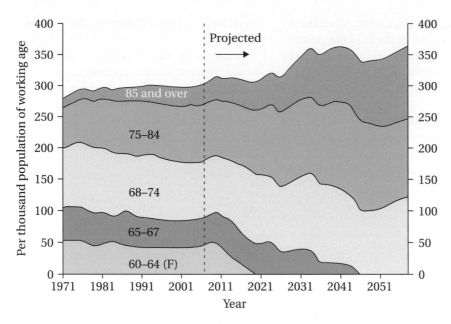

Figure 9.5 Actual and projected components of UK dependency ratio for population of pensionable ages, 1971–2058

Source: ONS (2010c: 18).

to the SPA projected into the 2050s. As the SPA increases are introduced, affecting those in the sixty to sixty-four and sixty-five to sixty-seven age bands, the overall dependency ratio will level off (and even fall slightly) around 2021, before rising again. Thus the demographic ageing trend remains the strongest long-run force shaping dependency ratios in the developed countries. In the UK, some 40 per cent of those of state pensionable age in 2008 were aged seventy-five or over, but by 2058 this age group will make up 67 per cent (ONS 2010c: 17–18). In France, the retirement age is planned to rise from sixty to sixty-two by 2018; Germany plans to move retirement from sixty-five to sixty-seven by 2029, and numerous other governments are seeking similar changes.

Some critics argue that all of this 'dependency talk' is unnecessarily alarmist and does not accurately depict the reality of demographic change. It also risks constructing negative interpretations of older people that stigmatize them and reinforce stereotypes. Mullan (2002) argued that those who believe the ageing population is a ticking time bomb about to bring about a series of devastating social problems are falling for a series of myths. For example, Mullan maintains that an ageing population will not necessarily mean an exponential rise in ill health and dependency. Ageing is not an illness; most older people are neither ill nor disabled, and many continue to work after the formal retirement age. People live longer because of the improvement in living conditions over the past century. Categorizing older people as a 'dependent population' alongside children merely constructs this social group as 'a problem'. And, though not all older people are uniformly fit and financially secure, later life has changed very much for the better for many people who now look forward to retirement (Gilleard and Higgs 2005).

For some sociologists, there are good reasons to believe that the very concept of dependency needs to be reconsidered (Arber and Ginn 2004). First, the age ranges used to define dependency in the past no longer reflect the patterns of employment in the developed

Global Society 9.2   China's ageing population

In October 2015, the Chinese government announced that it was ending its longstanding one child per family policy and couples would be allowed to have a second child. The one-child policy has been in place since 1979 and was designed to slow the birth rate. In 1979 the population was close to 1 billion, and the Communist Party saw continuing population growth as a brake on their attempts to increase productivity and economic growth.

Chinese couples who did not adhere to the policy were often fined; others lost their jobs and some women underwent forced abortions. Given the widespread preference for a male child, the policy is also held to be responsible for China's gender imbalance, as some couples gave up their first female child to an orphanage or aborted the pregnancy in order to try and ensure their only child was a boy. However, over time, some provinces, rural areas and regions had already effectively adopted a less rigid enforcement regime. For example, rural families were allowed a second child if the first was female.

The ending of the one-child policy seems to be a recognition that China has an ageing population (almost one-third are over fifty years old) and the country needs more young workers if the economy is to continue its previous rapid improvement. Yet one consequence of the one-child policy is that small families have now become normal, and, for many, the preferred choice, as couples look to enjoy the consumer benefits of the growing economy and its integration into the global capitalist system. After many years of trying to control and manage its population, China now faces similar demographic issues and dilemmas to those faced by other ageing societies around the world.

THINKING CRITICALLY

What might be the financial implications of the 'greying' of the world's population? How has the 2008 financial crash impacted on relations between younger and older generations?

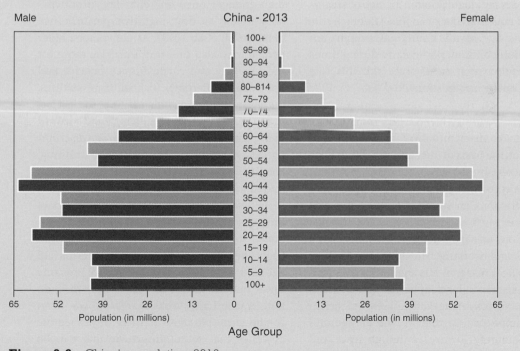

Figure 9.6   China's population, 2013

Source: US Census Bureau.

countries. Fewer young people enter the labour market to work full time at the age of sixteen, instead staying in formal education for much longer. Many workers also leave the labour market before the age of sixty-five or move into and out of work at various stages of the life course, and more women than ever before are now in paid employment, offsetting the shorter duration of employment for men.

Second, activity that benefits the economy is not confined to active participation in the formal sector. Evidence from the UK shows that, rather than being a burden, older people make many productive economic and social contributions. They provide unpaid and informal care to less able partners, reducing the cost to the state of providing health- and personal care. They are a major source of care provision for grandchildren, allowing their children to work, and are highly active in voluntary organizations. Older people are an important source of financial support for grown-up children, providing them with loans, educational fees, gifts and help for housing – especially significant in an 'age of austerity' and cuts to welfare benefits. Older parents continue to provide emotional support for their adult children, particularly during times of difficulty, such as divorce, and this role should not be underestimated.

Ageism

Ageism is discrimination against people purely on the basis of their age and is therefore akin to sexism or racism, though it does not apply only to older people. For example, there are restrictions on young people's rights and freedoms, such as forced schooling and age restrictions on sexual activity, smoking, taking alcohol and working. However, the bulk of sociological research has examined discrimination against older people. There is a crucial difference between ageism and sexism, racism and homphobia, in that we will all age and become older. However, although sexist and racist jokes are no longer publicly acceptable, jokes about old age remain widespread. Many people send birthday cards whose humour trades on ideas of increasing decrepitude with

every passing year. Such is the paradox of ageing in ageist societies.

Macnicol (2010: 3–4) argues that ageism can be seen in three areas of social life: social relations and attitudes, employment, and the distribution of goods and services. As we have seen, there are many stereotypes of older people in circulation in society. Many younger people believe that most people over seventy are in care homes or hospitals and that a high proportion of them suffer from dementia. In fact, most live in private dwellings and less than 10 per cent of those aged between sixty-five and eighty have symptoms of dementia. Although erroneous, such views feed negative attitudes and elder abuse in both domestic and institutional settings.

In employment, it is often believed that older workers are less able and competent than younger ones, though firms that have sought out older workers report superior productivity and attendance records compared with younger workers. Psychological research also suggests that older workers score more highly than younger ones on reliability, productivity and day-to-day cognitive performance (Schmiedek et al. 2013). As consumers, older people may also find that they pay more for their holiday and car insurance policies and are treated differently in healthcare settings, purely on grounds of their age. Over the last few decades many governments have put forward or implemented proposals to ban age discrimination, covering recruitment, job training, entry to higher education, promotion, pay, job retention and – importantly – retirement rights.

Bytheway's (1995) account of ageism draws on social constructionism (an approach introduced in chapter 8, 'Social Interaction and Daily Life'). Bytheway questions the terms 'old age' and 'the elderly', arguing that we presume these have a universal reality that they do not, in fact, have. What exactly do we mean by the term 'old age'? Is there any scientific evidence that something exists that can be called old age? If it does exist, how do people enter it and 'become' elderly? For Bytheway, the categories we use to describe the ageing process are themselves ageist. They are social

Older people often provide much-needed help to families and communities – for example, by becoming informal childminders for their working children.

constructions which legitimize the separation and management of people on the basis of their chronological age.

The ideological and value differences between older and younger people may contribute to a generation gap which some scholars argue has become wider. In this sense, ageism may be a unique form of discrimination, as older people were once young and younger people will become old. However, recognition of this fact does not appear to be enough, in itself, to prevent ageism. Some theorists also argue that a key reason for ageism lies in the perceived threat older people pose to younger generations.

For younger people, especially in Western cultures, with their valorization of youth and youthfulness, old age, with its unwanted physical changes, is something to be feared (known as *gerontophobia* – fear of ageing), and discussions of ageing are generally avoided. Old people therefore represent that fear for young people and are constant reminders of their own future (Greenberg et al. 2004). However, older people are also reminders of our own eventual mortality, and modern societies tend to hide the process of dying 'behind the scenes' to avoid having to face up to the inevitability of death. Therefore, a prerequisite for eliminating ageism would seem to be a more open, public, inter-generational discussion of issues around death, dying and bereavement. In the final section, we will see whether this is a realistic prospect.

Death, dying and bereavement

The sociology of death and dying

Sociologists have only recently become interested in the universal human experiences of

367

dying, death and bereavement. One reason why the study of death and dying has not been more central to sociology is that death marks the *end* of an individual's participation in the social world and therefore seems to lie outside sociology's main concerns. Societies continue to develop even though individuals die, and social development, rather than individual deaths, has been the focus of much sociology. Another reason is that, within modern societies themselves, death and dying have long been 'taboo subjects', not topics for polite conversation. One early research study was Glaser and Strauss's *Awareness of Dying* (1965), which looked at the experience of death and dying in a US hospital's cancer ward, but this was an exception rather than the norm.

Since the 1990s, the neglect of death and dying has been rectified by the development of a new research field – the sociology of death, dying and bereavement (Clark 1993). One of the founders of this field is the British sociologist Tony Walter (1994, 1999), whose work has focused on the ways in which societies organize death, dying and mourning. How do societies care for the hundreds of thousands of dying people? Practically, how do they deal with this number of dead bodies? What support is provided for bereaved relatives? What beliefs are held about the prospects for the dead when their earthly lives are over? The answers to such questions turn out to be quite varied. Anthropologists have long studied cultural differences in death rituals in small-scale societies and within developing countries, but the modern sociology of death and dying has concentrated primarily on the developed world. Yet even here there are many cultural differences. Nonetheless, sociologists have been struck by some key, *shared* features of modern industrial societies in relation to their handling of death.

Theorizing death in modern societies

One main aspect of modern societies is that, until quite recently, death tended to be hidden 'behind the scenes' of social life, while in previous times a majority of people experienced the final process of dying while at home, with family and friends in close attendance. This is still the case in many non-industrialized societies today. But in most modern societies death typically occurs in hospitals and nursing homes – relatively impersonal settings that are distanced from the mainstream of social life. Bodies are then moved to different parts of the buildings, thereby maintaining a physical distance between living patients, their families and the dead (Ariès 1965).

In *The Loneliness of the Dying* (1985: 8), Norbert Elias connects this hiding away of death and dying to the increasing life expectancy we looked at in earlier sections. He argues that

> The attitude to dying and the image of death in our societies cannot be completely understood without reference to this relative security and predictability of individual life and the correspondingly increased life expectancy. Life grows longer, death is further postponed. The sight of dying and dead people is no longer commonplace. It is easier in the normal course of life to forget death.

However, Elias sees that the modern way of death and dying presents emotional problems for people reaching this stage of their lives. Although hospitals provide the best available nursing care, scientific medicine and use of the latest technologies, the patient's contact with family members and friends is usually seen as inconveniencing treatment and care regimes, and is therefore restricted to short visits at specific times of day. This rational management of patients may well deny people the essential emotional comfort of being close to their loved ones, which they actually need most in the final period of life. In modern societies, says Elias, dying can be a very lonely process indeed.

Zygmunt Bauman (1992) offers another perspective on the distancing of modern people from death and dying. He argues that modern societies deny and defer death long into the future by turning the ultimate and inevitable ending of life into a multitude of smaller, 'non-ultimate' and potentially resolvable 'health

9.3 An ageless future?

In *Stories of Ageing* (2000), Mike Hepworth uses literature to encourage his readers to 'explore fiction as an imaginative resource for understanding variations in the meaning of the experience of ageing in society'. In the extract below, Hepworth discusses how science and technology could radically alter how we understand ageing:

Outside the realms of legend and the romantic imagination there was until very recently only one future of ageing in Western culture if one was lucky to live long enough to grow old: the Christian vision of the inevitable decline of the human body, death and an afterlife of either Heaven or Hell. The dualistic separation of the body from the soul in Christian thought regards the ageing of the body in the temporal world as a brief testing ground for eternal spiritual life beyond the veil. The corruption of the flesh frees the soul or essential self for an other-worldly existence out of time. Heaven is the compensation for graceful or virtuous ageing and not looking for pacts with the Devil to prolong a youthfully active life.

But times are rapidly changing and the emergence of modern scientific medicine and technology has offered an alternative promise to release from the ageing body in this world rather than the next (Katz 1996). One of the interesting features of this development is that contemporary models of an ageless future have become predominantly biological rather than essentially spiritual (Cole 1992). The prevailing belief now is that it is the science of the biological body, and not the religion of the eternal immaterial soul, which will arrest the process of ageing and extend the period of youthful life. . . . The widespread faith in the limitless potential of science to solve human problems encourages us to turn expectantly to medical science to transform ageing from the natural termination of the life course into a disease, which is 'potentially curable'. One of these days ageing will disappear from the human agenda when cures for the illnesses associated with growing older have been found and ailing and malfunctioning body parts can be replaced.

One way of defeating the ageing process is for humans to become cyborgs or to assume the 'post-human' bodies of partly biological and partly technological beings (Featherstone and Renwick 1995). . . . Any part of the internal body which causes distress in later life will be removed and replaced with a genetically engineered or transplanted substitute. The story of the ageing body will thus become not a story of how individuals cope or come to terms with its limitations but science fiction come true. The body will be a machine and the meaning of ageing may cease to be a matter of concern.

Source: Hepworth (2000: 124–5).

> **THINKING CRITICALLY**
>
> Is the desire for eternal youthfulness really just the product of an ageist society? What are some of the negative social consequences of the quest to eliminate physical signs of ageing?

hazards' and illnesses. Mortality is therefore effectively 'deconstructed', which brings the endless defensive battles against ageing and death right into the centre of daily life. People become used to treating, curing and managing their chronic illnesses, for example.

In particular, modern societies place a high value on youthfulness, and the quest to remain 'young' – both physically and emotionally (staying 'young at heart') – takes up a large part of many people's lives. As we noted above, as the demand for youthfulness increases, there are now huge markets for anti-ageing treatments, vitamin supplements, cosmetic surgery and fitness equipment. Bauman describes such actions as part of a 'life strategy', though,

FOR THE PERFECT AGE
LOOK REJUVENATED
IRRESISTIBLY RADIANT

BECAUSE YOU'RE WORTH IT.

AGE PERFECT

WITH
SOYA
PEPTIDES

TAILOR-MADE FOR YOUR SKIN
■ AGE SPOTS APPEAR REDUCED
■ SKIN FEELS NOURISHED
   WITH MOISTURE
■ COMPLEXION LOOKS
   MORE RADIANT

Grow another year better.
Helen Mirren

L'ORÉAL
PARIS

3 for 2 on L'oréal Paris Age Perfect
Shop online at Boots.com

Boots
let's feel good

Available at larger Boots stores. Cheapest product free. Offer valid from 13.05.15 - 09.06.15. Subject to availability.

Consumer societies promote a bewildering range of products aimed at 'delaying' or 'combating' the physical signs of ageing. Youthful ideals make the older idea of 'growing old gracefully' less socially acceptable, particularly for women.

of course, people may not always acknowledge that their attempts to stay young and fit are ultimately futile defensive actions to avoid acknowledging their own mortality.

Assisted dying – a developing debate

Since the mid-1990s, sociologists have noted some significant changes in the way that death, dying and bereavement are dealt with in modern societies. First, the hospice movement, which started in the 1960s, aims to offer an alternative to the impersonality of hospitals for terminally ill people. The first modern hospice was founded in London in 1967 by Dame Cicely Saunders, and many hospices in the UK and the USA have a Christian basis. The UK has some 231 hospices (twenty-nine

for children), which are based on the principle that death and dying are a natural part of life and that the quality of life for dying people should be as positive as possible. Hospices encourage family and friends to continue to play a part in the patient's life, even in the final stages. Saunders actually believed that the pain-relief regimes within hospices made euthanasia unnecessary. The growth of more personalized forms of care for terminally ill people may make the modern experience of dying much less impersonal than Elias thought.

Second, the issues of euthanasia, assisted dying and the 'right to die' have become more widely debated in the developed societies. Euthanasia refers to deliberate interventions (usually by doctors) to end life in order to relieve intractable suffering, while assisted dying (sometimes called 'assisted suicide') is when another person helps someone to take their own life by supplying them with the means to do so. That more people are now seeking a right to die is perhaps not surprising given the evidence presented earlier on the greying of societies, which, for some, brings with it extended periods of chronic illness or degenerative diseases such as Alzheimer's. For increasing numbers of people, the prospect of suffering and the loss of 'self' towards the end of life is not one they are prepared to accept.

In the USA in 1994, the state of Oregon passed the Death with Dignity Act, which allows medically diagnosed, terminally ill people (those with six months left to live) to request a lethal dose of medication. The legislation also includes some strict safeguards: only 'competent adults' can make the decision, patients themselves must make the request in writing, two witnesses must confirm the request, diagnosis must be confirmed by an independent professional, patients must administer the medication themselves, and any medical professionals can refuse to participate if they have moral objections. Euthanasia or assisted suicide has also been legalized or partially legalized in a growing number of countries, including Belgium, Switzerland,

Germany, Japan, Luxembourg and the Netherlands. A Swiss 'assisted suicide' organization, Dignitas, founded in 1998, has received much publicity for allowing foreign nationals to use their service. More than 100 people from the UK and over 500 from Germany have taken their own lives at Dignitas (*Der Tagesspiegel* 2008).

However, the issue of a right to die is controversial, and moral opinion is polarized. In September 2015, MPs in the UK Parliament debated a bill that would have allowed some adults to die under medical supervision if they had been diagnosed as having less than six months to live. The bill was rejected by 330 votes to 118. Many MPs argued that medics should focus on prolonging life, not helping to end it. Rather than promoting the right to die, better palliative care is suggested as a more humane or 'civilized' alternative (Forman 2008: 11–12). Others are concerned that legalizing assisted suicide may lead to undue pressure being placed on ill, mainly older people who want to avoid 'becoming a burden' on relatives and healthcare systems. In that situation, the idea that people 'freely choose' to take their own life is compromised. The concern is that assisted suicide, rather than being a last resort for people facing terminal illness and suffering, may spread to other, non-life-threatening conditions. For instance, disabled people may face increased discrimination and pressure if they come to be seen as a drain on society's resources.

Nonetheless, the demographic trends we have seen in this chapter suggest that the voices of those seeking change will grow stronger as larger numbers of people come into contact with the effects of degenerative and terminal illnesses within their families and among their friends. It therefore seems likely that some societies will legalize assisted suicide, while in others a *de facto* decriminalization will occur as authorities decide not to prosecute those who assist close relatives to die – at least in cases where that wish has been clearly stated.

Finally, there now seem to be ways of dealing with death and bereavement that are much more informal than those in the past. Some sociologists have described these as 'postmodern' developments (see chapter 3 for a discussion of postmodern social theory) in which more individualistic and diverse approaches to dealing with death are emerging (Bauman 1992; Walter 1994). For example, it is now common for people to personalize their own or their relatives' funerals: playing pop music, giving their own speeches and insisting on colourful clothing rather than relying on the traditional rituals of the churches. It is also becoming more commonplace for relatives to mark road-accident deaths with flowers at the scene of a crash as an individual way of remembering the dead rather than, or in addition to, the ritual of attending a cemetery to tend the grave. Web-based memorials and tribute sites are also gaining in popularity, and new debates have arisen concerning the ownership of people's online legacy and how their presence on social media should be dealt with after their death.

Since the 1980s, then, in many of the developed societies people have embarked on a quest for such new, more informal rituals in dying and mourning to extend or replace the older, more formal, religious ones (Wouters 2002). This development represents an attempt by people to find new public rituals which match their own individual and personal needs.

Along with the spread of the hospice movement and campaigns for and against the right to die, the informalization of mourning rituals may be one more sign that death and dying are finally moving out of their hidden location into a much more open, public discussion. Once this occurs, perhaps we may see the gradual erosion of the stigma and social taboos around ageing, dying and death. Future generations may well wonder why so many self-defined civilized societies took so long to come to terms with one of very few universal aspects of human existence.

Chapter review

1   How do children gain a 'social self' and come to see themselves as others see them? What makes Mead's theory a genuinely sociological theory of self-formation?

2   How well does Piaget's theory of development fit your own or your children's experience? What criticisms are made of the idea that there are *universal* stages of socialization?

3   Explain the concept of gender socialization and describe how people acquire a gender identity. What evidence is there that socialization is not a deterministic process but a series of opportunities for interaction which produce differential outcomes?

4   Explain how the concept of the life course differs from that of life cycle. Why might the former be said to be an advance on the latter?

5   What, if any, common life transitions still exist in the developed societies? Are even these common across gender, social classes and diverse ethnic groups?

6   Compare the idea of a cohort with that of a generation. What can we learn about social change from studying cohorts and generations?

7   What is *social ageing* and how can it be demonstrated that social ageing differs across both time and cultures?

8   What is meant by the *greying* of Western societies? What is the *dependency ratio* and what economic and social problems may be created as it increases? How have critics countered the pessimism of such accounts?

9   Compare and contrast functionalist theories of the desirable disengagement of older people from work with activity theories, emphasizing the importance of continuing engagement as a necessary source of vitality.

10 How do conflict theories differ from both of these perspectives? For example, how might older people be materially disadvantaged and how might the concept of intersectionality help us to understand the differential experience of old age?

11 What is meant by ageism? Provide some examples and explain why it occurs.

12 Many developed societies have hidden death and dying behind the scenes of social life. What is meant by the *informalization* of mourning rituals? How are the developed societies changing in relation to the handling of death, dying and bereavement?

Research in practice

Discussions of the increasing dependency ratio have been newsworthy for foregrounding the potential for intergenerational conflict as younger generations face a worse set of social and economic conditions than previous generations. Steep housing costs, reduced pension provision, university tuition fees and debt, insecure jobs and financial uncertainty combine to create a sense of a 'lost generation'. The following article takes issue with this argument, using a life course approach and a very specific father and son case study. Read it and address the questions below.

Nilsen, A., and Brannen, J. (2014) 'An Intergenerational Approach to Transitions to Adulthood: The Importance of History and Biography', *Sociological Research Online*, 19(2): www.socresonline.org.uk/19/2/9.html.

1   What is the main source used in this paper? How would you describe this analysis, which reinterprets research carried out by others?

2   In the authors' view, what is wrong with the idea of a 'lost generation' and arguments focused on intergenerational conflict?

3   The paper adopts a 'life course biographical' approach. What is this and what does it entail for researchers who use it?

4   The case study here is of a father and son, 'Geoff' and 'Adam'. With examples from the paper, list the main differences in the historical and social conditions of Geoff and Adam's biographical life courses.

5   What do we learn about life course transitions from this article's analysis? Is it legitimate to draw general theoretical conclusions from the study of this very specific case?

Thinking it through

The sociologies of childhood and the life course, like many other areas of the discipline, have become dominated by social constructionist analysis. This has carved out a clear remit for sociologists, different from the biologically oriented psychology of childhood and studies of the human life cycle. In this sense, constructionism has been essential in moving sociological studies away from erroneous ideas of human universality towards detailed historical accounts of changing conceptions of children, childhood and social aspects of the life course.

Yet some critics argue that social constructionism is also a political strategy used by activist groups and movements to undermine all apparently fixed social relations. Others contend that it has become 'more stupid' as it has become more radical, reducing all of social life to a 'mere' social construction (Heinich (2010), cited in Alanen (2015)).

Now read this editorial from the online journal *Childhood*: http://chd.sagepub.com/content/22/2/149?etoc. Write a 1,000-word essay on this piece, which outlines the main criticisms of social constructionism. Using evidence and material from this chapter, provide your own assessment of the continuing value of social constructionism in life course and childhood studies.

Society in the arts

1   The life course is marked by changing dress codes and bodily markings. For example, in most developed societies there are distinct, appropriate dress codes for adults and small children. Tattoos were previously viewed with disdain and suspicion, but in the last twenty-five years or so they have become widespread and fashionable for both men and women. Browse the body art and ornamentation in the 'Lifecycle Arts' section of the online collection of the Pitt Rivers Museum at the University of Oxford in the UK: http://web.prm.ox.ac.uk/bodyarts/.

Much of this material is quite old or collected from developing countries and small tribal groups. But do such recognizable, stage-specific forms of bodily adornment still exist in the contemporary developed societies? Carry out your own observations and suggest which body arts today (piercings, tattoos, ornaments or clothing) tend to be linked to specific life course stages. What can we learn about social changes in the life course from studying body art?

2   The biological ageing process and eventual death are inevitable, though there have been several unsuccessful attempts to delay the process, and religions promise an afterlife or reincarnation – though not an end to ageing as such. Watch the film *Cocoon* (1985), directed by Ron Howard, in which a group of older people discover a way of reversing the physical ageing process. The film is essentially science fiction, but it also asks whether immortality is really desirable anyway. What social and psychological aspects of ageing are covered in the film and how does it connect them? Does biological ageing always take precedence over the other forms? Would you say the film adopts a *life cycle* or a *life course* perspective? Does it come down on one side or the other on the issue of the desirability of human ageing?

Further reading

Two excellent introductions to the sociology of the life course are Lorraine Green's (2016) *Understanding the Life Course: Sociological and Psychological Perspectives* (2nd edn, Cambridge: Polity) and Stephen Hunt's (2016) *The Life Course: A Sociological Introduction* (2nd edn, Basingstoke: Palgrave Macmillan). Green's book attempts to combine insights from both psychology and sociology, while Hunt's is exactly what the title suggests it is.

Bill Bytheway's (2011) *Unmasking Age: The Significance of Age for Social Research* (Bristol: Policy Press) is a stimulating read, using a variety of sources to address the central question 'what is age'? Christopher Phillipson's (2013) *Ageing* (Cambridge: Polity) is an excellent introduction to current debates, while Virpi Timonen's (2008) *Ageing Societies: A Comparative Introduction* (Milton Keynes: Open University Press) sets current debates in a broader context.

A critical approach to ideas of inevitable social problems in an ageing society is taken in *The Myth of Generational Conflict: The Family and State in Ageing Societies* (2007), edited by Sara Arber and Claudine Attias-Donfut (London: Routledge). A comprehensive and worthwhile (if very large) book (770 pages) which can be approached for particular life course subjects is *The Cambridge Handbook of Age and Ageing* (2005), edited by Malcolm Johnson (Cambridge: Cambridge University Press).

Finally, anyone interested in sociological issues around death, dying and bereavement could try Glennys Howarth's (2006) *Death and Dying: A Sociological Introduction* (Cambridge: Polity). Then a very good collection edited by Sarah Earle, Carol Komaromy and Caroline Bartholomew is *Death and Dying: A Reader* (Milton Keynes: Open University Press, 2008), which also includes moral debates and policy matters.

For a collection of original readings on relationships and the life course, see the accompanying *Sociology: Introductory Readings* (3rd edn, Cambridge: Polity, 2010).

Internet links

@ Additional information and support for this book at Polity:
www.politybooks.com/giddens

@ Centre for Research on Families, Life course and Generations (FLaG)
at the University of Leeds, UK:
http://flag.leeds.ac.uk

World Health Organization – comprehensive international resources on ageing
and the life course:
www.who.int/ageing/en

@ UNICEF – United Nations Children's Fund; contains many useful resources
on children's experience around the world:
www.unicef.org

HelpAge International – a campaigning organization and a good source of
information on ageing across the world:
@ www.helpage.org

Centre for Policy on Ageing (UK) – charity promoting the interests of older people
through research and policy analysis:
www.cpa.org.uk

@ United Nations Programme on Ageing – focal point for the UN on all issues related
to ageing:
www.un.org/development/desa/ageing

Centre for Death and Society at the University of Bath, UK – since 2005, an
@ interdisciplinary centre for research into death and dying:
www.bath.ac.uk/cdas

British Sociological Association's (BSA) Study Group on the social aspects of death,
dying and bereavement:
@ www.britsoc.co.uk/groups/study groups/social aspects-of-death-dying-and-
bereavement-study-group

CHAPTER 10

Families and Intimate Relationships

Contents

Sir Elton John and David Furnish converted their 2005 civil partnership to a marriage in December 2014. They have two sons, Elijah and Zachary.

Almost twenty years ago I fell in love with a man called David who changed my life. He had worked in advertising, and then moved into film. I had come out as gay five years before, and met David at a dinner party I was hosting. We exchanged numbers, and I asked him to dinner the following night, which happened to be Halloween. Like any couple in the first flush of romance, there was the thrill of mutual attraction. Soon that developed into something much stronger, as we realised we had something that would last forever. Though there were ups and downs, looking back I feel like, even in those early days, we knew the other person was 'the one'. The rest, as they say, is history. (Sir Elton John, *The Independent* 2012).

Elton John's account of his developing relationship with his (now) husband will be familiar to anyone who has 'fallen in love'. A first meeting at a party, an exchange of phone numbers, followed by a date and a mutual attraction that developed into something stronger – feeling that this person 'was the one'. Yet this apparently 'natural' progression is in fact historically unusual. In early modern Europe, royal and aristocratic marriages were often arranged on political grounds or for reasons of enhancing or maintaining a family's social status. And, although 'arranged marriages' across the world are less common than once they were, among some South Asian communities they remain the norm. In all these cases, 'falling in love' is rarely thought of as having any necessary connection to marriage or starting a family, and material, status or pragmatic reasons take precedence.

Only in modern times have love and sexuality come to be seen as closely connected in the Western industrialized societies. During the Middle Ages, virtually no one in Europe married for love. There was even a medieval saying: 'To love one's wife with one's emotions is adultery.' As Boswell argues (1995: xxi):

> In premodern Europe marriage usually began as a property arrangement, was in its middle mostly about raising children, and ended about love. Few couples in fact married 'for love', but many grew to love each other in time as they jointly managed their household, reared their offspring, and shared life's experiences. Nearly all surviving epitaphs to spouses evince profound affection. By contrast, in most of the modern West, marriage begins about love, in its middle is still mostly about raising children (if there are children), and ends – often – about property, by which point love is absent or a distant memory.

Spouses may have become close companions, but this happened after marriage rather than being a necessary precursor to it. It was only in the late eighteenth century that the concept of romantic love became the basis for marriage. Romantic love – as distinct from the compulsion of passionate love – involved idealizing its object. The notion of romantic love more or less coincided with the emergence of the novel as a literary form and the spread of romantic novels played a vital part in advancing the idea (Radway 1984). For women in particular, romantic love involved telling stories about how relationships could lead to personal fulfilment. Romantic love, therefore, cannot be understood as a natural part of human life; rather, it has been shaped by broad social and historical influences.

For most people in the developed world, the couple – married or unmarried – is at the core of what family life is. Family forms today are very diverse indeed, as our opening example illustrates. Elton John and David Furnish became civil partners shortly after the relevant legislation was enacted in 2005. And while some within the LGBT (lesbian, gay, bisexual and transgender) community view marriage as tainted by its long history

as an exclusively heterosexual institution, others see things differently. Elton John said that, 'for this legislation to come through is joyous, and we should celebrate it. We shouldn't just say, "Oh, well we have a civil partnership. We're not going to bother to get married." We will get married' (cited in BBC News 2014d). The couple also have two children via surrogacy, and their family life displays many of the social changes and shifting attitudes that have transformed family and personal life today.

In the developed countries a 'good relationship' is thought to be one based on open, emotional communication or other forms of intimacy. The idea of intimacy, like so many other familiar notions we encounter in this book, is a recent one. In the past, marriage was never *based* on intimacy and emotional communication; while this was often seen as important to a 'good' marriage, it was not the foundation of it. Social change is a continuous thread running through all sociology, though there is also much continuity with the past. We live in a turbulent and rapidly changing world today and, whether we like it or not, we must come to terms with the mixture of opportunity and risks it presents. The discussion of romantic love shows that nowhere is this observation truer than in the domain of personal and family life.

In this chapter we start with the familiar idea of 'the family' – a social institution which appears to be timeless and universal. As we shall see, sociologists now acknowledge that this notion has often conflated empirical reality with a normative conception of family which allows little room for alternatives. We then outline an alternative approach which explores the actual practices – positive and negative – in which people engage and which they acknowledge as being in some way 'familial'. After looking at family diversity today, we explore the transformation of intimate relations and some of the main shifts in marriage, divorce and post-divorce families. The chapter ends with an assessment of the possible convergence of family forms across the world.

'The family' as institution and ideology

The sociology of the family has involved contrasting theoretical perspectives for more than a century. Most of these perspectives concentrated on studying the family as a central social institution that performs important functions for individuals, communities, society and the capitalist economic system. However, these conventional approaches seem much less convincing today in the light of trends towards heightened individualism and the diversification of family forms. This divergence is reflected in the increasing use of 'families' rather than 'family' in the contemporary literature. It is also evident in the disjunction between official discourses promoting the nuclear family as the norm and people's lived experience of diverse and changing family forms (Chambers 2012: 5–6). It is valuable to trace briefly the development of earlier theories before turning to more recent studies of families and family life.

Functions of the family

The functionalist perspective views society as constituted by a set of social institutions that perform specific functions, ensuring continuity and value consensus. Thus, the family performs important tasks that fulfil some of society's basic needs, helping to reproduce the social order. Sociologists working in the functionalist tradition have seen the nuclear family in particular as fulfilling certain specialized roles in developed Western societies. With the advent of industrialization and the separation of work and home, the family became less important as a unit of economic production and more focused on reproduction, child-rearing and socialization (see 'Classic Studies 10.1').

In Parsons's account, the nuclear family became the dominant type, at least in the

---

Classic Studies 10.1 | **Talcott Parsons on the functions of the family**

The research problem

Why is the family such an enduring feature within human societies? Do families do things that other social institutions cannot? Is the family really necessary for a well-ordered society? These questions have been part of ongoing debates within sociology from the discipline's earliest days, but the answers are still the subject of heated debate.

Parsons's explanation

According to the American functionalist sociologist Talcott Parsons, the family's two main functions are *primary socialization* and *personality stabilization* (Parsons and Bales 1956). Primary socialization is the process by which children learn the cultural norms of the society into which they are born. Because this happens during the early years of childhood, the family is the most important arena for the development of the human personality. Personality stabilization refers to the role that the family plays in assisting adult family

members emotionally. Marriage between adult men and women is the arrangement through which adult personalities are supported and kept healthy. In industrial society, the role of the family in stabilizing adult personalities is said to be critical. This is because the nuclear family is often distanced from its extended kin and is unable to draw on larger kinship ties as families could do before industrialization.

Parsons regarded the nuclear family as the unit best equipped to handle the demands of industrial society. In this 'conventional family', one adult can work outside the home, while the second cares for the home and children. In practical terms, the specialization of roles within the nuclear family involved the husband adopting the 'instrumental' role as breadwinner and the wife assuming the 'affective', emotional role in domestic settings.

Critical points

Today Parsons's view of the family comes across as inadequate and outdated. Functionalist theories of the family have come under heavy criticism for justifying the domestic division of labour between men and women as something 'natural' and unproblematic. We can also criticize functionalist arguments for overemphasizing the role of the family and neglecting the role that other social institutions, such as government, media and schools, play in socializing children. And Parsons had little to say about variations in family forms that do not correspond to the model of the nuclear family. Families that did not conform to the white, heterosexual, suburban, middle-class 'ideal' could then be seen as deviant. Finally, the 'dark side' of family life is arguably underplayed in functionalist accounts and therefore not given the significance it deserves.

Contemporary significance

Parsons's functionalist theory of the family is undoubtedly out of favour today, and it is fair to say that it must be seen as a partial account of the role of families within societies. Yet it does have historical significance. The immediate postwar years *did* see many women returning to gendered domestic roles and men reassuming positions as sole breadwinners, which was closer to Parsons's account. Social policy in the UK and the USA has also relied on some variant of the functionalist theory of the family and its role in tackling social problems. We should remember that a central tenet of functionalism is that, as societies change, social institutions must also change if they are to survive. It is possible to see some of the contemporary diversity of family forms as evidence of the adaptation of the family to a rapidly changing social life. If so, then Parsons's functionalist approach may retain some general relevance.

developed countries, because it was best adapted to the requirements of a mobile and flexible economic system. This approach highlights a significant problem that has dogged the sociology of the family. While analysing the positive functions of the nuclear family, the latter was also presented as *the best* family form against which all other families could be measured. In this way analytical detachment slipped into normative endorsement and functionalism tacitly endorsed an ideological version of 'the family'. This version was not dissimilar to that propounded by some political and religious groups, who argued that the family was under threat from poor parenting, liberal education policies and general moral decline. As divorce rates and single-parent families increased and same-sex relationships became more widely accepted, functionalism seemed ill-equipped to understand the increasing diversity of family life.

From a critical standpoint, Marxist theories of the family also saw the nuclear form as functional, but in ways that enabled capitalists to make profits at the expense of workers. In the late nineteenth century, Engels (2010 [1884]) argued that the spread of private property relations transformed a previously equal domestic division of labour. Managing the household, housework and child-rearing came to be seen as elements of the emerging *private sphere* of life, while men were needed in workplaces outside the home in the *public sphere*. The separation of public and private led to a growing gender inequality that has only recently been challenged as large numbers of women have moved into paid employment. Even so, this has not resulted in full equality, as women are still expected to shoulder the double burden of household chores as well as going out to work. The nuclear family enabled the workforce to be reproduced with the costs of doing so falling mainly on women and latterly, the state, rather than eating into capitalist profits. Engels also argues that, under capitalism, monogamous marriage became the ideal way of passing capital and wealth down generations, sustaining the class system.

Is the nuclear family really timeless and universal?

Functionalist and Marxist theories may seem very different and, in terms of their evaluation of the nuclear family's role in society, they are. However, the theories also share a 'family resemblance' (pun intended) in that they both explore the structural position of the family in society and point to the functions that this institution fulfils. This kind of approach is today seen as limited and often misleading.

For example, it focuses attention on just one type of family – the nuclear form – and has little to say about alternative types. There is also a tendency for normative or ideological biases to creep in. For instance, there is a simple heteronormativity embedded within these accounts. That is, structural theories assume that the family is an exclusively heterosexual institution, usually rooted in marriage. Functionalist studies tend to portray the nuclear family as ideally suited to modern societies, while Marxists view the bourgeois family as underpinning an exploitative capitalist economic system.

What these theories do not explore are the ways in which family life is actually lived and experienced. As we shall see later, more recent studies of 'family practices' and 'family displays' mark a significant shift in sociological research on families that takes the field in a different direction.

Feminist approaches

For many people, families provide a vital source of solace and comfort, love and companionship. Yet they can also be a locus for exploitation, loneliness and profound inequality. During the 1970s and 1980s, feminist theory had an enormous impact on sociology, challenging the functionalist view of the family as a harmonious institution. If previously the sociology of the family had focused on family structures, feminism succeeded in directing attention to familial relationships, examining the experiences of women in the domestic sphere.

Feminist research and writing emphasized a broad spectrum of topics, but three main themes are of particular importance. One – explored in chapter 7, 'Work and the Economy' – is the *domestic division of labour*: the way that tasks are allocated among family members. Among feminists there are differing opinions about the historical emergence of this division. Socialist feminists see it as the outcome of industrial capitalism, while others claim that it is linked to patriarchy and thus pre-dates industrialization. As Engels argued, a domestic division of labour did exist before industrialization, but capitalist social relations brought about a much sharper distinction between (private) domesticity and (public) work. This resulted in the crystallization of 'male and female spheres' and the model or ideal of the male breadwinner, though this has been eroded somewhat over recent decades.

Feminist studies of the way domestic tasks, such as childcare and housework, are shared between men and women have investigated the validity of claims that gender relationships are becoming more 'symmetrical' as the distribution of responsibilities is shared equally (Young and Willmott 1973). Feminist research has shown that women continue to bear the main responsibility for domestic tasks and enjoy less leisure time than men, despite the fact that more women are in paid employment outside the home than ever before (Sullivan 1997; de Vaus 2008: 394–6). Some sociologists have examined the contrasting realms of paid and unpaid work, focusing on the contribution that women's unpaid domestic labour makes to the overall economy (Oakley 1974b; Damaske 2011). Others have investigated the way in which resources are distributed among family members, particularly the unequal patterns of access to and control over household finances (Pahl 1989).

Second, feminists have drawn attention to the *unequal power relationships* that exist within family relations. One topic that has received increased attention as a result of this is the phenomenon of domestic violence. 'Wife battering', marital rape, incest and the sexual abuse of children have all received more public attention following feminists' discovery that the violent and abusive sides of family life have long been ignored in academic contexts and legal and policy circles. Feminist sociologists sought to understand how the family serves as an arena for the reproduction of male dominance through the oppression of women.

The study of *caring activities* is a third field to which feminists have made important contributions. This is a broad area that encompasses a variety of processes, from attending a family member who is ill to looking after an elderly relative over a long period of time. Sometimes caring means simply being attuned to someone else's psychological well-being, and some feminist writers have been interested in 'emotion work' within relationships. Not only do women tend to shoulder concrete tasks such as cleaning and childcare, but they also invest large amounts of emotional labour in maintaining familial personal relationships (Wharton 2012: 164–5). While caring activities are grounded in love and deep emotion, they are also a form of work which demands an ability to listen, perceive, negotiate and act creatively.

It would not be an exaggeration to say that 'the family' in sociology is not what it was before feminism. Feminist research and theorizing helped to produce a much more realistic and balanced appreciation of the institution of the family and of family life as it is lived. And as is the case with much good sociology, the reality of family life turns out to be far removed from political and normative ideals.

The family in decline or the way we never were?

Surveying the social changes of the past few decades, some commentators lament what they see as the demise of traditional family duties and obligations. They argue that we must recover a moral sense of family life and reinstate 'the traditional family', which was more stable and ordered than the tangled web of relationships in which we now find ourselves (R. O'Neill 2002). Proponents of an ideal of 'the traditional family' are unhappy with the increasing diversity of families and intimate relationships, which they see as undermining marriage and traditional family life. This argument draws on the idea that in some earlier period there really was a 'golden age' of family life. But when was this?

For some, the discipline and stability of nineteenth-century Victorian family life is held to be the ideal. Yet families at this time also suffered high death rates, the average length of marriages was less than twelve years, and more than half of all children saw the death of at least one parent by the time they were twenty-one. The discipline of the Victorian family was also rooted in the strict authority of parents over their children. Some middle-class wives were more or less confined to the home, as Victorian morality demanded that women should be strictly virtuous, but it was accepted that men would visit prostitutes and brothels. In fact, wives and husbands often had little to do with each other, communicating only through the children. Domesticity was not even an option for poorer social groups. In factories and workshops, working-class families worked very long hours with little time for a cosy home life, while child labour was commonplace. Coontz (1992) pointed out that, as with all visions of a previous golden age, the rosy light shed on the 'traditional family' dissolves when we look at the historical evidence.

Another suggestion is that the 1950s was the time of an ideal family life. This was a period when many women stayed at home to bring up children and maintain the home while men were the 'breadwinners' responsible for earning a 'family wage'. Women held paid jobs in large numbers during the Second World War as part of the war effort, which they then lost when men returned home. Yet large numbers of women did not want to retreat to a purely domestic role and felt miserable and trapped within it. Husbands were still emotionally distant from their wives and often observed a strong sexual double standard, seeking sexual adventure for themselves but expecting a strict monogamous code for their spouse.

The American author Betty Friedan's (1921–2006) best-selling book, *The Feminine Mystique* (1963), discussed women's lives in the 1950s and struck a chord with women. She described the 'problem with no name' – that is, the oppressive nature of domestic life bound up with childcare, domestic drudgery and a husband who only occasionally put in an appearance and with whom little emotional communication was possible. Even more severe than an oppressive home life were the alcoholism and violence suffered within many families during a period when domestic and intimate violence were seen as private matters. Again, the idea of a 1950s 'ideal family' appears to be another nostalgic myth.

> ### THINKING CRITICALLY
> If the traditional family, as described above, is 'a myth', why do so many people still believe in it? What political and personal consequences might follow from people's belief in and commitment to this mythical family form?

As sociologists, we cannot adjudicate between firmly held moral positions, but we can evaluate the proposals put forward. Returning to an older, traditional family is not realistic – not just because the traditional family was a mythical entity anyway or because people today consider it oppressive. It is not possible because the broad social changes that have transformed marriage, families and sexual partnerships are not easily reversible. Women will not return in large numbers to a domestic situation from which they have striven to extricate themselves. Sexual partnerships, emotional communication and marriage cannot return to the way they used to be. On the other hand, there is little doubt that trends affecting sexuality, marriage and the family do create deep anxieties for some at the same time as they generate new possibilities for satisfaction and self-fulfilment for others.

We must be careful not to let ideas of how society *ought to be* influence our understanding of society based on the evidence. As the older sociology of the family came to be seen as conflating what is with what ought to be, it became clear that alternative approaches were required. One of the more influential of these is rooted in the deceptively simple idea that, rather than studying the family as a social institution, sociologists should explore what people actually do that they recognize as being 'family-like'. This perspective is outlined next.

Family practices

Political debates on family policy are bound up with ideas of an ideal family form that should be promoted by governments. Today, there is no such single model of family life that is or could be more or less universal. The evidence is clear that there are many different family forms: heterosexual families, same-sex families, 'blended' or step-families, extended families, single-parent families, and more. Gittins (1993) argued that this diversity should be acknowledged by speaking of 'families' rather than 'the family'. In a similar vein, Gillis (1996) distinguished the 'families we live by' – the ideal family presented in social policy and the mass media – from the 'families we live with' – the daily family lives we actually create and experience.

As we will see later, the diversification of family is linked to wider social processes, including an increasing proportion of women in paid employment, more sexual freedom, and the movement towards gender and sexual equality. So, although we may discuss 'the family' as a key social institution, it is vital to remember the variety of forms this generalization covers. For some, understanding family as it is lived demands a new approach which builds from empirical research rather than theorizing the family's institutional role.

'Doing' family life

An alternative way of discussing family life is suggested by David Morgan, who argues that it is more productive to talk of family practices – that is, all of those activities engaged in by people which *they* perceive to be part of 'family life' (see 'Classic Studies 10.2'). Chambers et al. (2009) argue that there are several advantages in adopting this perspective. First, it helps researchers to explore the increasingly fluid character of family lives and networks, such as the criss-crossing of biological and step-families. Second, it focuses attention on the relatively neglected ways in which people 'do families' – or how they actually construct and live their familial relations. Third, it rebalances existing sociological work on the family as a social institution by looking at the agency of the individuals involved, who actively create their family roles and routines, thereby helping to explain changing family forms.

Family practices cover many activities eating together, holding 'family' events, organizing children's attendance in school, and much more. But studying these kinds of practices may not tell us the whole story of families. Following Finch's (2007) work, recent studies in this area have also looked at family displays – all of those ways in which people demonstrate to others that they are engaged in (appropriate) family practices and family relationships. Finch argues that people do not 'do family' in isolation from the rest of social life. As Dermott and Seymour (2011: 13) note, 'it is insufficient for practices associated with family life to be merely carried out; they must also be recognised *as* family practices by others.' These 'others' may be social workers and state officials, but more often family

Classic Studies 10.2 — From social institution to family practices

The research problem

Sociologists of the family tended to look at families through the lens of the nuclear family, which was seen as the dominant form after industrialization took hold. This set the nuclear family as the standard against which other family types were assessed. Chambers (2012: 41) argues that, from the 1990s, it became increasingly clear that it was more realistic and accurate to talk of *families* rather than *the family* and, as a result, the conventional sociology of family structure and functions lost ground. But what could replace it? David Morgan (1996, 1999, 2011) laid out an alternative approach which has been highly influential in shaping the field of family studies.

Morgan's explanation

For many twentieth-century sociologists, delineating what counts as 'family' was unproblematic. Family involved marriage and biologically related, emotionally close kinship groups. Seen in this way, it was relatively easy to differentiate family from non-family relationships. But numerous changes, including fewer marriages, high divorce rates, more step- or blended families, LGBT couples and families, single-parent families, and new reproductive technologies, highlighted the diversity rather than uniformity of family types. As Morgan (2011: 3) bluntly put it, 'there is no such thing as "The Family".'

Morgan's central innovation was to set out an alternative approach which promised an empirically adequate family sociology based on the actions or practices of families. Rather than continuing the sterile debate on the supposed decline of (the nuclear) family, he suggests that a more productive research agenda is to focus on how people 'do family'. That is, which of the many actions and activities in which people engage are seen by them as 'familial' and why? This theoretical shift means that '"Family" represents a constructed quality of human interaction or an active process rather than a thing-like object of detached social investigation' (Morgan 1999: 16).

For example, Mason (2011) asks what it means to say that people 'are related'. The answer may once have been obvious, but today it is not. A married heterosexual couple with children may divorce and both parents then take new partners, for whom the children become 'step-children'. But, if the new couples then separate, does this effectively end the new partners' relationship with their step-children? A family practices approach treats this as an empirical question, as the answer depends on the choices and decisions made by the actors involved. Who counts as kin or family is likely to change over time, thus illustrating Morgan's point that 'family' is not an entity but is always in process.

If kin relations change over time, then so too do the activities defined as familial. Taking children to school, attending family events such as celebrations, weddings and funerals, providing informal unpaid childcare, doing household chores, keeping in touch by daily phone calls, and lots more may all be perceived as 'family-like' activities. Yet these may involve people who are not biologically related, such as friends and neighbours, who themselves may be considered to be 'part of the family' and treated as such. Very often, family nomenclature such as 'uncle' or 'auntie' are applied to close friends who perform family-like activities as a recognition of their awarded status as a privileged family member. Morgan argues that none of this should lead to sociologists dispensing with the concept of family altogether. However complex understanding this concept has now become, he argues that 'family' continues to be meaningful for most people. May (2015: 482) suggests that 'Family practices also retain some distinctiveness that would be lost if we subsumed these under some broader term such as intimacy practices.'

Critical points

The family practices approach has been particularly influential in empirical British sociology, but less so elsewhere. For example, Heath et al. (2011) argue that, despite dealing with similar concerns, the language and concept of family practices have not been widely adopted in the more anthropologically oriented transnational studies of families that span national boundaries. One reason for this is the different ways in which these approaches view ideologies of 'the family'. In the study of migration to the European Union, families remain constrained by legal definitions which tend to be of the nuclear family. Kofman (2004: 245) notes that 'migrants cannot determine for themselves the persons who constitute their family.' This is a reminder that official ideas of the family as a key social institution retain their power to affect family life.

A second substantive criticism is that the attempt to avoid becoming bogged down in normative and political arguments about which family form best fits a particular society has not been wholly avoided. Family practices are not distinct from political discourses and moral ideals. Heaphy (2011) argues that alternative family practices and family displays (see below), such as those of single parents and gay couples, struggle to gain legitimacy from wider audiences, which are often unwilling to accept them as viable alternatives to the idealized 'normal' middle-class nuclear family form. Again,

the criticism is that a focus on family practices, however insightful, should not obscure the continuing power of the conventional idea of 'the family', which remains dominant in policy circles and among large sections of society.

Contemporary significance

Morgan's family practices approach set out the theoretical basis for British family studies (BFS) to move in a new direction – one that encourages detailed empirical research studies. This was a welcome move which reinvigorated the field of family studies, lifting it out of a theoretical malaise. Over time the perspective has also been expanded and developed to take in new areas such as family displays – the ways in which people show that they are doing appropriate 'family things' to relevant audiences. And it has connected the study of family life to other fields associated with understanding the everyday and personal, and doing so it promises to bridge the divide between family and non-family relations. The next stage for Morgan's approach will be to test its applicability beyond the British case and into different national and, indeed, transnational family practices.

displays are aimed at family members, other families, friends and onlookers. It is also likely that, as with other social interactions, displays involve multiple audiences.

A good example of this is Harman and Cappellini's (2015) qualitative research into the practice and display of middle-class mothers making their children's school lunchboxes. Preparing a packed lunch is a routine family practice for their small sample of eleven, but such a simple object carries numerous meanings and messages. For example, in the wake of a highly charged public debate about what constitutes a healthy diet for children, mothers had to take account of the child's requests but also of television programmes and media commentary, political debate, school rules and supermarket advertising. The authors argue that mothers used lunchboxes to display their competence as mothers not

only to other children, school staff and canteen supervisors but also to themselves. However, the key audience seemed to be the school staff, and most of the mothers adhered to school guidance in their preparations.

This small-scale study of just eleven mothers from a highly specific class grouping is not generalizable to the wider population, but we can see in it some links to the wider society. It is clear that gendered assumptions were operative, as preparing the lunchbox was clearly perceived as the mother's responsibility not the father's, even though all the mothers had paid employment too. Although the mothers described their lunchbox choices as individually tailored to their child, the study found that they were essentially similar. This suggests the continuing influence of widespread cultural norms governing what constitutes the basic structure of a 'balanced' and 'healthy' meal.

As members of white, middle-class families, these mothers felt anxious about being on display in the public setting of the school, which potentially opened them up to monitoring and criticism.

The family practices approach has proved to be an effective one which continues to develop. Yet there are good reasons to think that we should not be too eager to dispense with older structural perspectives altogether. As Edwards and her colleagues (2012) argue, much valuable statistical research remains committed to some concept of families as households, while tracking shifts in family life over time also requires an awareness of family structure(s) and the way these change. It is difficult to see how significant macrosociological questions – such as whether family structures are converging globally or whether economic systems lead to specific family forms – could be addressed unless some notion of 'family' as a social institution (as well as a set of practices) is retained.

In the next two sections we draw on research into family practices and statistical survey evidence on housework and gender inequality and intimate violence to illustrate the more comprehensive picture that emerges from combining micro and macro approaches.

The simple school lunchbox is an example of displaying 'family' to several audiences.

Balancing work and care

Family practices are not simply those that people enjoy or choose to engage in. As Morgan (1996) made clear, there are numerous family practices which people feel under pressure to perform or which have negative consequences for them. Gendered expectations put pressure on men to work full-time and women to prioritize domestic responsibilities, while the abuse of children, older people and women within family settings is much more common than was once thought. These aspects must be considered family practices too, as they are actions which involve people perceived to be family members and take place in family settings. The next two sections look in more detail at some of the inequalities and negative practices associated with families.

Gender inequalities vary across the world's societies. The World Economic Forum found that women had made most progress towards equal participation in Sweden, with Norway, Finland and Iceland also in the top four. Yemen came in last, and Chad, Pakistan and Nepal completed the bottom four positions (World Economic Forum 2007: 7). In addition, the average wage of employed women is below that of men, although the difference has narrowed over the past thirty years or so. In the countries of the European Union the gender pay gap (the difference between average gross hourly pay of men and women) in 2010 was still, on average, 17.5 per cent (Eurostat 2010: 303–4). One of the major factors affecting women's careers are *perceptions* that, for women, work comes second to having children and that looking after them is a natural and biologically determined role. Such beliefs directly impact on the work–care balance for men and women despite formal equal opportunities legislation (Crompton 2008).

 See chapter 15, 'Gender and Sexuality', for much more on issues of gender.

Many women find themselves struggling with two contradictory forces. They want and need economic independence, but at the same time they want to be 'good' mothers to their children. A major question is how the caring 'work', previously carried out by women in the domestic sphere without payment, will be performed now that more women have moved into paid employment. Crompton (2006: 17) suggests that this can be achieved only if the previous gendered division of labour is 'deconstructed' and men become rather more like women, combining employment and care-giving in their everyday lives. An increasing flexibility in employment and working life may be one part of the solution, but much more difficult is likely to be shifting the traditional attitudes of men.

Housework

Although there have been major changes in women's status in recent decades, including the entry of women into male-dominated professions, one area of work has lagged far behind: housework. As more married women entered the workforce, some presumed that men would begin to make a larger contribution to housework. On the whole, this has not been the case. Although men do more housework than in the 1970s and 1980s and women do slightly less (see table 10.1), the balance is highly unequal and varies widely across societies. In Greece, Turkey and Malta the female–male difference in time spent on housework is more than 70 per cent, but in Sweden and Denmark it falls to less than 30 per cent. The European average gender difference is around 53 per cent, which indicates that, in the area of housework, gender equality still has a long way to go.

Several UK surveys have found that women still do most of the housework and childcare. In the 2013 British Social Attitudes Survey, women reported spending an average of 13 hours per week on housework and 23 hours caring for family members. Men reported spending, on average, 8 hours on housework and 10 hours on caring activities (Park et al. 2013: 115). Some sociologists have argued that, where women are already working in the paid sector, this extra work amounts to a 'second shift' (Shelton 1992), leading Hochschild to call the state of relations between women and men a 'stalled revolution'. But why does housework remain largely 'women's work'? This question has been the focus of a good deal of research over recent years.

One possible explanation is that it is the result of gendered economic forces: female household work is exchanged for male economic support. Because women earn, on average, less than men, they tend to remain economically dependent on their husbands and thus perform the bulk of the housework. Hence, until the earnings gap is narrowed, women are likely to remain in a dependent position. Hochschild (1989) argued that women are thus doubly oppressed by men: once during the 'first shift' and then again during the 'second shift'. But, while it contributes to our understanding of the gendered aspects of housework, this exchange model breaks down in situations where the wife earns more than the husband.

Miller (2011) argues that, when heterosexual couples have children, the tendency is that they 'fall back into gender'. That is, although men may use the language of a 'new fatherhood', which emphasizes fathers' increased involvement and bonding with children, their practices continue to reflect an older discourse of family breadwinner. In Hochschild's study, even husbands who earned less than their wives did not do an equal share of housework. Mothers are also far more likely to take a career break after the birth of a child than fathers, and traditional gendered expectations continue

Table 10.1	People doing daily housework in Europe (percentages)			
Country	Sex respondent		Total	Female–Male difference
	Male	Female		
Finland	64	95	79	31
Sweden	65	90	77	25
Romania	60	93	76	33
Denmark	65	86	74	21
Hungary	46	93	70	47
Slovakia	47	92	70	45
Luxembourg	44	92	69	48
Belgium	44	91	68	47
Estonia	53	84	68	31
Bulgaria	33	95	66	62
Lithuania	44	90	66	46
Netherlands	47	86	66	39
Germany	36	90	64	54
Latvia	43	85	64	42
Portugal	27	96	62	69
France	32	86	61	54
Slovenia	30	96	61	66
Austria	28	89	59	61
Greece	18	94	59	76
UK	36	80	58	44
Italy	26	88	57	62
Turkey	15	91	57	76
Ireland	33	78	56	45
Malta	21	91	54	70
Cyprus	19	80	53	61
European average[a]	35	88	62	53

Note: [a] Sample weighted according to population size of each country.

Source: Voicu et al. (2007: 9).

to inform family practices in this area (Björnberg 2002). Women are expected to enjoy the motherhood role and to prioritize this over their role as a worker, while, for men, fatherhood is still seen as essentially a part-time role, secondary to their primary one of worker. Not only does this create problems for women wanting to pursue their career, it also means that men find it difficult to justify becoming the main care-giver for children without being criticized.

Sociologists have long seen the inequitable distribution of household tasks as rooted in the assumption that men and women operate in different spheres of life which then leads to gendered expectations of their roles. Men are expected to be providers while women are expected to tend to the family – even if they are 'breadwinners' as well as mothers. The persistence of such gendered assumptions demonstrates just how deeply embedded and consistently reproduced they are, even in the face of quite radical shifts in educational opportunity, employment and personal relationships.

THINKING CRITICALLY

List all of the reasons you can think of as to why men are not as involved in routine housework as women. What connections are there between these reasons and stereotypes associated with men and women? How might such gendered stereotypes be challenged?

Intimate violence

Since family and kin relations are part of everyone's existence, family life encompasses virtually the whole range of emotional experiences. Family relationships can be warm and fulfilling, but they can also contain the most pronounced tensions, driving people to despair or filling them with anxiety and guilt. This 'dark side' of families involves domestic violence, elder abuse and the abuse of children, belying the rosy images of harmony emphasized in TV adverts and the popular media.

The abuse of children

One section of the UK's Children Act 1989 speaks of 'significant harm' being caused to children by a lack of reasonable care, but what is 'significant' is left quite vague. The National

Families can be sites of violence and tensions as well as affection and support. Acknowledging the dark side of families has led to a more realistic, if disturbing, assessment of family life.

Society for the Protection of Cruelty to Children (NSPCC) defines four categories of abuse: neglect, physical abuse, emotional abuse and sexual abuse. Sexual abuse is defined as 'sexual contact between a child and adult for the purpose of the adult's sexual gratification' (Lyon and de Cruz 1993). The full extent of child sexual abuse is difficult to calculate accurately because of the many forms it can assume, but one recent 'informed estimate' suggests that some 10 to 20 per cent of children in Europe will be sexually assaulted. In one 1999 survey, only 1 per cent of Europeans had never heard of child sexual abuse within the family, while 97 per cent thought that child sexual abuse *was* a form of violence (May-Chahal and Herczog 2003: 3–4). The 1989 UN Convention on the Rights of the Child helped to raise awareness of child sexual abuse, but no fully agreed definitions of either child abuse or child sexual abuse have been arrived at, either by researchers or in the courts, which makes cross-national comparisons unreliable.

Incest refers to sexual relations between close kin, but not all incest is child sexual abuse. For example, sexual intercourse between brother and sister is incestuous but does not fit the definition of abuse. In child sexual abuse, an adult is essentially exploiting an infant or child for sexual purposes. Nevertheless, the most common form of incest is one that *is* also child sexual abuse – incestuous relations between fathers and young daughters.

Incest, and child sexual abuse more generally, is a phenomenon that has been 'discovered' only in the past few decades. Of course it has long been known that such sexual acts occur, but it was assumed by most that the strong social taboos against this behaviour meant that it must be very rare. This assumption has been shown to be false. Child sexual abuse has proved to be much more widespread than was thought. Research by the World Health Organization (WHO 2006a) into factors associated with a higher risk of child maltreatment include poverty and high levels of unemployment, though we need to be cautious about drawing such conclusions. It may be that, with a range of charities and

welfare services targeting poverty alleviation, more abuse among poorer families is reported as a result. Rather than there being a clear causal relationship between social class and domestic violence, differential levels of surveillance and reporting may better account for this finding (Hearn and McKie 2008).

Child sexual abuse exists at all levels of the social hierarchy as well as in institutional settings such as residential care, educational establishments and churches. The recent discovery of the extent of child abuse carried out by priests, nuns and monks in the Roman Catholic Church, along with attempts to cover this up, shows that no social institution is immune to the abuse of power by adults over the children in their care (Jenkins 2001).

Force or the threat of violence is involved in many cases of incest. Children are sexual beings and quite often engage in mild sexual play or exploration with one another. But children subjected to sexual contact with adult family members report finding the experience repugnant, shameful and distressing. Some studies point to correlations between child physical or sexual abuse and drug addiction, non-suicidal self-injury and other harmful behaviours. However, again, we must remember that correlation is not causation. Demonstrating that people in these categories have been sexually abused as children does not show that the abuse was a causal influence over their later behaviour. More research is needed to establish what consequences follow from childhood maltreatment.

Domestic violence

We may define domestic violence as physical abuse directed by one member of the family against another or several others. The main targets of physical abuse are children, especially small children. For example, in England, the murder of eight-year-old Victoria Climbié in February 2000 and a seventeen-month-old boy, known as 'Baby P', in 2007 brought extreme domestic violence against children to widespread public attention.

In the UK, Victoria Climbié died of hypothermia after months of torture and neglect inflicted by her great-aunt and the woman's boyfriend. Her abusers were jailed for life. During the trial, police and health and social services were all criticized for missing opportunities to intervene and a subsequent inquiry made recommendations as to how such a tragedy could be prevented in the future (Laming 2003). But in August 2007, Peter Connelly (known as 'Baby P') died just one day after police informed his mother they were dropping their investigation into reports of suspected child abuse. A post-mortem found many injuries consistent with a pattern of systematic physical abuse, and, again, social services, police and health professionals were criticized for failing the child. The serious case review found that Peter was failed by all the agencies involved, describing the practice of his doctor, social workers, managers and the police as individually and collectively incompetent. It is important to grasp just how serious such extreme cases of domestic child abuse can be.

Global Society 10.1 **Domestic violence – a global view**

According to a series of surveys by the World Health Organization in the 1990s, globally, domestic violence is widespread. The Commonwealth Fund estimated that almost 4 million women are physically abused each year in the United States, while a 1995 survey by the Beijing Marriage and Family Affairs Research Institute discovered that 23 per cent of husbands admitted to beating their wives. In 1993, 60 per cent of Chilean women involved in a relationship for two years or more were surveyed, and 60 per cent reported being abused by their male partner. In Japan, the Domestic Violence Research Group found that 59 per cent of 796 women questioned in 1993 reported having been physically abused by their partner, and surveys in 1992 found that 60 per cent of low-income women in Ecuador and 38 per cent of women in South Korea reported having been beaten by their spouse or partner in the previous year (Marin et al. 1998). More than 50 per cent of women in Bangladesh, Ethiopia, Peru and Tanzania and 71 per cent in rural Ethiopia reported physical or sexual violence by their partners (WHO 2005).

Levels of domestic violence in Eastern Europe were not really known about until after the break-up of the former Soviet Union in 1991, which brought with it a more open exchange of information. Surveys by the Astra Network (Central and Eastern European Women's Network for Sexual and Reproductive Health and Rights) in 1993 found that 29 per cent of women in Romania, 22 per cent in Russia, 21 per cent in Ukraine, and more than 42 per cent of married and cohabiting women in Lithuania said they had been victims of 'physical or sexual violence or threats of violence by their present partner'. In the same year, some 60 per cent of divorced women in Poland reported having been hit at least once by their former husbands (UNICEF 2000b).

On 27 November 2006, the Council of Europe launched a campaign to combat violence against women, including domestic violence. The campaign noted that:

> An overview of figures for the prevalence of violence against women suggests that one-fifth to one-quarter of all women have experienced physical violence at least once during their adult lives, and more than one-tenth have suffered sexual violence involving the use of force. Secondary data analysis supports an estimate that about 12% to 15% of all women have been in a relationship of domestic abuse after the age of 16. Many more continue to suffer physical and sexual violence from former partners even after the break-up. (Council of Europe 2006: 1)

THINKING CRITICALLY

The statistics show that violence within families and households is mainly by men against women and children. If we reject simple biological explanations of aggressive males and passive females, what social, economic or cultural factors may help us to explain this widespread pattern?

Violence by men against their female partners is the second most common type of domestic violence. In the UK, on average, two women per week are killed by their partners. At any time, 10 per cent of women are experiencing domestic violence, which affects between a third and a quarter of all women at some point in their lives. Domestic violence is the most common crime against women, who are at greater risk of violence from men in their own families or from close acquaintances than they are from strangers (Rawsthorne 2002).

The issue of domestic violence attracted public and academic attention during the 1970s as a result of the work undertaken by feminist groups with refuge centres for 'battered women'. Before that time, domestic violence, like child abuse, was a phenomenon that was tactfully ignored as a private matter. Feminist studies of patriarchy and domestic violence drew attention to the ways in which this privatization of violence and abuse worked to uphold the dominance of men in patriarchal societies. It was feminist studies which documented the prevalence and severity of violence against women in the home. Indeed, most violent episodes between spouses reported to the police involve violence by husbands against their wives. There are far fewer reported cases of women using physical force against their husbands. Feminists argue that domestic violence is a major form of male control over women.

> For theories and evidence of patriarchy, see chapter 15, 'Gender and Sexuality'.

However, some conservative commentators have claimed that violence in the family is not about male power, as feminists contend, but to do with 'dysfunctional families': violence against women is a reflection of the growing crisis of the family and the erosion of standards of morality. They question the finding that violence from wives towards husbands is rare, and suggest that men are less likely to report instances of domestic violence against them than vice versa (Straus and Gelles 1986).

This argument has been strongly criticized by feminists and other scholars. Violence by women, they say, is more restrained and episodic than that of men and much less likely to cause enduring physical harm. It is not sufficient to look at the 'number' of violent incidents within families. Instead, it is essential to look at the meaning, context and effect of violence. There is no real equivalent of 'wife battering' – the regular physical brutalizing of wives by husbands – committed by women against men. Research has found that violence by women against male partners is often defensive rather than offensive, with women resorting to violence only after suffering repeated attacks (Rawsthorne 2002). Men who physically abuse children are also much more likely to do so in a persistent manner, causing longstanding injuries, than are women.

Why is domestic violence so common? One factor is the combination of emotional intensity and personal intimacy that is characteristic of family life. Family ties are charged with strong emotions, often mixing love and hate, and quarrels which break out in domestic settings can unleash antagonisms that are not so potent in other social contexts. Minor incidents can precipitate full-scale hostilities between partners or between parents and children. A second factor is that a certain level of violence within the family is often tolerated or even approved of. For example, many children in Britain have at some time been slapped or hit, if only in a minor way, by one of their parents. Such actions quite often meet with general approval on the part of others and may not even be thought of as 'violence'. Today there is increasing pressure from campaigning groups for the UK to follow many of the other European countries and outlaw the physical punishment of children.

We should not overstate the dark side of family life because most people's experience of families is, on the whole, positive. Indeed, when asked what is the most important part of their lives, many people say that family is what matters most. Nevertheless, sociological studies of inequalities and violence within families have led to a more rounded and sober appreciation of the reality of these family practices.

Family diversity and intimate relations

In the 1980s, Rapoport et al. (1982: 476) argued that 'families in Britain today are in transition from coping in a society in which there was a single overriding norm of what a family should be like to a society in which a plurality of norms are recognised as legitimate and, indeed, desirable.' Substantiating this argument, they identified five types of diversity: *organizational, cultural, class, life course* and *cohort*. We could now add to this list *sexual* diversity. The diversity of family forms identified by Rapoport and his colleagues is even more obvious across European societies today than when these authors first wrote about Britain in 1982.

 Socialization and life stages are also discussed in chapter 9, 'The Life Course'.

Diverse family structures

Families organize their domestic duties and links with the wider social environment in a variety of ways. The contrast between 'orthodox' families – with the woman as 'housewife' and husband as 'breadwinner' – and dual-career (both working) or one-parent families illustrates this point. *Culturally*, there is also greater diversity of family arrangements and values today than in the first half of the twentieth century. Persistent *class* divisions between the poor, the skilled working classes and the various groupings within the middle and upper classes also sustain major variations in family structure. Variations in the individual experience of 'family' across the *life course* are fairly obvious. For instance, one individual might be born into a family in which both parents had stayed together and go on to marry and then divorce. Another person might be brought up in a single-parent family, be

married several times and have children from each marriage.

The term *cohort* refers to generations within families and, as more people live into very old age, it is becoming more common to find three 'ongoing' families existing in close relation to one another: married grandchildren, their parents and grandparents. There is also greater *sexual* diversity in family organizations than ever before. As homosexuality becomes increasingly accepted in most Western societies, families are formed based on same-sex partnerships as well as opposite-sex couples. The presence of minority ethnic groups, such as families of South Asian or West Indian origin, have also produced considerably variety in family forms, and we look at two instances of this cultural diversity next.

> Gay marriage and civil partnerships are discussed in chapter 15, 'Gender and Sexuality'.

South Asian families

The category of 'South Asian families' covers Indians, Bangladeshis, Pakistanis and African Asians (people of South Asian origin who had lived in Africa before migrating to the UK) (Smith and Prior 1997). There are clearly many differences between these varied national groups in relation to family structures and patterns of living, though there are also some distinctive similarities, especially when compared with the conventional nuclear family type. Migration began in the 1950s from three main areas of the Indian subcontinent: Punjab, Gujarat and Bengal. In Britain, these migrant groups formed communities based on religion, area of origin, caste and, most importantly, kinship. Many migrants found their ideas of honour and family loyalty largely absent among the white British population.

South Asian children born in Europe today are often exposed to two different cultures. At home, their parents continue to expect conformity to the norms of cooperation, respect and family loyalty, while, at school, academic success is rooted in a competitive and individualistic social environment. Most choose to organize their domestic and personal lives in terms of their ethnic culture, as they value the close relationships associated with traditional family life.

Yet involvement with Western culture has brought changes. The Western tradition of marrying 'for love' seems to be growing among young people, though this can be a source of tension with the traditional practice of arranged marriages within Asian communities. Such unions, arranged by parents and family members, are predicated on the belief that love comes from within marriage. However, some recent studies have found that compromises are being negotiated, with young people increasingly demanding greater consultation in the arrangement of their marriages, and many want to wait until their higher education is completed before marrying.

On the other hand, police forces in the UK report that they deal with 'forced marriages' in which mainly Pakistani and Bangladeshi young women are sent abroad to marry without their consent. One study estimated at least 3,000 such cases per year (Revill 2008). The Forced Marriages Unit (FMU) at the British High Commission in Islamabad was created to help young British women in forced marriages who often feel that simply returning to their families in the UK would not resolve their situation. The FMU reports that the problem is particularly acute in more remote, rural areas, and its role is to provide a supportive network for those who seek help. Forced marriage can be seen as one aspect of the 'darker side' of families, which also includes intimate violence and the abuse of children.

In the UK Policy Studies Institute's fourth national survey of ethnic minorities in 1997, Indians, Pakistanis, Bangladeshis and African Asians were the ethnic groups most likely to be married (Modood et al. 1997; Berthoud 2000). Table 10.2 shows there has been little change in this pattern. In 2009, 894,000 dependent children in Asian or Asian British families (some 86 per cent) lived in married couple families.

This remains relatively high compared with 62 per cent of dependent children (6.7 million) from white ethnic backgrounds and just 39 per cent (196,000) from black or black British backgrounds who lived in such families. conversely, some 56 per cent of black and black British children lived in single-parent households in 2009, compared with 23 per cent of white children and just 14 per cent of Asian and Asian British children. Cohabitation was also much less common among Asian and Asian British couples with children than among other ethnic groups. So, although there are some signs of change among South Asian families in Britain, including young people wanting a greater say in marriages and a small rise in divorces and single-parent households, overall South Asian ethnic groups in the UK, and across Europe more generally, continue to retain relatively strong familial bonds.

African-Caribbean families

Families of African-Caribbean descent in Europe have a different structure again. In the UK there are far fewer African-Caribbean women aged between twenty and forty-four living with a husband than white or South Asian women in the same age group. Rates of divorce and separation are higher among African Caribbeans than among other ethnic groups in Britain and, as a result, single-parent households are more commonly found. Yet, unlike other ethnic groups, single African-Caribbean mothers are more likely to be employed and to have more control over family finances (Modood et al. 1997). The high proportion of single-parent families, a majority of which are headed by the mother, among the British African-Caribbean population compared with other ethnic groups can be seen in table 10.2.

In the UK, the same factors seem to be at work among African-Caribbean families in the poorer neighbourhoods of London and other European cities. Many discussions concentrate on low rates of formal marriage, but some believe that this emphasis is misplaced. The marriage relationship does not necessarily form the structure of African-Caribbean

Table 10.2 **British families with dependent children,[a] by ethnic group, 2001–9 (thousands)**

	2001	2003	2005	2007	2009
Married couple[b]					
White	7,863	7,637	7,313	7,061	6,717
Mixed	125	126	151	167	188
Asian or Asian British	620	659	693	752	894
Black or black British	131	148	152	215	196
Chinese	33	23	33	36	25
Other ethnic group	45	108	142	148	181
Total dependent children with married parents[c]	8,997	8,772	8,577	8,441	8,290
Cohabiting couple[d]					
White	1,256	1,300	1,383	1,492	1,567
Mixed	27	26	29	50	55
Asian or Asian British	3	7	2	5	7
Black or black British	26	19	24	26	22
Chinese	2	*	*	2	3
Other ethnic group	*	4	5	7	12
Total dependent children with cohabiting parents[c]	1,339	1,366	1,455	1,597	1,682
Lone parent					
White	2,418	2,557	2,474	2,424	2,496
Mixed	127	128	133	134	150
Asian or Asian British	94	81	107	134	143
Black or black British	198	206	206	240	279
Chinese	12	9	6	10	6
Other ethnic group	5	24	47	73	40
Total dependent children with lone parents[c]	2,900	3,020	2,995	3,028	3,146

Notes:
[a] Children aged under 16 and those aged 16 to 18 who have never married and are in full-time education.
[b] Data for 2007 onwards include civil partnerships.
[c] Includes those who did not know or state their ethnicity.
[d] Data for 2007 onwards include same-sex couples.

Source: ONS (2010a: 18).

families in the same way that it does for families in other ethnic groups. Extended kinship networks are important in West Indian groups, for example, and tend to be much more significant, relative to marital ties, than in most white European communities. Therefore, a mother heading a single-parent family is likely to have a wider supportive network of relatives and friends to depend on (Berthoud 2000). Siblings also play an important role in many African-Caribbean families by helping to raise younger children (Chamberlain 1999). Such strong support networks provide the necessary foundation for the higher involvement of African-Caribbean women in paid employment than other ethnic groups.

The transformation of intimacy

Contemporary family life seems quite different from how it was just one or two generations ago. Attitudes towards sex and marriage, childcare, domestic tasks and emotional communication between couples have all undergone major change. Lawrence Stone (1980) charted some key developments in relation to England through a three-phase model of family, from the 1500s to the 1800s.

In the early 1500s people lived in fairly small households, but families were not as clearly separated from the wider community as many are today. Stone (1980) argues that the family at that time was not a major focus of *emotional* attachment or dependence. People did not experience, or look for, the emotional closeness associated with 'family' today. Sex within marriage was regarded not as a source of pleasure but as a necessity to propagate children. Outside aristocratic circles, where it was sometimes actively encouraged, moralists and theologians regarded erotic or romantic love as a sickness. As Stone (1980: 17) puts it, the family during this period 'was an open-ended, low-keyed, unemotional, authoritarian institution. . . . It was also very short-lived, being frequently dissolved by the death of the husband or wife or the death or very early departure from the home of the children.'

This type of family was succeeded by a 'transitional form' that lasted from the early seventeenth to the beginning of the eighteenth century. This type was confined largely to the upper reaches of society, but it was important as it transmitted attitudes that have since become almost universal. The nuclear family became more clearly separated from the community. There was a growing stress on the importance of marital and parental love, although there was also an increase in the authoritarian power of fathers.

In the third phase, the Western nuclear family gradually evolved, characterized by close emotional bonds, a high degree of domestic privacy and a preoccupation with the rearing of children. It is marked by the rise of affective individualism – the formation of marriage ties on the basis of personal selection, guided by sexual attraction or romantic love. The family became geared to consumption rather than production as a result of the increasing number of workplaces that were separate from the home, and women became associated with domesticity. Stone's three-phase history can be criticized for overstating the lack of love in English marriages before the eighteenth century, though the rise of affective individualism as the basis for intimate relationships is broadly in line with other studies.

Feminist perspectives also generated increasing interest in the family and intimate relationships in sociology, but, because they tended to focus on neglected aspects within the domestic realm, feminist studies did not always reflect larger trends and influences taking place *outside* the home. In the past two decades an important body of sociological work on the family has emerged that draws on feminist theory but is not strictly informed by it. The central concerns of this work are the formation and dissolution of families and households and the shifting expectations within personal relationships.

In *The Transformation of Intimacy* (1993), Anthony Giddens looked at how intimate relationships are changing in modern societies. He argues that the most recent phase of modernity has seen a major transformation in the nature of intimate relationships in the development of plastic sexuality. For many people in modern societies there is much greater choice than ever before over when, how often and with whom they have sex (see chapter 15, 'Gender and Sexuality'). With plastic sexuality, sex can be effectively 'untied' from reproduction. This is due partly to improved methods of contraception, which free women from the fear of repetitive pregnancies and childbirths, but also to the development of a sense that the self could be actively chosen in a kind of social reflexivity.

The emergence of plastic sexuality, according to Giddens, brings with it a change in the nature of love. The ideals of romantic love are fragmenting, being slowly replaced by confluent love. Confluent love is active and contingent. It jars with the forever, one-and-only qualities of romantic love. The emergence of confluent love goes some way towards explaining the rise of separation and divorce which we discussed earlier in the chapter. Romantic love meant that, once people had married, they were usually stuck with one another, no matter how the relationship subsequently developed. But now people have more choice: whereas divorce was previously difficult or impossible to obtain, married people are no longer bound to stay together if the relationship does not work for them.

Rather than basing relationships on romantic passion, people are increasingly pursuing the ideal of a pure relationship, in which couples remain together because they *choose* to do so. The pure relationship is held together by the acceptance of each partner that, 'until further notice', each gains sufficient benefits to make its continuance worthwhile. Love is based upon emotional intimacy that generates trust. Love develops depending on how much each partner is prepared to reveal their concerns and needs and to be vulnerable to the other. However, there is a diversity of forms of pure relationship, and some same-sex relationships, because of their open and negotiated status, come closer to the ideal of pure relationships than do married heterosexual ones.

Critics have argued that the instability of the pure relationship, which was thought of as a relationship between adults, contrasts with the complexities of family practices which include children. The concept also neglects the different experiences which men and women tend to have when a heterosexual relationship ends. By focusing on relationships between adults, the idea of a pure relationship actually reflects the marginalization of children and childhood in sociological thought (Smart and Neale 1999). Although it helps us to understand something of the changes in intimate relations, perhaps the thesis of the pure relationship does not give enough attention to issues of space and time that are required for its construction. For example, such relationships may still involve home-building and looking after children, both of which can be seen as practical 'joint projects' requiring material resources that also contribute significantly to the maintenance of intimate relationships (Jamieson 1998).

> The sociology of childhood is discussed in chapter 9, 'The Life Course'.

The 'normal chaos' of love

In *The Normal Chaos of Love*, Ulrich Beck and Elisabeth Beck-Gernsheim (1995) examine the tumultuous nature of personal relationships, marriages and family patterns against the backdrop of a rapidly changing world. They argue that the traditions, rules and guidelines which used to govern personal relationships no longer apply and that individuals are confronted with an endless series of choices as part of constructing, adjusting, improving or dissolving the unions they form with others. The fact that marriages are now entered into voluntarily, rather than for economic purposes or at the urging of family, brings both freedoms and new strains. In fact, the authors conclude, they demand a great deal of hard work and effort.

Beck and Beck-Gernsheim see the present age as one filled with colliding interests between family, work, love and the freedom to pursue individual goals. This collision is felt acutely within personal relationships, particularly when there are two 'labour market biographies' to juggle instead of one, as more women pursue a career. Previous gendered work patterns are less fixed than they once were, as both men and women now place

399

Modern relationships often involve dual-income families where mothers are in full-time work. This has led to the re-emergence of 'old-fashioned' institutions such as schools training professional nannies.

emphasis on their professional and personal needs. Relationships in the modern age are not just about relationships; they are also about work, politics, economics, professions and inequality. It is therefore not surprising that antagonisms between men and women are rising. Beck and Beck-Gernsheim claim that the 'battle between the sexes' is the 'central drama of our times', evidenced by the growth of the marriage-counselling industry, family courts, marital self-help groups and high divorce rates. Yet, even though they seem to be more 'flimsy' than ever before, marriage and family life remain very important to people. Divorce is more common, but rates of remarriage are high. The birth rate may be declining, but there is a huge demand for fertility treatment. Fewer people choose to get married, but the desire to live with someone as part of a couple holds steady. How do we explain such apparently competing tendencies?

Beck and Beck-Gernsheim's answer is simple: love. They argue that today's 'battle of the sexes' is the clearest possible indication of people's 'hunger for love'. People marry for the sake of love, divorce for the sake of love, and engage in an endless cycle of hoping, regretting and trying again. While, on the one hand, the tensions between men and women are high, there remains a deep hope and faith in the possibility of finding true love and fulfilment. This may appear too simple an answer, but Beck and Beck-Gernsheim argue that it is precisely because our world is so overwhelming, impersonal, abstract and rapidly changing that love has become increasingly important. Love is the only place where people can truly 'find themselves' and connect with others:

Love is a search for oneself, a craving to really get in contact with me and you, sharing bodies, sharing thoughts, encountering one another with nothing held back, making confessions and being forgiven, understanding, confirming and supporting what was and what is, longing for a home and trust to counteract the doubts and anxieties modern life generates. If nothing seems certain or safe, if even breathing is risky in a polluted world, then people chase after the misleading dreams of love until they suddenly turn into nightmares. (1995: 175–6)

Critics have attacked Beck and Beck-Gernsheim's exclusive focus on heterosexuality – the battle between the sexes is the 'central drama of our times' – which seems to marginalize LGBT relationships (Smart and Neale 1999). The thesis can also be criticized for its reliance on the concept of 'individualization', which plays down or fails to acknowledge the continuing importance of social class and community in structuring opportunities and shaping personal relationships. For instance, by no means do all women enjoy the kinds of lifelong, middle-class careers outlined by Beck and Beck-Gernsheim. Smart (2007) argues that the focus on the individual who makes free, rational choices fails to appreciate that personal life is necessarily 'relational'; that is, it takes place within networks of relationships. Hence, the individualization thesis, despite its insights, overstates the extent to which people can ever really be 'cut loose' from wider social structures and networks.

> ### THINKING CRITICALLY
>
> To what extent do you think *love* is capable of holding together the institution of the family? What problems could arise within families when there is such a high value on love to hold couple relationships together?

Liquid love?

As with Giddens and Beck and Beck-Gernsheim, Zygmunt Bauman (2003: viii) argues that, today, relationships are 'the hottest talk of the town and ostensibly the sole game worth playing, despite their notorious risks'. His book *Liquid Love* is about the 'frailty of human bonds', the feeling of insecurity to which this frailty leads, and our responses to it. Bauman writes that the hero of his book is 'the man or woman without bonds' (of family, class, religion or marriage) or at least without any fixed, unbreakable ties. The ties Bauman's hero does have are loosely knotted, so they can be released again with little delay if circumstances change. And, for Bauman, the circumstances will change and often. He uses the 'liquid' metaphor to describe modern society, which he sees as characterized by constant change and a lack of lasting bonds.

Bauman maintains that, in a world of rampant individualization, relationships are a mixed blessing, filled with conflicting desires, which pull in different ways. On the one hand, there is the desire for freedom, for loose bonds that we can escape from if we so choose. On the other, there is the desire for greater security that is gained by tightening the bonds between partners and ourselves. As it is, Bauman argues, people swing back and forth between the two polarities of security and freedom. Often they run to experts – therapists or columnists, for example – for advice on how to combine the two. Bauman (2003: ix) sees this as attempting 'to eat the cake and have it, to cream off the sweet delights of relationship while omitting its bitter and tougher bits'. The result is a society of 'semi-detached couples' in 'top pocket relationships'. By the phrase 'top pocket relationships', he means something that can be pulled out when needed but pushed into the pocket when no longer required.

One response to the 'frailty of human bonds' is to replace quality in our relationships for quantity. It is not the depth of our relationships, but the number of contacts that we have which then becomes important to us. That is partly why, Bauman argues, we are always talking on mobile phones, sending text messages to one another and even typing them in truncated sentences to increase the speed at which we can send them. It is not the message

401

itself that is important but the constant circulation of messages, without which we feel excluded. Bauman notes that people now speak more of connections and networks and less of relationships. To be in a relationship means to be mutually engaged, but networks suggest fleeting moments of being in touch.

Bauman's ideas are certainly insightful, but critics see their empirical basis as weak and not grounded in empirical research. For example, too much is perhaps made of magazines and the short-term impact on social relationships of new technologies such as mobile phones and computers. Like Giddens and Beck and Beck-Gernsheim, Bauman is accused of being too pessimistic about contemporary social change, especially the transformation of intimate relationships he identifies. Yet is his assessment realistic? Carol Smart (2007) thinks not. Indeed, she takes issue with all theories of individualization, seeing them as exaggerating the extent of family fragmentation and the decline of relationship commitment. Instead, she suggests that *personal life*, rather than 'the family' or 'the individual', is characterized by strong social and emotional bonds alongside the sharing of memories and experience.

Smart suggests that the concept of personal life encompasses people's pursuit of a 'life project' (as described in the work of Beck and Giddens, for example) but always relates such individual projects to the wider familial and social context within which they make sense. Smart (2007) argues that Beck's work, for instance, often gives the impression that individuals have been 'cut free' from social structures – a very unrealistic and anti-sociological notion. Instead, she says, 'meaning-constitutive traditions' are important here, as well as such structural factors as social class, ethnicity and gender. She attributes particular importance to collective memories transmitted across generations as well as the way that people are embedded within social structures and 'imagined communities'.

Studying personal life alerts sociologists to something that Smart sees missing in the theories discussed above – namely, *connectedness*.

By this, she means all the ways in which people maintain their social relationships and associations in different times and contexts, along with the memories, feelings and experiences of being connected to others. Studying connectedness rather than fragmentation allows macrosociological theories to reconnect with the large amount of empirical research on families and relationships and thus get closer to – and understand better – people's real-life experiences.

Clearly, these debates and the view we take of recent social change cover some of the big social and political questions of recent times, but what do they mean for the debate about the decline, or otherwise, of family values?

Marriage, divorce and separation

The normalization of divorce

For many centuries in the West and other parts of the world, marriage was regarded as virtually indissoluble. A divorce was granted only in very limited cases, such as the non-consummation of marriage. Today, however, legal divorce is possible in virtually all of the industrialized and developing societies of the world. Only in Malta and the Philippines is it still not legally recognized, though Maltese couples can obtain a 'foreign divorce' from another country if one or both partners are 'habitually resident' there. Seen in a global perspective, these are now isolated examples. Most countries have moved towards making divorce more readily available by moving to 'no fault' divorce laws, such as the UK's 1969 Divorce Reform Act.

Between 1960 and 1970 the divorce rate in England and Wales grew by a steady 9 per cent each year, doubling within that decade. By 1972 it had doubled again, partly as a result of the 1969 Act, which made it easier for people in marriages that had long been 'dead' to obtain a divorce. The annual number of divorces hit a peak of 165,000 in 1993, but since 2004 the number has fallen, to 126,700 in 2007. Of course, this figure remains very high compared with those of previous periods, and

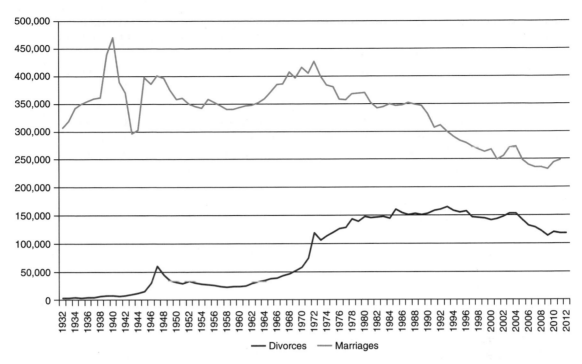

Figure 10.1 Number of marriages and divorces, 1932–2012, England and Wales

Source: ONS (2014g: 2).

around two-fifths of all marriages now end in divorce (ONS 2010b: 22). Since the 1970s, a rising number of divorces in England and Wales has gone hand in hand with a fall in the number of marriages (figure 10.1).

Taking a long-term view of European-wide marriage and divorce rates, figure 10.2 demonstrates a similar pattern. However, there are national exceptions in some Eastern European countries such as Romania and Croatia,

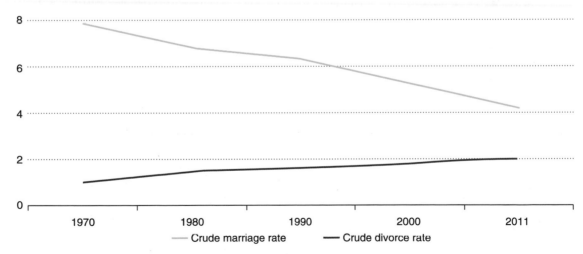

Figure 10.2 Crude marriage and divorce rates (per 1,000 inhabitants) in the EU-28, 1970–2011

Source: Eurostat (2015b).

where divorce rates have actually fallen. Marriage rates since the 1970s have steadily reduced across the twenty-eight EU countries apart from in the Nordic countries – Sweden, Denmark, Norway and Iceland – and some Eastern European states such as Latvia and Poland. Comparing national statistics shows that the patterns of marriage and divorce in the UK are far from unique but form part of broader, Europe-wide social trends.

Divorce rates are not a direct index of marital unhappiness. For one thing, rates of divorce do not include people who are separated but not legally divorced. Moreover, people who are unhappily married may choose to stay together – because they believe in the sanctity of marriage, worry about the financial or emotional consequences of a break-up, or wish to remain with one another to give their children a 'family' home.

USING YOUR SOCIOLOGICAL IMAGINATION

10.1 Diane Vaughan on 'uncoupling': the experience of breaking up

In *Uncoupling: The Turning Points in Intimate Relationships* (1990), Diane Vaughan analysed the relationships between partners during the course of separation or divorce. She carried out a series of interviews with more than 100 recently separated or divorced people (mainly from middle-class backgrounds) to chart the transition from living together to living apart. The notion of uncoupling refers to the break-up of a long-term intimate relationship. Vaughan found that in many cases, before the physical parting, there had been a social separation – at least one of the partners developed a new pattern of life, becoming interested in new pursuits and making new friends in contexts in which the other was not present. This usually meant keeping secrets from the other – especially, of course, when a relationship with a lover was involved.

According to Vaughan's research, uncoupling is often unintentional at first. One individual – whom she called the initiator – becomes less satisfied with the relationship than the other and creates a 'territory' independent of the activities in which the couple engages together. For some time before this, the initiator may have been trying unsuccessfully to change the partner, to get him or her to behave in more acceptable ways. At some point, the initiator feels that the attempt has failed and that the relationship is fundamentally flawed. From then onwards, he or she becomes preoccupied with the ways in which the relationship or the partner is defective. Vaughan suggests this is the opposite of the process of 'falling in love' at the beginning of a relationship, when an individual focuses on the attractive features of the other, ignoring those that might be less acceptable.

Initiators seriously considering a break notably discuss their relationship extensively with others, 'comparing notes'. In doing so, they weigh the costs and benefits of separation. Can I survive on my own? How will friends and parents react? Will the children suffer? Will I be financially solvent? Having thought about these and other problems, some decide to try again to make the relationship work. For those who proceed with a separation, these discussions and enquiries help make the break less intimidating, building confidence that they are doing the right thing. Most initiators become convinced that a responsibility for their own self-development takes priority over commitment to the other.

Of course, uncoupling is not always entirely led by one individual. The other partner may also have decided that the relationship cannot be saved. In some situations, an abrupt reversal of roles occurs. The person who previously wanted to save the relationship becomes determined to end it, while the erstwhile initiator wishes to carry on.

> **THINKING CRITICALLY**
>
> In any country of your choice, find out from official statistics whether men or women in heterosexual marriages initiated the most divorces in 2012. What social and practical factors would you suggest could account for the disparity?

Why has divorce become more common? Several factors linked to wider social changes have been identified. Except in the case of a very small proportion of wealthy people, marriage no longer has much connection with the desire to pass on property and status. Also, as women become more economically independent, marriage is less of a necessary economic partnership than it used to be. Greater overall prosperity and more women working means that it is easier than it used to be to establish a separate household if there is marital disaffection. As a result of these changes there is much less stigma attached to divorce, which adds momentum to the process. A further important factor is the growing tendency to evaluate marriage in terms of the levels of personal satisfaction it offers. Overall, high divorce rates do not seem to indicate deep dissatisfaction with the institution of marriage but, rather, show an increased determination to make marriage a rewarding and satisfying relationship.

Single-parent households

Single-parent households have become increasingly common in the developed countries since the early 1970s, and the pattern is quite varied even across a distinct region such as the European Union (see table 10.3). A relatively low percentage of dependent children (under eighteen years old) live in single-parent households in Greece (5.3 per cent), Spain (7.2 per cent) and Cyprus (7.2 per cent), with much higher proportions in Ireland (24.3 per cent), the UK (21.5 per cent) and Latvia (27.1 per cent) (Iacovou and Skew 2010: 14). The USA and New Zealand have even higher proportions of single parents, at 31 and 29 per cent respectively, while Japan has just 8 per cent (Institute for Child and Family Policy 2004).

It is important to note that single parenthood with dependent children is an overwhelmingly female category and that, on average, these households are among the poorest groups in contemporary societies. In addition, many single parents, whether they have ever been married or not, still face social disapproval as well as economic insecurity, though some of the more judgemental terms such as 'deserted wives', 'fatherless families' or 'broken homes' are slowly disappearing.

The category of single-parent household is also an internally diverse one. For instance, UK data show that more than half of widowed mothers are owner-occupiers, but the vast majority of single mothers who have never married live in rented accommodation. Single parenthood tends to be a changing state, and its boundaries are blurred by multiple paths both into and out of the status. In the case of a person whose spouse dies, the break is obviously clear-cut – although even here a person might have been living on his or her own in practical terms if the partner was in hospital for some while before they died. However, about 60 per cent of single-parent households today are brought about by separation or divorce.

Among single-parent families in the UK, the fastest growing category is that of single mothers who have never married, which constitutes around 9 per cent of the total number of families with dependent children. Of these, it is difficult to know how many have chosen to raise children alone – though most people do not wish to be single parents. The ongoing *Millennium Cohort Study*, which follows the lives of some 19,000 children born in 2000–1, has found that younger women are more likely to become solo mothers and that, the more highly educated the woman, the more likely she is to have a baby within marriage. The research also reveals that, for 85 per cent of solo mothers, their pregnancy was unplanned, in contrast to 52 per cent of cohabiting couples and 18 per cent of married women. For the majority of unmarried or never-married mothers, there is also a strong correlation between the rate of births outside marriage and indicators of poverty and social deprivation. However, a growing minority of women are now choosing to have a child or children without the support of a spouse or partner. 'Single mothers by choice' is an apt description of some single parents, usually those who possess sufficient resources to manage satisfactorily as a single-parent household.

Table 10.3 **Living situation of dependent children in Europe, by family type, 2007 (percentages)**

	Percentage of children living with:				% of children in multigenerational households
	0 parents	1 parent	2 parents, cohabiting	2 parents, married	
Sweden	1.3	**17.6**	**30.5**	*50.6*	*0.3*
Finland	0.9	14.4	**15.8**	68.9	*0.6*
Denmark	**1.5**	**17.9**	15.1	65.6	*0.4*
Netherlands	*0.3*	11.1	13.1	75.5	*0.3*
UK	1.4	**21.5**	12.6	*64.5*	3.4
France	0.9	13.5	**21.0**	*64.5*	*1.8*
Germany	1.3	15.0	*5.5*	**78.2**	*0.9*
Austria	**2.2**	14.3	7.4	76.1	7.5
Belgium	**2.5**	**16.2**	13.7	*67.7*	*2.2*
Luxembourg	*0.3*	*10.2*	6.9	**82.6**	*2.8*
Ireland	**1.9**	**24.3**	5.9	*67.9*	4.5
Italy	*0.8*	*10.2*	*5.2*	**83.9**	5.0
Spain	1.2	*7.2*	7.9	**83.7**	5.8
Portugal	**2.9**	11.9	9.7	75.5	**11.6**
Greece	1.2	*5.3*	*1.2*	**92.3**	6.5
Cyprus	*0.7*	*7.2*	*0.6*	**91.5**	3.0
Czech Republic	*0.6*	14.9	8.2	76.3	7.7
Hungary	*0.8*	15.4	9.9	73.9	**11.6**
Estonia	**1.9**	**21.8**	**23.9**	*52.5*	**12.0**
Latvia	**3.3**	**27.1**	**14.1**	*55.5*	**24.4**
Lithuania	**2.0**	**18.1**	*6.1*	73.8	**14.5**
Slovenia	*0.6*	*10.4*	**19.5**	69.4	**13.7**
Slovakia	1.1	*10.6*	*3.7*	**84.7**	**17.6**
Poland	*0.8*	*11.0*	9.2	**79.0**	**22.0**
EU25	1.2	14.1	11.0	73.8	5.4
EU15	1.2	14.3	11.3	73.2	3.1
EU10	0.9	13.1	9.2	76.7	17.4

Notes: 'Children' are defined as all those under age 18.
Bold type denotes the eight countries with the highest incidence, and italics denote the eight countries with the lowest incidence of each situation.

Source: Iacovou and Skew (2010: 14).

Some researchers have suggested a direct link between differential levels of welfare support for single parents and the diverse proportions of single-parent families seen across Europe (P. Morgan 1999). According to Morgan, the main reason why Sweden and the UK have relatively high proportions of single-parent families compared with, say, Italy, is because Italian family allowances have been very low and the primary source of support for young people is other family members. Morgan argues that, in states where it is not subsidized, single parenting is simply less prevalent. But is this overly simplistic? The diversity of 'pathways' into and out of single-parent families means that they do not constitute a uniform or cohesive group in the first place and, though single-parent families may share some material and social disadvantages, they do not have a collective identity. The plurality of routes means that, for the purposes of social policy, the boundaries of single parenthood are hard to define and needs are difficult to target.

Fathering and the 'absent father' debate

Political debate on the role of fathers has been dominated by the idea of the 'absent father' since at least the late 1930s. During the Second World War, many fathers, because of war service, rarely saw their children. In the period following the war, in a high proportion of families women were not in the paid labour force and stayed at home to look after the children. The father was the main breadwinner and, consequently, was at work all day and would see his children only in the evenings and at weekends.

However, with rising divorce rates since the 1970s and the increase in single-parent households, the theme of the absent father has come to mean something quite different. It has come to refer to fathers who, as a result of separation or divorce, have only infrequent contact with their children or who lose touch with them altogether. In both Britain and the United States, which have among the highest divorce rates in the world, there has been intense debate on what some see as the 'death of the dad'.

Writing from contrasting perspectives, sociologists and commentators have seized on the increasing proportion of fatherless families as the key to a whole range of social problems, from rising crime to mushrooming welfare costs for child support. Some have argued that children will never become effective members of society unless they are exposed to examples of negotiation, cooperation and compromise between adults in their immediate environment (Dennis and Erdos 1992). In particular, the argument suggests that boys who grow up without a father will struggle to be successful parents themselves. However, it is important to distinguish between fatherless families and fatherless households. In many cases of separation and divorce, fathers play a role throughout their children's lives despite not living in the same household, and in this sense, as parental involvement from both parties continues, the family is not 'fatherless'.

One outcome of high divorce rates has been the unexpected emergence of organizations lobbying for the rights of fathers after divorce. In the UK, the Netherlands and the USA, the pressure group Fathers 4 Justice (F4J) has gained a high profile as a result of some well-publicized stunts, protest marches and direct actions carried out by activists. In May 2004, F4J activists threw a condom filled with purple flour at the British prime minister in the House of Commons, and a few months later one campaigner scaled the walls of Buckingham Palace dressed as the comic-book hero Batman – 'every father is a superhero to his children'. The group claims that the law, which aims to serve 'the best interests' of the child, is biased in favour of mothers when couples split up, making it difficult for fathers to stay in contact with their children.

In *Fatherless America* (1995), David Blankenhorn argues that societies with high divorce rates face not just the loss of fathers but the erosion of the idea of fatherhood itself. One reviewer of Blankenhorn's book said that it was 'better to have a dad who comes home from a nasty job to drink beer in front of the television than no dad at all' (*The Economist* 1995). Yet, is it? The issue of absent fathers overlaps with that of the more general question of the effects of divorce on children – and there the implications of the available evidence are far from clear.

Some scholars have suggested that the key question is not whether the father is present but how engaged he is in family life and parenting. In other words, the make-up of the household may not be as important as the quality of care, attention and support that children receive from its members. For example, even in cases where the biological father neither lives in the household nor has any parental involvement, there may be a step-father or other father figure present who performs a similar role. Since the 1980s, issues of good parenting and, in particular, good 'fathering' have become more prominent in political debate and academic research (B. Hobson 2002).

As we have already noted, as women move into paid employment in larger numbers, men's contribution to domestic tasks and childcare does not seem to be increasing at the same pace. This suggests that an assumption of women as primary care-givers remains strong even in dual-earner families. In Europe, campaigns by the Equal Opportunities Commission have sought new ways to promote 'active fatherhood', including increasing paternity-leave entitlement, promoting family-friendly workplaces, and changing the long-hours culture of many European countries such as Britain and Greece.

European provision for fathers is diverse. In Sweden, both parents are entitled to 450 days of paid leave at the birth or adoption of a child – thirteen months at 80 per cent of salary for most parents and the rest at a lower rate – and employees are entitled to go back to their previous job or a similar one when they do return. However, in Greece, Italy and Spain, fathers do not normally take parental leave: in Spain it is unpaid; in Italy it is not a right; and in Greece such leave is not guaranteed in companies with fewer than fifty employees (Flouri 2005). These three countries also have the lowest female labour market participa-

tion in the EU, at around 40 per cent. The USA introduced maternity leave only in 1993; Australia introduced eighteen weeks of paid maternity or paternity leave at the minimum wage level from 1 January 2011; and, while New Zealand introduced paid maternity leave in 2002, it still has no provision for paid paternity leave. The UK introduced shared parental leave in 2105, allowing leave from work to be shared between the parents following a birth or adoption and offering more flexibility to share parental tasks in the first year of a child's life or adoption.

Even in Sweden, the most generous provider for fathers, it is still mothers who take 85 per cent of all parental leave. Many Swedish fathers are reluctant to take their 'papa leave' entitlement for fear of losing out to colleagues for promotion or upsetting their employer; in addition, women's wages lag behind those of men, and just two out of 282 listed companies have female chief executives. Therefore, we have to be cautious when drawing conclusions about national situations, as the introduction of particular policies does not necessarily mean they will be taken advantage of by the social groups they target (Lister et al. 2007).

It seems that, in the light of wider concerns about youth crime and the effects of 'bad' parenting or the absence of a 'father figure' in the lives of young men, there is a growing interest in fathering and parenting more generally. Such interest and concerns have led to new policies aimed at increasing fathers' engagement in childcare and domestic life. However, even where such policies have been introduced, wider social and economic factors and longstanding gendered assumptions about male and female roles continue to play a strong part in determining the extent to which government policy can shape the dynamics of family life. This means that families and households always need to be studied in relation to broader social changes and trends.

Changing attitudes to family life

There are some important class differences affecting reactions to the changing

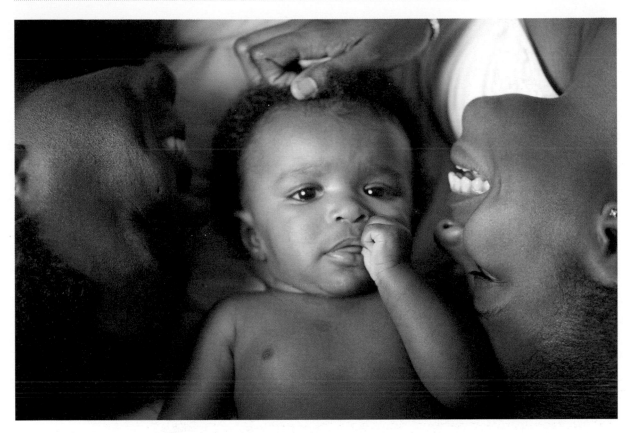

Globally, there exists a diversity of provision for maternity and paternity leave, though the long-term trend shows a movement towards the acceptance of paid maternity leave.

character of family life and continuing high levels of divorce. For example, Lillian Rubin (1994) interviewed the members of thirty-two working-class families in the USA and concluded that, compared with middle-class families, working-class parents tend to hold more traditional attitudes. The norms that many middle-class parents have accepted, such as the open expression of pre-marital sex, are more likely to be disapproved of by working-class people, even where they are not particularly religious. The young women were more ambivalent about marriage than their parents' generation and spoke of exploring available options and living life more fully and openly than was possible for their mothers. However, the generational shift in men's attitudes was not as great.

These changes are similar to those found in European studies. Wilkinson and Mulgan (Wilkinson 1994; Wilkinson and Mulgan 1995) carried out two large-scale studies of men and women in the UK aged eighteen to thirty-four. They found major changes occurring in the outlook of young women in particular and that the values of this age group contrasted with those of older generations in Britain. Among young women they found a desire for autonomy and self-fulfilment, through work as much as family, and an increased valuing of risk-taking and pursuit of excitement. Wilkinson and Mulgan argued that young women's attitudes have been shaped by their inheritance of freedoms that were unavailable to earlier generations – freedom for women to work and control their reproduction, freedom of mobility for both sexes, and freedom to define their own style of life.

10.2   Carol Smart and Bren Neale's *Family Fragments?*

Between 1994 and 1996, Carol Smart and Bren Neale carried out two rounds of interviews with a group of sixty parents from West Yorkshire who had either separated or divorced after the passage of the 1989 Children Act. This Act altered the situation facing parents and children on divorce by abolishing the old notions of 'custody' and 'access' so parents would no longer feel that they had to fight. It also encouraged parents to share child-rearing and required judges and others to listen more to the views of children. Smart and Neale were interested to know how patterns of parenting were initially formed after divorce and how they changed over time. They compared parents' expectations about post-divorce parenting at the point of separation with the 'reality' of their circumstances one year later.

Smart and Neale found that parenting after divorce involved a process of constant adjustment that many had not anticipated and for which they were ill-prepared. Skills which worked as part of a two-parent team were not necessarily successful in a single-parent household. Adults were forced to re-evaluate continuously their approaches to parenting, not only in terms of 'big decisions' affecting their children but also with regard to the everyday aspects of child-rearing occurring across two new households. Following divorce, parents faced two opposing demands – their own needs for separation and distance from their former spouse and the need to remain connected as part of co-parenting responsibilities.

Smart and Neale found that the lived experience of post-divorce parenting was extremely fluid and changed over time. When interviewed a year after separation, many re-evaluated their behaviour and actions in the light of their changing understanding. For example, many were worried about the harm their children would suffer as a result of divorce but were unsure how to transform their fears and sense of guilt into constructive action. This led some to hold on tightly to their children or to treat them like 'adult' confidants. In other

© Mike Baldwin / Cornered

"Thanks to separations, divorces and remarriages, I've got 20 grandparents."

cases it led to alienation, distance and the loss of meaningful connections.

In the media and some political contexts, the authors argued, there is an implicit – sometimes explicit – assumption that, after divorce, adults abandon family morality and begin to act more selfishly. Flexibility, generosity, compromise and sensitivity disappear, and the previous moral framework for making decisions about family and welfare is discarded. Smart and Neale's interviews led them to reject this argument. They claim that people do operate within a moral framework when parenting, but it is best understood as a 'morality of care' rather than an unambiguous moral reasoning. They argue that, as parents care for their children, so decisions emerge about 'the proper thing to do'. These decisions are highly contextual and parents must weigh many considerations, including the effects on the children, whether it is the appropriate time to act, and what harmful implications it might have on the co-parenting relationship.

Smart and Neale conclude that divorce unleashes changes in circumstances which can rarely be 'put straight' once and for all. Successful post-divorce parenting demands constant negotiation and communication. While the 1989 Children's Act has added necessary flexibility to contemporary post-divorce arrangements, its emphasis on the welfare of the child may overlook the crucial role played by the quality of the relationship between divorced parents.

> ### THINKING CRITICALLY
> Given the need to continue parenting across two households, is it inevitable that post-divorce parenting will involve conflict and disagreements? What measures could be introduced to assist parents in making the transition from being married to post-divorce living?

Of those in the sample, 29 per cent of women and 51 per cent of men wanted to delay having children. Statistics show that such attitudes do seem to have led to changed practices; by 2008, just 25 per cent of babies in the UK were born to mothers under the age of twenty-five compared with 47 per cent in 1971 (ONS 2010a: xxiv). Of women in the sixteen to twenty-four age group, 75 per cent believed that single parents can bring up children as well as a couple can, suggesting that marriage is losing its status as the primary socially sanctioned location for child-rearing.

New partnerships, 'blended' families and kin relations

LGBT partnerships

Many people today live in same-sex couples. Because most countries still do not sanction same-sex marriage (though this is changing), intimate relationships between gay men and between lesbians are grounded in personal commitment and mutual trust rather than in law. The term 'families of choice' has sometimes been applied to LGBT partnerships to reflect the positive and creative new forms of family life. Many traditional features of heterosexual partnerships – such as mutual support, care and responsibility in illness, the joining of finances, and so on – are becoming integrated into gay and lesbian relationships in ways that were not possible in earlier times.

A very significant recent trend in Western European countries, which has long been campaigned for by lesbian and gay movements, is the introduction of registered or civil partnerships and the extension of marriage rights for same-sex couples (see figure 10.3).

> Lesbian and gay social movements are discussed in chapter 21, 'Politics, Government and Social Movements'.

Civil partnerships are legally recognized unions between two people of the same sex, though technically they are not 'marriages' in any religious sense. Nonetheless, couples who become legally 'partnered' generally have the same legal rights as married couples on a range of issues. For example, civil partners can expect equal treatment on financial matters such as inheritance, pensions and child maintenance, and they have new rights as 'next of kin'. Immigration rules take account of civil partnerships and marriages in the same way. In Britain, new legislation came into force in December 2005, giving same-sex couples in civil partnerships similar rights to married couples. By mid-2009, some 34,000 civil partnerships had been formed in the UK, though the initial backlog of couples appears to have cleared by 2008, which saw a fall of some 18 per cent on the previous year (ONS 2010a: 22).

Denmark was the first state to grant same-sex partners the same rights as married couples, in 1989, followed in 1996 by Norway,

Map classifications as of 22 July 2016. The US territories of Guam, US Virgin Islands, American Samoa and the Northern Mariana Islands fall into the 'legal nationwide' category.

Figure 10.3 Countries and territories that permit same-sex marriage, as at 26 June 2015

Sweden and Iceland, and in 2000 by Finland. The Netherlands introduced full civil marriage rights in 2001. Belgium and Spain introduced gay marriage rights in 2003 and 2005 respectively, while England and Wales and Scotland legislated for same-sex marriage in 2014. The Pew Research Center (2015) notes that twenty-two countries allowed same-sex marriage by mid-2015. Although this is still a very small proportion of the world's societies, the trend looks likely to continue despite opposition from some religious groups, which see legal recognition of same-sex partnerships as legitimizing 'immoral' relationships.

Since the 1980s there has been a growing research interest in LGBT partnerships. Sociologists have seen homosexual relationships as displaying forms of intimacy and equality that are sometimes and in some respects quite different from those common among heterosexual couples. Because homosexuals have been excluded from the institution of marriage and because traditional gender roles are not easily applicable, homosexual

partnerships must be constructed and negotiated outside the norms and guidelines that govern heterosexual unions. Some have suggested that the 1980s AIDS epidemic was an important factor in the development of a distinctive culture of care and commitment among same-sex partners.

Weeks et al. (2004) point to three significant patterns within gay and lesbian partnerships. First, there is more opportunity for equality between partners because they are not guided by the gendered cultural assumptions that underpin heterosexual relationships. Gay and lesbian couples may choose to shape their relationships to avoid the inequalities and power imbalances characteristic of many heterosexual couples. Second, homosexual partners negotiate the parameters and inner workings of the relationship. If heterosexual couples are influenced by socially embedded gender roles, same-sex couples face fewer expectations about who should do what within the relationship. Women tend to do more of the housework and childcare in heterosexual marriages, but there are no such

Same-sex relationships have been sanctioned across much of the world, but the right of gay parents to adopt and bring up children remains a more controversial issue.

expectations within homosexual partnerships. Everything becomes a matter for negotiation, which may result in a more equal sharing of responsibilities. However, such negotiations can also be a source of disputes and disagreements. Third, LGBT partnerships demonstrate a particular form of commitment that lacks institutional backing. Mutual trust, a willingness to work at difficulties and a shared responsibility for 'emotional labour' seem to be the hallmarks of such partnerships (Weeks 1999). It will be interesting for sociologists to observe how the new civil partnerships and gay marriage rights affect such commitment and mutual trust as they become fully established.

A relaxation of previously intolerant attitudes towards homosexuality has been accompanied by a growing willingness in the courts to allocate custody of children to mothers living in lesbian relationships. Techniques of artificial insemination mean that lesbians may have children and become parents without any heterosexual contact, while a number of recent legal victories for homosexual couples indicate that their rights are gradually becoming enshrined in law. In Britain, a landmark 1999 ruling declared that a homosexual couple in a stable relationship could be defined as 'a family'. This classification of homosexual partners as 'members of the family' will affect legal categories in immigration, social security, taxation, inheritance and child support.

New legal rights for LGBT couples are discussed further in chapter 15, 'Gender and Sexuality'.

Remarriage

Remarriage can involve a variety of circumstances. Some remarried couples are in their early twenties, neither of them bringing a child to the new relationship. Couples that remarry in their late twenties, their thirties or their early forties might each take one or more children from the first marriage to live with them. Those who remarry at later ages might have adult children who never live in the homes that the new partners establish. There may also be children within the new marriage itself. Either partner of the new couple may previously have been single, divorced or widowed, adding up to eight possible combinations. Sociologically, this means that generalizations about remarriage must be made with considerable caution, though some general points are worth making.

In 1900 about nine-tenths of all marriages in the UK were first marriages and most remarriages involved at least one widowed person. With the rise in the divorce rate from the 1970s, the level of remarriage also began to climb, and an increasing proportion of remarriages now involve divorced people. In 1970, 18 per cent of UK marriages were remarriages (for at least one partner); by 1996 that figure was 42 per cent, and, though 2007 data show a fall to 38 per cent, the long-term trend is for remarriages to make up more than one-third of all marriages (as figure 10.4 shows). These statistics do not provide a full picture of post-divorce partnerships, however, as they do not take into account levels of cohabitation following divorce.

People who have been married and divorced are more likely to marry again than

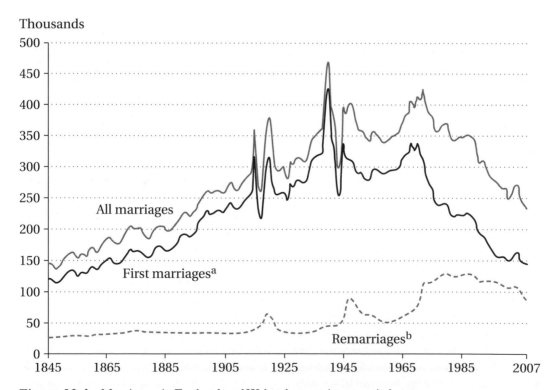

Thousands

Figure 10.4   Marriages in England and Wales, by previous marital status

Notes: [a] For both parties.
[b] For one or both parties.

Source: ONS (2010a: 20).

single people in comparable age groups are to marry for the first time. At all age levels, divorced men are more likely to remarry than divorced women: three in every four divorced women, but five in every six divorced men, remarry. Odd though it might seem, the best way to maximize the chances of getting married, for both sexes, is to have been married before! However, in statistical terms, remarriages are less successful than first marriages. Rates of divorce from second marriages are higher than those from first marriages. This does not show that second marriages are doomed to fail. People who have been divorced may have higher expectations of marriage than those who have not. Hence they may be more ready to dissolve a new marriage. It is quite possible that the second marriages which endure might be more satisfying, on average, than first marriages.

Blended families

The term 'step-family' refers to a family in which at least one of the adults has children from a previous marriage or relationship. Sociologists more often refer to such family groups as reconstituted families or blended families. There are clearly joys and benefits associated with blended families and the growth of the expanded families which result. But certain difficulties can arise. First, there is usually a biological parent living elsewhere whose influence over the child or children is likely to remain powerful.

Second, cooperative relations between divorced people are often strained when one or both remarry. Take the case of a woman with two children who marries a man who also has two children and they all live together. If the non-resident parents insist that children visit them at the same times as before the marriage, the tensions involved in melding such a newly established household together can be exacerbated. For example, it may prove impossible ever to get all the members together at weekends, leading to resentment and arguments.

Third, blended families involve children from different backgrounds, who may have varying expectations of what constitutes appropriate behaviour within the family. Since most of the children 'belong' to two households, the likelihood that there will be clashes in habits and outlook is high. Here is a step-mother describing her experience after the problems she faced with her step-child led to separation:

> There's a lot of guilt. You cannot do what you would normally do with your own child, so you feel guilty, but if you do have a normal reaction and get angry, you feel guilty about that, too. You are always so afraid you will be unfair. Her [step-daughter's] father and I did not agree and he would say I nagged if I disciplined her. The more he did nothing to structure her, the more I seemed to nag. . . . I wanted to provide something for her, to be an element of her life which was missing, but perhaps I am not flexible enough. (Quoted in Smith 1990)

There are few established norms which define the relationship between step-parent and step-child. Should a child call a new step-parent by name, or is 'Dad' or 'Mum' more appropriate? Should the step-parent discipline the children? How should a step-parent treat the new spouse of his or her previous partner when collecting the children? These and many other matters have to be resolved in practice through suggestion and negotiation. This is one area which is particularly suited to research rooted in Morgan's family practices approach, which could help us to understand how blended families manage their relationships.

Blended families are also developing new types of kinship connection and creating new difficulties and possibilities through remarriage after divorce. Members of these families are developing their own ways of adjusting to the relatively uncharted circumstances in which they find themselves. Some authors today speak of binuclear families, meaning that the two households which form after divorce still comprise one single family group on account of the shared responsibility for raising children.

In the face of such rich and often confusing familial transformations, perhaps the most appropriate conclusion to be drawn is a simple one: although marriages are broken up by divorce, family relationships continue. Especially where children are involved, many ties persist despite the reconstructed family connections brought into being through remarriage.

THINKING CRITICALLY

From your own experience, are blended families accepted as 'normal' in modern societies? What new problems, issues and opportunities might arise for children growing up in these families?

Cohabitation

Cohabitation – when two people live together in a sexual relationship without being married – has become increasingly widespread in the developed countries. Rather than focusing on marriage, today it may be more appropriate to speak of coupling and uncoupling, as we do when discussing the experience of divorce. A growing number of couples in committed long-term relationships choose not to marry but to reside together and raise children. It is also the case that many older people choose to cohabit following a divorce rather than or in advance of remarrying.

Across Europe, cohabitation was previously regarded as somewhat scandalous and attracted a social stigma. Until 1979, the UK *General Household Survey* – the main source of data on British households – did not even include a question on cohabitation. But, among young people in Britain and wider Europe, attitudes to cohabitation are changing quite rapidly. Presented with the statement that 'It is alright for a couple to live together without intending to get married', 88 per cent of British people aged between eighteen and twenty-four in 2004 agreed, while only 40 per cent of respondents aged sixty-five and over did so (ONS 2004b).

In recent decades, the number of unmarried men and women sharing a household has risen sharply. Only 4 per cent of UK women born in the 1920s cohabited and 19 per cent of those born in the 1940s did so, but among women born in the 1960s the proportion is almost half. By 2001–2, the proportion of cohabiting unmarried women and men under the age of sixty was 28 per cent and 25 per cent respectively (ONS 2004b). The prevalence of cohabitation was highest for women aged between twenty-five and twenty-nine and for men aged between thirty and thirty-four. Although cohabitation has become more popular, analysis of research data suggests that marriage tends to be more enduring. Unmarried couples who live together are three to four times more likely to split up than those who are married.

In 2001, of younger adults aged twenty-five to thirty-four, 39 per cent in Sweden were unmarried and cohabiting, 32 per cent in Denmark, 31 per cent in France and 30 per cent in Finland. Sizeable numbers had also cohabited previously. Young adults often find themselves living together because they drift into cohabitation rather than making a calculated plan to do so. Two people who are already having a sexual relationship spend more time together and eventually give up one of their homes. Young people living together tend to anticipate getting married at some point, but not necessarily to their current partner. Only a minority of such couples pool their finances while cohabiting. Cohabitation in most countries seems to be primarily an experimental stage before marriage, although the length of cohabitation prior to marriage is increasing and more couples are choosing it as an alternative to marriage. In this respect we may expect more young people to experience cohabitation in the future compared with their parents' generation.

Staying single

Recent trends in European household composition raise the question as to whether we are becoming a community of single people. The

10.3 Bean-pole families

Julia Brannen (2003) argues that the UK has entered an age of the 'bean-pole family'. She suggests that the family household is just one part of a network of kin relations that increasingly consists of several generations. This is largely because people are living longer. She notes that, at the age of fifty, three-fifths of the UK population have at least one parent still alive and just over a third are grandparents. There is also a rise in the number of four-generation families – families that include great-grandchildren.

As the 'vertical' links between family generations are extended by increasing life expectancy, so the 'horizontal' links within generations are weakening, as divorce rates rise, fertility rates fall and people have fewer children. Brannen therefore characterizes contemporary families as long and thin 'bean-pole structures' (see figure 10.5).

Brannen found that grandparents are increasingly providing intergenerational services, particularly informal childcare for their grandchildren. Demand for intergenerational support is particularly high among single-parent families, where older generations can also provide emotional support in times of need, such as during a divorce. In turn, the 'pivot generation', sandwiched between older and younger generations, will often become carers for their parents (as they become elderly), their children and perhaps even their grandchildren.

Bengtson's (2001) research in the USA found that more people are becoming involved in extended relationships as grandchildren or grandparents, while great-grandparenthood is also becoming more widely experienced. As older social structures of class, religion and marriage become weaker and less constraining on individuals, one consequence seems to be, paradoxically, the strengthening of multigenerational family bonds. As multigenerational 'co-survivorship' increases and people spend more years in effective relationships with parents and grandparents, so family stability and continuity is actually enhanced. Bengtson also counters the stereotype that older people are a drain

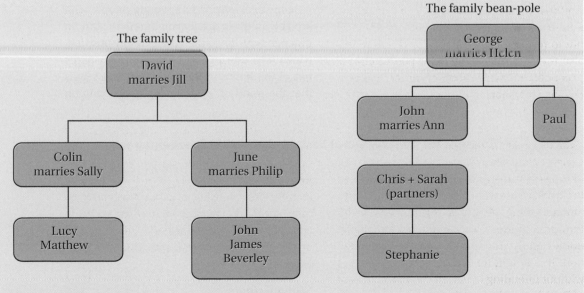

Figure 10.5 The family tree and the family bean-pole

Source: Brannen (2003).

on society's resources, pointing out that help and assistance within families flows mainly downwards from older generations to younger ones. This can take the form of financial assistance with house purchases or university fees but is just as likely to be help in times of emergencies. The nuclear family may well be in decline, but the significance of families is not.

> **THINKING CRITICALLY**
>
> Draw up a family tree for your own family, identifying which connections are more active and engaged than others – would you characterize it as a bean-pole structure? Is it inevitable that horizontal links between generations will lessen as vertical links grow closer?

proportion of one-person households in the UK increased from 14 per cent in 1971 to 29 per cent in 2001, but since then the rise has levelled off (see table 10.4). In 2014, one person households made up 28 per cent of UK households ONS (2015c: 10). Several factors have combined to increase the numbers of people living alone in modern Western societies. One is a trend towards later marriages – in 2001 people in the UK were marrying on average about six years later than was the case in the early 1970s, and by 2007 the average age at first marriage stood at thirty-two for men and thirty for women. Another, as we have seen, is the high rate of divorce. Yet another is the growing number of older people in the population whose partners have died (discussed in chapter 6). Indeed, nearly half of the one-person households in the UK single-pensioner households.

Being single means different things at different periods of the life course. A larger proportion of people in their twenties are unmarried than used to be the case. By their mid-thirties, however, only a small minority of men and women have never been married. The majority of single people aged thirty to fifty are divorced and 'in-between' marriages, while most single people over fifty are widowed.

> See chapter 9, 'The Life Course' for much more on this concept.

More than ever before, young people who are able to do so are leaving home to start an independent life rather than to get married, which was one of the most common paths out of the home in the past. Hence it seems that the trend of 'staying single' or living on

Table 10.4 Households by size, Great Britain, 1971–2011 (percentages)									
	1971	*1975*	*1981*	*1985*	*1991*	*1995*	*2001*	*2005*	*2011*
One person	17	20	22	24	26	28	31	31	31
Two people	31	32	31	33	34	35	34	35	32
Three people	19	18	17	17	17	16	16	15	16
Four people	18	17	18	17	16	15	13	13	14
Five people	8	8	7	6	6	5	4	4	5
Six or more people	6	5	4	2	2	2	2	2	2
Average household size	2.91	2.78	2.70	2.56	2.48	2.40	2.33	2.30	2.35

Source: ONS (2013c).

one's own may be part of a societal trend that values independence at the expense of family life. However, we should remember that most people do eventually marry, which suggests continuing support for the institution of marriage.

Kinship relations

As family structures become more fluid and diverse, sociologists are increasingly interested in understanding what is happening to relationships between family members. What ties exist among siblings and how do they perceive their obligations towards each other and to parents, grandparents and other family members? Indeed, who counts as kin anyway?

In an early study of kinship in the UK, Raymond Firth (1956) made a distinction between 'effective' and 'non-effective' kin. Effective kin are those with whom we have active social relationships; non-effective kin are those with whom we do not have regular contact but who form part of the extended family group. For example, we may be in contact with sisters and brothers every day but speak to certain cousins or uncles and aunts only at annual events such as birthdays. The distinction between effective and non-effective kin works with conventional family groups assumed to share biological forms of kinship, but it is less able to capture the diversity of contemporary familial relations.

It is also commonplace for people to describe certain non-family members in kinship terms. For example, close friends may

The family practice of 'sistering' changes over the life course and does not adhere to a fixed set of social norms.

be known as 'uncle' or 'aunt'. Anthropologists refer to such relationships as 'fictive kin'. An awareness of different categories of kinship blurs the boundary between family and non-family members, showing that what people perceive to be 'the family' is socially constructed. As a result, kin relations have come to be discussed in terms of the wider concept of 'relatedness', which allows cross-cultural comparisons to be made without imposing the Western idea (and ideal) of what constitutes kinship (Carsten 2000). Like David Morgan's (1996, 1999) idea of family practices, the focus of this research moves from the sociologist's descriptive categories onto people's own sense of 'relatedness'.

Mauthner's (2005) qualitative study of changing forms of 'sistering' – that is, how women perform the role of sister – interviewed thirty-seven women from nineteen sets of sisters and identified four 'discourses of sistering' that shaped the women's narratives. *Best friendship* is a discourse which identifies the sibling relationship as a very intimate one that is closer than other friendships. This comes close to the common-sense idea of the biological closeness of siblings. *Companionship* can take two forms. *Close companionship* is a type of relationship that is less actively engaged and intense than best friendships but still remains very close. *Distant companionship* represents those sibling relations characterized by low levels of contact and emotional closeness, leaving sisters' attitudes towards them somewhat ambivalent. Two related discourses – *positioned relations* and *shifting positions* – then describe the dynamics of power in sibling relations. Positioned relations are shaped largely by fairly fixed roles defined by families, including older sisters who assume responsibility for younger ones or those who become 'mother substitutes' when required. By contrast, shifting positions applies to the more fluid and egalitarian relations where the exercise of power is negotiated rather than assumed.

Mauthner concludes that the practices of sistering are varied and likely to change over

the life course as the dynamic of power shifts within relationships. Therefore we cannot assume that sibling relations are shaped by fixed biological and familial relations, even though the attitudes and ideals of many women (and men) may be influenced by society-wide discourses of women as primary care-givers. In short, the practice of sister*ing* implies an active and ongoing attempt to (re-) create sibling relations compared to sister*hood*, which can be seen as implying universal role expectations.

Families in global context

Today there is a diversity of family forms across the world's societies. In some areas, such as remote regions in Asia, Africa and the Pacific Rim, longstanding family patterns are little altered. In most developing countries, however, widespread changes are occurring. The origins of these changes are complex, but several factors can be picked out as important. One is the spread of Western culture through mass media such as television, film and, more recently, the Internet. Western ideals of romantic love have spread to societies in which they were previously unknown. Another factor is the development of centralized government in areas previously composed of autonomous smaller societies. People's lives become influenced by their involvement in a national political system, and governments make active attempts to alter traditional ways of life.

States frequently introduce programmes that advocate smaller families – as in China – the use of contraception, and so forth, as a way of tackling rapid population growth. A further influence is large-scale migration from rural to urban areas. Often men go to work in towns or cities, leaving family members in their home village. Alternatively, a nuclear family group will move as a unit to the city. In both cases, traditional family forms and kinship systems may become weakened as a result. Finally, employment opportunities away from the land and in organizations such as government bureau-cracies, mines and plantations, and – where they exist – industrial firms tend to have disruptive consequences for family systems previously centred on agricultural production in the local community.

The combination of these factors has generated a worldwide movement towards the breaking down of extended family systems and household kinship groups, though relations between kinspeople continue to be important sources of social bonds. William J. Goode (1963) argued that, as modernization spreads across the world, the nuclear family would become the dominant form, as it allows the kind of geographical mobility required by industrial capitalism. Since the late 1960s the pace of globalization and its impact on families has led to changes that Goode simply could not have foreseen, and families today are more notable for their diverse range of forms than any uniform character.

Merging or diversifying family patterns?

Recent empirical studies of family lives in a global perspective have reinforced the conclusion that diversity best characterizes family structures around the world. The Swedish sociologist Göran Therborn's *Between Sex and Power* (2004) is an extensive global history of the family over the entire twentieth century. Therborn discusses five major family types that have been shaped by particular religious or philosophical worldviews: sub-Saharan African (Animist); European/North American (Christian); East Asian (Confucian); South Asian (Hindu) and West Asian/North African (Islamic). Two others – South-East Asian and Creole American – are described as 'interstitial systems', combining elements from more than one of the five major types. The institution of the family, Therborn argues, has been structured by three central elements across all these types: patriarchy or male dominance, marriage and non-marriage in the regulation of sexual behaviour, and fertility and birth control measures in the production of demographic trends. Focusing on these three elements allows international comparisons to be made, and we can take each element in turn.

Patriarchal power *within* the family has generally declined over the twentieth century. And Therborn identifies two key periods of change. The first was during and after the First World War (1914–18), when women demonstrated by contributing to the war effort that there were no physical barriers to women's work, while the Russian Revolution of 1917 challenged the patriarchal ideology of women's 'natural' domestic role in favour of egalitarian ideals. The second was between the sexual revolution of the late 1960s and the 1975 'International Women's Year', when second-wave feminism reinforced the shifting position of women and legislative measures enabled them to participate more equally in public life.

Of course, the realities of life 'on the ground' are not suddenly transformed by the formal lifting of legal restrictions, and the extent of gender inequality remains a matter of research and debate. The second period of change, argues Therborn, was more noticeable in Europe and America, with less pronounced changes in the family situations of South Asia, West Asia and North Africa and sub-Saharan Africa. In more recent years, he sees evidence that the economic power of women has been growing in the textile and electronics industries in the developing world, which could reshape patriarchal family relations there too.

Marriage and family patterns changed across the world in the twentieth century, but Therborn's studies lead to a different conclusion from that reached by Goode. The different family types are *not* becoming increasingly similar, nor are they conforming to the Western nuclear family model, as suggested by structural functionalist theory (see the section on theories in this chapter). In most developed countries, intimate relationships have become more open and less bound by tradition, especially since the 1960s. The combination of increasing rates of divorce, high remarriage rates and more people living alone seems to disprove the thesis of a convergence of family structures, even in the West itself. Therborn also argues there is no evidence that such change and fluidity in family life is spreading globally. For example, in most of Asia people remain committed to monogamy within marriage, while in sub-Saharan Africa polygamous relationships continue to be the norm. The nuclear family, so important to functionalist theory, no longer looks set to dominate in the twenty-first century.

Finally, Therborn sees possibly the major change of the last century to be a falling global fertility rate, with the significant exception of sub-Saharan Africa. This is the product of more effective birth control methods, rising economic prosperity and the increasing movement of women into the workforce, thereby improving their own position. As we discuss in detail in chapter 9, 'The Life Course', such demographic changes will mean, for most countries, that population will decline and societies will 'age', with a higher proportion of older people living longer.

If diversity is the most notable feature of families across the world, are there *any* general patterns emerging? The most important general changes are that clans and other kin-based groups are declining in influence, there is a trend towards the free selection of a spouse, the rights of women are becoming more widely recognized at a formal level in both the initiation of marriage and within families, there are higher levels of sexual freedom for men and women, there is a general trend towards granting and extending children's rights and, finally, there is an increased acceptance of same-sex partnerships, though this is unevenly distributed across the world. We should not exaggerate the extent of these trends, as many are being fought for and are bitterly contested. The suppression of women's rights under the Taliban in Afghanistan (1996–2001) shows that these trends are not uniform or inevitable.

Conclusion

Therborn's study shows that, in spite of some convergence, families across the world are not being transformed in the direction suggested by theories of individualization and de-traditionalization. These theories seem to have most relevance to some of the developed industrial nations, where there has been an enormous amount of change in family structures and mores, attitudes to sex and intimacy, gender relations, marriage and divorce rates, and acceptance of LGBT relationships. How increasing levels of short- and long-term migration will alter the global situation cannot be forecast with any certainty.

What is clear is that the sociology of the family, which was for quite some time considered an increasingly moribund field of inquiry, has become a thriving specialism again. This is mainly a result of the major changes we have rehearsed in this chapter. These have prompted a new generation of sociologists to seek out fresh approaches and research methods that are adequate for the study of families and personal life as they are lived today. We can expect that process to continue into the future.

Yet many, perhaps most, people see family as the most significant part of their lives. And, as the movement for civil partnerships and equality of marriage for LGBT couples also demonstrates, 'family' still has an enormous attraction not just legally, but morally and emotionally too. Despite Parsonian functionalism appearing to be defunct, paradoxically it may still have an important insight to offer. Functionalism teaches that social institutions survive only if they are able to adapt to changing circumstances. In doing so, they may well look very different from previous incarnations while continuing to perform vital functions for individuals, communities and societies. However changed and diverse it may be today, the institution of 'family' (not 'the family') remains a fundamental part of most people's experience.

Chapter review

1. Outline the functionalist perspective on the family. How has this proved valuable and in what ways has it been criticized?
2. In what new directions did feminist theorizing take family studies?
3. What criticisms did David Morgan level at the conventional, institutional sociology of the family?

4. Describe what is meant by a 'family practices' approach to the study of families. In what ways is this said to be an advance on previous approaches?
5. How has the domestic division of labour changed and in which ways has it stayed the same? What evidence is there that increasing gender equality in the public sphere is not translating into the equal sharing of housework?
6. Does increasing family diversity mean the long-term demise of the nuclear family type? What grounds are there for thinking that the latter will survive?

7. Outline the main tenets of the theories of Giddens, Beck and Beck-Gernsheim, and Bauman on the contemporary transformation of intimacy. What do some think is wrong with the individualization thesis?
8. Describe the changing pattern of divorce, marriage and remarriage from the 1960s to the present day. On the basis of the available evidence, is marriage losing its value for younger generations?
9. In what ways do families of South Asian and African-Caribbean origin differ from the ideal-typical Western nuclear family?
10. The introduction of civil partnerships and same-sex marriage shows an increasing acceptance of LGBT relationships. Can these be described as extending the nuclear family model?
11. If diversification best describes families in a global context, what might this tell us about the globalization process?

Research in practice

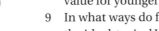

The individualization thesis in sociology argues that people are increasingly cut loose from social structures, thrown back on their own resources and forced to choose their own life paths. In the field of family studies, this thesis has come in for stern criticism from those who see it as positing an unrealistic, isolated and rational individual, detached from social relations. Read the article below, which looks at this debate from the point of view of Polish migrants to the UK. What role, if any, is left for the family in the lives of such free, mobile individuals?

Botterill, K. (2014) 'Family and Mobility in Second Modernity: Polish Migrant Narratives of Individualization and Family Life', *Sociology*, 48(2): 233–50.

1. What kind of study is this? What methods are adopted and are they appropriate for the research question?
2. How did EU membership impact on family life in Poland?
3. The authors suggest that the family plays three main roles in the young migrants' lives. What are these? Give examples of each.
4. Three 'ruptures to the individualization thesis' are identified. Discuss these in relation to the life course and migration decisions.

5   Do the conclusions drawn in the article tend to support or undermine the individualization thesis? Do you agree with the authors?

Thinking it through

 Study one of these aspects of your own family's 'family practices' as a participant observer: mealtimes, watching television/video together, a family day out, visiting relatives, performing household tasks. Write up the results as a short paper:

- describe the practice in detail
- explain its importance in sustaining family solidarity
- note any elements of family display

- discuss the influence of class, ethnicity, gender and disability on the performance.

Is it possible to separate out the structural from the agency elements of the family practice? Is either more explanatory than the other or is there a way of successfully combining structure/agency in your discussion?

Society in the arts

 1   The pleasures and conflicts of families have been documented in novels, documentaries, TV series, films and paintings over many years. Historical sociologists study these representations to gain insights into how societies reflect, promote or challenge society's mainstream moral rules and behavioural norms. Watch one week's episodes of two continuing dramas (known as 'soaps') on television. Using examples from the episodes as your evidence, consider the following questions.

To what extent do the families in these programmes accurately reflect the reality of contemporary family life that emerges from this chapter? For example, how are gender relations presented? How is the domestic division of labour dealt with? Is domestic violence a theme? How about step-families or LGBT relationships? In general, do these programmes have any underlying perspective on the thorny issue of 'family values'? Do they promote a certain view of 'the family' or is family diversity central to the stories? Do soaps merely *reflect* social reality or do they use an *idealized* or *ideological* version of it?

2   Read the novel *Intimacy* (1998) (London: Faber & Faber) by Hanif Kureishi or watch the film adaptation directed by Patrice Chéreau (2001). The book/film traces divorced Jay's weekly sexual encounters with a married woman, Claire, during which they do not speak or become emotionally involved at all. For Claire, the affair provides a type of intimacy that is missing from her marriage, but Jay becomes increasingly aware that mere sex is not enough for him, and he begins to want more from the relationship.

How might the book/film be seen as engaging with recent sociological theories of the transformation of intimacy, particularly the concepts of:

- plastic sexuality
- the pure relationship
- confluent love
- the 'normal chaos of love'

- individualization
- liquid love?

Do the people around the two main characters have any sense of contemporary 'family values'? If so, how would you characterize them?

Further reading

A good place to begin is with Deborah Chambers's (2012) *A Sociology of Family Life* (Cambridge: Polity), which is an excellent account of recent evidence and debates. An interesting comparative perspective on families is David Cheal's (2008) *Families in Today's World: A Comparative Approach* (New York: Routledge), which covers all the topics in this chapter.

Sociological theories can be approached via James M. White and David M. Klein's (2007) *Family Theories* (3rd edn, London: Sage), which also includes perspectives from other disciplines. David H. J. Morgan's (2011) *Rethinking Family Practices* (Basingstoke: Palgrave Macmillan) is probably the best introduction to family practices and associated ideas. Issues around blended families are covered in Graham Allan, Graham Crow and Sheila Hawker's (2011) *Stepfamilies* (Basingstoke: Palgrave Macmillan), and a comprehensive account of violence within families is Ola Barnett, Cindy Miller-Perrin and Robin D. Perrin's (2011) *Family Violence across the Lifespan: An Introduction* (3rd edn, New York: Sage).

Finally, you may want a resource covering the whole field and, if so, *The Blackwell Companion to the Sociology of Families* (2007), edited by Jacqueline Scott, Judith Treas and Martin Richards (Oxford: Wiley-Blackwell), has many insightful pieces.

For a collection of original readings on relationships and the life course, see the accompanying *Sociology: Introductory Readings* (3rd edn, Cambridge: Polity, 2010).

Internet links

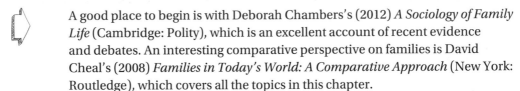

Additional information and support for this book at Polity:
www.politybooks.com/giddens

The Morgan Centre for Research into Everyday Lives is named after David Morgan. It was founded in 2005 at the University of Manchester, UK:
www.socialsciences.manchester.ac.uk/morgan-centre

Centre for Research on Families and Relationships (CRFR) is a research centre founded in 2001, based at the University of Edinburgh, UK:
www.crfr.ac.uk

425

@ **The Centre for Family Research at Cambridge University – a multidisciplinary centre which carries out research on children, parenting and families:** www.cfr.cam.ac.uk

@ **The Clearinghouse on International Developments in Child, Youth and Family Policies is based at Columbia University, New York; it provides cross-national information on family policies in the industrialized societies:** www.childpolicyintl.org

CHAPTER 11

Health, Illness and Disability

Contents

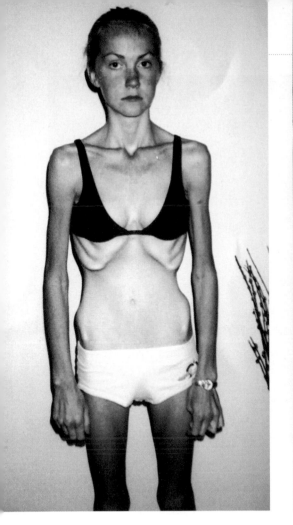 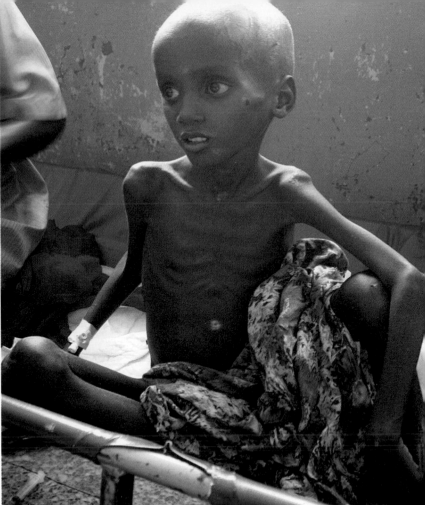

The similarities are striking in these two photographs. Both images show disturbingly thin, emaciated bodies. But the young Somalian child's life is at risk due to a desperate lack of food, while the young British woman's life is endangered because she eats so little, despite the ready availability of food. The social dynamics involved in each case could not be more different.

Starvation from lack of food is caused by factors outside the control of the individual, and today it affects only the world's poorest people. We will discuss this issue in detail in chapter 14, 'Global Inequality'. However, the British woman, living in one of the world's richest countries, is affected by anorexia, an illness with no known biological origin. Obsessed with an ideal of slimness linked to an image of the ideal body that differs from that seen by most others, she has developed a life-threatening health condition. Anorexia and other eating disorders are illnesses of the affluent societies, unknown in countries where food is scarce. Issues of health and medicine may be thought of as the exclusive province of medical science and biology, but, in fact, they are also central to an established field of inquiry known as the sociology of the body.

Sociology of the body

Throughout most of human history, a few people – saints or mystics, for example – have chosen to abstain from food for periods on religious grounds. Anorexia, on the other hand, has no specific connection to religious beliefs, and estimates suggest that about 90 per cent of people affected by it are women (Lask and Bryant-Waugh 2000). Anorexia was first identified as a disorder in France in 1874 but remained quite rare until the mid-twentieth century (Brown and Jasper 1993). Since then, along with bulimia (bingeing on food, followed by self-induced vomiting), it has become increasingly common and geographically widespread. As an illness of the body, we might think anorexia has a biological or physical cause, but a body of research has shown that social pressure to achieve a slim, 'attractive' body, especially for girls and women, is a key factor.

Before the modern era, many societies held that the ideal female shape was a rounded, fleshy one. Being slim was not desirable as it was associated with a lack of food and therefore with poverty. The social status of being 'thin' was low and, hence, not sought after. Even in seventeenth- and eighteenth-century Europe the ideal female shape was still well proportioned. Looking at paintings of this period, such as those by Rubens (see photograph), provides an illustration of what constituted female beauty at that time. The high value traditionally attached to plumpness can still be seen in some cultures, though this is rapidly changing as global communications

This Rubens painting, *The Toilet of Venus*, completed around 1613, depicts Venus, the goddess of love and beauty.

transmit images of slim, high-status celebrities from the worlds of film, music and fashion around the world (see 'Global society 11.1').

The ideal of slimness as *the* desirable female form originated among middle-class groups in the late nineteenth century but became generalized as a social ideal during the twentieth century. As Western images of 'feminine beauty' spread around the world via mass media and the Internet, so too have eating disorders. As the pace of globalization increased during the 1980s and 1990s, linking national economies closer together, eating problems surfaced among young, primarily affluent women in Hong Kong and Singapore, as well as in urban areas of Taiwan, China, the Philippines, India and Pakistan (Efron 1997). An increasing incidence has been reported

Global Society 11.1   Slim in Sudan: Female Fleshiness Loses its Allure

For centuries, female fleshiness has been prized in Sudan, with women encouraged to be plump. But many Sudanese women now aspire to being slim – and gyms are taking off in a big way.

Inside a large sweaty hall, about 20 women are taking an aerobics class. US dance-pop music blares from the speakers. You could be in just about any city in the world. Only there is not a man in sight. Sudan is a conservative country and just a few years ago, this kind of scene would have been virtually unthinkable. 'Many more people want to exercise', says fitness trainer Amal Ahmed. 'They all want to be slim . . . They want to slim their tummy', she adds. Sama Style health club is in an upmarket area of Khartoum. It's one of about 30 gyms that have sprung up in the capital in the past few years – most of them aimed exclusively at women.

[. . .]

Weight loss never used to be a priority here. As little as two generations ago, the custom was to fatten up Sudanese girls before their weddings. People living at the time of the ancient Kush civilization, which ended in AD350, favoured full bodies, says folklore historian Sadia Elsalahi – especially thick hips and thighs.

Until the 1930s, Sudanese parents would marry off their daughters as young as 11 or 12 years old, says Elsalahi, when their bodies hadn't fully developed. 'To make a girl seem older, they made her bigger and fatter.' When a girl got engaged, her family would cut a large hole in the centre of a bed. The girl would sit in the hole for a whole year being fed fatty foods and drinks. When she grew big enough to fill the hole, she would be considered ready for the wedding. There was an economic incentive to fattening

up too – a bigger bride would mean a larger payment of gold for her family. That was then.

'The idea of being fat is our fathers' and grandfathers'', says Nusaiba Abdelaziz, a student studying at Afhad University for Women in Khartoum. 'I like my body, but if I can get skinnier I will', adds her friend Marwa Salahadeen. 'I want to be really skinny.' Most men, they agree, now want to be with a woman who is slim. 'They see superstars on TV like Rihanna and Beyonce, and so we want to be like that', says Tibyan Yaseen. In recent years, a new term 'style' has entered the vocabulary in Sudan. The word is used – in English – to refer to a woman who is slim and pretty. And these young women all want to be 'style'.

There has been a significant shift in the way that young women feel about their bodies, says Nafisa Bedri, a professor at Afhad University for Women who has researched obesity and body image in Sudan. Her studies show that many have a skewed view of themselves – describing themselves as overweight, when they are underweight, and vice-versa. When you turn on the TV in Sudan, you're bombarded with adverts for weight-loss products, with images of svelte Lebanese and Egyptian women flashing across the screen, and this undoubtedly has an effect, says Bedri. 'The media has created this image among young women that they have to be very thin – they want to be skinny like the models they see in magazines and on satellite television.' Just as in the West, it's now very common for women to lose weight – rather than gain it – in time for their wedding day, she says.

Source: Adapted from Baba (2013).

in Argentina, Mexico, Brazil, South Africa, South Korea, Turkey, Iran and the United Arab Emirates (Nasser 2006). In a study reported in *Medscape General Medicine* (Makino et al. 2004), the prevalence of bulimia nervosa in women in Western countries ranged from 0.3 to 7.3 per cent, compared with 0.46 to 3.2 per cent in the non-Western world. Some sociologists argue that the proliferation of eating disorders is due to the spread of modern lifestyles around the world (S. Lee 2001).

Once again, something that may seem to be a purely personal trouble – a problem with food and unhappiness or despair over one's appearance – turns out to be a public issue. If we include not just anorexia and bulimia, but also widespread dieting and worries about bodily appearance, eating disorders are now part of the lives of millions of people around the world.

The rapid growth of eating disorders brings home the influence of social factors on health. The sociology of the body investigates the ways in which our bodies are affected by social influences, and many scholars adopt a social constructionist approach that emphasizes the ways in which meaning is created in social interactions. We all possess a physical body, but this does not exist outside social relations. Our bodies are deeply affected and shaped by social experience as well as by the norms and values of the groups to which we belong. But, conversely, social interactions cannot be reduced simply to conversations or discourse; they are also embodied. That is, they involve physical humans who use their bodies, read the body language and appearance of others, and experience the world as both a material and a social environment.

Understanding the rise of eating disorders demands an awareness of social change, a theme that runs throughout this book. The increasing prevalence of eating disorders coincides with the globalization of food production. The invention of new modes of refrigeration and container transport allows food to be stored for longer periods and to be delivered around the world without being ruined. Since the 1950s, supermarkets have stocked foods from all over the world, available to everyone who can afford them, and most foods are available all year round, not just when they are in season locally. The continuous availability of food and its relatively low cost marks a genuine revolution, potentially ending the historic problem of food scarcity and impacting on the length of the individual life course.

Over the last thirty years or so, many people in the developed countries have begun to think more carefully about diet, and not just because they want to be thinner. When all foods are available more or less all the time, we have to decide what to eat and construct a diet for ourselves – where 'diet' means the foods we habitually consume. To help construct that diet, there are many types of information – medical, scientific, family, and many more – that now bombard us. For example, while genetically modified (GM) foods are grown routinely in the USA, Brazil and Argentina, and to a lesser extent in South America and Asia, in most of Europe, GM trials are strictly regulated and consumers are anxious about their 'man-made' status. Conversely, the trend towards organically grown food shows a willingness to 'buy natural' – at least, for those who can afford to do so. Eating disorders have their origins in the opportunities, choices and profound tensions this situation generates.

Not all those affected by eating disorders are women; globally around 10 per cent are men (Nasser 2006). One intriguing question, then, is why do eating disorders affect women in particular and young women most acutely? One reason is that social norms stress the importance of physical attractiveness more for women than for men. Although men *are* increasingly presented in magazines and marketing as sex objects, such images tend to combine muscularity and leanness. As traditional male jobs have become scarce and service-sector jobs have rapidly expanded, muscularity remains a potent symbol of masculinity, while the individual body is an aspect of life over which men still have control (Elliott and Elliott 2005: 4). Drawing on the diaries of American girls over the last two centuries, Joan Jacobs Brumberg (1997) found that, when adolescent girls in the USA ask themselves the questions 'Who am I?' and 'Who do I want to be?', the answer, far more than it was a century ago, is likely to involve the body. Young American women and girls, like their counterparts elsewhere, are subject to routine media representations of idealized, thin female bodies.

Anorexia and other eating disorders also reflect the fact that women play a much larger part in the wider society than previously, yet they are still judged as much by their appearance as by their achievements. The individual feels herself to be inadequate or imperfect, and anxieties about how others perceive her become focused on feelings about the body. Ideals of slimness can then become obsessive and losing weight brings a sense of being in control. Anorexia is an extreme example of attempts to shape the body, but it is not an isolated one. People are able to modify the body through technological interventions too. From anti-wrinkle creams, hair removal procedures and botox injections to more invasive procedures such as liposuction, breast augmentation, rhinoplasty (reshaping the nose) and abdominoplasty (tummy tuck), people of all ages are now able to change their bodies according to personal preference. Techniques such as these are part of a broad range of health technologies, and their use is burgeoning in modern healthcare systems.

Innovative health technologies

The social context within which eating disorders can spread has been explored by sociologists through the concept of the socialization of nature. This refers to the fact that phenomena previously seen as 'natural', including the body, have become 'social' because they are shaped by human actions. One theme across this chapter is the creation of new dilemmas brought about by the increasing separation of the human body from 'nature', the natural environment and the body's biological rhythms via the increasing application of science and technology. Cosmetic surgery enabling people to mould and shape their bodies is an obvious example, but modern healthcare also involves a plethora of widely differing medical technologies, including blood pressure monitors, prosthetic limbs, replacement joints, ultrasound and MRI scanning, telemedicine, reproductive technologies such as IVF, organ transplants, drug treatments, surgical instruments, acupuncture needles, gene therapies, and many more.

Even this range is quite narrowly focused on *material* technologies, but we must also take account of what Michel Foucault (1988) called *social technologies* affecting the body. By this he means that the body is increasingly something we have to create rather than just accept. A social technology is any kind of regular intervention into the functioning of our bodies in order to alter them in specific ways, such as fasting, purging, choosing specific types of food (such as organics) and dieting to achieve 'good health' or a specific body size and shape. Modern life, it seems, offers more ways to intervene and mould our own bodies than ever before.

Novel health technologies also offer the potential for new approaches to the prevention and treatment of disease, and one of the most recent is experimental gene therapy. In 1990 an international research programme, the Human Genome Project, was launched, aiming to map the entire human DNA sequence – all of the genes that make up human beings. In 2003 it was announced that the project had been successfully completed – an astonishing scientific achievement with revolutionary potential. The new knowledge underpins a 'biotechnological revolution' in medicine that could see applications and bodily interventions that will genuinely transform the delivery of healthcare. Gene therapy – the use of genes (rather than drugs, surgery or medicines) to treat or prevent the onset of disease – carries perhaps the greatest potential. For example, where a mutated or non-functioning gene causes illness, gene therapy can be used to create a healthy copy that can be implanted into the body to replace it. Genes could also be introduced into bodies to help fight disease or to deactivate faulty genes that cause health problems.

A good example of the enormous potential of gene therapy was demonstrated recently in an experimental trial to treat a rare condition

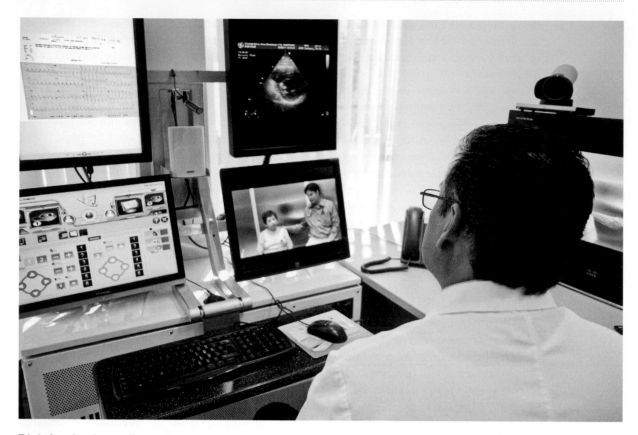

Digital technology offers great potential for taking medical expertise into hard-to-reach rural areas via Internet-based telemedicine. Here a cardiologist in Sonora, Mexico, engages in a pre-op consultation with a patient 400 miles away. However, such technology reshapes the lay–professional relationship in medicine as one of 'remote doctors and absent patients' (Mort et al. 2003).

in which the child has no functioning immune system, leaving the body unable to deal with disease. Severe combined immunodeficiency – X-linked (X-SCID) – is a genetic condition affecting only boys, and treatment usually involves stem cell transplants in bone marrow from donors; however, gene therapy is less intrusive and can avoid the use of chemotherapy. The latest reported trial involved nine children in five cities in the USA, the UK and France, seven of whom were said to be doing well up to forty-three months after the first treatment (Marcus 2014; Stephens 2014).

Clearly, successful examples of gene therapies raise the tantalizing prospect of being able to cure other inherited conditions, such as sickle cell anaemia, but they also have

enormous commercial potential. In 2012, the European Union became the first regulatory authority to approve a 'one-off' gene therapy, with the brand name Glybera, for patients with familial lipoprotein lipase deficiency (LPLD), a rare inherited metabolic condition which produces multiple debilitating pancreatitis attacks. In 2014, a genetic testing company, 23andMe, was launched in the UK. It sells testing kits which enable screening for genetic diseases and allow customers to explore their personal genome. Yet the prospect of gene testing and therapies has also raised serious concerns.

Genetic testing offers the possibility of more accurate forecasting of health risks. A good example is testing for a genetic predisposition to develop breast cancer, which identifies which people are at risk of developing the disease so they can make better-informed decisions about treatment. However, as Nettleton (2013: 220) observes, genetic testing – such as that offered by 23andMe – can create more uncertainty, turning a healthy individual into 'a "patient without symptoms", a body that has greater likelihood of developing a condition: a kind of partial diagnosis'. There may also be significant impacts on everyday life if test results indicating a heightened risk of serious conditions are shared with financial institutions, insurance companies, government departments and employers.

For some, the very language of the 'new genetics' is an issue, as it has begun to dominate debates on health and illness, leading to an individualized, medicalized and reductionist notion of what constitutes 'health' and 'illness' extracted from their social and cultural context (Conrad 2002). As a result, simple biological explanations are becoming more commonplace and, in a reversal of the recent trend towards a more equal lay–professional relationship, the medical profession is regaining its powerful position as the only legitimate source of expertise in this expanding field.

On the other hand, sociological studies have found that those with a shared biological status have also formed groups providing mutual support, lobbying governments for research funding and working with medics and scientists to understand better the specific condition and its consequences (Rabinow 1999). Patients also tend to locate genetic test results within their wider framework of understanding and may not even view them as especially significant, seeing family history as a better indicator of their health prospects. Similarly, doctors may have more confidence in, say, cholesterol readings and symptoms as described by patients than in genetic test results (Will et al. 2010).

So, despite legitimate concerns about the impact of new health technologies, the way these are understood and integrated into the existing social contexts of people's everyday lives means we cannot assume that people are simply at the mercy of a newly 'imposed' technology. Empirical studies will be necessary to uncover exactly how new technologies are used and understood.

> **THINKING CRITICALLY**
>
> Would you be prepared to take part in a programme of genetic testing? What positive results might you expect and what problems could widespread testing generate? On balance, is genetic testing a positive development for the population as a whole?

The sociology of health and illness

In Britain, a common ritual when two friends meet is to ask, 'How are you?', with the expectation that the reply will be, 'I'm well, thank you. How are you?' Once it is established that both parties are healthy, social interaction and conversation can begin. But the obvious concept of health assumed in this habitual exchange is not quite so clear once we start to ask exactly what 'health' is and how we know we are healthy. The sociology of health and illness has demonstrated that health is every bit a social as it is a biological or physiological phenomenon.

Defining health

Sociologists studying the social meanings attributed to the concepts of health and illness have found several different versions, the main ones being health as the absence of illness, disease as deviance, health as balance and health as function (Blaxter 2010). We will outline these briefly in turn.

For much of the twentieth century, health and illness were seen as opposites. Health was simply *the absence of illness*. If we are not ill, then we must be healthy. The medical profession saw illness, especially long-term illness, as leading to 'biological disadvantage' by reducing the lifespan or individual fertility, while being healthy (without illness) was seen as the normal human condition. A closely related second definition is *illness as a form of deviance*, which requires monitoring and legitimization by medical professionals to prevent the disruption of society. Such definitions came to be seen as problematic because they suggest that what is in fact a highly unusual situation – the complete lack of any illness at all – is the norm. Today there is a greater awareness that chronic illness is very widespread and that perhaps a majority of people have some form of illness, disease or impairment and yet still perceive themselves as normal and healthy and able to lead productive lives.

By contrast, many cultures around the world contain a belief that *health is a kind of balance*, both between the individual and their environment and within the individual organism. Modern scientific medicine has shown that the human body does, in fact, contain such homeostatic or 'self-regulating' elements, including the regulation of the blood supply and the triggering of the immune system when the body is attacked. Recent concern with the work–life balance in fast-moving modern societies also suggests that health can be promoted or damaged by the social environment. Although widespread, this definition has its critics. Not only is the idea of health as balance almost impossible to measure accurately, it is also highly subjective. Some people feel they have achieved a good, healthy balance in situations that others perceive as highly stressful and detrimental to their health. How can a general definition of health be distilled from such disparate experiences?

A fourth definition of health sees it as lying in people's ability to carry out their normal tasks. This is *health as function*. If individuals are able to perform the activities or functions that provide them with a good living, a satisfying life and enjoyable leisure time, then we can say they are healthy. But, if illness or injury interferes with their capacity to do these things, both the individual and society suffer as a result of their loss of functional ability. While this definition is initially attractive, the main problem is that people live very differ-

ent lives and perform a range of very different activities. Some people are engaged in hard, physical work while others sit in comfortable, heated offices. Some enjoy paragliding and rock climbing and others visit museums and spend their leisure time reading and web-surfing. Consequently, it is difficult to set down any universal concept of 'health' based on functional ability. Functional definitions of health have also been the subject of attacks from the disabled people's movement, as they are too individualistic and fail to appreciate that barriers erected by society's organization can 'disable' those with certain impairments (Blaxter 2010: 9).

An attempt at a more holistic definition of health combining social and biological aspects was devised in 1946 by the World Health Organization (WHO), which defined health as 'a state of complete physical, mental and social well-being, and not merely the absence of disease or infirmity' (WHO 2006b: 1). This comprehensive definition offers a rounded account of what it means to be healthy, but it is open to the charge that it is too utopian to be helpful. However, it does offer the possibility of comparing health across social groups within a society, and between nations across the world, along each of the dimensions listed. It is then possible to devise policies and make interventions to improve the state of public health. The definition, which has remained unchanged since it was first published in 1948, remains the basis on which the WHO operates.

Nonetheless, in spite of these definitional problems and challenges, in practice there is one perspective on health and illness that has tended to dominate all others. This is the biomedical model originating within the medical profession and on which professional medicine has long been based.

Biomedicine and its critics

For some 200 years, dominant Western ideas about medicine have been expressed in the biomedical model of health. This understanding developed alongside the growth of modern societies and can be considered one of their main features. The biomedical model was closely linked to the rise of science and reason, which took over many traditional or religious-based explanations of the world (see the discussion of Max Weber and rationalization in chapter 1). It was also a product of the social, political and historical context of the time, out of which arose state involvement in the health of whole populations.

Public health

Many societies before the modern era relied largely on folk remedies, treatments and healing techniques passed down over generations. Illnesses were frequently regarded in magical or religious terms and were attributed to the presence of evil spirits or 'sin'. For peasants and average town-dwellers, there was no larger authority concerned with their health in the way that states and public health systems are today. Health was much more a private matter, not a public concern.

The rise of both the nation-state and industrialization utterly transformed the situation. The emergence of nation-states with defined territories produced a shift in attitudes as local people were no longer simply inhabitants of the land but a population under the rule of a central authority. Therefore they were a resource to be used for maximizing national wealth and power. The health and well-being of the population affected the nation's productivity, prosperity, defensive capabilities and rate of growth. The study of demography – the size, composition and dynamics of human populations – now assumed a much greater importance. For instance, the national census in the UK was introduced in 1801 and repeated every ten years in order to record and monitor changes occurring in the population. Statistics were collected on birth rates, mortality rates, average ages of marriage and childbearing, suicide rates, life expectancy, diet, common illnesses, causes of death, and much more.

Michel Foucault (1926–84) (1973) drew attention to the regulation and disciplining of human bodies by European states. He argued that sex was both the way in which the population could reproduce and grow and, paradoxi-

cally, a potential threat to its health. Sexuality not linked to reproduction had to be repressed and controlled by the state through the regular collection of data about marriage, sexual behaviour, legitimacy and illegitimacy, contraceptive use and abortions. This surveillance went hand in hand with the promotion of strong public norms on sexual morality and acceptable forms of sexual activity. For example, homosexuality, masturbation and sex outside marriage were all labelled 'perversions' and condemned.

 See chapter 15, 'Gender and Sexuality', for a discussion of different forms of sexuality.

The idea of public health took shape in the attempt to eradicate diseases from the population or 'social body'. The state also assumed responsibility for improving the conditions in which the population lived. Sanitation and water systems were developed to protect against disease, roads were paved and attention was devoted to housing. Regulations were imposed on slaughterhouses and facilities for food processing. Burial practices were monitored and a whole series of institutions, including prisons, asylums, workhouses, schools and hospitals, emerged as part of the move towards monitoring, controlling and reforming the people. What Foucault describes is the emergence of a public health system that was concerned just as much with surveillance and discipline as it was with health promotion.

Over recent decades a 'new' public health model has emerged which shifts the emphasis from the state back onto the individual. This model puts the emphasis on self-monitoring, illness prevention and 'care of the self', so that staying healthy has come to be a responsibility attached to citizenship (Petersen and Lupton 2000). This can be seen in health-promotion messages encouraging people to stop smoking, take regular exercise, and cut down on the consumption of products containing high levels of sugar and in 'five-a-day' campaigns promoting the routine consumption of fruit and vegetables. Nonetheless, such campaigns remain firmly underpinned by advice and targets produced by medical professionals who retain much of their power to define and legitimize illness and disease.

The biomedical model

Medical practice was closely intertwined with the social changes described above. The application of science to medical diagnosis and cure was a central aspect in the development of modern healthcare. Disease came to be defined objectively, in terms of identifiable 'signs' located in the body, as opposed to mere symptoms experienced by the patient. Formal medical care by trained 'experts' became the accepted way of treating both physical and mental illnesses, and medicine became a tool of reform for behaviours or conditions perceived as 'deviant' – from crime to homosexuality and mental illness.

There are three main assumptions on which the biomedical model of health is predicated.

First, disease is viewed as a breakdown within the human body that diverts it from its 'normal' state of being. The germ theory of disease, developed in the late 1800s, holds that there is a specific identifiable agent behind every disease. In order to restore the body to health, the cause of the disease must be isolated and treated.

Second, the mind and body can be treated separately. The patient represents a sick body rather than a rounded individual, and the emphasis is on curing the disease rather than on the individual's overall well-being. The biomedical model holds that the sick body can be manipulated, investigated and treated in isolation. Medical specialists adopt a 'medical gaze', a detached approach to viewing and treating the sick patient, and treatment is to be carried out in a neutral, value-free manner, with information collected and compiled, in clinical terms, in the patient's official file.

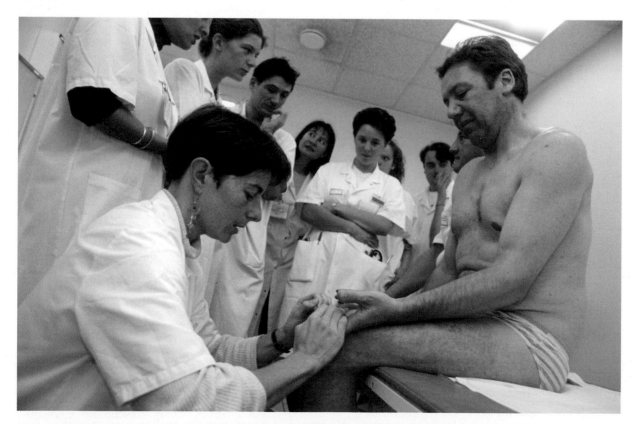

According to the biomedical model of health, to the medical profession patients represent 'sick bodies', to be observed and 'fixed', rather than 'people' in the round.

Third, trained medical specialists are considered the only experts in the diagnosis and treatment of disease. The medical profession adheres to a recognized code of ethics and is made up of accredited practitioners who have successfully completed their long-term training. There is no room for self-taught healers or unscientific treatments. The hospital represents the appropriate environment in which to treat serious illnesses, as these often require a combination of technology, medication and/or surgery.

THINKING CRITICALLY

List as many of the positive benefits of biomedicine as you can think of, then list some health problems that biomedicine has *not* been very effective in tackling. Why do you think this is the case?

Criticisms of the biomedical model

Since the 1970s, the biomedical model has been subjected to growing criticism. First, social historians argue that the effectiveness of scientific medicine has been exaggerated. In spite of the prestige that modern medicine has acquired, improvements in public health should be attributed primarily to social, economic and environmental changes. Effective sanitation, more and cheaper food, better nutrition and improved sewerage and personal hygiene were more influential in reducing infant mortality rates than medicine (McKeown 1979). Drugs, advances in surgery, and antibiotics did not significantly impact on death rates until well into the twentieth century, when public health had already improved. Antibiotics used to treat bacterial infections first became available in the 1930s and 1940s, while immunizations against diseases such as polio were developed even later. This conclusion has significant consequences for the development of health systems in developing countries.

Second, Ivan Illich (1975), a radical cultural critic and philosopher, argued that modern medicine has done more harm than good because of iatrogenesis, or 'physician-caused' illness, and its impact on people to take care of their own health. Illich asserted that there are three types of iatrogenesis: clinical, social and cultural. *Clinical iatrogenesis* occurs when medical treatment makes the patient worse or creates new problems. For example, some treatments have serious side effects, patients contract deadly infections in hospitals (such as MRSA or *Clostridium difficile*) and misdiagnosis or negligence leads to patient deaths. For example, it was reported that hospital patient deaths in England due to medical errors rose by 60 per cent between 2005 and 2009, mainly as a result of medical procedures, infections, medication errors, abuse by staff and the mixing up of patient files (*Nursing Times* 2009).

Social iatrogenesis, or medicalization, occurs when medicine expands into more and more areas of life, creating an artificial demand for its services, medicines and treatments as well as new technologies and ever-increasing healthcare costs for society. Illich maintained that social iatrogenesis leads to *cultural iatrogenesis*, where people's ability to cope with the challenges of everyday life is progressively reduced, making them more reliant on medicine and doctors and creating unnecessary dependency. In this way, people are deskilled in relation to looking after their own bodies and health, and Illich argued that the scope of modern medicine should be dramatically reduced.

Third, modern medicine has been accused of discounting the opinions and experiences of patients. Because biomedicine looks for an objective understanding of the causes and cures of specific physical ailments, there is little need to listen to the individual interpretation of patients. Patients exist as 'sick bodies' to be treated and cured. Critics argue that effective treatment can take place only when the patient is treated as a thinking, capable being with their own understanding and interpretation of health and illness. For instance, many prescription medicines are never taken, as patients either do not understand why they need them or are unconvinced of their efficacy.

USING YOUR SOCIOLOGICAL IMAGINATION

11.1 Complementary or Alternative Medicine?

Earlier in her life Jan Mason enjoyed vibrant health. But, when she began experiencing extreme tiredness and depression, she found that her regular doctor was unable to provide her with much relief:

> Before, I was a very fit person. I could swim, play squash, run, and suddenly I just keeled over. I went to the doctor but nobody could tell me what it was. My GP said it was glandular fever and gave me antibiotics which gave me terrible thrush. Then he kept saying that he did not know what it was either. . . . I went through all the tests. I was really very poorly. It went on for six months. I was still ill and they still did not know what it was. (Quoted in Sharma 1992: 37)

Jan's doctor suggested she try anti-depressants, concluding that she was suffering from the effects of stress. Jan knew that anti-depressants were not the answer for her, even though she acknowledged that her undiagnosed condition had become a great stress in her life. After listening to a radio programme, she suspected that her lethargy might be a result of post-viral fatigue syndrome. On the advice of a friend, she sought out the assistance of a homeopath – an alternative medical practitioner who assesses the state of the whole body and then, using minuscule doses of substances, treats 'like with like', on the assumption that the symptoms of a disease are part of a body's self-healing process. On finding a homeopath whose approach she was comfortable with, Jan was pleased with the treatment she received (Sharma 1992).

Jan is one of a growing number of people who are incorporating non-orthodox medical practices into their health routines. It has been estimated that as many as one in four Britons have consulted an alternative practitioner. The profile of the typical individual who seeks out

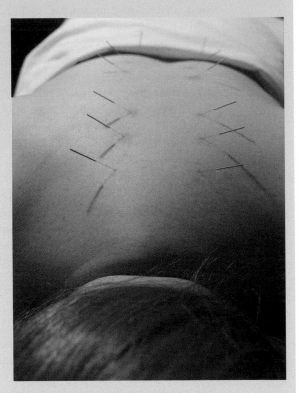

Acupuncture, a form of traditional Chinese medicine, is one of many complementary and alternative therapies which do not conform to the principles of scientific biomedicine.

alternative forms of healing is female, young to middle-aged, and middle class.

THINKING CRITICALLY

Have you or members of your family ever tried complementary or alternative therapies? What led you or them to do so? How did their approach to health differ from the biomedical model? Does it matter that they are not 'scientifically tested'?

Fourth, there has been a backlash against the belief that scientific medicine is superior to all other forms of healing, which are considered 'unscientific' and therefore inferior. As we have seen, this belief is being eroded by the growing popularity of complementary and alternative forms of medicine, particularly in situations where biomedicine has proved ineffective. This challenge is likely to grow as the 'disease burden' continues to shift towards chronic illness, which demands a collaborative relationship between physicians and patients.

Before the mid-twentieth century, the major illnesses were infectious diseases such as tuberculosis, cholera, malaria and polio, which could take on epidemic proportions and threaten a whole population. In the developed countries today, these acute diseases have been substantially eradicated. The most common causes of death today are non-infectious, chronic diseases such as cancer, heart disease, diabetes or circulatory disease. This shift is referred to as the 'health transition' (see figure 11.1). In pre-modern Europe the highest rates of death were among infants and young children, but today death rates rise with increasing age and people live longer with chronic degenerative diseases. There is also increased emphasis on 'lifestyle choices' which influence the onset of illness. Following the health transition, the biomedical model looks increasingly outdated. After all, many people who live with chronic conditions are likely to become experts in the management of the condition. Thus, the power gradient between doctor and patient becomes less steep and loses much of its previous asymmetrical character.

Many people see the rise of alternative therapies such as reflexology, hypnotherapy, chiropractic or light therapy treatments as posing a real challenge to the dominance of biomedicine, but we should be cautious about this assessment. Most people who turn to alternatives do so not as a simple substitute for, but in combination with, orthodox treatment, and will try alternatives only *after* they have been through the mainstream system and gained a medical diagnosis. The dominance of biomedicine remains firmly established within modern healthcare systems and, for this reason, most sociologists see non-orthodox techniques as *complementary* rather than genuine alternatives (Saks 1992). Indeed, some complementary therapies, such as acupuncture, have become part of many mainstream healthcare systems and are offered alongside biomedical diagnosis and treatment.

Table 11.1 Assumptions and critiques of the biomedical model

Assumptions	Critiques
Disease is a breakdown of a human body part or system, caused by a specific biological agent.	Disease is socially constructed, not something that can be revealed through 'scientific truth'.
The patient is a passive being whose 'sick body' can be treated separately from his or her mind.	The patient's opinions and experience of illness are crucial to the treatment. The patient is an active, 'whole' being whose overall well-being – not just physical health – is important.
Medical specialists possess 'expert knowledge' and offer the only valid treatment of disease.	Medical experts are not the only source of knowledge about health and illness. Traditional remedies and complementary therapies are seen by many as valid alternatives.
The appropriate arena for the treatment of complex conditions is the hospital, where medical technology is concentrated and best employed.	Healing does not need to take place in a hospital. Treatments utilizing technology, medication and surgery are not necessarily superior and may, in fact, result in more harm than health benefits.

There are a number of reasons why people turn to a complementary or alternative practitioner. Some perceive orthodox medicine as deficient or incapable of relieving chronic, nagging pain or the symptoms of stress and anxiety (as in Jan's case in 'Using your sociological imagination 11.1'). Others are dissatisfied with the way in which healthcare systems function and are fed up with long waiting lists, referrals through chains of specialists, financial restrictions, and so on. Many more are concerned about the harmful side effects of medication or the intrusiveness of surgery, both of which are mainstays of modern medicine. The asymmetrical power relationship between doctors and patients is also a problem for some patients, who feel their knowledge of their own body is not taken seriously enough during consultations and diagnosis, leaving them dissatisfied. Finally, some people have religious or philosophical objections to orthodox medicine, which tends to treat the mind and body separately. They believe that a more holistic approach involving the spiritual and psychological dimensions of health is more likely to be part of alternative therapies.

The growth of alternative medicine reflects some of the social changes occurring within modern societies. We live in an information-rich age where more and more information is available from a variety of sources, not least the Internet, that are taken into account when making lifestyle and health choices. Individuals are increasingly becoming 'health consumers', adopting an active stance towards their own health that is at odds with the passive bearing required by conventional medicine. Not only are people able to make choices about which practitioners to consult, but they also demand more involvement in their care and treatment. The number of self-help groups is increasing, and people are more likely to seize control of their lives and actively reshape them rather than relying only on the instructions or opinions of medical experts.

Some of the strongest criticisms of biomedicine have come from women, who argue that the processes of pregnancy and childbirth

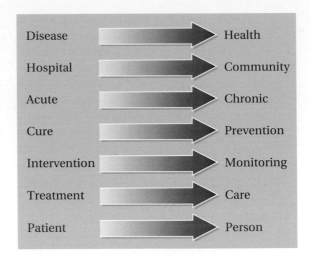

Figure 11.1 Contemporary transformations in health and medicine

Source: Nettleton (2013: 10).

have been medicalized. The medical profession has the power, as the arbiter of 'scientific truth', to bring more areas of human life under the medical gaze (see 'Using your sociological imagination 11.2' for the role of pharmaceutical companies in defining illness). Rather than remaining in the hands of women – with the help of midwives – in the home, most childbirths occur in hospitals under the direction of predominantly male specialists. Pregnancy, a common and natural phenomenon, is treated in similar ways to an 'illness', laden with risks and dangers. Feminists argue that women have lost control over the process and that their opinions and knowledge are deemed irrelevant by male 'experts' who oversee reproductive processes (Oakley 1984).

Similar concerns about the medicalization of previously 'normal' conditions have been raised in relation to unhappiness or mild depression, tiredness (frequently labelled 'chronic fatigue syndrome') and ADHD ('attention deficit hyperactivity disorder') in children. In the United States, some 2 million prescriptions per month are written for ADHD drugs (mainly Ritalin) for children, and between 3 and 5 per cent of America's children live with the condition. In Britain, 361,832

11.2 Psychopharmaceuticals: from treatment to enhancement?

Sociologists have shown that medical professionals play a key role in defining what constitutes 'illness' and how it should be treated. Yet it is also clear that pharmaceutical companies take the lead in developing treatments for emerging health problems. One recently identified health issue is fatigue or excessive sleepiness, and there are medically recognized sleep disorders such as narcolepsy – a brain disorder which causes 'sleep attacks' where people fall asleep without warning. One drug, Modafinil, made by the pharmaceutical company Cephalon in Pennsylvania, USA, was licensed ostensibly for the treatment of narcolepsy, as it helps people to stay awake. However, over time it has been used in the treatment of other conditions, such as obstructive sleep apnoea (OSA) (temporary blockage of the airway) and shift-work sleep disorder (SWSD).

The extension into more general usage for a whole new range of 'disorders' raises concerns about the power of psychopharmaceutical companies. Williams (2010: 538) argues that 'concerns have recently been expressed about the role of the pharmaceutical industry not simply in the manufacturing and marketing and manufacturing of drugs, but also in the manufacturing and marketing of disorders for these drugs to treat . . .'. If this is true, then the process of medicalization has to be seen in a wider social context, taking in the development, manufacture and marketing of medicines as well as the undoubted power of the medical profession.

Modafinil seems to be a rational solution to some of the problems generated by our 24/7 society, which demands job flexibility, long working hours and extended periods of intense concentration. Williams (2010: 540) suggests that the legitimacy of using drugs to promote 'wakefulness' rests on safety concerns: 'Would you, for example, feel safer in the hands of a chemically-enhanced physician or pilot, whose performance at the operating table or in the cockpit will not be affected by sleepiness?' But is using the drug in these situations really a 'treatment' for a real health problem, or is it best seen as a performance enhancer that enables workers to perform the range of tasks that employers now demand of them?

> ### THINKING CRITICALLY
>
> Critics challenge the power of the medical profession to redefine lifestyle matters as illnesses. Does the brief discussion above support the contention that the medical profession has great power in society? Is 'fatigue' or 'sleepiness' a health problem that demands pharmaceutical intervention in a 24/7 society?

prescriptions for Ritalin and similar drugs were issued in 2005, most of them for children with diagnosed ADHD (Boseley 2006). Ritalin has been described as 'the magic pill' which helps children to focus, calms them down and helps them to learn more effectively. Critics argue that the 'symptoms' of ADHD reflect the growing pressures and stresses on children – an increasingly fast pace of life, the overwhelming effect of information technology, lack of exercise, high-sugar diets and the fraying of family life. For critics, the widespread use of Ritalin has, in effect, medicalized child hyperactivity and inattentiveness, rather than drawing attention to the social causes of the observed symptoms.

Clearly we are living through a period of significant and rapid reform in modern medicine and people's attitudes towards the care of their own health. But whether the transformations in healthcare discussed in this section will result in a new 'health paradigm' to replace the biomedical model is unlikely. As the next section demonstrates, epidemics and pandemics pose global public health threats that will not be successfully tackled and prevented without the involvement of scientific medicine.

Pandemics and globalization

A disease epidemic can be defined as an infection that spreads beyond that which is expected within a particular community, while a pandemic is said to be 'an epidemic occurring worldwide, or over a very wide area, crossing international boundaries and usually affecting a large number of people' (Last 2001). In our era of intensified global connections and communications, pandemics may become more commonplace. If we take the whole of humanity to be a single community then the difference between epidemics and pandemics collapses, but the distinction is still helpful in order to differentiate those disease outbreaks which do not 'travel' from those that do. We focus in this section primarily on pandemics.

Disease epidemics and pandemics are nothing new. For instance, in the early fourteenth century, bubonic plague broke out in China when the bacterium *Yersinia pestis* was transmitted to humans by rat fleas, which spread the disease via merchant ships and major trading routes into Asia and Europe. In just five years, from 1347 to 1352, it is estimated that at least 25 million people in Europe died – between one-third and half of the entire population (Cunningham 2011: 101). New outbreaks continued to develop around the world until the seventeenth century. In 1918–19, at the end of the First World War, an influenza pandemic known as 'Spanish flu' (Spain was the first country to declare an epidemic) spread across Europe and other parts of the world, killing around 50 million people and disproportionately affecting young adults between twenty and forty years old – many more than had died in the war (Barry 2005: 4–5).

In recent years there have also been several potentially serious pandemics. SARS (severe acute respiratory syndrome) – a type of coronavirus that can develop into life-threatening pneumonia – emerged in Guandong Province, China, in 2003 and infected around 8,000 people around the world, killing more than 750. SARS was brought under control within nine months or so, and there have been no reported outbreaks since 2004 (Centers for Disease Control 2014). 2009 saw the spread of 'swine flu', in which the infectious agent, a new type of the H1N1 'common' influenza virus, was a combination of genetic material from humans, birds and swine 'mixed' within Mexican pigs to create a new strain. Swine flu was first detected in April and quickly spread to most countries around the world, though in many regions infection produced only mild symptoms and very few deaths. By the end of 2010 the World Health Organization announced that the pandemic was at an end. Although the original estimate of deaths from swine flu was around 18,000, the latest analyses suggest that some 280,000 people died, with South-East Asia, Africa and South America the worst affected regions (Dawood et al. 2012). Both the swine flu and Spanish flu pandemics disproportionately killed those under sixty-five, unlike common seasonal influenza, which has the most severe impact on older people.

If pandemics can be traced all the way back to the medieval period, we may think there is nothing different about the global spread of disease today. However, globalization processes, particularly more fluid population movements across nation-states and regional boundaries, may be leading to a new 'pandemic age' in which viruses are able to combine more readily, spread more rapidly and travel further than at any time in the past. With each development in transportation, from horse-drawn carriages to boats and ships, road networks and air travel, the human population has moved itself, other animals and products around the world in increasingly efficient and systematic ways. The virologist Nathan Wolfe (2011: 118) argues that, today, globalization also facilitates the widespread transmission of infectious agents, giving them 'a truly global stage on which to act'. It also means the more rapid spread of disease, because 'humans can literally have their boots in the mud of Australia one day and in the rivers of the Amazon the next.'

Globalization is not the only cause of the new age of pandemics. One factor in the initial process of animal–human transmission of some viruses is that, in parts of Africa, bushmeat – wild animals from rainforests – is widely consumed, enabling viruses to move from animals into human populations. In addition, continuing urbanization and the growth of cities has created dense human populations in which infectious agents can be spread to large numbers of people very rapidly, while industrial farming on a large scale opens up the possibility for viruses and other infectious agents to combine, producing novel forms which pose serious threats to public health. Taken together, these factors produce the conditions for more pandemics in the future. Yet globalization also enables the sharing of expertise, data from many sources, medical facilities and new treatments which could make those pandemics much less severe than in the past. Two examples illustrate the pros and cons of contemporary globalizing trends.

Preventing an Ebola pandemic

In 1976 a viral disease caused the deaths of 280 people in Zaire, now the Democratic Republic of the Congo (DRC). As it originated in Yambuku, a village close to the Ebola River, the illness was called Ebola virus disease (EVD). In the same year, EVD also led to the deaths of 151 people in Nzara in Sudan. The virus is brought into the human population by contact with wild animals and spreads through contact with bodily fluids, secretions, organs and contaminated environments such as the clothing and bedding of infected people. While fatality rates very widely, on average across numerous outbreaks, EVD proves fatal in 50 to 60 per cent of infected people. There is no approved vaccine, though some recent experimental treatments have proved successful in a small number of patients. Treatment of the symptoms can help to improve the individual's chances of survival, but, left untreated, patients are unlikely to survive. Since 1976 the WHO has identified more than twenty Ebola outbreaks, mostly in Central Africa, but none has been as deadly as that which began in Guinea, West

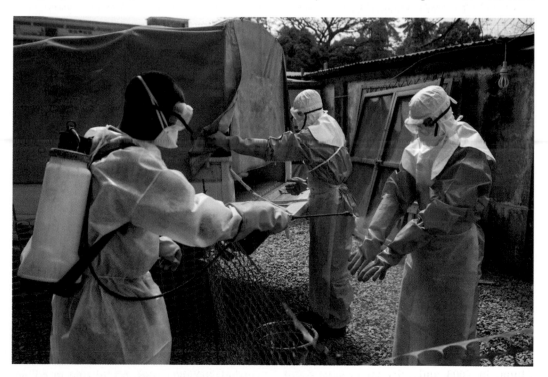

The Ebola virus enters the body through contact with fluids from infected people, so healthcare workers in West Africa donned full protective clothing to avoid catching and potentially spreading the virus. Essential protection such as this was not readily available in Sierra Leone and Liberia during the 2014 outbreak.

Africa, in December 2013, first reported in March 2014.

By 12 October 2014, the World Health Organization (WHO 2014a) estimated that around 4,500 people had died of EVD: 2,458 in Liberia, 1,183 in Sierra Leone, 843 in Guinea, eight in Nigeria and one in the USA. However, the US Centers for Disease Control (CDC) suggested that, as people were dying of the disease without attending health centres, the true figure could be at least double that total. The 2014 epidemic was thought to be the result of the virus being transmitted in bushmeat, which is a delicacy in Guinea. Monkeys, antelope and other animals, especially fruit bats, are eaten in Central and West Africa, and fruit bats are thought to be a possible 'natural reservoir' for the Ebola virus. Previous Ebola outbreaks have tended to occur in remote rural villages, but the latest episode spread quickly to urban centres such as the capital of Guinea, Conakry. Health facilities were overstretched, and a lack of basic equipment and protective clothing contributed to at least 440 healthcare workers themselves becoming infected.

Some governments in the developed world, including Canada, the USA and the UK, introduced airport screening to try to prevent the spread of Ebola, though most of the relatively wealthy countries have the advanced health facilities and resources available to control the spread of an infection. Therefore it was unlikely that a pandemic with mass fatalities would occur in all parts of the world. Outbreaks in Nigeria and Senegal were brought under control quickly, and in Guinea – which has a stronger healthcare system – the situation was stabilizing by mid-October. But in Sierra Leone and Liberia the virus spread into densely populated urban areas and became much more difficult to halt (BBC News 2014a).

Understanding Ebola (and other pandemics) is not simply about biological facts – infectious agents, transmission routes and the spread of infection; it also takes us to the heart of why global inequality remains, quite literally, a matter of life and death. As Doherty (2013: xxxvi) puts it,

> when it comes to pandemics, the pathogen – the infectious cause – is only half the equation: the other half is who we are and what we do. Thinking that way should also cause us to extend our concern about pandemics to a much greater challenge – that of achieving a more equitable and environmentally sustainable earth. In the long term, it is on this achievement that our survival as a species will depend. Pandemics are only part of the story, and perhaps not even the scariest part.

Much of the loss of life to EVD in West Africa can be attributed to poorly resourced health provision and a lack of basic services and infrastructure, such as safe, clean water and accessible roads. In Sierra Leone and Liberia, civil wars in the 1990s damaged both countries' infrastructure, leaving them without a properly functioning healthcare system and thus making them more vulnerable to a rapid transmission of the virus.

How best to bring an EVD under control before it spreads globally led some to suggest the use of big data analytics as a useful tool. One simple example was the surveillance of mobile phone data from phone masts during the outbreak to map calls to helplines, showing where treatment centres could be most effectively set up. Phones themselves could be targeted with health advice. Big data analytics could also be used in future for contact tracing (of those infected or at risk), observing population movements into and out of 'hot zones', tracking movements across borders using data from airports, ports, railways and vehicle identification systems, and collating mobile phone and social media activity. All of these sources provide essential information for health agencies and governments trying to understand the shape of an outbreak in order to bring it under control. Big data analytics is able to collate an enormous amount of data from multiple sources to build a more comprehensive picture, adding to existing methods of information gathering (Wall 2014).

Of course, big data cannot, in itself, control potential pandemics, which will always require concerted international efforts from a range of government and non-governmental agencies on the ground, but it does have the potential to make a significant contribution, which was simply not available before the digital revolution in communications. So, while globalizing processes have increased the potential for health epidemics to turn more quickly into dangerous pandemics, the same processes of global communication create the possibility that this trend can be countered. This point reminds us of Karl Marx's (1970 [1859]: 21) maxim that 'Mankind thus inevitably sets itself only such tasks as it is able to solve, since closer examination will always show that the problem itself arises only when the material conditions for its solution are already present or at least in the course of formation.'

Whether the potential of big data analytics is realized in helping to control disease pandemics depends on several factors, not least whether the global political community has the will to help. Seven months after the 2014 Ebola outbreak began, the international response was still being criticized as too slow, with a shortage of at least 3,000 healthcare beds identified in Liberia and Sierra Leone. The former UN General Secretary Kofi Anna declared himself 'bitterly disappointed' at the response from developed countries, suggesting that international assistance picked up pace only once the virus had reached the USA and Western Europe (BBC News 2014b). One conclusion we can draw is that the socio-economic situation of the countries affected has a direct impact on the scale, the severity and, ultimately, the control of any

disease outbreak. But the Ebola epidemic also demonstrates the stark disparity in available healthcare between developed and developing countries and, consequently, the differing levels of risk for people based only on their location.

See chapter 18, 'The Media', for a more detailed discussion of the digital revolution.

The HIV/AIDS pandemic

A powerful reminder that the general shift from acute to chronic conditions is not absolute came in the early 1980s, with the emergence of a new epidemic – HIV – which rapidly became a pandemic leading to the deaths of millions of adults and young people alike as HIV infections developed into AIDS. A person is said to have 'acquired immunodeficiency syndrome' (AIDS) when the number of immune cells in the body falls below a designated minimum required to fight off infections. Once that point is reached, the individual is susceptible to opportunistic infections which the body is unable to fight off, leading to serious, life-threatening diseases such as pneumonia, tuberculosis and skin cancers. AIDS is the result of damage caused by a previous infection with the human immunodeficiency virus (HIV). There is still no cure for either HIV infection or AIDS, nor is there a vaccine to prevent infection. In this situation health professionals concentrated on turning HIV infection from a potentially fatal acute illness into a chronic condition that can be safely managed. The focus has been on slowing down infection rates through public health education and developing drug treatments which delay the onset of AIDS. Transmission of HIV occurs in four main ways:

- from unprotected penetrative sex with an infected person
- from injection or transfusion of contaminated blood or blood products such as skin grafts or organ transplants from infected people

THINKING CRITICALLY

Provide some specific examples of ways in which smartphones, apps, the Internet and other digital devices and programs could be used to help prevent the global spread of disease. What problems do you foresee in relying on these during a health crisis?

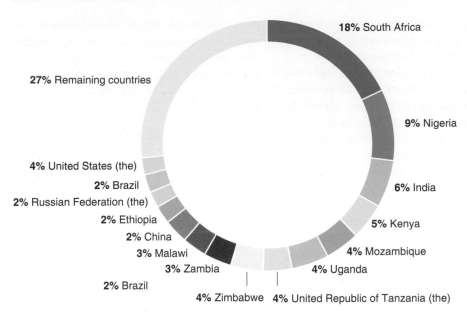

Figure 11.2 People living with HIV by country, 2013

Source: UNAIDS (2014: 17).

- from infected mothers to their babies during pregnancy, at birth or through breastfeeding
- sharing unsterilized injection equipment used by an infected person.

The WHO estimates that, at the end of 2012, some 35.3 million people around the world were living with HIV, and sub-Saharan Africa accounted for 71 per cent of those. Indeed, just fifteen countries accounted for around 75 per cent of all those living with HIV in 2013 (see figure 11.2). Since the pandemic began in the 1980s, around 75 million people have been infected with HIV and 36 million have died of HIV/AIDS-related conditions (www.who. int/gho/hiv/en/). Such bald statistics mean that this is one of the deadliest pandemics in human history, and HIV/AIDS has become a major cause of death in many parts of Africa (UNAIDS 2008). Although there is some evidence of a rising trend in the USA (where the disease was first identified in 1981), parts of Asia and Eastern Europe, the global rise in the number of people living with HIV has slowed.

New HIV infections have fallen by 38 per cent since 2001 and AIDS-related deaths have fallen by 35 per cent since 2005. However, 2.1 million people were newly infected in 2013 and the number of people living with the virus continues to rise, partly as a result of the effectiveness of anti-retroviral treatments (ART) in delaying the onset of AIDS (UNAIDS 2014: 4). Yet the drugs are expensive and, while there has been progress in widening their distribution since 2010, many people with HIV in developing countries still do not have access to the most effective treatments. For example, at the end of 2013, around 12.9 million people were receiving antiretroviral therapy, but this constitutes just 37 per cent of all those living with HIV around the world (ibid.: 14). Clearly there is some way to go before HIV can be said to be 'under control' globally, but the UN suggests that we may be at the 'beginning of the end' of the pandemic.

What are the *sociological* lessons to be learned from the HIV/AIDS pandemic? Erving Goffman (1963) argued that stigma is a rela-

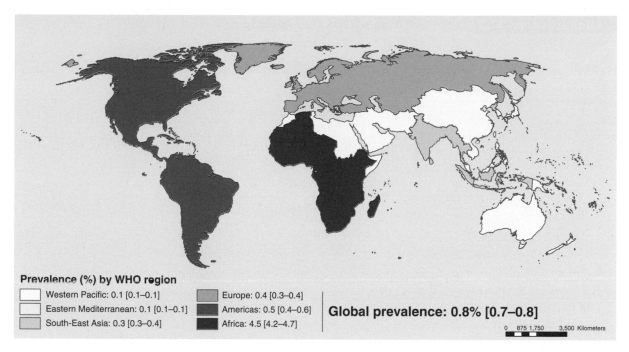

Figure 11.3   Global adult HIV prevalence (those aged 15 to 49), 2014, by WHO region

Source: WHO (2016b).

tionship of devaluation in which one individual or group is disqualified from full social acceptance. Stigmas are rarely based on valid understanding but spring from stereotypes or false perception, which may be only partially correct. In some cases the stigma is never removed and the person is never fully accepted into society. Certainly this was true of early AIDS patients, and it continues in parts of Africa.

Because HIV/AIDS was first discovered among gay men in the USA, some commentators referred to the disease as GRID – 'gay related immune deficiency' – as a 'fast-lane' gay lifestyle was said to *cause* the disease (Nettleton 2013: 57). The supposed connection between particular lifestyles and risk of infection initially led to the stigmatizing of gay men and certain lifestyles. Nettleton points out that research findings soon discredited such beliefs, showing that it was specific *practices*, such as injecting with non-sterilized needles or unprotected penetrative sex, that

transmitted the virus. Nevertheless, epidemiological interpretations of gay men as a 'high-risk group' tended to reinforce their separation from the 'heterosexual general public', thus lulling the latter into a dangerous sense of false security.

HIV/AIDS also raises important issues in relation to social inequalities. In many countries, heterosexual norms of masculinity reject the use of condoms, favouring unprotected sex as a way of 'being a man', but the consequences could hardly be more serious for heterosexual women. Like Ebola, global inequality between the developed and developing countries is emphasized by the HIV/AIDS pandemic, as HIV-infected people in the wealthy countries have a much higher chance of survival than those in poorer ones. Attempts to make anti-retroviral drugs more widely available in developing countries have had some success in recent years, though the disparity in healthcare provision remains starkly unequal.

Global Society 11.2 Is South Africa's AIDS Plan Working?

Table 11.2 AIDS in South Africa

End of Thabo Mbeki's term (2008)	Since Jacob Zuma's U-turn in 2009 (effective from April 2010)
678,550 people on Anti-Retroviral Drugs (ARVs)	**1.5 million** people on ARVs
10.3% of the population were living with HIV; this equates to **5.2 million** people	**10.6%** of the population are living with HIV; this equates to **5.38** million people
HIV-infected mothers put on treatment from **28 weeks** of pregnancy to prevent mother-to-child transmission	HIV-infected mothers put on treatment from **14 weeks** of pregnancy to prevent mother-to-child transmission
1.5 million AIDS orphans	**2.1 million** AIDS orphans

South Africa has one of the world's highest HIV rates but for many years was accused of ignoring the problem. Two years ago, President Jacob Zuma introduced some radical changes to the country's Aids policy.

Moses Sechedi lives in Soweto, one of South Africa's biggest townships. Outside the Chris Hani Baragwanath Hospital – the largest hospital in Africa – Mr Sechedi, 62, tells me that he has seen the benefits of the new policy. 'A few months ago, my younger sister became gravely ill and we rushed her to hospital. After a number of tests the doctor told us she had Aids', he says.

The family was devastated.

His 39-year-old sister suffers from mental illness and had been raped when she was younger by a local traditional healer who had promised the family he could cure her. The healer recently died of Aids-related complications but Mr Sechedi's family had not thought to have her tested until she became sick. Mr Sechedi says his sister would have died were it not for the Aids drugs she receives. 'Those pills are the reason she is alive today. She is getting stronger by the day – it is like looking at a miracle daily', he says.

'Doing the right thing'

Under President Zuma's new policy, the number of HIV-positive people like Mr Sechedi's sister receiving live-saving anti-retroviral (ARV) drugs has more than doubled from 678,500 to 1.5 million. The government of former President Thabo Mbeki, who denied the link between HIV and Aids, said it could not afford to roll out this treatment to all the South Africans who needed it.

Cost of life

Following the changes, South Africa now runs the world's largest anti-retroviral programme but some have expressed concerns about how much these drugs are costing the country. Mr Motsoaledi says his department has managed to halve spending on ARVs. Instead of paying out 8.8bn rand ($104.5m; £67.2m) on the drugs over the next two years, South Africa will now spend just 4.2bn – less than 4% of the 2011 health budget of 112.6bn rand.

But despite the progress, Aids remains South Africa's leading cause of death. Last year it killed more than 260,000 people – almost half of all those who died in the country. The TAC says it will monitor the government to makes sure that it builds on its progress. 'We need to make sure that the government stays committed to this programme', says Mr Low.

Source: Extracted from Fihlani (2011).

The winner of Botswana's 'Miss HIV Stigma-Free Beauty Pageant', 2007, which sought to end the stigmatizing of HIV-positive women and encourage discussion of HIV/AIDS.

 See chapter 14, 'Global Inequality', for a wider discussion of these issues.

The concept of 'risk' has become a central one in sociological research into lifestyles, health and medicine since the late twentieth century, and the emergence of HIV/AIDS was instrumental in creating a more 'risk-aware' population. Indeed, Ulrich Beck (1999) argued that we are moving into a 'world risk society' in which people will spend more effort and use more resources dealing with risks than ever before. If this is the case, then anticipating pandemics and planning for them must be one of the most important tasks for all governments and international governmental organizations such as the European Union, WHO and United Nations.

Sociological perspectives on health and illness

Sociologists ask how illness is experienced and interpreted by the sick person and those with whom they come into contact. The patterns of everyday life are temporarily modified by illness and interactions with others become transformed. This is because the 'normal' functioning of the body is a vital, but often unnoticed, part of our lives. We depend on our bodies to operate as they should, and our very sense of self is predicated on the expectation that our bodies will facilitate, not impede, social interactions and daily activities.

Illness has both personal and public dimensions. When we become ill, not only do we experience pain, discomfort and confusion, but others are affected too. People in close contact may extend sympathy, care and support or they may struggle to make sense of our illness or to find ways to incorporate it into the pattern of their own lives. Others with whom we come into contact may also react to illness, and their reactions help to shape our own interpretation, even posing a challenge to our sense of self.

Two ways of understanding the experience of illness have been particularly influential in sociological research. The first, associated with the functionalist school, sets out the norms of behaviour which individuals adopt when they are ill (see 'Classic studies 11.1'). The second perspective, favoured by symbolic interactionists, is the attempt to reveal the interpretations ascribed to illness and how these meanings influence people's actions and behaviour.

> For more on functionalist theory see chapter 1, 'What is Sociology?', and chapter 3, 'Theories and Perspectives'.

Illness as 'lived experience'

Many sociologists have applied a symbolic interactionist approach to health and illness in order to understand how people experience being ill or perceive the illness of others. How do people react and adjust to news about a serious illness? How does having a chronic illness affect the way people are treated by others and thus their self-identity? People in industrialized societies are now living longer but, as a result, develop more chronic illnesses, and a growing number of people are faced with the prospect of living with illness over a long period of time. Sociologists have studied how illness in such cases becomes incorporated into an individual's personal biography.

Certain illnesses demand regular treatments or maintenance which can affect daily routines. Dialysis, insulin injections or taking large numbers of pills all demand that individuals adjust their schedules in response. Other illnesses can have unpredictable effects on the body, such as the sudden loss of bowel or bladder control or violent nausea. Individuals affected by such conditions are forced to develop strategies for managing their illness in day-to-day life. These include both practical considerations – such as always noting the location of the toilet in unfamiliar places – as well as skills for managing interpersonal relations, both intimate and routine. Although the symptoms of the illness can be embarrassing and disruptive, people develop coping strategies to live life as normally as possible (Kelly 1992).

At the same time, the experience of illness can bring about transformations in people's sense of self. These develop through the reactions of others to the illness and through imagined or perceived reactions. For the chronically ill or disabled, social interactions which are routine for many people become tinged with risk or uncertainty. The shared understandings that underpin standard, everyday interactions are not always present when illness or disability is a factor, and interpretations of common situations may differ substantially. An ill person may be in need of assistance but not want to appear dependent, for example. An individual may feel sympathy for someone who has been diagnosed with an illness but be unsure whether to address the subject directly. The changed context of social interactions can precipitate transformations in self-identity.

Illness can place enormous demands on people's time, energy, strength and emotional reserves. Sociologists have investigated how individuals manage their illness within the overall context of their lives (Jobling 1988; Williams 1993). Corbin and Strauss (1985) studied the regimes of health which the chronically ill develop in order to organize their daily lives and identified three types of 'work' contained in people's everyday strategies. *Illness work* refers to those activities involved in managing their condition,

Classic Studies 11.1 Talcott Parsons on society's 'sick role'

The research problem

Think of a time when you have been ill. How did other people react to you? Were they sympathetic? Did they try to help you get well again? Did you feel they expected you to get better too quickly? The American theorist Talcott Parsons (1952) argued that illness has a clear social as well as an individual dimension. People are not only individually sick, they also have to learn what society expects of them when they are sick; and, if they fail to conform, they may be stigmatized as engaging in deviant behaviour.

Parsons's explanation

Parsons argued that there exists a sick role – a concept he used to describe the patterns of behaviour which the sick person adopts in order to minimize the disruptive impact of illness to society. Functionalism holds that society usually operates in a smooth and consensual manner, but a sick person might not be able to perform all their normal responsibilities or might be less reliable and efficient than usual. Because sick people are not able to carry out their normal roles, the lives of those around them are disrupted: work tasks go unfinished, causing stress for co-workers; responsibilities at home are not fulfilled; and so on.

According to Parsons, people *learn* the sick role through socialization and enact it – with the cooperation of others – when they fall ill. There are three pillars of the sick role.

1 The sick person is not personally responsible for being sick. Illness is seen as the result of physical causes and the onset of illness is unrelated to the individual's actions.
2 The sick person is entitled to certain rights and privileges, including withdrawal from normal responsibilities, since they bear no responsibility for being ill. For example, they might be 'released' from normal duties around the home, and behaviour that is not as polite or thoughtful as usual is excused. The sick person gains the right to stay in bed or to take time off from work.

"We're running a little behind, so I'd like each of you to ask yourself, 'Am I really that sick, or would I just be wasting the doctor's valuable time?'"

3 The sick person must work to regain health by consulting a medical expert and agreeing to become a 'patient', so the sick role is a temporary and 'conditional' one, contingent on the sick person actively trying to get well. The patient is expected to cooperate and follow 'doctor's orders', but a sick person who refuses or does not heed medical advice puts the legitimacy of their sick role status in jeopardy.

Parsons's concept has been refined by later sociologists, who have found that the experience of the sick role varies with type of illness. Thus, the added rights and privileges which are part of the sick role may not be uniformly granted. Freidson (1970) identified three versions of the sick role, which correspond to different types and degrees of illness.

The *conditional* sick role applies to people affected by a temporary condition from which they can recover. For example, someone with bronchitis would reap more benefits than those with a common cold. The *unconditionally legitimate* sick role refers to individuals with incurable illnesses. Because the sick person cannot 'do' anything to get well, they are entitled to occupy the sick role in the long term. The unconditionally legitimate role would apply to those affected by alopecia (hair loss) or severe acne. In both cases there are no special privileges but, rather, an acknowledgement that the individual is not responsible for their illness. The onset of cancer or Parkinson's disease may result in important privileges and the right to abandon many or most duties.

The final sick role is the *illegitimate role*, which occurs when an individual has a disease or condition that is stigmatized by others. In such cases, there is a sense that the individual might somehow bear responsibility, and rights and privileges are not necessarily granted. Alcoholism, smoking-related illness and obesity are possible examples of stigmatized illnesses which affect a person's right to assume the sick role.

Critical points

Parsons's concept of the sick role has been very influential. It reveals clearly how the sick person is an integral part of their larger social context. But there are a number of important criticisms which can be levelled against it.

Some writers have argued that the sick role 'formula' is unable to capture the *experience* of being ill. Others point out that it cannot be applied universally. For example, it does not account for instances when doctors and patients disagree about a diagnosis or have opposing interests. Furthermore, taking on the sick role is not always a straightforward process. Some individuals have symptoms that are repeatedly misdiagnosed and are denied the sick role until a clear diagnosis is made. In other cases, social factors such as race, class and gender can affect whether, and how readily, the sick role is granted. In sum, the sick role cannot be divorced

from the social, cultural and economic influences which surround it, and the realities of illness are more complex than the model suggests.

The increasing emphasis on lifestyle and health means that individuals are seen as bearing ever greater responsibility for their own well-being, which contradicts the first premise of the sick role – that individuals are not to blame for their illness. Moreover, in modern societies, the shift away from acute infectious disease towards chronic illness has made the sick role less applicable. Whereas it has been useful in understanding acute illness, it is less useful today in the case of chronic illness, as there is no single role for chronically ill or disabled people to adopt.

Contemporary significance

The concept of a 'sick role' remains valuable as it allows us to link individual illness to wider healthcare systems. Bryan Turner (1995) argues that most societies *do* develop sick roles but that these differ. In Western societies, an individualized sick role exists, which means that hospital stays for non-life-threatening conditions are generally quite short, visiting hours are limited and the number of visitors is strictly controlled. However, in Japan, a more communal sick role is the norm. Patients tend to stay in hospital longer after their medical treatment is completed, and the average hospital stay is much longer than in Western societies. Hospital visits are also more informal, with family and friends often eating together and staying for longer periods. Turner suggests that we can still learn much about the social aspects of health and illness from such a comparative sociology of sick roles.

such as treating pain, doing diagnostic tests or undergoing physical therapy. *Everyday work* pertains to the management of daily life – maintaining relationships with others, running household affairs and pursuing professional or personal interests. *Biographical work* involves activities that the ill person does as part of building or reconstructing their personal narrative, incorporating the illness

into their life, making sense of it and developing ways of explaining it to others. This process can help people restore meaning and order to their lives after coming to terms with the knowledge of chronic illness.

Studies of the way illness is experienced by individuals have been extremely valuable in showing how illness can disrupt personal biographies and require the rebuilding of relationships. However, perhaps the most significant finding of the sociology of health is the discovery of broad patterns of illness and health which are consistently related to the social inequalities of social class, gender and ethnicity.

The social basis of health

The twentieth century saw a significant rise in life expectancy for the industrialized countries, and the WHO suggested a rise in average life expectancy at birth for the global population to seventy years by 2012. Of course, such blunt averages hide major inequalities of health (see chapter 9, 'The Life Course'). Many of the advances in public health have been attributed to the efficacy of modern medicine, and there is a widely held assumption that medical research will continue to be successful in finding the biological causes of disease and developing effective treatments. On this view, as medical knowledge and expertise grow, we will see sustained improvements in public health. Although this perspective has been extremely influential, it is unsatisfactory for sociologists. Improvements in public health over the past century cannot conceal the fact that health and illness are not distributed evenly. Some social groups enjoy much better health than others, and health inequalities are linked to larger socio-economic patterns.

Sociologists and specialists in social epidemiology – the study of the distribution and incidence of disease and illness within populations – try to explain the link between health and variables such as social class, gender, race, age and geography. Although most scholars acknowledge the correlation between health and social inequalities, there is no agreement about the nature of this connection or how health inequalities should be addressed. One of the main areas of debate concerns the relative importance of *individual variables*, such as lifestyle, behaviour and diet, and *environmental* or *structural* factors, such as social class position, income distribution and poverty. In this section we look at health variations according to social class, gender and ethnicity and review some competing explanations for their persistence.

Social class and health

Research studies consistently report a clear relationship between patterns of mortality and morbidity (illness) and social class. In fact, Cockerham (2007: 75) argues that 'Social class or socioeconomic status (SES) is the strongest predictor of health, disease causation, and longevity in medical sociology.' In the UK, an influential nationwide study – the Black Report (DHSS 1980) – was important in publicizing the extent of class-based health inequalities, which many people found shocking in such a wealthy country. Although there was a trend towards better health in society as a whole, significant disparities existed across classes, affecting health indicators including birth weight, blood pressure, risk of chronic illness and death from accidents. People from higher socio-economic groups are, on average, healthier, taller and stronger and live longer than those in lower socio-economic positions (Drever and Whitehead 1997).

An analysis by the Office for National Statistics (ONS 2011e) looked at health inequality in England and Wales over a twenty-five-year period from 1982 to 2006, when the general life expectancy of all class groups was rising (see figures 11.4 and 11.5). Surprisingly, perhaps, the study found that inequalities in male life expectancy actually *widened* with the gap in life expectancy between routine workers (class 7) and higher management/professionals (class 1), rising from 4.9 years in the period 1982–6 to 6.2 years in 1997–2001. In 2002–6, average life expectancy at birth for men in class 1 was 80.4 years, compared to just 74.6 years for those in class 7. Life expectancy differences between women in the top and bottom classes changed little over the period, with the gap remaining stable at around four years – 83.9 years for those with parents in the highest class group and 79.7 years for those in routine occupations.

A recent analysis of 2011 Census data also found a large 'health gap' between class 1 and class 7 based on self-reported health condition (figure 11.7, p. 459). More than 30 per cent of men and women in class 7 reported their own health as 'not good', with less than 15 per cent of those in class 1 doing the same (ONS 2013a). This is, of course, a subjective measure of people's health, but it gains support from other studies showing a clear class gradient in male deaths from lung cancer, drug dependency, diabetes and accidents (White et al. 2003). A similar class gradient is evident in mental health, with research finding that 'those in the lowest social class are over twice as likely to suffer from a neurotic disorder as those in the highest social class' (Nettleton 2013: 159).

Clairvoyants may not be able to predict exactly when we will die, but social scientists have established that the class position into which we are born is a major determinant of how long, on average, we can expect to live. Studies from other developed countries also consistently report a clear class gradient to health and life expectancy. Yet, despite a growing amount of research, scholars have not been entirely successful in locating the actual mech-

anisms that connect the two. Several competing explanations have been advanced for the causes behind the well-established correlation.

The Black Report adopted a *materialist* explanation, which sees the cause of health inequalities in large social structures, such as poverty, wealth and income distribution, unemployment, housing and poor working conditions. Health inequalities are therefore understood as the result of material deprivation, and reducing them requires addressing these root causes. Consequently, the Black Report suggested the need for a comprehensive anti-poverty strategy and improvements in education.

The Conservative government (1979–90) was dismissive of the Black Report's findings and shifted the focus onto cultural and behavioural explanations, emphasizing the importance of freely chosen individual lifestyles. For example, lower classes tend to engage in unhealthy behaviours such as smoking, eating a poor diet and consuming high levels of alcohol. Some proponents of this approach argue that individual behaviours are embedded within their social class context and are not entirely 'free' choices, but,

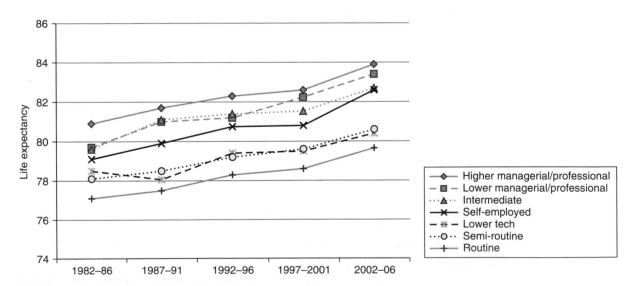

Figure 11.4 Life expectancy in England and Wales by National Statistics socio-economic classification, males at birth, 1982–2006

Source: ONS (2011e: 2).

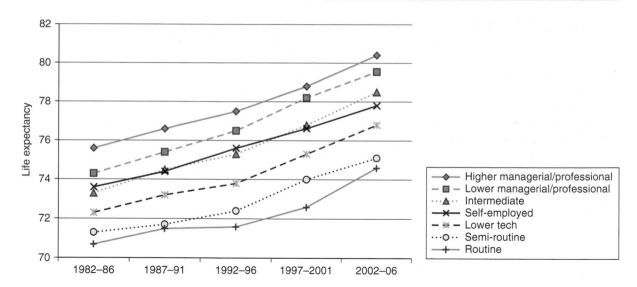

Figure 11.5   Life expectancy in England and Wales by National Statistics socio-economic classification, females at birth, 1982–2006

Source: ONS (2011e: 3).

even so, there has been continuing emphasis on public health campaigns to influence lifestyles. Anti-smoking initiatives, healthy eating and exercise programmes are examples of efforts to change behaviour, exhorting individuals to take responsibility for their own health. Yet critics argue that the structural constraints of low incomes and class position are not given enough weight. Fresh fruit and vegetables, for instance, which are central to a good diet, are more expensive than many foods that are high in fat and cholesterol. The highest consumption of 'healthy' food is, unsurprisingly, among high-income groups.

The 1997 Labour government (1997–2010) acknowledged both cultural and material influences on people's health and commissioned another study – the Acheson Report (Acheson 1998) – which confirmed that, for many aspects of health, inequality had worsened since the 1970s. Drawing on this evidence, the government's White Paper *Saving Lives: Our Healthier Nation* (DoH 1999) emphasized the many diverse influences – social, economic, environmental and cultural – which work together to

produce ill health (illustrated in figure 11.6). It also proposed new initiatives linking health with unemployment, substandard housing and education in order to address not just the symptoms of poor health but its causes.

In 2003, the government launched its 'Spearhead Initiative', targeting areas with the highest levels of deprivation, which covered 28 per cent of the national population and 44 per cent of black and other minority ethnic groups. The aim was to achieve a 10 per cent reduction in class-based health inequality in infant mortality and life expectancy by 2010 (DoH 2003). By early 2009 it was announced that only 19 per cent of the selected areas were on target to achieve this aim, while, in 66 per cent, the health inequality gap was actually widening compared with the national average (Health Inequalities Unit 2009). Why should the health inequality gap widen at the same time that the general health of the nation was improving? The explanation seems to be that wealthier social classes are more likely to act on the messages of public health-promotion campaigns and so their health

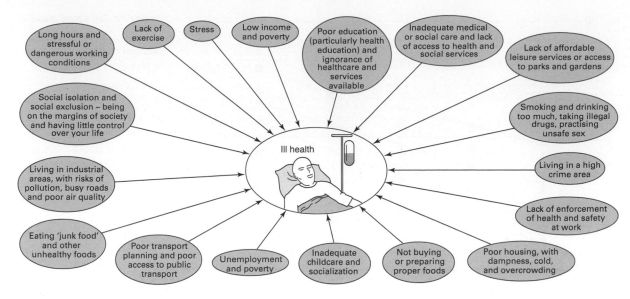

Figure 11.6 The cultural and material influences on health

Source: Browne (2005: 410).

is improving faster than that of less well-off social classes. Paradoxically, therefore, it appears that general health-promotion campaigns may widen rather than narrow health inequalities.

In February 2010, another government-commissioned report, *Fair Society, Healthy Lives* (led by Sir Michael Marmot), was published. The research team was charged with assembling evidence to advise the government on a health inequalities strategy for England. Looking at statistical evidence on both life expectancy and 'disability-free-life-expectancy', the report yet again confirmed that there existed a steep class gradient in health and that reducing this would be beneficial for society as a whole. However, it rejected the idea that this could be achieved by focusing on the most deprived areas alone. Instead, the report argued that 'proportionate universalism' was needed – that is, universal measures across all social groups, but with the scale and intensity varying according to the level of disadvantage experienced.

The Marmot Review called for action across a range of social and economic inequalities that impact on health, including people's material circumstances, social environment, psychosocial and biological factors, as well as education, occupation, income, gender, ethnicity and race (Marmot 2010: 10). The authors argued that it is time to put sustainability and well-being before economic growth, though critics point out that government action across such a broad front seems unlikely, particularly in difficult economic circumstances. However, the early years of life were identified as the main priority for laying down a strong foundation for future health, and the report said that the proportion of government expenditure should increase in this area to give children the best possible start.

> **THINKING CRITICALLY**
>
> If the general state of health is improving for all social classes, does it matter that some classes are doing better than others? List some of the potential social and economic consequences of a widening class-based health gap which might persuade governments that narrowing the gap is a worthwhile policy priority.

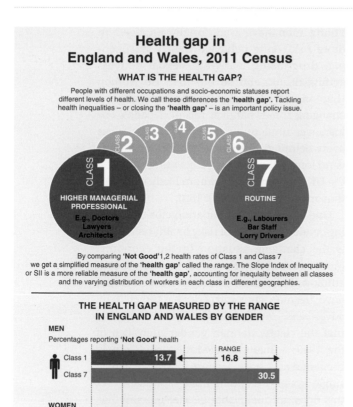

Figure 11.7   The 'health gap' in England and Wales from 2011 Census data

Source: Browne ONS (2013a).

Gender and health

Disparities in health between men and women have been noted in many research studies. For example, women generally enjoy a longer life expectancy than men in almost every country in the world (UNDP 2004), while causes of death and patterns of illness in men and women exhibit key differences. In the developed world, although it affects men more than women, heart disease is still the most frequent killer of both sexes under the age of sixty-five. Men have higher rates of death as a result of accidents and violence and are also more prone to drug and alcohol dependency.

Material circumstances influence women's health status, but this has traditionally been a difficult factor to gauge as the evidence on women's health is not as extensive as that on men. Many studies classify women according to the social class of their husbands, thereby producing a distorted picture of women's health (see chapter 12, 'Stratification and Social Class'). We do know, however, that women are more likely to seek medical attention and have higher rates of self-reported illness than men. Yet this pattern is not repeated across the life course. Using ONS data for England and Wales, in 2002 twice as many women as men aged sixteen to forty-four visited a doctor in the two weeks prior to the survey, but this gap virtually disappeared in the forty-five to sixty-four age range (Nettleton 2013: 168). It has been suggested that much of the gender difference among those aged sixteen to forty-four can be accounted for by routine health visits related to reproduction rather than indicating more ill health (MacFarlane 1990).

The gendered pattern is different in South Asian countries such as Afghanistan, Bangladesh, India and Pakistan, where the life expectancy differential is greatly reduced (Arber and Thomas 2005). Explanatory factors here include conflict and wars, nutritional deficiencies, disadvantages related to lower social status, and limited access to medical services for women (Cockerham 2007).

Women in the developed countries report twice as much anxiety and depression as men. According to some scholars, the multiple roles which women perform – domestic work, childcare and professional responsibilities – increase their levels of stress, contributing to higher rates of illness. Doyal (1995) suggested that women's lives are inherently different from men's in terms of domestic work, sexual reproduction, childbearing and mothering, and regulating fertility through birth control, though this may be changing as more women enter the workforce. Doyal argues that what matters in the shaping of women's health is the cumulative effect of these tasks. Therefore, any analysis of women's health should focus on the interaction between social, psychological and biological influences.

Heather Graham (1987, 1994) studied the effects of stress on the health of white working-class women, highlighting the fact that women at the lower socio-economic end of the spectrum have less access to support networks in times of life crisis than do middle-class women. Working-class women tend to encounter life crises such as job loss, divorce, eviction from housing or the death of a child more often than other groups but, generally, have weaker coping skills and fewer outlets for their anxiety. Not only is the resulting stress harmful both physically and psychologically, but some of the coping strategies adopted are damaging. For example, smoking is a way of reducing tension when personal and material resources are stretched to breaking point. Thus it increases the health risk for women and their children while simultaneously allowing them to cope under difficult circumstances.

Ann Oakley and her colleagues (1994) studied the role of social support in the health of socially disadvantaged women and children in four English cities. They found that the relationship between stress and health applies both to major life crises and to smaller problems, and that it is felt particularly acutely in the lives of working-class people. Oakley notes that social support – such as counselling services, hotlines or home visits – can act as a 'buffer' against the negative health consequences of stress commonly experienced by women. Other studies have shown that social support is an important factor that can help people adjust to disease and illness and that women are more likely to form and maintain self-help communities, including female communities in cyberspace, such as the mothers' forum mumsnet. com (Ell 1996; Drentea and Moren-Cross 2005).

There is some research that shows men are not as vigilant about their own health and tend to ignore health problems for longer.

Young men have traditionally engaged in more risk-taking behaviour, such as speeding, drug-taking, early-age sexual activity, getting drunk, and so on, than do women (Lupton 1999). However, this pattern has been changing somewhat over recent decades. For instance, until quite recently smoking was overwhelmingly associated with men, but this is no longer the case; among young adults in the UK, women are now more likely to smoke than men (Nettleton 2013: 169).

One of the main explanations for the shifting gendered pattern of risky health behaviour is the changing situation in the economy. More women have moved into the same employment sectors as men and, as a result, have become consumers to be targeted by advertisers. Annandale (2009: 8–9) suggests that the clearly defined gender identities of the 1950s – male breadwinners and female homemakers – have become blurred in a 'new single system' of patriarchal capitalism. Yet this does not mean that gender equality has been or is being achieved. Rather, the argument is that the old binary system of men's and women's roles has broken down, leaving a complex, uncertain situation with many new freedoms for women but also new controls. For example, as more young women participate in the night-time economy, consume more alcohol and smoke, they are redefined as irresponsible and unattractive 'ladettes' determined to outdo their male counterparts in bad behaviour. Hence, increasing diversity and fluidity in gender relations is tempered by the continuing salience of the old ideology of 'different spheres'.

One area where women's health *has* been found to be worse than men's is in some minority ethnic groups. Not only is self-reported illness higher among ethnic minority groups than in the general population, but within some groups, notably Pakistani and Bangladeshi communities, women report more ill health than men (Cooper 2002). Such findings illustrate some of the complexity produced by intersecting social inequalities of class, gender and ethnicity, and we can expect future research on health inequalities to become increasingly sensitive to intersectionality.

Ethnicity and health

Although health in the developed societies is ethnically patterned, our understanding of the relationship between ethnicity and health is partial at best. An increasing number of sociological studies are being conducted in this area, but the evidence remains inconclusive. In some cases, trends that have been attributed to membership of an ethnic group may have ignored other factors, such as class or gender, which may also be highly significant.

Nevertheless, the incidence of certain illnesses is higher among individuals from African-Caribbean and Asian backgrounds. Mortality from liver cancer, tuberculosis and diabetes is higher among these populations than among whites. African Caribbeans have higher than average rates of hypertension and sickle-cell anaemia (an inherited disorder affecting red blood cells), while people from the Indian subcontinent experience higher mortality from heart disease.

Some scholars have turned to cultural and behavioural accounts to explain ethnic health patterning. In a similar way to cultural explanations of class-based health inequalities, emphasis is placed on individual and group lifestyles that are considered to result in poorer health. These are often seen as linked to religious or cultural beliefs, such as dietary and cooking habits or consanguinity (the practice of intermarriage within families at the level of second cousins). Critics argue that cultural explanations fail to identify the real problems facing ethnic minorities in the industrialized societies – namely, the structural inequalities and the racism and discrimination encountered in healthcare systems.

Social-structural explanations for ethnic patterning in health in many European societies focus on the social context in which African Caribbeans and Asians live. These groups frequently experience multiple disadvantages which can be harmful to their health, among them poor or overcrowded housing conditions, high rates of unemployment, and over-representation in hazardous, low-paying occupations. Such material factors are then compounded by the effects of racism, experienced either directly in the form of violence, threats or discrimination or in 'institutionalized' forms. In short: 'Ultimately, what makes race important in a causal sense for health is its close association with class circumstances. Subtract affluence or lack thereof from considerations of race and the causal strength of race in health and disease is severely minimized' (Cockerham 2007: 143).

Nonetheless, institutional racism has been found in the provision of healthcare (Alexander 1999). Ethnic groups may experience unequal or problematic access to health services. Language barriers can present difficulties if information cannot be relayed effectively; culturally specific understandings of illness and treatment are often not considered by professionals within the health service. The National Health Service has been criticized for not requiring more awareness of cultural and religious beliefs among its staff and for paying less attention to diseases that occur predominantly in the non-white population.

 Institutional racism is discussed in detail in chapter 16, 'Race, Ethnicity and Migration'.

There is no consensus on the connection between ethnicity and health inequality, and much research still remains to be done. Yet it is clear that this issue must be considered in relation to larger social, economic and political factors which affect the experience of ethnic minority groups in the developed societies.

Health and social cohesion

In chapter 1 we saw that, for Durkheim, social solidarity is one of society's most crucial features. In his study of suicide, for example, he found that individuals and groups that were well integrated into society were less likely to take their own lives than others. In trying to unravel the causes of health inequalities today, a growing number of sociologists are turning their attention to the role of social cohesion in promoting good health.

Richard Wilkinson (1996) argues that it is not the richest societies in the world that are the most healthy, but those in which income is distributed most evenly and levels of social integration are highest. In surveying empirical data from countries around the world, he notes a clear relationship between mortality rates and patterns of income distribution. Inhabitants of countries such as Japan and Sweden, which are some of the most egalitarian in the world, enjoy better levels of health on average than do citizens of countries where the gap between the rich and the poor is more pronounced, such as the United States and the UK.

In Wilkinson's view, the widening gap in income distribution undermines social cohesion and makes it more difficult for people to manage risks and challenges. Heightened social isolation and the failure to cope with stress are reflected in health indicators. Social factors – the strength of social contacts, ties within communities, the availability of social support, a sense of security – are the main determinants of the relative health of a society. During the 2010 British election campaign, the Conservative Party leader David Cameron drew on the theme of Britain as a 'broken society' that needed fixing. But according to Wilkinson and Pickett (2010: 5):

> Long before the financial crisis which gathered pace in the later part of 2008, British politicians commenting on the decline of community or the rise of various forms of anti-social behaviour would sometimes refer to our 'broken society' . . . and while the broken society was often blamed on the behaviour of the poor, the broken economy was widely attributed to the rich . . . But the truth is that both the broken society and the broken economy resulted from the growth of inequality.

Wilkinson and Pickett's thesis was enthusiastically received by some politicians and academics. The argument that too much emphasis has been placed on market relations and the drive towards economic growth has failed many members of society is one of the main points made by the Marmot Review (Marmot 2010).

Others criticize Wilkinson's work on the grounds that, again, it fails to demonstrate a causal relationship between income inequality and poor health. Judge (1995) reanalysed Wilkinson's earlier data, employing standard measures of inequality in use at the time, and found that the apparent connection between levels of inequality and life expectancy simply did not exist. It is also argued that Wilkinson and Pickett's choice of countries for comparison is highly selective and methodologically flawed. For example, Japan is included but not Singapore or Hong Kong. The latter two countries are more unequal than Japan, yet they experience similar health and well-being benefits. Similarly, Wilkinson and Pickett put Portugal's relatively poor health performance down to its high level of inequality, but Snowdon (2010: 14) argues that it is, in fact, the poorest country in their analysis, and what it really suffers from is a lack of material prosperity. Some recent evidence also shows that the suggested pattern does not hold within developing countries either. The 'Wilkinson thesis' has been described, perhaps a little unfairly, as 'a doctrine in search of data' (Eberstadt and Satel 2004: 118) rather than as a thesis that is well supported by the evidence. Wilkinson continues to respond to his critics, and this debate looks set to continue for some time yet.

THINKING CRITICALLY

Examine figures 11.4, 11.5 and 11.7 above. How would a concerted attempt to tackle poverty help to reduce such inequality? Could education campaigns on healthy diet and lifestyles reduce health inequality?

The sociology of disability

The biomedical model of health has long underpinned the way that disability has conventionally been understood – as an illness or abnormality that is a personal tragedy for the individual. Recent social trends leading to a backlash against the biomedical model have also been part of a strong challenge to medical and individualistic understandings of disability. In this section, we explore the dominant 'individual model' of disability and see how it has been challenged, notably by disabled people themselves, through the development of a 'social model' of disability. But a good place to start is with the language of disability.

Sociologists argue that our awareness and understanding of social issues is partly shaped by the very words we use and the way in which we discuss disability. The word 'handicapped', for example, has largely fallen out of use because it was previously associated with 'cap in hand' – charity and begging. Other words used originally to describe certain impairments are rejected because they became hurtful insults – terms such as 'spastic' or 'cripple' are examples. And some metaphors in everyday use, such as 'turning a blind eye' or 'a deaf ear', have been criticized because they imply a sense of social exclusion from the mainstream. As we shall see, even the way we use the term 'disability' is subject to criticism.

The individual model of disability

Historically, an individual model of disability has been dominant in Western societies. This contends that individual mental and bodily impairments are the main causes of the problems experienced by disabled people. Bodily 'abnormality' is seen as causing functional limitation, which then leads to 'disability'. Underpinning the individual model is a 'personal tragedy approach' in which disabled people are seen as unfortunate victims of chance events. Medical specialists play a central role in the individual model because it is their job to offer curative and rehabilitative diagnosis. For this reason, the individual model is often described as a 'medical model', as it illustrates the power of the medical expert over disabled people's lives. Over recent decades, the individual model of disability has come under fierce challenge.

The social model of disability

An important early challenge to the individual model was Paul Hunt's *Stigma: The Experience of Disability*, in which he argued that 'the problem of disability lies not only in the impairment of function and its effects on us individually, but also in the area of our relationship with "normal" people' (1966: 146). Hunt was a leading activist in the early years of the disability movement in Britain and became a founding member of the Union of Physically Impaired Against Segregation (UPIAS). In its manifesto, UPIAS (1976: 14) developed a radical alternative to the individual model, stating that there was a crucial distinction between 'impairment' and 'disability':

- *Impairment*: Lacking part or all of a limb, or having a defective limb, organ or mechanism of the body.
- *Disability*: The disadvantage or restriction of activities caused by a contemporary social organization, which takes no or little account of people who have physical impairments and thus excludes them from participation in the mainstream of social activities.

UPIAS largely accepted the definition of physical 'impairment' as a biomedical property of individuals, though this was later extended to include non-physical, sensory and intellectual forms of impairment. Disability, however, was defined in social terms, which challenged the conventional understanding of the term. Disability was now understood not as an individual problem but in terms of the social barriers that people with impairments faced as a result of society's organization. Factors such as building construction, inaccessible public transport systems, and the discriminatory attitudes of employers and the non-disabled population effectively 'disable' people with a range of impairments.

Is this Paralympic sprinter 'disabled'? Where do Paralympians fit into the various definitions of health and illness at the start of this chapter?

Mike Oliver turned the assumptions in the individual model of disability around by rewriting the questions used by the UK Office of Population, Censuses and Surveys (OPCS) in the 1980s to assess 'disability' (see 'Using your sociological imagination 11.3'). Oliver (1983) was the first theorist to make explicit the distinction between the individual and the social model of disability (summarized in table 11.3). The social model was given further academic credibility in the work of Vic Finkelstein (1980, 1981), Colin Barnes (1991) and Oliver himself (1990, 1996).

Social model theorists are interested in explaining how the social and cultural barriers faced by disabled people have developed. Some theorists, influenced by Marx, argue that a historical materialist understanding of disability is needed (see chapters 1 and 3 for more on materialism). Oliver, for example, argues that the severe restrictions placed on disabled people's full participation in society can be traced back to the Industrial Revolution, when they were excluded from the labour market. The first capitalist workshops based payment on individual waged labour and, as the process developed, 'so many [disabled people] were unable to keep or retain jobs that

Table 11.3 Two models of disability

Individual model	Social model
Personal tragedy model	Social oppression theory
Personal problem	Social problem
Individual treatment	Social action
Medicalization	Self-help
Professional dominance	Individual and collective responsibility
Expertise	Experience
Individual identity	Collective identity
Prejudice	Discrimination
Care	Rights
Control	Choice
Policy	Politics
Individual adjustment	Social change

Source: Adapted from Oliver (1996: 34).

11.3   Applying the social model to assumptions in the OPCS questions

OPCS question	Oliver's question
'Can you tell what is wrong with you?'	'Can you tell me what is wrong with society?'
'What complaint causes you difficulty in holding, gripping or turning things?'	'What defects in the design of everyday equipment like jars, bottles and tins causes you difficulty in holding them?'
'Are your difficulties in understanding people due mainly to a hearing problem?'	'Are your difficulties in understanding people due mainly to their inability to communicate with you?'
'Do you have a scar, blemish or deformity which limits your daily activities?'	'Do other people's reactions to any scar, blemish or deformity you may have limit your daily activities?'
'Have you attended a special school because of a long-term health problem or disability?'	'Have you attended a special school because of your education authority's policy of sending people with your health problem/disability to such places?'
'Does your health problem/disability prevent you from going out as often or as far as you would like?'	'What is it about the local environment that makes it difficult for you to get about in your neighbourhood?'
'Does your health problem/disability make it difficult for you to travel by bus?'	'Are there any transport or financial problems which prevent you from going out as often or as far as you would like?'
'Does your health problem/disability affect your work in any way at present?'	'Do you have problems at work because of the physical environment or the attitudes of others?'
'Does your health problem/disability mean that you need to live with relatives or someone else who can help or look after you?'	'Are community services so poor that you need to rely on relatives or someone else to provide you with the right level of personal assistance?'
'Does your present accommodation have any adaptations because of your health problem/disability?'	'Did the poor design of your house mean that you had to have it adapted to suit your needs?'

Source: Oliver (1990: 7–8).

THINKING CRITICALLY

Exactly what changes would be needed to bring about the full participation of disabled people in relation to communication, schooling, employment, public services and housing? Can you make an *economic* as well as a moral case for such changes?

they became a social problem for the capitalist state whose initial response to all social problems was harsh deterrence and institutionalization' (Oliver 1996: 28). Even today, disabled people's presence in the workforce remains small, though there are now legal measures in place aimed at preventing discrimination on grounds of disability.

Evaluation of the social model

The social model has been enormously influential in shaping the way that we think about disability today. It has gained global influence and is described as 'the big idea' of the British disability movement (Hasler 1993). In focusing on the removal of social barriers to full participation, the social model redefines disability as the result of oppression, a move that many disabled people found liberating (Beresford and Wallcraft 1997). This political strategy led some to argue that disabled people had formed 'a new social movement' (Oliver and Zarb 1989).

> New social movements are discussed further in chapter 21, 'Politics, Government and Social Movements'.

Since the late 1980s, several criticisms have been made of the social model from those working in disability studies and mainstream sociology. First, it is seen as neglecting the often painful or uncomfortable *experience* of impairment, which is a central part of many disabled people's lives. Shakespeare and Watson (2002: 11) argue that 'We are not just disabled people, we are also people with impairments, and to pretend otherwise is to ignore a major part of our biographies.' Against this criticism, defenders of the social model say that, rather than denying everyday experiences of impairment, it merely seeks to shift the focus of attention onto the social barriers raised against disabled people.

Second, many people accept they have impairments but do not wish to be labelled as 'disabled'. In a UK survey of people claiming disability benefits, fewer than half chose to define themselves as disabled. Many rejected the label because they perceived their health problems as illnesses, not disabilities, or because they did not think that they were ill enough to be so categorized (DWP 2002). However, Barnes (2003) points out that, in a society where disability is still associated with abnormality and social deviance, it is not surprising that people with impairments reject the label 'disabled', which carries a stigma. Indeed, the social model has been influential in challenging the stigmatizing of disability.

Third, many medical sociologists reject the social model, arguing that the distinction between impairment and disability on which it rests is false. They argue that *both* disability *and* impairment are socially constructed and interrelated. Shakespeare and Watson (2002) claim that the division between impairment and disability collapses when one asks the question 'Where does impairment end and disability start?' In some cases it may be straightforward – a failure to design suitable wheelchair access in a building clearly creates a disabling barrier for wheelchair users. However, there are many more instances where it is impossible to remove all the sources of disability because they are not caused by oppressive conditions in society. For example, to be impaired by constant pain or significant intellectual limitation disables the individual from full participation in society in a way that cannot be removed by modifications or social changes. Therefore, any full account must take into account disability caused by the impairments themselves and not just those created by the organization of society.

Supporters of the social model argue that this last claim blurs the distinction between disability and impairment and is rooted in the biomedical model underlying the older, individual model of disability. The social model does not deny that impairment can be the cause of pain or that there are things an individual may not be able to do solely because of a specific impairment. Indeed, Carol Thomas (1999, 2002), an advocate of the social model, uses the idea of 'impairment effects' to bring in the ensuing psycho-emotional implications of impairment for disabled people.

Criticism of the social model from within the disabled people's movement may seem strange, given that this model originated in discussions among movement activists themselves. But this internal controversy is perhaps best seen as the maturing of debate and the success of the social model in reshaping the meaning of disability as a political rather than a medical concept.

11.4 'Why I want you to look me in the face'

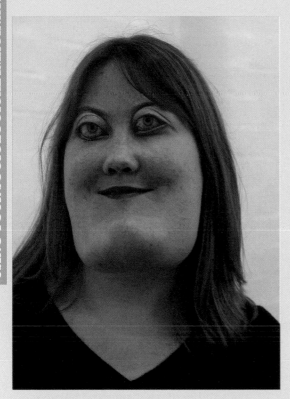

Instead of people looking away, gasping or shuddering, Vicky Lucas wants them to know that her face is integral to who she is. And, as she explains, she likes who she is.

I have a rare genetic disorder called Cherubism, which affects my face. I was diagnosed when I was about four years old. I was too young to remember what happened, but visiting hospitals became a regular part of my life. Although it was only when I was about six that my face started to really change shape, I don't remember a time when I didn't look different. Growing up with a facial disfigurement wasn't easy. When puberty kicked in, it included all the usual developments with a little bit extra – my face became very large and my eyes were more affected too.

Double take
My teenage years were difficult. People would sometimes stare or do a double take. Some people would be downright nasty and call me names. Even when people said 'Oh you poor thing!' their pity also hurt me and that hurt would stay with me for a long time. I became very withdrawn, afraid of how I might be treated if I went out. But over time, I gradually started to develop my self-esteem and self-confidence and I started to feel that I shouldn't waste my life just because of other people's attitudes towards me.

At the age of 16 I went to college and studied subjects such as film, media studies and photography. I started to research the representation of disfigured people in the media. When I looked at how people with facial disfigurements are portrayed in films, well, no wonder people don't know how to react to us! Freddy Krueger in Nightmare on Elm Street, the Joker in Batman, the various scarred villains in gangster films – the list is endless.

Bad assumption
With stereotypes like that, it's hardly surprising that people assume that if you have a facial difference, there must be something 'different' or 'bad' about you in the inside too. This was a huge turning point for me because I realised that facial disfigurement was not just a medical issue, but a social issue as well. I realised that the reason why I was so unhappy was not because of my face, but the way some people would react to it. I decided that it wasn't my face that I wanted to change, but social attitudes. I'm not against plastic surgery. It's just that my personal choice is to not have it.

Now, at the age of 24, I'm used to seeing my face reflected back at me in the mirror and I'm okay with it. Though I could quite happily do without the headaches and double vision. I also dislike being physically unable to wink, but I've overcome this particular disability by doing a nice line in fluttering and blinking. But my face is integral to who I am. The way people treat me and the way I've had to learn to live my life has created the person I am today.

Lack of imagination

I love the good genuine friends my face has brought me and I appreciate the way it's made me want to be a better person. I also have a boyfriend who thinks I look like a cat. I'm not quite sure if I agree with him, but I'm certainly not complaining! Now, whenever a person says I'm ugly, I just pity them for their lack of imagination. For every person who calls me fat chin, I think 'Nah! It's just that you've got a really small weak one. Talk about chin envy!' For every naturally curious stare I get, I give a friendly smile. And if they don't smile back within my 10-second time limit, I give them a very effective scowl.

Last week, walking in the street with my boyfriend, a man walked towards me and went 'Urghhhhhoooooh!'

Confrontation

It wasn't so much a word as a strange guttural sound, and the kind that only funny looking people could understand the subtext to. I was so angry that I confronted him. I won't go into details of what I did but let's just say it's probably the last time he ever gives a strange guttural sound to a funny looking woman in the street ever again.

Two minutes later, as we were walking home, a homeless man came up to me asking for change. He asked me how I was. 'Fine', I said and I told him what had just happened. There was a short pause. Then he smiled and said 'I hope you hurt him!' We all laughed.

It's funny how some strangers can be so cruel and hurtful, and yet others, the ones you'd least expect, the ones you would usually ignore and think nothing of, can be so warm and kind. That pretty much sums up my life. I go from experiencing the worst in people to the very best, and often within the same five minutes! It makes my life more challenging, but also very interesting. I wouldn't want to change that for the world.

Source: BBC (2003).

THINKING CRITICALLY

Are people with facial disfigurements 'disabled' according to the UPIAS definition? Does Vicky's story tell us anything about the validity of the distinction between impairment and disability?

Disability, law and public policy

Given that the social model of disability emerged in the UK, it is instructive to look at the way British legislation has developed, partly as a result of the campaigns of the disabled people's movement.

The Disability Discrimination Act (DDA) was passed in 1995, giving disabled people legal protection from discrimination in several areas, including employment and access to goods and services. Further legislation was introduced in 1999 that led to the creation of the Disability Rights Commission (DRC), set up to work towards 'the elimination of discrimination against disabled people', and a new DDA covering more areas and activities was introduced in 2005. On 1 October 2007, the DRC was subsumed under a new national human rights body, the Equality and Human Rights Commission. Then, in 2010, a more general Equality Act was passed which replaced most of the previous DDA and included new rights for the carers and parents of disabled people not to be discriminated against.

The 1995 DDA defined a disabled person as 'anyone with a physical or mental impairment which has a substantial and long-term adverse effect upon their ability to carry out normal day-to-day activities', and this definition was carried forward into the 2010 Equality Act. It covers, for example, people with mental health problems as well as those with facial disfigurements and avoids the common misconception that disability is primarily the result of genetically transmitted impairments and/or diseases. In fact,

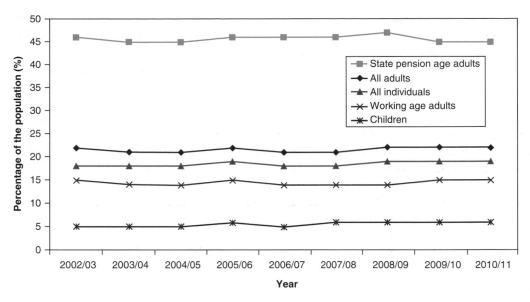

Figure 11.8   Disability prevalence in the UK by age, 2002/3–2010/11 (percentage of age group)

Source: DWP (2012: 79).

only around 17 per cent of disabled people in the UK were born with impairments, and the percentage of the population that is disabled increases with age (Papworth Trust 2013; see figure 11.8).

Under the Equality Act definition, in 2011–12 some 11.6 million people in the UK were disabled – about 19 per cent of the population, the same proportion as in 2002–3. Of these, 5.7 million were adults of working age, 5.1 million were over state pension age and 800,000 were children (DWP 2014). People with impairments linked to disability still belong to one of the most disadvantaged groups in the UK. They are more likely to be out of work than the able-bodied, and those who are employed tend to earn less. In 2005, the DRC reported that the average gross hourly pay of disabled employees was 10 per cent less than that of non-disabled employees. Yet disability-related expenditure by governments is high compared with spending in many other areas. The wealthiest countries spend at least twice as much on disability-related programmes as they do on unemployment benefits (OECD 2005).

Disability around the world

In 2011, the World Health Organization estimated that over 1 billion people around the world lived with some form of disability, some 15 per cent of the total global population. This is a significantly higher proportion than 1970s estimates of around 10 per cent (WHO 2011: 7–8). The global prevalence of disability is rising as a result of ageing populations and the increase in chronic conditions. The main causes of disability in the developed countries are chronic disease and long-term impairments, while in developing countries the main causes are poverty, inadequate sanitation, poor diet and bad housing. Injuries, such as broken bones, will often result in long-term impairment in developing countries, which would not occur if treatment and rehabilitation facilities had been available. Iron deficiency (anaemia) and chronic infections of the pelvis are major causes of impairment that lead to disability in women in many developing countries. It is estimated that around 250,000 children lose their sight each year because their diet lacks Vitamin A (found in green vegetables) and that up to half of the world's impairments could be prevented by improving policies on poverty reduction, malnutrition, sanitation, drinking water and employment conditions (Charlton 1998). War and its aftermath – such as uncleared landmines – is another major cause of impairments. Furthermore, in poorer countries, disabled children are more likely to receive a lower level of education, which exacerbates their poverty later in life. From this evidence, we can see that poverty in the developing world creates impairments and shapes disability in ways that are very different from the situation in the relatively rich countries.

In 2006, the UN noted that only a minority of countries – forty-five – had introduced legislation to protect the rights of disabled people. In the majority of countries, disabled people did not have equal rights with the rest of the population. In India (a country with anti-discrimination laws), of around 70 million people with disabilities, only 100,000 or so were in employment in 2004. In the USA, just 35 per cent of working-age people with disabilities were employed, compared with 78 per cent of the non-disabled population (UN Convention on the Rights of Persons with Disabilities 2006: preamble).

Clearly, anti-discriminatory laws and policies are unevenly distributed across the world, and many disabled people continue to be denied full citizenship in their own country. In an attempt to 'level up' provision for disabled people, the UN launched the first human rights treaty of the twenty-first century – the 2006 UN Convention on the Rights of Persons with Disabilities – which aims to contribute to a global 'paradigm shift' in attitudes towards disabled people. On the opening day for signatures – 30 March 2007 – ninety-nine countries signed the Convention; by 2010, 147 countries had signed and ninety-five had ratified it.

The Convention commits national governments to 'develop and carry out policies, laws and administrative measures for securing the rights recognized in the Convention and to abolish laws, regulations, customs and practices that constitute discrimination'. It also guarantees that disabled people enjoy a right to life on an equal basis, ensures equal rights and advancement for women and girls with disabilities, and protects children with disabilities. And it sets out, for the first time, a global policy agenda to promote equal rights for disabled people. Disability politics has clearly moved a very long way in a short period of time. However, the modern world also makes demands that were unknown in the past and which can create new disabling barriers. For example, most employers now require high levels of written communication, literacy and numeracy, which effectively 'disables' some people with learning difficulties.

Health and disability in a changing world

The very different experiences of health, illness, impairment and disability encountered by people around the world illustrate an idea reflected in this chapter: that our experience of our own bodies and interactions with others – whether able-bodied or disabled, sick or healthy – are shaped by shifting social contexts. Today, of course, we are more keenly aware of the global dimension of human existence, which brings home the gross inequalities of condition and opportunity, particularly between the developed and the developing countries. Nowhere is this more evident than in the impact of pandemics such as HIV/AIDS or Ebola.

From the divergent impact of HIV/AIDS to the widely differing access to healthcare and the experience of disability, comparative sociological research provides some of the necessary evidence and understanding for governments and policy-makers. Interventions aimed at raising health standards demand reliable evidence, and sociologists can play their part by pointing out where spending and assistance are most needed. But sociology also fulfils its promise by helping all citizens to understand the modern world better, relating health challenges, such as the spread of eating disorders, the emergence of genetic screening and the onset of frightening epidemics, to globalizing social processes.

Chapter review

1   Outline three competing definitions of *health*.
2   Give a concise description of the Western *biomedical model* that includes at least three of its main elements.
3   Provide examples of three recent *health technologies* and suggest some applications for each. What are the benefits and possible social problems we might expect to develop as a result of these?

4   Outline what is meant by *medicalization* and *iatrogenesis* and explain how they differ.
5   What social changes are said to be responsible for the rise of complementary and alternative therapies?
6   What is the difference between an *epidemic* and a *pandemic*? What *social changes* do virologists believe will lead to more pandemics in the future?

7   Describe the main ways in which people can be infected with HIV. Which countries and regions have been most badly affected? How have sociologists tried to explain this?
8   What are the three 'main pillars' of the *sick role*? How has Parsons's thesis been defended against its critics?
9   Using specific examples, describe how *social class* and *health* are closely related. How do the findings on class also help us to understand the poorer health of some minority ethnic groups in the UK?

10 'The pattern of women's health is strongly linked to female biology.' Explain why sociologists do not accept this statement.
11 Compare the *individual* and the *social model of disability*, noting down the main differences between them. What are the implications of the social model for the reorganization of society?

12 What are the main differences in *patterns of disability* in the developing and developed countries?

Research in practice

Doctor–patient confidentiality is key to medical consultations, and intimate examinations are often necessary if an accurate diagnosis is to be made. However, over recent years, reports of the abuse of patients in this clinical setting have become more commonplace, and it is clear that the intimate examination raises difficult issues of embarrassment and emotional control/distancing for both parties. Read the following article, which explores the attitudes of doctors in the UK: Hine, P., and Smith, H. (2014) 'Attitudes of UK Doctors to Intimate Examinations', *Culture, Health & Sexuality*, 16(8): 944–59.

1   This study made use of a software package called 'NVivo9'. What is this and how has it been used here?
2   How would you characterize the research method(s) adopted for this study? What do the authors mean by 'a constructivist approach'?
3   What reasons are given for the variability in the use of intimate examinations among doctors?
4   Describe some of the main methods used by doctors to help them to handle the emotional aspects of the intimate examination.

5   According to this paper, how have recent medical scandals influenced doctors' attitudes towards the value of conducting intimate examinations?

6   Put together a research proposal for a follow-up study exploring the attitudes of *patients* to intimate examinations. What difficulties do you foresee in gathering a sample for this study and how could these be overcome?

Thinking it through

It is well established that there is a social class gradient in health, with lower classes, on average, having poorer health and shorter life expectancy than higher ones. Some sociologists have argued that tackling poverty and its related material environments should be at the heart of government policy. However, a 2012 report by the King's Fund in the UK found that people with no educational qualifications were five times more likely to smoke and drink large amounts of alcohol and to shun exercise and advice on a healthy diet.

Why should there be a correlation between lack of educational qualifications and unhealthy lifestyle choices? Suggest some theoretical links that might exist, focusing on why key health and lifestyle messages are more likely to be taken seriously and acted on by higher, middle-class socio-economic groups. Could health-promotion messages be made more effective, or should governments simply accept that some social groups are just not accessible via this route?

Society in the arts

Consider the following comment from Rosemarie Garland Thompson's (1997) *Extraordinary Bodies: Figuring Physical Disability in American Culture and Literature* (New York: Columbia University Press), pp. 9–10.

Disabled literary characters usually remain on the margins of fiction as uncomplicated figures or exotic aliens whose bodily configurations operate as spectacles, eliciting responses from other characters or producing rhetorical effects that depend on disability's cultural resonance. . . . From folktales and classical myths to modern and postmodern 'grotesques,' the disabled body is almost always a freakish spectacle presented by the mediating narrative voice. . . . Take as a few examples Dickens' pathetic and romanticized Tiny Tim of *A Christmas Carol*, J. M. Barrie's villainous Captain Hook from *Peter Pan*, Victor Hugo's gothic Quasimodo in *The Hunchback of Notre Dame* . . .

Choose one of the three characters below. To what extent does Thompson's gloomy assessment apply to your character and storyline? In what ways do these twenty-first-century representations of disability diverge from 'otherness' and negative stereotyping?

- 'John Nash' in the film *A Beautiful Mind* (2001), directed by Ron Howard
- 'Artie Abrams' in the TV series *Glee* (2009), Season 1, Episode 9, 'Wheels', directed by Paris Barclay
- 'Tyrion Lannister' in the TV series *Game of Thrones* (2011–), various directors

Further reading

The sociology of health and illness is a well-established field, and there are many introductory textbooks. Two very good ones are Mildred Blaxter's (2010) *Health* (2nd edn, Cambridge: Polity), which has an excellent discussion of the concepts of health and illness, and Anne-Marie Barry and Chris Yuill's (2016) *Understanding the Sociology of Health: An Introduction* (4th edn, London: Sage), which provides an up-to-date overview.

From here, try something that covers key debates, evidence and policy in more detail. For example, Sarah Nettleton's (2013) *The Sociology of Health and Illness* (3rd edn, Cambridge: Polity) and Ellen Annandale's (2014) *The Sociology of Health and Medicine* (2nd edn, Cambridge: Polity) are both reliable and engagingly written.

Critical reviews of the sociology of the body can be found in Alexandra Howson's (2012) *The Body in Society: An Introduction* (2nd edn, Cambridge: Polity) and Bryan S. Turner's (2008) *The Body and Society* (3rd edn, London: Sage). For disability studies in sociology, see Colin Barnes and Geof Mercer's (2010) *Exploring Disability: A Sociological Introduction* (2nd edn, Cambridge: Polity) and John Swain, Sally French, Colin Barnes and Carol Thomas's (2013) very useful edited collection *Disabling Barriers – Enabling Environments* (3rd edn, London: Sage).

A useful reference work covering the field of health and illness is *Key Concepts in Medical Sociology* (2013), edited by Jonathan Gabe and Lee Monaghan (2nd edn, London: Sage).

For a collection of original readings on the sociology of health and the body, see the accompanying *Sociology: Introductory Readings* (3rd edn, Cambridge: Polity, 2010).

Internet links

@ **Additional information and support for this book at Polity:**
www.politybooks.com/giddens

European Observatory on Health Systems and Policies – monitors and studies healthcare systems in Europe:
@ www.euro.who.int/en/about-us/partners/observatory

The World Health Organization – exactly what it says: a good source of data on health and illness across the world:
www.who.int/en

@ **UNAIDS – United Nations AIDS programme with lots of resources and statistics:**
www.unaids.org/en

Innovative Health Technologies – a research programme at the University of York, UK. See 'Projects by Theme':
@ www.york.ac.uk/res/iht/introduction.htm

@ **The Wellcome Library, UK – resources on the history of medicine and its role in society:**
http://wellcomelibrary.org

@ **The Disability Archive at the University of Leeds, UK – a large resource of material covering all aspects of disability:**
http://disability-studies.leeds.ac.uk/library

@ **The European Disability Forum – a non-governmental organization that is run by disabled people promoting equal rights in the EU:**
www.edf-feph.org

@ **The UK's Equality and Human Rights Commission – web resources that contain much information and a useful set of publications:**
www.equalityhumanrights.com

@ **United Nations Convention on the Rights of Persons with Disabilities – site of the UN Convention with the latest news on signatories, but also resources on disability across the world:**
www.un.org/development/desa/disabilities/convention-on-the-rights-of-persons-with-disabilities.html

CHAPTER 12

Stratification and Social Class

Contents

Mark Zuckerberg, the co-founder of Facebook, turned his computer programming talent into a multi-billion dollar Internet business.

Everyone loves a rags to riches story. The plucky individual starts with nothing but, through hard work and dedication, overcomes all obstacles and rises to the top ranks of society or builds a business and gets rich. This timeless story was updated for the digital age in the 2010 film *The Social Network,* based on the creation of Facebook and its co-founder, Mark Zuckerberg, whose talent for computer programming and business acumen made him a billionaire at the age of twenty-three; by 2015 he had ammassed a personal wealth of more than $33 billion (*Forbes* 2015). Capitalist economies seem to encourage and reward such entrepreneurship, offering the enticing prospect that anyone might achieve success whatever their family background or place of birth. The biography of another entrepreneur, Sir Gulam Noon, perfectly illustrates this.

Noon was born in 1936 in Bombay (now Mumbai), India, where his Muslim family owned a small market sweet shop. Following the death of his father when Gulam was just seven years old, life was a struggle, and he helped out in the shop as well as going to school. In 1954, at the age of seventeen, he joined the family business, which he expanded and diversified into property and manufacturing. In 1964 he went to England to gain experience and in 1972 returned to establish a confectionery company, Bombay Halwa, in London. In the growing Asian communities of London and Leicester the business expanded, and today the chain has fifty-one shops, most of them in Britain, with a few in Mumbai and Paris. Since 1982 the business has also provided services to the airline catering industry.

In 1989 another company, Noon Products Ltd, was established. Gulam had spotted a gap in the market: 'All the pre-packaged Indian ready meals available from the supermarkets were insipid and frankly unacceptable. I thought I could do better.' The business began with just eleven employees, but was soon selling 'authentic' Indian food to the frozen food company Birds Eye, and then to the supermarket chains Waitrose, Morrisons and Sainsbury's. The business almost failed when a fire destroyed the original factory in 1994, but Noon rebuilt quickly and continued to expand the business.

Noon Products now has a range of more than 500 ready meals produced by some 1,200 employees, with 1.5 million curries per week supplied to supermarkets. Noon sold the company to the Irish food business Kerry Group in 2005, and his personal fortune is estimated at £85 million. However, he did not come from a particularly wealthy family, describing himself as a 'self-made man'. Reflecting on what motivated him at such an early age, he says: 'I was restless, I had a hunger to get out of the poverty trap, not be poor. My elder brother was more like my father, more calm. He's retired now and thinks I am bloody

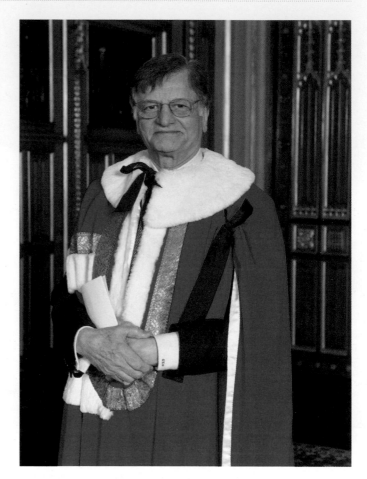

Sir Gulam Noon received a peerage in 2010.

working like a dog. He will never understand my philosophy' (interview in *Management Today*, 27 November 2008). Noon was knighted in 2002 and joined the House of Lords in November 2010.

Noon's rags-to-riches story raises some interesting questions. What chance does someone from a poor background really have of gaining such high social status and personal wealth? For every Gulam Noon, how many others work in his businesses and are they paid their 'fair share' for helping the company to succeed? The issues of wealth and poverty raised here also lead us to broader questions. What factors influence our economic position in society? Are life chances different if you are a woman or a member of a minority ethnic group? Is globalization opening up opportunities for advancement or closing them down?

A large body of sociological research over many years shows that societies are patterned or structured and that the individual's position in that structure significantly shapes their life chances. For example, in Britain, the chances of someone from a working-class background making it into the 'top jobs' and positions of power are slim: 'In every single sphere of British influence, the upper echelons of power in 2013 are held overwhelmingly by the privately educated or the affluent middle class.' This is the view not of a Marxist revolutionary, but of Sir John Major, a former Conservative prime minister (cited in Social Mobility and Child Poverty Commission 2014: 6). The same study found that, although just 7 per cent of British people attend private schools, 71 per cent of senior judges, 62 per cent of senior armed forces officers, 50 per cent of the House of Lords, 44 per cent of the *Sunday Times* rich list and 36 per cent of the coalition government's cabinet were educated in such schools. Similarly, less than 1 per cent of people attend Oxford or Cambridge University ('Oxbridge'), yet, in 2014, 75 per cent of senior judges, 59 per cent of the cabinet, 50 per cent of diplomats and 38 per cent of the House of Lords did so (ibid.: 10). For sociologists, this regularly reproduced pattern is every bit as interesting and demanding of an explanation as the individual biographies of Gulam Noon or Mark Zuckerberg.

> For an extended discussion of schooling and the reproduction of inequalities, see chapter 19, 'Education'.

We begin by scrutinizing what sociologists mean when they talk about stratification and social class before examining some influential theories of class and attempts to measure it. Then we move on to take a more detailed look at social classes and lifestyles in the developed societies. The chapter closes with a discussion of social mobility – how far up or down the social scale it is possible to move and how much mobility there is today. Given the sheer scale of research studies into class systems, these will necessarily take up the bulk of the chapter, and readers will be able to explore the other forms of stratification we discuss briefly through the readings at the end of the chapter.

Systems of stratification

Sociologists use the concept of social stratification to describe inequalities between individuals and groups within societies. Often we think of stratification in terms of assets or property, but it can also occur because of other attributes, such as gender, age, religious affiliation or military rank. Individuals and groups enjoy differential (unequal) access to rewards based on their position within the stratification scheme. Thus, stratification can be defined as structured inequalities between different groupings of people. It is useful to think of stratification as rather like the geological layering of rock in the Earth's surface. Societies can be seen as consisting of 'strata' in a hierarchy, with the more favoured at the top and the less privileged nearer the bottom. All socially stratified systems of this kind share three basic characteristics.

1 The rankings apply to social categories of people who share common characteristics without necessarily interacting or identifying with one another. For example, women may be ranked differently from men or wealthy people differently from the poor. Individuals from a particular category may move between ranks, but the category itself continues to exist.

2 People's life experiences and opportunities depend on the relative ranking of their social category. Being male or female, black or white, upper class or working class makes a big difference in terms of life chances – often as large as personal effort or good fortune.

3 The ranks of social categories tend to change only slowly. In the industrialized societies, for example, women have begun to achieve equality with men in many spheres of life only recently.

> Gender issues and theories are discussed more fully in chapter 15, 'Gender and Sexuality'.

Stratified societies have changed considerably throughout history. In the earliest human societies, based on hunting and gathering, there was very little social stratification – mainly because there were very few resources to be divided or fought over. The development of settled agriculture produced considerably more wealth and resources and an increase in stratification. Social stratification in agricultural societies increasingly came to resemble a pyramid, with a large number of people at the bottom and a smaller number towards the top. Today, industrial and post-industrial societies are extremely complex and their stratification is more likely to resemble a teardrop, with a large number of people in the middle and lower-middle ranks, a smaller number at the bottom and very few people at the top.

THINKING CRITICALLY

Stratification systems are widespread and remarkably persistent. Should we then assume that some form of stratification is 'natural' and inevitable? In what ways is a system of stratification functional for society as a whole?

Historically, four basic systems of stratification can be distinguished: slavery, caste, estates and class. These are sometimes found in conjunction with one another and, though modern class systems are found right across the globe today, there is no simple chronology through the four types. For example, as we will see, in recent years modern forms of slavery have emerged even within the class-based societies of the developed world.

Slavery

Slavery is an extreme form of social inequality, in which some people are owned as property by others. The legal conditions of slave-ownership have varied considerably across societies. Sometimes slaves were deprived of almost all rights by law, as on the Southern plantations in the pre-Civil War United States. In other societies their position was closer to that of servants, and in the ancient Greek city-state of Athens some slaves occupied positions of great responsibility. Some were literate and worked as government administrators, and a number were trained in craft skills. They were excluded from political positions and the military but were accepted in most other occupations, though many began and ended their days in hard labour in the mines.

Throughout history, slaves have fought back against their subjection; the black slave rebellions in the American South before the Civil War are an example. Because of such resistance, systems of slave labour have tended to be unstable. High productivity could be achieved only through constant supervision and brutal punishments. Slave-labour systems eventually broke down, partly because of the struggles they provoked and partly because economic or other incentives motivate people to produce more effectively than direct compulsion. Slavery is not particularly economically efficient.

From the eighteenth century onwards, many people in Europe and America came to see slavery as *morally* wrong in what they perceived to be 'civilized societies', and the practice of transporting people as slaves gradually came to be outlawed. Today slavery is illegal in every country of the world, yet recent research confirms that many people continue to be taken by force, trafficked across national borders and held against their will. From enslaved brick-makers in Pakistan to sex slaves in Thailand and domestic slaves in wealthy countries such as the UK and France, what is termed modern slavery remains a significant human rights violation across the world.

Modern slavery is not legitimized by the state and does not constitute a legally recognized system of stratification, but it does seem to be growing and spreading geographically. Precisely because modern slavery is a hidden form of exploitation and its forms are diverse,

Human trafficking, forced labour, slavery and domestic servitude are growing problems in the twenty-first century, attracting the interest of academics and politicians.

it is very difficult to arrive at an accurate estimate of how many people are affected. However, one recent government report argued that there are likely to be between 10,000 and 13,000 victims of slavery in the UK alone (Silverman 2014). Best estimates suggest that almost 36 million people are victims of slavery, bonded labour or domestic servitude around the world (Global Slavery Index 2014). Of these, 61 per cent are in just five countries: China, India, Pakistan, Russia and Uzbekistan. Against the expectations of many, and contrary to more optimistic assessments of globalization, the process also facilitates the forced movement of people across the world and into modern forms of enslavement (Bales et al. 2009).

Caste

A caste system is a form of stratification in which one's social position is given for a lifetime. In caste societies, all individuals must remain at the social level of their birth. Everyone's social status is based on personal characteristics, such as perceived race, ethnicity, skin colour, parental religion or parental caste, that are accidents of birth and are therefore believed to be unchangeable. In a sense, caste societies can be seen as a special type of class society in which one's position is ascribed at birth (Sharma 1999). They have typically been found in agricultural societies such as in rural India or in South Africa before the end of white rule in 1992.

Before the modern period, caste systems were found throughout the world. In Europe, for example, Jews were frequently treated as a separate caste, forced to live in restricted neighbourhoods and barred from intermarrying and, in some instances, even interacting with non-Jews. The term 'ghetto' is said to derive from the Venetian word for 'foundry', the site of one of Europe's first official Jewish ghettos, established by the government of Venice in 1516. The term eventually came to refer to those sections of European towns where Jews were legally compelled to live, long before it was used to describe minority neighbourhoods, with their caste-like qualities of racial and ethnic segregation.

In caste systems, intimate contact with members of other castes is strongly discouraged. Such 'purity' of a caste is often maintained by rules of endogamy – marriage within one's social group as required by custom or law.

Caste in India and South Africa

The Indian caste system reflects Hindu religious beliefs and is at least 2,000 years old. According to Hindu scholars, there are four major castes, each roughly associated with broad occupational groupings: the *Brahmins* (scholars and spiritual leaders) at the top, followed by the *Ksyatriyas* (soldiers and rulers), the *Vaisyas* (farmers and merchants) and the *Shudras* (labourers and artisans). Beneath the four castes are those known as the 'untouchables', or *Dalits* ('oppressed people'), who – as their name suggests – are to be avoided at all costs. Untouchables are limited to the worst jobs in society, such as removing human waste, and they often resort to begging and searching garbage for food. In traditional areas of India, some members of higher castes still regard physical contact with untouchables to be so contaminating that a mere touch requires cleansing rituals. Following independence in 1947, India made it illegal in 1949 to discriminate on the basis of caste, though elements of the system remain in full force today, particularly in the more rural areas.

As India's modern capitalist economy brings people of different castes together, whether in the same workplace, on an aeroplane or in restaurants, it is increasingly difficult to maintain the rigid barriers required to sustain the caste system. As more and more of India is influenced by globalization processes, it seems reasonable to assume that the caste system will weaken further in the future.

Before its abolition in 1992, the South African caste system – termed apartheid – rigidly separated black Africans, Indians, 'coloureds' (people of mixed races) and Asians from whites. In this case, caste was based entirely on racial identification. Whites, who made up only 15 per cent of the total population, controlled virtually all the country's wealth, owned most of the usable land, ran the principal businesses and industries, and had a monopoly on political power, since blacks could not vote. Black people – who made up three-quarters of the population – were segregated into impoverished *bantustans* (homelands) and were allowed out only to work for the white minority.

The apartheid system, with its widespread discrimination and oppression, created intense conflict between the white minority and the black, mixed-race and Asian majority. Decades of often violent struggle finally proved successful in the 1990s. The most powerful black organization, the African National Congress (ANC), mobilized an economically devastating global boycott of South African businesses, forcing South Africa's white leaders to dismantle the system, which was abolished by popular vote among white South Africans in 1992. In the country's first multiracial elections in 1994, Nelson Mandela – the ANC leader who had spent twenty-seven years in jail – was elected president. South Africa's version of a caste system came to an end and the government adopted policies aimed at empowering black people and creating a 'patriotic' and 'productive' black capitalist class, as it seeks closer integration into the global capitalist economy (Southall 2004: 313).

In India's caste system, the *dalits* (or 'untouchables') occupy the lowest rung of the ladder and were traditionally limited to the lowest occupations and posts in society.

Estates

Estates were part of European feudal societies, though they also existed in many other traditional civilizations. The feudal estates consisted of social strata with differing obligations towards one another and unequal sets of rights, some of these differences being established in law. In Europe, the highest estate was composed of the *aristocracy* and gentry. The *clergy* formed another estate, having lower status but possessing some distinctive privileges. Those in what came to be called the 'third estate' were the *commoners* – serfs, free peasants, merchants and artisans. In contrast to castes, a certain degree of intermarriage and mobility was tolerated between the estates. Commoners might be knighted, for example, in payment for special services given to the monarch, and merchants could sometimes purchase titles. Remnants of the estates system persist in Britain, where hereditary titles are still recognized and sought, though since 1999 peers are no longer automatically entitled to vote in the House of Lords. Similarly, business leaders, civil servants and others may be honoured with knighthoods for their services.

In the past, estate systems tended to develop wherever there was a traditional aristocracy based on the concept of noble birth. In feudal systems, such as in medieval Europe, estates were closely bound up with the manorial community – that is, they formed a local, rather than a national, system of stratification. In the centralized traditional empires, such as China or Japan, they were organized on a more national basis. Sometimes the differences between estates were justified by religious beliefs, although rarely in as strict a way as in the Hindu caste system.

Class

Though social class is a contested concept, a general definition is that a class is a large-scale grouping of people who share common economic resources, which strongly influence the type of lifestyles they are able to lead. Ownership of property and wealth and occupation are the chief bases of class differences. Classes differ from other forms of stratification in four main respects.

1 *Class systems are fluid.* Unlike other types of strata, classes are not established by legal or religious provisions. The boundaries between classes are never clear-cut and there are no formal restrictions on intermarriage between people from different classes.
2 *Class positions are in some part achieved.* An individual's class is not simply given at birth, as is the case in the other types of stratification systems. Social mobility – movement upwards and downwards in the class structure – is more common than in other systems.
3 *Class is economically based.* Classes are created in economic differences between groups of individuals – inequalities in the possession of material resources. In other stratification systems, non-economic factors tend to be more important.
4 *Class systems are large scale and impersonal.* Class systems operate mainly through large-scale, impersonal associations such as exist between businesses and their employees. Class differences occur in inequalities of pay and working conditions. In other systems of stratification, inequalities are expressed in personal relationships of duty or obligation, as between master and slave or between lower- and higher-caste individuals.

Most official caste systems have already given way to class-based ones in industrial capitalist societies (Berger 1986). Industrial production demands that people move around freely to take up work they are suited or able to do and to change jobs frequently according to economic conditions. The rigid restrictions found in caste systems are at odds with this necessary freedom. As globalization reshapes the world into a single economic system, remaining caste-like relationships will become increasingly vulnerable to the pressure for change. The next section looks at theories of social class, which has become the dominant form of social stratification globally.

> **THINKING CRITICALLY**
>
> If social class becomes the dominant form of stratification in all countries, would this be a generally positive or negative development? How would life improve for those currently living in other systems of stratification and what new problems would be created?

Theorizing social class

The theories developed by Karl Marx and Max Weber form the basis of most sociological analyses of class and stratification. We shall begin by examining these theories before analysing the neo-Marxist ideas represented by the American sociologist Erik Olin Wright. The section ends with an introduction to intersectionality, a concept that helps to capture the ways in which diverse social inequalities intertwine in social life.

Chapter 1, 'What is Sociology?', contains an introduction to Marx and Weber, while chapter 3, 'Theories and Perspectives', covers these in more detail.

Karl Marx's theory of class conflict

Most of Marx's work was concerned with stratification and, above all, with social class, yet surprisingly he failed to provide a systematic discussion of the concept itself. The manuscript on which Marx was working at the time of his death (subsequently published as part of his major work, *Capital* (1867)) breaks off just at the point where he posed the question 'What constitutes a class?'. This means that Marx's concept has to be reconstructed from his writings as a whole. There have been numerous interpretations of his work and many disputes about 'what Marx really meant'. Nevertheless, his central ideas are quite clear and are discussed in 'Classic studies 12.1'.

Max Weber: class, status and party

Weber's approach to stratification built on the analysis developed by Marx, though Weber reached very different conclusions about capitalism and the fate of the working classes. Like Marx, he regarded society as characterized by conflicts over power and resources. But, where Marx saw polarized class relations and economic issues at the heart of major social conflicts, Weber developed a more complex, multidimensional view of society. Social stratification is not a matter simply of class, according to Weber, but is shaped by two further aspects: status and party. These three overlapping elements produce an enormous number of possible positions within society, in contrast to the bipolar model proposed by Marx.

Although Weber accepted Marx's view that social class is founded on objectively given economic conditions, he saw a larger variety of economic factors as important in class formation. According to Weber, class divisions derive not just from ownership or lack of ownership of the means of production, but from economic differences that have nothing directly to do with property. These include the skills and credentials, or qualifications, which affect the types of work that people are able to obtain. Weber argued that an individual's *market position* strongly influences their life chances. Those in managerial or professional occupations earn more and have more favourable conditions of work, for example, than people in working-class or 'blue-collar' jobs. The qualifications they possess, such as degrees, diplomas and the skills they have acquired, make them more 'marketable' than others without such qualifications. Similarly, among blue-collar workers, skilled craft workers are able to secure higher wages than the semi- or unskilled.

In Weber's work, status refers to differences between groups in the social honour or prestige they are accorded by others. In traditional societies, status was often determined on the basis of first-hand knowledge of a person gained through interactions in different contexts over a period of years. But, as societies grew more complex, it became impossible for status always to be accorded in this way. Instead status came to be expressed through people's *styles of life*. Markers and symbols of status – such as type of housing, dress, manner of speech and occupation – all shape an individual's social standing in the eyes of others. People sharing the same status then form a community in which there is a sense of shared identity.

While Marx maintained that status distinctions are the result of class divisions, Weber argued that status often varies independently of class. Possession of wealth can confer high status, but this is not universally the case. The term 'genteel poverty' refers to one example. In Britain, for example, people from aristocratic families continue to enjoy considerable social esteem even when their fortunes have been lost. Conversely, many bankers may be wealthy, but their social status has rarely been lower – the result of a widespread perception that their reckless lending caused the 2008 global economic crisis while their annual bonuses are excessive and have not been earned.

In modern societies, Weber pointed out, party formation is an important aspect of *power* and can influence stratification

485

Classic Studies 12.1   Karl Marx and the theory of class conflict

The research problem

Nineteenth-century European industrialization transformed societies, in many ways for the better. But it also led to protests and revolutionary movements. Later, as industrial societies developed in the twentieth century, strikes and militant activity by workers continued to occur. Why did workers protest even as societies became wealthier? Karl Marx (1818–83) studied class societies in an attempt to understand how they operated. His crucial argument was that industrial societies were rooted in capitalist economic relations. But Marx was no detached academic observer; he was a key figure in communist politics and an activist in workers' movements. For Marx, industrial capitalism, for all its progressive elements, was founded on an exploitative system of class relations and had to be overthrown.

Marx's explanation

For Marx, a social class is a group of people who stand in a common relationship to the means of production – the means by which they gain a livelihood. In this sense, all societies have a central class system. Before the rise of modern industry, the means of production in estate systems consisted of land and the instruments used to tend crops or pastoral animals. The two main classes were those who owned land (aristocrats, gentry or slave-holders) and those engaged in producing from it (serfs, slaves and free peasantry). In industrial societies, factories, offices, machinery and the wealth or capital needed to buy them have become more important. The two main classes consist of those who own the new means of production – industrialists or capitalists – and those who earn their living by selling their labour to them – the working class or, in the term Marx used, the proletariat.

According to Marx, the relationship between classes is exploitative. In feudal societies, exploitation took the form of the direct transfer of produce from the peasantry to the aristocracy. Serfs had to give a proportion of their production to their masters or to work a number of days each month to produce crops for the master's household. In industrial capitalist societies, the source of exploitation is less obvious. Marx argued that workers produce more than is actually needed by employers to repay the cost of hiring them. The surplus is the source of profits, which capitalists are then able to put to their own use. Say a group of workers in a clothing factory produce 100 suits a day. Selling seventy-five suits covers the cost of paying workers' wages and the cost of plant and equipment, so income from the remaining twenty-five suits can then be taken as profit.

Marx was struck by the gross inequalities created by capitalism. Although aristocrats had lived a life of luxury, completely different from that of the peasantry, agrarian societies were relatively poor. Even if there had been no aristocracy, standards of living would inevitably have been meagre. With the development of modern industry, wealth is produced on a scale far beyond anything ever seen, but workers remain relatively poor, while the wealth accumulated by the propertied class grows. Marx used the term pauperization to describe the process by which the working class grows increasingly impoverished in relation to the capitalist class. Even if workers become more affluent in absolute terms, the gap separating them from the capitalist class continues to stretch ever wider. Recent protests against the vast wealth owned by the '1 per cent' at the top express something of this point.

The inequalities between capitalists and the working class were not strictly economic in nature. Marx saw that the mechanization of production means that work frequently becomes tedious, dull and unsatisfying and workers become alienated from their own labour and its products. Instead of being fulfilling in itself, work becomes simply a means of making money to survive. As large numbers of workers are gathered together in factories, Marx argued that a collective class consciousness would develop, as workers became acutely aware that, to improve their situation over the long-term, a revolution would be necessary to overthrow the exploitative social relations of capitalism.

Critical points

Sociological debates on Marx's ideas have continued for more than 150 years, and it is impossible to do justice to them here. Instead, we can point to some major themes in Marxist criticism. First, Marx's characterization of capitalist society as splitting into 'two main camps' has been seen as too simple. Even within the working class there are divisions between skilled and unskilled workers, and such divisions have become more complex, with gender and ethnicity also factors leading to diverse life chances. As a result, critics argue, concerted action by the entire working class is very unlikely.

Second, Marx's forecast of a communist revolution led by the industrial working class in the advanced societies has not materialized, which calls into question his analysis of the dynamic of capitalism. Some contemporary Marxists still consider capitalism as eventually doomed, but critics see little evidence of this. Indeed, the majority of the working class have become increasingly affluent property-owners, with more of a stake in the capitalist system than ever before.

Third, although Marx saw class-consciousness arising from the increasingly shared experiences of the working class, today people identify rather less with their social class position. Instead, there are multiple sources of identification, and class is not necessarily the most important. Without a developing and widespread class-consciousness, there can be no concerted class action and, hence, no communist revolution. Again, critics see long-term social trends moving away from Marx's theoretical forecasts.

Contemporary significance

Marx's influence – not just in sociology, but on the world – has been enormous. Numerous regimes across the world have considered themselves 'Marxist', and opposition movements routinely draw on Marx's ideas for inspiration. Even though his major predictions have not proved correct, the analysis of capitalism he pioneered continues to inform our understanding of globalization. Indeed, it could be argued that the widespread recognition of rapid globalization may give fresh impetus to Marxist studies, particularly with the recent emergence of international anti-capitalist movements.

 See chapter 21, 'Politics, Government and Social Movements', for a discussion of anti-globalization movements.

independently of class and status. Party, in Weber's sense, refers to a group of individuals who work together because they have common backgrounds, aims or interests. Often a party works in an organized fashion towards a specific goal which is in the interest of its membership. Marx explained both status differences and party organization in terms of class, but neither, in fact, can be reduced to class divisions. Weber reasoned that, even though both are influenced by class, each can in turn influence the economic circumstances of individuals and groups, thereby affecting their class. Parties may appeal to concerns cutting across class differences. For example, parties may be based on religious affiliation or nationalist ideals. Marxists may explain the conflict between Catholics and Protestants in Northern Ireland in class terms, since more Catholics than Protestants are in working-class jobs. But Weberians would argue that this explanation is ineffective, as the parties to which people are affiliated express religious as well as class differences.

Weber's writings on stratification are important, because they show that other dimensions of stratification besides class strongly influence people's lives. Weber drew attention to the complex interplay of class, status and party as distinct aspects of social stratification, creating a more flexible basis for empirical studies of people's life chances.

Bringing Marx and Weber together?

The American sociologist Erik Olin Wright developed the Marxist theory of class to include elements of Weber's approach (Wright 1978, 1985, 1997). In doing so, he shifted away from a strict focus on the relationship to means of production and looked instead at the issue of how much control members of different social classes have in the production process. According to Wright, there are three dimensions of *control over economic resources* in modern capitalist production that allow us to identify the major classes that exist:

- control over investments or money capital
- control over the physical means of production – land or factories and offices
- control over labour power.

As Marx argued, those who belong to the capitalist class have control over each of these dimensions in the production system. Members of the working class have control over none of them. But in between these two main classes are groups whose position is ambiguous – managers and white-collar workers, for example. These groups are in *contradictory class locations*, because they are able to influence some aspects of production but are denied control over others. White-collar and professional employees have to sell their labour power to employers in order to make a living, just as manual workers do. But at the same time they have a greater degree of control over their work than most blue-collar workers. Wright calls these class positions 'contradictory', because the individuals concerned are neither capitalists nor workers, yet they share certain common features with each.

A large section of the population – 85 to 90 per cent according to Wright (1997) – falls into the category of those who are forced to sell their labour. Yet within this population there is great diversity, from the traditional, manual working class to white-collar workers. In order to differentiate class locations Wright takes two factors into account: relationship to authority and the possession of skills and expertise.

First, he argues that many middle-class workers, such as managers and supervisors, enjoy relationships towards authority that are more privileged than those of the working class. They assist in controlling the working class yet at the same time remain under the control of capitalist owners – they are both exploiters and exploited. Second, Wright argues that middle-class employees with skills that are in demand can exercise a specific form of power and can demand higher wages. This point is illustrated, for example, by the lucrative positions available to some information technology specialists in the emerging knowledge economy.

By combining elements from the perspectives of both Marx and Weber, Wright effectively shows that they are not necessarily diametrically opposed. He also demonstrates that, as capitalist societies have become more complex, sociology theories which try to understand them must also develop. One recent perspective which aims to connect inequalities of class with other major social divisions is intersectionality, and a brief discussion of this idea follows.

> **THINKING CRITICALLY**
>
> In what ways are the theories of class of Marx and Weber at odds with each other and how can they be seen as complementary? Does the concept of 'contradictory class locations' support Weber's idea that working-class revolution is highly unlikely or Marx's contention that revolution is inevitable?

Intersecting inequalities

In the latter half of the twentieth century, sociological studies of inequality shifted away from an almost exclusive focus on social class to explore other inequalities of gender, ethnicity, sexuality and disability. It thus became increasingly clear that the theories and concepts used to study class were not easily transferable to other forms of inequality.

In recent years it has also been argued that, if we are to understand the lives of people

Intersectional theory questions whether we can ever assume the 'shared experience' of, say, 'white people', 'women' or 'the working class'. Such overarching categories hide the diverse life experiences of individuals such as one would find around this table of professionals.

in contemporary societies, sociologists will need to find ways of connecting class with other inequalities (Andersen and Collins 2009; Rothman 2005). One influential attempt to do so has been via the concept of intersectionality – the complex interweaving of diverse social inequalities which shapes individual lives and complicates the earlier, comparatively simple class analysis. As McLeod and Yates (2008: 348) argue, 'To only analyse class (or gender, or race . . .) is now understood as a political and analytical act of exclusion.'

Research into intersecting inequalities typically involves seeking to understand the real lives of individuals within their social context, though there is also an interest in the operation of power as it is maintained and reinforced through the main axes of class, gender and ethnicity (Berger and Guidroz 2009). But intersectional research is more than just 'class +' race, gender or other social divisions. Such an approach would privilege

class over the other forms, theorizing the latter as somehow secondary to a primary focus on class. Instead, 'intersectionality posits that race, class, gender, sexuality, ability, and various aspects of identity are constitutive. Each informs the other, and taken together they produce a way of experiencing the world as sometimes oppressed and marginalized and sometimes privileged and advantaged depending on the context' (Smooth 2010: 34).

For example, when sociologists discuss and debate the experience of 'the working class', what exactly are they referring to? We cannot assume that social class forms the primary source of identity for all or even a majority of, say, working-class people, nor are their experiences necessarily similar. The lives of white, heterosexual, working-class men may be very different from those of black, working-class, lesbian women, and only empirical research will establish which of these constitutive forms of identity is more important in specific socio-historical contexts. As this example implies, intersectional research tends to adopt qualitative methods that are able to tap into people's real-life experiences, and this is one significant difference from conventional quantitative social class research.

There are some problems with intersectionality research. How many inequality and identity categories are there to be studied? This is often called the '*et cetera*' problem, as some scholars simply add 'etc.' onto class, gender and 'race' to indicate there are many other sources (Lykke 2011). But, if this is so, how do researchers know that they have covered all of them in order to validate their findings? A second issue is the relative weight afforded to the different categories. Should we theorize them all as being broadly similar, or are there reasons to suppose that social class is in some way more important in shaping lives, especially in what remain capitalist societies?

Such questions are still being worked through in a growing body of intersectional research. But what we can conclude is that many social scientists today are seeking ways of better understanding the complexities of multicultural societies and, in doing so, are moving beyond conventional forms of class analysis.

> Discussions of intersectionality can also be found in the following chapters: 3, 'Theories and Perspectives'; 7, 'Work and the Economy'; 9, 'The Life Course'; 13, 'Poverty, Social Exclusion and Welfare'; 15, 'Gender and Sexuality'; and 16, 'Race, Ethnicity and Migration'.

Mapping the class structure

Both theoretical and empirical studies have investigated the link between class position and other dimensions of social life, such as voting patterns, educational attainment and physical health. Yet, as we have seen, the concept of class is far from clear-cut. In both academic circles and common usage, the term 'class' is understood and used in a variety of ways. How can sociologists and researchers measure such an imprecise concept in their empirical work?

When an abstract concept such as class is transformed into a measurable variable, we say that the concept has been *operationalized*. This means that it has been defined clearly and concretely enough to be tested in empirical research. Sociologists have operationalized class through a variety of schemes which attempt to map the class structure of society. These schemes provide a theoretical framework by which individuals are allocated to social class categories.

A common feature of most class schemes is that they are based on the occupational structure. Sociologists have seen class divisions as corresponding to material and social inequalities linked to types of employment. The development of capitalism and industrialism has been marked by a growing division of labour and an increasingly complicated occupational structure. Although it is no longer as true as it once was, occupation plays an important part in determining social position, life chances and level of material comfort. Social scientists have used occupation extensively as an indicator of social class because of the finding that individuals in the same occupation tend to experience similar degrees of social advantage or disadvantage, maintain comparable lifestyles, and share similar opportunities.

Class schemes based on the occupational structure take various forms. Some are largely descriptive, reflecting the shape of the occupational and class structure in society without addressing relations between social classes. These models have been favoured by scholars who see stratification as unproblematic and part of the natural social order, such as those working in the functionalist tradition.

> Functionalism was introduced in chapter 1, 'What is Sociology?', and chapter 3, 'Theories and Perspectives'.

John H. Goldthorpe on social class and occupation

The research problem

What is the connection between the jobs we do – our occupations – and our class position? Is class simply the same thing as occupation? Do we then move *between* classes when we change jobs? And, if we retrain, move into higher education or become unemployed, does our class position also change? As sociologists, how should we carry out research into social class?

Many sociologists have been dissatisfied with *descriptive* class schemes, as these merely *reflect* existing social and material inequalities between classes but do not seek to *explain* the social processes that created them. With such concerns in mind, the British sociologist John Goldthorpe created a scheme for use in empirical research on social mobility. The *Goldthorpe class scheme* was designed not to describe a hierarchy of classes, but as a

representation of the 'relational' nature of the contemporary class structure.

Goldthorpe's explanation

Goldthorpe's ideas have been highly influential, and other sociologists have often pointed to his classification as an example of a neo-Weberian class scheme. This is because the original scheme identified class location on the basis of two main factors: *market situation* and *work situation*. An individual's market situation concerns their level of pay, job security and prospects for advancement; it emphasizes material rewards and general life chances. The work situation, by contrast, focuses on questions of control, power and authority within the workplace. An individual's work situation is concerned with the degree of autonomy and the overall relations of control affecting employees.

Table 12.1 **Goldthorpe/CASMIN and UK ONS-SEC social class schemes alongside more commonly used sociological categories**

Goldthorpe/CASMIN schema	National Statistics Socio-Economic Classification	Common descriptive term
I Professional, administrative and managerial employees, higher grade	1 Higher managerial and professional occupations ab	Salariat (or service class)
II Professional, administrative and managerial employees, lower grade; b technicians, higher grade	2 Lower managerial and professional occupations b	
IIIa Routine non-manual employees, higher grade	3 Intermediate occupations	Intermediate white collar
IV Small employers and self-employed workers	4 Employers in small organizations, own account workers	Independence (or petty bourgeoisie)
V Supervisors of manual workers; technicians, lower grade	5 Lower supervisory and lower technical occupations	Intermediate blue-collar
VI Skilled manual workers	6 Semi-routine occupations	Working class
IIIb Routine non-manual workers, lower grade	7 Routine occupations	
VII Semi- and unskilled manual workers		

Source: Goldthorpe and McKnight (2004).

In the 1980s and 1990s, Goldthorpe's comparative research encompassed a project on social mobility known as the CASMIN project (Comparative Analysis of Social Mobility in Industrial Nations). The outcomes of this project are significant, as the resulting classification was incorporated into the UK Office of National Statistics' own Socio-Economic Classification (ONS-SEC) and is widely used across Europe (Crompton 2008). The Goldthorpe/CASMIN and UK ONS-SEC schemes are shown in table 12.1, alongside the more commonly used sociological terms (on the right-hand side).

Originally encompassing eleven class locations, reduced to eight in the CASMIN research, Goldthorpe's scheme remains more detailed than many others. Yet, in common usage, class locations are still compressed into just three main class strata: a 'service' class (classes I and II), an 'intermediate class' (classes III and IV) and a 'working class' (classes V, VI and VII). Goldthorpe acknowledges the presence of an elite class of property-holders at the very top of the scheme but argues that it is such a small segment of society that it is not meaningful as a category in empirical studies.

In his more recent work, Goldthorpe (2000) has emphasized *employment relations* within his scheme rather than 'work situation', as described above. In doing so, he draws attention to different types of employment contract. A *labour contract* supposes an exchange of wages and effort which is specifically defined and delimited, while a *service contract* has a 'prospective' element, such as the possibility of salary growth or promotion. According to Goldthorpe, the working class is characterized by labour contracts and the service class by service contracts; the intermediate class locations experience intermediate types of employment relations.

Critical points

The chapter gives an extended evaluation of Goldthorpe's work, but here we can note two major criticisms. Although this scheme is clearly a useful one for empirical researchers, it is not so clear that it can tell us much about the position of those social groups, such as students and the unemployed, that lie outside social class boundaries. It has also come under fire for underplaying the significance of the gross disparities in wealth within capitalist societies. In a sense, such criticisms are a reflection of the longstanding debate between Marxist and Weberian scholars on social class.

Contemporary significance

Goldthorpe's work has been at the centre of debates on social class and occupations for quite some time. In spite of some highly pertinent criticisms, his class scheme, while remaining within the broadly Weberian tradition of sociology, has been constantly updated and refined. With the latest version set to become the standard class scheme across the European Union, it would seem that Goldthorpe's ideas and categories are likely to become more rather than less influential in the future.

Other schemes are more theoretically informed, drawing on the ideas of Marx or Weber and concerned with explaining relations between classes in society. 'Relational' class schemes are favoured by sociologists working within conflict paradigms in order to demonstrate the divisions and tensions in society. Erik Olin Wright's theory of class, discussed above, is an example of a relational class scheme, because it seeks to depict the processes of class exploitation.

John Goldthorpe's influential work, originally rooted in Weberian ideas of class (see 'Classic studies 12.2'), is another example of a relational scheme.

Evaluating Goldthorpe's class scheme

As 'Classic studies 12.2' notes, Goldthorpe's class scheme has been widely used in empirical research. It has been useful in highlighting class-based inequalities, such as those related to health and education, as well as in reflecting the class dimension in voting patterns, political outlooks and general social attitudes. Yet it is important to note several significant limitations to all such schemes, which caution us against applying them uncritically.

Occupational class schemes are difficult to apply to the *economically inactive*, such as the unemployed, students, pensioners and children. Unemployed and retired individuals are often classified on the basis of their previous work activity, but this can be problematic with the long-term unemployed or people with sporadic work histories. Students can sometimes be classified according to their subject, but this is likely to be successful only where the field of study correlates closely to a specific occupation, such as engineering or medicine.

Class schemes based on occupational distinctions are also unable to reflect the importance of property-ownership and wealth. Occupational titles alone are not sufficient indicators of an individual's wealth and overall level of assets. This is particularly true among the richest members of society, including entrepreneurs, financiers and the 'old rich', whose occupational titles of 'director' or 'executive' place them in the same category as many professionals of much more limited means. In other words, class schemes derived from occupational categories do not accurately reflect the enormous concentration of wealth among the 'economic elite'. Marxist scholars see this as a crucial failing.

By classifying the richest members of society alongside upper-class professionals, the occupational class schemes dilute the relative weight of property relations in social stratification and fail to take account of extreme inequality. For example, John Westergaard has disputed Goldthorpe's view that, because they are so few in number, the rich can be excluded from schemes detailing class structure. As Westergaard (1995: 127) argues:

> It is the intense concentration of power and privilege in so few hands that makes these

Where do unemployed people and jobseekers fit into a social class scheme? How should we assess their class location?

people top. Their socio-structural weight overall, immensely disproportionate to their small numbers, makes the society they top a class society, whatever may be the pattern of divisions beneath them.

Clearly there are complexities involved in devising schemes that can reliably 'map' the class structure of society. Even within a relatively 'stable' occupational structure, measuring and mapping social class remains fraught with difficulty. The rapid economic transformation since the 1970s has made the measurement of class even more problematic, leading some to question the usefulness of class itself as a central concept. New occupational categories are emerging, there has been a general shift away from manufacturing towards services and knowledge work, and a very large number of women have entered the workforce. Occupational class schemes are not necessarily well suited to capturing such dynamic processes of class formation, mobility and change.

Class divisions in the developed world

The question of the upper class

Is there still a distinctive upper class in the developed societies, founded on the ownership of property and wealth? Or should we talk of a broader service class, as Goldthorpe suggests? Of course, Goldthorpe also recognizes an elite upper class, but this is so small it is difficult to build into representative social surveys. On the other hand, the elite upper class today is not the same as the landed aristocracy of the estates systems. Instead, it is a capitalist class whose wealth and power is derived from profit-making in global markets.

One way of approaching this issue is to see how far wealth and income are concentrated in the hands of a few people. Reliable information about personal wealth is difficult to obtain, as the affluent do not normally publicize the full range of their assets, and some governments hold more accurate statistics than others. It has often been remarked that we know far more about the poor than we do about the wealthy. What is certain is that large amounts of wealth are concentrated in the hands of a small minority whose personal wealth is tracked annually by the *Forbes* magazine 'rich list' in the USA.

> Chapter 14, 'Global Inequality', discusses both the 'rich list' and extreme global inequality in more detail.

In Britain, for example, in 2002 the top 1 per cent of the population owned around 23 per cent of all marketable wealth (ONS 2010a: 62). Even during the 2008 banking and credit crisis and its aftermath, the richest individuals have been able to protect their wealth. In 2009–10, the total wealth of the 1,000 richest individuals in the UK actually rose by £77 billion, to £335.5 billion, equivalent to over one-third of the country's national debt (*Sunday Times* 2010). Indeed, the wealthiest 10 per cent of the population has consistently owned around 50 per cent of the total marketable wealth in the country, while the least wealthy half consistently owns less than 10 per cent (see table 12.2). Since the early 1990s, the wealthiest 10 per cent have actually owned *more* than 50 per cent of all marketable wealth in the UK.

Ownership of stocks and bonds is even more unequal than holdings of wealth as a whole. The top 1 per cent in the UK own some 75 per cent of privately held corporate shares; the top 5 per cent own over 90 per cent of the total. But there has also been more change in this respect. Around 25 per cent of the population own shares, compared with 14 per cent in 1986 and just 5 per cent in 1979. Many people bought shares for the first time during the privatization programme of the Conservative government that came to power in 1979. However, the bulk of these holdings are small, and institutional share-ownership – shares held by companies in other firms – has grown faster than individual ownership.

Historically, it has been very difficult to arrive at an overall picture of global wealth distribution because of the problems of data-gathering in some countries. However, a 2007 study by the World Institute for Development Economics Research of the United Nations University covers all the countries of the world, looking at household wealth, shares and other financial assets, as well as land and buildings, making it the most comprehensive global survey of personal wealth undertaken to date. The survey found that the richest 2 per cent of the global population own more than half of global household wealth. It also found that, while the richest 10 per cent of adults owned 85 per cent of global wealth, the bottom 50 per cent owned just 1 per cent (Davies et al. 2007). Clearly, the global pattern of wealth distribution is even more unequal than a single national case, reflecting the gross

12.1 The death of class?

In recent years there has been a vigorous debate within sociology about the usefulness of 'class'. Some sociologists, such as Ray Pahl, have even questioned whether it is still a useful concept in attempting to understand contemporary societies. Australian academics, Jan Pakulski and Malcolm Waters, have been prominent among those who argue that class is no longer the key to understanding contemporary societies. In their book *The Death of Class* (1996), they argue that contemporary societies have undergone profound social changes and are no longer to be accurately seen as 'class societies'.

A time of social change

Pakulski and Waters argue that industrial societies are now undergoing a period of tremendous social change. We are witnessing a period in which the political, social and economic importance of class are in decline. Industrial societies have changed from being organized class societies to a new stage, which Pakulski and Waters call 'status conventionalism'. They use this term to indicate that inequalities, although they remain, are the result of differences in status (prestige) and in the lifestyle and consumption patterns favoured by such status groups. Class is no longer an important factor in a person's identity, and class communities . . . [are becoming] a thing of the past. These changes in turn mean that attempts to explain political and social behaviour by reference to class are also out of date. Class, it seems, is well and truly dead . . .

Increase in consumer power

These changes have been accompanied by an increase in consumer power. In ever more competitive and diverse markets, firms have to be much more sensitive in heeding the wishes of consumers. There has thus been a shift in the balance of power in advanced industrial societies. What marks out the underprivileged in contemporary society – what Pakulski and Waters refer to as an 'ascriptively disprivileged underclass' – is their inability to engage in 'status consumption' – which is to say, their inability to buy cars, clothes, houses, holidays and other consumer goods. For Pakulski and Waters, contemporary societies are stratified, but this stratification is achieved through cultural consumption, not class position in the division of labour. It is all a matter of style, taste and status (prestige), not of location in the division of labour.

Is status-based consumption, rather than social class position, now the main form of stratification in modern societies?

Processes of globalization

The shift from organized class society to status conventionalism is explained as being the result of processes of globalization, changes in the economy, technology and politics. Pakulski and Waters argue that globalization has led to a new international division of labour, in which the 'first world' is increasingly post-industrial – there are simply fewer of the sort of manual working-class occupations which characterized the previous era of 'organized class society'. At the same time, in a globalized world, nation-states are less self-contained and are less able to govern either their population or market forces than they once were. Stratification and inequality still exist, but they do so more on a global than a national basis; we see more significant inequalities between different nations than we do within a nation-state . . .

Nothing but a theory?

John Scott and Lydia Morris argue for a need to make distinctions between the class positions of individuals – their location in a division of labour – and the collective phenomena of social class through which people express a sense of belonging to a group and have a shared sense of identity and values. This last sense of class (a more subjective and collective sense) may or may not exist in a society at a particular time – it will depend on many social, economic and political factors.

It is this last aspect of class that appears to have diminished in recent years. This does not mean that status and the cultural aspects of stratification are now so dominant that the economic aspects of class are of no significance; indeed, mobility studies and inequalities of wealth indicate the opposite. Class is not dead – it is just becoming that bit more complex!

Source: Extracted from Abbott (2001).

> **THINKING CRITICALLY**
>
> To what extent do you feel your identity has been shaped by the things and experiences you consume and use? Are there any ways in which your family's class position has influenced your life chances? Is consumerism changing the way older family members perceive their position in society?

inequalities between the industrialized countries and those in the developing world.

Despite the concentration of wealth in relatively few hands, 'the rich' do not constitute a homogeneous group. Nor is this a static category, as people follow varying trajectories into and out of wealth. Like poverty, wealth must be regarded in the context of life cycles. Some individuals become wealthy very quickly, only to lose much of it, while others experience a gradual growth or decline in assets over time. Some rich people were born into families of 'old money' – wealth passed down several generations – while other affluent individuals are 'self-made', having successfully built up their wealth from more humble beginnings. Next to members of longstanding affluent families are music and film celebrities, top athletes, and representatives of the 'new elite' who have made fortunes through the development and promotion of computing, mobile telecommunications and the Internet.

Some other noteworthy trends have arisen in recent years, which we can observe from UK data. First, 'self-made millionaires' make up a larger proportion of the very wealthiest individuals, including some who made their fortunes in the digital revolution. For example, King Digital Entertainment saw four of its members make the list, largely on account of the phenomenal success of the game Candy Crush Saga, while Sam and Dan Houser, owners of Rockstar Games, which created Grand Theft Auto, just made the list with their combined fortune of £90 million (*Sunday Times* 2010). More than 75 per cent of the 1,000 richest Britons in 2007 made their own wealth rather than inheriting it. Second, in 2014, the wealth of Britain's richest 1,000 people had risen by 15 per cent in a single year and their

Table 12.2	UK distribution of wealth, 1976–2005					
	Most wealthy percentages of population					
	1	2	5	10	25	50
Year	Percentages of wealth owned					
1976	21	27	38	50	71	92
1977	22	28	39	50	71	92
1978	20	26	37	49	71	92
1979	20	26	37	50	72	92
1980	19	25	36	50	73	91
1981	18	24	36	50	73	92
1982	18	24	36	49	72	91
1983	20	26	37	50	73	91
1984	18	24	35	48	71	91
1985	18	24	36	49	73	91
1986	18	24	36	50	73	90
1987	18	25	37	51	74	91
1988	17	23	36	49	71	92
1989	17	24	35	48	70	92
1990	18	24	35	47	71	93
1991	17	24	35	47	71	92
1992	18	25	38	50	73	93
1993	18	26	38	51	73	93
1994	19	27	39	52	74	93
1995	19	26	38	50	72	92
1996	20	27	40	52	74	93
1997	22	30	43	54	75	93
1998	22	28	40	52	72	91
1999	23	30	43	55	74	94
2000	23	31	44	56	75	95
2001	22	29	41	54	72	93
2002	21	28	41	54	72	92
2003	19	27	40	53	73	93
2004	n/a	n/a	n/a	n/a	n/a	n/a
2005	21	28	40	54	77	94

Source: HMRC (2010).

combined fortune of £520 billion amounted to about one-third of Britain's entire GDP (*The Independent* 2014). This rise contrasts sharply with the UK government's 'austerity' policies and public-sector cuts in the wake of the 2008 financial crash. Third, a small but growing number of women are entering the ranks of the rich. In 1989, there were only six women among the wealthiest Britons, but by 2007 that number had risen to ninety-two. Fourth, ethnic minorities, particularly those of Asian origin, have been increasing their presence among the super-rich (*Sunday Times* 2007). Finally, many of the richest people in Britain were not born in the country but decided to make it their place of residence for a variety of reasons, including relatively low rates of tax for the super-rich.

With such a fluid situation it may be thought that there is no longer a distinct upper class, but this assumption is questionable. The upper class today has certainly changed its shape, but it still retains its distinctive position. John Scott (1991) pointed to three particular groups that together form a constellation of interests controlling and profiting from big business: senior executives in large corporations, industrial entrepreneurs and 'finance capitalists'. Senior executives may not actually own the businesses they run, but their shareholdings connect them to industrial entrepreneurs. Policies encouraging entrepreneurship during the 1980s and the information technology boom of the 1990s led to a new wave of entry into the upper class of people who have made fortunes from business and technological advances.

Finance capitalists, a category that includes the people who run the insurance companies, bankers, investment fund managers and managers of other organizations that are large institutional shareholders, are, in Scott's view, among the core of the upper class today (see 'Global Society 12.1'). At the same time, the growth of corporate shareholding among middle-class households has broadened the profile of corporate ownership. Yet the concentration of power and wealth in the upper class remains intact. While corporate-ownership patterns may be more diffuse

today, it is still a small minority who benefit substantially from shareholding.

The Bank of England's deputy governor noted that the situation in private equity and hedge funds was similar to that in English premiership football, where individual pay is set according to a world market, not a national one (Crompton 2008: 145). JPMorgan Chase is the largest manager of hedge funds, with more than US$53 billion worth of assets under its management, while the twenty-five largest managers had assets of around US$520 billion in 2009 (Pensions and Investments 2010).

We can conclude that we do need the concepts of the upper class and the service class. The upper class consists of a small minority of individuals who have both wealth and power and are able to transmit their privileges to their children. This class can be roughly identified as the top 1 per cent of wealth-holders. Below them are the service class and the intermediate class, consisting, as Goldthorpe says, of professionals, managers and many non-manual, higher grade occupations. In common usage, the latter two categories are part of the middle class, and it is to this class that we now turn.

The expanding middle class

The 'middle class' covers a broad spectrum of people working in many different occupations, from employees in the service industries to school teachers and medical professionals. Some authors prefer to speak of 'middle classes' in order to take account of this diversity, which also includes status situations and life chances. The middle class now encompasses the majority of the population in Britain and other industrialized countries. This is largely because the proportion of white-collar jobs rose markedly relative to blue-collar ones over the course of the twentieth century.

 See chapter 7, 'Work and the Economy', for more on the rise of white-collar jobs.

Global Society 12.1   Masters of the universe: meet the world's best-paid men

There are some in this world who look upon bankers' pay as small change. They wouldn't even consider getting out of bed for the $13m (£8m) Goldman Sachs' boss Lloyd Blankfein was paid last year. Such a trifling pay packet represents just a few days' work for these staggeringly well-paid financial executives. If bankers inhabit a different world, says London-based headhunter John Purcell, 'these guys are out on their own in a different universe'.

'Private bunch'

So just how much do these guys – for the vast majority are men – earn each year? At the very top of the pile, we're talking $4bn. Just in case that hasn't quite registered yet – that's four billion dollars. This does, of course, include bonuses and fees as well as salary. In fact, the salary is a tiny fraction of their overall pay.

And who are these men? They are called hedge fund managers – in other words, they are investors who buy and sell all manner of financial instruments with the express aim of making money for their clients, and for themselves. Finding out much about them is notoriously difficult. 'They're a very private bunch', Mr Purcell explains, 'largely because they earn so much. They are highly secretive in every aspect of what they do.' Discovering how they make their money is a little easier.

Popular myths

Hedge funds are actually one of the most misunderstood of all financial products. . . . What sets them apart from most investment funds is the range of instruments they can use and the strategies they can employ. Whereas traditional fund managers buy shares and bonds in the hope that they will rise in value, or occasionally dabble in financial derivatives, their hedge fund counterparts can do so much more. For example, they can take advantage of movements in interest rates and currencies, company restructuring and bankruptcies, and pricing anomalies across different markets. One of their most important strategies is shorting – borrowing shares to sell into the market in the expectation that they will fall, then buying them back at the lower price. This means they can make money when markets fall.

[. . .]

Celebrity pay

It's also important to bear in mind that the very best-paid hedge fund managers – the John Paulsons and George Soroses of the industry – own their own companies. They take a cut on all the assets under management across a number of funds run by their firm. In other words, George Soros owns Soros Fund Management. By contrast, Lloyd Blankfein does not own Goldman Sachs.

And while it's relatively easy to find out what the boss of a public company owns, it's far harder to discover what the owner of a private company pays him or herself. Individual hedge fund managers actually earn a fraction of what their employers earn – on average $4.9m in 2007, the last year for which figures are available. Still, nice work if you can get it.

[. . .]

Charitable giving

[. . .]

Many also donate vast sums to charity and have become well-known philanthropists. Carl Icahn, for example, who earned $1.3bn in 2009, recently signed up to the Giving Pledge, a club of billionaires who have promised to give large chunks of their wealth to charity. Still, whichever way you look at it, $4bn sure is a lot of dough for one man to be earning over many lifetimes, let alone one year. Are they worth it? No doubt a good number of their clients, which include many of the world's biggest pension funds, will say that they are. Their tailors may well agree. Others may take a slightly different view.

Source: Extracted from Anderson (2011).

THINKING CRITICALLY

Successful hedge fund managers can reap spectacular financial rewards and become very wealthy. How would Marxist theory categorize them in social class terms? Do they own and control any 'means of production', for instance? Which class do they fit into in Goldthorpe's scheme?

David Beckham was born into a working-class family in East London and went on to have a successful football career, diversifying into fashion and making a large fortune in the process, not least as the face (and body) of many advertising campaigns across the globe. But has Beckham moved into the upper class?

Members of the middle class, via their educational credentials or technical qualifications, occupy positions that provide them with greater material and cultural advantages than those of manual workers. Unlike the working class, members of the middle class can sell their mental *and* physical labour power to earn a living. While this distinction is useful in forming a rough division between the middle and working classes, the dynamic nature of the occupational structure and the possibility of upward and downward social mobility make it difficult to define the boundaries of the middle class with any precision.

The middle class is not internally cohesive and is unlikely to become so, given the diversity of its members' interests (Butler and Savage 1995). It is not as homogeneous as the working class, nor do its members share a common social background or cultural outlook, as do the top layers of the upper class. The relatively 'loose' composition of the middle class has been its abiding feature since the early nineteenth century (Stewart 2010).

Professional, managerial and administrative occupations have been among the fastest growing sectors of the middle class. There are several reasons why this is so. The first is that the spread of post-1945 bureaucracies has created opportunities and a demand for employees to work within institutional settings. Doctors and lawyers, who might have been self-employed in earlier times, now tend to work in institutional environments. Second, the increase in the number of professionals is a reflection of the expanding number of people who work in sectors of the economy where the government plays a major role. The creation of the welfare state led to an enormous growth in professions such as social work, teaching and healthcare. Finally, with the deepening of economic and industrial development, there has been an ever-rising demand for the services of experts in the fields of law, finance, accounting, technology and information systems. In this sense, professions can be seen both as a product of the modern era and as central to its evolution and expansion.

Professionals, managers and higher-level administrators gain their position largely from their possession of credentials – degrees, diplomas and other qualifications. As a whole, they enjoy relatively secure and well-paid careers, and their separation from people in routine non-manual jobs has grown more pronounced in recent years. Some authors have seen professionals and other higher white-collar groups as forming a specific class – the 'professional/managerial class' (Ehrenreich and Ehrenreich 1979; Glover and Hughes 1996) – or what Goldthorpe calls 'the service class'. Others argue that the degree of division between them and white-collar workers is not deep or clear-cut enough to make such a position defensible.

There has been interest in how white-collar professionals join together to maximize their interests and secure high levels of material reward and prestige. The medical profession clearly illustrates this process (Hafferty and Castellani 2011). Some groups within the medical profession, particularly doctors, have successfully organized themselves to protect their status, ensuring a high level of material rewards. Three main dimensions of *professionalism* have enabled this to happen: entry into the profession is restricted to those who meet a strict set of criteria (qualifications); a professional association, such as the British Medical Association, monitors and disciplines members' conduct and performance; and it is generally accepted that only members of the profession are qualified to practise medicine. As a result, self-governing professional asso-

ciations are able to exclude unwanted individuals and so enhance the market position of their own members – a key characteristic of middle-class occupations.

The changing working class

Marx forecast that the working class would become progressively larger – the basis for his thesis that the working class would realize their shared, exploited situation and rebel. But, in fact, the working class has reduced in size as the middle class has grown. In the 1960s, some 40 per cent of the working populations of developed societies were employed in blue-collar work. Today this has reduced to around 15 per cent. Moreover, the conditions under which working-class people live and the styles of life they follow have substantially improved.

The developed countries do have significant numbers of people living in poverty. But the majority of those in working-class occupations no longer live in poverty. The income of manual workers has increased considerably since the early twentieth century, and the rising standard of living is expressed in the increased availability of consumer goods to all classes. Cars, washing machines, televisions, computers, mobile phones, and much more are owned by a very high proportion of working-class households. Similarly, many working-class families own their own homes and regularly take foreign holidays.

 We examine this issue more closely in chapter 13, 'Poverty, Social Exclusion and Welfare'.

The phenomenon of working-class affluence suggests yet another possible route towards a 'middle-class society'. As blue-collar workers grow more prosperous, do they become middle class? This idea is known as the embourgeoisement thesis – simply, the process through which more people become 'bourgeois', or middle class, as a result of increasing affluence. In the 1950s, when the thesis was first advanced, it was argued that many well-paid blue-collar workers would also adopt middle-class values, outlooks and lifestyles. Economic development was having a powerful effect on the shape of social stratification.

In the 1960s, John Goldthorpe and his colleagues in the UK carried out a study designed to test the embourgeoisement hypothesis. They argued that, if the thesis was correct, affluent blue-collar employees should be virtually indistinguishable from white-collar employees in terms of attitudes to work, lifestyle and politics. The research, known as *The Affluent Worker* study (Goldthorpe 1968–9), was based on interviews with workers in the car and chemical industries in Luton: 229 manual workers were interviewed, together with fifty-four white-collar workers for purposes of comparison. Many of the blue-collar workers had migrated to the area specifically in search of well-paid jobs and, compared with most other manual workers, were highly paid, even earning more than most lower-level white-collar workers.

The Affluent Worker study focused on three dimensions of working-class attitudes but found very little support for the embourgeoisement thesis. First, it found that many workers had acquired a 'middle-class' standard of living in their incomes and ownership of consumer goods. Yet this relative affluence was gained in jobs characterized by poor benefits, low chances of promotion and little job satisfaction. The affluent workers saw their job simply as a means to gaining good wages, but the work was repetitive and uninteresting and they had little commitment to it.

Second, the affluent workers did not associate with white-collar workers in their leisure time and did not aspire to climb the class ladder. Their socializing was done at home with immediate family members and kin or with working-class neighbours. There was little indication that they were adopting middle-class norms and values. And, third, there was a negative correlation between working-class affluence and support for the Conservative Party. Supporters of the embourgeoisement thesis predicted that growing affluence would weaken the affluent workers' traditional support for the Labour Party.

The results of this study were clear-cut: the embourgeoisement thesis was wrong. However, Goldthorpe and his colleagues did concede the possibility of some convergence between the lower middle class and upper working class. Affluent workers shared similar patterns of consumption, a privatized, home-centred outlook, and support for instrumental collectivism (joining unions to improve wages and conditions) at the workplace.

No strictly comparable research has been carried out in the intervening years, and it is not clear how far the conclusions reached by Goldthorpe's team remain true now. However, it is generally accepted that older, traditional, working-class communities have become fragmented with the decline of manufacturing industry and the impact of consumerism. But how far this fragmentation has proceeded remains a matter of evidence and debate.

> **THINKING CRITICALLY**
>
> List the main changes that have taken place within the working, middle and upper classes since the late nineteenth century. Explain how it is possible for the working class to become more affluent at the same time that social inequality is increasing.

Is there an underclass?

The term 'underclass' has been used to describe the segment of the population located at the very bottom of – literally underneath – the class structure. Members of the underclass have significantly lower living standards than the majority, and many are among the long-term unemployed or drift in and out of paid work. Some are homeless or have no permanent place in which to live. They may spend long periods of time dependent on state welfare benefits. Such people are frequently described as 'marginalized' or 'socially excluded' from the way of life of the bulk of the population.

The underclass is often associated with underprivileged minority ethnic groups. The underclass debate originated in the United States, where the preponderance of poor black communities living in inner-city areas prompted talk of a 'black underclass' (Wilson 1978; Murray 1984, 1990; Lister 1996). In Britain, black and Asian people are disproportionately represented in the underclass, and, in some European countries, migrant workers who found jobs in times of prosperity also make up a large part of this group. This is true, for instance, of Algerians in France and Turkish immigrants in Germany.

The term 'underclass' is a contested one that has been at the centre of a furious sociological debate since the late 1980s. Although it has entered everyday speech, many scholars and commentators are wary of using it at all, as it encompasses a broad spectrum of meanings that are politically charged and carry negative connotations. Many researchers in Europe prefer the notion of 'social exclusion', which is a broader concept and has the advantage that it emphasizes social processes – mechanisms of exclusion – rather than individual situation, though not all agree.

> Social exclusion is discussed in detail in chapter 13, 'Poverty, Social Exclusion and Welfare'.

Background to the underclass debate

An influential contribution to the debate was made by Charles Murray (1984), who argued that African Americans in the USA are at the bottom of society as a result of the unintended consequences of state welfare policies. This is similar to the 'culture of poverty' thesis, which sees people becoming dependent on welfare and having little incentive to find work, build solid communities or make stable marriages. A dependency culture is then created that is transmitted across generations.

In response to Murray's claims, in the 1990s William Julius Wilson revisited his own earlier structural explanation of underclass formation from *The Declining Significance of Race* (1978). Drawing on research in Chicago, he argued that the movement of many whites from cities to the suburbs, the decline of urban industries and other urban economic problems had led to high rates of unemployment among African-American men. He explained the aspects of social disintegration to which Murray pointed, including the high proportion of unmarried black mothers, in terms of the shrinking available pool of 'marriageable' (that is, employed) men. Wilson (1999) examined the role of these processes in creating spatially concentrated pockets of urban deprivation populated by a so-called ghetto poor of predominantly African-American and Hispanic people. These groups experienced multiple deprivations, from low educational qualifications and poor health to high levels of criminal victimization. They were also disadvantaged by a weak urban infrastructure with inadequate public transport, community facilities and educational institutions, which further reduced their chances of integrating into society socially, politically and economically.

Wilson's focus on the structural and spatial aspects of underclass formation were mirrored in the UK in Lydia Morris's (1993, 1995) research into long-term unemployment in the wake of the decline of heavy industries in North-East England that were once major sources of employment. Nevertheless, she concluded that 'there is no direct evidence in my study of a distinctive culture of the "underclass"' (1993: 410). What she did find was that even the long-term unemployed (those without a job for more than a year) were actively seeking work and had not adopted an anti-work culture. What they lacked were the social contacts that many employed respondents had. This research again moves away from exploring individual motivations in isolation from wider social processes (Crompton 2008). However, the study was restricted to a region that lacks significant minority ethnic

Does the American theory of an underclass make sense in the context of European societies? Consider these Muslims outside a mosque in Whitechapel in East London: is it race, class or something else that keeps them living there?

populations, and its findings cannot simply be generalized to the national level.

The underclass, the EU and migration

Debates on the underclass in the United States centred on the ethnic dimension, and this is increasingly the case in Europe, where discussion of 'the underclass' is closely tied to questions of race, ethnicity and migration. In major cities such as London, Manchester, Rotterdam, Frankfurt, Paris and Naples, there are neighbourhoods marked by severe economic deprivation. Hamburg is Europe's richest city, with the highest proportion of millionaires in

Germany, but it also has the highest proportion of people on welfare and unemployment benefits – 40 per cent above the national average.

The majority of poor and unemployed people in Western European countries were born in those countries, but there are also many first- and second-generation immigrants living in poverty, trapped in deteriorating inner-city neighbourhoods. Sizeable populations of Turks in Germany, Algerians in France and Albanians in Italy, for example, have grown up in each of these countries. Migrants in search of a better standard of living are often found in casual jobs with low wages and few career prospects (see 'Global society 12.2'). Furthermore, migrants' earnings are frequently sent home to support family members, and the standard of living of recent immigrants can be precariously low.

Evaluation

How can we make sense of the contrasting approaches to the underclass? The concept was created in the United States and continues to be more useful there. In the USA, extremes of rich and poor are more marked than in Western Europe. Particularly where economic and social deprivation converge with racial divisions, social groups find themselves locked out of the wider society. However, the concept is less effective in European countries. There is not the same level of separation between those who live in conditions of marked deprivation and the rest of the society.

Nonetheless, even in the USA, some studies have suggested that accounts of a 'defeated and disconnected underclass' are exaggerated. Research into fast-food workers and homeless street traders have found that the separation between the urban poor and the rest of society is not as great as scholars of the underclass believed (Duneier 1999; Newman 2000).

Class and lifestyles

In analysing people's class location, sociologists have conventionally relied on indicators such as market position, occupation and relationship to the means of production. However, more recently it has been argued that we should evaluate class location not only, or even mainly, in terms of economics and employment but also in relation to cultural factors such as lifestyle and consumption patterns. According to this 'cultural turn' in stratification research, contemporary societies are marked by the significance of 'symbols' and markers of consumption, which play a greater role in daily life. Individual identities are structured to a larger extent around lifestyle choices – such as how we dress, what

---

Global Society 12.2 | The creation of a 'Muslim underclass' in Germany?

'Berlin integration plan attacked'

Demonstrators from the large Turkish community in Germany have protested in Berlin outside a summit on integration convened by Chancellor Angela Merkel. Four Turkish groups are boycotting the meeting, saying a new immigration bill treats Turkish-origin people and other immigrants as 'second-class citizens'. The forum will examine ways to improve community relations, including teaching German in nursery schools.

About 15 million people with immigrant backgrounds are living in Germany. The BBC's Tristana Moore in Berlin says the situation of Germany's 3.2 million Muslims, most of whom are of Turkish origin, has generated some anxiety, with fears that a lack of job prospects and the language divide risk creating an embittered Muslim underclass. Ministers have long been concerned that ghettos are springing up in German cities, she reports.

New rules

Chancellor Merkel has invited members of the Muslim community and other immigrant groups to the conference. But several Turkish community groups want the government to change the controversial immigration bill. It stipulates that an immigrant who wants to bring a spouse to Germany has to prove the partner can earn a living and has some knowledge of German. The new rules do not apply to German nationals who have foreign partners. The government has ruled out making any changes to the new bill, which has already been approved by both houses of parliament. The Turkish-German groups boycotting the forum have threatened to take the matter to the constitutional court.

Source: BBC (2007b).

we eat, how we care for our bodies and where we relax – and less around conventional class indicators such as the type of work we do.

The French sociologist Pierre Bourdieu (1930–2002) argued that lifestyle choices are an important indicator of class. He saw that *economic capital* – material goods such as property, wealth and income – was important, but he argued that it could provide only a partial understanding of social class as it is lived (Crompton 2008). He identifies four forms of 'capital' that characterize class position, of which economic capital is only one: the others are cultural, social and symbolic capital (Bourdieu 1986).

 See chapter 19, 'Education', for an extended discussion of Bourdieu's theoretical scheme.

Bourdieu argues that people increasingly distinguish themselves from others not on economic criteria, but on the basis of *cultural capital* – including education, appreciation of the arts, consumption and leisure pursuits. They are aided in the process of accumulating cultural capital by a proliferation of 'need merchants' selling goods and services – either symbolic or actual – for consumption. Advertisers, marketers, fashion designers, style consultants, interior designers, personal trainers, therapists, web designers, and many others seek to influence cultural tastes and promote lifestyle choices among communities of consumers.

Also important in Bourdieu's analysis of class is *social capital* – our networks of friends and other contacts. Bourdieu (1992) defined social capital as the resources that individuals or groups gain through their long-lasting networks of relationships with friends, mutual acquaintances and other contacts. The concept of social capital has since become an important and productive one in contemporary sociology. Lastly, Bourdieu argues that *symbolic capital* – which includes possession of a 'good reputation' – is an important indication of social class. The idea of symbolic capital

is similar to that of social status, being based on other people's assessment of us.

In Bourdieu's account, each type of capital is related, and being in possession of one can help in the pursuit of others. A businesswoman who earns a large amount of money (economic capital) may not have much knowledge of the arts, but she can pay for her children to attend private schools where these pursuits are encouraged, so the children gain cultural capital. The businesswoman's money may lead her to make contacts with senior people in business and her children will meet others from wealthy families, so she, and they, will gain in social capital. Similarly, someone with a large group of well-connected friends (social capital) might be quickly promoted to a senior position in a company where they do well, thus gaining economic and symbolic capital.

Other scholars agree that class divisions can be linked to distinctive lifestyle and consumption patterns. Thus, speaking of groupings within the middle class, Mike Savage and his colleagues (1992) identified three sectors based on cultural tastes and 'assets'. Professionals in public service, who are high in cultural capital and low in economic capital, tend to pursue healthy, active lifestyles involving exercise, low alcohol consumption, and participation in cultural and community activities. Managers and bureaucrats, by contrast, are typified by 'indistinctive' patterns of consumption, which involve average or low levels of exercise, little engagement with cultural activities, and a preference for traditional styles in home furnishings and fashion. The third grouping, the 'postmoderns', pursue a lifestyle that lacks any defining principle and may contain elements not traditionally enjoyed together. Thus, horse-riding and an interest in classical literature may be accompanied by a fascination with extreme sports such as rock-climbing and a love of raves and illicit use of the drug Ecstasy (MDMA).

Le Roux and her colleagues (2007), who investigated the cultural tastes and participation of a stratified, random sample of just over 1,500 people in areas such as sport, television, eating out, music and leisure, found that class boundaries were being redrawn in quite unexpected ways:

> Our findings suggest that class boundaries are being redrawn through the increasing interplay between economic and cultural capital. Those members of the 'service class' who do not typically possess graduate level credentials, especially those in lower managerial positions, are more similar to the intermediate classes than they are to the other sections of the professional middle class. Boundaries are also being re-drawn within the working class, where lower supervisory and technical occupations have been downgraded so that they have become similar to those in semi-routine and routine positions. (2007: 22)

However, this does not mean that social class is no longer relevant. In fact, the authors conclude, class divisions are central to the organization of cultural tastes and practices in the UK.

In 2011, the BBC conducted a web-based survey of social class in the UK which drew 161,400 respondents, making it the largest survey of class ever conducted. Mike Savage and his colleagues (2013) analysed these data alongside a national representative survey. Using Pierre Bourdieu's theory of social, cultural and economic capital, and taking in occupation, leisure interests, food preferences, social relationships and more, the research team derived a 'new model' of the class system.

The new model found a fragmentation of the conventional working and middle classes but also suggested that an elite exists at the top of society which enjoys very high economic capital, high social capital and very high cultural capital. Among this elite are barristers, judges, chief executive officers and PR directors with mean household incomes of £89,000 per annum. But at the bottom of the class system is what Savage and his colleagues call a 'precariat', around 15 per cent of the population which has poor economic capital (mean household income of £8,000 per annum) and low social and cultural capital, including cleaners, caretakers, cashiers and care workers. Members of the precariat tend to be located in old industrial areas; they are very unlikely to have attended university and their work brings high levels of insecurity. With an elite group at the top and an insecure, precariously situated class at the bottom, this analysis illustrates the polarization of inequality in twenty-first century Britain.

It would be difficult to dispute that stratification *within* classes, as well as *between* classes, has come to depend not only on occupational differences but also on differences in consumption, lifestyles and social relationships. This is borne out by looking at trends in society as a whole. The rapid expansion of the service sector and the entertainment and leisure industries, for example, reflects an increasing emphasis on consumption. Modern societies have become consumer societies geared to the desiring and acquisition of material goods. And, though such mass consumption might suggest a growing uniformity of products, since the 1970s there has been an increasing differentiation of production and consumption patterns running alongside class differences, which Bourdieu (1986) suggests can intensify class distinctions through fine variations in lifestyle and 'taste'.

Despite this, we should not ignore the critical role played by economic factors in the reproduction of social inequalities. For the most part, people experiencing extreme social and material deprivations are not doing so as part of their lifestyle choices. Rather, their circumstances are constrained by factors relating to the economic and occupational structure (Crompton 2008). In the present period, when economies across the world are still recovering from recession and a rapid global economic downturn, lifestyle choices may be increasingly constrained by economic situation and class position.

Gender and stratification

For many years, research on stratification was 'gender-blind' – written as though women did not exist or as though, for purposes of studying divisions of power, wealth and prestige, women were unimportant. Yet gender itself is one of the most profound examples of social stratification, and all societies are structured in ways which reproduce gender inequality and privilege men over women in terms of wealth, status and influence.

One of the main problems posed by the study of gender and stratification is whether we can understand gender inequalities today in terms of class divisions. Inequalities of gender are more deep-rooted historically than class systems; men have superior standing to women even in hunter-gatherer societies, where there are no distinct classes. Yet class divisions are so fundamental to modern capitalist societies that they 'overlap' substantially with gender inequalities. The material position of most women tends to reflect that of their fathers or male partners, and it can be argued

USING YOUR SOCIOLOGICAL IMAGINATION

12.2 'Disidentifying' with the working class?

Bourdieu's work on class and status distinctions has been highly influential, and many sociologists have drawn on it in their own studies of social class. One notable example is the British sociologist Beverley Skeggs, who used Bourdieu's account of class and culture to examine the formation of class and gender in her study of women in North-West England.

Over a twelve-year period, Skeggs (1997) followed the lives of eighty-three working-class women who had all enrolled, at some point, in a course for carers at a local further education college. Following Bourdieu's terminology, Skeggs found that the women she studied possessed low economic, cultural, social and symbolic capital. They were poorly paid, had limited success in formal education and few relationships with people in powerful positions that they could draw upon; they also possessed low status in the eyes of higher social classes. Skeggs argues that this lack of capital reflects the wider lack of positive identities for working-class women in the UK. Working-class men, by contrast, do not have the same difficulty gaining a positive identity, and Skeggs suggests this has often been provided through participation in the trade union movement. For women, therefore, to be called 'working class' is to be labelled dirty, valueless and potentially dangerous.

It is this theoretical background, Skeggs argues, that explains why the women in her study were so reluctant to describe themselves as working class. They were well aware of cultural jibes aimed at working-class women about 'white stilettos', 'Sharons' and 'Traceys'. In the interviews, Skeggs found that the women tended to 'disidentify' with a perception of themselves as working class. When discussing sexuality, for example, they were keen to avoid the accusation that they were 'tarty', which would devalue the limited capital they did possess as young, marriageable women. It was important among the group that they were sexually desirable and could 'get a man' if they wanted to. Marriage offered the best chance of respectability and responsibility. The choice to pursue a course in caring emphasized these concerns: training to be a carer taught the women good parenting and offered the possibility of respectable paid work over unemployment after qualification.

Although the women tried to disidentify with a view of themselves as working class and often saw class as of marginal importance in their lives, Skeggs argues it is actually fundamental to the way they lived, and their attempts to distance themselves from a working-class identity made it even more so. Skeggs's account of the lives of a group of women in North-West England shows how class is closely interlinked with other forms of identity – in this case, gender.

THINKING CRITICALLY

The women in this study saw class as marginally important to them, but, actually, it shaped their life chances. Given the gap between the women's understanding and that of the sociologist, is this a case of a sociologist treating 'ordinary people' as 'cultural dopes' (Garfinkel 1963)? What practical steps could the sociologist take to enhance the validity of her conclusions?

that gender inequalities can still be explained, at least in part, in class terms.

Determining women's class position

The view that class inequalities govern gender stratification was an unstated research assumption until the late twentieth century. Feminist critiques and the undeniable changes in women's economic position in the developed countries made this an issue for debate.

The 'conventional position' in class analysis was that women's paid work is relatively insignificant compared with that of men, so we can assume that women are effectively in the same class as their fathers, male partners or husbands (Goldthorpe 1983). According to Goldthorpe, whose own class scheme was originally predicated on this assumption, this is not sexist. On the contrary, it is a recognition of the subordinate position in which most women find themselves. Women are more likely to have part-time jobs than men and to have an intermittent experience of paid employment, because they are forced to withdraw for lengthy periods to bear and care for children or to look after relatives.

See chapter 7, 'Work and the Economy', for more about the differences between women and men's working patterns.

However, Goldthorpe's position has been criticized. First, in a substantial number of households, the income of women, even if lower than that of male partners, is essential to maintaining the family's economic position and lifestyle. If so, then women's paid employment, in part, determines the class position of the household and cannot be discounted. Second, a woman's occupation may set the social class for the household, even when she earns less than her partner or husband. This could be the case where the man is an unskilled or semi-skilled worker and the woman is the manager of an office or shop. Third, in 'cross-class' households – where the work of the man is in a different category from that of the woman – it may be more

realistic to treat men and women as being in different class positions. Fourth, the proportion of households in which women are sole breadwinners is increasing, and here women are, by definition, the determining influence on the class position of the household, except in cases where child maintenance payments put a woman on the same economic level as her ex-partner/husband (Stanworth 1984; Walby 1986).

Goldthorpe and others have defended the conventional position against their critics, but some important changes have been incorporated into Goldthorpe's scheme. For research purposes, the partner in the higher class position can now be used to classify a household, whether that person is a man or a woman. Rather than assuming a 'male breadwinner', household classification is now determined by what is called the 'dominant breadwinner'. Furthermore, class III in Goldthorpe's scheme has been divided into two subcategories to reflect the preponderance of women in low-level, white-collar work. When the scheme is applied to women, class IIIb – non-manual workers in sales and services – is treated as class VII. This is seen as a more accurate representation of the position of unskilled and semi-skilled women in the labour market.

The impact of women's employment on class divisions

The entry of women into paid employment has had a significant impact on household incomes. But this impact has been experienced unevenly and may be accentuating class divisions between households. A growing number of women are moving into professional and managerial positions and earning high salaries, contributing to a polarization between high-income 'dual-earner households' and 'single-earner' or 'no-earner' households.

Research has shown that high-earning women tend to have high-earning partners, and that the wives of men in professional and managerial occupations have higher earnings than other employed female partners. Therefore, marriage tends to produce partnerships where both individuals are relatively privileged or disadvantaged in terms of occupational attainment (Bonney 1992). The impact of dual-earner partnerships is heightened by the fact that the average childbearing age is rising, particularly among professional women. The growing number of dual-earner, childless couples is fuelling a widening gap between the highest and lowest paid households.

Social mobility

Scholars of stratification study not just the differences between economic position or occupations but also what happens to the individuals who occupy them. The term 'social mobility' refers to the movement of individuals and groups between socio-economic positions. Vertical mobility means movement up or down the socio-economic scale. Those who gain in property, income or status are said to be *upwardly mobile*, while those who move in the opposite direction are *downwardly mobile*. In modern societies there is also a great deal of lateral mobility, which refers to geographical movement between neighbourhoods, towns or regions. Vertical and lateral mobility are often combined – for instance, where someone working in a company in one city is promoted to a higher position in a branch of the firm located in another town, or even in a different country.

There are, broadly, two ways of studying social mobility. First, we can look at individual careers – how far people move up or down the social scale in the course of their working lives. This is called intragenerational mobility. Alternatively, we can analyse how far children enter the same type of occupation as their parents or grandparents. Mobility across generations is called intergenerational mobility.

Comparative mobility studies

The amount of vertical mobility in a society is a major index of its 'openness', indicating how far talented individuals born into lower

Today's generation enjoys a higher material standard of living than their grandparents at a similar age, including car-ownership, holiday travel and (despite a recent reversal of the trend due to the 2008 financial crisis) home-ownership.

strata can move up the socio-economic ladder. In this respect, social mobility is a political issue, particularly in societies committed to the liberal vision of equality of opportunity for all. But how 'open' are the industrialized countries?

Studies of social mobility cover a period of more than fifty years and frequently involve international comparisons. An important early study was conducted in America by Peter Blau and Otis Dudley Duncan (1967).

Global Society 12.3 Is inequality declining in class-based societies?

There is some evidence that, at least until recently, the class systems in mature capitalist societies were increasingly open to movement between classes, thereby reducing the level of inequality. In 1955, the Nobel Prize-winning economist Simon Kuznets proposed a hypothesis that has since been called the Kuznets Curve: a formula showing that inequality increases during the early stages of capitalist development, then declines, and eventually stabilizes at a relatively low level (Kuznets 1955; figure 12.1).

Studies of European countries, the United States and Canada suggested that inequality peaked in these places before the Second World War, declined through the 1950s, and remained roughly the same through the 1970s (Berger 1986; Nielsen 1994). Lowered postwar inequality was the result in part of economic expansion in industrial societies, which created opportunities for people at the bottom to move up, and also of government health insurance, welfare and other programmes, which aimed to reduce inequality. However, Kuznets's prediction may well turn out to apply only to industrial societies. The emergence of the post-industrial society has brought with it an increase in inequality in many developed nations since the 1970s (see chapter 13), which calls into question Kuznets's theory.

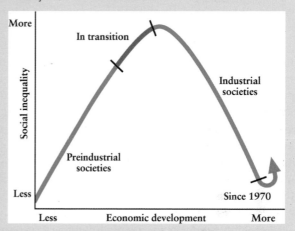

Figure 12.1 The Kuznets Curve

Source: Nielsen (1994).

Theirs remains the most detailed investigation of social mobility yet carried out in a single country, though, as with most others in this field, all the subjects were men, reinforcing the point that social mobility studies lack gender balance.

Blau and Duncan collected information on a national sample of 20,000 males. They concluded that there was much vertical mobility in the USA, but nearly all of this was between occupational positions quite close to one another. 'Long-range' mobility was found to be rare. Although downward movement did occur, both within the careers of individuals and intergenerationally, it was much less common than upward mobility. The reason is that the numbers of white-collar and professional jobs have grown much more rapidly than blue-collar ones, creating new openings for the sons of blue-collar workers to move into white-collar positions. Blau and Duncan emphasized the importance of education and training on an individual's chances for success. In their view, upward social mobility is characteristic of industrial societies as a whole and contributes to their stability and social integration.

Perhaps the most celebrated *international* study of social mobility was carried out by Seymour Martin Lipset and Reinhard Bendix (1959). They analysed data from nine industrialized societies – Britain, France, West Germany, Sweden, Switzerland, Japan, Denmark, Italy and the United States – concentrating on the mobility of men from blue-collar into white-collar work. Contrary to their expectations, they discovered no evidence that the United States was more open than European societies. Total vertical mobility across the blue-collar–white-collar line was 30 per cent in the United States, with the other societies varying between 27 and 31 per cent. Lipset and Bendix concluded that all the industrialized countries experienced similar changes in their occupational structure, which led to an 'upward surge of mobility' of comparable dimensions in all of them. However, some have questioned their findings, arguing that significant differences between countries are found if more attention is given to downward mobility and if long-range mobility is also considered (Heath 1981; Grusky and Hauser 1984).

Most studies of social mobility have focused on the 'objective' dimensions of mobility – that is, how much mobility exists, in which directions and for which sections of the population. Marshall and Firth (1999) took a different approach in their comparative study of social mobility, investigating people's 'subjective' feelings about changing class positions. The authors designed their research in response to what they call 'unsubstantiated speculation' among sociologists about the likely effects of social mobility on an individual's sense of well-being. While some have argued that social mobility produces a sense of disequilibrium and isolation, others have taken a more optimistic view, suggesting that a gradual process of adaptation to the new class location takes place.

Using survey data from ten countries – Bulgaria, the Czech Republic, Slovakia, Estonia, Germany, Poland, Russia, Slovenia, the USA and the UK – Marshall and Firth examined whether class mobility was linked to a heightened sense of satisfaction or dissatisfaction in relation to family, community, work, income and politics. On the whole, they found little evidence of an association between class experience and overall life satisfaction. This was true for both upward and downwardly mobile individuals.

Downward mobility

Although downward mobility is less common than upward mobility, it is still a widespread phenomenon. Downward intragenerational mobility is also common. Mobility of this type is quite often associated with psychological problems and anxieties, where individuals become unable to sustain the lifestyles to which they have become accustomed. Redundancy is a main source of downward mobility. Middle-aged people who lose their jobs can find it hard to gain new employment or can obtain work only at a lower level of income than before.

Thus far, there have been few studies of downward mobility in the UK. However, it is probable that, in both inter- and intragenerational terms, it is increasing in Britain, as it is in the United States. In the USA over the 1980s and early 1990s, for the first time since the Second World War, there was a general downturn in the average real earnings (earnings after adjusting for inflation) of people in middle-level, white-collar jobs. Thus, even if such jobs continue to expand relative to others, they may not support the lifestyle aspirations they once did.

Corporate restructuring and 'downsizing' are the main reasons for these changes. In the face of increasing global competition, and because of the 2008 global recession, many companies cut their workforces. White-collar as well as full-time blue-collar jobs have been lost, many replaced by relatively poorly paid, part-time occupations and short-term contracts. Downward mobility is particularly common among divorced or separated women with children. Women who enjoyed a comfortable middle-class way of life when married can find themselves living 'hand-to-mouth' after divorce. In many cases, women attempting to juggle work, childcare and domestic responsibilities find it difficult to make ends meet (Schwarz and Volgy 1992).

Social mobility in Britain

Overall levels of mobility have been extensively studied in Britain over the postwar period, and there is a wealth of empirical evidence and research studies on the British case. For this reason, in this section we will look at UK evidence, remembering that, until very recently, virtually all of this research concentrated on the experience of men.

One important early study was directed by David Glass (1954). Glass's work analysed intergenerational mobility for a long period up to the 1950s. His findings correspond to those noted above in respect of international data, with around 30 per cent mobility from blue-collar into white-collar jobs. On the whole, he concluded that Britain was not a particularly 'open' society. While a good deal of mobility occurred, most of it was short range. Upward mobility was much more common than downward mobility and was concentrated at the middle levels of the class structure. People at the bottom tended to stay there, while almost 50 per cent of sons of workers in professional and managerial jobs were in similar occupations. Glass also found a high degree of 'self-recruitment' into the elite positions within society.

Another important piece of research – the Oxford Mobility Study – was carried out by Goldthorpe and his colleagues (1987 [1980]), based on findings from a 1972 survey. They investigated how far patterns of social mobility had changed since Glass's work and concluded that the overall level of mobility of men was in fact higher, with more long-range movement. The main reason for this was not that British society had become more egalitarian but on account of the acceleration in the growth of higher white-collar jobs relative to blue-collar ones. The researchers found that two-thirds of the sons of unskilled or semi-skilled manual workers were themselves in manual occupations. About 30 per cent of professionals and managers were of working-class origin, while 4 per cent of men in blue-collar work were from professional or managerial backgrounds.

Despite finding higher rates of absolute social mobility in Britain, the Oxford Mobility Study concluded that the relative chances for mobility remained highly unequal, and that inequalities of opportunity remained squarely grounded within the class structure.

The original Oxford study was updated on the basis of new material collected about ten years later (Goldthorpe and Payne 1986). The major findings of the earlier work were corroborated, but some new developments were found. The chances of men from blue-collar backgrounds getting professional or managerial jobs, for example, had increased.

Once again this was traced to changes in the occupational structure, producing a reduction of blue-collar occupations relative to higher white-collar jobs. Such findings reinforce the argument that much social mobility is generated by structural shifts in the economy rather than increasing equality of opportunity.

In the Essex Mobility Study (Marshall et al. 1988), about a third of people in higher white-collar or professional jobs were from blue-collar backgrounds, demonstrating a substantial amount of fluidity in British society. Yet the scales were still tilted against women, whose mobility chances are hampered by their over-representation in routine non-manual jobs. The fluid character of modern societies derives mostly from their propensity to upgrade occupations. The study by Marshall and his colleagues (1988: 138) concluded that 'More "room at the top" has not been accompanied by great equality in the opportunities to get there.' However, we should bear in mind that social mobility is a long-term process, and, when society is becoming more 'open', the full effects may not be seen for a generation.

A study by Jo Blanden et al. (2002) at the London School of Economics found a reversal of this process, comparing intergenerational mobility in Britain between two groups, the first born in March 1958 and the second in April 1970. Even though the age difference between the people involved was only twelve years, the study documented a sharp fall in intergenerational mobility between them. The economic status of the group born in 1970 was more strongly connected to the economic status of their parents than the group born in 1958. The authors suggested that one of the reasons for the fall in intergenerational mobility from the earlier to the later group was that the general rise in educational attainment from the late 1970s onwards benefited children of the wealthy more than children of the less well-off.

More recently, Jackson and Goldthorpe (2007) studied intergenerational class mobility in the UK by comparing previous

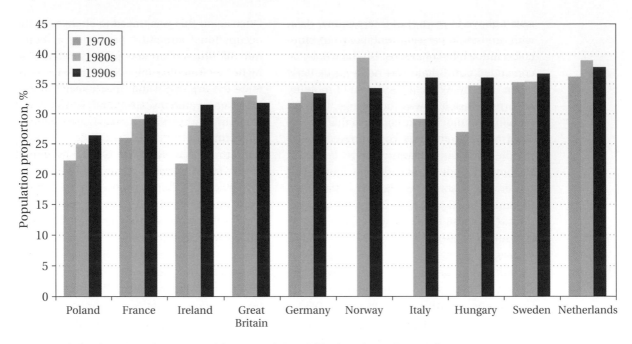

Figure 12.2 Absolute (intergenerational) social mobility in selected countries, men (proportion of men getting better jobs than their parents)

Source: National Equality Panel (2010: 323).

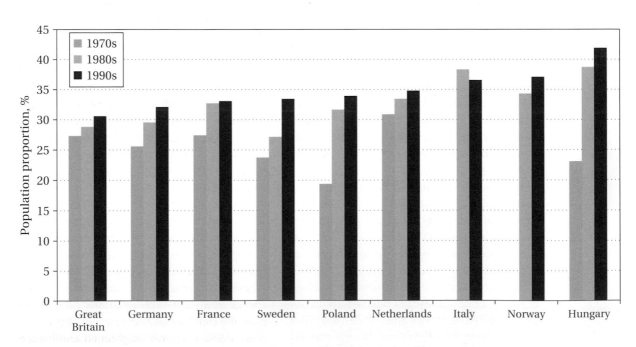

Figure 12.3 Absolute (intergenerational) social mobility in selected countries, women (proportion of women getting better jobs than their parents)

Source: National Equality Panel (2010: 323).

and more recent datasets. They found no evidence that intergenerational mobility was falling in an absolute sense: relative social mobility rates for both men and women remained fairly constant, but there was some indication of a decline in long-range mobility. However, the authors also found a generally less favourable balance between downward and upward mobility emerging for men, which is the product of structural class change. They conclude that there can be no return to the rising rates of upward mobility experienced in the mid-twentieth century.

In 2010, the British government's National Equality Panel reported on the current state of economic inequality. They found that absolute (intergenerational) upward social mobility had changed little since the 1970s. But, when parental income is included, upward mobility for men fell in the 1990s and is lower than in most other European countries, while women's mobility shows a gradual improvement since the 1970s (figures 12.2 and 12.3). However, the rate of increase for women is also at the bottom of the range internationally. The report concludes that the main reason for these relatively low levels of social mobility is that Britain has a high level of social inequality. This matters, the authors say, because 'moving up a ladder is harder if the rungs are further apart . . . it matters more in Britain who your parents are than in many other countries' (National Equality Panel 2010: 329–30). More than fifty years after David Glass's research, this finding demonstrates that Britain is still 'not a particularly "open" society' and shows how firmly established its class boundaries are.

> **THINKING CRITICALLY**
>
> Is social mobility important? If intergenerational social mobility *has* fallen, does it matter? What social consequences are likely to follow from falling levels of social mobility? What can governments do to promote upward social mobility?

Gender and social mobility

Although so much research into social mobility has focused on men, in recent years more attention has been paid to patterns of mobility among women. At a time when girls are 'outperforming' boys in school and females are outnumbering males in higher education, it is tempting to conclude that longstanding gender inequalities in society may be relaxing their hold. Has the occupational structure become more 'open' to women, or are their mobility chances still guided largely by family and social background?

 See chapter 19, 'Education', for a more detailed discussion of higher education.

An important cohort study funded by the UK's Economic and Social Research Council (ESRC), published as *Twenty-Something in the 1990s* (Bynner et al. 1997), traced the lives of 9,000 Britons born during the same week in 1970. In 1996, it was found that, for both men and women at the age of twenty-six, family background and class of origin remained powerful influences. The study concluded that the young people who coped best with the transition to adulthood were those who had obtained a better education, postponed children and marriage, and had fathers in professional occupations. Individuals who had come from disadvantaged backgrounds tended to remain there.

The study also found that, on the whole, women today have more opportunities than their counterparts in the previous generation. Middle-class women have benefited most from the shifts described above: they are just as likely as their male peers to go to university and to move into well-paid jobs on graduation. The trend towards greater equality is also reflected in women's heightened confidence and self-esteem compared with those of a similar cohort of women born just twelve years earlier. As table 12.3 shows, women are now moving into some of the high-status positions

Table 12.3 **Percentage of women in Britain's top jobs, 2010–11**

Occupation/role	Female	Occupation/role	Female
MP (House of Commons)	22.2	Senior judiciary	12.9
MSP (Holyrood, Scottish Parliament)	34.9	FTSE 100 company director	12.5
MEP (Strasbourg, European Parliament)	31.9	University vice chancellor	14.3
MWA (Cardiff, Welsh Assembly)	41.7	Senior ranks in the armed forces	1
Local authority council leader	13.2		

Source: Collated from EHRC (2011).

in British society, as they are in many developed countries, though not in particularly large numbers. For example, only 7.8 per cent of directors across the FTSE 250 companies in the UK are female (EHRC 2011: 4), and almost half of these companies still have all-male boardrooms (McVeigh 2010). One way of expressing this change is to say that women have cracked the 'glass ceiling' but, as yet, it has not been broken.

Women's chances of gaining a good career are improving, but two major obstacles remain. Male managers and employers have been found still to discriminate against women applicants. They do so, at least partly, because of a belief that women are not really interested in careers and are likely to leave when they start a family. Having children does indeed have a significant effect on the career chances of women. This is not because they are uninterested in a career; rather, they are effectively forced to choose between a career and having children. This is on account of the fact that men are rarely willing to share full responsibility for domestic work and childcare. And, though more women than before are organizing their domestic lives in order to pursue a career, this is still a challenging situation.

Is Britain a meritocratic society?

Peter Saunders (1990, 1996, 2010) is one of the most vocal critics of the whole British tradition of social mobility research encompassing most of the studies described above. For Saunders, Britain really is a meritocratic society, because the biggest rewards go to those who 'perform' and achieve. In his view, intelligence, ability and effort are the key factors in occupational success, not class background. Saunders (1996) used empirical data from the National Child Development Study to show that children who are bright and hard-working succeed regardless of their social advantages or disadvantages. Britain may be an unequal society, he argues, but it is a fair one. This conclusion may well be a widely held assumption among the populations of developed countries.

In response, Breen and Goldthorpe (1999) criticize Saunders on theoretical and methodological grounds. They accuse him of introducing bias into his analysis of the survey data, such as excluding respondents who were unemployed. Breen and Goldthorpe provide an alternative analysis of the same data, arriving at radically different conclusions, showing that there are significant class barriers to social mobility. They concede that individual merit is a contributory factor in determining class position but maintain that 'class of origin' remains a powerful influence. They argue that children from disadvantaged backgrounds must show more merit than those who are advantaged if they are to acquire a similar class position.

A more recent international and comparative study of inequality and social mobility, by Dan Andrews and Andrew Leigh (2009), also takes issue with Saunders's claim that societies can be both unequal and fair. Their empirical survey used occupational data on men aged twenty-five to fifty-four in sixteen countries around the world (excluding the UK), concentrating on the comparative earnings of fathers and their sons. Their main conclusion was that 'Sons who grew up in more unequal countries in the 1970s were less likely to have experienced social mobility by 1999' (ibid.: 1491–2). In unequal societies around the world, there is less social mobility, and the movement from 'rags to riches' becomes much more difficult for those who start from the lower positions. Thus, inequality actually seems to impede 'fair' outcomes (based on ability and effort), and in order to move to a genuine meritocracy it will be necessary to reduce inequality.

Conclusion: the enduring significance of class

People's lives are never completely determined by class divisions, and many people do experience social mobility. The expansion of higher education, the growing accessibility of professional qualifications, and the emergence of the Internet and the 'new economy' all present important new channels for upward mobility. Such developments may further erode old class and stratification patterns, contributing to a more fluid social order.

However, inequality between the poor and the more affluent has actually expanded in Britain and elsewhere over the past thirty years or so, and concerns continue to grow about the impact of wealth concentration at the very top of the social hierarchy. Is increasing class inequality a price that has to be paid to secure a more general economic development? Since the 1980s, the pursuit of wealth has been seen as generating economic development because it is a motivating force encouraging innovation and drive. Today many argue that globalization and the deregulation of economic markets have led to a widening of the gap between rich and poor and a 'hardening' of class inequalities.

Although the traditional hold of class may well be weakening in some respects, particularly as multiple sources of identification and consumerism have become more significant, class divisions remain at the heart of core economic inequalities. Social class continues to exert a large influence on life chances and class membership correlates strongly with a variety of inequalities, from life expectancy and physical health to access to education, workplace remuneration and social mobility. Hence, the balance of the available evidence leads us to conclude that reports of the death of class are, at best, premature.

Chapter review

1 Four major types of stratification system can be identified: slavery, caste, estates and class. Outline the distinctive characteristics of each.
2 What is meant by 'modern slavery'? Why is it increasing today?
3 Explain Marx's theory of class conflict, including his definition of class. How satisfactory is this theory and how can it be criticized?

4 Weber distinguished class from status and party. What is social status? What does he mean by 'party'? If Weber's view of modern stratification is correct, is a class-based revolution likely?
5 Occupation is often used as an indicator of class. What are occupational class schemes good at identifying and what do they miss out or underplay?

6 The upper class is a small minority that enjoys significant advantages in society. What are these advantages? Do members of the upper class wield real power in society or are they merely extremely wealthy?

7   List some occupations considered 'middle class' today. What is required to gain access into these and why did the middle class expand rapidly over the twentieth century?

8   What do sociologists mean by 'the working class'? What social and economic factors account for the shrinking of this class from the mid-twentieth century?

9   Describe the main elements attributed to 'the underclass'. How has this concept been criticized by sociologists?

10 Some authors have argued that cultural factors, such as lifestyle and consumption patterns, are important influences on class position. What evidence is there in support of this view?

11 In social mobility studies, a distinction is made between intragenerational and intergenerational mobility. What is the difference? Why have mobility studies not adequately accounted for the position of women?

Research in practice

Since the 1990s, sociologists have debated the shifting power of social class to shape individual identities. As gender, ethnicity, religion and consumerism have all become stronger sources of identity, class appears to be in long-term decline. Indeed, Ulrich Beck argued that class has become a 'zombie category' which no longer performs a useful role in sociology. Read the following article and try to answer the questions below: Loveday, V. (2014) '"Flat-Capping It": Memory, Nostalgia and Value in Retroactive Male Working-Class Identification', *European Journal of Cultural Studies*, 17(6): 721–35.

1   What is the central research question in this paper?

2   How has the sample of research participants been selected? Is this sample appropriate for the research question?

3   What do the authors mean by 'mnemonic imagination', 'flat-capping it' and 'family folklore'?

4   What conclusions are drawn about the participants' continuing identification with social class?

5   Why do the authors argue that looking nostalgically to the past may not be as regressive today as it may have seemed previously?

Thinking it through

Social mobility is generally assumed to be a good thing, both for the individual and for society as a whole. It may be easier to see this in the case of an individual looking to enjoy a long career and reap the benefits of it both financially and in terms of status. However, it is more difficult to see why mobility is good for society. After all, there are many routine and fairly mundane manual jobs which have to be filled, and these are not noted for having a career ladder or high wages.

Review the evidence on social mobility in the chapter, thinking about how far the rhetoric of encouraging mobility matches the available evidence. Write a short briefing paper for government ministers exploring the question of whether government policy should continue to promote social mobility. In particular, address their concerns about the impact of this policy on the take-up of routine manual jobs in the economy. Also comment on the issue of whether an increasing concern with social mobility devalues this type of work, making it harder to fill the jobs.

Society in the arts

There has been an enormous amount of sociological research into the lives and experiences of the working class but much less interest in documenting middle- and upper-class life. Many people's ideas of 'how the other half live' are shaped by the way they have been represented in film, in novels and on television. The most successful of recent times is the British series *Downton Abbey* (2010–15, various directors), which represents upper-class norms, values and lifestyles, as well as class relations. If you have not already seen it, watch one or two episodes and answer the questions below.

1   How are the upper-class characters portrayed? Are there clear gender differences?
2   What values do they hold and how do these differ from the values of those 'downstairs'?
3   How are the attitudes of the domestic staff towards those 'upstairs' presented? For example, is workers' deference to their social superiors presented as necessary?
4   This series is extremely popular and attracts large audiences around the world. How can this popularity be explained during a so-called age of austerity and when extreme inequality at the top is causing much political concern and protest? Discuss this with reference to the show's portrayal of class relations.

Further reading

A good place to start is with Will Atkinson's (2015) *Class* (Cambridge: Polity), which is an engaging introduction to contemporary debates. Lucinda Platt's (2011) *Understanding Inequalities: Stratification and Difference* (Cambridge: Polity) is a nicely balanced and broader discussion of inequalities and stratification.

Kath Woodward's edited collection (2004) *Questioning Identity: Gender, Class, Ethnicity* (London: Routledge) is very good, with substantial chapters on the main social divisions. Finally, for the British experience of class, Ken Roberts's (2011) *Class in Contemporary Britain* (2nd edn, Basingstoke: Palgrave Macmillan) is an up-to-date review of the latest evidence and trends.

Moving beyond introductory texts, Mike Savage's (2000) *Class Analysis and Social Transformation* (Buckingham: Open University Press) brings class debates into contact with recent theories of individualization in the work of Beck and Giddens, providing a fresh interpretation. Similarly innovative is Fiona Devine, Mike Savage, John Scott and Rosemary Crompton's edited collection (2004) *Rethinking Class: Cultures, Identities and Lifestyles* (Basingstoke: Palgrave Macmillan), focusing on the links between class analysis and culture.

For a collection of original readings on social inequalities, see the accompanying *Sociology: Introductory Readings* (3rd edn, Cambridge: Polity, 2010).

Internet links

@ **Additional information and support for this book at Polity:**
www.politybooks.com/giddens

@ **Social Inequality and Classes – many useful links from Sociosite at the University of Amsterdam:**
www.sociosite.net/topics/inequality.php#class

@ **The Great British Class Survey – results from this survey as well as readers' comments on them:**
www.bbc.co.uk/science/0/21970879

@ **Social Mobility Foundation – a UK charity promoting social mobility for young people from low-income backgrounds:**
www.socialmobility.org.uk

@ **Explorations in Social Inequality – lots of resources, mainly American, based at Trinity University, San Antonio, USA:**
www.trinity.edu/mkearl/strat.html

@ **Marxists Internet Archive – exactly what it says: all things Marx and Marxism:**
www.marxists.org

@ **BBC Working Class Collection – visual and audio materials on the history of British working-class life:**
www.bbc.co.uk/archive/working

CHAPTER 13

Poverty, Social Exclusion and Welfare

Contents

In 2009–10 the Trussell Trust's fifty-six foodbanks provided enough food for 41,000 people in need for three days. By 2015, the trust had 445 foodbanks across the UK distributing enough food to feed 1.1 million people for the same period. The rapid expansion of foodbanks shows that poverty remains a key issue in one of the world's richest societies.

Jennie worked as a hairdresser when she left school, but when her son became visually impaired as a result of meningitis she left work to care for him. At forty-one years old, and having separated from her husband when her children were quite young, Jennie was living in temporary accommodation in North London as a single parent with three disabled children over the age of ten. In fact, she has only known various forms of temporary accommodation and has not had a permanent place of her own over that period.

Jennie and the boys do get welfare benefits, most of which goes on food, school clothes, fuel and travel. Their rent is paid by housing benefit. While they have a television, washing machine and fridge, they don't go out much and have never been on holiday together. Jennie says she often struggles to provide enough food for all the family, though the boys do not go hungry. Instead, she will have just one meal a day to make sure the food budget ekes out. She often runs out of money to pay for the essentials and saving money for a rainy day is impossible.

Can Jennie's family be seen as living 'in poverty'? Are they poor? Jennie herself thinks they are: 'I mean, in a way, yes, I am poor. Poor – it means you can't afford anything. You can't afford what you need.' However, Jennie's youngest son, eleven-year-old Michael, thinks not. He says, 'We're not actually poor like in a living on the streets way. We ain't got the perfect clothes in the world, clothes that other people's kids have, but we're happy with what we've got as long as we can live.' Thirteen-year-old Mark says, 'We've got this house; we've got friends and stuff like that. So I don't think we are actually poor. Sometimes I think we're poor, because like, we can't get money to spend on like things we want, so I kind of think and I kind of don't think we're poor.' We will spend some time looking at definitions of poverty, as these have a direct impact on sociological research into the phenomenon and on policies to tackle it.

Our abridged version of Jennie's situation is taken from Lansley and Mack's (2015) survey of poverty in Britain in the twenty-first century. Contrary to common-sense views, studies such as this show that poverty in the UK is not in decline but is actually increasing. And yet, in common with other developed societies, the UK has an established welfare state which provides free healthcare and education and aims to help people to improve their lives. If Jennie really is poor, or can be said to be living in conditions of poverty, it is not the same type of poverty that exists in many developing countries, where even the basic necessities such as clean water, free education and easily accessible healthcare are just not available for many millions of people. What we think of as poverty differs according to the norms of life for the majority of people in their own national context.

As we shall see in this chapter, even across the developed world, welfare states differ, both in the type and level of benefits they provide and in their underlying philosophies – that is, in what they are trying to achieve. Some welfare states provide a basic 'safety-net' while others are rooted in an ideal of 'cradle to the grave' provision. Still others, such as the USA, have minimal welfare provision which links benefits to people's commitment to work. These differing philosophies are reflected in welfare expenditure, which is relatively high in Denmark, Sweden and France and relatively low in South Korea, the USA and Japan.

In the UK, Germany and the Netherlands, dealing with the 2008 global financial crisis and economic downturn has brought about a 'politics of austerity', which demands that governments cut public spending levels and welfare provision. Welfare states such as the UK remain committed to mitigating the impact of poverty, but increasingly there is a shift towards 'conditionality' – linking the right to receive benefits to individual responsibilities, especially to take paid employment. However, even where people are in work and receiving top-up or 'in-work' benefits, many still live in conditions of poverty.

Many people who encounter someone like Jennie make assumptions about her life. They might see her poverty and relatively low position in society as a result of her upbringing. Others might blame her for not working hard enough or suggest that living on welfare benefits is too comfortable and an easy option. In the mid-1990s, Carol Walker (1994: 9) found no evidence for such commonplace views: 'Despite sensational newspaper headlines, living on social assistance is not an option most people would choose if they were offered a genuine alternative.'

In sociology, we can rarely, if ever, be satisfied with individualistic explanations. Poverty is not just a 'personal trouble' but a persistent 'public issue', and it is the sociologist's task to develop a broader view of society that can make sense of the experiences of the many people who are in a similar position to Jennie. In this chapter, we examine the idea and experience of poverty more closely and also consider the broader concept of social exclusion. In the final section, we look at how and why welfare states came into being and at attempts to reform them. Readers should note that chapters 13 and 14 are quite closely related. This chapter focuses primarily on poverty, exclusion and welfare in the developed countries, using the UK as a case study throughout, with European comparisons. However, chapter 14, 'Global Inequality', widens the focus to take in issues of poverty and inequality in a global context, with a specific focus on developing countries.

Poverty

Defining poverty

While everyone seems intuitively to understand what poverty is, arriving at an agreed definition for social scientific use has proved difficult. The World Bank (2000: 15) defines poverty as 'pronounced deprivation in well-being'. This pithy statement is a start, but it raises the question of what constitutes well-being? Is it the ability to maintain good health, to have a good education or to have sufficient food? Is it all of those things? In the relatively wealthy developed societies, enjoying these things means having the resources to do so and is usually measured by income. Conversely, being 'in poverty' or 'pronounced deprivation' means not having enough income to gain such resources.

Sociologists usually distinguish between two types of poverty: absolute poverty (often called 'extreme' poverty) and relative poverty. Absolute poverty is grounded in the idea of subsistence – the basic conditions that must be met in order to sustain a physically healthy existence. People who lack these fundamental requirements – such as sufficient food, shelter and clothing – are said to live in absolute poverty. It is held that standards of human subsistence are more or less the same for all people of equivalent age and physique,

so any individual, anywhere in the world, can be said to live in absolute poverty if this universal standard is not met.

On this definition, large sections of the population in many developing countries can be said to be living in relative poverty. Indeed, just over 122 million people in the twenty-eight countries of the European Union were 'at risk of poverty or social exclusion' in 2012, almost one-quarter of the population of the EU (Eurostat 2015a: 1) (The concept of social exclusion is discussed fully later in the chapter.) However, in the more developed countries, with their well-established welfare systems, absolute poverty is rare.

In terms of economic inequality *within* countries, the share of national revenue which goes to the bottom fifth of the population is often not so different. For example, in Rwanda, 5.3 per cent of national revenue goes to the poorest fifth of the population, and in the USA the figure is 5.4 per cent (IBRD/World Bank 2007). As we will see in chapter 14, 'Global Inequality', chronic inequality still exists within the *developed* countries in spite of their elimination of extreme forms of poverty. Poverty and inequality are related, but they are not the same.

Many scholars do not accept that it is possible to identify a universal standard of absolute poverty. It is more appropriate, they argue, to use the concept of relative poverty, which relates deprivation to the overall standard of living in a particular society. Human needs are not everywhere identical but differ both within and across societies. Things seen as essential in one society might be regarded as luxuries in another. For example, in most industrialized countries, running water, flush toilets and the regular consumption of fruit and vegetables are regarded as basic necessities, so people without them could be said to live in relative poverty. Yet, in many developing societies, these elements are not standard among the majority of the population, and it would not make sense to measure poverty according to their presence or absence. It is also the case that the accepted definition of absolute poverty has changed over time according to the existing knowledge that is available in particular periods (Howard et al. 2001). In short, even the definition of absolute poverty proves to be relative to time and place, which undermines the concept's supposed universality.

> For much more on issues of inequality and poverty in developing countries, see chapter 14, 'Global Inequality'.

The concept of relative poverty presents complexities too. As societies develop, so understandings of relative poverty also change and, as societies become more affluent, criteria of relative poverty are gradually adjusted upwards. At one time, for example, refrigerators, televisions, central heating and mobile phones were all considered luxury goods, but in the developed countries today they are seen as necessities for leading a full and active life. Families which do not have or cannot afford such items may be considered to be in relative poverty because they are not able to live the kind of lifestyle enjoyed by the majority in their society. Yet their parents and grandparents may not have had such items but would not have been considered to be in poverty according to the criteria of that period.

Can we really say that 'poverty' exists in the wealthy societies, where consumer goods such as central heating, televisions and dishwashers sit in practically every home? To illustrate these debates, the next section examines some of the official methods of measuring poverty in the UK and sociological attempts to improve on these.

Measuring poverty

Official measurements of poverty

Until around 1999, successive British governments, unlike most other European countries, did not recognize an official 'poverty line', preferring instead to use a range of separate indicators. This meant that researchers had to rely on statistical indicators, such as eligibility for certain welfare benefits, to gauge poverty levels. However, since the 1980s, most EU states have defined poverty as living in a household with an income on or below 60 per cent of the national median household income, usually after direct taxes but excluding housing costs. This is often abbreviated to HBAI (Households Below Average Income'), though we have to remember that the median is not a simple arithmetic average but the midpoint of the income range.

This measure was adopted by Tony Blair's Labour government from 1999 in its attempt to halve child poverty within a decade and eliminate it within twenty years (Lansley and Mack 2015). Using the HBAI measure, in 2013, rates

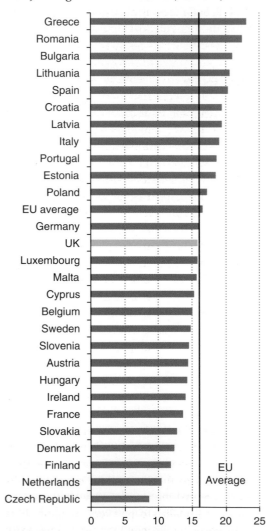

Figure 13.1 Poverty rates across the EU, 2013

Source: ONS (2015a: 5).

of poverty across the twenty-eight countries of the EU differed quite widely. For example, in Greece and Romania, over one-quarter of the population lived in relative poverty, while, in Denmark, the Netherlands and the Czech Republic, less than 15 per cent did so (ONS 2015a: 5–6; see figure 13.1).

It is important to recognize that HBAI is a measure of relative poverty. Consistent use of this measure allows poverty levels to be tracked over time. For instance, the number of people living in poverty in the UK increased dramatically throughout the 1980s, peaking in 1991–2, before falling back from the mid-1990s onwards. In 2009–10, the Department for Work and Pensions reported that 10.4 million people – 17 per cent of the population – were living in poverty according to this measure (DWP 2011: 11). That percentage has been remarkably stable since 1994–5: it rose briefly to around 19 per cent following the 2008 financial crash but had fallen back to 16 per cent by 2013 (ONS 2015a: 4).

The EU has adopted a similar but not identical measure, known as the 'at risk of poverty or social exclusion' rate (AROPE). This involves three measures: people at risk of (income) poverty, those in material deprivation, and those living in households with a very low 'work intensity' (Eurostat 2015a). Combining poverty and social exclusion in this way allows for a broader comparison of cross-national disadvantage and inequality, but it also adds a layer of complexity to comparative statistical analyses.

The 'at risk of poverty' measure refers to individuals with an equivalized disposable income below 60 per cent of the national median income. Note that this does not measure 'poverty' as such, but low income relative to the median, which then leaves people 'at risk' of falling into poverty. Material deprivation refers to the inability to pay for goods such as a washing machine, TV or car and an enforced inability to pay rent or utility bills or to cover unexpected expenses. Low work intensity means that a household's members collectively work less than one-fifth of the time they could have done in a given year. Clearly, given the differing and changing definitions of

relative poverty that exist, comparing poverty rates across time and countries, though not impossible, is fraught with difficulties.

The picture is even more complex, though, as other organizations use their own poverty indicators in addition to income poverty. One independent think tank, the New Policy Institute (NPI), looks at fifty indicators of poverty and social exclusion across income, housing, employment (and unemployment), benefits and services. It defines poverty as a 'state where people are far below the norms of everyday life', effectively covering issues of both poverty and social exclusion (MacInnes et al. 2014: 6). The thirteenth NPI *Monitoring Poverty and Social Exclusion* report, in 2010, found that overall poverty levels in the UK in 2008–9 were unchanged from the previous year, but the number of people in households experiencing 'deep poverty' – less than 40 per cent of median incomes – had continued to rise and now stood at 5.8 million, or 44 per cent of all those in poverty. This was the highest proportion since 1979 (NPI 2010: 23).

The NPI's 2015 report (MacInnes et al. 2015) noted that half of all those in poverty live in families where someone is in paid work. This finding shows that we must be careful not to perpetuate social stereotypes of poverty as linked only to welfare benefit claimants and unemployed people. As we shall see later in the chapter, more recent research studies in this area demonstrate that people move into and out of poverty over the life course as their work and overall situation changes.

Poverty and relative deprivation

Some researchers argue that official measures of the kind discussed above do not give an accurate picture of poverty. Several important studies have been carried out which define poverty as a type of deprivation. One pioneer of this approach was Peter Townsend, whose work from the late 1950s onwards increased public awareness of what 'living in poverty' actually entails (see 'Classic studies 13.1').

Building on Townsend's definition of poverty as deprivation, Mack and Lansley

Who is poor? These children in a refugee camp . . .

carried out two highly influential studies of relative poverty in the UK, the first in 1983 and a second in 1990 (published in 1985 and 1992 respectively). For a television programme in 1983 called *Breadline Britain*, they conducted an opinion poll to determine what people considered 'necessities' for an 'acceptable' standard of living, creating a list of twenty-two basic necessities that more than 50 per cent of respondents considered important for a normal life. By asking respondents what *they* thought to be necessities, Mack and Lansley avoided the criticism directed against Townsend's original survey – namely, that his choice of items for the deprivation index was arbitrary. The 1983 survey estimated around 7.5 million people in the UK living in poverty – about 14 per cent of the population. Mack and Lansley repeated the exercise in 1990 and found a significant *growth* in poverty during

the 1980s, with the number of people living in poverty at around 11 million.

In 2000, David Gordon and his colleagues carried out a similar survey, the Millennium Survey of Poverty and Social Exclusion (known as the PSE survey). The research team used a questionnaire to determine what people considered 'necessities' for an acceptable standard of life in the UK. Based on the responses, they created a list of thirty-five items that more than 50 per cent of respondents considered necessary for a normal life (see table 13.2, p. 531). The team then set a threshold for deprivation, based on an enforced lack of *two or more* necessities, combined with a low income.

The PSE survey found that 28 per cent of the sample lacked two or more necessities, although this included 2 per cent whose incomes were high enough to suggest they had

. . . or these children from a dilapidated housing estate?

Classic Studies 13.1 **Peter Townsend on poverty and deprivation**

The research problem

Sociologists can understand the extent of poverty in society by collating income and other statistics, but what is it like to experience poverty? How are low incomes juggled to make ends meet and what do people have to go without? Peter Townsend's studies concentrated on just this issue of people's subjective experience and understanding of poverty, trying to ascertain exactly what poverty means in terms of deprivation – the lack of or denial of material benefits considered essential for life in a society. In his classic study *Poverty in the United Kingdom* (1979), Townsend examined the responses to more than 2,000 questionnaires filled in by households across the UK during the late 1960s. Respondents provided detailed information about their lifestyles, including their living conditions, eating habits, and leisure and civic activities, as well as their income.

Townsend's explanation

From the information collected, Townsend selected twelve items which were relevant across the sample population, rather than to particular social groups, and calculated the proportion of the population that were deprived of these items (see table 13.1, p. 530). He gave each household a score on a deprivation index – the higher the score, the more deprived the household – then compared the position of households on the index to their total income, making allowances for factors such as the number of people in each household, whether the adults were working, the ages of

529

Table 13.1 Townsend's deprivation index (1979)

Characteristics	Percentage of the population
1 Has not had a holiday away from home in the past twelve months.	53.6
2 Adults only. Has not had a relative or a friend to the home for a meal or snack in the past four weeks.	33.4
3 Adults only. Has not been out in the past four weeks to a relative or friend for a meal or snack.	45.1
4 Children only (under fifteen). Has not had a friend to play or to tea in the past four weeks.	36.3
5 Children only. Did not have a party on last birthday.	56.6
6 Has not had an afternoon or evening out for entertainment in the past two weeks.	47.0
7 Does not have fresh meat (including meals out) as many as four days a week.	19.3
8 Has gone through one or more days in the past fortnight without a cooked meal.	7.0
9 Has not had a cooked breakfast most days of the week.	67.3
10 Household does not have a refrigerator.	45.1
11 Household does not usually have a Sunday joint (three in four times).	25.9
12 Household does not have sole use of four amenities (flush WC; sink or washbasin and cold water tap; fixed bath or shower and gas/electric cooker).	21.4

Source: Townsend (1979: 250).

the children, and whether any members of the house were disabled.

Townsend concluded that his survey had revealed a threshold for levels of income below which social deprivation rose rapidly. It was these households which he described as suffering from poverty, and he calculated that they formed 22.9 per cent of the population – far higher than previous figures had suggested. Townsend's study showed that, as household income falls, so families withdraw from taking part in quite ordinary family-type activities: in short, they become 'socially excluded'.

Critical points

Although Townsend's approach was highly influential, it was also criticized by some commentators, and one particular criticism stands out. Among several critics, David Piachaud (1987) argued that the items selected by Townsend for his deprivation index have an arbitrary quality. That is, it is unclear exactly how they relate to 'poverty' or on what basis they were selected. Some of the items seem to have more to do with social or cultural decisions than with poverty and deprivation. If someone chooses not to eat meat or to have cooked breakfasts, or decides not to socialize regularly or holiday away from home, it is not immediately obvious that the person is suffering from poverty.

Contemporary significance

The cultural critique is an important one, but, over the long term, Townsend's approach to the study of poverty and deprivation has retained its significance. Indeed, it has formed the basis for numerous sociological studies, which have tried to avoid the cultural criticism levelled against Townsend's original study. The attempt to construct a deprivation index based on specific factors remains valuable in our efforts fully to understand how poverty and deprivation are inextricably linked. Townsend's studies were also instrumental in moving contemporary debates on poverty towards an appreciation of the underlying processes of social exclusion, which deny full citizenship to people in poverty.

Table 13.2 **Perception of adult necessities and how many people lack them (percentage of adult population)**

	Items considered		Items that respondents	
	necessary	not necessary	don't have, don't want	don't have, can't afford
Beds and bedding for everyone	95	4	0.2	1
Heating to warm living areas of the home	94	5	0.4	1
Damp-free home	93	6	3	6
Visiting friends or family in hospital	92	7	8	3
Two meals a day	91	9	3	1
Medicines prescribed by doctor	90	9	5	1
Refrigerator	89	11	1	0.1
Fresh fruit and vegetables daily	86	13	7	4
Warm, waterproof coat	85	14	2	4
Replace or repair broken electrical goods	85	14	6	12
Visits to friends or family	84	15	3	2
Celebrations on special occasions such as Christmas	83	16	2	2
Money to keep home in a decent state of decoration	82	17	2	14
Visits to school, e.g., sports day	81	17	33	2
Attending weddings, funerals	80	19	3	3
Meat, fish or vegetarian equivalent every other day	79	19	4	3
Insurance of contents of dwelling	79	20	5	8
Hobby or leisure activity	78	20	12	7
Washing machine	76	22	3	1
Collect children from school	75	23	36	2
Telephone	71	28	1	1
Appropriate clothes for job interviews	69	28	13	4
Deep freezer/fridge freezer	68	30	3	2
Carpets in living rooms and bedrooms	67	31	2	3
Regular savings (of £10 per month) for rainy days or retirement	66	32	7	25
Two pairs of all-weather shoes	64	34	4	5
Friends or family round for a meal	64	34	10	6
A small amount of money to spend on self weekly, not on family	59	39	3	13
Television	56	43	1	1
Roast joint/vegetarian equivalent once a week	56	41	11	3
Presents for friends/family once a year	56	42	1	3
A holiday away from home once a year	55	43	14	18
Replace worn-out furniture	54	43	6	12
Dictionary	53	44	6	5
An outfit for social occasions	51	46	4	4

Source: Gordon et al. (2000: 14).

Table 13.3   **Results of the poverty and social exclusion survey, UK, 2000**

Poverty classifications	Percentage (to the nearest whole number)
Poor	26
Vulnerable to poverty	10
Risen out of poverty	2
Not poor	62

Source: Gordon et al. (2000: 18).

now risen out of poverty, leaving 26 per cent of the survey population classified as being in relative poverty (see table 13.3). Because the researchers in the PSE survey adopted a similar method to that used by Mack and Lansley, they were able to use their data to compare how the UK poverty level had changed over time. The number of households lacking three or more socially perceived necessities (set as the poverty threshold in Mack and Lansley's studies) increased substantially, from 14 per cent in 1983 to 21 per cent by 1990, and to 24 per cent by 1999. Thus, although the British population as a whole had become wealthier since the early 1980s, by 2000 there had also been a dramatic rise in levels of poverty.

A 2006 study reanalysed some of the data from Gordon's PSE survey (Palmer et al. 2006). Combining similar items from the thirty-five 'essential items' scale, they found that the bulk of essential items were directly 'money-related' – that is, the respondents simply did not have a high enough income to afford them (figure 13.2). Drawing on a Family Resources Survey from 2004–5, the team was then able to compare low-income households with those on average incomes in relation to ten selected essential items (see figure 13.3).

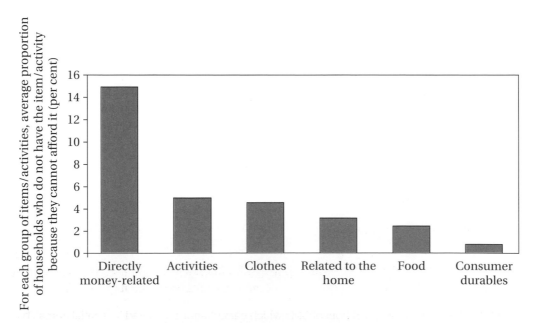

Figure 13.2   Essential items most commonly lacking, by category

Source: Palmer et al. (2006).

Again, significant proportions of low-income households reported they could not afford these items. Almost 60 per cent could not make savings of £10 or more per month, over 50 per cent could not afford an annual holiday, and one-third could not afford to insure their household contents.

However, Palmer's team point out that a significant minority of households on average incomes reported that they could not afford these items either. The report is therefore critical of the use of subjectively defined measures, which are of limited value in providing a reliable and valid measure of 'real' poverty. For instance, if almost one-third of people on average incomes cannot afford to make 'savings of £10 per month or more' and one-quarter cannot afford 'holidays away from home one week a year', does that mean they also live 'in poverty'? What is needed in addition is qualitative information about exactly

why households cannot afford such items. This would enable us to assess the extent to which the lack of each item is an example of 'enforced poverty' caused by socio-economic circumstances or the result of personal choice, where other things simply take priority.

> **THINKING CRITICALLY**
>
> Does the concept of 'relative poverty' accurately capture the real experience of people living with multiple disadvantages and deprivation? How else might such conditions be characterized?

Who are the poor?

Many individuals move into and out of poverty throughout their lives, which may create the impression that poverty is too fluid to

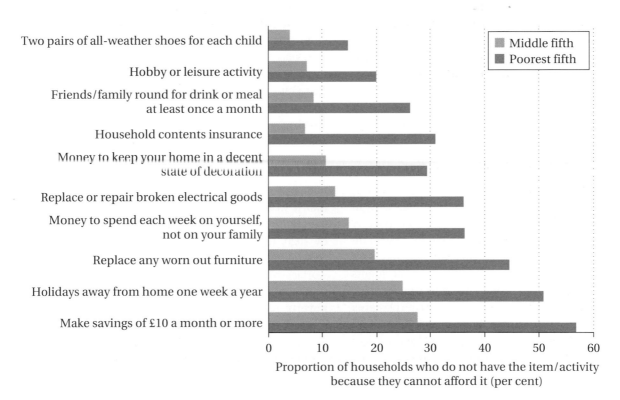

Figure 13.3 Percentage of UK households which cannot afford selected 'essential items', by average and low-income household

Source: DWP (2005).

be patterned. However, what we also know is that the *risk* of being in poverty is higher for some social groups than for others. For example, children, women, some minority ethnic groups and older people are among the high-risk groups. In particular, those who are disadvantaged or discriminated against in other aspects of life have an increased chance of being poor. Recent migrants from outside the European Union, for example, have higher poverty rates than longstanding European populations. In Belgium, more than half of non-EU citizens live in poverty, as do 45 per cent of those in France and Luxembourg. Not only are migrants more at risk of poverty, they also face a higher risk of being exploited at work (Lelkes 2007). And, while this section focuses primarily on the UK, these patterns are repeated to varying degrees across the developed societies.

> Poverty and inequality in developing societies is covered in chapter 14, 'Global Inequality'.

Children

Platt (2013: 328) maintains that 'Children not only face higher risks of poverty but they are particularly vulnerable to its negative consequences, particularly when these persist over time. Effects are both long-term (into adulthood) and have been shown to emerge early in life.' For example, children who live in poverty tend to have worse health than those who do not. They are also more likely to be of low birth weight, to be injured or killed in road accidents (because they are more likely to be pedestrians and less likely to have access to a safe play area or garden), to suffer abuse and self-harm, and to attempt suicide. Poorer children are less likely to do well at school and are far more likely to become poor as adults (Lister 2004). But how big is the problem of child poverty in a developed country like the UK?

The proportion of *all people* in the UK living in households below average income (before housing costs) rose steadily between 1979 and 1991–2, reaching 22 per cent. However, after 1991–2, the trend was downwards, and by 2007–8 this figure had fallen to 18 per cent. The proportion of *children* living in poverty stood at 27 per cent in 1990–1, then fell to 21 per cent in 2004–5 (ONS 2010a: 71). The Labour government elected in 1997 set ambitious targets of reducing child poverty by 50 per cent between 1998 and 2010–11 and eliminating it 'within a generation', but even the former has not been achieved. In 2009–10, child poverty still stood at 19.7 per cent, 900,000 children short of the target.

Labour's 2010 Child Poverty Act set a legal requirement for the eradication of child poverty by 2020, and though the Conservative–Liberal Democrat coalition government (2010–15) confirmed this as a policy goal, in practice the commitment was not actively pursued in its social policies (Lansley and Mack 2015). An analysis by the New Policy Institute (NPI) (Aldridge et al. 2015) suggested that, since 2013, poverty has been rising and child poverty has actually increased by some 300,000, with 29 per cent of UK children living in poverty. Some forecasts now see that child poverty is likely to rise to around 25.7 per cent by 2020–1 (Browne and Hood 2016).

The aim of eliminating child poverty by 2020 was ambitious, but all the signs are that it will not be achieved. Indeed, the Conservative government elected in 2015 announced that it would remove the legal requirement (set out in 2010) of eliminating child poverty by 2020, replacing it with a simpler duty to report on levels of educational attainment, worklessness and addiction. In January 2016, the House of Lords voted to keep the child poverty target, forcing the government to reconsider its plans, and at the time of writing it is unclear whether the child poverty target will be maintained (Cooper 2016). What we can say is that eliminating child poverty cannot be achieved by short-term economic and social policies, but requires consistently applied measures over a long period. This seems unlikely given the five-year electoral cycle of British politics.

Women

As we see at several points throughout this chapter, women are more likely to be poor than men. The PSE survey carried out by Gordon and his colleagues (2000) found that women comprised 58 per cent of all adults living in poverty. However, the causes of this are complex, as female poverty has often been masked behind studies which focused on 'male-headed households' (Ruspini 2000). This presents problems for sociologists when they try to make use of such studies.

One important element concerns the gendered division of labour both inside and outside the home. The burden of domestic labour and the responsibility of caring for children and relatives still fall disproportionately on women, and this has an important effect on their ambitions and ability to work outside the home. It means that they are far more likely than men to be in part-time paid employment and earn less as a result. For example, the UK's Low Pay Commission (2009: 15) found that around two-thirds (64.3 per cent) of all jobs covered by the National Minimum Wage were held by women. Although more women have entered paid work in the UK than ever before, occupational segregation – what is considered 'a man's job' and 'women's work' – in the labour force remains entrenched. Women are disproportionately represented in less well-paid industries, which has a negative effect on income from private pensions later in life (Flaherty et al. 2004).

Minority ethnic groups

Higher rates of poverty exist in the UK for all black and minority ethnic groups than for the white majority population (Barnard and Turner 2011). Minority ethnic groups in the UK are also more likely to have poorly paid jobs, to struggle at school, to live in deprived areas and in poor quality housing, and to suffer health problems (Salway et al. 2007).

A recent study of pre- and post-2008 recession poverty levels shows clearly the disparities across ethnic groups in the UK. Before 2008, relative poverty levels (after housing costs (AHC)) were highest among Bangladeshi (67 per cent), Pakistani (58 per cent) and black African groups (47 per cent), but lowest among the white majority population (20 per cent), Indian (27 per cent) and other white groups (28 per cent) (Fisher and Nandi 2015: 25–8; see figure 13.4). Most European governments prefer the before housing costs (BHC) measure, which allows regional comparisons to be more readily made. However, an AHC measure is also useful, especially where housing costs vary widely across regions. In London, for instance, the number of people living in poverty almost doubles once housing costs are factored in (Tunstall et al. 2013: 34). Figure 13.4 includes both measures to illustrate the impact of the different measures on poverty levels.

The 2008 recession had no impact on the three most disadvantaged groups. In fact, relative poverty levels for Bangladeshi, Pakistani and black Africans actually fell along with those of the white majority and black Caribbean groups. However, levels rose for Indians, Chinese, other white groups and those of mixed parentage.

The report argues that, in absolute terms, the position of the most disadvantaged ethnic groups did not change during and after the financial crash, but other groups saw their situation worsen. However, between 2009 and 2012, Pakistanis and Bangladeshis experienced more persistent poverty (in at least two of three observed years) than other groups, while during the same period 72 per cent of the white majority were never observed to be in poverty.

Part of the reason for ethnic differences in income poverty levels can be found in the high unemployment and low employment rates for minority ethnic groups in the UK. In 2006, Indian and black Caribbean groups had relatively high employment rates, of 70.2 and 67.8 per cent respectively, while Pakistani and Bangladeshi groups had the lowest employment rates among minority ethnic groups – 44.2 and 40.2 per cent respectively. In the same year, the unemployment rate for African and Pakistani/Bangladeshi people, for example,

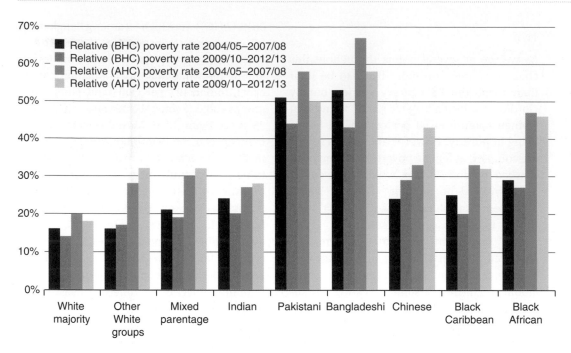

Note: AHC – after housing costs; BHC – before housing costs

Figure 13.4   Relative poverty levels by ethnic group, pre- and post-2008 recession, UK (excluding Northern Ireland)

Source: Fisher and Nandi (2015: 26).

was 11.2 per cent compared with an overall rate of 5.2 per cent, and minority ethnic groups are still twice as likely to be unemployed as white people (Ethnic Minority Employment Taskforce 2006).

There is also a high degree of labour market segregation. Pakistani groups are largely concentrated in the former heavy manufacturing and textile industry areas, such as Yorkshire and Birmingham – industries that fell into recession in the late 1970s and 1980s. Black Caribbean men are over-represented in manual occupations, particularly within the transport and communications industries, while Chinese and Bangladeshi people are particularly concentrated in the catering industry. Some of this occupational segregation has occurred because minority ethnic groups perceive certain industries or employers as 'white', though there is also evidence of racial discrimination during some recruitment processes (Wood et al. 2009).

Over recent years, the concept of intersectionality has become more important in attempts to understand the differentiated experience not just of poverty, but also of social life as a whole. Intersectionality refers to the way that the varied aspects of an individual's identity – such as class, ethnicity, gender, disability and location – interact to produce complex patterns of inequality, poverty and discrimination. As one recent report puts this,

> The experience of a middle class, third generation, Indian, Hindu woman with a degree, living in Milton Keynes may have little in common with a second generation, Indian, Muslim woman, with a level three qualification, living in Bradford with a disabled husband and two children.
> (Barnard and Turner 2011: 4)

Analysing the ways in which the varied elements of individual identities intersect

Minority ethnic groups are among the poorest in Western societies, often, as this poster by the Commission for Racial Equality suggests, because of discrimination and limited work opportunities.

to produce widely differing outcomes in relation to poverty is likely to become more commonplace in sociological and policy studies. However, it is also important to remember that there are structured patterns of disadvantage involving minority ethnic groups in the UK and elsewhere, which influence the life chances of individuals and the choices they are able to make to shape their futures.

 Intersectionality is discussed in more detail in chapter 12, 'Stratification and Social Class'.

Older people

As life expectancy increases, so too does the number of older people in the population. Between 1961 and 2008, the proportion of people in the UK of pensionable age (sixty for women, sixty-five for men) more than doubled, to 11.8 million, some 19 per cent of the total population (ONS 2010a: 3). However, this will change as the state pension age is raised to sixty-five for all by 2018 and eventually to sixty-eight and perhaps higher in the future. At the age of sixty-five, men can expect to live, on average, to 81.6 years and women to 84.4 years, the highest levels ever (Palmer et al.

Percentages

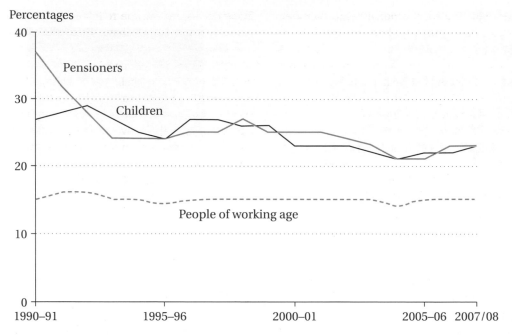

Figure 13.5 Individuals in UK households below average income

Note: 1994–5 to 2000–1 data are for Great Britain only.

Source: ONS (2010a: 71).

2007). Traditionally, many people who may have been quite well paid in their working lives experience a sharp reduction in income and status when they retire, with a large proportion falling into relative poverty. However, there is now increasing evidence that this historic situation has changed.

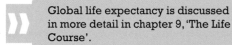

Global life expectancy is discussed in more detail in chapter 9, 'The Life Course'.

Over recent years, several studies have shown that poverty among pensioners has been reducing since 1990 (see figure 13.5). Based on the HBAI (after housing costs) measure, the proportion of pensioners living in poverty decreased from around 40 per cent in 1990 to 15.6 per cent (1.8 million) in 2009–10 (IFS 2011: 55). Between 1996–7 and 2009–10, pensioner poverty declined particularly rapidly, by 46 per cent over the period.

The main reason for this steady improvement seems to be increases in benefit entitlement when inflation was relatively low for an extended period.

The number of pensioners on low income does tend to increase with age, though not for all groups. For example, those with additional private pension provision are less likely to experience poverty, and there is a clear gender dimension to this: only 30 per cent of women have an additional private pension, compared with more than 70 per cent of men (Wicks 2004). In recent decades, older women and those from ethnic minorities are more likely to experience poverty than other pensioner groups, which, as described above, points to the need to be sensitive to issues of intersectionality in the analysis of poverty and its alleviation.

Explaining poverty

Explanations of poverty can be grouped under two main headings: theories that see poor individuals as responsible for their own poverty and theories that view poverty as produced and reproduced by structural forces in society. These competing approaches are sometimes described as 'blame the victim' and 'blame the system' theories, respectively. We will briefly examine each in turn.

There is a long history of social attitudes that hold the poor responsible for their own disadvantaged position. Early efforts to address the effects of poverty, such as nineteenth-century workhouses, were grounded in a belief that poverty was the result of individual inadequacy or pathology. The poor were unable to succeed in society because of a lack of skills, moral or physical weakness, absence of motivation or below-average ability. Those who deserved to succeed did so; others less capable were doomed to fail. The existence of 'winners' and 'losers' was regarded simply as a fact of life.

Accounts that explain poverty as primarily an individual failing lost ground during the mid-twentieth century, but by the 1970s and 1980s they enjoyed a renaissance. One influential version of this thesis was put forward by the American sociologist Charles Murray. Murray (1984) argued that there was an emerging underclass who must take personal responsibility for their own poverty. This group forms part of a dependency culture of people who rely on government welfare provision rather than entering the labour market. Murray contends that the growth of the welfare state has created this subculture, which undermines personal ambition and people's capacity for self-help. In short, welfare, which was meant to provide a safety net, has eroded people's incentive to work, though Murray exempts those who are poor through 'no fault of their own', such as widows or disabled people.

> Murray's work is examined in more detail in chapter 12, 'Stratification and Social Class'.

Murray's views resonated in many developed countries, especially the UK. Yet these ideas do not reflect the reality of poverty for many people. As we have seen, the oldest and youngest members of society have often been the poorest, and they are either not in a position to work or are legally prevented from doing so. Many others in receipt of welfare benefits are actually in work but do not earn enough to take them over the poverty threshold. There is no convincing evidence linking poverty to an underclass of workshy people. Nonetheless, in the UK and the USA at least, the idea of an underclass has taken root. For example, in a speech to the Conservative Party conference in 2011, the government's work and pensions secretary, Iain Duncan Smith, again returned to the 1980s language of the 'underclass' when discussing the perpetrators of that summer's English riots.

The second perspective emphasizes larger social processes which produce conditions of poverty that are difficult for individuals to overcome. Structural forces within society, such as social class position, gender, ethnic group or occupational position, shape the way that resources are distributed. On this view, the apparent lack of ambition among the poor, which is often taken for a 'dependency culture', is in fact one *consequence* of people's constrained situation, not the *cause* of it.

An early exponent of this type of argument was R. H. Tawney (1964 [1931]), who saw poverty as an aspect of social inequality. For Tawney, social inequality led to extremes of both wealth and poverty, and both were dehumanizing. Extreme poverty limited life to mere subsistence, while extreme wealth led to a pampering of the rich. Both were reprehensible, but the key to tackling poverty was to reduce structural social inequality, not simply to blame individuals for their situation (Hickson 2004). Reducing poverty is not simply a matter of changing individual outlooks; it requires policy measures aimed at distributing income and resources more equally throughout society.

Will Hutton's (1995) *The State We're In* argued that processes of economic restructuring during the 1970s and 1980s created new social divisions between the *disadvantaged*

The decline of manufacturing jobs in the 1970s and 1980s eliminated many forms of traditionally male-dominated work. As a result, the urban economy was restructured and poverty levels increased.

(out of work but seeking employment), the *marginalized insecure* (in work but on fixed or short-term contracts with low income) and the *privileged* (in more secure full-time employment or self-employed with higher incomes). Hutton concluded that levels of poverty cannot be explained by individual motivations or personal attitudes. Instead, they have to be seen as intimately connected to structural, socio-economic shifts in society. As capitalist firms look to keep production costs down, manufacturing has moved to other parts of the globe where labour is cheaper and trade unions are weaker. As a new global division of labour takes shape, older working patterns are also transformed.

Standing (2011) argues that the 2008 financial crisis drew attention to the recent emergence of the precariat, a global 'class-in-the-making', which lies outside of the conventional social class schemes of sociology. This term has been coined by combining *proletariat* – Marx's working class – with the increasingly *precarious* and insecure situation in which many groups of workers find themselves under conditions of 'flexible working', neo-liberal economics and globalization. Standing sees the precariat as making up around 25 per cent of the adult population of many countries that lack several or all of the main aspects of security afforded by citizenship in the industrial economies: adequate labour market opportunities, employment protections (including health and safety and regulations and protection against arbitrary dismissal), job security (including opportunities for advancement), opportunities to gain skills, income security and trade union representation.

While the industrial working classes fought for and still enjoy the many benefits of these opportunities and protections, those working on short-term or zero-hours contracts, who are in and out of employment, unemployed or underemployed, are denied the security and stability that they bring. Yet the precariat is not a homogeneous or unified class. Standing (2011: 13–14) notes that

> The teenager who flits in and out of the internet café while surviving on fleeting jobs is not the same as the migrant who uses his wits to survive, networking feverishly while worrying about the police. Neither is similar to the single mother fretting where the money for next week's food bill is coming from or the man in his 60s who takes casual jobs to help pay medical bills. But they all share a sense that their labour is instrumental (to live), opportunistic (taking what comes) and precarious (insecure).

Like Hutton, Standing adopts an economic restructuring explanation for the rise and growth of the precariat. Globalization processes since the early 1970s brought newly industrializing countries with relatively low labour costs into the global market, intensifying competitive pressures and leading to the movement to introduce more flexible labour market practices. The latter required sources of collective solidarity – such as trade unions – to be more tightly regulated and controlled, and governments (led by those with a neoliberal economic agenda such as the USA and the UK) introduced a raft of new legislation to achieve this. As China, India, Vietnam, Thailand, Indonesia and other countries have been drawn into the global economic system, firms have built or moved their production facilities into these countries and the global labour supply has grown enormously. One crucial result has been a serious weakening of workers' bargaining position in the developed countries and the parallel growth of chronic insecurity.

The two broad perspectives at the start of this section – poverty as individual choice and poverty as structurally caused – represent both sides of the agency–structure debate in sociology. However, it is not necessary to take sides. As the discussion in chapter 3 argues, structure and agency are inevitably intertwined, and the sociologist's task is to explore the significance of each in specific research studies. The decisions and choices made by individuals always take place within social contexts that are not entirely of their own making, and we need to understand those 'decisions in context' if we are to make sense of the interplay between human agency and social structure in the production of poverty.

Poverty and social mobility

Most research into poverty in the past focused on people's entry into poverty and measured aggregate levels year by year. Less attention has traditionally been paid to the 'life cycle' of poverty – people's trajectories into and out of (and often back into) poverty over time. Stephen Jenkins (2011) likens the distribution of income to a multi-storey apartment building. The poorest are in the basement and the richest in the penthouse, with the majority on the floors in between. Many 'snapshot' research studies tell us how many people are on each floor at a particular time, but they do not give us any information about movement between the floors.

Similarly, a widely held, common-sense view of poverty is that it is a constraining condition from which escape is unlikely. However, longitudinal research and panel studies (which track the same households or people over time) can provide useful information on whether people do move out of the basement and, if so, whether they stay out or return. Of course, they can also tell us about movement the other way, from the penthouse down to the lower floors. The British Household Panel Survey (BHPS) was just such a longitudinal study, which tracked 16,000 individuals across 9,000 households between 1991 and 2008.

In the decade of the 1990s, BHPS data showed that just over half of the individuals who were in the bottom fifth (quintile) by income in 1991 were in the same category in 1996. This does not necessarily mean they stayed there over the entire five-year period. Some may have done so, while others are likely to have risen out of the bottom quintile and returned to it again. As figure 13.6 shows, only around 18 per cent of those who spent some time in the poorest fifth between 2004 and 2007 were persistently in that quintile. Three-quarters made one or two moves in and out of the bottom fifth over the period. The BHPS survey shows that many families which move out of poverty have a higher risk of re-entering the category later. These findings have led to a new understanding of the quite fluid patterns into and out of poverty, which have also been found in other developed societies (Leisering and Leibfried 1999).

Using data from the UK's New Earnings Survey Panel Dataset and other sources, McKnight (2000) analysed trends in *earnings* mobility in Britain between 1977 and 1997. By tracking groups of low-paid workers, McKnight found a significant amount of persistence in low pay. Her survey showed that around a fifth of employees in the lowest earnings quartile (quarter) were still there six years later. She also found that people who are unemployed, who are among the poorest in Britain, are most likely to gain employment in the lowest-paid sectors when they do find work, and that low-paid employees are more likely to go on to experience unemployment than higher-paid employees.

Jenkins (2011: 3) draws similar conclusions from his analysis of the UK BHPS data on the fluidity of poverty:

> there is substantial movement between floors each year, but most residents only make short distance moves. Few take the lift from the basement to the penthouse and few make the reverse trip. Fewer than one in ten people are long-term residents of the basement, stuck at the bottom. About one-half of the basement residents in a given year move out the following year, but there is also a significant probability of returning

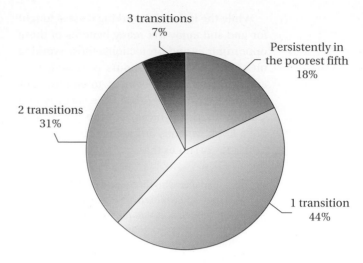

Figure 13.6 Number of moves into and out of the poorest fifth in the period 2004–7 among those with at least one year in the bottom fifth

Source: The Poverty Site, 2011, www.poverty.org.uk/08/index.shtml.

there within the following one or two years. Getting a new job or higher pay is closely associated with transitions upwards from the bottom, and losing a job is closely associated with downward moves to the basement. Demographic events such as divorce, death of a partner, or the birth of a child are also important correlates of changes in fortunes, though more relevant for downward moves than upward ones.

Longitudinal research shows that poverty is not simply the result of social forces acting on passive individuals. Even those who are severely disadvantaged can seize opportunities to improve their economic position, illustrating the power of human agency to bring about change. Nonetheless, moving out of poverty is clearly fraught with challenges and obstacles, and staying out of poverty over the long term seems to be especially difficult. Although being poor does not necessarily mean being permanently mired in poverty, effective social policies which maximize the power of human agency will be a key part of any solution.

Social mobility is discussed more fully in chapter 12, 'Stratification and Social Class', and chapter 19, 'Education'.

Social exclusion

The concept of social exclusion has been used by politicians in various ways to frame their own welfare policies. For example, the British Labour government adopted the concept in 1997, when it established a multidisciplinary Social Exclusion Unit. However, the concept originated in France and became embedded within the social policies of the European Union (Pierson 2010: 8). It has been used by sociologists to refer to new sources of inequality and continues to inform applied social research into multiple sources of disadvantage.

Social exclusion refers to ways in which individuals may become cut off from full participation in the wider society. For instance, people who live in a dilapidated housing estate, with poor schools and few employment opportunities in the area, may effectively be denied the opportunities for self-betterment available to most people in society. The concept of social exclusion also implies its opposite – *social inclusion* – and attempts to foster inclusion of marginalized groups have now become part of the agenda of modern politics, though *how* this is done differs across societies (Lister 2004).

Social exclusion raises the question of personal responsibility. After all, the word 'exclusion' implies a process in which some people are 'left out'. Individuals can find themselves excluded as a result of decisions taken by others. Banks might refuse to give a current account or credit card to people living in a certain area; insurance companies might reject a policy application because of an applicant's personal history or background; an employee made redundant later in life may be refused further jobs on the basis of their age. But social exclusion is not only the result of people being excluded; it can also result from people excluding themselves. Some people choose to drop out of education, to turn down a job offer and become economically inactive, or to abstain from voting in elections. In considering the phenomenon of social exclusion, we must again be conscious of the interaction between human agency and the role of social forces in shaping people's circumstances.

A useful way of thinking about social exclusion is to differentiate between 'weak' and 'strong' versions of the concept (Veit-Wilson 1998). Weak versions see the central issue simply as one of trying to ensure the inclusion of those who are currently socially excluded. Strong versions also seek social inclusion, but, in addition, try to tackle some of the processes through which relatively powerful social groups 'can exercise their capacity to exclude' (Macrae et al. 2003: 90). This is a significant distinction, as the version adopted by governments will shape their policies towards social exclusion.

For example, in debates on rising levels of school exclusions for bad behaviour, a weak approach would focus on how individual children can be brought back into the mainstream education system, while a strong approach would also look at potential problems within the education system itself and the role of powerful groups within it which have the power to exclude. Fairclough (2000: 54) argues that the Labour government's approach was essentially a 'weak' version: 'In the language of New Labour social exclusion is an outcome rather than a process; it is a condition people are in rather than something that is done to them.' The problem with this version is it runs the risk – as with the concept of poverty – that those who are excluded will be blamed for their own situation.

Dimensions of social exclusion

Social exclusion focuses attention on a broad range of factors that prevent individuals or groups from having the same opportunities that are open to the majority of the population.

Lister (2004) argues that this broad concept is a useful one for social scientists, provided that it is not seen as an alternative to poverty, which, she contends, remains central to any understanding of inequality and disadvantage. The 2000 PSE survey distinguished four dimensions of social exclusion: poverty or exclusion from *adequate income* or resources (which we discussed above), *labour market* exclusion, *service* exclusion and exclusion from *social relations* (Gordon et al. 2000).

For the individual, work is important not just because it provides an adequate income, but also because involvement in the labour market is an important arena of social interaction. Thus, labour market exclusion can lead to poverty, service exclusion and exclusion from social relations. Consequently, increasing the number of people in paid work has been seen by politicians as an important way to reduce social exclusion. However, to be in a 'jobless household' should not necessarily be associated with unemployment. The largest group of those who are not active in the labour market are, in fact, retired people. Other groups include those involved in domestic and caring activities, people who are unable to work, perhaps because of disability, and students. Labour market inactivity cannot in itself be seen as a sign of social exclusion, but it can significantly increase the risk of wider social exclusion.

Another important aspect of social exclusion is lack of access to basic services, whether these are in the home (such as power and water supplies) or outside it (including access to transport, shops or financial services). Service exclusion can be individual, when someone cannot use a service because they cannot afford to do so or because they are not told it exists, or collective, when services are unavailable to whole communities. The latter occurs, for instance, when shops, banks and other services move out of disadvantaged housing estates, leaving communities without access to consumer goods and financial services enjoyed by the majority.

There are numerous ways in which people can be excluded from wider social relations.

Individuals may be unable to participate in common social activities, such as visiting friends and family, celebrating special occasions, having friends round for a meal or taking holidays. They can be isolated from friends and family or face a lack of practical and emotional support in times of need – someone to help around the house, to talk to when depressed or to get advice from about important life changes. People are excluded from social relations through a lack of *civic engagement*, including voting, getting involved in local or national politics, or being able to campaign on an issue they feel strongly about.

The multiple aspects of social exclusion can be seen most forcibly in the case of people seeking asylum in a country other than their own. Indeed, the very term 'asylum-seeker' has become stigmatized over recent years following sensationalist tabloid press reporting of the issue. But, as Pierson (2010: 7) points out, asylum-seekers face 'barriers to the jobs market, thin or non-existent support networks of their own, extreme difficulties in obtaining the safety net benefits of the welfare state, children facing poverty and marginalisation in the school system'. This example also illustrates that social exclusion is not 'natural' or inevitable and that there are things governments, individuals and communities can do to tackle the problems.

Examples of social exclusion

Sociologists have conducted research into the different ways that individuals and communities experience exclusion. Investigations have focused on topics as diverse as housing, education, the labour market, crime, young people and the elderly. We now look briefly at three examples of social exclusion in the UK.

Housing and neighbourhoods

The nature of social exclusion can be seen clearly within the housing sector. While many people in industrialized societies live in comfortable, spacious homes, others reside in dwellings that are overcrowded, inadequately heated or structurally unsound. When entering the housing market, individuals are able to secure accommodation on the basis of their existing and projected resources. Thus, a dual-earning childless couple will have a greater chance of obtaining a mortgage. In countries where people tend to buy rather than rent, in recent decades house prices have risen considerably faster than inflation, ensuring that owner-occupiers realize large profits on their property, while those not already on the housing ladder find it increasingly difficult to buy a first home. By contrast, households whose adults are unemployed or in low-paying jobs may be restricted to less desirable options in the rented or public housing sector.

Stratification within the housing market occurs at both the household and the community level. Just as disadvantaged individuals are excluded from desirable housing options, so whole communities can be excluded from opportunities and activities that are norms for the rest of society. Exclusion can take on a spatial dimension: neighbourhoods vary greatly in terms of safety, environmental conditions and the availability of services and public facilities. For example, low-demand neighbourhoods tend to have fewer basic services such as banks, food shops and post offices than do more desirable areas. Community spaces such as parks, sports grounds and libraries may also be limited. Yet people living in disadvantaged places are often dependent on what few facilities are available. Unlike residents of more affluent areas, they may not have access to transport (or funds) which would allow them to shop and use services elsewhere.

In deprived communities, it can be difficult for people to overcome exclusion and to take steps to engage more fully in society. Social networks may be weak; this reduces the circulation of information about jobs, political activities and community events. High unemployment and low income levels place strains on family life; crime and juvenile delinquency undermine the overall quality of life in the neighbourhood. Low-demand housing areas often experience high household turnover rates, as many residents seek to move on to more desirable housing while new, disadvantaged entrants to the housing market continue to arrive.

Homelessness

Homelessness is one of the most extreme forms of exclusion (Tipple and Speak 2009: 195). People lacking a permanent residence may be shut out of many everyday activities, such as going to work, having a bank account, entertaining friends and even getting letters in the post. Most homeless people are in some form of temporary accommodation, staying with friends and family for short periods or sleeping in hostels, in nightshelters or in places where they have no legal right to stay, such as squats. A minority of people do choose to sleep on the streets, free from the constraints of property and possessions, but the majority of rough sleepers have been pushed into homelessness by domestic violence, unemployment, the loss of a partner, being evicted, on leaving the armed forces or being released from prison (Daly 2013).

Who sleeps rough on the streets in Britain? The answer is complicated. Surveys have consistently shown that about a quarter of people who sleep rough have spent time in mental health institutions or have had a diagnosis of mental illness. Hence changes in healthcare policy are likely to have a disproportionate effect on the incidence of homelessness. However, most people who are homeless do not have mental ill health, nor are they alcoholics or regular consumers of illegal drugs. They are people who find themselves on the streets because they have experienced personal crises.

Becoming homeless is rarely the outcome of a direct 'cause–effect' sequence. A number of misfortunes may occur in quick succession, resulting in a powerful downward spiral. A woman may get divorced, for instance, and at the same time lose not only her home but also her job. A young person may have trouble at home and take off for a big city without any means of support. Those who are most vulnerable to homelessness are people from lower-working-class backgrounds who have no specific job skills and very low incomes.

Homelessness is one of the most complicated and often extreme forms of social exclusion.

Long-term joblessness is a major indicator, though family and relationship breakdown also appear to be key influences.

Although the vast majority of people who are homeless manage to find a place in a shelter or other temporary accommodation, those who find themselves sleeping rough are often in danger. The British Crime Survey, the leading statistical indicator of crime in Britain, does not include homeless people among its respondents. A survey of homelessness in Glasgow, Swansea and London (IPPR 1999) revealed that four out of five rough sleepers had been the victims of crime at least once. Almost half had been assaulted, yet only one-fifth chose to report the crimes to the police. The picture that emerges is one of homeless people who are victims of high levels of violence on the streets, but who are excluded from the systems of legal and police protection that might possibly offer assistance.

Even though it is not the complete answer, most sociologists who have studied the issue agree that the provision of more adequate forms of housing is of key importance in tackling the multiple problems faced by homeless people, whether the housing is directly sponsored by the government or not. As Jencks (1994) concludes, 'Regardless of why people are on the streets, giving them a place to live that offers a modicum of privacy and stability is usually the most important thing we can do to improve their lives. Without stable housing, nothing else is likely to work.'

Others disagree, stressing that homelessness is only 20 per cent about 'bricks and mortar' and 80 per cent about social work and outreach to counter the effects of family breakdown, violence and abuse, drug and alcohol addictions, and depression. Mike, a homeless man in his late fifties, concurs: 'I think that for most people the situation is much more complicated than it seems. Often the problem is about their own belief in themselves, their self-worth. A lot of people on the street have low self-esteem. They do not believe they can do anything better' (quoted in Bamforth 1999).

Crime and social exclusion

Some sociologists have argued that, in many industrialized societies, there are strong links between crime and social exclusion. There is a trend in modern societies, they maintain, away from inclusive goals (based on citizenship rights) and towards arrangements that accept and even promote the exclusion of some citizens (Young 1998, 1999). Crime rates may be reflecting the fact that a growing number of people do not feel valued by – or feel they have an investment in – the societies in which they live.

Currie (1998) investigated the connections between social exclusion and crime in the United States, particularly among young people. He argues that, faced by the seductive lure of the market and consumer goods, they are confronted by diminishing opportunities in the labour market to sustain a livelihood. In fact, economic restructuring has led to feelings among young people of a profound sense of relative deprivation and a willingness to turn to illegitimate means of sustaining a desired lifestyle.

In a more recent ethnographic study of a deprived community in the North of England, Robert McAuley (2006) investigated the links between social exclusion and crime among young people. McAuley maintains that the dominant explanation for persistent youth crime is that some communities are 'intolerant of work' – that is, many arguments suggest that a growing underclass – or the experience of social exclusion – gives rise to poor communities in which a number of people are turning to crime to get what they want. However, most of the young people to whom McAuley spoke still valued work but, because of the stigma attached to the place in which they lived, felt abandoned by the rest of society and 'victimized' both at school and when applying for jobs.

McAuley argues that, as the UK's industrial base contracted, service industries provided the main work, and, like many other developed societies, the UK became a consumer society. In fact, he says, it is consumer societies rather than the urban poor that have devalued work, because consumerism promotes the acquisition of material goods rather than a work ethic. What McAuley's research points to are some of the consequences for young people growing up in deprived communities. However, for McAuley, it is not just a period of economic restructuring but the affluent consumer society itself which effectively 'socially excludes' the poor.

The welfare state

In most developed countries, poverty and social exclusion at the bottom are alleviated to some degree by the welfare state. But how did welfare states develop and how can we explain the variations in national welfare models? The face of welfare is different from country to country and welfare states have changed over time. In the present period of post-recession planning, spending cuts and debt reduction policies, governments around the world are having to rethink what the welfare state should provide and, in some cases, whether in its present form it even remains affordable.

Theories of the welfare state

Most developed and developing countries in the world today are welfare states. By this is meant that the state plays a central role in the provision of welfare, which it does through a system that offers services and benefits to meet the basic needs of citizens for healthcare, education, housing and income. An important role of the welfare state involves managing the risks faced by people over the course of their lives: sickness, disability, job loss and old age. The services provided by the welfare state and the levels of spending on it vary from country to country. Some have highly developed systems and devote a large proportion of the national budget to them. In Sweden, for example, tax revenues in 2005

13.1 Social exclusion at the top?

The examples of exclusion that we have considered thus far all concern individuals or groups who, for whatever reason, are unable to participate fully in institutions used and activities undertaken by the majority of the population. Yet not all cases of exclusion occur among those who are disadvantaged at the bottom of society. In recent years, new dynamics of 'social exclusion at the top' have been emerging. By this, it is meant that a minority of individuals at the very top of society can 'opt out' of participation in mainstream institutions by merit of their affluence, influence and connections.

Such elite exclusion at the top of society can take a number of forms. The wealthy might retreat fully from the realm of public education and healthcare services, preferring to pay for private services and attention. Affluent residential communities are increasingly closed off from the rest of society – the so-called gated communities located behind tall walls and security checkpoints. Tax payments and financial obligations can be drastically reduced through careful management and the help of private financial planners. Particularly in the United States, active political participation among the elite is often replaced by large donations to political candidates who are seen to represent their interests. In a number of ways, the very wealthy are able to escape from their social and financial responsibilities into

Elite social exclusion can physically separate the rich from the rest of society.

a closed, private realm largely separate from the rest of society. Just as social exclusion at the 'bottom' undermines social solidarity and cohesion, so exclusion at the 'top' is detrimental to an integrated society.

> ### THINKING CRITICALLY
>
> What are the main differences between social exclusion at the 'bottom' and at the 'top' of society? Is it sensible to use the concept of social exclusion to describe the actions of small groups of rich people? Can you devise an alternative concept for these actions?

represented 51.1 per cent of the gross domestic product (GDP), while in Belgium this figure was 45.4 per cent and in Austria it was 49.7 per cent. By comparison, other industrialized nations take far less in tax. In the UK, tax revenues in 2006 were 37.2 per cent of GDP, in Germany 34.7 per cent, and in the USA just 26.8 per cent (OECD 2006).

Numerous theories have been advanced to explain the evolution of the welfare state. Marxists have seen welfare as necessary for sustaining a capitalist market-based society by ensuring the reproduction of a healthy, well-educated workforce, while functionalists held that welfare systems helped to integrate society in an orderly way under conditions of industrial development. While these general perspectives have been useful points of orientation, the ideas of T. H. Marshall in Britain and of the Danish sociologist Gøsta Esping-Andersen have been particularly influential contributions to theories of the welfare state. Marshall's persuasive arguments are outlined in 'Classic studies 13.2', and you should read through this before moving on to later arguments on welfare and citizenship.

Classic Studies 13.2   T. H. Marshall and the evolution of citizenship in Britain

The research problem

You may have been described as a 'citizen' of a particular country, implying a certain 'belonging'. But when did the idea of national 'citizenship' emerge and how did it develop? What exactly is citizenship anyway, and what rights and responsibilities does it confer on citizens? How is citizenship related to the state's provision of welfare? One important theorist who tackled these questions was Thomas Humphrey Marshall (1893–1981), whose ideas have been very influential in shaping debates on welfare and citizenship rights. Writing from the late 1940s, Marshall saw citizenship as emerging alongside industrialization as a fundamental feature of modern society.

Marshall's explanation

Taking a historical approach, Marshall (1973) traced what he described as the 'evolution' of citizenship in Britain (specifically England) and identified three key stages, each one expanding the meaning of 'citizenship'. The eighteenth century, according to Marshall, was the time when civil rights were obtained. Among these were important personal liberties such as freedom of speech, thought and religion, the right to own property, and the right to fair legal treatment. Building on these rights, in the nineteenth century, *political rights* were gained. These included the right to vote, to hold office and to participate in the political process. The third set of rights – *social rights* – were obtained in the twentieth century, notably the right of citizens to economic and social security through education, healthcare, housing, pensions and other services, all of which became enshrined in the welfare state.

The incorporation of social rights into the notion of citizenship meant that everyone was entitled to live a full and active life and had a right to a reasonable income, regardless of their position in society. In this respect, the rights associated with social citizenship greatly advanced the ideal of equality for all, and Marshall's account is often described as an optimistic one, seeing a growing range of rights for all citizens.

Critical points

One immediate problem with Marshall's explanation is that it is based on a single case study – Britain – and critics have shown that his evolutionary approach cannot be applied to other national cases such as Sweden, France or Germany (Turner 1990). Marshall's 'evolutionary' explanation is also not entirely clear. Is it really just a description of *how* citizenship actually developed in Britain, rather than a causal explanation of *why* it did so? Critics argue that Marshall tends to *assume* the progressive development of types of rights but does not explain the links between them or how, say, civil rights lead inevitably to political and then to social rights.

In more recent times, critics have asserted that the awareness of globalization makes Marshall's theory – which is based on the influence of the nation-state – rather outdated, as it seems to assume that citizenship develops from the internal dynamics of national societies. Today, however, sociologists are much more sensitive to the relationships and influences between and across the world's societies. Finally – as we will see later in the chapter – Marshall's evolutionism is severely challenged by the attempts since the late 1970s to 'roll back' welfare provision in many developed societies, which does not appear to fit his historical thesis. Rather than witnessing a growing set of rights, citizens may find their right to state welfare support becomes more tightly restricted.

Contemporary significance

Marshall's views influenced debates about the nature of citizenship and, in recent years, informed political questions and academic research on social inclusion and exclusion. His central idea that rights and responsibilities are tightly intertwined with the notion of citizenship is enjoying renewed popularity in discussions about how to promote an 'active citizenship'. And, although his explanation is certainly too state-centred to be entirely satisfactory in a globalizing age, the notion of an evolution of rights and responsibilities continues to inform our understanding of what citizenship is. For example, a relatively new type of citizenship now seems to be emerging – environmental or ecological citizenship – based on the rights and responsibilities of people towards the natural environment (M. J. Smith 1998; Dobson and Bell 2006). Hence, despite its flaws, there may yet be a little more life in Marshall's general approach.

> The concept of environmental citizenship is discussed in chapter 5, 'The Environment'.

Gøsta Esping-Andersen: three worlds of welfare

Gøsta Esping-Andersen's *The Three Worlds of Welfare Capitalism* (1990) brings a comparative perspective to the earlier theories of the welfare state. In so doing, Esping-Andersen can be seen to have taken seriously the criticism levelled at Marshall's general evolutionary perspective – namely, that different national societies followed different paths towards citizenship rights and, accordingly, created different 'welfare regimes'. In this important work, Esping-Andersen compares Western welfare systems and presents a three-part typology of their regimes.

In constructing this typology, Esping-Andersen evaluated the level of decommodification – a term which simply means the degree to which welfare services are free from the market. In a system with high decommodification, welfare is provided publicly and is not in any way linked to one's income or economic resources. In a commodified system, welfare services are treated more like commodities – that is, they are sold on the market like any other good or service. By comparing policies on pensions, unemployment and income support among countries, Esping-Andersen identified the following three types of welfare regime.

1 *Social democratic* Social democratic welfare regimes are highly decommodified. Welfare services are subsidized by the state and available to all citizens (universal benefits). Most Scandinavian states such as Sweden and Norway have social democratic welfare regimes.

2 *Conservative-corporatist* In conservative-corporatist states, such as France and Germany, welfare services may be highly decommodified, but they are not necessarily universal. The amount of benefit to which a citizen is entitled depends on their position in society. This type of regime may be aimed not at eliminating inequalities but at maintaining social stability, strong families and loyalty to the state.

3 *Liberal* The United States provides the best example of a liberal welfare regime. Welfare is highly commodified and sold through the market. Means-tested benefits are available to the very needy but become highly stigmatized. This is because the majority of the population is expected to purchase its own welfare through the market.

The United Kingdom does not fall cleanly into any of these three 'ideal types'. Formerly, it was closer to a social democratic model, but a series of reforms since the 1970s have brought it much closer to a liberal welfare regime with higher levels of commodification, which continues into the present period. The shift from one model to another makes the UK an interesting case study.

The UK welfare state

One of the main differences between welfare models is the eligibility criteria for receipt of benefits. A simple divide is between universality and means-testing. In systems with universal benefits, welfare is seen as a right to be enjoyed equally by all, ensuring that citizens' basic welfare needs are met. An example in the UK has long been the provision of child benefit, which goes to the parent or guardian of children under the age of sixteen regardless of income or savings. Systems based on means-testing are designed to provide a basic, usually short-term safety net for people who find themselves in difficulty and need help to get by. In the UK, universal child benefit was effectively ended in 2013 as part of the coalition government's squeeze on public spending and was limited to those with incomes below £50,000 per year. The Swedish system has a higher proportion of universal benefits than that of the UK, which today increasingly provides means-tested benefits.

The distinction between universal and means-tested benefits is expressed at a policy level in two contrasting approaches to welfare. Supporters of an *institutional* view argue that access to welfare services should be provided as a right for everyone. Those taking a *residualist* view argue that welfare should be available only to people who truly need help and are unable to meet their own needs. The debate between institutionalists and residualists is often presented as a dispute about tax levels, as welfare services are funded through taxation.

Residualists advocate a 'safety-net welfare state' in which only those most in need – to be demonstrated through means-testing – should be in receipt of benefits. They also see the welfare state as expensive, ineffective and too bureaucratic. On the other hand, institutionalists argue that tax levels should be high because the welfare state needs to be properly funded. They say that the welfare state must be maintained and even expanded to counter the harsh, polarizing effects of the market, even though this means a high tax burden. They claim that it is the responsibility of any civilized state to provide for and protect its citizens.

This difference over institutional and residual models has been at the heart of UK debates on welfare reform since the mid-1970s. Today, in all developed countries the future of the welfare state is under intense examination as never before, as governments deal with large national debts following the 2008 financial crisis, recession and its aftermath. Similarly, as globalization changes national societies, new patterns of migration, and shifts in the family, personal life, and employment, the nature of welfare is changing too. We will briefly trace the history of the welfare state in the UK and recent attempts to reform it.

Founding the British welfare state

The welfare state in the UK was created during the twentieth century, though its roots stretch back to the Poor Laws of 1601 and the dissolution of the monasteries. The monasteries had provided for the poor; without this provision, extreme poverty and a near complete absence of care for the sick resulted. With the development of industrial capitalism and the transition from an agricultural to an industrial society, traditional forms of informal support within families and communities began to break down.

In order to maintain social order and reduce the inequalities brought about by capitalism, it was necessary to offer assistance to those members of society who found themselves on the periphery of the market economy. This resulted in 1834 in the Poor Law Amendment Act. Under this Act, workhouses were built, offering a lower standard of living than anything available outside. The idea was that the living conditions in the workhouses would make people do all they could to avoid poverty. With time, as part of the process of nation-building, the state came to play a more central role in administering to the needy. Legislation which established the national administration of education and public health in the late 1800s was a precursor of the more extensive programmes which would come into being in the twentieth century.

The welfare state expanded further under the pre-First World War Liberal government, which introduced pensions and health and unemployment insurance. The years following the Second World War witnessed a further powerful drive for the reform and expansion of the welfare system. Rather than concentrating solely on the destitute or ill, the focus of welfare was broadened to encompass all

The 1942 Beveridge Report identified five evils that had to be eliminated: Want, Disease, Ignorance, Squalor and Idleness. Beveridge's ideas are seen as foundation stones of the modern welfare state in the UK.

members of society. The war had been an intense and traumatic experience for the entire nation – rich and poor. It produced a sense of solidarity and the realization that misfortune and tragedy were not restricted to the disadvantaged alone.

This shift from a selective to a universalist vision of welfare was encapsulated in the Beveridge Report of 1942, often regarded as the blueprint for the modern welfare state. The report was aimed at eradicating the five great evils: Want, Disease, Ignorance, Squalor and Idleness. A series of legislative measures under the postwar Labour government began to translate this vision into concrete action. Several main acts lay at the core of the new universalist welfare state. The wartime national government had already introduced the Education Act in 1944, which tackled lack of schooling, while the 1946 National Health Act was concerned with improving the quality of health among the population. 'Want' was addressed through the 1946 National Insurance Act, which set up a scheme to protect against loss of earnings as a result of unemployment, ill health, retirement or widowhood. The 1948 National Assistance Act provided means-tested support for those who were not covered under the National Insurance Act and finally abolished the old Poor Laws. Other legislation addressed the needs of families (1945 Family Allowances Act) and the demand for improved housing conditions (1946 New Towns Act).

The British welfare state came into being under a set of specific conditions and alongside certain prevailing notions about the nature of society. The premises on which it was built were threefold. First, it equated work with paid labour and was grounded in a belief in the possibility of full employment. Welfare would meet the needs of those who were located outside the market economy through the mischance of unemployment or disability. Connected to this, the vision for the welfare state was predicated on a patriarchal conception of families – the male breadwinner was to support the family, while women tended to the home. Welfare programmes were designed around this traditional family model.

Second, the welfare state was seen as promoting national solidarity. It would integrate the nation by involving the entire population in a common set of services. Welfare was a way of strengthening the connection between the state and its citizens. Third, the welfare state was concerned with managing risks that occurred as a natural part of the life course. In this sense, welfare was viewed as a type of insurance that could be employed against the potential troubles of an unpredictable future. Unemployment, illness and other misfortunes in the country's social and economic life could thus be managed.

These principles underpinned the enormous expansion of the welfare state in the three decades after 1945. As the manufacturing economy grew, the welfare state represented a successful class 'bargain' that met the needs of the working class as well as those of the economic elite who depended on a healthy workforce. But by the 1970s the splintering of political opinion into institutional and residualist camps became increasingly pronounced. However, by the 1990s both the left and the right acknowledged that the welfare state was in need of significant reform.

Reforming the welfare state: 1979–1997

The political consensus on welfare broke down in the 1980s when the administrations of Margaret Thatcher in the UK and Ronald Reagan in the USA attempted to 'roll back' the welfare state. Several criticisms were at the heart of attempts to reduce welfare. The first concerned mounting financial costs. General economic recession, growing unemployment and the emergence of enormous bureaucracies meant that expenditure continued to increase steadily – and at a rate greater than that of overall economic expansion. A debate over welfare spending ensued, with advocates of a 'roll-back' pointing to the ballooning financial pressure on the welfare system. Policy-makers emphasized the potentially overwhelming impact of the 'demographic time bomb': the number of people dependent on welfare services was growing as the population aged, yet the number of young people of working age paying into the system was declining. This signalled a potential financial crisis.

The 'greying' of the global population is discussed in chapter 9, 'The Life Course'.

A second line of criticism was related to the notion of *welfare dependency*. Critics of existing welfare systems, such as Charles Murray in the USA, whose work was discussed earlier, argued that people become dependent on the state assistance that is meant to allow them to forge an independent and meaningful life. They become not just materially but psychologically dependent on the arrival of the welfare payment, adopting a resigned and passive approach to life. The work of Murray and others on the creation of a growing, welfare-dependent underclass framed the political and policy debates on welfare provision in the 1980s and 1990s.

The Conservative government implemented a number of reforms that began to shift responsibility for public welfare away from the state and towards the private sector, the voluntary sector and local communities. Services which were formerly provided by the state at highly subsidized rates were privatized or made subject to more stringent means-testing. One example of this can be seen in the privatization of council housing in the 1980s. The 1980 Housing Act allowed rents for council housing to be raised significantly, laying the groundwork for a large-scale sell-off of stock. This move towards residualism in provision was particularly harmful to those located just above the means-tested eligibility line for housing benefit, as they could no longer get access to public housing but could ill-afford to rent accommodation at market rates. Critics argue that the privatization of council housing contributed significantly to rising homelessness in the 1980s and 1990s.

Another attempt to reduce welfare expenditure and increase its efficiency came through the introduction of market principles in the provision of public services. The Conservative government argued that injecting a degree of competition into services such as healthcare and education would provide the public with greater choice and ensure higher quality. Consumers could, in effect, 'vote with their feet' by choosing among schools or healthcare providers. Institutions providing substandard services would be obliged to improve or be forced to close down, just like a business. Critics charged that 'internal markets' within public services would lead to lower quality and a stratified system of provision rather than protecting the value of equal service for all citizens.

To what extent did the Conservative governments of the 1980s actually succeed in rolling back the welfare state? In *Dismantling the Welfare State?*, Christopher Pierson (1994) compared the process of welfare 'retrenchment' in the UK and the USA and concluded that welfare states emerged from the Conservative era relatively intact. Although both administrations came into office with the express intent of slashing welfare expenditure, Pierson argued that the obstacles to rolling back welfare were ultimately more than either government could overcome. The reason lies in the way in which social policy had unfolded over time. Since its inception, the welfare state and its institutions had given rise to specific constituencies – such as trade unions and voluntary agencies like the Child Poverty Action Group – which actively defended benefits against political efforts to reduce them. Social spending stayed fairly constant and all the core components of the welfare state remained in place.

The theory underlying the policies of Margaret Thatcher's and successive Conservative administrations (1979–97) was that cutting tax rates for individuals and corporations would generate high levels of economic growth, the fruits of which would then 'trickle down' to the poor. Similar policies were implemented in the USA. But the evidence does not support the 'trickle-down' thesis. Such an economic policy may generate an acceleration of economic development, but it also tends to expand the differential between the poor and the wealthy and increase the numbers living in poverty.

> ### THINKING CRITICALLY
>
> From your reading so far, does a comprehensive welfare state tend to create a dependency culture? With reference to Esping-Andersen's (1990) three types of welfare regime (discussed above), which countries would you expect to have the highest levels of welfare dependency? What evidence can you find that these societies have been particularly damaged by state welfare?

Reforming the welfare state: 1997–2010

Welfare reform was a top priority for the Labour government which came to office in 1997. Agreeing in some respects with Conservative critics of welfare (and thus breaking with traditional left politics), 'New' Labour argued that new policies were needed to cope with poverty and inequality as well as to improve health and education. It saw the welfare state as often part of the problem, creating dependency and offering a 'hand-out' instead of a 'hand-up'.

Instead, Labour wanted to tackle the roots of poverty, arguing that it was pursuing a Third Way – beyond the politics of the 'old' left and that of the Thatcher government's 'new' right. In doing so – initially at least – Labour drew on some of the ideas of Anthony Giddens (1994, 1998), which were aimed at modernizing the politics of the left for a global age. These included the strengthening of civil society, decentralizing power away from the nation-state, a focus on social exclusion rather than inequality, and the use of the private sector to add a dynamic element into public service provision, thereby creating a 'social investment state'.

Initially rejecting the policies of the old left as outdated in an era of individualism, consumerism and globalization, Labour looked to create a 'new left' political position and programme. For example, the party argued that one of the main difficulties with the welfare system was that the conditions under which it had been created no longer existed: it had been inaugurated at a time of full employment when many families could rely on men to work and bring in a 'family wage'. However, changes in family structures had, by the 1990s, rendered such a patriarchal view of the male breadwinner inapplicable. An enormous number of women had entered the workforce and the growth of lone-parent households placed new demands on the welfare state. Women's earnings have become integral to household income and the impact of their earnings can carry enormous weight. Indeed, the success of dual-earner households, particularly those without children, is one of the most important factors in the shifting pattern of income distribution.

From the outset, Labour focused on a type of 'positive welfare', involving a new 'welfare contract' between the state and citizens based on both rights *and* responsibilities. It saw the role of the state as helping people into work and thereby a stable income, not just supporting them financially through periods of unemployment. At the same time, it expected citizens to take responsibility for trying to change their own circumstances rather than waiting for hand-outs. Employment became one of the cornerstones of Labour's social policy, as it was believed that getting people into work was one of the main steps in reducing poverty. Among the most significant reforms introduced under Labour were so-called welfare-to-work programmes (see 'Using your sociological imagination 13.2').

As well as the welfare-to-work programmes, Labour used measures to raise the income of those in low-paid jobs. A minimum wage was introduced in 1999 and a commitment was made to reduce child poverty by 50 per cent by 2010 and to abolish child poverty entirely by 2020. By 2006, 600,000 children had been moved out of poverty, but, as we saw earlier in this chapter, by 2010 child poverty had been reduced only by about one-quarter. Even if the ten-year target of halving child poverty by 2010 had been met, levels would still have been higher than in 1979 when Margaret Thatcher became prime minister (Flaherty et al. 2004). Clearly, far more radical measures would be needed if the targets in the Child Poverty Act 2010 are to be met.

Even critics accept that some of Labour's welfare policies had successes: helping many people – particularly young people – into work and raising levels of funding for public services. However, Labour's approach to welfare has been more harshly judged. The attempt to make benefits dependent on a commitment actively to seek work or attend interviews has been described as a 'creeping conditionality' which erodes the principle of a citizen's 'entitlement' (Dwyer 2004). Labour's work-focused programmes (and others in some European countries) were promoted through the language of 'social inclusion'. However, it is not clear how exclusion relates to underlying problems of social *inequality*, which, historically, formed the basis of Labour's policy programmes when in government.

In *The Inclusive Society*, Ruth Levitas (2005) studied three main discourses, or ways of discussing and framing welfare policy, used by Labour since 1997. First, Labour adopted a *redistributionist* discourse, which viewed social exclusion as a *consequence*, not a cause, of poverty and social inequalities. Second, she identified a *moral* discourse on the underclass (as we saw in the discussion of Charles Murray earlier). This tends to blame those who are socially excluded, seeing them as responsible for their own situation and, sometimes, as a separate social group with specific characteristics. Third, Levitas notes a *social integrationist* discourse that ties social exclusion and inclusion firmly to employment, encouraging labour market participation as a solution to social exclusion.

The main issue for Levitas is that Labour discourse and policy drifted away from the party's historically dominant, redistributionist approach to welfare, becoming little different from the previous approach by the Conservatives. This separated social exclusion from social inequality and concentrated on the divide between the excluded and the included rather than that between rich and poor, allowing the rich successfully to evade their responsibilities to the wider society. Similarly,

13.2   Evaluating welfare-to-work programmes

From 1997, the Labour government put forward a number of policies and targets to move people from welfare into work. 'New Deal' programmes were introduced for certain groups such as disabled people, the long-term unemployed, young people and those aged over fifty. Similar programmes have existed for some time in the United States, and their implications have been studied.

Daniel Friedlander and Gary Burtless (1994) studied four different US government-initiated programmes designed to encourage welfare recipients to find paid work. The programmes were roughly similar: they provided financial benefits for those who actively searched for jobs, as well as guidance in job-hunting techniques and opportunities for education and training. The target populations were mainly single-parent heads of households who were recipients of Aid to Families with Dependent Children, the largest cash welfare programme in the country. Friedlander and Burtless found that the programmes did achieve results. People involved in them were able either to enter employment or to start working sooner than those who did not participate. In all four programmes, the earnings produced were several times greater than the net cost of the programme. They were least effective, however, in helping those who needed them the most – those who had been out of work for a lengthy period, the long-term unemployed.

Although welfare-to-work programmes have succeeded in reducing American welfare claims by approximately 40 per cent, some statistics suggest that the outcomes are not wholly positive. In the USA, approximately 20 per cent of those who cease to receive welfare do not work and have no source of independent income; nearly one-third who do get jobs return to claim welfare again within a year. Between a third and a half of welfare leavers who are in work find that their incomes are lower than their previous benefit levels.

In Wisconsin, the US state which was one of the first to introduce welfare-to-work programmes, two-thirds of welfare leavers live below the poverty line (Evans 2000). Pointing to such findings, critics argue that the apparent success of such initiatives in reducing the absolute number of cases conceals some troublesome patterns in the actual experiences of those who lose their welfare.

Others question the effectiveness of local empowerment 'zones' for combating social exclusion. They argue that poverty and deprivation are not concentrated in those designated areas alone, yet many government programmes are targeted as if all the poor live together. In the UK, the findings of the government's own Social Exclusion Unit showed that, in 1997, when Labour came to power, two-thirds of all unemployed people lived in areas outside the forty-four most deprived boroughs of the country. Localized initiatives, sceptics point out, cannot replace a nationwide anti-poverty strategy, because too many people fall outside the boundaries of the designated empowerment zones.

THINKING CRITICALLY

Is it realistic to expect welfare-to-work programmes to help *all* social groups to find employment? Why do you think these programmes fail to help the long-term unemployed to find work? List the obstacles facing those who have been unemployed for more than a year. What can governments do to remove these obstacles?

MacGregor (2003: 72) argued that Labour dealt mainly with the unacceptable behaviour of the poor – separating out the 'deserving' from the 'undeserving' unemployed, the genuine 'asylum-seeker' from the 'economic migrant', and so on: 'This concentrates on the bad behaviours among the poor, ignoring the drug taking, infidelities, frauds and deceptions and

The drug-taking of celebrities can be a source of entertainment for glossy magazines. But the negative aspects of addiction are associated with the poor and socially excluded and can lead to these groups being targeted in police searches.

other human frailties found among the rich, the better off and the not-quite-poor.'

The welfare state in an age of austerity: 2010–

The 2010 UK election resulted in a 'hung' or 'balanced' parliament that produced no clear winner, but the Conservatives had most MPs. A coalition government was formed by the Conservative and Liberal Democrat parties, based on an agreement outlining the new government's direction and key policies. At the top of the agenda was reduction of government debt, in part by fundamentally reforming public services and welfare provision. Of course, welfare reform had also been central to the previous Labour governments, but the

2008 financial crisis, the ensuing recession and the perceived need to cut government spending rapidly gave extra impetus to the coalition's rethinking of the welfare state. Taylor-Gooby (2013) argues that the UK welfare state faces a double crisis as a result of harsh spending cuts and a restructuring programme which is leading to the fragmentation of services and increasing private provision throughout the public sector.

Underpinning the coalition's reforms was the central idea that 'work should pay'. That is, people should always be better off in work than if they stayed out of work and lived on welfare benefits. The secretary of state for work and pensions, Iain Duncan Smith, had been working on welfare reform through a think tank he founded in 2004, the Centre for Social Justice (CSJ). One influential CSJ publication, *Dynamic Benefits* (2009), helped to shape the new government's welfare policy (King 2011: 105). Following a period of consultation (see the DWP's *21st Century Welfare*, published in July 2010), the centrepiece of current welfare reform was set out by Duncan Smith in his idea of a new Universal Credit (DWP 2010).

Duncan Smith argued that the new system should always reward, not penalize, those who pursue work. Universal Credit allows people moving from benefit into work to keep more of their earnings by reducing their benefits gradually. A related aim was to simplify the benefits system, making it easier to understand and less expensive to administer, which would help individuals to receive the benefits to which they are entitled and reduce the opportunities for people to 'play the system' or commit fraud. To achieve this, the new Universal Credit was to be phased in for new claimants from 2013, replacing six income-related benefits (DWP 2010: 14). Because Universal Credit is income-related, the government argued that it would reduce poverty levels among working families.

A raft of other changes were made in the Welfare Reform Act (2012). A benefit cap of £26,000 per year limited the total amount of welfare any household could receive. This was aimed at ensuring that households cannot receive more in welfare than the median (after-tax) earnings of those in work. However, the cap takes no account of the cost of rent and living expenses in different parts of the country, with London being particularly expensive. Child benefit would continue to be paid to families where anyone earns over £50,000 per year, but it would be effectively 'reclaimed' by an increase in income tax. Indirectly, this move ends the universality of this longstanding benefit. Disability benefits were changed, with a new Personal Independence Payment (PIP) replacing Disability Living Allowance from 2013. PIPs remain non-means tested, but recipients face new 'objective assessments' of their individual needs.

One of the most controversial new measures was a change to housing benefit paid to council and housing association tenants. The government argued that social housing tenants with spare bedrooms were effectively being paid a 'spare room subsidy'. It therefore reduced the amount of housing benefit if tenants had 'too many' bedrooms. For example, the benefit is reduced by 14 per cent for one bedroom and 25 per cent for two or more 'unused bedrooms', forcing people to pay part of their rent. Critics and the Labour opposition dubbed this an unfair 'bedroom tax' that would have a particularly severe impact on older people, whose relatives may use their spare room(s) intermittently, and disabled people who need spare bedrooms for the storage of equipment and overnight stays by carers and helpers.

The election of a majority Conservative government in the 2015 UK general election has ensured that the central thrust of welfare reform pursued by the previous coalition government will continue. It came to office with a plan to cut a further £12 billion from the welfare budget, continuing the strategy of shrinking the welfare state. In outlining its policy to allow private housing association tenants to buy their rented properties at below market value and to force councils to sell off their most valuable homes, the new government established a clear line of continuity with Margaret Thatcher's privatization agenda. The announcement of an increased minimum wage, rebadged as a 'national living wage', rising from £7.20 per hour to £9 per hour in 2020, also continues the Conservatives' key theme of 'making work pay' (Stewart 2015).

Remodelling the welfare state

Modern, post-1945 welfare states were created at a time of economic reconstruction and industrial development when men were perceived as 'breadwinners' requiring a 'family wage'. In the twenty-first century, European societies have moved far away from such conditions, and as a result their welfare states have been incrementally changing for quite some time. Hemerijck (2013: 15) argues that five main socio-economic changes are pushing governments to look for a welfare state model that will be adequate for the new global context: exogenous, endogenous, historical, supranational and political.

The main *exogenous* factor is intensified international competition, especially from emerging economies, which presents new challenges for the stability of Europe's redistributive welfare states. *Endogenous* factors include the economic shift away from manufacturing and towards services, the 'feminization' of work, high-skill labour markets and the fragmentation of employment relations, and increasing life expectancy and ageing populations, which brings a higher demand for health services and long-term care. The *historical* legacy of 'old social risks' means that large sums of public money are still directed at unemployment insurance, disability benefits and relatively generous old-age pensions, thus limiting the available resources to deal with the new policy challenges in the era of austerity politics. The *supranational* institutions of the European Union also impact on the ability of national welfare states to manage their domestic demands. In a very real sense, welfare states have become 'semi-sovereign' (Ferrera 2005). The *political* challenges come from the well-established decline in party loyalty, electoral volatility and the increasingly widespread antipathy to rising EU integration alongside anti-immigration sentiment; all were significant factors in the UK's 2016 referendum decision to leave the European Union. One result of these changes is a developing climate of an inward-looking defence of national welfare state provision.

What these five elements collectively produce is a growing push for fundamental reform of the welfare state. The UK case illustrates how a politics and discourse of austerity has garnered broad public support for measures aimed at reducing welfare spending, limiting numbers of eligible claimants, and moving people off welfare and into fragmented and increasingly destabilized labour markets. However, it has also been noted that, despite a seemingly continuous process of welfare reform over several decades, welfare states have actually proved to be remarkably resilient to fundamental change (Pierson 2011). This is largely because welfare policy creates interest communities which defend the status quo and make experimentation with radical policy changes electorally risky – a kind of in-built inertia.

Nevertheless, the post-2008 debt crises in EU nation-states and widespread declining government revenues have created the conditions for a political discourse which overtly criticizes state welfare, demonizes benefit 'scroungers', privileges private over public provision and actively promotes the rolling back of state involvement. Lister (2011) argues that we have entered an 'age of responsibility' in which social policy is increasingly used to encourage the poorest in society to feel and fulfil their obligations as 'responsible' citizens. Perhaps we are witnessing the historical moment when the welfare state's resistance to change is at its weakest and countries such as the UK are moving in a genuinely new direction, 'rolling back the state to a level of intervention below that in the United States – something which is unprecedented' (Taylor-Gooby and Stoker 2011: 14).

Chapter review

1. Explain the differences between an *absolute* and *relative* definition of poverty. Provide some real-world examples to illustrate these.

2   What is meant by a *poverty line*? Describe some problems associated with this concept by comparing the European Union and UK government definitions.

3   What are the main advantages and disadvantages of allowing members of the public to define what constitutes poverty? What can we expect subjective measures to add to our understanding of poverty?

4   Child poverty has proved to be a persistent social problem. What are the consequences of poverty in childhood and why is it so difficult to eliminate?

5   Outline the two main competing explanations for poverty in the developed countries today. Are these alternative explanations or could elements of them be combined to create a more powerful explanatory framework?

6   Define *social exclusion* and outline the main aspects associated with it. How is social exclusion related to poverty? With examples, explain how the concept of *intersectionality* may enable us to better understand social exclusion in the real world.

7   What is a 'welfare state' and why did the welfare state model spread? What are the differences between *institutionalists* and *residualists* in debates on the welfare state.

8   Trace the key moments in the formation and development of the UK welfare state. How does the UK model differ from other European versions?

9   In the 1970s, the post-1948 period of welfare consensus broke down. What has happened in debates on the future of the welfare state since 1979?

10 Given the election of the Conservative Party in 2015 and its focus on austerity politics, can we now say that the residualist perspective has definitively won the argument on welfare reform in the UK?

Research in practice

As we have seen in the chapter, there are two main explanations for poverty: the individualistic and the social-structural. However, it is not just social scientists who hold to one or other of these views. Everyone in society has an opinion as to why some people are poor and what could and should be done to help them out of poverty. But is there a connection between general public attitudes towards the poor and types of national welfare state regime? The following article explores this question. Read it and have a go at the questions: Kallio, J., and Niemelä, M. (2014) 'Who Blames the Poor? Multilevel Evidence in Support for and Determinants of Individualistic Explanation of Poverty in Europe', *European Societies*, 16(1): 112–35.

1   What kind of research is this? What is meant by 'multilevel evidence'?

2   North America and Europe have long been seen as different in their attitudes towards poverty. In what ways? On what basis do the authors criticize this standard view?

3   How is 'poverty' measured here? What factors are included in the definition of poverty?

4   Which countries tend to blame the individual for their poverty most and which the least? Is there a pattern to this cross-national distribution of public opinion?

5   The authors say that 'attitudes towards the poor can be seen as a part of the moral economy of the welfare state.' Explain what this means and suggest why some countries, such as Italy, Spain and Hungary, are exceptions to the pattern established in the paper.

Thinking it through

Since the 2008 financial crisis, many commentators and politicians have argued that we have entered an age of 'austerity politics', characterized by cuts in public spending and services, a reduction in welfare benefits and a focus on getting unemployed people into paid work. Yet, in the UK, this has gone hand in hand with a commitment to eliminating child poverty by 2020. An analysis by the New Policy Institute (NPI) in 2015 suggested that, since 2013, poverty has been rising; child poverty has actually increased by some 300,000, with 29 per cent of UK children living in poverty. Some

now think child poverty will be higher in 2020 than it is now. Download the NPI report here: http://npi.org.uk/files/5214/3031/5186/What_happened_to_poverty_under_the_Coalition_FINAL.pdf.

Provide a 1,000-word assessment of this report for ministers, focusing on the issue of how the authors define and use the concept of 'poverty'. In particular, discuss ways in which academic definitions of relative poverty may not accord with public understand-

ing of what it is to be 'in poverty'. In your conclusion, suggest how the government might frame its explanation of why the 2020 target may now be missed.

Society in the arts

In recent years, some policy researchers and sociologists have argued that poverty barely features in the visual media, especially television, and that, when it does, poverty and 'the poor' are represented through lazy stereotypes. Owen Jones's (2011) *Chavs: The Demonization of the Working Class* (London: Verso) takes issue with hateful representations and discussions of the working class as uneducated, workshy benefit recipients. Read the Introduction to this book, pp. 1–13.

Although Jones is making a wider argument about misleading perceptions of a classless society, the well-known 'chav' representations on television – Kelly Bailey in *Misfits*

(Channel 4), the Chatsworths in *Shameless* (Channel 4), Lauren Cooper in the *Catherine Tate Show* (BBC), and so on – are mainly of a poor, unemployed underclass, living lives of poverty. But are such representations of poverty any worse than earlier versions in literature or art?

Do your own research into how the poor and poverty are represented in mid- to late nineteenth-century paintings and fictional characters. What kinds of images and imagery are used? Are the poor presented as sympathetic characters? Construct an argument – using examples – suggesting that contemporary television characterizations, such as those noted above, are in some ways an improvement on earlier repre-

sentations of the poor. In what ways are they more positive?

Further reading

For an introduction to issues of poverty and social exclusion, Pete Alcock's (2006) *Understanding Poverty* (3rd edn, Basingstoke: Palgrave Macmillan) is very well written and reliable. Ruth Lister's (2004) *Poverty* (Cambridge: Polity) covers all the basics and includes a discussion of social exclusion and inclusion. The latest Breadline Britain survey is Stewart Lansley and Joanna Mack's (2015) *Breadline*

Britain: The Rise of Mass Poverty (London: Oneworld), which provides an up-to-date account of poverty and public perceptions of it.

The concept of social exclusion can then be further explored in an edited volume by Ann Taket et al. (2009), *Theorising Social Exclusion* (London: Routledge), a guide to theories and covering many types of exclusion. A useful book which uses case studies and scenarios to put flesh on the bones of the theories is John Pierson's (2009) *Tackling Social Exclusion* (2nd edn, London: Routledge).

For a very reliable and widely used account of the development of welfare in the UK, see Derek Fraser's (2009) *The Evolution of the British Welfare State* (4th edn, Basingstoke: Palgrave Macmillan). From here, a broader, comparative view of welfare states in Europe is provided in Mel Cousins's (2005) *European Welfare States: Comparative Perspectives* (London: Sage). Finally, *The Welfare State Reader* (2013), edited by Christopher Pierson, Francis G. Castles and Ingela K. Naumann (3rd ed, Cambridge: Polity), is a very useful resource.

Internet links

Additional information and support for this book at Polity:
www.politybooks.com/giddens

Eurostat on Poverty and Social Exclusion – contains statistical data on poverty and social exclusion across the EU:
http://ec.europa.eu/eurostat/statistics-explained/index.php/People_at_risk_of_poverty_or_social_exclusion

Joseph Rowntree Foundation – UK organization funding research aimed at understanding and eradicating poverty and social exclusion.
www.jrf.org.uk

The Townsend Centre for International Poverty Research, based at Bristol University, UK – some very useful resources on poverty and social exclusion here:
www.bristol.ac.uk/poverty

The Child Poverty Action Group, UK – a respected campaigning group; this site has lots of information and publications on child poverty:
www.cpag.org.uk

The Governance and Social Development Resource Centre – established by the UK Department for International Development (DfID) in 2005; covers all aspects of social exclusion:
www.gsdrc.org/topic-guides/social-exclusion

OECD site on Social and Welfare Issues – covers poverty reduction plans and OECD targets:
www.oecd.org/dac/povertyreduction.htm

The World Bank's Poverty Reduction and Equity site – lots of reading lists, information and more:
www.worldbank.org/en/topic/poverty

CHAPTER 14

Global Inequality

Contents

'Occupy Seoul' protesters in South Korea, 2011. The placards say 'Tax the 1%, welfare for the 99%'.

In the wake of the 2008 global financial crisis, self-styled 'Occupy' movements protesting against corporate greed and corruption emerged in many countries, starting with the Occupy Wall Street demonstrations in the USA in September 2011. Campaigners occupied city centres around the world to protest about a variety of issues, but the central and recurring theme has been the grossly unequal distribution of wealth, both within individual societies and at the global level. A symbolic way of representing this has been the slogan 'We are the 99 per cent'. The notion is that global inequality is worsening and just 1 per cent of the world population holds more wealth than the 99 per cent majority collectively.

The development charity Oxfam produced two reports, published in 2014 and 2015, which gave further credence to the '99 per cent' campaign. Oxfam calculated that the eighty-five richest people in the world owned as much wealth as the bottom 50 per cent of the global population and that over the past thirty years the rich have been getting richer (Oxfam 2014). Using data from the financial services company Credit Suisse, they argued that 1 per cent of people owned 48 per cent of global wealth, with the remaining 99 per cent owning just 52 per cent. In addition, 'Almost all of that 52% is owned by those included in the richest 20%, leaving just 5.5% for the remaining 80% of people in the world.' The report forecast that, by 2016, the wealthiest 1 per cent would own more than the remaining 99 per cent (Oxfam 2015: 2).

It is not just protest movements and international development charities that see increasing inequality as socially destabilizing and unsustainable. Warren Buffett, the fourth richest person in the world in 2014, with a net worth of US$58.2 billion, also argued that governments should 'stop coddling the rich'. In relation to the USA, he argued that

> Our leaders have asked for 'shared sacrifice.' But when they did the asking, they spared me. I checked with my mega-rich friends to learn what pain they were expecting. They, too, were left untouched. While the poor and middle class fight for us in Afghanistan, and while most Americans struggle to make ends meet, we mega-rich continue to get our extraordinary tax breaks. . . . These and other blessings are showered upon us by legislators in Washington who feel compelled to protect us, much as if we were spotted owls or some other endangered species. It's nice to have friends in high places. (Buffett 2011)

Buffett also argued that the current situation, in which the wealthiest people pay less in tax than the majority on low and middle incomes, cannot continue. He suggested an immediate increase in income tax for anyone in the US earning over $1 million (236,883 people in 2009) and additional increases for anyone earning $10 million or more (8,274 in 2009).

However, Bill Gates, founder of Microsoft and the world's wealthiest individual, with a personal fortune of $82.8 billion in 2014, reportedly said (in 2010) that 'Capitalism has worked very well' and that 'Anyone who wants to move to North Korea is welcome.' Gates's wealth increased by an immense $9 billion in just the year 2013–14 (*Forbes* 2014a).

See chapter 7, 'Work and the Economy', for a discussion of the 2008 crisis and chapter 13, 'Poverty, Social Exclusion and Welfare', for some of the recovery policies.

Twenty-first-century capitalism certainly has 'worked well' for billionaires – those with a personal wealth of at least US$1 billion. In 2014, *Forbes* magazine found that the world's 1,645 billionaires held $6.4 trillion, almost $2 trillion more than in 2011, higher than the national GDP of Germany and the largest total ever recorded. The USA still dominates *Forbes*'s rich list, with 492 billionaires compared to second placed China's 152 and Russia in third with 111, but smaller numbers of billionaires can be found on every continent.

THINKING CRITICALLY

Is the existence of 1,645 billionaires the sign of a successful global economy? If the poor living and working standards of people in many developing countries could be improved, would it be acceptable for the number of billionaires and the totality of their collective wealth to carry on growing?

How have a small number of individuals and families accumulated such fabulous wealth? In the past, aristocrats passed wealth and property down through the family, but far fewer people get rich this way today. Two-thirds of the 2014 billionaires' list can describe their fortunes as 'new entrepreneurial wealth', made rapidly in the course of a single lifetime; 13 per cent inherited their wealth, while another 21 per cent have built on

Denise Coates made her $1.6 billion fortune with the success of the online gambling site Bet365.com, which launched in 2001. She is one of a small minority of women – just 172 billionaires – on *Forbes*'s 2014 rich list, though the number of super-rich women is increasing. Of 268 new billionaires in 2014, forty-two were women.

the businesses passed down to them (*Forbes* 2014b). Many newly made billionaires have benefited from globalization and the digital revolution in communications. For example, Mark Zuckerberg, Sheryl Sandberg and Jeff Rothschild of Facebook all appear on the billionaires list, as do Jan Koum and Brian Acton, founders of WhatsApp. The success of Internet companies such as these illustrates

Gates's point. For some, capitalism continues to work extremely well.

However, the extreme inequalities of wealth and income across the world have caused consternation. Even as billionaires see their wealth rising rapidly and seemingly inexorably, millions of workers have been drawn into the global workforce in developing countries, working long hours for little pay. According to the 2014 United Nations *Human Development Report* (UNDP 2014: 19), some 1.2 billion people live on less than $1.25 per day. Such oppressive conditions would be unimaginable in the relatively rich countries. How can 'fairness' be calculated for individuals when there is such an unimaginable gulf between the highest- and lowest-paid people in the global economy? For sociologists, these issues are matters of structured social inequality that cannot be understood simply by tracing the individual biographies of the super-rich.

> It would be a good idea to refer to chapter 4, 'Globalization and Social Change', for a refresher on 'globalization'.

Moving towards equality?

It is a commonplace assumption in the developed world that each generation will be financially better off than the previous one as the economy expands. For much of the twentieth century this assumption was quite accurate. Hence, we might also believe that economic inequality has been continually shrinking as the lives of working-class people have significantly improved. Yet, in recent years, fresh concerns have been expressed about what is now called 'extreme inequality', particularly (as illustrated above) the rapid growth of wealth accumulating at the top of global distribution. Concerns about extreme inequality fit into and have become part of the *Zeitgeist* – the spirit of the age – which is shaped in large measure by reactions to the 2008 financial crisis.

Global Society 14.1 Where do the wealthiest 1% live?

As the business and political elite met at the World Economic Forum in Davos this week, there was much talk of rising inequality, and many references to the 'wealthiest 1%'. The phrase conjures up images of billionaires living on private islands – but is that who the 1% really are?

Obviously billionaires like Bill Gates, Warren Buffett and Mark Zuckerberg are part of the 1%. But who else is? According to Credit Suisse, another 47m people – everyone with wealth of $798,000 (£530,000) or more. That includes many people in rich countries who may not regard themselves as particularly wealthy, but who simply own their house outright or have paid off a significant chunk off their mortgage. Among them are:

- 18m people in the US
- 3.5m people in France
- 2.9m people in the UK
- 2.8m in Germany
- 4m in Japan
- 1.6m in China

But Credit Suisse's report doesn't tell the whole story. It doesn't take into account how much it costs to buy goods in each country, for example. Half a million pounds might buy a one-bedroom flat in central London, but in other countries it could buy a mansion. It also doesn't take into account income. As a result, many well-paid young people in Western countries may fall into the bottom 50% of wealth – either because they still have student debt to pay off, or because they know how to live well, and spend all their income.

If entry into the 1% does not guarantee a jet-set lifestyle, this is even truer when it comes to the cut-off point for the wealthiest 10% – for this you only need $77,000 (£50,000) of assets. And the figure required to be in the top half of the world's wealthiest is just $3,650 (£2,400).

Source: Extracted from Moore (2015).

> ### THINKING CRITICALLY
> Given the level of wealth required to be part of the world's wealthiest 10 per cent, what exactly can we learn about global inequality a) between individuals across the world and b) between relatively rich and relatively poor countries? If poverty is relative to the social context, can the same be said of wealth?

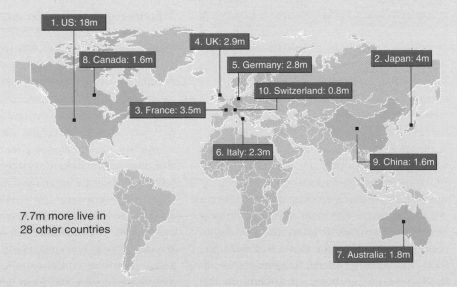

Figure 14.1   Share of the wealthiest 47 million people, by country

Source: Data from Credit Suisse Global Wealth Database, 2014.

But there is a paradox here. Why, during a period of slow or zero economic growth, swingeing cuts to public spending, and static or falling living standards, is the number of billionaires increasing along with the continuous growth of their personal fortunes? How have these people managed not just to hold onto their wealth but rapidly to increase it in such trying times? Arguably, the most satisfactory answer to date comes from the French economic historian Thomas Piketty, whose 696-page book *Capital in the Twenty-First Century* (2014) became an unlikely bestseller.

Piketty analysed long-term trends in the distribution of wealth in the developed economies since the eighteenth century, focusing particularly on those countries – such as Britain, Sweden, France, the USA and Germany – where the available data cover a very long period. In doing so, he produced an alternative account of and explanation for the persistence of striking inequality as well as a strong critique of the way that contemporary economics is practised. Piketty's work has proved controversial, but it also reshaped the debate on capitalism and the apparent drive towards increasing economic equality since the nineteenth century.

Piketty takes issue with two important but opposing theories of capitalist development: the 'catastrophist' version of Karl Marx and the 'cornucopian' one laid out by Simon Kuznets. In the mid-nineteenth century, Marx saw capitalism as an exploitative economic system which contained an internal dynamic leading inexorably to class conflict. This is because the working class would become increasingly poor or 'immiserated', while capitalists became richer and more powerful. At some point, class consciousness would develop and a revolution would overthrow the ruling capitalist class. Although Marx was right about the long-term tendency towards increasing inequality, economic growth and the spread of knowledge and skills have significantly offset any revolutionary fervour. On the other hand, in the 1950s – a postwar period of strong economic growth – Kuznets maintained that industrial capitalist economies initially produce stark

inequality. But as they develop and average incomes rise, inequality is gradually reduced, as the history of European and North American societies demonstrates. He argued that this developmental process would also apply to developing countries as they follow a similar path (see chapter 12, 'Stratification and Social Class', for the 'Kuznets Curve'). Though Kuznets's model seemed to fit 1950s economic development quite well, Piketty's data do not bear out his thesis, but tell an altogether different story.

Capitalist economies did indeed exhibit a stark inequality, which continued to increase until the early twentieth century, although the period from the start of the First World War to the mid-1970s saw a counter-trend towards the flattening out of gross disparities of income and wealth. Since the 1980s, however, there has been a reversal of that trend, and inequality is now increasing again (Piketty calls this 'divergence'). So is the latter just a temporary 'blip' in the 'normal' movement towards more equality? Not so, argues Piketty. In fact, the real 'blip' was the twentieth-century movement towards equality (Piketty calls this 'convergence'), and that was due to specific events. The destruction wrought by two world wars, large-scale bankruptcies during the 1930s depression, the nationalization of key industries and the growing strength of trade unions combined to compress inequality. But, by the 1980s, capitalism returned to its long-term trend for capital accumulation at the top, and we should expect that to continue unless concerted action is taken by the people and governments of the world.

One key reason for persistent accumulation at the top lies in the difference between economic growth rates (g) and net returns on capital investment (r). Seen in long-term perspective, returns on capital consistently outstrip economic growth rates, expressed in the pithy equation $r > g$. This means that those individuals and families which accumulated wealth and capital in the past will see their fortunes grow faster than those gaining their wealth purely from income. For instance, 'Between 1990 and 2010, Bill Gates saw his fortune grow from $8 billion to $50 billion. During the same period, Liliane Bettencourt, heiress of L'Oreal the cosmetics company, saw her fortune rise from $2 to $25 billion. After inflation, both enjoyed a real return on their capital of 10–11 per cent per annum.' Hence, 'Liliane Bettencourt, who never worked a day in her life, saw her fortune grow exactly as fast as Bill Gates, the high-tech pioneer, whose wealth has incidentally continued to grow just as rapidly since he stopped working. Once a fortune is established, the capital grows according to a dynamic of its own' (Piketty 2014: 439–40).

In a sense, Piketty's study puts empirical flesh on the commonplace truism that 'money makes money' or, as he puts it himself, 'money tends to reproduce itself'. So why is this a problem? Piketty (2014: 1–2) expresses deep disquiet about the social consequences of extreme inequality. He argues that, 'When the rate of return on capital exceeds the rate of growth of output and income, as it did in the nineteenth century and seems quite likely to do again in the twenty-first, capitalism automatically generates arbitrary and unsustainable inequalities that radically undermine the meritocratic values on which democratic societies are based.' Contemporary capitalism, a system ostensibly rooted in creativity, entrepreneurship and hard work, actually rewards idleness and inherited wealth. How long will the 99 per cent put up with this contradiction?

Nonetheless, Piketty offers some policy solutions that could halt the trend and promote the general interest over individual gain. Chief among these is a progressive annual tax on global wealth (not income), ideally in all countries of the world. The primary aim of this tax is not to fund welfare or social services (though it may be used for these ends) but to end the limitless expansion of global inequality and better regulate the global financial system. Yet Piketty is not naïve enough to think that international agreement is remotely close or that the wealthiest would comply willingly. His argument is that, however difficult or fanciful it sounds, only by tackling the increasing concentration of wealth can potentially disas-

trous social conflict be avoided. Despite being widely perceived as radical and utopian by media commentators, in fact Piketty's proposals are best seen as an attempt to save capitalism from exactly the kind of social uprising that Marx envisaged.

Global inequality

Piketty's study is fascinating and, though primarily an economic thesis, has a place within broader sociological studies of class-based inequality. Social inequality is one of sociology's foundational issues, with the classical sociologists focusing on inequalities of class, status and power within the emerging industrial capitalist societies. However, similar issues of class, status and power exist on an even larger scale at the global level. Just as we can speak of the rich and poor, high and low status, or the powerful and powerless *within a single country*, we can also see these and investigate their causes *within the global system as a whole*. In the rest of this chapter, we look at global inequality in the late twentieth and early twenty-first centuries (see chapter 4 for globalization in a longer timescale).

Economic inequality is a major source of the world's problems of poverty, hunger and health, and for that reason it forms the central focus of this chapter. However, as we noted above, there are also major inequalities of social status and global inequalities of power both within and between nation-states. The latter remains an important source of many entrenched conflicts, some of which are discussed in chapter 22, 'Nations, War and Terrorism'. For a broader analysis of inequalities of status and power, readers should consult the relevant chapters identified above.

Global economic inequality refers primarily to the systematic differences in wealth, incomes and working conditions that exist *between* countries. The challenge for social scientists is not merely to identify such differences but to explain *why* they occur and what are the social consequences. First,

Millions of workers across the world, many of them children, are employed in 'sweatshops', working long hours for little financial reward. Has globalization been beneficial for these individuals?

though, we must clarify some key terms that are used in the literature in this area.

The language of global inequality

The language used to discuss economic development and global inequality is contentious and has changed several times over the past 100 years. Until the late twentieth century, it was common to use a three worlds model, of first, second and third worlds, embodying the idea that each developed relatively separately. Although it is useful as a basic description of the rich first world, the middle-income second world and the relatively poor third world, there are two main problems with this typology.

First, it is recognized today that there exists a global level of reality covering all the societies of the world which compromises the idea that the three worlds are effectively separate entities. In a globalizing world, the first, second and third worlds are tightly interconnected, and it is just not possible to grasp the situation in one 'world' without understanding its position in the global system as a whole. Second, labelling relatively rich countries as the 'first world' has been seen as a value judgement which stigmatizes the (lower) 'third world' as an undeveloped and economically stagnant region. This characterization also 'blames the victims', as it portrays the people and governments of poorer countries as responsible for their often desperate situation. As we shall see later, the three worlds model takes no account of the impact of colonialism or Western multinational corporations' exploitation of 'third world' natural and human resources.

Because of the flaws in the three worlds model, social scientists began to discuss the world as divided into 'developed' and 'underdeveloped' societies, with the developed societies being those that, broadly defined, are in the northern hemisphere of the globe with the underdeveloped societies in the southern hemisphere. However, most sociologists dropped the concept of 'underdeveloped', which again gave the impression of economic backwardness, in favour of 'developing countries'. The latter is a more dynamic concept, implying movement and ongoing economic progress rather than unchangeable underdevelopment. The exceptions are those scholars working within the Marxist tradition, who link underdevelopment in the South to development in the North. That is, the rich countries are seen as actively underdeveloping the countries of the global South in order that Western capitalism can continue to expand. This perspective is discussed in more detail later.

However, for some, even this move remains too close to Western ideas of what economic development actually entails. Some recent scholarship has adopted the term majority world to describe (broadly) the relatively poor countries of the southern hemisphere and minority world for the relatively wealthy countries of the North. One benefit of this conceptualization is that it reminds us that a small number of countries encompassing a minority of the global population enjoy comfortable lifestyles, while the majority of the world's people still live in relatively poor conditions that severely reduce their life chances. However, it gives little impression of the economic situation in different regions of the world.

As we are concerned primarily (though not exclusively) with economic inequality, in this chapter we will generally use 'developed' to refer to those countries that have arrived at a relatively high level of income and economic development and 'developing' when discussing those countries that have a lower level of income but are in the process of development. In this sense, the 'developing countries' include most 'second' and all 'third' world countries on the older model, though the discussion throughout will draw on national case studies and make clear which regions and countries are being referred to. Whichever concepts are used, it is important to understand how the very different economic situations of countries around the world fit into such classification schemes.

Measuring economic inequality

One way to classify countries in terms of global inequality is to compare their economic productivity. An important measure of economic productivity is a country's gross domestic product (GDP), which is made up of all the goods and services on record as being produced in a particular year. Income earned abroad by individuals or corporations is not included in GDP. An important alternative measure is gross national income (GNI). Unlike GDP, GNI includes income earned by individuals or corporations outside the country. Measures of economic activity, such as GDP or GNI, are often given per person, which allows us to compare the wealth of an average inhabitant of a country. Also, in order to compare different countries, we need to use a common currency, and most international institutions, such as the World Bank and the United Nations, use the US dollar.

The World Bank is an international lending organization that provides loans for development projects in poorer countries. It uses per person GNI to classify countries as high income, upper middle income, lower middle income or low income. This system of classification will help us to understand why there are such vast differences in living standards between countries. For the sake of simplicity, we will usually merge the upper-middle and lower-middle categories into one category: middle income.

The World Bank (2011a) divides 155 countries into the three economic classes. There are fifty-eight other economies in the world for which the World Bank does not provide data, either because information is lacking or because the economies have fewer than 1 million people. In 2013, countries with a GNI per capita of $1,045 per annum were classified as 'low income', those between $1,045 and $12,746 were 'middle income', and those with a GNI of $12,746 or more were labelled 'high income'. However, we should bear in mind that this classification system is based on *average income* for each country and therefore does not tell us about income inequality *within* each country. This can be significant in assessing inequalities, though we do not focus on intra-country inequalities in this chapter. For example, the World Bank reclassified India from a low-income to a lower-middle-income country after its GNI per capita had risen from just $450 in 1999 to $1,220 in 2009 (World Bank 2011a: 11). Yet, despite India's large and growing middle class and recently developed space exploration programme, large numbers of its people still live in poverty. Similarly, China was reclassified in 1999 from low to middle income, and in 2009 its GNI per capita was $3,650. As with India, the average income figure confers middle-income status on China, but hundreds of millions of its people still live in poverty.

Comparing countries on the basis of income alone may be misleading, since GNI takes account only of goods and services produced for cash sale. Many people in low-income countries are farmers or herders who produce for their own families or for barter involving non-cash transactions, and these crops and animals are not taken into account. Countries also possess unique and widely differing languages and traditions. Poor countries are no less rich in history and culture than their wealthier neighbours, even though the lives of their people may be harsher. Social and cultural assets such as social solidarity, strong cultural traditions, or systems of familial and community assistance do not lend themselves to statistical measurement.

Many environmental campaigners have argued that GDP and GNI are blunt quantitative measures that tell us nothing about the *quality* of life. Even those economic activities that damage the natural environment are counted as part of a country's total economic output and seen as contributing to economic well-being. From the perspective of long-term environmental sustainability, this method is completely irrational. If we took account of some of the social and cultural aspects of life noted above, we may arrive at a radically different view of the apparent benefits of pursuing continuous increases in GDP/GNI.

Even if we do compare countries solely on the basis of economic statistics, the statistics we choose for our comparisons are likely to make a difference to our conclusions. For example, if we choose to study global inequality by comparing levels of household consumption (of food, medicine or other products) rather than GNI, we might reach a different conclusion. Similarly, a comparison of the GNI of several countries does not take into account how much things *actually* cost. If two countries have a more or less equal GNI but, in the first, an average family meal costs a few pence, whereas in the second it costs several pounds, it may be misleading to argue that the countries are equally wealthy. People get considerably more for their money in the first. Instead, researchers tend to use *purchasing power parities* (PPP) that eliminate the difference in prices between two countries. In this chapter we generally use comparisons of GNI between countries, but both GDP and PPPs are included where necessary.

High-income countries

The *high-income countries* are generally those that were first to industrialize, starting with the UK some 250 years ago and spreading to Europe, the United States and Canada. It was only some forty years ago that Japan joined the ranks of such high-income industrialized nations, while Singapore, Hong Kong and Taiwan moved into this category only in the 1980s and 1990s. The reasons for the success of these Asian latecomers are much debated by sociologists and economists, and we will look at these debates later in the chapter.

High-income countries account for around 15 per cent of the world's population, yet they lay claim to over 75 per cent of the world's annual output of wealth. High-income countries offer good housing, adequate food, safe water supplies and other comforts unknown in many other parts of the world. Although these countries often have large numbers in poverty, most of their inhabitants enjoy a standard of living unimaginable for the majority of the world's people.

Middle-income countries

The *middle-income countries* are found primarily in East and South-East Asia, the oil-rich countries of the Middle East and North Africa, the Americas (Mexico, Central America, Cuba and other countries in the Caribbean, and South America) and the once-communist republics that formerly made up the Soviet Union and its East European allies. Most of these countries began to industrialize relatively late in the twentieth century and are therefore not yet as industrially developed (or wealthy) as the high-income countries.

Although many people in middle-income countries are substantially better off than their neighbours in low-income countries, most do not enjoy the high standard of living of the high-income countries. The ranks of the world's middle-income countries expanded when China – with 1.34 billion people – was reclassified from low to middle income as a result of its rapid economic growth. This reclassification is somewhat misleading, as China's average per person income of $3,650 per year in 2009 is at the lower end of the middle-income category, and a large majority of its population fall within the World Bank's low-income category (World Bank 2011a).

Low-income countries

Finally, the *low-income countries* take in much of eastern, western and sub-Saharan Africa, Cambodia and some other East Asian countries, and Nepal and Bangladesh in South Asia. Many of these countries have agricultural economies and only recently began to industrialize. However, as the cases of Pakistan, India and China show, average income levels are rising in some previously low-income countries and regions as they become part of the global economic system.

Fertility rates are higher in low-income countries than elsewhere, as large families provide additional farm labour or otherwise contribute to family income. In wealthy industrial societies, where children are more likely to be in school than on the farm, the economic benefit of large families declines and people tend to have fewer children. Because of this, in the early twenty-first century the populations of low-income countries grew more than three times as fast as those of the high-income countries (World Bank 2004).

See chapter 6, 'Cities and Urban Life', for a wider discussion of urbanization.

> **THINKING CRITICALLY**
>
> Which aspects of life does the measure of 'average income' help us to understand? Which aspects is this method likely to miss? How else could we compare the living conditions of countries with such different cultures, social structures and economies?

Is global economic inequality increasing?

The question of whether global inequality is increasing or diminishing has polarized opinion in recent years. Those who see global inequality expanding argue that, since the mid-1970s, globalization has exacerbated the trend towards inequality that began with capitalist industrialization. Critics cite statistics from the UN *Human Development Report 2007/2008*, which noted that the 40 per cent of the human population living on less than US$2 a day accounted for just 5 per cent of global income. In particular, 48 per cent of people in sub-Saharan Africa live in poverty, and this region accounts for just over one-quarter (26 per cent) of world poverty, up from one-fifth in 1990 (UNDP 2007a: 25; UNSDSN 2012). The wealthiest 20 per cent accounted for three-quarters of global income. At the global level as well as within many countries, inequality is increasing along with globalization.

By contrast, others point out that over the past few decades the overall standard of living in the world as a whole has actually risen. Many indicators measuring the living standards of the world's poorest people show improvements. There has been a reduction in illiteracy, infant death rates and malnutrition are falling, people are living longer, and global poverty – commonly defined as the number of people living on less than US$1.25 a day – has also declined (see table 14.1, p. 595). Tracking purely economic inequality does not provide us with the full picture of what is happening across the world.

However, there are substantial differences between countries. Many of the gains have been in the high- and middle-income countries, while living standards in some of the very poorest countries have declined. Indeed, although the 1990s was a time of economic boom for the world's richest country, the United States, the UN *Human Development Report 2003* (UNDP 2003) found that more than fifty countries, located mainly in sub-Saharan Africa, suffered falling living standards during that decade as a result of famine, deaths from the HIV/AIDS epidemic, conflicts and failed national economic policies. Atkinson (2003) reminds us that increasing inequality cannot be explained entirely by general reference to rapid globalization, as national taxation and other economic policies play an important role. For example, in Scandinavian countries such as Sweden, where the welfare state operates in a redistributive way, global trends towards widening social inequality have been more effectively mitigated than in others, such as the UK, which have adopted a more neo-liberal, free-market approach to welfare reform.

> See chapter 13, 'Poverty, Social Exclusion and Welfare', for a discussion of welfare state regimes.

As this dispute shows, the way we choose to measure global inequality makes a big difference to the likely conclusions that we reach. The economist Stanley Fischer compared two ways of looking at global income inequality:

the first simply compares income inequality between countries, while the second takes into account the number of people living in those countries as well. The first is shown in the top chart of figure 14.2. This shows the average income of a selection of poor and rich countries between 1980 and 2000, with each country represented on the graph by a uniform dot. The figure demonstrates that, during this period, the average income of the poorest nations grew much more slowly than the average income of the world's richest nations. Hence, the trend (indicated by the black line) reveals inequality increasing as the economies of the richer countries grow more quickly than those of the poorer countries (on the left). If the poorest countries had grown faster than the richest, the black trend line would slope down from left to right. The gap between the richest and the poorest of the world's countries therefore appears to be growing.

The bottom chart, which takes into account population, presents a rather different view of global inequality. The same chart is shown here, but this time the dots that represent each country have been drawn in proportion to the size of the number of people living in that country. Two of the world's most populous countries – India and China, which between them account for well over one-third of global population – have increased the size of their economies considerably since 1980. Because of their size, a population-weighted line of best fit drawn through the second chart would slope downwards, implying that global inequality is falling as, on average, the populations of the poorest countries catch up. Those countries that have done well since 1980 – India, China and Vietnam, for example – also tend to be those that have integrated most successfully into the global economy.

Trends in the Human Development Index

An enormous gulf in living standards separates most people in rich countries from their counterparts in poor ones. Wealth and poverty make life different in a host of ways.

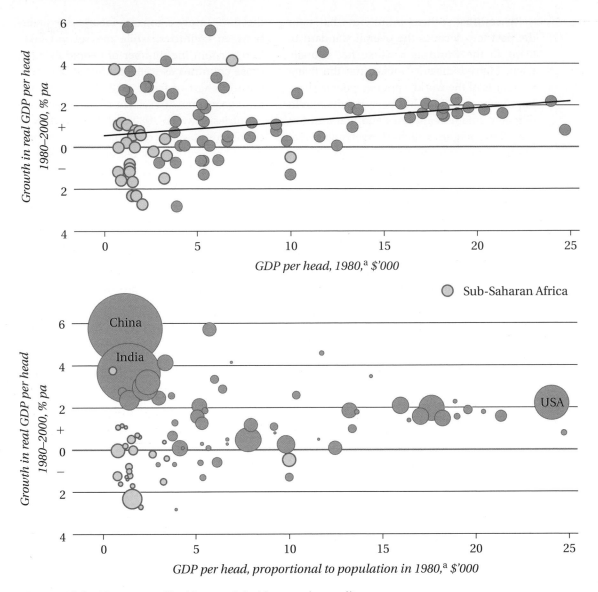

Figure 14.2 Two ways of looking at global income inequality

Note: [a]1996 prices.
Source: The Economist (2004b) © The Economist Newspaper Limited, London.

For instance, about one-third of the world's poor are undernourished and almost all are illiterate, lacking access to basic primary school education. There is a gender dimension here, as educating girls has traditionally been seen as unnecessary or secondary to the education of boys. While most of the world is still rural, within a decade there are likely to be more poor people in urban than in rural areas.

> Urbanization in developing countries is discussed in more detail in chapter 6, 'Cities and Urban Life'.

Yet conditions have undoubtedly improved in many low- and middle-income countries since the 1980s. For example, between 1990–1 and 2004–5 the global infant mortality rate dropped from sixty-five (per 1,000 live

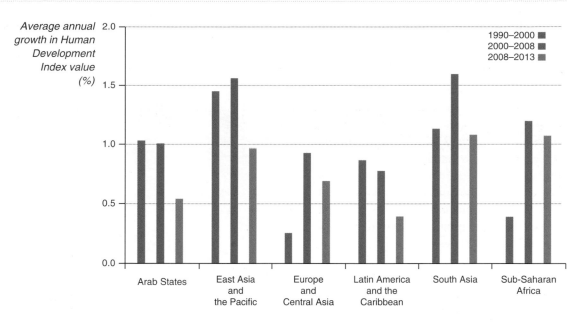

Figure 14.3 Improving quality of life trend in the UN HDI, 1990–2013

Source: UNDP (2014: 34).

births) to fifty-two, alongside an increase in the proportion of births attended by medical personnel, from 47 to 59 per cent. The UNDP has demonstrated that a range of other measures have also showed continuing improvement, despite a slowdown in annual improvement growth rates following the 2008 global financial crash (see Figure 14.3).

The United Nations Development Programme (UNDP 2010) produced a

forty-year trend analysis based on their Human Development Index (HDI), which combines economic and non-economic indicators of 'human development'. The HDI covers three dimensions – health, education and living standards – using four indicators – life expectancy at birth, mean years of schooling, expected years of schooling and GNI per capita (figure 14.4). In 2010 three new indicators were added, taking account of the impact

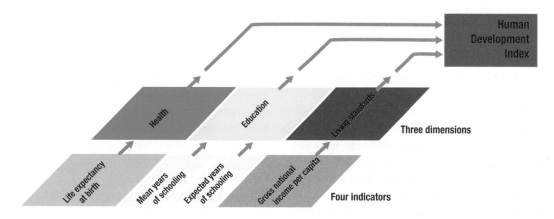

Figure 14.4 Components of the Human Development Index

Source: UNDP (2010: 13).

of social inequality, gender inequality and a multidimensional index of poverty.

Since the first *Human Development Report* in 1990, these annual reports have consistently argued that there is no 'automatic link' between economic growth and human progress. What is more significant is how the benefits of economic growth are used by governments and shared across national populations. In general, between 1970 and 2010 there was progress in HDI measures across all regions of the world, though not in all countries. East Asia showed the fastest progress, followed by South Asia and the Arab states.

Of the 135 countries in the comparison, only three – the Democratic Republic of the Congo, Zambia and Zimbabwe – had a lower HDI in 2010 than in 1970. Figure 14.5 traces a selection of the 135 countries from their original score in 1970. Oman (an oil-rich state) made the most progress, followed by China, Nepal and Indonesia. Ethiopia was eleventh on the list of countries making the fastest development, despite having the fourteenth *lowest* GNI per capita, illustrating that a broader definition of 'development' produces very different outcomes compared to purely economic measures. Among the top ten performing countries – Oman, China, Nepal, Indonesia, Saudi Arabia, the Lao People's Democratic Republic, Tunisia, South Korea, Algeria and Morocco – only China's overall HDI score was largely a result of progress in economic growth as measured in GNI per capita.

Progress made in human development means that life in developing countries today is generally 'more similar' to life in the developed countries than it was in 1970. But the gross inequality of life conditions in 1970 means that this progress is relative, and global inequality remains the most striking feature of international comparisons. For example, the 2010 report (UNDP 2010: 29) notes that, in 1970, life expectancy at birth in Norway was seventy-four years and in Gambia just forty-one years. By 2010 the gap had narrowed, with Norway at eighty-one years and Gambia at fifty-seven years, but a life expectancy of only fifty-seven places strict limitations on the life chances and freedoms of people born in Gambia today. So,

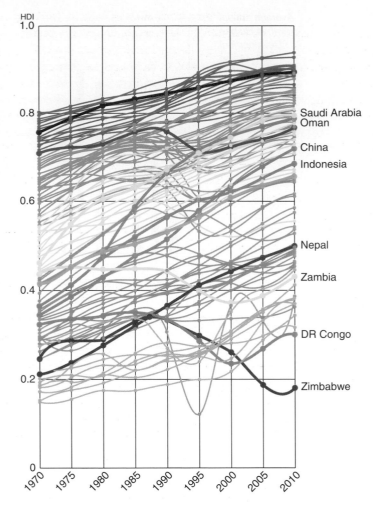

Figure 14.5 National trends in the HDI, selected countries, 1970–2010

Note: Top movers are Oman, China, Nepal, Indonesia and Saudi Arabia. Bottom movers are the DR Congo, Zambia and Zimbabwe.
Source: Adapted from UNDP (2010: 27).

despite a progressive general trend in human development, the process of developing countries 'catching up' with the developed world will take a very long time indeed.

Unequal life chances

Sociologists have long studied the ways in which inequalities of class, ethnicity and gender affect the overall life chances of individuals. Being born male or female, working class or middle class, or part of an ethnic majority or minority group can shape how healthy we are, what level of education we will reach or the kind of work we can expect to do. International comparisons of developed and developing societies show that inequality is even starker across countries than among social groups within countries. In this section we briefly outline some key inequalities in relation to health, nutrition and education as well as looking at the continued use of child labour.

Health

People in high-income countries are generally healthier than their counterparts in low-income countries. Low-income countries generally suffer from inadequate health facilities, and where these exist they seldom serve the poorest people. Those living in low-income countries also lack proper sanitation, put up with polluted water and run greater risk of contracting infectious diseases. They are more likely to suffer malnourishment, starvation and famine. These factors all contribute to physical weakness and poor health, making people in low-income countries susceptible to illness and disease. There is growing evidence that high rates of HIV/AIDS infection found in many African countries are due, in part, to the weakened health of impoverished people (Stillwaggon 2000).

Between 1970 and 1990, health conditions improved across the world, and by 2010 life expectancy even for people in the poorest region of the world – sub-Saharan Africa – had risen by an additional eight years from that in 1970. In developing countries, infant mortality rates fell by fifty-nine per 1,000 live births between 1970 and 2005, though the developed countries saw a higher percentage decline, thus widening the global inequality gap. In 2010, there were still eight times more infant deaths per 1,000 live births in developing countries than in developed ones, and less than 1 per cent of all child deaths are in the developed world (UNDP 2010: 32).

Maternal mortality rates have also improved, though at a much slower pace, and progress

Every year hunger, arising from both natural and social causes, disease and lack of healthcare result in the deaths of about 12 million children.

seems to have slowed since 1990. The HIV/AIDS epidemic has had a dramatic impact on the countries of sub-Saharan Africa, where HIV prevalence rates remain higher than 15 per cent and life expectancy in the worst affected countries is fifty-one years – about the same as in the UK before the Industrial Revolution in the mid-eighteenth century.

Hunger, malnutrition and famine

Hunger, malnutrition and famine are major sources of poor health, though these are

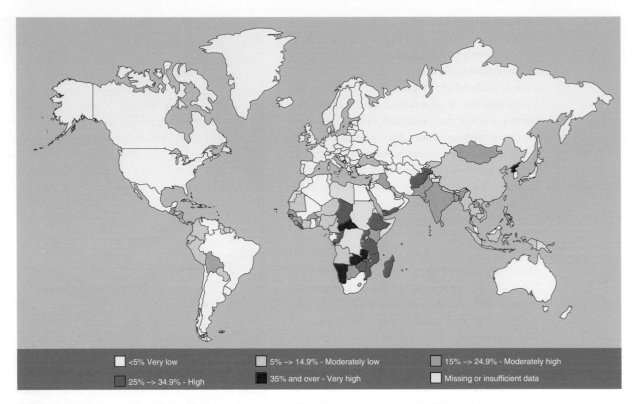

Figure 14.6 Prevalence of undernourishment in developing countries, 2015

Source: UNFAO (2015).

longstanding issues rather than new problems. What seems to be new is the extent of hunger and undernourishment – the fact that so many people in the world today appear to be on the brink of starvation (see figure 14.6). The United Nations World Food Programme (UNWFP 2001) defines 'hunger' as a diet of 1,800 or fewer calories per day – an amount insufficient to provide adults with the nutrients required for active, healthy lives. The number of malnourished people globally has remained quite stable since 1980, at around 800 million, though this is down from a peak of 1 billion in the early 2000s (UNDP 2010). According to the World Food Programme study, 200 million of the world's hungry are children under the age of five, who are underweight because they lack adequate food. Every year hunger kills an estimated 12 million children.

Yet more than three-quarters of all malnourished children under the age of five in the world's low- and middle-income countries live in countries that actually produce a food surplus (Lappe 1998). In the developed countries, it is not too little but, rather, too much food that has become a problem, as obesity rates have developed into an increasing cause for concern. Indeed, some experts suggest that, in the USA, life expectancy may begin to fall by 2050 on account of obesity-related health problems such as diabetes, strokes and cardiovascular disease (Olshansky et al. 2005).

Famine and hunger are the result of a combination of natural and social forces. Drought alone affects an estimated 100 million people in the world today. In countries such as Sudan, Ethiopia, Eritrea, Indonesia, Afghanistan, Sierra Leone, Guinea and Tajikistan, the combination of drought and internal warfare has devastated food production, resulting in starvation and death for millions of people. In Latin America and the Caribbean at the start of the twenty-first century, 53 million people (11 per cent of the population) were malnourished, along with 180 million (33 per cent) in sub-Saharan Africa and 525 million (17 per cent) in Asia (UNWFP 2001).

The countries affected by famine and starvation are, for the most part, too poor to pay for new technologies that would increase their food production. Nor can they afford to purchase sufficient food imports from elsewhere in the world. At the same time, paradoxically, as world hunger grows, food production continues to increase. Between 1965 and 1999, for example, world production of grain doubled. Even allowing for the substantial world population increase over this period, the global production of grain per person was 15 per cent higher in 1999 than it was thirty-four years earlier. This growth, however, is not evenly distributed around the world. In much of Africa, for example, food production per person has declined in recent years. Surplus food produced in high-income countries such as the United States is seldom affordable to the countries that need it most.

Education, literacy and child labour

Education contributes to economic growth, since people with advanced schooling provide the skilled work necessary for high-wage industries. Education also offers the only hope of escaping from the cycle of harsh working conditions and poverty, since poorly educated people are condemned to low-wage, unskilled jobs. It is also the case that educated people are less likely to have large numbers of children, thus slowing down the global population growth that contributes to poverty. But, here again, developing countries are disadvantaged, since they can seldom afford high-quality public education systems. As a consequence, children in developed countries are much more likely to get schooling than are children in developing countries, and adults in the high-income countries are much more likely to be able to read and write.

Nevertheless, there has been much improvement in education provision and enrolment since the 1980s. Primary school enrolment has become the norm in both developed and developing countries since around 1990, and the global proportion of people who have received some form of education rose from 57 per cent in 1960 to 85 per cent by 2010. Levels of youth literacy also rose to more than 95 per cent in developing countries as a result of increases in the average length of years at school (UNDP 2010). We might expect that, as a result, illiteracy will become far less of a problem for developing countries and individuals in the future.

One reason for the disparities in education is that developed countries spend a much larger percentage of their gross domestic product on education than low-income countries, which means large inequalities in funding per pupil (World Bank 2001). For instance, in 2010, the average spend per pupil on education was forty times higher in developed countries than in sub-Saharan Africa, where it was just $184 per annum. There is also a significant gender gap in primary school enrolment. Of the 156 countries surveyed for the HDI report in 2010, only eighty-seven had comparable primary school enrolments for girls and boys. In rural areas of some developing countries, the gender gap for secondary-age children is striking. In Bolivia and Guinea, for example, only around 35 per cent of older rural girls are enrolled compared with 71 per cent and 84 per cent, respectively, of urban boys (UNDP 2010: 36–8). While virtually all secondary school-aged males and females in the developed world were in full-time education in 2007, only 64 per cent of children in developing countries enjoyed this benefit. In tertiary education the situation is even more unequal, though the overall direction of travel is upwards (see figure 14.7, p. 584).

A major cause of the relatively low levels of young people in secondary and tertiary education in developing countries is their involvement in work. Children are often forced to work because of a combination of family poverty, lack of education provision, and

Global Society 14.2 What does the world eat? What should the world eat?

In 2000, the photojournalist Peter Menzel and the journalist Faith D'Alusio set out to record what a culturally diverse range of families across the world ate in one week, the result being their 2005 book *Hungry Planet: What the World Eats*. They visited thirty families in twenty-four countries looking at food purchases, costs and recipes, and photographing families with their typical weekly food items. Two examples from their book are reproduced here.

THINKING CRITICALLY

Compare the two family diets on the basis of cost, quantity of food, diversity of food items and fresh versus pre-packaged items. Is it possible to say which diet is healthier? Why might it be argued that the Earth's natural environment could not sustain the current global human population (7.5 billion in 2016) if every society adopted the US family's diet?

Republic of Chad: the Aboubakar family of Breidjing Camp
Food expenditure for one week: 685 CFA francs, or $1.23
Favourite foods: soup with fresh sheep meat

USA: the Revis family of North Carolina
Food expenditure for one week: $341.98
Favourite foods: spaghetti, potatoes, sesame chicken

traditional indifference to the plight of those who are poor or who belong to ethnic minorities (UNICEF 2000a). Child labour has been legally eliminated in the high-income countries but still exists in many parts of the world. According to the United Nations International Labour Organization (ILO) there were about 215 million child labourers between the ages of five and seventeen in 2008, a reduction of 7 million since 2004. Around 115 million of these children were working in hazardous conditions (ILO 2010: v). The highest incidence of child labour is in sub-Saharan Africa and the largest number of child workers is found in the Asia-Pacific region.

Some 68 per cent of child labourers in 2008 were involved in unpaid family labour, 21 per cent were in paid employment and 5 per cent were self-employed; 60 per cent worked in agriculture, 7 per cent in industry, and 26 per cent in services, such as restaurants and hotels, and as servants in wealthy households (ILO 2010). At best, these children work long hours with little pay and are unable to go to school and develop the skills that might eventually enable them to escape their lives of poverty. However, simply enforcing an immediate ban on all child labour, even if it were possible, might be counter-productive. Child labour is a better alternative to child prostitution or chronic undernourishment, for example. The challenge is not just to end child labour but also to move children from work into education and to ensure that

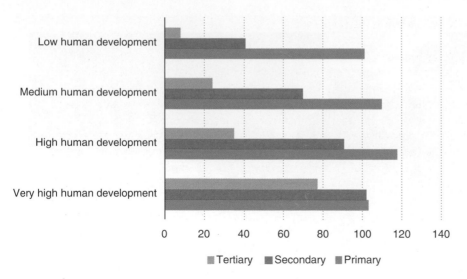

Figure 14.7 Gross enrolment ratios by level of education and human development index, 2015

Note: Ratios can exceed 100 per cent where enrolment is of students who are not of school age (on account of late entry or repeat study).
Source: UNDP (2015: 245).

they are properly provided for during their school years.

One form of child labour today that is close to slavery is 'bonded labour'. In this system, children as young as eight or nine are pledged by their parents to factory-owners in exchange for small loans. These children are paid so little that they never manage to reduce the debt, condemning them to a lifetime of bondage. One case of bonded labour that attracted international attention was that of Iqbal Masih, a Pakistani child who, at the age of four, was sold into slavery by his father in order to borrow 600 rupees (roughly US$16) for the wedding of his first-born son. For six years, Iqbal spent most of his time chained to a carpet-weaving loom, tying tiny knots for hours on end. After fleeing the factory at the age of ten, he began speaking to labour organizations and schools about his experience. Iqbal paid a bitter price for his outspokenness: when he was thirteen, while riding his bicycle in his hometown, he was gunned down by agents believed to be working for the carpet industry (Bobak 1996).

Abolishing such exploitative child labour will require countries around the world to enact strong laws against the practice and be willing to enforce them. International organizations such as the ILO have outlined a set of standards for such laws to follow, and in June 1999 it adopted Convention 182, calling for the abolition of the 'worst forms of child labour', including slavery, the sale and trafficking of children, forced labour, prostitution, pornography, drugs trafficking and work that harms the health, safety or morals of children (ILO 1999). Countries must also provide free public education and require that children attend school full time (UNICEF 2000a). Part of the solution also lies with the global corporations manufacturing goods using child labour, trade unions that organize the workforce, agricultural cooperatives whose values are opposed to child labour and, ultimately, the consumers who buy the goods.

The changing human population

The United Nations estimates that the Earth's six-billionth inhabitant was born on 20 January

Global Society 14.3 Child labour in agriculture

Instead of attending school, millions of girls and boys in rural areas worldwide are child labourers. They are everywhere, but often hidden, on farms, on fishing boats, in plantations, in mountain areas, herding livestock or toiling as domestic servants. Child labour perpetuates a cycle of poverty for the children involved, their families and communities. Without education, these rural boys and girls are likely to be the poor of tomorrow. Policies must address the root causes of child labour and promote decent work for adults in rural areas.

Around sixty per cent of working children are in agriculture – more than 129 million girls and boys aged 5–17 years old. The vast majority of the world's child labourers are not toiling in factories and sweatshops or working as domestics or street vendors in urban areas; they are working on farms and plantations, often from sun up to sun down, planting and harvesting crops, spraying pesticides, and tending livestock on rural farms and plantations. These children play an important role in crop and livestock production, helping supply some of the food and drink we consume, and the fibres and raw materials we use to make other products. Examples include cocoa/chocolate, coffee, tea, sugar, fruits and vegetables, along with other agricultural products like tobacco and cotton.

Around 70 million of these girls and boys carry out 'hazardous child labour', which is work that can threaten their lives, limbs, health, and general well-being. Irrespective of age, agriculture – along with construction and mining – is one of the three most dangerous sectors in which to work in terms of work-related fatalities, non-fatal accidents and occupational disease. Bangladesh is a primarily rural country and for many children working to help grow, harvest, transport or sell farm products is a normal, everyday role from the earliest days of childhood. They are regularly exposed to farm machinery and tools that often result in devastating injuries. About 50 children a day

are injured by machines, and three of them are injured so severely that they become permanently disabled.

In Zimbabwe, the wheels of a tractor which had been standing over night had become bogged down in the mud. The following morning, a 12-year-old boy started the tractor, revved up the engine to free the wheels, trying to move in a forward direction (when the safe procedure would have been to try to reverse out). The wheels remained stuck, that is, resisted movement, and the tractor reared up on its front wheels and overturned backwards, fatally crushing the boy beneath it.

In 2000, an 11-year-old girl, illegally employed on a farm in Ceres, Western Cape, South Africa, fell off a tractor, resulting in the amputation of her left leg.

In 1990, a 15-year-old migrant farm worker in the USA was fatally electrocuted when a 30-foot section of aluminium irrigation pipe he was moving came into contact with an overhead power line. Two other child labourers with him sustained serious electrical burns to their hands and feet.

Child labourers are susceptible to all the hazards and risks faced by adult workers when placed in the same situation. They are at even greater risk from these dangers because their bodies are still growing and their minds and personalities still developing, and they lack work experience. So the effects of poor to non-existent safety and health protection can often be more devastating and lasting for them. Also, a feature of agriculture that sets it apart from most other forms of child labour is that the children usually live on the farms or plantations where they work. This exposes them to additional risks.

Source: Selections from ILO (2007b, 2011b) and FAO/IFAD/ILO (2010).

THINKING CRITICALLY

Should *all* child labour around the world be banned? What consequences – positive and negative – would be likely to follow from such a ban? What forms of 'child labour' are still seen as acceptable in the developed countries? What makes the latter more acceptable than those discussed in the ILO report here?

1999 and the seven-billionth on 26 August 2011. The global population has more than doubled since 1965. In the 1960s, Paul Ehrlich calculated that, if the 1960s rate of population growth were to continue, in 900 years time there would be 60,000,000,000,000,000 (60 quadrillion) people on the face of the Earth. The physicist J. H. Fremlin worked out that housing that population would need a continuous 2,000-storey building covering the entire planet (Fremlin 1964). Such a picture, of course, is just a nightmarish fiction designed to drive home the cataclysmic consequences of unlimited population growth.

Some of the more catastrophist predictions of global population have proved inaccurate. In the 1960s and 1970s, there were estimates suggesting a population of around 8 billion people by 2000, but in fact the figure was just over 6 billion. Today the UN's 'medium variant' forecast (between the extremes of low and high) is that there will be 9.3 billion people on the planet by 2050, with the bulk of the increase coming from high fertility rates in thirty-nine countries in Africa, nine in Asia, six in Oceania and four in Latin America (UN 2011). In low-fertility countries (including Japan, China, the Russian Federation and Brazil) the number of people is forecast to reach a peak by 2030, after which it will slowly fall. By 2100, the population of the low-fertility countries should be 20 per cent lower than it is today. The population of intermediate-fertility countries (such as the USA, India, Bangladesh and Indonesia) is forecast to peak by 2065, leaving only that of the high-fertility group still increasing by 2100 (ibid.: 1–2; see figure 14.8).

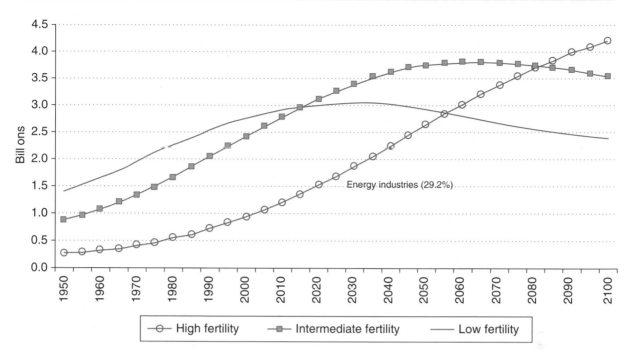

Figure 14.8 Population for countries grouped by fertility level, medium variant, 1950–2100

Source: UN (2011: 3).

On the latest UN forecast, then, global population growth is starting to slow down and by 2100 should be tailing off, perhaps leading to a gradual reduction in the numbers of people in the twenty-second century. Nevertheless, the rapid growth of the human population, from about 1 billion early in the nineteenth century to 7 billion today, is still quite staggering. Is this level sustainable? Can 7 billion people be adequately fed and housed, or are large sections to be condemned to a life of poverty? What would the spread of Western lifestyles to the global population mean for the condition of the natural environment? Can the planetary ecosystem cope with the pollution and waste of global consumerism? Small changes in fertility levels can have very large consequences, and it is not inconceivable that a higher variant forecast could prove more accurate. If so, then these questions would become even more urgent.

Population analysis: demography

If global inequality is one of the most important problems facing people today, then a related issue is the dramatic increase in world population. Global poverty and population growth are tied together, for it is in some of the world's poorest countries that population growth is greatest. It is to a discussion of this phenomenon that we now turn.

The study of population is called demography. The term was invented about 150 years ago when governments began to collect official statistics on the nature and distribution of national populations. Demography is concerned with measuring the size of populations and explaining their rise or decline. Population patterns are governed by three factors: births, deaths and migration. Demography is customarily treated as a branch of sociology, because the factors that influence the level of births and deaths in a given group or society, as well as migrations of population, are largely social and cultural.

Demographic work tends to be principally statistical. All the developed nations gather and analyse basic statistics on their populations by carrying out censuses – systematic surveys designed to find out about the population. Rigorous as the modes of data collection now are, even in these nations demographic statistics are not wholly accurate. In the UK, there has been a population census every ten years since 1801, though the coalition government elected in 2010 has been exploring alternative methods that would be less expensive, and the 2011 census may have been the last of this long series. The census aims to be as accurate as possible, though some people – illegal immigrants, homeless people, transient workers and others who for various reasons avoid registration – are not registered in the official statistics. In many developing countries, particularly those with recent high rates of population growth, demographic statistics are far less reliable.

Dynamics of population change

Rates of population growth or decline are measured by subtracting the number of deaths per 1,000 from the number of births per 1,000 – this is usually calculated annually. Some European countries have negative growth rates – in other words, their populations are declining. Virtually all the industrialized countries have growth rates of less than 0.5 per cent. Rates of population growth were high in the eighteenth and nineteenth centuries but have since levelled off. Many developing countries today have rates of between 2 and 3 per cent. These may not seem very different from the rates of the industrialized countries but, in fact, the consequences are enormous.

The reason for this is that growth in population is exponential. Starting with one item and doubling it, doubling the result, and so on, rapidly leads to huge numbers – 1:2:4:8:16:32:64:128, and so on. Exactly the same principle applies to population growth, and we can measure this effect by the doubling time – the period it takes for the population to double in size. A population growth of 1 per cent will produce a doubling of numbers in seventy years. At 2 per cent growth, a population will double in thirty-five years, while at 3 per cent it will double in just twenty-three years. It took the whole of human history

until just after 1800 for the global population to reach 1 billion. By 1930 it had doubled to 2 billion, by 1975 (just forty-five years) it had doubled again to 4 billion, and today it has reached 7.4 billion.

Malthusian concerns

In pre-industrial times, birth rates were very high by the standards of the contemporary developed world. However, population growth remained low until the eighteenth century because there was a rough balance between births and deaths. The general trend was upward and there were periods of marked population increase, but these were followed by increases in death rates. In medieval Europe, for example, when harvests were bad, marriages tended to be postponed and the number of conceptions fell, while deaths increased. No society was able to escape from this self-regulating rhythm (Wrigley 1968).

During the rise of industrialism, many looked forward to a new age in which scarcity would be a thing of the past. But, in his celebrated *Essay on the Principle of Population* (1976 [1798]), Thomas Malthus criticized such assumptions, initiating a debate about the connection between population and food resources that continues today. In 1798 the population in Europe was growing rapidly, and Malthus pointed out that, while population increase is exponential, food supply depends on fixed resources that can be expanded only by developing new land. Population growth therefore tends to outstrip the means of support and the inevitable outcome is famine, which, combined with the influence of war and plagues, acts as a natural limit on population increase. Malthus predicted that, unless they practised 'moral restraint', human beings would always live in circumstances of misery and starvation. His cure for excessive population growth was strict limits to the frequency of sexual intercourse, as he saw contraception as a 'vice'.

In the developed countries, Malthusianism was seen as overly pessimistic, since the population dynamic followed a quite different pattern from that which he anticipated.

14.1   Demography – the key concepts

Among the basic concepts used by demographers, the most important are crude birth rates, fertility, fecundity and crude death rates. Crude birth rates are expressed as the number of live births per year per 1,000 of the population. They are called 'crude' rates because of their very general character. They do not, for example, tell us what proportion of a population is male or female or what the age distribution of a population is (the relative proportions of young and old people). Where statistics are collected that relate birth or death rates to such categories, demographers speak of 'specific' rather than 'crude' rates. For instance, an age-specific birth rate might specify the number of births per 1,000 women in different age groups.

If we wish to understand population patterns in any detail, the information provided by specific birth rates is normally necessary. Crude birth rates, however, are useful for making overall comparisons between different groups, societies and regions. Thus, in 2006 the crude birth rate in Australia was 12.4 (per

year, per 1,000 population), in Nicaragua 24.9, in Mozambique 39.5 and, highest of all, in the Democratic Republic of the Congo it was 49.6 (UN 2006). The industrialized countries tend to have low rates, while, in many other parts of the world, crude birth rates are much higher (figure 14.9).

Birth rates are an expression of the fertility of women. Fertility refers to how many live-born children the average woman has, and a fertility rate is usually calculated as the average number of births per 1,000 women of childbearing age. Fertility is distinguished from fecundity, which means the potential number of children women are biologically capable of bearing. It is physically possible for a normal woman to bear a child every year during the period when she is capable of conception. There are variations in fecundity according to the age at which women reach puberty and menopause, both of which differ among countries as well as among individuals. While there may be families in which a woman bears twenty or more children, because of limiting social and cultural factors,

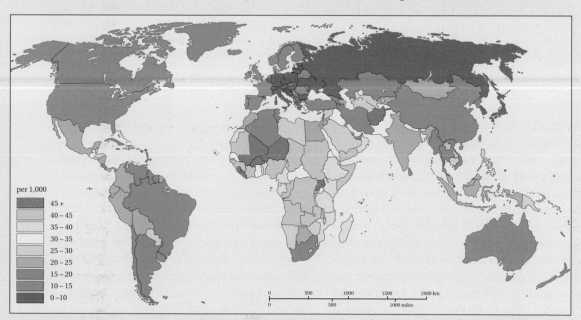

per 1,000

45 +
40 – 45
35 – 40
30 – 35
25 – 30
20 – 25
15 – 20
10 – 15
0 – 10

Figure 14.9   Global crude birth rates

Source: Based on CIA (2007).

fertility rates in practice are always much lower than fecundity rates.

Crude death rates (also called 'mortality rates') are calculated in the same way as birth rates – the number of deaths per 1,000 of population per year. Again, there are major variations among countries, but death rates in many societies in the developing world are falling to levels comparable to those in developed nations. The death rate in the United Kingdom in 2002 was ten per 1,000, in India it was nine per 1,000, and in Ethiopia it was eighteen per 1,000. A few countries had much higher death rates. In Sierra Leone, for example, the death rate was thirty per 1,000. Like crude birth rates, crude death rates provide only a very general index of mortality (the number of deaths in a population). Specific death rates give more precise information. A particularly important specific death rate is the infant mortality rate: the number of babies per 1,000 births in any year who die before reaching their first birthday. One of the key factors underlying the population explosion has been reductions in infant mortality rates.

Declining rates of infant mortality are the most important influence on increasing life expectancy – that is, the number of years the average person can expect to live. In 2007, life expectancy at birth for women born in the UK was 81.3 years, compared with 76.23 years for men (CIA 2007). This contrasts with forty-nine and forty-five years respectively at the turn of the twentieth century. This does not mean, however, that most people born in 1901 died when they were in their forties. When there is a high infant mortality rate, as there is in many developing nations, the average life expectancy – which is a statistical average – is brought down. Illness, nutrition and the influence of natural disasters are other factors that influence life expectancy. Life expectancy has to be distinguished from life span, which is the maximum number of years that an individual could live. While life expectancy has increased in most societies in the world, life span has remained unaltered, with a very small proportion of people living to 100 or more.

> **THINKING CRITICALLY**
>
> Demographic studies provide much useful quantitative data on broad trends in human populations, and this is invaluable for comparative analysis. But is there any role for qualitative methods in demography? Consider some of the qualitative methods in chapter 2 and suggest what some might add to our understanding of population dynamics.

Rates of population growth tailed off in the late nineteenth and twentieth centuries. Indeed, in the 1930s there were major worries about population decline in many developed countries. The rapid global population growth of the twentieth century has made Malthus's views seem more palatable to some, though few would support them in the original version. Modern Malthusians see the population expansion in developing countries as outstripping the resources those countries can generate to feed their people, resulting in undernourishment and widespread poverty. However, as we have seen, progress is being made in many aspects of human development in even the poorest countries.

The demographic transition

Demographers often refer to changes in the ratio of births to deaths in the industrialized countries from the nineteenth century onwards as the demographic transition. This thesis was first outlined by Warren S. Thompson (1929), who described a three-stage process in which, as a society reached an advanced level of economic development, one type of population stability would eventually be replaced by another. This thesis is discussed in 'Classic Studies 14.1'.

Demographic transition theory is based on the assumption – also held by Karl Marx – that industrial capitalism would spread across

| Classic Studies 14.1 | Demographic transition theory |

The research problem

As societies industrialized from the mid-eighteenth century onwards, their populations increased rapidly. But a century or so later population growth had slowed, and in the twenty-first century many developed societies are barely replacing their populations. Why did this happen? Is there a pattern to this long-term transformation and, if so, is it likely to be repeated in the developing countries? How will it affect the size of the global human population in the future? Warren S. Thompson (1887–1973), an American demographer, was the first to identify a pattern to such developments, and his work was developed by later demographers who linked demographic trends to industrialization.

The Demographic Transition Model

Thompson recognized that, although changes to birth and death rates shape population growth and size, there are important *transitions* in such rates which have a profound impact on a country's population. Later demographers refined and developed his ideas into a model, usually referred to as the *Demographic Transition* *Model* (DTM), which identifies a series of stages as societies go through industrial development (refer to the model, illustrated in figure 14.10, as you read the next section).

Stage 1 refers to the conditions characterizing most non-industrial societies, in which birth and death rates are high and the infant mortality rate is especially high. Population grows little, if at all, as the large number of births is more or less balanced by the number of deaths. This stage covers most of human history, as epidemics, disease and natural disasters kept human numbers down. In *Stage 2*, which began in most of Europe and the United States in the early part of the nineteenth century, the death rate fell but fertility remained high. The consequence was a phase of long-term population growth. Improvements in food quality together with higher crop yields, safe water supplies, and more efficient sewerage and waste disposal produced a fall in the death rate and a rise in population. In *Stage 3* the birth rate also fell to a level such that the population gradually became fairly stable, though at a much higher absolute level than in Stage 1.

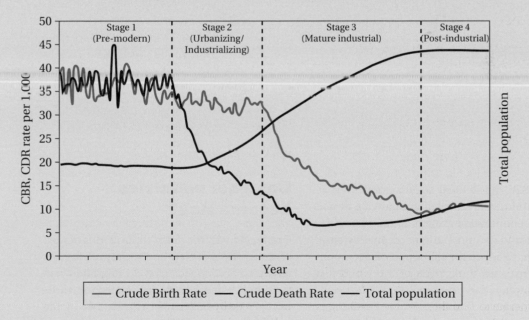

Figure 14.10 The Demographic Transition Model

Source: Wikimedia Commons.

Several possible reasons have been put forward for this change, including increasing literacy levels (particularly among women), leading to the challenging of traditional ideas on women solely as childbearers; compulsory education, which removed children from the workforce; and urbanization, which removed the need (in rural areas) for large families to work on the land.

Somewhat later, improved contraceptive technologies also played a major part in enabling people to control their fertility. Some demographers identify a *Stage 4*, in which populations stabilize, thus completing the demographic transition. However, some countries, among them Greece, Italy and Japan, have recently been reproducing below replacement levels, and we might speculate about a stage in which population levels in advanced industrial societies decline. However, so far this stage remains a theoretical possibility rather than reality.

Critical points

Although it is generally accepted that the sequence accurately describes a major transformation in the demographic character of modern societies, there are considerable differences across the developed countries. When the model is applied to developing countries, critics point out that the emergence of HIV/AIDS in the 1980s has been a major factor, slowing or even halting some countries' progress, as death rates and infant mortality rates have risen rather than fallen. Sub-Saharan Africa has suffered most as a result of the spread of HIV/AIDS (see chapter 11, 'Health, Illness and Disability').

The DTM has been widely seen as anti-Malthusian. It suggests that, rather than exponential growth leading to mass hunger and widespread famine, human populations are likely to settle into comfortable stability. One objection to this optimism is that the spread of Western-style consumerism to the global population would seriously threaten the planet's ecosystem, and on present population forecasts things can only get worse. Environmentalists argue we should not be so sanguine about high absolute human numbers but should be aiming for a managed *reduction* in the global population.

Contemporary significance

The DTM has been perhaps the most influential perspective on long-term population trends ever devised, and it continues to inform research in the field of demography. Demographers do not agree about how the sequence of change predicted by the model should be interpreted, though, nor how long Stage 3 is likely to last. Nevertheless, the great virtue of the model is that it encourages us to take a long-term view of human development in a global perspective and provides a point from which to start doing so.

the world. As it does so, economies grow, birth and death rates fall and, after a period of rapid population growth, national populations stabilize and perhaps even decrease. But what happens if economic development is uneven and some parts of the world just do not follow the proposed stages? Is it realistic to suggest that all the world's societies can become equally wealthy? This much-disputed issue is the subject of our next section.

Can poor countries become rich?

One reason why the older 'three worlds model' of the world's societies lost ground was its failure to account for global integration and the movement of countries between the 'three worlds'. This problem became clearer by the mid-1970s, when a number of low-income countries in East Asia were undergoing a rapid process of industrialization (Amsden 1989; see chapter 4 for a discussion of this

14.2   Raising the 'bottom billion' out of poverty

As we have seen, significant progress has been made in tackling disadvantage and poverty in many developing countries. Even so, that progress has been unevenly distributed across the developing world and some countries continue to struggle. Paul Collier's (2007) *The Bottom Billion* argues that the focus of development aid should now be on those poorest developing countries that have not made solid economic progress over recent decades. This would cover some sixty or so countries with a combined population of about 1 billion people. However, this view is not shared by all, and other research calls into question the conventional view that a majority of those people and families in absolute poverty live in the very poorest countries.

For example, a report for the Institute for Development Studies in the UK shows that 72 per cent of the 1.33 billion people living on less than US$1.25 a day are actually in middle-income countries (Sumner 2010). India and China still have very large numbers living in poverty (about 50 per cent of the global total), but, on account of rapid economic development over the last twenty years, both countries have been reclassified by the World Bank as 'middle-income countries' (Kanbur and Sumner 2011). Sumner notes that India, Indonesia, Pakistan and Nigeria have been similarly reclassified, but collectively they still account for most of the global poor whose home countries have moved into middle-income status.

This is an important interpretation of the data because it suggests that the conventional form of development assistance – aid targeting particular *countries* – may be becoming much less productive. Instead, assistance would

Despite having one of the fastest growing economies in the world, poverty remains widespread in India, mostly in rural areas, but also in urban slums.

be better aimed at *poor people*, regardless of the economic situation of the countries in which they live. If large numbers of citizens in middle-income countries still live in poverty, then tackling inequality within those countries becomes a major issue, both for their governments and for foreign aid donors.

development). The process began with Japan in the 1950s but quickly extended to the newly industrializing countries (NICs), or rapidly growing economies, of the world, particularly in East Asia but also in Latin America. The East Asian NICs included Hong Kong in the 1960s and Taiwan, South Korea and Singapore in the 1970s and 1980s. Other Asian countries began to follow in the 1980s and the early 1990s, most notably China, but also Malaysia, Thailand and Indonesia.

Figure 14.11 compares the average economic growth rates of the low-, middle- and high-income countries of the world. Economists have tended to assume that the developing countries, collectively, would experience higher average rates of economic growth than the developed high-income ones as their development starts to catch up. However, until quite recently this was often not the case, and only a few developing countries managed to out-perform the average growth rates of the developed economies.

This has changed since the mid-1990s, though, as the *average* growth rates of low- and middle-income countries have been higher than those in the developed world. Indeed, thirteen countries have been reclassified by the World Bank as 'developed economies', as their economic growth rates have propelled them into the ranks of the relatively wealthy countries: Antigua and Barbuda, Bahrain, Greece, Guam, the Isle of Man, the Republic of Korea, Malta, New Caledonia, the Northern

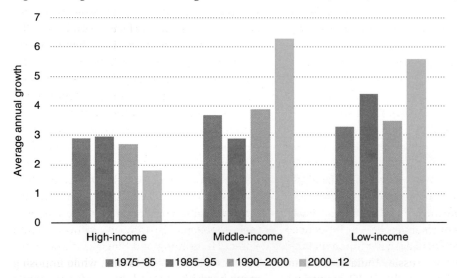

Figure 14.11   Average economic growth in the low-, middle- and high-income countries, 1975–2008

Source: Data from various *World Development Indicators* reports of the World Bank.

Table 14.1 Cross-country, within-country and global inequalities

Concept of income inequality	Cross-country inequality	Within-country inequality	Global inequality
What it measures	Inequality of *average* income across countries	Differences between incomes of the rich and the poor within a country	Differences between incomes of the rich and the poor, ignoring the country to which they belong
What the evidence shows	Divergence	Increasing inequality in many countries (for example, Brazil, China, United States), but low and stable levels in many others (for example, Canada, France, Japan)	Convergence

Source: Loungani (2003).

Mariana Islands, Puerto Rico, Saudi Arabia, San Marino and Slovenia (World Bank 2007). These are all places that were considered 'poor' just two generations ago. By 1999, the GDP per person in Singapore was virtually the same as that in the USA, while China has one of the most rapidly growing economies on the planet. With an average annual growth rate of 10 per cent between 1980 and 1999, the Chinese economy doubled in size.

Comparing countries on the basis of their average income level shows a wide divergence, particularly between the developed and developing countries. Comparing the incomes of rich and poor people *within* a single country shows that, over recent years, some countries have experienced widening income inequality (the USA, the UK, Brazil), while others have remained fairly stable (France, Canada).

If we measure global inequality since 1970 at the *individual* level, regardless of country of residence, the average 'global citizen' has become richer and global income distribution has become more equal (Loungani 2003). However, this conclusion is heavily influenced by the rapid growth of a small number of large countries – Brazil, Russia, India and China (known collectively as the BRIC countries). Leaving aside China, India and Vietnam, the thirteen countries recategorized by the World Bank as 'developed economies', whose combined population totals only around 2 per cent of the global population, represent a small minority of all developing countries. Clearly, economic growth rates remain very unevenly distributed. The share of global output over the decade 1995–2005 did not improve for most developing regions, with the notable exception of East Asia and the Pacific (see figure 14.12), which increased its share by some 6 per cent.

The economic expansion in East Asia has not been without its costs. These have included the sometimes violent repression of labour and civil rights, terrible factory conditions, the exploitation of an increasingly female workforce, the exploitation of immigrant workers from impoverished neighbouring countries, and widespread environmental degradation. Nonetheless, thanks to the sacrifices of past generations of workers, large numbers of people in these countries are now prospering.

How do social scientists account for the rapid economic growth of the East Asian NICs? The answers may hold some crucial lessons for developing countries hoping to follow in their footsteps. Historically, Taiwan, South Korea, Hong Kong and Singapore were once part of colonial regimes that, while imposing many hardships, paved the way for economic growth. Taiwan and Korea were tied to the Japanese Empire; Hong Kong and Singapore were former British colonies. Japan eliminated

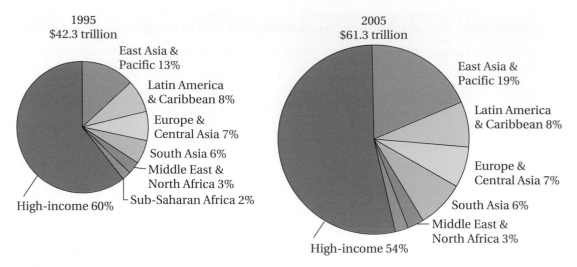

1995
$42.3 trillion

East Asia &
Pacific 13%

Latin America
& Caribbean 8%

Europe &
Central Asia 7%

South Asia 6%
Middle East &
North Africa 3%
Sub-Saharan Africa 2%

High-income 60%

2005
$61.3 trillion

East Asia &
Pacific 19%

Latin America
& Caribbean 8%

Europe &
Central Asia 7%

South Asia 6%

Middle East &
North Africa 3%

High-income 54%

Figure 14.12 Share of global output by region, 1995 and 2005

Source: World Bank (2007).

large landowners who opposed industrialization, and both Britain and Japan encouraged industrial development, constructed roads and transportation systems, and built relatively efficient governmental bureaucracies. Britain also actively developed both Hong Kong and Singapore as trading centres (Gold 1986; Cumings 1987). Elsewhere in the world – for example, in Latin America and Africa – countries that are poor today did not fare so well in their dealings with the richer, more powerful nations.

The East Asian region also benefited from a long period of world economic growth. Between the 1950s and the mid-1970s, the growing economies of Europe and the United States provided a substantial market for the clothing, footwear and electronics that were increasingly made in East Asia, creating a 'window of opportunity' for economic development. Periodic economic slowdowns in the United States and Europe forced businesses to cut their labour costs, and companies relocated their operations to the lower-wage East Asian countries (Henderson and Appelbaum 1992). A study by the World Bank (1995) found that, between 1970 and 1990, annual wage increases averaged 3 per cent in developing countries where economic growth was led by exports

to wealthier countries, while wages failed to increase elsewhere in the developing world.

Economic growth in East Asia took off at the high point of the Cold War, when the United States and its allies provided generous economic and military aid as a barrier to communist expansion in the region. Direct aid and loans fuelled investment in new technologies such as transistors, semiconductors and other electronics, contributing to the development of local industries. Military assistance frequently favoured strong, often military governments that were willing to use repression to keep labour costs low (Mirza 1986; Cumings 1987, 2005; Castells 1992).

Some sociologists argue that the economic success of Japan and the East Asian NICs is due in part to internal cultural traditions – in particular, their shared Confucian philosophy (Berger 1986). More than a century ago, Max Weber (1992 [1904–5]) argued that the Protestant belief in thrift, frugality and hard work helped to explain the rise of capitalism in Western Europe, and his argument has been applied to Asian economic history. Confucianism, it is argued, inculcates respect for one's elders and superiors, education, hard work and proven accomplishments as the key to advancement, as well as a willingness to sacrifice today to

From a Weberian perspective, traditions of respect and submission to authority embedded in Japanese culture can be used to help explain the history of the country's economic development.

earn a greater reward tomorrow. As a result of these values, this Weberian argument goes, Asian workers and managers are highly loyal to their companies, submissive to authority, hardworking and success-oriented. Workers and capitalists alike are said to be frugal and, instead of living lavishly, are likely to reinvest their wealth in further economic growth.

This explanation has merit, but it overlooks the fact that businesses are not always revered and respected in Asia. During the late 1950s, pitched battles occurred between workers and capitalists in Japan, as they did in South Korea in the late 1980s. Students and workers throughout the East Asian NICs have opposed business and governmental policies they felt to be unfair, often at the risk of imprisonment

and sometimes even their lives (Deyo 1989; Ho 1990). Furthermore, Confucian cultural values such as thrift appear to be declining in Japan and the NICs, as young people – raised in the booming prosperity of recent years – increasingly value conspicuous consumption over austerity and investment.

A final factor in the rapid economic growth of the NICs is the intentional actions of the East Asian governments which adopted strong policies favouring economic growth. Governments played a very active role in keeping labour costs low, encouraging economic development through tax breaks and other economic policies, and offering free public education. We shall return to East Asian government policies later in the chapter.

In 1997–8, a combination of poor investment decisions, corruption and world economic conditions brought these countries' economic expansion to an abrupt halt. Their stock markets collapsed, currencies fell and the entire global economy was threatened. The experience of Hong Kong was typical: after thirty-seven years of continuous growth, the economy stalled and its stock market – the Hang Seng Index – lost more than half its value. By 2004, economists noted that Hong Kong's economy was again growing and the property market was rising.

In the aftermath of the 2008 financial crisis and economic recession that spread outwards from the USA to most of the developed countries, East Asian NICs have shown some resilience. In spite of the impact of the crisis, the 2011 Japanese earthquake and higher oil prices from the Middle East, the South-East Asian economies of Singapore, Thailand, Malaysia and the Philippines all returned to economic growth of between 5 and 7 per cent per year by 2015 (Fensom 2015). However, the slowdown in economic growth in China and India alongside China's housing bubble and growing debt burden – largely the result of local government spending on infrastructure projects – led to concerns of a new crash that could impact negatively on East Asia (Elliott 2013; Evans-Pritchard 2015). Nonetheless, we can conclude that the NICs were not just a 'flash in the pan' but have broadly continued along their path of economic development.

Theories of development

Describing the extent and shape of global inequality is useful, but explaining its causes and assessing whether it could ever be overcome require theories that are able to link the evidence to types of society, international relations and socio-economic change. In this section, we look at different types of theory that seek to explain economic development – market-oriented theories, dependency and world-systems theories, state-centred theories, and recent post-development critiques. Theories are necessary if we are to make sense of the huge amount of data collected from across the world's societies.

Market-oriented modernization theories

The most influential theories of global inequality advanced by British and American economists and sociologists forty years ago were market-oriented theories. These assume that the best possible economic consequences will result if individuals are free – uninhibited by any form of governmental constraint – to make their own economic decisions. Unrestricted capitalism, if it is allowed to develop fully, is said to be the avenue to economic growth. Government bureaucracy should not dictate which goods to produce, what prices to charge or how much workers should be paid. According to market-oriented theorists, governmental direction of the economies of low-income countries results in blockages to economic development. In this view, local governments should get out of the way of development (Rostow 1961; Warren 1980; Ranis 1996).

Dependency and world-systems theories

During the 1960s, a number of theorists questioned market-oriented theories of global inequality such as modernization theory. Many of these critics were sociologists and economists from the low-income countries of Latin America and Africa, who drew on Marxist ideas to reject the idea that their countries' economic underdevelopment was owing to their own cultural or institutional faults. Instead, they build on the theories of Karl Marx, who argued that world capitalism would create a class of countries manipulated by more powerful countries, just as capitalism within countries leads to the exploitation of workers. Dependency theorists, as they are called, argue that the poverty of low-income countries stems from their exploitation by wealthy countries and the multinational corporations that are based in wealthy countries (Peet and Hartwick 2009: ch. 5). In their view, global capitalism locked their countries into a downward spiral of exploitation and poverty.

According to dependency theories, this exploitation began with colonialism,

Classic Studies 14.2 Walt Rostow and the stages of economic growth

The research problem

Why have some countries and regions experienced rapid economic development while others continue to struggle? Is the problem of underdevelopment essentially an internal one (rooted within particular countries), or is it the consequence of external forces? What can we learn about the process of development from the already developed societies? The answers given by Walt Rostow (1916–2003), an economic adviser to former US president John F. Kennedy who became an influential economic theorist, helped to shape US foreign policy towards Latin America during the 1960s.

Rostow's explanation

Rostow's explanation is a market-oriented approach, which came to be described as modernization theory. Modernization theory says that low-income societies *can* develop economically, but only if they give up their traditional ways and adopt modern economic institutions, technologies and cultural values, which emphasize savings and productive investment. According to Rostow (1961), the traditional cultural values and social institutions of low-income countries impede their economic effectiveness. For example, he argued that many people in low-income countries lack a strong work ethic; they would rather consume today than invest for the future. Large families are also seen as partly responsible for 'economic backwardness', since a breadwinner with many mouths to feed can hardly be expected to save money for investment purposes.

But, for Rostow and other modernization theorists, the problems in low-income countries run much deeper. The *cultures* of such countries tend to support 'fatalism' – a value system that views hardship and suffering as an unavoidable part of normal life. Acceptance of one's lot thus discourages people from working hard and being thrifty in order to overcome their fate. On this view, then, a country's economic underdevelopment is due largely to the cultural failings of the people themselves. Such failings are reinforced by government policies that set wages and control prices, generally interfering in the operation of the economy. So how can low-income countries break out of their poverty? Rostow saw economic growth as moving through several stages, which he likened to the journey of an aeroplane (see figure 14.13):

1 *The traditional stage* is the stage just described, characterized by low rates of savings, the (supposed) lack of a strong work ethic and the 'fatalistic' value system. We could say that this aeroplane is stuck on the runway.

2 *Take-off to economic growth.* The traditional stage *can* give way to a second one: economic take-off. This occurs when poor countries begin to jettison their traditional values and institutions and people start to save and invest money for the future. The role of wealthy countries is to facilitate and support this take-off. They can do this by financing birth control programmes or providing low-cost loans for electrification, road and airport construction, and starting new industries.

3 *Drive to technological maturity.* According to Rostow, with the help of money and advice from high-income countries, the aeroplane of economic growth would taxi down the runway, pick up speed and become airborne. The country would then approach technological maturity. In the aeronautical metaphor, the plane would slowly climb to cruising altitude, improving its technology, reinvesting its recently acquired wealth in new industries, and adopting the institutions and values of the high-income countries.

4 *High mass consumption.* Finally, the country would reach the phase of high mass consumption. Now people are able to enjoy the fruits of their labour by achieving a high standard of living. The aeroplane (country) cruises along on automatic pilot, having entered the ranks of the high-income countries.

Rostow's ideas remain influential. Indeed, neo-liberalism, which is perhaps the prevailing view among economists today, can be seen as rooted

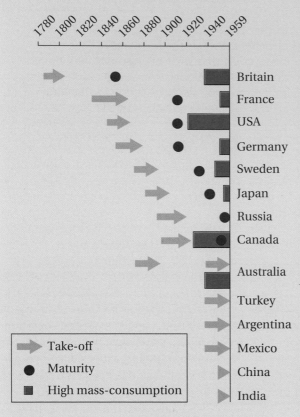

Figure 14.13 Rostow's stages of economic growth for selected countries, 1750–1959

Source: www.agocg.ac.uk/reports/visual/casestud/southall/trajecto.htm.

in modernization theory. Neo-liberals argue that free-market forces, achieved by minimizing governmental restrictions on business, provide the route to economic growth, holding that global free trade will enable all the countries of the world to prosper. Eliminating governmental regulation is seen as necessary for economic growth to occur. However, Rostow's model does allow for governmental action to promote development, something that free-market enthusiasts treat with suspicion.

Critical points

Supporters of modernization theory point to the success of the newly industrializing economies of East Asia as proof that development really

is open to all. However, it can be objected (as we saw above) that the reasons for this success are partly accidental, involving Cold War political expediency and the historical legacy of colonialism. Such a conjunction of conditions is unlikely to apply to other low-income countries in the post-Cold War world. Indeed, even in the twenty-first century, many low-income countries, in spite of external assistance, have not passed through Rostow's stages and remain very far from becoming economically developed.

A further criticism is that Rostow saw high-income countries playing a key role in helping low-income ones to grow. But this fails to take proper account of the long-term consequences of colonialism, which benefited the militarily powerful European societies at the expense of those in Asia and Latin America, thus dealing the latter's economic development a devastating early blow. Finally, by pointing to 'fatalistic' cultural values as a causal factor in underdevelopment, Rostow can be seen as ethnocentric, holding up Western values, ideals and models of 'progress' as superior. As chapter 5, 'The Environment', shows, the Western pursuit of untrammelled economic growth has, perhaps irrevocably, damaged the global natural environment, leading some to question whether this kind of 'progress' can be sustainable over the long term.

Contemporary significance

Rostow's theory of 'evolutionary' stages towards self-sustaining economic growth has suffered in the light of continued global poverty, hunger and underdevelopment, leading many to abandon it altogether. Certainly any notion of *inevitable* progress through the Rostovian stages finds little support almost half a century later, and his 'non-communist manifesto' has attracted as much opposition and criticism as the original communist version of Marx and Engels (1848). But, as we have already seen in this chapter, recent *global* indicators do present a more positive picture of an improving situation for many, though by no means all, populations in the low- and middle-income countries of the world.

This may show that economic development is not exclusive to the high-income societies and that, as Rostow argued, the process of modernization remains a possibility for all in an era of rapid globalization and the intensification of international trade.

THINKING CRITICALLY

Karl Marx said that the industrialized countries presented to the less developed countries an image of their own future. What are the main differences between Marx's version of modernization theory and that of Walt Rostow? Which version, if any, is best supported by the historical evidence to date?

a political-economic system under which powerful countries, for their own profit, established rule over weaker peoples or countries. Powerful nations have colonized other countries usually to procure the raw materials needed for their factories and to control markets for the products manufactured in those factories. Under colonial rule, for example, the petroleum, copper, iron and food products required by industrial economies are extracted from low-income countries by businesses based in high-income countries. Although colonialism typically involved European countries establishing colonies in North and South America, Africa and Asia, some Asian countries (such as Japan) had colonies as well.

Even though colonialism ended in most of the world after 1945, exploitation did not: transnational corporations continued to reap enormous profits from their branches in low-income countries. According to dependency theory, global companies, often with the support of powerful banks and governments in rich countries, established factories in poor countries, using cheap labour and raw materials to maximize production costs without governmental interference. In turn, the low prices set for labour and raw materials precluded poor countries from accumulating the profit necessary to industrialize, and local businesses were prevented from competing with Western companies. On this view, poor countries are forced to borrow and become

indebted to the rich countries, thus increasing their economic dependency.

Low-income countries are thus seen as *misdeveloped* rather than underdeveloped (Frank 1966; Emmanuel 1972). Peasants are forced to choose between starvation and working at near-starvation wages on foreign-controlled plantations and in foreign-controlled mines and factories. Since dependency theorists argue that exploitation has prevented economic growth, they typically call for revolutionary changes that would push foreign corporations out of these countries altogether (Frank 1969).

While market-oriented theorists usually ignore political and military power, dependency theorists regard the exercise of power as central to enforcing unequal economic relationships. Whenever local leaders question such unequal arrangements, their voices are quickly suppressed, unionization is usually outlawed, and labour organizers are jailed and sometimes killed. When people elect a government opposing these policies, that government is likely to be overthrown by the country's military, often backed by the armed forces of the industrialized countries. Dependency theorists point to examples such as the role of the CIA in overthrowing the Marxist governments of Guatemala in 1954 and Chile in 1973 and in undermining support for the leftist government in Nicaragua in the 1980s. For dependency theorists, global economic inequality is backed up by military force. Economic elites in poor countries, backed by their counterparts in wealthy ones, use police and military power to keep the local population under control.

The Brazilian sociologist Fernando Henrique Cardoso, once a prominent dependency theorist, argued more than twenty-five years ago that some degree of 'dependent development' was nonetheless possible, though only in ways shaped by their reliance on the wealthier countries (Cardoso and Faletto 1979). In particular, the governments of these countries could play a key role in steering a course between dependency and development (Evans 1979). However, as president of Brazil from 1995 to 2003, Cardoso changed his thinking and called for greater integration of Brazil into the global economy.

During the last thirty years, sociologists have increasingly seen the world as a single – though often conflict-ridden – economic system. Although dependency theories hold that individual countries are economically tied to one another, world-systems theory argues that the capitalist economic system is not merely a collection of independent countries engaged in diplomatic and economic relations but must instead be understood as a single system. The world-systems approach is most closely identified with the work of Immanuel Wallerstein and his colleagues (Wallerstein 1974, 1980, 1989, and elsewhere).

See 'Classic studies 4.1', in chapter 4, 'Globalization and Social Change', for a discussion of Wallerstein's pioneering role in world-systems theory.

Wallerstein argued that capitalism has long existed as a global economic system, beginning with the extension of markets and trade in Europe in the fifteenth and sixteenth centuries. The world system is seen as comprising four overlapping elements (Chase-Dunn 1989):

- a world market for goods and labour
- the division of the population into different economic classes, particularly capitalists and workers

- an international system of formal and informal political relations among the most powerful countries, whose competition with one another helps shape the world economy
- the carving up of the world into three unequal economic zones, with the wealthier zones exploiting the poorer ones.

World-systems theorists term these three economic zones the 'core', the 'periphery' and the 'semi-periphery'. All countries in the capitalist world system fall into one of the three categories. Core countries are the most advanced industrial nations, taking the lion's share of profits from the world economy. These include Japan, the United States and Western Europe. Peripheral countries comprise most of the developing world, largely agricultural economies manipulated by the core countries for their own economic advantage. Peripheral countries are found throughout Africa and to a lesser extent in Latin America and Asia, where natural resources flow from periphery to core along with profits. The core, in turn, sells finished goods back to the periphery, also at a profit.

World-systems theorists argue that core countries have become wealthy through this unequal trade and, at the same time, limit the economic development of the periphery. Finally, the semi-peripheral countries occupy an intermediate position. These are semi-industrialized, middle-income countries that extract profits from peripheral countries and in turn yield profits to the core countries. Examples are Mexico, Brazil, Argentina and Chile and the newly industrializing economies of East Asia. The semi-periphery, though to some degree controlled by the core, is able to exploit the periphery, and its greater economic success holds out to the peripheral countries the promise of similar development.

Although the world system tends to change very slowly, once-powerful countries eventually lose their economic power and others can take their place. Some five centuries ago the Italian city-states of Venice and Genoa dominated the world capitalist economy. But first

Western transnational corporations have often been seen as exploiting the poorest countries and people to increase their profits. Dependency theory holds that this is an active process of underdevelopment designed to prevent developing countries from competing on equal terms.

the Dutch, then the British and currently the United States superseded them. Today, in the view of some theorists, American dominance is giving way to a more 'multipolar' or 'multiplex' situation where the world order is shaped by several power centres, including the USA, Europe and Asia (Acharya 2014).

State-centred theories

Some of the more recent explanations of successful economic development emphasize the role of state policy in promoting economic growth. Differing sharply from market-oriented theories, state-centred theories argue that appropriate government policies do not negatively interfere with economic development but, rather, can play a key role in bringing it about. A large body of research

now suggests that, in some regions of the world, such as East Asia, successful economic development has been state-led. Even the World Bank, long a strong proponent of free-market theories of development, has changed its thinking about the role of the state. In its 1997 report *The State in a Changing World*, the World Bank concluded that, without an effective state, 'sustainable development, both economic and social, is impossible.'

Strong governments contributed in various ways to economic growth in the East Asian NICs during the 1980s and 1990s (Appelbaum and Henderson 1992; Amsden et al. 1994; World Bank 1997). For example, some East Asian governments acted aggressively to ensure political stability while keeping their labour costs low. This was achieved by acts of repression, such as outlawing trade unions, banning strikes, jailing labour leaders and, in general, silencing the voices of workers. The governments of Taiwan, South Korea and Singapore in particular have engaged in such practices as a way of encouraging inward investment.

Similarly, East Asian governments have frequently sought to steer economic development in their desired directions. State agencies provided cheap loans and tax breaks to businesses that invested in favoured industries. Sometimes this strategy backfired, resulting in bad loans held by the government – one cause of the region's economic problems in the late 1990s. Some governments prevented businesses from investing their profits in other countries, forcing them to invest in economic growth at home. In some cases, governments have owned and controlled key industries. The Japanese government has owned railways, the steel industry and banks, South Korea has owned banks, and the government of Singapore has owned airlines and the armaments and ship-repair industries.

Governments in East Asia have also created social programmes such as low-cost housing and universal education. The world's largest public housing systems outside former communist countries have been in Hong Kong and Singapore, where government subsidies keep rents extremely low. As a result, workers do not require high wages to pay for their housing, which means that they can compete with American and European workers in the emerging global labour market. The Singaporean government also requires businesses and individual citizens alike to save a large percentage of their income for investment in future growth.

Post-development critiques

In the early 1990s, the dominant concept of 'development' came under severe criticism from scholars and activists, many of them working in developing countries. Drawing on Foucault's ideas on how powerful discourses in society limit and shape knowledge on crime, mental health and sexuality, the 'develop-

ment discourse' which became established after 1945 was also seen as limiting how global poverty and inequality are understood. Sachs (1992: 1) argued that 'The last forty years can be called the age of development. This epoch is coming to an end. The time is ripe to write its obituary.' For some, this statement marked the start of a new era of post-development which bears some similarity to ideas of post-industrialism and postmodernism.

The categorizing by US president Harry S. Truman in 1949 of Africa, Asia and Latin America as 'underdeveloped' effectively belittled the diverse countries of these regions, marking them out as inferior to the industrialized societies (Esteva 1992). In doing so, the ensuing development discourse is seen by post-development theorists as a central element in maintaining the power of the minority world over the global majority (Escobar 1995). In the post-1945 period, when colonial regimes were giving way to the demands for national independence and autonomy in the so-called third world, development discourse, policy and institutions 'helped a dying and obsolete colonialism to transform itself into an aggressive – even sometimes an attractive – instrument able to recapture new ground' (Rahnema 1997: 384).

Post-development theory has gained ground for several reasons. First, the ending of the Cold War after 1989 changed the relationship between developing countries and the two competing superpowers of the USA and the USSR, both of which had offered 'development' in order to expand their geopolitical influence. The apparent superiority of industrial civilization was also undermined by a growing environmentalist critique, which called into question why this model, which has been so ecologically destructive, should be imported into the developing world. Finally, many argued that the evidence from forty years of development was that the global inequality gap had actually widened, and in this sense the development project had clearly failed its recipients (Ziai 2007: 4). But, if the industrial model of modernization has run into the sand, what alternative model should be pursued?

Some suggest this is simply the wrong question. Escobar (1995) argues that post-development is not about finding 'development alternatives' but, rather, concerns alternatives *to* development, as conventionally defined. And it is more likely that these alternatives will be found in indigenous local cultures, grassroots movements and community initiatives. Instead of becoming another overarching discourse, post-development theory is closer to a motivating ideology which legitimizes the practical solutions of local people, who are closer to the social and economic problems of their own countries. This approach is seen as preferable to relying on development 'experts' with little knowledge of local knowledge and traditions.

Critics assert that post-development theory, like postmodernism, is much better at criticism than practical, constructive suggestions for change. The risk of their stringent, generalized critique of modern, scientific development perspectives is that the latter's genuinely progressive aspects will also be rejected. Kiely (1999: 47) argues that rejecting development initiatives on the basis of their origin rather than their effectiveness in tackling serious problems, such as high infant mortality rates, 'expresses the view, not of the consistent multiculturalist, but of the patronising tourist'. Others suggest that post-development theory fails to see that an outright rejection of modernity could allow patriarchal local elites and anti-democratic fundamentalists the space to become politically powerful (Nanda 2004).

However, although the post-development critique has not displaced existing development perspectives, it has been successful in forcing all those working in development and development studies to be more reflexive in both their analyses and practices.

Evaluating theories of development

The development theories discussed above have particular strengths and weaknesses, but, together, they give us a better grasp of the causes and possible solutions to global inequality. Market-oriented theories recommend the adoption of modern capitalist institutions to promote economic development, as the East Asia NICs have done successfully. They also argue that countries can develop economically only if they open their borders to trade. But market-oriented theories fail to take account of the various economic ties between poorer countries and wealthier ones – ties that can impede or enhance economic development. They tend to blame low-income countries for their poverty rather than looking to the influence of outside factors, such as the business operations of more powerful nations. Market-oriented theories also ignore the ways government can work with the private sector to generate economic development, and they do not explain why some countries take off economically while others cannot.

However, dependency theories address some of the issues that market-oriented theories neglect, such as considering how wealthy countries have developed by economically exploiting poorer ones. But dependency theories are unable adequately to explain the successes of low-income countries, such as Brazil and Argentina, or the rapidly expanding economies of East Asia. In fact, some countries that were once in the low-income category have risen economically even with the presence of Western multinational corporations. Former colonies, such as Hong Kong and Singapore, previously dependent on Great Britain, also count as economic success stories. World-systems theory sought to overcome these shortcomings by analysing the world economy as a whole, exploring the complex global web of political and economic relationships that influence development and inequality.

State-centred theories focus on the governmental role in fostering economic growth. They thus offer a useful alternative to both the prevailing market-oriented theories, with their emphasis on the state as a hindrance, and dependency theories, which view states as allies of global business elites. When combined with the other theories – particularly world-systems theory – state-centred theories can help to explain many of the changes transforming the world economy.

The post-development critique is a significant reminder that the very concept of 'development' is a contested one which runs the risk of privileging the experience of the relatively rich countries, leading to an exclusive focus on crude economic measures. The Nobel Prize winning economist Amartya Sen argues that, as well as understanding global inequality, theories of development have to recognize that 'development' is ultimately a matter of human freedom. If so, then individual agency must be at the centre of the process.

In particular, Sen (2001: 36) holds that the expansion of freedom is both the 'primary end' and the 'principal means' of development. Pursuing development means attempting to remove 'unfreedoms' (such as tyranny, famine or poverty) which prevent individuals from being able to make real choices and to 'do things one has reason to value' (ibid.: 18). More freedom also means that people are able to help themselves and therefore to have more influence on society's development.

Moving towards a focus on 'development as freedom' does not mean ignoring the very real obstacles to greater global equality, nor does it mean ignoring mainstream issues of comparative GNI per capita or other economic criteria. Concentrating on the expansion of individual freedoms does require states and multilateral organizations – such as the IMF, World Bank and United Nations – to review their public policies *from the perspective* of freedom. In short, Sen's argument suggests that individual freedom needs to become a social commitment in order to bridge the divide between structure and agency and give a new direction to the process of 'development'.

Global inequality in a changing world

Today the social and economic forces leading to a global capitalist economy appear irresistible. The main challenge to this outcome – socialism/communism – ended with the collapse of the Soviet Union in 1991, and the largest remaining communist country in the world, the People's Republic of China, is rapidly adopting capitalist economic institutions and is the fastest-growing economy in the world. It is too soon to tell how far the future leaders of China will take the country down the capitalist road. Will they move to a full market-oriented economy or some combination of state control and capitalist institutions?

Most experts agree that, as China continues to engage with the global capitalist system, its impact will increasingly be felt around the world. With an enormous workforce, mostly well trained and educated, which receives extremely low wages compared with workers in similar jobs in the developed world, China is extremely competitive, potentially forcing down wages in the wealthy countries.

What does rapid globalization mean for global inequality? No sociologist can know for certain, but two contrasting scenarios exist. In one, the global economy might be dominated by large, global corporations, with workers competing against one another for a living wage. On this scenario we could forecast falling wages for large numbers of people in the high-income countries and rising wages in low-income countries. There would be a general levelling out of average income around the world, but at a lower level than that currently enjoyed in the developed countries. Polarization between the 'haves' and the 'have-nots' within countries would grow, and the world would be increasingly divided into those who benefit from the global economy and those who do not. This may fuel conflict between ethnic groups, and even nations, as those suffering from economic globalization would blame others for their plight (Hirst and Thompson 1992; Wagar 1992).

A second scenario would see greater opportunities for everyone as the benefits of modern technology stimulate worldwide economic

The fast-growing Chinese economy seems to be leading to a widening internal gap between rich and poor as the country becomes part of the global capitalist economy. Does Piketty's analysis at the start of this chapter lead you to expect such an outcome?

growth. The more successful East Asian NICs, such as Hong Kong, Taiwan, South Korea and Singapore, may be a sign of things to come. Other NICs, such as Malaysia and Thailand, will follow, along with China, Indonesia, Vietnam and more. India, the world's second most populous country, already boasts a middle class of some 200 million people, about a quarter of its total population, showing that positive development is already being generated for some countries (Kulkarni 1993).

However, one crucial factor that may make the second scenario less likely is the widen-

ing technology gap between rich and poor countries, which makes it difficult for poor countries to catch up. Poor countries cannot easily afford modern technology – yet, in the absence of it, they face major barriers in overcoming poverty and are caught in a vicious downward spiral. Jeffrey Sachs (2000), director of the Earth Institute at Columbia University in New York, claims that the world is becoming divided into three classes: technology innovators, technology adopters and the technologically disconnected. Technology innovators are those regions that provide nearly all of the world's technological inventions, accounting for less than 15 per cent of the world's population. Technology adopters are those regions that are able to adopt the technologies invented elsewhere, applying them to production and consumption; they account for 50 per cent of the world's population. Finally, the technologically disconnected are those regions that neither innovate nor adopt technologies and account for 35 per cent of the world's population. Sachs uses regions for comparison rather than countries because technologies do not always respect national frontiers.

Sachs says that technologically disconnected regions include southern Mexico, parts of Central America, the Andean countries, tropical Brazil, sub-Saharan Africa, most of the former Soviet Union, landlocked parts of Asia, landlocked Laos and Cambodia, and the deep-interior states of China. These impoverished regions lack access to markets or major ocean trading routes and have become caught in what Sachs terms a 'poverty trap', plagued by diseases, low agricultural productivity and environmental degradation. Ironically, these problems demand technological solutions.

Innovation requires a critical mass of ideas and technology to become self-sustaining. 'Silicon Valley', near San Francisco in the United States, provides an example of how technological innovation tends to be concentrated in regions rich in universities and high-tech firms. Silicon Valley grew up around Stanford University and other educational

607

and research institutions located south of San Francisco. Developing countries are ill-equipped to develop such regions; they are too poor to import computers, mobile phones, computerized factory machinery and other kinds of high technology. Nor can they afford to license technology from foreign companies that hold the patents. Sachs urges governments of wealthy countries, along with international lending institutions, to provide loans and grants for scientific and technological development to help bridge the technology divide.

Prospects for the twenty-first century

Forecasting the future – often called futurology – does not have a good track record. For example, catastrophist demographers have been predicting that the world's oil resources would run out 'in the next decade' for the last forty years or so. Similar forecasts in the 1960s of the mass starvation of hundreds of millions of people in the 1970s as a result of population growth did not materialize either, despite continuing malnutrition in some regions. Part of the reason for the failures of futurology is that forecasts are based on trends that are active in the present, and these are amenable to both intentional and unintentional change. Zygmunt Bauman (1982) once noted that social science ends at the point at which prediction begins. However, we can at least summarize something of what we have learned from this chapter.

In the twenty-first century the human world remains a grossly unequal one, where place of birth is perhaps the largest influence on an individual's life chances. If you happen to be born in a relatively wealthy developed country, chances are you will not be at risk of starvation, will be housed in some degree of comfort and will have many opportunities for work and careers. You also have a decent prospect of becoming part of the wealthiest 1 per cent of people on the planet. If you are

born into a poorer country, especially outside the middle classes, gaining an education may well be a struggle, work opportunities will be limited and life expectancy will be lower. This is exactly what global inequality means – radically different life chances rooted in the simple fact of being born. This knowledge is also what motivates some people to try to understand better how global inequality is (re)produced and others to try and eliminate it.

But the chapter is also clear that there are some very positive examples of development in some of the poorest countries and regions of the world. Real and significant global progress has been made in health, education and life expectancy over just the last half century. China, India, Brazil and Russia have made enormous economic progress, and a raft of countries, including Ethiopia, Gambia, Nepal and Indonesia, have made positive improvements according to the UNDP's broader HDI. Of course development on the HDI measure, very welcome though it is, may do little to bridge the economic equality gap if the developed countries continue to reap more rewards from the world economy. But perhaps this illustrates something of the point that post-development theorists seek to make – namely, that what constitutes 'development' or 'progress' cannot simply be lifted out of the context of the developed countries and used as a universal measure.

Indeed, concerns with the work–life balance, downsizing, living simpler lifestyles and 'treading softly on the Earth', which have surfaced in the developed societies, indicate a growing dissatisfaction with purely economic criteria of well-being. If so, then they may be early signs of a possible convergence towards something closer to the UN Human Development Index with its multiple indicators of 'development'. It is more visible today than fifty years ago to see that people in the developed world might have things to learn from alternative forms of human development that are being pursued in some developing countries.

Chapter review

1. What is meant by 'extreme inequality'? How does 'global inequality', as defined in this chapter, differ from extreme inequality?

2. Explain the differences between a) the three worlds model; b) the contrast between developed/developing countries and c) the idea of majority/minority worlds. Are these differences largely semantic or do they have real consequences?

3. Is the classification of high-, middle- and low-income countries an improvement on the 'three-worlds' model. In what ways?

4. What factors make up the UNDP concept of 'human development'? Can 'human development' be achieved in developing countries without substantially reducing global economic inequality?

5. List some of the practical advantages that being born into a high-income country confers on individuals. How are life chances related to country of birth?

6. What lessons can be learned about the process of 'development' from the experience of the newly industrializing countries of East Asia? What obstacles exist which might prevent other countries following this path?

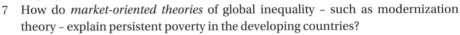

7. How do *market-oriented theories* of global inequality – such as modernization theory – explain persistent poverty in the developing countries?

8. What are *dependency theories* and how does Wallerstein's *world-systems theory* depart from some of the assumptions of the dependency perspective?

9. *State-centred theories* emphasize the role that governments play in generating economic development. Using specific examples, how have governments actually promoted growth and development and how successful have such measures been?

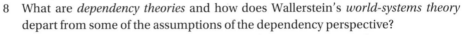

10. What is demography and in what ways is it relevant to the study of global economic inequality? How might it be argued that Malthusian ideas are still relevant in social science today?

11. The most rapid population growth over the twenty-first century will occur in the developing world. Why should this be so? Does the DTM adequately account for the population dynamic in developing countries?

Research in practice

The world's billionaires are often held to be part of the global inequality problem, since they hold vast reserves of wealth that could be used more productively to alleviate poverty. However, many rich individuals also see themselves as philanthropists and use some of their fortune for charitable purposes to tackle social problems. The following article examines two such foundations and the role they have played in tackling the scourge of malaria in developing countries. Read the study and answer the questions: Eckl, J. (2014) 'The Power of Private Foundations: Rockefeller and Gates in the Struggle Against Malaria', *Global Social Policy*, 14: 91–116.

1. How would you characterize this research? How was it actually carried out?

2. How does the author conceptualize power for use in the study? What is the basis of the power of these two private foundations?

3. What evidence is provided to show that the foundations have the power to shape global health and social policy in this area?

4   How do the foundations manage disagreements and conflict over their preferred approach to tackling malaria?

5   Provide some examples from the piece illustrating the claim that both foundations promote a biomedical model of health. Why might this be problematic for the countries in which they operate?

6   On balance, are developing countries better or worse off for the interventions of private foundations?

Thinking it through

The evidence on global inequality can be somewhat contradictory. On the one hand, the disparities between developed and developing countries are quite stark and, while the number of billionaires increases, absolute poverty remains a real issue for many millions of people. On the other hand, there have been some major successes in the last thirty years or so and the direction of change now appears positive. As we saw earlier, UNDP reports show that 'development' can occur in health, education and employment with little relation to crude measures of growth in national GDP. But how can positive 'human development' in the developed world coexist with increasingly extreme global inequalities of wealth?

Using evidence from the chapter, write a 500-word briefing paper, aimed at informing government ministers, summarizing the present global development situation. In the conclusion, give your assessment of Piketty's (2014) proposal for an annual wealth tax as a key instrument for halting the runaway accumulation of capital among a small number of individuals and families.

Society in the arts

Watch both of the following films:

- *The Agronomist* (2003), directed by Jonathan Demme
- *Lumumba* (2000), directed by Raoul Peck.

Lumumba is a biographical drama following Patrice Lumumba, the first prime minister of Congo (now the Democratic Republic of the Congo), before and after independence from Belgium in 1960 until his assassination in 1961. *The Agronomist* is a documentary film about Jean Leopold Dominique, a Haitian radio DJ and human rights activist who was assassinated in 2000.

In relation to the political situation in both countries and the wider international context at the time(s), what do these films have to say about the role of the USA and other developed countries in enabling or constraining independence and autonomous development? For example, what role did the US and Belgian governments play in Congolese independence and the assassination of Lumumba? Why was Dominique considered a threat to the Haitian dictators? Which do you find more powerful – the dramatized account or the documentary? Why is this?

For more information on these cases, see Ludo de Witte (2002) *The Assassination of Lumumba* (New York: Verso) and Jeb Sprague (2007) 'Haiti and the Jean Dominique Investigation: An Interview with Mario Joseph and Brian Concannon', *Journal of Haitian Studies*, 13(2): 136–50.

Further reading

A good place to begin is with Jeffrey Haynes's (2008) *Development Studies* (Cambridge: Polity), which covers a lot of ground and deals with globalization and its impact. *Global Inequality: Patterns and Explanations* (2006), edited by David Held and Ayse Kaya (Cambridge: Polity), offers exactly what it says: a discussion of patterns of inequality and the explanations and theories which try to account for it.

A good account of what 'development' means today and has meant in the past can be found in Katie Willis's (2011) *Theories and Practices of Development* (2nd edn, Abingdon: Routledge), which also looks at attempts to put theory into practice. Alastair Greig, David Hulme and Mark Turner's (2007) *Challenging Global Inequality: Development Theory and Practice in the 21st Century* (Basingstoke: Palgrave Macmillan) presents another up-to-date alternative.

Theories of development are comprehensively covered in Richard Peet and Elaine Hartwick's (2009) *Theories of Development: Conditions, Arguments, Alternatives* (2nd edn, London: Guilford Press), which takes in recent poststructuralist, feminist and critical modernist ideas. Anyone interested in the measurement of inequality should try Branko Milanovic's (2007) *Worlds Apart: Measuring International and Global Inequality* (Princeton, NJ: Princeton University Press), which is a stimulating read. Finally, do not be put off reading Thomas Piketty's (2014) *Capital in the Twenty-First Century* (Cambridge, MA, and London: Harvard University Press). The author says the book was written for a wide audience, which it certainly got.

Internet links

Additional information and support for this book at Polity:
www.politybooks.com/giddens

Inequality.org – based at the Institute for Policy Studies, Washington, USA. The site tracks inequality and is full of useful resources:
http://inequality.org/global-inequality

The UC Atlas of Global Inequality – based at the University of California, this has some good visual sources and lots more:
http://ccrec.ucsc.edu/news_item/uc-atlas-global-inequality-0

Forbes **magazine – everything you always wanted to know about the super-rich, including who they are and how much they own. It's a lot:**
www.forbes.com/billionaires

The International Monetary Fund – the official IMF site:
www.imf.org

The World Bank – search the site for the latest *World Development Report:*
www.worldbank.org

@ **Global Call to Action Against Poverty – a global coalition of groups campaigning on issues of poverty and inequality:**
www.whiteband.org

United Nations Development Programme – much information on inequality, home to the HDI reports and the Millennium Development Goals:
@ www.undp.org

CHAPTER 15
Gender and Sexuality

Contents

Kellie Maloney, formerly the boxing promoter and manager Frank Maloney.

As a high-profile fight promoter and manager, Frank Maloney developed a highly successful career in the macho world of professional boxing. Maloney has also been married twice and has three children. But in August 2014, at the age of sixty-one, he shocked the boxing world when he announced that he was transitioning to become a woman and would now be known as Kellie Maloney. The gender reassignment process, involving extensive surgery and medical treatments, was completed in mid-2015. Kellie explained her reasons for making the transition in her autobiography (2015: 12–13):

As Frank Maloney I had made my life in boxing as the tough-talking, wise-cracking, cockney promoter and manager. I came from a macho working class background and I managed Lennox Lewis when he was heavyweight champion of the world. I was a man's man, someone who wouldn't take any nonsense and who was always up for a night out with the boys. . . . But behind the public face another person had always lurked: Kellie, the woman I always wanted to be. In fact, it wasn't just a case of her being the woman I always wanted to be, it was more a case of Kellie being the real me. The truth was I had always been a woman trapped inside the body of a man, but in order to protect and hide that truth I had lived a lie all my life.

What Maloney describes is her previous gender dysphoria – the disjunction between her self-identity as female and her male, physical body. Kellie's solution was transitioning to become a trans woman – someone assigned as male at birth whose self-identity is female. The term transgender covers a variety of people exhibiting 'gender variance', including those whose gender identity and/or performance of gender diverges from that assigned at birth or expected according to dominant social norms of femininity and masculinity. Cisgender is the term often used to describe people whose assigned gender at birth does coincide with their self-identity and gender performance.

One high-profile example of gender variance is Thomas Neuwirth, a gay man and drag queen, who won the 2014 Eurovision Song Contest for Austria as Conchita Wurst. Conchita's appearance involves female clothing, make-up and a broadly feminine manner along with a beard, thereby confounding the conventional binary male–female distinction (see photo, right). Conchita's involvement was opposed by the Russian Orthodox Church, President Vladimir Putin and many other Eastern European politicians, who saw it as 'homosexual propaganda'. A petition was organized urging Russian national television stations to edit out her performance on the night, but it was not successful in doing so.

Conchita's resounding win was widely seen as symbolizing the very different attitudes towards sexuality in Western and Eastern Europe, though we should note that the views of political leaders and clergy do not necessarily reflect those of the wider public. Attempts to organize a parade in Moscow to celebrate Conchita's win were banned by officials on security grounds and the need to 'respect morality'. Even so, the support for Conchita both during and after the competition does show how far and how rapidly attitudes towards sexuality and gender have shifted in Western Europe as well as in other developed countries.

In recent years a range of films and television series centred on transgender characters and some high-profile celebrities, including Kellie Maloney, have brought transgender issues to the attention of the wider public. The Olympic Games decathlon gold medallist Bruce Jenner transitioned to become Caitlyn Jenner, the transgender actor Laverne Cox starred in the successful Netflix series *Orange is the New Black*, and Andreja Pejic was the first transgender model to be profiled in fashion the magazine *Vogue*. More broadly, in many developed countries, the numbers of people being referred to gender identity clinics or seeking gender reassignment are growing rapidly. For instance, in 2009 the UK's Gender

Eurovision Song Contest winner of 2014, Conchita Wurst

Identity Research and Education Society (GIRES) reported that numbers were growing by about 15 per cent per year and close to 50 per cent per year among young people (*The Guardian* 2015).

For sociologists, Kellie Maloney's story takes us to the heart of some key issues in the study of sex, gender and sexuality. What is the relationship between biological sex and identifying as 'male' or 'female'? How is sexuality connected to human biology and self-identity? Are there just two sexes – male and female – or are there more, and, if so, how many? Asking such questions suggests that fundamental aspects of our personal identities may not be as fixed or secure as many previously thought. Instead, gender and sexual identities are fluid, shifting and unstable, and this chapter attempts to show how sociological research and theorizing in this area has developed alongside this recognition. We should note at the outset that this is a complex field of study replete with major disagreements, both theoretical and political, and the body of research relates primarily to the developed world.

Many of the themes in this chapter overlap with questions raised in chapter 10, 'Families and Intimate Relationships', as sex, gender and sexuality are closely linked to love, intimacy and personal relationships. In this chapter we begin by looking at what we mean by sex, gender and sexuality, noting some of the difficulties of carrying out research into such highly personal and intimate aspects of people's lives. The thoroughgoing social constructionism of sociological approaches today is then contrasted with commonly held biological ideas of sex and sexuality, some of which permeated early sociological work. We move on to look at theories of gender identity and the existence of a gender order in society that is dominated by heterosexuality and heterosexual norms, before outlining the role of feminist and LGBT social movements in transforming cultures. Finally we set out changing theories of gender inequality and examine the impact of globalization on sex trafficking and the diversity of sex work today.

Sex, gender and sexuality

First, we must start with the basic contrast in sociology between sex and gender. 'Sex' is an ambiguous term. It can mean sexual activity, as in to 'have sex' with someone. But it can also refer to the physical characteristics (such as the female uterus and male/female genitalia) that distinguish males and females. Gender, by contrast, concerns the psychological, social and cultural differences between men and women. Gender is linked to socially constructed notions of masculinity and femininity and is not necessarily or inevitably a direct product of biological sex. For instance, as our opening example of Kellie Maloney illustrates, some people feel they have been born into the 'wrong' physical body and seek to 'put things right' by changing their physical body. In sociology, contrasting approaches have been taken to explain the formation of gender identities, with some scholars giving more prominence than others to social influences.

In many countries, but especially in the developed world, important aspects of people's sexual lives have been altered in fundamental ways since the 1960s. The previously dominant view that sexuality was tied to the process of reproduction is today undermined as it is clear that, for many people, sexuality and reproduction are not necessarily linked. Gender and sexuality are dimensions of life for each individual to explore and shape, and the widespread assumption of heteronormativity – the widespread assumption that heterosexuality is 'normal' and 'right' while other sexualities are in some way deviant – is fast losing ground. If sexuality was once 'defined' in terms of heterosexuality and monogamy in the context of marital relations, there is today a growing acceptance of diverse forms of sexuality, sexual identities and sexual activity. In spite of this, many discussions of gender differences and sexuality still make biological assumptions that there are basic or 'natural' differences between men and women.

Are the readily observable differences between women and men the result of biological differences? Is it metaphorically true that

Global Society 15.1 Gender and sexuality in the eighth edition

Hardly any subject has been left untouched by the recognition that there has been a persistent male bias in social scientific research and theorizing. It is therefore important to note that we cannot cover the entirety of gender-related issues in this chapter, but readers can use the guide below to find other relevant sections.

Chapter 1 – Introduction to feminist theorizing in sociology
Chapter 3 – Extended discussion of feminist critiques of 'malestream sociology'; the significance of gender inequality in social science
Chapter 6 – Gender inequality in the city
Chapter 7 – The feminization of work; gender inequality at work; a history of women's employment; housework, the housewife role and changes in the domestic division of labour
Chapter 8 – Gender in verbal and non-verbal communication; gender identities and the body; gender inequality in social interaction situations
Chapter 9 – Extended discussion of gender socialization, stereotyping and the feminization of later life
Chapter 10 – Extended discussion of gender inequalities; work, housework and the domestic division of labour; intimate violence and the 'dark side' of family life; feminist approaches to family studies
Chapter 11 – The medicalization of pregnancy and childbirth; global gender inequalities in health; the impact of HIV on sexual behaviour
Chapter 12 – Extended discussion of gender inequality and stratification; gender and social mobility
Chapter 13 – Gender inequality and poverty; pension inequalities
Chapter 17 – Christianity, gender and sexuality
Chapter 18 – Representations of gender in the global mass media
Chapter 19 – Extended discussion of gender inequality and heterosexual sexism in schools; the reproduction of gender divisions
Chapter 20 – The gendered pattern of crime and deviance; feminist criminology; gender, sexuality and hate crimes
Chapter 21 – Feminist and LGBT movements

'men are from Mars and women are from Venus' (Gray 1993)? For example, evolutionary psychology draws attention to the fact that, in almost all cultures, men rather than women take part in hunting and warfare. Does this indicate that men possess a natural tendency for aggression that women lack? Sociologists are not convinced by such arguments, which tend to be reductionist – reducing complex human activities and social relations to a single biological 'cause'. For instance, the level of male aggressiveness varies widely between different cultures, while women are expected to be more passive or gentle in some cultures than in others (Elshtain 1987). Anthropological and historical evidence actually reveals much variation over time and place. Even where a trait appears more or less universal, it does not follow that it is biological in origin. In the majority of human societies, most women spend a significant part of their lives caring for children and could not readily take part in hunting or war, but this does not mean that male aggression causes this difference.

Although the hypothesis that biological factors determine behavioural patterns in men and women continues to inform some scientific work, a century of research to identify the physiological origins of this influence has been unsuccessful. There is no evidence of the mechanisms which would link biological forces with the complex social behaviour exhibited by human beings (Connell 1987). Theories that see individuals as complying with some kind of innate predisposition neglect the vital role of social interaction in shaping human behaviour.

> ### THINKING CRITICALLY
>
> If gender differences are not rooted in human biology, why are the majority of people heterosexual? What social and cultural factors can you suggest that might give us a starting point from which to pursue an answer?

Gender identity

Since heterosexuality is the majority sexual orientation, it has tended to be ignored or taken for granted, and a good deal of research has focused on why some people are *not* heterosexual. There are parallels here with the way that gender was once seen as almost entirely about the experience of women (men represented the ungendered norm) and, in the sociology of 'race' and ethnicity, 'whiteness' was not seen as a form of ethnic identification at all (Back and Ware 2001). Some argued that biological influences predispose a minority to become gay or lesbian from birth (Bell et al. 1981). Biological explanations for homosexuality include differences in the brain characteristics of gay men (Maugh and Zamichow 1991) and the impact on foetal development of the mother's *in utero* hormone production during pregnancy (McFadden and Champlin 2000). Such studies, based on a small number of cases, produce inconclusive results, as it is virtually impossible to separate biological from early social influences in generating a person's sexual orientation (Healy 2001).

In sociology, one important early approach was gender socialization – the learning of gender roles via social agencies such as the family, state and mass media. This approach distinguishes biological sex from social-cultural gender – an infant is born with the first but develops the second. Through contact with various agencies of socialization, both primary and secondary, children gradually internalize the social norms and expectations that, according to dominant ideas, correspond to their biological sex. Hence, gender differences are not biologically determined but culturally produced as men and women are socialized into different roles.

Theories of gender socialization see boys and girls learning 'sex roles' and the male and female identities – involving masculine and feminine norms – that accompany them. They are guided in this process by positive and negative sanctions, socially applied forces which reward or restrain behaviour. For example, a small boy could be positively sanctioned in his behaviour ('What a brave boy you are!') or be the recipient of a negative sanction ('Boys don't play with dolls'). Positive and negative reinforcements aid boys and girls in learning and conforming to socially expected sex roles. If an individual engages in practices which do not correspond to his or her biological sex, the explanation may be inadequate or irregular socialization.

Social influences on gender identity flow through many diverse channels and tend to be largely indirect and unnoticed. Even parents committed to raising their children in 'non-sexist' ways find existing patterns of gender learning difficult to combat (Statham 1986). Studies of parent–child interactions have shown distinct differences in the treatment of boys and girls even when the parents believe their reactions to both are the same. The toys, picture books and television programmes experienced by young children all tend to emphasize differences between male and female attributes. Male characters generally outnumber females in most children's books, magazines, television programmes and films, and they tend to play more active, adventurous roles, while females are portrayed as passive, expectant and domestically oriented (Zammuner 1986; Davies 1991; Grogan 2008).

Feminist researchers have demonstrated how cultural and media products aimed at young audiences embody stereotypical, gendered representations of girls and boys and their expected ambitions. For example, in

Breaking the gendered expectations of daily life can bring opprobrium. What is 'wrong' with this image?

a series of four projects, Smith and Cook (2008) found persistent disparities in the presentation of male and female characters. In popular G-rated (for general or 'family' viewing) films between 1990 and 2005, only 28 per cent of the active speaking characters were female, while 85 per cent of narrators were male. A wider study of 400 films across the rating scale also found two contrasting representations of women: the traditional parent in a committed relationship or the attractive, alluring woman with an unrealistic body shape, including thin, small waist and 'hourglass' figure (ibid.: 12–14).

Unrealistic body proportions were much more likely to be found in animated female characters in television programmes and cartoons for the under-elevens than in 'live action' ones, as was 'sexually revealing clothing' (that which reveals body parts between the neck and knees). Male animated characters also tended to have a large chest size, small waist and overly muscular physique. Even in the twenty-first century, therefore, gender stereotyping remains a persistent feature of media output aimed at children. This has been seen as having a significant impact on young people's attitudes towards their own bodies.

A growing body of evidence has found a widespread dissatisfaction among girls and young women with their own bodies, partly as a result of comparing themselves with the airbrushed, perfected female role models which predominate in glossy magazines, on television and in film (American Psychological Association 2010). The spread of new digital technologies, which allow for the manipulation of bodies in photographs and on video, means that young people now face even more idealized and unrealistic media representations than did previous generations. This problem is especially acute in magazines, which have a powerful impact on the attitudes of regular readers (Grogan 2008: 108–9; see also Wykes and Gunter 2005).

A more detailed discussion of gender socialization is in chapter 9, 'The Life Course'.

Nonetheless, gender socialization and sex role theories have been heavily criticized. Many interactionist researchers argue that socialization is not a smooth process; different 'agencies', such as the family, schools and peer groups, may be at odds with one another and do not produce a homogeneous socializing experience. Just as seriously, socialization theories underplay the ability of individuals to reject or modify social expectations in their actual practices (Stanley and Wise 1993, 2002). It is more accurate to say that socializing agencies offer opportunities for people to take part in gendered practices, but this does not mean that gender identity is *determined*. Children do resist such pressures: boys mix masculine and feminine aspects, while some girls determinedly pursue competitive sports, and both boys and girls may behave differently in private to the gendered face they present in public (Connell 1987). The interactionist critique is an important one. Human beings are not passive, unquestioning recipients of gender 'programming' but actively engage with their social world, often modifying or rejecting pre-scripted gender roles, however powerful these may appear.

For a discussion of the social construction of bodies, see chapter 11, 'Health, Illness and Disability'.

Theories based on the separation of sex and gender implicitly accept that there is a biological basis beneath surface gender differences. In the socialization approach a biological distinction between the sexes provides a framework which becomes 'culturally elaborated' in society. By contrast, social constructionist theorists increasingly reject any biological basis for gender differences. Gender identities emerge in relation to *perceived* sex differences in society and in turn help to shape those differences. For example, a society in which ideas of masculinity are characterized by physical strength and 'tough' attitudes will encourage men to cultivate a specific body image and set of mannerisms different from those of societies with other norms of masculinity. In short, gender identities and sex differences are inextricably linked within individual lived bodies (Connell 1987; Scott and Morgan 1993; Butler 1990).

Not only is gender a social creation that lacks a fixed 'essence', but the human body itself is subject to individual choices and social forces which shape and alter it in numerous ways. People give their bodies meanings which challenge what is usually thought of as 'natural', choosing to construct and reconstruct them using exercise, dieting, piercings and cosmetic surgery. Transgender people may undergo gender reassignment operations to reshape the physical body, facilitating the performance of their gender identity. Medical and technological interventions blur the boundaries of the physical body, opening it to quite radical changes. However, these apparently 'free' individual choices are still linked to wider social norms of the ideal body size and shape, social trends and commercial pressures associated with marketing and the fashion industry.

Biology, sexuality and sexual identities

Sexuality has long been considered a highly personal subject. Until recently, much of what is known about sexuality came from sociobiologists, medical researchers and 'sexologists'. Sociobiologists such as David Barash (1979) argued that there is an evolutionary explanation for the widely reported sexual promiscuity of males. Men produce millions of sperm during a lifetime and can be seen as biologically disposed to impregnate as many women as possible. However, women produce only a few hundred eggs over a lifetime and have to carry the foetus within their body for nine months, which, says Barash, explains why they focus more on emotional commitment and are not as sexually promiscuous. This argument finds some support in studies of the sexual behaviour of animals, which claim to show that males are normally more promiscuous than females of the same species.

However, many scholars are dismissive of the evolutionary approach. Steven Rose (Rose et al. 1984: 145) notes that, unlike most animals, 'The human infant is born with relatively few of its neural pathways already committed', illustrating that human behaviour is shaped more by the environment than by genetically programmed instincts. Similarly, Norbert Elias (1987a) argues that the human capacity to learn *is* an evolutionary development but that, in humans, learned behaviour has become more significant than non-learned behaviour. The consequence is that humans not only *can* learn more than other species, they *must* learn more in order to participate successfully in increasingly diverse and complex societies. Biological evolution is overlain with social development in human societies, and all attempts to explain the latter by reference to the former are reductionist and inadequate.

Sexual orientation concerns the direction of one's sexual or romantic attraction, but sexual orientation results from the complex interplay of biological and social factors. It may be better to think of sexuality as involving, to varying degrees, both orientation and preference. The most commonly found sexual orientation is heterosexuality, the sexual or romantic attraction for persons of the opposite sex. Homosexuality involves the sexual or romantic attraction for persons of the same sex. Today, the term *gay* is also used to refer to male homosexuals, lesbian for female homosexuals, and *bi* as shorthand for bisexuals, people who experience sexual or romantic attraction for persons of either sex.

In some non-Western cultures, same-sex relations are accepted and even encouraged among certain groups. The Batak people of northern Sumatra, for example, permit male sexual relations before marriage. Boys leave the parental home at puberty and sleep in a dwelling with a dozen or so older males who initiate the newcomers into same-sex practices. But, in many societies, same-sex relationships are not so openly accepted and lesbian and gay people face prejudice and discrimination. In the Western world, sexuality is linked to individual identity, and the prevailing idea of 'a homosexual' or 'a heterosexual' is of a person whose sexual orientation lies within themselves and is a very personal matter.

Mary McIntosh (1968) was among the first to suggest that homosexuality was not a universal 'medical condition' but a social role that did not even exist in some societies. For instance, she maintained that, in England, 'the homosexual role' came into being only at the end of the seventeenth century. McIntosh also argued that evidence from Kinsey's research projects in the 1940s and 1950s into the varied sexual practices of adults in the USA (see 'Classic Studies 15.1') showed that the apparently distinct identities of 'heterosexual' and 'homosexual' were not as polarized as this contrast implies. For example, many 'heterosexual' men reported they had also engaged in same-sex activities with other men.

In his studies of sexuality, Michel Foucault (1978) showed that, before the eighteenth century, the notion of a homosexual identity seems barely to have existed in Europe. The act of 'sodomy' was denounced by Church authorities and the law, and in England and several other European countries it was punishable by death. However, sodomy was not defined exclusively as a homosexual offence; it also applied to relations between men and women or men and animals. The term 'homosexuality' was coined only in the 1860s, and, from then on, lesbians and gay men were increasingly regarded as being distinct types of people with a particular sexual aberration (Weeks 1986).

Homosexuality became part of a 'medicalized' discourse, spoken of in clinical terms

In ancient Greece, same-sex relationships were not prohibited, though they were governed by social codes. Only since 1967, after centuries of condemnation, has homosexuality been legal in the UK.

as a psychiatric disorder or perversion rather than as a religious 'sin'. 'Homosexuals', along with other 'deviants' such as paedophiles and transvestites, were seen as suffering from a biological pathology that threatened the wholesomeness of mainstream society. Until just a few decades ago, same-sex relations remained a criminal activity in virtually all Western countries. The movement of lesbians and gay men from the margins of society to the mainstream is not yet complete, but rapid progress has been and is being made.

Sexuality and sexual practices

Until Alfred Kinsey's research in the USA in the 1940s and 1950s, sexuality and sexual behaviour were seen as private matters and had been largely ignored by sociologists. Many were shocked and surprised at Kinsey's research findings, which revealed a wide divergence between public understanding, social norms and actual sexual practices (see 'Classic studies 15.1'). We can speak much more confidently about public values concerning sexuality than we can about private practices, which, by their nature, go mostly undocumented. But

why should sexuality be particularly difficult to research compared to, say, family relationships?

Until quite recently, sex was a taboo subject, not something to be discussed in the public realm of society or, for many, even in private. Perhaps more so than in any other area of life, many, maybe even most, people see sexual behaviour as a purely personal matter and are unwilling to discuss such an intimate subject with strangers. This may mean that those who *are* prepared to come forward for interview are essentially a self-selected sample, and so are unrepresentative of the general population.

The reticence in relation to sexual matters has changed somewhat since the 1960s, a time when social movements associated with 'hippie' lifestyles and counter-cultural ideas of 'free love' challenged existing attitudes and broke with established sexual norms. But we must be careful not to exaggerate their impact. Once the movements of the 1960s had become assimilated into mainstream society, some of the older norms relating to sex and sexuality continued to exert an influence. However, some have argued that a 'new fidelity' emerged in the late 1980s, partly as a result of concerns about the risks associated with the transmission of HIV/AIDS and other sexually transmitted infections (Laumann 1994). One important lesson from Kinsey's studies is that publicly stated attitudes may reflect people's understanding of prevailing public norms rather than accurately describing their private beliefs.

> **THINKING CRITICALLY**
>
> Kinsey's research was conducted over sixty-five years ago. Discuss this research with a sample of your friends and relatives across the age range and gauge their reactions. Were the younger people less surprised than older ones? What would you expect to discover given Kinsey's findings?

Sources of evidence on sexual activity

The validity of surveys of sexual behaviour has been the focus of much debate (Lewontin 1995). Critics argue that surveys simply do not generate reliable information about sexual practices. For instance, a survey of the sexual activities of young people in rural northern Tanzania compared data collected using five different methods: biological markers, such as the presence of a sexually transmitted disease (STI), a face-to-face questionnaire, an assisted self-completed questionnaire, in-depth interviews, and participant observation (Plummer et al. 2004). The research found many inconsistencies across the different methods. For example, five out of six young women with an existing STI reported during in-depth interviews having had sex, but only one out of the six in the questionnaires did so. Overall, in either of the two questionnaires, only 58 per cent of young men and 29 per cent of young women with biological markers of sexual activity reported any sexual activity.

The researchers found that, although the self-reporting data were 'fraught with inconsistencies', in-depth interviews seemed most effective in generating accurate information from the young women, while participant observation was the most useful method for uncovering the nature, complexity and extent of sexual activity in this particular population.

However, in many developed countries where public discussion of sexual matters has become more acceptable, questionnaires may yield more reliable data.

Many studies of sexual behaviour have taken the form of attitude and behaviour surveys using postal questionnaires or face-to-face interviews. But evidence in this area can also be collected through the analysis and interpretation of documentary materials such as personal diaries, oral history, magazines, newspapers and other published and unpublished historical materials. These research methods are not mutually exclusive, of course, and, as the two studies below show, they can be combined to produce a richer account of sexuality within societies.

Lillian Rubin's (1990) large-scale survey interviewed 1,000 Americans between the ages of thirteen and forty-eight to discover what changes had occurred in sexual behaviour and attitudes since the Kinsey studies. Rubin found that there had been some significant shifts. Sexual activity was typically beginning at a younger age than in the previous generation, and the sexual practices of teenagers tended to be as varied and comprehensive as those of adults. There was still a gendered sexual double standard, but it was not as powerful as it once had been.

One of the most important changes was that women had come to expect, and actively pursue, sexual pleasure in their relationships. They expected to receive, not only to provide, sexual satisfaction. Rubin discovered that women were more sexually liberated than previously, but most men in the survey found such female assertiveness difficult to accept, often saying they 'felt inadequate', were afraid they could 'never do anything right' and thought it was 'impossible to satisfy women these days'. This finding seems to contradict much of what we have come to expect about gender relations. Men continue to dominate in most spheres, and they are, in general, more violent towards women than the other way round. Such violence is substantially aimed at the control and continuing subordination of women. Yet a number of research studies have

Classic Studies 15.1 Alfred Kinsey discovers the diversity of sexual practices

The research problem

Do public norms of sexuality really govern people's actual sexual behaviour? Are sexually 'deviant' practices limited to just a tiny minority? To address these issues, Alfred Kinsey (1894–1956) and his research team set out to collect evidence from the white population of 1940s America. The team faced condemnation from religious organizations and their work was denounced as immoral in newspapers and even in Congress. But they persisted and eventually obtained sexual life histories from 18,000 people, a reasonably representative sample of the white American population (Kinsey 1948, 1953).

Kinsey's findings

Kinsey's research findings were surprising because they did indeed reveal a large difference between the public expectations of sexual behaviour and actual sexual conduct as described by people in the sample. The survey found that almost 70 per cent of men had visited a prostitute and 84 per cent admitted to premarital sexual experiences (quite a shocking figure at the time). Yet, following the sexual double standard, 40 per cent of men also expected their wives to be virgins on marriage. More than 90 per cent of males said they had engaged in masturbation and nearly 00 per cent in some form of oral sexual activity. Among women, around 50 per cent had had premarital sexual experiences, although mostly with prospective husbands, while 60 per cent had masturbated and the same percentage had engaged in oral–genital contact. The study also showed much higher levels of male same-sex activity than expected.

The gap between publicly accepted attitudes and actual behaviour that Kinsey's findings demonstrated was especially great in that particular period, just after the Second World War. A phase of sexual liberalization had begun rather earlier, in the 1920s, when many younger people felt freed from the strict moral codes that had governed earlier generations. Sexual behaviour probably changed a good deal, but issues concerning sexuality were not openly discussed in ways with which people today are now familiar. Individuals participating in sexual activities that were still strongly disapproved of on a public level concealed them, not realizing the full extent to which many others were engaging in similar practices.

Critical points

Kinsey's research was controversial in the USA and was attacked by conservative and religious organizations. For example, one aspect of the studies explored the sexuality of children under sixteen years of age, and many critics objected to their involvement as research subjects. Religious leaders also claimed that open discussion of sexual behaviour would undermine Christian moral values. Academic critics argued that Kinsey's positivist approach collected much raw data, but the study failed to grasp either the complexity of sexual desire underpinning the diverse behaviour he uncovered or the meanings people attach to their sexual relationships. Later surveys also found lower levels of same-sex experience than did Kinsey, suggesting that his sample may have been less representative than the team first thought.

Contemporary significance

Kinsey is widely seen as a founder of the scientific study of sex and sexuality. His findings were instrumental in challenging the widespread view that homosexuality was a form of mental illness requiring treatment. It was only in the more 'permissive' era of the 1960s, which brought openly declared attitudes more into line with the reality of behaviour, that Kinsey's findings came to be accepted as providing a more realistic picture. Kinsey died in 1956, but the Institute for Sex Research, which he headed, continues its research today and has produced much valuable information about contemporary sexual behaviour. In 1981 it was renamed the Kinsey Institute for Research in Sex, Gender and Reproduction to celebrate his contribution to scientific research in this field.

argued that masculinity is a burden as well as a source of rewards, and, were men to stop using sexuality as a means of control, they would benefit as much as women.

The Studies by Rubin and Wouters (see 'Global society 15.2') share some similarities. Both are concerned with changes over time in gender relations, norms of sexual behaviour, and private and public attitudes towards sexuality. While Rubin's study tells us something of how people *today* feel about such changes and what impact they have on contemporary lifestyles, Wouters's analysis of primary documents sets the contemporary findings into historical and comparative perspective. Bringing together the findings from studies using such different methods, which also focus on different aspects of changing sexual behaviour, gives sociologists more confidence in their conclusions in this difficult to research area.

Social constructions of gender and sexuality

Scholars who subscribe to the 'natural differences' school of thought tend to argue that social inequalities of class, gender and 'race' are rooted in biological differences. Similarly, the existing division of labour must be 'natural', with women and men performing those tasks for which they are best suited. Thus, the anthropologist George Murdock saw it as both practical and convenient that women should concentrate on domestic and family responsibilities while men work outside the home. On the basis of a cross-cultural study of more than 200 societies, Murdock (1949) concluded that the sexual division of labour is present in all cultures. While this is not the result of biological 'programming', it is the most logical basis for the organization of society.

Talcott Parsons was particularly interested in the socialization of children and argued that stable, supportive families are the key to successful socialization (Parsons and Bales 1956). In Parsons's view, the family operates most efficiently with a clear-cut sexual division of labour in which females act in *expressive*

roles, providing care and security to children and offering them emotional support. Men, on the other hand, should perform *instrumental* roles – namely, being the breadwinner in the family. This complementary division of labour, springing from a biological distinction between the sexes, would ensure the solidarity of the family unit.

Feminists have sharply criticized claims of a biological basis to the sexual division of labour, arguing that there is nothing natural or inevitable about the allocation of tasks in society. Parsons's view on the 'expressive' female has also been attacked by feminists and other sociologists who see such views as condoning the domination of women in the home. There is no basis to the belief that the 'expressive' female is necessary for the smooth operation of the family – rather, it is a social role promoted largely for the convenience of men.

Sociologists today do not accept that complex human behaviour can be explained by reference to a fixed 'human nature' or the biological 'essence' of men and women. The attempt to do so is known as essentialism, and the history of sociological theories from the early twentieth century onwards has been the steady movement away from essentialist assumptions. However, essentialist arguments continually resurface in scientific work. In the 1990s, a scientific study comparing male 'gay', male 'straight' and 'female' brains claimed to have discovered that one of the four anterior regions of the hypothalamus area tended to be smaller in gay men than in straight men, resembling that of the female brain (LeVay 1993). The study was seen as suggesting a biological foundation to homosexuality and was widely reported in the media – also bringing positive comment from some gay rights campaigners, who saw this as supportive of their claim for equal civil rights.

Rahman and Jackson (2010) argue that this study illustrates the deep flaws embedded within essentialist thinking. How did the researchers know that the 'straight brains' were from 'straight men'? It seems this was simply an assumption based on the lack of any contrary self-reporting by the men or evidence

Global Society 15.2 · Sex and manners in comparative perspective

The use of documentary materials to study changing forms of sexual behaviour is well demonstrated in *Sex and Manners*, by the Dutch sociologist Cas Wouters (2004), a comparative study of shifting gender relations and sexuality in England, Germany, the Netherlands and the USA. Wouters studied books on 'good manners' from the end of the nineteenth century to the end of the twentieth, particularly as these pertained to gender relations and 'courting behaviour' – the opportunities for and limitations on meetings and 'dating' between men and women. Manners books offer advice on how such meetings should be conducted, providing codes of manners on how to meet and behave in relations with 'the opposite sex'.

For instance, in England, a 1902 publication, *Etiquette for Women*, advised that 'It is the man's place to pay for what refreshments are had, if the ladies do not insist on paying their share; and if he invited the ladies with him to go in somewhere and have some, then the case is simple enough.' But by the 1980s the practice of 'going Dutch' – sharing the cost of a date – was commonplace and well established. A manners book from 1989, reflecting on the old practice of men always paying for women, noted that 'some still do, but women can't dine endlessly without offering a crust in return' (Wouters 2004: 25–7). This example seems fairly trivial, but in fact it shows that shifting gender relations in the wider society, with more women moving into paid employment and the public sphere more generally, were also leading to changing behavioural norms in relations between men and women.

Wouters's research provides many examples in relation to sexual behaviour and courtship.

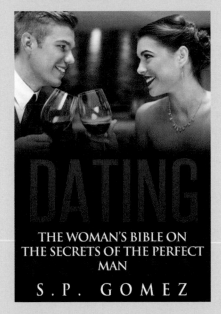

Etiquette manuals are not merely of historical interest for sociologists. Today there are many more books, magazine and newspaper columns, and websites devoted to dating etiquette and the art of 'finding the right man'.

By analysing manners books over the course of a century and relating the advice given in these to sociological theories of social change, Wouters argues that the four countries all exhibit a long-term trend, away from very formal and rigid codes of manners and towards much more informal codes that allow for a wider range of acceptable courtship behaviour. Hence, those critics of 1960s 'permissiveness' fail to appreciate that such changes are part of a much longer and deeper process of social transformation.

from their medical records. Yet what we have learned from Kinsey's 1950s research and Laud Humphreys's (1970) study of American 'tearooms' (see chapter 2) is that a not insignificant number of publicly 'straight' men also engage in same-sex sexual activity which they keep hidden: 'In a classically essentialist mode of thinking, Le Vay conflates identity with behaviour, without knowing anything about the actual behaviour exhibited by these subjects' (Rahman and Jackson 2010: 121). Similarly, the brains of 'gay' men were taken from men who had died of AIDS-related illnesses, and the researchers could not have known what these men's patterns of sexual behaviour had been either.

What makes essentialism initially plausible is the apparently incontrovertible 'fact' that there are two biological sexes – men and women – which form the basis for understanding gender differences and sexuality. But historians and sociologists have shown this assumption to be false. Before the mid-eighteenth century, Western cultures held a presumption that there was only *one sex*, which varied along a behavioural continuum from femininity to masculinity, and the perception of two distinct sexes emerged only from the mid-eighteenth century (Laqueur 1990). Some people have an intersex condition, in which their reproductive or sexual anatomy 'doesn't seem to fit the typical definitions of male or female' (ISNA 2015). But which of these variations 'counts' as intersex is socially constructed and therefore not purely biological. These examples show that what it means to be a 'man' or a 'woman', and to be 'gay' or 'straight', is not fixed by biology.

Sexuality, religion and morality

Attitudes towards sexual behaviour are not uniform across the world's societies, and even within one national society they undergo significant changes over time. For example, Western attitudes to sexuality for nearly 2,000 years were moulded primarily by Christianity. Although different Christian sects and denominations have held divergent views about the proper place of sexuality in life, the dominant view has been that all sexual behaviour is suspect except when connected with reproduction. In some periods, this view produced an extreme prudishness in society at large. At other times many people ignored or reacted against the teachings of the Church, commonly engaging in practices (such as adultery) forbidden by religious authorities.

In the nineteenth century, religious assumptions about sexuality were partly replaced by medical ones. Most of the early writings by doctors about sexual behaviour were as stern as the views of the Church. Some argued that any type of sexual activity unconnected with reproduction would cause serious physical harm. Masturbation was said to bring on blindness, insanity, heart disease and other ailments, while oral sex was claimed to cause cancer. In Victorian times, sexual hypocrisy abounded. Virtuous women were believed to be indifferent to sexuality, accepting the attentions of their husbands only as a duty. Yet in the expanding towns and cities, where prostitution was rife and often openly tolerated, 'loose' women were seen as being in an entirely different category from their respectable sisters.

Many Victorian men who were, on the face of things, sober, well-behaved citizens, devoted to their wives, also regularly visited prostitutes or kept mistresses. Such behaviour was treated leniently, whereas 'respectable' women who took lovers were regarded as scandalous and, if their behaviour came to light, shunned in public society. The different attitudes towards the sexual activities of men and women formed a double standard which has long existed and whose residues still linger on today (Barret-Ducrocq 1992).

Today traditional attitudes exist alongside a much more liberal approach to sex and sexuality, which developed particularly strongly from the 1960s. Sexual scenes in films and plays are shown that would previously have been unacceptable, and pornographic material is readily available online to most adults who want it. Those with strong religious beliefs still see premarital sex as wrong and generally frown on all forms of sexual behaviour which departs from heterosexuality. Yet it is more commonly accepted that sexual pleasure is a desirable and important feature of intimate relations. Sexual attitudes have undoubtedly become more liberal since the mid-twentieth century in most Western countries, though there are significant differences globally. Religious beliefs and traditional norms relating to sexuality have not simply been swept aside by the incoming tide of modernity but continue to exert an influence on many people's attitudes and values.

> **THINKING CRITICALLY**
>
> In what ways are your attitudes towards sex and sexuality different from those of your parents and older relatives? Is there any connection between such attitudes and religious beliefs? Do changing attitudes towards sexuality provide evidence for secularization?

Forms of sexuality

Most people, in all societies, are heterosexual, and heterosexuality has historically been the basis for child-rearing and family life. Yet there are numerous sexual orientations and identities. Judith Lorber (1994) distinguishes as many as ten sexual identities: straight woman, straight man, lesbian woman, gay man, bisexual woman, bisexual man, transvestite woman (a woman who regularly dresses as a man), transvestite man (a man who regularly dresses as a woman), transsexual woman (a man who becomes a woman) and transsexual man (a woman who becomes a man). She also discusses the variety of sexual practices. For example, a man or woman can have sexual relations with women, with men or with both. This can happen one at a time or with three or more participating. One can have sex with oneself (masturbation) or with no one (celibacy). One can have sexual relations with transsexuals or with people who erotically cross-dress, use pornography or sexual devices, practise sado-masochism (the erotic use of bondage and the inflicting of pain), have sex with animals, and so on (ibid.).

In all societies there are sexual norms that approve of some of these practices while discouraging or outlawing others. Members of a society learn these norms through socialization. Over the last few decades, for example, sexual norms in Western cultures have been linked to ideas of romantic love and family relationships. Such norms, however, vary widely between different cultures. Same-sex relations are a case in point. Some cultures have either tolerated or actively encouraged same-sex relations in certain contexts. Among the ancient Greeks, for instance, the love of men for boys was idealized as the highest form of sexual love.

The most extensive study was carried out nearly sixty years ago by Ford and Beach (1951), who surveyed anthropological evidence from more than 200 societies. Striking variations were found in what is regarded as 'natural' sexual behaviour and in norms of sexual

Increasingly the toned, muscular and sexualized male body is used as an ideal type in fashion and advertising campaigns. How might this development be linked to the changing position of men and women in contemporary societies?

attractiveness. In the West a slim, small body is admired, while in other cultures a much more generous shape is regarded as most attractive. Some societies placed great store on the shape of the face, while others emphasized the shape and colour of the eyes or the size and form of the nose and lips. The variety of accepted types of sexual behaviour is one important piece of evidence that most sexual responses are learned rather than innate.

The gender order

In *Gender and Power* (1987), *The Men and the Boys* (2001) and *Masculinities* (2005), Raewyn Connell set out one of the most complete theoretical accounts of gender, which has become something of a 'modern classic' (see 'Classic studies 15.2'). Her approach has been particularly influential because it integrates the concepts of patriarchy – the socially organized dominance of men over women – and masculinity into an overarching theory of gender relations. According to Connell, masculinities are a critical part of the gender order and cannot be understood separately or from the femininities which accompany them.

Connell argues that empirical evidence on gender is not simply a 'shapeless heap of data', but reveals the basis of an 'organized field of human practice and social relations' through which women are kept in subordinate positions to men (Connell 1987). In Western capitalist societies, gender relations are still defined by patriarchal power. From the individual to the institutional level, various types of masculinity and femininity are arranged around a central premise: the dominance of men over women. Gender relations are the product of everyday interactions and practices, though the actions and behaviour of people in their personal lives are directly linked to collective arrangements in society. These arrangements are continuously reproduced over lifetimes and generations, but they are also subject to change.

Connell suggests there are three aspects which interact to form a society's gender order – patterns of power relations between masculinities and femininities that are widespread throughout society – namely, labour, power and cathexis (personal/sexual relationships). These three realms are distinct but interrelated and represent the main sites in which gender relations are constituted and constrained. *Labour* refers to the sexual division of labour both within the home (such as domestic responsibilities and childcare) and in the labour market (issues such as occupational segregation and unequal pay). *Power* operates through social relations such as authority, violence and ideology in institutions, the state, the military and domestic life. *Cathexis* concerns dynamics within intimate, emotional and personal relationships, including marriage, sexuality and child-rearing.

Gender relations, as they are enacted in these three areas, are structured on a societal level in a particular gender order. Connell uses the term gender regime to refer to the play of gender relations in smaller settings, such as a specific institution. Thus, a family, a neighbourhood and a state all have their own gender regimes. (One such gender regime is explored by Máirtín Mac an Ghaill in 'Using your sociological imagination 15.1'.)

Change in the gender order: crisis tendencies

Although Connell's account sees a clearly organized gender hierarchy, gender relations are the outcome of an ongoing process and are therefore open to challenge and change. Connell sees the gender order in dynamic terms. If sex and gender *are* socially constructed, then it must be possible for people to change their gender orientation. This does not necessarily mean that people can switch their sexuality with ease, but that gender identities are constantly being adjusted. Women who once subscribed to 'emphasized femininity' might develop a feminist consciousness which leads to a change in identity and behaviour. This possibility of change means that patterns of gender relations are open to disruption and subject to the power of human agency.

While some sociologists believe that Western society is undergoing a 'gender crisis',

Classic Studies 15.2 Connell on the dynamics of the gender order

The research problem

Why do some people become male and female role models? What characteristics and actions do role models display and how do those characteristics and actions (and not others) come to be widely seen as desirable? Connell (1987, 2001, 2005) explored such questions in her studies of the 'gender order' in societies. In particular, she developed a theory of the *gender hierarchy.*

Connell's explanation

Connell argues that there are many different expressions of masculinity and femininity. At the level of society, these contrasting versions are ordered in a hierarchy which is oriented around one defining premise – the domination of men over women (figure 15.1). Connell uses stylized 'ideal types' of masculinities and femininities in this hierarchy.

At the top of the hierarchy is hegemonic masculinity, which is dominant over all other masculinities and femininities in society. 'Hegemonic' refers to the concept of hegemony – the social dominance of a certain group, exercised not through brute force but through a cultural dynamic which extends into private life and social realms. Thus, the media, education, ideology, even sports and music can all be channels through which hegemony is established. According to Connell, hegemonic masculinity is associated first and foremost with heterosexuality and marriage, but also with authority, paid work, strength and physical toughness. Examples of men who embody hegemonic masculinity are film stars such as Arnold Schwarzenegger, rappers such as 50 Cent and the entrepreneur Donald Trump.

Although hegemonic masculinity is held up as an ideal form of masculinity, only a few men in society can live up to it. A large number of men, however, still gain advantage from its dominant position in the patriarchal order. Connell refers to this as the 'patriarchal dividend' and to those who benefit from it as embodying complicit masculinity.

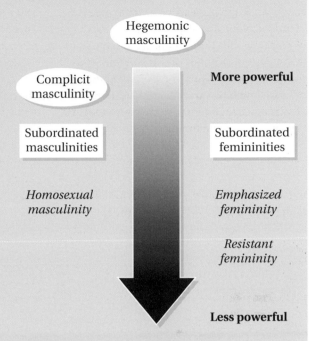

Figure 15.1 The gender hierarchy

Existing in a subordinated relationship to hegemonic masculinity are a number of subordinated masculinities and femininities. Among subordinated masculinities, the most important is that of homosexual masculinity. In a gender order dominated by hegemonic masculinity, the homosexual is seen as the opposite of the 'real man', he does not measure up to the hegemonic masculine ideal and often embodies many of its 'cast off' traits. Homosexual masculinity is stigmatized and ranks at the bottom of the gender hierarchy for men.

Connell argues that femininities are all formed in positions of subordination to hegemonic masculinity. One form – emphasized femininity – is an important complement to hegemonic masculinity. It is oriented to accommodating the interests and desires of men and is characterized by 'compliance, nurturance and empathy'. Among young women it is associated with sexual receptivity, while among older women it implies motherhood. Connell refers to Marilyn Monroe as both 'archetype and satirist' of emphasized femininity and stresses that images of emphasized femininity remain highly prevalent in the media, advertising and marketing campaigns.

Finally, there are subordinated femininities, which reject the version of emphasized femininity outlined above. But, on the whole, the overwhelming attention devoted to maintaining emphasized femininity as the conventional norm in society means that other subordinated femininities which resist convention are not given voice. Among women who have developed non-subordinated identities and lifestyles are feminists, lesbians, spinsters, midwives, witches, prostitutes and manual workers. The experiences of these resistant femininities, however, are largely 'hidden from history'.

Critical points

Several critics have argued that, although hegemonic masculinity appears to be fairly obvious, Connell does not really present a satisfactory account of it. This is because she does not specify what would count as 'counter-hegemonic'. For example, with more men now involved in childcare and parenting, is this part of or a trend against hegemonic masculinity? Unless we know what actions would challenge it, how can we know what actions constitute

hegemonic masculinity in the first place? Some social psychologists also wonder *how* men come to 'embody' complicit masculinity; if they do not live up to the hegemonic masculine ideal themselves, what does this failure mean for them psychologically and what do they actually do? In short, 'What is missing is more fine-grain work on what complicity and resistance look like in practice' (Wetherell and Edley 1999: 337). Finally, Connell did not theorize the gender order at the global level, though this was the subject of a later work.

Contemporary significance

Given that Connell's work is relatively recent, sociologists are still working through all of its implications. Her early writings are notable for their wider focus on men and masculinities as well as women in the field of gender studies. However, so far she has been enormously influential in shaping gender studies and especially in our understanding of how particular gender regimes are stabilized and, potentially, destabilized. As Connell's ideas show that the gender order is never fixed or static, they have influenced not just sociologists but also political activists within LGBT social movements.

Connell suggests there are powerful *tendencies* towards crisis. First, there is the *crisis of institutionalization*. Institutions that have traditionally supported men's power – the family and the state – are gradually being undermined. The legitimacy of men's domination over women is being weakened through legislation on divorce, domestic violence and rape, and economic questions such as taxation and pensions. Second, there is a *crisis of sexuality*, in which hegemonic heterosexuality is less dominant than it once was. The growing strength of women's sexuality and gay sexuality puts traditional hegemonic masculinity under pressure. Finally, there is a *crisis of interest formation*. Connell argues that there are new foundations for social interests that contradict the existing gender order. Married

women's rights, gay movements and the growth of 'anti-sexist' attitudes among men all pose threats to the current order.

Of course, threats to the gender order do not have to be negative for men. More men today are becoming fully involved in child-rearing and a minority have enthusiastically embraced the relatively new social role of 'house-husband'. Similarly, the idea of the 'new man', who self-consciously rejects older forms of behaviour associated with hegemonic masculinity in favour of a more caring and emotionally open disposition, brings with it the possibility of new types of relationship. The crisis tendencies already in evidence within the existing order could be exploited in order to bring about the eradication of gender inequality (Connell 1987, 2005).

See chapter 10, 'Families and Intimate Relationships', for a more detailed discussion of changes to gender roles within family life.

Masculinities

Feminist sociologists from the 1970s onwards produced many empirical studies of inequalities between men and women which laid bare the real extent of women's unequal position in society. But little effort was expended trying to understand masculinity – the experience of being a man – or the formation of male identities. However, since the late 1980s this has altered significantly. Quite fundamental changes for women in relation to paid employment and the public realm of society, along with the diversification of families, have raised new questions about the position of men. What does it mean to be a man in the twenty-first century? How are the traditional expectations of men being transformed in a rapidly changing age? Are traditional norms of masculinity losing their grip on younger generations?

In recent years, sociologists have become increasingly interested in the positions and experiences of men within the larger 'gender order'. This shift in the sociology of gender and sexuality has led to studies of men and masculinity within the overarching context of gender relations – the societally patterned interactions between men and women. Sociologists have tried to understand how male identities are constructed and what impact socially prescribed roles have on men's behaviour.

More recently, Connell (2011) has examined the effects of globalization on the gender order. She maintains that gender itself has become globalized, with interactions between previously distinct, local gender orders as well as the creation of new arenas of gender relations. Connell argues that there are several new global arenas of gender relations: transnational and multinational corporations with a masculine management culture; international non-governmental organizations, which are also gendered and run mainly

This young Wodaabe man from the Gerewol in Niger is participating in a formal dance. His make-up, decorative dress and accessories, combined with his facial expressions, give him sex appeal to young Wodaabe women. In what ways does this form of 'expressed masculinity' differ from Western norms?

by men; the international media, which disseminate particular understandings of gender; and, lastly, global markets in capital, commodities, services and labour, which tend to be strongly gender-structured and can increasingly reach into local economies. Hence, it is now possible to talk of a 'world gender order' which provides the context for future discussions of gender and sexuality.

Gender inequality

Gender differences are rarely neutral and gender is a significant form of social

15.1   Education and the formation of masculinities and sexualities

In *The Making of Men* (1994), Máirtín Mac an Ghaill presented the findings from a piece of ethnographic research which explored the 'gender regime' – the way gender relations play out – at an English state secondary school. Drawing on Connell's work, Mac an Ghaill was interested in how schools actively create a range of masculinities and femininities among students. Although he was particularly curious about the formation of heterosexual masculinities, he also investigated the experiences of a group of gay male students. His findings revealed that the school itself is an institution characterized by gendered and heterosexual patterns.

The prevailing 'regime' encourages the construction of gender relations among students which coincide with the larger gender order – that is, a hierarchy of dominant and subordinate masculinities and femininities could be detected within the confines of the school. Social influences and practices as diverse as disciplinary procedures, subject allocation, teacher–student and student–teacher interactions, and surveillance all contribute to the formation of heterosexual masculinities.

Mac an Ghaill notes four emergent types of masculinity in the school setting. The *macho lads* are a group of white working-class boys who are defiant of school authority and disdainful of the learning process and student achievers. Mac an Ghaill concludes that they are undergoing a 'crisis of masculinity', as the manual and unskilled/semi-skilled jobs which they once saw as defining their future identities are no longer available. This leaves the lads in a psychological and practical dilemma about their futures which is difficult for them to comprehend and even harder to resolve.

The second group is made up of *academic achievers*, who see themselves as future professionals. These boys are stereotyped by the 'macho lads' (and teachers) as effeminate, 'dickhead achievers'. The most common route taken by the achievers in handling the vicious stereotyping, according to Mac an Ghaill, is to retain confidence that their hard work and academic credentials will grant them a secure future. This forms the basis of their masculine identities.

The third group, the *new enterprisers*, are boys who gravitate towards subjects in the new vocational curriculum, such as computer science and business studies. Mac an Ghaill sees them as children of the new 'enterprise culture' that was cultivated during the Thatcher years. For these boys, success in A-level exams is relatively useless for their emphasis on the market and their instrumental planning for the future.

The *real Englishmen* make up the final group. They are the most troublesome of the middle-class groups, as they maintain an ambivalent attitude towards academic learning but see themselves as 'arbiters of culture', superior to anything their teachers can offer. Because they are oriented towards entry into a career, masculinity for this group involves the appearance of effortless academic achievement.

In his study of gay male students, Mac an Ghaill found that a distinctly heterosexual set of norms and values – based on traditional relationships and nuclear families – is taken for granted in all classroom discussions that touch on gender or sexuality. This leads to difficult 'confusions and contradictions' in the construction of gender and sexual identities for young gay men, who can feel simultaneously ignored and categorized by others.

THINKING CRITICALLY

Do you recognize the subcultures in this study from your own experience? If same-sex relationships have become more widely accepted in society, why is heteronormativity still so strong in schools? How might individual teachers change the prevailing gender order of the school?

stratification. Gender is also a key factor in structuring the types of opportunities and life chances faced by individuals and groups and strongly influences the roles they play within social institutions, from the household to the state. The prevailing division of labour between the sexes has led to men and women assuming unequal positions in terms of power, prestige and wealth. Despite the advances that women have made in countries around the world, gender differences continue to serve as the basis for inequalities. Investigating and accounting for gender inequality has become a central concern of sociologists, and several theoretical perspectives have been advanced to explain men's enduring dominance over women. This section focuses on theoretical approaches, as the empirical evidence of gender inequality in specific settings and institutions is covered in other chapters.

> Evidence on gender inequality is introduced and discussed in chapter 12, 'Stratification and Social Class', chapter 14, 'Global Inequality', and chapter 16, 'Race, Ethnicity and Migration'.

Feminist approaches

The feminist movement has given rise to a large body of theory which attempts to explain gender inequality. These feminist theories contrast markedly with each other. Competing schools have sought to interpret gender inequalities through a variety of deeply embedded social processes, such as sexism, patriarchy and capitalism. We begin by looking at the major strands of feminism in the West during the twentieth century: liberal, socialist (or Marxist) and radical feminism. The distinction between these has never been clear-cut, though it provides a useful introduction. In recent decades new forms have also emerged – such as postmodern feminism – which cut across the earlier strands (Barker 1997).

Liberal feminism

Liberal feminism looks for explanations of gender inequalities in social and cultural attitudes. An important early contribution to liberal feminism came from the English philosopher John Stuart Mill, in his essay *The Subjection of Women* (1869), which called for legal and political equality between the sexes, including the right to vote. Unlike radical and socialist feminists, liberal feminists do not see women's subordination as part of a larger system or structure. Instead, they draw attention to many separate factors. For example, since the early 1970s, liberal feminists have campaigned against sexism and discrimination against women in the workplace, educational institutions and the media. They tend to focus on establishing and protecting equal opportunities for women through legislation and other democratic means. In the UK, legal advances such as the Equal Pay Act (1970) and the Sex Discrimination Act (1975) were actively supported by liberal feminists, who argued that enshrining equality in law is an important step in eliminating discrimination against women. Liberal feminists work through the existing system to bring about reforms in a gradual way. In this respect, they are more moderate in their aims and methods than many radical and socialist feminists, who call for an overthrow of the existing system.

While liberal feminists have contributed greatly to the advancement of women over the past century, critics charge that they are unsuccessful in dealing with the root causes of gender inequality and do not acknowledge the systemic nature of women's oppression in society. By focusing on the independent deprivations which women suffer – sexism, discrimination, the 'glass ceiling', unequal pay – liberal feminists draw only a partial picture of gender inequality. Radical feminists accuse liberal feminists of encouraging women to accept an unequal society and its competitive character.

Socialist and Marxist feminism

Socialist feminism developed from Marx's conflict theory, although Marx himself had little to say about gender inequality. It has been critical of liberal feminism for its perceived inability to see that there are powerful interests in society that are hostile to equality for women (Bryson 1993). Socialist feminists have sought to defeat both patriarchy and capitalism (Mitchell 1966). It was Marx's friend and collaborator Friedrich Engels who did more than Marx to provide an account of gender equality from a Marxist perspective.

Engels argued that, under capitalism, material and economic factors underlay women's subservience to men, because patriarchy (like class oppression) has its roots in private property. Engels maintained that capitalism intensifies patriarchy by concentrating wealth and power in the hands of a small number of men. Capitalism intensifies patriarchy more than earlier social systems because it creates enormous wealth which confers power on men as wage-earners as well as possessors and inheritors of property. Second, for the capitalist economy to succeed, it must define people – in particular women – as consumers and persuade them that their needs will be met only through ever-increasing consumption of goods and products. Last, capitalism relies on women to labour for free in the home, caring and cleaning. To Engels, capitalism exploited men by paying low wages and women by paying no wages.

> Payment for housework is an important component of many feminist arguments, and is discussed further in chapter 7, 'Work and the Economy'.

Socialist feminists have argued that the reformist goals of liberal feminism are inadequate. They have called for the restructuring of the family, the end of 'domestic slavery', and the introduction of some collective means of carrying out child-rearing, caring and household maintenance. Following Marx, many argued that these ends would be achieved through a socialist revolution, which would produce true equality under a state-centred economy designed to meet the needs of all.

Radical feminism

At the heart of radical feminism is the belief that men are responsible for and benefit from the exploitation of women. The analysis of patriarchy – the systematic domination of females by males – is of central concern to this branch of feminism. Patriarchy is viewed as a universal phenomenon that has existed across time and cultures. Radical feminists often concentrate on the family as one of the primary sources of women's oppression in society. They argue that men exploit women by relying on the free domestic labour that women provide in the home. As a group, men also deny women access to positions of power and influence in society.

Radical feminists differ in their interpretations of the basis of patriarchy, but most agree that it involves the appropriation of women's bodies and sexuality in some form. Shulamith Firestone (1970), an early radical feminist writer, argued that men control women's roles in reproduction and child-rearing. Because women are biologically able to give birth to children, they become dependent materially on men for protection and livelihood. This 'biological inequality' is socially organized in the nuclear family. Firestone wrote of a 'sex class' to describe women's social position and claimed that women can be emancipated only through the abolition of the family and the power relations which characterize it.

Other radical feminists point to male violence against women as central to male supremacy. According to such a view, domestic violence, rape and sexual harassment are all part of the systematic oppression of women rather than isolated cases with their own psychological or criminal roots. Even interactions in daily life – such as non-verbal communication, patterns of listening and interrupting, and women's sense of comfort in public – contribute to gender inequality. Moreover, popular conceptions of beauty and sexuality are imposed by men on women in order to produce a certain type of femininity. Social and cultural norms that emphasize a slim body and a caring, nurturing attitude towards men help to perpetuate

Does the concept of patriarchy adequately capture the diverse experiences and life chances of women across social class and ethnic groups? Is the category 'women' too broad to allow any useful work in social science?

women's subordination. The 'objectification' of women through the media, fashion and advertising turns women into sexual objects whose main role is to please and entertain men. Because patriarchy is a systemic phenomenon, they argue, gender equality can be attained only by overthrowing the patriarchal order.

Perhaps the main objection to radical feminism is that the concept of patriarchy is inadequate as a general explanation for women's oppression. Radical feminists have tended to claim that patriarchy has existed throughout history and across cultures – that it is a universal phenomenon. Such a conception does not leave room for historical or cultural variations. It also ignores the important influence that race, class or ethnicity may have on the nature of women's subordination. In other words, it is not possible to see patriarchy as a universal phenomenon; doing so risks biological reductionism – attributing all the complexities of gender inequality to a simple distinction between men and women.

Sylvia Walby has advanced an important reconceptualization of patriarchy (see 'Using your sociological imagination 15.2'). She argues that the notion of patriarchy remains a valuable and useful explanatory tool, providing that it is used in certain ways.

Black feminism

Do the versions of feminism outlined above apply equally to the experiences of both white and non-white women? Many black feminists and feminists from developing countries claim they do not. They argue that the main feminist schools of thought paradoxically incline towards essentialism, debating the experience of 'women' as a general category, while being oriented to the white, predominantly middle-class women in developed societies. It is not valid to generalize about women's subordination as a whole from the experience of one specific group. Moreover, the very idea that there is a 'unified' form of gender oppression experienced equally

15.2   Theorizing patriarchy

Sylvia Walby reasoned that the concept of patriarchy is essential to any analysis of gender inequality but agreed that many criticisms of the concept are valid. In *Theorizing Patriarchy* (1990), she presented a way of understanding patriarchy that is more flexible than its predecessors. It allows room for change over historical time and for consideration of ethnic and class differences.

For Walby, patriarchy is 'a system of social structures and practices in which men dominate, oppress and exploit women' (1990: 20). She sees patriarchy and capitalism as distinct systems which interact in different ways – sometimes harmoniously, sometimes in tension – depending on historical conditions. Capitalism, she argues, has generally benefited from patriarchy through the *sexual division of labour*. But, at other times, capitalism and patriarchy have been at odds with one another. For example, in wartime, when women have entered the labour market in great numbers, the interests of capitalism and patriarchy have not been aligned.

Walby recognizes that a weakness of early feminist theory was the tendency to focus on one 'essential' cause of women's oppression, such as male violence or women's role in reproduction. Because she is concerned with the depth and interconnectedness of gender inequality, she sees patriarchy as composed of six structures that are independent but interact with one another.

1 *Production relations in the household* Women's unpaid domestic labour, such as housework and childcare, is expropriated by her husband (or cohabitee).
2 *Paid work* Women in the labour market are excluded from certain types of work, receive lower pay, and are segregated in less skilled jobs.
3 *The patriarchal state* In its policies and priorities, the state has a systematic bias towards patriarchal interests.

4 *Male violence* Although male violence is often seen as composed of individualistic acts, it is patterned and systematic. Women routinely experience this violence and are affected by it in standard ways. The state effectively condones the violence with its refusal to intervene, except in exceptional cases.
5 *Patriarchal relations in sexuality* This is manifested in 'compulsory heterosexuality' and in the sexual double standard between men and women, in which different 'rules' for sexual behaviour apply.
6 *Patriarchal cultural institutions* A variety of institutions and practices – including media, religion and education – produce representations of women 'within a patriarchal gaze'. These representations influence women's identities and prescribe acceptable standards of behaviour and action.

Walby distinguishes two distinct forms of patriarchy. *Private patriarchy* is domination of women which occurs within the household at the hands of an individual patriarch. It is an exclusionary strategy, because women are essentially prevented from taking part in public life. *Public patriarchy*, on the other hand, is more collective in form. Women are involved in public realms, such as politics and the labour market, but remain segregated from wealth, power and status. Walby contends that, at least in Britain, there has been a shift in patriarchy – both in degree and in form – from the Victorian era to the present day. If at one time women's oppression was found chiefly in the home, it is now woven through society as a whole. As Walby quips: 'Liberated from the home, women now have the whole of society in which to be exploited.'

In recent years, Walby and other feminist theorists have suggested that the concept of patriarchy has become too easy for opponents of feminism to misrepresent as an ahistorical, unchanging theory of male domination. Instead, she suggests its replacement with the concept of 'gender regimes' (discussed in 'Classic Studies 15.2', p. 631), which 'means the same as the term "patriarchy"' (Walby 2011: 104), but more readily suggests changes over time, can be used to analyse local, national and international institutions, and is therefore less likely to be misinterpreted.

> **THINKING CRITICALLY**
>
> Taking each of Walby's six 'structures of patriarchy' in turn, what evidence is there of a shift towards public forms of patriarchy? What evidence is there that the movement of women into the public sphere has actually been *beneficial* for the majority of them?

by women across ethnic groups and social classes is problematic, and more recent studies have adopted an intersectional approach to inequality taking in gender, class and ethnic dimensions (Taylor and Hines 2012).

Dissatisfaction with existing forms of feminism has led to the emergence of a strand of thought which concentrates on the particular problems facing black women. For example, the American black feminist bell hooks (1997 – her name is written in lower-case) argues that some white feminist writers have seen black girls as having higher self-esteem than white girls, evidenced by their more confident and assertive manner. But hooks points out that these traits were instilled in girls by parents and teachers as a means of 'uplifting the race', and it does not follow that black girls who appear confident do not also feel worthless because of the social stigma attached to their skin colour or hair texture. Such apparently simple misunderstandings illustrate the underlying flaws in much mainstream feminist thinking, which black feminism aims to correct.

Black feminist writings tend to emphasize history – aspects of the past which inform the current problems facing black women. The writings of American black feminists emphasize the influence of the powerful legacy of slavery, segregation and the civil rights movement on gender inequalities in the black community. They point out that early black suffragettes supported the campaign for women's rights but realized that the question of race could not be ignored: black women were discriminated against on the basis of their race and gender. In recent years, black

women have not been central to the women's liberation movement in part because 'womanhood' dominated their identities much less than did concepts of race.

hooks has argued that explanatory frameworks favoured by white feminists – for example, the view of the family as a mainstay of patriarchy – may not be applicable in black communities, where the family represents a main point of solidarity against racism. In other words, the oppression of black women may be found in different locations compared with that of white women.

Black feminists contend that any theory of gender equality which does not take racism into account cannot be expected adequately to explain black women's oppression. Class dimensions are another factor that cannot be ignored in the case of many black women. Some black feminists hold that the strength of black feminist theory is its inherent intersectionality (Crenshaw 1991). Patricia Hill Collins (2000: 18) describes intersectionality as 'particular forms of intersecting oppressions, for example, intersections of race and gender, or of sexuality and nation'. Intersectionality can also be seen as a methodology, bringing into focus the interplay between race, class, gender, disability, and so on, which aims to generate more comprehensive and valid accounts of differently positioned women's divergent experiences. Black women may then be seen as multiply disadvantaged, on the basis of their colour, gender and social class position. When these three factors interact, they may reinforce and intensify one another (Brewer 1993).

Postmodernism and queer theory

Like black feminism, postmodern feminism challenges the idea that there is a unitary basis of identity and experience shared by all women. This strand draws on the cultural phenomenon of postmodernism in the arts, architecture, philosophy and economics which has its roots in the ideas of Jean-François Lyotard (1984), Jacques Derrida (1978, 1981) and Jacques Lacan (1995). Postmodern feminists reject the claim that there is a grand or overarching theory that can explain the position of women in society or, indeed, that there is a universal category of 'woman'. Consequently, they reject other theories of gender inequality based on patriarchy, race or class as 'essentialist' (Beasley 1999).

> Postmodernist approaches in sociology were introduced in chapter 3, 'Theories and Perspectives'.

Instead, postmodernism encourages the acceptances of many different standpoints as equally valid. Rather than an essential core to womanhood, there are many individuals and groups, all of whom have very different experiences (heterosexuals, lesbians, black women, working-class women, and more). This 'otherness' of different groups and individuals is celebrated in all its diverse forms, and the emphasis on the positive side of 'otherness' is a major theme. Postmodern feminism accepts that there are many truths and social constructions of reality.

As well as the recognition of difference, postmodern feminists stress the importance of 'deconstruction'. In particular, they have sought to deconstruct male language and masculine views of the world. In its place is an attempt to create fluid, open terms and language which more closely reflect women's experiences. Many postmodern feminists argue that men see the world in terms of pairs or binary distinctions ('good versus bad', 'right versus wrong', 'beautiful versus ugly').

Men, they argue, have cast male as normal and female as a deviation. Sigmund Freud, for example, saw women as effectively men who lacked a penis, maintaining that they envied males for possessing one. In this masculine worldview, the female is always cast in the role of 'other'. Deconstruction attacks all binary concepts, recasting their opposites in a new and positive manner.

> Freud's views on gender socialization are discussed in chapter 9, 'The Life Course'.

The idea that, theoretically, it is possible to separate gender from sexuality altogether marks the starting point for queer theory, which breaks with many conventional sociological ideas on identity. Queer theory is heavily influenced by poststructuralist thought, particularly that associated with Judith Butler (1990) and Michel Foucault (1978). In particular, queer theorists challenge the very concept of 'identity' as something that is relatively fixed or assigned to people by socializing agents. Drawing on Foucault, queer theorists argue that gender and sexuality, along with all of the other terms that come with these concepts, constitute a specific *discourse* rather than referring to something objectively real or 'natural'.

For example, in his work on the history of sexuality during the 1970s and 1980s, Foucault argued that the male homosexual identity today associated with gay men was not part of the dominant discourse on sexuality in the nineteenth century or previously. Therefore, this form of identity just did not exist for people until it became part of, or was created within, the discourses of medicine and psychiatry. Identities can then be seen as pluralistic, unstable and subject to change over time.

This radical perspective is also applied to the identities of 'gay' and 'lesbian', which, like all other forms of identification, have become 'essentialized' in society. Queer theory therefore challenges all fixed or apparently 'authentic' identities, including those which appear to be opposed to the dominant heterosexual norm. Although concepts such as 'gay' and 'lesbian' may well have been politically useful in pressing claims for equal rights, queer theorists argue that they remain tied to the binary opposition, as the 'other' to the norm of heterosexuality, which consistently favours the powerful 'heteronormative discourse' in society (Rahman and Jackson 2010: 128).

Queer theorists are also interested in all forms of unconventional sexuality – prostitution, bisexuality, transgender, and so on – many of which are 'heterosexual' rather than, or as well as, 'homosexual'. In this way, queer theory can be viewed as a radical social constructionism that explores the process of *identity creation* and re-creation insofar as this relates to sexuality and gender. Some theorists argue that every major sociological topic as well as other subjects should bring queer voices to the centre to challenge the heterosexual assumptions that underlie much contemporary thought (Epstein 2002).

Sociological critics argue that queer theory tends to study cultural texts (film, novels, and so on) and lacks empirical support. It also fails to explain the social-structural grounding of sexual and gender categories in the material life created by capitalist economics and male dominance represented by the concept of patriarchy. Jackson (2001) argues that a materialist feminism which focuses on social structures, relations and practices still offers a better perspective for understanding gender inequalities than culturally oriented postmodernism or queer theories. It may also be that many, maybe most, people do not experience their identity as being as fluid or shifting as queer theory suggests but, rather, as something quite firm and fixed (Edwards 1998). If so, then the radical constructionism of queer theorists perhaps overestimates the degree to which identities are open-ended and subject to change.

Similarly, despite the criticism that the basic two-sex, male/female divide is inaccurate and theoretically unsustainable, many areas of social life remain rooted in the distinction between men and women. For example, Woodward (2015: 50) notes that 'in the field of sport there are two sexes'. She argues that sport is structured by a sex/gender system that influences all aspects, from athletic prowess to regulatory authorities. Most sports have separate competitions for men and women (including tennis singles, athletics and golf) and, until 2000, the International Olympic Committee adopted universal sex testing designed to prevent the unfairness of men passing as women. Since 2000, any 'suspicious' athlete can be requested to have a medical examination as part of a 'gender verification' process.

Woodward argues that women who do not conform to conventional feminine appearance, behaviour and athletic performance are likely to be deemed 'suspicious'. The muscular physique and strong performances of an eighteen-year-old South African 800m runner, Caster Semenya, fell foul of these criteria, and she was subject to medical testing by a gynaecologist, a gender expert, an endocrinologist and a psychologist. The results were made public by the International Federation of Athletics Associations (IAAF), causing her much distress. Semenya was from a relatively poor, rural village with few sports facilities, and her school friends insisted there has never been any question of her being anything but a girl. The head of South African athletics suggested that this case was not only about gender but also involved racism: 'Who are white people to question the makeup of an African girl?' (cited in *The Guardian* 2009). Woodward (2015: 54) concludes that 'Gender-verification testing has largely failed to recognize the possibility of women's athletic achievement; if they are any good they must be men.'

Gender verification is a good example of the complex issues involved when trying to unravel sex and gender today. On the one hand, it demonstrates that the binary oppositions of sex/gender and male/female are not adequate for understanding the diversity of physical, social and cultural factors in play. Yet, on the other hand, the testing regime shows that these binary oppositions remain deeply embedded within many social institutions which continue to shape and reproduce conventional social norms and expectations.

Feminism and LGBT movements

The sociology of gender and sexuality did not pave the way for feminist and LGBT social movements; rather, the reverse is true. For a very long period sociology had very little to say about gender relations and sexuality, and it was not until feminist campaigns and movements began to raise new issues and, crucially, feminist and LGBT activists made their way into university departments that the discipline began to examine issues of sex, gender and sexuality. This section provides a whistle-stop tour of the chronological development of feminist and LGBT activism since the late nineteenth century.

Feminist movements

The long-term development of feminist thought and social movements seeking to promote the rights of women is convention-ally seen as passing through a series of three 'cycles of protest' or 'waves' (Whelehan 1999; Krolløke and Sørensen 2006). First-wave feminist movements arose in the context of industrialization in the late nineteenth and early twentieth centuries. First-wave femin-ism sought equal access to political power by extending voting rights to women on the same basis as men. The first wave also involved campaigns for equal opportunities for women and access to all of society's institutions, including higher education. Ideas and activi-ties of the first wave continued throughout the first half of the twentieth century.

Second-wave feminism originated within a broader movement for civil rights in the 1960s and 1970s, which involved students, black people's movements, lesbian and gay move-ments, and disabled people's movements (Valk 2008). It focused on ideas of women's 'liberation' and 'empowerment'. If the first-wave movement was influenced by liberal and socialist political ideals of equality before the law, the second wave was a more 'radical' movement for change. The idea that women as

a social group were oppressed by their male-dominated, patriarchal society and its institu-tions was a radical shift. A keynote slogan for second-wave feminism was 'the personal is political' – a challenge to the common-sense notion that the private world of family life and domesticity was just as much a political arena as the realm of public policy and formal poli-tics (David 2003).

Second-wave feminism was closely linked to academic feminist research and theoriz-ing, which produced a vibrant, activist move-ment that engaged in many public protests and demonstrations. Feminists campaigned, among many other things, against beauty contests, the use of (hetero)sexist language, male violence, both in the home and in aggres-sive national politics, and in favour of payment for housework as a valuable contribution to society. Such activism was underpinned by key feminist works, including Betty Friedan's (1963) *The Feminine Mystique*, Juliet Mitch-ell's (1971) *Women's Estate* and Shulamith Firestone's (1970) *The Dialectic of Sex: The Case for Feminist Revolution*. The second wave also gave rise to attempts to connect feminism with existing political positions and ideologies such as socialism, Marxism and liberalism and to find ways of bringing feminist issues into discourses of class exploitation, capitalism and equal legal rights.

The second wave of feminism focused on the similarities among all women, promot-ing the idea that women as a group (or a 'class') had much in common with one another, regardless of social class position or geographical location in the world. However, from the early 1980s onwards, the insistence on a universal women's experience came under challenge from within the movement. A new focus on difference emerged as black, working-class women and lesbian feminists asked whether it made sense to think that differently situated groups of women really could share essentially similar interests (hooks 1981). The early second-wave femin-ism was seen as the product mainly of white, middle-class women with a particular view of the world which should not be illegitimately portrayed as universal. Gayatri Spivak (1987) argued that it was naïve to suggest that relatively wealthy women in the developed countries could claim to speak on behalf of women in the much poorer regions of the developing world. By the mid-1990s, the universal ambition of early second-wave activists and theorists had effectively been ended by a new recognition that the fundamental characteristic of women's experience around the world was, in fact, difference.

Third-wave (or 'new') feminism developed in a very different social context to that faced by second-wave feminists (Gillis et al. 2007). Between the mid-1990s and the early twenty-first century, the world underwent major changes: globalization, the demise of Eastern European ('actually-existing') communism, multiculturalism, global terrorism, religious fundamentalisms, the digital revolution in communications, the spread of the Internet, and genetic biotechnologies. A new generation of women was growing up in a less ordered and predictable world than the previous one and embraced cultural diversity and difference.

> This new 'new' feminism is characterized by local, national and transnational activism, in areas such as violence against women, trafficking, body surgery, self-mutilation, and the overall 'pornofication' of the media. While concerned with new threats to women's rights in the wake of the new global world order, it criticizes earlier feminist waves for presenting universal answers or definitions of womanhood and for developing their particular interests into somewhat static identity politics. (Krolløke and Sørensen 2006: 17)

One recent theme is the attempt to reclaim the derogatory terms used to describe women – such as 'bitch' and 'slut' – rather than to try to prevent their use altogether. In 2011, for example, a series of large-scale protests called 'SlutWalks' spread from Canada across the world following comments from a Toronto police officer that, in order to be safe, women should stop 'dressing like sluts'. The protesters

Protests reclaiming words such as 'slut' and countering assumptions about what constitutes the 'correct' dress code for women is one example of third-wave feminist activism.

made extensive use of the word 'slut' in their banners and badges, effectively reclaiming the word as representing independent women who claim the right to dress however they like without being sexually harassed or raped. In this way, activists aim radically to alter the social meaning of the word, thereby completely reversing its previously negative meaning and defusing its stigmatizing impact.

Third-wave feminism is even more diverse than late second-wave forms, but it is important to acknowledge that many third-wave feminists have grown up with the benefit of the achievements of the second-wave movement. In this sense there is a line of development between the waves. In developed countries such as Britain, France and the USA, women's movements achieved many successes over the twentieth century during the first two waves of insurgent social movement activity. But some have argued that these countries have now moved into a 'post-feminist' phase (Tasker and Negra 2007) or that feminism is in a state of abeyance (but not dissolution), during which the movement maintains itself by engaging in educational and intellectual action aimed at becoming firmly established within the political system (Bagguley 2002; Grey and Sawyer 2008).

However, Walby claims that these are misreadings of contemporary feminist activism. There are many movements and groups around the world that actively campaign to mainstream gender equality into government policies, even though many of them do not identify themselves as 'feminist'. Because of this, they tend to be influential but relatively invisible compared with the spectacular direct actions of second-wave feminism. Walby (2011: 1) insists that 'Feminism is not dead. This is not a postfeminist era. Feminism is still vibrant, despite declarations that it is over. Feminism is a success, although many gender inequalities remain. Feminism is taking powerful new forms, which make it unrecognizable to some.'

One example of the kind of feminism Walby alludes to is the UK-based online Everyday Sexism Project (http://everydaysexism.com/), which enables women to post their personal experiences of sexist language, behaviour and harassment in their daily life. The site includes many posts from girls and young women in school settings, on public transport, at work and when simply walking around their home towns. In cataloguing everyday sexism, the project reminds us that moves towards formal gender equality have not yet fundamentally changed an existing sexist culture of male dominance. Similarly, male sexual harassment and rape of women on university campuses in the UK and the USA have been

the focus of research and campaign groups. A 2015 documentary film, *The Hunting Ground*, highlighted these issues using interviews with victims and university administrators from several US institutions. The film proved controversial as it suggested that some universities were slow to act when rape claims were made. Campaigns such as these show that third-wave feminism remains vibrant and continues to involve many young women who may not even consider themselves and their activity as 'feminist' in some traditional sense of that term.

The influence of feminist ideas and women's movements has been profound in Western societies but is increasingly challenging gender inequality in other areas of the world. Feminism is not merely an academic exercise, nor is it restricted to Western Europe and North America. In today's increasingly globalized world, there is a good chance that those who become active in the British women's movement will come into contact with women pursuing other feminist struggles overseas.

> Women's movements are discussed in chapter 21, 'Politics, Government and Social Movements'.

Although participants in women's movements have, for many years, cultivated ties to activists in other countries, the number and importance of such contacts have increased with globalization. A prime forum for the establishment of cross-national contacts has been the United Nations Conference on Women, held four times since 1975. Approximately 50,000 people – of whom more than two-thirds were women – attended the last conference, held in Beijing, China, in 1995. Delegates from 181 nations attended, along with representatives from thousands of non-governmental organizations. One attendee, Mallika Dutt, wrote in the journal *Feminist Studies*: 'For most women from the United States, Beijing was an eye-opening, humbling, and transformative experience. US women were startled by the sophisticated analysis and well-organized and powerful voices of women from other parts of the world' (Dutt 1996). The Platform for Action finally agreed to by the conference participants called on the countries of the world to address such issues as:

- the persistent and increasing burden of poverty on women
- violence against women
- the effects of armed or other kinds of conflict on women
- inequality between men and women in the sharing of power and decision-making
- stereotyping of women
- gender inequalities in the management of natural resources
- persistent discrimination against and violation of the rights of the girl child.

The 1995 conference heard that, in China, for example, women are working to secure equal rights, employment, a role in production and participation in politics, and that South African women played a major role in the fight against apartheid and are now working to improve conditions for the poorest groups of people in the country. Peruvian activists told delegates that they have been working for decades to create more opportunities for women to participate in public life, and, in Russia, women's protest was responsible for blocking the passage of legislation that would have encouraged women to stay home and perform 'socially necessary labour' (Basu 1995).

As the UN Conference shows, the uneven development of regions and societies means that many of the equal rights measures that people in the developed world now take for granted have yet to be won in the developing countries. It also illustrates how the global dimension of contemporary social life offers new opportunities for women's movements to join together in the ongoing campaign for gender equality.

LGBT civil rights

A good deal of recent research has explored the shifting social and legal position of same-sex relations in the world's societies, though there is a growing appreciation of the wider diversity of sexual minorities, including bisexual and transgender people. This section focuses on the changing position of lesbian and gay people and attitudes towards same-sex relations since the late 1960s.

Kenneth Plummer (1975) distinguished four types of homosexuality within modern Western culture. *Casual homosexuality* is a passing encounter that does not substantially structure a person's overall sexual life. Schoolboy crushes and mutual masturbation are examples. *Situated activities* refer to circumstances in which same-sex acts are regularly carried out but do not become an individual's overriding preference. In settings such as prisons or military camps, where men live without women, same-sex behaviour of this kind is common, regarded as a substitute for heterosexual behaviour rather than as preferable. *Personalized homosexuality* refers to individuals who have a preference for same-sex activities but are isolated from groups in which this is easily accepted. Same-sex relations here are secretive activities, hidden away from friends and colleagues. *Homosexuality as a way of life* refers to individuals who have 'come out' and made associations with others of similar sexual tastes a key part of their lives. Usually this involves belonging to subcultures in which same-sex activities are integrated into a distinct lifestyle. Such communities often provide the possibility of collective political action to advance the rights and interests of lesbians and gay men.

The proportion of the population (both male and female) who have had same-sex experiences or experienced strong inclinations towards the same sex is larger than those who follow an openly *gay* lifestyle. The term 'gay' has been used primarily to refer to male homosexuals, as in the widely used phrase 'gay and lesbian' people, though it is becoming increasingly used to describe lesbians.

Attitudes of intolerance towards lesbians and gay men have been so pronounced in the past that it is only during recent years that some of the myths surrounding the subject

THINKING CRITICALLY

Are you a feminist? What does this label mean in the twenty-first century? Is it possible to square the argument from queer theory that there is no universal experience or identity of 'woman' with the practical global feminist solidarity illustrated by the UN Conference on Women?

have been dispelled. Homophobia, a term coined in the late 1960s, refers to an aversion to or hatred of homosexuals and their lifestyles, along with behaviour based on these. Homophobia is a form of prejudice that is reflected not only in overt acts of hostility and violence but also in verbal abuse. In Britain, for example, terms such as 'fag' or 'queer' are used to insult heterosexual males. Although gay and lesbian relations are becoming more accepted, homophobia remains ingrained in many areas of Western societies, and 'hate crimes' such as violent assault and even the murder of gay men still occur.

See also the issues raised in the section 'Sexual orientation hate crimes' in chapter 20, 'Crime and Deviance'.

In 2008, a survey of teachers in the UK reported that the word 'gay' was the most widely heard term of abuse among schoolchildren of all ages, meaning 'lame' or 'rubbish' (BBC 2008a). Over recent decades, many governments have introduced legislation to punish and combat hate crimes. Hate crimes are attacks on members of social groups, such as gay men, lesbians, disabled people, homeless people and religious groups, purely on the basis of their group membership (Gerstenfeld 2010). A body of empirical research has shown that 'lesbians and gay men experience a wide spectrum of heterosexist violence, from physical assault to harassment and verbal abuse on a day-to-day basis' (Moran et al. 2004: 1). While such levels of violence were previously largely hidden from view, the concept of hate crime has helped to draw attention to continuing homophobic attitudes and abuse – a necessary first step to dealing with it.

There are enormous differences between countries in the degree to which homosexuality is legally punishable (see figure 15.2). In Africa, for example, male same-sex relations have been legalized in only a handful of countries, while lesbian relations are seldom mentioned in the law at all. In Asia and the Middle East, the situation is similar: gay sex is banned in the vast majority of countries, including all those that are predominantly Islamic. Europe, meanwhile, has some of the most liberal laws in the world: same-sex relationships have been legalized in nearly all countries, and many legally recognize same-sex partnerships or marriages.

THINKING CRITICALLY

Same-sex relationships seem to be more widely accepted today than in the past. Conduct a participant observation at a football match or in a nightclub or other public place, noting instances where 'gay', 'lesbian', and so on, are used as terms of abuse. What do you conclude from your evidence about same-sex acceptance?

Today there is a growing global movement for the rights of sexual minorities. The International Lesbian, Gay, Bisexual, Trans and Intersex Association (ILGA), founded in 1978, has more than 1,100 member organizations across every continent. It holds international conferences, supports lesbian and gay social movements around the world, and lobbies international organizations. For example, it convinced the Council of Europe to require all its member nations to repeal laws banning homosexuality. In general, active lesbian and gay social movements tend to thrive in countries that emphasize individual rights and liberal state policies (Frank and McEneaney 1999).

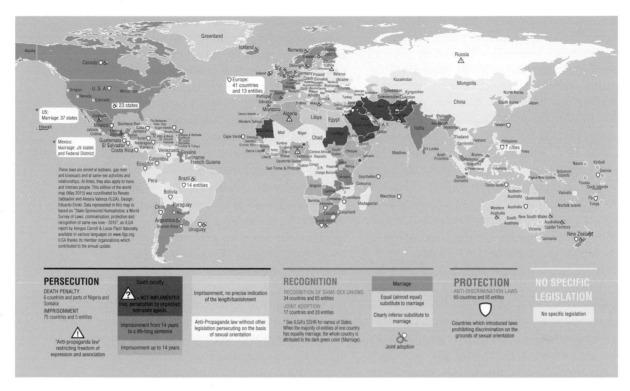

Figure 15.2 Legal status of lesbian, gay and bisexual people across the world

Source: Data from ILGA (2015).

Some kinds of gay male behaviour might be seen as attempts to alter the usual connection of masculinity with power – one reason, perhaps, why some in the heterosexual community find them threatening. Many gay men reject the image of 'effeminacy' popularly associated with them and deviate from this in two ways. One is through cultivating outrageous effeminacy – a 'camp' masculinity that parodies the stereotype and is often seen at Gay Pride events around the world. The other is by developing a 'macho' image. This also is not conventionally masculine; men dressed as motorcyclists or cowboys are again parodying masculinity, by exaggerating it, as in the 1970s band the Village People and their globally recognized anthem *YMCA* (Bertelson 1986).

Sociological research into the impact of the HIV/AIDS epidemic suggests that it challenged some of the main ideological foundations of

heterosexual masculinity. Sexuality and sexual behaviour became topics for public discussion, from safe-sex campaigns backed by government funds to media coverage. Most of all, the media-driven moral panic linking HIV infection to 'gay lifestyles' – however misguided and factually incorrect – increased the visibility of gay men and lesbians. Thus the epidemic called into question the universality of heterosexuality, demonstrating that alternatives exist to the traditional nuclear family (Redman 1996). In many ways, same-sex relations have become an accepted part of everyday society, with many countries passing legislation to protect the civil rights of LGBT people.

When South Africa adopted its new constitution in 1996, it became one of very few countries at that time constitutionally to guarantee the rights of homosexual people. Many countries in Europe now permit same-sex partners to register with the state in a civil ceremony, and the increasing trend is to extend marriage rights to same-sex couples. Such rights are important, as both civil partnerships and marriage grant rights to social security and pension benefits, tenancy rights, possible parental responsibility for a partner's children, full recognition for life

assurance, responsibility to provide reasonable maintenance for partners and children, and visiting rights in hospitals. The opportunity to make such a public demonstration of personal commitment has been popular. For example, in the twelve months following the introduction of the UK's civil partnership legislation in 2005, 18,059 gay and lesbian couples became civil partners, though since this initial surge of enthusiasm the number of civil partnerships contracted have fallen year on year (figure 15.3). This trend seems likely to continue, as England, Wales and Scotland legislated for same-sex marriage in 2014 and many couples now choose marriage rather than a civil partnership.

Nevertheless, public attitudes towards equal marriage rights differ widely within societies as well as across the world. Even within one geographical region such as Europe, a wide divergence of national opinion exists (see figure 15.4). When a Eurobarometer survey (European Commission 2006) asked respondents if they agreed with the statement 'Homosexual marriages should be allowed throughout Europe', 82 per cent in the Netherlands agreed, along with 71 per cent of Swedes, 69 per cent of Danes and 62 per cent of Belgians. However,

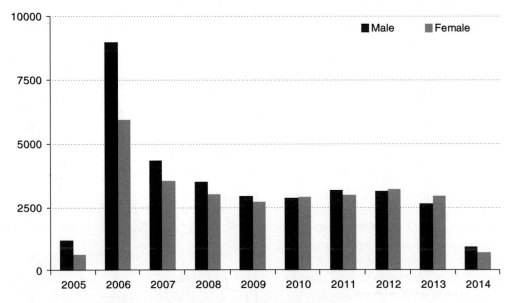

Figure 15.3   Number of UK civil partnerships, 2005–2014

Source: ONS (2015e).

in most of Eastern Europe, only a minority of people agreed – just 11 per cent in Romania, 15 per cent in Bulgaria and 17 per cent in Poland. In only eight of the then twenty-five European Union countries surveyed did 50 per cent or more agree with the statement – an interesting finding in a period when more and more governments are moving in the direction of equalizing marriage rights.

As 'public opinion' on sexuality is really quite diverse, with strong disagreements rooted in religious and political beliefs, legislative change and social policy do not always *follow* public opinion but can also contribute to *changing* it. For many LGBT people, the introduction of civil partnerships did not represent progress but instead reinforced the distinction between heterosexual and homosexual partnerships. Real progress requires legal marriage to be available for all on an equal basis, with full equality of status, rights and obligations. By mid-2015, twenty-two countries had introduced full marriage rights for same-sex couples, including the USA, Spain, the Netherlands, Norway and Sweden (Pew Research Center 2015).

Before the late 1960s, most gay men and lesbians hid their sexual orientation for fear that 'coming out' would cost them their jobs, families and friends and leave them open to discrimination and hate crime. Since the 1960s, though, many people have acknowledged their homosexuality openly, and in some areas the lives of lesbians and gay men have to a large extent been normalized (Seidman 1997). Manchester, New York, San Francisco, Sydney and many other large metropolitan areas around the world have thriving gay and lesbian communities. 'Coming out' may be important not only for the person who does so but for others in the larger society, as previously 'closeted' lesbians and gay men come to realize they are not alone and heterosexuals are forced to recognize that celebrities and friends they may have admired and respected are lesbian or gay.

It is clear that significant strides have been made, although discrimination and outright homophobia remain serious problems for many lesbian, gay, bisexual, transgender and intersex (LGBTI) people.

Globalization, human trafficking and sex work

In this chapter, most of our discussion has focused on issues within Western industrialized societies. But, in a global age, social movements are forging international networks and a global orientation in order to remain effective and combat continuing exploitation. In parts of the developing world, feminism means working to alleviate absolute poverty and to change traditional male attitudes, which favour large families and oppose contraception, while in the developed countries it means continuing campaigns for equality in employment, adequate childcare provision, and the ending of male violence towards women. One area which connects the concerns of women's movements in the global South and the North is the exploitation of women, particularly young women, in the global sex industry.

The global sex trafficking industry

'Sex tourism' exists in several areas of the world, including Thailand and the Philippines. Sex tourism in the Far East has its origins in the provision of prostitutes for American troops during the Korean and Vietnam wars. 'Rest and recreation' centres were built in Thailand, the Philippines, Vietnam, Korea and Taiwan. Some still remain, particularly in the Philippines, catering to regular shipments of tourists as well as to the military stationed in the region.

Today, package tours oriented towards prostitution draw men to these areas from Europe, the United States and Japan, often in search of sex with minors. However, such tours are illegal in more than thirty countries, among them the UK, Australia, Canada, Japan and the USA, under laws dealing with the 'extraterritorial accountability' of their citizens. Enforcement is patchy, though, and by 2004 Japan had made no prosecutions under its legislation, whereas

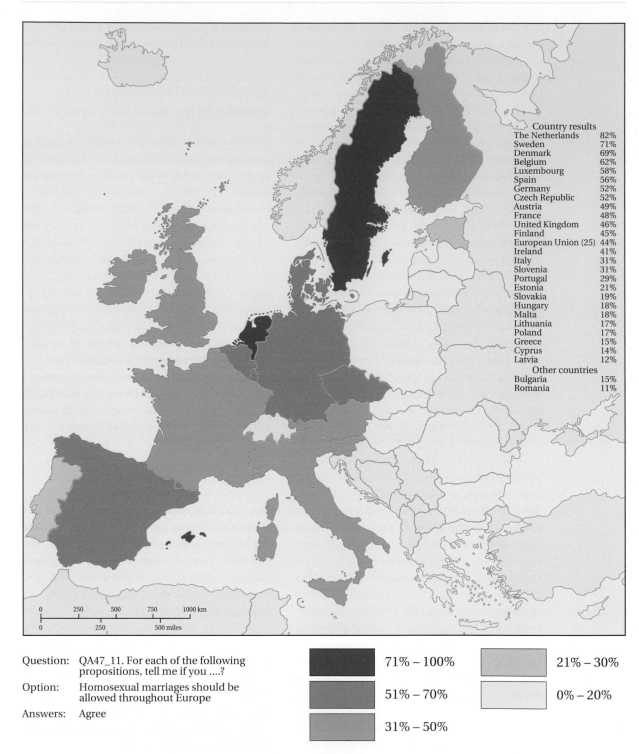

Country results
The Netherlands	82%
Sweden	71%
Denmark	69%
Belgium	62%
Luxembourg	58%
Spain	56%
Germany	52%
Czech Republic	52%
Austria	49%
France	48%
United Kingdom	46%
Finland	45%
European Union (25)	44%
Ireland	41%
Italy	31%
Slovenia	31%
Portugal	29%
Estonia	21%
Slovakia	19%
Hungary	18%
Malta	18%
Lithuania	17%
Poland	17%
Greece	15%
Cyprus	14%
Latvia	12%
Other countries	
Bulgaria	15%
Romania	11%

Question:	QA47_11. For each of the following propositions, tell me if you ....?
Option:	Homosexual marriages should be allowed throughout Europe
Answers:	Agree

71% – 100%   21% – 30%

51% – 70%   0% – 20%

31% – 50%

Figure 15.4 European attitudes to 'homosexual marriage', by country, 2006

Source: European Commission (2006).

the USA had made at least twenty prosecutions for sex tourism (Svensson 2006).

Cheaper global travel and the large differential in exchange rates between Asian and international currencies have made sex tourism more affordable and attractive to foreigners. Some desperate families force their own children into prostitution; other young people are unwittingly lured into the sex trade by responding innocently to advertisements for 'entertainers' or 'dancers'. Migration patterns from rural to urban areas are an important factor in the growth of the sex industry, as many women eager to leave their traditional and constraining hometowns grasp at any opportunity to do so (Lim 1998). One study of trafficking in South-Eastern Europe found that, in 2003–4, the majority of victims of trafficking were sexually exploited, though they were also used for labour, begging, delinquency and adoption (Surtees 2005: 12).

Governments have made some moves to legislate against trafficking. In the UK, the Nationality, Immigration and Asylum Act 2002 made trafficking for prostitution a criminal offence for the first time (extended to trafficking for domestic servitude and forced labour in 2004). Clearly, globalization enables the more rapid movement of people across national boundaries, and new patterns of movement are emerging. Relatively rich Westerners make short trips into developing countries to buy sex from relatively poor people, while relatively powerless Eastern European women are being forced into 'sex work' in Western Europe by organized gangs of, mostly male, people traffickers. The lives of many victims of the global sex industry are very far removed indeed from the 'liberated' and 'empowered' lap dancers and other sex workers often interviewed in tabloid newspapers.

Prostitution and sex work

Prostitution can be defined as performing sexual acts for monetary gain, and the word 'prostitute' began to come into common usage in the late eighteenth century. A key aspect of modern prostitution is that women and their

clients are generally unknown to one another. Although men may become 'regular customers', the relationship is not initially established on the basis of personal acquaintance. Prostitution is directly connected to the break-up of small-scale communities, the development of large impersonal urban areas, and the commercializing of social relations. In the newly developed urban areas, anonymous social connections were more easily established.

A United Nations resolution passed in 1951 condemned those who organize prostitution or profit from the activities of prostitutes, but it did not ban prostitution as such. Legislation on prostitution varies widely. In some countries, prostitution itself is illegal, while in other countries only certain types, such as street soliciting or child prostitution, are banned. Some national or local governments license officially recognized brothels or sex parlours – such as the 'Eros centres' in Germany or sex houses in Amsterdam. In October 1999 the Dutch Parliament turned prostitution into an official profession for the estimated 30,000 women who work in the sex industry. All venues where sex is sold can now be regulated, licensed and inspected by local authorities. However, only very few countries license male prostitutes.

Legislation against prostitution rarely punishes clients. In many countries, those who purchase sexual services are not arrested or prosecuted, and in court procedures their identities may be kept hidden. However, in Sweden (since 1999), Norway and Iceland (since 2009), legislation has been enacted which criminalizes the *buying* of sexual services, pimping, procuring and operating a brothel but does not criminalize the *selling* of sexual services. This is intended to shift the burden of stigma away from female prostitutes and onto the men who buy their services, which, it is hoped, will reduce the demand for prostitution in the long term.

There are far fewer studies of buyers than sellers of sexual services (but see Sanders 2008), and it is rare for anyone to suggest – as is often stated or implied about prostitutes – that clients are psychologically disturbed. The imbalance

Global Society 15.3   The global trade in female sex workers

International human trafficking, mostly of women and girls, has become a much more significant issue in recent years. For example, the trafficking of women into Western Europe to become prostitutes and sex workers is expanding rapidly. Although it not known exactly how many people become victims of human trafficking, the UN Office on Drugs and Crime estimates that there were some 140,000 trafficking victims in Europe in 2010 (UNODC 2010: 4). As EU borders expand with the entry of new countries such as Bulgaria and Romania, more transit routes become available for entry into wealthy Western European states or the new border countries become final destinations themselves for a growing sex industry.

Victims of human trafficking may also experience 'retrafficking' – being trafficked again (many within two years) after moving out of their original situation (Surtees 2005). Estimates of retrafficking vary widely and tend to be derived from relatively small-scale studies. Stephen-Smith (2008) suggested a rate of 21 per cent for women trafficked for sexual exploitation into the UK, while in India the comparable figure was 25.8 per cent in 2003 (Sen and Nair 2004). However, other studies have found retrafficking rates as low as 3 per cent in some regions of South-Eastern Europe but as high as 45 per in the case of trafficked people in Albania for forced labour (Surtees 2005).

Retrafficking can occur while victims are exiting or after they have escaped from a trafficked situation. This can mean a second episode of international trafficking across borders or internal trafficking within the country of origin on their return. Jobe's (2010: 11–12) analysis of seventy-nine cases of trafficked women, from the International Organization for Migration's (IOM) Human Trafficking Database, found that women, young adults and children were most vulnerable to retrafficking. This study also found that retrafficking was more likely when victims return home and face problems integrating into society, which is more probable:

- where trafficked people returned home and were members of minority ethnic groups, subject to discrimination
- where significant gender inequality exists in the country of origin
- where victims are from countries with ongoing or recent conflicts, or
- are refugees or displaced persons, or
- are between fifteen and twenty-five years old and lack family support, or
- have alcohol or drug dependency problems, or
- have psychological or psychosocial problems as a result of their trafficking experiences.

Although human trafficking affects both men and women, the available evidence from research studies shows a clear gendered pattern, with most of its victims being young women and girls. There is a need for much more research in this area, but it seems clear that trafficking and retrafficking is a particularly severe and harmful dimension of global gender inequality in the twenty-first century.

in research expresses an uncritical acceptance of orthodox stereotypes of sexuality, according to which it is 'normal' for men actively to seek a variety of sexual outlets, while those who cater for those 'needs' are condemned.

Sex work

Today, prostitution is more widely seen by sociologists as just one form of sex work. Sex work can be defined as the provision of sexual services in a financial exchange between consenting adults, though, of course, children (and adults) have historically been – and still are – forced into exploitative sex work. Sex workers, like prostitutes, are mostly female, and sex work includes at least all of the following: actors in pornographic films, nude modelling, striptease and lap dancers, live sex show workers, providers of erotic massage, phone sex workers, and home-based 'webcam sex' via the Internet, if this involves a financial exchange (Weitzer 2000).

A 2012 demonstration for the decriminalization of sex work in Kenya, which campaigners see as the key to better conditions for sex workers. Can feminists ever support the idea that prostitution and sex work are 'professions'?

The original 1970s concept of the sex worker aimed to destigmatize the working practices of prostitutes and other women in the sex industry. Provided that sexual services were exchanged between freely consenting adults, it was argued that such work should be treated like any other type of work and that prostitution, in particular, should be decriminalized. Prostitutes around the world today come mainly from poorer social backgrounds, as they did in the past, but they have now been joined by considerable numbers of middle-class women operating across the range of sex work described above, and many see what they do as providing useful and respectable sexual services. As 'Rona', a sex worker with ten years' experience, insists:

Yes, it is a profession – I believe a perfectly respectable profession, and should be viewed as such in the same way as a teacher, accountant or anyone else. . . . Why should the fact that I have chosen to work as a prostitute be considered any different from that of being a nurse, which I once was? There should be no social stigma attached. I work in clean comfortable surroundings, have regular medical check-ups and pay taxes like anyone else. ('Rona' 2000)

The idea of a trade union for sex workers may appear strange, but, in the context of ensuring health and safety at work, legal support in disputes over pay and conditions, and access to training or retraining for those who wish to leave the industry, these issues lie at the centre of mainstream trade union activity. Sex workers point out that union collectivization may help to root out exploitation and abuse. For example, formed in 2000 and based in London, the International Union of Sex Workers (IUSW) sees unionization as the first step towards the professionalization of sex work. In 2002 it became affiliated to the GMB, a large general trade union in the UK. The IUSW campaigns for the decriminalization of sex work involving consenting adults and the right of workers to form professional associations or unions.

Nevertheless, the concept of sex work remains controversial. Many feminists actively campaign against the sex industry, seeing it as degrading to women, strongly linked to sexual abuse and drug addiction, and ultimately rooted in women's subordination to men. Yet, more recently, sex work has been reappraised by some feminists, who argue that many, though by no means all, women sex workers earn a good living, enjoy what they do, and do not fit the stereotype of the poor, sexually abused drug addict forced into prostitution by their circumstances (O'Neill 2000). For these women, sex work provides worthwhile jobs that are relatively well paid. Many sex workers see themselves as independent women who have taken control of their lives, which makes them little different from successful women in other employment sectors (Chapkis 1997).

In a study of lap dancers in England, Teela Sanders and Kate Hardy (2011) found that 87 per cent were educated to at least further education level, about one-quarter had a university degree and a third were students. For 60 per cent, dancing was their sole form of income, though almost 40 per cent had other forms of work and income. Sanders and Hardy report that job satisfaction was 'strikingly high', with a large majority (76.4 per cent) of the women saying they felt 'happy' or 'very happy' with their work. More than 70 per cent also reported positive aspects of the job as the ability to choose the hours of work, earning more money than in other jobs, getting paid immediately, allowing

them to become independent and keep fit, and with the job combining 'fun' and 'work'. One dancer summed up the benefits as 'Better money. No commitment. Leave when you want to leave. Drink what you want.'

However, significant proportions of dancers in the study also reported negative aspects, such as uncertainty of income, a lack of career prospects, having to keep the job a secret, rude and abusive customers, losing respect for men, and feeling bad about themselves. Some also found the job emotionally difficult to handle and reported that some clubs were dangerous or exploitative. Clearly, the experience of lap dancers is not uniform or wholly positive, but, for most, the positive aspects do seem to outweigh the negatives, giving credence to the idea that, in some forms of sex work at least, the stereotypical image of young women from poor backgrounds being forced into paid sexual activity in order to survive is no longer an accurate description.

Lap dancing, however, unlike prostitution, does not usually involve physical contact with customers and may therefore not be representative of the experience of other sex workers. Indeed, given the wide diversity of sex work, it would be unwise to try to generalize about its apparently exploitative or empowering character. Rather, it will be necessary for researchers to investigate and compare the different types if we are to understand better the attractions and risks of sex work in the twenty-first century.

> **THINKING CRITICALLY**
>
> If female sex workers express a general satisfaction with sex work, explain why it is legitimate for feminists to argue that it is exploitative and to campaign against it.

Conclusion

Getting to grips with debates on sex, gender and sexuality today is undoubtedly more difficult than it was just thirty years ago.

Theoretical positions and arguments seem to be in constant flux, as is the language and terminology within the field of gender studies. For new students to sociology, this situation can be off-putting. But we have to remember that the reason why this field has become so complex is not because sociologists are a naturally argumentative group of academics (though they are). Rather, it is because the pace of social change has forced sociologists to devise new concepts and theories to try to understand the shifting situation on the ground.

To take just one example, the separation of sex and gender which characterized the second-wave feminism of the 1970s appeared to offer a radical solution to the identification of men and women purely on the basis of their biological sex at birth. Recognizing that social norms of femininity and masculinity changed over time and differed across societies allowed sociologists to trace their development and demonstrated that gendered behaviour was not merely the product of biology. For a while the sex/gender distinction provided a settled paradigm for researchers which produced some valuable findings. But today this previously radical approach is itself viewed as falling into essentialism, uncritically accepting that sex is biologically given while only gender is subject to change. Perspectives and concepts in this field can seem dated very quickly.

As our final example of sex work and human trafficking shows, though, not everything in the global social world is fluid and changing. Male dominance and the exploitation of children and young women continues apace in the twenty-first century, but now on a truly global scale. The progress towards gender and sexual equality that has been made in the developed world – and this is considerable – has generally not been mirrored in developing countries. While theories of gender and sexuality must adapt to a rapidly changing world, empirical sociology needs to maintain its focus on longstanding issues of power, inequality and discrimination if we are to understand the impact of global processes on gender inequalities across the relatively rich and poor countries of the world.

Chapter review

1   What is the difference between sex and gender?

2   'Sex and gender are *both* socially constructed *and* can be shaped and altered in various ways.' With examples, explain the consequences for people's gender identity.

3   With examples, explain what is meant by gender socialization. What problems are there with conventional accounts of gender socialization?

4   In your own words, explain Connell's theory of the gender order. What evidence is there that this order is changing in our global age?

5   'Same-sex relationships are now widely accepted in society.' What evidence is there from the chapter to support or refute this statement?

6   Explain the difference between transgender and cisgender. How has the heightened public profile of transgender people challenged the embedded heteronormativity of modern societies?

7   Mainstream feminist approaches all reject the idea that gender inequality is somehow 'natural'. What are the main differences between liberal feminism, socialist feminism and radical feminism? How do these three positions make use of the concept of patriarchy?

8   Why are postmodern and poststructural feminism and queer theory seen as radically different from earlier theories of gender and gender inequality?

9   What are the main differences between second- and third-wave feminism? Does the third wave represent 'post-feminism' or a reinvigoration of feminist activism?

10   What is 'sex work'? Discuss the debate within feminism as to whether it should be accepted as a form of work or challenged because it is exploitative of women.

Research in practice

One longstanding aspect of gender inequality that has proved very resistant to change is the gendered division of domestic labour. Even in the age of post-feminism, housework, it seems, is still considered to be 'women's work'. As more women move into paid employment, some earning more than their male partners, will men finally do their share of household tasks? Read the following article, which looks at this issue, then answer the questions: Lyonette, C., and Crompton, R. (2015) 'Sharing the Load? Partners' Relative Earnings and the Division of Domestic Labour', *Work, Employment and Society*, 29(1): 23–40.

1   What type of research is this? Describe the research methods used. Was the sample appropriate for the questions asked?

2   What do the authors conclude from the existing literature about the relationship between earnings and domestic labour in dual-earner couples?

3   How many men and women reported that the man was 'mainly responsible for housework'?

4   What are 'the myth of male incompetence' and 'gender essentialism'? How do these ideas impact on both the 'undoing' and the 'doing' of gender?

5   What do the authors conclude about the relationship between women's earnings and the gendered division of domestic labour?

Thinking it through

The development of postmodern feminism and queer theory can be seen as part of a more general 'cultural turn' in sociology. The latter saw radical forms of social constructionism rooted in the idea of the power of discourses in shaping social life gaining ground over the older, materialist sociological theories such as Marxism. However, not everyone sees this turn as positive, and Stevi Jackson argues, in the article below, that culturalist perspectives are, in some ways, inferior to materialist analyses. Read the article, noting the paper's main criticisms of cultural theories: Jackson, S. (2001) 'Why a Materialist Feminism is (Still) Possible – and Necessary', *Women's Studies International Forum*, 24 (3–4): 283–93.

Explain what the author means by 'materialist feminism', why she considers a 'sociological perspective' to be fruitful, and how she redefines 'social constructionism'. Overall, do you think this paper is theoretically persuasive?

Society in the arts

1   In recent years there has been a trend for television programmes about or involving transgender people and characters, particularly in the USA. On the surface this appears to be one sign of the acceptance of transgender people in society. However,

some critical voices warn that the 'marriage' of transgender celebrities and actors with the medium of television may not be altogether productive for the wider transgender community. Read this piece on the subject: www.huffingtonpost.com/terri-lee-ryan/are-there-too-many-transg_b_7845150.html.

What exactly is the problem, according to this author, with television's representations of transgender people and issues? Watch one or two episodes from the various series identified. Are issues of social class ignored? Do they deal with transphobic hate crimes or conflict with non-trans people? Are any transgender actors involved? Are there common themes across the different series? What is your overall assessment of the way transgender people are represented on television?

2   Watch the documentary film *Miss Representation* (2011), directed by Jennifer Siebel Newsom (official trailer on YouTube here: www.youtube.com/watch?v=Nw_QEuAvn6I). This movie looks at gender inequality in the US media and society, asking questions about the impact of persistent one-dimensional images and representations of women and the underpresentation of women within the media industry. Write a 1,000-word review of the film, linking its main evidence to sociological theories from this chapter. Make sure the conclusion comes to an overall evaluation of the central thesis that the mass media make a significant contribution to reproducing gender inequality in society. Is this the case?

Further reading

A reliable introduction to the study of gender and sexuality in sociology is Momin Rahman and Stevi Jackson's (2010) *Gender and Sexuality: Sociological Approaches* (Cambridge: Polity). Amy S. Wharton's (2011) *The Sociology of Gender: An Introduction to Theory and Research* (2nd edn, Oxford: Wiley-Blackwell) looks at gender through individual, interactional and institutional perspectives. Victoria Robinson and Diane Richardson's (2015) *Introducing Gender and Women's Studies* (4th edn, Basingstoke: Palgrave Macmillan) offers a comprehensive and up-to-date guide to issues of gender alongside the full range of feminist theorizing.

Judith Lorber's (2012) *Gender Inequality: Feminist Theories and Politics* (5th edn, Oxford: Oxford University Press) provides an excellent chronological account of the development of feminist theories of gender inequality. Raewyn Connell (2014) offers a rigorous yet very accessible overview of the social scientific study of gender in *Gender: In World Perspective* (3rd edn, Cambridge: Polity). A stimulating assessment of the main achievements and future of feminism as a movement for change is provided in Sylvia Walby's (2011) *The Future of Feminism* (Cambridge: Polity).

Finally, anyone looking for a reference work could consult *Gender: The Key Concepts* (2012), edited by Mary Evans and Carolyn H. Williams (Abingdon: Routledge).

For a collection of original readings on social inequalities, see the accompanying, ***Sociology: Introductory Readings*** **(3rd edn, Cambridge: Polity, 2010).**

Internet links

@ **Additional information and support for this book at Polity:**
www.politybooks.com/giddens

@ **The Women's Library – has lots of electronic and other resources on women's history in the UK:**
www.lse.ac.uk/library/collections/featuredcollections/womenslibrarylse.aspx

@ **The Centre for Women's Studies – a research centre based at the University of York, UK:**
www.york.ac.uk/inst/cws

The Weeks Centre for Social and Policy Research – based at London's South Bank University. Covers a lot of areas including gender and sexuality:
www.lsbu.ac.uk/research/research-interests/sites/weeks-centre

@ **Queer Resource Directory – a gateway to many resources on religion, youth, health and more:**
www.qrd.org

@ **Eldis – gender issues in developing countries:**
www.eldis.org/gender

Voice of the Shuttle – many gender and sexuality studies resources at the University of California:
http://vos.ucsb.edu/browse.asp?id=2711

ILGA – the International Lesbian, Gay, Bisexual, Trans and Intersex Association:
http://ilga.org

@ **Feminist.com – US site with lots of resources and ideas:**
www.feminist.com

CHAPTER 16

Race, Ethnicity and Migration

Contents

Twenty-year-old Ariana Miyamoto (in the centre above) was delighted to be crowned Miss Universe Japan in 2015. Ariana was born in Japan, has lived there all her life, and Japanese is her first language, but her success was not universally welcomed in Japan. For many Japanese people her skin colour and appearance mean she is not an appropriate person to represent Japan at the Miss Universe contest. Ariana's mother is Japanese, while her black father is from Arkansas in the USA. In Japan this makes her 'hafu' or 'half' rather than 'fully' Japanese. Some Twitter users openly asked, 'Is it OK to select a hafu as Miss Japan?' Another said, 'It makes me uncomfortable to think she is representing Japan.' Ariana also says she is more likely to be congratulated in the streets by non-Japanese tourists than by local Japanese people (Wingfield-Hayes 2015).

Derogatory terms for people of mixed race are not unusual and have been used in many other cultures. Until the 1970s in Britain, for example, the term 'half-caste' was widely used with reference to the children of white and black parents. Half-caste was also commonly used in British colonies around the world. In Australia the term was used to describe children born to white colonists and indigenous Aboriginals. And although these instances may appear to be simply descriptive, they were associated with ideas of racial purity ('caste' is derived from the Latin word *castus*, meaning 'pure') and the weakening of the supposedly superior white race through racial mixing. Thus, the concept of half-caste was used in negative ways and mixed-race children were stigmatized and treated as outsiders.

Ariana Miyamoto recounts how her best friend at school – also hafu – committed suicide, in part, she says, because his 'foreign' appearance meant that he was always considered an outsider in his own country: 'We used to talk a lot about how hard it was to be hafu. He wanted to talk about why we are excluded from others three days before he died. He used to say it was very difficult for him to live.' Despite this, Miyamoto argues that, in the relatively homogeneous Japanese society, the concept of hafu has allowed her to better understand and embrace her own identity: 'There is no word like hafu outside Japan, but I think we need it here. In order for us mixed kids to live in Japan, it is indispensable and I value it.' We also have to remember that she did win the Japanese contest, which suggests that the stigma associated with hafu status may be starting to break down.

Miyamoto's experience illustrates something of the complexity of ideas of race, ethnicity, nationality and identity that circulate within and across societies. Her mixed-race parentage is perceived as a 'problem', but is 'Japanese' a racial category, an ethnic group or simply a type of nationality? What are the differences between 'race', 'ethnicity' and 'nationality'? Hafu seems to refer to a small group of mixed-race people within a homogeneous majority population, but is this true? Given the long history of cross-cultural contact and the continuous mixing of peoples, is it more accurate to say that most of us are, in some way, 'hafu', while racially pure groups are in fact the tiny minority?

As we will see in this chapter, discrimination on grounds of 'race' or ethnicity has long been and remains a major social problem around the world, in both the developed and the developing countries. It is not possible to do justice to the many forms of ethnicity and ethnic divisions around the world in such a short chapter. Hence, our primary focus will be on the situation in the UK, though we will draw on a range of examples from other countries where necessary. After considering the ways in which the concepts of race and ethnicity are used in academic sociology and the wider society, we look at prejudice, discrimination and racism and then outline sociological theories that help to explain their persistence. One question we address is why racial and ethnic divisions can turn into conflict. From there, the chapter covers ethnic diversity, models of integration – including multiculturalism – and examples of ethnic conflict. The final section takes in the increasing scale and significance of global migration and geographical mobility, which are continually reshaping relations between ethnic groups as well as increasing society's cultural diversity (Vertovec 2007).

Key concepts

Race

Race is one of the most complex concepts in sociology, not least because its supposedly 'scientific' basis is now rejected by most scholars. Despite this, there remains widespread, everyday use of the term, as many people still accept that human beings can be separated into biologically distinct 'races'. Since the late eighteenth century, there have been numerous attempts by scholars and governments to establish categories of people based on skin colour or racial type. These schemes have never been consistent, with some identifying just four or five major races and others recognizing as many as three dozen. This diversity does not provide a reliable basis for social scientific research.

In many ancient civilizations, distinctions were often made between social groups on visible skin colour differences, usually lighter and darker skin tones. However, before the modern period, it was more common for perceived distinctions to be based on tribal or kinship affiliations. These groups were numerous and the basis of their classification was relatively unconnected to modern ideas of race, with its biological or genetic connotations. Instead, classification rested on cultural similarity and group membership. Theories of racial difference linked to supposedly scientific methods were devised in the mid- to late eighteenth and early nineteenth centuries and used to justify the emerging social order, as Britain and other European nations became imperial powers ruling over subject territories and overseas populations.

Count Joseph Arthur de Gobineau (1816–82), sometimes called the 'father' of modern racism, proposed the existence of just three races: white (*Caucasian*), black (*Negroid*) and Yellow (*Mongoloid*). According to de Gobineau, the white race possessed superior intelligence, morality and willpower, and these inherited qualities underpinned the spread of Western influence across the world. The black race, by contrast, was the least capable, marked by an animal nature, a lack of morality and emotional instability. Such wild generalizations seem implausible and racist today, but they have been influential. For example, race supremacy ideas were part of the ideology of the German National Socialist Party as well as racist groups such as the Ku Klux Klan in the USA. Race may be a thoroughly discredited scientific concept, but the material consequences of people's belief

in distinct races are a telling illustration of W. I. Thomas's (1928) famous theorem that, 'when men [*sic*] define situations as real, then they are real in their consequences.'

Many biologists report that there are no clear-cut races, just a range of physical variations in the human species. Differences in physical type arise from population inbreeding, which varies according to the degree of contact between different groups. The genetic diversity *within* populations that share visible physical traits is just as great as the diversity *between* those populations. As a result of such findings, the scientific community has virtually abandoned the concept of race. UNESCO (1982: 3) recognized these findings in its 1978 Declaration on Race and Racial Prejudice, which noted that 'All human beings belong to a single species and are descended from a common stock. They are born equal in dignity and rights and all form an integral part of humanity.'

Some social scientists argue that race is nothing more than an ideological construct whose use in academic circles perpetuates the commonly held belief that it has a basis in reality (Miles 1993). It should therefore be abandoned. Others disagree, claiming that 'race' still has meaning for many people and cannot be ignored. In historical terms, 'race' has been an extremely important concept used by powerful social groups as part of their strategies of domination (Spencer 2014). For example, the contemporary situation of African Americans in the USA cannot be understood without reference to the slave trade, racial segregation and persistent racial ideologies (Wacquant 2010). Racial distinctions are more than ways of describing human differences – they are also important factors in the reproduction of patterns of power and inequality. Hence, 'race' remains a vital, if highly contested concept, which sociologists have to explore wherever it is in use. For this reason you will come across sociological papers and books that use the word 'race', but placed in inverted commas to reflect its unscientific, problematic, but still commonplace usage in society.

Peace processes are discussed in detail in chapter 22, 'Nations, War and Terrorism'.

THINKING CRITICALLY

How is the term 'race' used in your society? Examine some newspaper and other media content noting how 'race' is used. Is it used with reference to biological characteristics, for instance, or aspects of particular cultures?

The process through which understandings of race are used to classify individuals or groups of people is called racialization.

Global Society 16.1 Racial segregation in apartheid South Africa

From 1948 until the first free multiracial election in 1994, South Africa was governed by apartheid – a state-enforced regime of racial segregation. The apartheid system classified people into one of four categories: *white* (descendants of European immigrants), *black* (native South African people), *coloured* (those of mixed race) and *Asian* (immigrants from China, Japan and elsewhere). The white South African minority – about 13 per cent of the population – ruled over the non-white majority. Non-whites could not vote and therefore had no representation at national level. Racial segregation – which had been introduced in the late nineteenth century – was now enforced at all levels of society, from public places such as washrooms, beaches and railway carriages to residential neighbourhoods and schools. Millions of black people were corralled into so-called homelands, well away from the main cities, and worked as migrant labourers in gold and diamond mines.

Apartheid was encoded in law but enforced through violence and brutality. The governing National Party used law enforcement and security services to suppress all resistance to the apartheid regime. Opposition groups were outlawed, political dissidents were detained without trial and often tortured, and peaceful demonstrations frequently ended in violence. After decades of international condemnation, economic and cultural sanctions, and growing internal resistance, the apartheid regime began to weaken. When F. W. de Klerk became president in 1989, he inherited a country already deep in crisis. In 1990, de Klerk lifted the ban on the main opposition party, the African National Congress (ANC), and freed its leader, Nelson Mandela, who had been imprisoned for twenty-seven years. Following a series

Two players from the multi-race South African national football team. Today's South Africa was a natural choice to host the 2010 FIFA World Cup, welcoming diverse teams from across the world on the basis of equality.

of complex negotiations, South Africa's first national election took place on 27 April 1994; the ANC won, with 62 per cent of the vote. Nelson Mandela became South Africa's first post-apartheid president.

But South Africa was a deeply divided society after decades of white rule. Ethnic tensions flared up in violent outbreaks and the country was in desperate need of reconciliation. Unemployment and poverty were also widespread: 20 million people lived without electricity, more than half of the black population was illiterate, and infant mortality rates were about ten times higher among blacks than whites. A new constitution was produced in 1996 which outlawed discrimination on the basis of race, ethnic or social origin, religion and belief, sexual orientation, disability or pregnancy. The new government also brought dissenting political groups, such as the Zulu-based Inkatha Freedom Party (IFP), into government to reduce ethnic and political tension.

From 1996 to 1998, the Truth and Reconciliation Commission (TRC) held hearings across South Africa to expose and examine human rights abuses under apartheid. More than 21,000 testimonies were recorded during the process, laying bare the brutal apartheid regime. However, those who had committed crimes were offered amnesty in return for honest testimony and the 'full disclosure' of information. The apartheid government was identified as the main perpetrator of human rights abuses, though transgressions by other organizations, including the ANC, were also noted. Mandela stood down in 1999, but the ANC won the next four national elections, in 1999, 2004, 2009 and 2014, and has been continuously in government since the apartheid era was ended.

Historically, some groups of people came to be labelled as distinct on the basis of naturally occurring physical features. From the fifteenth century onwards, as Europeans came increasingly into contact with people from different regions of the world, attempts were made to categorize and explain both natural and social phenomena. Non-European populations were racialized in opposition to the European 'white race'. In some instances, this racialization took on codified institutional forms, as in the case of slavery in the American colonies and apartheid in South Africa. More commonly, however, everyday social institutions became racialized in a *de facto* manner.

Racialization has also occurred *within* Europe – for example, in relation to the discrimination against and exclusion of Roma populations in European nation-states. In a racialized system, aspects of individuals' daily lives – employment, personal relations, housing, healthcare, education and legal representation – are shaped and constrained by their own positions within that system.

Ethnicity

While the idea of race implies something fixed and biological, ethnicity is a source of identity whose basis lies in society and culture. Ethnicity refers to a type of social identity related to ancestry (perceived or real) and cultural differences which become effective or active in certain contexts. It has a longer history than 'race' and is a concept closely related to those of nation and 'race', as all three refer to some idea of a class or category of people (Fenton 2010: 14–15). Like nations, ethnic groups are 'imagined communities' whose existence depends on the self-identification of their members. Members of ethnic groups may see themselves as culturally distinct from other groups and are seen by them, in return, as different. In this sense, 'Ethnic groups always co-exist with other ethnic groups' (Pilkington 2015: 73). Several characteristics may serve to distinguish ethnic groups, but the most usual are language, a sense of shared history or ancestry, religion, and styles of dress or adornment. We should also note that both minority and majority groups in a society are 'ethnic groups'. Failure to acknowledge the ubiquity of ethnicity results in more powerful groups perceiving themselves as simply the 'natural' norm from which all other minority ethnic groups diverge.

Ethnic differences are learned, a point that seems self-evident until we remember how often some groups are regarded as 'born to rule' or 'naturally lazy', 'unintelligent', and so on. Indeed, when people use the term 'ethnicity', very often they do so (as with 'race') when referring to ascriptive characteristics such as skin colour, blood ties or place of birth. Yet there is nothing innate about ethnicity; it is a social phenomenon that is produced and reproduced over time. For many people, ethnicity is central to their individual and group identity, but for others it is irrelevant and, for still others, seems significant only during times of conflict or social unrest. Ethnicity can provide an important thread of continuity with the past and is often kept alive through the practices of cultural traditions. For instance, third-generation Americans of Irish descent may proudly identify themselves as Irish American despite having lived their entire lives in the United States.

Sociologists favour the concept of 'ethnicity' over 'race' because it carries no inaccurate biological reference. However, 'ethnicity' can also be problematic if it implies a contrast with some 'non-ethnic' norm. In Britain, for example, 'ethnicity' is commonly used in the press and among the wider white British population to refer to cultural practices and traditions that differ from 'indigenous' (that is, 'non-ethnic') British practices. The term 'ethnic' is applied in this way to cuisine, clothing, music and neighbourhoods to designate practices that are 'non-British'. Using ethnic labels in this manner risks producing divisions between 'us' and 'them', where certain parts of the population are seen as 'ethnic' while others are not. In fact, ethnicity is an attribute possessed by *all* members of a population, not just certain segments of it.

There is a further problem with the concept of ethnicity as it has come to be used in sociol-

ogy. Although the concept is widely preferred, in practice, many studies make use of the idea of actually existing and identifiable 'ethnic groups'. This is particularly the case in studies of ethnic conflicts, such as that between Serbs, Albanians and Croats in the former Yugoslavia. This 'groupism' represents 'the tendency to take discrete, bounded groups as basic constituents of social life, chief protagonists of social conflicts, and fundamental units of social analysis' (Brubaker 2006: 8). It also suggests that such conflicts are actually *caused by* ethnic or cultural differences.

Yet if ethnicity really is entirely a social creation which becomes effective only in certain situations and at certain times, then we cannot accept the notion of an ethnic group as a 'primordial' or essential thing in itself, unrelated to social context (A. D. Smith 1998). Of course, in real-world conflicts, participants may well perceive that they are acting on behalf of or to defend a cohesive and objectively real ethnic group. However, the sociologist's task is not to accept these perceptions at face value but to understand how and why this hardening of ethnic identification happens, under what circumstances and with what consequences.

> The concept of 'identity' is introduced and discussed in chapter 8, 'Social Interaction and Daily Life'.

Minority ethnic groups

The notion of minority ethnic groups (often 'ethnic minorities') is widely used in sociology and is more than a merely numerical distinction. There are many minority groups in a statistical sense, such as people over 6 feet tall or those wearing shoes bigger than size 12, but these are not minority ethnic groups according to the sociological concept. In sociology, members of a minority ethnic group are disadvantaged when compared with the dominant group – a group possessing more wealth, power and prestige – and have some sense of *group solidarity*, of belonging together. The experience of being the subject of prejudice

16.1 Black identity and the 'new ethnicities'

Use of the term 'black' to describe individuals and groups has undergone fundamental transformation since the 1960s and remains highly contested. In the UK until the 1960s, non-white people were conventionally described as 'coloured', and, for some time after that, 'black' was a derogatory label assigned by whites as a term of abuse. Only in the mid-1960s did Americans and Britons of African descent begin to reclaim the term 'black' for themselves. The slogan 'black is beautiful' and the motivational concept of 'black power' were central to the black liberation movement in the USA. These ideas were used to counter the symbolic domination of 'whiteness' over 'blackness'.

In the UK, the concept of 'black' as a collective identity became increasingly used in relation to various African, Caribbean and South Asian communities. Hall (2006 [1989]) argues that adopting a black identity was the first stage in a cultural politics of resistance that referenced a common experience of racism across various minority ethnic groups in Britain. This 'moment' or stage produced a certain unity of experience, a 'necessary fiction' that was and continues to be politically useful in struggles against racism and discrimination. According to Hall (1991: 55),

> That notion [black identity] was extremely important in the anti-racist struggles of the 1970s: the notion that people of diverse societies and cultures would all come to Britain in the fifties and sixties as part of that huge wave of migration from the Caribbean, East Africa, the Asian subcontinent, Pakistan, Bangladesh, from different parts of India, and all identified themselves politically as Black.

Nonetheless, this conception of 'black' *is* a fiction that simply reverses the racist message that 'white is good, black is bad' without moving beyond the polarization (Procter 2004: 123). Modood (1994) argued that 'black' was used too loosely and overemphasized oppression based on skin colour, implying an 'essential' identity which does not exist in people's real experience. From the late 1980s, some scholars and members of minority ethnic groups saw this unified black identity as silencing the experience of South Asian people who sought to draw on their own traditions and cultural resources: 'just as "Black" was the cutting edge of a politics vis-à-vis one kind of enemy, it could also, if not understood properly, provide a kind of silencing in relation to another. These are the costs, as well as the strengths, of trying to think of the notion of Black as an essentialism' (Hall 1991: 56).

Hall (2006 [1989]: 200) sees a second stage or 'moment' beginning in the mid-1980s. In this stage there is a recognition that a sense of solidarity can be achieved, 'without being dependent on certain fixed notions of racial and ethnic identity' (Davis 2004: 183–4). In this second moment, 'new ethnicities' break apart the previous monolithic representations of white and black cultures as bad and good respectively. In short, this stage is one in which differences between ethnic groups and differences within specific groups are acknowledged and a range of new voices are heard.

For example, Hanif Kureshi's 1985 film *My Beautiful Laundrette* rejects simple oppositions of black/white and good/bad. Instead, it shows some Asians to be materialistic and exploitative businessmen, aspiring to middle-class status, and others as drug dealers – not typical victims of a white, racist culture. The film 'refuses a positive, "right-on" version of black culture', showing many internal divisions and differences (Procter 2004: 129). It also deals with sexualities, gender and class as multiple sources of identity, refusing to prioritize any single form of identification over the others. Cultural products such as this are part of the construction of a more diverse conception of ethnicity which works to 'demarginalise and validate ethnic forms in the experiences of the ethnic communities from which it draws its strength' (Rojek 2003: 181).

and discrimination tends to heighten feelings of common loyalty and interests.

Thus sociologists frequently use the term 'minority' in a non-literal way to refer to a group's subordinate position within society rather than its numerical representation. There are many cases in which a 'minority' is in fact in the numerical majority. In some geographical areas, such as inner cities, minority ethnic groups make up the majority of the population but are nonetheless referred to as 'minorities'. This is because the term 'minority' captures their disadvantaged positions. Women are sometimes described as a minority group, while in many countries of the world they form the numerical majority. Yet, because women tend to be disadvantaged in comparison with men (the 'majority'), the term is also applied to them.

Some scholars have favoured speaking of 'minorities' to refer collectively to groups that have experienced prejudice at the hands of the 'majority' society. The term 'minorities' draws attention to the pervasiveness of discrimination by highlighting the commonality of experience of various subordinate groups. As an example, disablist attitudes, anti-Semitism, homophobia and racism share many features in common and reveal how oppression against different groups can take similar forms. At the same time, speaking collectively of 'minorities' can result in generalizations about discrimination and oppression that do not accurately reflect the experiences of specific groups. Although homosexuals and Pakistanis are both minority groups in London, the way they experience discrimination in society is not identical. Frequently, physical differences such as skin colour are the defining factor in designating an ethnic minority.

Prejudice and discrimination

Prejudice and discrimination have been widespread in human history, and we must distinguish clearly between them. Prejudice refers to opinions or attitudes held by members of one group towards another. A prejudiced person's preconceived views are often based on hearsay rather than on direct evidence, and are resistant to change even in the face of new information. People may harbour favourable prejudices about groups with which they identify and negative prejudices against others. Someone who is prejudiced against a particular group may not deal with its members impartially.

Prejudices are frequently grounded in stereotypes – fixed and inflexible characterizations of a social group. Stereotypes are often applied to minority ethnic groups, such as the idea that all black men are naturally athletic or that all East Asians are hard-working, diligent students. Some stereotypes contain a grain of truth; others are simply a mechanism of displacement, in which feelings of hostility or anger are directed against objects that are not the real origin of those feelings. Stereotypes become embedded in cultural understandings and are difficult to erode, even when they are gross distortions of reality. The belief that single mothers are dependent on welfare and refuse to work is an example of a persistent stereotype that lacks empirical grounding. A large number of single mothers do work, and many who receive welfare benefits would prefer to work but have no access to childcare.

Scapegoating is common when ethnic groups come into competition with one another for economic resources. People who direct racial attacks against ethnic minorities, for example, are often in a similar economic position. A recent poll found that half of all people who felt 'hard done by' believed that immigrants and ethnic minorities were taking priority over them, blaming ethnic minorities for grievances whose real causes lie elsewhere (Stonewall 2003; *The Economist* 2004a). Scapegoating is normally directed against groups that are distinctive and relatively powerless, because they make an easy target. Protestants, Catholics, Jews, Italians, black Africans, Muslims, gypsies and others have played the unwilling role of scapegoat at various times throughout Western history.

If prejudice describes attitudes and opinions, discrimination refers to actual behaviour towards another group or individual. A report by the European Union Fundamental Rights Agency on racism and xenophobia (EUFRA 2007) listed numerous examples of continuing discrimination in some European countries, including poor housing provision for minority ethnic groups, a lack of adequate educational provision for Romany children, and rising levels of racist violence and crime in eight European member states – Denmark, Germany, France, Ireland, Poland, Slovakia, Finland, and England and Wales. A key problem identified in the report is the 'paucity of adequate comparable official statistical or quantitative research data' on which anti-discriminatory policy could be founded. Such evidence covers a range of types of discrimination: direct (racist attacks), indirect (inappropriate education) and structural (a lack of adequate housing).

Discrimination can be seen in activities that disqualify members of one group from opportunities open to others; although prejudice is often the basis of discrimination, the two may exist separately. For example, white house-buyers might steer away from purchasing properties in predominantly black neighbourhoods, not because of attitudes of hostility they might have towards those who live there, but because of worries about declining property values. Prejudiced attitudes in this case influence discrimination, but in an indirect way.

> **THINKING CRITICALLY**
>
> Is it possible for people to be prejudiced and yet not behave in discriminatory ways? Should we be prepared to accept prejudice as 'normal' if it does not turn into discrimination?

An anti-Semitic attack on a Jewish cemetery in Germany.

The persistence of racism?

One widespread form of prejudice is racism – prejudice based on socially significant physical distinctions. A racist is someone who believes that some individuals or groups are superior or inferior to others on the basis of racialized differences. Racism is commonly thought of as behaviour or attitudes held by certain individuals or groups. An individual may profess racist beliefs or may join in with a group, such as a white supremacist organization, which promotes a racist agenda. Yet many have argued that racism is more than simply the ideas held by a small number of bigoted individuals.

The concept of institutional racism was developed in the USA in the late 1960s by civil rights campaigners, who saw that racism underpinned American society rather than merely representing the opinions of a small minority of people (Omi and Winant 1994). The concept suggests that racism pervades all of society's structures in a systematic manner. According to this view, institutions such as the police, the health service and the education system all promote policies that favour certain groups while discriminating against others.

A highly significant investigation into the practices of the London Metropolitan Police Service (the Stephen Lawrence Inquiry – see 'Classic studies 16.1') used and built on a definition of institutional racism devised by Stokely Carmichael, a US civil rights campaigner in the 1960s: 'the collective failure of an organisation to provide an appropriate and professional service to people because of their colour, culture or ethnic origin which can be seen or detected in processes; attitudes and behaviour which amount to discrimination through unwitting prejudice, ignorance, thoughtlessness and racist stereotyping which disadvantages minority ethnic people' (Macpherson 1999: 6.34). The Macpherson Inquiry found that institutional racism did exist within the police force and the criminal justice system. Institutional racism has also been revealed in culture and the arts, in spheres such as television broadcasting (negative or limited portrayal of ethnic minorities in programming) and the international modelling industry (an industry-wide bias against non-white fashion models).

From 'old' to 'new' forms of racism

Just as the concept of biological race has been discredited, so too is old-style 'biological' racism, based on differences in physical traits, rarely openly expressed in society today. The end to legalized segregation in the United States and the collapse of apartheid in South Africa were important turning points in the rejection of biological racism. In both these cases, racist attitudes were proclaimed by directly associating physical traits with biological inferiority. Such blatantly racist ideas are rarely heard today, except in the cases of violent hate crimes or the platforms of certain extremist groups. But this is not to say that racist attitudes have disappeared from modern societies. Rather, as some scholars argue, they have been replaced by a more subtle, sophisticated new racism (or *cultural racism*), which uses the idea of cultural differences to exclude certain groups (Barker 1981).

Those who argue that a 'new racism' has emerged claim that cultural arguments are now employed instead of biological ones in order to discriminate against certain segments of the population. According to this view, hierarchies of superiority and inferiority are constructed according to the values of the majority culture. Those groups that stand apart from the majority can become marginalized or vilified for their refusal to assimilate. It is alleged that new racism has a clear political dimension. Prominent examples can be seen in efforts by some American politicians to enact official English-only language policies and in the conflict in France over girls who wish to wear Islamic headscarves to school. The fact that racism is increasingly exercised on cultural rather than biological grounds has led some scholars to suggest that we live in an age of 'multiple racisms', where discrimination

Classic Studies 16.1 Institutional racism – the Stephen Lawrence Inquiry

The research problem

The overwhelming majority of 'Classic studies' chosen for this book are pieces of research or theoretical studies conducted by professional sociologists. Sometimes, however, research conducted by public bodies or investigators on behalf of government has such a far-reaching impact that it takes on the status of a classic. The Stephen Lawrence Inquiry carried out by Sir William Macpherson (1999) is a good example.

In 1993, a black teenager, Stephen Lawrence, was murdered in a racially motivated attack by five white youths as he was waiting at a bus stop with a friend in south-east London. The attackers stabbed him twice and left him on the pavement to die. At the time, no one was convicted of his murder. However, in November 2011, eighteen years after Stephen Lawrence died, two men were finally found guilty after new forensic evidence was uncovered.

Macpherson's explanation

As a result of the perseverance of Stephen Lawrence's parents, three of the suspects were brought to trial in 1996, but the case collapsed when a judge ruled that the evidence presented by one witness was inadmissible. Jack Straw, then home secretary, announced a full inquiry into the Lawrence case in 1997; its findings were published in 1999 in the Macpherson Report. The commission concluded that the police investigation into Stephen Lawrence's murder had been mishandled from the very start (Macpherson 1999).

Police arriving on the scene made little effort to pursue the attackers and displayed a lack of respect for his parents, denying them access to information about the case to which they were entitled. An erroneous assumption was made that Lawrence had been involved in a street brawl rather than being an innocent victim of an unprovoked racist attack. Police surveillance of the suspects was poorly organized and conducted with a 'lack of urgency'; searches of the suspects' dwellings, for example, were not performed thoroughly, despite tips describing where weapons might be concealed. Senior officers who were in a position to intervene in

the case to correct such mistakes failed to do so. During the course of the investigation and subsequent inquiries into it, police withheld vital information, protected one another, and refused to take responsibility for mistakes. The authors (Macpherson 1999: 46.1) of the report were unequivocal in their findings:

> The conclusions to be drawn from all the evidence in connection with the investigation of Stephen Lawrence's racist murder are clear. There is no doubt but that there were fundamental errors. The investigation was marred by a combination of professional incompetence, institutional racism and a failure of leadership by senior officers.

The charge of *institutional racism* was one of the most important outcomes of the inquiry. Not just the Metropolitan Police Service, but many other institutions, including the criminal justice system, were implicated in this collective failure. The Macpherson Report (1999: 46.27) concluded that 'it is incumbent upon every institution to examine their policies and the outcome of their policies' to ensure that no segment of the population be disadvantaged. Seventy recommendations were set forth for improving the way in which racist crimes are policed. Among these were 'race-awareness' training for police officers, stronger disciplinary powers to remove racist officers, clearer definitions of what constitutes a racist incident, and a commitment to increasing the total number of black and Asian officers in the police force. In 2015, the National Crime Agency began an inquiry into claims that corrupt police officers acted to shield Stephen Lawrence's murderers (Dodd 2015).

Critical points

Although the report's conclusions were welcomed by many, some thought it did not go far enough. Stephen Lawrence's mother, Doreen Lawrence, said at the time that the police had investigated her son's murder like 'white masters during slavery', and, although she was positive about the report's honest appraisal of police failings, she said it had 'only scratched the surface' of racism within the police force. The most contentious part of the report was its central finding, that not just the Metropolitan Police Service but the criminal justice system as a whole was 'institutionally racist'. The Police Complaints Commission (PCC) found 'no evidence' of racist conduct by the police, and the idea of 'unwitting racism' in the report's definition of institutional racism has been criticized as too general. Echoing the PCC's conclusions, Michael Ignatieff wrote that the real issues from the case were not 'race' and 'race awareness', but 'institutionalized incompetence' and 'equal justice before the law' (cited in Green 2000).

Contemporary significance

The Macpherson Report did not deliver justice for Stephen Lawrence. However, it did help to change the way that people in the UK and elsewhere think about racially motivated crime and its prosecution. The concept of institutional racism, devised in the civil rights struggles of late 1960s America, was accepted in an official report commissioned by government and led to a statutory duty for all public bodies to pursue racial equality. In this way, the Lawrence Inquiry not only imposed new demands on the criminal justice system; it also marked a significant change in discourses of race in British society.

is experienced differently across segments of the population (Back 1995).

The persistence of racism

Why has racism persisted into the twenty-first century? There are several possible reasons. One important factor leading to modern racism was simply the invention and diffusion of the concept of race itself. Quasi-racist attitudes have been known to exist for hundreds of years. But the notion of race as a set of fixed traits emerged with the rise of 'race science', discussed above. Belief in the superiority of the white race, although completely without value factually, remains a key element of white racism.

A second reason lies in the exploitative relations that Europeans established with non-white peoples. The slave trade could not have been carried on had it not been widely believed by Europeans that blacks belonged to an inferior, even subhuman, race. Racism helped justify colonial rule over non-white peoples and denied them the rights of political participation that were being won by whites in their European homelands. Some sociologists argue that exclusion from citizenship remains a central feature of modern-day racism as well.

A third reason lies in the response of some social groups within countries that encouraged inward migration in the post-1945 period, such as Britain, Europe and North America. As the postwar economic boom faltered in the mid-1970s, and most Western economies moved from being short of labour (and having relatively open borders) to having large numbers of unemployed, some began to believe that immigrants were responsible for the shortage of work and were illegitimately claiming welfare benefits. In practice this widely held fear is a myth. Migrant workers tend to complement local workers by doing the work that local people reject, providing valuable additional skills and creating new jobs. Similarly, migrant workers generally make a net contribution to society as taxpayers.

Sociological theories of racism

Some of the concepts discussed above – such as stereotypical thinking and displacement – help explain prejudice and discrimination through psychological mechanisms. They provide an account of the nature of prejudiced and racist attitudes and why ethnic differences matter so much to people, but they tell us little about the social processes involved in racism. To study such processes, we must call on sociological ideas.

Ethnocentrism, group closure and allocation of resources

Sociologists have used ideas of ethnocentrism, group closure and resource allocation to understand why racism persists. Ethnocentrism is a suspicion of outsiders combined with a tendency to evaluate the culture of others in terms of one's own culture. Virtually all cultures have been ethnocentric to some degree, and it is easy to see how ethnocentrism combines with stereotypical thought discussed above. Outsiders are thought of as aliens, barbarians or morally and mentally inferior. This was how most civilizations viewed the members of smaller cultures, for example, and the attitude has fuelled innumerable ethnic clashes in history.

Ethnocentrism and group closure, or ethnic group closure, frequently go together. 'Closure' refers to the process whereby groups maintain boundaries separating themselves from others. These boundaries are formed by means of exclusion devices, which sharpen the divisions between one ethnic group and another (Barth 1969). Such devices include limiting or prohibiting intermarriage between the groups, restrictions on social contact or economic relationships such as trading, and the physical separation of groups (as in the case of ethnic ghettoes). African Americans have experienced all three exclusion devices: racial intermarriage has been illegal in some states, economic and social segregation was enforced by law in the South, and segregated black ghettos still exist in most major cities.

Sometimes, groups of equal power mutually enforce lines of closure: their members keep separate from each other, but neither group dominates the other. More commonly, however, one ethnic group occupies a position of power over another. In these circumstances, group closure coincides with resource allocation, instituting inequalities in the distribution of wealth and material goods.

Some of the fiercest conflicts between ethnic groups centre on the lines of closure between them precisely because these lines signal inequalities in wealth, power or social standing. The concept of ethnic group closure helps us understand both the dramatic and the more insidious differences that separate communities of people from one another – not just why the members of some groups are murdered, attacked and harassed, but also why they do not get good jobs, a good education or a desirable place to live. Wealth, power and social status are scarce resources – some groups have more of them than others. To hold on to their distinctive positions, privileged groups sometimes undertake extreme acts of violence against others. Similarly, members of underprivileged groups may turn to violence as a means of trying to improve their own situation.

Conflict theories

Conflict theories, by contrast, are concerned with the links between racism and prejudice, on the one hand, and relationships of power and inequality, on the other. Early conflict approaches to racism were heavily influenced by Marxist ideas, which saw the economic system as the determining factor for all other aspects of society. Some Marxist theorists held that racism was a product of the capitalist system, arguing that the ruling class used slavery, colonization and racism as tools for exploiting labour (Cox 1959).

Later, neo-Marxist scholars saw these early formulations as too rigid and simplistic and suggested that racism was not the product of economic forces alone. A set of articles published in 1982 by the Birmingham Centre for Contemporary Cultural Studies, *The Empire Strikes Back*, takes a broader view of the rise of racism. While agreeing that the capitalist exploitation of labour is one factor, contributors point to a variety of historical and political influences which led to the emergence of a specific brand of racism in Britain in the 1970s and 1980s. They argue that racism is a complex and multifaceted phenomenon involving the interplay of minority ethnic and working-class identities and beliefs. Racism is much more than simply a set of oppressive ideas enacted against the non-white population by powerful elites (Centre for Contemporary Cultural Studies 1982).

From the mid-1980s, a new conflict perspective called critical race theory (CRT) began to develop in the field of legal studies in the USA, and this spread into studies of education, ethnic relations and political science during the 1990s and sport in the 2000s (Hylton 2009). CRT diverged from earlier theories of race and ethnicity in some important ways. In particular, critical race theorists are not just detached analysts of 'race relations' but activists, seeking to intervene to transform unequal relations between ethnic groups. The perspective emerged as a reaction to and critique of mainstream legal theory, which was rooted in a broadly liberal position that saw a steady incremental progress towards equality in the development of the law and legal systems (Brown 2007). CRT rejects this linear story, arguing that the gains made by the 1960s civil rights movements were quickly eroded and positive legal precedents have not been followed through.

Delgado and Stefancic (2001: 7–10) outline the key aspects of CRT. First, racism, they contend, is not a deviation from the non-racist norm: racism is in fact the everyday 'normal' experience for 'people of colour' in the USA and, by extension, in many other societies. Racism is therefore not 'exceptional' but, rather, is deeply embedded within legal systems and other social institutions, which is why it is so persistent. Because of this, formal ideas of equal treatment before the law deal only with very explicit types of racism, while everyday or micro forms continue without redress. Second, both white elites and the white working class stand to benefit materially from the operation of this 'normal' racism, hence large parts of the population have no real interest in working to alter the situation. This makes real change towards equality even harder to achieve.

CRT is also strongly social construction-ist, noting that (as we saw above) 'races' are not immutable biological facts but social creations which perpetuate inequality. For example, during periods when there is a shortage of unskilled or semi-skilled labour and immigration is encouraged, black people may be depicted as hard-working and reliable. However, when unemployment levels are high, the same 'racial' group can be described in the mass media and by politicians as essentially lazy and prone to criminality. Such differential racialization illustrates how power is woven into ethnic relations.

Finally, critical race theorists argue that, given their history and experience, minority ethnic groups are uniquely able to articulate what racism means to its victims. For this reason, CRT tends to make extensive use of narrative and biographical methods to give voice to those who experience racism and thus bring this to the attention of scholars of law and other disciplines (Zamudio et al. 2011: 5; see Denzin et al. 2008). However, the ultimate goal of critical race theorists is an intensely practical one – to make their own necessary contribution to all of those social movements that try to move societies in the direction of greater social equality.

> ### THINKING CRITICALLY
> Give some contemporary examples of how racism may be related to group closure, ethnocentrism, resource allocation or social class. What does the perspective of critical race theory add to our understanding of the chosen examples?

Ethnic diversity, integration and conflict

Many states in the world today are characterized by multi-ethnic populations. Some Middle Eastern and Central European states, such as Turkey or Hungary, are ethnically diverse as a result of long histories of changing borders, occupations by foreign powers and regional migration. Other societies have become multi-ethnic more rapidly, as a result of policies encouraging migration or through the legacy of colonialism and imperialism. In an age of globalization and rapid social change, the benefits and complex challenges of ethnic diversity confront many nation-states. International migration is accelerating with the further integration of the global economy, and the movement and mixing of human populations seems sure to intensify in years to come. Meanwhile, ethnic tensions and conflicts continue to flare up in societies around the world, threatening to lead to the disintegration of some multi-ethnic states and protracted violence in others.

Ethnic diversity

Britain, like most developed countries, is an ethnically diverse society, home to people with a variety of cultures and ethnic backgrounds. This ethnic diversity is an increasingly common feature of most developed societies and, as we shall see later, is key to understanding the policy of multiculturalism, which numerous governments have adopted to ensure that minority ethnic groups can enjoy the full benefits of citizenship. The population of England and Wales has become steadily more diverse, particularly since the early 1990s, and around 14 per cent identified themselves as 'non-white' in the 2011 census (see figure 16.1). The 1991 census reported 94.1 per cent of the population identified themselves as being in the white ethnic group, but this fell to 91.3 per cent

in 2001 and, again, to 86 per cent in the 2011 census. Among the white ethnic group, 'white British' had similarly decreased, from 87.5 per cent in 2001 to 80.5 per cent in 2011.

'Non-white' ethnic groups all saw increases in their populations over the same period (see table 16.1). For example, both Indians and Pakistanis increased by around 400,000 between 2001 and 2011, making up 2.5 and 2 per cent of the total population respectively (ONS 2012b: 1–5). The largest growth was in the 'any other white' category, rising by 1.8 per cent between 2001 and 2011, an increase of 1.1 million people. This group is primarily people migrating from European countries, but also from Australia, Canada, New Zealand and South Africa. Between 2002 and 2009, the strongest growth was in the Chinese population, averaging an 8.6 per cent increase per year (ONS 2011c).

It is important to note that immigration is now responsible for a declining proportion of minority ethnic populations in Britain. This marks an important shift away from an 'immigrant population' to a 'non-white British' population with full citizenship rights. Since the 1991 UK census was the first to ask respondents to classify themselves in ethnic terms, comparing data across studies can be difficult (Mason 1995). The number of people self-identifying as belonging to the main minority ethnic groups is shown in table 16.1, though it is necessary to be cautious about these estimates. For example, respondents' understanding of their own ethnicity may be more complex than the options offered (Moore 1995). This is particularly true in the case of individuals identifying as 'mixed ethnic groups', which have grown considerably to make up 2.2 per cent of the population in 2011, largely as a result of more 'ethnic mixing' rather than through increasing birth rates.

The 'non-white' population in England and Wales is concentrated in some of the most densely populated urban areas of England. London is easily the most ethnically diverse region, though over the last decade or so many people of minority ethnic descent have left

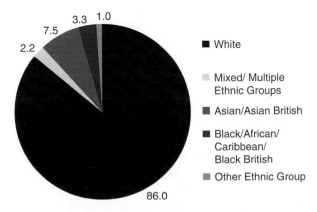

Figure 16.1 Ethnic groups, England and Wales, 2011

Source: ONS (2012b: 3).

Table 16.1 **Population change by ethnic group, England and Wales, 2001 and 2009 (thousands)**

Ethnic group	Mid-2001 population	Natural change	Net migration and other changes	Mid-2009 population	Average annual percentage growth
All groups	**52,360.0**	**1,093.8**	**1,355.3**	**54,809.1**	**0.6**
White: British	45,718.9	359.9	−396.7	45,682.1	0.0
White: Irish	646.6	−51.3	−21.1	574.2	−1.5
White: other white	1,379.7	38.6	514.3	1,932.6	4.3
Mixed: white and black Caribbean	240.4	72.8	−2.6	310.6	3.3
Mixed: white and black African	80.7	35.6	15.5	131.8	6.3
Mixed: white and Asian	192.3	82.8	26.5	301.6	5.8
Mixed: other mixed	158.6	61.8	22.2	242.6	5.5
Asian: Indian	1,053.9	88.8	291.5	1,434.2	3.9
Asian: Pakistani	728.4	138.4	140.6	1,007.4	4.1
Asian: Bangladeshi	287.0	55.5	49.7	392.2	4.0
Other Asian	247.3	35.5	102.9	385.7	5.7
Black Caribbean	572.4	22.3	20.5	615.2	0.9
Black African	494.9	89.5	214.4	798.8	6.2
Other black	98.1	21.9	6.1	126.1	3.2
Chinese	233.3	22.6	195.6	451.5	8.6
Other	227.6	19.1	175.9	422.6	8.0
Non-'white British'	**6,641.2**	**733.9**	**1,752.0**	**9,127.1**	**4.1**

Note: Figures may not sum due to rounding.

Source: ONS (2011c: 2).

London for other parts of England. One reason for this is the relatively younger age profile of the 'non-white' groups, as younger people in general tend to move around more than those beyond their mid-twenties, who settle into employment and communities. There are also concentrations of specific minority groups in certain cities and regions. For example, in the East Midlands city of Leicester, the Asian Indian population makes up 19 per cent of the total; in Bradford, Asian Pakistanis make up 13 per cent of the population; while the British African Caribbean population is concen-

trated in some London boroughs (such as Lewisham) and the city of Birmingham (ONS 2011c).

At this point it is worth stopping to consider the ethnic categories we have used in this section, which are those devised for the official 2001 census of England and Wales. What kind of categories are they? Is it legitimate to discuss Chinese, white British, black Caribbean, black African, Asian Indian and 'mixed: white and Asian' as 'ethnic groups'? Is Chinese an ethnic group or a nationality? Does the scheme confuse 'race' with 'ethnicity'? Also, the ONS classification divides 'Asian' into Pakistani, Bangladeshi, Indian and 'other', but the 'mixed' category (introduced for the first time in 2001) dispenses with this variation in favour of simply 'white and Asian'. Some categories appear to be loosely based on skin colour, some on geographical region and others on nationality. And why is 'white British' the only category to include 'Britishness'? What are we to make of such an apparently inconsistent scheme?

Ethnic group classification schemes do not simply describe an external social world 'out there' but in some ways also contribute to the social construction of 'ethnicity' and 'race' and our understanding of what these terms mean. This is particularly the case with official government schemes, which form the basis for policy-making in important areas such as housing, welfare, immigration and employment. The current highly charged discourse on immigration is replete with references to growing minority ethnic populations and the drain on health and social services. Hence, the ONS classification scheme reflects not just certain characteristics of the population of England and Wales but also the current political framework of debate on immigration and British identity.

Since the mid-2000s, some sociologists and official bodies have become keenly aware that ethnic diversity has changed. In particular, it can no longer be assumed (if ever it could) that members of specific ethnic groups and communities share the same life chances. Vertovec (2006, 2007) coined the term super-diversity to describe the increasingly complex level of diversity that is emerging in the UK. He argues that Britain can now be characterized by 'super-diversity, a notion intended to underline a level and kind of complexity surpassing anything the country has previously experienced' (Vertovec 2006: 1). Post-1945 migration to Britain was state-led and intended primarily to fill labour market gaps by drawing large groups from South Asian and African-Caribbean communities in the former colonies of the Commonwealth. But recent demographic changes and shifting patterns of migration have produced a much more complex situation, as smaller groups of people from a wider range of countries move away from their country of origin for a variety of reasons.

The phenomenon of super-diversity involves complex combinations of country of origin, channel or route of migration, age and gender profile, legal status (and therefore legal rights), migrants' human capital (such as qualifications and skills), access to employment (linked to legal status), locality, transnationalism (connections to people and places around the world) and the response of authorities, service providers and local residents to migrant groups (Vertovec 2006: 31). This is illustrated in the example of Somalis living in the UK. Some Somalis are British citizens, while others are 'refugees, asylum-seekers, persons granted exceptional leave to remain, undocumented migrants, and people granted refugee status in another country but who subsequently moved to Britain' (ibid.: 18). These varied routes into Britain and the different legal statuses and associated rights shape access to employment, public services, housing, place of residence and much more. Super-diversity involves not simply diverse experiences *across* different ethnic groups; it also alerts us to the diversity *within* particular ethnic groups. The task for sociologists will be to find ways of exploring, writing about and understanding the interplay of the many variables which characterize this emerging diversity of lifestyles and experiences.

Any attempt to discuss the social world and its diversity necessarily has to make distinctions and, in doing so, carves up reality into meaningful categories. Sociologists as well as government statisticians cannot avoid this. In the case of ethnic diversity, we have to acknowledge the limitations of these categories to capture the reality of people's experience and try not to confuse our categories with existing, cohesive social groups. To do so would be to fall into the trap of 'groupism' highlighted by Brubaker (2006) above. Increasingly, sociologists recognize that the differential experiences of ethnic

677

USING YOUR SOCIOLOGICAL IMAGINATION

16.2 Ethnic diversity versus social solidarity?

In a controversial article published in February 2004, David Goodhart, the editor of *Prospect* magazine, argued that there is a trade-off between an ethnically diverse society and one that has the solidarity among citizens that allows it to have a decent welfare system to protect those in need. To Goodhart, people are willing to pay taxes – to go towards pensions or unemployment benefit, for example – if they believe that they are paying to help people who are in some way like themselves: people who share at least common values and assumptions. Goodhart called this trade-off 'the progressive dilemma', which faces all those who want both a diverse and a solidaristic society.

As evidence of this trade-off, Goodhart pointed to the Scandinavian countries, such as Sweden and Denmark, which historically have the world's most generous welfare states. He argued that it has been possible to build large welfare systems in these countries because they are fairly socially and ethnically homogeneous, so people are prepared to pay more in taxes. In contrast, welfare states have been weaker in ethnically more divided countries such as the United States.

Goodhart asked if there is a 'tipping point' that occurs somewhere between the proportion of the population in Britain that belongs to a minority ethnic group and that of the United States, where a wholly different US-style society is created – that is, one with sharp ethnic divisions and a weak welfare state. He suggested that, for this tipping point to be avoided and for feelings of solidarity towards incomers not to be overstretched, it is important that there are limits to the number of people allowed to enter the country and that the process of asylum and immigration is seen to be transparent and under control (Goodhart 2004).

Goodhart's thesis has been heavily criticized. Saskia Sassen (2004) has argued that, in the long run, integration of immigrants does happen

and that, broadly speaking, immigrants face the same sort of difficulties in becoming accepted today as they did in previous centuries. Historically, all European societies have over time incorporated many, if not all, of the major foreign immigrant groups. Past experience shows that it has often taken no more than a couple of generations to turn 'them' into 'us' – the community that can experience solidarity in Goodhart's analysis.

The political theorist Bhikhu Parekh (2004) also attacked Goodhart's thesis, suggesting that he gets the relationship between solidarity and the redistribution of the welfare state the wrong way round. Goodhart is convinced that solidarity is a necessary precondition of redistribution. That is a half truth, according to Parekh: one could just as plausibly say that redistribution generates loyalty, creates common life experiences, and so on, and therefore paves the way for solidarity. The relation between the two is far more complex than Goodhart suggests in his article.

Bernard Crick (2004), another political theorist, asked Goodhart: 'Solidarity of what?' Goodhart discusses solidarity in *Britain*, but, Crick noted, if he had talked of the 'United Kingdom', it might have reminded him that the UK has been a multinational and a multi-ethnic state for a long time. Today, the dual status of being British and Scottish, Welsh, Irish or English is an established fact. The question, then, concerns neither solidarity *nor* loss of identity: identity lies partly in being a member of more than one group.

> **THINKING CRITICALLY**
>
> In your experience, is Crick right: are dual identities widely accepted within the UK and Europe? What does Scottish, Irish and Welsh nationalism tell us about the acceptance of dual nationality in the UK?

groups that are more and more varied and the diversity within them make broad generalizations less valid. An awareness of such problems is at least a first step towards a better understanding of how the concepts of 'race' and ethnicity are deployed, understood and experienced today.

Models of ethnic integration

How can ethnic diversity be accommodated and the outbreak of ethnic conflict averted? What should be the relationship between minority ethnic groups and the majority population? There are three primary models of ethnic integration that have been adopted by multi-ethnic societies in relation to these challenges: assimilation, the 'melting pot' and, finally, cultural pluralism, or multicultural-ism. It is important to realize that these three models are ideal types and are not easy to achieve in practice.

> Max Weber's use of 'ideal types' is discussed in chapter 1, 'What is Sociology?'.

The first model is assimilation, mean-ing that immigrants abandon their original customs and practices and mould their behav iour to the values and norms of the majority. An assimilationist approach demands that immigrants change their language, dress, lifestyles and cultural outlooks as part of integrating into a new social order. In the United States, generations of immigrants were subjected to pressure to become 'assimi-lated' in this way, and many of their children became more or less completely 'American' as a result. Of course, even if minorities try to assimilate, many are unable to do so if they are racialized or if their attempts are rebuffed – whether it be in employment or dating or any other context.

A second model is that of the melting pot. Rather than the traditions of the immigrants being dissolved in favour of those domi-nant among the pre-existing population,

they become blended to form new, evolving cultural patterns. The USA has been seen as exhibiting the pattern associated with the idea of a melting pot. Not only are differing cultural values and norms 'brought in' to a society from the outside, but diversity is created as ethnic groups adapt to the wider social envi-ronments in which they find themselves. One often-cited literal example of a melting-pot culture is the dish chicken tikka masala, said to have been invented by Bangladeshi chefs in Indian restaurants in the UK. Chicken tikka is an Indian dish, but the masala sauce was an improvised addition. In 2001, the dish was described by the former foreign secretary Robin Cook (1946–2005) as a 'British national dish'.

Many have believed that the melting-pot model is the most desirable form of ethnic inte-gration. Traditions and customs of immigrant populations are not abandoned but contribute to and shape a constantly transforming social milieu. Hybrid forms of cuisine, fashion, music and architecture are manifestations of the melting-pot approach. To a limited degree, this model is an accurate expression of aspects of American cultural development. Although the 'Anglo' culture has remained the pre-eminent one, its character in some part reflects the impact of the many different groups that now compose the American population.

The third model is cultural pluralism, in which ethnic cultures are given full validity to exist separately yet participate in the larger society's economic and political life. A recent and important outgrowth of pluralism is multiculturalism, which refers to state poli-cies that encourage cultural or ethnic groups to live in harmony with one another. The United States and other Western countries are pluralistic in many senses, but ethnic differ-ences have for the most part been associated with inequalities rather than with equal but independent membership in the national community. It does seem at least possible to create a society in which ethnic groups are distinct but equal, as is demonstrated by Swit-zerland, where French, German and Italian groups coexist in the same society.

One advocate of multiculturalism, the political scientist Bhikhu Parekh (2000: 67), puts forward its central argument:

> The cultural identity of some groups ('minorities') should not have to be confined to the private sphere while the language, culture and religion of others ('the majority') enjoy a public monopoly and are treated as the norm. For a lack of public recognition is damaging to people's self-esteem and is not conducive to encouraging the full participation of everyone in the public sphere.

Parekh (2000) argues that there are three 'insights' in multicultural thinking. First, human beings are embedded within a culturally structured world, which provides them with a system of meanings. And, though individuals are not entirely determined by their cultures, they are 'deeply shaped' by them. Second, cultures contain visions of what constitutes 'a good life'. But, if they are not to stagnate or become irrelevant, each culture needs other, different cultures with alternative visions, which encourages critical reflection and the expansion of horizons. Finally, cultures are not monolithic but internally diverse, with continuing debates between different traditions. The crucial task for multicultural societies in the twenty-first century, according to Parekh (2000: 78), is 'the need to find ways of reconciling the legitimate demands of unity and diversity, of achieving political unity without cultural uniformity, and cultivating among its citizens both a common sense of belonging and a willingness to respect and cherish deep cultural differences.'

Amartya Sen (2007) argues against a 'solitarist approach' to understanding human identities. Solitarism, such as that found in some religious and civilizationist approaches, perceives a person's national, civilizational or religious adherence to be their primary form of identity and places them into just one main 'identity group'. However, Sen (2007: xii) claims that this approach generates much mutual misunderstanding. In reality, we see ourselves and each other as belonging to a variety of identity groups and have little problem doing so:

> The same person can be, without any contradiction, an American citizen, of Caribbean origin, with African ancestry, a Christian, a liberal, a woman, a vegetarian, a long-distance runner, a historian, a schoolteacher, a novelist, a feminist, a heterosexual, a believer in gay and lesbian rights, a theater lover, an environmental activist, a tennis fan, a jazz musician, and someone who is deeply committed to the view that there are intelligent beings in outer space with whom it is extremely urgent to talk (preferably in English). Each of these collectivities, to all of which this person simultaneously belongs, gives her a particular identity. None of them can be taken to be the person's only identity or singular membership category.

The assumption of one unique or primordial identity that dominates all others breeds mistrust and often violence. Solitarist identities which generate an 'illusion of destiny' – such as that of a national people's unique identity that gives them an ancient right to hold territory – come into conflict. Sen maintains that a more widespread recognition of the plurality of individual identities holds out the hope of a genuine multiculturalism, set against the divisiveness of a model based on the imposition of singular identities.

Critics of multiculturalism raise concerns about the potential for ethnic segregation if states enable, for example, separate schooling and curricula. Some countries, including France, Norway and Denmark, have drawn back from recognizing multiculturalism as official policy, and there is something of a backlash in sections of most European societies. In July 2010, following a passionate and divisive public debate about foreign cultures and French political ideals, French MPs voted to ban the wearing of the burka and niqab in public places. In the Netherlands, the Party for Freedom won nine seats in 2006 but twenty-four in 2010. Its leader declared that 'More security, less crime, less immigration, less Islam – this is what Holland chose.' In a similar vein, a book by the German Bundesbank executive Thilo Sarrazin (2010) argued that foreigners were breeding rapidly and that Muslim migrants were linked to criminal activity and welfare dependency. In 2010, the German chancellor, Angela Merkel, said that, when Germany encouraged foreign workers into the country in the early 1960s it was assumed 'they won't stay and that they will have disappeared again one day. That's not the reality.'

We must remember that all of these societies are already 'multi-cultural', in the sense that they are constituted by a diversity of ethnic groups and cultures. Current debates are really concerned with 'political multiculturalism' – that is, whether facilitating and encouraging ethnic and cultural diversity should be official state policy. In many developed societies, the community leaders of most minority ethnic groups have emphasized the path of cultural pluralism, though achieving 'distinct but equal' status seems a distant option at present. Minority ethnic groups are still perceived by ethnic majorities as a threat – to their jobs, to their safety and to their 'national culture' – and the scapegoating of minority ethnic groups is a persistent tendency. This is increasingly likely in societies characterized by economic recession and austerity plans alongside tensions and anxieties about immigration and national identities.

However, many people confuse multiculturalism with *cultural diversity* – they talk about living in a 'multicultural society' when, in reality, they mean that society is made up of people from different ethnic backgrounds. Others think that multiculturalism is about separatism. According to this view, we simply have to accept that there are many different cultures across the world and within particular societies, and that none can have primacy over others. This naïvely implies leaving all social groups to follow whatever norms they like, regardless of the consequences for the wider society.

More 'sophisticated' versions of multiculturalism are concerned with social solidarity, not, as critics claim, with separateness, where different groups have equality of status and diversity should be openly respected (Giddens 2006: 123–4; Rattansi 2011: 57). But equality of status does not mean the uncritical acceptance of all practices. Charles Taylor (1992) argues that all people in society have an equal right to respect, but if they have equal rights they also have responsibilities, including a fundamental responsibility to obey the law. Thus, although the issues are not clear-cut, it is the fostering of open dialogue that is an important element of multiculturalism.

> **THINKING CRITICALLY**
>
> If cultural diversity is inevitable in a globalizing world, why do 'solitarist' identities retain their power? In particular, can you see any evidence of national identities declining?

Employment, housing and criminal justice

Work, housing and criminal justice are three areas which have been investigated by sociologists to monitor the very real effects of social and economic disadvantage resulting from the major social inequalities of gender, class and ethnicity. In this section we will briefly outline some key issues and themes in relation to the experiences of different ethnic groups in the UK. However, we also illustrate how 'race' and ethnicity intersect with other forms of inequality to produce diverse patterns of advantage and disadvantage in employment opportunities, housing status and criminal justice.

Trends in employment

The earliest national survey of ethnic minorities in Britain, conducted by the Policy Studies Institute (PSI) in the 1960s, found that most recent immigrants were clustered disproportionately in manual occupations within a small number of industries. Even those recent arrivals with qualifications from their countries of origin tended to work in jobs that were incommensurate with their abilities.

Discrimination on the basis of ethnic background was a common and overt practice, with some employers refusing to hire non-white workers, or agreeing to do so only when there was a shortage of suitable white workers.

By the 1970s, employment patterns had shifted somewhat. Members of many minority ethnic groups continued to occupy semi-skilled or unskilled manual positions, but a growing number were employed in skilled manual work. However, very few were represented in professional and managerial positions. Regardless of changes in legislation to prevent racial discrimination in company hiring practices, social scientific research found that whites were consistently offered interviews and job opportunities in preference to equally qualified non-white applicants.

The third PSI survey in 1982 found that, with the exception of African-Asian and Indian men, minority ethnic groups had rates of unemployment twice as high as whites. This was due primarily to the economic recession, which had a strong impact on the manufacturing sector in which large numbers of minority ethnic workers were employed. Qualified non-whites with fluent English, however, were increasingly entering white-collar positions, and on the whole there was a narrowing in the wage gap between ethnic minorities and whites. A growing number took up self-employment, contributing to higher earnings and lower levels of unemployment, especially among Indians and African Asians.

Some scholars suggested that 1980s and 1990s de-industrialization had a disproportionate impact on minority ethnic groups (Iganski and Payne 1999). However, this conventional view was challenged by findings from the PSI surveys and comparisons of Labour Force Survey and census statistics. These demonstrated that some minority ethnic groups in fact attained high levels of economic and occupational success in much the same way as successful white workers. Using data from three decades of Labour Force Surveys and censuses (1971, 1981 and 1991), Iganski and Payne (1999) found that, as a whole, minority ethnic groups experienced

lower levels of job loss than did the rest of the industrial labour force.

The fourth PSI survey in 1997 (Modood et al. 1997) also found employment patterns varied among non-white women. Black Caribbean women were much less likely to be in manual work than white women, while Indian and Pakistani women tended to be in manual jobs. There was a much higher level of economic activity among black Caribbean and Indian women, but Pakistani and Bangladeshi women were less active in the labour market. On average, Caribbean and Indian women tended to have slightly higher full-time earnings than white women, although among Indian women there was a sharp polarization between those on relatively high incomes and those on low incomes. Figure 16.2 shows how much the employment rates for men and women have varied over time according to different ethnic background.

However, the substantial gains made by certain minority ethnic groups should not be mistaken for the end of occupational disadvantage. Such 'collective social mobility' demonstrates that the forces of post-industrial restructuring are stronger than those of racial discrimination and persistent disadvantage. More recent investigations have revealed the divergent employment trajectories of different ethnic groups. For example, the UK government's Strategy Unit (2003) found that Indians and Chinese were, on average, outperforming whites in the labour market, though other groups were doing less well. Pakistanis, Bangladeshis and black Caribbeans experienced, on average, significantly higher unemployment and lower earnings than whites.

In 2010, the National Equality Panel reported that about 80 per cent of white and Indian men and between 50 and 70 per cent of men in other ethnic groups were in paid work (Hills et al. 2010). However, unemployment was relatively high (between 10 and 16 per cent) for black African, black Caribbean and other groups of black men. Around one-quarter of Pakistani and Bangladeshi women were in paid employment compared with about 50 per cent of women in all other groups.

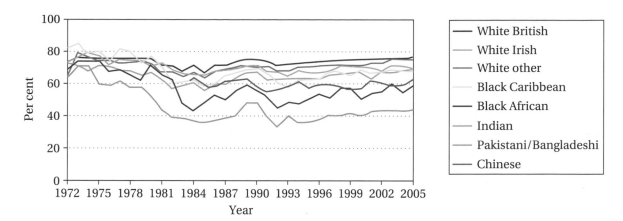

Figure 16.2 Probability of employment by ethnic group, UK, 1972–2005 (men aged 16–64; women aged 16–59)

Source: Li and Heath (2007: 2).

The survey also found similar differences in relation to income levels between ethnic groups. The median net weekly income for white British men was £288, which was 30 per cent higher than that for black and black British Caribbean men. The incomes of the top 10 per cent of white British men were 22 per cent higher than those of the top 10 per cent of black or black British Caribbean men (Hills et al. 2010: 161). Similarly, across the overall income distribution, white men were some thirty places higher (out of 100) in the distribution than Asian or Asian British Bangladeshi men. Clearly, although there are different experiences between minority ethnic groups, white men continue to enjoy significant economic advantages over most black and Asian minority groups in Britain.

Housing

Minority ethnic groups in Britain, as elsewhere in the developed world, tend to experience discrimination, harassment and material deprivation in the housing market. Since the early calls for immigration controls, housing has been at the forefront of struggles over resources between groups, and tendencies towards ethnic closure are evident. As with employment patterns, differentials in the quality and type of housing vary across ethnic groups. Although the non-white population as a whole tends to be disadvantaged compared with whites in terms of housing, there are some important exceptions. Certain groups, such as those of Indian origin, have attained very high levels of home-ownership, while other ethnic minority groups are disproportionately housed in sub-standard accommodation and tend to be over-represented among the homeless (but not rough sleepers) (Law 2009: 178).

Several factors contribute to housing differentials between non-white and white populations and across non-white groups. Racial harassment or violent attacks, which are still frequent in European countries, are likely to encourage a certain degree of ethnic segregation in housing tenure. In many European countries, evidence shows that Roma communities face the worst discrimination in relation to available and affordable housing (EUFRA 2007). Non-white families with the means to move into more affluent, predominantly white neighbourhoods may be dissuaded from doing so because they face hostility.

Another factor relates to the physical condition of housing. A high proportion of Pakistanis and Bangladeshis live in accommodation that is overcrowded – partly because of the large average size of households – and their housing tends to be susceptible to damp and more likely to lack central heating. By contrast, people of Indian origin are just as likely as whites to occupy detached or semi-detached homes and are less likely than other ethnic groups to reside in inner-city neighbourhoods. African-Caribbean households, on the other hand, are much more likely to rent accommodation in the social housing sector rather than becoming home-owners. This may be related to the high proportion of lone-parent families within this ethnic group. Poor housing is a significant factor leading to higher levels of poor health among some minority ethnic groups, though such health inequalities are strongly correlated with social class position (Cockerham 2007).

See also chapter 11, 'Health, Illness and Disability', for a wider discussion of health inequalities.

Understanding the intersecting social inequalities of class, ethnicity and gender has formed the basis of much recent sociological research, and intersectionality has informed attempts to improve public services for ethnic minorities. The complex intertwining of inequalities of age, sexuality, disability, class, ethnicity and gender produces a wide variety of social positions and identities in society. Intersectional research in sociology is helping policy-makers to understand better the diversity of contemporary social inequalities and to produce social policy that is more attuned to the different needs of social groups and individuals.

Intersectionality is discussed in detail in chapter 12, 'Stratification and Social Class', and is also covered in chapters 3, 'Theories and Perspectives', 7, 'Work and the Economy', 9, 'The Life Course', 13, 'Poverty, Social Exclusion and Welfare', and 15, 'Gender and Sexuality'.

Awareness of discrimination can also become an impetus for creative action. This is important, as one independent health service report argued: 'At present, people from the

black and minority ethnic communities . . . are not getting the service they are entitled to. Putting it bluntly, this is a disgrace' (Blofeld 2003: 58). An additional factor for minority ethnic groups is racist attitudes within society, which, as is shown by the Macpherson Report (1999) discussed above, are institutionally embedded in many public services (Karlsen 2007). We can see this in relation to the operation of the criminal justice system.

The criminal justice system

Since the 1960s, members of minority ethnic groups have been represented in ever greater numbers in the criminal justice system, both as offenders and as victims. Compared with their distribution in the overall population, minority ethnic groups are over-represented in the prison population. In 2008, 11 per cent of male prisoners and 9 per cent of female prisoners in England and Wales were 'black or black British', around five times greater than their proportion in the overall population (ONS 2010a: 134). Young black men are also far more likely than whites to be in youth custody. In 2010, black and other minority ethnic young men made up 39 per cent of the population of youth jails in England and Wales, a rapid rise from 23 per cent in 2006 (Travis 2011).

There is good reason to believe that members of minority ethnic groups suffer discriminatory treatment within the criminal justice system. The number of 'stop-and-search' procedures of black and ethnic minority groups fell after the publication of the Macpherson Report in 1999, but rose again as police forces became more sensitive to terrorism associated with the al-Qaeda network. This has led to a hike in the number of cases where British Asians, many of whom are Muslims, have been stopped and searched, with police using new powers granted to them under the 2000 Terrorism Act.

However, black people, particularly young black men, are disproportionately subject to stop and search – seven times more than white people in 2009–10. And, while the proportion of stop and searches involving whites fell between 2006–7 and 2009–10, the proportion involving black people rose, from 22 to 33 per cent. And there is a higher rate of custodial sentencing among non-whites, even in cases where there are few or no previous convictions, and ethnic minorities are more likely to experience discrimination or racial attacks once imprisoned. The administration of criminal justice is overwhelmingly dominated by whites. In 2010, less than 5 per cent of police officers were from black or other minority ethnic backgrounds, and only a similar proportion were part of the judiciary (Ministry of Justice 2011: 14–15 and 19).

Minority ethnic groups are vulnerable to racism of varying kinds – including racially motivated attacks. Most escape such treatment, but for a minority the experience can be disturbing and brutal. It has been estimated that racially motivated incidents represented 12 per cent of all crime against minority ethnic

people in 2002, compared with just 2 per cent for white people (ONS 2002b). The British Crime Survey also found that emotional reactions to racially motivated incidents were generally more severe than they were for non-racially motivated incidents.

The experience of many people from minority ethnic groups, particularly young men, is that it is they who are the 'objects of violent exploitation' in their encounters with whites and, to some extent, with the police. Roger Graef's (1989) study of police practice concluded that the police were 'actively hostile to all minority groups', frequently using stereotypes and racial slurs when speaking about ethnic minorities. The racist murder of Stephen Lawrence in 1993 and subsequent inquiry found that racism can pervade whole institutions (see 'Classic studies 16.1', p. 671). In the first year after the report, more

A Muslim man being questioned by police at Stansted airport. In 2015, black people in the UK were up to 17.5 times more likely to be stopped and searched than white people, with the largest disparities found in rural rather than urban areas.

than one-third of police forces had not hired any additional black or Asian officers, and the number of minority ethnic officers had actually fallen in nine out of forty-three forces in England and Wales.

How can we account for these patterns of crime and victimization? Crime is not evenly distributed among the population. Areas that suffer from material deprivation generally have higher crime rates and people living in such regions run a greater risk of falling victim to crime. The deprivations to which people exposed to racism are subject both help to produce and are produced by the decaying environment of inner cities (see chapter 6, 'Cities and Urban Life'). Here, there are clear correlations between 'race', unemployment and crime, which tend to centre on the position of young males from minority ethnic backgrounds. Through the political and media creations of moral panic about crime, a public link has been established between 'race' and crime.

> The theory of moral panic is discussed in chapter 20, 'Crime and Deviance'.

Ethnic conflict

Ethnic diversity can greatly enrich societies. Multi-ethnic societies are often vibrant and dynamic places, strengthened by the varied contributions of their inhabitants. But they can also be fragile, especially in the face of internal upheaval or external threat. Differing linguistic, religious and cultural backgrounds can become fault-lines for open antagonism. Sometimes societies with long histories of ethnic tolerance and integration can rapidly become engulfed in ethnic conflict – hostilities between different ethnic groups or communities. This was the case in the 1990s in the former Yugoslavia, a region renowned for its rich multi-ethnic heritage. Centuries of migration and the rule of successive empires produced a diverse, intermixed population composed predominantly of Slavs

(such as the Eastern Orthodox Serbs), Croats (Catholic), Muslims and Jews. After 1991, alongside major political and social transformations following the fall of communism, deadly conflicts broke out between ethnic groups in several areas of the former Yugoslavia.

The conflicts in former Yugoslavia involved attempts at ethnic cleansing – the creation of ethnically homogeneous areas through the mass expulsion of other ethnic populations. More recently, government-backed Arab militias have been accused of ethnic cleansing in Sudan, following an uprising by some of the black population of the Western Sudanese region of Darfur in 2003. Reprisals by the militia led to at least 70,000 deaths and left around 2 million people homeless. It has been noted that violent conflicts around the globe are increasingly based on ethnic divisions and that only a tiny proportion of wars now occur between states. The vast majority of conflicts are civil wars with ethnic dimensions. In a world of increasing interdependence and competition, international factors become even more important in shaping ethnic relations, while the effects of 'internal' ethnic conflicts are felt well outside national borders.

> Changing forms of warfare are discussed in chapter 22, 'Nations, War and Terrorism'.

As we have seen, ethnic conflicts attract international attention and have sometimes provoked physical intervention. International war crimes tribunals have been convened to investigate and try those responsible for the ethnic cleansing and genocide in Yugoslavia and Rwanda. Responding to and preventing ethnic conflict have become key challenges facing both individual states and international political structures. Although ethnic tensions are often experienced, interpreted and described at the local level, they are increasingly taking on national and international dimensions.

Global Society 16.2 | Genocide in Rwanda

Between April and June 1994, an estimated 800,000 Rwandans were killed in the space of 100 days. Most of the dead were Tutsis – and most of those who perpetrated the violence were Hutus. Even for a country with such a turbulent history as Rwanda, the scale and speed of the slaughter left its people reeling.

The genocide was sparked by the death of the Rwandan president Juvenal Habyarimana, a Hutu, when his plane was shot down above Kigali airport on 6 April 1994. A French official report blamed the then current Rwandan president, Paul Kagame. The report – extracts of which appeared in the daily newspaper *Le Monde* – said French police had concluded that Mr Kagame gave direct orders for the rocket attack. Rwanda rejected the report, describing it as a 'fantasy'.

Within hours of the attack, a campaign of violence spread from the capital throughout the country and did not subside until three months later. But the death of the president was by no means the only cause of Africa's largest genocide in modern times.

History of violence

Ethnic tension in Rwanda is nothing new. There have been always been disagreements between the majority Hutus and the minority Tutsis, but the animosity between them has grown substantially since the colonial period. The two ethnic groups are actually very similar – they speak the same language, inhabit the same areas and follow the same traditions.

But when the Belgian colonists arrived in 1916, they saw the two groups as distinct entities, and even produced identity cards classifying people according to their ethnicity. The Belgians considered the Tutsis as superior to the Hutus. Not surprisingly, the Tutsis welcomed this idea, and for the next twenty years they enjoyed better jobs and educational opportunities than their neighbours. Resentment among the Hutus gradually built up, culminating in a series of riots in 1959. More than 20,000 Tutsis were killed, and many more fled to the neighbouring countries of Burundi, Tanzania and Uganda. When Belgium relinquished power and granted Rwanda independence in 1962, the Hutus took their place.

Building up to genocide

This was still the case in the years before the genocide. The economic situation worsened and the incumbent president, Juvenal Habyarimana, began losing popularity. At the same time, Tutsi refugees in Uganda – supported by some moderate Hutus – were forming the Rwandan Patriotic Front (RPF). Their aim was to overthrow Habyarimana and secure their right to return to their homeland. Habyarimana chose to exploit this threat as a way to bring dissident Hutus back to his side, and Tutsis inside Rwanda were accused of being RPF collaborators.

In August 1993, after several attacks and months of negotiation, a peace accord was signed between Habyarimana and the RPF, but it did little to stop the continued unrest. When Habyarimana's plane was shot down at the beginning of April 1994, it was the final nail in the coffin. Exactly who killed the president – and with him the president of Burundi and many chief members of staff – has not been established. Whoever was behind the killing, its effect was both instantaneous and catastrophic.

Mass murder

In Kigali, the presidential guard immediately initiated a campaign of retribution. Leaders of the political opposition were murdered and, almost immediately, the slaughter of Tutsis and moderate Hutus began. Within hours, recruits were dispatched all over the country to carry out a wave of killing. The early organizers included military officials, politicians and businessmen, but soon many others joined in the mayhem.

Encouraged by the presidential guard and radio propaganda, an unofficial militia group called the Interahamwe (meaning 'those who attack together') was mobilized. At its peak, this group was 30,000 strong. Soldiers and police officers encouraged ordinary citizens to take part. In some cases, Hutu civilians were forced by military personnel to murder their Tutsi neighbours. Participants were often given incentives, such as money or food, and some were even told they could appropriate the land of the Tutsis they killed.

On the ground at least, the Rwandans were largely left alone by the international community. UN troops withdrew after the murder of ten of their soldiers. The day after Habyarimana's death, the RPF renewed their assault on government forces, and numerous attempts by the UN to negotiate a ceasefire came to nothing.

Aftermath

Finally, in July, the RPF captured Kigali. The government collapsed and the RPF declared a ceasefire. As soon as it became apparent that the RPF was victorious, an estimated 2 million Hutus fled to Zaire (now the Democratic Republic of Congo). Back in Rwanda, UN troops and aid workers then arrived to help maintain order and restore basic services.

On 19 July a new multi-ethnic government was formed, promising all refugees a safe return to Rwanda. But, although the massacres are over, the legacy of the genocide continues, and the search for justice has been a long and arduous one. About 500 people have been sentenced to death, and another 100,000 are still in prison. But some of the ringleaders have managed to evade capture, and many who lost their loved ones are still waiting for justice.

Source: Adapted from BBC (2011).

Migration in a global age

While we may think of immigration as a phenomenon of the twentieth century, the process has its roots in the earliest stages of written history, and migration is accelerating as part of the process of global integration. As we saw earlier, the recent 'new migration' has produced an intensified super-diversity of situation and experience within as well as across ethnic communities. In some areas, such as Hackney in London or parts of New York, the experience of cultural diversity is so ordinary that people pay it little attention. Wessendorf (2014: 3) notes that 'Commonplace diversity thus results from a saturation of difference whenever people step out of their front door.' The new migration patterns which have helped to transform social life in the last twenty-five years or so are one aspect of the rapidly growing economic, political and cultural ties between countries.

It has been estimated that one in every thirty-three people in the world today is a migrant. In 2012, about 214 million people resided in a country other than where they were born, and the International Organization for Migration (2012) estimates that this number may almost double by 2050, to 405 million, prompting some scholars to label this the 'age of migration' (Castles and Miller 2009). In this section we recount the experience of immigration in Britain, which has played a crucial role in the movement of people around the world, during the period of both imperialist expansion and the demise of the British Empire.

Immigration, the movement of people into a country to settle, and emigration, the process by which people leave one country to settle in another, combine to produce global migration patterns linking *countries of origin* and *countries of destination*. Migratory movements add to ethnic and cultural diversity in many societies and help to shape demographic, economic and social dynamics. The intensification of global migration since the Second World War, and particularly in more recent decades, has transformed immigration into an important and contentious political issue.

Four models of migration have been used to describe the main global population movements since 1945. The *classic model* applies to countries such as Canada, the United States and Australia, which have developed as 'nations of immigrants'. In such cases, immigration has been largely encouraged and the promise of citizenship has been extended to newcomers, although restrictions and quotas help to limit the annual intake. The *colonial model*, pursued by countries such as France and the United Kingdom, tended to favour immigrants from former colonies over those from other countries. The large number of immigrants to Britain in the years after the Second World War from Commonwealth countries, such as India or Jamaica, reflected this tendency.

Countries such as Germany, Switzerland and Belgium have followed a third policy – the *guest workers model*. Under such a scheme, immigrants are admitted into the country on a temporary basis, often to fulfil demands within the labour market, but they do not receive citizenship rights even after long periods of settlement. Finally, *illegal forms* of immigration are becoming increasingly common. Immigrants who are able to gain entry into a country either secretly or under a 'non-immigration' pretence are often able to live illegally outside the realm of official society. Examples can be seen in the large number of Mexican 'illegal aliens' in many Southern American states and in the growing international business of smuggling refugees across national borders.

The spread of industrialization dramatically transformed migration patterns. The growth of opportunities for work in urban areas coupled with the decline of household production in the countryside encouraged a trend towards rural–urban migration. Demands within the labour market also gave new impetus to immigration from abroad. In Britain, Irish, Jewish and black communities had existed long before the Industrial Revolution, but the surge of new opportunities altered the scale and scope of international immigration. New waves of Dutch, Chinese, Irish and black immigrants transformed British society.

A large wave of immigration to Britain occurred in the 1930s when the Nazi persecutions sent a generation of European Jews fleeing westwards to safety. It has been estimated that some 60,000 Jews settled in the UK between 1933 and 1939, but the real figure may well have been higher. In the same period, around 80,000 refugees arrived from Central Europe, and a further 70,000 entered during the war itself. By May 1945, Europe faced an unprecedented refugee problem: millions of people had become refugees, and many settled in Britain.

Following the Second World War, Britain experienced immigration on a large scale as people from Commonwealth countries were encouraged and facilitated to come to the UK, which had a marked shortage of labour. In addition to rebuilding the country and economy following the destruction of the war, industrial expansion provided British workers with unprecedented mobility, creating a need for labour in unskilled and manual positions. Government, influenced by ideas of Britain's imperial heritage, encouraged people from the West Indies, India, Pakistan and other former colonies in Africa to settle in the UK. The 1948 British Nationality Act granted favourable immigration rights to citizens of Commonwealth countries.

With each wave of immigration, the religious make-up of the country changed. British cities, in particular, are now multi-ethnic and religiously diverse. In the nineteenth century, immigrants from Ireland swelled the number of Catholics in cities such as Liverpool and Glasgow, where many settled. In the postwar period, large-scale immigration from Asia increased the number of Muslims, many from the largely Muslim countries of Pakistan and Bangladesh, and Hindus, mainly from India. Immigration brought new questions about what it means to be British and how ethnic and religious minorities can integrate fully into British society.

> Religious diversity is discussed in more detail in chapter 17, 'Religion'.

Migration and the decline of empire: Britain since the 1960s

The 1960s marked the start of a gradual rolling back of the idea that inhabitants of the British Empire had the right to settle in Britain and claim citizenship. Although changing labour markets played a role in the new restrictions, they were also the response to a backlash

There was a rise in Commonwealth immigrants coming to Britain after the Second World War in response to a national labour shortage, but they often faced racism. Immigration was later restricted.

against immigrants by groups of white Britons. In particular, working people living in poorer areas, to which the new immigrants gravitated for their work, were sensitive to the 'disruption' to their own lives. Attitudes to the newcomers were often hostile. The 1958 Notting Hill riots, in which white residents attacked black immigrants, were testament to the strength of racist attitudes.

Many anti-racist campaigners have argued that British immigration policy is racist and discriminatory against non-white groups. Since the Commonwealth Immigrants Act 1962, a series of legislative measures have been passed, gradually restricting entry and settlement rights for non-whites, while protecting the ability of whites to enter Britain relatively freely. For example, among citizens of Commonwealth states, immigration laws discriminated against the predominantly non-white 'New Commonwealth' states, while preserving the rights of mainly white immigrants from 'old Commonwealth' countries such as Canada and Australia. The British Nationality Act of 1981 separated 'British citizenship' from citizenship of British dependent territories. Legislation introduced in 1988 and 1996 increased these restrictions even further.

The Nationality, Immigration and Asylum Act 2002 set requirements for people wanting British citizenship, including a basic knowledge of life in the UK, citizenship ceremonies and a pledge of allegiance. In 2008, a new points-based immigration system was introduced, in which points were awarded for workplace skills, age, educational qualifications and UK experience. The aim was to manage migration better and link migration to the needs of the economy. The government imposed a temporary cap on immigration from outside the European Union in 2010, with a permanent annual cap of 20,700 skilled workers from April 2011. Very wealthy individuals and those of 'exceptional talent' (such as some sports stars) are still allowed to enter.

The stated intention was to reduce net immigration to the UK to 'tens of thousands' rather than 'hundreds of thousands'. However, business organizations expressed concerns that reducing the number of skilled workers could damage the economy, while human rights groups have opposed proposals to tighten the rules on immigration for family members. In practice, the target was not met and, when the government left office in 2015, net long-term immigration in the previous year was 318,000, significantly higher than the 2013 figure of 209,000 (ONS 2015b: 1).

Many European countries have reduced the possibility for asylum-seekers to gain entry. To be granted asylum, individuals must claim that being forced to leave the country would break obligations that the government has under the United Nations Convention and Protocol relating to the Status of Refugees (1951). Since 1991, there have been more stringent checks on people claiming refugee status, including fingerprinting, reduced access to free legal advice, and the doubling of fines levied on airlines which bring in passengers not holding valid visas. As more measures were introduced, an increased number of refusals resulted in a larger number of asylum-seekers being held in detention centres for long periods of time.

In the last twenty years or so, issues of 'race' and immigration have again become more important in public opinion surveys across the developed societies. Despite periodic spikes of increased interest, immigration and race relations barely registered in UK surveys until around 1993, when a steadily rising trend began (Duffy and Frere-Smith 2014). Of course, key events can also affect public opinion, and the so-called race riots in parts of the UK also played a part. Following the al-Qaeda attacks on the USA in September 2001, the trend has been towards rising concerns about race and ethnicity, not just in Britain but across the developed world.

But, as may be seen in figure 16.3, as annual net migration to the UK increases, opinion polls show migration rising to the top of 'issues of concern'. Across the other countries of the EU there appears to be no such correlation, which points to the importance of the national social and political context in generating concerns about particular issues. As opportunities for migrants to enter Britain were cut off, there was a sharp rise in the number of people seeking asylum. Depictions of 'bogus' asylum-seekers 'swamping' the UK have served to create a distorted image of immigration and asylum. The coordinated terrorist suicide bombings in London on 7 July 2005, which killed fifty-two civilians and injured 700 others, promoted lurid headlines in British newspapers suggesting a direct link between terrorism and asylum-seekers. This sensationalist reporting proved to be entirely inaccurate. In addition, the emergence and electoral successes of the United Kingdom Independence Party (UKIP), which focuses on the negative aspects of EU membership and a society-wide political discourse of immigration as a problem, have provided a specific lens through which migration statistics are interpreted. The UK voted to leave the EU in June 2016 after migration became a key issue in the 'Vote Leave' campaign.

In Europe, concerns about 'race' and immigration have also been rising, though with national differences. In Germany only a minority, 34 per cent, thought immigration from the Middle East and North Africa was 'a good thing', while 57 per cent thought it was 'a bad thing'; two-thirds of Germans in the survey disapproved of immigration from Eastern Europe. Public opinion in the Netherlands was rather more split, with roughly equal percentages approving and disapproving of immigration from the Middle East and North Africa and Eastern Europe (50 per cent and 47 per cent). In France, a small majority actually approved of immigration from these areas; in Spain, 67 per cent saw immigration from the Middle East and North Africa as a good thing, and 72 per cent approved of Eastern European immigration (Pew Research Centre 2005).

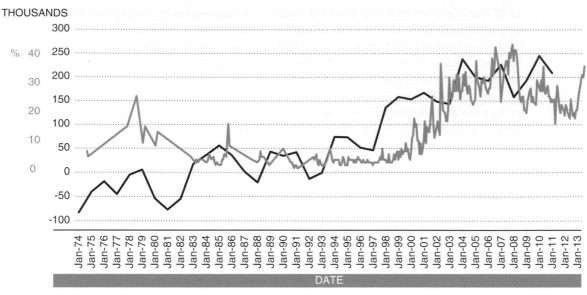

THOUSANDS

Figure 16.3 Immigration as an important issue, by UK net migration, 1974–2013

Source: Duffy and Frere-Smith (2014: 8).

Given the 2008 financial crisis, the 2009 global recession and post-recession austerity programmes across the countries of the developed world, it is unsurprising that immigration remains at the forefront of media commentary and political debate. In testing economic periods, there is a tendency to apportion blame, which often means that visible minority ethnic groups become convenient scapegoats. In such times, rational analysis of the pros and cons of immigration often struggle to be heard. Nonetheless, conducting such rational analyses as the basis for policy-making is fundamental to social scientific work and will be even more important than ever in the coming years.

THINKING CRITICALLY

Given the increasing mobility of the global age, is rising concern about immigration inevitable in the developed countries? Does this also mean increasing success for anti-immigration political parties?

Migration and the European Union

Not just Britain, but most other European countries were profoundly transformed by migration during the twentieth century. Large-scale migrations took place in Europe during the two decades after the Second World War. The Mediterranean countries provided the nations in the North and West with cheap labour. Migrants moving from areas such as Turkey, North Africa, Greece and southern Spain and Italy were, for a period, actively encouraged by host countries facing acute shortages of labour. Switzerland, Germany, Belgium and Sweden all have considerable populations of migrant workers. At the same time, former colonial powers experienced an influx of immigrants from their former colonies: this applied primarily to France (Algerians) and the Netherlands (Indonesians), as well as the UK.

Since the end of Eastern European communism, the EU has witnessed new migration marked by two main events. First, the opening of borders between East and West led to the migration of several million people into EU countries between 1989 and 1994. Second, war and ethnic strife in the former Yugoslavia resulted in a surge of approximately 5 million refugees into other regions of Europe (Koser and Lutz 1998). The geographical patterns of European migration have also shifted, with the lines between countries of origin and countries of destination becoming increasingly blurred. Countries in Southern and Central Europe have become destinations for many migrants, a notable departure from earlier immigration trends. As part of the move towards European integration, many of the earlier barriers to the free movement of commodities, capital and employees have been removed. This has led to a dramatic increase in regional migration, as

Figure 16.4   The Schengen Area, March 2016

EU citizens have the right to work in any other EU country.

As the process of European integration continues, a number of countries dissolved internal border controls with neighbouring states as part of the Schengen agreement, which came into force in 1995. By 2001, the agreement had been implemented by twenty-five countries, and their external borders are only monitored, as they allow free entry from neighbouring member states (see figure 16.4). This reconfiguration of European border controls has had an enormous impact on illegal immigration into the EU and cross-border crime. Illegal immigrants able to gain access to a Schengen state can move unimpeded throughout the entire Schengen area.

Migration into the EU from non-EU countries has become one of the most pressing issues for a number of European states. Many of the key issues were thrown into sharp relief in 2014–15, when thousands of people arrived in Southern Europe having crossed by boat from Libya. Some migrants were escaping conflicts in Syria, Iraq and parts of Africa, while many others were trying to improve their life chances. The involvement of human trafficking groups profiting from such desperate movements of people around the world only added to the controversy. The EU's border management agency, Frontex, estimated that around 63,000 migrants arrived in Greece, 62,000 in Italy, with some 10,000 on the Hungary–Serbia border. These numbers represented almost a 150 per cent increase from 2013 (BBC News 2015a).

Many migrants die at sea while trying to make the Mediterranean crossing to Europe from Libya. In 2014 over 3,000 people lost their lives in this way, and in just the first four months of 2015 more than 1,700 people were killed, often when their hugely overcrowded boats capsized and sank at sea. A majority of these migrants had travelled from Syria and some of the poorest countries of sub-Saharan Africa, including Mali, Eritrea, Sudan, Gambia,

The collapse of national government in Libya after 2011 allowed human traffickers to exploit the thousands of people escaping conflict in Syria and persecution and hardship in parts of Africa. In 2014–15, Italy and Greece were the main entry points from Libya.

Senegal and Somalia, plus a smaller number of Palestinians (Malakooti and Davin 2015). EU rules state that those seeking asylum should be fingerprinted and make their application in the first EU country they enter. That would mean countries such as Greece and Italy shouldering the entire administrative burden as well as taking in the very large numbers involved.

In June 2015 the European Commission proposed a quota system to distribute around 40,000 of the new migrants to other EU countries and set out a plan to break up the human traffickers' networks. Agreement proved difficult on both aspects. Some EU countries objected to mandatory migration quotas, while UN authorization for operations in Libya and its territorial waters brought objections from Russia. The crisis illustrates the truly global nature of migration and mobility, suggesting that irregular mass movements of humanity may become more frequent as long as internal conflicts and gross global inequality continue to characterize the world's societies.

Globalization and migration

So far we have concentrated on recent immigration into Europe, but European expansion centuries ago also initiated large-scale movement of populations, which formed the basis of many of the world's multi-ethnic societies today. Since these initial waves of global migration, human populations have continued to interact and mix in ways that have fundamentally shaped the ethnic composition of many countries. In this section we shall consider concepts related to global migration patterns.

Many early theories about migration focused on so-called push and pull factors. 'Push factors' referred to dynamics within a country of origin which forced people to emigrate, such as war, famine, political oppression or population pressures. 'Pull factors', by contrast, were those features of destination countries which attracted immigrants: prosperous labour markets, better overall living conditions and lower population density, for example, could 'pull' immigrants from other regions.

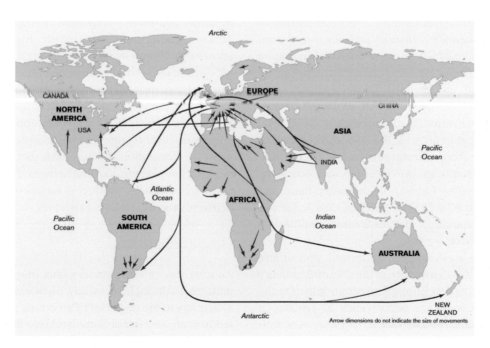

Figure 16.5 Global migrations, 1945–73

Source: Castles and Miller (1993: 67).

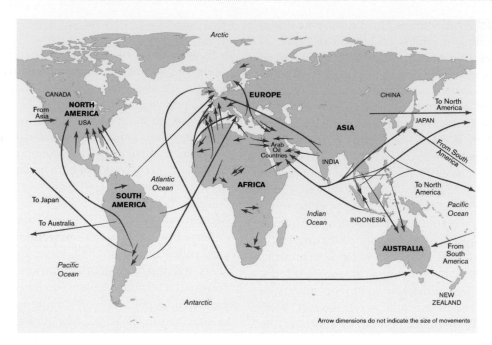

Figure 16.6   Global migrations from 1973

Source: Castles and Miller (1993: 67).

Recently, 'push and pull' theories of migration have been criticized for offering overly simplistic explanations of a complex and multifaceted process. Instead, scholars of migration are increasingly looking at global migration patterns as 'systems' which are produced through interactions between macro- and micro-level processes. Macro-level factors refer to overarching issues such as the political situation in an area, the laws and regulations controlling immigration and emigration, or changes in the international economy. Micro-level factors, on the other hand, are concerned with the resources, knowledge and understandings that the migrant populations themselves possess.

The intersection of macro and micro processes can be seen in the case of Germany's large Turkish immigrant community. On the macro level are factors such as Germany's economic need for labour, its policy of accepting foreign 'guest workers' and the state of the Turkish economy, which prevents many Turks from earning at the level they would wish. At the micro level are the informal networks and channels of mutual support within the Turkish community in Germany and the strong links to family and friends who have remained in Turkey. Among potential Turkish migrants, knowledge about Germany and 'social capital' – human or community resources that can be drawn on – help to make Germany one of the most popular destination countries. Supporters of the migration systems approach emphasize that no single factor can explain the process of migration. Rather, each particular migratory movement, like that between Turkey and Germany, is the product of an interaction of macro- and micro-level processes.

Global diasporas

Another way to understand global migration patterns is through the study of diasporas. This refers to the dispersal of an ethnic population from an original homeland into foreign areas, often in a forced manner or under traumatic circumstances. References are often made to the Jewish and African diasporas to describe the way in which these populations

Classic Studies 16.2 | Understanding the new age of migration

The research problem

People have always moved around the world for better job prospects or to flee persecution. But today, as globalization takes hold, patterns of migration have changed as people take advantage of global transport and travel systems and new opportunities for tourism. How will global migration affect the composition and solidarities within the societies of the twenty-first century? Stephen Castles and Mark Miller's (1993) book on the subject was into its fourth edition by 2009, suggesting that the authors' analysis successfully framed and redefined the field of migration studies. In short, their analysis of 'the new migration' has become a modern classic.

Castles and Miller's explanation

Castles and Miller acknowledge that international migration is certainly not new; it has existed from the earliest times. What has changed today, though, is the sheer size, speed and scope of migration, all of which have the potential to transform societies. Examining recent trends in global migration patterns, the authors identify four tendencies which they claim will characterize migration in the coming years.

First there is a tendency towards the *acceleration* of migration across borders as people move in greater numbers than ever before. Second is the tendency towards *diversification*. Most countries now receive immigrants from many different places with a variety of motivations, in contrast with earlier times when particular forms of immigration, such as labour immigration or refugees fleeing persecution, were predominant. Third, there is a tendency towards *globalization*. Migration has become global in character, involving a larger number of countries as both 'senders' and 'recipients' of migrants. Finally, there is a tendency towards the *feminization* of migration. A growing number of migrants are women, making contemporary migration much less male-dominated than in previous times.

Taking these together, Castles and Miller argue that, in the 'new age of migration', there will be much more movement of people, many

of them women, and particular countries will experience a more diverse range of immigrant groups. Migration is also very likely to become normalized as a central feature of the world in which we live; people, governments and international bodies (such as the United Nations) will have to find new ways of managing it.

Critical points

Some have suggested that the analysis presented by Castles and Miller remains quite conventional and does not do enough to link with emerging and potentially overlapping fields, such as the new studies of mobilities (see Sheller and Urry 2004; Larsen et al. 2006). Others argue that their book is centred on states and their fate in the age of mass migration, rather than moving beyond states to explore large urban regions. Finally, the inclusion of terrorist activity has been seen by some critics as somewhat forced, rather than flowing from their general analytical framework.

Contemporary significance

Castles and Miller have made a significant contribution to the new migration studies by effectively showing how globalization influences patterns of migration and how migration has much greater potential to reshape societies. They have helped, too, to reshape the field of migration studies by adopting a more comparative perspective than usual and exploring migration from the developed to the developing countries as well as in the other direction. They also manage to link migration patterns to theories of globalization, thus bringing the study of migration into the mainstream of sociology.

THINKING CRITICALLY

Castles and Miller suggest that migration will become 'normalized' as a consequence of globalization. Using examples from this chapter, why might they be right? What counter-examples are there that may mean increasing migration is likely to be resisted?

---

have become redistributed across the globe as a result of slavery and genocide. Although members of a diaspora are by definition scattered geographically, they are held together by factors such as shared history, a collective memory of the original homeland, or a common ethnic identity which is nurtured and preserved.

Although we are more familiar with diaspora as the involuntary movement of people resulting from persecution and violence, Cohen (1997) argues that the dominant meaning has changed over time. Adopting a historical approach to the dispersal of people, Cohen identifies five categories of diaspora. The ancient Greeks used the word to describe the dispersal of populations which resulted from *colonization*. *Victim* diasporas, such as those of the African slave trade, along with Jewish and Armenian population movements, are those in which people suffer forced exile and long to return to their homelands. *Labour* diasporas

are typified by the indentured labour of Indian workers during British colonialism. Cohen sees movements of Chinese people to South-East Asia during the creation of a *trading* diaspora as an example of a voluntary movement for the buying and selling of goods, not the result of some traumatic event. *Imperial* diasporas are those where imperialist expansion into new lands takes with it people who subsequently make new lives; the British Empire would be the most well-known example. Finally, Cohen makes a case for viewing the movement of people from the Caribbean as an instance of *cultural* diaspora – 'cemented as much by literature, political ideas, religious convictions, music and lifestyles as by permanent migration' (ibid.). In reality though, as Cohen admits, these categories are overlapping and diasporas occur for a variety of reasons.

Despite the diversity of forms, however, all diasporas share certain key features. Cohen suggests that they all meet the following criteria:

The Jewish community represents one of the most historical and dispersed examples of a global diaspora.

- a forced or voluntary movement from an original homeland to a new region
- a shared memory about the original homeland, a commitment to its preservation and belief in the possibility of return
- a strong ethnic identity sustained over time and distance
- a sense of solidarity with members of the same ethnic group living in areas of the diaspora
- a degree of tension in relation to the host societies
- the potential for valuable and creative contributions to pluralistic host societies.

This typology is a simplification (which Cohen readily admits) and may therefore be criticized for being imprecise. However, the study is valuable because it shows how the meaning of diaspora is not static but relates to the ongoing processes of maintaining collective identities and preserving ethnic cultures in the context of a rapid period of globalization. The concept of a 'diaspora' has been applied to a rapidly expanding number of possible cases from national groups such as Scottish, Estonian or Iraqi diasporas to suggested diasporas of 'fundamentalists' and 'rednecks'. This expansion has led some to argue that, 'If everyone is diasporic, then no one is distinctively so. The term loses its discriminating power – its ability to pick out phenomena, to make distinctions. The universalization of diaspora, paradoxically, means the disappearance of diaspora' (Brubaker 2005: 3). Brubaker proposes that one way to retain the concept in social scientific work is to treat 'diaspora' as a form of practice or a project rather than as an existing 'bounded group'. Doing so would enable researchers to explore the extent to which any diasporic 'project' has support from those said to be its members.

Conclusion

In our global age, ideas, goods and people flow across borders in greater volumes than ever before. These processes are profoundly altering the societies in which we live. Many societies are becoming ethnically diverse for the first time; others are finding existing patterns of multi-ethnicity are being transformed or intensified. In all societies, individuals are coming into regular contact with people who think differently, look different and live differently from themselves. These interactions are happening in person, as well as through the images that are transmitted through the media, especially the Internet.

Global migration patterns form one element within an increasing interest in 'mobilities' in sociological research and theorizing (Sheller and Urry 2004; Urry 2007; Benhabib and Resnik 2009). The mobilities research agenda explores issues of 'movement' across a very wide range of social phenomena, including the physical movement of goods, movements of people across the world, information and monetary transfers in cyberspace, and much more. Urry (2007: 6), a key figure in this field, observes that

> Issues of movement, of too little movement for some or too much for others, or of the wrong sort or at the wrong time, are it seems central to many people's lives and to the many operations of many small and large public, private and non-governmental organizations. From SARS to plane crashes, from airport expansion controversies to SMS texting, from slave trading to global terrorism, from obesity caused by the 'school run' to oil wars in the Middle East, from global warming to slave trading, issues of what I term 'mobility' are centre-stage on many policy and academic agendas. There is we might say a 'mobility' structure of feeling in the air . . .

For Urry (2000), the focus on mobilities may mean that we need a new type of sociology which goes 'beyond societies' – that is, a sociology which investigates social processes, networks and movement across the boundaries of nation-states and effectively dispenses with the previously foundational concept of (a national) 'society' itself. In some ways, the emerging mobilities paradigm captures some crucial dynamics of global migration.

For example, many migrants today do not simply leave one home to forge a new one in a far-flung location. More easily accessible, faster and relatively cheaper travel means that people can physically revisit their original home or attend family reunions and keep in touch via email, social networks and mobile telephony (Larsen et al. 2006: 44–5). Emigration, for some, has become much less of a one-way, once-and-for-all movement.

But exploring mobilities need not entail a commitment to the thesis that social life is inevitably becoming more and more fluid or liquid, or that movement and mobility are certain to increase in the future. As our discussion of ethnic conflicts over resources and territory, public hostility to increasing immigration in Europe, and opposition to multiculturalism as state policy all suggest, increasing mobilities also prompt resistance. It is precisely the growing perception that, to paraphrase Karl Marx, 'all that is solid is melting into air' in an increasingly mobile world which gives rise both to optimistic notions of a global or cosmopolitan citizenship and fears of the loss of national and ethnic identity in the global melting pot.

Chapter review

1 What is meant by 'race' today? Why do sociologists continue to refer to 'race' even though it has no scientific basis?

2 How does the concept of ethnicity differ from 'race'? How are boundaries between ethnic groups generated and reinforced?

3 Provide some examples of minority ethnic groups and describe the types of discrimination they face. Does racial prejudice inevitably lead to discrimination?

4 What is 'racism'? How is the so-called new racism different from older forms? Are the consequences for minority ethnic groups any different?

5 What is institutional racism? Give some examples of this and explain how it affects social integration.

6 Describe the three main models of ethnic integration: assimilation, the melting pot and cultural pluralism/multiculturalism. Which of the models best fits the different situations in Britain, the USA, Germany and Australia? Why does multiculturalism draw negative responses from some European political leaders?

7 Outline some of the main movements of people into the UK which have led to its present ethnic diversity. Which ethnic groups tend to be disadvantaged compared to the white majority population and which do as well or better? How can we explain such differences?

8 What are the main patterns that characterize the 'age of migration'? List some of the national social and political consequences of global migration.

9 What are diasporas? Outline the main types and their social consequences.

10 How does the thesis of expanding 'mobilities' help us to understand global migration?

Research in practice

Migrants and asylum-seekers have often been scapegoats for the ills and problems of society. In majority white cultures, the readily observable difference of skin colour has been a marker for prejudice and discrimination against black and Asian groups. But what if those disrupting social norms do not fit neatly into identifiable ethnic categories but cut across them? How does society make sense of the apparent contradiction? In 2010 a former Kosovan refugee killed five people, including his ex-girlfriend, in a Finnish shopping centre before killing himself. Read the following article, which analyses the impact of this event on Finland's self-image: Keskinen, S. (2014) 'Re-constructing the Peaceful Nation: Negotiating Meanings of Whiteness, Immigration and Islam after a Shopping Mall Shooting', *Social Identities*, 20(6): 471–85.

1   What kind of a study is this? What are the main sources of evidence used here?
2   How does the author characterize Finland's 'imagined national identity'?
3   How did 'whiteness' act as both a source of difference and similarity in media reporting of the killings?
4   The author suggests that the threat of violence to Finnish society was eventually defused. Trace the steps in this process, noting the key turning points.
5   List the main actors in the social process which resolved the dilemma of extreme violence in a peaceable society. In what ways did this process bear similarity to a 'moral panic' and in what ways did it differ?

Thinking it through

The increasing normality of mobility and migration raises the question of how people's identities are formed in the more fluid or 'liquid' social world today. Read Zygmunt Bauman's (2011) theoretical paper 'Migration and Identities in the Globalized World', *Philosophy and Social Criticism*, 37(4): 425–35, which discusses how societies hold together in this situation.

In your own words, describe the three stages outlined in the transformation of modern societies. What does Bauman mean by 'gardening' in the first stage? How does he characterize contemporary multiculturalism? Explain how 'continuity' and 'discontinuity' may combine to provide the glue that holds modern societies together. What criticisms might be levelled at Bauman's arguments in this piece?

Society in the arts

There are many representations of relations between ethnic groups, races and cultures in film and television series, some based directly on real events, others entirely fictional. *District 9* (2009), directed by Neill Blomkamp, is ostensibly a science fiction movie about aliens arriving on Earth and the way they are received by humans. However, as the aliens are housed in the squalor of a makeshift camp in South Africa (District 9), the film calls to mind both apartheid-era segregation and the situation of human migrants and refugees in various sites around the world.

Watch the film and note down all of the relevant parallels between the plight of the aliens and that of real-world migrants and refugees. For example, are there prejudice, discrimination and racism towards the aliens? How is this manifested in the behaviour of the humans? What are the responses of groups of aliens? The story turns on the gradual transformation of one human operative into an alien. Given the way this tale unfolds, what, if anything, is the central message of the film? What are the advantages and disadvantages of using science fiction rather than documentary as a way of presenting issues of migration, segregation and asylum?

Further reading

A good place to start your reading is with Steve Fenton's (2010) *Ethnicity* (2nd edn, Cambridge: Polity), which is an introductory text pitched at the right level. Ian Law's (2009) *Racism and Ethnicity: Global Debates, Dilemmas, Directions* (Harlow: Pearson Education) is also very good. Khalid Koser's (2016) *International Migration: A Very Short Introduction* (2nd edn, Oxford: Oxford University Press) also covers key issues at an introductory level.

From here, you can move on to something like Stephen Spencer's (2014) *Race and Ethnicity: Culture, Identity and Representation* (2nd edn, London: Routledge), which covers a lot of ground. For debates and issues around multiculturalism, see Michael Murphy's (2011) *Multiculturalism: A Critical Introduction* (New York: Routledge). Stephen Castles, Hein de Haas and Mark J Miller's (2013) *The Age of Migration: International Population Movements in the Modern World* (5th edn, Basingstoke: Palgrave Macmillan) is a key work on migration which now includes material on climate change too.

For reference works, *Theories of Race and Racism* (2009), edited by Les Back and John Solomos (2nd edn, London: Routledge), is an excellent collection of theories. Alice Bloch and John Solomos's (2009) *Race and Ethnicity in the Twenty-First Century* (Basingstoke: Palgrave Macmillan) is also a very useful and comprehensive edited collection. Nasar Meer's (2014) *Key Concepts in Race and Ethnicity* (London: Sage) is a comprehensive text that goes well beyond the material in this chapter.

For a collection of original readings on social inequalities, see the accompanying *Sociology: Introductory Readings* (3rd edn, Cambridge: Polity, 2010).

Internet links

@ **Additional information and support for this book at Polity:**
www.politybooks.com/giddens

@ **CRER – the Centre for Research in Ethnic Relations at the University of Warwick, UK – archived material on varied subjects:**
www2.warwick.ac.uk/fac/soc/crer

@ **FRA – the European Union Agency for Fundamental Rights – themes include minorities, racism and xenophobia, Roma and travellers:**
http://fra.europa.eu

@ **The Runnymede Trust – an independent UK race equality think tank with many useful reports:**
www.runnymedetrust.org

@ **Black History Pages – a US site with useful links and news reports:**
http://blackhistorypages.com

@ **UNHCR – the United Nations Refugee Agency – news about and resources on refugees:**
www.unhcr.org/cgi-bin/texis/vtx/home

@ **IRR – the Institute of Race Relations, UK – much research and library material:**
www.irr.org.uk

The Migration Observatory, University of Oxford, UK – news and resources on migration issues:
www.migrationobservatory.ox.ac.uk

@ **DARE – Democracy and Human Rights Education in Europe, launched in Antwerp, 2003 – promoting citizen participation across Europe:**
www.dare-network.eu

CHAPTER 17

Religion

Contents

Creation museums – the majority of which are in the USA – present a biblical creationist account of the origins of life on Earth in opposition to Darwinian evolutionary theory and geological evidence.

Question: Did human beings live with dinosaurs? Answer: 'God made Adam and Eve on the same day as land animals. So dinosaurs and people lived at the same time.' 'Mastodons and mammoths are related to modern elephants, and all of them appear to be descendants of the original elephant "kind" that God created around six thousand years ago.' These and many similar statements are presented as facts among the exhibits in the Creation Museum in Kentucky, one of a number of 'creation museums', most of which are in the USA.

For creationists, the sheer complexity of life, and the human body in particular, strongly suggests an intelligent design rather than random mutation or undirected evolutionary development. Arguments for an 'Intelligent Design' (Meyer 2013) are rooted in a critique of certain aspects of Charles Darwin's ground-breaking book *On the Origin of Species* (2008 [1859]), which presented his evidence for the unplanned, natural evolution of life on Earth.

The 'young Earth' notion that the planet is just 6,000 years old, with humans and dinosaurs living contemporaneously, appears as pure fantasy to geologists, biologists and other natural scientists. The evolutionary biologist Richard Dawkins (1986, 2006) argues that the evidence for 'blind' evolutionary processes is overwhelming and requires no recourse to an intelligent designer or God. He sees religious belief as essentially 'a delusion' and has become a spokesperson for atheism, secularism and rationalist thought. The physicist Brian Cox (cited in Farndale 2011) is even less charitable, asserting that, 'if you believe the world was created 6,000 years ago, as the creationists do, then you're an idiot.'

The scientific view is that planet Earth is around 4.5 billion years old and dinosaurs were wiped out some 65 million years ago, while the earliest evidence of human types can be traced back only between 6 and 7 million years ago in Africa. The Earth is very old, humans did not live with dinosaurs, and evolutionary processes, not Gods, are responsible for the long-term development of the planet's varied life forms.

Quite often, religion and science appear to be at odds with each other, and the dispute between creationists and mainstream natural scientists is a particularly stark example. You might think that, given the spectacular successes of modern science in many fields, from medicine to space exploration, the number of people adopting a creationist view of the universe must be tiny. However, opinion polls in the USA since 1982 consistently show that more than 40 per cent of adult

Americans believe the creationist account and that God created humans in their present form sometime within the last 10,000 years (see figure 17.1). Only 19 per cent agree with scientists that humans evolved over millions of years from less developed life forms without the involvement of God (Gallup 2014). However, the same poll also found a developing generational change, with 30 per cent of those aged between eighteen and twenty-nine agreeing with the scientific view compared with just 11 per cent of those aged fifty to sixty-four.

A secular, scientific perspective has been part of the expansion and deepening of modernity, yet reactions against science and rationalist thought continue. Some suggest this is because scientists and rationalists remain silent on fundamental questions such as the meaning and purpose of life. Religion remains a major aspect of human experience and, in one form or another, is found in all known human societies. The very earliest societies, of which the only evidence is archaeological remains, show clear traces of religious symbols and ceremonies. Cave drawings suggest that religious beliefs and practices existed more than 40,000 years ago. Throughout subsequent history, religion has continued to be central in human affairs.

But what exactly is 'religion' and why is it so pervasive in human societies? Under what conditions does it unite or divide communities? How do individuals make sense of religion and put their individual beliefs into practice? These are some of the issues we consider in this chapter. In order to do so, we shall look at some of the varied religious beliefs, practices and organizations as well as the main sociological theories of religion and empirical studies of religious practice. Throughout, we will consider the fate of religion primarily, though not exclusively, in relation to the developed countries, as it is here that it is said to be in long-term decline. Two key questions are whether the developed world really is becoming a secular space and, if it is, whether some form of religion will survive.

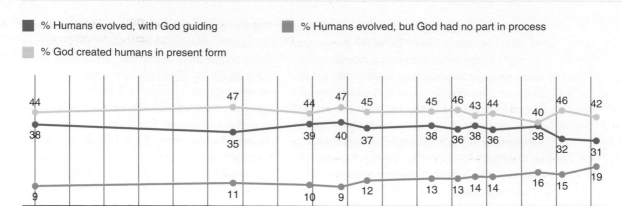

■ % Humans evolved, with God guiding ■ % Humans evolved, but God had no part in process

■ % God created humans in present form

Figure 17.1 Proportion of US adults favouring creationist or evolutionary explanations of human origin

Source: Gallup (2014).

The sociological study of religion

The study of religion is a challenging enterprise which places special demands on our sociological imagination. In analysing religious practices, we have to make sense of the diversity of beliefs and rituals found in human cultures. This means we have to be sensitive to the ideals that inspire profound conviction in believers, yet at the same time we must take a balanced view. We have to confront ideas that seek the eternal, while recognizing that religious groups also promote quite mundane goals, such as acquiring finance or soliciting for followers. We need to recognize the diversity of religious beliefs and modes of conduct but also probe into the nature of religion as a general social phenomenon.

What is religion?

What is religion? For most people, this is a simple question which hardly merits deep thought. Religions are commonly defined by a belief in God or gods and perhaps an afterlife, but they also involve worship in religious buildings such as chapels, synagogues or mosques and doing 'religious things' such

as praying and eating or not eating certain foods. However, for sociologists trying to set limits to their field of study, reaching general agreement on such a basic matter has proved extraordinarily difficult. Indeed, Aldridge (2007: 30) argues that 'We cannot expect to agree on a definition and then debate matters of substance, since matters of substance are built into any definition. There is not, and never will be, a universally agreed definition of religion.' But why not?

One reason is that sociology contains a plurality of general theoretical perspectives, and these differ in how they construe the nature of social reality. As a consequence, they also disagree about how that reality can and should be studied. For example, many macro-level studies adopt a realist view which sees religion as a fundamental social institution that transmits values, a moral code and norms of behaviour across generations. Hence 'religion' exists objectively and has real effects on individuals. Alternatively, several other micro-level studies are rooted in a more social constructionist position, which focuses on the ways in which what constitutes 'religion' is continually reproduced and changed in everyday interaction processes.

> Social constructionism is discussed in more detail in chapter 5, 'The Environment', and chapter 15, 'Gender and Sexuality'.

In general terms, competing sociological definitions of religion can be divided into three types: *inclusive definitions*, *exclusive definitions* and *definitions in use*. Inclusive definitions tend to be functionalist in orientation, viewing religion as central to human life as such and, in some ways, as functionally necessary for society. An example is the following: 'religion is a system of beliefs and practices by means of which a group of people struggles with the ultimate problems of human life' (Yinger 1970: 7). Others refer to religion as all those beliefs about the forces that shape human destiny (Lenski 1963). On this view, religion provides people with answers to enduring questions of existence, offers hope, and helps to bind people together in solidarity.

The main problem with inclusive definitions is they tend to include *too* much. That is, they imply that everyone is implicitly religious, whether or not they acknowledge it. As all humans face the same 'ultimate problems' of dying, death and the search for meaning, then they should all 'be' religious in some way. Even apparently secular political ideologies and regimes such as communism or leisure pursuits such as supporting football have been interpreted as forms of 'religion', because they represent systems of belief and practice that help people to find meaning in the world. However, critics suggest this stretches the definition of religion to everyone and removes key questions such as whether religion is growing or secularization is advancing (Aldridge 2007).

By contrast, *exclusive* definitions reject the functionalism of inclusive ones, instead looking to define religions by reference to the substance of their varied beliefs. In particular, exclusive definitions are rooted in the idea that all religions make a distinction between a worldly empirical reality and a 'super-empirical' or transcendent reality (Robertson 1970). Adopting this distinction means that many groups and institutions – such as football supporters or secular political ideologies – are effectively excluded on the grounds that they make no reference to a transcendent reality. This has the benefit of limiting what counts as religion, allowing sociologists to address the extent of secularization through empirical research. However, the attempt to produce a single definition to encompass all known religions relies on a very broad concept of the 'super-empirical', which is less applicable to new religious movements as well as to some Eastern religions. The distinction between empirical and super-empirical realities reflects its origins in Western social science.

The third type of definition is one described as a 'definition in use' and is similar to what today we call social constructionism. For many sociologists, a social constructionist approach to the study of religion offers a better starting point than the previous two types. Rather than assuming that there is a real phenomenon called religion and then exploring the varied ways in which it is manifest in society, constructionism sees it as more productive to investigate all of those situations in which people themselves make reference to 'religion' or 'religious meaning' and engage in self-defined 'religious' practices. This means that sociologists do not need to wrestle with the problem of devising their own universal definition; it is enough to investigate how religion has been and is used by a whole range of individuals, groups and organizations and how those uses have been challenged. Constructionist studies look at how the meaning of religion has changed over time, how people use the concept for their own purposes, and whether that use is increasing or diminishing.

However, one problem associated with all 'definitions in use' is that they do not set out a clear boundary between religious and non-religious phenomena, accepting that all of those things considered 'religious' by people themselves are legitimate

Large crowds of football supporters exhibit some of the characteristics attributed to religions, as these Manchester United supporters illustrate before a 2008 European Champions League game. But how does football supporting differ from religion?

subjects for research. Yet, for social constructionists, this lack of definitional clarity is not debilitating for empirical sociological research. On the contrary, Beckford (2008: 21) argues that

> uncertainty about what religion really is does not pose a problem to social scientists: it merely challenges them to understand how so many human beings still manage to navigate life without achieving certainty about religion or religious issues. . . . Social scientists therefore search for clear and robust reasons for the strong religious convictions that they observe in some cases. Neither religious confusion nor religious certainty can be regarded as natural or given in the nature of things.

Over time, both inclusive and exclusive definitions have lost ground to more social constructionist approaches to the study of religion. As you read through the different theories outlined in the section that follows, consider which of the three types of definition are being used. You should also think about what the different perspectives have contributed to our overall understanding of religion and religions.

Sociologists and religion

When sociologists study religion, they do so as professional sociologists, not as believers or unbelievers. This means that, *as sociologists*, they are not concerned with whether specific religious beliefs are true or false. For example, they may ask how a religion is organized, what its principal beliefs and values are, how religious organizations are related to the larger society, and what explains their successes and failures in recruiting and retaining members. The issue of whether a particular belief is 'good' or 'true', however important that may be to those involved, is not something sociologists can address. Of course, as private individuals, they may well have strong views, but as sociologists they try to prevent these from influencing their research and its findings.

In practice, sociologists have been especially concerned with religious organizations, which are some of the most important in society. Within Christianity and Judaism, religious practice often occurs in formal organizations – churches and synagogues – though this is not necessarily true of Asian religions such as Hinduism and Buddhism, where religious practices are just as likely to occur in the home and other informal settings. In the developed societies today, many religions have become established through bureaucratic organization. We will also see later that some sociologists view religions as essentially similar to business organizations, competing for members and resources (Warner 1993).

Sociologists have often seen religions as important sources of social solidarity. Religious beliefs, rituals and collective worship help to create a 'moral community' in which all the members know how to behave towards one another. However, religion has also been a factor in destructive social conflicts, such as struggles between Sikhs, Hindus and Muslims in India, clashes between Muslims and Christians in Bosnia, and 'hate crimes' against Jews, Muslims and other religious minorities in the United States and Europe. The question of whether religion *per se* produces harmony or conflict is, for contemporary sociologists, a historical and empirical one, and the classical founders were the first to tackle such questions in a sociological manner.

THINKING CRITICALLY

Should the sociology of religion be interested in adjudicating between competing beliefs? Give some reasons why sociologists cannot or should not take on this role.

Religion in classical sociology

Sociological approaches to religion have been influenced by the ideas of Marx, Durkheim and Weber. None of the three was devout, and all thought that traditional religions would be eroded as science and reason effectively 'disenchanted the world'. However, their detailed explanations of how and why disenchantment would progress are markedly different, and their central ideas are outlined in turn.

Karl Marx: religion and inequality

Karl Marx did not study religion in any detail and his ideas were derived mainly from several early nineteenth-century theological and philosophical writers. One of these was Ludwig Feuerbach (1804–72), whose most famous work was translated as *The Essence of Christianity* (1957 [1853]). According to Feuerbach, religion consists of ideas and values produced by human beings in the course of their cultural development, which they mistakenly project onto divine forces or gods. Because human beings do not fully understand their own history, they tend to attribute long-established, socially created values and norms to the activities of supernatural beings or 'spirit'. For instance, in Christianity, the story of the ten commandments given to Moses by God is a mythical version of the origin of moral precepts which govern the lives of Jewish and Christian believers.

If we fail to understand the origins of the religious symbols we have created, Feuerbach argues, we are condemned to be prisoners of forces we do not control. Feuerbach uses the term alienation to describe the creation of gods or divine forces distinct from human societies. The result is that human values and ideas become transferred onto gods and spirits. Feuerbach saw that understanding religion as a form of alienation promises great hope for the future. Once human beings recognize that religious powers are really their own, those values become capable of realization on Earth, rather than being deferred to an afterlife.

Marx accepted Feuerbach's view that religion represents human self-alienation.

And though it is often thought that Marx was entirely dismissive of religion, this is far from true. Religion, he writes, is the 'heart of a heartless world' – a haven from the harshness of the daily realities of capitalism. In Marx's view, religion in its traditional form will, and should, disappear; yet this is because the positive values embodied in religion can become guiding ideals for improving the lot of humanity on Earth, not because those ideals and values are themselves mistaken.

Marx declared, in a famous phrase, that religion is the 'opium of the people'. Religions such as Christianity defer happiness and rewards to the afterlife, teaching the resigned acceptance of existing conditions in this life. Attention is thus diverted away from inequality and injustice by the promise of what is to come. Hence, religion has a strong ideological element: religious beliefs and values often provide justifications for inequalities of wealth and power. For example, the teaching that 'the meek shall inherit the Earth' suggests an attitude of humility and an acceptance of worldly oppression.

> **THINKING CRITICALLY**
>
> Are there any examples from across the world where religions have opposed rather than supported the dominant social order? What do such cases tell us about Marx's perspective on religion?

Emile Durkheim: functionalism and religious ritual

In contrast to Marx, Emile Durkheim spent a good part of his later career studying religion. Durkheim's sociological theory of religion, like his work on suicide (see chapter 1), was of immense significance in establishing the discipline of sociology. It demonstrated that any subject could be approached from a sociological perspective but also that, without sociology, we are likely to misunderstand social life. This perspective on religion is discussed in 'Classic studies 17.1'.

Durkheim's functionalist approach focuses our attention on the relationship between religion and other social institutions, and this was taken forward in the twentieth century by the founder of structural functionalism, Talcott Parsons. Parsons was interested in the role and fate of religion in modern societies, and his central ideas are covered in chapter 3, 'Theories and Perspectives'.

Max Weber: world religions and social change

While Durkheim based his arguments on a very small number of cases, Max Weber embarked on an enormous project, studying the major religions of the world. No scholar before or since has undertaken such a huge task. Most of his attention was concentrated on what he called the *world religions* – those that have attracted very large numbers of believers and decisively affected the course of global history. He made detailed studies of Hinduism, Buddhism, Taoism and ancient Judaism (1951, 1952, 1958, 1963), and, in *The Protestant Ethic and the Spirit of Capitalism* (1992 [1904–5]) and elsewhere, he wrote extensively about the impact of Christianity on the history of the West. He did not, however, complete his projected study of Islam, which was left to later Weberian scholars (Turner 1974, 1993).

Weber's writings concentrate on the connection between religion and social change, something to which Durkheim paid little attention. Weber also disagreed with Marx, arguing that religion is not principally or necessarily a conservative force. On the contrary, religiously inspired movements have often produced dramatic social transformations. For example, Protestantism – particularly in its Puritan forms – was the original source of the capitalistic outlook found in the modern West, and it revolutionized attitudes towards profit-making and tradition. The early entrepreneurs were mostly Calvinists, and their drive to succeed, which helped initiate economic development, was originally prompted by a desire to serve God. Material success was for them a sign of divine favour.

Weber saw his research on the world religions as a single project. His discussion of the impact of Protestantism on the development of

Classic Studies 17.1 Emile Durkheim on the elementary forms of religion

The research problem

There are many religions across the world, some very old, such as Christianity and Hinduism, and some more recently developed, such as Scientology, which dates only from the 1950s. What, if anything, do they all have in common? What is it that allows us to discuss them as 'religions' rather than, say, philosophies? And how should we try to answer such questions sociologically? Emile Durkheim (1965 [1912]) suggested that the most productive method for discovering the essential character of religion was to investigate its simplest form, within small-scale, traditional societies – hence the title of his classic study, *The Elementary Forms of the Religious Life* (1912), one of the most influential studies in the sociology of religion.

Durkheim's explanation

Unlike Marx, Durkheim does not connect religion primarily with social inequality or power but, instead, relates it to the overall nature of the institutions of a society. He based his work on a study of totemism as practised by Australian Aboriginal societies, arguing that totemism represents religion in its most 'elementary' form. In this quite uncluttered form, it becomes easier to discern the crucial defining features of religion.

A 'totem' was originally an animal or plant taken as having particular symbolic significance for a social group. Totems are sacred objects, regarded with veneration and surrounded by various ritual activities. Durkheim defines religion in terms of a distinction between the sacred and the profane. Sacred objects and symbols, he holds, are treated as being apart from the routine aspects of existence, which constitute the realm of the profane. Eating the totemic animal or plant, except on special ceremonial occasions, is usually forbidden, and, as a sacred object, the totem is believed to have divine properties which separate it from other animals that might be hunted or crops that are gathered and consumed.

But *why* is the totem sacred? According to Durkheim, it is because it is a symbol representing the social group itself which stands for the central values of the community. It follows that the reverence which people feel for the totem actually derives from the respect they hold for central social values. In religions, the real object of worship is society itself.

Durkheim emphasized that religions are never just matters of belief. All religions involve regular ceremonial and ritual activities in which the group of believers meets together. In collective ceremonials, a sense of group solidarity is heightened and affirmed in what Durkheim called collective effervescence – the heightened feeling of energy generated in collective gatherings and events. Ceremonials take individuals away from the concerns of their profane social lives and into an elevated sphere in which they feel in contact with higher forces. These higher forces – attributed to totems, divine influences or gods – are in reality the expression of the influence of the collectivity over the individual. Nonetheless, people's religious *experience* should not be dismissed as mere self-delusion, for it is indeed the *real* experience of social forces.

In Durkheim's view, ceremony and ritual are essential in binding members of social groups together. This is why they are found not only in regular situations of worship but also in the various life crises, when major social transitions such as birth, marriage and death are experienced. In virtually all societies, ritual and ceremonial procedures are observed on such occasions. Durkheim reasons that collective ceremonials reaffirm group solidarity at a time when people are forced to adjust to major changes in their lives. Funeral rituals demonstrate that the values of the group, and the group itself, outlive the passing of particular individuals, thus providing a means for bereaved people to adjust to their altered circumstances. Mourning is not simply the spontaneous expression of grief, though of course it is for those personally affected by a death. Mourning is also a duty imposed by the group.

In small, traditional cultures, Durkheim argued, almost all aspects of life are permeated by religion. Religious ceremonies do reaffirm existing social values, but they can also be the source of new ideas and categories of thought.

Durkheim argues that rituals, such as Buddhist Wesak ceremonies, mark out the spiritual from the mundane, but in doing so they reinforce key social values.

Religion is not just a series of sentiments and activities, but actually conditions the modes of thinking within traditional cultures. Even the most basic categories of thought, including how time and space are thought of, were first framed in religious terms. The concept of 'time', for instance, was originally derived from counting the intervals involved in religious ceremonies.

With the development of modern societies, the influence of traditional religion begins to wane. Scientific explanations increasingly replace religious ones and ceremonial and ritual activities shrink, coming to occupy a much smaller part of people's lives. Durkheim agrees with Marx that the older forms of religion are slowly disappearing. He wrote that 'The old gods are dead.' Yet he also says that religion, in somewhat different forms, is very likely to continue. Even modern societies depend for their cohesion on rituals that reaffirm their values, and new rituals can be expected to emerge. Durkheim is quite vague about what these might be, but it seems he has in mind the celebration of the individual in humanist and political values such as freedom, equality and cooperation.

Critical points

One strand of criticism of Durkheim's thesis focuses on the argument that it is possible to understand the essential character of all religions by generalizing from a few small-scale societies. But critics maintain that it seems unlikely that Aboriginal totemism is typical of the large-scale, multinational world religions, casting doubt on what can be learned about the latter by studying the former. Over the course of the twentieth century many of the world's societies became culturally more varied, with a diverse range of religions existing within a single national society. Some think that Durkheim's thesis of religion as a source of the continual re-creation of social solidarity is less persuasive in multi-faith societies and does not properly account for intra-society conflicts involving competing religious beliefs.

Finally, we may take issue with the basic idea that religion is essentially the worship of society rather than deities or spirits. This has been seen as a reductionist argument that religious experience can be brought down to social phenomena, thus rejecting even the possibility of a 'spiritual' level of reality. Therefore, for people with strong religious beliefs and commitment, Durkheim's argument will probably always appear inadequate.

Contemporary significance

By locating religions firmly *within* the social realm rather than outside it, Durkheim effectively demystified religious experience and laid the ground for later empirical studies of religions. As we will see later in this chapter, the emergence of new religious movements and alternative forms of spirituality bear out the functionalist theory that, although the old gods may be dying, new ones are being created as societies undergo significant change. If so, then we may well agree with Durkheim that 'there is something eternal in religion which is destined to survive all the particular symbols in which religious thought has successively enveloped itself' (1965 [1912]: 427).

> ### THINKING CRITICALLY
>
> Is Durkheim's definition of religion *inclusive*, *exclusive* or *social constructionist*? How accurate has been his forecast that 'the old gods [traditional world religions] are dead'? What examples are there which suggest the 'old gods' have survived rather better than he thought they would?

the West is part of a comprehensive attempt to understand the influence of religion on social and economic life in different cultures. Analysing the Eastern religions, Weber concluded that they provided insuperable barriers to the development of industrial capitalism. This is not because Eastern civilizations are 'backward'; they have simply developed values that are different from those which came to dominate in Europe.

Weber notes that in traditional China and India there was, in certain periods, significant development of commerce, manufacture and urbanism, but this did not generate the radical patterns of social change produced by the rise of industrial capitalism in the West. Religion in the East was therefore a major influence inhibiting such change, seen, for instance, in Hinduism. Weber called Hinduism an 'other-worldly' religion – that is, its highest values emphasize escape from the toils of the material world onto a higher plane of spiritual existence. The religious feelings and motivations produced by Hinduism do not focus on controlling or shaping the material world. On the contrary, Hinduism sees material reality as a mere veil hiding the true concerns to which humankind should be oriented. Confucianism also acted to direct effort away from economic development, as this came to be understood in the West, emphasizing harmony with the world rather than promoting an active mastery of it. Although China was, for a long time, the most powerful and culturally most developed civilization in the world, its dominant religious values were a brake on any commitment to economic development purely for its own sake.

Weber regarded Christianity as a 'salvation religion', involving a belief that human beings can be 'saved' if they adopt the beliefs of the religion and follow its moral tenets. The ideas of sin and being rescued from sinfulness by God's grace are important in this, as they create a tension and emotional dynamism that is absent from the Eastern religions. Salvation religions have a 'revolutionary' aspect. While the religions of the East cultivate an attitude of passivity towards the existing order, Christianity involves a constant struggle against sin which can stimulate revolt against the existing order of things. Religious leaders – such as Jesus – emerge, who reinterpret existing doctrine in such a way as to challenge the prevailing power structure. This conclusion is quite different from Marx's perspective on the ideological role of Christianity under capitalism.

Critical assessment of the classical theories

Marx, Durkheim and Weber looked for general characteristics of religion as such, something that most sociologists of religion today now see as a somewhat misguided enterprise. Yet we can learn something quite generic about religions from all three founders. Marx's view that religion often has ideological implications, justifying the interests of ruling groups at the expense of others, can be seen in the influence of Christianity on European colonialism. Christian missionaries who sought to convert 'heathen' peoples to Christian beliefs were no doubt sincere, but the effect of their teachings was to reinforce the destruction of traditional cultures and impose colonial rule. The various Christian denominations almost all tolerated, or endorsed, slavery in the United States and other parts of the world up to the nineteenth century. Doctrines were developed claiming that slavery was based on divine law, with disobedient slaves being guilty of an offence against God as well as their masters.

Yet Weber was also right to emphasize the unsettling and often revolutionary impact of religious ideals on the established social order. Despite their early support for slavery in the United States, many church leaders later played a key role in the fight to abolish it. Religious beliefs have motivated people to join social movements seeking to overthrow unjust systems of authority. Religion played a prominent part in the civil rights movements of the 1960s in the United States and the Solidarity movement in 1980s Poland, which opposed and helped eventually to overthrow communist rule.

Among the most valuable aspects of Durkheim's writings is his stress on ritual and ceremony. All religions involve regular assemblies of believers during which rituals and rules are observed. As he rightly points out, ritual activities also mark the major transitions of life – birth, entry to adulthood (rituals associated with puberty are found in many cultures), marriage and death. The use of ritual and ceremony can be seen, too, in many aspects of what are otherwise secular events and occasions, such as the state opening of Parliament or university graduations.

All three of the classical founders forecast that religion, or at least the traditional world religions, would lose ground over time and the modern world would be an increasingly secular place. However, as we shall see below, this pithy statement has proved to be deceptively simple, and the 'secularization debate' continues to rumble on after more than a century of research and theorizing.

Into a secular age?

Secularization in sociological debates is the process or processes through which religion gradually loses its influence over various spheres of social life. For example, an apparently simple measure of secularization is declining weekly church attendance. While in Britain, France and the Netherlands this fell steadily and significantly over the twentieth century, it seems to have stabilized at around 5 per cent of national populations (Kaufman 2007). Large numbers of people within most European countries report that they never attend church services other than on special occasions such as weddings and funerals (see figure 17.2). On the other hand, numerous surveys have consistently shown that religious belief has not fallen as dramatically as church attendance, which might support the characterization of Western Europe as a region of 'believing without belonging' (Davie 1994).

Davie has since suggested that, where a small, active minority perform religious activities on behalf of and with the tacit approval of the non-active majority, this is better described as vicarious religion. Vicarious religion describes the position in the Nordic countries, which traditionally have high levels of church membership but low levels of attendance (Bäckström and Davie 2010: 191). But this concept has also come in for criticism. Bruce and Voas (2010) argue that it does not give any insight into how those who are not involved in organized religion (and are not 'for' or 'against' it) actually perceive religion. They also argue that the mounting evidence of secularization is not challenged by vicarious religiosity.

What are we to make of such different and often contradictory pieces of evidence? In the most basic terms, the debate on weekly church attendance is typical of the disagreement between supporters of the thesis, who see religion diminishing in power and importance, and opponents, who argue that religion remains a significant force, albeit often in new and unfamiliar forms. This debate is fleshed out in more detail in the next section.

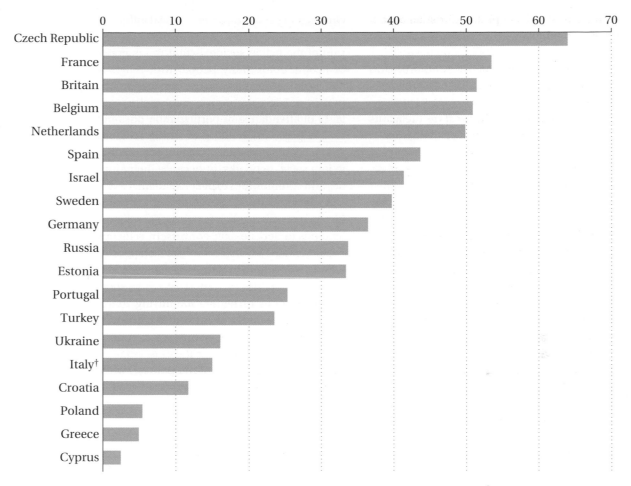

Figure 17.2 Percentage of respondents who never attend church services, selected European countries

Note: [†]2008.
Source: *The Economist* (2010).

The sociological debate

Secularization is a complex concept, in part because there is little consensus about what exactly should be measured and how. Should we focus on attendance in church, expressed religious beliefs, the power and influence of church leaders, or something else? And how can these be accurately measured? Moreover, as we have seen, sociologists employ differing definitions of religion, and these inevitably influence arguments for and against secularization.

Secularization can be evaluated on several aspects or dimensions. Some of them are quantitative measures, such as the *level of membership* of religious organizations. Statistics and official records can show how many people belong to a church or other religious body and are active in attending services and other ceremonies. With the exception of the USA, most of the industrialized countries have experienced considerable secularization according to this index. The pattern of religious decline seen in Britain is found in much of Western Europe, including Catholic countries such as France and Italy. More Italians than French attend church regularly and participate in the major rituals, such as

Easter communion, but the overall pattern of declining religious observance is similar in both cases.

A second dimension of secularization concerns how far churches and other religious organizations maintain their *social influence*, *wealth* and *prestige*. In earlier times, religious organizations wielded considerable influence over government and commanded respect in the community. Over the twentieth century, religious organizations progressively lost much of the social and political influence they had previously held. The trend is also global, but with some exceptions. Church leaders can no longer assume their views will be influential with powerful political groups. While some established churches remain very wealthy and new religious movements may rapidly build up fortunes, the material circumstances of many longstanding religious organizations are quite insecure. As attendance and membership has fallen, churches and other places of worship have been sold or remain in a state of disrepair.

The third dimension of secularization concerns beliefs and values. We can call this the dimension of *religiosity*. Levels of churchgoing and the degree of social influence of churches are not necessarily a direct expression of the beliefs or ideals that the majority of people hold. Many people with religious beliefs do not regularly attend services or take part in public ceremonies; conversely, regularity of attendance or participation does not always imply the holding of strong religious views. People may attend church out of habit, to join social networks, or because their families and communities expect it of them.

As socio-economic development generates increasingly higher living standards, religiosity tends to decline and, conversely, religious belief remains stronger in circumstances of deprivation and hardship. We can see this illustrated in tables 17.1 and 17.2, which show the proportions of people identifying themselves as 'a religious person' and 'a convinced atheist' across a sample of fifty-seven nations (excluding the UK). Some of the most religious countries are also some of the poorest, while a majority of the most atheistic are based in some of the world's wealthiest developed economies (WIN-Gallup 2012: 3).

Alongside other dimensions of secularization, we need an accurate understanding of

Table 17.1 **Most religious populations based on self-identification as 'a religious person'**

Countries	A religious person	Not a religious person	A convinced atheist	Don't know/no response
Ghana	96%	2%	0%	1%
Nigeria	93%	4%	1%	2%
Armenia	92%	3%	2%	2%
Fiji	92%	5%	1%	2%
Macedonia	90%	8%	1%	1%
Romania	89%	6%	1%	3%
Iraq	88%	9%	0%	3%
Kenya	88%	9%	2%	1%
Peru	86%	8%	3%	3%
Brazil	85%	13%	1%	1%

Source: WIN-Gallup International (2012: 4).

Table 17.2 **The ten most atheistic populations, based on self-identification as 'a convinced atheist'**

Countries	A religious person	Not a religious person	A convinced atheist	Don't know/no response
China	14%	30%	47%	9%
Japan	16%	31%	31%	23%
Czech Republic	20%	48%	30%	2%
France	37%	34%	29%	1%
South Korea	52%	31%	15%	2%
Germany	51%	33%	15%	1%
Netherlands	43%	42%	14%	2%
Austria	42%	43%	10%	5%
Iceland	57%	31%	10%	2%
Australia	37%	48%	10%	5%
Ireland	47%	44%	10%	0%

Note: There are eleven countries listed here because of four tying at 10 per cent.

Source: WIN-Gallup International (2012: 4).

the past to see how far religiosity has declined. Supporters of the secularization thesis argue that, in the past, religion was far more important in people's daily lives than it is today and that the church was the centre of local life. Critics of the thesis contest this idea, arguing that, in medieval Europe, commitment to religious belief was actually weaker and less important in daily life than has previously been supposed. Research into English history, for example, shows that ordinary people had only a lukewarm commitment to religion, while religious sceptics have been found in most cultures, particularly in the larger traditional societies (Ginzburg 1980).

Yet there is also much evidence that the hold of religious ideas today is less than was generally the case, particularly if we include the whole range of the supernatural and magical. Most people in the developed world do not experience the everyday environment as permeated by divine or spiritual entities which intervene directly in their lives. Taylor argues that some advanced societies may be entering a genuinely secular age in which many or even a majority of their populations see no need for religion or spirituality. In Taylor's (2007: 19) words, 'A secular age is one in which the eclipse of all goals beyond human flourishing becomes conceivable; or better, it falls within the range of an imaginable life for masses of people.' However, it seems unlikely that the mass of people will shift directly from religious belief to secular atheism. Rather, the transition to a wholly secular age may involve a period in which traditional religions are in decline but people still have a sense that 'there is something out there'.

Exploring Christian beliefs and atheism in Britain, Sweden and the USA, Heelas (2002) found that atheists and agnostics made up only 24 per cent (1990), 15 per cent (2000) and 6 per cent (1986) of adults respectively. Only 10 per cent (Britain), 2 per cent (Sweden) and 20 per cent (USA, 2000) were regular church attenders. But the large majorities between these two poles – what Heelas calls 'betwixt and between' – included those who believed in 'a higher power', held 'New Age' beliefs or were simply indifferent to questions of religious belief. At best, people in this middle zone could be described as exhibiting a 'fuzzy fidelity' to Christian beliefs and traditions (Voas 2009). Yet just as likely is that these 'fuzzies' may hold opinions about the world rather than recognizable religious beliefs. If so, then against Davie's (1994) notion of Britain being a nation of 'believing without belonging', it may be that a majority of people in Britain and elsewhere in Europe neither believe *nor* belong (Voas and Crockett 2005: 14).

> ### THINKING CRITICALLY
>
> Design a small research study which aims to test the theory that people do not shift directly from religious belief to atheism. What would be your sample population and how would you recruit them? What questions would you ask of your participants to gather the relevant data?

Beyond secularization

Although the thesis of secularization in Europe and other developed countries is well supported, both theoretically and empirically, there have been many criticisms of it. For example, it has been suggested that sociology has tended to elide the analytical concept of secularization with a predictive version that sees the process as globally inevitable. While the analytical concept remains useful, the predictive version has faltered in the face of many empirical examples – not least the USA – of the continuing strength of religious affiliation (Pérez-Agote 2014).

Here, we introduce two alternative perspectives which neither query nor reinterpret the statistical evidence. Instead, both suggest that sociology has focused too heavily on the formal, institutional aspects of established religions and, in so doing, has tended to ignore or downplay religion and spirituality as it is practised and experienced in everyday life. Once we shift our focus onto the latter, a quite different picture of 'religion' emerges. Looking at 'religious practices' among voluntary associations and individuals calls into question some of the basic assumptions underlying the sociology of religion and offers a different way of thinking about what religion is.

The rise of the tribes?

The French sociologist Michel Maffesoli suggests an alternative assessment of secularization. Drawing on Durkheim's ideas of religion as a form of worship of society and its moral rules, Maffesoli (1995) theorizes that, although traditional religions may be in decline, people in large urban areas increasingly live in the 'time of the tribes'.

Maffesoli argues against sociological theories of a growing individualization, as in the work of Giddens and Beck. Individualization refers to the process through which people identify less with collective bodies and instead are 'cut loose' from social structures such as trade unions, social classes and even families. In this situation, personal choice becomes a key value and individuality is prized, as seen in the practice of consumerism, as people buy 'identity kits' in the form of clothing, music, interior décor, and so on, all of which help them to forge an individual identity (Bauman 2007).

However, Maffesoli also argues against older theories of a mass society, which suggested an increasing social uniformity and the loss of individual differences. Instead, he suggests that modern societies are characterized by the rapid growth of small groupings of people who voluntarily band together on the basis of shared musical tastes, ideas, consumer preferences, leisure pursuits, and so on. He calls these groups 'neo-tribes' ('new' tribes). They are quite like traditional tribal groups, because they have a shared identity, but unlike them because they do not last as long. People's commitment to neo-tribes tends to be quite weak and short-lived, which makes them very fluid and fragile social entities.

Maffesoli's point is that the continual creation of neo-tribes demonstrates that there remains a very strong human need and a quest for close social contact and interaction, which does not support either the theories

Skateboarding is a popular activity among young people, but, according to Maffesoli, the subculture it generates can also be seen as a 'neo-tribe' which fulfils the members' need for sociability.

of heightened individualization or those of a mass society. And this deep, underlying search for human sociability is, in Durkheim's terms, a religious search. With this in mind, Maffesoli argues that the old gods may well be dead but, as Durkheim (1965 [1912]: 427) put it, there is still 'something eternal in religion'. Maffesoli's ideas suggest that the debate on secularization need not be quite as polarized as it has become. Secularization does seem to be impacting on the older world religions, but new forms of religious expression are also emerging, if sociologists know where to look.

Everyday 'lived religion'

Much of the research and theorizing has focused on organized religion and its functions in society. This body of work is discussed throughout the rest of this chapter. However, some recent empirical studies of individual religious practice show that, in the pursuit of generic definitions and theories of religion, sociologists may have largely ignored the creative blending of 'religious' and 'secular' elements by individuals trying to make sense of their place in the world. When they have looked into individual religious practices, sociologists have tended to view their apparently contradictory internal diversity as illustrative of the problems brought by excessive individualism in society.

The most often cited example of such studies is the survey of 'privatized' religion in the USA by Robert Bellah and his colleagues (2008 [1985]). The authors argue that America has seen a long-term movement away from a unified, public form of religion, which helped to bind people together, towards extraordinarily diverse and private forms of religion. The latter reflect a wider social process of individualization. This study presents the case of a young nurse called Sheila Larson as indicative of this shift in religious practice. Sheila explained that her personal 'faith' was very important to her, but it was not the kind of coherent, church-oriented religion we might expect. She said: 'I believe in God. I'm not a religious fanatic. I can't remember the last time I went to church. My faith has carried me a long way. It's Sheilaism. Just my own little voice. . . . It's just try to love yourself and be gentle with yourself. You know, I guess, take care of each other. I think He would want us to take care of each other' (ibid.: 221).

Bellah et al. note that, on the basis of such individualized expressions of faith, there could be '220 million American religions'. However, they argue, such a radically privatized situation does not contribute to social solidarity, nor can it support a unified public realm. The danger is that it will produce very abstract and shallow forms of religious life. But is this assessment coloured by the institutional focus of the conventional sociology of religion? Meredith Maguire (2008) argues that it is. In particular, the assumption underlying the critique is that religions are or should be unified and organized and embody a consistent set of beliefs and rituals. Maguire sees this as a Western image of what religions are, which prevents sociologists from properly understanding the apparently randomly selected collages of belief and practice that characterize many individual lives, such as that of 'Laura' in 'Global society 17.1'.

Maguire (2008) suggests that, to an outsider, Laura's choices may appear to lack any internal logic or religious coherence. However, to the individual concerned, each element fits logically into a personally meaningful whole. For example, the substance of Sheila Larson's 'Sheilaism' was clearly connected to personal crises in relation to her health and her experience as a nurse caring for dying patients. In advance of major surgery, for instance, Sheila claims to have heard reassurances directly from God, and the fact that 'caring for each other' was central to her faith is explicable in relation to such information. For Maguire (and others) there is a need to attend to the complexities of such everyday lived religion

if we are to grasp the changing relationship between religion, society and the individual.

Evaluating the secularization thesis

There is little dispute among sociologists that, considered as a long-term trend, religion in the traditional churches has declined in most Western countries – a notable exception is the USA. The influence of religion in these countries has diminished along each of the three dimensions of secularization, much as nineteenth-century sociologists predicted it would. However, as we have seen, individuals and groups still practise 'religion', but in ways that have remained largely invisible to the predominantly quantitative research methods in sociological surveys.

What we can conclude, therefore, is that the position of religion in the developed countries is much more complex than the secularization thesis originally suggested. Religious and spiritual belief remain powerful and motivating forces in many people's lives, even if they do not choose to worship formally through the framework of the traditional church organizations. Many people do have religious beliefs but prefer to practise and develop their faith outside institutionalized forms of religion. And, even if secularization could be measured according to membership figures alone, this should also include the growing role of non-Western faiths and new religious movements. In Britain, for example, active membership within traditional churches is falling, yet participation among Muslims, Hindus, Sikhs, Jews and evangelical 'born-again' Christians remains dynamic.

There is also less evidence of secularization outside the developed societies. In many areas of the Middle East, Asia, Africa and India, fundamentalist Islamist groups challenge Westernization. When the pope toured South America, millions of Catholics enthusiastically followed his progress. Eastern Orthodoxy has been re-embraced by many people in parts of formerly communist societies of Eastern Europe, even after decades of repression of the Church. It seems that the secularization thesis may be most powerful in terms of explaining the declining power and influence in society

Global Society 17.1 | Religious practice in individual lives

Consider the case of 'Laura' below, a well-educated woman in her late thirties who worked from home as an author and part-time reading consultant for schools in the area. Laura was one of the individuals interviewed by Meredith Maguire (2008: 9–11) as part of an empirical research project in the USA looking at religious practices and beliefs.

Laura

Laura . . . was raised Catholic and considered herself to be Catholic still, although she seldom attended Mass and then just to please her mother when visiting her several times a year. At the same time, however, she spoke of nurturing her spiritual life, and she described how she set aside at least an hour daily for meditation as the first priority for her morning as soon as her children left for school.

Her home altar held several traditional religious items, including a family heirloom cross brought from Mexico three generations ago, pictures of several deceased or distant loved ones, eighteen candles of all sizes, a small bouquet of wildflowers, and an amulet (*milagro*) attached to the frame of one grandmother's photo . . . There were numerous and prominent non-traditional items as well: amethyst crystals used in healing meditations, Asian incense and a Tibetan prayer bell, a large colourful triptych of Frida Kahlo [a Mexican painter], and a modern representation of the Virgin of Guadalupe as a young Chicana in running shoes . . .

Laura described deeply important practices that produced a comfortable blend of elements of her identity. For example, she explained that she respects her mother's more traditional Mexican American religious practices, including popular religious practices such as devotions to *la virgincita* (the dear Virgin), but she identifies with them in a transmuted form. . . .

At the same time, however, Laura's own religion was very different from her mother's . . . She was an avowed feminist, proud of her Mexican heritage and her bilingual fluency and closely linked with her extended family, and she cared a lot about the well-being and education of children (her own children, her students, and those who read her books). All these commitments and concerns were interwoven into her religious practices, at home, in church, or while going about her everyday activities, including her writing and her frequent interactions with her extended family.

THINKING CRITICALLY

Is Laura still 'a Catholic' in terms of her religious practice? If she is entirely comfortable with this blend of beliefs and practices, what does this tell us about the relationship between institutional, organized religion and individual religious commitment?

---

of the traditional churches, which are trying to adapt to equal rights movements.

Above all, religion in the contemporary world should be evaluated against a backdrop of globalization, instability and increasing diversity. It is not surprising, then, that during times of rapid change many people look for and find answers in religion. Fundamentalism is perhaps the clearest example. Yet, increasingly, religious responses to change occur in new and unfamiliar forms: new religious movements, neo-tribes, cults, 'New Age' activities

and individual 'bricolage'. While most of these may not look much like conventional forms of religion, they may more accurately reflect some major transformations which are occurring in religious belief and practice today.

Religious organizations and movements

Although there may be important changes under way in religious beliefs and practices in

17.1 Migration and religion?

'Migrants fill empty pews as Britons lose faith'

The rate of decline in church attendance has been slowed by an unexpected factor – the influx of Christians from Africa and Europe. One of the biggest surveys among Britain's 37,000 churches . . . finds that the growth of immigrant-led churches has partly offset dwindling congregations elsewhere [Brierley 2006]. The news will cheer Church leaders. The Archbishop of Canterbury, Dr Rowan Williams, said the phenomenon was having a healthy impact on mainstream churches.

But the survey also shows that congregations are getting older as young people continue to abandon the pews, which could have a devastating impact in a decade. The 2005 English Church Census, carried out by the independent Christian Research organisation, finds that, between 1998 and 2005, half a million people stopped going to a Christian church on Sunday. The figure is lower than expected because a million left in the previous nine years.

The survey finds that black-led Pentecostal churches in immigrant communities gained about 100,000 worshippers since 1998. Although churches of all denominations and sizes have stemmed their losses, most growth has occurred in the larger charismatic and evangelical churches. The research shows that black people now make up 10 per cent of all Sunday churchgoers in England, while other non-white ethnic groups add a further 7 per cent. In inner London, fewer than half the worshippers are white, with black Christians accounting for 44 per cent of churchgoers and non-white ethnic groups 14 per cent. The impact of Roman Catholic Croatians and Poles and Orthodox Russians and Greeks has been significant.

The findings will give the churches hope that they are pulling out of the decline they have been in for decades. Overall, however, they are losing far more than they are gaining. While 1,000 new people are joining a church each week, 2,500 are leaving. Just 6.3 per cent of the population goes to church on an average Sunday, compared with 7.5 per cent in 1998, although more people are going midweek.

Dr Williams, who wrote the foreword to the research, said one of its most striking findings was the number of thriving churches started by immigrant communities. 'This is having a big impact on our major cities, where the black majority churches are growing fast', he said. 'People from ethnic minorities are also bringing new life and energy into churches from established denominations such as the Church of England. This is one of the reasons why the Anglican Diocese of London, for example, is now growing steadily.' However, the Archbishop acknowledged that the mainstream denominations faced serious problems as the average worshipper was getting older.

The research, based on questionnaires from 19,000 churches, finds that 29 per cent of churchgoers are 65 or over compared with 16 per cent of the population. It also finds that 9 per cent of churches have no one under the age of 11 in their congregations. 'The last English Church Census, carried out in 1998, showed an alarming decline in the number of children and young people in church', said Dr Williams. 'These latest results suggest we have yet to reverse this, but at least the rate of change has slowed.'

Source: Petre (2006).

THINKING CRITICALLY

Why do migrant groups often display higher levels of religiosity and church attendance than the rest of the population? What factors might explain the 'alarming decline in the number of children and young people in church'?

the developed world, the bulk of sociological studies of religion have focused on the functions of religion and the role played by religious groups and organizations. It is therefore important to look at how sociologists have understood the various types of organization and movements that are rooted in religious belief.

Organizing religion

Although sociologists of religion have been interested in non-European religions, there has frequently been a tendency to view all religions through concepts and theories that grew out of the analysis of the European experience. For example, concepts such as *denomination* or *sect* presuppose the existence of formally organized and established religious institutions. This leads some scholars to argue that such concepts are of limited use. In recent decades, there has been an effort to create a more systematic, comparative sociology of religion which seeks to understand religious traditions from within their own frames of reference (Wilson 1982; Van der Veer 1994).

Early theorists such as Max Weber (1963), Ernst Troeltsch (1981 [1931]) and Richard Niebuhr (1929) described religious organizations as falling along a continuum, based on the degree to which they are established and conventional. Churches lie at one end, as they are conventional and well established, while cults lie at the other, as they are neither conventional nor established. Sects fall somewhere between these two opposites. These distinctions were based on the study of European and North American religions, and there is much debate about how well they apply to the non-Christian world.

Although we introduce the concepts of *sect* and *cult* in our historical sketch below, these terms were used by early sociologists of religion; today they have acquired negative connotations in society, and most contemporary sociologists try to avoid using them. Instead the tendency is to use the phrase *new religious movements* to characterize novel religious organizations which lack the respectability

that comes with being well established over a long period of time (Hexham and Poewe 1997; Hadden 1997).

THINKING CRITICALLY

Should sociologists avoid using the concepts of 'cult' and 'sect', just because they have acquired a negative meaning in society? Is it possible for sociologists to avoid making value judgements during the research process?

Churches and sects

All religions involve communities of believers, but there are many different ways in which these are organized. One way of classifying religious organizations was first suggested by Max Weber and his colleague the religious historian Ernst Troeltsch. Weber and Troeltsch distinguished between churches and sects. A church is a large, well-established religious body – such as the Catholic Church or the Church of England. A sect is a smaller, less well-organized group of committed believers, usually created in protest against what a church has become, as was the case with Calvinists and Methodists in the past. Churches normally have a formal, bureaucratic structure with a hierarchy of religious officials and tend to represent the conservative face of religion, since they are integrated into the existing institutional order of society. Most of their adherents become members of the church.

Sects are comparatively small; they usually aim at discovering and following 'the true way', and tend to withdraw from the surrounding society into their own form of community life. Sect members regard the established churches as corrupt. Most have few or no officials, as all members are regarded as equal participants. A small proportion of people are born into sects, but most actively join them. A tragic example of a sect built around an inspirational leader came to light in the USA in 1993. David Koresh led the Branch Davidian sect, claiming to be a 'messiah'. He was also allegedly stockpiling illegal weapons in the group's compound in Waco, Texas. Up to eighty members of the Davidians, including nineteen children, burned to death as fire engulfed their complex when it came under assault by officials from the US government after a lengthy armed stand-off. Controversy remains over whether the fire was ordered by Koresh, who reportedly preferred mass suicide to surrender, or whether the actions of the federal authorities caused the tragedy.

Denominations and cults

Other authors have further developed the church/sect typology. Howard Becker (1950) added two further types: the denomination and the cult. A denomination is a sect which has 'cooled down' to become an institutionalized body rather than an active protest group. Sects which survive over a period of time often, though not always, become denominations. Thus Calvinism and Methodism were sects during their early formation, when they generated great fervour among members, but over the years they became gradually more 'respectable'. Denominations are recognized as more or less legitimate by churches and quite often cooperate harmoniously with them.

Cults resemble sects, but have different emphases. Cults are the most loosely knit and transient of all religious organizations, being composed of individuals who reject what they see as the main values of the wider society. Their focus is on individual experience, bringing like-minded individuals together. People do not formally join but follow particular theories or prescribed ways of behaving, and members are usually allowed to maintain their other religious connections. Like sects, cults quite often form around an inspirational or charismatic leader. Instances of cults in the West today would include groups of believers in spiritualism, astrology or transcendental meditation.

It is worth noting that what is seen as a cult in one country may well be an established religious practice in another. When Indian gurus (religious teachers) bring their beliefs into Europe, what might be considered an established religion in India is regarded as a cult in the UK. Christianity began as an indigenous cult in ancient Jerusalem, and, in many Asian countries today, Evangelical Protestantism is regarded as a cult imported from the West. We should therefore try to avoid seeing cults *per se* as somehow strange and alien. One leading sociologist of religion, Jeffrey K. Hadden (1997), points out that *all* of the 100,000 or so religions that humans have ever devised were once new, and most, if not all, were initially despised cults from the standpoint of respectable religious beliefs of the time. After all, Jesus was crucified because his ideas were so threatening to the established order of the Roman-dominated religious establishment of ancient Judaea.

Religious movements

Religious movements are associations of people who join together to spread a new religion or to promote a new interpretation of an existing religion, and we can see them as a special form of social movement. They are larger than sects and have a less exclusive membership, though, like the church/sect distinction, movements and sects (or cults) are not always clearly distinct from one another. In fact, all sects and cults can probably be classified as types of religious movement. Examples of religious movements include groups that founded and spread Christianity in the first century, the Lutheran movement that split Christianity in Europe about 1,500 years later, and the groups involved in the more recent Islamic Revolution (discussed later in the chapter).

Religious movements tend to pass through certain phases of development. In the first phase, the movement derives its life and cohesion from a powerful leader. Max Weber classified such leaders as *charismatic* – that is, they are perceived as having inspirational qualities capable of capturing the imagination and devotion of followers. Charismatic leaders in Weber's formulation could be political as well as religious figures – revolutionary China's

Mao Tse-tung as well as Jesus and Muhammad. The leaders of religious movements are usually critical of the religious establishment and seek to proclaim a new message. In their early years, religious movements are fluid; they do not have an established system of authority. Their members are normally in direct contact with the charismatic leader, and together they spread the new teachings.

The second phase occurs following the death of the leader. Rarely does a new charismatic leader arise from the masses, so this phase is crucial. The movement is now faced with what Weber termed the 'routinization of charisma', a process that often begins while the original charismatic leader is still alive. To survive, it has to create formalized rules and procedures, since it can no longer depend on the individual qualities of the leader in organizing followers. Many movements fail to achieve this and fade away when their leaders die. A movement that survives and takes on a permanent character tends to develop into a church. In other words, it becomes a formal organization of believers with an established authority system and established symbols and rituals. The church itself might, at some later point, become the established norm against which other movements that question its teachings set up in opposition or from which they break away completely. In this way, we can see a dynamic cycle of religious development.

> Social movements are discussed in more detail in chapter 21, 'Politics, Government and Social Movements'.

New religious movements

Although traditional churches have experienced a decline in membership over recent decades, we will see below that other forms of religious activity have been growing. Sociologists use the term new religious movements to refer collectively to the broad range of religious and spiritual groups, cults and sects that have emerged in Western countries alongside the larger mainstream religions. New religious movements encompass an enormous diversity of groups, from spiritual and self-help groups within the New Age movement to exclusive sects such as the Hare Krishnas (International Society for Krishna Consciousness). The latter worship the Hindu deity, Krishna, as the source of all forms of 'God'.

Many new religious movements are derived from the major traditions of Hinduism, Christianity and Buddhism, while others have emerged from traditions virtually unknown in the West. Some new religious movements are essentially the creations of the charismatic leaders who lead their activities. This is the case, for example, with the Unification Church, led by the Reverend Sun Myung Moon, who is seen by his supporters as a messiah and whose church claims 4.5 million members (though this is more likely to be in the hundreds of thousands). Adherents of new religious movements consist mostly of converts rather than individuals brought up within a particular faith; in the West they tend to be relatively well educated and from middle-class backgrounds.

New religious movements can be seen as falling into three broad categories: world-affirming, world-rejecting and world-accommodating movements (Wallis 1984). Each is based on the relationship of the individual group to the larger social world, and, though they are relatively small compared with the world religions, the rise of these movements can be seen as reflecting some aspects of wider social changes, such as the decline in automatic deference to experts and established authorities among younger generations. Sociological interest in new religious movements stems from the 1960s and 1970s, when they were seen as challenging mainstream social values. In particular, the fact that young people tended to be disproportionately attracted to them was associated with a moral panic about the 'brainwashing' of society's youth, which was similar in tone to panic around spectacular youth subcultures.

> See chapter 9, 'The Life Course', for more on youth culture.

World-affirming movements

World-affirming movements are more akin to self-help or therapy groups than to conventional religious groups. They often lack rituals, churches and formal theologies, turning their focus on members' spiritual well-being. As the name suggests, world-affirming movements do not reject the outside world or its values. Rather, they seek to enhance their followers' abilities to perform and succeed in that world by unlocking human potential.

The Church of Scientology is one example, widely known today because of the involvement of the actor Tom Cruise. Founded by L. Ron Hubbard, a successful science fiction novelist in the early 1950s, the Church of Scientology has grown from its original base in California and has a large membership around the world. Scientologists believe we are all spiritual beings but we have neglected our spiritual nature. Through training that makes them aware of their real spiritual capacities, people can recover forgotten supernatural powers, clear their minds and achieve their full potential.

Many strands of the New Age movement come under the category of world-affirming movements. The New Age movement emerged from the counter-culture of the 1960s and 1970s and encompasses a broad spectrum of beliefs, practices and ways of life. Pagan teachings (Celtic, Druidic, Native American and others), shamanism, forms of Asian mysticism, Wiccan rituals and Zen meditation are only a few of the activities that are thought of as 'New Age'.

On the surface, the mysticism of the New Age movement stands in stark contrast to the modern societies in which it is popular. Yet New Age activities should not be interpreted as simply a radical break with the present society or mainstream religions. They are part of a larger cultural trajectory. In the developed societies, individuals possess unparalleled degrees of autonomy and freedom to chart their own lives. As Maguire (2008) found in her extensive interviews, many people now combine aspects of New Age spirituality and practices such as meditation and healing with conventional religious tenets drawn from Christianity, Buddhism and other world religions. In this respect, the aims of the New Age movement coincide closely with the modern age: people are encouraged to move beyond traditional values and expectations and to live their lives actively and reflexively.

World-rejecting movements

In contrast to world-affirming groups, world-rejecting movements are highly critical of the outside world and often demand significant lifestyle changes from their followers. Members may be expected to live ascetically, to change their dress and hairstyle, or to follow a certain diet. World-rejecting movements are frequently exclusive in contrast to world-affirming movements, which tend to be inclusive in nature. Some display similar characteristics to total institutions; members are expected to subsume their individual identities into that of the group, to adhere to strict ethical codes and rules, and to withdraw from activity in the outside world.

Many world-rejecting cults and sects have come under the intense scrutiny of state authorities, the media and the public. Certain extreme sects have attracted much concern. For example, the Japanese group Aum Shinrikyo ('supreme truth') released deadly sarin gas into the Tokyo subway system in 1995, injuring hundreds of commuters and killing twelve people. Its leader, Shoko Asahara, was sentenced to death in 2004 for ordering the attacks, and many countries now designate the group as a terrorist organization.

World-accommodating movements

The third type of new religious movement is closer to a traditional religion. World-accommodating movements emphasize the importance of the inner religious life above worldly concerns. Members of such groups seek to reclaim the spiritual purity that they believe has been lost in traditional religious settings. Where followers of world-rejecting and world-affirming groups alter their lifestyles in accordance with their religious activity, many adherents of world-accommodating movements carry on in their everyday lives and careers with little visible change. One example of a world-accommodating movement is Pentecostalism, which emphasizes the individual's direct experience of God. Pentecostalists believe that the Holy Spirit can be heard through individuals who are granted the gift of 'speaking in tongues'.

THINKING CRITICALLY

How do religious movements, such as those discussed above, differ from secular social movements, such as socialism, feminism and environmentalism? Are there any 'religious' elements in secular social movements?

Various theories have been advanced to explain the popularity of new religious movements. Some scholars have argued that they should be seen as a response to the process of liberalization and secularization. People who feel that traditional religions have become ritualistic and devoid of spiritual meaning may find comfort and a greater sense of community in smaller, less impersonal religious movements. Others point to new religious movements as an outcome of rapid social change (Wilson 1982). As traditional social norms are disrupted, people search for both explanations and reassurance. The rise of groups which emphasize personal spirituality, for example, suggests that many individuals feel a need to connect with their own values or beliefs in the face of instability and uncertainty.

New religious movements are one recent development, but not the only one. In many national contexts, religious beliefs and practices have undergone changes as a result of new challenges such as the development of religious fundamentalism, globalization and multiculturalism, internal movements for gender and sexuality equality, and, of course, secularization. The next section traces some of these shifts, focusing on Europe and North America.

Trends in contemporary religion

The influence of Christianity was a crucial element in the development of Europe as a political unit. One possible border to what we now define as Europe is the first great split in Christian thought in the eleventh century, between Catholic and Eastern Orthodox forms of Christianity. Orthodox Christianity is still the dominant religion in many Eastern European countries, including Bulgaria, Belarus, Cyprus, Georgia, Greece, Romania, Russia, Serbia and Ukraine.

Religion in Europe

In Western Europe the division of the continent into Catholic and Protestant in the sixteenth century marked a second great rupture in Christian thought. This process, known as the Reformation, is inseparable from the division of Western Europe into the relatively stable patchwork of modern nation-states that we still see on the map today. Very broadly, it became divided into a Protestant North (Scandinavia and Scotland), a Catholic South (Spain, Portugal, Italy and France, as well as Belgium and Ireland further north) and several more or less denominationally mixed countries (Britain and Northern Ireland, the Netherlands and Germany). The Reformation took different forms in different countries, but was unified by the attempt to escape the influence of the pope and the Catholic Church. However, a variety of Protestant denominations and relations between church and state emerged within Europe.

The *Nordic countries* (Norway, Denmark, Finland and Iceland) have a state church (the Lutheran State Church of Northern Europe), and their populations are characterized by a high rate of church membership but a low level of both religious practice and acceptance of Christian beliefs. These countries have therefore been characterized as 'belonging without believing' (Skeie 2009: 7). In Sweden the close relationship between the Lutheran Church and the state was being seriously questioned in the late twentieth century, and, in 2000, state and Church officially separated after 469 years. Many people had found the idea of a church that is specially privileged by the state inappropriate in an increasingly ethnically and culturally diverse country.

Germany can still be characterized as divided between Catholicism and Protestantism, though this is now changing as there is a growing Muslim population and an increase in the number of people claiming no religious allegiance. The latter may be partly explained by the reunification of East and West Germany after the fall of the Berlin Wall in 1989 and the suppression of Christianity in the former communist countries of Eastern Europe.

France is largely a Catholic country but is far more like the Protestant countries of Northern Europe in exhibiting low levels of religious belief and practices. Of all the countries of Western Europe, France has the most rigorous separation between church and state. The French state is strictly secular and refuses to privilege any religion or denomination, which includes no discussion of religion and a ban on religious education and religious dress and symbols in state institutions. A controversial ban on 'conspicuous' religious items in French schools was introduced in September 2004, particularly affecting Muslim girls who wore headscarves. In September 2010, the French Senate also ratified a decision to ban the wearing in public places of full-face Islamic veils – the burka and niqab.

The *United Kingdom* is a predominantly Protestant country. The 2011 national census for England and Wales reported that some 59 per cent of people still described themselves as Christians (33 million), a fall from 71.7 per cent in 2001. Islam is the next most common faith, with 4.8 per cent of the population (2.7 million people) describing themselves as

Muslims. Other significant groups are Hindus (1.5 per cent) and Sikhs, Jews and Buddhists, each accounting for less than 1 per cent. However, 25 per cent (14 million) said they had 'no religion', a significant increase on the 14.8 per cent in 2001, making this the second largest grouping (ONS 2012a). Although 59 per cent of the UK population describe themselves as Christian, a much smaller number attend church regularly. The 1851 census of religion found about 40 per cent of adults in England and Wales attended church each Sunday, but by 1900 this had dropped to 35 per cent, by 1950 to 20 per cent, and by 2000 to just 8 per cent. There are now signs that this trend is slowing, and the general decline in church attendance is unevenly spread. Among ethnic minority populations, attendance at church and religious services has been rising, and a number of 'new religious movements' have also attracted followers in Britain.

Italy, *Spain* and *Portugal* are largely Catholic countries, demonstrating higher levels of religious belief and practice than most other Western European states, especially those in the north. The Catholic Church, based inside Italy, enjoys a high level of influence in all these countries. In Italy, Catholicism is privileged above other denominations and religions. In Spain, there is no official link between state and church, though the Catholic Church is privileged by its dominance in terms of numbers. In Portugal, despite some constitutional reform in the 1970s, the Catholic Church still has a degree of influence in law (Davie 2000).

Religious minorities

Europe is also home to sizeable non-Christian religious minorities. Although Jews have been present in Europe for centuries, their recent history has been bound up with anti-Semitic discrimination and genocide.

The mass murder of European Jews during the Second Word War, and the fact that many of those who survived the Holocaust left Europe for the newly created state of Israel after 1945, meant a dramatic decline in the

Global Society 17.2 | In Poland, a Jewish revival thrives – minus Jews

Krakow, Poland. There is a curious thing happening in this old country, scarred by Nazi death camps, raked by pogroms and blanketed by numbing Soviet sterility: Jewish culture is beginning to flourish again.

'Jewish-style' restaurants are serving up platters of pirogis, klezmer bands are playing plaintive oriental melodies, derelict synagogues are gradually being restored. Every June, a festival of Jewish culture here draws thousands of people to sing Jewish songs and dance Jewish dances. The only thing missing, really, are Jews. 'It's a way to pay homage to the people who lived here, who contributed so much to Polish culture', said Janusz Makuch, founder and director of the annual festival and himself the son of a Catholic family.

Jewish communities are gradually reawakening across Eastern Europe as Jewish schools introduce a new generation to rituals and beliefs suppressed by the Nazis and then by communism. At summer camps, thousands of Jewish teenagers from across the former Soviet bloc gather for crash courses in Jewish culture, celebrating Passover, Hanukkah and Purim – all in July.

. . . in Poland, there are now two Jewish schools, synagogues in several major cities and at least four rabbis. But, with relatively few Jews, Jewish culture in Poland is being embraced and promoted by the young and the fashionable. Before Hitler's horror, Poland had the largest Jewish population in Europe, about 3.5 million souls. One in ten Poles was Jewish. More than 3 million Polish Jews died in the Holocaust. Postwar pogroms and a 1968 anti-Jewish purge forced out most of those who survived.

The Hasidic 'dance of happiness', here at a wedding in New York, is one of the mainstays of the annual Jewish festival in Krakow celebrating the music and cultural traditions of the 3.5 million Jews who lived in Poland before the Holocaust. Thousands of people attended, though few of them are Jewish.

Probably about 70 per cent of the world's European Jews, or Ashkenazi, can trace their ancestry to Poland – thanks to a fourteenth-century king, Casimir III, the Great, who drew Jewish settlers from across Europe with his vow to protect them as 'people of the king'. But there are only 10,000 self-described Jews living today in this country of 39 million.

Source: Adapted from Smith (2007).

number of Jews living in Europe, from 9.6 million in 1937 to fewer than 2 million by the mid-1990s (as table 17.3 shows).

Racism and discrimination are discussed in chapter 16, 'Race, Ethnicity and Migration'.

In the twentieth century, global migration, partly shaped by Europe's colonial history, also led, for the first time, to the development of sizeable non-Judeo-Christian minorities across the whole of the European continent. Of these, Islam is by far the largest non-Christian faith, with 15 to 20 million Muslims living in the European Union in 2009 (Open Society Institute 2010). The colonial links between France and North Africa account for a sizeable French Muslim population of 3 to 4 million. Germany, by contrast, has large numbers of Muslim migrant workers from Turkey and South-Eastern Europe. Britain's Muslim population comes largely from the former British Empire countries of the Indian subcontinent (Davie 2000).

Religion in the United States

Compared with other developed countries, Americans are unusually religious. With few exceptions, 'the United States has been the most God-believing and religion-adhering, fundamentalist, and religiously traditional country in Christendom[, where] more new religions have been born . . . than [in] any other country' (Lipset 1991: 187). Certainly there is a body of evidence to suggest that America is generally more religious than Europe, though there are differences in national European societies as well as between states and regions in the USA (Berger et al. 2008).

Around three out of every five Americans say that religion is 'very important' in their lives, and, at any given time, around 40 per cent will have been to church in the previous week (Gallup 2004), though other estimates suggest the true figure may be around half that, at less than 22 per cent (Hadaway and Marler 2005). A 2010 poll of 3,412 adults found that 86 per cent of Americans said they believed in God 'or a higher power' (Grossman 2010). However, there is evidence that things may be changing. A 2010 survey of eighteen- and nineteen-year-olds – the so-called Millennial Generation – found this group to be less likely to be committed to a faith than their parents, with 25 per cent unaffiliated to a church, declaring themselves to be atheists or to believe in 'nothing in particular'. They were also more liberal in their attitudes towards homosexuality and saw Darwinian evolutionary theory as 'the best explanation of life'. Nevertheless, they maintained a strong belief in God, heaven and hell in similar numbers to previous generations (Pew Forum on Religion and Public Life 2010) – another example of 'believing without belonging' perhaps?

Some 51 per cent of Americans identify themselves as Protestant and 25 per cent as Catholic. Other significant religious groups are Mormons, Muslims and Jews (Kosmin and Keysar 2009). The Catholic Church has had by far the largest increase in membership, partly because of the immigration of Catholics from Mexico and Central and South America. Yet the growth in Catholic Church membership has also slowed in recent years, as some have drifted away. One survey found that 50

Table 17.3   Jewish populations in Europe, 1937–94

	1937	1946	1967	1994
Austria	191,000	31,000[a]	12,500	7,000
Belgium	65,000	45,000	40,500	31,800
Bulgaria	49,000	44,200	5,000	1,900
Czechoslovakia	357,000	55,000	15,000	7,600[b]
Denmark	8,500	5,500	6,000	6,400
Estonia[c]	4,600	–	–	3,500
Finland	2,000	2,000	1,750	1,300
France	300,000	225,000	535,000	530,000
Germany	500,000	153,000[a]	30,000	55,000
Great Britain	330,000	370,000	400,000	295,000
Greece	77,000	10,000	6,500	4,800
Hungary	400,000	145,000	80,000	56,000
Ireland (Republic)	5,000	3,900	2,900	1,200
Italy	48,000	53,000[a]	35,000	31,000
Latvia	95,000	–	–	18,000
Lithuania[c]	155,000	–	–	6,500
Luxembourg	3,500	500	500	600
Netherlands	140,000	28,000	30,000	25,000
Norway	2,000	750	1,000	1,000
Poland	3,250,000	215,000	21,000	6,000
Portugal	n/a	4,000	1,000	300
Romania	850,000	420,000	100,000	10,000
Spain	n/a	6,000	6,000	12,000
Sweden	7,500	15,500	13,000	16,500
Switzerland	18,000	35,000	20,000	19,000
Turkey[d]	50,000	48,000	35,000	18,000
USSR/CIS[d]	2,669,000	1,971,000	1,715,000	812,000
Yugoslavia[e]	71,000	12,000	7,000	3,500[e]
Total	9,648,100	3,898,350	3,119,650	1,980,900

Notes: These figures, collated from many sources, are of varying reliability and in some cases are subject to a wide margin of error and interpretation. This warning applies particularly to the figures for 1946, a year in which there was considerable Jewish population movement. It must also be borne in mind that the boundaries of many European countries changed between 1937 and 1946.

n/a = not available.

[a] Includes 'Displaced Persons'.
[b] Total for Czech Republic and Slovakia.
[c] Baltic States included in USSR between 1941 and 1991.
[d] Excludes Asiatic regions.
[e] Total for former Yugoslavia.

Source: Wasserstein (1996).

per cent of American Catholics now reject the notion that the pope is infallible on matters of morals, such as birth control and abortion (Gallup 2004).

In recent decades, the composition of the Protestant Church in America has changed too. Membership of liberal or mainstream American churches, such as the Lutherans, Episcopalians (Anglicans), Methodists and Presbyterians, has been in decline. But there has been an increase in the membership of conservative, non-traditional Protestant churches, such as Pentecostalists and Southern Baptists (Roof and McKinney 1990; Jones et al. 2002). Conservative Protestants emphasize a literal interpretation of the Bible, morality in daily life and conversion through evangelizing.

The Protestant Church in the USA has seen a huge rise in evangelicalism, the belief in spiritual rebirth or being 'born again'. Evangelicalism can be seen, in part, as a response to growing secularism, religious diversity and, in general, the decline of once core Protestant values in American life (Wuthnow 1988). Many Protestants are clearly seeking the more direct, personal and emotional religious experience promised by evangelical denominations. Evangelical organizations are highly effective in mobilizing resources to help achieve their religious and political objectives. In the business-like language used by religious economists, they have proved to be extremely competitive 'spiritual entrepreneurs' in the 'religious marketplace' (see 'Using your sociological imagination 17.2').

The USA has seen a dramatic growth in evangelicalism, widely seen as helping to elect George W. Bush as president in 2000 and 2004. Republican presidential nominees do much to try to win the favour of evangelical Christian groups.

Radio and television have provided important new marketing technologies, enabling evangelists to reach a much wider audience than was previously possible.

Called 'televangelists' because they conduct their evangelical ministries via television, these ministers depart from the path of many earlier evangelicals by preaching a 'gospel of prosperity': God wants the faithful to be financially prosperous and satisfied rather than to sacrifice and suffer. This differs considerably from the austere emphasis on hard work and self-denial ordinarily associated with traditional conservative Protestant beliefs (Bruce 1990). Theology and fundraising are the staples of televangelism, which must support not only the television ministries but also schools, universities, theme parks and, sometimes, the lavish lifestyles of its preachers. Televangelism has increased in Latin America too, where North American television programmes are shown, resulting in Protestant movements, mostly of the Pentecostal kind, making a dramatic impact in predominantly Catholic countries such as Chile and Brazil (Martin 1990).

In the debate on secularization, the United States represents an important exception to the view that religion is generally declining in the developed world. On the one hand, the USA is one of the most thoroughly 'modernized' countries, but, on the other, it is characterized by some of the highest levels of religious belief and membership in the world. How can we account for American exceptionalism? Steve Bruce (1996) argues that the persistence of religion in the USA can be understood in terms of *cultural transition*. In cases where societies undergo rapid and profound demographic or economic change, religion can play a role in helping people adjust to their new situation. Industrialization came relatively late to the United States, which then developed very quickly among a population composed of a great diversity of ethnic groups. Religion was thus important in stabilizing people's identities, allowing a smoother cultural transition into the emerging American 'melting pot'.

Christianity, gender and sexuality

Churches and denominations are religious organizations with defined systems of authority. In these hierarchies, as in many other areas of social life, women are mostly excluded from positions of power. This is very clear in Christianity, but it is characteristic of the other major religions as well.

Elizabeth Cady Stanton (1815–1902), an American campaigner for women's rights, argued that the deity had created women and men as beings of equal value, and the Bible should fully reflect this fact. Its 'masculinist' character, she believed, reflected not the authentic word of God but the fact that the Bible was written by men. In 1870, the Church of England established a committee to revise and update the biblical texts, but Cady Stanton pointed out that it contained not a single woman. She asserted that there was no reason to suppose that God is a man, since it was clear in the Scriptures that all human beings were fashioned in the image of God. When a colleague opened a women's rights conference with a prayer to 'God, our Mother', there was a fierce reaction from church authorities. Yet she pressed on, organizing a Women's Revising Committee in America, composed of twenty-three women, to advise her in preparing *The Woman's Bible*, which was published in 1895.

More than 100 years later, the Anglican Church is still largely dominated by men, though recently this has been changing. In the Church of England, between 1987 and 1992, women were allowed to be deacons but not permitted to be priests. Although they were officially part of the clergy, they were not allowed to conduct certain basic religious rituals, such as pronouncing blessings or solemnizing marriages. In 1992, after increasing pressure, particularly from women inside the Church of England, the Synod (governing assembly) voted to open the priesthood to women, and the first women priests were ordained in 1994. The decision is still opposed by many conservatives in the Church, who

17.2 Competition in the religious economy?

One quite recent and influential approach to the sociology of religion is tailored to Western societies, which offer many different faiths from which to choose. Taking their cue from economic theory, sociologists who favour this religious economy approach argue that religions can be fruitfully understood as organizations in competition with one another for followers (Stark and Bainbridge 1987; Finke and Stark 1988, 1992; Moore 1994).

Like economists who study businesses, these sociologists argue that competition is preferable to monopoly when it comes to ensuring religious vitality. This position is exactly opposite to that of the classical theorists. Marx, Durkheim and Weber assumed that religion weakens when it is challenged by different religious or secular viewpoints, whereas the religious economists argue that competition increases the overall level of religious involvement in society. Why should this be so? First, competition makes each religious group try that much harder to win followers. Second, the presence of numerous religions means that there is likely to be something for just about everyone. In culturally diverse societies, a single religion will probably appeal to a strictly limited range of followers, while the presence of Indian gurus and fundamentalist preachers, for example, in addition to more traditional churches, is likely to encourage a high level of religious participation.

This analysis is adapted from the business world, in which competition encourages the emergence of highly specialized products that appeal to very specific markets. In fact, the religious economists borrow the language of business in describing the conditions that lead to the success or failure of a particular religious organization. According to Finke and Stark (1992), a successful religious group must be well organized for competition, have eloquent preachers who are effective 'sales reps' in spreading the word, offer beliefs and rituals that are packaged as an appealing product, and develop effective marketing techniques. Religion, on this view, is a business much like any other.

Thus religious economists do not see competition as undermining religious beliefs and contributing to secularization. Rather, they argue that modern religion is constantly renewing itself through active marketing and recruitment. Although there is a growing body of research which supports the notion that competition is good for religion (Stark and Bainbridge 1980, 1985; Finke and Stark 1992), not all have reached this conclusion (Land et al. 1991).

The religious economy approach overestimates the extent to which people rationally pick and choose among religions, as if they were shopping around for a new car or pair of shoes. For deeply committed believers it is not obvious that religion is a matter of rational choice. Even in the United States, where the religious economy approach originated, sociologists may overlook the spiritual aspects of religion. A study of baby boomers in the USA – the generation born in the two decades after the end of the Second World War – found that one-third had remained loyal to their childhood faith, while another third continued to profess their childhood beliefs although they no longer belonged to a religious organization. Thus only one-third were looking to make the kind of selection assumed by the religious economy approach (Roof 1993).

> ### THINKING CRITICALLY
> How might the religious economy approach help us to understand the process of secularization in the industrialized world? What does religious economy tell us, if anything, about the role of spirituality in human affairs?

argue that full acceptance of women is a blasphemous deviation from revealed biblical truth and a move away from eventual reunification with the Catholic Church. Some church members withdrew from the Church of England in protest, and a number converted to Catholicism.

By 2009, around one-fifth of priests in the Church of England were women, and the numbers look set to increase. In July 2005, the Church of England voted to begin the process that would allow women to become bishops, a decision strongly opposed by several senior Church figures. In July 2008, the ruling General Synod rejected proposals for separate structures aimed at accommodating traditionalists, and in 2010 it agreed to allow women bishops. The first female bishop was finally ordained in January 2015.

The Catholic Church has been far more conservative in its attitude to women and continues formally to support inequalities of gender. Calls for the ordination of women have been consistently turned down by Catholic authorities. In 1977 the Sacred Congregation for the Doctrine of the Faith, in Rome, declared formally that women were not admissible to the Catholic priesthood. The reason given was that Jesus did not call a woman to be one of his disciples. In January 2004, seven women who had been ordained as priests by the rebel Argentinian Bishop Romulo Antonio Braschi were excommunicated from the Church and their ordinations overturned. Pope John Paul II (1920–2005) encouraged women to recall their roles as wives and mothers, attacked feminist ideologies which assert that men and women are fundamentally the same, and supported policies prohibiting abortion and the use of contraception, which place further limitations on women's freedom (Vatican 2004).

Libby Lane was ordained at York Minster as the first female bishop in the Church of England.

Controversy in the Anglican Church in recent years has shifted away from gender to the issue of homosexuality and the priesthood. Gay men have long served in the Christian Church, but with their sexuality suppressed, ignored or unobserved. The Catholic Church still holds to the position set out in 1961 that those 'affected by the perverse inclination' (towards homosexuality) must be barred from taking religious vows or being ordained. Other, Protestant denominations have introduced liberal policies towards homosexuality, and openly gay clergy have been admitted to the priesthood in some of the smaller denominations. In 1972, the Evangelical Lutheran Church in the Netherlands was the first European Christian denomination to decide that lesbians and gays could serve as pastors. The United Church of Canada (in 1988) and the Norwegian Church (in 2000) followed suit.

The controversy over the admission of gay men to the priesthood came to the fore in the UK in June 2003, when Dr Jeffrey John, an openly gay man living a celibate life, was appointed bishop of Reading. He eventually declined to take the post after his appointment caused a bitter row within the international Anglican Church. In August 2003 the rank and file of the Anglican Church in America voted to elect an openly gay bishop, Reverend Canon Gene Robinson of New Hampshire. A conservative lobby group, Anglican Mainstream, was created to lobby against the appointment of gay clergy, and the issue remains unresolved.

Issues of gender and sexuality have been at the centre of some recent controversies within the Anglican Church as well as other traditional religions. What we may conclude from these controversies is that religions cannot ignore social changes in the wider society of which they are a part. As the impetus towards equality, a key feature of modernity, brings about increasing tolerance and acceptance of homosexuality and gender equality, religious organizations are having to respond accordingly. And, as the culture of modernity spreads globally, we can expect religions in the developing countries to face similar challenges.

See chapter 15, 'Gender and Sexuality', for a wider discussion of sexuality and identities.

Fundamentalism

The growth of religious fundamentalism is another indication that we have not yet entered a secular age. The term fundamentalism can be applied in many different contexts to describe strict adherence to a set of principles or beliefs. Religious fundamentalism describes an approach calling for the literal interpretation of basic scriptures or texts and that the doctrines which emerge should then be applied to all aspects of social, economic and political life.

Religious fundamentalists believe that only one view of the world is true, so there is no room for ambiguity or multiple interpretations. Within religious fundamentalist movements, access to the exact meanings of scriptures is restricted to a set of privileged 'interpreters' – priests, clergy or other religious leaders. This gives these leaders a great amount of authority in both religious and secular matters. Religious fundamentalists have become powerful political figures in opposition movements, in mainstream political parties and even as heads of state.

Religious fundamentalism is a relatively new phenomenon that has arisen largely in response to globalization since the 1970s. As the forces of modernization progressively undermine traditional elements of the social world – such as the nuclear family and the domination of women by men – fundamentalism has arisen in defence of traditional beliefs. In a globalizing world which demands rational reasons, fundamentalism insists on faith-based answers and references to ritual truth: fundamentalism is tradition defended in a traditional way.

Although fundamentalism sets itself in opposition to modernity, it also employs modern approaches in spreading its beliefs. Christian fundamentalists in the USA, for example, were among the first to use television as a medium for spreading their doctrines, while Hindutva militants in India have used the Internet and email to promote feelings of 'Hindu identity'. In this section we will examine two of the most prominent forms of religious fundamentalism: Islamic and Christian. In the past thirty years, both have grown in strength, shaping the contours of national and international politics alike.

Islamic fundamentalism

Of the early sociological thinkers, only Weber might have suspected that a traditional religion like Islam could undergo a major revival and become the basis of important political developments in the late twentieth century. Yet this is exactly what has occurred since the Iranian Revolution (1978–9), which brought about the end of monarchical rule and introduced an Islamic republic with Ayatollah Khomeini at its head. In recent years, Islamic revivalism has spread, with a significant impact on other countries including Egypt, Iraq, Syria, Lebanon, Algeria, Afghanistan and Nigeria. What explains this large-scale renewal of Islam?

To understand the phenomenon, we have to look to aspects of Islam as a traditional religion and to secular changes that have affected modern states where its influence is pervasive. Islam, like Christianity, is a religion that has continually stimulated activism. The Koran – the Islamic holy scripture – contains many instructions to believers to 'struggle in the way of God'. This struggle is both within the individual and against unbelievers and those who introduce corruption into the Muslim community. Over the centuries there have been successive generations of Muslim reformers, and Islam has become as internally divided as Christianity.

Shia Islam diverged from *Sunni Islam* after the death of the Prophet Muhammad in 632 ce. It has also been the official religion of Iran (earlier known as Persia) since the sixteenth

The three most prominent leaders of the Islamic revolution in Iran – Ayatollah Khomeini (in the foreground), Ayatollah Ali Khamenei and the then president, Hashemi Rafsanjani – look down from a poster over a street in Tehran.

century and was the source of the ideas behind the Iranian Revolution. Shia Islam traces its origins to Imam Ali, a seventh-century religious and political leader who is believed to have shown qualities of personal devotion to God and virtue outstanding among the worldly rulers of the time. Ali's descendants came to be seen as the rightful leaders of Islam, since, unlike the dynasties in power, they were held to belong to the Prophet Muhammad's family.

Shiites believed that the rule of Muhammad's rightful heir would eventually be instituted, doing away with the tyrannies and injustices associated with existing regimes. Muhammad's heir would be a leader directly guided by God, governing in accordance with the Koran. There are large Shia populations in other Middle Eastern countries, including Iraq, Turkey and Saudi Arabia, as well as in India and Pakistan. Islamic leadership in these countries, however, is in the hands of the majority, the Sunni.

In the last thirty years, arguably the most important development has been the spread of *Salafism* – a revivalist, Sunni reform movement that seeks to base Islamic practice on the example set by the first three generations of Muslim leaders after Muhammad's death (Wiktorowicz 2006). In particular, Salafism advocates that Muslims today should live and behave, as far as is possible, just like the 'pious forefathers' of that early, golden age of Islam in order to purify the religion. In this sense, Salafism is 'fundamentalist' (seeking a return to fundamental principles) but by no means necessarily violent.

Meijer (2009: 2–6) argues that Salafism can be seen as Islam's 'new religious movement', though it is not a unified movement and contains many strands and internal disagreements. Chief among these is the tension between the doctrine of complete submission to God and what believers should do to comply with this demand in societies that are not rooted in *Sharia* law. For some Salafists, in that situation the focus should be on persuasion, education and spreading the Islamic faith. For others, this is not enough, and believers must be prepared to criticize and seek peaceful reform. Still others advocate uprisings against leaders and regimes that do not adopt Sharia law.

The activist interpretation of Salafism has received much attention since it combined with Saudi *Wahhabism* and other ideologies, influencing movements that engage in terrorist activity. Wahhabism originated in the eighteenth century through the ideas of Muhammad ibn Abd-al-Wahhab. He focused initially on reforming Muslim societies, which he believed had moved away from true Sunni

Islam and lost their way (DeLong-Bas 2004). He also saw Shiism as heresy, as it places 'infallible' imams between the individual and God and rejects three of the four Rightly Guided Prophets (known as the *Rashidun*) who were close companions of Muhammad. Wahhabism considers all those who do not believe in the Oneness of God (i.e., strict monotheism) to be apostates or unbelievers, justifying a coercive and often violent *jihad* against them.

Though it is the extreme violence and terrorism of groups with global expansionary aims – such as al-Qaeda and IS – which generates most publicity and, hence, public awareness, we must remember that Salafism remains a multifaceted religious movement with numerous quietist and apolitical elements too. What unites all Salafists is the central belief that Muslims should be guided by the example of Islam's earliest exponents if the religion is to prosper in the future.

Islam and the West

During the Middle Ages, there was a more or less constant struggle between Christian Europe and the Muslim states, which controlled large sections of what became Spain, Greece, Yugoslavia, Bulgaria and Romania. Most of the lands conquered by the Muslims were reclaimed by European Christians, and many of their possessions in North Africa were in fact colonized as Western power grew in the eighteenth and nineteenth centuries. These reverses were catastrophic for Islamic religion and civilization, which Muslim leaders held to be the highest and most advanced possible, transcending all others. In the late nineteenth century, the inability of the Muslim world effectively to resist the spread of Western culture led to reform movements seeking to restore Islam to its original purity and strength. A key idea was that Islam should respond to the Western challenge by affirming the identity of its own beliefs and practices (Sutton and Vertigans 2005).

This idea was developed in various ways in the twentieth century and formed a backdrop to the Islamic revolution in Iran of

1978–9. The revolution was fuelled initially by internal opposition to the shah of Iran, who had accepted and tried to promote forms of modernization modelled on the West – for example, land reform, extending the vote to women, and developing secular education. The movement that overthrew the shah brought together people of diverse interests, by no means all of whom were attached to Islamic fundamentalism, but a dominant figure was Ayatollah Khomeini, who provided a radical reinterpretation of Shiite ideas.

Following the revolution, Khomeini established a government organized according to traditional Shia law, and religion, as specified by that interpretation of the Koran, became the direct basis of political and economic life. Under this interpretation of Islamic law – Sharia – as it was revived, men and women were kept rigorously segregated, women were obliged to cover their bodies and heads in public, practising homosexuals were sent to the firing squad, and adulterers were stoned to death. The aim of the Islamic Republic in Iran was to Islamize the state – to organize government and society so that Islamic teachings would become dominant in all spheres. The process was by no means completed, however, and forces emerged to act against it.

Three groups now struggle with one another (Zubaida 1996). *Radicals* want to carry on with and deepen the Islamic revolution and believe that revolution should be actively exported to other Islamic countries. *Conservatives* are made up mostly of religious functionaries, who think that the revolution has gone far enough, having given them a position of power which they wish to hold on to. *Pragmatists* favour market reforms and opening up the economy to foreign investment and trade. They tend to be opposed to the strict imposition of Islamic codes on women, the family and the legal system.

The death of Ayatollah Khomeini in 1989 was a blow to radical and conservative elements in Iran. His successor, Ayatollah Ali Khamenei, retained the loyalty of Iran's powerful mullahs (religious leaders) but became increasingly unpopular with Iranian citizens, who resented the repressive regime and persistent social ills. The fault-lines between pragmatists and others came to the surface under the reform-minded presidency of Mohammad Khatami (1997–2005). Khatami's administration was characterized by disputes with conservatives, who managed to hamper his attempts at reforming Iranian society.

In 2005, the election of Tehran's deeply conservative mayor, Mahmoud Ahmadinejad, as president of Iran decreased tensions within the country's religious and political leaderships. Although he was re-elected in 2009 – amid protests over suspected electoral fraud – Ahmadinejad's time in office was characterized by tensions with the West, not least because of his commitment to Iran's nuclear power programme. He was replaced as president in 2013 by Hassan Rouhani – a critic of Ahmadinejad's pro-nuclear stance – widely seen as a moderate and pragmatist, whose stated aim was to end Iran's international isolation. To that end, in 2015 an agreement was reached that will see cuts to Iran's nuclear programme in return for a gradual lifting of economic sanctions against the country (Graham-Harrison 2015).

The spread of Islamic revivalism

Although the ideas underlying the Iranian Revolution were meant to unite the whole of the Islamic world against the West, governments of countries where Shiites are in a minority did not align themselves closely with Iran. Islamic fundamentalism has still achieved significant popularity in many other states, and various forms of Islamic revivalism elsewhere have been stimulated by it.

Though Islamic fundamentalist movements have gained influence in many countries in North Africa, the Middle East and South Asia, they have succeeded in coming to power in only two other states: Sudan was ruled by the National Islamic Front from 1989 and the fundamentalist Taliban regime consolidated its hold on the fragmented state of Afghanistan in 1996. The latter was ousted from power at the end of 2001 by Afghan opposition forces and the USA. In many other countries, Islamic fundamentalist groups have gained influence but have been prevented from coming to power. In Egypt, Turkey and Algeria, for example, Islamic fundamentalist uprisings have been suppressed by the state or the military. The most recent group, Islamic State (IS), has gained territory and several cities in Iraq and Syria and is well funded and armed. In 2014 IS declared a new worldwide caliphate and encouraged people from around the world to travel and join their campaign. More recently, however, the group has been losing ground in both Iraq and Syria as government forces, backed by international air strikes, have retaken territory.

Some scholars have been concerned that 'the Islamic world' is heading for confrontation with those parts of the world that do not share its beliefs. Most notable among these is the political scientist Samuel Huntington (1996), who argued that, with the ending of the Cold War and increasing globalization, struggles between Western and Islamic cultures might become part of a worldwide 'clash of civilizations'. According to Huntington, the nation-state is no longer the main actor in international relations. Instead, rivalries and conflicts will occur between larger cultures or civilizations which he sees as the basis for people's basic identities and commitments. In particular, Huntington suggests, religion is

Pro-secular Turks in the city of Izmir protest against the Islamist-based government. Around 98 per cent of Turkey's population are Muslim, though its independent constitution laid the foundations for a secular state.

the most important aspect which differentiates and divides civilizations.

Possible examples of such conflicts were seen during the 1990s in the former Yugoslavia, in Bosnia and in Kosovo, where the Bosnian Muslims and Albanian Kosovars fought against the Serbs, who represent an Orthodox Christian culture. Such events have heightened awareness of Muslims as a world community; as observers have noted: 'Bosnia has become a rallying point for Muslims throughout the Muslim world. . . . [It] has created and sharpened the sense of polarization and radicalization in Muslim societies, while at the same time increasing the sense of being a Muslim' (Ahmed and Donnan 1994).

The wars in the former Yugoslavia are discussed in more detail in chapter 22, 'Nations, War and Terrorism'.

In the same way, the American-led invasion of Iraq became a rallying point for radical Muslims after 2003. As an explanation of the causes of terrorist attacks on New York and Washington on 11 September 2001, the American decision to oust the Islamic regime in Afghanistan and the revival of religious resistance to the US presence in Iraq after 2003, Huntington's thesis gained widespread media attention.

However, critics point out that there are many political and cultural divisions *within* civilizations and that the forecast of conflict between civilizations is unlikely and alarmist. For example, in 1990 Saddam Hussein's Sunni regime in Iraq invaded Kuwait, which also has a majority Sunni population, and between 1980 and 1988 Iraq and Iran (with majority Shia populations) were engaged in armed conflict with each other. The number of 'civilizational conflicts' in the past can also be exaggerated, as many apparently cultural conflicts have been more centrally focused on access to scarce resources and the struggle for political power and military dominance (Russett et al. 2000; Chiozza 2002). In such conflicts, it has

been, and still is, more common to see alliances forming across the boundaries of large-scale civilizations.

The phenomenon of terrorism is discussed further in chapter 22, 'Nations, War and Terrorism'.

Christian fundamentalism

The growth of Christian fundamentalist organizations in Europe, and particularly in the United States, is one of the most notable features of the past few decades. Fundamentalists believe that the Bible is a guide to all spheres of social life, from family and business to politics and government (Capps 1995). The Bible is taken as infallible and its contents are expressions of Divine Truth, as we saw in our opening example of creationist arguments against evolution. Fundamentalist Christians believe in the divinity of Christ and the possibility of salvation for the soul through the acceptance of Christ as personal saviour. They are committed to spreading their message and converting those who have not yet adopted the same beliefs.

Christian fundamentalism is a reaction against liberal theology and supporters of 'secular humanism' – those who 'favour the emancipation of reason, desires and instincts in opposition to faith and obedience to God's command' (Kepel 1994: 133). The movement sets itself against the perceived moral crisis of modernization – the decline of the traditional family, the threat to individual morality and the weakening relationship between humans and God.

In the United States, beginning with Reverend Jerry Falwell's 'Moral Majority' in the 1970s, some fundamentalist groups became increasingly involved in what has been termed the 'New Christian Right' in national politics, particularly in the conservative wing of the Republican Party (Simpson 1985; Woodrum 1988; Kiecolt and Nelson 1991). Falwell identified five issues to be tackled: abortion, homosexuality, pornography, humanism, and the fractured family (Kepel 1994). Fundamentalist religious organizations are a powerful force in the USA and helped to shape Republican Party policies and rhetoric during the Reagan and both Bush administrations.

Falwell initially blamed the 9/11 terrorist attacks in 2001 on 'sinners' in the USA, saying on live television:

> I really believe that the pagans, and the abortionists, and the feminists, and the gays and the lesbians who are actively trying to make that an alternative lifestyle, the [American Civil Liberties Union], People For the American Way [both liberal organizations], all of them who have tried to secularize America. I point the finger in their face and say 'you helped this happen'. (CNN 2001)

Although he later apologized, he caused further controversy by stating that 'Moham-mad was a terrorist. I read enough by both Muslims and non-Muslims [to decide] that he was a violent man, a man of war' (BBC 2002). Again, he apologized for the remark, but it was too late to stop sectarian rioting between Hindus and Muslims in Solapur, Western India, reacting against his claims. His comments led to widespread condemna-tion from Islamic leaders around the world. Another Christian fundamentalist preacher, pastor Terry Jones from Florida, tried to organ-ize an international 'burn a Koran' day on the anniversary of 9/11 in 2010, though this did not materialize after pressure from President Obama and the defense secretary. However, in March 2011, the pastor did stage a mock trial and burning of his copy of the Koran in front of a small group at his own church in Gainesville.

Many of America's best-known and most influential evangelists are based in the South-ern and Midwestern states of Virginia, Okla-homa and North Carolina. The most influ-ential fundamentalist groups in the United States are the Southern Baptist Convention, the Assemblies of God and the Seventh-Day Adventists. Prominent preachers on the New Christian Right have founded a number of universities in the United States to produce a new generation 'counter-elite', schooled in fundamentalist Christian beliefs and able to take up prominent positions in the media, academia, politics and the arts. Liberty University (founded by Falwell), Oral Roberts University, Bob Jones University and others confer degrees in standard academic disci-plines, taught within the framework of biblical infallibility. On campus, strict ethical stand-ards are maintained in students' private lives (accommodation is single sex and students can be expelled for engaging in unmarried sex) and sexuality is channelled towards marriage (Kepel 1994).

> **THINKING CRITICALLY**
> Religious fundamentalism seems to have increased during a period of rapid globalization. How are these two phenomena related? What evidence is there that religious fundamentalism may become a permanent feature of modern societies?

Conclusion

In a globalizing age that is in desperate need of mutual understanding and dialogue, religious fundamentalism can be a destructive force. Yet one of fundamentalism's continuing attrac-tions is its ability to provide certainty on how to live a moral life based on clear religious texts and teachings. Such clarity is arguably lacking in secular thought and science, which accept that knowledge is always changing in the light of new findings. If Taylor (2007) is right, that a secular age is gradually emerging as traditional religions decline, the question of how people can or should live fulfilling lives will become more significant. Could a secular perspective really come to dominate such a quest?

Heelas (2015: 442) expresses serious doubts: 'Secularity is not exactly all-conquering. Atheism has not come to rule the roost.' He also notes that those who are indifferent rather than opposed to religion are unlikely to become the majority. In recent years some philosophers and social theorists have introduced the concept of the 'post-secular society' – a notion designed to capture the rising public consciousness of religion and religion-related issues in the public life of most developed countries. Habermas (2008) argues that this rising consciousness is related to the linking of religion to global conflicts, the involvement of various religious 'voices' in debates on civil and political matters, and the political focus on issues around increasing levels of migration. Taken together, these call into question the longstanding sociological forecast that secularity – over the long term – will probably become dominant. If this forecast is accepted as incorrect, then sociologists will have to rethink the role of religion in modern societies (Moberg et al. 2014).

Yet, so far, the thesis of post-secularism does not refer to the contemporary condition of social life or to the emergence of a new type of society. Instead, post-secular ideas occur in scholarly discussion about what the requirements are for the coexistence of religious and secular perspectives and where each accepts the other on equal terms. What sociologists can bring to these essentially philosophical debates is an empirical focus that examines the contexts and practices of coexistence in the various spheres of social life. Turning philosophical and theoretical speculation into empirical research studies has long been a crucial part of sociology's role. Only in this way can the prospects for any 'new accommodation' between religious and secular groups in a putative post-secular society be realistically evaluated.

. . . .

Chapter review

1 Dissect Emile Durkheim's famous definition of religion, noting which elements it includes. On this definition, is football supporting 'religious'? If not, why not?

2 Briefly outline the three classical theories of religion. Provide some contemporary examples from around the world which demonstrate the continuing relevance of Marx, Durkheim and Weber's ideas on religion.

3 What is meant by the process of secularization? List three ways in which this process can be measured. What counter-evidence is there in this chapter? On the balance of available evidence, is the twenty-first century likely to usher in a 'secular age'?

4 Explain what is meant by 'neo-tribes' and 'everyday lived religion'. Does this research challenge or support the secularization thesis?

5 Which of these are monotheistic religions: Hinduism, Judaism, Christianity, Confucianism, Islam? How would you categorize those that are *not* monotheistic?

6 A church is a large and established religious body with a formal bureaucratic structure and hierarchy of religious officials. But how can we characterize sects, cults and denominations?

7 Write a 500-word summary of the major trends in religious observance in Europe over the last fifty years or so. Include reference to issues of religious diversity, gender, sexuality and the impact of migration.

8 What are new religious movements? Explain the differences in emphasis and practice of world-affirming movements, world-rejecting movements and world-accommodating movements.

9 Religious 'fundamentalists' believe in returning to the fundamentals of religious doctrine and practice. In what ways is the growth of fundamentalism reliant on modern science and technology?

Research in practice

From the classical theorists to Taylor, in his *A Secular Age* (2007), sociologists seem convinced that modernity, capitalism, science and technology must, at some point, generate levels of secularization that will reduce religion to a relatively insignificant aspect of people's everyday lives. Yet in recent years there have been numerous religious 'revivals', and even within developed societies new forms of 'religious quest' continue to surface. Why? Have sociologists just got this one wrong?

An insight into this issue is provided by Mark Jennings's (2014) 'An Extraordinary Degree of Exaltation: Durkheim, Effervescence and Pentecostalism's Defeat of Secularisation', *Social Compass*, 62(1): 61–75. Read the paper and try the questions below.

1   What is Pentecostalism? Outline its central elements and historical development.
2   What does Durkheim mean by 'collective effervescence'? How did he think modern societies would appropriate this phenomenon to secular ends?
3   In what ways has Pentecostalism made use of 'effervescence' and how significant has it been for its expansion?
4   On the basis of this paper's argument, would it be possible for other religions to adopt a similar approach to worship?
5   Do you agree with the author that Pentecostalism really has 'bucked the trend' towards the secular? What evidence would you draw on to argue against this contention?

Thinking it through

Some scientists also have a religious faith, and many religious people accept that Darwinian evolutionary theory, for instance, is the best explanation we have of the development of life on Earth. On the other hand, some scientists, such as Richard Dawkins, argue that science is necessarily a secular enterprise and that scientists ought to be atheists or, at least, agnostics. Religion has no place in a scientific culture.

Watch this Al-Jazeera interview with Dawkins from December 2012 on YouTube: https://www.youtube.com/watch?v=U0Xn60Zw03A.

1   How does Dawkins define 'religion'? How does this definition fit with those at the start of this chapter? Is his definition satisfactory?
2   List Dawkins's main criticisms of religions and religious faith. Looking at the evidence in this chapter, are these criticisms legitimate or one-sided?
3   Dawkins spends a fair amount of time discussing the *content* of religious belief systems such as Islam and Christianity. As we have seen, sociologists tend not to do so. But is Dawkins right? If sociologists are 'agnostic' towards the content of religions, can their assessments only ever be partial? Are there compelling reasons why sociologists should not engage with the truth claims of all religions?

Society in the arts

The genre of science fiction mixes the latest scientific inventions and theories with some of the oldest religious ideals and themes. However, science fiction does tend to foreground the science and technology, leaving the religious or spiritual hidden beneath the surface. This has led some to suggest that science fiction doesn't 'do' religion because it jars with the basic scientific underpinning that defines the genre.

- *Star Wars: The Force Awakens* (2015), directed by J. J. Abrams
- *Avatar* (2009), directed by James Cameron
- *2001: A Space Odyssey* (1968), directed by Stanley Kubrick

Watch one or more of the films above, paying close attention to the religious themes of belief, faith, ritual, salvation and the supernatural. On the basis of your observations, do these examples of science fiction 'do' religion as well as they 'do' science? Does science fiction provide evidence that science and religion inhabit two distinct cultures?

Further reading

The sociology of religion is one of the oldest specialist fields in sociology. As a result there are lots of good introductory texts. However, Alan Aldridge's (2013) *Religion in the Contemporary World: A Sociological Introduction* (3rd edn, Cambridge: Polity) is very well written. Then a comprehensive and contemporary edited collection is Peter B. Clarke's (2011) *The Oxford Handbook of the Sociology of Religion* (Oxford: Oxford University Press). Both books cover all of the issues discussed in this chapter in more detail and take readers deeper into the subject. After these, Grace Davie's (2013) *The Sociology of Religion: A Critical Agenda* (London: Sage) is a very good assessment by a renowned expert.

Steve Bruce's (2013) *Secularization: In Defence of an Unfashionable Theory* (Oxford: Oxford University Press) does exactly what it says. For an alternative view, try Peter Berger's (2003) *Questions of Faith: A Skeptical Affirmation of Christianity* (Oxford: Blackwell). Berger see his earlier support of secularization as a mistake, and this is an interesting book by a sociologist with a religious faith.

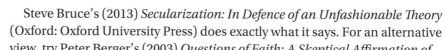

Finally, two useful, if large, edited collections of essays by scholars of religion are Bryan S. Turner's (2010) *The New Blackwell Companion to the Sociology of Religion* (Oxford: Blackwell) and James Beckford and N. Jay Demerath III's (2007) *The Sage Handbook of the Sociology of Religion* (London: Sage).

For a collection of original readings on social institutions, see the accompanying *Sociology: Introductory Readings* (3rd edn, Cambridge: Polity, 2010).

Internet links

@

Additional information and support for this book at Polity:
www.politybooks.com/giddens

@

Sociology of Religion – **a peer-reviewed quarterly journal with many articles covering this field:**
http://socrel.oxfordjournals.org

@ **The Religious Studies Project** – an international project covering social scientific studies of religion – lots of interviews and other interesting material here:
www.religiousstudiesproject.com

@ **Sociology of Religion Resources** – exactly what it says, based at the University of Aberdeen, UK:
www.sociologyofreligion.net

@ **Sociology of Religion Study Group of the British Sociological Association** – very helpful 'faith guides' and much more available:
http://socrel.org.uk

Religion and Society Research Programme – British research programme with information on seventy-five research projects on the relationship between society and religion:
www.religionandsociety.org.uk

@ **BBC Religion** – BBC's UK-based site on all things religious:
www.bbc.co.uk/religion

British Religion in Numbers – exactly what you might think, lots of quantitative data on the state of religion in Britain:
www.brin.ac.uk

@ **The Association of Religion Data Archives** – American site aiming to 'democratize access to the best data on religion':
www.thearda.com

@ **The Immanent Frame** – US site which publishes essays on secularism, religion and the public sphere, and much more:
http://blogs.ssrc.org/tif

CHAPTER 18

The Media

Contents

In July 2015, immediately after the Greek government had won a referendum vote to reject the harsh terms of a new economic bailout package, the finance minister Yanis Varoufakis announced on Twitter that he was resigning. He tweeted, 'Minister No More!' On 12 April 2015, Hillary Clinton posted a video on YouTube and released a tweet announcing that, as many predicted, she *would* be running a presidential campaign for the 2016 election. In May 2010, during sensitive coalition negotiations between the Conservative and Liberal Democrat parties, the former Conservative leader William Hague tweeted updates on the state of the parties' discussions. Politicians today are just as likely to use social media to make important announcements as they are to speak to TV stations, book press conferences or give interviews to print journalists – a small sign of big changes in modern communications.

Both the immediacy and global reach of online social media and the ability of the audience to comment and interact with the message sender directly contrast sharply with previous media forms. In 1865 the actor John Wilkes Booth assassinated US President Abraham Lincoln in a Washington theatre. It took twelve days before a ship carrying the news reached London. A small boat off the south coast of Ireland met the ship carrying the message from the United States and the news was telegraphed to London from Cork, beating the ship by three days. This is a singular and rather stark example, but, as we will see in this chapter, the Internet and new digital media have already changed the way that people routinely communicate with each other.

In the twenty-first century, communication technologies enable information to be shared instantaneously and simultaneously with many millions of people almost anywhere in the world. Communication – the transfer of information from one individual or group to another, whether in speech or through the media – is crucial to any society. Today a wide variety of mass media exist, including radio, television, newspapers and magazines, film and the Internet. These are referred to as 'mass' media because they communicate with very large numbers of people.

The Canadian media theorist Marshall McLuhan (1964) famously argued that media forms have distinct effects on society. His dictum is that 'the medium *is* the message'. That is, society is influenced much more by the *type* of media than by the content or messages which that media conveys. Everyday life is experienced differently in a society in which the Internet and social media communicate instantaneously from one side of the globe to the other, compared to one that relies on horses, ships or telegraph cables.

McLuhan forecast that modern electronic media would lead to the creation of a global village in which a majority of people can witness major events unfolding. In that, he was surely correct. Globalization and information communications technology (ICT) allow people on all continents to receive the same music, news, films and television programmes. Twenty-four-hour news channels report on stories in real time, films made in Hollywood or Hong Kong reach worldwide audiences, and sports stars such as Usain Bolt and Serena Williams are global household names. The human world is becoming ever more integrated into a single 'community of fate'.

Even thirty years ago, forms of communication were relatively self-contained spheres, but today they have become intertwined to a remarkable degree. This is often described as media convergence, the process through which apparently distinct media forms merge in new ways. Television, radio, newspapers and telephones have undergone profound transformations as a result of advances in technology and the rapid spread of the Internet. Newspapers can be read online, radio stations are accessed on digital televisions, and smartphones enable Internet access. With the expansion of technologies such as voice recognition, broadband, web casting and cable links, the Internet may already have become the primary conduit in the developed countries for the delivery of information, entertainment, advertising and commerce.

We start with this relatively recent digital revolution, focusing on the Internet and worldwide web. We then provide a brief account of selected forms of mass media – film, television, music and newspapers – before considering some of the main theoretical approaches to the media and their role(s) in society. Media representations of social groups and the effects of mass media on the audience follow, and the chapter ends with a discussion of the concentrated ownership of the global media and emerging alternatives and resistance to it.

Media diversity in the global age

For most of human history the main means of communication was speech, and face-to-face communication was the norm. In such oral

How many people in the world would not know who these people are?

cultures, information, ideas and knowledge are transmitted across generations by word of mouth, and the kind of repositories of useful knowledge we are used to – such as books, libraries and archives – just did not exist. Once speech could be written down and stored, initially on stone, the first writing cultures emerged, initially in China around 3,000 years ago. Religions have played a major part in the development of communication by finding ways of producing manuscripts and texts for study and transportation, literally to 'spread the word'.

An important precursor to the modern mass media was the invention in the mid-fifteenth century of the Gutenberg movable type printing press, which enabled texts to be reproduced. Gutenberg made use of existing technologies – paper and woodblock printing – which originated in Asia much earlier. Although technological advances and new uses of older technologies played a crucial part in the development of mass media, the influence of social, cultural and economic factors must be taken into account. For instance, mass forms of printed media could develop only in societies where access was relatively cheap and an educated population was able to take advantage of them.

In the late twentieth century, digital technology facilitated new media such as the mobile and smartphone, video games, digital television and the Internet which enable interactivity and user participation. We will look first at this 'digital revolution' before examining ways in which digitization impacts on older forms such as film, television, music and newspapers.

> For more on the Internet and mobile phones, see chapter 4, 'Globalization and Social Change'.

The digital revolution

The digitization of information or data is widely seen as revolutionizing modern communications. Digitization is at the origin of the development of multimedia: what used to be different media needing different technologies (such as visuals and sound) is now combined on a single medium (such as DVDs and PCs). The processing power of computers has increased continuously and Internet speeds have become faster, making it possible to stream or download music, movies and live sport. Digitization also permits the development of interactive media such as blogs and social media in which people actively participate in or structure what they see or hear (Negroponte 1995).

One fundamental aspect of media is the infrastructure through which information is communicated and exchanged. Some important technological advances over the second half of the twentieth century completely transformed the face of telecommunications – the communication of information, sounds or images at a distance. For example, ICT stands behind profound changes in the world's money systems and stock markets. Money is no longer physical cheques or cash in your pocket. Money has become electronic, 'stored' in computers in the world's banks. The value of whatever cash you do have is determined by the activities of traders on electronically

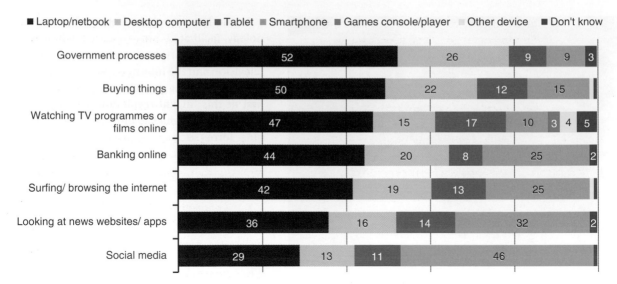

Figure 18.1 Device used most often for specific internet activities

Source: Ofcom (2015: 74).

linked money markets, and these markets are the product of the last few decades, a marriage between computers and satellite communication.

Four technological trends have led to such developments: first, the constant improvement in the *capabilities of computers*, together with declining costs; second, the *digitization of data*, making possible the integration of computer and telecommunications technologies; third, *satellite communications*; and, fourth, *fibre optics*, which allow many different messages to travel down a single cable. The dramatic communications explosion of recent years shows no sign of slowing down. Indeed, since our 6th edition in 2008, there has been a rapid take-up of the (then) new smartphones and tablet PCs, made possible by the spread of wireless technology (Wi-Fi), which enables Internet access almost anywhere. Smartphones (such as the iPhone, HTC and Blackberry) – which integrate the functions of computers into small, hand-held devices – have become widespread and are used for an ever wider range of activities. In 2007, smartphone sales overtook laptop PCs for the first time, though laptops and netbooks remain the device of choice for most

online activities with the exception of social media (figure 18.1).

Ofcom (2015: 8–9), the UK communications regulator, reports that 66 per cent of adults used smartphones both inside and outside the home and 39 per cent used a tablet PC for Internet access. Among those aged twenty-five to thirty-four, 88 per cent reported having a smartphone (ibid.: 28). In 2011, Ofcom found that 37 per cent of adult users and 60 per cent of teenagers said they were 'highly addicted' to their smartphone, with 81 per cent of all users leaving them switched on for twenty-four hours every day (Ofcom 2011).

The remarkably rapid take-up of smartphones and tablets shows just how far computing has come. The first computing era began with large mainframe machines taking up entire rooms. The second era saw the personal computer become a fixture in workplaces and homes. The current miniaturization of the computer takes us into the third era of 'ubiquitous computing' in which computers are mobile and part of almost every social environment (Maier 2011: 143–4). As the Ofcom research shows, digital technology is quickly becoming normalized, and new social norms are evolving both online and in physical environments where they are used. Fundamental to all of these changes is the Internet.

> ### THINKING CRITICALLY
>
> Conduct a participant observation of smart/mobile phone use over one week, noting how people use them in public places. What, if any, social norms govern their acceptable use in public spaces?

The Internet and worldwide web

In the early 1990s, it became clear that the future lay not with personal computers (PCs) but with a global system of interconnected computers – the Internet. Although many computer users may not have realized it at the time, the PC was becoming little more than a point of access to a network stretching across the planet that is not owned by any individual or company.

> The potential of the Internet for the growth of international political activism is explored in chapter 21, 'Politics, Government and Social Movements'.

The Internet was created during the Cold War period, developed from a system used in the Pentagon, headquarters of the American military, from 1969. This system was named the ARPA net, after the Pentagon's Advanced Research Projects Agency. ARPA sought to enable scientists working on military projects in different parts of the USA to pool their resources and share expensive equipment. Almost as an afterthought, its originators thought of a way to send messages, and electronic mail – 'email' – was born. Universities began using the system for their own purposes, and by 1987 the Internet had 28,000 host computers in universities and research labs. By 1994, business companies overtook universities as the main users of the developing network.

The best-known use of the Internet is the worldwide web – in effect, a global multimedia library. It was invented by a British software engineer, Tim Berners-Lee, at a Swiss physics lab in 1990. Users conventionally navigate the web with a 'web browser', but the increasing popularity of 'apps' – software applications for use mainly with smartphones – removes the need for a browser altogether. Websites have grown in sophistication, and many now integrate graphics and photographs, video and audio files, and the web is also the main interface for 'e-commerce' – business transactions conducted online.

Internet use continues to grow as more people have smartphones and other mobile devices. The UK Office for National Statistics estimates that 60 per cent of UK adults accessed the Internet every day in 2010, double the 2006 figure (ONS 2011a). Some 73 per cent of all households (19.2 million) had their own Internet connection. Increasing numbers of people were shopping online, with 62 per cent of all adults (31 million) having bought goods and services online in the previous twelve months. Social networking is growing rapidly, and social media were most popular among the sixteen- to 24-year-old age group. There is also a trend towards watching television and listening to radio over the Internet, with 17.4 million adults doing so in 2010, compared with just 6.4 million in 2006. This survey suggests that more people are accessing and using the Internet and doing so for a wider variety of activities.

> Online social networks and social media are also discussed in chapter 8, 'Social Interaction and Daily Life'.

However, ONS data also reveal that Internet access and use is marked by inequalities, known today as digital divides (Andreasson 2015; Ragnedda and Muschert 2013). Nationally, around 8.7 million people (17.5 per cent) had never used the Internet. Of these, 5.1 million were women, 3.6 million were men, two-thirds were aged sixty-five or over,

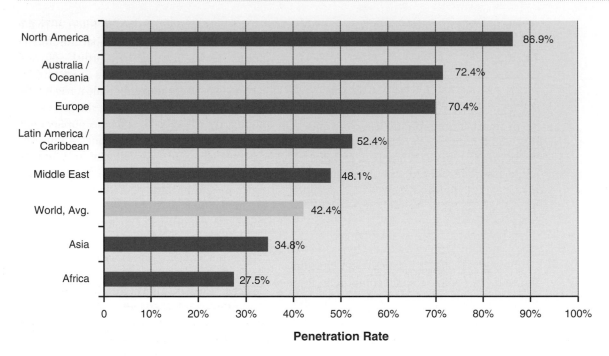

Figure 18.2 World Internet penetration rates by geographic region, 2014

Note: Penetration rates are based on a world population of 7,264,623,793 and 3,079,339,857 estimated internet users on 31 December 2014.
Source: Internet World Stats (2015).

and almost half (48.3 per cent) were disabled. Indeed, just over one-third of disabled people had never been online compared with just 11.9 per cent of people with no disability. There were also significant regional differences. Over one-fifth of the populations of Northern Ireland, Merseyside, south-west Scotland and Northumberland and Tyne and Wear had never been online, but in the wealthier counties of Berkshire, Buckinghamshire and Oxfordshire this figure was only 10.2 per cent (ONS 2011b).

How many people are connected to the Internet globally is not known with any certainty, but in 2015 the best estimate was just over 3 billion (Internet World Stats 2015). Access remains geographically uneven, reflecting global inequalities. Around 27.5 per cent of the population of Africa and 34.8 per cent in Asia were Internet users in 2014 compared with 85.9 per cent in North America and 70 per cent in Europe (see figure

18.2). One development which may lead to a faster spread of the Internet is the advent of cloud computing. In essence, this enables computing to be delivered to end users as a service rather than as a product, eliminating the need for every individual to have the same platforms and software installed on their devices. This may not appear particularly significant, but many experts insist that 'cloud computing is revolutionary, even if the technology it is built on is evolutionary' (Sosinsky 2011: 3).

The revolutionary aspect is that cloud computing makes potentially unlimited computing resources universally and continuously available. Applications, programs, file storage and operating systems are based in large datacentres whose locations are unknown to end users and made available usually on a pay-as-you-go basis. Individuals can access the services they need on whatever device they have, such as a laptop, tablet, notebook or smartphone, again without installing software on each device. There are also issues of privacy, confidentiality and data security: as more information travels across wireless connections and material is stored in datacentres, users cede control to cloud providers. Nonetheless, we may be moving towards an 'intercloud' – an interconnected, global 'cloud of clouds' (Rothenberg 2010). This may sound fanciful but, if pay-as-you-go, utility computing takes off globally, the intercloud may become as normal as the Internet.

The impact of the Internet

Many see the Internet as exemplifying an emerging, networked, global society (Castells 2006). Interactions on the Internet take place in the virtual world of cyberspace. Cyberspace means the space of interaction formed by the global network of computers that make up the Internet. In cyberspace, we cannot know with any certainty the details of people's identity, whether they are male or female, or where in the world they are. Indeed, cyberspace often feels rather like an alternative form of reality and a type of medium which gives users more control than in earlier media forms. Kolker (2009: 253) argues that:

> In our relationship with traditional media, we are always aware that what we read, hear, and see has some kind of authorship behind it: someone writing and editing the newspaper column; producing, directing, and distributing a recording, a radio or TV show, or a movie. Advertising reminds us continuously that someone wants something from us . . . But at the keyboard and online, we seem to be in control and in intimate connection with something or someone, in a world both internal and external simultaneously.

Opinions on the effects of the Internet fall into two broad categories. Some see the online world as fostering electronic relationships that either enhance or supplement existing face-to-face interactions. For example, while travelling or working abroad, people use the Internet to communicate with friends and relatives back home, making distance and separation more tolerable. The Internet also allows the formation of new types of relationship, such as 'anonymous' online users who meet on social networks, chatrooms and blog sites to discuss topics of mutual interest. Many Internet users become part of lively online communities that are qualitatively different from those they inhabit in the physical world. Scholars who see the Internet as a positive addition to human life argue that it expands and enriches our social networks.

On the other hand, some are less enthusiastic. As people spend more time communicating online and performing daily tasks in cyberspace, they spend less time interacting in the physical world. Some sociologists fear that the spread of Internet technology will lead to increasing social isolation. They argue that one effect of increasing Internet access in households is that people are spending less 'quality time' with their families and friends. The Internet is encroaching on domestic life as the lines between work and home are blurred: many employees continue to work at home after hours – checking email or finishing tasks that they were unable to complete during the day. Personal relationships suffer, traditional forms of entertainment such as theatre and books fall by the wayside, and the fabric of social life is weakened. Very similar fears were expressed in relation to television. In *The Lonely Crowd* (1961), David Riesman and his colleagues expressed concern about the impact of TV on family and community life. And while some of their fears were well founded, television has enriched the social world in many ways too.

In *The Virtual Community* (2000), Howard Rheingold acknowledges the positive potential of computer-mediated communication while accepting that its darker side cannot be wished away. Rheingold (2000: 5) is particularly interested in virtual communities, which he defines as 'social aggregations that emerge from the Net when enough people carry on . . . public discussions long enough, with sufficient human feeling, to form webs of personal relationships in cyberspace'. He provides an extended description and analysis of a virtual community – a parenting conference – on the WELL (Whole Earth 'Lectronic Link), a computer conferencing system that enables people across the world to engage in public discussions and to exchange private emails. Rheingold says that being a part of the WELL is very much like being part of the real physical world, but in disembodied form:

> People in virtual communities use words on screens to exchange pleasantries and argue, engage in intellectual discourse, conduct commerce, exchange knowledge, share emotional support, make plans, brainstorm, gossip, feud, fall in love, find friends and lose them, play games, flirt, create a little high art and a lot if [sic] idle talk. People in virtual communities do just about everything people do in real life, but we leave our bodies behind. You can't kiss anybody and nobody can punch you in the nose, but a lot can happen within those boundaries. (www.rheingold.com/vc/book/intro.html)

Nevertheless, there is a less palatable side of the Internet. For example, the so-called dark web – a hidden and encrypted part of the worldwide web where access requires authorization – has been used for distributing child pornography and other criminal activities. The Internet may also become dominated by business corporations which view virtual communities along with social media and social networking services (SNS) as commodities, gathering and selling personal details for profit to anyone who wants them, and it offers opportunities for intensified state surveillance and monitoring. This 'nightmare vision' owes something to Foucault's (1975) ideas on the eighteenth-century Panopticon, a prison design based on the principle of continuous monitoring of prisoners by guards (see chapter 20, 'Crime and Deviance' for a discussion of the Panopticon). There are no magic solutions, but Rheingold suggests that such criticisms have to be kept in mind by all Internet enthusiasts working to create a human-centred virtual world.

Questions of personal identity and new forms of community are discussed in chapter 8, 'Social Interaction and Daily Life'.

Manuel Castells (2001) argues that the Internet will enable new combinations of work and self-employment, individual expression, collaboration and sociability. For political activists, it will be possible for networks of individuals to combine and cooperate to spread their message around the world. Arguably the so-called 'Arab Spring' of 2010–12 was one example, as activists shared their ideas, concerns and experiences on globally accessible blogs and social media, using the latter to organize protests. Mainstream news outlets also relied on citizens' reports of a rapidly changing situation, effectively turning members of the public into citizen-journalists and participants in the production of news. Similarly, WikiLeaks, which publishes intact and online the secret and confidential political, corporate and military documents supplied by whistleblowers, has opened up debates on the extent and legitimacy of complete freedom of information in a dramatic way (see 'Society in the Arts' in the chapter review).

Social media such as Twitter, Pinterest, Instagram and Facebook, along with video-sharing sites such as YouTube, show just how popular web-based communications are becoming for all age groups, though people in higher socio-economic groups with higher levels of education are most likely to be involved (Kagan 2011). Playing on McLuhan's idea that 'the medium is the message', Castells maintains that, today, 'the network is the message'.

THINKING CRITICALLY

If the message of television is be passive and watch, is this also the message of the Internet as people endlessly watch YouTube videos and online content? How else might we read the message of 'networks'?

Film

The first movie to be shown to paying customers was in 1895 in Paris, France, where the Lumière brothers' *Arrival of the Train in La Ciotat Station* caused viewers to flee their seats as the screen slowly filled with an oncoming steam engine heading towards them. While the print media developed slowly over decades, film and cinema arrived much faster. The first cinema in the UK opened in 1896 and by 1914 there were more than 500 in London alone. Cinema tickets could be afforded by all classes, and the decline in working hours and rise in unemployment in the late 1920s meant cinema-goers soon formed a mass audience in the developed countries.

By 1925, the vast majority of commercially successful films were American in origin, and they still are (table 18.1). Cinemas were increasingly controlled by American studios, which owned the distribution rights to films. The studios could oblige cinemas to bulk-buy future productions, effectively freezing out competitors. As with the print media, ownership became concentrated among a few large corporations. The obvious dominance of American film production, partly the result of its large domestic market, raises questions about 'cultural imperialism' as American values, products and culture are promoted through the worldwide distribution of film.

There are different ways to assess the globalization of cinema. One is to consider *where* films are produced and the sources of financing that support them. By such criteria, there has unquestionably been a process of globalization in the cinema industry. According to studies by the United Nations Educational, Scientific and Cultural Organization

Around 1 billion more tickets per year are sold for Indian Bollywood films than for Hollywood blockbusters. Yet US films are better known around the world and generate more revenue.

Table 18.1 Highest grossing films of all time by worldwide box office sales, at 9 August 2015

Rank	Title	Year	Country of origin	Total gross revenue (US$)
1	Avatar	2009	USA	2,783,918,992
2	Titanic	1997	USA	2,207,615,668
3	Jurassic World	2015	USA	1,565,122,588
4	The Avengers	2012	USA	1,519,479,547
5	Fast and Furious 7	2015	USA	1,513,906,673
6	The Avengers: Age of Ultron	2015	USA	1,398,442,728
7	Harry Potter and the Deathly Hallows: Part 2	2011	USA	1,341,511,219
8	Frozen	2013	USA	1,274,234,980
9	Iron Man 3	2013	USA	1,215,392,272
10	The Lord of the Rings: Return of the King	2003	USA	1,141,408,667

Source: The Numbers (2015).

(UNESCO), many nations possess the capacity to produce films. However, only a handful of countries – the United States, India, Nigeria and Hong Kong – dominate global film production (UNESCO 2009b).

Another criterion used to assess globalization is the extent to which nationally produced films are *exported* to other countries. In the 1920s, Hollywood made four-fifths of all films screened in the world. But in 2006, India, with its growing Bollywood film productions, produced more films than any other country (1,091); Nigeria's 'Nollywood' was in second place (872) and the United States third (485) (UNESCO 2009b). But many Indian and Nigerian films are not shown internationally and, though governments do provide subsidies for their own film industries, the USA continues to be the largest exporter. As table 18.1 shows, the top-grossing films of all time worldwide are all American produced.

Hollywood studios generate well over half of their revenues from the overseas distribution of films. In an effort to increase the size of foreign audiences further, the studios are involved in building multiplex cinemas around the world. Global box-office revenues

rose in 2010 to $31.8 billion, nearly double the 1995 total, as audiences increased (Bloomberg 2011). The spread of video, DVD players and video-on-demand has also increased the number of people who are able regularly to watch films.

The digital revolution is rapidly transforming the filmmaking and distribution process. Conventionally, movies were produced by the analogue recording of images and associated sound onto celluloid film strips, which could then be cut and spliced in an editing suite to produce the final version. Today, more films are recorded in digital files that can easily be manipulated and changed, but films are also leaked or stolen and widely circulated over the Internet. Cinema theatres are converting to digital projection, which will eventually finish off the previous age of celluloid. The film director George Lucas pointed out that, for his Star Wars movie *The Revenge of the Sith* (2005), some 95 per cent was computer designed and animated (Kolker 2009: 249).

As digital technology advances, filmmaking is becoming possible for more amateurs, who are able to create their own movies, edit them and make them available online via

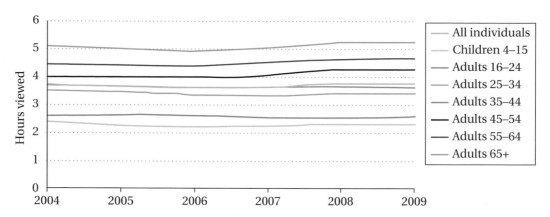

Figure 18.3   Average hours of television viewing per day, by age, all UK homes, 2004–9

Source: Ofcom (2010: 160).

file-sharing websites such as YouTube. Critics may question the quality of this 'do-it-yourself' output. However, in accord with the ongoing digital revolution in other media forms, the technology enables people who might previously have remained passive consumers to become active producers and consumers – 'prosumers' (Bruns 2009) – something that would have been unthinkable just twenty-five years ago.

Television

The interaction between television and the audience is different to that between the cinema and its audience. Television enters the household in a way that the cinema cannot, and it doesn't demand the same level of focused attention. Television also has an immediacy which film does not, since it can report events as they happen from almost anywhere in the world to a mass audience.

The number of television sets in the developed countries and the amount of time that people spend viewing increased dramatically from the 1950s onwards. If current trends in TV watching continue, the average child born today will have spent more time watching television by the age of eighteen than in any other pursuit except sleep. Virtually every household now possesses a TV set. In the UK, most people watch some television every day,

and the average set is switched on for between three and six hours per day (figure 18.3).

Television and social life

Television is ingrained in the routines of daily life; we watch TV, talk about it with friends and family, and build TV viewing into the routines of our daily lives. The 'box in the corner' is switched on while we get on with other things and appears to provide an essential backdrop to our lives. As Silverstone (1994: 3) explains:

> Television accompanies us as we wake up, as we breakfast, as we have our tea and as we drink in bars. It comforts us when we are alone. It helps us sleep. It gives us pleasure, it bores us and sometimes it challenges us. It provides us with opportunities to be both sociable and solitary. Although, of course, it was not always so and although we have had to learn how to incorporate the medium into our lives we now take television entirely for granted.

Television contributes to people's emotional and cognitive well-being and helps them design their routines and habits. As a result it creates a stronger sense of 'ontological security' – feelings or order and continuity in daily life – which helps to explain its persistent popularity. However, this does not mean that the dominant position of TV is inevitable or unassailable. The technological dimension of television does not determine its social and cultural reception. As 'Using your sociological imagination 18.1' shows, young people's everyday routines and habits today may well be significantly different from those of their parents, with significant consequences for the future of television.

Several media theorists have been highly critical about the seemingly ever-increasing diet of television. Neil Postman's (1931–2003) tellingly titled *Amusing Ourselves to Death* (1986) argues that television fails to present or handle serious issues because 'the form excludes the content'. By this he means that television is a medium that is incapable of sustaining serious content. For Postman, rational argument is best carried in the form of the printed word, which can sustain complex and serious content. He harks back to the nineteenth century as an 'age of reason', when the written word was dominant. For Postman, the medium of print creates a rational population, whereas the medium of television creates an entertained one. News, education and politics are all reduced to TV entertainment, so that, as the book title says, we are simply 'amusing ourselves to death'.

In a similar vein, Putnam (1995) has argued that, in the USA, the significant decline in social capital – mutual obligations and trust – correlates well with the rise of the television. TV viewing, he argues, is strongly and negatively related to trust and group membership. One reason for this is the effect of programme content on viewers. For example, heavy watchers of TV tend to be sceptical about the benevolence of others – by overestimating crime rates, for instance. Putnam concludes that the erosion of America's social capital was recognized only several decades after the process had begun.

However, television watching habits are changing, particularly among younger people, as 'on-demand' services become popular, Internet use increases and video-sharing websites provide interactive ways of viewing. Many social networking sites, such as Twitter and Facebook, may also show that Putnam's thesis is too pessimistic. There is

some evidence that young people favour interactive forms of media and, if so, this is likely to mean changes in television production and output as well.

Putnam's thesis on the decline of social capital is examined in more detail in chapter 8, 'Social Interaction and Daily Life'.

On the other hand, television remains very popular. Livingstone and Bovill's (1999) survey of children's media use in the UK – the first for forty years – found a developing 'bedroom culture', with two out of three working-class children and 54 per cent of middle-class children having a TV in their bedroom. By 2009, around 77 per cent of all five- to sixteen-year-olds had their own TV in the bedroom, 56 per cent of which were multi-channel sets. Such personal ownership by children is not restricted to TV, as 73 per cent also had their own mobile phone, 69 per cent had a DVD player, MP3 player and games console, and 55 per cent had a laptop or PC (Livingstone 2009). By contrast, in other parts of Europe, children's TV ownership is much lower. However, the popularity of TV still seems to be rooted in its ability to provide a broad range of 'gratifications': excitement, overcoming boredom, relaxation and overcoming the threat of feeling 'left out'.

Digital television

Since the start of the twenty-first century, television broadcasting technology has undergone a revolution with the transfer of programme transmission from analogue to digital. Analogue TV is the 'old' system of broadcasting, used to transmit signals to television sets since the 1940s. It converts sound and pictures into waves, which are transmitted through the air and picked up by the aerial on the roof of a house or on top of the television. Digital TV works by transforming pictures and sound into information that is potentially understood by a computer.

Digital transmissions are received in three ways: through the TV aerial and a decoder

18.1 Is the Internet killing television?

In August 2010, the end of the age of television as we know it was widely predicted. The US pay-TV market had suffered its first ever drop in subscribers. In the end the economy was roundly found to blame, with cable packages being sacrificed as families were forced to tighten their belts. But some commentators pointed to this as the inevitable result of the growth of on-demand and over the top offerings available on the internet.

So is technology killing what we think of as traditional television – and taking pay-TV operators with it? It's a confusing picture. Nielsen, who track US television viewing habits, have reported a drop in television ownership – albeit from 98.9% to 96.7%. DVD sales are falling, while Netflix recently overtook cable operator Comcast to become the biggest subscription video service in North America. IMS Research however is predicting digital cable TV subscribers in the US will increase by 7.8m between 2010 and 2015.

YouTube, Hulu, iPlayer, Netflix and other 'over the top' (OTT) services, not to mention illegal downloading, all offer alternatives. Apple and Google have both launched OTT services that let consumers play online content through their televisions, although Google's service is only available in the US. We're watching more video than ever before this way. But we're also watching more television. What is less clear is where the broadcast industry is ultimately headed.

Ask the experts

So what do those in the industry think lies in store? Neil Gaydon is the chief executive of pay-TV technology developer Pace. They manufacture set-top boxes and other technology for some of the world's biggest cable and satellite operators. He points to a rise in subscription figures over the last two quarters as proof that pay TV is healthier than ever. 'All the latest evidence is zero cord-cutting [using devices like laptops and tablets instead of TV sets] – and actually all over the top is doing is providing other services', he says. 'And if

you look at TV viewing figures, it's the highest it's ever been.' He also points to what he sees as the failure of Apple TV and Google TV to take off. 'The challenge to pay-TV is greatly exaggerated – OTT has certainly pointed to the desire people have to watch what they want, when they want.'

Mr Gaydon doesn't see pay-TV standing still. In his view, OTT has sounded a wake-up call to operators to develop hybrid services. 'The set-top box will morph into a media gateway', he says. 'If you fast-forward, and you think about the home of the future, you will have to have a hub, a media gateway, some form of device that's going to manage a suite of services.'

On demand

Not everyone is quite so confident the set-top box will survive the change. Suranga Chandratillake is the founder of blinkx, a video search engine and aggregator. 'Every device will have an internet connection as standard, that's increasingly the case already. I think set-top boxes are a temporary business at this stage', he says. Despite this, Mr Chandratillake is not predicting the end of television as we know it. 'I think that the device will live on, I think that we'll continue to have large screen devices whether we call them TVs or not. But while linear will remain popular, I think you will see massive growth in on demand. I don't know to what extent these two things are cannibalistic.'

The success of services like Netflix, he says, is proof consumers are willing to pay for reasonably priced services. 'I think partly we'll pay for it through small upgrades to our satellite, cable or broadband bills. The other way is through advertising – there'll be software or cloud services, you'll use a lot of them for free, but you'll be shown ads in the middle of them. I think though there are certain aspects of linear consumption that will remain with us. We'll all still watch the World Cup final at the same time.'

Source: Adapted from Fiona Graham (2011).

THINKING CRITICALLY

Where and how do you watch TV programmes: live or 'on demand' and on which device? Give some reasons why the television set is likely to survive in the long term.

(often a set-top box), via a satellite dish or via cable. The television acts like a computer and converts this information back into pictures and sound. Digital TV offers the possibility of interactive TV, the Internet, and home shopping and banking.

Digital television has largely replaced analogue in most developed countries and the demise of analogue TV is proceeding rapidly. The number of television channels available has increased as a result of advances in satellite, cable and digital technology. It is now usual to see digital service providers offering monthly subscription packages that give viewers the choice of a staggering 200+ TV, radio and data channels. Analogue TV in the UK provided just five. This increase extends more opportunities for content providers and, crucially, for advertisers, while pay-per-view and monthly subscription services are likely to increase the amount consumers spend. Of course the originality, creativity and quality of what they will be watching is another matter entirely.

Music

Music is as old as human societies and its use pre-dates the development of complex language. The first music is assumed to have come from the human voice, with instruments developing later along with different forms of material culture. Some of the oldest musical instruments have been found in parts of India and China and some of the earliest functional uses of music were in religious rituals and practices. But while these rituals and practices have tended to diminish in modern societies, music has continued to flourish.

Theodor Adorno (1976 [1950]) of the Frankfurt School of critical theory argued that musical forms tend to reflect the society within which they exist. Many musical forms in industrial capitalist societies, for example, take on predictable structures and offer easy gratification. They train people to expect uniformity and repetition, and they require little effort on the part of the listener to be enjoyed. In his own time, Adorno saw jazz and other popular music as guilty of this. However, although music can promote conformity, it can also foster critical enlightenment and is therefore, at least potentially, an active force in social life. Some forms of 'progressive' music (such as the experimental music of Schoenberg) defy standard musical conventions and, in 'breaking the rules', challenge people's assumptions and force them to think more critically.

See chapter 3, 'Theories and Perspectives', for discussion of the Frankfurt School.

Like Adorno, the music theorist Jacques Attali (1985) argues that music holds up a mirror to society, as its social organization and forms reflect society's mode of organization. For example, in industrialized societies, music is listened to primarily in recorded form on vinyl records, CDs and digital downloads. Music's hallmark in such societies is therefore repetitive mass production and the erosion of difference. Music becomes background noise in supermarkets, railway stations, restaurants and many other public and private spaces. Echoing Max Weber's comments on music in the bureaucratic age, Attali notes that the endless repetition of recorded music reflects the industrial society that enabled it.

However, Attali's thesis goes one step further. He maintains that music not only *mirrors* social organization, it also carries a *prophecy* of the future. Music can do this, he says, because musicians rapidly explore and exhaust all the possibilities within a given code (the 'rules of the game', as it were) much more quickly than in other forms of cultural output. Music changes more quickly and is not bound so much to material things such as projectors or TV sets. As musical organization is pushed to its internal limits, it is forced to break the bounds of the existing system in order to continue moving forward. An example is the current battle over downloading and free sharing of copyrighted music. The commercial element of music-making is desperately struggling to keep pace with an emergent form which continually pushes and breaks the existing commercial 'rules of the game'.

What Attali saw emerging from industrialized music was a form of music-making based on the erosion of boundaries between the composer, the performer and the audience. Instead, people were starting to make music for their own and their friends' pleasure, with little or no commercial motivation. Music was becoming, once again, localized and made for smaller communities of people. The paradox of Attali's argument is that the movement towards the localization of music is occurring at a time when we seem to be caught up in a much more rapid globalization of the world's societies.

In contrast to such large-scale social structural theories, the 1970s and 1980s saw the emergence of a new approach, known as the 'production of culture' perspective (Peterson 1976; Becker 1982). Here, music and other cultural products are viewed as social activities that have to be analysed in relation to the processes and contexts in which they are produced.

For example, Peterson and Berger (1975) studied pop music by looking at 'Number 1' hits in the USA between 1948 and 1973, comparing the number of performers and lyrics. They found that competition between large and small recording companies in the production of music was a key factor in explaining innovations. In periods of high market concentration (when just four companies produced almost 75 per cent of all hit singles), there was little innovation because there was no need to look for novelty or to introduce new products. However, as the large companies lost their monopoly on radio promotion of music and smaller companies were able to gain a foothold, innovation increased.

What Peterson and Berger were able to show through their careful analysis of how pop music is *actually produced* (the production of culture) is that innovation and increasing diversity *followed* changes in market concentration, they did not lead it. Thus, innovation was not down to the creative genius or powerful consumers demanding new music but more to do with the prevailing conditions of the music industry (see also Negus 1999).

Music is also part of people's self-identity, something that is readily seen in fan subcultures. It would be easy to dismiss the activities of pop music fans, from The Beatles to One Direction, as trivial and fleeting. Yet studies of 'fandom' show that the 'thousands of fan discussion groups, web sites, and mailing lists populating the Web are only eclipsed in presence by pornography (which, of course, has its own thriving fan base' (Gray et al. 2007: 7). In these online forums and offline events, participatory fan subcultures develop which are intense sources of identification and belonging. Moving online has also demonstrated that fans cannot be dismissed as brainless and uneducated dupes and are perfectly capable of engaging in creative practices and intelligent discourse. As Duffett (2014: 4) argues, 'fandom seems to be at the forefront of an astute, techno-savvy consumer culture.'

Tia DeNora's *Music in Everyday Life* (2000) adopts an interactionist approach, exploring the way individuals use music in the construction of the self and personal experience. The book is based on in-depth interviews with women in the USA and the UK and participant observation of 'music in action' in aerobics classes, karaoke evenings and music therapy sessions in retail settings. Music is not only something to be used, according to DeNora, it can also influence people's actions. For instance, a routine car journey to the shops

For most people, music forms a key aspect of their personal identity.

can easily become a secondary aim to listening to music on the car stereo. Hearing a particular opening chord or melody can reorientate people's actions, turning them away from their previous course.

DeNora argues that people often behave rather like disc jockeys to their own selves, choosing music to create or change their mood and to alter the way they experience social life. And though sociology has lagged behind other disciplines in the academic study of music, DeNora (2000: x) notes that music is 'a dynamic material, a medium for making, sustaining and changing social worlds and activities', though this cannot be understood in the abstract and has to be explored within the different contexts in which music is used. In this way, empirical studies could bring together the structural sociological theories of music and individual experience of it in order to enhance our understanding of its 'social powers'.

Globalization and the digitization of music

David Held and his colleagues (1999: 351) argued that 'the musical form is one that lends itself to globalization more effectively than any other.' This is because music is able to transcend the limitations of written and spoken language to reach and appeal to a mass audience. The global music industry, dominated by a small number of multinational corporations, has been built on the ability to find, produce, market and distribute the musical abilities of thousands of artists to audiences around the world. Over recent decades, an 'institutional complex' of companies has developed as part of the global marketing and distribution of music. Direct downloading of music via the Internet is the present state-of-the-art practice exemplified by Spotify, Apple Music and other streaming services.

The global industry in recorded music is one of the most concentrated. The four largest companies – EMI, Universal, Warner and Sony/BMG – control between 80 and 90 per cent of all music sales internationally (Herman and McChesney 1997). The global music industry experienced substantial growth during the mid-1990s, with sales in developing countries particularly strong, prompting many of the top companies to sign up more local artists in anticipation of further market growth. The growth of the global music industry in the postwar period was primarily a result of the success of popular music – originating mainly in America and Britain – and the spread of youth cultures that identify with it (Held et al. 1999). Processes of globalization have therefore been one of the main forces in the diffusion of American and British music genres to international audiences.

Yet the growing popularity of 'world music' – such as the phenomenal success of Latin-inspired sounds in the USA – shows that globalization may lead to cultural diffusion in more than one direction. Similarly the growing popularity of Korean pop music – 'K-pop' – which was popularized by the success of Psy's 2012 single 'Gangnam Style', owes much to community networks on social media rather than to conventional, top-down corporate marketing (Jung and Shim 2014). Although the music industry has become more concentrated, it has proved particularly vulnerable to Internet file-sharing and illegal downloads. If Internet distribution does not need a complex production and distribution network of shops, factories and warehouses, what will be left of the music business?

In 2000, the record industry filed several lawsuits against the small company behind Napster – a software program that allows people to trade files over the Internet – forcing it to stop providing the software. In 2003, the Recording Industry Association of America (RIAA) sued 261 individuals for music piracy, having found that, on average, each had downloaded about 1,000 songs. A landmark case in 2007 saw a single individual – Jammie Thomas-Rasset from Minnesota – taken to court for music-sharing online and fined US $222,000. In 2009, she was found guilty of copyright violation on twenty-four songs, and the companies involved were awarded $1.92 million. In 2012 the original fine was reinstated. While Thomas-Rasset petitioned the Supreme Court, in 2013 it refused to hear the case, though the RIAA said it is open to a much lower settlement. In 2008 the RIAA dropped charges against thirty-five other people, saying that it would look to reach agreements with service providers to control piracy by persuading them to cancel the accounts of illegal file-sharers (Biagi 2011).

Wikström (2009) argues that the digital music revolution is characterized by three central features: connectivity, music as a service and amateur production. First, while the 'old' music industry centred on the corporate control of music to maximize revenue, the new digital business is about *connectivity* – the links between producers and their audience. The Internet has (potentially) enabled everyone in the producer–audience network to upload music, not merely passively to receive it. This means the new industry is high in connectivity but low in producer control. Second, the old industry was based on sales of physical products such as vinyl records, cassettes and CDs, but the digital industry shifts to the provision of *access to music services*. As soon as music is uploaded onto the web it becomes freely available, thus reducing its commercial value. However, people may still be prepared to pay for services that help them to find what they want amid the vast amount of online music.

Third, music audiences today can become *amateur producers*, creatively remixing their favourite professionally recorded music and publishing online. If these amateur producers are also the ones who attend concerts and buy merchandise, then it is in the interests of music companies not to challenge them or their practices but to work with and encourage them (Wikström 2009: 7–8). What Wikström (and 'Using your sociological imagination 18.2') describes are some of the practical realities, conflicts and trade-offs as digitization transforms the music industry.

18.2   'Free' music and copyright infringement in the Internet age

Because of the Internet, music can be shared globally in an instant, which is a huge benefit for artists and consumers. Yet the Internet also makes music piracy so easy that many people consider it a harmless act, and the economic implications for recording artists are substantial. In 2007 RIAA [Recording Industry Association of America] estimated the industry had lost nearly £1 billion in revenue just from illegal music downloads. In 2009, RIAA announced that music sales were down 18 per cent worldwide from 2007 to 2008 – the lowest level ever. In 2010, RIAA estimated that 'globally only one of 20 downloads is authorized, and online piracy rates in many markets is in the vicinity of 99 per cent.'

No industry could survive for long on such a rapid loss of income. So the recording companies have no choice but to pursue copyright infringement wherever they find it. Licenced music is governed by national and international copyright law, and the recording industry continues to aggressively pursue all the legal remedies available to curtail illegal music downloads in the United States and reduce piracy, especially overseas. The industry, of course, also encourages all legal music download services, such as iTunes, and subscription sites, such as Spotify.

By April 2008, the iTunes store had become the largest music retailer in the United States. By 2010, according to Apple, customers had downloaded 10 billion songs. Spotify has 7 million users in Britain, Spain, France, Sweden, Norway and Finland. Because of the Internet, music artists today can find a bigger audience than Thomas Edison [inventor of the phonograph or 'record player' in 1877] could ever have imagined – through music downloads and subscription services. However, the music business cannot escape the challenges of the Internet. The recording companies must learn how to produce music consumers want to hear using a format and/or a service they're willing to buy.

Source: Biagi (2011: 106).

THINKING CRITICALLY
Given the enormous numbers of people who have illegally downloaded music, what reasons can you offer as to why they do not feel like criminals? Should music piracy be decriminalized, pursued with more vigour or is there another solution to the problem?

The corporate music industry is trying to come to terms with the consequences of digitization. Global music sales have been falling: between 2000 and 2009, annual record sales were down from $40 billion (£22 billion) to $17 billion (Gammons 2011: xix). The sector has undergone large-scale redundancies and been forced to restructure. Many in the music industry claim that the swapping of music files (such as MP3s) over the Internet is one of the major causes of lost revenue. Although attempts are being made to impose tighter controls on the replication of legally purchased music, the pace of technological change eclipses the industry's ability to curtail piracy (see 'Using your sociological imagination 18.2').

Broadcasting music on radio was also initially described by the music industry as 'piracy'. Record labels worried that if people could hear the latest releases over their radios they would not buy records and the business would be undermined. Eventually, rather than maintaining outright opposition, the labels incorporated radio use of copyright material into their business models with royalties paid by radio stations (Marshall 2015). In a similar process, the music industry today has begun to offer *legal* download services – Spotify being the most notable example to date. This downloading is legal because royalties are paid on the songs to record labels and artists. By the end of 2004, more than 125 million

Despite the welter of online news and sports sites, physical newspapers remain popular.

legal downloads of songs had been purchased and an official 'music download chart' had been established (BBC 2004). After the music industry's initial rejection of the Internet, its successful adaptation is now perceived to be crucial to its future.

Newspapers

The development of the press during the nineteenth century occurred at a time of political and social unrest in Europe. The UK government, for example, exerted its control over the emerging newspaper industry through strict laws on libel and sedition, which prevented political agitation; at the same time, a stamp tax was imposed to ensure that newspapers could be afforded only by the well-off. The stamp tax had unintended consequences, as there emerged illegal and inexpensive pamphlets such as William Cobbett's weekly *Political Register*, spreading radical views among the newly industrial working class (Dyck 1992).

The stamp tax – condemned by its opponents as a 'tax on knowledge' – was finally repealed in 1855 after a series of reductions, leading many writers to hail a golden era of British journalism marked by a 'transition from official to popular control' (Koss 1973). An alternative view is put forward by Curran and Seaton (2003), who argue that the repeal of the stamp tax was an attempt to break the popularity of the radical press and to boost the sales of more 'respectable' newspapers funded by private owners and advertisers. The repeal of the stamp tax introduced not a new era of press freedom but a time of repression and ideological control, this time by market forces rather than government.

The newspaper was a fundamentally important development in the history of modern media, because it packaged many different types of information in a limited and easily reproducible format. Newspapers contained, in a single package, information on current affairs, entertainment and consumer goods. The cheap daily press was pioneered in the United States with the 'one-cent daily' paper in New York. The invention of cheap newsprint was the key to the mass diffusion of newspapers from the late nineteenth century onwards.

By the early twentieth century, ownership of much of the UK newspaper industry was concentrated in the hands of a few rich entrepreneurs. By the 1930s, Lords Beaverbrook, Camrose, Kemsley and Rothermere owned 50 per cent of British national and local daily papers and 30 per cent of the Sunday papers. Critics have claimed that the 'press barons', as they became known, used their ownership of national newspapers to promote their own political causes and ambitions (Curran and Seaton 2003).

For half a century or more, newspapers were the chief way of conveying information quickly and comprehensively to a mass public. But their influence waned with the rise of radio, cinema and – much more importantly – television and, increasingly, the Internet. Figures for newspaper readership suggest that the proportion of people who read a national daily paper in Britain has been in terminal decline since the early 1980s. At the end of the twentieth century those men who read daily newspapers fell from 76 per cent in 1981 to 60 per cent in 1998–9; readership levels are lower among women, but a similar drop – from 68 per cent to 51 per cent – also took place (ONS 2000).

Newspapers, particularly the *tabloid* press (which targets a mass audience, in contrast to the so-called *broadsheets*), have become focused less on providing news and more on reporting, creating and sustaining a celebrity culture to combat falling circulation (Cashmore 2006). The role of newspapers and television in creating a climate in which celebrity culture can flourish alerts us to what some sociologists, following the 'production of culture' approach (discussed below), have

called the 'celebrity industry' (Turner 2004). But what is a celebrity? In the early 1960s, Daniel Boorstin (1961: 58) noted that 'the celebrity is a person who is well known for their well-knownness.' Although many celebrities today are film stars or sportspeople, they may be known more for their media personalities and private lives than for their achievements. Others become celebrities just by regularly making it into magazines and newspapers or appearing on television.

Of course, the celebrity culture in newspapers and on television requires an appreciative and demanding audience. As consumers, we also participate in the production of celebrity culture and we do it in knowing ways (Gamson 1994). We know that many of our celebrities have no major achievements to offer and that their fame will probably be short-lived. When we get bored with them we simply move on to the next one. In this way, celebrities have become commodities for our consumption via their media representations. Nonetheless, despite the apparent public addiction to celebrity, the continuing decline in newspaper sales indicates that celebrity news will probably not be enough to save conventional newspapers.

Indeed, online communication might well bite further into newspaper circulation. News information and celebrity gossip is available online via numerous websites almost instantaneously and is constantly updated during the course of the day. Many newspapers themselves can also be accessed and read online free of charge, though some are trialling pay-per-view and subscription services. In the longer term it would seem that the age of paper-only newspapers may be drawing to a close as companies are already diversifying their output into new media forms in order to survive.

The pressures on the newspaper industry show how the digital revolution is transforming modern communications. Newspapers may survive into the future if they can adapt to online news services, but the Internet, worldwide web and digitization tend to canalize earlier media forms, undermining previous business models. Having reached this conclusion, it is now time to look at some theories of media which will help to set the changes discussed so far in a broader perspective.

THINKING CRITICALLY

Can paper-based newspapers survive the Internet revolution? How could the newspaper business change, and what new practices could it adopt to maximize its opportunities of gaining and holding on to readers?

Theorizing the media

In this section we examine four influential theoretical approaches to the study of the mass media: functionalism, conflict theory, symbolic interactionism and recent postmodern media theory. As we will see, there are widely divergent views on the role and functions of the media within societies, and our fourfold categorization here is not an exhaustive one in the field of media studies.

Functionalism

In the mid-twentieth century, functionalist theorists focused on the ways in which the media help to integrate and bind societies together. Following the media theorist Denis McQuail (2000), we can identify several important social functions of the media that may work to stabilize the social system.

1 *Information* The media provide a continuous flow of information from webcams and radio reports alerting us to traffic jams, rolling weather reports, the stock market, and news stories about social and political issues.
2 *Correlation* The media help us to understand the meaning of the information they provide. In this way they provide support for established social norms and have an important role in the socialization of children, contributing a shared framework for the interpretation of events.

3 *Continuity* The media have a certain function in expressing the dominant culture, recognizing new social developments but also forging common values.
4 *Entertainment* The media provide amusement and a diversion from work, thus reducing social tensions. Entertainment acts as a release valve for society's problems and conflicts.
5 *Mobilization* The media can be used to persuade and encourage people to contribute to economic development, to uphold moral rules and to mobilize the population in times of war. This can be via direct public campaigns but is usually more subtle in the morality tales of soap operas and films.

Functionalist theories of the media – along with the functionalist approach in general – have fallen into decline. There are several reasons why sociologists have moved away from functionalism. First, it appears to do little more than describe the media's current roles rather than explaining why these exist. Second, functionalist accounts have had little or nothing to say about the audience reception of media products, tending to assume that people are relatively passive rather than active interpreters of media messages. Third, the functions above appear wholly positive, but others see the media as a much less benign force. In particular, conflict approaches influenced by Marxism see the modern mass media as destructive of society's cultural vitality.

> Functionalism was introduced in chapter 1, 'What is Sociology?', and discussed in chapter 3, 'Theories and Perspectives'.

Conflict theories

In Europe, conflict approaches to the mass media have had more impact than functionalism. We look at two of the most important theories of the media from a broadly Marxist standpoint: the political economy approach, which concentrates on the ownership and control of media, and the 'culture industry' approach of the Frankfurt School of critical theory. The important research of the Glasgow University Media Group is also rooted in Marxist theory and is discussed below.

Political economy approaches

Political economy approaches view the media as an industry and examine the way in which the major means of communication have come to be owned by private interests. Media ownership has often been concentrated in the hands of a few wealthy magnates. In the pre-war era of mass newspaper readership, a handful of 'press barons' owned a majority of newspapers and were able to set the agenda for news and its interpretation. In our increasingly global age, the ownership of media crosses national borders, and media magnates now own transnational media corporations, giving them international recognition and influence. Perhaps the best known of these is Australian-born Rupert Murdoch, the owner of Sky Digital, Fox Broadcasting Company and other media organizations.

Advocates of a political economy view argue that economic interests in media ownership work to exclude less powerful voices. Moreover, the voices that *do* survive are those least likely to criticize the prevailing distribution of wealth and power (Golding and Murdock 1997). This view was famously advanced by the American linguist and radical writer Noam Chomsky (1991). Chomsky is highly critical of the dominance of large corporations over the American and global media and the tight control of information provided to the public. During the Cold War, for example, these corporations controlled information to create a climate of fear in the West about the Soviet Union. Since the collapse of the USSR, Chomsky maintains that corporately owned media have exaggerated people's fears of global terrorism. This prevents the airing and proper discussion of other issues that are, arguably, more significant, such as the unaccountability of corporations or the lack of democracy. Chomsky sees the mass media as disseminating propaganda in support of ruling groups.

Ideology and bias in the media

The study of the media is closely related to the impact of ideology in society. Ideology refers to the influence of ideas on people's beliefs and actions, and the concept has been widely used in media studies. The term was first coined in the late 1700s by a French writer, Destutt de Tracy, who used it to refer to a 'science of ideas', which he thought would be a branch of knowledge. De Tracy's view has been seen as a 'neutral' conception of ideology. Neutral conceptions discuss phenomena as being ideological, but this does not imply they are misleading or biased in favour of particular social classes or groups.

In the hands of later authors, 'ideology' was used in a more critical way. Karl Marx, for example, saw ideology as important in the reproduction of relations of class domination. Powerful groups are able to control the dominant ideas circulating in society to justify their own position. Thus, according to Marx, religion is often ideological: it teaches the poor to be content with their lot. The social analyst should uncover the distortions of ideology to allow the powerless to gain a true perspective on their lives. Critical notions of ideology 'convey a negative, critical or pejorative sense' and carry within them 'an implicit criticism or condemnation' (Thompson 1990: 53–4).

Thompson argues that the critical notion is preferable because it links ideology with power. Ideology is about the exercise of symbolic power – how ideas are used to hide, justify or legitimate the interests of dominant groups in the social order. In their numerous studies, the Glasgow University Media Group analyse the ideological aspects of TV news reporting and how it systematically generates bias. For example, news reports on industrial disputes tend to favour government and management rather than striking workers. In general, Thompson claims that mass media – including not only the news but all varieties of programme content and genre – greatly expand the scope of ideology in modern societies. They reach mass audiences and are, in his terms, based on 'quasi-interaction' – that is, audiences cannot answer back in a direct way.

In media and communication studies, a particular type of analysis – discourse analysis – has been widely used to study media products. Discourse analysts begin from the premise that language is a fundamental part of social life which is related to all other aspects (Fairclough 1992). Discourse analysis is used to examine texts of many kinds, though there are different versions of it (van Dijk 1997). For example, some studies engage in a detailed analysis of texts and documents, while others, drawing on Foucault's ideas, connect texts to theories of society, exploring the way that discourses construct and shape social life itself. Fairclough argues that 'text analysis is an essential part of discourse analysis, but discourse analysis is not merely the linguistic analysis of texts' (2003: 3).

Texts can be newspaper articles and personal diaries, but they can also be transcripts of interviews, ethnographic conversations and focus groups, films, television programmes and web pages. *Discourses* are 'systems of thought' or ways of thinking about and discussing the world within a particular framework. Discourses erect boundaries around subjects, which limit what can sensibly be said about them.

The recent discourse on 'Islamic terrorism' sets the terms of debate for discussion of this phenomenon, ruling out alternative conceptions of those involved, as 'freedom fighters' or 'terrorists using Islam to justify their acts', for example. In *critical discourse analysis*, such discursive practices are linked to wider social structures of inequality and power relations, so that the ideological aspects can be identified and opened up for examination. According to Fairclough (1989: 15), 'language connects with the social through being the primary domain of ideology, and through being both a site of, and a stake in, struggles for power.' As we see in 'Classic studies 18.1', the work of the Glasgow University Media Group shows what critical content analysis can add to our understanding of news reporting in conflict situations.

The culture industry

Members of the Frankfurt School of critical theory (see chapter 3 for a discussion), such as Theodor Adorno (1903–69), were critical of the effects of mass media on the population and on culture. The Frankfurt School was established during the 1920s and 1930s and consisted of a loose group of theorists inspired by Marx, who nevertheless saw that the latter's views needed radical revision. Among other things, they argued that Marx had not given enough attention to the influence of culture in modern capitalist societies.

Members of the Frankfurt School argued that leisure time had effectively been industrialized. Their extensive studies of the 'culture industry' – such as the entertainment industries of film, TV, popular music, radio, newspapers and magazines – have been very influential in the field of cultural studies (Horkheimer and Adorno 2002 [1947]). They claimed that, in mass societies, the production of culture had become just as standardized and dominated by the desire for profit as in other industries. In a mass society, the leisure industry was used to induce appropriate values among the public: leisure was no longer a break from work, but a preparation for it.

Members of the Frankfurt School maintained that the spread of the culture industry, with its undemanding and standardized products, undermined the capacity of individuals for critical and independent thought. Art disappears, swamped by commercialization – 'Mozart's greatest hits', for example, or student posters of the great works of art – and culture is replaced by simple and undemanding entertainment.

> **THINKING CRITICALLY**
>
> Why should a poster of da Vinci's *Mona Lisa* or Van Gogh's *The Starry Night* be described as 'undemanding' when the original is not? Is there a positive side to mass reproduction of this kind?

Classic Studies 18.1   'Bad News' from the Glasgow University Media Group

The research problem

As we have seen, a substantial proportion of the population no longer reads newspapers. However, for many people, TV news is their key source of information about the world. Can it be trusted to give a true and accurate picture of events? Why would the news *not* provide accurate information and what are the consequences if it does not?

Some of the best-known research studies concerned with television news have been carried out by the Glasgow University Media Group (GMG) in the UK. The group has published a series of studies that are highly critical of the presentation of the news. Their early studies, including *Bad News* (1976), *More Bad News* (1981), *Really Bad News* (1983) and *War and Peace News* (1985) were very influential, setting out a research strategy for critical content analysis. Their strategy was essentially similar in each of these studies, though the focus of their investigations differed.

The Glasgow Group's explanation

Bad News (1976), the Glasgow Group's first and most influential book, was based on an analysis of TV news broadcasts between January and June 1975 on the three UK terrestrial channels available at that time. The objective was to provide a systematic and dispassionate analysis of the content of the news and how it was presented. *Bad News* concentrated on the portrayal of industrial disputes, while the later work concentrated more on political coverage, including the Falklands War of 1982.

The conclusion of *Bad News* was that reporting of industrial relations was typically presented in a selective and biased fashion. Terms such as 'trouble', 'radical' and 'pointless strike' suggested anti-union views. The effects of strikes, causing disruption for the public, were much more likely to be reported on than their underlying or immediate causes.

Film material used very often made the activities of protesters appear irrational and aggressive. For example, film of strikers stopping people entering a factory would focus on any confrontations that occurred, even if these were infrequent.

Bad News also pointed out that those who construct the news act as 'gatekeepers' for what gets onto the agenda – in other words, what the public hears about at all (McCoombs 2014). Strikes in which there were active confrontations between workers and management, for instance, might get widely reported, while more consequential and long-lasting industrial disputes tend to be largely ignored. The views of news journalists, the authors suggested, tend to reflect their middle-class backgrounds and support the views of the dominant groups in society, who inevitably see strikers as dangerous and irresponsible.

In recent years, members of the Glasgow Group have carried out a range of further studies. *Bad News From Israel* (Philo and Berry 2004) examined television news reporting of the Israeli–Palestinian conflict. The study was carried out over a two-year period, supported by several senior television news broadcasters and journalists who were involved in panel discussions with members of an 800-person sample audience. As well as looking at the television coverage of the conflict and its production, the authors were interested in how the coverage related to the understanding, beliefs and attitudes of the audience.

The research concluded that television news coverage of the conflict confused viewers and substantially featured Israeli government views. There was little devoted to the history or origins of the conflict which would have provided a relevant context, and there was a bias towards official 'Israeli perspectives', particularly on BBC1, where Israelis were interviewed or reported more than twice as often as Palestinians. In addition, American politicians who supported Israel were often featured. The study found that the news gave a strong emphasis to Israeli casualties relative to Palestinians (although two to three times more Palestinians than Israelis died).

There were also differences in the language used by journalists to describe Israeli and Palestinian attacks. Journalists would often describe Palestinian acts as 'terrorism', but when an Israeli group was reported as trying to bomb a Palestinian school they were referred to as 'extremists' or 'vigilantes' (Philo and Berry 2004). The message of this body of work is that news reporting can never be thought of as neutral or 'objective'. Rather, it reflects the unequal societies within which it exists and, as such, should be seen as systematically biased.

Critical points

The work of the Glasgow Media Group is much discussed in media circles as well as in the academic community. Some news producers accused the researchers of exercising their own biases, which lay with workers and strikers rather than with government and management. They pointed out that, while *Bad News* contained a chapter entitled 'The trade unions and the media', there was no chapter on 'management and the media'. This should have been discussed, because news journalists are often accused by management of bias against them in disputes rather than against the strikers.

Academic critics made similar points. Martin Harrison (1985) gained access to transcripts of ITN news broadcasts for the period covered by the original 1976 study and argued that those five months were not typical. There was an abnormal number of days lost because of industrial action over the period and, as it would have been impossible for the news to report all of these, the tendency

to focus on the more dramatic episodes was understandable.

In Harrison's view, the Glasgow Group was wrong to claim that news broadcasts concentrated too much on the effects of strikes. After all, many more people are affected by strikes than take part in them. Sometimes millions of people find their lives disrupted by the actions of just a handful of people. Finally, according to Harrison's analysis, some of the assertions made by the group were simply false. For example, contrary to what the group stated, news reports did normally name the unions involved in disputes and did say whether or not the strikes were official or unofficial.

Contemporary significance

The central point made in the Glasgow Group studies holds – the news is never a mere description of what 'actually happened'. It is a complex construction and the process of construction regularly influences what 'the news' is. For example, when a politician appears on a news programme and makes a comment about a controversial issue – say, the state of the economy and what should be done about it – that comment itself becomes 'news' in subsequent programmes.

John Eldridge (1993), editor of one volume of the Glasgow Group's research, points out that what counts as objectivity in news reporting will always be difficult. Against those postmodernists who say that the idea of objectivity is irrelevant, Eldridge affirms the importance of continuing to look at media products with a critical eye. Accuracy in news reporting can and must be studied. The work of the Glasgow Group forcefully reminds us that issues of truth and truthfulness are always involved in news reporting, and the latter is certainly worthy of sociological research.

Does mass reproduction equal cultural destruction?

Conflict theories remain popular in media studies, though they are subject to some of the same criticisms as functionalist theories. There is a tendency to assume that people are unable to resist media propaganda and are easy prey for it. Like functionalists, the early critical theorists paid little or no attention to audience reception of media messages, focusing instead on the production of culture. The Frankfurt School's damning critique of mass culture has also been seen as linked to their defence of the high culture – classical music, opera, painting and the arts – favoured by social elites (Swingewood 1977). This is somewhat paradoxical, of course, given the Marxist origins of critical theory. As we will see later, this distinction between high and 'low' or popular culture was seized upon and attacked by postmodern media theorists in the 1980s and 1990s.

Jürgen Habermas was one of several theorists to assert that the public sphere in society was in trouble (see the discussion of Habermas's ideas in 'Classic studies 18.2'). In *The Fall of Public Man* (2003 [1977]) Richard Sennett sought to explain the origins of the separation of public and private spheres, arguing that these have become disconnected, both physically – with the separate development of residential housing estates, workplaces and leisure developments (including shopping arcades) – and philosophically, in the way we think about our distinct private lives. However, over time, the private sphere has tended to take over the public sphere. For instance, politicians are judged more on their personal characteristics, such as honesty and sincerity, than on their ability to perform public roles. The advent of modern visual media, especially television, has led to a highly

Classic Studies 18.2 | Jürgen Habermas – the rise and fall of the public sphere

The research problem

Modern democracies developed alongside the mass media, particularly newspapers and other types of publication. In a very real sense, the mass media enabled and encouraged democracy. Yet today the mass media are often seen negatively, as trivializing the democratic process and creating a climate of general hostility to politics. How did such a radical shift happen? Could it be reversed or are the mass media inevitably failing democracies? The German philosopher and sociologist Jürgen Habermas (1929–), one of the last influential intellectuals of the Frankfurt School, took up these questions in a series of important works.

Habermas's explanation

Habermas (1981, 1985, 1989 [1962]) developed themes from the Frankfurt School in different directions, rooted in his abiding interest in language and the process of democracy. He analysed the emergence and development of the mass media from the early eighteenth century to the present, tracing the creation and subsequent decay of the 'public sphere'. For Habermas, the public sphere is an arena of public debate in which issues of general concern can be discussed and opinions formed, which is necessary for effective democratic participation and oils the wheels of the democratic process.

According to Habermas, the public sphere developed in the salons and coffee houses of seventeenth- and eighteenth-century London, Paris and other European cities. People would meet to discuss issues of the moment, with political debate being a matter of particular importance. Although only small numbers of the population were involved in the salon cultures, Habermas argues salons were vital to the early development of democracy because they introduced the idea of resolving political problems through public discussion. The public sphere – at least in principle – involves individuals coming together as equals in a forum for public debate.

However, the promise offered by the early development of the public sphere has not been fully realized. Democratic debate is now stifled by the development of the culture industry. The spread of mass media and mass entertainment causes the public sphere to shrink and become a sham. Politics is stage-managed in Parliament and the mass media, while commercial interests triumph over those of the public. 'Public opinion' is no longer formed through open, rational discussion but through manipulation and control – as, for example, in advertising. On the other hand, the spread of global media can put pressure on authoritarian governments to loosen their hold over state-controlled broadcasting outlets, and many 'closed' societies such as China are discovering that the media can become a powerful force in support of democracy.

As the global media become increasingly commercialized, they encroach on the public sphere. Commercialized media are beholden to the power of advertising revenue and compelled to favour content that guarantees high ratings and sales. As a result, entertainment will necessarily triumph over controversy and debate, weakening citizen participation in public affairs and shrivelling the public sphere. The media, which promised so much, have now become part of the problem with democracy. Yet Habermas remains optimistic. He argues that it is still possible to envisage a political community beyond individual nation-states in which issues can be openly debated and where public opinion will influence governments.

Critical points

Habermas's ideas have been subject to an important critique. The salon culture that he holds up as an arena of civilized, rational debate was strictly limited to the higher social classes and was beyond the reach of the working class. In short, it was an elitist pastime that bore little real resemblance to the needs of mass democratic participation. Habermas's view that the modern mass media are destructive of the public sphere has also been seen as misguided. As we will see below, Thompson (1995) argues that the media actually enable *more* public debate by airing a variety

777

of public matters and encouraging wider discussions. The Internet, with its innumerable blogs, forums and chatrooms, is just the latest example of this.

Contemporary significance

Habermas's ideas have provoked a good deal of debate and much controversy. Currently, it appears that they have lost some ground in the wake of critique from those who defend the mass media as, on balance, a positive force in society, but also from postmodern thinkers who see Habermas as working within the older Frankfurt tradition, with its fear and mistrust of the 'mass' public. There is some truth in such critiques. And yet Habermas is a powerful reminder that the rational, modernist project that we can trace back to the Enlightenment still has much to offer sociological or social theories of the media.

developed presentation of self by politicians aimed at matching such expectations. Sennett sees this as destructive of an effective political life and representative of the fall of the dedicated public official.

However, there are some problems with the way the 'the public sphere' is presented and idealized in these accounts. The public sphere was constituted by excluding certain social groups, notably women, ethnic minorities and non-property-owners, and, in being limited in this way, the notion of a public sphere allowed middle-class men to perceive themselves and their role and to present it to others as universal. Feminist scholars argue that Habermas did not pay enough attention to the *gendered* nature of the public sphere. In separating the public from the domestic, private sphere, many issues that were important for women were simply excluded. As Nancy Fraser says, 'The view that women were excluded from the public sphere turns out to be ideological; . . . In fact, . . . the bourgeois public was never *the* public' (1992: 116).

This alerts us to another important point, namely that some 'publics' – such as women – were *intentionally* blocked from participating, demonstrating that conflictual social relations underpinned the idealized conception of a common public sphere. What critics suggest, therefore, is that the 'bourgeois concept' of the public sphere was a male-dominated one that helped to legitimize systematic social inequalities.

> ### THINKING CRITICALLY
>
> In what ways are social networking sites such as Twitter or Facebook similar to and different from the kind of salon culture discussed by Sennett and Habermas? How representative of 'the public' are social media? Who is likely to be included or excluded?

Symbolic interactionism

Interactionist media studies have not been as numerous as functionalist and conflict theories, though they have increased over recent years. Herbert Blumer's 1930s study of the impact of cinema on the audience was an early attempt to allow people themselves to inform sociological understandings of media influence. Blumer asked 1,500 American high school and college students to record their experiences of watching films in 'autobiographies', which he presented in his book *Movies and Conduct* (1970 [1933]). Although pioneering in some ways, the study has been seen as rather naïve, both in believing that the respondents' views could 'speak for themselves' and in its rather simple approach to cinematic 'texts'.

Perhaps the most influential interactionist approach to the media is moral panic theory, which emerged from the labelling perspectives of Charles Lemert and Howard Becker. Stan Cohen's (2003 [1972]) famous study of clashes between Mods and Rockers in the UK showed how exaggerated and sensational media representations contribute to recurring moral panics in society. Such panics serve to scapegoat social groups, including immigrants and ethnic minorities, taking attention away from structural problems such as unemployment and poverty.

See chapter 20, 'Crime and Deviance', for a discussion of the labelling perspective and also for a detailed discussion of moral panic theory, which you may want to refer to.

Drawing partly on the work of Habermas, Thompson (1990, 1995) analysed the relationship between the media and industrial societies from early forms of print through to electronic communication. He argues that the main founders of sociology – Marx, Weber and Durkheim – paid little attention to the role of media in shaping even the early development of modern society. Sympathetic to some of the ideas of Habermas, Thompson is also critical of him, as he is of the Frankfurt School and of Baudrillard's postmodern position. In common with the Frankfurt School, Thompson (1995: 42–3) says, too often Habermas tends to treat people as the passive recipients of media messages rather than active agents:

Media messages are commonly discussed by individuals in the course of reception and subsequent to it. . . . [They] are transformed through an ongoing process of telling and retelling, interpretation and reinterpretation, commentary, laughter and criticism. . . . By taking hold of messages and routinely incorporating them into our lives . . . we are constantly shaping and reshaping our skills and stocks of knowledge, testing our feelings and tastes, and expanding the horizons of our experience.

Thompson's theory of the media rests on a distinction between three types of interaction (see table 18.2). *Face-to-face* interaction, such as people talking at a party, is rich in the cues used by individuals to make sense of what others say. *Mediated interaction* involves the use of technology such as paper, electrical connections or electronic impulses. Mediated interaction is stretched out in time and space and goes way beyond the contexts of face-to-face interaction. It takes place between individuals in a direct way – say, two people talking on a phone – but there is no opportunity for non-verbal cues.

A third type is *mediated quasi-interaction*. This refers to the sort of social relations created by the mass media. Such interaction is stretched across time and space but does

Interactional characteristics	Face-to-face interaction	Mediated interaction	Mediated quasi-interaction
Space–time constitution reference system	Context of co-presence; shared spatial-temporal time and space	Separation of contexts; extended availability in time and space	Separation of contexts; extended availability in time and space
Range of symbolic cues	Multiplicity of symbolic cues	Narrowing of the range of symbolic cues	Narrowing of the range of symbolic cues
Action orientation	Oriented towards specific others	Oriented towards specific others	Oriented towards an indefinite range of potential recipients
Dialogical/ monological	Dialogical	Dialogical	Monological

Table 18.2 Types of interaction

Source: Thompson (1995: 465).

not link individuals directly – hence the term 'quasi-interaction'. The two previous types are 'dialogical' – individuals communicate in a direct way – but mediated quasi-interaction is 'monological'. A TV programme, for example, is a one-way form of monological communication. People watching the programme may discuss it and perhaps shout at their set, but it does not answer back.

Thompson's point is that all three types of interaction intermingle in our lives today and that the media change the balance between the public and the private. Unlike Sennett and Habermas, Thompson argues that this shift brings *more* into the public domain than before, not less, and often leads to more debate and controversy. Postmodern theorists see things rather differently: some consider that mediated quasi-interaction dominates the other two types, with dramatic and negative consequences for social life.

More people today appear on television to discuss moral and political issues on audience discussion shows, such as those of Oprah Winfrey in the USA or Jeremy Kyle in the UK, and in so-called 'reality television', such as *Big Brother* and numerous others. In addition, millions of people watch at home and discuss their content at work, in coffee shops, pubs and other gathering places. In the case of the global phenomenon of *Big Brother*, audiences interact with the show, voting for evictions of participants and commenting in online forums and spin-off shows. But are such programmes really providing new public spaces for engagement in a vibrant public sphere, or is this just cheap, trashy TV for the masses?

In an empirical study of audience discussion shows, Livingstone and Lunt (1993) used a multi-method approach involving focus group discussions, individual interviews, textual analysis of the programmes and a survey questionnaire to gather the views of studio audiences and home viewers. They argue that these programmes do deal with current issues as they affect people's everyday experiences, but they are not 'documentaries' and tend to construct viewers as community members. Hence, such programmes do not easily fit into any existing TV genre (Gregori Signes 2000). As types of participation depend largely on the conventions of the genre involved, they are particularly open and undefined. Some involve lay people and experts sitting together while the host moves around with a microphone. Here experts can be questioned and challenged and thus made accountable. In this sense, they are public spaces for the exercise of democracy, which is reinforced through the systematic prioritization of the lay rather than the expert perspective (Livingstone and Lunt 1993).

However, this positive conclusion can be questioned as the study did not explore the 'interactional dynamics' of the actual discussions (Hutchby 2005). This is an important criticism because the issue of *who* speaks and when is a fundamental part of shaping conversations in particular directions. For example, audience discussions follow a formulaic progression, usually dominated and steered by the host, which means that the programmes may not be such open, public forums as they appear in audience and participants' accounts of them (Tolson 2005).

There have also been allegations of actors being hired and paid to take part in discussion programmes, such as that of Jerry Springer in the USA and Vanessa Feltz's show in the UK. The latter was cancelled in 1999 when it was revealed that an agency had been used to source several audience members. These episodes are reminders of Neil Postman's argument that television is primarily an *entertainment* medium, to which all of its other potentially useful functions are subordinated.

> **THINKING CRITICALLY**
>
> How satisfactory is Thompson's threefold schema? How might it be argued that television is becoming less monological and more dialogical in the digital age?

Postmodern theory

Since the publication of Jean-François Lyotard's *The Postmodern Condition* (1984), sociology has had to contend with a set of ideas about science, knowledge and culture that are at odds with the progressive, modernist ideals of modern life since the Enlightenment period. Lyotard argued that the great metanarratives of modernity – scientific truth, human progress and historical development – are in decline. Science continues, but, in the wake of global warming and nuclear weapons, who now believes it leads inexorably to a better life for all? Technologies develop, and more of us have smartphones and digital TVs, but, in the light of recent terrorism, wars and persistent undernourishment and famine, does anyone still believe in continuous human progress? For postmodern thinkers the demise of metanarratives may be a positive development. It means that we live in a period when people are forced to face modernity head-on with no grand illusions. We live in a time of 'self-conscious modernity' or postmodernity (Bauman 1992, 1997).

The postmodern world is marked by a lack of certainty, a mixing and matching of styles and genres, and a playfulness in relation to cultural products. In pop music, there is sampling, the mixing of original tracks with new rhythms and rap, mash-ups – songs created by blending two or more recorded songs – and many more hybrid forms. In film, David Lynch's seminal *Blue Velvet* (1986) merged time periods and historical eras seamlessly, with vehicles from the 1950s, 1960s and 1970s driving the same 1980s streets. And, in art, postmodern trends reject the idea of a progressive 'avant-garde', instead mixing high and popular forms in playful 'post-progressive' ways. Lyotard saw such playful mixing as marking the end of specific genres. As Western culture has run into the sand, he said, all that is left to do is 'play with the pieces'.

Baudrillard and hyperreality

One of the most influential contemporary media theorists is the French postmodernist thinker Jean Baudrillard (1929–2007), whose work was strongly influenced by the ideas of Marshall McLuhan. Baudrillard regarded the impact of modern mass media as being quite different from, and much more profound than, that of any previous media technology. The coming of the mass media, particularly electronic media such as television, has transformed the very nature of our lives. TV does not just 'represent' the world to us; it increasingly defines the world in which we live.

Baudrillard's postmodern ideas can be hard to grasp, but a relatively simple way of doing so is as follows. There was a time – not so long ago – when it was possible to separate reality, or the real world of events, from media representations of that world. So, for instance, in the real world there may be a war with real and terrible consequences for the combatants and civilians caught up in it. The media report on this war and inform us of what is happening. These two aspects – the reality and the representations – were seen as quite separate things.

But Baudrillard (1983) argues that the border between reality and its representations has collapsed and we can no longer separate representations from reality. But why not? After all, there are still wars and there are still reporters sending back images and reports on them. Baudrillard argues that media representations are, in fact, *part of* the hyperreal world and cannot be seen as separate from it. As the vast majority of people only ever 'know' about foreign wars, celebrities, politicians, and much more via media representations of them, their reality is shaped, determined even, by media representations. Hyperreality is a world in which the ultimate guarantor of authenticity and reality is precisely that we have seen it on TV or other media, which makes it 'more real than the real'. This may be part of an explanation for the growth of celebrity culture, where the only acceptable sign of significance is to appear on TV or in newspapers or magazines.

Just before the outbreak of hostilities in the first Gulf War in 1991, Baudrillard wrote a newspaper article entitled 'The Gulf War Will Not Take Place'. When war was declared and a bloody conflict took place, it might seem obvious that Baudrillard was wrong. Not a bit of it. After the war, Baudrillard (2004 [1991]) then wrote, *The Gulf War Did Not Take Place*. What could he possibly mean? His argument is that this war was not like others across history. It was a war of the media age, a televisual spectacle, in which, along with millions of viewers throughout the world, US President George Bush Senior and the president of Iraq, Saddam Hussein, watched the coverage on CNN to see what was actually 'happening'.

Baudrillard argues that, in a media-saturated age a new reality – hyperreality – is created, composed of the intermingling of people's behaviour and media representations. The world of hyperreality is constructed of simulacra – images which only get their meaning from other images and hence have no grounding in an 'external reality'. A long-running series of advertisements for the insurance comparison website Comparethemarket.com, for example, barely refers to insurance at all. Instead it alludes to previous adverts in the series, building characters and storylines concerning an anthropomorphized family of meerkats. Similarly, no political leader today can hope to win an election if they do not appear constantly on television. And the TV version of the leader is the one most viewers know – a hyperreal person who is 'more real than the real'.

Baudrillard's theory is seductive in an age of the global mass media and certainly has to be taken seriously. However, it can be objected that, once again, it treats the mass of people as passive recipients of media messages rather than as active participants able to engage with and even resist them. Many social movement

In what way was the 2003 invasion of Iraq a hyperreal event?

organizations, such as Greenpeace, do try to compete with the mass media to create an alternative (hyper)reality which will motivate the uncommitted to environmental activism. It is also the case that many real-world conflicts, famines and events fail to attract sufficient Western media interest and therefore fall outside hyperreality. In short, there is still a real world beyond the hyperreality of postmodern theory.

Many of the theories discussed above fail to appreciate the active part played by audiences in the reception of media content and forms. Because they look to theorize 'the media', there has been a tendency to downplay or ignore the diverse ways in which audiences make sense of and use different media products. However, scholars working in the field of audience research have changed this situation somewhat, and we look at some key ideas from this body of work in the next section.

> **THINKING CRITICALLY**
>
> Provide three recent examples of 'hyperreality'. Explain exactly what makes each one 'hyperreal'. Why should it matter if we can understand the world only through the lens of the global mass media?

Audiences and media representations

The effect that media representations may have on the audience cannot be inferred from media theories but requires a range of empirical research studies. The next section provides a brief summary of some of this research alongside a sketch of the chronological development of audience studies.

Audience studies

One of the earliest and most straightforward models of audience response is the *hypodermic model*. This compares the media message to a drug injected by syringe. The model is based on the assumption that the audience passively and directly accepts the message and does not critically engage with it. It also assumes that the message is received and interpreted in more or less the same way by all members of society. On this view, the media is seen as 'drugging' the audience, destroying its ability to think critically about the wider world (Marcuse 1964). The hypodermic model is now seen as rather simplistic and was often little more than an unstated conjecture in early studies. However, its assumptions can still be found in some contemporary theories – for instance, those suggesting that violent video games lead directly to violent actions – that are overly critical of media effects on society.

Critics of the hypodermic model point out that it takes no account of the very different responses that audiences have to the media. There is also general agreement that audience responses go through various stages. In their work on this question, Katz and Lazarsfeld (1955) drew on studies of political broadcasts during US presidential elections, arguing that audience response is formed through a two-step flow: the first step is when the message reaches the audience; the second comes when the audience interprets the message through their social interaction with influential people – 'opinion leaders' – who further shape the response.

More recent theories began to acknowledge the active role of the audience. The *gratification model* looks at ways in which different audiences actually use the media to meet their own needs (Lull 1990). Audiences may use the media to learn more about the world, finding out about the weather or stock markets, for example. Others may get help with their relationships or feel part of a fictional community (by watching TV soaps), or use these to get on with friends and colleagues who watch the same programmes. This was an advance on the hypodermic model, though the 'needs' of the audience are thought already to exist, while critics suggest that the media may, in fact, create new 'needs'.

Reception theories, such as that advanced by Stuart Hall (1980), focus on the way in which the class and cultural background of the members of an audience affect the way in which they make sense of different media 'texts' – a term that encompasses various media from books to films and music. Some individuals may simply accept the 'preferred reading' that is encoded in a text – such as a news bulletin – by the producer. This preferred reading is likely to reflect the dominant or mainstream position or ideology. However, Hall argues that the understanding of a text also depends on cultural and class background. Other audience members may take an 'oppositional' reading of a text because their social position places them in conflict with the mainstream reading. For example, a worker involved in strike action or members of minority ethnic groups are likely to make an oppositional reading of a news story on industrial or race relations rather than accept the dominant one.

Audiences also tend to filter information through their own life experience and may link different media 'texts' (programmes or genres, for example) or use one type of media to engage with another – questioning what they are told on television compared to newspapers (Fiske 1989). This *interpretative model* views the audience response as shaping the media through engagement or rejection of its output. Here the audience has a more powerful role, far removed from the early hypodermic model and almost a reversal of its main tenets.

In recent years media theorists and researchers have drawn attention to the emergence of participatory cultures, particularly among young people who have grown up with digital technology and social media. A participatory culture can be defined as one 'with relatively low barriers to artistic expression and civic engagement, strong support for creating and sharing one's creations, and some type of informal mentorship whereby what is known by the most experienced is passed along to novices . . . also one in which members believe their contributions matter, and feel some degree of social connection with

The hypodermic model is often implicit in arguments about the negative impact of television on children.

one another' (Jenkins et al. 2016: 4). Participatory cultures tend to break down the previous separation of active cultural producers from passive media audiences/consumers. Instead, there are new opportunities for people to be both producers and audience/consumers – prosumers – within communities of interest stretched across the world.

Participatory cultures involve their members actively in a variety of ways, and the Internet, digital media and mobile devices have made involvement much easier than in the past. Jenkins (2009: xi–xii) argues that such forms of participation include *affiliations* (membership of online communities such as Facebook and Twitter, gaming sites and message boards), *expressions* (including the creative production and sharing of music, video, images, mash-up and digital sampling), *collaborative problem-solving* (mentoring and team-working to develop knowledge or complete tasks, as found on Wikipedia or in alternative reality gaming) and *circulations* (shaping the flow of media via podcasting or blogging). On this characterization, many readers of this book may recognize their own activities as part of participatory cultures.

Empirical research and attempts to theorize the impact of participatory cultures on individuals, groups, communities and societies are ongoing. For example, how vulnerable are such cultures to commercialization and systematic data-gathering by corporate interests? Will the 'lowering of barriers to artistic creation' enhance our lives and improve understanding or lead to the so-called dumbing down of modern cultures? These questions and more will be the subject of the next wave of research studies in this field.

What we can see in this brief sketch of audience research is the steady movement, away from a simplistic understanding of the relationship between media output and the audience and towards increasingly more sophisticated models that place greater emphasis on the participation of an active audience. We can also see a shift away from one-way models (from media to audience) in favour of two-way models that allow room for audiences to shape media output rather than simply being passive sponges soaking up whatever messages they are fed. Indeed, theories of an emergent participatory culture are about as far removed from the early hypodermic model of audience reception as it is possible to imagine.

Representing class, gender, ethnicity and disability

An issue that has received much attention in media studies is the problem of media representations, particularly in television fiction. Which social groups should the mass media represent and which groups are absent from our TV screens? We look briefly at the way in which representations of social class, gender, ethnicity and disabled people serve to reinforce stereotypes, noting some more recent evidence suggesting that this may now be changing, at least in some cases.

Representations of the working class on UK television appear to be ubiquitous (Kendall 2005), from continuing TV dramas (soap operas) such as the long-running *Coronation Street* (1960 to the present) and *EastEnders* (1985 to the present) to films exploring working-class life such as *Billy Elliott* (2000) or *Vera Drake* (2004) and comedy/drama series such as *Clocking Off* (2000–3) and *Happy Valley* (2014). Some think soaps provide a means of escape from people's mundane lives, though this is not particularly convincing as many soaps feature characters whose lives are just as unexciting. A more plausible explanation is that soap operas explore dilemmas anyone may face and help viewers to think creatively about their own lives. Rather than providing an escape, in fact soaps must connect with the audience's experience if they are to be successful (D. Hobson 2002).

Nonetheless, it may be objected that the majority of these representations reflect a middle-class view of what working-class life is like. This is mainly because the production of TV drama and film is dominated by middle-class professionals and consequently represents their understanding. The working class tend to be shown in northern industrial cities; people work in manual jobs (or are unemployed) and are seldom shown making a living in other ways. The environments in which they live are usually hard and unforgiving, but, paradoxically, also involve strong communities exhibiting social solidarity. This stereotypical presentation has been remarkably enduring and persists well into the twenty-first century. So, although working-class life is represented, it is the accuracy of the portrayals that is at issue.

Research studies have repeatedly demonstrated that representations of girls and women in the mass media overwhelmingly involve traditional stereotypes of gender roles. Women are seen in domestic roles as housewives and homemakers, as objects of male sexual desire, or in working situations that extend the domestic role such as nurses, carers or office workers. Generally, such representations have been quite consistent across news reports, drama and entertainment programming, leading Gaye Tuchman (1978) to refer to 'the symbolic annihilation of women' on television. For example, in 1973 some 72 per cent of all characters on American prime-time television were male, and, though still the majority, this had fallen only to 65 per cent by 1993 (Gerbner 1997).

More recent research concludes that things are changing, albeit slowly, with an increasing variety, including that of the strong, independent woman (Glascock 2001; Meyers 1999). New female heroines in programmes such as *Buffy the Vampire Slayer*, *La Femme Nikita* and *Lara Croft*, alongside strong female characters such as high-powered lawyers (*Silk*, 2010–14), police chiefs (*The Killing*, 2011–14) and other professions in TV drama, all attest to changing representations of women. Yet many of these characters still conform to longstanding feminine norms. Buffy and Lara Croft are young, slim and conventionally attractive, appealing to the mainstream 'male gaze'. And many of the older, successful, professional women have disastrous or empty personal lives, illustrating Faludi's (1991) argument of a subtle backlash (both in reality and fiction) against women who break conventional gender roles – it will all end in tears eventually.

> See chapter 15, 'Gender and Sexuality', for a detailed discussion of gender issues.

Media representations of ethnic minorities and disabled people have been seen as reinforcing rather than challenging stereotypes. Black and Asian people were noticeably absent from mainstream television until quite recently; even when present – for example, in news reports and documentaries – they tended to be represented as problematic social groups. Media coverage of the 1970s moral panic around 'mugging' by black youths (Hall et al. 1978) and the inner-city 'race' riots of the 1980s and early twenty-first century was extensive.

Jack Shaheen's *The TV Arab* (1984) and *Reel Bad Arabs: How Hollywood Vilifies a People* (2001) examined the portrayal of Arabs on television and in Hollywood films (mostly American made) respectively. The 1984 study looked at more than 100 television shows between 1975 and 1984 featuring Arab characters. According to Shaheen, TV depictions depend on four myths: '[Arabs] are all fabulously wealthy; they are barbaric and uncultured; they are sex maniacs with a penchant for white slavery; they revel in acts of terrorism' (1984: 179). They are usually dressed strangely, reinforcing the view that Arabs do not look or act like Americans. Such portrayals were just as easy to find in children's cartoons and educational programmes, though more recent documentaries had attempted to provide more accurate accounts.

In the overwhelming majority of Hollywood film characterizations, Shaheen found that Arab characters were the 'bad guys'. Out of around 1,000 films, just twelve involved positive depictions, fifty-two were quite balanced, and the other 900+ portrayed Arabs in negative ways. This was the case irrespective of whether the film was a blockbuster or low-budget feature and whether the character was central to the plot or played a minor part. Shaheen shows that Arab stereotypes have existed in film since 1896 and generally depict Arab people as 'brutal, heartless, uncivilized religious fanatics and money-mad cultural "others" bent on terrorizing civilized Westerners, especially Christians and Jews'. He argues that such stereotypes are useful for writers and filmmakers as they make their jobs that much easier. Shaheen suggests this situation will only change when the Arab-American community is powerful enough to influence the film industry in the same way that women and African Americans have done in the past.

Ethnic minority cultures have also been commonly presented as different from an indigenous, white British culture and, often, as presenting problems for it (Solomos and Back 1996). Recent attempts to produce more representative imagery, such as in *EastEnders*, may offer a way forward. The serial drama provides a format which allows a variety of ethnic groups to be shown as ordinary members of society with similar lives and the same personal troubles as everyone else. It may be through such mundane representations that stereotypes can be avoided in future.

If ethnic minorities have been defined as *culturally* different, then the representations of disabled people in the media have routinely been as *physically* or *bodily* different, based on the 'personal tragedy' model of disability (Oliver 1990; also see chapter 11). News stories involving disabled people are more likely to be aired if the story can be fitted into this dominant framing. Typically this means showing disabled people as dependent, rather than as living independent lives (Karpf 1988).

Disabled people have been all but invisible in TV drama and entertainment and, when they are included, are over-represented among criminals and mentally unstable characters – 'the bad, mad and sad'. This situation has a very long history. Think of the evil Captain Hook in *Peter Pan*, the tragic Quasimodo in *The Hunchback of Notre Dame* or John Merrick in *The Elephant Man*. Disabled characters are never incidental to a storyline but are included precisely because of their disability. In a content analysis of six weeks of UK television, Cumberbatch and Negrine (1992) found just 0.5 per cent of fictional characters were disabled people and almost all of these were wheelchair users – not an accurate representation of disabled people in the UK, the overwhelming majority of whom do not use a wheelchair.

The 1990s saw some more positive representations, particularly in American drama series, which tried to present disabled people as living 'normal' lives and playing down impairments. However, Barnes (1991: 19) sees that simply ignoring impairments is not the answer. Instead, he maintains:

> The only solution with any hope of success is for all media organisations to provide the kind of information and imagery which, firstly, acknowledges and explores the complexity of the experience of disability and a disabled identity and, secondly, facilitates the meaningful integration of all disabled people into the mainstream economic and social life of the community.

Media representations are not the direct *cause* of discrimination and exclusion. Nevertheless, stereotypical representations can *reinforce* existing negative ideas of social groups and are therefore part of the wider social problem. Despite some signs of growing awareness and some evidence of positive changes in recent years, there is a way to go yet before media representations make a significant contribution to actually challenging damaging social stereotypes.

Ownership, power and alternatives to the global media

Sociological theories of the media show us that media forms can never be assumed to be politically neutral or socially beneficial. A key problem is the increasing concentration of ownership of different types of media within large conglomerates that have come to be known as 'supercompanies'. If politicians were alarmed at the ownership of a single national newspaper by one of the big press barons, then how much more serious is ownership of transnational media companies? As we have seen throughout this book, the Internet is one of the main contributors to – and manifestations of – current processes of globalization. Yet globalization is transforming the international reach and impact of other forms of media as well.

Although the media have always had an international dimension – such as gathering news stories and the distribution of films

Global Society 18.1 Censoring the media in China

The contradictory nature of globalization is illustrated clearly in China, a country that is undergoing rapid cultural and economic transformation under the Chinese Communist Party.

In the 1980s, the Chinese government oversaw the expansion of a national television system and encouraged the purchase of televisions by citizens. It saw television broadcasting as a means of uniting the country and promoting party authority. Television, however, can be a volatile medium. Not only is it not possible for television broadcasting to be tightly controlled in an age of satellite-based channels, but Chinese audiences have demonstrated their willingness to interpret TV content in ways that run contrary to government intentions (Lull 1997).

In interviews with 100 Chinese families, Lull found that audiences were 'masters of interpretation, reading between the lines in order to pick up the less obvious messages'. He noted that respondents described not only what they watched but how they watched it: 'Because viewers know that the government often bends and exaggerates its reports, they become skilled at imagining the true situation. What is presented, what is left out, what is given priority, how things are said – all these modes are noticed and interpreted sensitively.' Lull concluded that many of the messages seen by Chinese audiences on TV – primarily in imported films and commercials – run contrary to the way of life and opportunities available in China. Seeing television content emphasizing individuality and consumerism, many viewers felt their own options were constrained. Television conveyed to Chinese audiences that other societies seemed to offer greater freedom than their own.

More recently, the Internet and other new communication technologies have posed fresh challenges for the Chinese government. Many Western sites are blocked to Chinese Internet users, and a veritable army of institutional, paid and volunteer censors monitor blog posts, bulletin boards and web content. Such an authoritarian approach has been labelled the 'great firewall of China', though on occasion an even more radical approach has been taken. For example, following ethnic protest and riots, the Chinese authorities closed down the Internet altogether for six months in the province of Xinjiang.

Some think that the new media will enable people to circumvent state controls, but others maintain that state censors will keep pace with technological advances. In 2006, the leading Internet company Google announced that, in order to gain access to China's vast market, it would censor search results to satisfy the Chinese authorities. The BBC website was blocked, and critics warned that sensitive subjects, such as the 1989 Tiananmen Square massacre and sites promoting independence for Taiwan, would be restricted. However, in 2010, after a hacking attempt came to light, Google moved its China-compliant service to Hong Kong, and in 2014 another row broke out when Google refused recognition for the Chinese authorities' certificates of trust for websites. Nonetheless, Google's underlying cooperation with the Chinese on censorship suggests that profit-making rather than promoting American values is the main driver for US media companies.

THINKING CRITICALLY

What similarities and differences are there in censoring the Internet and television? What comparative evidence from other countries might make China's censorship practices seem less extraordinary?

– until the 1970s most media companies operated within domestic markets in accordance with regulations from national governments. The media industry was also differentiated into distinct sectors and, for the most part, cinema, print media, radio and television operated independently. But since then profound transformations have taken place. National markets have given way to a fluid global market, while new technologies have led to the fusion of media forms that were once distinct. By the start of the twenty-first century, the global media market was dominated by a group of about twenty multinational corporations whose role in the production, distribution and marketing of news and entertainment could be felt in almost every country in the world.

In their work on globalization, David Held and his colleagues (1999) point to five major shifts that have contributed to bringing about the global media order.

1 *Increasing concentration of ownership* The global media is now dominated by a small number of powerful, centralized media conglomerates.

2 *A shift from public to private ownership* Traditionally, media and telecommunications companies were partially or fully owned by the state. But liberalization of the business environment and relaxation of regulations led to the privatization and commercialization of media companies.

3 *Transnational corporate structures* Media companies no longer operate strictly within national boundaries and, likewise, media ownership rules have been loosened to allow cross-border investment and acquisitions.

4 *Diversification over a variety of media products* The media industry has diversified, and enormous media conglomerates produce and distribute a mix of media content, including music, news, print media and television programming.

5 *A growing number of corporate media mergers* There has been a distinctive trend towards alliances between companies in different segments of the media industry. Telecommunications firms, computer hardware and software manufacturers, and media 'content' producers are increasingly involved in corporate mergers.

If traditional media forms ensured that communication occurred within the boundaries of nation-states in a 'vertical' fashion, globalization is leading to the horizontal integration of communications. Communications and media can now more readily extend beyond the confines of individual countries (Sreberny-Mohammadi et al. 1997). Yet the new information order has developed unevenly and reflects divisions between the developed and developing societies. Some scholars suggest that the new order would be better described as 'media imperialism'.

Media imperialism?

The paramount position of the industrialized countries, above all the United States, in the production and diffusion of media has led many observers to speak of media imperialism (Herman and McChesney 2003). According to this view, a cultural empire has been established. Less developed countries are held to be especially vulnerable, because they lack the resources to maintain their own cultural independence. However, others argue that American media domination is not as simple as the above sketch suggests. What *exactly* is media imperialism? Does it exist when people from other cultures watch, and perhaps accept as superior, Western cultural products imbued with Western values? Or does media imperialism lie in the export of particular technologies such as television and mobile phones, which disrupt and transform local cultures? Or does it exist when one country or region's media industries become so powerful they take over or force out of existence local media outlets? Can we speak of domination at all when people across the world have chosen to purchase TV sets and smartphones and claim to find uses and pleasures in them (Tomlinson 1991)?

The headquarters of the world's twenty largest media conglomerates are located in industrialized nations, the majority in the USA. Media empires such as Time Warner, Disney/ABC and Viacom are all US-based. Among other large media corporations are Sony Music Entertainment (one of the 'big 4' music companies), which owns numerous record labels and distributes many independent labels, and Mondadori, Italy's largest publishing house controlled by the television

Does the smartphone help to spread Western culture around the world?

corporation owned by the former prime minister Silvio Berlusconi.

Through the electronic media, Western cultural products have become widely diffused round the globe. As we have seen, American films are ubiquitous, as is Western pop music. In 2005 a new Disney theme park was opened in Hong Kong which replicates largely American attractions rather than reflecting local cultures. For example, the 'themed lands' in Hong Kong included Main Street (USA), Adventureland, Fantasyland and Tomorrowland, with all the usual characters, among them Mickey Mouse, Donald Duck and Buzz Lightyear. It is not only the more popular entertainment forms that are at issue. Control of the world's news by the major Western agencies, it has been suggested, means the predominance of a 'First World outlook' in the information conveyed. Attention is given to the developing world mainly in times of disaster, crisis or military confrontation, which sustains a negative discourse on developing countries and their prospects.

Nonetheless, there are also some counter-trends which may support a more pluralistic theory of the media at a global level. One trend is that of 'reverse flows', where media products in, for example, former colonies become popular and are sold to the previous colonizers. Reverse flows suggest that media imperialism is not absolute or unchallengeable. An example of a reverse flow is the success of the Hindi-language Bollywood, based in Mumbai. Bollywood films are becoming more popular in the UK (the former colonial power), the USA and Russia, and come second only to Hollywood films in Australia.

A second criticism is that the thesis of media imperialism rests implicitly on the 'hypodermic needle' model (discussed earlier), which assumes that Western cultural products carry within them Western values that are 'injected' into passive consumers around the globe. However, as we have already seen, consumers are active rather than passive watchers and listeners and may reject, modify or reinterpret the messages in media output. Liebes and Katz (1993) studied a range of subcultural audiences in Israel and their responses to the American series *Dallas*. Russians in Israel saw the programme as embodying a form of capitalist manipulation that children should not be allowed to watch. For Israeli Arabs, the sexual themes in *Dallas* were potentially embarrassing and, as a result, the show ought not to be watched in mixed-sex groups. They also saw a domineering villain such as J. R. Ewing as reflecting similar figures within the Israeli establishment.

In a similar vein, Roland Robertson (1995) has argued that a better concept for understanding global processes is *glocalization* (the mixture of globalizing and localizing forces) rather than globalization (see chapter 4 for discussion). This is because American corporations have to take cognizance of local cultures if they are to market their products successfully in other countries. They certainly cannot ignore them. In this process, the products are often significantly altered. The thesis of glocalization suggests that the simple one-way flow process suggested by media imperialism is likely to be the exception rather than the rule.

The titles of two studies by Jeremy Tunstall, thirty years apart, tell a similar story. In *The Media Are American* (1977), he argued that the industrialization of mass media in America enabled it to dominate global media production. But, in *The Media Were American* (2007), his thesis is that the USA has lost its global dominance. The rise of India and China as media producers and consumers along with stronger national cultures and media systems has weakened the position of America in relation to the rest of the world. Even so, the logic of capital accumulation remains an effective force: 'In the global media system, it is as if

anything can be said, in any language, at any location, as long as it can be said profitably' (Hackett and Zhao 2005: 22). In that sense, it is capitalistic values rather than American national values that characterize the exchange of media products.

> ### THINKING CRITICALLY
>
> Is 'media imperialism' an accurate description of the global influence of Western media and culture? How does media imperialism fit with Lyotard's postmodern thesis of the collapse of Western culture? Which view is best supported by the evidence?

Ownership of media 'supercompanies'

In January 2000, two of the most influential media companies joined together in what was the largest corporate merger the world had ever seen. In a deal worth $337 billion, the world's biggest media company, Time Warner, and the world's largest Internet service provider, America Online (AOL), announced their intention to create the 'world's first fully integrated media and communications company for the Internet Century'. Yet, even more than for its size, the deal attracted great attention as the first major union between 'old media' and 'new media'.

The origins of Time Warner date back to 1923 when Henry Luce founded *Time* magazine. The overwhelming success of *Time* was followed by the creation of the business magazine *Fortune* in 1930 and the photographic magazine *Life* in 1936. Over the twentieth century, Time Inc. grew into a media corporation embracing TV and radio stations, the music industry, the vast Warner Brothers movie and cartoon empire, and the world's first 24-hour news channel, CNN.

The rise of America Online is typical of the 'new media' of the information age. Founded in 1982, AOL initially offered dial-up Internet access charged at an hourly rate. By 1994, it had 1 million subscribers. After introducing unlimited Internet use for a standard monthly fee in 1996, its membership soared to 4.5 million. As the number of users continued to grow – 8 million people were using AOL by 1997 – the company embarked on a series of mergers, acquisitions and alliances which consolidated its position as the pre-eminent Internet service provider.

The merger between the two companies was set to create a US$350 billon media supercompany, AOL-Time Warner, bringing 24 million AOL subscribers, 120 million magazine readers and the television channels CNN, HBO and Warner Brothers all under one corporate roof. Yet the merger failed. AOL was never able to meet its ambitious subscriber or revenue targets, and the technological spin-offs from combining film and Internet technologies were slow to materialize. In 2002, the company posted a loss of almost $100 billion, resulting in the company dropping 'AOL' from its name in 2003. Plans to sell off AOL were mooted in 2007, and it was sold on 9 December 2009. The companies that did succeed were not those looking to merge the old and the new but others such as Google, which had a clear focus on the worldwide web and its huge global potential.

Not everyone agrees that the idea of media supercompanies is one that should be aspired to. Where enthusiasts see a dream, critics sense a nightmare. As media corporations become ever more concentrated, centralized and global in their reach, there is reason to be concerned that the important role of the media as a forum for free speech, expression and debate will be curtailed. A single company that controls both the content – TV programmes, music, films, news sources – and the means of distribution is in a position of great power. It can promote its own material (the singers and celebrities it has made famous), it can exercise self-censorship (omitting news stories that might cast its holdings or corporate supporters in a negative light) and it can 'cross-endorse' products within its own empire at the expense of those outside it. The vision of the Internet in the hands of several media conglomerates stands in stark contrast to the idea of a free and unrestricted electronic realm held out by Internet enthusiasts just a few years ago.

But it is important to remember that there are few inevitabilities in the social world. Attempts at total control of information sources and distribution channels rarely succeed, either because of anti-trust legislation preventing monopolies or through the persistent and creative responses of media users who seek out alternative sources. Media consumers are not 'cultural dopes' who can be manipulated effortlessly by corporate interests. As the scope and volume of media forms and content expand, individuals are becoming more, not less, skilled in interpreting and evaluating the messages and material they encounter.

Resistance and alternatives to the global media

While the power and reach of the global media are undeniable, there are attempts to counter global media empires by using new technologies to facilitate alternative forms of news gathering. One of the more successful is the Independent Media Centre, or Indymedia, a global collective of independent media outlets associated with the anti-globalization movement. Since its creation in 1999, during a protest against the World Trade Organization in Seattle, Indymedia has sought to create open access online platforms, enabling political activists and citizens to upload their own videos, images and reports as well as live streaming of protest events. It is thought to have some 150 local centres across thirty countries.

Indymedia seeks to break down the barrier between media professionals and the public, encouraging people to participate in the production of news rather than being passive consumers of corporate and state broadcast news. Although the Internet is clearly central to the Indymedia project, local groups also produce publications, community radio stations, video, email lists, a wiki site and even TV stations in public access slots. However, the emergence and increasing popularity of individual blogs (which did not exist when Indymedia was created) has to some extent

Global Society 18.2 Media empires – News Corporation

Rupert Murdoch is an Australian-born entrepreneur who is the head of one of the world's largest media empires. News Corporation holds nine different media operating on six continents. By 2001 its turnover was £16.5 billion and it employed 34,000 staff (BBC 2001). In October 2004, ABC News reported the annual turnover as £29 billion.

Murdoch established News Corporation in Australia before moving into the British and American markets in the 1960s. His initial purchases of the UK *News of the World* and *The Sun* in 1969 and the US *New York Post* in the mid-1970s paved the way for a dramatic expansion in later acquisitions. Murdoch turned many of his newspapers towards sensationalistic journalism, building on the three themes of sex, crime and sport. *The Sun*, for example, became highly successful, with the highest circulation of any daily English-language newspaper in the world.

In the 1980s Murdoch started to expand into television by establishing Sky TV, a satellite and cable chain that proved commercially successful. He also owns 64 per cent of the Star TV network based in Hong Kong. Its declared strategy is to 'control the skies' in satellite transmission over an area from Japan to Turkey, taking in the gigantic markets of India and China. It transmits five channels, one of which is BBC World News. In 1985, Murdoch bought a half interest in 20th Century Fox films. His Fox Broadcasting Company started up in 1987 and became the fourth major television network in the United States.

In recent years, Murdoch invested heavily in the profitable digital satellite television industry, particularly through his ownership of Sky and coverage of live sporting events such as basketball and live premiership football. According to Murdoch, sports coverage is News Corporation's 'battering ram' for entering new media markets (Herman and McChesney 1997). Because sporting events are best viewed live, they lend themselves to the 'pay-per-view' format that is profitable both for Murdoch and for advertisers.

On 13 July 2011, Murdoch's News Corporation bid of £8 billion to take full control of BSkyB was abandoned in the wake of police and parliamentary inquiries into illegal mobile phone hacking by journalists and private investigators hired by the *News of the World*. The scandal led to the closure of the paper three days earlier after 168 years in print. However, James Murdoch suggested that the *News of the World* constituted less than 1 per cent of News Corp business – a reflection of the declining readership, profitability and influence of newspapers in the digital era. On 19 July, both Rupert and James Murdoch appeared at a live, televised session of the House of Commons Culture, Media and Sport Committee, answering questions on phone hacking. A judicial inquiry into the scandal was ordered by the prime minister, and the affair has been widely seen as the biggest setback the expanding Murdoch empire has ever had.

Governments can cause trouble for Murdoch because, at least within their own boundaries, they can introduce legislation limiting media cross-ownership – that is, a situation where the same firm owns several newspapers and TV stations. The European Union has also expressed concern about the dominant position of very large media companies. Yet Murdoch's power is not easily contained, given its global spread. He is weighty enough to influence governments, but it is in the nature of the telecommunications business that it is everywhere and nowhere. Murdoch's power base is very large but also elusive.

Murdoch was, for a while, head of the largest media organization the world has known. In 1995, however, he was overtaken when the Disney Company and ABC merged. Disney's chairman at the time, Michael Eisner, made it clear that he wanted to compete with Murdoch in the rapidly expanding markets of Asia. Murdoch's response to the merger was: 'They are twice as big as me now.' Then he added: 'A bigger target.' The chief executives of Disney, Time Warner and Viacom have all noted that Murdoch is the media executive they respect and fear the most – and whose moves they study most carefully (Herman and McChesney 1997).

undermined its originality and functions (Ritzer 2011: 142–3). Anyone can now create and manage their own blog – the ultimate form of decentralization – and get their views and opinions published online.

Paradoxically, Indymedia has suffered from its democratic, open access approach, which allows many different individuals and groups to make use of the network, sometimes bringing heightened governmental surveillance and intervention. In 2004, its Internet provider took down two hard drives from its server at the request of the FBI, effectively closing down twenty websites in thirteen countries. The FBI had received a request from the Public Prosecutor's Office in Bologna, Italy, based on their claim that a violent Italian anarchist group involved in planting bombs and sending letter bombs to politicians had used Indyme-dia to claim responsibility for the attacks. It is unclear whether this was, in fact, the case. But it does highlight some of the problems with the loosely organized, networked model of Indymedia, which seems ill-equipped to resist the demands of states and security forces (Mueller 2011: 18–22).

Religion, tradition and popular outlooks can also be a brake on media globalization, while local regulations and domestic media institutions can play a role in limiting the impact of global media (see 'Global Society 18.2', p. 793). The case of new media in the Middle East is an interesting one. In investigating the response of Islamic countries to the forces of media globalization, Ali Mohammadi (2002) found that resistance to the incursion of outside media forms has ranged from muted criticism to the outright banning of Western satellites.

In spite of being banned in some Middle East countries and its broadcast centres in Afghanistan and Iraq being attacked by the American military, Al Jazeera continues to prosper in the digital age.

The reaction to media globalization and the action taken by individual countries in large part reflect their overall responses towards the legacy of Western colonialism and the encroachment of modernity.

Until the mid-1980s, most television programming in the Islamic world was produced and distributed within national borders or through Arabsat – the pan-Arab satellite broadcasting network composed of twenty-one states. The liberalization of broadcasting and the power of global satellite TV have transformed the contours of television in the Islamic world. The events of the 1991 Gulf War made the Middle East a centre of attention for the global media industry and significantly affected television broadcasting and consumption within the region as well. Satellites spread rapidly, with Bahrain, Egypt, Saudi Arabia, Kuwait, Dubai, Tunisia and Jordan all launching satellite channels by 1993. By the end of the decade, most Islamic states had established their own satellite channels, as well as accessing global media programmes.

Al Jazeera is the largest Arabic news channel in the Middle East, offering news coverage twenty-four hours a day. Founded in 1996, and based in Qatar, Al Jazeera is the fastest growing news network among Arab communities and Arabic-speaking people around the world. Some Western critics have argued that it is overly sensational and shows too much violent and emotionally charged footage from war zones, as well as giving disproportionate coverage to fundamentalist and extremist groups (Sharkey 2004). Its political programmes are popular, but other shows covering culture, sport and health help to increase the channel's audience share. However, many, perhaps most, TV stations use sensational stories to capture audiences, and it may be objected that Al Jazeera is simply reflecting its audience in the same way that Western outlets do.

Recent academic studies argue that Al Jazeera has played an influential role in breaking open state control of the Middle East media, encouraging open debate on important issues such as the invasion of Iraq, the situation in Palestine and Arab identities (Lynch 2006; Zayani 2005; Miles 2005). The news channel has helped to change political and social debates not only in the Middle East but also in the West, where digital viewers can tune in for an alternative perspective on global events. Al Jazeera now broadcasts from London and Washington, DC, as well as from Doha and Kuala Lumpur.

In some Islamic states, the themes and material dealt with on Western television have created tensions. Programmes relating to gender and human rights issues are particularly controversial; Saudi Arabia, for example, no longer supports BBC Arabic because of concerns over its coverage of human rights issues. Three Islamic states – Iran, Saudi Arabia and Malaysia – have banned satellite access to Western television, while Iran has been the staunchest opponent of the Western media, branding it a source of 'cultural pollution' and a promoter of Western consumer values.

Such strong responses are in the minority. Mohammadi (2002) concluded that, although Islamic countries have responded to media globalization by attempting to resist or provide an alternative, most have found it necessary to accept certain modifications to their culture in order to maintain their own cultural identity. The 'traditionalist approach', such as that favoured by Iran and Saudi Arabia, is losing ground to responses based on adaptation and modernization.

Conclusion

Contemporary mass media are comprised of a complex variety of different forms, from print and newspapers to radio, television and film, smartphones and interactive cyberspace. Understanding the social impact of the new digital media is an important task for sociologists. In particular, a new generation who have experienced socialization processes incorporating the new media may be better placed to appreciate just how embedded they are in the routines of everyday life. However, the task still requires that same struggle for sociological detachment and methodological rigour that characterizes the discipline's best research studies.

As individuals, we do not control techno-logical change, and some critics perceive that the sheer pace of the contemporary changes threatens to lead to either a Big Brother-style surveillance state or, alternatively, social chaos. Undoubtedly, the Internet, wireless networks, smartphones, etc., are leading to changes in behaviour, but they do not entirely determine it. So far, at least, the overwhelmingly negative scenarios predicted by sceptics have failed to materialize. Not only has the surveillance state not emerged, but, on the contrary, the Internet has facilitated decentralization, new forms of social networking and an opening up of opportunities for ordinary people to produce their own music, film, news, and much more. Conventional books and other 'pre-electronic' media also look unlikely to disappear. Bulky as it is, the book you are reading is actually handier to use than a digitized version and is much more flexible and portable, requiring no power source. Even e-book readers, such as the Kindle, Nook and Cybook, require a power source and cannot be handled and manipu-lated like a conventional book.

On the other hand, the new media are steadily canalizing or 'giving direction to' older media forms. Newspapers have moved online and are experimenting with subscrip-tions and payment methods to counter continuously falling sales. Music downloads have fatally undermined sales of music CDs and, probably sometime in the future, DVD film sales too. Even the future of that most successful global medium, television, is not immune. The development and rapid take-up of on-demand television accessed via the Internet over the last decade shows that the days of national populations watching TV shows and events 'live' together may already have ended.

It is often easier to appreciate revolution-ary changes from a distance, long after their impact is known and, thus, proven. However, it is safe to say that those of us alive today are currently experiencing a digital revolution that is changing the media landscape forever. But that revolution is not just happening somewhere 'out there'. We are all part of it, and how we respond to and make use of the new technologies and media outlets will be just as important in determining their social impact.

Chapter review

1 What do sociologists mean by 'mass media'? What are their key characteristics?

2 In what ways is digitization a 'revolution'? What kinds of technologies and devices have emerged from the digital revolution?

3 How does the Internet differ from older media forms? What impact is the Internet likely to have on relationships, communities and global inequality?

4 What positive and negative aspects of television have been found? How are digital television services different from analogue services?

5 What issues have arisen as a result of sharing music files over the Internet? How have companies and authorities tackled these, or how could they best do so in the future? What are the short- and long-term benefits of music sharing for audiences?

6 A range of different theories of the media have been developed. Briefly outline each of the four main ones presented in the chapter, bringing out their similarities and differences.

7 The Frankfurt School saw modern mass media as part of the 'culture industry'. What is the latter and why was it perceived to be a negative development?

8 What does John Thompson mean by 'mediated quasi-interaction'? Provide some examples.

9 Compare the theories of Habermas (on the decline of the public sphere) and Baudrillard (on hyperreality). Which do you think best fits the contemporary mix of media forms and their social consequences?

10 What have we learned about media messages and their reception from audience research studies?

11 The ownership of media is increasingly concentrated in the hands of large conglomerates. What, if anything, is wrong with this concentration? Do current alternatives really challenge this pattern of ownership?

Research in practice

Much has been prophesied or assumed about the potential of new digital media to transform the way that people make, distribute and consume music, video, television and news. But will the dominance of large media companies really be challenged by groups of cultural producers and audiences making use of the subversive potential of the Internet?

Read Sun Jung and Doobo Shim's (2014) 'Social Distribution: K-pop Fan Practices in Indonesia and the "Gangnam Style" Phenomenon', *International Journal of Cultural Studies*, 17(5): 485–501. This article explores one instance which may provide an insight into how this challenge might develop in relation to pop music.

1 What kind of study is this? How did the authors conduct the research into fan behaviour?

2 Using examples from the paper, what is meant by a 'social distribution network'?

3 How powerful are K-pop fans in making the phenomenon a global success? Provide examples from the paper to illustrate this.

4 What role do top-down, corporate interests play in the creation and distribution of K-pop? Is it likely that such interests may become dominant in the production, distribution and consumption of Korean pop music?

Thinking it through

Sociologists have long sought to understand the relationship between the emergence and spread of new technologies and their social context. Do some technologies 'take off' because they fulfil a need or are they devised and marketed to *create* newly perceived 'needs'? Do technological devices shape and transform societies or do societies bring into being appropriate technologies at particular times?

Read the article by Ben Agger (2011) entitled 'iTime: Labour and Life in a Smartphone Era', *Time and Society*, 20(1): 119–36, which looks at the emergence of the smartphone. Consider the way the author addresses and answers the questions noted above. How does the paper theorize the social impact of the smartphone and what conclusions does it draw? What kind of theoretical position would you say this is? How satisfactory do you find the paper's discussion of smartphone use and the 'transforming potential' of this device in society?

Society in the arts

One of the most controversial uses of the Internet has been the release of large swathes of confidential political and military documents by WikiLeaks – a group that enables whistleblowers to anonymously leak secret information into the public domain. The co-founder of WikiLeaks, Australian computer programmer Julian Assange, was granted asylum in the Ecuadorian Embassy in London in 2012 to avoid extradition to Sweden for alleged sexual offences.

The Fifth Estate (2013), directed by Bill Condon, is a film detailing the founding and development of WikiLeaks. Watch the film and then provide answers to the following questions.

- How did WikiLeaks come into being? What were the founders' original intentions?
- Looking at the material it has released, does WikiLeaks have a political philosophy? If so, what is it?
- During the discussions over the Bradley Manning Iraq and Afghan War logs, what was the relationship between WikiLeaks and mainstream newspapers? To what extent did news journalists influence the released material?
- Do your own research into WikiLeaks. Assange says the film is 'a propaganda attack on WikiLeaks'. List the aspects of the film that may support his view. Overall, is the film even-handed or biased?

Further reading

An excellent introductory text is Danielle Albertazzi and Paul Cobley's (2009) *The Media: An Introduction* (3rd edn, Harlow: Longman), which is logically structured and well written. James Slevin's (2000) *The Internet and Society* (Cambridge: Polity) covers the social impact of the Internet. For new forms of media, try Martin Lister, John Dovey, Seth Giddings, Iain Grant and Kieran Kelly's (2008) *New Media: A Critical Introduction* (London: Routledge), which does exactly what it says.

On media theories, a good place to start is Dan Laughey's (2007) *Key Themes in Media Theory* (Maidenhead: McGraw-Hill), which is a comprehensive survey going beyond this chapter. A useful discussion can then be found in David Hesmondhalgh and Jason Toynbee's (2008) edited collection *The Media and Social Theory* (London: Routledge).

John L. Sullivan's (2012) *Media Audiences: Effects, Users, Institutions and Power* (Thousand Oaks, CA: Sage) is an up-to-date survey of the field. On problems of global media ownership, a good guide is Gillian Doyle's (2002) *Media Ownership: The Economics and Politics of Convergence and Concentration in the UK and European Media* (London: Sage).

Those pursuing media studies further could try Gill Branston and Roy Stafford's (2010) *The Media Student's Book* (5th edn, London: Routledge). A good resource for designing your own media research is David Deacon, Michael Pickering, Peter Golding and Graham Murdock's (2007) *Researching Communications: A Practical Guide to Methods in Media and Cultural Analysis* (2nd edn, London: Hodder Arnold).

For a collection of original readings on communication and the media, see the accompanying *Sociology: Introductory Readings* (3rd edn, Cambridge: Polity, 2010).

Internet links

@   Additional information and support for this book at Polity:
www.politybooks.com/giddens

@   Glasgow University Media Group's own website:
www.glasgowmediagroup.org

Ofcom – the UK's independent media regulator site, which has some useful surveys:
www.ofcom.org.uk

@   The Foundation for Information Policy Research – UK-based think tank studying the interaction between ICT and society:
www.fipr.org

@   OECD, ICT Homepage – lots of comparative data on the 'Internet economy':
www.oecd.org/internet/ieconomy

@   Theory.org – playful postmodern site on links between media and identities:
www.theory.org.uk

@   Indymedia UK – British-based 'grassroots' site providing an alternative platform to mainstream news:
www.indymedia.org.uk

@   The UK Broadcasters' Audience Research Board – lots of research and surveys on audiences here:
www.barb.co.uk

CHAPTER 19

Education

Contents

This image of girls in a school classroom may appear quite mundane and uncontroversial, but, in some regions of the world, educating girls is viewed as unnecessary or even morally wrong. Malala Yousafzai lived in the Swat valley in north-west Pakistan and had spoken out for the right of girls to education and schooling, and at just eleven years old in 2009 had even written an anonymous blog for the BBC. At the time, the Taliban were attempting to occupy the valley and banned schooling for girls. When government troops moved into the valley to clear it of Taliban fighters, who had already destroyed dozens of schools, Malala's family temporarily moved out to escape the conflict. When they finally moved back, Malala attended a school founded by her father, but by then she had become an identifiable target and faced threats from

Taliban activists, who saw her as promoting secular education for Pakistan (BBC News 2014c).

On 9 October 2012, fifteen-year-old Malala went to school with her friends by bus as usual. The school itself was disguised and bore no signage that would alert Taliban supporters to its existence. On the way home, the bus was stopped just short of an army checkpoint and a young man got on board. Malala's autobiography describes what happened next (Yousafzai 2013: 6):

> 'Who is Malala?', he demanded. No one said anything, but several of the girls looked at me. I was the only girl with my head not covered. That's when he lifted up a black pistol. I later learned it was a Colt 45. Some of the girls screamed. Moniba tells me I squeezed her hand. My friends say he fired three shots, one after another. The first went through my left eye socket and out under my left shoulder. I slumped forward onto Moniba, blood coming from my left ear, so the other two bullets hit the girls next to me. One bullet went into Shazia's left hand. The third went through her left shoulder and into the upper right arm of Kainat Riaz. My friends later told me that the gunman's hand was shaking as he fired. By the time we got to hospital my long hair and Moniba's lap were full of blood.

Malala survived and was flown to the UK for surgery and rehabilitation. The family now lives in Birmingham, though Malala has always expressed a desire one day to return to the Pashtun region of Pakistan. She now works with a fund in her name that helps children into education around the world, and in October 2014 she was jointly awarded the Nobel Peace Prize (with Kailash Satyarthi, an Indian children's rights campaigner).

Malala's personal experience is clearly exceptional, but it highlights the fact that the value attributed to 'getting an education' is both culturally and socially variable as well as politically contested. What kind of education is appropriate in the context of agricultural communities with high levels of rural poverty? Should education systems challenge

Malala receiving the jointly awarded 2014 Nobel Peace Prize in Oslo, alongside Kailash Satyarthi.

traditional gender divisions and roles or serve to reproduce them? Is schooling always the most appropriate form of education for young people?

In some countries and regions, large numbers of children do not attend school at all. In particular, sub-Saharan Africa accounts for around 52 per cent of all children in this category globally, with 22 per cent of primary-age children not in school. Nigeria has the highest proportion of children who are not in education of any country in the world, with almost one in three primary-age (six- to eleven-year-olds) and one in four junior secondary-age children (twelve- to fourteen-year-olds) not in formal schooling. In 2008, more than 10 million children in Nigeria were not in basic education (UNICEF 2012: vi–xii). However, in rural areas there can also be pronounced gender differences. As Malala records (Yousafzai 2013: 9),

I was a girl in a land where rifles are fired in celebration of a son, while daughters are hidden away behind a curtain, their role in life simply to prepare food and give birth to children . . . For most Pashtuns it's a gloomy day when a daughter is born. My father's cousin . . . was one of the few who came to celebrate my birth and even gave a handsome gift of money. Yet, he brought with him a vast family tree of our clan, the Dalokhel Yousafzai, going right back to my great-great-grandfather and showing only the male line.

Rural families in very poor situations often educate their boys rather than girls. David Archer, of the charity ActionAid, says that there are numerous reasons why they may do this:

Some are to do with traditional attitudes, which hold that investing in the education of girls is not worthwhile because they won't be able to bring the economic return to the household that boys will, and also because they're likely to get married and leave the family home. There are also issues around early pregnancy, fears of violence towards girls on the way to and at school, inappropriate teaching and an absence of basic facilities like toilets for girls. It's a gamble sending a child to school when you are poor and need support in the household, and it's often girls who lose out. (*The Independent* 2007)

In relatively wealthy, urbanized and industrialized countries such as Sweden, Canada and the UK, the situation is very different. The main issue exercising parents is not *whether* their children – girls and boys – will be able to go to school, but *what kind* of schooling their children will receive. Will it be in a school that is highly regarded? Should it be a faith school, a state school or a fee-paying, private one? The diversity of provision in the education systems of developed countries means that education involves a large measure of consumer choice. Yet, despite very different national contexts, the connection between education and social inequalities of class, gender, ethnicity and disability remains central in education

systems right across the world and has been the subject of much research and debate in sociology.

Education is one of sociology's founding subjects, seen as crucial for the transmission of society's values and moral rules to new members. Indeed, Emile Durkheim's first professorial post was as professor of education at the Sorbonne in Paris. As education is one of the oldest sociological subjects, there exists a huge body of research and scholarship on the subject. Clearly, we cannot hope to cover this body of work here, but the chapter offers an overview of some of the most important themes and recurring issues that have helped to shape the sociology of education.

We begin with the deceptively simple question: what is education for? The answer is not as straightforward as it may appear. Is 'education' the same thing as 'schooling', for instance? Not surprisingly, there are several ways to answer these questions, and we look at some influential sociological theories. We then explore the links between the major social divisions of class, gender and ethnicity in education and evaluate contentious debates around intelligence and IQ. The final sections look at education and literacy levels around the world and the impact of digital technology in the classroom, and the UK education system is used as a guide to wider social changes such as consumerism and demands for more parental choice. The chapter ends with digital developments in the delivery of higher education. Universities are charged with meeting the demands of the global knowledge economy, and yet, in many countries, they seem to be in crisis, as government deficit reduction plans mean severe cutbacks in public spending and increasing student indebtedness. Does the e-university offer a possible solution?

Education, schooling and culture

Education, like health, is often seen as an unproblematic social good to which all individuals are entitled as their right. Who would not be in favour of it? Indeed, most people who have been through an education system and emerged literate, numerate and reasonably knowledgeable would probably agree that education has been beneficial. However, there is a difference between education and schooling. Education can be defined as a *social institution* which enables and promotes the acquisition of skills, knowledge and the broadening of personal horizons. Education can take place in many social settings. Schooling, on the other hand, refers to the formal process through which certain types of skill and knowledge are delivered, normally through a pre-designed curriculum in specialized settings – schools. Schooling in most countries is typically divided into stages such as primary and secondary and is mandatory for all young people up to a specified age.

Some sociologists see education as crucial for individuals to fulfil their potential, but they also argue that education is not confined to or defined by what is delivered in schools. Mark Twain is reported to have said: 'I never let my schooling get in the way of my education' – the implication being that schools are not the best educators and may even be obstacles to useful learning, such as that gained from wise adults, within families or from personal experience. In this chapter we will deal with both education and schooling and will often refer to the latter as taking place within organized 'education systems' to reflect common usage.

Education is a complex political, economic, social and cultural issue. Should education systems be paid for by the state through taxation and delivered free to all, or should we expect to pay directly for our own family's education? These are important *political and economic* decisions and matters of continuing public debate. What *kind* of education should be delivered and how? Should it cover history, politics or astrology, for example? Should we aim for the same basic education for all, regardless of inequalities of wealth, gender or ethnicity, in comprehensive education systems? Or should the wealthy be allowed to buy their children's education outside the state system? Should schools be able to select pupils on the

basis of ability? These *social* issues combine with the political and economic in increasingly complex arguments. Should education involve the compulsory teaching of religion? Should faith-based schools be allowed and even encouraged? What kinds of values should underpin education systems? These *cultural* issues are of enormous political significance in multicultural societies.

Education has become an important site for a whole range of debates, which are not simply about what happens within schools. They are debates about the direction of society itself and how we can best equip young people for life in an increasingly global world. Sociologists have been involved in debates about education ever since the work of Durkheim in the late nineteenth century, and this is where we begin our review of theories of education.

Education as socialization

For Emile Durkheim, education plays an important role in the socialization of children because they gain an understanding of the common values in society, uniting a multitude of separate individuals. Common values include religious and moral beliefs and a sense of self-discipline. Durkheim argues that schooling enables children to internalize the social rules that contribute to the functioning of society. He was particularly concerned with shared moral values in late nineteenth-century France, as he saw the emergence of a creeping individualism that threatened social solidarity and considered there was a key role for schools in teaching mutual responsibility and the value of the collective good. As a 'society in miniature', the school could impart discipline and respect for authority.

In industrial societies, Durkheim wrote (2011 [1925]), education has another socialization function; it teaches the skills needed to perform roles in increasingly specialized occupations. In traditional societies, occupational skills could be learned within the family, but as the extended division of labour led to a more complex society, an education system developed to pass on the skills required to fill the various specialized, occupational roles.

Durkheim's functionalist approach to sociology was introduced in chapter 1, 'What is Sociology?', and chapter 3, 'Theories and Perspectives'.

Talcott Parsons outlined a different structural functionalist approach to education in mid-twentieth century America. Unlike Durkheim, Parsons was not worried about increasing individualism, arguing instead that a central function of education was to instil in pupils the value of individual achievement. This was crucial to the functioning of industrialized societies, but it could not be learned in the family. A child's status in the family is ascribed – fixed from birth. By contrast, a child's status in school is largely achieved and, in schools, children are assessed according to universal standards through tests and exams. For Parsons, the main function of education is to enable children to move from the particularistic standards of the family to the universal standards that operate in modern society. According to Parsons, schools, like the wider society, operate on a meritocratic basis where children achieve their status according to merit, or worth, rather than on the basis of their sex, race or class (Parsons and Bales 1956). However, as we shall see, the idea that schools are meritocratic has been much criticized.

There is little doubt that functionalist theory does tell us something significant about education systems. They do aim to provide individuals with the skills and knowledge needed to participate in societies, and schools do teach children some of the values and morals of the wider society. Yet functionalist theory also overstates the case for a single set of society-wide values. There are many cultural differences within a single society, and the notion of a set of central values that should be taught to all may not be accurate or well received. This highlights a recurring problem within functionalist accounts, namely the concept of 'society' itself. Functionalists see education

Education systems in developed societies celebrate individual achievement.

systems as serving several functions for society as a whole, but the problem is that this assumes society is relatively homogeneous and that all social groups share similar interests. Is this really true? Critics from the conflict tradition in sociology point out that, in societies marked by major social inequalities, education systems which support them must also reinforce those social inequalities. In that sense, schooling works in the interests of the ruling groups.

The importance of education and peer relations in socialization is discussed further in chapter 9, 'The Life Course'.

Schooling for capitalism?

In a highly influential study of education in the USA, Bowles and Gintis (1976) concluded that schools are 'agents' of socialization, but only because they help to produce the right kind of workers for capitalist businesses. Their Marxist thesis argued that the close connection between the worlds of work and education was not simply a matter of the school curriculum teaching knowledge and skills that employers need. The education system helps to shape whole personalities.

> The structure of social relations in education not only inures the student to the discipline of the workplace, but also develops the types of personal demeanour, modes of self-presentation, self-image, and social class identifications, which are the crucial ingredients of job adequacy. Specifically, the social relationships of education – the relationships between administrators and teachers, teachers and students, students and students, and students and their work – replicate the hierarchical divisions of labor. (Ibid.: 131)

Bowles and Gintis maintained that the structure of schooling is based on a 'correspondence principle' – that is, the structures of school life *correspond* to the structures of working life. In both school and work, conformity to rules is rewarded, teachers and managers dictate tasks, pupils and workers perform these tasks, school staff are organized hierarchically – as is company management – and this situation has to be accepted as inevitable. Bowles and Gintis's theory challenged the widespread idea at the time that education was 'a great leveller' which treats people equally and thus widens opportunities for all. They argued that education under capitalism was, in fact, a great divider which reproduces social inequality.

In some ways this orthodox Marxist theory represents a kind of 'conflict functionalism', which sees society as riven with conflict and the education system within it as performing important functions that help to maintain inequality. Other Marxist critics saw the main

flaw in the thesis as its correspondence principle, which was too simple and reductionist. For example, it relied on the social structure shaping and determining individuals and did not give enough significance to the possibility of active pupil and student resistance (Giroux 1983; Brown and Lauder 1997). The thesis is also too generalized and was not developed from empirical research within schools themselves. Later researchers found a diversity of practice in schools, and, in many cases, it may be possible for school heads and teachers to generate an ethos that encourages working-class pupils to be more ambitious than the theory allows for. After all, in many capitalist countries today, employers complain that schools are actually *failing* to produce workers with the skills and knowledge they require.

> **THINKING CRITICALLY**
>
> On Bowles and Gintis's account, are successful middle-class children also subject to the 'hierarchical division of labour' in schools? In what ways could a 'correspondence principle' work in schools based in mainly middle-class areas?

The hidden curriculum

In focusing on the *structure* of schooling rather than simply its content, Bowles and Gintis showed that a hidden curriculum exists within education systems, through which pupils learn to accept discipline, hierarchy and passivity towards the status quo. One of the most controversial and interesting theorists of education to explore the hidden curriculum is the Austrian anarchist and philosopher Ivan Illich (1926–2002). Illich is noted for his staunch opposition to the culture of industrial capitalism, which he saw as gradually deskilling the population as they come to rely more on the products of industry and less on their own creativity and knowledge. In the sphere of health, for example, traditional remedies and practices are lost as bureaucratic health systems lead to a reliance on doctors and hospitals – a pattern that is repeated in all areas of life, including education.

Illich (1971) argued that the very notion of compulsory schooling should be questioned. According to Illich, schools have developed to supply four basic functions: the provision of custodial care, the distribution of people within occupational roles, the learning of dominant values, and the acquisition of socially approved skills and knowledge. Schools, like prisons, have become custodial organizations because attendance is compulsory and young people are 'kept off the streets' between early childhood and their entry into work. Much is learned in school that has nothing to do with the formal content of lessons. By the nature of the discipline and regimentation they involve, schools inculcate what Illich called 'passive consumption' – an uncritical acceptance of the existing social order. The hidden curriculum teaches young people that their role in life is 'to know their place and to sit still in it' (Illich 1971: 74).

Illich advocated the *deschooling of society*. Since schools do not promote equality or the development of individual creativity, why not do away with them altogether? Illich did not mean that all forms of educational organization should be abolished, but that everyone who wants to learn should be provided with access to available resources at any time in their lives and not just during childhood. Such a system should make it possible for knowledge to be widely diffused and shared rather than confined to specialists. Learners should not have to submit to a standard curriculum but should have personal choice over what they study.

What all this means in practical terms is not wholly clear. In place of schools, however, Illich suggested several types of educational framework. Material resources for formal learning would be stored in libraries, rental agencies, laboratories and information storage banks, accessible to any student. 'Communications networks' would be set up, providing data about the skills possessed by different individuals and whether they would be willing to train others or engage in mutual learning activities. And students would be provided with vouchers, allowing them to use educational services as and when they wished.

Are these proposals unrealistic? Many think so. Yet if, as looks possible, paid work is substantially reduced or restructured in the future and courses can be delivered remotely over the Internet, perhaps without charge, they may appear more realistic and perhaps even attractive. Education would not just be a form of early training in special institutions but would become available to whoever wished to take advantage of it. Illich's 1970s ideas became interesting again with the rise of digital technology and ideas of learning throughout the life course. We will return to these recent developments towards the end of this chapter.

John Taylor Gatto (2002), a retired schoolteacher with thirty years' experience, reached a similar conclusion, arguing that the hidden curriculum in the USA teaches seven basic lessons. This curriculum involves a fairly random mix of information on a variety of subjects, which produces *confusion* rather than genuine knowledge and understanding. Schools teach children to accept the status quo, to know their place within the *class hierarchy* and to defer to their betters. The rule of the class bell at the start and end of lessons teaches *indifference*; no lesson is ever so important that it can carry on after the bell sounds. Students are taught to be both *emotionally dependent* and *intellectually dependent* on authority figures, namely teachers who tell them what to think and how to feel. They also learn that their own *self-esteem is provisional*, reliant on the opinion that officials have of them, and that opinion is based on a battery of tests, report cards and grades. The final lesson is that being under *constant surveillance* is normal, as evidenced by the culture of homework, which effectively transfers school discipline into the home environment. Gatto concluded that the compulsory state school system in the USA (and, by implication, everywhere else) delivers 'compulsory subordination for all' and is 'structurally unreformable'. Instead, he argued for home education where children can take control of their own learning, using parents and other adults as 'facilitators' rather than as teachers.

Education and cultural reproduction

As many sociological studies have shown, education and inequality are closely related. This section reviews the ways in which sociological theorists have attempted to account for social inequalities within education systems. Basil Bernstein's classic study emphasizes the significance of language (see 'Classic studies 19.1'), Paul Willis looks at the effects of cultural values in shaping attitudes to education and work, while Pierre Bourdieu examines the relationship between the cultures of school and home life. What all of these key studies are concerned with is cultural reproduction – the generational transmission of cultural values, norms and experience and the mechanisms and processes through which this is achieved.

Learning to labour – by failing in school?

Paul Willis's (1977) research in a school in Birmingham, UK, is now forty years old, but it remains a classic study of investigative sociology. The research problem Willis set himself was how cultural reproduction actually occurs – or, as he succinctly put it, 'how working-class kids get working-class jobs'. It is often thought that, during the process of schooling, many young people from working-class or ethnic minority backgrounds come to recognize that they are just not clever enough to get highly paid or high-status jobs in the future. This experience of academic failure teaches them to acknowledge their individual intellectual limitations, and, having accepted this 'inferiority', they move into jobs with limited prospects.

Willis pointed out that this interpretation does not conform at all to the reality of people's lives and experiences. The 'street wisdom' of those from poor neighbourhoods may be irrelevant to academic success, but it does

involve a set of abilities just as subtle, skilful and complex as any intellectual skills taught in school. Few, if any, young people leave school thinking, 'I'm so stupid it's fair and proper for me to be stacking boxes in a factory all day.' So, if children from less privileged backgrounds accept manual jobs without feeling themselves to be failures, other factors must be involved.

Willis looked at a particular group of boys in the Birmingham school, spending a lot of time with them. Members of the gang, who called themselves 'the lads', were white, though the school also contained many young people from West Indian and Asian backgrounds. Willis found that the lads had an acute and perceptive understanding of the school's authority system but used this knowledge to fight it instead of to work with it. They saw the school as an alien environment but one they could manipulate to their own ends. They derived positive pleasure from the constant conflict and minor skirmishes they carried on with teachers and were adept at seeing the weak points of the teachers' claims to authority, as well as where they were vulnerable as individuals.

In classrooms, for instance, young people were expected to sit still, be quiet and get on with their work. But the lads were forever on the move, except when the teacher's stare might freeze one of them momentarily; they would gossip surreptitiously or pass open remarks that were on the verge of direct insubordination but could be explained away if challenged. The lads recognized that future work would be much like school, but they actively looked forward to it. They expected no direct satisfaction from work but were impatient for wages. Far from taking the jobs they did – in tyre-fitting, carpet-laying, plumbing or decorating – from feelings of inferiority, they held an attitude of dismissive superiority towards work, just as they had towards school. They enjoyed the adult status that came from working but were not interested in 'making a career'. As Willis points out, work in blue-collar settings often involves similar cultural features to those the lads actually created in their counter-school culture – banter, quick

Classic Studies 19.1 | Basil Bernstein on social class and language use

The research problem

It is a well-established finding that working-class children tend not to do as well in school as their middle-class peers. But this is a deceptive statement which demands a more detailed answer. Why do working-class children not do so well? Are they, on average, less intelligent? Are they lacking the motivation to do well at school? Do they not get enough support from their parents? Alternatively, is there something about schools that prevents working-class children from doing well?

Bernstein's explanation

The British sociologist Basil Bernstein (1924–2000) was interested in the connection between class inequality and education. Drawing on conflict theory, Bernstein (1975) examined the problem through an analysis of children's linguistic skills. He found that, during their early lives, children from varying backgrounds develop different *language codes*, or forms of speech, which affect their subsequent school experience. But he was not concerned with differences in vocabulary or verbal skills; rather, his interest was in systematic differences in ways of *using* language.

The speech of working-class children, Bernstein argued, represents a *restricted code* – a way of using language containing many unstated assumptions that speakers expect others to know. A restricted code is a type of speech tied to its cultural setting. Many working-class people live in strong familial or neighbourhood cultures in which values and norms are taken for granted and not explicitly expressed, and parents tend to socialize children directly by the use of rewards or reprimands to correct their behaviour. Language in a restricted code is more suitable for communication about practical experience than for discussion of abstract ideas, processes or relationships. Restricted-code speech is thus oriented to the norms of the group, without anyone being able to explain why they follow the patterns of behaviour they do.

By contrast, the language development of middle-class children involves the acquisition of an *elaborated code* – a style of speaking in which the meanings of words can be individualized to suit the demands of particular situations. The ways in which children from middle-class backgrounds learn to use language are less bound to particular contexts and the child is able more easily to generalize and express abstract ideas. Thus middle-class parents, when controlling their children, frequently explain the reasons and principles that underlie their reactions to the child's behaviour. While a working-class parent might tell a child off for wanting to eat too many sweets simply by saying 'No more sweets for you!', a middle-class parent is more likely to explain that eating too many sweets is bad for their health and teeth.

Children who have acquired elaborated codes of speech are more able to deal with the demands of academic education systems than those with restricted codes. This does not imply that working-class children have an 'inferior' type of speech or that their codes of language are 'deprived'. Rather, the way in which they use speech clashes with the academic culture of schools, and those who have mastered elaborated codes fit more easily into the school environment.

Joan Tough (1976) found that working-class children had less experience of having their questions answered at home and were less able to ask questions in classroom situations, while a study by Barbara Tizard and Martin Hughes (1984) came to similar conclusions. It is generally accepted that Bernstein's thesis has been a productive one (Morais et al. 2001). His ideas help us to understand why those from certain socio-economic backgrounds underachieve in school. Working-class children find the classroom situation difficult to cope with, especially when middle-class children appear so comfortable with it. The majority of teachers are from middle-class backgrounds and their language use makes the elaborated code appear normal and the restricted code inferior. The child may attempt to cope with this by translating the teacher's language into something she or he is familiar with – but may then fail to grasp the principles the teacher intends to convey. And, while working-class children experience little difficulty with rote or 'drill' learning, they may have major difficulties grasping conceptual distinctions involving generalization and abstraction.

Critical points

Some critics of Bernstein's thesis argue that it is one of several 'deficit hypothesis' theories which see working-class culture as lacking something essential (Boocock 1980; Bennett and LeCompte 1990). In this case the deficit is an elaborated language code which enables middle-class children to express themselves more fully. For these critics, Bernstein takes the middle-class code to be superior, and the theory is therefore an elitist one. It is not just that those of working-class backgrounds *perceive* the higher social classes as somehow their betters – as in many theories of ideological dominance; in Bernstein's theory, the elaborate code is *objectively* superior to the restricted code. Critics have also claimed that the theory of language codes is not supported by enough empirical research to be accepted as it does not tell us enough about the reality of life inside schools.

Contemporary significance

Bernstein's theory of language codes has been enormously influential in the sociology of education and many studies have been conducted which draw heavily on his methods (Jenkins 1990). More recent studies have taken his ideas into new areas such as gender and pedagogy, and his reputation as an educational theorist has spread internationally (Sadovnik 1995; Arnot 2001). Bernstein's work successfully linked language and speech with education systems and wider power relations in society as a whole. Rejecting the charge of elitism, he said that his thesis 'draws attention to the relations between macro power relations and micro practices of transmission, acquisition and evaluation and the positioning and oppositioning to which these practices give rise' (Bernstein 1990: 118–19). Understanding these relations better, he hoped to find ways of preventing the wastage of working-class children's abilities.

wit and the skill to subvert the demands of authority figures.

In this way, Willis shows that the lads' subculture, created in an active process of engagement with school norms and disciplinary mechanisms, mirrors the shop-floor culture of the work they expect to move into. Only later in life might they come to see themselves as trapped in arduous, unrewarding labour. By the time they have families, they may look back on education retrospectively, and see it – hopelessly – as having been the only escape route. Yet, if they try to pass this assessment on to their children, they are likely to have no more success than their own parents did. Willis's study succeeds in demonstrating the process of cultural reproduction and the way inequalities are linked to education systems. Willis's study shows that educational research can be both empirically oriented and, at the same time, theoretically informed. However, its focus is explicitly on the educational experiences of white, working-class boys, and it is not possible to generalize from this to the experiences of other social classes, girls or minority ethnic groups.

Reproducing gender divisions

Until the 1970s, the issue of gender was not central to the sociology of education and research on the experience of girls was limited (Gilligan 1982; Griffin 1985). This situation was not uncommon, as most other sociological subjects lacked a female perspective. Sociologists working from a feminist theoretical perspective explored the socialization of girls into feminine norms during their school careers, and a series of studies established that schools systematically disadvantaged girls from across social classes.

Angela McRobbie (1991) and Sue Lees (1993) argued that schooling in the UK helped to reproduce 'appropriate' feminine norms

Paradoxically, the apparently rebellious anti-school counter-cultures serve to produce the right kind of attitudes to work which routine, lower-paid jobs demand.

among girls. Schools saw their task as preparing girls for family life and responsibilities and boys for future employment, thus reinforcing traditional gender stereotypes within the wider society (Deem 1980). Michelle Stanworth (1983) studied the classroom experiences of a mixed group of children in a comprehensive school and discovered that, although comprehensives were intended to provide equal opportunities, girls tended to receive less attention from teachers than did boys. She concluded that this differential teaching pattern undermined the girls' confidence in their own abilities and contributed to their underachievement. This was a self-fulfilling prophecy, in which teachers' initial expectations (boys will do better than girls) shape their behaviour towards the pupils, which then brings about the outcome they (perhaps wrongly) assumed at the start.

The culture of schools has been found to be permeated with a general heterosexual sexism, particularly in the playground, corridors and other spaces outside the classroom (Wood 1984). As Willis (1977) found, boys routinely use sexist language and refer to girls using derogatory terms. This creates an atmosphere of aggressive masculinity that degrades girls and women while corralling boys' acceptable identities into a very narrow, masculine range. One consequence is that homosexuality is made invisible, and gay and lesbian young people find that the school environment does not allow them openly to express their emerging identities. If they do, they run the risk of teasing, harassment and even physical assault (Burbridge and Walters 1981; see chapter 15, 'Gender and Sexuality', for a wider discussion of sexuality).

Feminist scholars also investigated the *content* of the school curriculum. The

19.1 Learning *not* to labour

Some twenty years after Willis studied 'the lads' in Birmingham, Máirtín Mac an Ghaill (1994) investigated the experiences of young working-class men at the Parnell School, also in the West Midlands. He was interested in how male students develop specific forms of masculinity in school as part of their passage into manhood. Unlike Willis's lads, the boys at the Parnell School were growing up with high unemployment, the collapse of the manufacturing base in the region, and cutbacks in government benefits for young people.

Mac an Ghaill found that the transition to adulthood was more fragmented than that experienced by Willis's lads in the 1970s. There was no longer a clear trajectory from school into waged labour. Many of the boys saw the post-school years as characterized by dependency (on family in particular), 'useless' government training schemes, and an insecure labour market unfavourable to young manual workers. There was widespread confusion as to how education was relevant to their futures, which manifested itself in very different responses. While some of the male peer groups tried to chart upwardly mobile paths for themselves as academic achievers or 'new enterprisers', others were openly hostile to schooling altogether.

Of the four school peer groups Mac an Ghaill identified, the 'macho lads' were the most traditionally working class. The macho lads had coalesced as a group by the time they became teenagers, and members were in the bottom two academic 'sets' for all subjects. Their attitudes towards education were openly hostile, and they shared a view that school was part of an authoritarian system that placed meaningless study demands on captive students. Where Willis's 'lads' had found ways to manipulate the school environment to their advantage, the macho lads were defiant about their role within it.

The macho lads were seen by the school administration as the most dangerous anti-school peer group at Parnell School.

Teachers were encouraged to deal with them using overtly authoritarian means, and the lads' symbolic displays of working-class masculinity – such as certain clothing, hairstyles and earrings – were banned. Teachers were involved in the 'surveillance' of students, constantly monitoring them in hallways, instructing them to 'look at me when I'm talking to you' and telling them to 'walk properly down the corridor'.

Secondary school for the macho lads was an 'apprenticeship' in learning to be tough. School was not about the 3 Rs (reading, writing and arithmetic), but about the 3 Fs (fighting, fucking and football). 'Looking after your mates' and 'sticking together' were key values, and school became a contested territory, just like the streets. The macho lads regarded teachers in the same way as law enforcement – with open disdain – believing they were the main source of conflict within the school. They refused to accept teachers' authority and were convinced they were constantly being 'set up' to be punished, disciplined or humiliated.

Like Willis's 'lads', the macho lads associated academic work and achievement with being inferior and effeminate. Students who excelled were labelled 'dickhead achievers' and schoolwork was rejected out of hand as inappropriate for real men. As one macho lad, Leon, commented: 'The work you do here is girls' work. It's not real work. It's just for kids. They [the teachers] try to make you write down things about how you feel. It's none of their fucking business' (Mac an Ghaill 1994: 59).

Mac an Ghaill's study shows how the 'macho lads' were undergoing a particular 'crisis of masculinity'. This is because they were actively developing an 'outdated' working-class masculinity centred on manual waged labour at a time when a secure future in manual labour had all but disappeared. They continued to fantasize about a 'full-employment' society which their fathers and uncles had inhabited, so, despite some of their actions appearing hypermasculine and defensive, in fact they were grounded in a working-class worldview they had inherited from previous generations.

 The changing forms of masculinity are discussed in chapter 15, 'Gender and Sexuality'.

THINKING CRITICALLY

Both Willis and Mac an Ghaill's studies focused on working-class 'lads', but have you witnessed girls' subcultures in schools? How might the processes of exclusion and gang formation found among girls and young women differ from those of boys and young men ?

Australian sociologist Dale Spender (1982) reported that many subjects were thoroughly imbued with an unwitting sexism, which made them unattractive to girls. Science texts, for example, routinely ignored the achievements of female scientists, making them invisible to students. In this way, science offers girls no positive role models and fails to engage them with the subject. Sue Sharpe (1994) saw schools steering girls' choices towards more 'feminine' subjects such as health studies and the arts and away from the more 'masculine' ones such as mathematics and ICT (information communication technologies).

Nonetheless, as we will see later, over recent years there has been a significant change in this traditional pattern of disadvantage and exclusion, one of the most striking being the way that girls and young women now outperform boys and young men in almost every subject area and at every level of education. This shift has led to new debates on the problems boys face amid an apparent 'crisis of masculinity' (Connell 2005).

Education, cultural capital and the formation of 'habitus'

The most systematic general theory of cultural reproduction to date is, arguably, that of the French sociologist Pierre Bourdieu (1930–2002). Bourdieu (1986, 1988; Bourdieu and Passeron 1977) devised a broad theory of cultural reproduction which connects economic position, social status and symbolic capital with cultural knowledge and skills.

Education is a central element of this perspective, but it is necessary to outline Bourdieu's theory of forms of capital in order to grasp its significance for educational sociology.

The central concept in Bourdieu's theory is *capital*, which he takes from Marx's ideas on capitalism. Marx saw ownership of the means of production as the crucial division in society, conferring many advantages on capitalists, who are able to subordinate workers. But, for Bourdieu, this economic capital is just one of several forms of capital which individuals and social groups can use to gain advantages. Bourdieu identifies social capital, cultural capital and symbolic capital in addition to economic capital. Social capital refers to membership of and involvement in elite social networks or moving within social groups which are well connected and influential. Cultural capital is that gained within the family environment and through education, leading to increased knowledge and skills, along with qualifications such as degrees and other credentials. Symbolic capital refers to the prestige, status and other forms of social honour which enable those with high status to dominate those with lower status.

The important aspect of this scheme is that forms of capital can be exchanged. For example, those with high *cultural capital* may be able to trade it for *economic capital*. During interviews for well-paid jobs, their superior knowledge and credentials, gained mainly during schooling, can give them an advantage over other applicants. Similarly, those with high *social capital* may 'know the right people' or 'move in the right social circles' and be able effectively to exchange this *social capital* for *symbolic capital* – respect from others and increased social status – which increases their power chances in dealings with other people.

Bourdieu's second concept is that of the field – various social sites or arenas where competitive struggles take place. It is through fields that social life is organized and power relationships operate, with each field having its own 'rules of the game' that may not be transferred to other fields. For example, in art and aesthetics, cultural capital is most highly prized, and those who are able to converse knowledgeably about the history of art or music become powerful within the field – hence the power of critics in literature or cinema to make or break a book or film with their reviews. But these criteria do not apply in the field of production, where economic capital holds sway.

Finally, Bourdieu uses the concept of habitus, which can be described as the learned dispositions, such as bodily comportment, ways of speaking or ways of thinking and acting, that are adopted by people in relation to the social conditions in which they exist. Examples of aspects of habitus would be Bernstein's language codes and Mac an Ghaill's macho boys' displays of working-class masculinity. The concept of habitus is important, as it allows us to analyse the links between social structures and individual actions and personalities.

But what has all of this to do with education? Bourdieu's (1986) concept of cultural capital is at the heart of the matter, and he identifies three forms in which it can exist. Cultural capital can exist in an *embodied state* – that is, we carry it around with us in our ways of thinking, speaking and bodily movement. It can also exist in an *objectified state* – for example, in the material possession of works of art, books or clothes. Finally, cultural capital is found in *institutionalized forms*, such as those held in educational qualifications, which are nationally accepted and easily translated into economic capital in the labour market. It is easy to see how the embodied and institutionalized forms are acquired through education,

forming resources to be used in the specific fields of social life. In this way, education can be a rich source of cultural capital which potentially benefits many people.

However, as Bernstein, Willis and Mac an Ghaill all saw, the education system itself is *not* just a neutral field divorced from the wider society. Rather, the culture and standards within the education system reflect that society, and, in doing so, schools systematically advantage those who have already acquired cultural capital in the family and through the social networks in which they are embedded (a crucial form of social capital). Middle-class children fit into the culture of schools with ease; they speak correctly, they have the right manners and they do better when it comes to exams. But, because the education system is portrayed and widely perceived as being open to all on the basis of talent, many working-class children come to see themselves as intellectually inferior and accept that they, rather than the system itself, are to blame for their failure. In this way, the education system plays a key role in the cultural reproduction of social inequalities.

Acquiring cultural capital

In an ethnographic study of twelve diverse families in the USA, Annette Lareau (2003) used Bourdieu's ideas, particularly the concept of cultural capital, to conduct an 'intensive "naturalistic" observation' of parenting styles across social classes. In the working-class and poorer families, parents did not try to reason with children but simply told them what to do and what not to do. Children were also expected to find their own forms of recreation and not to rely on parents to create it for them. Working-class children did not talk back and accepted that the family's financial situation imposed limits on their own aspirations. Working-class parents perceived a clear difference between adults and children and did not see a need to engage with their children's feelings and opinions, preferring to facilitate a 'natural growth'. This parenting style, says Lareau, is 'out of synch' with the current standards of social institutions. But working-class parents and children still come into contact with social institutions such as schools, and children therefore begin to develop a growing sense of 'distance, distrust and constraint'.

On the other hand, middle-class children in the study were talkative, good at conversation and adept at social mores such as shaking hands and making eye contact when talking. They were also very good at getting other family members, especially parents, to serve their needs and were comfortable with adults and authority figures. Lareau argues that middle-class parents are constantly interested and involved in their children's feelings and opinions and jointly organize their leisure activities, rather than leaving them to make their own. Continual discussion between parents and children marks out the middle-class parenting style, which is based on a *concerted cultivation of the child*. The result is that the middle-class children had a clear sense of personal entitlement rather than feeling distant and constrained. Lareau's study shows us some of the practical ways in which cultural capital is passed on across generations and how styles of parenting are strongly linked to social class.

Lareau notes that both parenting methods have their advantages, but some of the middle-class families she studied were exhausted by constant efforts to fulfil their children's demands, while the children were more anxious and stressed than the working-class children, whose family ties were closer and who experienced much less sibling rivalry. Lareau's conclusion is that parenting methods tend to vary much more by social class than by ethnicity and that, as we have seen, the middle-class children in the study were much better prepared for success at school than those children from working-class families.

Summary

Bourdieu's theory has stimulated much sociological research into education, inequality and processes of cultural reproduction. However, it has its critics. One issue is that it appears almost impossible for the working classes to succeed in a middle-class education system, but, of course, a fair number actually do so. In an age of mass higher education, many more working-class people are entering universities and acquiring the kinds of institutionalized cultural capital that enables them to compete with the middle classes. Also, we should not mistake the resigned acceptance of their situation by working-class children with a positive legitimation of schools and their outcomes. After all, there is ample evidence of resistance and rebellion among working-class pupils through truancy, bad behaviour in classrooms and the formation of school gangs, which generate alternative standards of success. Nevertheless, Bourdieu's theoretical framework remains the most systematic synthesis yet produced for understanding the role of schooling in the reproduction of social inequality.

> Bourdieu's view on class and social capital are discussed in more detail in chapter 12, 'Stratification and Social Class'.

Evaluation

The sociological theories explored in this chapter illustrate two important aspects of education. On the one hand, a good quality education is something that can change people's lives for the better, and, in many parts of the world, children like Malala and her friends are desperate for schooling as the route to a better life. Education is highly sought after and has often had to be fought for against opposition. Yet sociological research consistently finds that education systems not only create new opportunities but are also experienced differently by a range of social groups. Education systems are part of the societies within which they are embedded, and, when society is riven with inequalities, schools help reproduce them, even against the best intentions of the people who work within them. As the works of Bernstein, Willis and Bourdieu (among others) demonstrate, cultural reproduction in unequal societies leads to recurring patterns of educational inequality. The next section looks at such

19.2 The British public schools

The public schools in Britain are an oddity in more ways than one. They are not 'public' at all, but private, fee-paying institutions. The degree of independence they have from the rest of the education system and the key role they play in the society at large marks them out from schools in other countries. There are some private schools, often linked to religions, in Western societies, but nowhere are private schools as exclusive or important as in the UK.

The public schools are nominally subject to state supervision, but, in reality, few major pieces of educational legislation have affected them. They were left untouched by the 1944 Act, as they were by the setting up of the comprehensive schools, and until quite recently the large majority were still single-sex institutions. There are about 2,300 fee-paying schools in England, educating some 6 per cent of the population. They include a diversity of different organizations, from prestigious establishments such as Eton, Rugby or Charterhouse, through to so-called minor public schools whose names would be unknown to most people.

The term 'public school' is limited by some educationalists to a group of the major fee-paying schools. Among these are those that are members of the Headmasters' Conference (HMC), originally formed in 1871. Initially there were just fifty schools in the conference but the number has expanded to more than 240 today. Individuals who have attended HMC schools still tend to dominate the higher positions in British society. A study by the Social Mobility and Child Poverty Commission (2014: 10) found that those who attended fee-paying schools made up 71 per cent of senior judges, 62 per cent of senior armed forces officers, 55 per cent of the most senior civil servants, 50

Eton College boys in their very traditional school uniform

per cent of the House of Lords, 36 per cent of the cabinet and 53 per cent of senior diplomats. The Conservative prime minister at the time, David Cameron, went to Eton College, and his deputy in 2014, Nick Clegg, studied at Westminster School: both schools are members of HMC. The commission noted that the survey had found 'elitism so stark that it could be called "Social Engineering"'.

THINKING CRITICALLY

Drawing on Bourdieu's theory, what kinds of cultural capital do the British public schools transmit to their students? Could the state sector ever perform the same function for the mass of pupils in the British education system?

patterns and how far they have changed in recent times.

Social divisions and education

Much of our discussion of education and inequality so far has focused on social class and education. The reason for this is quite simply that a large number of empirical studies over a very long period have consistently reported a clear connection between social class and educational attainment, and sociologists have looked for theories which explain this. In very blunt terms, probably the best established finding in the sociology of education is that children at the lower end of the socio-economic scale do less well in school and get fewer qualifications than those at the upper end, at all levels of the education system.

Fairly typical of this body of work is a UK study which used a measure of socio-economic position constructed from parental income, social class, housing tenure and self-reported financial difficulties, in order to examine differential educational achievement up to the age of sixteen. The study found that class-based differences in cognitive ability were already large in infants of just three years old and had widened significantly at the age of five (Goodman and Gregg 2010: 5–6). The gap continued to widen through the primary school years (figure 19.1). By the time children reached secondary school, the achievement gap seems to have become embedded, with the result that only 21 per cent of the poorest fifth (or quintile) of children gained five A to C grades at age sixteen compared with 75 per cent of the top fifth (figure 19.2). This represents a gap between the highest and lowest socio-economic classes of an enormous 54 percentage points.

The authors note that children from poorer backgrounds experience worse health and well-being, less advantageous home 'learning environments', fewer parent–child interactions, such as reading together, and less

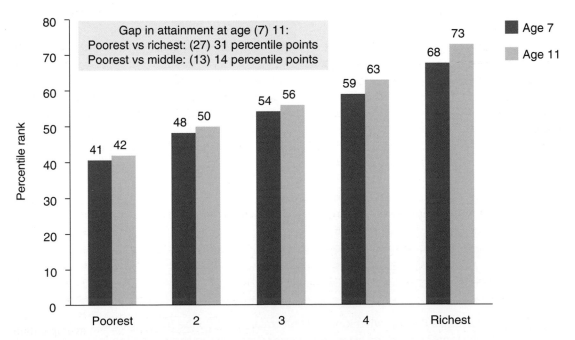

Figure 19.1 Average test score rank, by socio-economic position quintile at age seven and eleven

Source: Gregg and Washbrook (2010: 27).

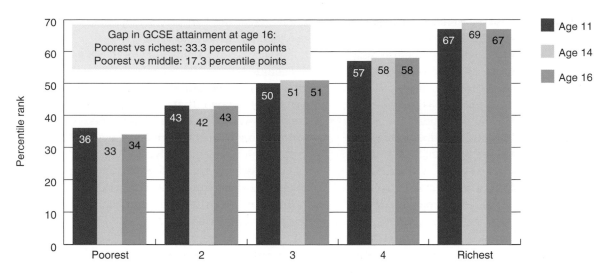

Figure 19.2 Key Stage test scores at ages eleven, fourteen and sixteen by socio-economic quintile

Source: Chowdry et al. (2010: 35).

'mother–child closeness' than those from better-off backgrounds. They also point to differing attitudes towards the value of education and divergent educational aspirations. In short, like many others, this study finds that social class position at birth has wide-ranging consequences for children's educational opportunities and life chances. In Bourdieu's terms, findings such as these illustrate how the intergenerational transmission of cultural (and economic) capital continues to structure educational attainment in the twenty-first century.

However, social class is not the only form of inequality which affects educational achievement. The rest of this section looks at the longstanding and highly contentious debate on IQ and human intelligence, before moving on to look at other educational inequalities involving gender and ethnicity. This will help us to see how education systems are changing as societies themselves undergo significant restructuring.

The IQ debate

For many years, psychologists have debated whether there exists a single human ability which can be called *intelligence* and, if so, how far it rests on innate differences. Intelligence is difficult to define because it covers many different, often unrelated, qualities. We might suppose that the 'purest' form of intelligence is the ability to solve abstract mathematical puzzles. Yet people who are very good at these sometimes have low ability in other areas, such as grasping the narrative of history or understanding works of art. Since the concept has proved resistant to a generally accepted definition, it may be supposed that intelligence can simply be regarded as 'what IQ tests measure' (IQ means 'intelligence quotient').

'The bell curve'

Scores on IQ tests do correlate well with academic performance, which is not surprising, since the tests were originally developed to predict success in school. They also correlate closely with social, economic and ethnic differences, since these are associated with variations in levels of educational attainment. White students score better, on average, than black students or members of other disadvantaged minorities, and this has led some to suggest that IQ differences are, in part, due to genetic variation (Jensen 1969, 1979).

Pinning down the reasons for educational underachievement must take into account the influence of education systems themselves, as these are not neutral sites where those with the highest intelligence simply do best.

Herrnstein and Murray (1994) reopened the debate about IQ and education in a controversial way. They argued that intelligence within the population is 'normally distributed' in the shape of a bell curve, and differences in average IQ between racial and ethnic groups can be explained by reference to *both* environmental and hereditary factors. Asian Americans, for example, particularly Japanese and Chinese Americans, tend to have a higher IQ than whites, though the difference is not large. The average IQ of Asians and whites, however, is substantially higher than that of blacks. The authors claim that such hereditary racial differences contribute to social divisions in society. Those at the top are there partly because they are more intelligent than the rest of the population and those at the bottom are there because, on average, they are not so intelligent. Critics disagree that IQ differences between racial and ethnic groups have a genetic component, arguing that they are the result of social and cultural influences.

Social psychological studies have found that the 'stereotype threat' – the fear of confirming a negative social stereotype as a self-characteristic – can impair people's performance in intelligence tests (Steele and Aronson 1995; Steele 1997). Steele and Aronson tested white and African-American students, with half of each ethnic group being told that their intelligence was being measured. The white students' performance was not noticeably affected, but African-American students who thought their IQ was being tested performed well below their previous level. Fear of confirming the stereotype that African Americans have a lower IQ than whites raised anxiety levels, producing poorer performance. Similar research into gender stereotyping and test performance has found physiological evidence of stress and anxiety such as changes in surface skin temperature and diastolic blood pressure (Osborne 2007). Social and cultural stereotypes can play a large part in people's performance in test situations.

Some scholars see the bell curve thesis as a dangerous form of 'racist pseudoscience' (Fraser 1995). The biologist Stephen Jay Gould (1941–2002) argued that Herrnstein and Murray are wrong on four major counts. A single IQ score cannot describe intelligence; people cannot be meaningfully ranked along a single intelligence scale; intelligence does not derive substantially from genetic inheritance; and 'intelligence' can be altered and improves with age. Gould concluded that:

> We must fight the doctrine of The Bell Curve both because it is wrong and because it will, if activated, cut off all possibility of proper nurturance for everyone's intelligence. Of course, we cannot all be rocket scientists or brain surgeons, but those who can't might be rock musicians or professional athletes (and gain far more social prestige and salary thereby). (Quoted in Fraser 1995: 22)

The 'new IQism'

According to Gillborn and Youdell (2001), measuring IQ is rarely used today, but educationalists use the term 'ability' in a very similar way. The authors carried out surveys in two London schools over two years in the mid-1990s, interviewing and observing teachers and pupils in their third and final years at secondary school. Both schools were aiming to get as high a proportion of pupils as possible to obtain five or more A to C grades at GCSE level. This was the government benchmark and a key criterion on which schools were rated in official league tables. Although this was a legitimate aim, Gillborn and Youdell saw that it put teachers under pressure to spend more time on those pupils they thought were able to achieve the requisite grades. The effect was that staff time and effort was rationed according to each student's perceived ability. From their interviews and observations, Gillborn and Youdell found that 'ability' was viewed by teachers as fixed, which determined the potential of pupils. One headteacher remarked, 'You can't give someone ability can you? You can't achieve more than you're capable of, can you?'

Teachers often believed that ability could be measured objectively. At one school, pupils were given a 'cognitive ability' test when they arrived, which teachers took as a good indication of future GCSE performance. Not surprisingly, pupils with the highest 'ability' tended to be white and middle class. The authors also noted many occasions when black pupils received differential, negative treatment in class. Hence, beliefs about which pupils had ability constituted an unwitting discrimination against black and working-class children.

The main consequence of the 'new IQism' was that fewer black and working-class pupils gained five GCSEs above grade C, thus reinforcing the teachers' belief in 'fixed ability'. In one school, 16 per cent of black pupils attained five or more GCSEs above C level, compared with 35 per cent of white pupils. These results are typical of the UK national pattern, which sees black and working-class pupils doing worse academically than the average. Gillborn and Youdell's conclusion is that, though most educationalists oppose ideas of hereditary racial differences in intelligence, the British education system has come to adopt the kind of assumptions proposed by Herrnstein and Murray, albeit under the guise of a focus on 'ability' rather than 'intelligence'

> **THINKING CRITICALLY**
>
> Critics of IQ tests say that they do not really measure 'intelligence'. If this is true, what do they measure and why do they get such diverse results? Are IQ tests inherently racist or should governments fund them in the future?

Emotional intelligence

Since the 1990s, there have been many popular books and psychological studies that have sought to add emotional awareness and competence into our understanding of what 'intelligence' means. The idea was popularized by Daniel Goleman's (1996) best-selling book *Emotional Intelligence*. Goleman argued that emotional intelligence can be as important as IQ in determining people's life chances. Emotional intelligence (EI) is seen as the ability to recognize emotions both in ourselves and others, to evaluate them when they arise and to be able to manage them. Unlike IQ, though, EI qualities are not perceived to be inherited and, the more that children can be taught EI, the better their chances of using the full range of intellectual capabilities. According to Goleman, 'The brightest among us can founder on shoals of unbridled passion and unruly impulses; people with high IQs can be stunningly poor pilots of their private lives' (1996: 34).

Theories of emotional intelligence have become popular among educationalists through the related concept of 'emotional literacy', which, as the term implies, suggests that emotional competence can be taught as a way of giving pupils the emotional resources to cope with a range of social pressures. As the concept of 'intelligence' broadens to take in IQ, EI and interpersonal factors, schooling may become less narrowly focused and look to produce rounded individuals with a range of social and life skills. Yet the chances of success at school are heavily influenced by broad patterns of social inequality which are deeply rooted in the social structure of societies.

Gender and schooling

Education and the formal school curriculum in the developed societies have long been differentiated along gendered lines. For example, in late nineteenth-century Britain, girls were taught the skills to prepare them for domesticity, while boys took basic mathematics and were expected to gain the skills needed for work. Women's entry into higher education was similarly gradual, and they were not able to gain degree-level qualifications until 1878. Even so, the number of women studying for degrees remained very low – a situation that began to change significantly only in the 1960s and 1970s. This state of affairs has been utterly transformed in the present period of mass higher education.

Today, the secondary school curriculum no longer distinguishes explicitly between boys

19.3 Teaching emotional literacy?

Behaviour lessons for teenagers

Secondary schools are to teach lessons in 'emotional intelligence' in an attempt to improve classroom behaviour. . . . the 'social and emotional aspects of learning' (Seal) project will be available to secondary schools in England. It teaches skills such as resolving conflicts, managing anger, respecting others and playing fairly.

The Department for Education and Skills says pilot schemes have had very positive results in primary schools. A DFES spokesperson said that support would be available for secondary schools wanting to use this approach to improving how children behave.

Confrontation

Teachers' union conferences at Easter heard a series of warnings about the levels of violence and abuse faced by teachers from badly behaved pupils. And this 'Seal' project is designed to teach pupils about the need to show respect to others and to give them the skills to avoid aggression and confrontation.

The DFES says that primary schools have reported a decrease in problems such as bullying and fighting where the emotional intelligence lessons have been taught. The type of subject areas covered would include developing empathy – such as showing how someone else might feel or another point of view – managing strong feelings such as anger and recognising the rights of others.

Among the primary schools to have taken part in a pilot was Vicarage Park in Kendal, Cumbria – with the head teacher Anne Hallam saying that the scheme had a 'significant impact' on helping boys to articulate their emotions. And more contented pupils are more likely 'to be able to focus on their learning', she says.

Pelham Primary School in Wimbledon also introduced the emotional intelligence lessons and reported that it helped to defuse the everyday arguments that could otherwise escalate. 'What we're doing in class seems to spill out into the playground. Problems continue to happen, but now the kids are more articulate and better at seeing things from the other person's point of view', said teacher Justine Green.
Source: BBC (2007a).

> **THINKING CRITICALLY**
>
> Do you recognize *emotional intelligence* in yourself and friends? Is it feasible to suggest that our emotions can be brought completely under rational control?

and girls in any systematic way, apart from participation in sports. However, there are various other 'points of entry' for the development of gender differences in education. These include teacher expectations, school rituals and other aspects of the hidden curriculum. Although rules are gradually loosening, regulations which compel girls to wear dresses or skirts in school are one of the more obvious ways in which gender-typing occurs. The consequences go beyond mere appearance. As a result of the clothes they wear, girls lack the freedom to sit casually, join in rough-and-tumble games or to run as fast as they are able.

School textbooks also perpetuate gendered images. Until very recently, it was common for storybooks in primary schools to portray boys as showing initiative and independence, while girls, if they appeared at all, were far more passive. Stories written especially for girls often have an element of adventure in them, but this usually takes the form of intrigues or mysteries in domestic or school settings. Boys' adventure stories are more wide-ranging, have heroes who travel to distant places or who are sturdily independent in other ways. At the secondary level, females have tended to be 'invisible' in most science and maths textbooks, suggesting that these are really 'male subjects'.

Gender differences in education are also clear when considering subject choice in schools. The view that some subjects are more

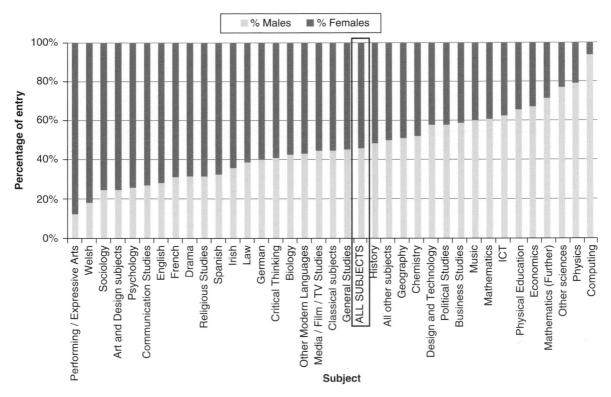

Figure 19.3   Gender differences in student A-level choice, selected subjects, 2013

Source: Joint Council for Qualifications (2013).

suited to boys or to girls is very common. Becky Francis (2000) has argued that girls are more likely to be encouraged into less academically prestigious subjects than boys, and there is certainly a marked difference in the subjects they choose to pursue, especially at the higher levels. In 2013, over 90 per cent of students in the UK who entered for an A-level or equivalent examination (the standard university entry qualification) in computing were male, as were almost 80 per cent of those taking physics and science subjects (with the exception of biology). Conversely, an overwhelming majority of those choosing the expressive and performing arts, psychology, sociology and art and design were female (figure 19.3). Although over the past two decades the British government and business organizations have encouraged young women to take STEM subjects (science, technology, engineering and mathematics), the stark gender gap at A-level remains. A similarly gendered pattern can be found across the twenty-eight countries of the European Union, where engineering, science and computing graduates are predominantly male, while women form the majority in social sciences, health and welfare and the humanities (figure 19.4). Nonetheless, as we will see, the actual achievement of girls and women in education systems around the world has now surpassed that of boys at all levels.

Gender and achievement

Throughout the twentieth century, girls tended to outperform boys in terms of school results until they reached the middle years of secondary education. They then began to fall behind and, by the age of sixteen to eighteen as well as at university, boys did consistently better. For example, in the UK until the late 1980s, girls were less likely than boys to attain the three A-levels necessary for admission to university and were entering higher education in smaller numbers than boys. Concerned about such unequal

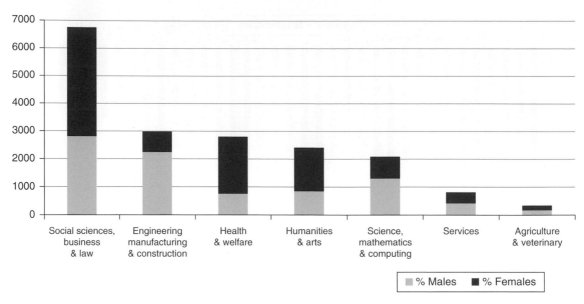

Figure 19.4 Students in tertiary education, by field of education and gender (EU-28), 2011

Source: Eurostat (2014).

outcomes, feminist researchers undertook a number of important studies into how gender influences the learning process. They found that school curricula were often male-dominated and that teachers were devoting more attention to boys than girls in the classroom.

Since the 1990s, the debate on gender in schools has undergone a dramatic and unexpected reversal. 'Underachieving boys' are now one of the main concerns of educators and policy-makers as girls began to outperform boys in all subject areas, including science and mathematics, and at all levels of education. Table 19.1 clearly shows this trend for pupils in England between the ages of five and fourteen (Key stages 1–3). Although boys' Key Stage results have improved in many subjects, so have those of girls, and only in Key Stage 2 mathematics has the gendered achievement gap been closed over the decade 1999–2009. Similar findings have been reported in America and many other developed countries. Young women in the USA are more likely than young men to go further in school, get a college education and to go on to a postgraduate degree.

The problem of 'failing boys', which Keddie and Mills (2007) termed 'the boy turn' in policy

discourses, is seen as linked to a host of social problems such as crime, unemployment, drug abuse and lone parenthood. In combination, these factors have produced what has been described as a 'crisis of masculinity' (discussed in chapter 15, 'Gender and Sexuality'). Boys who leave school early or with poor educational results are less likely to find good jobs and create stable families, because, in the post-industrial economies of the developed world, fewer unskilled manual jobs are available for young men without a solid education and qualifications. Meanwhile, a large proportion – up to 70 per cent – of jobs that are created in the rapidly growing service sector are filled by women. However, Mac an Ghaill (1996) points out that, although many more women are entering employment, the jobs they are moving into by no means always provide well-paid professional careers. In fact, women still make up the overwhelming majority of part-time workers, and the service-based work they do is often relatively poorly paid and low in status.

Explaining the gender gap

Why do boys now do less well than girls in education systems? No single theory is

Table 19.1 **Pupils reaching or exceeding expected standards in England, teacher assessment by key stage and sex, 1999 and 2009 (percentages)**

	1999		2009	
	Boys	Girls	Boys	Girls
Key Stage 1				
English				
Reading	78	86	81	89
Writing	75	85	75	87
Mathematics	84	88	88	91
Science	85	88	87	91
Key Stage 2				
English	62	74	75	84
Mathematics	69	70	80	80
Science	75	76	85	87
Key Stage 3				
English	55	73	71	84
Mathematics	63	66	79	80
Science	59	62	76	79

Source: ONS (2010a: 37).

Girls are outperforming boys at every level of education, and in most subjects.

generally accepted and several explanations have been advanced. One significant factor is the influence of women's movements on the self-esteem and expectations of girls and young women. Many girls presently in school have grown up surrounded by examples of women working outside the home. Exposure to these positive role models during socialization increases girls' awareness of their own opportunities and challenges traditional stereotypes of women as housewives. Teachers and educationalists have also become more aware of gender discrimination, and many schools have taken steps to avoid gender stereotyping in the classroom, encouraging girls to explore traditionally 'male' subjects and promoting educational materials that are free of gender bias.

Some theories centre on the difference in learning styles between boys and girls. Girls are often regarded as more effectively organized and motivated than boys and they mature earlier. One manifestation of this is that girls tend to relate to one another by talking and using their verbal skills – an aspect of emotional intelligence, perhaps. Boys, on the other hand, socialize in a more active manner through sport, computer games or just hanging out in the playground and streets, and tend to be more disruptive in the classroom. These broad patterns of behaviour may be reaffirmed by teachers in the classroom, who then hold lower expectations for boys than girls and indulge boys' disruption by paying more attention to them.

Other scholars question the enormous amount of attention and resources being directed at underachieving boys, which amounts to something of a moral panic which ignores the fact that, beyond school, 'maleness' continues to confer significant economic and cultural advantages on young men that are denied to women (Keddie and Mills 2007). The gender gap in language skills is actually longstanding and has been found the world over, but differences that used to be ascribed to boys' 'healthy idleness' are now provoking controversy and frantic attempts to improve their results. As national performance targets, league tables and international literacy comparisons proliferate, thus bringing differences out into the open, 'equal outcomes' in education have become a top priority.

All the attention given to boys, critics argue, serves to hide other forms of inequality within education. Although girls have forged ahead in many areas, they are still less likely than boys to choose subjects in school leading to careers in science, technology, engineering or mathematics. Boys pull ahead in science by about the age of eleven and continue to outperform girls through to university: in subjects such as chemistry and computer science they continue to dominate. So, though women may be entering higher education in greater numbers, they continue to be disadvantaged in the job market in comparison with men holding the same level of qualification (Epstein 1998).

It has also been argued that factors such as class and ethnicity actually produce the greatest inequalities within the education system. For example, UK comparisons in achievement by pupils across social classes reveal that 70 per cent of children from the top professional class receive five or more pass grades, compared with only 14 per cent from working-class backgrounds. Concentrating on 'failing boys' is therefore misleading, since men continue to dominate the positions of power in society. The underachievement of working-class boys may have less to do with their gender than with the disadvantages of their class position.

Gender and higher education

One significant aspect of the expansion in higher education is the increase in the number of female students. For example, since the 1970s, the UK has seen much faster growth rates for women entering further and higher education than for men (table 19.2). By 1990 there were more women than men in further education, and by 2005 the same was true of higher education. This is a reversal of the position in the 1970s, when there were far more male than female students. By 2007 there were seven times as many female students in further and higher education than in 1970, but only around two and a half times as many male students. However, the choice of subjects is

Table 19.2 **UK students in further and higher education, by type of course and sex, 1970–2008 (thousands)**

	Men				Women			
	1970/71	*1980/81*	*1990/91*	*2007/08*	*1970/71*	*1980/81*	*1990/91*	*2007/08*
Further education								
Full-time	116	154	219	520	95	196	261	534
Part-time	891	697	768	984	630	624	986	1,432
All further education	1,007	851	986	1,503	725	820	1,247	1,966
Higher education								
Undergraduate								
Full-time	241	277	345	574	173	196	319	717
Part-time	127	176	148	255	19	71	106	422
Postgraduate								
Full-time	33	41	50	124	10	21	34	125
Part-time	15	32	46	109	3	13	33	150
All higher education	416	526	588	1,063	205	301	491	1,414

Source: ONS (2010a: 32).

still marked by conventional gender expectations (see figure 19.3 for EU data).

The earlier pattern of subject choice in the developed countries saw women pursuing degrees in education and the health professions, which led into somewhat lower-paid careers than those following from computer science and engineering subjects, which were dominated by male students. Women have made some inroads into the latter subjects, though they remain male-dominated today. On the other hand, many degree subjects previously dominated by men, including the social sciences, history, life sciences and business management, have become predominantly 'female' subjects. What does *not* appear to be happening is a move by men into the university subjects that were previously considered 'female'.

Women are still heavily under-represented among the academic staff in colleges and universities, especially in senior positions. In 2010/11 for example, although women made up 44.5 per cent of academic staff in the UK (80,775), just 20 per cent of professors were female (3,790) and 38.6 percent were senior lecturers and researchers (HESA 2010). Similarly, some 72 per cent of senior managers and 80 per cent of university principals and vice-principals were men (Parr 2014). More female academics than their male colleagues also work part-time. In 2013, almost 55 per cent of all part-time academic staff were women (Equality Challenge Unit 2013: 34). Nonetheless, the longer-term trend is towards greater gender equality in higher education, and the number of female professors, though still relatively low, is at an all-time high. The number of female academics and professors is increasing, albeit not at a particularly rapid rate.

Given the unequal situation with regard to type of contract, seniority and the likelihood of high-level promotion, women in higher education are, on average, paid less than men. Even at the same professional position, the level of pay is unequal. The UK's Higher Education Statistics Agency reported that, in 2008, male professors were paid 13.9 per cent more than female professors.

What we may conclude from this brief survey is that girls and women have made significant headway within education systems over the three decades. But there remain significant inequalities once highly educated women move into the workforce, with men maintaining their traditionally better rates of pay and improved promotion prospects. Even within the institutions of twenty-first-century higher education, it seems that men have been able to maintain their longstanding domination of positions of seniority and high status.

> **THINKING CRITICALLY**
>
> List some reasons why the achievement of boys in the developed countries is now falling behind that of girls. What social consequences might there be for communities in the future and should we really be concerned? If we should, what can be done to change the situation?

Ethnicity and education

Sociologists have carried out a good deal of research into the educational trajectories of minority ethnic groups. Governments also monitor educational trends by social class, gender and ethnicity and sponsor their own investigations. For example, the 1985 Swann Report found significant differences in average levels of educational success between groups from different ethnic backgrounds (Swann Committee 1985). However, by the early twenty-first century, members of minority ethnic groups were not, on the whole, under-represented in British higher education.

People from Indian and Chinese backgrounds were, on average, significantly more likely than those from other ethnic backgrounds to have a degree qualification or higher. However, men who defined themselves as 'mixed race' and women who defined themselves as 'black/black British' and 'Asian/Asian British' were slightly less likely than the national average to have gained a degree or higher qualification (ONS 2004b: 46–7).

In 2010, *Race into Higher Education*, a report by the charity Business in the Community, analysed data from HESA's student record statistics for 1995–6 and 2007–8. The report found that the proportion of UK resident students from minority ethnic groups in higher education rose from 8.3 per cent in 1995–6 to 16 per cent by 2007–8, or about one in six of all UK students. This is broadly in line with the rise in the ethnic minority population over the period, from 7.7 per cent in 1995–6 to 14.2 per cent in 2007–8. However, there were some large differences between minority groups (figure 19.5). British Indians, mixed ethnic groups and black British Africans were best represented in universities, with the latter tripling their university presence over the twelve-year period. British Bangladeshi and Pakistani students were under-represented in the 1990s and remained so in 2007–8. There were also many differences according to type and status of institution, geographical region and subject choice. In addition, black, Asian and other minority ethnic groups found it more difficult in the labour market, with 56 per cent in work within a year of graduation compared with 66 per cent of white students (Business in the Community 2010: 5).

Inequality is also quite pronounced among minority ethnic academic staff groups. For example, in 2011/12, although 13.8 per cent of UK Chinese academic staff were professors, only 4.1 per cent of black academics had made professorial status, the lowest of any ethnic group. Among full-time academics, 24.5 per cent of white UK staff earned more than £50,000 per year compared with 13.6 per cent of staff from UK minority ethnic groups. A higher proportion of UK white academics were also employed on open or permanent contracts (81.4 per cent) than other minority ethnic academics. Full-time Asian academic staff had the lowest percentage (69.7 per cent) on open or permanent contracts (Equality Challenge Unit 2013: 72–80). The pattern of inequality shares some similarities with that of women in higher education. However,

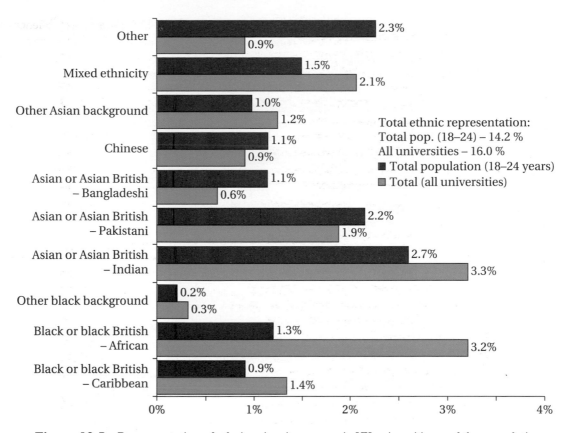

Figure 19.5 Representation of ethnic minority groups in UK universities and the population aged eighteen to twenty-four, 2007–8

Source: Business in the Community (2010: 6).

there is also a diversity of experience among ethnic groups, with some enjoying better employment conditions, pay and promotion prospects than others.

School exclusions and ethnicity

Social exclusion has become a topic of great interest over the last twenty-five years as sociologists have explored the ways in which some people become excluded from key areas of mainstream social life. A more specific concern is with the number of young people outside the formal education system, many of whom are children from minority ethnic groups. Connections are often made between the exclusion of students from school and truancy, delinquency, poverty, limited parental supervision and a weak commitment to education.

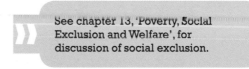

See chapter 13, 'Poverty, Social Exclusion and Welfare', for discussion of social exclusion.

Permanent school exclusions in England, as in many other developed countries, increased rapidly during the 1990s, to a peak of 12,668 (twelve exclusions per 10,000 students) in 1996–7 (ONS 2007: 29). In the twenty-first century, the number of permanent exclusions has been falling, down to eleven exclusions per 10,000 enrolments by 2007–8 and just six per 10,000 enrolments in 2012/13 (ONS 2010a: 31; DfE 2014a: 1). An overwhelming majority of permanent exclusions, some 78 per cent, are of boys, and rates also differ according to ethnicity. It is important to consider how rates of

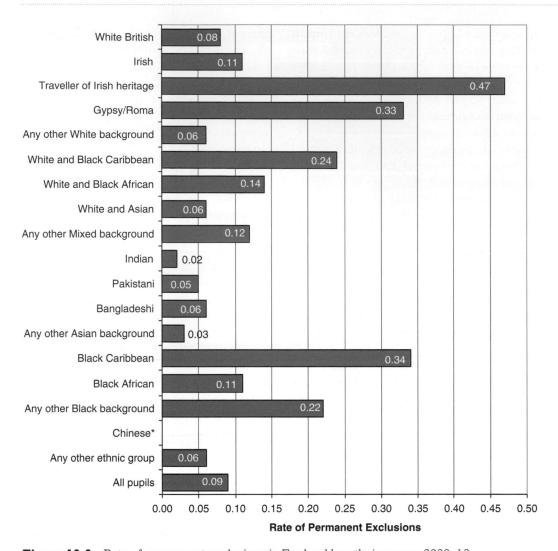

Figure 19.6 Rate of permanent exclusions in England by ethnic group, 2009–10

Note: * Some figures have been omitted as figures were very small and suppressed.

The number of permanent exclusions per 10,000 pupils of compulsory school age in each ethnic group in primary, secondary and special schools (excluding dually registered pupils in special schools). Dual registration is when a pupil is registered at more than one school.

Source: DfE (2012: 32).

school exclusion may reflect broader patterns of exclusion and disadvantage within society. Many young people are growing up under very challenging conditions, with a relative lack of adult guidance and support, while traditional norms of masculinity are undergoing change, leading to uncertainty and anomie that is particularly acute for working-class boys and young men. In this social environment, schools may appear irrelevant and authoritarian rather than as a site for opportunity and advancement.

In 2009–10, the highest permanent exclusion rates in England were among pupils of Irish traveller heritage, black Caribbean and Gypsy/Roma backgrounds. However, the small numbers of pupils from Irish traveller and Gypsy/Roma backgrounds means that we have to be cautious in drawing conclusions from these figures. Children from Chinese and Indian families and all Asian groups were the least likely to be permanently excluded from school (figure 19.6). Findings from America exhibit a similar pattern between black pupils and students from other ethnic backgrounds. Why should school children from some ethnic backgrounds come to be excluded more than others?

Like other institutions and organizations, education systems harbour the potential for institutional racism (Rattansi 1992). In education systems, this concept refers to the way that school life is structured, the dress codes are deemed appropriate and the curriculum is adopted. Teachers may interpret the behaviour and dress styles of black pupils as evidence of their 'disruptive' behaviour, leading to more temporary and permanent exclusions. However, some non-white ethnic groups, including Chinese and Indian students, have relatively low rates of school exclusions. This differential experience suggests to some that ethnocentrism – a focus on one's own familiar culture and a lack of interest in others – rather than institutional racism may be a better characterization of some – though not all – forms of discrimination in schools (Mason 2000).

> Institutional racism was introduced in chapter 16, 'Race, Ethnicity and Migration', in relation to the Stephen Lawrence case (Macpherson 1999).

Nonetheless, racism within schools may be a contributory factor in the relatively high rates of exclusion among mixed-race and black pupils. In one UK study of race relations in primary schools, Cecile Wright (1992) studied relationships in four inner-city primary schools over a three-year period. She found that teachers tended to assume that African-Caribbean boys were disruptive and were quick to reprimand and control their behaviour. Asian pupils were perceived as likely to struggle with language skills but were willing to learn and compliant with the teachers' instructions. Social stereotypes were leading to a certain level of fear among staff, which then fed into the reinforce-

ment of stereotypes. Wright acknowledged that the teachers were committed to equal treatment but were simply caught up in wider social processes leading to discrimination.

Racial harassment was part of the daily experience of black and Asian pupils, who were often victimized by white children, and social processes leading to racism and discrimination in the wider society were also found within schools. Wright (1992: 103) explains that 'staff, like most other people, do treat people differently on the basis of perceived "racial" characteristics. Further, many nursery and primary staff are still reluctant to accept that younger children can hold incipient racist attitudes and exhibit hostility towards members of other groups.'

However, recent sociological work suggests that, although educational policy-makers are sensitive to issues of underachievement among some minority ethnic groups, the dominant explanatory framework is one which 'naturalizes' ethnic differences and blames the individual. Underachievement among black Caribbean and Asian Muslim students, for example, tends to be explained in terms of ethnic cultures, family practices and personal beliefs, while the relative success of British Chinese students lies in their personal commitment or parents' ambition. In this way, policy discourses sidestep the more controversial issue of racism in the school system and its effects, despite many reports from students that they experience racism on a daily basis (Archer and Francis 2007).

Such findings have led some to advocate multicultural forms of education requiring curriculum change to bring currently ignored national histories, religions and cultures into the classroom (Mahalingam and McCarthy 2000; Race 2010). This has happened to a limited extent in religious education, where pupils are introduced to the diversity of religious beliefs and practices. Yet there are some problems with multicultural initiatives. Historical facts never 'speak for themselves' and history still has to be interpreted. How should the history of colonialism and imperial expansion be taught and where should the emphasis lie?

An alternative approach is to include anti-racist education. Anti-racist education

Social stereotypes may affect the way teachers treat children from different ethnic groups. For example, African-Caribbean children are often assumed to be 'disruptive'.

involves multicultural teaching but goes further, to challenge inequalities by helping both staff (during staff training) and young people to understand how racist attitudes and stereotypes develop and how they can deal with them when they arise. Anti-racist education attempts actively to identify and challenge discriminatory language, actions and policies *within* the school. The main issue raised by critics is the potential for such teaching to reinforce divisions and to contribute to the 'racialization' of conflicts within the school community. While multiculturalist and anti-racist approaches are somewhat different, it has been argued that a 'critical multiculturalist' approach may offer the best way forward (May and Sleeter 2010).

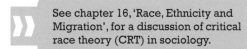

See chapter 16, 'Race, Ethnicity and Migration', for a discussion of critical race theory (CRT) in sociology.

THINKING CRITICALLY

In your experience, is there any evidence that schools are *institutionally* racist, or is it more accurate to say that there is racism within schools? Did your school have an anti-racist curriculum? If it did, what did it include and how did this help to combat racism? If it did not, should it create one?

Evaluation

Inequalities within education systems have proved remarkably persistent, particularly in relation to social class divisions. Even in the twenty-first century, it remains the case that 'social class is the strongest predictor of educational achievement' (Perry and Francis 2010: 6). However, class intersects with gender and ethnicity to produce quite complex patterns of inequality and 'success'. For example, a recent study of the attainment and progress of more than 14,500 students aged eleven and fourteen found that, although socio-economic variables explained the attainment gap for black African, Pakistani and Bangladeshi students compared with white British students, it did not do so for black Caribbean students (Strand 2011). Similarly, girls outperform boys within each social class grouping.

As we have seen in relation to gender inequalities, there can be quite radical changes too. Educational opportunities for women opened up considerably over the second half of the twentieth century, though they have taken time to become firmly established. Economic restructuring, which reduced the need for heavy manual work in favour of post-industrial employment in the service sector, has been a major structural factor favouring a better trained and educated female workforce. Nonetheless, differences in the educational experiences of ethnic groups also shows that inequality in education is as strongly linked to social and cultural factors as it is to economic ones.

Education in global context

Before the mid-nineteenth century, and even more recently in some regions, children of the wealthy were educated by private tutors. Some still are. However, until the first few decades of the nineteenth century – when systems of primary schooling were created in Europe and North America – most people had no formal schooling at all. Industrialization and the growth of cities increased the demand for specialized schooling. People worked in many different occupations, and work skills could no longer be passed on directly from parents to children. The acquisition of knowledge was increasingly based on abstract learning in subjects such as maths, science, history and literature rather than on the practical transmission of very specific skills. In modern societies, people have to be furnished with basic skills, such as reading, writing and calculating, as well as a general knowledge of their physical, social and economic environment. It is also important that they know *how to learn*, so they are able to master new, and often very technical, forms of information.

In our increasingly global context today, the diversity of educational provision across the world is a striking feature. As we saw in the chapter introduction, many people in the developing world struggle to gain access to education and illiteracy is widespread, while in the developed countries issues of choice and consumerism are more likely to exercise parents and governments. If inequalities *within* countries are proving difficult to tackle, then the inequalities *between* the countries of the developed and developing worlds are an even bigger challenge.

One way of comparing the world's national education systems is to look at government spending on education. Figure 19.7 shows the broad picture of the percentage of Gross Domestic Product (GDP) spent by the countries and regions of the world. Yet given the diversity of local currencies, comparing national spending is not a simple task. In order to compare cost per student and the size of national education budgets, local currencies have to be converted into a standard measure. According to UNESCO's Institute for Statistics, 'purchasing power parities' (PPPs) best reflect the real value of educational investment by governments and families. PPPs are rates of currency conversion that eliminate differences in price levels among countries. So, a given sum of money,

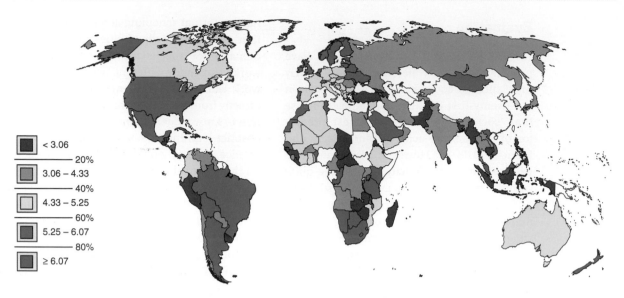

Figure 19.7   Public education expenditure as percentage of GDP, 2006–12

Source: World Bank (2013).

converted into US dollars at PPP rates, will buy the same basket of goods and services in all countries.

Table 19.3 includes PPPs to compare world regions, showing that the various governments spent 5.1 per cent of global Gross National Product (GNP) on education in 2011, up from 4.6 per cent in 1999. The highest levels of spending were in North America and Western Europe, with 6.2 per cent of regional GNP. The lowest levels of spending were in South and West Asia and sub-Saharan Africa. However, UNESCO reports that thirty low- and middle-income countries actually increased their education spending by at least 1 per cent between 1999 and 2011. Yet only forty-one of 150 countries had hit the UNESCO target of allocating 6 per cent of GNP for education spending, which means there is a very long way to go at present rates. In the Arab countries and South and West Asia, education spending as a percentage of GNP actually fell between 1999 and 2011.

For developing countries, the credit crisis of 2008 and global economic downturn followed rapid rises in world food prices between 2003 and 2008. As a result, poor families were forced to cut back on spending for their children's education in order to buy food. In Bangladesh, for instance, around one-third of poor households reported doing just that (UNESCO 2010: 7). The developed countries established recovery plans aimed at restoring economic growth, which allowed public spending on primary and secondary education to be prioritized and protected. But in the developing countries, the main source of expanding 'fiscal space' in the short term lies in increased levels of foreign aid. Yet UNESCO reports that government commitments on aid levels made in 2005 at the Gleneagles Summit in Scotland have not been met, falling short by some $20 billion, $18 billion of which was for Africa. Aid for basic education fell by 6 per cent between 2010 and 2011, hitting the poorest countries hardest. Thirteen of nineteen countries whose education aid was cut were in sub-Saharan Africa (UNESCO 2014a: 111). Clearly, unless international aid is significantly increased, the global gap in education spending between the developed and developing countries looks set to grow even wider (UNESCO 2010: 32).

Table 19.3 Public spending on education by world region, 1999 and 2011

| | Public education spending | | | | | |
| | % of GNP | | % of goverment expenditure on education | | Per capita (primary education) (PPP constant 2010 US$) | |
	1999	*2011*	*1999*	*2011*	*1999*	*2011*
World	**4.6**	**5.1**	**15.0**	**15.5**	**2,149**	**3,089**
Low income	3.1	4.1	16.4	18.3	102	115
Lower middle income	4.6	5.1	15.9	16.9	356	545
Upper middle income	4.8	5.1	15.8	15.5	1,117	1,745
High income	5.3	5.6	13.3	13.2	4,752	6,721
Sub-Saharan Africa	4.0	5.0	17.1	18.7	345	468
Arab States	5.3	4.8	21.0	18.1	822	1,338
Central Asia	3.4	4.1	15.4	12.3	...	...
East Asia and the Pacific	3.9	4.4	15.0	16.6	2,216	3,245
South and West Asia	3.9	3.7	14.5	15.0	297	573
Latin America and the Caribbean	5.0	5.5	14.4	16.2	1,142	1,753
Central and Eastern Europe	4.8	5.2	12.4	12.2	1,813	3,845
North America and Western Europe	5.6	6.2	13.3	13.1	5,990	8,039

Source: UNESCO (2014: 111).

> **THINKING CRITICALLY**
>
> Education spending is directly linked to literacy levels and educational achievement. In a grossly unequal world, is foreign aid the only realistic way to raise the level of education spending in the poorest countries? How might it be argued that the wealthy countries benefit from high illiteracy rates in poorer countries?

Global primary school enrolment

An important aspect of global education is the number of children who are in some form of primary education. A simple but useful measure of this is primary school enrolment. Between 1999 and 2004, this improved spectacularly, to around 86 per cent, with the largest increases in sub-Saharan Africa (27 per cent) and South and West Asia (19 per cent) (UNESCO 2008). Yet by 2007 there were still 72 million primary-age children not in any form of education, three-quarters of these in sub-Saharan Africa and South and West Asia (see figure 19.8). This is inevitably an underestimate, however, as not all those who are enrolled actually attend regularly or at all, as Bruneforth's (2006) analysis in figure 19.9 shows in relation to some of the countries facing the biggest challenge.

An analysis of factors revealed that slightly more boys than girls were out of school, but gender was not the key factor. Residence was significant: 18 per cent of primary-age children were out of school, but almost a third (30 per cent) of the total were rural children. Household wealth was also important:

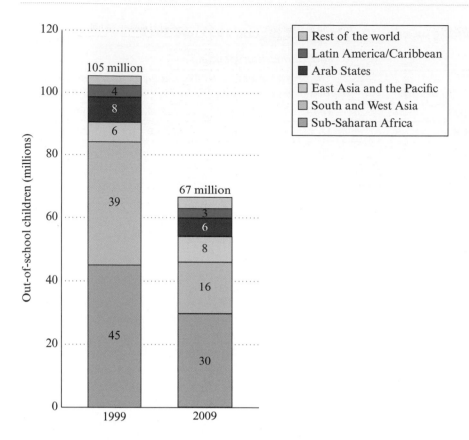

Figure 19.8 Number of out-of-school children (not enrolled in primary school) by region, 1999 and 2007 (millions)

Source: UNESCO (2010: 12).

38 per cent of children in the poorest fifth of households were not in primary education compared with 25 per cent of the middle fifth and just 1 per cent of the wealthiest fifth. Once again, we can see the issue of social class and educational inequality arising, this time at the global level. The final factor is whether mothers had been involved in education themselves. Whereas just 16 per cent of children whose mothers had some education were not in primary school, the figure for those whose mothers had had no education was 38 per cent (UNESCO 2008). This may indicate that the value families place on education and the existence of positive role models are crucial elements in raising attendance levels. Clearly, primary school attendance is fundamental if global levels of basic literacy are to be improved.

Literacy and illiteracy

In 2012, some 781 million adults across the world did not have even basic literacy skills, and almost two-thirds of these were women, the majority living in sub-Saharan Africa, South and West Asia and East Asia (UNESCO 2014b). However, illiteracy exists in every society, including those in the developed world. In England, for example, about 5 per cent of adults aged between sixteen and sixty-five perform below the literacy level expected of seven-year-old children. National literacy rates below 60 per cent are recorded in twenty-two countries, fourteen of which are in sub-Saharan Africa (figure 19.10). Yet just four countries – Bangladesh, China, India and Pakistan – account for more than half of all illiterate adults in

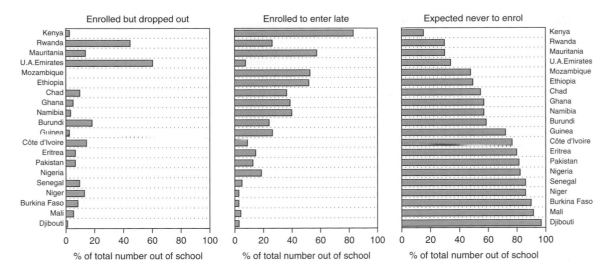

Figure 19.9 Distribution of out-of-school children in selected countries with the most difficulties in enrolment

Source: Bruneforth (2006).

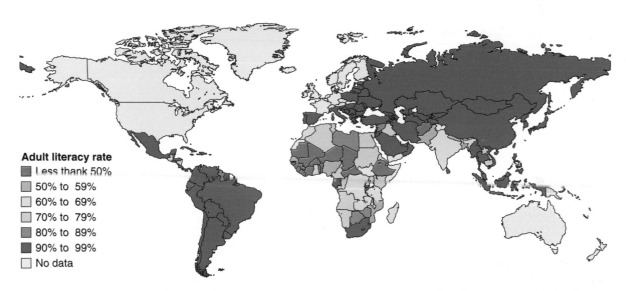

Figure 19.10 Adult illiteracy rate (age fifteen and older), 2012 (or latest year with data)

Source: UNESCO (2014b).

the world population. In Morocco, Ethiopia, Pakistan and Bangladesh, although literacy *rates* have increased, the absolute *number* of illiterate adults has increased on account of the growth of their populations, while India has remained fairly static. With expanding populations and large numbers of illiterate adults, these countries face a formidable obstacle in the competitive global economy. Global literacy rates have been improving in the twenty-first century, but the proportion of illiterate females has remained steady at around 64 per cent (UNESCO 2014b).

Some have suggested that a new kind of illiteracy may be emerging as information technology becomes commonplace in work environments. This could see large numbers of people who have no regular access to information technology or training for its use, and no familiarity with the specialized language of computing, becoming disadvantaged in new ways. We will return to this issue in the final part of the chapter.

See chapter 4, 'Globalization and Social Change', for more detail on the global spread of ICT.

Creating literate environments

There are clear links between educational expenditure, primary school attendance and literacy. Levels of government and

---

Global Society 20.1 | **The threat of literacy in colonial regimes**

During the period of colonialism, colonial governments regarded education with some trepidation. Until the twentieth century, most believed indigenous populations to be too primitive to be worthy of educating. Later, education was seen as a way of making local elites responsive to European interests and ways of life. But, to some extent, the result was to foment discontent and rebellion, since the majority of those who led anti-colonial and nationalist movements were from educated elites who had attended schools or colleges in Europe. They were able to compare at first hand the democratic institutions of the European countries with the absence of democracy in their lands of origin.

The education that the colonizers introduced usually pertained to Europe, not to the colonial areas themselves. Educated Africans in the British colonies knew about the kings and queens of England and read Shakespeare, Milton and the English poets, but they learned next to nothing about their own countries' history or past cultural achievements. Policies of educational reform since the end of colonialism have not completely altered the situation, even today.

Partly as a result of the legacy of colonial education, which was not directed towards the majority of the population, the educational system in many developing countries is top-heavy: higher education is disproportionately developed relative to primary and secondary education. The consequence is a correspondingly overqualified group who,

having attended colleges and universities, cannot find white-collar or professional jobs. Given the low level of industrial development, most of the better-paid positions are in government, and there are not enough of those to go around.

In recent years, some developing countries, recognizing the shortcomings of the curricula inherited from colonialism, have tried to redirect their educational programmes towards the rural poor. They have had limited success, because usually there is insufficient funding to pay for the scale of the necessary innovations. As a result, countries such as India have begun programmes of self-help education. Communities draw on existing resources without creating demands for high levels of finance. Those who can read and write and who perhaps possess job skills are encouraged to take on others as apprentices, whom they coach in their spare time.

The links between literacy and development are discussed in chapter 14, 'Global Inequality'.

THINKING CRITICALLY

In what ways could the restriction of educational opportunity under colonial regimes have affected future economic development? How should the former colonial powers help their former colonies to catch up in today's global economy? What practical assistance could they offer?

other expenditure on education not only bring children and young people into free schooling but can also help to create 'literate environments'. Literate environments are those spaces which provide numerous opportunities for the newly literate to exercise their skills, offering, for example, a range of printed and visual materials such as newspapers, magazines and books; easy access to continuing education such as in schools and training centres; opportunities to be involved in organizations where literacy skills can be used, such as local government or agricultural cooperatives; and chances to work in businesses or not-for-profit organizations that allow the exercise of literate skills (Easton 2006). Primary and other schools are obviously literate environments, which benefit very young children and young people, but literate environments can also be created in libraries and other public spaces, as well as in workplaces and even private homes.

Apart from providing opportunities for the exercise of literacy skills, the main significance of literate environments may be in their impact on people's *motivation* to become literate or improve their levels of literacy. What is clearer today, however, is that literate environments will have to be able to provide access to electronic forms of communication, as well as more conventional forms, if they are to be successful in tackling illiteracy in the future.

Technology in the classroom

The spread of information technology is already influencing education in schools. The knowledge economy demands a computer-literate workforce, and it is increasingly clear that education will play a critical role in meeting this need. While household computer-ownership has risen sharply in recent years, many children still do not have access to a computer at home. For this reason, schools are a crucial forum for young people to learn about and become comfortable with the capabilities of computers and online technology.

As we saw earlier, the rise of education systems was connected to a number of other major changes happening in the nineteenth century. One was the development of printing and the arrival of 'book culture'. The mass distribution of books, newspapers and other printed media was as distinctive a feature of the development of industrial society as were machines and factories. Education provided the skills of literacy and numeracy, giving access to the world of printed media. Nothing is more characteristic of the school than the schoolbook or textbook.

In the eyes of many, all this is set to change with the growing use of computers and multimedia technologies in education. Will digital media such as tablets, e-book readers and smartphones replace the schoolbook? Will schools exist in anything like the form they do today? The new technologies, it is said, will not just add to the existing curriculum but will undermine and transform it. Young people today are already growing up in an information age in which they are more comfortable with ICT than most adults – including teachers.

A 2003 OECD study assessed the educational performance of fifteen-year-old students and found that regular computer use led to better scores, particularly in mathematics. Students who had used computers for several years generally performed better at maths than the OECD average, while those with infrequent access to computers, or who had used them only for a short time, lagged behind their class year group (OECD 2005). Of the sample of students, 10 per cent had used computers for less than a year, and their average score was well below the OECD average in mathematics. Almost three out of four students in the OECD countries frequently used a computer at home, but only 44 per cent did so at school. These are the kind of data which some social scientists see as evidence of the growing divide between IT-rich and IT-poor households. If schools do not provide better access to computing, then the social class divide in education looks likely to become wider.

Over recent years, the use of technology in education has been utterly transformed. In most of the developed countries, education systems have been modernized and computerized. Some observers now talk of a 'classroom revolution' – the arrival of 'desk-top virtual reality' and the classroom without walls. There is little question that computers have expanded opportunities in education. They provide the chance for children to work independently, to research topics with the help of online resources, and to benefit from educational software that allows them to progress at their own pace. Yet the vision of classrooms of children learning exclusively through individual computers has not yet come to pass. In fact, the 'classroom without walls' looks some way off.

Although the number of students with regular access to a computer is rising, the picture is quite uneven, even across the relatively wealthy countries of the OECD (see figure 19.11). Pupils can use computers to complete tasks within the standard curriculum, such as producing a research project or investigating current events, but few teachers see information technology as a medium that can substitute for learning from and interacting with human teachers. The challenge for teachers is learning how to integrate the new information technologies into lessons in a way that is meaningful as well as educationally sound. Internet access has, arguably, already become the new line of demarcation between the rich and the poor.

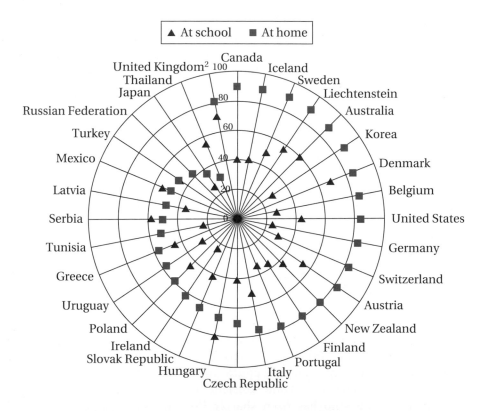

Figure 19.11 Percentage of students who frequently use a computer at home or school, OECD countries, from 2003 data

Note: Countries are ranked in descending order of percentage of students frequently using computers at school. [2]Response rate too low to ensure comparability.

Source: OECD (2005).

Global Society 19.2 The lifelong learning environment

New technologies and the rise of the knowledge economy are transforming traditional ideas about work and education. The sheer pace of technological change is creating a much more rapid turnover of jobs than was once the case. Training and the attainment of qualifications is now occurring throughout people's lives rather than in just the early years, as mid-career professionals are choosing to update their skills through continuing education programmes and Internet-based learning. Many employers now allow workers to participate in on-the-job training as a way of enhancing loyalty and improving the company skills base.

As societies continue to change, the traditional beliefs and institutions that underpin it are also undergoing transformation. The idea of schooling as the structured transmission of knowledge within formal institutions is giving way to a broader notion of 'learning' in a diversity of settings and at different times. The shift from 'education' to 'learning' is not inconsequential. Learners are active, curious social actors who can derive insights from a multiplicity of sources. Learners acquire skills and knowledge through many types of encounter – with friends and neighbours, at seminars and museums, in conversations at the local pub, through the Internet and other media, and so forth.

The shift in emphasis towards lifelong learning can already be seen within schools themselves, where there is a growing number of opportunities for pupils to learn outside the confines of the classroom. The boundaries between schools and the outside world are breaking down, not only via cyberspace but in the physical world as well. 'Service learning', for example, has become a mainstay of many American secondary schools. As part of their

Continuing professional development (CPD) and lifelong learning can continue over a person's lifetime.

graduation requirements, pupils devote a certain amount of time to volunteer work in the community. Partnerships with local businesses have also become commonplace in many countries, fostering interaction and mentor relationships between adult professionals and pupils.

Lifelong learning should play a role in the move towards a knowledge society (Longworth 2003). Not only is it essential to a well-trained, motivated workforce, but learning should also be seen in relation to wider human values. Learning is both a means and an end to the development of a rounded and autonomous self-education in the service of self-development and self-understanding. There is nothing utopian in this idea; indeed, it reflects the humanistic ideals of education developed by educational philosophers. An example already in existence is the 'university of the third age', which provides retired people with the opportunity to educate themselves as they choose, developing whatever interests they care to follow.

> **THINKING CRITICALLY**
>
> How realistic is the suggestion that formal schooling will give way to a less formal and structured form of lifelong learning? Will employers really support the concept of lifelong learning and facilitate it? What benefits might accrue for them if they do?

The future of education and schooling

Education systems across the world today are changing quite quickly. One reason for this is the digital revolution and the spread of information communication technologies (ICTs). However, education systems face other challenges too, such as how to accommodate an increasing focus on consumerism and choice in education and how schools should be funded in the future. These are especially pertinent during a period of public spending cutbacks and austerity politics. To get a sense of the way that education systems in the developed countries changed over the twentieth century, we will take a brief look at British education and its development. Although education systems are diverse, a single case can reveal some key issues arising at different historical moments.

Transformations in education – the UK case

The UK education system, more accurately the system in England and Wales (Scotland has a different system), has developed through several stages. In its early development, provision was quite diverse and strongly religious in orientation. After 1945 the state became centrally involved and, gradually, the system moved towards compulsory universal education for all – first through a three-part system based on perceived intelligence, and later in a comprehensive education system. However, from the 1990s there has been a steady movement away from uniform provision towards a consumer choice model with increasingly diverse school types, which privileges parental choice rather than local authority control. The brief sketch below highlights some key developments in the process.

Between 1870 (when compulsory education was first established) and the Second World War, successive British governments increased expenditure on education. The minimum school-leaving age rose from ten to fourteen and more schools were built, but education was not considered to be a major area for government intervention. Private and church authorities under the supervision of local government boards ran schools, most of which would today be described as 'faith schools' with a strong religious content. The Second World War (1939–45) changed this situation, as recruits to the armed forces startled the authorities by showing a low level of educational skills. Concerned about the prospects for postwar recovery, the government began to rethink education provision and settled on a tripartite system of grammar, secondary technical and secondary modern schools, which sifted pupils on the basis of an examination at the age of eleven (Halsey 1997).

By the 1960s, it was clear that the system established in 1947, of selecting pupils considered more intelligent for a grammar school education at the age of eleven, had not reached expectations. Only 12 per cent of pupils continued in school until the age of seventeen, and early leaving was shown to be more closely related to class background than to academic performance (CACE 1959). In 1965 the Labour government moved towards a more standardized and uniform comprehensive education for the state sector. From the early 1970s, educational expansion, which characterized the whole of the postwar period, was suddenly replaced by contraction and efforts to reduce government expenditure.

Education has long been a political battleground, and one protracted debate has centred on the impact of comprehensive schooling and its results. The architects of comprehensive education believed that the new schools would provide for more equality of opportunity. But the 1979 Conservative government under Margaret Thatcher criticized comprehensive schooling, believing that selective grammar schools should be saved. In the late 1980s, the government sought to dismantle the comprehensive system and reduce the power of local education authorities that were responsible for running them. The 1988 Education Act introduced a universal national curriculum for the state sector. It also introduced local management of schools, devolving their administration to balance the inevitable centralization involved in the national curriculum.

A new group of city technology colleges (CTCs) and grant-maintained schools was also promoted. The latter could 'opt out' of local authority control and receive funding directly from the state – effectively becoming businesses funded from central government – with the right to select up to 50 per cent of their student intake on the basis of ability. The government hoped all schools would opt out and eventually become grant-maintained. By 1995, however, only 1,000 state schools out of a total of 23,000 had done so. Gewirtz and her colleagues (1995) found that, for many parents, the choice of school was severely limited, as the real extent of school choice depended largely on parents' social class position.

The Labour government of 1997 put education at the top of its agenda. In a White Paper, *Excellence in Schools* (1997), Labour committed itself to defending and modernizing comprehensive schools. The White Paper also called for intervention in all schools assessed as having chronically sub-standard performance. The government emphasized the importance of good teaching methods and strong leadership as the keys to educational reform. In primary schools, literacy and numeracy programmes were introduced which were extended to form a primary strategy, setting out standards in English, mathematics and science. Grant-maintained schools became 'foundation schools', retaining a high degree of independence and focusing on technology, arts or maths, for example. These schools were allowed to select up to 10 per cent of their intake according to ability in these specialist areas.

Diversification and choice

City academies were created in deprived areas and became heavily oversubscribed. Sponsors from the private or charitable sector provided 20 per cent of the start-up costs, up to a maximum of £2 million, and the state paid the rest. Critics claimed that the generous funding of academies drained resources from other schools. The government was also rigorous in its policy of school inspections. Where a school was deemed to be failing, government agencies intervened directly to take it over. In some cases, failing schools reopened as city academies. Education action zones were created in areas of high deprivation using money from government and the private sector to attract teachers and tackle social exclusion. By 2005 there were seventy-three education action zones across England.

In 2010, a new Conservative-led coalition government set out its approach to UK education with a central focus on returning to 'traditional' educational values, encouraging 'blazer and tie' uniforms, discipline, good spelling and grammar. The size of the compulsory national curriculum was to be slimmed down, head teachers would be given more powers and pupils would be encouraged to take the traditionally more 'rigorous' STEM subjects – sciences, technology, engineering and mathematics.

A 'pupil premium' was also introduced: a fixed annual sum per pupil (£1,300 for primary and £935 for secondary pupils in 2014/15) paid to schools for those in receipt of free school meals to provide extra resources to help poorer students increase their attainment (DfE 2014b). The government also encouraged all schools to become academies free of local authority control. By 2013 there were 3,613 academy schools. Some 56 per cent of state secondary schools had become academies, though a much smaller proportion, 11 per cent, of primary schools. A 2014 report suggested that state schools that convert to become academies are more likely than other schools to raise their overall status from 'good' to 'outstanding' and to see more pupils achieving the higher grades at GCSE level. However, critics see academies as reducing democratic accountability and carrying forward the gradual privatization of the state system (BBC News 2012b).

The most controversial coalition reform has been the policy of 'free schools', based on the 'charter schools' in the USA and Sweden's own free school model. Free schools are privately governed but state-funded academies set up and run by parents, charities, businesses, teachers or religious groups. Estimates suggest that, by 2015, around 250,000 pupils were studying in free schools (higher than forecast in 2010) and 102 were approved for opening from 2014, forty-six of these in London (*The Guardian* 2014). Critics argue that this type of school will be most attractive to wealthier middle-class groups and will create a two-tier

system in which money and the best teachers will gravitate towards free schools, leaving state schools as the poor relation. For example, initial data suggests that only 9.4 per cent of free school pupils received free school meals compared to the national average of 16.7 per cent (Florack 2014: 220–1).

Because free schools can choose to limit their intake to create smaller class sizes, some critics are concerned about their cost, both in strict financial terms and for the education system as a whole. In 2012 the shadow education minister pointed to problems with one free school in Suffolk (Twigg, cited in Florack 2014: 221): '£2m has been spent on a school which will serve only 37 pupils, in an area with over 10,000 spare secondary places. 3,000 people signed a petition against the school.' Concerns have also been raised about the break-up of the national education system and problems in some free schools. For instance, in 2014, E-Act, a private sponsor of a chain of free schools, pulled out due to concerns about low standards.

It is too early to reach firm conclusions about free schools and whether they will thrive and spread, as there has as yet been almost no research on them. However, what is clear is that the post-1945 movement towards a unified national education system of comprehensive schooling for all is over. Since the mid-1990s, successive governments have introduced reforms that have led to an increasing diversity of provision, geographical disparities, a consumer choice model, and the gradual removal of local authority control and accountability. Indeed, the emerging situation begins to look more like that which existed before the 1870 Education Act, with a variety of providers, relatively unconnected to each other.

As the onus shifts increasingly onto parental choice, it seems likely that existing social inequalities will be reinforced, as middle-class families are better placed to negotiate and, in the case of free schools, help to create the fragmented educational landscape:

> Not all families have the skills, time or resources to decode and work the system; and some are simply unable to afford to

move their children long distances to school. Bluntly, this fuzzy system of unclear and uneven provision offers the opportunity for well-informed, well-resourced, confident and persistent parents, many of whom are middle class, to seek social advantage for their children. (Ball 2013)

Higher education

The system of higher education (HE) in Britain has, as in many other countries, expanded rapidly since the 1980s. There were twenty-one universities in Britain in the 1950s, but most were very small by today's standards. Between 1945 and 1970 the UK higher education system grew to be four times larger. Older universities expanded and new ones, such as at Sussex, Stirling and York – labelled 'red-brick' – were built. A binary system was set up with the creation of polytechnics, which concentrated more on vocational courses. Today, UK higher education has a 'standard coinage' – a degree from Leicester or Leeds, at least in theory, is of the same standard as one from Cambridge, Oxford or London. Yet Oxford and Cambridge are noted for their highly selective intake, about half of whom come from fee-paying schools. An Oxford or Cambridge degree confers a greater chance of a profitable career than a qualification from most other universities, and it is clear that major social divisions are not confined to the compulsory education sector.

In 1900–1 there were a mere 25,000 students in full-time higher education in the UK, but by 1971 this had increased to 457,000, and by 2008–9 there were more than 1.5 million (Universities UK 2010: 7). Social class background influences the likelihood of participation in higher education, and, though involvement of those with working-class backgrounds has increased, it remains well below that of students from non-manual classes. The debate about access to education for the children of working-class parents has been central to the debates about how higher education is and should be funded.

While the number of students in higher education has expanded enormously, government spending has not increased at the same rate. Funding per student fell by 29 per cent in real terms between 1976 and 1989, and by a further 38 per cent between 1989 and 1999. The National Committee of Inquiry into Higher Education (1997) concluded that the expansion and improvement of higher education would be impossible under existing funding arrangements. The result has been a crisis in funding for higher education, made more acute by the UK government's debt reduction measures following the global downturn since 2008. But then, who should pay?

> The 2008 credit crisis and recession are discussed in chapter 7, 'Work and the Economy'.

The two main sources of large-scale investment in universities are taxation and those who experience and benefit from higher education – students. Some argue that, given the social and economic benefits that higher education provides for society, university funding should be met by the taxpayer. Where would we be without doctors, teachers and other professional groups? Others maintain that those taxpayers who do not go to university should not have to pay for those who do. Graduates enjoy many career advantages, earning, on average, significantly more over a lifetime than non-graduates, and it would be unfair to expect non-graduates to pay for the rewards of others. There now seems to be a widespread acceptance that students should pay a greater share of their university costs.

In 2010, the Browne Report, an independent review into higher education in England and Wales, commissioned by the previous Labour government, was published. In *Securing a Sustainable Future for Higher Education*, Lord Browne recommended slashing the teaching budget by some 80 per cent and shifting costs onto students by sharply raising tuition fees. Government support for the arts, humanities and social sciences would be all but wiped out. Increasing tuition fees would open up the university sector to competition between subjects and institutions, said the report, thus

Cuts in higher education funding and rising tuition fees for students led to protests in the UK. Government policies have continued, however, and, so far, raising tuition fees has not led to a reduction in numbers of students applying. Does this demonstrate the changing attitudes to education in the UK?

targeting resources on the better institutions and 'more relevant' subjects.

The new coalition government accepted the report's main recommendations, and, in December 2010, MPs voted to raise tuition fees from just over £3,000 per year to £6,000, with a maximum of £9,000 if certain criteria on widening access were met. The policy was met with large-scale student marches, sit-ins at universities, and confrontations between police and students in London. Student leaders argued that students should not have to suffer because of the reckless actions of bankers and politicians that led to the 2008 financial crash.

Critics argued that raising fees so steeply would deter under-represented groups, such as working-class students, who would baulk at the prospect of incurring a large debt.

However, this has not happened, and student numbers, including those from working-class groups, have not fallen. Student fee loans do not have to be paid back until graduates earn £21,000 a year and not at all if that salary is not achieved, as debts are written off after thirty years. So far, the new system appears not to have created an obstacle to participation in higher education.

A second criticism concerned the impact on universities themselves. John Holmwood, chair of the Heads and Professors of Sociology group, argued that a three-tier system might emerge. A small upper tier of research-intensive universities will continue to do well, a larger middle tier of teaching-only universities will struggle to survive, and a third tier of teaching-only universities will be forced into mergers or even to close down altogether (Holmwood 2010). Again, though, as most universities have chosen to charge the maximum £9,000 course fees, it may be that this will protect university funding, thus avoiding the worst-case scenario of division and closures. However, some question whether the new system is sustainable in the long term, particularly if a majority of student loans are eventually written off (Higher Education Commission 2014).

What we can see in the example of the British case is something of the changing face of education systems. The twentieth century saw compulsory schooling become established across the developed world and years spent in education rose for all social classes. Strict selection on the basis of testing gave way, in the 1960s and 1970s, to more comprehensive models of schooling, but by the 1990s that trend had gone into reverse. In higher education, universities have slowly opened their doors to a wider section of the population, but, as the elite system became a mass system, the thorny question of who pays became a serious problem. The next big challenge for education systems will be how to make effective use of the new possibilities created by digital technology, and we now turn to this issue.

Higher education in a digital age

Back in 1971, Britain's Open University pioneered the use of television in distance learning. Its programmes were broadcast by the BBC in the early morning and late at night. Students combined these with written materials, work by correspondence, meetings with a personal tutor, and summer courses with other students. In this way they could take high-quality degree courses from home – and often while still in work. The OU has become the UK's largest university and has added the Internet to its range, though it remains committed to a mix of encounters with students. Today many, perhaps most, universities offer some distance learning courses, which depend on the Internet for email communication, chatrooms, online assess-

ment or web-based course materials such as podcasts and videos.

The Internet now appears to be transforming education in an even more profound way than television did. This approach was, and is being, pioneered by the University of Phoenix in the United States. Founded in 1989, it is a private institution and the second largest accredited university in the USA. Yet, unlike most large US universities, it cannot boast a grassy campus, a sprawling library, a football team or a student centre. The 420,000 students enrolled at the university meet and interact predominantly across the Internet – the University of Phoenix's eCampus – or at one of its 'learning centres' located in forty US states.

The University of Phoenix offers more than a dozen degree programmes which can be completed entirely online, making students' actual geographical location irrelevant. Online 'group mailboxes' substitute for physical classrooms: rather than making presentations or discussing ideas in person, students post their work in the electronic classroom for other students and the instructor to read. An electronic library is available for students to complete their research and reading assignments. At the start of each week, the course instructor distributes the week's reading list and discussion topics electronically. Students complete the required work according to their own schedules – they can access the 'electronic classroom' at any hour of day or night – and instructors mark assignments and return them to students with comments.

It is not simply the medium of learning that is distinctive at the University of Phoenix. The university only admits students who are over twenty-three years of age and are employed at a workplace. Both the structure and the content of the university's offerings are aimed at adult professionals who want new skills and qualifications but need to complete this continuing education in a way that does not conflict with their busy personal and professional lives. For this reason, courses are taught in intensive five- to eight-week blocks and are run continuously throughout the year, rather than according to an academic calendar.

There is one more important way in which the University of Phoenix is different from traditional universities – it is a for-profit institution owned by a corporation called Apollo Communications. A decade after its creation, the university was making an average profit of US$12.8 million a quarter. A growing number of educational institutions are drawing on private rather than public management. Outside organizations with expertise in management, or in the production and distribution of technology, are becoming involved in the educational system as consultants or administrators.

The flexibility and convenience of Internet-based learning cannot be denied, but the approach is not without its critics. Many argue that there is no substitute for face-to-face learning in a truly interactive environment with other students. Will future generations of learners be little more than networks of anonymous students known only by their online user names? Will skills-oriented, practical studies undermine the importance of abstract reasoning and learning 'for learning's sake'?

Globalization and technological advancement have also enabled the creation of a global market in higher education and the logical development of the Massive Open Online Course, or MOOC. These are online courses which are available to anyone, usually without charge, and could potentially lead to large online learning communities. Currently, MOOCs are in an experimental phase, and it is unclear whether they will be able to offer full degree schemes or university accreditation and how they will be funded in the long term.

Although higher education has always had an international dimension – thanks to overseas students, cross-national research projects and international scholarly conferences – radically new opportunities are emerging for collaboration among students, academics and educational institutions scattered round the globe. Through Internet-based learning and the formation of MOOCs and 'e-universities', education and qualifications are becoming

more accessible to a global audience. Credentials, certificates and degrees can now be acquired outside the world of physical classrooms and traditional educational establishments. A range of competing institutions and companies – some commercially based – are rapidly entering the global education market. More than ever before, knowledge and learning are 'up for grabs'.

Even conventional universities are taking steps to become 'e-universities' – consortia of institutions are sharing their academic resources, research facilities, teaching staff and students online. Universities around the world are acknowledging the benefits of these partnerships with other institutions whose offerings complement their own. As scholarship and technological innovation proliferate, it is impossible for even the most elite institutions to stay on top of advances in all disciplines. Through online partnerships, they can pool their expertise and make it available to students and researchers within the consortium. Students in Brisbane, for example, can access online libraries in San Francisco, email specialized academic staff elsewhere to have questions clarified, and collaborate on research projects.

Conclusion

New communication technologies open up enormous new possibilities in education. They potentially allow formal education to escape the confines of the classroom or lecture hall and reach new students anywhere in the world, regardless of age, gender or class. However, critics have pointed out that, rather than being a liberating and egalitarian force, new information and communication technologies may reinforce educational inequalities. Information poverty might be added to the material deprivations and inequalities that education can serve to reproduce. The sheer pace of technological change and the demand of employers for computer-literate workers may mean that those who are technologically competent 'leapfrog' over people who have little experience with computers. This threat of a divide between those who are technologically qualified and those who are not reinforces the importance of lifelong learning to cope with the new challenges of life in the information age.

IT enthusiasts claim that the strength of digital technology lies in its ability to draw people together and to open up new opportunities. Schools in Asia and Africa that are lacking textbooks and qualified teachers can benefit from online communications. Distance learning programmes and collaboration with colleagues overseas could be the key to overcoming poverty and disadvantage. When technology is put in the hands of smart, creative people, they argue, the potential is limitless.

Yet others already fear the emergence of a 'computer underclass'. As the global economy becomes increasingly knowledge-based, there is a real danger that poorer countries will become even more marginalized because of the gap between the information rich and the information poor. Similarly, in the developed countries, information technology may well increase the gap in performance between the middle and working classes, given the financial investment required.

While new technologies can certainly open up access for some, it has to be recognized that there is no such thing as an easy 'techno-fix' for the problems facing education systems across the world. Many developing countries are struggling with high levels of illiteracy and lack telephone lines and electricity. They will need an improved educational infrastructure before they can truly benefit from new technologies that enable distance learning programmes.

As we have seen throughout this chapter, education systems are implicated in the processes of cultural reproduction, reproducing and reinforcing social inequalities. New information and communication technologies may serve to exacerbate these divisions while also creating new ones. However, if managed properly, they also offer some exciting, liberating and potentially egalitarian outcomes for education systems around the world.

Chapter review

1 How and why did modern education systems develop? List the main reasons why industrial capitalism demanded a better educated workforce.

2 Compare and contrast the main aspects of functionalist and Marxist theories of education and schooling. Explain what is meant by a 'correspondence theory' of schooling and the 'hidden curriculum'.

3 What is meant by 'cultural reproduction'? Illustrate this with examples of gender and social class from the work of Willis, Mac an Ghaill and Bernstein.

4 Provide an account of Pierre Bourdieu's general theory of forms of 'capital', including his ideas on 'fields' and 'habitus'. Give two examples showing how this theory is relevant to the study of education.

5 Trace the historical pattern of gender differences in education and explain why girls now generally outperform boys.

6 Which minority ethnic groups do least well in the UK education system and which do best? How can such inequalities and differences be explained?

7 How would you characterize the *global* situation regarding literacy, illiteracy and public spending on education? How has the 2008 economic downturn affected educational development in the developing countries?

8 What can be learned about overall trends in education in the developed world from the UK case study in this chapter?

9 Higher education has expanded significantly since the Second World War, and many societies now have mass higher education with large student numbers. What issues and problems has this expansion produced?

10 With specific examples, explain what is meant by the theory and practice of lifelong learning. Does this signal the end of conventional education and schooling?

11 Information technology is being integrated into educational processes in various ways and at all levels. How is the digital revolution likely to affect employment in the university sector?

Research in practice

Everyone who has been through formal schooling will know that school is a key site for the bullying of some pupils by their peers. But why are some pupils bullied and not others? What is it that makes some school pupils 'legitimate' targets in the eyes of peers? This article looks into the question of victimization: Lehman, B. (2014) 'Gender Differences in Bullying Victimization: The Role of Academics and School Context', *Sociological Spectrum*, 34: 549–70.

1 What research methods were used in this research? How would you characterize the study?

2 What does the author mean when he says that bullying is 'a multifaceted phenomenon'? Provide some examples to illustrate this.

3 Specifically, which aspects of intellectualism, hard work or 'being a "nerd"' tend to lead to bullying victimization? How do these factors influence the different experiences of boys and girls?

4 From the paper's analysis and conclusions, how might the bullying of successful students be tackled within the school context?

5 Devise a small-scale, qualitative study aimed at understanding bullying victimization from the standpoint of those who bully others. What ethical and practical problems do you foresee and how might you overcome them?

Thinking it through

One central issue in all sociological work is balancing the relative influences of social structure and individual agency – the so-called structure–agency problem. This issue is evident in some of the theories of education and schooling in this chapter:

- Bowles and Gintis's Marxist correspondence theory of schooling
- Bourdieu's theoretical framework covering the acquisition and use of cultural capital
- feminist theories of the reproduction of gender inequality in schools.

Compare and contrast these theories, showing how they handle structure and agency. Could they be effectively combined? Are there areas where their analyses overlap? How successful are they in connecting education systems to the wider society and its shifting social structure? Which theoretical perspective deals with the structure–agency problem in the most satisfactory way?

Society in the arts

1   Watch the 2009 film *Precious* (directed by Lee Daniels) and/or read the 1996 novel on which it is based, *Push*, by Sapphire (Chicago: Alfred A. Knopf), retitled *Precious* from 2009. The novel/film follows the life of Claireece Precious Jones, a sixteen-year-old black girl living in an American ghetto. 'Precious' is the victim of parental sexual, physical and emotional abuse and faces multiple disadvantages which severely restrict her life chances. The film follows her as she tries to change her circumstances.

Write a 1,000-word review of the film. You should discuss events and issues in the film using sociological concepts such as class, poverty, ethnicity, gender and intersectionality, and theories such as Marxism, interactionism, feminism and cultural reproduction. Your conclusion should reflect on what fictional representations such as this, based on the life of a single individual, might add to existing sociological work on education and disadvantage.

2   There are many films and novels which portray troubled teenagers whose lives are turned around by a special teacher who takes them under their wing. Such stories help to promote the notion that schooling is the route to happiness and fulfilment. However, as this chapter has shown, there is a large body of sociological work which demonstrates that schooling also reproduces inequalities and can be restrictive just as much as it is enabling.

Watch Davis Guggenheim's 2010 documentary *Waiting for 'Superman'* with this thought in mind. The film follows several students as they try to get into much sought-after places in 'charter' schools in the USA – schools that receive state funding but also have a large measure of organizational independence. What are the main criticisms of the public education system in the USA made in the film? Which of these criticisms finds support from sociological theories and critiques of schooling described in the chapter? What solutions does the film have to offer and how realistic are these?

Now watch a counter-documentary – *The Inconvenient Truth about Waiting for Superman* – which was made by the Grassroots Education Movement as a critique of Guggenheim's film, available here: http://gemnyc.org/our-film/. This documentary sets out to defend public education from business and political interests which, the makers argue, seek to undermine and privatize education. List the main criticisms of Guggenheim's film. How far do you agree with these? Why would the potential privatization of education exacerbate the intersecting social inequalities of class, race and ethnicity? Does the 'Grassroots' analysis fit into any of the sociological perspectives discussed in this chapter?

Further reading

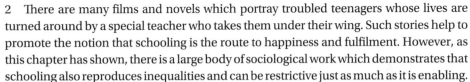

To deepen your knowledge of the sociology of education, you might want to start with a good introductory text such as Rob Moore's (2004) *Education and Society: Issues and Explanations in the Sociology of Education* (Cambridge: Polity). Sharon Gewirtz and Alan Cribb's (2009) *Understanding Education: A Sociological Perspective* (Cambridge: Polity) is also an excellent account of what sociology has to offer and is very good on inequalities in education.

The sociology of education is a well-established field within the discipline, so consulting an edited collection on specific topics is a good idea. To this end you could try Michael W. Apple, Stephen J. Ball and Luis Armando Gandin's (2011) *The Routledge International Handbook of the Sociology of Education* (London: Routledge), which contains a very comprehensive range of subjects, from theories to masculinities and inequalities. *Contemporary Debates in the Sociology of Education* (2013), edited by Rachel Brooks, Mark McCormack and Kalwant Bhopal (Basingstoke: Palgrave Macmillan), is an up-to-date set of sharp essays covering key issues.

On the transformation of education in Britain over the past decades, see Ken Jones's (2015) *Education in Britain: 1944 to the Present* (2nd edn, Cambridge: Polity). In the global age, Hugh Lauder, Phillip Brown, Jo-Anne Dillabough and A. H. Halsey's (2006) edited collection *Education, Globalization and Social Change* (Oxford: Oxford University Press) provides an effective mix of classic and contemporary readings. The concept of the digital university is explored in F. Bryce McCluskey and Melanie Lynn Winter's (2012) *The Idea of the Digital University: Ancient Traditions, Disruptive Technologies and the Battle for the Soul of Higher Education* (Washington, DC: Westphalia Press). There is an illuminating discussion of digital impacts on education in Neil Selwyn's (2016) *Is Technology Good for Education?* (Cambridge: Polity).

For a collection of original readings on social institutions, see the accompanying *Sociology: Introductory Readings* (3rd edn, Cambridge: Polity, 2010).

Internet links

@ **Additional information and support for this book at Polity:**
www.politybooks.com/giddens

@ **Sociosite on Education – lots of links to educational resources, not all of them sociological:**
www.sociosite.net/topics/education.php

@ **The Global Campaign for Education – lots of useful education resources:**
www.campaignforeducation.org

@ **21st Century Learning Initiative – UK-based archive of new ideas on education:**
www.21learn.org

@ **UNESCO Education Homepage – UN Educational, Scientific and Cultural Organization:**
http://en.unesco.org/themes/education-21st-century

@ **Lifelong Learning – a UK site promoting this concept:**
www.lifelonglearning.co.uk

CHAPTER 20

Crime and Deviance

Contents

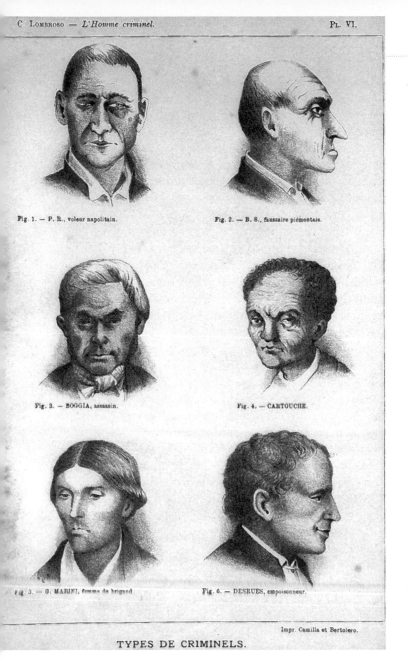

C. LOMBROSO — *L'Homme criminel.* PL. VI.

Fig. 1. — P. R., voleur napolitain.

Fig. 2. — B. S., faussaire piémontais.

Fig. 3. — BOGGIA, assassin.

Fig. 4. — CARTOUCHE.

Fig. 5. — O. MARINI, femme de brigand

Fig. 6. — DESRUES, empoisonneur.

Impr. Camilla et Bertolero.

TYPES DE CRIMINELS.

Criminal types, as presented in the French edition of his book *L'uomo delinquente*, by Cesare Lombroso (1836–1909): a robber from Naples, a forger from Piedmont, an assassin, Cartouche, whose criminal tendency is not specified, a robber's wife and a poisoner.

I n visual media such as film, theatre and television, criminals and villains are often easy to spot. In Hollywood Westerns, for instance, the bad guys tend to wear black and have distinguishing features such as tattoos or facial scars. Criminals just look different to law-abiding people. But in the real world it would be ridiculous to suggest we could identify tendencies to criminality purely on the basis of people's appearance. Or would it?

During the police investigation into the murder of Joanna Yeates in late 2010 and early 2011, the British tabloid press seemed convinced that a man they described as a 'strange' 'oddball', a 65-year-old retired schoolteacher and the victim's landlord, was the prime suspect. *The Sun* newspaper (and others) used a thirty-year-old photograph of Christopher Jefferies to make the point that he was 'a loner with blue rinse hair' (Cathcart 2011). But Mr Jefferies was innocent. A neighbour, Vincent Tabak, later pleaded guilty to manslaughter but was found guilty of murder at his trial in October 2011 and sentenced to life imprisonment with a minimum term of twenty years. The *Daily Mirror* was fined £50,000 and *The Sun* £18,000 for contempt of court for their coverage of the case, while Mr Jefferies won significant libel damages from eight newspapers for their untrue and damaging stories.

Even in the twenty-first century, then, the notion persists that criminals must somehow look unlike law-abiding people. This idea is well established. In his book *L'uomo delinquente* (1876) ('Criminal Man'), the Italian scientist Cesare Lombroso argued that criminal types *could* be identified by their visible, anatomical features. Lombroso investigated the physical characteristics of convicted criminals in prisons, such as the shape of the skull and forehead, jaw size and arm length, as well as skin markings such as tattoos. He concluded that criminals displayed clear signs of atavism. That is, they exhibited traits from earlier stages of human evolution, which 'civilized' human beings did not. Criminals were essentially uncivilized, evolutionary throwbacks and, as their criminality was inherited, they could not be held responsible for their nefarious tendencies.

In a later work on female criminals, Lombroso (with Guglielmo Ferrero) was forced to rely on photographs, as men were not allowed into women's prisons. Critics attacked his work for its lack of reliable evidence and questionable methodology, but at the time it was actually innovative, as Lombroso insisted that crime could and should be studied in a scientific manner – the basis for the discipline of criminology. Physiological and biological explanations of crime and deviance have continually resurfaced.

For example, William Sheldon's (1949) theory of 'somatotypes' distinguished three main types of human physique, each linked to individual personality, one of which was associated with delinquency and crime. Muscular active types (mesomorphs) tend to be more physical and aggressive, which means they are more likely to become delinquent than those of thin physique (ectomorphs) or more round, fleshy people (endomorphs). Sheldon also based his theory on the study of photographs, this time of some 4,000 young men, comparing their body shapes. Sheldon's critics argued that, even if there was a correlation between bodily type and delinquency, this would not necessarily show that heredity was the determining influence. People of the muscular type may be drawn towards criminal activities because these offer opportunities for the physical display of their athleticism. There is no decisive evidence that any traits of personality are inherited in this way, and, even if they were, their connection to criminality would be a distant one at best.

Scientists continue to be attracted to biological ideas. In 2011, researchers argued that their analysis of twin studies suggested that criminal tendencies exist in children as young as four years old as a result of an abnormal brain make-up. 'Callous unemotional traits' could be identified in very young infants which could predict future adult criminality. Early screening may therefore offer the possibility of interventions such as drugs to boost the brain. One researcher said, 'I believe we have to pursue the causes of crime at a biological and genetic level as well as at a social' (cited in *The Telegraph* 2011).

Biological and many psychological approaches presume that crime and deviance are signs of something 'wrong' within the individual person. By contrast, for sociologists, any satisfactory account of the nature of crime must take account of how some actions come to be categorized as 'crimes' in the first place.

Since Durkheim turned his attention to crime and deviance in the 1890s, sociological theories have focused on the social and cultural context in which crime takes place. Hence, a full answer to the question of why people commit crimes must start by questioning the question: What exactly do we mean by 'crime' and 'deviance'?

The basic concepts

Deviance is defined as non-conformity to a given set of norms that are accepted by a significant number of people in a community or society. No society can be divided in a simple way between those who deviate from norms and those who conform to them. Most people, most of the time, follow social norms because, as a result of socialization, we are used to doing so. Yet most of us, on occasion, transgress – or deviate from – generally accepted rules of behaviour. For example, we may have shoplifted in our youth or taken stationery from the workplace. Some may have exceeded speed limits, made prank phone calls or experimented with illegal drugs. As we will see, sociologists distinguish between these initial acts of primary deviance and secondary deviance, which involves the development of a deviant or criminal identity and, potentially, a criminal 'career'.

All social norms are accompanied by sanctions promoting conformity and protecting against non-conformity. A sanction is any reaction from others to the behaviour of an individual or group that is meant to ensure compliance with a given norm. Sanctions may be positive (offering rewards for conformity) or negative (punishing behaviour that does not conform). They can be levied informally or formally. *Informal sanctions* are less organized, more spontaneous reactions to non-conformity. A studious pupil who is teased by classmates for being a 'nerd' when they refuse to go out at night experiences a type of informal sanction. Informal sanctions might also occur, for example, when an individual who makes a sexist or racist comment is met with

disapproving responses from friends or work colleagues.

Formal sanctions are applied by a specific body of people or an agency to ensure that a particular set of norms is followed. The main types of formal sanction in modern societies are those represented by the courts and prisons. A law is a formal sanction defined by government as a rule or principle that its citizens must follow and is used against people who do not conform.

> **THINKING CRITICALLY**
>
> Have you or your friends committed acts that broke social norms or laws? Did you think of yourselves afterwards as 'deviants'? Why do most of us *not* see ourselves this way?

Deviance and crime are not synonymous, though in many cases they overlap. The concept of deviance is much broader than that of crime, which refers only to the breaking of laws. Many forms of deviant behaviour are not sanctioned by law. Thus, studies of deviance investigate phenomena as diverse as naturism, 1990s rave culture and the lifestyles of 'New Age' travelling groups. The concept of criminalization is also fundamental to the study of patterns of crime in criminology. When a social group or certain activities are targeted for intensified monitoring, redefinition and, ultimately, prosecution, this process is known as criminalization. For example, stalking, hate crime and knowingly passing on HIV have all undergone processes of criminalization. In recent years, Internet piracy has come under increasing scrutiny and monitoring, while some types of antisocial behaviour have also been criminalized (Croall 2011: 5).

Two distinct but related social science disciplines study crime and deviance. Criminology is 'the scientific study of crime', though this is rather too general. More accurately, criminology is 'the study of crime, attempts to control it, and attitudes to it' (Walsh and Poole 1983: 56). Criminologists are interested in techniques for measuring crime, trends in crime rates, and policies aimed at reducing crime. The

The annual 'Tomatina' festival in Buñol in Spain is a huge tomato fight in the town centre. While clearly a deviant form of behaviour, it is promoted by the authorities as a local tradition and tourist attraction.

sociology of deviance draws on criminological research but also investigates conduct which lies outside the criminal law. Sociologists studying deviance seek to understand *why* certain actions are regarded as deviant in the first place and how the concepts of deviance and normality are socially constructed. The study of deviance directs our attention to issues of power, the influence of social class and divisions between rich and poor. When we look at deviance from or conformity to social rules or norms, we always have to bear in mind the question: *whose* rules are they?

Theories of crime and deviance

In the sociology of crime and deviance, no single theory has become dominant, and diverse theoretical perspectives remain relevant and useful today. However, four broad sociological approaches have been influential in the sociology of crime and deviance: *functionalist theories*, *interactionist theories*, *conflict theories* and *control theories*. It should be noted that the development of feminist theories has had a significant impact on research in this field and that these generally fall within the broad category of 'conflict theories'. In particular, feminist research explores the gendered pattern of crime and deviance and the ways in which social norms of masculinity and femininity impact on the operation of the criminal justice system. As we have included an extended discussion of 'gender and crime' later in the chapter, feminist theorizing is embedded within that section rather than being incorporated below as an example of conflict theory.

The functions of crime

Functionalist theories see crime and deviance resulting from structural tensions and a lack of moral regulation within society. If the aspirations of individuals and groups do not coincide with society's stock of available rewards, then a disparity between desires and their fulfilment will be witnessed in the deviant motivations of some of society's members.

Crime and anomie: Durkheim and Merton

The concept of anomie was first used by Emile Durkheim to describe the undermining of traditional norms and standards in modern societies. Anomie occurs when there are no clear standards to guide behaviour in a given area of social life. Under such circumstances, people can feel deeply disoriented and anxious. People in the modern age are less constrained than in previous times and, because there is more room for individual choice, it is inevitable there will be non-conformity or deviance. In any society it is highly unlikely that there could ever be complete consensus about the norms and values that govern it.

But Durkheim went further. He claimed that deviance is actually necessary for society, as it fulfils two important functions. First, deviance has an *adaptive* function; it can introduce new ideas and challenges into society and can therefore be an innovative force, bringing about social and cultural change. Second, it promotes *boundary maintenance* between 'good' and 'bad' behaviours; a deviant or criminal act can provoke a collective response that heightens in-group solidarity and clarifies social norms.

Although Durkheim is considered a typically 'conservative' functionalist thinker, we should remember that his ideas were crucial in pointing up the limits of individual explanations and the need for properly sociological studies of social forces and relations. Durkheim's ideas on crime and deviance were considered radical at the time, running against the grain of conservative opinion. Indeed, even today his suggestion that a certain amount of deviance is functional and useful is politically controversial.

An attempt to update Durkheim's ideas on crime for the mid-twentieth century was Merton's analysis of class and crime in the USA. Adapting the concept of anomie, Merton showed that America's self-image as a relatively open, meritocratic and classless society was far from accurate. His study is discussed in detail in 'Classic studies 20.1'.

Following Merton's work, Albert Cohen also saw the contradictions within American society as the main structural cause of acquisitive crime. But, while Merton emphasized individual adaptive responses, Cohen saw the latter as occurring collectively through the formation of subcultures. In *Delinquent Boys* (1955), Cohen argued that boys in the lower working class who are frustrated with their position in life often join together in delinquent subcultures, such as gangs. These subcultures reject middle-class values, replacing them with norms that celebrate defiance and acts of non-conformity.

Normalizing deviance

As we have seen, Emile Durkheim argued that deviance has an important part to play in a well-ordered society. By defining what is deviant, we become aware of what is not deviant and thereby learn the shared standards of society. Rather than eliminating deviance completely, it is more likely that society needs to keep the level of deviance within acceptable limits.

In 'Defining Deviancy Down', Moynihan (1993) argued that deviance in the USA had increased beyond the point that society could handle or accept. But, rather than strengthening the agencies of social control and trying to cut deviance levels, deviance had been redefined so that previously unacceptable behaviours had become 'normalized'. One example was the deinstitutionalization of mental health patients that began in the 1950s. Instead of being forced into institutions, the mentally ill were treated with tranquillizers and then released. As a result, the number of psychiatric patients in New York dropped from 93,000 in 1955 to just 11,000 by 1992. Many former patients became homeless, sleeping rough across New York City, and were redefined as persons lacking affordable housing.

At the same time, the 'normal' or acceptable level of crime had risen. Moynihan points out that, after the St Valentine's Day massacre in 1929, in which seven gangsters were murdered, the public and government were outraged. Yet, today, the number of murders in the USA is much higher than in the 1920s, and they are so often reported in the media that they hardly provoke a reaction at all. Moynihan also sees the under-reporting of crime as another way in which it becomes 'normalized'. However, he did not see redefining deviance down as a positive development: instead, he argued that many normalized behaviours have negative consequences both for the individual and for society as a whole.

Evaluation

Functionalist theories rightly emphasize the links between conformity and deviance in

Classic Studies 20.1   Robert Merton and the failing American dream

The research problem

Why have crime rates remained relatively high in the developed societies? Does increasing affluence lead to less criminality? To answer these questions, the American sociologist Robert K. Merton (1957) used Durkheim's concept of anomie to construct an influential theory which located the sources of crime within the social structure of American society. Merton tried to explain a well-established observation from official statistics at the time, that a high proportion of crimes for immediate financial gain are committed by the 'lower working class' – those from manual, blue-collar families. Why should this be so?

Merton's explanation

Merton used the concept of 'anomie' to describe the *strain* which occurs when widely accepted cultural values conflict with people's lived social reality. In American society – and, by extension, in similarly developed countries – generally held values emphasize material success, achieved through self-discipline, education and hard work. Accordingly, people who work hard can succeed no matter what their starting point in life – an idea known as 'the American dream', as it has proved so attractive to immigrant groups. Merton argued that, for many social groups, it really is just a dream, because disadvantaged groups have only limited conventional opportunities for advancement or none at all. Yet those who do not 'succeed' find themselves condemned for their inability to make material progress. In this situation, there is great pressure or 'strain' to try to get ahead by any means. Deviance and crime are the products of the strain between cultural values and the unequal distribution of legitimate opportunities.

The idea of the American dream – an open society where people will always succeed by their own efforts – has motivated people from across the world to live and work in the USA.

Table 20.1 Adaptive responses to social strain

	Approved values	Approved means
Conformity	+	+
Innovation (crime)	+	−
Ritualism	−	+
Retreatism	−	−
Rebellion	replacement	replacement

Merton identified five possible responses to the tension between socially endorsed values and the limited means for achieving them (see table 20.1). *Conformists* accept both generally held values and the conventional means for realizing them; a majority of the population fall into this category. *Innovators* also accept socially approved values but, finding legitimate avenues blocked, turn to illegitimate means to follow them. Criminals who acquire wealth through illegal activities exemplify this type. *Ritualists* conform to social values despite not being particularly successful, following the rules purely for their own sake. Someone who dedicates themselves to a boring job, even though it has no career prospects and few rewards, is an example. *Retreatists* have abandoned the values and the legitimate means, effectively 'dropping out' of mainstream society. Finally, *rebels* reject both the existing values and legitimate means but, instead of dropping out, work actively to transform the system and institute new values. Members of radical political groups fall into this category.

Merton's scheme is designed to capture some of the main responses of social groups to their differing location in the social structure. In particular, it suggests a deeply felt relative deprivation among 'lower-working-class' groups, which explains their over-representation in the prison population.

Critical points

Critics point out that, in focusing on individual responses, Merton failed to appreciate the significance of subcultures in sustaining deviant behaviour, an omission he later sought to rectify in his work on reference groups. His reliance on official statistics is problematic, because these are inevitably partial and may tell us more about the process of collection than the true extent of crime. Merton's thesis also overestimates the amount of 'lower-working-class' criminality, implying that everyone in this class fraction should experience the strain towards crime. But, as the majority never become involved in crime, we have to ask, why not? Similarly, the model underestimates middle-class crime. More recent research has found unexpectedly high levels of white-collar and corporate crime, which is not predicted by Merton's model.

Contemporary significance

Merton's study retains its significance because it addresses a central research problem: when society as a whole is becoming more affluent, why does acquisitive crime (for financial or material gain) not rapidly fall? In emphasizing the social strain between rising aspirations and persistent structural social inequalities, Merton points to relative deprivation among manual working-class groups as an important motivator for deviant behaviour. His research was also an effective sociological critique of biological and psychological explanations of crime and deviance. He shows that individual choices and motivations are always made within a wider social context, which shapes them according to the differential opportunities available to social groups.

  The idea of relative deprivation is discussed in chapter 13, 'Poverty, Social Exclusion and Welfare'.

different social contexts. Lack of opportunity to succeed can be a key differentiating factor between those who engage in criminal behaviour and those who do not. But we should be cautious about the idea that people in poorer communities aspire to the same level of success as more affluent groups. Most tend to adjust their aspirations to what they see as the reality of their situation, and only a minority ever turn to crime. It would also be wrong to suppose that a mismatch of aspirations and opportunities is confined to the less privileged. There are opportunities for criminal activity among other groups too, as indicated by the 'white-collar crimes' of embezzlement, fraud and tax evasion, which we deal with later in the chapter.

Interactionist perspectives

Sociologists working from an interactionist perspective focus on the social construction of crime and deviance, rejecting the notion that there are types of conduct that are inherently or objectively 'deviant'. Interactionists ask how such behaviours come to be defined as deviant and why certain groups and not others are likely to be labelled as deviant. For example, over recent years there has been an increasing focus on recipients of welfare benefits that, arguably, amounts to a redefinition of their status in society from legitimate to illegitimate claimants. The concept of criminalization was devised by criminologists to capture such processes of definition and redefinition in relation to crime and offending behaviour.

Labelling perspectives

One of the most important interactionist approaches has been the labelling perspective. Labelling theorists interpret deviance as the product of interaction processes between deviants and non-deviants. Therefore, if we are to understand the nature of deviance, we must discover why some people come to be tagged with a 'deviant' label.

Labelling processes tend to express the power structure of society. By and large, the rules in terms of which deviance is defined are framed by the wealthy for the poor, by men for women, by older people for younger people, and by ethnic majorities for minority groups. For example, many young university students experiment with legal and illegal drugs, which is accepted by authorities as a 'normal' part of the move into adulthood. However, young people's drug use on a deprived, inner city housing estate may be viewed as evidence of delinquency and future criminality. The primary act is the same but is assigned different meanings depending on the context.

Howard Becker's (1963) work showed how deviant identities are produced through labelling processes rather than through deviant motivations. Becker argued that 'deviant behaviour is behaviour that people so label.' He was highly critical of criminological approaches that saw a clear distinction between the 'normal' and the 'deviant'. For Becker, deviant behaviour is not the determining factor in why people take on the identity of 'deviant'. Rather, there are processes which are more influential in determining whether or not someone is so labelled. A person's dress, manner of speaking or country of origin could be the key factors that determine whether or not a deviant label is applied.

Labelling theory came to be associated with Becker's (1963) studies of marijuana smokers. In the early 1960s, smoking marijuana was a marginal activity within subcultures rather than the lifestyle choice it has become today. Becker found that becoming a marijuana smoker depended on one's acceptance into the subculture – close association with experienced users who taught new members how to use and enjoy the drug and adopt in-group attitudes towards non-users. It did not depend simply on the objective act of smoking.

Labelling not only affects how others perceive an individual, it also influences that individual's own sense of self-identity. Edwin Lemert (1972) devised a model for understanding how deviance can either coexist with or become central to one's identity. He argued that, contrary to common-sense ideas, deviance is actually quite commonplace and most

THINKING CRITICALLY

Both of these people are engaged in deviance. Which one is more likely to be *labelled* as 'a deviant'? List the consequences for the individual that may follow from being so labelled.

people usually get away with it. For example, traffic violations rarely come to light and small-scale theft is often tolerated or 'overlooked'.

Lemert called the initial act of transgression primary deviance. In most cases, these acts remain 'marginal' to the person's self-identity and the deviant act becomes normalized. But in other cases normalization does not occur, and the person is labelled a criminal or deviant. Lemert used the term secondary deviance to describe the cases where individuals come to accept the deviant label for themselves. The new label can then become a master status, overriding all other indicators of status, becoming central to the person's sense of self-identity and leading to a continuation or intensification of their deviant behaviour.

Longitudinal studies of the development of 'criminal careers' have led to an increasing

focus on early interventions with children and young people. These aim to tackle a series of risk factors for offending in order to prevent the development of extended secondary deviance. Farrington (2003: 2) argues that the typical age at the onset of offending is between eight and fourteen, and early onset is a good predictor of a long criminal career. Early interventions may be able to prevent young people from taking this first step. Farrington and Welsh (2007: 4) report that there is good evidence that preschool enrichment programmes, child skills training and parental education schemes can be effective in preventing later offending.

The process of 'learning to be deviant' can also be accentuated by prisons and other control agencies, the very organizations charged with correcting deviant behaviour. For labelling theorists, this is a clear demonstration of the 'paradox of social control', described by Wilkins (1964) as deviancy amplification. Wilkins was interested in how deviant identities are 'managed' and integrated into daily life. He suggested that the outcome of this process is often deviancy amplification. This refers to the unintended consequence of an agency of control provoking more of the deviant behaviour it set out to stop. If the labelled person incorporates the label into his or her identity through secondary deviance, this is likely to provoke more responses from agencies of control. In other words, the behaviour that was seen as undesirable becomes more prevalent, and those labelled as deviant become more resistant to change.

Evaluation

Labelling perspectives are important because they begin from the assumption that no act is intrinsically 'deviant' but becomes so through the formulation of laws and their interpretation by police, courts and correctional institutions. Critics of labelling argue that certain acts – such as killing others, rape and robbery – *are* universally and consistently prohibited across all societies. Yet this view is surely incorrect. Killing, for example, is not always regarded as murder. In times of war, killing the enemy is positively approved of and rewarded. Similarly, until the second half of the twentieth century, laws in much of Europe and North America did not recognize sexual intercourse forced on a woman by her husband as 'rape'. Clearly the same act can be relabelled and its meaning in society can change.

However, we can criticize labelling on more convincing grounds. First, in focusing on secondary deviance, labelling theorists downplay the significance and fail to explain acts of primary deviance. The labelling of activities as deviant is not completely arbitrary; differences in socialization, attitudes and opportunities all influence how far people are likely to engage in behaviour branded as deviant or criminal. Second, it is not clear whether labelling really does have the effect of increasing deviant conduct. Deviant behaviour tends to escalate following conviction, but is this the result of labelling? Other factors, such as greater interaction with other offenders or learning about new criminal opportunities, may also be involved. Nonetheless, although not a comprehensive account, the labelling perspective remains one part of any satisfactory explanation of why deviant identities are adopted.

Conflict theories

In 1973, publication of *The New Criminology* marked an important break with earlier theories of crime and deviance. Taylor, Walton and Young (1973) drew on Marxist theory, arguing that deviance is deliberately chosen and often political in nature. They rejected the idea that deviance is 'determined' by biology, personality, anomie, social disorganization or labelling. People actively choose to engage in deviant behaviour as a response to the inequalities of the capitalist system. Thus, members of counter-cultural groups regarded as 'deviant' – such as the Black Power or gay liberation movements – were engaging in political acts which challenged the existing social order. Theorists of this new criminology framed their analysis in terms of the structure of society and the protection of ruling class power.

This broadly Marxist perspective was developed by others. Stuart Hall and his colleagues at the Birmingham Centre for Contemporary Cultural Studies in the UK carried out an important study of the apparently new 1970s offence of 'mugging'. In fact, mugging was a term used in the press to refer to street robberies with the threat of violence. Several high-profile muggings were publicized in the mass media, fuelling widespread popular concerns of an explosion of violent street crime. Muggers were overwhelmingly portrayed as young, black men, contributing to the view that immigrants were responsible for a breakdown in society.

In *Policing the Crisis* (1978), Hall and his colleagues maintained that the criminalization of young black men was a moral panic, encouraged by both the state and the media

Classic Studies 20.2 Stan Cohen's folk devils and moral panics

The research problem

Youth subcultures can be colourful, spectacular and, for authorities, quite alarming. But how are they created and how do societies react to youthful creativity? The process of *deviancy amplification* was examined in a highly influential study conducted by Stanley Cohen, published in 1972 as *Folk Devils and Moral Panics*. Cohen examined labelling processes in relation to the emergence and control of youth cultures in the UK. As a young postgraduate student, he observed some minor clashes between 'Mods' and 'Rockers' in the seaside town of Clacton in 1964, but could not reconcile what he saw with newspaper reports the following day. Had he just missed the violence they reported or was there another explanation?

Cohen's explanation

Lurid newspaper headlines, such as 'Day of Terror by Scooter Groups' and 'Wild Ones Invade the Seaside', described the young people at Clacton as 'out of control'. Though Cohen says this was wide of the mark, the tone was set. In carefully sifting the documentary evidence from newspapers, court reports and arrest records, Cohen reconstructed the events at Clacton, showing that, apart from a few minor skirmishes, nothing out of the ordinary had happened. In fact, far worse disturbances had occurred in the years before the Mods and Rockers emerged. In presenting young people's activities in a sensationalist way, the press contributed to a climate of fear and a panic that society's moral rules were under threat.

Attempts to control youth subcultures in the UK during the 1960s succeeded in drawing attention to them and made them more popular. The process of labelling a group as *outsiders* – or 'folk devils' – in an attempt to control them, backfired. Future seaside gatherings attracted much larger crowds, including some youths just looking for a fight, potentially creating larger problems for law enforcement – a classic instance of the paradox of social control. Exaggerated media coverage was part of a new moral panic – a concept used by sociologists to describe societal over-reaction towards a certain social group or type of behaviour. Moral panics often emerge around public issues that are taken as symptomatic of general social disorder.

Critical points

Critics claim that the main problem with the theory was how to differentiate between an exaggerated moral panic and a serious social problem. For example, would the societal response to recent 'Islamist' terrorist acts be part of a moral panic, or is this so serious that extensive media coverage and new laws are appropriate? Where does the boundary lie between an unnecessary panic and a legitimate response? Similarly, in diverse, multicultural societies, are there still clearly defined shared values that delineate normal from deviant behaviour? A further criticism is that, in recent years, persistent moral panics have arisen over matters such as 'welfare scroungers', immigration and youthful crime and drug use. This has led some to argue that moral panics are no longer confined to short bursts of intense activity but are chronic features of everyday life in modern societies and, as such, have become 'institutionalized'.

Contemporary significance

Cohen's early study is particularly important because it successfully combined theories of deviant labelling with ideas of social control and the creation of deviant identities. In doing so, it created the framework for a productive research agenda in the sociology of deviance which has shed light on moral panics around 'black criminality', welfare 'scroungers', refugees and asylum-seekers and young people's drug use (Cohen 2003; Marsh and Melville 2011). Cohen's study also reminds us that, as sociologists, we cannot take events at face value or accept journalists' reports as accurate. Instead, we have to dig beneath the surface if we are better to understand societies and social processes.

THINKING CRITICALLY

Do your own research into media reporting of a) immigration statistics and b) Internet 'grooming' of children. Do either of these fit the criteria for a moral panic?

---

as a way of deflecting attention away from rising unemployment, declining wages and other deep structural flaws within society. As we will see in the section on victimization below, a notable feature of the patterning of crime and deviance is that some social groups, such as young people within black and South Asian communities, are much more likely to be victims of crime, or seen as a social problem, than others. Around the same time, other conflict criminologists examined the formation and use of the law, arguing that laws are tools used by the powerful to maintain their own privileged positions. As inequalities increase between the ruling class and the working class, law becomes a more important instrument which the powerful use to maintain order. This dynamic could be seen in the workings of the criminal justice system, which had become more oppressive towards working-class 'offenders', or in tax legislation, which disproportionately favoured the wealthy.

Powerful individuals also break laws, but they are rarely monitored and caught. Corporate crime, for example, is arguably far more economically harmful than the everyday crime and delinquency which attracts most attention. But, fearful of the difficulty and implications of pursuing corporate offenders, law-enforcement agencies focus their efforts on less powerful members of society, such as prostitutes, drug users and petty thieves (Pearce 1976; Chambliss 1978; Box 1983).

These studies and others associated with the 'new criminology' were important in widening the debate about crime and deviance to include questions of relative harm, social justice, power and politics. They emphasized that crime occurs at all levels of society and must be understood in the context of inequalities and competing interests. Indeed, the new criminology led to a new sub-field known as zemiology – the study of social harm focused on economic and social inequalities and their damaging impact. For scholars working within this perspective, social harm is of greater significance than crime or deviance (Hillyard et al. 2004).

> ### THINKING CRITICALLY
> Imagine you have been paid to carry out a research study into the use of so-called legal highs and harm. How would you measure the level of harm to individuals, communities and society caused by these products?

Left Realism

By the 1980s, partly in response to perceived inadequacies of the new criminology, a perspective emerged which became known as 'New Left Realism' or just 'Left Realism'. Left Realism drew on ideas from the 'new criminology', but its proponents distanced themselves from so-called left idealists, whom they saw as romanticizing deviance as a form of rebellion. For Left Realists, crime is a real problem that is especially harmful to working-class communities and its significance should not be downplayed. Many criminologists on the political left had tended to minimize the importance of official crime statistics, arguing that these were not reliable but were used by the mass media to create fear and to scapegoat working-class youth and minority ethnic groups.

Left Realists did not agree. They emphasized that there was reliable evidence that crime had increased and the public was right to be concerned. Rather than focusing on theoretical arguments, Left Realists saw that criminology had to engage with the 'real' issues of crime control and social policy (Lea and Young 1984; Matthews and Young 1986). In particular, they were interested in the victims of crime, not just the perpetrators. They argued that victim surveys can provide a more valid picture than official statistics of the extent of crime (Evans 1992). Successive surveys revealed that crime was indeed a serious problem, particularly in impoverished inner-city areas. Left Realists pointed out that rates of crime and victimization were concentrated in marginalized neighbourhoods and that poorer social groups in society were at a much greater risk of becoming victims of crime than the wealthy.

Left Realists emphasize the real and very harmful effects of crime on the lives of the poorest people and communities in society.

Left Realism draws on Merton's work on social strain and subcultural theories, suggesting that criminal subcultures develop in the inner cities. However, these do not derive directly from conditions of poverty but from political marginalization and relative deprivation – people's experience of being deprived of things to which they and everyone else is entitled. Since the 1990s these ideas have increasingly been discussed using the concept of social exclusion – the processes that operate effectively to deny some social groups full citizenship. Criminalized youth groups, for example, operate at the margins of 'respectable society' and pit themselves against it. The fact that rates of crime carried out by black youths have risen over recent years is attributed to the fact that policies of racial integration have failed.

 The ideas of relative deprivation and social exclusion are discussed in chapter 13, 'Poverty, Social Exclusion and Welfare'.

Left Realists advanced what they saw as 'realistic' proposals for changes in policing to make law enforcement more responsive to communities, rather than relying on 'military' techniques which reduce public support for the police. They proposed 'minimal policing', where locally elected police authorities would be accountable to citizens, who would have a larger say in setting priorities for their area. Furthermore, by spending more time investigating and clearing up crimes and less time on routine administration, the police could regain the trust of local communities. On the whole, Left Realism represents a more pragmatic and policy-oriented approach to crime than many of the criminological perspectives which preceded it.

However, while critics accept the importance placed on victimization, they see the focus on individual victims in political and media-driven discussions of 'the crime problem' as too narrow. The focus on only the most visible forms of crime, such as street crimes, neglects other offences, such as those carried out by the state or large corporations that are not so obvious (Walton and Young 1998). In this sense, many Marxists argued, Left Realism concedes too much ground to mainstream criminology, which calls into question the 'radicalism' of the new criminology.

Controlling crime

Control theories see crime occurring as the result of an imbalance between the impulse towards criminal activity and the social or physical controls that deter it. Control theorists are interested less in individual motivations to commit crimes. They assume that people act rationally and instrumentally, so, if deviant acts would benefit an individual, then, given the opportunity, most people would commit them. Many types of crime, it is argued, are the result of such 'situational decisions', when a person sees an opportunity and is motivated to take advantage of it.

An early control theorist, Travis Hirschi (1969), argued that humans are fundamentally selfish beings who make calculated decisions about whether or not to commit crime by weighing the potential benefits against the risks of doing so. Hirschi proposed four types of social bond linking people to society and, hence, to law-abiding behaviour: attachment (to parents, peers and institutions), commitment (to conventional lifestyles), involvement (in mainstream activities) and beliefs (respect for the law and authority). When sufficiently strong, these bonds help to maintain social control by tying people into conforming behaviour. But, if the bond with society is weak, delinquency and deviance may result. Hirschi's approach suggests that delinquents are often individuals with low levels of self-control as a result of inadequate socialization at home or in school (Gottfredson and Hirschi 1990).

Hirschi's control theory shifts the focus away from the question of why people commit crimes to ask, instead, why do people *not* break the law? Talcott Parsons (1937) had already provided a sociological solution to this question: most people conform positively; they want to be law-abiding citizens, which is a consequence of socialization and their desire for sociability. Tom Tyler (2006) fleshed out this idea with his empirical research in the USA on why people obey the law.

Tyler suggests that people's compliance with laws is closely related to their personal morality and perception that the law is legitimate. For example, people may evaluate each law according to their personal moral code. If so, they will obey those laws which accord with that morality but not ones that do not. Many middle-class people are generally law-abiding but may also use cannabis, break the speed limit on motorways, and help themselves to stationery from the workplace. They do these things because they do not see them as 'immoral'. At the same time, they may castigate others who shoplift or spray graffiti in public places as criminals lacking a moral code.

On the other hand, people may obey the law because they believe that law-making and enforcing bodies are legitimate and have the right to enact and enforce the law. Where this is the case, people tend to obey all the laws. But Tyler notes that negative experiences with the police or courts – such as young black men being repeatedly stopped and searched – may challenge people's attitude to legitimate authority. However, in both cases – compliance via personal morality and compliance via legitimacy – people obey laws because of their internalized norms of fairness and justice, not because they fear punishment. This 'procedural justice' perspective means that, even where people disagree with particular decisions or outcomes, provided the procedures used are seen as just, then the authorities should retain their legitimacy.

Tyler's research suggests that lengthening jail sentences or sending more young people to prison will most likely not prevent future offending. What authorities could do is ensure that the procedures used in the criminal justice system operate in ways that are just, which would sustain respect for the law among the public. However, another influential perspective on crime in the 1980s, similarly focused on individual and familial morality, sought to tackle crime by strengthening policing and taking a harder line on sentencing. This approach was known as 'Right(-wing) Realism'.

Right Realism

The late 1970s election successes of Margaret Thatcher in Britain and Ronald Reagan in the USA led to vigorous 'law-and-order' approaches to crime in both countries, often described as Right Realism. They saw the perceived escalation of crime and delinquency as linked to moral degeneracy, the decline of individual responsibility due to welfare dependency and liberal education, the decentring of the nuclear family model, and the wider erosion of traditional values (Murray 1984). Public debates and extensive media coverage centred on the crisis of violence and lawlessness which threatened social order.

For Right Realists, deviance is a problem of individuals who *choose* destructive, lawless behaviour and lack self-control and morality. Right Realism was dismissive of other 'theoretical' approaches, especially those that linked crime to poverty and class-based inequality. Conservative governments in the UK and the USA began to intensify law-enforcement activities. Police powers were extended, funding for the criminal justice system was expanded, new prisons were built, and long prison sentences were increasingly used as the most effective deterrent against crime.

In the USA, 'three strikes laws' were introduced by state governments in the 1990s to tackle 'habitual' offenders. Third-time offenders were given mandatory jail terms to keep the public safe from their activities. Of course, one major consequence of such policies has been the enormous growth of prison populations.

In the USA the prison population more than doubled, from around 774,000 in 1990 to more than 1.6 million by 2008 (US Census Bureau 2011). In England and Wales, there were 46,400 people in prison in 1990, a figure that had risen to 85,590 by May 2015 (Ministry of Justice 2015). An increasing prison population may be seen as a good thing as it takes criminal activity off the streets. However, it can also be seen as a policy failure, which represents an acceptance that more people will inevitably turn to crime.

Environmental criminologies

Modern control theory sees rises in crime as an outcome of the increasing number of opportunities and targets in contemporary societies. As the population becomes more affluent, consumerism becomes central to people's lives, and televisions, DVD players, computers, cars and designer clothing are owned by more and more people. A larger number of residential homes are left empty during the daytime as more women take on employment outside the home, and 'motivated offenders', interested in committing crimes, can then select from a range of 'suitable targets'.

Since the 1980s, a raft of pragmatic measures have been tried aimed at 'designing out crime' rather than reforming criminals. Collectively, such measures have come to be known as environmental criminology. Although environmental criminologies appear novel, they can be seen as extending the 'ecological' ideas of the Chicago School of Sociology in 1920s and 1930s America. Chicago School sociologists saw modern cities as productive of 'social disorganization' – the weakening of primary social relations through poverty and transient populations – and crime flourished in such environments, as neighbourhoods were not able effectively to defend themselves. An echo of this approach can be heard in environmental criminologies.

The Chicago School's ideas are discussed in chapter 6, 'Cities and Urban Life'.

Recent government policy on crime prevention in the UK has focused on limiting the opportunities for the commission of crimes in an approach known as situational crime prevention (SCP), a type of environmental criminology (Hughes 1998; Colquhoun 2004). SCP and other environmental criminologies are distinctive in concentrating on changing environments rather than trying to reform offenders – justified by acknowledging that rehabilitation programmes have been tried over many years with very limited success. Moving away from transforming people to transforming the contexts within which they live was seen as a novel move.

Central to such policies are the ideas of *surveillance* and *target hardening*. Surveillance involves communities 'policing' themselves via Neighbourhood Watch schemes and often makes use of closed circuit television (CCTV) systems in city centres and public spaces to deter criminal activity. Modifying the local environment has become a more widespread technique, making it more difficult for crimes to take place by intervening directly into potential 'crime situations'.

Target hardening involves strengthening the security of potential targets, making them more difficult to steal. For example, factory-fitted vehicle immobilizers, alarms and better locks are intended to reduce the opportunities for car thieves, while gaming machines are fitted with tougher coin boxes to deter opportunistic vandals. SCP theorists based their ideas on a widespread feeling that previous policies which had tried to reform criminals had all failed.

Target-hardening techniques, combined with zero-tolerance policing, have gained favour among politicians in recent years and have been successful in reducing crime in some contexts. Zero tolerance in the USA targets petty crime and forms of disruptive conduct, such as vandalism, loitering and public drunkenness, in order to prevent more serious forms developing. However, although the language of zero tolerance has become quite popular in the UK, especially among politicians, in practice, British policing has not

been significantly changed as a result (Jones and Newburn 2007).

Target hardening and zero-tolerance policing do not address the underlying causes of crime, but they do protect and defend certain social groups. The growing popularity of private security services, car alarms, house alarms, guard dogs and gated communities has led some people to feel that we are heading towards an 'armoured society' or 'military urbanism', where segments of the population feel compelled to defend themselves against others (Graham 2010). This tendency is occurring not only in Britain and the United States, as the gap between the wealthiest and most deprived widens, but is particularly marked in the former Soviet Union, South Africa and Brazil, where a 'fortress mentality' has emerged among the privileged (Davis 2006).

There is another unintended consequence of such policies: as popular crime targets are 'hardened', patterns of crime shift from one domain to another. For example, strengthening the security of new cars left older models relatively more vulnerable. The result was that car theft shifted from newer models to older ones. Target-hardening and zero-tolerance approaches run the risk of displacing criminal offences from better protected areas into more vulnerable ones and, as Left Realists point out, victimization is likely to fall even more disproportionately on poorer communities. Neighbourhoods that are poor or lacking in social cohesion may well experience a growth in crime and delinquency as affluent areas succeed in defending themselves.

Target hardening and zero-tolerance policing are based on a theory known as 'broken windows' (Wilson and Kelling 1982). This is rooted in a 1960s study by Philip Zimbardo (1969), who abandoned cars without licence plates and with their bonnets raised in the wealthy community of Palo Alto, California, and a poor neighbourhood in the Bronx, New York. In both places, as soon as passers-by, regardless of class or race, sensed that the vehicles were abandoned and that 'no one cared', the cars were vandalized. The authors argued that small signs of social disorder,

The widespread use of CCTV in urban environments (and elsewhere) is one example of the intensified surveillance that is typical in situational crime prevention initiatives.

even the appearance of a broken window, will encourage more serious crime to flourish. As a result, minor acts of deviance can lead to a spiral of crime and social decay (Felson 1994).

Since the late 1980s, the broken windows theory has had some impact on policing strategy in some areas, focusing on 'minor' crimes, such as drinking or using drugs in public and traffic violations. In the UK, antisocial behaviour orders and contracts were introduced to deal with a range of low-level disorder, while,

in the USA, new control measures such as Stay Out of Drug Areas (SODA) and Off-limits Orders have been used to remove individuals from public parks or shopping centres for littering, drinking alcohol in public and other unwanted activities. This spatial exclusion has been described as the reintroduction into contemporary criminal justice systems of the very old punishment of banishment (or exile) (Beckett and Herbert 2010).

One flaw with the broken windows theory is that defining 'social disorder' and what behaviour is likely to lead to it is left largely to police forces. But, without a systematic, shared definition, a wide variety of behaviour could be interpreted as threat to social order. In fact, as crime rates fell throughout the 1990s, the number of complaints of police abuse and harassment went up, particularly from young, black men in urban areas who fitted the profile of a potential criminal.

Theoretical conclusions

What can we conclude from this survey of theories of crime? First, we must recall a point made earlier: even though crime is only one type of deviant behaviour, it covers such a variety of activities – from shoplifting a bar of chocolate to intentional, planned murder – that it is highly unlikely any single theory could ever account for all criminal conduct. Sociological theories of crime emphasize the continuity between criminal and 'normal' behaviour. The contexts in which particular types of activity are seen as criminal and punishable by law vary widely and are linked to broader questions of power and inequality in processes of criminalization, which draw some social groups disproportionately into the criminal justice system.

Nonetheless, the growth of criminology since the late 1960s has lent support to many more pragmatic and policy-oriented perspectives, which seek not just to understand crime or to explain why it occurs but to intervene to prevent it. This more applied focus has become the dominant one in social science and, to a large extent, has today overshadowed the earlier sociology of deviance. Criminology

"We find that all of us, as a society, are to blame, but only the defendant is guilty."

is now a distinctive enterprise which makes use of sociological ideas but is not simply another specialism in sociology. Its research studies are often funded by government agencies, and criminology is today a key element of the 'discourse' of crime within society, which shapes how this phenomenon is understood.

We now turn to recent crime trends and discuss the thorny issue of crime statistics, which form the basis for political debates about the extent of crime and whether it really is increasing or declining. As we will see, finding answers to such apparently simple questions is far from easy.

Patterns of crime in the United Kingdom

As measured by the number of crimes reported to the police, rates of crime in the developed countries increased enormously over most of the twentieth century before the trend went into reverse from the 1990s. While politicians and media commentators often discuss rising or falling crime rates as though the statistics are accurate representations of crime in society, sociologists approach them with great care. We must bear in mind that no international standard exists for the recording of crimes and that national legal systems differ

widely, which greatly reduces the scope for the direct comparison of crime rates. Crime statistics have proved to be the least reliable and most contentious type of information in social research. Indeed some have suggested that they are entirely useless and should be abandoned altogether (Box 1983). This section focuses on the UK, mainly England and Wales, in order to examine some of the general issues and problems associated with crime statistics through a single national case.

Before the 1920s there were fewer than 100,000 offences recorded each year in England and Wales. This figure rose to around 500,000 by 1950 and peaked at 5.6 million in 1992 (ONS 2014a). Levels of recorded crime more than doubled between 1977 and 1992. However, since the mid-1990s, the overall number of crimes committed in England and Wales has levelled off, with both recorded police and additional victim surveys, such as the Crime Survey for England and Wales (CSEW), showing a considerable fall (see figure 20.1). This is consistent with the trend in most other European countries. The risk of becoming a victim of crime in England and Wales in the twenty-first century is at its lowest for at least two decades (Clegg et al. 2005). The end of continually rising crime figures took many experts by surprise and its causes are still not clear. But can we take such a statistical shift at face value?

Despite falling crime figures, there remains a widespread public perception that crime has actually become *more* prevalent (Nicholas et al. 2007). And while concerns about some types of police recorded crime have lessened, anxiety over antisocial behaviour – such as littering, groups of teenagers hanging around and drug dealing – has remained quite stable (ONS 2014d: 112–13). In the postwar years of the 1950s, crime was seen as marginal to people's everyday lives, but today it is a prominent concern for many. Numerous surveys have shown that people experience heightened anxiety about going out after dark, having their homes burgled or becoming victims of violence.

How much crime actually exists and how vulnerable are people to becoming victims?

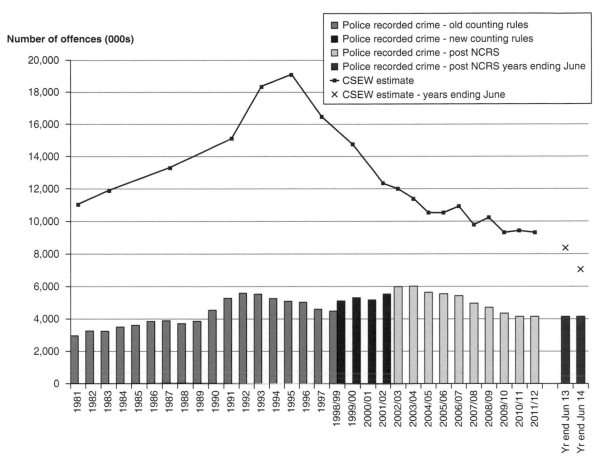

Number of offences (000s)

Legend:
- Police recorded crime - old counting rules
- Police recorded crime - new counting rules
- Police recorded crime - post NCRS
- Police recorded crime - post NCRS years ending June
- CSEW estimate
- CSEW estimate - years ending June

Figure 20.1 Trends in police recorded crime and the CSEW, 1981–June 2014

Note: The National Crime Recording Standard (NCRS) was introduced in 2002 to improve consistency across police forces by applying standard legal definitions to victim reports. *Source*: ONS (2014b: 6).

What can be done to prevent crime? These questions have become highly political as media coverage has risen along with public outrage, and as governments have promised to be 'tough on crime and tough on the causes of crime'. Untangling the nature and distribution of crime, let alone designing policies to address it, has proved to be far from straightforward, and we need to begin our exploration by looking at how crime is reported and recorded.

Understanding crime statistics

How can we determine the extent of crime and the most common forms of offence? One

obvious answer is to examine the official statistics on the number of crimes committed, which are recorded by the police. Since these recorded crime statistics are published regularly, it may appear that there is a readily available, reliable source of information that allows us to gauge the true extent of crime. Yet this assumption is quite erroneous, as there are significant limitations to all such official statistics.

The most basic limitation of statistics based on reported crime is that the majority of crimes are not reported to the police at all. For example, in 2009–10, just 43 per cent of crimes reported by victims to the British Crime Survey

(BCS) were known to the police, which means that 57 per cent had not come to their attention. There are many reasons why people do not report crimes (see table 20.2). Victims may see the offence as a private matter which they have to deal with themselves or they might think their account will not be believed. Even when a victim is wounded, more than half of these cases are not reported to the police.

Crime may go unreported for other reasons. Some forms of criminal violence, for example, are more 'hidden' than others. Physical

Table 20.2	**Reasons for not reporting crime, by crime category, England and Wales, 2009–10 (percentages)**							
	Vandalism	Burglary	Thefts from vehicles & attempts[a]	Other household theft	Other personal theft	All violence[b]	Comparable crime[c]	All BCS crime
Trivial/no loss/ police would not/could not do anything[d]	85	67	88	84	67	52	74	75
Private/dealt with ourselves	8	14	8	8	10	36	16	15
Inconvenient to report	4	7	6	7	9	4	5	6
Reported to other authorities	3	4	1	2	17	9	4	6
Common occurrence	2	1	1	2	1	3	2	2
Fear of reprisal	2	6	0	3	1	4	2	2
Dislike or fear of the police/ previous bad experience with the police or courts	2	2	1	1	1	2	2	2
Other[e]	4	10	5	3	9	8	6	6
Unweighted base	*2,006*	*280*	*932*	*1,260*	*492*	*633*	*4,522*	*6,274*

Notes:
[a] Theft of vehicles not shown as very few incidents were not reported.
[b] All violence includes wounding, assault with minor injury, assault without injury, and robbery (and is equivalent to comparable violence in previous publications).
[c] 'Comparable crime' includes vandalism, burglary, vehicle-related theft, bicycle theft, theft from the person, wounding, assault with minor injury, assault without injury, and robbery.
[d] Too trivial/no loss/would not have been interested/police could not do anything/attempt at offence was unsuccessful are merged due to the similarity in their definition, for example: a respondent who thinks the incident was too trivial may code the incident as 'too trivial. no loss' or 'the police would not be interested' as these two codes may be understood as meaning the same.
[e] This category includes: something that happens as part of job; partly my/friend's/relative's fault: offender not responsible for actions; thought someone else had reported incident/similar incidents; tried to report but was not able to contact the police/police not interested; other. Figures may add to more than 100 as more than one reason could be given.

Source: Flatley et al. (2010: 44).

and sexual abuse often takes place behind closed doors in the home, in care institutions or in prisons. Victims may fear they will not be believed by the police or that the abuse will get worse if they report it. For example, victims of domestic violence, overwhelmingly women, are often reluctant to report crimes to the police as they may believe the abuser will take revenge or that police will not take it seriously. In the UK, many victims of sexual abuse perpetrated by former DJ Sir Jimmy Savile did not come forward until after his death, as many thought the police and public would never believe that such a well-respected figure could also be a serial sex offender (Gray and Watt 2013: 5). For other types of offence, people may assume that the crime is too trivial to be reported or that the police would not be able to do anything about it anyway. On the other hand, almost all car thefts are reported, because owners need to have done so in order to claim on their insurance policies.

Second, of crimes that *are* reported to the police, many are not actually recorded. It has been estimated that, while 43 per cent of crimes in the UK are *reported* to the police, just 29 per cent are *recorded*, though this figure does vary depending on the type of crime (Simmons and Dodds 2003). The police may be sceptical of the validity of the information supplied, or the victim may decide not to lodge a formal complaint after reporting an incident. The overall effect of such partial reporting and recording of crimes is that the official crime statistics reflect only a proportion of all criminal offences.

Those not captured in official statistics are collectively referred to as the *dark figure* of unrecorded crime and are often described as the much larger portion of the 'crime iceberg' that is effectively hidden from view. However, in England and Wales, National Crime Recording Standards were introduced in 2002 which aimed to increase the consistency across police forces of recording crimes. Since then the trends in police recorded figures and the CSEW have tracked each other quite well.

Perhaps a more accurate picture of crime comes from the annual Crime Survey for England and Wales (before April 2012, known as the British Crime Survey (BCS)), which measures levels of crime by asking people directly about their experiences. As a result, the CSEW includes crimes that are not reported to or recorded by the police and is an important source of data. The survey interviews around 35,000 people (since 2013) aged sixteen and over who live in private households, asking about their experience of crime in the previous twelve months. Although there are differences in the rates of growth and decline for different offences, the overall trend since the mid-1990s in both the BCS/CSEW and the recorded crime figures has been downwards.

Surveys such as the CSEW are known as victimization studies and, though they are valuable indicators and are not prone to changes in police recording practices, data from these must also be treated with some caution. There are strengths and limitations to all crime statistics (see table 20.3). In certain instances, the methodology of the study itself may result in significant underreporting. The CSEW is conducted by means of interviews in respondents' homes. This might result, for example, in a victim of domestic violence not reporting incidents in the presence of the abuser or where the abuse has taken place.

The survey also excludes those under the age of sixteen. Since January 2009, the annual CSEW *has* interviewed around 4,000 children aged between ten and fifteen (3,000 from 2013), but these data are considered 'experimental'. The survey also omits those who are homeless or live in institutions such as residential care or care homes with nursing. This is particularly important, as these groups can be particularly prone to becoming victims of crime. Just as significantly, the CSEW does not cover businesses or workplaces, which leaves out corporate offending, white-collar crimes such as fraud, and most cybercrimes, including credit card fraud. This means that our information on the extent and significance of these types of crime relies on the police-recorded crime statistics.

Another potentially important source of information about crime is self-report studies,

Table 20.3 Strengths and limitations of the CSEW and police recorded crime figures

Crime Survey for England and Wales	Police recorded crime
STRENGTHS	STRENGTHS
- Large nationally representative sample survey which provides a good measure of long-term trends for types of crime and the population it covers (that is, those resident in households) - Consistent methodology over time - Covers crimes not reported to the police and is not affected by changes in police recording practice; is therefore a better measure of long-term trends - Independent collection of crime figures	- Has wider offence and population coverage than the CSEW - Good measure of offences that are well reported to the police - Is the primary source of local crime statistics and for lower-volume crimes (e.g., homicide) - Provides whole counts (rather than estimates that are subject to sampling variations) - Time lag between occurrence of crime and reporting results tends to be short, providing an indication of emerging trends
LIMITATIONS	LIMITATIONS
- Survey is subject to error associated with sampling and respondents recalling past events - Excludes crimes against businesses and those not resident in households (e.g., residents of institutions and visitors) - Headline estimates exclude offences that are difficult to estimate robustly (such as sexual offences) or that have no victim who can be interviewed (e.g., homicides and drug offences)	- Excludes offences that are not reported to, or not recorded by, the police and does not include less serious offences dealt with by magistrates courts (e.g., motoring offences) - Trends can be influenced by changes in recording practices or police activity - Not possible to make long-term comparisons due to fundamental changes in recording practice introduced in 1998 and 2002/3

Source: ONS (2014a: 124).

in which people are asked to admit anonymously if they have *committed* any offences. The Offending, Crime and Justice Survey was introduced for England and Wales in 2003 and interviewed 12,000 people aged between ten and sixty-five. Subsequent surveys in 2004, 2005 and 2006 targeted young people between the ages of ten and twenty-five in order to uncover the extent of offending, antisocial behaviour and drug use. Such surveys are a useful addition to victimization surveys and police records. Of course, they could suffer from under-reporting, as participants might be unwilling to admit an offence for fear of the consequences. Over-reporting could also take place, perhaps because of a bad memory or through a desire to show off.

What we may legitimately conclude from this brief survey is that crime statistics can be very useful for sociologists. We can learn much about patterns of crime, their change over time and which groups tend to be victims. However, we should always remember that the official crime statistics as published are the end point of a long production process and that that process also requires investigation.

Victims and perpetrators

Are some individuals and groups more likely to commit crimes, or to become the victims of crime? Social science research and crime statistics show that crime and victimization are not randomly distributed across the population. For example, men are more likely than women to commit crimes and the young are more often involved, both as perpetrators and as victims, than older people.

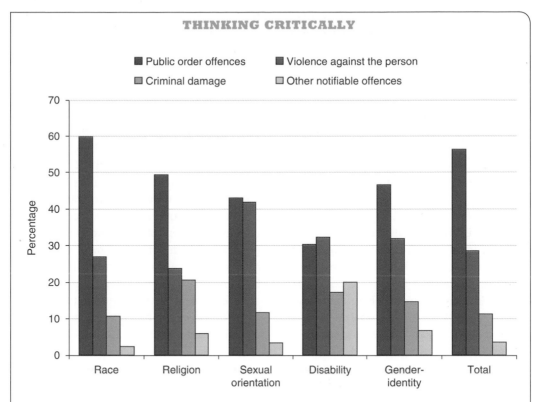

THINKING CRITICALLY

Figure 20.2 Proportion of hate crimes by recorded offence type, seventeen police forces in England and Wales, 2012–13

Source: Home Office, ONS and Ministry of Justice (2013: 20).

Figure 20.2 gives a snapshot of the types and distribution of hate crimes in England and Wales. Why should religious hate crimes and those against disabled people involve a higher proportion of criminal damage than other types? Are there other types of hate crime that are not accounted for here?

The likelihood of someone becoming a victim of crime is also closely linked to the area in which they live. Areas suffering from greater material deprivation generally have higher crime rates, and higher proportions of minority ethnic groups tend to live in such areas. People living in inner-city neighbourhoods have a much greater risk of becoming victims of crime than do residents of more affluent suburban areas. That minority ethnic groups are concentrated disproportionately in inner-city areas also appears to be a significant factor in their higher rates of victimization.

An extended discussion of racial discrimination and minority ethnic groups in the criminal justice system can be found in Chapter 16, 'Race, Ethnicity and Migration'.

Gender, sexuality and hate crime

Before the 1970s, criminology had generally ignored half the population. Feminists criticized the subject as a male-dominated enterprise in which women were largely 'invisible', both in theoretical considerations and in empirical studies. Since the 1970s, many important feminist studies have drawn attention to the way in which criminal acts by women occur in different contexts from those of men. Women's experience of the criminal justice system has also been found to be influenced by certain gendered assumptions regarding 'appropriate' male and female roles. Feminists have played a critical role in highlighting the prevalence of violence against women, both in the home and in public settings.

Male and female crime rates

Statistical evidence consistently shows the most striking and well-established pattern of crime across all developed and developing countries: criminal offences are committed overwhelmingly by males. For instance, in November 2014 there were 81,959 males in prison in England and Wales and just 3,943 females (Ministry of Justice 2014). There is a similar imbalance in the ratio of male to female prisoners in all the industrialized countries. However, over recent years the number of women in prison in the UK has risen rapidly,

from an average of 1,560 in 1993 to an all-time high of 4,672 in May 2004. Yet, despite this, women still constitute a tiny percentage of prisoners: just 4.5 per cent of the prison population at the end of 2014.

There are some differences in the types of crime that men and women commit. As figure 20.3 illustrates, women are much more likely to commit theft, usually from shops, than to be involved in crimes of violence and burglary. On the other hand, theft and handling stolen goods are the most common indictable offences committed by both men and women, accounting for 31 per cent of all male and 53 per cent of all female offending. For men, the second most common offence involves drugs, while for women it was violence against other people.

Of course, the true gender difference in crime rates *could* be much less than the official statistics show. In the mid-twentieth century, Otto Pollak (1950) suggested as much. He saw women's primary domestic role as providing them with the opportunity to commit 'secret' crimes, such as poisoning, in the home. Pollak regarded women as 'naturally' deceitful and

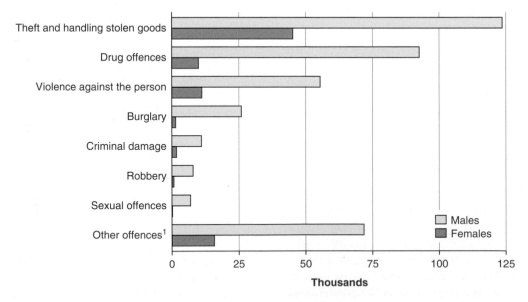

Figure 20.3 Persons found guilty of, or cautioned for, indictable offences in England and Wales: by sex and type of offence, 2010

Note: [1]The category 'Other offences' includes fraud, forgery and indictable motoring offences.
Source: ONS (2011f: 13).

highly skilled at covering up their crimes, which they had learned from having to hide the pain and discomfort of menstruation from men. Pollak also argued that female offenders are treated more leniently by the police and courts, as the men involved adopted a 'chivalrous' attitude towards them. Pollak's stereotypical portrayal of women has no basis in evidence from research studies and seems frankly laughable today. However, the suggestion that women may be treated more leniently by the criminal justice system has been taken more seriously.

First, it is possible that the police and other justice officials regard female offenders as less dangerous than men and ignore some activities for which males would be arrested. Second, studies of sentencing suggest that women are less likely to be imprisoned than men. One possible reason for differential sentencing may simply be that women commit less serious and violent offences than men. If so, then a gender dimension clearly exists, but it is unrelated to the 'chivalry' of officials. Another major difficulty is assessing the relative influence of gender compared to other factors, such as age, class and race. For example, older women offenders tend to be treated less forcefully than their male counterparts, while some studies have shown that black women receive worse treatment from the police than white women (Player 1989; Britton 2011: 66–8). Evidence of this kind illustrates the complexity of untangling the independent effects of what are, in reality, intersecting social inequalities.

Feminist criminologists have examined how widespread ideas of appropriate 'femininity' can shape women's experience in the criminal justice system. Frances Heidensohn (1996) has argued that women are treated more harshly in cases where they have allegedly deviated from feminine norms. For example, young girls who are perceived to be sexually promiscuous are more often taken into custody than promiscuous boys. In such cases, women are seen as 'doubly deviant': not only have they broken the law, they have also flouted 'appropriate' norms of female behaviour.

Heidensohn and others point to the double standard within the criminal justice system: male aggression and violence are seen as natural or 'normal' phenomena, while an explanation of female offending is often sought in 'psychological' imbalances. In an effort to make female crime more visible, feminists have conducted a number of detailed investigations of female criminals, from girl gangs to female terrorists and women in prison. These have shown that violence is not exclusively a characteristic of male criminality. Women *are* much less likely than men to participate in violent crime, but they *do* commit similar acts of violence.

But why are rates of criminality so much lower for women than for men? There is some evidence that female lawbreakers are brought to courts less often, as they can persuade the police and authorities to interpret their actions in a particular way. They invoke what has been called the 'gender contract' – a stereotypical assumption that to be a woman is to be erratic and impulsive, on the one hand, and in need of protection, on the other (Worrall 1990). On this view, the police and courts *do* act chivalrously and do not punish women for behaviour which would be considered unacceptable for men. Other research suggests that women who do not live up to the norms of femininity may be perceived as 'bad mothers', for example, and receive *more* severe penalties from the courts for not fulfilling their part of the gender contract (Carlen 1983).

However, differential treatment by courts and police could not account for the vast difference between male and female rates of crime. The reasons for this are almost certainly the same as those that explain gender differences in other spheres. There are, of course, certain crimes that are perceived to be specifically 'female crimes' – most notably prostitution – for which women are convicted while their male clients are not. 'Male crimes' remain 'male' because of differences in socialization and because men's activities and involvements are generally non-domestic compared with those of women. In the 1950s and 1960s, gender differences in crime were explained by innate biological or psychological differences, such as strength, passivity or a preoccupation with reproduction.

Today, 'feminine' qualities are seen as socially created, in common with the traits of 'masculinity'. Many women are socialized to value different qualities, such as caring for others and fostering personal relationships, from those valued by males. Equally important, through the influence of ideology and other factors – such as ideas of what it means to be a 'nice girl' – women's behaviour is often constrained and controlled in ways that male activities are not. Ever since the late nineteenth century, criminologists have predicted that gender equalization would reduce or eliminate the differences in criminality between men and women, but, so far, this has not happened and crime remains a robustly gendered phenomenon.

Crimes against women

There are certain categories of crime where men are overwhelmingly the aggressors and women the victims. Domestic violence, sexual harassment, sexual assault and rape are crimes in which males use their social status and physical strength against women, though the CSEW found that a smaller percentage of men also experience some form of non-sexual domestic abuse. In 2012–13, some 30 per cent of women and 16 per cent of men reported having experienced some form of domestic abuse since the age of sixteen. The CSEW estimates that this equates to almost 5 million women and 2.7 million men having experienced domestic abuse since the age of sixteen. The most commonly reported type was non-sexual abuse by a partner, which was reported by more than twice as many women (23.8 per cent) as men (11.1 per cent) (see figure 20.4). Feminist sociologists point out that the persistent threat of physical and intimate violence by men affects all women, whether or not they have direct experience of it.

However, the 2012–13 CSEW survey found that far more women than men reported having experienced sexual assault – a finding

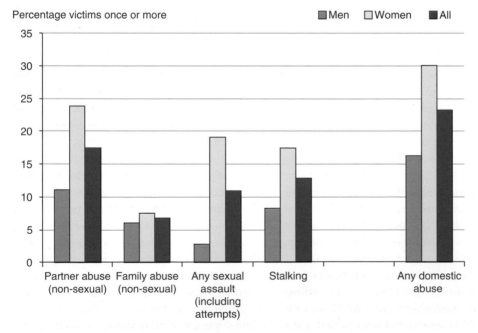

Figure 20.4 Percentage of adults aged sixteen to fifty-nine having experienced intimate violence since age sixteen, by gender and category, 2012–13

Source: ONS (2014c: 5).

that remains consistent with earlier reports. Some 19 per cent of women reported being victims of sexual assault compared with just 2.7 per cent of men (ONS 2014c: 4–5). For many years, these types of offence were largely ignored by the criminal justice system, and victims had to persevere to gain legal redress against offenders. Until 1991, rape within marriage was not recognized as an offence in Britain. In a 1736 ruling, Sir Matthew Hale declared that a husband 'cannot be guilty of rape committed by himself upon his lawful wife, for by their mutual matrimonial consent and contract the wife hath given up herself in this kind unto her husband which she cannot retract' (quoted in Hall et al. 1984: 20). This formulation remained the law in England and Wales until 1994, when an amendment brought 'marital rape' (and 'male rape') within the legislative framework. Even today, the prosecution of crimes of intimate violence against women remains far from straightforward, though feminist criminology has done much to raise awareness and integrate such offences into mainstream debates on crime. In this section we shall focus on the crime of rape in the UK context, leaving domestic violence and sexual harassment to other chapters.

> See chapter 10, 'Families and Intimate Relationships', for a wider discussion of domestic violence.

The extent of rape is very difficult to assess accurately as only a small number of rapes are actually reported to and then recorded by the police. Although police figures show a general reduction in crime since the mid-1990s, sexual offences are an exception. In 2009–10, police recorded a 7 per cent increase in the most serious sexual offences over the previous twelve months. Serious sexual crimes constituted 80 per cent of total recorded sexual offences, and rapes of females increased by 15 per cent (almost 14,000 cases) in the same period (Flatley et al. 2010: 57). In 2012–13, police forces in England and Wales recorded around 10,000 cases of the rape of adults and 6,000 of children alongside a 9 per cent increase in all sexual offences (including rape). The police inspectorate noted that the number of recorded rape cases had been steadily increasing since 2008 (HMIC 2014). Yet a detailed analysis of the 2001 BCS estimated around 47,000 female victims of rape or attempted rape in the previous year (Walby and Allen 2004). In all likelihood, therefore, the police recorded figures seriously underestimate the prevalence of female rape.

Rapes of males also increased by 22 per cent between 2008–9 and 2009–10, though this was from a low base of reporting and recording so the numbers involved were much smaller (1,174 cases). An analysis of CSEW findings between 2009 and 2012 estimated that around 85,000 women per year were victims of rape or sexual assault by penetration compared to 12,000 men (Ministry of Justice 2013: 6). One important point is that, following the introduction of the Sexual Offences Act (2003) in May 2004, there have been changes in police recording practice for all sexual offences which led to their redefinition, thus making long-term trends harder to establish (Flatley et al. 2010). 'Operation Yewtree', which was instigated in late 2012 – the police investigation into the extent of Jimmy Savile's sexual offending and associated historic sexual offences – has also led to an increased willingness of victims to come forward and report sexual offences. Clearly, establishing the true extent of sexual offences is a much more complex task than many media headlines might suggest.

There are also many reasons why a woman might choose not to report sexual violence to the police. The majority of women who are raped either wish to put the incident out of their minds or are unwilling to participate in the process of medical examination, police interrogation and courtroom cross-examination. The legal process often takes a long time and can be intimidating. Courtroom procedure is public and the victim must come face to face with the accused. Proof of penetration, the identity of the rapist and the fact that the act occurred without the woman's consent all have to be established. A woman may feel that *she* is the one on trial, particularly if her own sexual history is examined publicly, as often happens in such cases (Soothill and Walby 1991; Abbott et al. 2005: 291–5).

Women's groups have pressed for change in both legal and public thinking about rape. They stress that rape should be seen not as a sexual offence but as a type of violent crime. It is not just a physical attack but an assault on an individual's integrity and dignity. Rape is clearly related to the association of masculinity with power, dominance and toughness. It is for the most part not the result of overwhelming sexual desire but of the ties between sexuality and feelings of power and superiority. The campaign has had some real results in changing legislation, and rape is today generally recognized in law to be a specific type of criminal violence. Yet some recent studies suggest that these changes have not had a major impact so far and that the prevalence of reporting of rape has not significantly increased since the 1990s (Wolitzky-Taylor et al. 2010).

There is a sense in which all women are victims of rape. Women who have never been raped often experience similar anxieties to those who have. They may be afraid to go out alone at night, even on crowded streets, and may be equally fearful of being on their own in a house or flat. Emphasizing the close connection between rape and orthodox male sexuality, Brownmiller (1975) argued that rape is part of a system of male intimidation that makes all women more cautious than men in daily life.

Sexual orientation hate crimes

Feminists have pointed out that understandings of violence are highly gendered and influenced by 'common-sense' perceptions about risk and responsibility. Because women are seen as less able to defend themselves, common sense holds that they should alter their behaviour to reduce the risk of becoming a victim of violence. For example, not only should women avoid walking in 'unsafe' neighbourhoods alone and at night, but they should be careful not to dress provocatively or behave in a manner that could be misinterpreted by men. Women who fail to do so can be accused of 'asking for trouble'. In a court setting, their behaviour can be taken as a mitigating factor in considering the perpetrator's violent act (Dobash and Dobash 1992; Richardson and May 1999).

It has been suggested that a similar 'blame-the-victim' logic applies in the case of violent acts against lesbians, gay men, bisexuals and transgender people (LGBT). Richardson and May (1999) argued that, because they remain stigmatized and marginalized, there is a greater tendency for homosexuals to be seen as 'deserving' of crime rather than as innocent victims. Homosexual relationships are still seen as belonging to the private realm, while heterosexuality is the norm in public spaces. According to Richardson and May, lesbians and gay men who deviate from this private–public contract by displaying their homosexual identities in public are often blamed for making themselves vulnerable to crime.

Victimization studies reveal that homosexuals experience a high incidence of violent crime and harassment. A UK national survey of 4,000 gay men and women in the mid-1990s found that, in the previous five years, 33 per cent of gay men and 25 per cent of lesbians had been the victim of at least one violent attack. In all, one-third had experienced some form of harassment, including threats or vandalism, and an overwhelming 73 per cent had been verbally abused in public (Mason and Palmer 1996).

In 2009–10, lesbian, gay or bisexual people were also more likely to have experienced domestic abuse in the last year (13 per cent compared with 5 per cent of heterosexuals), while 17 per cent of lesbian or bisexual women reported domestic abuse compared with just 9 per cent of gay or bisexual men (Roe 2010: 63). One reason for this difference may be the higher proportion of younger gay, lesbian and bisexual couples (37 per cent compared with 21 per cent of heterosexual couples), as intimate violence has been found to be particularly associated with the sixteen to twenty-four age group (Povey et al. 2009).

Crimes against gay men in the UK led to calls for the adoption of 'hate crime' legislation to protect the human rights of those who remain stigmatized in society. The Criminal Justice Act of 2003 allowed judges in England and Wales to increase a sentence if an assault was motivated by 'homophobia' – the hatred or fear of homosexuals. Following lobbying in relation to extreme, anti-homosexual websites and some song lyrics advocating violence against gay men, the 2003 Act was extended in the Equality Act 2010 to outlaw incitement to homophobic hatred. However, the introduction of same-sex civil partnerships in 2004 and more positive portrayals of homosexual relationships in TV drama may be signs of changing social attitudes.

Young people as offenders and victims

Popular fears about crime in developed countries centre on offences such as theft, burglary and assault – 'street crimes' – that are perceived to be committed primarily by young working-class males. Media coverage of crime rates often focuses on the 'moral breakdown' of youth, highlighting issues such as vandalism, school truancy and drug use. Yet the discourse linking young people with criminal activity and deviance is not a recent development.

The idea of delinquency can be found in England in the sixteenth century and recurred through the seventeenth and eighteenth centuries. In the early nineteenth century, one report noted an 'alarming increase' in juvenile delinquency in London. It identified the main causes as poor parenting, lack of education and suitable employment, and 'violation of the Sabbath' (Muncie 2009). Excluding this last, such causes seem remarkably contemporary, illustrating society's persistent concern with young people's moral and social development. Industrialization led to urban squalor for many poor families and an increase in both petty theft and property crime. The mid-nineteenth century also saw the emergence of 'child saving' movements, comprised mainly of middle-class philanthropists seeking to tackle truancy and delinquency by regulating the behaviour of young people. Criminologists argue that the nineteenth-century concern with juvenile crime was not a simple response to rising crime levels but was also the product of shifting attitudes towards young people, who now had to be managed by agencies beyond the family (Banks 2013: 3).

As we saw earlier, by the mid-twentieth century, young people were again the focus of a series of moral panics around consumerism and spectacular subcultures involving popular music, dress styles and fashion, attitudes towards sex and sexuality, and, increasingly, recreational drug use (Muncie 2015). One of the more recent concerns relates to young people's use of digital devices and their presence on online social media, which has been presented as unhealthy, antisocial and potentially dangerous. The recurring theme of young people as a social problem in media reports and political commentary shows that the state of youth is often seen as an indicator of the health of society itself.

Official statistics do show relatively high rates of offending among young people, with more boys than girls admitting to having committed an offence. In the Offending, Crime and Justice Survey (OCJS) carried out in England and Wales between 2003 and 2006, 5,000 young people between ten and twenty-six years of age formed a panel study and were interviewed four times over the period. Some 49 per cent of the sample reported committing one or more offences over the four years, 27 per cent had used drugs, and 72 per cent admitted some form of harmful or antisocial behaviour (Hales et al. 2009). The peak age for offending was in the late teens, for both males and females, while that for violent offences was fourteen to fifteen (figure 20.5).

According to data of this kind, it may appear that offending by young people is a major social problem. Yet we must be cautious in making this assumption. The OCJS analysis identified a small number of 'prolific offenders' who accounted for a disproportionate number of the offences reported, while more than half of the sample did not admit to committing any offences over the four-year period. Muncie

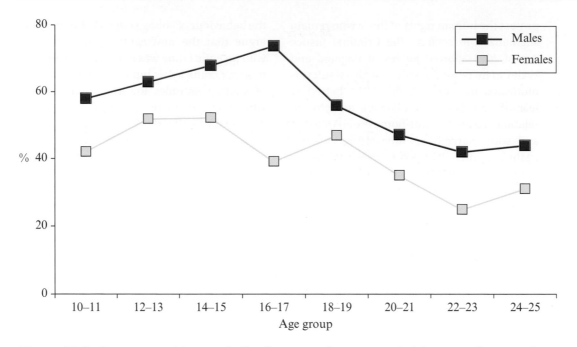

Figure 20.5 Percentage of the panel offending over a four-year period, by age at the start of the period and gender

Source: Hales et al. (2009: 9).

(2009) has noted that an isolated event involving young people and crime – such as the murder of two-year-old James Bulger in 1993 by two ten-year-old boys, can deflect attention away from larger social issues.

Similar caution can be expressed about the popular view that most youth crime in developed countries is drug-related. A 2006 UK Department of Health survey of more than 10,000 school children aged between eleven and fifteen revealed that 9 per cent were regular smokers, 25 per cent had drunk alcohol in the past week, 21 per cent had taken drugs in the past year, and 4 per cent had used 'Class A' drugs such as cocaine or heroin (DoH 2006). However, trends in drug use have shifted away from 'hard' drugs, such as heroin, towards combinations of substances such as amphetamines, 'legal highs', alcohol and Ecstasy. Ecstasy in particular has become a 'lifestyle' drug associated with club subcultures rather than the basis of an expensive, addictive habit pushing young people into lives of crime.

The other side of the association between youth and crime is that young people are more likely to be *victims* of crime than older age groups (see figure 20.6). The increasing political focus on victims and the development of 'victimology' as a specialist field of inquiry have helped to produce a more balanced understanding of young people's involvement in crime and deviance. In 2013–14, 25 per cent of young people aged sixteen to twenty-four in England and Wales had been a victim of at least one crime in the past year, compared to 17 per cent of those aged forty-five to fifty-four and just 14 per cent of those aged fifty-five to sixty-four (ONS 2014h). Similarly, those aged sixteen to twenty-four were more likely to be victims of violent crime than any other age group, with young men being most likely to be victims of violence and young women most likely to be victims of sexual assault (ONS 2015d).

In recent years the abuse of children and young people by adults has become a major issue in the UK. Following the uncovering of

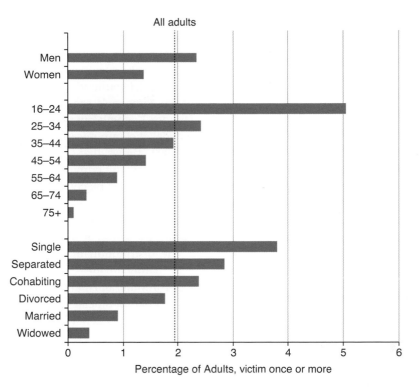

All adults

Figure 20.6 Characteristics associated with being a victim of violence, CSEW, 2013–14

Source: ONS (2015d: 19).

serious sexual abuse committed by the TV personality Jimmy Savile, victims have been more willing to come forward. Previously children's voices were largely ignored and their allegations about the behaviour of adults were not believed. For example, a series of inquiries revealed the widespread abuse of children in care homes and other institutional settings in the 1970s and 1980s. One of the most serious involved abuse against children in numerous care homes in the counties of Clwyd and Gwynedd, North Wales, in the 1970s and 1980s. By mid-2014, 283 people had come forward with allegations of abuse, eleven people had been charged with offences, and another fifty-six had been identified by police as potential suspects (Wales Online 2014).

The organized sexual abuse of children and young people by adults cannot be consigned to historic cases. In Rochdale, UK, nine men were convicted of sexual offences in 2012, including rape and child trafficking. The offences took place in 2008–9, and forty-seven vulnerable young girls were identified by police as victims of grooming. Members of the trafficking gang knew one another and were otherwise seen as 'ordinary' members of the local community; most of them were married with children of their own. Similar sex trafficking gangs were found to be operating in Derby, Oxford, Bristol and elsewhere.

In Rotherham, at least 1,400 children aged between ten and sixteen, overwhelmingly girls, were sexually abused by an organized trafficking gang between 1997 and 2013 (Jay 2014). The scale and brutality of the abuse shocked everyone:

> They were raped by multiple perpetrators, trafficked to other towns and cities in the north of England, abducted, beaten, and intimidated. There were examples of children who had been doused in petrol and threatened with being set alight, threatened with guns, made to witness brutally violent

rapes and threatened they would be next if they told anyone. Girls as young as 11 were raped by large numbers of male perpetrators. This abuse is not confined to the past but continues to this day. (Ibid.: 1)

The abuse in Rotherham highlighted many failures in the social care system and policing. In particular, despite a majority of victims describing the perpetrators as 'Asian', care workers told the inquiry they were 'nervous' about discussing the perpetrators' ethnicity for fear of being seen as 'racist', while councillors just hoped the 'problem' would go away.

The common-sense connection between youth and delinquency is clearly inaccurate. As the sexual abuse cases show, the crimes committed by older adults can be far more serious than those engaged in by young people. Youth criminality is often associated with activities that, strictly speaking, are not really 'crimes'. Antisocial behaviour, subcultural activity and non-conformity may be regarded as delinquency, but none of these is *criminal* conduct and may be considered quite ordinary, borderline-nuisance behaviour that, for many young people, is part of 'growing up'. Only in recent years has the image of young people as 'folk devils' been shown as stereotypical and highly misleading. As we have seen, the analysis of youth involvement in crime, whether as perpetrators or victims, is rarely straightforward.

'White-collar', corporate and state crime

The term white-collar crime was first introduced by Edwin Sutherland in 1949. It refers to crime that is carried out by those in the more affluent sectors of society, often against the interests of the companies for which they work. Croall (2001: 17) defines it as 'an abuse of a legitimate occupational role which is regulated by law'. White-collar crime therefore covers many types of activity, including tax fraud, illegal sales practices, securities and land frauds, embezzlement, and the manufacture or sale of dangerous products, as well as straightforward theft.

The world's largest energy trading company, Enron, collapsed in 2001 after the discovery that false accounting was disguising huge debts. Bankruptcy caused the loss of thousands of jobs around the world, and several of the company's senior staff, including the founder, Kenneth Lay, were arrested. A similar scandal at communications giant WorldCom, in 2002, shows that wealthy and powerful people carry out crimes whose consequences can be more far-reaching and damaging than the crimes of the poor. Of course, most white-collar crime is not as grand as that which occurred at Enron or WorldCom.

The distribution of white-collar crime is even harder to measure than that of other types of crime, and many white-collar offences are not part of official statistics at all. We can distinguish between white-collar crime and crimes of the powerful. The former mainly involves the use of a middle-class or professional position to engage in illegal activities for personal gain. The latter are those in which the authority conferred by a position is used in criminal ways – as when an official accepts a bribe to favour a particular policy.

Although some white-collar crime is tolerated by companies and police forces do not routinely come into contact with the sites where possible offences are committed, the cost of such crime is enormous. Far more research has been carried out on the subject in the United States than in Britain and Europe. The crude economic cost of white-collar crime (including insurance fraud, employee theft and embezzlement) is estimated to be at least US$200 billion a year, far greater than 'street' crimes such as robberies, burglaries, larceny, forgeries and car thefts, which the FBI calculated at between US$10 billion and $13.5 billion (Potter and Miller 2002: 2–3).

Corporate crime

In contrast to white-collar crime for personal gain, corporate crime refers to offences committed by large corporations and includes illegal pollution, mislabelling of products, and violations of health and safety regulations. The increasing power and influence of large

Eric Illsley was the first MP to be convicted as a result of the 2011 expenses scandal. Powerful business leaders and bank bosses rarely find themselves in court, even though their actions can have very serious consequences.

corporations and their global reach mean that our lives are touched by them in many ways. Corporations are involved in producing the cars we drive and the food we eat. They also have an enormous impact on the natural environment and financial markets. Corporate crimes show us that crime is not always something committed exclusively by individuals against other individuals.

Stephen Box (1983) argued that, in capitalist economies, where companies are in competition with one another, corporations are inherently 'criminogenic' – that is, they are forced to consider criminal actions if these lead to a competitive advantage. They also tend to see the harm they cause in simple calculations of financial risk. Gary Slapper and Steve Tombs (1999) reviewed both quantitative and qualitative studies of corporate crime and concluded that a large number of corporations do not adhere to the legal regulations which apply

to them. Like Box, they claim that corporate crime is not confined to a few 'bad apples' but is pervasive and widespread. Other studies have revealed six types of violation linked to large corporations: administrative (paperwork or non-compliance), environmental (pollution, permits violations), financial (tax violations, illegal payments), labour (working conditions, hiring practices), manufacturing (product safety, labelling) and unfair trade practices (anti-competition, false advertising).

> ### THINKING CRITICALLY
> List as many factors as you can think of which make the monitoring, detection and prosecution of corporate criminality so difficult for police forces. Based on this, write a short policy briefing suggesting how these obstacles could be removed.

The effects of corporate crime are often experienced unevenly. Those who are disadvantaged by other types of socio-economic inequalities tend to suffer disproportionately. For example, safety and health risks in the workplace tend to be concentrated most heavily in low-paying occupations, while many of the risks from healthcare products and pharmaceuticals have had a greater impact on women than on men. Flouting regulations concerning the preparation of new drugs or ignoring safety in the workplace or environmental pollution may cause physical harm or death to large numbers of people. Deaths from hazards at work far outnumber murders, although precise statistics about accidents at work are difficult to obtain, and we cannot assume that all, or even most, of these are the direct result of employer negligence. Nevertheless, there is some basis to suppose that many are due to the neglect of legally binding safety regulations by employers or managers.

Victimization patterns in corporate crime are not straightforward. Sometimes there are 'obvious' victims, as in the case of the gas poisoning of workers and residents in and around the Bhopal chemical plant in India (1984) or the health dangers posed to women by silicone breast implants. Recently, where companies have been negligent, those injured in rail crashes in the UK or relatives of those who were killed have called for the company executives responsible for the track and trains to be brought to trial.

Yet in many cases the victims of corporate crime do not see themselves as victims at all. This is because, in 'conventional' crimes, the physical proximity between victim and offender is much closer – it is difficult not to recognize that you have been mugged. But, in the case of corporate crime, greater distances in time and space mean that people may not realize they have been victimized, or may not know how to seek redress for the crime. It is also more difficult to know who to blame when harmful decisions are made by groups of boardroom executives rather than by single individuals. For legal systems founded on the principle of individual responsibility, corporate offences pose some specific problems that have proved difficult to solve.

State crime

One other form of criminality, which has not received as much attention as other types, is state crime – 'crime by and for the benefit of the state' (Doig 2011). This pithy working definition may seem admirably simple and clear, but in fact it hides some difficult definitional problems. For example, there are disagreements about both parts: what do we mean by 'the state' and are the wrongdoings of the state really 'crimes'?

Some researchers see 'the state' as government, the police, the military and various 'state-funded' public bodies. But should these include companies carrying out government-funded contracts such as arms manufacture and private military work? Also, is the concept of 'the state' too general and monolithic? Given the different departments of state, the relatively autonomous decision-making within them and decisions taken on the ground by officials, managers and commanders, unpacking the ultimate decision-makers is not easy.

Similarly, state *crime* could be restricted to the actions of states and state officials that break either the state's own laws or international law. For example, an official inquiry into the involvement of the Netherlands in the 2003 invasion of Iraq concluded that the Dutch government *had* breached international law. In the UK, some suggested that taking the country into an 'illegal war' in Iraq made the then prime minister, Tony Blair, a war criminal who should be tried as such. Domestically, the Saville Inquiry was set up in 1998 to investigate 'Bloody Sunday' – the shooting of British citizens on a protest march in Derry, Northern Ireland, in 1972. Was the decision to shoot made by a senior officer on the day or was it part of a deliberate state policy devised by high-level politicians? In all these cases the focus is on whether domestic or international law has been broken.

But, as the state is gatekeeper of the boundary between crime and legality and can define and redefine what constitutes 'crime', this definition may be too narrow. Consequently, some criminologists look to extend the definition. Ross (2000: 5–6) defines state crimes as 'coverups, corruption, disinformation, unaccountability, and violations of domestic and/or international laws. It also includes those practices that, although they fall short of being officially declared illegal, are perceived by the majority of the population as illegal or socially harmful (eg; worker exploitation).' This definition takes in 'acts of omission' (such as non-enforcement of workplace regulations) alongside the active commission of crime and covers publicly defined 'harm' as well as crime.

Others see this kind of definition as too broad to be useful. Sharkansky (2000: 39) argues that the term 'state crime' has been used so indiscriminately by researchers that it has become 'just another epithet for *undesirable activities*'. These definitional disputes have dogged the study of state crime and served to restrict the growth of this sub-field. As Doig (2011: 44) suggests, 'it is true that the study of state crime continues to be a niche activity. Even within that niche, however, there are divergences on a number of issues.'

Prisons, punishment and rehabilitation

From our discussion so far, it is clear that much effort is expended in an attempt to control and reduce offending behaviour. However, when prevention fails, societies punish offenders and, in most legal systems, imprisonment remains a widely used method of formal punishment, during which offenders are deprived of the freedoms they previously enjoyed. This section explores the use of prisons as institutions for the control, reform and rehabilitation of criminals.

What is prison for?

The underlying principle of modern prisons is to 'improve' or rehabilitate individuals and prepare them, once released, to play a fit and proper part in society. Prison, with a reliance on long sentences, is also seen as a powerful deterrent to others. For this reason, many politicians eager to 'get tough' on crime have favoured a more punitive justice system and the expansion of prison facilities. But do prisons have the intended effect of 'reforming' convicted criminals and preventing new crimes from being committed? It is a complex question, but the evidence seems to suggest that, in the main, they do not.

The criminal justice system of England and Wales has become much more punitive since the 1980s, when the then home secretary said that 'prison works' – it removes offenders from society and deters others from crime. In January 2013 there were 84,430 people in prison service facilities in England and Wales – an all-time high. England and Wales has a larger proportion of their population imprisoned – 148 per 100,000 – than any other country in Western Europe, though this is far fewer than in some Eastern European countries. Poland imprisons 217 per 100,000 and Russia 475 per 100,000. By contrast, Germany has a prison population of just 79 per 100,000 and Norway, 72 per 100,000 (see table 20.4). English and Welsh courts also tend to assign longer prison sentences to offenders than do courts in other European countries. Some critics fear that Britain is following too closely in the path of the United States – by far the most punitive among developed nations.

Prisoners are no longer routinely physically maltreated, as was once common practice, but they do suffer many other types of deprivation. They are deprived not only of their freedom but also of the means of earning an income, the company of their families and friends, heterosexual relationships, their own clothing and personal items. They may have to live in overcrowded conditions and have to accept strict disciplinary procedures and the regimentation of their daily lives (Stern 1989). Living in these conditions tends to divide prison inmates and the outside society, as they cannot adjust their behaviour to the norms of that society.

Prisoners have to come to terms with an environment quite distinct from 'the

Table 20.4 **World prison population, selected countries, 2013**

Continent	Country	Prison population total (including pre-trial detainees)	Prison population rate (per 100,000 of national population)
Africa	South Africa	156,370	294
	Zimbabwe	16,902	129
	Kenya	452,000	121
	Algeria	60,000	162
	Ethiopia	112,361	136
	Nigeria	54,144	32
	Burkina Faso	4,899	28
Americas	USA	2,239,751	716
	Mexico	246,226	210
	Brazil	548,003	274
	Jamaica	4,201	152
	Colombia	118,201	245
	Haiti	9,936	96
Asia	Israel	17,279	223
	Iran	217,000	284
	Thailand	279,854	398
	China	1,640,000[a]	121[a]
	India	385,135	30
	Japan	64,932	51
Europe	Russian Federation	681,600	475
	Poland	83,610	217
	England & Wales	84,430	148
	Italy	64,835	106
	Germany	64,379	79
	Norway	3,649	72
Oceania	New Zealand	8,597	192
	Fiji	1,537	174
	Australia	29,383	130
	Tonga	158	150
	Papua New Guinea	3,467	48

Note: [a] Sentenced prisoners only.

Source: Adapted from Walmsley (2013).

outside'. For instance, they may develop a grudge against ordinary citizens, learn to accept violence as normal, gain contacts with seasoned criminals (which they maintain when freed) and acquire criminal skills about which they previously knew little. For this reason prisons are sometimes referred to as 'universities of crime'. It is not too surprising that rates of recidivism – repeat offending by those who have been in prison before – are disturbingly high. More than 60 per cent of all men set free after a serving prison sentence in the UK are rearrested within four years of their original crimes, a figure that rises to 70 per cent for those who have served at least two previous sentences (Councell and Simes 2002).

While the evidence seems to show that prisons do not succeed in rehabilitating offenders, there remains enormous pressure to increase the number of prisons and to toughen sentences. Yet critics argue not only that prison-building programmes are an unreasonably expensive burden for taxpayers to bear but that any new prisons will have little impact on crime rates.

The restorative justice movement

Some campaigners for penal reform argue that there should be a shift away from punitive justice towards restorative justice. Restorative justice seeks to raise awareness among offenders of the impact of their crimes on victims through 'sentences' served within the community. Offenders might be required to contribute to community service projects or to engage in mediated reconciliation sessions or 'conferences' with victims and their families (Rossner 2013). Rather than being separated from society and shielded from the aftermath of their criminal acts, offenders need to be exposed to the costs of crime in a meaningful way that helps them to reintegrate into mainstream social relationships (Graef 2001).

John Braithwaite (1999) claims that the most effective forms of restorative justice are built around the principle and practice of 'reintegrative shaming'. That is, those committing criminal acts are confronted not just with

their victim but also with society's disapproval of their behaviour in ways which shame them into 'freely chosen compliance'. He argues that 'shaming is conceived in this theory as a means of making citizens actively responsible, of informing them of how justifiably resentful their fellow citizens are toward criminal behaviour which harms them' (Braithwaite 1999: 10).

However, Braithwaite is keen to point out that the process of shaming can develop into stigmatization, which may turn offenders into 'outsiders', pushing them towards criminal careers in deviant subcultures. It is therefore important to treat perpetrators with respect, to build interdependent relationships which enable shaming to be effective, and to facilitate community involvement in the criminal justice system (Strang and Braithwaite 2001). The use of an emotion such as shame as a tool for crime prevention may appear more suitable for some kinds of offender than others – opportunist burglars and 'joyriders', for example, but perhaps not gangsters or rapists? However, Braithwaite's theory proposes that, given high levels of recidivism, this type of 'moralizing social control' is more likely to succeed where repressive measures and prisons have already failed.

There are no easy answers to the debate as to whether or not prisons 'work'. While those who have been imprisoned do not seem to be deterred on release, the unpleasantness of prison life might well deter others. There is an almost intractable problem here for prison reformers: making prisons thoroughly unpleasant places probably helps deter potential offenders, but it makes the rehabilitating goals of prisons extremely difficult to achieve. On the other hand, the less harsh prisons are, the more imprisonment may lose its deterrent effect.

A sociological understanding of crime makes it clear that there are no quick fixes. The causes of crime are bound up with structural conditions of society, including poverty, the condition of the inner cities, and the deteriorating life circumstances of many young men. While short-term measures – for

20.1   Suicide in prison: the case of Adam Rickwood

A teenage boy who became the youngest inmate to die behind bars in the UK wrote a suicide letter to his mother before he died, an inquest has heard. Adam Rickwood, 14, from Burnley in Lancashire, was said to have a history of self-harm and threatening to commit suicide, the coroner's court was told. Adam was found hanging in his room at the Hassockfield secure training centre in County Durham in August 2004.

In his last letter to his mother he said he would kill himself at the unit. He described how he could not cope with life in the unit and how he wanted to be 150 miles back home. The letter,

It is commonly held that regimes in prisons and young offender institutions, such as the Feltham Youth Offender Institute pictured here, are too 'soft'. However, in 2013, there were seventy self-inflicted deaths across the prison estate in England and Wales.

read to the jury, said: 'I need to be at home with you. I need to be at home in my own bed or my head will crack up. I will probably try to kill myself and I will probably succeed this time. I can't stay in here.'

The inquest opened at Chester-le-Street Magistrates Court, in County Durham, where the 11-strong jury were told they had to decide how the teenager died but not to apportion any blame.

'Fullest scrutiny'

Durham Coroner, Andrew Tweddle, said: 'What happens behind prison walls is outside of the scrutiny of normal members of the public. If there is a death within those walls it is right and proper there needs to be the fullest scrutiny to ascertain what was going on there. Nobody is on trial here and we are not here to blame anyone. Adam was only 14 and as far as I know is the youngest person ever to die in some sort of penal institution.'

The teenager's mother, Carol Pounder, of Burnley, told how her son had been a 'fit and healthy young lad' but went off the rails when his grandfather died. She added: 'After I learned how Adam had died I was shocked but then disgusted because I had warned staff that Adam was suicidal. Staff said he was being watched constantly but I am accusing them of lying.'

The inquest heard how Adam had been involved with social services for a number of years, right up until he was sent to the County Durham unit, but staff did not feel he was a suicide risk. Gill Rigg, from Lancashire County Council, said: 'Adam was a vulnerable young man who was very troubled and that manifested itself in a whole range of ways but I would have thought he was not at the most severe end of the scale.' She added that a previous suicide attempt, in 2002, had been seen more as a cry for help.

Secure accommodation

Home Office pathologist, Dr Mark Egan, said the cause of death was pressure to the neck due to hanging and told the jury: 'There was nothing to suggest he was anything other than a willing participant.' The youngster's family and friends demonstrated outside the court with placards and banners ahead of the hearing. His sister Sharon, 19, said: 'We are here to hopefully see justice done and to make sure this does not happen again.'

Secure training centres are privately run children's prisons which are contracted and monitored by the Youth Justice Board on behalf of the Home Office to supply secure accommodation for children. Hassockfield STC, which opened in September 1999, in Medomsley, County Durham, is run by Premier Training Services Ltd (SERCO).

Source: BBC (2007c).

> **THINKING CRITICALLY**
>
> Should incarceration be used for vulnerable young offenders? What restorative justice alternatives could be considered and how would these potentially reduce repeat offending?

example, making prisons places of rehabilitation or experimenting with alternatives such as community work schemes – need to be further explored, for solutions to be effective they must address the long term (Currie 1998).

Crime in global context

Organized crime

Organized crime refers to illegal forms of activity that have many of the characteristics of orthodox business. Among other activities, it embraces smuggling, illegal gambling, the drug trade, prostitution, large-scale theft and protection rackets, and it often relies on violence or the threat of violence. While organized crime has traditionally developed within individual countries in culturally specific ways, it has become increasingly transnational in scope.

The reach of organized crime is felt in many countries, but historically it has been particularly strong in just a handful. In America, for example, it is a massive business, rivalling any of the major orthodox sectors of economic enterprise. National and local criminal organizations provide illegal goods and services to mass consumers. Illicit gambling on horse races, lotteries and sporting events represents the greatest source of income generated in the United States. Organized crime has probably become significant in American society because of an early association with – and in part a modelling on – the activities of the industrial 'robber barons' of the late nineteenth century. Many of the early industrialists made fortunes by exploiting immigrant labour, largely ignoring legal regulations on working conditions and often using a mixture of corruption and violence to build their industrial empires.

Although we have little systematic information on organized crime in the UK, it is known that extensive criminal networks exist in parts of London and other large cities. Some of these have international connections. London in particular is a centre for criminal operations based around the world. 'Triads' (Chinese gangsters, originally from Hong Kong and South-East Asia) and 'Yardies' (drug dealers with links to the Caribbean) are two of the largest criminal networks, but other organized groups from Eastern Europe, South America and West Africa are involved in money-laundering, drug-trafficking and fraud schemes.

Organized crime is much more complex than it was even thirty years ago. There is no single national organization linking different criminal groups, but organized crime has become more sophisticated than ever before. Some of the larger organizations find ways of

Global Society 20.2   Mexico's 'war' on drugs

Mexico's drugs problem is growing, and not for want of trying by the federal government. Three and a half years ago, Felipe Calderon was sworn in as president and immediately declared 'war' (his word) on drugs. Since then, about 23,000 people have been killed in drug-related violence, and a majority of Mexicans – according to surveys – believe their president is losing that war. That is despite the huge number of federal forces sent into the cities where the cartels are operating. . . . It is despite the social programmes set up to try to combat the poverty that encourages many to enter the lucrative drugs trade. And it is despite the eradication attempts the military carry out almost every day.

[. . .]

Multi-billion dollar industry

The army hierarchy insists its eradication efforts are bearing fruit. So far this year [2010] in this area they say they have destroyed exactly 28,321 marijuana plants and a total of 10,466 poppy plants.

In a warehouse, soldiers display plastic cool-boxes full of the acrid semi-liquid/semi-solid chemical mixture that would be sold on the streets as crystal-meth. Plastic buckets hold $17m (£11.7m) worth of opium. Here, too, the smell is somewhat overwhelming. Such seizures, though welcome, represent just a tiny part of the multi-billion dollar drug industry. Tackling that industry is proving to be very difficult indeed. 'As the government itself has said, the drug cartels are probably more powerful than anybody thought', says Jorge Castaneda, a former foreign minister.

[. . .]

Government tactics

So far, the war has been fought by pumping troops and police into cities like Juarez, which sits on the main smuggling route into the United States. It could be seen as a 'shock and awe' attempt by the president to bring down the murder rate. It has – officials say – forced the drug cartels to find other smuggling routes. Even so, the mayor of Juarez, Jose Reyes Ferriz, still uses a heavily armoured vehicle. More than 1,000 people have been killed in drugs-related violence in this – Mexico's murder capital – this year alone. 'We've already lost a generation. About 60 to 70% of those being killed right now are between 14 and 24 years old', Mayor Ferriz says.

The reason, says Mr Ferriz, is 'all social'. Unemployment has been rising. Assassins are paid $45 a week by the local drug gangs, he says, 'not to become rich, simply to put food on the table'. The Mexican government insists its approach is working, and that programmes to curtail corruption among the police and army are working. But there seems to be a growing realisation here that perhaps defeating the drug cartels is too ambitious a goal. Mr Ferriz says the approach in Juarez is simple: try to move the cartels elsewhere, to other cities in Mexico, even outside the country. Make it someone else's problem.

And he has a warning. 'If Mexico is successful in moving the flow of drugs, especially cocaine, into the US, into other countries, it's going to affect many small countries, like Guatemala, El Salvador, Honduras, Costa Rica, who don't have the economics of Mexico and are very likely not going to be successful in stopping the flow of drugs through their places.'

Source: Adapted from Price (2010).

laundering money through the big clearing banks, in spite of the procedures intended to foil them, then, using their 'clean' money, invest in legitimate businesses. Police believe that between £2.5 and £4 billion of criminally generated money passes through UK banks each year.

The changing face of organized crime

In *End of Millennium* (1998), Manuel Castells argues that the activities of organized crime groups are now international in scope. He notes that the coordination of criminal activities across borders – with the help of new

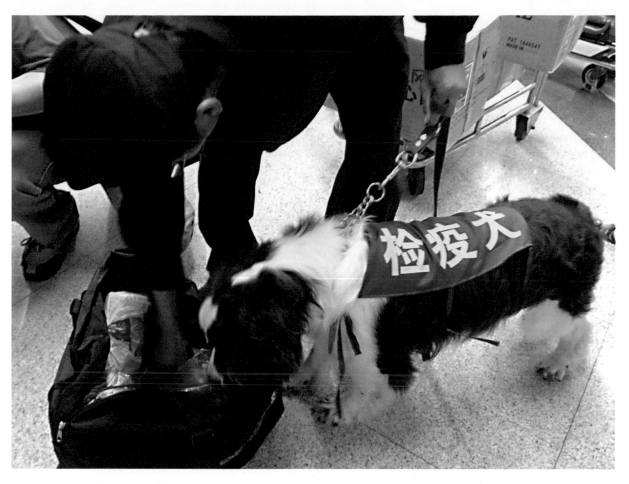

Customs officials spend much of their time tracking and attempting to intercept the movement of drugs across national borders.

information technologies – is becoming a central feature of the new global economy. Involved in activities ranging from the narcotics trade to counterfeiting to smuggling immigrants and human organs, organized criminal groups now operate in flexible international networks rather than within their own territorial realms.

According to Castells, criminal groups set up strategic alliances with one another. The international narcotics trade, weapons-trafficking, the sale of nuclear material and money-laundering have all become 'linked' across borders and crime groups. Criminal organizations tend to base their operations in 'low-risk' countries where there are fewer threats to their activities. The former Soviet Union has been one of the main points

of convergence for international organized crime. The flexible nature of this networked crime makes it relatively easy for groups to evade the reach of law-enforcement initiatives. If one criminal 'safe haven' becomes more risky, the 'organizational geometry' can shift to form a new pattern.

Despite numerous campaigns by governments and police forces, the narcotics trade is one of the most rapidly expanding criminal industries, with an annual growth rate of more than 10 per cent in the 1980s and early 1990s, and in 2009 the UN estimated that global drugs trafficking was worth around $US322 billion (UN 2009). Heroin networks stretch across the Far East, particularly South Asia, and are also located in North Africa, the Middle East and Latin America. Supply lines pass through Paris and Amsterdam, from where drugs are commonly supplied to Britain.

Cybercrime

Not only is international organized crime facilitated by recent advances in information technology, the information and telecommunications revolution is changing the face of crime in fundamental ways. Advances in technology have provided exciting new opportunities and benefits, but they also heighten vulnerability to crime. While it is difficult to quantify the extent of cybercrime – criminal acts committed with the help of information technology – it is possible to outline some of the major forms it appears to be taking. Grabosky and Smith (1998) identified nine main types of technology-based crime.

1 Illegal interception of telecommunications systems means that eavesdropping has become easier, with implications ranging from 'spouse-monitoring' to espionage.
2 Heightened vulnerability to electronic vandalism and terrorism, as interference with computerized systems – from hackers or computer viruses – can pose serious security hazards.
3 The ability to steal telecommunications services means that people can conduct illicit business without being detected or manipulate telecom and mobile phone services to receive free or discounted telephone calls.
4 Telecom privacy is a growing problem. It has become relatively easy to violate copyright rules by copying materials, software, films and CDs.
5 Sexually explicit material, racist propaganda and instructions for making incendiary devices can all be placed on, and downloaded from, the Internet. 'Cyberstalking' can pose not only virtual, but very real, threats to online users.
6 A growth in telemarketing fraud has been noted. Fraudulent charity schemes and investment opportunities are difficult to regulate.

7 There is an enhanced risk of electronic funds-transfer crimes. The widespread use of cash machines, e-commerce and 'electronic money' heightens the possibility that such transactions will be intercepted.
8 Electronic money-laundering can be used to 'move' the illegal proceeds from a crime in order to conceal their origins.
9 Telecommunications can be used to further criminal conspiracies. Because of sophisticated encryption systems and high-speed data transfers, it is difficult for law-enforcement agencies to intercept information about international criminal activities.

There are indications that cybercrime is rising, though it is difficult to reach firm conclusions. A 2005 YouGov poll of UK Internet users found that one person in twenty had lost money in online scams, while a 2001 survey revealed that 52 per cent of companies interviewed said Internet fraud posed real problems for them (Wall 2007). Credit and debit card fraud increased rapidly since the 1990s, peaking at almost £610 million in 2008. However, the introduction of new fraud screening tools by retailers and heightened online authentication processes led to a large fall, down to £341 million in 2011, before losses began to rise again (see figure 20.7).

As businesses take steps to prevent known card fraud, criminals devise new methods. For instance, there has been a large rise in 'deception fraud' in which card holders are tricked, either by phone or face to face, into giving out their card security details or even handing over the card and PIN number by fraudsters posing as bank staff or police. Other growing types are 'card-not-present' fraud, where cardholders' details are stolen and used to make 'remote purchases' online or by phone or email, and malware attacks on personal computers and smartphones. As more people move to shop and bank online, it seems likely that opportunities for this kind of fraud will continue to increase.

David Wall (2007) argues that there have been three successive phases of cyber-

Figures in orange show percentage change on previous year's total

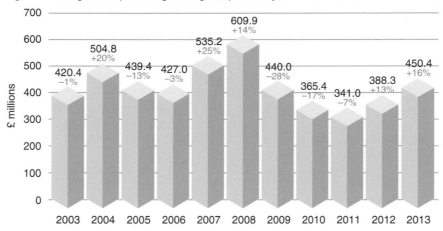

Figure 20.7 Fraud losses on UK-issued cards, 2003–13 (gross)

Source: Financial Fraud Action UK (2014: 8).

crime, closely tied to the development of communications technology. *First-generation cybercrimes* are those that make use of computers to assist traditional types of offending. Drug dealers, for instance, employ whatever forms of communication exist and, even in the absence of computers, would continue to buy and sell drugs. Similarly, finding information on how to build weapons or bombs may be easier on the Internet, but there have been, and still are, conventional sources available. *Second-generation cybercrimes* are those where the Internet has opened up new global opportunities for fairly conventional crimes. Examples are the global trade in online pornography, international fraud and theft, and deception via Internet auction sites. Second-generation cybercrimes are therefore 'hybrids' – traditional offences but within a new global networked environment.

Third-generation or *'true' cybercrimes* are those that are solely the product of the Internet and which can take place only within cyberspace. Examples are the illegal downloading of music and film, vandalism of virtual environments, and 'phishing' or spam emails containing virus attachments. This last is an example of the automation of cybercrime, where 'botnets' can enable control

over the infected computer, thus allowing the personal information to be gathered for future identity theft. Third-generation cybercrimes have been greatly facilitated by faster and cheaper broadband Internet access, which allows people to remain online for much longer periods and opens up new criminal opportunities.

> **THINKING CRITICALLY**
> Place each of Grabosky and Smith's (1998) nine types of cybercrime, listed above, into one of David Wall's (2007) three phases of cybercrime. How many of these are 'pure' or 'third-generation' cybercrimes? In what ways are the latter very different from conventional crimes?

The global reach of telecommunications crime poses particular challenges for law enforcement. Criminal acts perpetrated in one country have the power to affect victims across the globe, and this has troubling implications for detecting and prosecuting crimes. It becomes necessary for police from the countries involved to determine the jurisdiction in which the act occurred and to agree on extraditing the offenders and providing the

20.2   The future of crime and criminology?

Imagine a world in which physical cash no longer exists, all personal possessions are tagged with electronic chips and your personal identity is your most valuable asset. According to a report, *Just Around the Corner*, published by the British Department of Trade and Industry (DTI 2000), crime will soon be thoroughly transformed by advances in technology. Within two decades, the report suggests, many goods such as cars, cameras and computers will become less attractive targets for theft because they will be programmed to operate only in the hands of their legal owners. Personalized 'identities' – such as computer chips, PIN numbers and security codes – will become ubiquitous. They will be essential for conducting online transactions, using 'smart cards' (virtual cash) and passing through security systems. According to the report, cases of 'identity fraud' and thefts of personal identities will proliferate as more and more aspects of life become based in high technology.

A dramatic example came to light in March 2007, when the US retailer TJX – which owns the fashion outlet TK Maxx – announced that computer hackers had stolen information from at least 45.7 million payment cards used by their customers. TJX said that it did not know the full extent of the theft or its effect on customer accounts but revealed that information had been accessed over a sixteen-month period since July 2005. With the introduction and roll-out of replacement 'chip-and-pin' cards, many of the stolen details of UK cards would be worthless as the physical cards no longer exist. However, the case highlights the potentially huge scale of 'virtual' theft and identity fraud in the global information age.

Such developments have prompted a rethinking of mainstream criminology, as outlined by Jaishankar (2011: 411).

> Cyberspace presents myriad potential opportunities for society in the new millennium. In the 1990s, a new era was ushered in, in which Internet technology reigned supreme. However, the increase in the netizens has dwarfed the technology to a mere medium. Additionally the perpetrators who attacked machines through machines have started attacking real humans through the machines. This radical development led criminologists to address the need for a discipline to study and analyze criminal behavior in cyberspace. The crimes, offender behavior, and victimization that occur in cyberspace needed to be studied from a social science versus a technological perspective. Thus, *cyber criminology* as an academic discipline was born . . .

THINKING CRITICALLY

How accurate have the changes forecast in this report from the year 2000 proved to be? Give some reasons why cybercrimes may require a new discipline of cyber criminology. Alternatively, suggest why this proposed new discipline may not actually get off the ground.

---

necessary evidence for prosecution. Although police cooperation across national borders may improve with the growth of cybercrime, at present, cybercriminals have a great deal of room for manoeuvre.

At a time when financial, commercial and production systems in countries around the world are being integrated electronically, rising levels of Internet fraud and unauthorized electronic intrusions, and the constant threat of computer viruses are serving as potent warnings of the vulnerability of existing computer security systems. From the US Federal Bureau of Investigation (FBI) to the Japanese government's anti-hacker police force, governments are scrambling to contend with new and elusive forms of cross-national computer activity.

Conclusion: deviance, crime and social order

It would be a mistake to regard crime and deviance in a wholly negative light. Any society which recognizes that people have diverse values and concerns must find space for those whose activities do not conform to the norms followed by the majority. People who develop new ideas, in politics, science, art or other fields, are often regarded with suspicion or hostility by those who follow conventional rules. The political ideals developed in the French Revolution – individual liberty and equality – were fiercely resisted, yet they are widely accepted around the world today. To deviate from dominant norms takes courage and resolution, but it is often crucial in securing processes of change that are later seen to be in the general interest.

So is 'harmful deviance' the price a society must pay when it allows considerable freedom for people to engage in non-conformist pursuits? Are high rates of criminal violence inevitable if citizens are allowed so much personal freedom? Some have certainly suggested as much, arguing that developed societies have perhaps become too liberal. Yet this view does not stand up to close scrutiny. In some societies that recognize a wide range of individual freedoms and tolerate deviant activities (such as the Netherlands), rates of violent crime are, in fact, low. Conversely, in other countries where the scope of individual freedom is restricted (such as some Latin American societies), higher levels of violence exist.

A society that is tolerant towards deviant behaviour need not suffer major social disruption. A sensible outcome can probably be achieved only where individual liberties are joined to social justice, in a social order where inequalities are not glaringly large, and in which everyone has a chance to lead a full and satisfying life. If freedom is not balanced with equality and many people find their lives largely devoid of self-fulfilment, then deviant behaviour is likely to be channelled towards socially destructive and criminal ends.

Chapter review

1 What are the main differences between the sociology of crime and deviance and criminology? If scholars are happy to use the concepts of 'deviance' and 'crime', why are they cautious about using the concept of 'normal'?

2 Provide some sociological criticisms of biological and individualistic theories and explanations of crime and deviance.

3 Durkheim suggests that a certain level of deviance is not only inevitable but functional for society. What criteria can be used to assess the level at which deviance becomes 'dysfunctional'?

4 Outline Robert Merton's 'strain theory' of crime, explaining how he modified Durkheim's anomie concept in doing so.

5 Explain the difference between primary and secondary deviance. Which type does the labelling perspective focus on and why? Describe the interactional process through which deviant self-identities and criminal careers are forged.

6 Why did some Marxists see crime as working-class rebellion? Which types of crimes might support this position? What innovations did the 'new criminology' introduce into criminological studies?

7 Environmental criminologies focus on the design of crime-resistant environments. By decentring human intention in the study and prevention of crime, has sociology become redundant?

8   What type of survey is the Crime Survey for England and Wales and how is it conducted? Is this survey more reliable than police-recorded crime figures? List the main reasons why people do not report crimes committed against them and explain why the police do not record some of the crimes reported to them.

9   How has the overwhelming gender difference in the commission of crimes been explained sociologically? Describe the gendered pattern of crime over the last thirty years or so using evidence from criminal statistics.

10 Explain the difference between white-collar crime and corporate crime. How might it be argued that corporate crime is more harmful to society than 'street crime'? How can we define 'state crime'?

11 What is the available evidence that a) prisons work and b) prisons do not work? Explain what is meant by restorative justice and why its advocates believe it is more likely to reduce levels of reoffending.

12 Define what is meant by a 'true cybercrime' and provide some examples. How has globalization facilitated the growth of organized crime?

Research in practice

Representations of crime in fiction are ubiquitous and varied. But there is a more limited range of detectives who always seem to catch criminals through painstaking police work, restoring the social order and reassuring readers that crime never pays. The following article suggests that some recent 'noir procedurals' have broken with this representation as detectives become critical analysts of political and social issues of the day: Macleod, A. (2014) 'The Contemporary Fictional Police Detective as Critical Security Analyst: Insecurity and Immigration in the Novels of Henning Mankell and Andrea Camilleri', *Security Dialogue*, 45: 515–29. Read the article and answer the following questions.

1   Why should sociologists study popular cultural forms such as crime novels? What reasons are given by the authors?

2   In what ways do Wallander and Montalbano 'disavow reassurance by revising the syntax of the police procedural'?

3   Both novels deal with issues of immigration and border security. How do the novelists explain why people in their respective countries harbour strong fears of migrants?

4   In these books, the central crimes are still solved in a more-or-less conventional way. Yet the article suggests the books do not provide the conventional reassurance of standard police procedurals. Why not?

Thinking it through

Most established penal systems are based on the principle of retributive justice. Over recent years restorative justice has been advocated and practised as both complementary and an alternative to the retributive approach. Can these two approaches coexist or is restorative justice merely a minority adjunct to established systems? Read the following article, which tackles this issue: Armstrong, J. (2014) 'Rethinking the Restorative–Retributive Dichotomy: Is Reconciliation Possible?', *Contemporary Justice Review*, 17(3): 362–74.

1   The author is pessimistic about the possibility of reconciling the different restorative and retributive philosophies. Explain, with examples from the article, why there may be good grounds for such pessimism.

 2   Practical applications of restorative justice have 'run ahead' of a clear definition of the term. Armstrong sees this as a problem, wondering whether restorative justice is 'an alternative to punishment' or 'an alternative punishment'. Drawing on real-world examples from this chapter and elsewhere, write a short essay which contains your own conclusion about the underlying philosophy of the restorative approach to punishment.

Society in the arts

 1   Zahid Mubarek, a nineteen-year-old British Asian, was sentenced in January 2000 to three months in Feltham Young Offenders Institute, London, after being found guilty of stealing razor blades valued at £6 and interfering with a motor vehicle. He was placed in a cell with Robert Stewart, a white skinhead known to prison officers as a dangerous psychopath with racist tendencies. On the night before his release, Mubarek was attacked by Stewart and later died in hospital of his injuries. An official inquiry found 186 separate failings in this case and that Feltham was plagued with institutional racism. Consult the inquiry report here: https://www.gov.uk/government/publications/report-of-the-zahid-mubarek-inquiry

Watch a film about this case, *We Are Monster* (2014), directed by Antony Petrou. This film focuses on how Robert Stewart came to be the perpetrator of this murderous hate crime. Consider the following issues.

- Does the device of inventing an alter-ego for Stewart help or hinder understanding his motivation?
- What do we learn about the inmate assessment process and the institutional context of the murder?
- Given that an inquiry report is already available, how might it be argued that this dramatized version adds to our understanding of the case?

2   Watch Peter Mullan's 2010 film *NEDS*, which tells the story of John McGill growing up in 1970s inner-city Glasgow. McGill's journey takes him from school 'swot' to gang member, involved in violence, knife culture, crime and what today would be called antisocial behaviour. What does the film have to say about the following themes:

- the seriousness of the harm caused by antisocial behaviour
- the role of the police and social control agencies in preventing or increasing levels of crime and deviance
- the deterrent effect of the prison system on young people's choices and decisions
- the interactional process of labelling and its role in creating deviant identities
- theories of young people's crime and deviance?

Is this purportedly 'socially realistic' movie actually supported by research evidence from criminology and the sociology of deviance?

Further reading

A good place for beginners to the subject is with Tony Lawson and Tim Heaton's (2009) *Crime and Deviance* (2nd edn, Basingstoke: Palgrave Macmillan) and *Shades of Deviance: A Primer on Crime, Deviance and Social Harm* (2014), edited by Rowland Atkinson (London: Routledge), which includes many useful chapters. Sandra Walklate's (2016) *Criminology: The Basics* (3rd edn, Abingdon: Routledge) is a very useful textbook dealing with criminological theories and research. Robert Reiner's (2016) *Crime* (Cambridge: Polity) provides a concise guide to the different meanings and interpretations of 'crime' and its effects on society.

For crime in the British context, Hazel Croall's (2011) *Crime and Society in Britain* (2nd edn, London: Longman) is an excellent survey of the issues covered in this chapter. Another very worthwhile book covering criminology from a sociological perspective is *Criminology: A Sociological Introduction* (2014), by Eamonn Carrabine, Pamela Cox, Pete Fussey, Dick Hobbs, Nigel South, Darren Thiel, and Jackie Turton (3rd edn, London: Routledge).

If you intend to pursue crime and deviance studies further, then David Downes, Paul Rock and Eugene McLaughlin's (2016) *Understanding Deviance* (7th edn, Oxford: Oxford University Press) is a very good, challenging read. There are also two reference works you should consider: *The Sage Dictionary of Criminology* (2012), edited by Eugene McLaughlin and John Muncie (3rd edn, London: Sage), is exactly what it says it is. The most authoritative text is Mike Maguire, Rod Morgan and Robert Reiner's (2012) indispensable collection of essays in *The Oxford Handbook of Criminology* (5th edn, Oxford: Oxford University Press).

For a collection of original readings on crime and deviance, see the accompanying *Sociology: Introductory Readings* (3rd edn, Cambridge: Polity, 2010).

Internet links

@ **Additional information and support for this book at Polity:**
www.politybooks.com/giddens

@ **The British Journal of Criminology – one of the world's top criminology journals:**
http://bjc.oxfordjournals.org

Critical Criminology (USA) – for the 'new' criminology and its later development:
http://critcrim.org

@ **An independent 'public interest charity' promoting the centrality of social justice, based in London, UK:**
www.crimeandjustice.org.uk

@ **World Prison Brief – now based at the University of London:**
www.prisonstudies.org

@ **The Howard League for Penal Reform – a UK penal reform charity:**
http://howardleague.org

@ **NACRO – UK charity concerned with crime prevention and the welfare of offenders:**
www.nacro.org.uk

@ **United Nations Office on Drugs and Crime – coverage of crime internationally:**
www.unodc.org

CHAPTER 21

Politics, Government and Social Movements

Contents

The 2011 uprising in Libya, which ended Colonel Gaddafi's forty-two years of authoritarian rule, was part of the wider unrest across the Middle East and North Africa.

In August 2011, ecstatic rebel forces entered the military compound of the Libyan leader, Colonel Gaddafi, in the capital, Tripoli. Most could not believe they were actually there. The regime had seemed so stable and powerful, having been in place since 1969. Live television pictures of rebel forces celebrating in and around the deposed leader's highly fortified house and gardens was a symbolic event which showed that Gaddafi's rule was at an end.

Colonel Muammar Gaddafi's authoritarian system of rule was ended by a popular uprising in Benghazi and eastern Libya – supported by UN-sanctioned NATO air strikes and intelligence – which spread across the country. A new interim governing body, the National Transitional

Council, took effective control of most of Libya in 2012, promising to rebuild both the country and its institutions of government.

But, by 2015, a range of armed tribal groups were fighting each other for their own interests and control of the country's oil resources, Islamic State (IS)/Daesh was making headway in Derna, attracting many young fighters, and two competing governments existed. One, based in Tripoli, involves 'Libya Dawn', an Islamist coalition of the Muslim Brotherhood, Berbers and other armed militias. The other government, elected in 2014, is recognized internationally as the Libyan government and is based in Tobruk and Beida, supported by the military offensive 'Operation Dignity' (Al Jazeera 2015). Clearly, the optimism of the popular revolution is long gone and Libya has descended into a complex and violent civil war.

>> Terrorism, including that of IS/Daesh, is discussed Chapter 22, 'Nations, War and Terrorism'.

The Libyan revolution was part of the so-called Arab Spring protests, across Tunisia, Egypt, Bahrain, Syria and other countries in the Middle East and North Africa, calling for political freedom, democracy, economic development, poverty reduction and an end to corruption. Long-established regimes crumbled, taking many by surprise – President Mubarak in Egypt, President Ben Ali in Tunisia and Gaddafi in Libya were all removed. But the democratic wave was forcibly quelled in Syria, Bahrain, Algeria and Yemen as authorities clamped down hard. Syria has also become a battleground for rival groups seeking to overthrow President Assad's brutal authoritarian regime and take control of the state.

This chapter discusses many of the political themes emerging from the Libyan revolution and its aftermath. For example, how are globalization processes transforming national politics and government along with the theories and concepts of political sociology? The

rapid, global communications and transmission of images had a profound impact in Egypt, Tunisia, Libya, Bahrain and Syria. But is the digital revolution also influencing the conduct of 'normal', not just 'revolutionary' politics? The overthrow of Gaddafi's regime raises questions of power – one of the most contested, yet essential concepts in political sociology. What exactly is power and how does it operate? What are social movements and are they able to exert more influence today than they did in the past?

The desire and demand for democratic participation in Libya is not unusual. In fact, there has been a remarkable global spread of democracy over the last thirty years or so following the demise of Soviet communism and the end of the Cold War. Can authoritarian regimes resist this apparently inexorable democratization? On the other hand, why are so many voters in the established democracies now apathetic towards democratic participation? What has gone wrong with democracy in the developed world? Have elected politicians lost the trust of their people?

Military intervention by France, the UK and others in support of Libyan opposition groups brings issues of global governance into focus. Without a global government, how are international affairs and conflicts dealt with? Why was intervention deemed right in Libya, for example, but not, at that time, in Syria or Bahrain? All of these issues – and more – are central to both this chapter and chapter 22. Taken together, they provide an introduction to some central themes in political sociology, and we begin with a brief outline of some of this field's key concepts.

Political sociology

Many people believe that politics is either remote from their lives or uninteresting, but probably both. Until quite recently, formal politics seemed to be the exclusive preserve of middle-aged, middle-class men who dominated the world's parliaments and assemblies. The situation has changed quite significantly today as more women and people from minority ethnic groups have become members of parliamentary bodies and government ministers. But the belief persists that it is government and political party competition that constitute the main arena of what constitutes politics.

Yet politics is a contested concept, and the proper sphere of 'the political' goes well beyond the formal processes of governments and electoral party rivalries. The 2003 anti-war movement in Britain mobilized more than 1 million people who were protesting with an overtly political goal – to prevent governments invading Iraq. Similarly, many of the groups, networks and organizations discussed elsewhere in this book may be viewed as 'political'. Wherever people band together to change society, to amend or defend existing laws or otherwise to exert an impact, we can say that their activities are, at least in part, political.

Whether we like it or even realize it, all our lives are touched by what happens in this political sphere. Even in the narrow sense, government decisions affect quite personal activities and, in times of war, can even order us to lay down our lives for aims that others deem necessary. The sphere of government is the sphere where state power is exercised, though political life more generally is about power: who holds it, how they achieve it and what they do with it.

Where there is a political apparatus of government with institutions such as a parliament and an administration (or civil service) that rules over a given territory and whose authority is backed by a legal system and the capacity to use military force, we can say that a state exists. A majority of modern societies are nation-states in which the mass of the population consists of citizens who regard themselves as part of a single nation. Nation-states have been regularly created around the world – for example, the United States in 1776, the Czech Republic in 1993 and South Sudan in 2011. The following aspects characterize nation-states.

- *Sovereignty* Before the emergence of nation-states, the territories governed by ruling regimes were poorly defined and central government control was relatively weak. But nation-states are sovereign states with supreme authority over a more distinct, bounded territory.

- *Citizenship* Most of the people ruled by kings and emperors in earlier times had little awareness of those who ruled and had no political rights or influence. Only the dominant classes or wealthy social groups belonged to a political community. In nation-states, people within the borders of a political system are citizens with common rights and duties. Almost everyone in the world today belongs to a national political order.

- *Nationalism* Nation-states are associated with the rise of nationalism – a set of symbols and beliefs creating a consciousness of being part of a shared political community. Individuals feel a sense of pride and belonging in being French, Ghanaian, Russian, and so on. Nationalism is the main expression of identification with a large cultural and sovereign community – a nation.

We explore the phenomenon of nationalism in detail in chapter 22, 'Nations, War and Terrorism'. Citizenship is covered in chapter 13, 'Poverty Social Exclusion and Welfare'.

Power

The meaning, nature and distribution of power are central issues for political sociologists. Max Weber (1979 [1925]: 53) defined power as 'the probability that one actor within a social relationship will be in a position to carry out his own will despite resistance, regardless of the basis on which this probability rests'. For Weber, power is about getting your way, even against opposition from others. Many sociologists have followed Weber in distinguishing forms of power that are *coercive*

ideologies on people's desires. But how can sociologists study things that do *not* happen or that they cannot observe? Finally, it may be objected that Lukes's three-dimensional view is not really a theory of power at all, but an acknowledgement of the influence of social structures on individuals. If this is so, then it amounts to a theory of structural determination rather than the *exercise* of power.

Contemporary significance

Lukes's 1974 work was quite a short analytical piece, and in 2004 he published a second edition containing two new essays, bringing his arguments up to date. In particular, he discusses Foucault's theory of power, defending the three-dimensional view against more general (Foucauldian) ideas of power as running through all social relations in equal measure. However, following feminist theories of how male domination is established through the closing down of women's expectations and Amartya Sen's (1999) work on the concept of 'development' as lying in the *capacities* of people to 'live the kind of lives they value – and have reason to value', Lukes argues that power is similarly a 'capacity' or set of human 'capabilities', drawing attention to the way in which these can be denied or enhanced. His influential argument in favour of a radical view of power seems set to continue as the standard reference point for debates on the subject.

> **THINKING CRITICALLY**
>
> Think of some real-world political examples where power is exercised *without* the use of force. Can people and groups be said to be 'powerful', even if they have no means of force and violence?

power in Libya for forty-two years? It may be that, in this case (and others), the Gaddafi regime was successful because it concentrated power in the hands of a small political and military elite which violently suppressed all opposition. This debate is fleshed out in the next section, where we turn from theories of power to the exercise of power in contrasting political systems.

Authoritarianism and democratic politics

A variety of political systems have been found throughout history, and twenty-first-century societies around the world are organized according to different patterns and configurations. While most societies now claim to be democratic – that is, they involve the mass of people in decision-making as citizens – other forms of political rule also exist. In this section we shall profile democracy and authoritarianism, two of the basic types of political system.

Authoritarianism

If democracies encourage the active involvement of citizens in political affairs, in *authoritarian states* popular participation is denied or severely curtailed. In such societies, the needs and interests of the state are prioritized over those of average citizens, and no legal mechanisms exist for opposing the government or removing a leader from power.

Authoritarian governments exist today in many countries, some of which profess themselves to be 'democratic'. Iraq, under the leadership of Saddam Hussein until 2003, was an example of an authoritarian state where dissent was smothered and an inordinate share of national resources were diverted for the benefit of a select few. Powerful monarchies in Saudi Arabia and Kuwait and the leadership in Myanmar (Burma) strictly curtail citizens' civil liberties, denying them meaningful political participation. Myanmar has seen significant change since the release from house arrest of the opposition leader Aung San

Suu Kyi in 2010, demonstrating that authoritarian regimes do not have total control.

In 2015, Suu Kyi's political party, the National League for Democracy, won around 80 per cent of the seats in a national election, giving it 387 out of 478 seats (BBC News 2015b). President Thein Sein promised a smooth transfer of power, though the constitution reserves 25 per cent of seats for army personnel. The military remains an important factor in Myanmar and retains a veto on all future constitutional changes. This is important, as the constitution currently prohibits anyone with a foreign partner or children from becoming president. As Suu Kyi falls foul of this rule, conflict is again likely if she becomes *de facto* leader.

Singapore is often cited as an example of so-called soft authoritarianism. This is because the ruling People's Action Party maintains a tight grip on power but also ensures a high quality of life for its citizens by intervening in almost all aspects of society. Singapore is notable for its safety, its civil order and the social inclusion of all citizens. It is economically successful, the streets are clean, people are employed and poverty is virtually unknown. Yet, despite the high standard of living, even minor transgressions, such as dropping litter or smoking in public, are punishable by stiff fines; there is tight regulation of the media, Internet access and ownership of satellite dishes. The police possess extraordinary powers to detain citizens for suspected offences, and the use of corporal and capital judicial punishments is common.

Despite this strict authoritarian control, popular satisfaction with the government is relatively high and social inequalities are minimal in comparison with many similar countries. Although Singapore may be lacking democratic freedoms, the country's brand

A show of military strength at a May Day parade in North Korea, perhaps the most politically isolated country in the world and one of the most authoritarian.

of authoritarianism is different from those of more dictatorial regimes. Singapore has been described by the novelist William Gibson (1993) as, 'Disneyland with the death penalty'. Clearly, economically successful authoritarian regimes need not breed mass disaffection and revolt, though they are in the minority compared to democracies.

Democratic politics

The word democracy has its roots in the Greek term *demokratia*: *demos* ('people') and *kratos* ('rule'). Democracy is therefore a political system in which it is the people, not monarchs or aristocracies, who rule. This sounds straightforward enough, but it is not. Democratic rule has taken contrasting forms at varying periods and in different societies. For example, 'the people' has been variously understood to mean all men, all owners of property, all white educated men, and all adult men and women. In some societies the officially accepted version of democracy is limited to the political sphere, but in others it is extended to broader areas of social life.

The form that democracy takes in a given context is largely the outcome of how its values and goals are understood and prioritized. Democracy is generally seen as the political system most able to ensure political equality, the protection of liberty and freedom, defence of the common interest, and meeting citizens' needs, while promoting moral development and effective decision-making (Held 2006: 2–3). The weight that is granted to these various goals may influence whether democracy is regarded as a form of popular power (self-government and self-regulation) or whether it is seen as a framework for supporting decision-making by others (such as elected representatives).

In participatory democracy ('direct' democracy), decisions are made communally by all those affected by them. This was the original form practised in ancient Greece. Citizens – a small minority of the society – regularly assembled to consider policies and make major decisions. But participatory democracy is of limited importance in modern societies with very large populations, though some aspects still play a part.

Small communities in New England, in the north-eastern part of the United States, continue the traditional practice of annual 'town meetings'. On designated days, residents gather to discuss and vote on local issues. Another example of participatory democracy is the holding of referenda, when the people express their views on a particular issue. For example, Scotland held a referendum in September 2014 to decide whether the country should become independent from the UK, and the UK held a national referendum on EU membership in June 2016, which produced a vote to leave. Referenda have also been used to decide contentious issues of secession in ethnic nationalist regions such as Quebec, the predominantly French-speaking province of Canada.

> ### THINKING CRITICALLY
> Could more use be made of referenda to make decisions? Are there ways in which information technology could facilitate the expansion of referenda? What pitfalls can you foresee?

Representative democracy

Today representative democracy is the more common form. Representative democracy is a political system in which decisions are taken, not directly by members, but by others who have been elected for this purpose. In national governments, representative democracy takes the form of elections to congresses, parliaments or similar bodies. Representative democracy also exists at other levels such as in provinces or regions, cities, counties, boroughs and smaller regions. Many large organizations also run their affairs using representative democracy by electing a small executive committee to take key decisions.

Countries in which voters can choose between two or more political parties and the mass of the adult population has the right to vote are usually called liberal democracies.

Britain and other Western European countries, the USA, Japan, Australia and New Zealand, all fall into this category. Many countries in the developing world, such as India, also have liberal democratic systems, and, as we shall see later, their number is growing. But before we explore the spread of democracy, we consider elite theory and the role of bureaucracies in ostensibly democratic systems.

Elites and bureaucracies against democracy?

Democratic politics appears to be the dominant form in the world today, and it seems obvious that politicians are public officials who serve their constituents and citizens. But is this just the surface appearance? For some, societies continue to be ruled by small elites, despite all outward appearances. For others, democracy is undermined by large bureaucracies which wield far more power than the common idea of a 'neutral' administration might suggest. In this section we look at both elite theory and ideas of bureaucratic domination.

Elites and elite theory

An influential perspective on politics and a critique of democratic ideals comes from theories of political and social elites. Elite theorists view democracy as a sham or mirage which masks the fundamental fact that rule by a minority over the majority has been, is and always will be the case. In particular, and against Marxist theory, societies are ruled by powerful political elites rather than a coherent, economic ruling class.

The classical elite theories are found in the work of Gaetano Mosca (1858–1941), Vilfredo Pareto (1848–1923) and Robert Michels (1876–1936) (Berberoglu 2005: 29). Their key works were published in the late nineteenth and early twentieth centuries, a time of rising trade unions and other working-class organizations in the industrializing countries. To varying degrees, elite theories were influenced by this development, which some viewed with trepidation and others as promising a utopian but completely unrealistic image of a democratic future.

Pareto used the concept of 'elite' to describe governing or ruling groups, and he saw societies as divided into two: a small elite and a large 'non-elite' or 'mass'. But the elite group is also divided into those who govern or rule and those who, although part of the elite, play no part in actually governing. For Pareto, elites are characterized by the superior intelligence, knowledge and skills of the individuals who comprise them. Hence, a governing elite must draw from different strata, including from the masses, if it is to be successful. Elites that restrict membership – to, say, only men of a certain social class – fail to make use of the available human resources and are unable to reinvigorate themselves. The circulation of top individuals between elite and non-elite helps to keep an elite vibrant and to stave off challengers. Yet history shows that, while particular governing elites may rule for a time, it is inevitable that they will eventually be replaced: 'History is a graveyard of aristocracies' (Pareto 1935 [1916]: 1430).

This is the second aspect of the 'circulation of elites' – that established elites inevitably become decadent or stagnant and give way to rising groups. In this process the entire elite group changes, but what never changes is the principle of elite rule itself. All notions of 'rule by the people for the people', power-sharing and social equality are pipe dreams. In reality, power is always monopolized by small, highly organized elites. And, even though one elite may collapse or be overthrown, the result will be the installation and establishment of a new elite better equipped to rule.

Mosca's (1939 [1896]) ideas have a family resemblance to those of Pareto. He also sees society divided into two classes: a small ruling class and a large ruled class. And though he uses the term 'class', in fact, his concepts are far removed from Marxist or sociological definitions and lie much closer to the concept of broader elite theory. In this sense his theory pre-dates Pareto's (Marshall 2007: 10). Mosca argued that elite rule is inevitable and that Marx's vision of a classless society is untenable,

The state opening of parliament in the UK. Is this group part of a ruling class or is it a political elite?

disproven by the facts of history. Ruling elites are essentially coalitions of people drawn from the military, religious organizations, academia and other social groups with their own special talents or power bases. The elite is then a political elite which monopolizes power and dominates the masses. For both Mosca and Pareto, the 'mass' constitutes an incoherent majority, easily swayed by simple ideas and ideals (such as 'equality' or 'freedom') and subject to manipulation by elite groups. Neither theorist saw any potential for a working-class revolution as predicted by Marx.

A third theorist of elites was Robert Michels (1967 [1911]), whose ideas competed with those of Weber. Michels was a disillusioned former member of the social democratic party (SPD) in Germany who saw that not only do elites rise to the top of the state apparatus, but the process also operates in all organizations, right across society (Slattery 2003: 52–3). In particular, Michels argued that, even in apparently radical political parties, trade unions and other democratically inspired organizations, a small elite dominates and rules in its own interests. He called this process the iron law of oligarchy, the inevitable 'rule by the few'. The flow of power towards the top is just one aspect of our increasingly organized and bureaucratized world. But was Michels right?

It is surely correct that many large-scale organizations involve the centralization of power and routine decision-making by a few. Yet there is good reason to suppose that the 'iron law of oligarchy' is not quite so hard and fast as Michels (or Mosca and Pareto) thought. First, as organizations expand in size, power relationships can become looser. Those at the middle and lower levels may have little influence over general policies forged at the top, but power is often delegated downwards as corporate heads are so busy coordinating, coping with crises and analysing budgets that they have little time for original thinking. Many corporate leaders frankly admit that, for the most part, they simply accept the conclusions given to them.

Since the 1970s sociologists have recognized the increasing significance of 'weak ties' and technologically advanced, loosely connected social networks in economic, political and social life (Granovetter 1973; Castells 1996).

In a digital age, when globalization continues to reshape business organization and political decision-making, power seems to have become more fluid and powerful networks are potentially open to a broader range of individuals from across the social spectrum. Hence, it may be becoming more difficult for small elites to gain power and to retain it.

On the other hand, recent research into the powerful positions in UK society – top judges, MPs and cabinet members, members of the House of Lords, senior army officers, and so on – revealed that these continue to be dominated by those who are privately educated at a small number of independent schools (Social Mobility and Child Poverty Commission 2014). Sociological studies since the 1950s have also found elite formation in the USA (Mills 1956), France and the UK (Maclean et al. 2006; Scott 1991), as well as at the transnational level (Carroll 2004).

It seems likely that 'elite' is still the most accurate description of certain powerful groups of people, despite the rise to prominence of new social networks. But assessing whether such elites are really coherent or as powerful in shaping social life today as they were in, say, the nineteenth century is an ongoing task for empirical researchers.

A discussion of social networks can be found in Chapter 7, 'Work and the Economy'.

Bureaucracy against democracy?

The word bureaucracy was coined in 1745 by the French economist Jean Claude Marie Vincent de Gournay, by adding 'bureau' (an office and a writing table) to the Greek *kratos*, meaning 'rule'. Bureaucracy is thus 'the rule of officials'. From the beginning, the concept was used in a disparaging way. The French novelist Honoré de Balzac saw bureaucracy as 'the giant power wielded by pygmies', while the Czech author Franz Kafka gave a nightmarish depiction of an impersonal and unintelligible bureaucracy in his novel *The Trial* (1925).

This view persists: bureaucracies are widely seen as powerful yet irrational, and the image of the 'faceless bureaucrat' is someone who lacks sensitivity and compassion (Lune 2010: 5). In sociology, the potential for bureaucracy to usurp democracy was most clearly expressed by Max Weber.

Modern life needs some kind of formal organization if things are to run smoothly. But many people see organizations in a negative light as stifling individual creativity and obstructive when we need their help. How can organizations be perceived as both necessary and yet unhelpful? Is this a relatively minor problem of perceptions or something much more deep-rooted and serious? Max Weber developed the first systematic interpretation of the rise of modern organizations, emphasizing that they depend on the control of information, and he stressed the importance of writing in this process. Organizations need *written* rules to function and files in which organizational 'memory' is stored. But Weber detected a clash, as well as a connection, between modern organizations and democracy which has far-reaching consequences for social life.

A limited number of bureaucratic organizations existed in traditional civilizations. For example, there was a bureaucratic officialdom in imperial China, responsible for the overall affairs of government. But it is only in modern times that bureaucracies have developed fully. According to Weber, the expansion of bureaucracy is inevitable in modern societies; bureaucratic authority is the only way of coping with the administrative requirements of large-scale social systems. Yet he also argued that bureaucracy has a number of failings which have important implications for freedom and democracy.

In order to study the origins and nature of the expansion of bureaucratic organizations, Weber constructed an ideal-typical bureaucracy. 'Ideal' here refers not to the most desirable but to a 'pure' form. An ideal type is an abstract description constructed by accentuating certain features of real cases so as to pinpoint their most essential characteristics (see chapter 1). Weber (1979 [1925]) listed several characteristics of the ideal type of bureaucracy.

1 There is a clear-cut hierarchy of authority, such that tasks in the organization are distributed as 'official duties'. A bureaucracy looks like a pyramid with the positions of highest authority at the top. Each higher office controls and supervises the one below it.

2 Written rules govern the conduct of officials at all levels. This does not mean that bureaucratic duties are just a matter of routine. The higher the office, the more the rules encompass a wide variety of cases and demand flexibility in their interpretation.

3 Officials are full time and salaried. Each job has a definite and fixed salary attached and individuals are expected to make a career within the organization. Promotion is based on capability and seniority, or a mixture of the two.

4 There is a separation between the tasks of officials within the organization and their life outside. Home life is distinct from activities in the workplace and the two are physically separated.

5 No members of the organization own the material resources with which they work. Officials do not own the offices in which they work, the desks at which they sit or the office machinery they use.

Weber often likened bureaucracies to sophisticated machines operating via the principle of rationality. But he also recognized that bureaucracies could be inefficient and accepted that many bureaucratic jobs are dull, offering little opportunity for creativity. While Weber feared that the rationalization of society could have negative consequences, he concluded that bureaucratic routine and the authority of officialdom over our lives are prices we pay for the technical effectiveness of bureaucratic organizations. On the other hand, the diminishing of democracy with the advance of bureaucratic organization was something that worried Weber a great deal. How can democracy be anything other than a meaningless slogan in the face of the increasing power that bureaucratic organizations wield in society?

Some maintain that Weber's account is a *partial* one. It concentrates on the formal aspects of organizations and has little to say about their informal life, which introduces a welcome flexibility into otherwise rigid systems (Blau 1963). Meyer and Rowan (1977) argued that formal rules are often 'myths' that have little substance in reality. They serve to legitimize ways in which tasks are carried out, even while these diverge from how the rules state things are 'supposed to be done'. Similarly, workers entering organizational settings need to 'learn the ropes', and informal methods can be more important than training as the idealistic expectations of new entrants are adjusted to the complex, mundane reality of their position (Watson 2008: 213).

Others claim that Weber let bureaucracy off too lightly – that its consequences are actually *more* damaging than he thought. For example, in different ways, both George Ritzer's thesis of the McDonaldization of society and Zygmunt Bauman's account of the mass murder of Jews and other groups during the Second World War show that bureaucratic systems have been and still are much more damaging and potentially destructive than Weber ever considered. Finally, some see Weber's perspective as *too negative*. Many problems commonly attributed to an abstract concept of 'bureaucracy' are really caused by specific attempts to *bypass* or circumvent the rules and guidelines of bureaucratic management. Bureaucratic rules, if adhered to, may contain important safeguards which prevent, rather than facilitate, abuses of power by political leaders.

We should not expect Weber to have foreseen all of the consequences of bureaucratization, and some criticisms of the direction of social change can be conceded. But a majority of later studies of bureaucracy have been forced either to engage in debates with his influential interpretation or attempt to take his ideas further. This probably demonstrates that he put his finger on a crucial aspect of what it is like to live in the modern world.

Even in democratic countries, government organizations hold enormous amounts of information about people, from records of our date of birth, schools and universities attended and jobs held, to data on income used for tax-collecting and information used for issuing drivers' licences and allocating National Insurance numbers. Since we do not always know what information is held and which agencies are holding it, people fear that surveillance activities undermine the principle of democracy. These fears formed the basis of George Orwell's famous novel *1984*, in which the state bureaucracy, 'Big Brother', uses surveillance to suppress internal criticism and differences of opinion that are normal in any democracy.

Proposals to introduce identity cards, partly to help tackle global terrorism and protect citizens against identity theft, have focused these concerns. ID cards usually contain a photograph of the card-holder, their name, address, gender and date of birth, but also a microchip which holds biometric information, such as fingerprints, iris image or facial dimensions. Critics have expressed concerns that national central databases, which contain information about people's identities, will not be secure and will pose a threat to people's rights to privacy and freedom from discrimination. Supporters of identity cards argue that some types of surveillance may actually protect the principle of democracy, by allowing easier surveillance of those who are trying to destroy it.

Defending bureaucracy

Paul du Gay admits that 'These are not the best days for bureaucracy.' As we have seen, 'bureaucracy' still carries negative connotations. In an influential book, *In Praise of Bureaucracy* (2000), du Gay resists this characterization. While recognizing that bureaucracies can and do have flaws, he seeks to defend bureaucracy against the most common lines of criticism.

Were Nazi concentration camps, such as Auschwitz, reliant on bureaucratization or was the bureaucratic public ethos overridden?

First, du Gay argues against the idea that bureaucracies are 'faceless', purely administrative and lacking ethical foundations. He singles out Zygmunt Bauman's book *Modernity and the Holocaust* (1989) as an important example of this view. Bauman argues that the development of modern bureaucratic institutions made the Holocaust during the Second World War practically possible. The planned genocide of millions by the Nazis could only happen once organizations were in place that distanced people from taking moral responsibility for their actions. Rather than being a barbaric breakdown of modern civilized conduct, Bauman contends that the Holocaust was possible only because modernity's rational, bureaucratic institutions separated discrete tasks from their consequences. German bureaucrats followed orders and carried out their allotted tasks to the best of their abilities – making sure that a railway line had been built or that a group of people was moved from one part of the country to another – rather than questioning the purpose of the whole system.

However, du Gay states that quite the opposite was the case. For the Holocaust to happen, he argues, the Nazis actually had to *overcome* legitimate and ethical procedures that are integral to the bureaucratic operation. One aspect of this was the demand for unquestioning allegiance to the Führer ('leader') rather than to the objective codes of bureaucracy. Du Gay holds that bureaucracies have an important public ethos, which includes the equal and impartial treatment of all citizens. For du Gay, the Holocaust became possible when the racist convictions of Nazis *overcame* that impartial application of rules.

Du Gay also defends bureaucracy against a second line of attack, rejecting what he sees as the currently fashionable talk of the need for entrepreneurial reform of bureaucracies, especially public services. He stresses that the ethos of bureaucratic impartiality is being undermined by an increasingly politicized civil service, which is enthusiastic to get the job done in the way that pleases politicians. Yet the bureaucratic framework itself ensures

an administrative responsibility for the public interest as well as constitutional legitimacy. In sum, what really threatens democracy is not bureaucracy but the illegitmate overriding of conventional bureaucratic norms.

> **THINKING CRITICALLY**
>
> Think of a time when you dealt with a bureaucracy, maybe a university admissions system, health service, mobile phone provider or bank. List the *negative* and *positive* aspects of the encounter. Could that task be organized any more efficiently than via a bureaucracy?

Political ideologies

An inescapable aspect of political sociology is the study of political ideas, ideologies and political theory and their impact in shaping societies. *Political ideas* and concepts such as equality, justice, freedom and individual rights are used in a variety of ways even by people who would never see themselves as 'political'. *Political theory* is very old indeed, traceable to ancient Greece and its philosophers, who not only tried to understand the world, they also tackled thorny moral and normative questions, such as which actions constitute a good moral life? What are the elements that make up a 'good society'? How can we know that actions are 'just' and 'fair'? Such questions are still asked by political theorists today. 'Ideology' is clearly related to political ideas and political theory, but its meaning is more complex.

When an idea or statement is described as 'ideological', the implication is that it is in some way false, misleading or partial rather than being 'true'. This meaning was popularized in Marx's work and that of later Marxists. For Marx, ideology is produced by ruling classes as a means of mystifying social life, thus distorting the exploitative reality faced by subordinate classes. This is a 'negative' conception of ideology. As Marx famously argued (Marx and Engels 1970 [1846]: 64), 'The class which has the material means of production at its disposal, has control at the same time over the means of mental production, so that thereby, generally speaking, the ideas of those who lack the means of mental production are subject to it.'

Yet this meaning is very far from the term's origins. 'Ideology' was first used in late eighteenth-century revolutionary France by Destutt de Tracy to describe a potential science of ideas and knowledge. De Tracy intended ideology to be the systematic study and comparison of ideas in much the same way as other sciences studied their subject matter. This version is known as a 'neutral' conception, which doesn't suggest that ideas are biased or misleading (Heywood 2012: 5).

This neutral conception was revived in the 1930s and 1940s when Karl Mannheim developed a sociology of knowledge that linked particular modes of thought to their social class bases. Mannheim argued that people view the world from a particular perspective rooted in their material life and therefore the ideas and knowledge they produce can be only partial. The sociology of knowledge would bring the differing perspectival interpretations together to produce a more comprehensive understanding of society as a whole. Over time, Mannheim's version lost out to the negative version of ideology that has dominated sociological work since the 1950s.

Political ideologies are perhaps best seen as coherent sets of ideas which explain the existing society but also include a vision of a better, future society and a means of how to get there. In this sense ideologies are worldviews that also contain guides to political action. Most ideologies actually critique the existing social order, though some seek to defend it against such critiques. Most of the ideologies discussed in this section feature elsewhere in the book, and a search of the index will guide readers to the relevant chapters and sections.

The three 'classical' political ideologies of conservatism, liberalism and socialism were developed as a consequence of the American and French revolutions of the late eighteenth century. All were attempts to deal with the collapse of feudal social relations and the emergence of industrial society with its attendant social problems. Heywood (2012: 16) notes that conservatives sought to defend the status quo and resist radical change, liberals promoted individualism, free markets and a small state, while socialists looked towards a new society rooted in cooperation and community. In Mannheim's terms, conservatism was the ideology of the embattled aristocracy, liberalism the ideology of rising capitalist groups, and socialism an emergent ideology of the rapidly growing working classes.

At its root the divisions between these groups was primarily economic, based on their approach to the creation and distribution of socially created wealth. Groups on the left conventionally favour equality and community, are optimistic about the possibility of managed progress (hence are often called 'progressives') and are prepared to use the resources of the state to achieve their goals. Those on the right value order and stability, are suspicious of ideas of a mutable human nature and view free markets as preferable to state intervention, at least in terms of the economy. This ideological positioning is the basis of the left/right distinction in politics, which continues today, albeit in modified form. With the emergence of the ideologies of communism and fascism in the nineteenth and twentieth centuries, a linear political spectrum can be drawn (figure 21.1). Because twentieth-century communist and fascist regimes developed into brutal authoritarian regimes, some prefer to see the spectrum as a circle or horseshoe shape which brings the far left and far right closer together.

This scheme does not exhaust the ideological variety in society, as anarchism and nationalism, for example, also have long histories. Neither does it do justice to the internal differences within the basic positions. For example, there have been many varieties of socialism which bear a family resemblance to one another, but are also different in crucial ways. These include Christian socialism, utopian socialism, democratic socialism,

Figure 21.1 The linear political spectrum

Source: Heywood (2012: 16).

social democracy and eco-socialism. But it does allow us to see why, for instance, Tony Blair's New Labour electoral project in the mid-1990s sought to move the Labour Party into the centre ground of British politics after more than fifteen years out of government in order to attract more middle-class votes. Similarly, the left–right linear spectrum makes sense of Labour's internal divisions when the more left-wing Jeremy Corbyn became leader in 2015 following a disastrous general election defeat. Many established Labour MPs were already further to the right of Corbyn's own position and therefore found themselves at odds with the direction he wanted to take. Similar left–right divisions exist within most political parties.

Since the 1960s, several ideologies have risen to prominence that are less easily located on the left–right spectrum. Arguably, the most important of these are feminism, environmentalism (also called 'ecologism') and various religious fundamentalisms with overtly political aims and programmes. Whether these should all be described as 'new' is arguable, as older forms of feminism, environmentalism and religious fundamentalism can certainly be identified. Nonetheless, they are seen as having had renewed impact in the current period.

There are several reasons why new ideologies have emerged. First, as industrial societies have moved into a post-industrial stage, the economic basis of established ideologies has been eroded and a series of 'new' social movements (discussed later) have emerged, whose basis lies in culture and identity every bit as much as wealth creation and distribution. For example, feminist ideology focuses on gender equality, taking in equal pay, childcare and breaking the corporate 'glass ceiling', but it also promotes the category 'woman' as a fundamental identity and challenges the 'pornification' of images of women and girls in the mass media and the routine sexual harassment of women by men in public places. Similarly, environmentalist ideology contains a swingeing critique of capitalist economics and its ethos of continual economic growth, but it also promotes the welfare and rights of animals and localism as an alternative to untrammelled globalization.

Second, since the collapse of a discredited Soviet communism in the early 1990s and a rapid process of globalization, socialist and communist ideologies have lost ground. Contemporary anti-globalization and anti-capitalist movements may share some similarities with the socialist critique of capitalism, but they do not necessarily accept the socialist/communist alternative either. This erosion of socialism as the 'natural' alternative to capitalism has had profound effects on social movements and political ideologies that are not yet fully understood.

Third, globalization has brought different societies and cultures into contact with one another in more systematic ways. As Western cultural products, tourists and values have spread around the world and migration from developing into developed countries has increased, there has been a reaction against the perceived decadence and moral decline of modern life from fundamentalist religious groups whose ideologies are rooted in particular interpretations of religious texts. The most visible of these has been the Wahhabi/Salafist fundamentalism associated with a range of terrorist groups, including the Taliban in Afghanistan, al-Qaeda and its affiliates and, most recently, Islamic State

(IS)/Daesh, which aims to create a world-wide 'caliphate' expanding from its base in Syria and Iraq. Christian fundamentalists, especially in the USA, who base their beliefs on a specific reading of the Bible, reject evolutionary theories of life on Earth. They are opposed to aspects of modern life, such as homosexuality and abortion, and have carried out violent attacks on family planning clinics.

There is one final point to note. Mannheim argued that ideologies do not exist in isolation but change and develop in relation to one another. At any given time the shape of the ideological landscape and the content of particular ideologies is partly determined by the relations between social movements and their ideologies. A good example is the long-established socialist ideology, which took on board the issue of gender equality from feminism and a concern for the impact of industry on the planet from environmentalism. In the process, socialist ideology was modified and expanded. Most other ideologies are engaged in a similar, dynamic process of accommodation, assimilation and change.

Conclusion

Today the concept of ideology is not as popular in sociology as it was before the 1990s. It is more likely that sociologists with an interest in the power of ideas will draw on the Foucauldian concept of discourses and their effects, which has shifted the focus away from ideas and beliefs towards language, speech and documentary sources. 'Ideology' has historically been associated with Marxism, but, with the collapse of Soviet communism and the apparent triumph of neo-liberal capitalism since the 1980s, the concept has lost ground. We should also remember that, since the 1970s, a series of writers have pronounced that we are at the 'end of ideology' in post-industrial, consumer-oriented societies. Yet the concept has a habit of bouncing back with each rising social movement, and it seems likely that the concept of ideology will be part of the architecture of political sociology for some time yet.

The global spread of democracy

Since the 1980s, one political development stands out: the democratization of many of the world's societies. Since then, countries in Latin America, such as Chile, Bolivia and Argentina, have undergone the transition from authoritarian military rule to thriving democracy. Similarly, with the collapse of the communist bloc, many Eastern European states – Russia, Poland and Czechoslovakia, for example – became democratic. And in Africa, a number of previously undemocratic nations, including Benin, Ghana, Mozambique and South Africa, have come to embrace democratic ideals.

In the mid-1970s, more than two-thirds of all societies in the world could be considered authoritarian. Since that time, the situation has shifted markedly, and now fewer than one-third are authoritarian in nature. Democracy is no longer concentrated primarily in Western countries but is endorsed, at least in principle, as the desired form of government in most areas of the world. As the Arab Spring of 2010–12 demonstrated, the desire for democracy and mass political participation has become perhaps the main standard of political legitimacy in the twenty-first century.

In this section we will consider the global spread of democracy and look at some explanations for the popularity of democratic systems, before moving on to examine some of the main problems faced by democracies today.

The fall of communism

For much of the twentieth century, a large proportion of the world's population, mainly in the Soviet Union, China and Eastern Europe, lived under political systems that were communist or socialist in orientation. The 100 years following Marx's death in 1883 seemed to bear out his prognosis of the spread of socialism and workers' revolutions around the globe. Communist states regarded themselves as democratic, although their systems did not operate under liberal democratic principles. Communism was essentially a system of one-party rule. Voters could choose only between different candidates of the same party – the Communist Party, which was easily the most dominant power in Soviet-style societies, controlling not just the political system but the economy as well.

Almost everyone in the West believed that communist systems were deeply entrenched and had become a permanent feature of global politics. Very few predicted the dramatic course of events that began to unfold in 1989 as one communist regime after another collapsed in a series of 'velvet revolutions'. What had seemed like a solid and established system of rule throughout Eastern Europe was rapidly overthrown.

Communists lost power in an accelerating sequence in countries they had dominated for half a century: Hungary, Poland, Bulgaria, East Germany, Czechoslovakia and Romania. Eventually, the Communist Party within the Soviet Union itself lost control. When the fifteen constituent republics of the USSR declared their independence in 1991, Mikhail Gorbachev, the last Soviet leader, was rendered a 'president without a state'. Even in China, students and others protesting in Tiananmen Square in 1989 seemed to shake the Communist Party's grip on power until they were brutally dispersed by the army.

Since the fall of the Soviet Union, processes of democratization have continued to spread. Signs of democratization can be detected even among some of the world's most authoritarian states. Afghanistan was controlled by the Soviet Union after the latter's troops invaded in 1979. But the USSR's occupation ended ten years later following fierce resistance from the mujahidin (Muslim guerrilla warriors). During the early 1990s the country was the site of in-fighting between warlords composed of mujahidin factions. By 1996 the Taliban had seized control of most of the country and began the creation of a 'pure Islamic state'. They introduced an extreme interpretation of Islamic law, brought in public executions and amputations, forbade girls from going to school and women from working and banned all 'frivolous' entertainment.

In 2001 the USA led efforts to topple the Taliban, which it linked to the terrorist training camps of al-Qaeda. In June 2002 Hamid Karzai became president and set about gaining approval for a new constitution. This was signed in January 2004 and provides a strong executive branch, a moderate role for Islam and basic protections for human rights. The first elections in Afghanistan were held in October and resulted in Karzai winning a five-year mandate as president. But by 2007 the Taliban had regrouped and attacked US and other foreign troops and Afghan government officials. Only in 2015 did Taliban leaders agree to meaningful peace talks. Hence, in spite of its fledgling democracy, Afghanistan is not yet a viable democratic state.

In China, which contains about a fifth of the world's population, the communist government faces pressure to become more democratic. Although thousands of people remain in prison in China for the non-violent expression of their desire for democracy, there are still groups, resisted by the government, working actively to secure a transition to a democratic system. In recent years, other authoritarian Asian states, such as Myanmar, Indonesia and Malaysia, have also seen growing democratic movements. Some of these calls for greater freedom have been met with violent responses. Although the spread of democracy continues, the general trend towards democracy is not inevitable. And, to the extent that democratization is tied to globalizing processes, it seems likely to continue for some time yet.

Democratization and its discontents

Why has democracy become so widespread? One explanation is that other types of political rule have been attempted and failed. It may seem clear that democracy is a 'better' form of political organization than authoritarianism, but this alone does not adequately explain the recent democratizing wave. While a full explanation requires detailed analysis of the social

21.1   Politics at the 'end of history'?

One scholar who theorized the triumph of capitalist democracy in the Cold War – and thus the 'end of history' – is Francis Fukuyama (1992). In the wake of the revolutions in Eastern Europe, the dissolution of the Soviet Union and a movement towards multiparty democracy, Fukuyama argued that the ideological battle was over. The end of history is the end of alternatives. No one any longer defends monarchism, fascism is a phenomenon of the past, and so is communism, which had long been the major rival of Western democracy. Capitalism has won in its long struggle with socialism, contrary to Marx's prediction, and liberal democracy stands unchallenged. We have reached, Fukuyama asserts, the end point of mankind's ideological evolution.

Fukuyama's thesis provoked much criticism. It smacks of triumphalism and is based primarily on the post-Cold War situation rather than genuine comparative historical research. It also closes off any possible future developments. It is at least theoretically feasible that a global economic crisis, nuclear conflict or natural catastrophe could undermine democratic politics and lead to more authoritarian systems of government.

And yet, it is clear that Fukuyama highlighted a key phenomenon of our time. The uprisings in countries of the Middle East and North Africa in 2010–12 tend to support his argument that democratic political systems provide a standard by which non-democratic systems are assessed and found wanting. Long before the so-called Arab Spring, Fukuyama (1992: xiii) saw the weakness of authoritarian regimes:

The most remarkable development of the last quarter of the twentieth century has been the revelation of enormous weaknesses at the core of the world's seemingly strong dictatorships . . . From Latin America to Eastern Europe, from the Soviet Union to the Middle East and Asia, strong governments have been failing over the last two decades. And while they have not given way in all cases to stable liberal democracies, liberal democracy remains the only coherent political aspiration that spans different regions and cultures around the globe.

But why do people pursue democracy at great risk to themselves? Fukuyama suggests that democracy gives ordinary people something they crave: simply, recognition. Rather than being passive recipients, people are turned into active citizens capable of having their say in how nation-states behave. Such a basic demand should not be underestimated. Yet it seems doubtful that history has come to an end in the sense that all alternatives have been exhausted. Who can say what new forms of economic, political or cultural order may emerge in the future? Just as the thinkers of medieval times had no inkling of the industrial society that emerged in the mid-eighteenth century, so we cannot anticipate with any certainty what may change over the coming century.

> **THINKING CRITICALLY**
>
> What evidence is there from party politics that Fukuyama may be right – that the old ideological battles around capitalism, communism and socialism are now over? What is replacing them?

and political situations in each country, there can be little doubt that globalizing processes have played an important role.

First, the growing number of cross-national cultural contacts have invigorated democratic movements. The global media, along with advances in communications technology, have exposed inhabitants of non-democratic nations to democratic ideals, increasing internal pressure on political elites to hold

Demolishing the Berlin Wall separating East and West Germany in 1989 was a symbolic moment heralding an unprecedented spread of liberal democratic institutions.

elections. Of course, such pressure does not automatically result from the diffusion of the notion of popular sovereignty. More important is that, with globalization, news of democratic revolutions and accounts of the mobilizing processes that lead to them are quickly spread on a regional level.

Second, international organizations such as the United Nations and the European Union have put external pressure on non-democratic states to move in democratic directions. In some cases, these organizations have been able to use trade embargoes, conditional provision of loans for economic development, and diplomatic manoeuvres of various kinds to encourage the dismantling of authoritarian regimes. For example, the United Nations Development Programme (UNDP) and UN Mission in the Democratic Republic of the Congo (DRC) supported a new Independent Electoral Commission to monitor and administer the 2006 national election, in which there was an 80 per cent participation rate. This was a real achievement in a society that had experienced around 4 million deaths as a result of civil war and had not held elections for forty years. UNDP has focused particularly on improving the participation rates of women in elections, both as voters and as candidates, in, for example, Kuwait, Morocco and Mauritania (UNDP 2007b).

| Global Society 21.1 | Does the Internet promote democratization? |

Vietnam's bid to tame the internet boom

Vietnam is one of the fastest growing economies in Asia, spurred by a policy of rapid liberalisation in the Communist state. Shops are packed with the latest designs, from watches to iPads and MP3 players. The country is opening up to the outside world – and that presents a challenge to the authorities. Nowhere is that more clear than over the use of the internet. More than a third of Vietnam's young population now regularly goes online. Almost every cafe in central Hanoi, it seems, offers free WiFi.

Safeguard or censorship?

I met Minh, a 26-year-old lawyer, and Ngan, who has just graduated from university, at one of their favourite haunts. Minh was surfing the internet on his iPhone and Ngan was checking Facebook on her laptop. 'Whenever I have free time I often come here to surf the internet and hang out with my friends', Ngan told me over a cup of Vietnam's famous coffee.

The government has responded to the internet boom with a new law obliging any place that provides public access to the internet – cafes, hotels, businesses – to install monitoring software. The law, announced in April, will enable the authorities to track who is doing what online, and that worries Minh and Ngan. 'Sure, there are some bad websites and malicious information on the web', Minh said. 'But on the other hand, if they overdo it, then it will be like restricting access to information for Vietnamese people.'

[. . .]

But a recent report from Human Rights Watch alleged that the Vietnamese government was deliberately targeting independent bloggers. 'That's not true', Ms Nga [a Foreign Ministry spokesperson] said. 'In Vietnam we have more than a million bloggers. Bloggers are not arrested because of the expression of their opinions. Only those who break the law are dealt with according to the law.'

Same problems

An awful lot of political dissidents seem to fall into that category. It is not blogging as such that causes the problem, rather it is the choice of subjects that can land someone in jail. Writing about corruption, religious freedom, land seizures, or unpopular government deals with China can result in an unwanted knock on the door from the police. Le Thi Cong Nhan is a prominent human rights lawyer, who has openly campaigned for multiparty democracy, often using the internet to get her message out. She was sentenced in 2007 to three years in prison for 'spreading propaganda against the state'. Now she is under house arrest.

But despite the potential risk, Le Thi Cong Nhan agreed to meet me, under cover of dark, and on condition that I was able to lose my government-appointed minder. Ms Nhan's internet connection has been cut off, but somehow she still manages to use email, although she would not tell me how. Internet censorship, she told me, is just a new version of an old problem. 'The most basic thing in human rights is freedom of speech', she said emphatically. 'We can have nothing if we don't have freedom of speech.'

The internet it seems is helping to fuel that demand, in part because controlling the flow of information on the web is increasingly difficult. Inevitably perhaps, the tension between a centralised state and a globalised world is growing.

Source: Adapted from Harvey (2010).

THINKING CRITICALLY

If the Internet is helping to spread democratic ideals, is it also promoting Western cultural values? How likely is it that the prohibitions imposed in Vietnam will be effective in the long term?

Third, democratization has been facilitated by the expansion of capitalism. Although transnational corporations are notorious for striking deals with dictators, corporations generally prefer to do business in democratic states – not because they value freedom and equality, but because democracies are generally more stable, and stability is essential for maximizing profits. Because elites are often anxious to increase levels of international trade and encourage transnationals to set up in their countries, they have sometimes pursued a democratic agenda of their own – in what Barrington Moore (1966) once called 'revolutions from above'.

It is true that, if globalization was the sole cause of the most recent wave of democratization, all countries today would be democratic. The persistence of authoritarian regimes in such countries as China, Cuba, Nigeria, Vietnam and elsewhere suggests that globalizing forces are not always sufficient to force a transition to liberal democracy. But democratic movements exist in many of these countries, leading some sociologists to argue that many more nations will become democratic in the years to come.

Democracies in trouble?

Between 1974 and 2000, largely the result of newly independent countries introducing democratic systems, the proportion of democracies to non-democracies in the world increased from 27 per cent to 62 per cent (Linz 2000). By 2009 around half of the global population (some 3 billion people) lived in democratic countries with a high degree of political and civil freedom (Nobelprize.org 2012). However, the apparently inexorable expansion of democracy across the world seems to have stalled in recent years, and established democracies face voter apathy and political corruption.

In 2005 an assessment by the influential US-based NGO Freedom House found 123 'electoral democracies' in the world, the highest number ever. But by 2010 this had fallen back to the 1995 level, at 115 countries. The Philippines, Tanzania and Tonga were among those with the status of electoral democracy as a result of recent elections, but others, such as Burundi, Guinea-Bissau and Haiti, were removed from the classification because of intimidation, corruption, pre-election misuse of state resources and persecution of opposition candidates (Puddington 2011). However, even in countries with long-established democratic systems, democracy is not universally valued amid increasing evidence of voter apathy and a widespread mistrust of elected politicians.

One sign of disaffection with established democracies lies in reduced election turnout. In elections to the European Parliament, average turnout across the EU fell from around 62 per cent in 1979 to just 42.6 per cent by 2014. There is a qualification here, though. In 1979, just nine countries participated, while in 2014 there were twenty-eight, including some in Eastern Europe which recorded spectacularly low turnouts. This skews the average downwards. In 2014 turnout was just 13 per cent in Slovakia, 18.2 per cent in the Czech Republic, 23.8 per cent in Poland and 24.5 per cent in Slovenia (European Parliament 2014). However, most of the long-established member states have also seen turnout fall dramatically over the period, including Germany, France, Italy and the Netherlands. In the traditionally more Eurosceptic UK, turnout has struggled to get above one-third at any time (see table 21.1).

In a regional authority such as the European Parliament we might expect turnout to be lower than in national elections, as that parliament often appears more remote. Yet, as the experience of the UK shows, voter turnout has been falling at the national level too, particularly since the early 1990s (see figure 21.2). From a peak of over 80 per cent in the early 1950s, it fell below 60 per cent in 2001 before a modest recovery in 2005 and 2010. In 2015, turnout was 66.2 per cent (Rallings and Thrasher 2015). There does appear to be a generational shift driving reduced turnout. In the 2015 UK election, around 78 per cent of those over sixty-five and 77 per cent of those aged fifty-five to sixty-four voted, compared

The 2014 national independence referendum in Scotland engaged large numbers of people, with a voter turnout on the day of 84.6 per cent, the highest since universal suffrage was introduced. Yet in the 2011 Scottish parliamentary election turnout was just 50.6 per cent (Denver 2011: 1). What factors explain this very large difference?

with just 43 per cent of those aged eighteen to twenty-four (Ipsos MORI 2015). Such apathy stands in stark contrast to the enthusiasm displayed by voters in more recently created democracies.

The global picture of voter turnout is varied, though there is a general global decline from the mid-1980s. It has been suggested that the type of voting system adopted may explain the variety at the national level (see table 21.2). For example, it may be that election turnout is highest in those countries with compulsory voting and lowest where voting is entirely voluntary. This seems to be an effective argument in parts of Europe. Liechtenstein's average turnout of almost 93 per cent since 1945 can be attributed partly

to that country's compulsory voting system, whereas Switzerland, which has a voluntary system, has a low average of just 56.5 per cent. This cannot be the complete explanation of cross-national voting patterns, though, as the Bahamas has averaged a turnout of close to 92 per cent since 1945 in a *non-compulsory* system. Clearly there must be other factors at work as well.

Comparative statistics on voter turnout tell us very little about the state of democracy *within* countries. What is not revealed in such bald figures are the different national contexts within which the turnout figures were achieved. This is a pertinent point when comparisons are made between the 'new' and 'old' democracies, which are often very different political

Table 21.1	Turnout in European Parliament elections, by member state, 1979–2014 (percentages)							
	1979	*1984*	*1989*	*1994*	*1999*	*2004*	*2009*	*2014*
Belgium*	91.4	92.1	90.7	90.7	91.0	90.8	90.4	89.6
Luxemburg*	88.9	88.8	87.4	88.5	87.3	91.3	90.8	85.5
Malta						82.4	78.8	74.8
Greece*		77.2	79.9	73.2	71.5	63.2	52.6	60.0
Italy	84.9	83.4	81.0	73.6	69.8	71.7	65.1	57.2
Denmark	47.8	52.4	46.2	52.9	50.4	47.9	59.5	56.3
Ireland	63.6	47.6	68.3	44.0	50.2	58.6	57.6	52.4
Sweden					38.8	37.9	45.5	51.1
Germany	65.7	56.8	62.3	60.0	45.2	43.0	43.3	48.1
Lithuania						48.4	21.0	47.4
Austria					49.0	42.4	46.0	45.4
Cyprus*						72.5	59.4	44.0
Spain			54.6	59.1	63.0	45.1	44.9	43.8
EU	61.8	59.0	58.3	56.7	49.5	45.6	43.0	42.6
France	60.7	56.7	48.7	52.8	46.8	42.8	40.6	42.4
Finland					30.1	39.4	40.5	41.0
Netherlands	58.1	50.6	47.2	35.7	30.0	39.3	36.8	37.3
Estonia						26.8	43.9	36.5
Bulgaria							38.9	36.1
UK	32.5	32.6	36.2	36.4	24.0	39.2	34.5	35.4
Portugal			51.2	35.5	39.9	38.6	36.8	33.7
Romania							27.7	32.4
Latvia						41.3	53.7	30.2
Hungary						38.5	36.3	29.0
Croatia								25.2
Slovenia						28.4	28.3	24.5
Poland						20.9	24.5	23.8
Czech Republic						28.3	28.2	18.2
Slovakia						17.0	19.6	13.0

Notes:
*Compulsory voting (in Italy, voting was also compulsory for the 1979, 1984 and 1989 elections).
Lowest turnout.
Highest turnout without compulsory voting.

Source: European Parliament (2014).

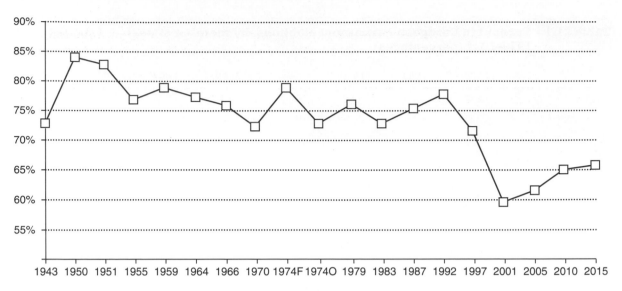

Figure 21.2 Voter turnout in British general elections, 1945–2015 (percentages)
Note: Two elections took place in 1974, in February and October (74F and 74O); 2015 turnout added.
Source: UK Political Info (2010).

environments. For example, in many established democracies, such as the USA, there are other means through which people's interests can be represented, such as in the courts under equal rights legislation (Pintor and Gratschew 2002), which may partly explain low turnout in elections. So, although turnout gives us a basic guide to the proportions of people voting in elections across the world, it may be more informative to look at the changing voting patterns over time within particular national contexts, as in our UK example in table 21.1. Addressing the important question of *why* people do or do not vote requires statistical evidence to be related to the societal context within which politics takes place.

Some have argued that people are increasingly sceptical of all established forms of authority, as there has been a shift in political values in democratic nations from 'scarcity values' to 'post-material values' (Inglehart 1997). This means that, after a certain level of economic prosperity has been reached, voters become concerned less with economic issues than with the quality of their individual (as opposed to collective) lifestyles. As a result, voters are generally less interested in national politics, except for issues involving personal liberty.

Many scholars and political commentators now argue that the decline in voting shows that people in the developed countries are losing trust in politicians and all of those in positions of power. Onora O'Neill (2002: 9) sees this as a crisis of trust in Western political leaders and other authorities:

> Mistrust and suspicion have spread across all areas of life, and supposedly with good reason. Citizens, it is said, no longer trust governments, or politicians, or ministers, or the police, or the courts, or the prison service. Consumers, it is said, no longer trust business, especially big business, or their products. None of us, it is said, trusts banks, or insurers, or pension providers. Patients, it is said, no longer trust doctors . . . and in particular no longer trust hospitals or hospital consultants. 'Loss of trust' is, in short, a cliché of our times.

Survey evidence seems to confirm a loss of trust in politicians and formal party politics,

Table 21.2 Vote/registration ratio league table, by world region, selected countries: ranking of average turnout, 1945–2001 (percentages)

Oceania		Central and South America	
Australia (22)	94.5	Guyana (7)	88.5
New Zealand (19)	90.8	Chile (11)	78.9
Fiji (3)	81.0	Nicaragua (6)	75.9
Tonga (4)	56.3	Colombia (18)	47.6
Average	**83.1**	**Average**	**71.5**
Western Europe		Asia	
Liechtenstein (17)	92.8	Singapore (8)	93.5
Sweden (17)	87.1	Japan (22)	69.6
United Kingdom (16)	75.2	India (13)	59.4
Switzerland (14)	56.5	Pakistan (6)	45.3
Average	**82.6**	**Average**	**74.0**
North America		Middle East	
Bahamas (6)	91.9	Israel (15)	80.3
Canada (18)	73.9	Iran (1)	77.3
United States of America (17)	66.5	Jordan (3)	51.8
Haiti (3)	47.1	Lebanon (3)	39.5
Average	**69.6**	**Average**	**72.2**
Africa		Central and Eastern Europe	
Burundi (1)	91.4	Uzbekistan (3)	93.5
Morocco (5)	71.2	Czech Republic (4)	82.8
Zimbabwe (3)	48.7	Russia (3)	58.4
Mali (2)	21.3	Poland (5)	50.3
Average	**64.5**	**Average**	**71.9**

Note: Number of elections in parentheses.

Source: Pintor and Gratschew (2002).

highlighted by political attempts to tackle the financial crisis in the eurozone economies and bring down national debt. A 2011 *Guardian/ICM* opinion survey of five EU countries – Poland, Britain, France, Germany and Spain – asked people if they trusted politicians to 'act with honesty and integrity'. Overall, only 9 per cent said they did trust politicians to act this way – 12 per cent in the UK, 10 per cent in Germany, 11 per cent in France, 8 per cent in Spain and just 3 per cent in Poland. The poll also asked whether people trusted their

"Apparently, I can't claim for the wheelbarrow."

government 'to deal with the country's problems'. Overall, 78 per cent said they did *not* trust their government – 66 per cent in the UK, 80 per cent in Germany, 82 per cent in France, 78 per cent in Spain and 82 per cent in Poland (Glover 2011).

In 2009, the growing rift between what is increasingly described as the democratically elected 'political class' or 'elite' and the citizens they serve was dramatically symbolized in an expenses scandal involving elected members of the UK Parliament. The *Daily Telegraph* newspaper began publishing leaked details of the expense claims of Members of Parliament, which further damaged trust in politicians. MPs are allowed to claim expenses to cover travel from constituencies, the cost of staff, necessary accommodation in London, and other legitimate expenses associated with their role. But there was public outrage at the use of public funds on a wide variety of small personal items (such as chocolate bars or DVDs) to large ones (such as plasma televisions, mortgages and inflated housing costs). Attempts by some MPs to exempt their expenses from the Freedom of Information Act (2000) were also seen as a disreputable bid to cover up wrongdoing.

The expenses system was changed in the wake of the scandal, and there is some polling evidence that public opinion on 'confidence in the operation of Parliament' returned to pre-scandal levels quite quickly (Bartle and Allen 2010: 132–3). Nevertheless, attitudes towards politicians have probably never been less favourable. Across the European Union since the financial crisis there have been mass public protests against corrupt and ineffectual politicians and their austerity plans. Greece, Italy, Ireland, Portugal and Britain have all seen demonstrations by trade unions, students and other social groups.

In the next section, we take a look at the changing situation of the nation-state, which some see as incapable of maintaining its pre-eminent political position in our global age. This may be yet one more reason why democratic participation seems less vital to younger generations.

Global governance: prospects and reality

The American sociologist Daniel Bell (1987) observed that national government is *too small* to respond to the big questions – such as the influence of global economic competition or the destruction of the world's environment – but it is *too big* to deal with the small questions – issues that affect particular cities or localities. The suggestion is that national politics is caught in a pincer movement of globalization and localization, which partly explains why many people, as we saw earlier, are just not enthused enough to participate.

National governments have little power over the activities of giant business corporations, the main actors within the global economy. For instance, a British corporation may decide to shut down its plants in the UK and shift production to Malaysia, as the vacuum-cleaner manufacturer Dyson did in 2002, in order to lower costs and compete more effectively with other corporations. British workers losing their jobs in such cases are likely to want the government to 'do something'. But national governments are unable to control globalizing processes. All they can do is try to soften the blow by providing unemployment benefits or job retraining.

Globalization has created new risks – the spread of weapons of mass destruction, pollution, terrorism and international financial crises, for example. These issues cannot be managed by nation-states alone, and international governmental organizations (IGOs) such as the World Bank, the World Trade Organization and the United Nations have been created as a way of pooling global risks.

These organizations form the basis for discussions about global governance. Global governance is not about creating government on a global level. Rather, it is concerned with the framework of rules needed to tackle global problems and the diverse set of institutions, including both international organizations and national governments, needed to guarantee this framework of rules.

Many of the international or global organizations already in place to tackle these problems lack democratic accountability. For example, the UN Security Council has fifteen members, of which five are permanent – the USA, Britain, France, China and Russia – some of the world's most powerful countries. For any resolution to be passed, the council requires nine votes, including those of all five permanent members. The UN did not back a resolution explicitly allowing force against Iraq in 2003, for example, because France threatened to veto it. This was one of the main grounds cited by critics of the war, who condemned it as an illegitimate use of power. The views of the majority of the world's poorer countries were largely irrelevant in the debate.

As a positive example of regional cooperation and integration, the European Union has often been seen as a potential model for successful international politics and global governance. The expansion of the EU to twenty-eight nation-states integrated into a union of cooperation within an institutional and legal framework stands in sharp contrast to the devastating conflicts of the past. It is also seen as probably the greatest achievement of postwar European politics. The historical roots of the EU lie in the Second World War and the idea of European integration was conceived to prevent such destruction from ever happening again. The British wartime prime minister, Winston Churchill, called for a 'United States of Europe' in 1946, and practical moves towards European unity were proposed by the then French foreign minister, Robert Schuman, in a speech on 9 May 1950. This date is celebrated annually as 'Europe Day'. However, in a 2016 referendum, the UK became the first EU state to vote to leave the EU, reducing the

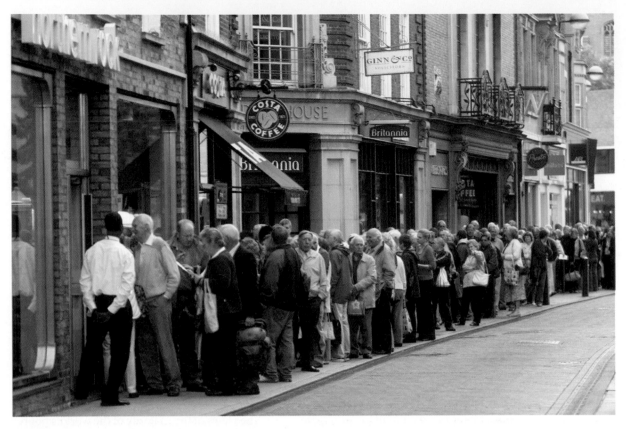

In early 2008, the financial crisis almost led to the collapse of a well-known UK high-street bank. Such crises lend weight to arguments in favour of global regulation.

union to twenty-seven countries. Nationalist movements in the Netherlands, France and elsewhere in the EU were emboldened as a result and called for their own citizens to demand a similar 'in–out' referendum.

Initially, the EU consisted of just six countries: Belgium, Germany, France, Italy, Luxembourg and the Netherlands. Denmark, Ireland and the United Kingdom joined in 1973, Greece in 1981, Spain and Portugal in 1986, and Austria, Finland and Sweden in 1995. The biggest ever enlargement took place in 2004, when ten new countries joined: eight from Eastern Europe – the Czech Republic, Estonia, Latvia, Lithuania, Hungary, Poland, Slovenia and Slovakia – plus Cyprus and Malta. Bulgaria and Romania joined in 2007 and Croatia in 2013, bringing the total to twenty-eight countries (European Commission 2015b).

In the early years, much of the cooperation between EU countries was about trade and the economy, but now the Union also deals with many other subjects of direct importance to daily life. EU agencies deal with areas as diverse as citizens' rights, security, job creation, regional development and environmental protection. In the UK referendum, the argument that membership of the EU undermines national sovereignty – that is, the independence and ability for self-government – was a crucial argument put forward by the Vote Leave campaign. Some people, especially in the UK, are concerned that membership of the EU undermines national sovereignty – that is, the independence and ability for self-government – while others argue that the EU is merely another international body like the United Nations or the World Trade Organization (*The Economist* 2005). However, defenders of the EU see both these accounts as inaccurate. They argue that it is an organization whose member states have set up common institutions to which they delegate some of their power so that decisions on specific matters of joint interest can be made democratically at European level. All decisions and procedures are based on the treaties, which are agreed by all the member countries. This pooling of sovereignty is also called 'European integration'.

EU supporters argue that the Union has delivered half a century of stability, peace and prosperity, helped to raise living standards, built a single Europe-wide market, launched the single European currency (the euro), and strengthened Europe's voice in the world. However, the sovereign debt crisis which began in 2009 not only raised issues of supra-national governance but also led some to question seriously whether a pan-European currency can actually survive in the long term.

THINKING CRITICALLY

Why might institutions such as the EU be better equipped than the nation-state to deal with politics in a global age? If nation-states promote national identities, will the EU have to challenge national identities in order to be successful?

The economic crisis which engulfed the eurozone countries (those within the single European currency) pointedly called into question the suitability of the EU model for governance of the global economy (Della Salla 2011: 152). In particular, as McNamara (2010: 22) argues,

> At base, the problem is simple: the EU is an outlier in political and economic history, and markets do not know what to expect from its unique combination of a single currency and separate nation-states. The Eurozone crisis reveals the challenges of the EU's *sui generis* political status – no longer a mere collection of nation-states, yet not a fully-fledged federal entity.

The huge bailout packages agreed for Greece, Ireland and Portugal may look like good evidence of concerted, multinational political action. However, apart from a general consensus that a better system of financial regulation is now needed, there seems little political agreement on how the EU should develop its governance structures to prevent a repeat of the crisis. Some leaders see a desperate need for closer political (and fiscal) union, while others, notably those outside the single currency, view the crisis as evidence that closer integration is undesirable. Which way the EU will develop remains uncertain at present, but, in the absence of effective regional and global governance, it is likely that economic markets and ratings agencies (whose assessments impact on national governments' ability to borrow money) will continue to exert a strong influence on events.

> The 2008 financial crisis and its aftermath are discussed in chapter 7, 'Work and the Economy', with some relevant material in chapter 4, 'Globalization and Social Change', chapter 6, 'Cities and Urban Life', and chapter 13, 'Poverty, Social Exclusion and Welfare'. The eurozone crisis is covered in chapter 7, 'Work and the Economy'.

What, then, is the fate of democracy in an age when democratic governance at the nation-state level seems ill-equipped to deal with events? Successive British Conservative Party leaders and some economists suggest there is little to be done: governments cannot hope to control the rapid changes occurring around us, and the most prudent course is to reduce the role of government and allow market forces to guide the way. However, the global financial crisis has demonstrated that this is a potentially hazardous path. Bootle (2011: 3) argues that, 'From the events of 2007/9, it seems plain that the financial markets have *not* worked to promote the common weal, and they have caused, rather than absorbed, chaos and instability. Ironically, they have had to be bailed out by governments.'

David Held (2004) argues that, in a

global age, we are in need of *more*, not less, governance. Yet effective governing demands a deepening of democracy, at the level of the nation-state, above it and below it. This means making global organizations accountable, in the same way that democratically elected governments are accountable to their electorate in national elections. The International Criminal Court, which prosecutes and brings to justice those responsible for genocide, crimes against humanity and war crimes, and the United Nations both provide good foundations. These institutions foster a vision of a world in which basic human rights are protected and a peaceful process for resolution of difference is agreed.

In Held's view, global social democracy will be achieved through multi-layered governance in which many organizations operate together at different levels: local, national and global. Where states were once the main actors in international politics, today these include administrative agencies, courts and legislatures. A former secretary-general of the UN, Kofi Annan, has been highly influential in international politics, for example. Non-governmental organizations, such as Oxfam and Amnesty International, as well as social movements, can also play an important role. Below, we look in more detail at the increasing significance of social movements and how sociologists have understood them.

Social movements and social change

Political life, as our discussion above shows, is by no means carried on only within the orthodox framework of political parties, voting systems and governmental bodies. Despite the spread of democracy, the persistence of authoritarian regimes reminds us that effecting change within existing political structures is not always easy or possible. Sometimes change can be brought about only through recourse to non-orthodox forms of political action, such as revolutions or social movements.

What are social movements?

The most dramatic and far-reaching example of non-orthodox political action is revolution – the overthrow of an existing socio-political order by means of a mass movement, often involving violence. Revolutions are tense, exciting and fascinating events; understandably, they attract great attention. Yet, for all of their high drama, revolutions occur relatively infrequently.

> See chapter 2, 'Asking and Answering Sociological Questions', for a discussion of Theda Skocpol's work on social revolutions.

The most common type of non-orthodox political activity is the social movement – a collective attempt to further common interests or secure common goals through action outside the sphere of established institutions. A variety of social movements have existed in modern societies, some enduring, some transient. While some carry on their activities within the laws of the society in which they exist, others operate as networks of illegal or underground groups. It is characteristic of protest movements, however, that they operate near the margins of what is defined as legally permissible by governments at any particular time or place. Social movements often arise with the aim of bringing about change on a public issue, such as expanding civil rights for a segment of the population. In response, counter-movements sometimes emerge in defence of the status quo. The campaign for women's right to abortion, for example, has been vociferously challenged by anti-abortion, 'pro-life' activists, who argue that abortion should be illegal.

Often, laws or policies are altered as a result of the action of social movements. For example, it used to be illegal for groups of workers to call their members out on strike. As a result of the actions of trade unions, laws were amended, making the strike a permissible tactic of industrial conflict. Similarly, lesbian and gay movements have been largely successful in raising the issue of equal rights, and many countries around the world have equalized their laws on the legal age of sexual activity for heterosexuals and homosexuals. The American civil rights movement succeeded in pushing through important pieces of legislation outlawing racial segregation in schools and public places, while feminist movements secured important gains for women in terms of economic and political equality. Environmental movements have campaigned in unconventional, direct ways to promote sustainable development and change attitudes towards the natural world.

> See chapter 5, 'The Environment', for a much wider discussion of environmental issues.

Social movements are as evident a feature of the contemporary world as are the formal, bureaucratic organizations they often oppose, and some scholars suggest that we may be moving towards a global 'social movement society' which provides fertile ground for this type of collective action. For this reason, we need to explore sociological theories of social movements.

Theorizing social movements

For most of the twentieth century, social movements were seen by sociologists as rather unusual phenomena. As with other forms of collective behaviour, such as riots, crowds and revolutions, they seemed to be marginal to the discipline (Tarrow 1998). This began to change from the 1960s with the emergence of a fresh wave of movements, which attracted a new generation of sociologists looking to understand and explain them. When they did so, they found the existing theories seemed inadequate for the task. To see why, we must take a brief tour through the field of social movement theories.

Collective behaviour and social unrest

The Chicago School of Sociology is often seen as the first systematically to chart forms of collective behaviour and, from the 1920s, to turn these into a specialist field of inquiry (Della Porta and Diani 2006). Scholars in the Chicago tradition, including Robert E. Park, Ernest W. Burgess and Herbert Blumer, saw social movements as *agents* of social change, not merely as *products* of it. In this sense, they began to theorize social movements in more productive ways.

Herbert Blumer was the foremost social movement analyst in the Chicago tradition of symbolic interactionism. He devised a theory of social unrest to account for the unconventional protest activities of social movements outside the sphere of formal party politics and interest representation. Essentially, he saw social movements of all kinds as motivated by dissatisfaction with some aspects of current society, which they sought to rectify. In doing so, they were trying to build a 'new order of life'. Blumer (1969: 8) argued that

> Social movements can be viewed as collective enterprises to establish a new order of life. They have their inception in a condition of unrest, and derive their motive power on the one hand from dissatisfaction with the current form of life, and on the other hand from wishes and hopes for a new scheme of living. The career of a social movement depicts the emergence of a new order of life. In its beginning, a social movement is amorphous, poorly organized, and without form; the collective behavior is on the primitive level. . . . As a social movement develops, it takes on the character of a society. It acquires organization and form, a body of customs and traditions, established leadership, an enduring division of labor, social rules and social values – in short, a culture, a social organization, and a new scheme of life.

Blumer's theory of social movements as social unrest makes some important points. He saw that movements can be 'active' or outwardly directed, aiming to transform society, or 'expressive' or inwardly directed, trying to change the people who become involved. An example of the former would be the labour movement, which aimed radically to change capitalist societies in egalitarian ways, while the latter would include 'New Age' movements, which encourage people to transform their inner selves. In practice, most social movements involve both active and expressive elements as activists and supporters undergo changes in their self-identity as a result of campaigns to change society. Many environmental campaigns, for example, are aimed at preventing environmental damage, but they often generate an increasing identification with the natural world, transforming people's perception of self.

Blumer also argued that social movements have a 'life cycle', involving four consecutive stages. First, there is 'social ferment', when people are agitated about an issue but are relatively unfocused and disorganized. This develops into a stage of 'popular excitement', during which the sources of dissatisfaction are more clearly defined and understood. In the third stage, formal organizations are normally created which bring about a higher level of coordination and a more effective campaigning structure. Finally comes 'institutionalization', in which the movement comes to be accepted as part of the wider society and political life. Of course, some movements partially succeed, while others completely fail. Some endure over quite long periods of time, while others simply run out of finance or enthusiasm, thus ending their life cycle. This idea of a life cycle has proved to be extremely productive and has been central to many recent studies, particularly in the USA, which shows that Blumer's work continues to influence social movement studies (Goodwin and Jasper 2002).

One problem with this interactionist approach is that, although it treats movements as meaningful phenomena – a clear breakthrough at the time – its studies tend not to explore the rational decisions and strategies of movement activists. This aspect was left for later scholars to pursue. Second, although the approach produced some detailed case studies

of particular movements, critics argued that these were largely descriptive accounts that did not pay enough attention to explanations that connected social movement activity to changes in the social structure (Della Porta and Diani 2006).

Resource mobilization

Traditions of social movement research in the USA and Europe have tended to be quite different. In the USA, social movements have been studied using some form of rational choice theory, which assumes that individuals make rational decisions, weighing up the choices facing them. In Europe, though, as we will see later, the focus has been much more on the connections between social movements and social classes. It has been suggested that American approaches concentrate mainly (though by no means exclusively) on the question of *how* movements become organized, while European approaches consider *why* social movements emerge when they do (Melucci 1989).

One of the most influential American perspectives is resource mobilization theory (RMT). RMT developed in the late 1960s and the 1970s, partly as a reaction to social unrest theories, which portrayed social movements as 'irrational' phenomena. Against this view, advocates of RMT argued that movement participants behaved in rational ways and that movements were purposeful, not chaotic (Oberschall 1973; Tilly 1978; Zald and McCarthy 1987). RMT theorists argued that capitalist societies produce chronic discontent among sections of the public, which renders social unrest theories problematic. If social unrest is always present, the emergence of movements cannot be explained by reference to it. What turns discontent into mobilizations and social movements is the availability of the necessary *resources* to mount effective campaigns. This point is nicely illustrated by Storr (2002: 82):

> The central insight of resource mobilization theory is actually very basic: social movements need resources. Suppose you and I are members of a social movement.

Classic Studies 21.2 Neil Smelser on understanding social movements

The research problem

Social movements have become very common, and you may well be part of one or more. They often appear unannounced, taking sociologists by surprise, but they can also collapse in much the same way. Does this mean that their emergence is entirely random, the product of chance and unpredictable circumstances? How might they be linked to wider social changes? Can we develop a general theory of movement emergence and development that would help us to understand the process better? The sociologist Neil J. Smelser worked with Talcott Parsons and studied collective behaviour from a structural functionalist perspective, aiming for just such a general theory of social movements.

Smelser's explanation

Smelser (1962) devised a theory of *structural strain* to account for the emergence of social movements, though one thing that marks out his perspective is that it amounts to a 'value-added model'. This idea is taken from economic theory and suggests that social movements emerge through a process with identifiable stages, with each successive stage 'adding value'. The model sees each stage adding to the probability that collective behaviour or a social movement will be created. In this sense, Smelser's argument is multi-causal, rejecting all notions of a single cause of social movements. This was a very important moment in the study of social movements.

Smelser proposed six 'value-added' elements as necessary for a social movement to develop.

1 *Structural conduciveness* All social movements take place within a wider social context, and this structural context has to be conducive to movement formation. For example, in authoritarian societies there may be very little scope for people to gather together in large groups or to demonstrate legally against things they oppose. Therefore, opponents of a regime have to find other, less open, ways to pursue change. The situation is not structurally conducive to social movement activity.

In recent years, social movement scholars have used the concept of 'political opportunity structure' to describe the ways in which political systems create or deny opportunities for movements to develop (Tarrow 1998), and this concept clearly owes much to Smelser's earlier idea (Crossley 2002).

2 *Structural strain* If the social structure is conducive to collective behaviour, then there needs to be a strain between people's expectations and social reality. When people expect, or have been led to expect, certain things from society and these expectations are not met, frustrations arise and people look for other ways to meet them.

3 *Generalized beliefs* Smelser argues that, if the first two conditions are met, it is necessary for generalized beliefs about the causes of strain to develop and spread in order to convince people of the need to join or form a social movement. He sees such generalized beliefs as often quite primitive and based on wish fulfilment rather than being thought through rationally.

4 *Precipitating factors* These are essentially events that act as sparks to ignite the flame of protest action. A good example of this would be in the USA in 1955, when Rosa Parks was removed from a racially segregated bus, an action which triggered protests and became a key event in the black civil rights movement. Precipitating factors help to make social strains more immediately visible for potential supporters. Without them, the process of movement formation may be stalled for a long period.

5 *Mobilization for action* Having witnessed a precipitating event, the next element is effective communication via the formation of an active social network which allows activists to perform some of the functions necessary for successful protest and organization-building – writing and distributing pamphlets, organizing demonstrations, taking membership fees, and so on. All of this activity requires a higher level of communication and social networking.

The response of governments and authorities to movement protests can be instrumental in encouraging or discouraging further activism.

6   *Failure of social control* The final factor in Smelser's model is the response of the forces of social control. The response of authorities can be crucial in closing down an emergent social movement or creating opportunities for it to develop. Sometimes an over-reaction by authorities can encourage others to support the movement, especially in our media-dominated age. For example, the widespread media reports of heavy-handed treatment of Greenpeace activists aboard the *Greenpeace III* in 1972 served to create the impression of a David and Goliath confrontation, which attracted many onto the side of the underdog. However, severe repressive measures can sometimes bring emergent social networking to a halt if people perceive the risks of continuing to be too great.

Critical points

Smelser's theory was subjected to critical attacks. In focusing attention on generalized beliefs, his model implied that individuals are motivated to start social movements for irrational reasons, rooted in misleading ideas about their situation. This fell back into an older tradition that saw movements as unusual or marginal phenomena. Social movement studies since Smelser have moved towards seeing activists as rational actors who weigh the costs and benefits of their actions (see Olson 1965) and social movements as part and parcel of social life rather than marginal to it. Smelser's theory was also structural functionalist in orientation, setting social movements in the context of their adaptive function during periods of rapid social change. Movements reassure people that something is being done to deal with their concerns. But the theory suffered indirectly from attacks on Parsonian functionalism and, probably unfairly, was not built on until quite recently.

Contemporary significance

Smelser's work on social movements has deservedly received more attention in recent years and is undergoing something of a resurgence. It still offers a multi-causal model of movement formation, and even critics have extracted elements from it – such as ideas within resource mobilization theory, political opportunity structures and frame analysis – which have proved very productive (Crossley 2002). Similarly, his model connects movement activism to social structures and may provide insights into the rise of new social movements. Revisiting these stimulating ideas is long overdue.

If we want to call a meeting, we need to have somewhere to hold it. If we want to publicize a protest action such as a demonstration, we need to be able to make leaflets, posters or fliers and to reproduce large numbers of them, and to distribute them widely. If we want to book our meeting space or contact our printer, we are probably going to need a telephone – and some money to pay for it all. As well as these material resources, we are more likely to be successful if we can call on other, less tangible resources – an address book full of useful contacts, practical know-how in poster design or web-site construction, and even just the time and energy to devote to our activism. According to resource mobilization theory, the more of these resources we can mobilize, the more likely we are to be successful in our pursuit of social change.

In RMT, political dissatisfaction is not enough, in itself, to bring about social change. Without resources, dissatisfaction does not become an active force. RMT does have something of an economistic feel, drawing similarities between social movements and the competitive market economy. That is, the theory pictures social movements as operating within a competitive field of movements – a 'social movement industry' – within which they compete for scarce resources, not least members and activists. Social movement organizations (SMOs) therefore find them-selves in competition with other SMOs, some of which may appear to share their aims.

Although RMT helped to fill the gap left by social unrest theories, producing detailed studies of how movements and movement organizations acquire resources and mobilize campaigns, critics still see these as partial accounts. In particular, RMT underplays the effects of broad social changes, such as the trend towards post-industrialism or globali-zation processes, on social movements. For example, the increasingly global political context has meant that traditional UK conser-vation organizations such as the National Trust have been challenged by newer environ-mental organizations such as Greenpeace, whose ideology and international campaigns seem to fit the changing context more closely.

RMT also has little explanation for social movements that achieve success with very limited resources. Piven and Cloward (1977) analysed 'poor people's movements' in the USA, such as unemployed workers in the 1930s, black civil rights in the 1950s and welfare movements of the late 1960s and the 1970s. Surprisingly, they found that their main successes were achieved during the formative stage, before they became properly organ-ized. This was because activists in the early stages were very enthusiastic and took part in many direct actions such as strikes and sit-ins. However, once they became more effectively organized, direct actions became fewer, the 'dead hand of bureaucracy' (described by Max Weber and Robert Michels) took over, and movements lost momentum and impact. This is quite the reverse of what we would expect according to RMT and shows that, sometimes, a lack of resources can be turned to a move-ment's advantage.

THINKING CRITICALLY

Choose a social movement from the ones discussed so far and research its history, development and successes. Analyse this material using RMT, showing *how* the movement became organized and *why* it succeeded or failed. What aspects does RMT *not* address?

New social movements

Since the late 1960s there has been an explosion of social movements around the globe. Among these are student movements of the 1960s, civil rights and feminist movements of the 1960s and 1970s, anti-nuclear and ecological movements of the 1980s, gay rights campaigns of the 1990s – and many more. Collectively, this group of movements is often referred to by European scholars as new social movements (NSMs). This is because they are seen as ushering in a new *type* of social movement (Touraine 1971, 1981). NSM theories try to address the question of why this happened when it did, and, in some ways, this approach complements that of RMT on how movements garner resources and make use of them. However, 'new' in this context means more than just 'contemporary'. There are four main ways in which NSMs are said to differ from 'old' movements, which we will now outline.

New issues

NSMs have introduced new issues into political systems, many of which are relatively unrelated to simple material self-interests. Instead, these issues are concerned with the 'quality of life', including the state of the global environment, animal welfare and animal rights, peaceful (non-nuclear) energy production, and the 'identity politics' associated with gay rights and disabled people's movements.

For NSM theorists, these movements reflect a very broad social transformation from an industrial to a post-industrial society. While industrial politics centred on wealth creation and its distribution, post-industrial politics centres on post-material issues. Ronald Inglehart (1977, 1990) conducted surveys of social values in more than twenty-five industrialized countries and found that younger generations exhibited post-material values. That is, they took for granted a certain material standard of well-being and were more likely to be concerned with the quality rather than the quantity of life.

This 'glacial', generational shift in values, Inglehart argued, could be explained by several factors. Those born after 1945 did not experience the depression and hardship of their parents' generation, nor did they have personal experience of war. Rather, they became used to postwar peace and affluence, being raised in the context of a 'post-scarcity socialization', in which the historic obstacle of food scarcity at least appeared to have been solved for good. This generation also had a different experience of work as a growing service sector took over from the old industrial workplaces. These enormous social changes led to the demise of an 'old' politics, which was rapidly giving way to a 'new', post-industrial form of politics.

New organizational forms

NSMs also appeared to be different in the way they organized. Many of them adopted a loose form that rejected the formal organization that earlier social movement theorists argued was necessary for success. NSMs looked much more like loose networks of people. In addition, they seemed to have no single centre or headquarters, preferring a polycephalous, or 'many-headed', structure. This meant that, should one local group break the law and face prosecution, the rest of the network could carry on, but this structure also suited the emotional needs of activists, who tended to be younger and imbued with post-material values and identities.

Alberto Melucci (1989) saw that this organizational form itself carried a message, namely the symbolic rejection of the aggressively masculine, bureaucratic power politics of the industrial age, typified by trade unions and party politics. The first president of the Czech Republic, Vaclav Havel (1988), described this as anti-hierarchical and 'anti-political politics'. What marked out this new form was a self-imposed limitation. NSMs did not seek to take over the state and use its power to change society; instead, they appealed directly to the public. This strategy has been described as a 'self-limiting radicalism' that contrasts sharply with the state-centred politics of socialism and the labour movement (Papadakis 1988).

New action repertoires

Like other social movements, NSMs make use of a range of protest actions, from political lobbying to sit-ins and alternative festivals, but one thing that characterizes their 'action repertoire' is non-violent, symbolic direct actions. Many actions aim to present to the public aspects of society that were previously unseen and unknown. For example, campaigns against toxic waste dumping in the UK, the culling of seal pups in Newfoundland, the destruction of woodlands for road-building, or the existence of disabling environments all showed people things they may not have been aware of. NSMs use new digital media to generate support – filming protests, showing videos on the Internet, organizing campaigns via social media and text messaging, and encouraging ordinary people to become involved in politics. Such efforts illustrate well the point made by Melucci (1985) that NSMs are forms of communication – 'messages' to society which present symbolic challenges to the existing political system.

New social constituencies

Finally, many studies of NSM activists have shown a predominance of the 'new' middle class which works in post-1945 welfare state bureaucracies, creative and artistic fields, and education (including many students). This finding led some to describe NSM activism as a form of 'middle-class radicalism' (Cotgrove and Duff 1980). Many of the large demonstrations – against nuclear weapons, in favour of animal welfare, and so on – attract a 'rainbow coalition' of retired people, students, first-time

protesters, feminists, anarchists, socialists, traditional conservatives, and many more. However, it seems that the working classes are not involved in significant numbers. Again, this marks a significant change from the industrial period with its working-class-based movements (Eckersley 1989).

Many observers argue that NSMs are a unique product of post-industrial society and are profoundly different to the collective action of earlier times. We can view new social movements in terms of a 'paradox of democracy'. While trust in traditional politics seems to be waning, the growth of NSMs is evidence that people are not apathetic or uninterested in politics, as is sometimes claimed. Rather, there is a belief that direct action and participation is more useful than reliance on politicians. More than ever before, people are supporting social movements as a way of highlighting complex moral issues and putting them at the centre of social life. In this respect, NSMs may be revitalizing democracy and are at the heart of a strong civic culture or civil society (Habermas 1981).

NSM theory has come in for some sharp criticism. All the supposedly 'new' features identified above have been found in 'old' social movements. For example, post-material values were evident in some small-scale communes in the nineteenth century (D'Anieri et al. 1990). And a focus on identity creation was also a crucial, perhaps defining, aspect of all nationalist movements and early women's movements. Such historical evidence led Calhoun (1993) caustically to describe these old movements as 'new social movements of the early nineteenth century'.

Others see NSM theorists as too quick to draw radical conclusions from weak empirical evidence. Over time, some NSMs have developed formal organizations and become more bureaucratic than the theory allows for. Greenpeace is the most notable example. Originally a loose network of like-minded individuals involved in numerous direct actions, Greenpeace has become a very large business-like organization with a mass membership and huge financial resources. Indeed, it seems to

21.2   The birth of gay liberation

The following article, celebrating thirty years of gay liberation, appeared in 2000.

The formation of the Gay Liberation Front (GLF) in London in 1970 was the defining watershed moment in queer history. For the first time ever, thousands of lesbians and gays stopped hiding in the closet and suffering in silence. We came out and marched in the streets, proclaiming that we were proud to be gay and demanding nothing less than total equality. That had never happened before. Lots of gay people in 1970 were ashamed of their homosexuality and kept it hidden. They wished they were straight. Some went to quack doctors to get 'cured'. Many accepted the bigot's view that being 'queer' was second rate.

Thirty years ago, the state branded gay sex as 'unnatural, indecent and criminal', the Church condemned homosexuality as 'immoral and sinful' and the medical profession classified us as 'sick' and in need of 'treatment'. Queers were routinely sacked from their jobs, arrested for kissing in the street, denied custody of their children, portrayed in films and plays as limp-wristed figures of ridicule, and only ever appeared in the news as murderers, traitors and child molesters. Straights vilified, scapegoated and invisibilised us – with impunity. And very few gay people dared question heterosexual supremacy.

Indeed, prior to GLF, most gay rights campaigners masqueraded as straight, and pleaded for 'tolerance' rather than acceptance. Some argued that we needed 'help', not criminalisation. They urged heterosexuals to show 'compassion' for those 'afflicted' by the 'homosexual condition'. This apologetic, defensive mentality was shot to pieces by GLF. It transformed attitudes towards homosexuality – among both gay and straight people.

Inspired by the Black Power slogan 'Black is Beautiful', GLF came up with a little slogan of its own, which also had a huge impact: 'Gay Is Good!'. Back then, it was absolutely outrageous to suggest there was anything good about being gay.

Even liberal-minded heterosexuals mostly supported us out of 'sympathy' and 'pity'. Many reacted with revulsion and horror when GLF proclaimed: '2–4–6–8! Gay is just as good as straight!' Those words – which were so empowering to queers everywhere – frightened the life out of smug, arrogant straight people, who had always assumed they were superior.

This challenge to heterosexual supremacism kick-started a still ongoing revolution in cultural values. GLF overturned the conventional wisdom on matters of sex and human rights. Its joyous celebration of gayness contradicted the straight morality that had ruled the world for centuries. The common-sense, unquestioned assumption had always been that queers were bad, mad and sad. All that prejudiced nonsense was turned upside down in 1970. While politicians, doctors, priests and journalists saw homosexuality as a social problem, GLF said the real problem was society's homophobia. Instead of us having to justify our existence, we forced the gay-haters to justify their bigotry.

Like many others of my generation, GLF changed me for the better – and forever. When I heard about the formation of the Gay Liberation Front, I could not wait to get involved. Within five days of my arrival in London from Australia, I was at my first GLF meeting. A month later I was helping organise many of its witty, irreverent, defiant protests. Being part of GLF was a profound personal liberation – arguably the most exciting, influential period of my life.

GLF's unique style of 'protest as performance' was not only incredibly effective, but also a lot of fun. We had a fabulous collection of zany props and costumes, including a whole wardrobe of police uniforms and bishop's cassocks and mitres. Imaginative, daring, humorous, stylish and provocative, our demonstrations were both educative and entertaining. We mocked and ridiculed homophobes with wicked satire, which made even the most hard-faced straight people realise the stupidity of bigotry.

A Gay Liberation Front (GLF) demonstration

A 12 foot papier-mache cucumber was delivered to the offices of Pan Books in protest at the publication of Dr David Reuben's homophobic sex manual, *Everything You Always Wanted To Know About Sex*, which implied that gay men were obsessed with shoving vegetables up their arses. Christian morality campaigner Mary Whitehouse had her Festival of Light rally in Central Hall Westminster invaded by a posse of gay nuns, who proceeded to kiss each other when one of the speakers, Malcolm Muggeridge, disparaged homosexuals, saying 'I just don't like them' (the feeling was mutual). On the night of the Miss World contest at the Royal Albert Hall, GLF's legendary street theatre group staged an alternative pageant on the pavement outside, starring 'Miss Used', 'Miss Conceived' and 'Miss Represented', plus a starving 'Miss Bangladesh' and a bloody bandaged 'Miss Ulster'.

There were also more serious acts of civil disobedience to confront the perpetrators of discrimination. We organised freedom rides and sit-ins at pubs that refused to serve 'poofs' and 'dykes'. A lecture by the psychiatrist Professor Hans Eysenck was disrupted after he advocated electric-shock aversion therapy to 'cure' homosexuality.

As well as its feisty protests, GLF pioneered many of the gay community institutions that we now take for granted. It set up the first help-line run by and for gay people (which later became Gay Switchboard), the first pro-gay psychiatric counselling service (Icebreakers), and the first gay newspaper (*Gay News*). These and many other trail-blazing institutions helped shape the gay community as we know it today, making a huge positive difference to the lives of lesbians and gay men.

Thirty years on, we've come a long way baby! As we look back at the giant strides for freedom that lesbian and gay people have made since 1970, let us also remember with pride that GLF was where it all started.

Source: Tatchell (2000).

THINKING CRITICALLY

What evidence is there in Tatchell's account to suggest that the GLF was part of a new social movement? Thinking back to Blumer's distinction between 'active' and expressive movements, how would you characterize the gay and lesbian movement?

conform much more to the long-term process of change identified by Blumer and RMT. Finally, even some apparently 'new' issues have been seen as much older. Environmental politics, for instance, can be traced back to the European and North American nature defence organizations of the mid-nineteenth century and is perhaps best understood as an enduring social movement which has passed through various stages of growth and decay (Sutton 2000; Paehlke 1989).

Globalization and the 'social movement society'

Despite the critical barrage aimed at NSM theory, it is apparent that social movements now operate in a very different set of historical circumstances to previous movements. In particular, processes of globalization mean that systematic and much more immediate connections across national boundaries become possible and, with this, the feasibility of genuinely transnational or global social movements.

The rise of NSMs also reflects some of the changing risks now facing human societies. The conditions are ripe for social movements as increasingly traditional political institutions find it harder to cope with the challenges before them, such as climate change. These new problems and challenges are ones that existing democratic political institutions seem unable to fix, and as a result they are frequently ignored until a full-blown crisis is at hand.

The cumulative effect of these new challenges and risks may be a growing sense that people are 'losing control' of their lives in the midst of rapid change. Individuals feel less secure and more isolated – a combination that leads to a sense of powerlessness. By contrast, corporations, governments and the media appear to be dominating more and more aspects of people's lives, heightening the sensation of a runaway world (Giddens 2002). There is a growing sense that, left to its own logic, globalization will present ever greater risks to citizens' lives.

In the midst of the digital revolution, social movements are able to join together in huge regional and international networks comprising non-governmental organizations, religious and humanitarian groups, human rights associations, consumer protection advocates, environmental activists, and others who campaign in the public interest. These electronic networks have the unprecedented ability to respond immediately to events as they occur, to access and share sources of information, and to put pressure on corporations, governments and international bodies as part of their campaigning strategies.

The enormous protests against the invasion of Iraq in cities around the world in February 2003, for example, were organized in large part through Internet-based networks, as were the protests against the World Trade Organization in Seattle in 1999 and outside the meeting of world leaders in Genoa in 2001. Similarly, the emergence of the World Social Forum in Porto Allegre, Brazil, in 2001 (see Global Society 21.2) was one element of an 'even newer social movement' (Crossley 2003) that aims to provide a global space for debates on

Global Society 21.2 The three faces of the World Social Forum

Anthony Barnett's openDemocracy article here dates from 2007.

The World Social Forum (WSF) is about three things, a young Frenchman told me. We were coming back from Kenya together. He had been to most of them since they first began in Porto Alegre in Brazil in January 2001. They are, he said, about protesting, networking and proposing.

Protesting power

When they began, before 9/11, the protest was against the World Economic Forum (WEF) at Davos, which appeared to celebrate the end of government and the triumph of market-driven, 'neo-liberal' capitalism and its rampant inequality. It was in the wake of the battle of Seattle in November 1999 that disrupted the world trade talks. The creation of the WSF as anti-Davos ensured that the new century began with a multinational stand in the name of the peoples of the world against the presumptions of the world economic order.

Since 2001, until this year [2007], the WSFs have grown and, undoubtedly, shifted the agenda, making sure that the big battalions have not had it all their own way. It has been a remarkable achievement. In 2004 the WSF was held in Mumbai with an enormous mobilisation of Indian organisations. In 2005 it returned to Porto Alegre. In 2006 it went regional or 'polycentric': to Caracas in Venezuela, Karachi in Pakistan and Bamako in Mali. One reason for this was that the decision had been taken to hold the next full world forum in Kenya, giving the organisers plenty of time to prepare against the backdrop of poor infrastructure. . . . unlike the mere protest mobilisations such as Seattle in 1999 (or the one being planned for the G8 meeting in June 2007 in Germany's remote Baltic resort of Heiligendamm), WSFs are designed as a form of positive protest, exemplary sites of solidarity with the struggles of the poor, to give voice to the 'have-nots'.

[. . .]

Networking Africa

In its second role, as an event for networking, I was impressed. In his account of his disappointment with what he felt was a lack of politics, Firoze Manji in *Pambazuka News* considers whether Nairobi's WSF was 'just another NGO fair'. But where else can the far-flung universe of all those who are working for a better world come together? In advance, the organisers boasted that 150,000 would attend. When it opened they claimed 50,000. I doubt if more than 20,000 participated, including Kenyans (but not including the water-vendors).

But still, to get 20,000 people from around the world to equatorial Africa is an achievement. A wonderful, friendly variety of views, arguments, dress, interests, beliefs and backgrounds came together in many conversations – such as Susan Richards and Solana Larsen described in their openDemocracy reports and blogs from previous WSFs.

[. . .]

Thinking beyond

This brings us to the third role of the WSF. After the protests and the networking, what does it propose? Thomas Ponniah (who gave an interview to openDemocracy on the nature of the WSF in February 2003) put this question to a small session on the future of politics: 'For seven years we have built a global consciousness. The question is, what next?'

[. . .]

But an answer to Ponniah's question came there none. In the different specialist areas there was strategic thinking. In smaller sessions there were arguments for engagement. Emira Woods of the Institute for Policy Studies in Washington, DC, insisted that 'grassroots campaigns, national campaigns and global campaigns can influence government'. In a dedicated session on implementing United Nations resolution 1325 to enhance the role of women (which I blogged), Cora Weiss called for 'participation, critical thinking and a holistic approach that engages with the issues'. There was participation in Nairobi. The holistic approach was often just knee-jerk 'oppose all forms of exploitation'. At that overall, movement level, there was little if any strategic thinking.

[. . .]

Larry Elliott, the economics editor of *The Guardian*, sensed at Davos 'more than a hint of a return to the future: a scramble for Africa, a sidelining of civil society, and geopolitical concerns trumping human rights'. If so, there needs to be a World Social Forum that continues to set out its different claim on the global future in a way the world notices. Its international

committee should be very concerned that this is slipping away.

Source: Barnett (2007).

> ### THINKING CRITICALLY
>
> The World Social Forums (WSFs) are said to have been more successful in protesting and networking than proposing solutions. Why? What evidence is there that the WSF may be an early harbinger of a global form of democracy beyond national states?

what progressive politics now means. More recently, a now famous Facebook video blog by Egyptian activist Asmaa Mahfouz – posted one week before thousands of Egyptians occupied Tahrir Square in January 2011 – has been credited with encouraging many young people to become involved in the uprising.

While rejecting some of the claims to novelty of NSM theory, Tarrow (1998: 207–8) argues that 'What *is* new is that they have greater discretionary resources, enjoy easier access to the media, have cheaper and faster geographic mobility and cultural interaction, and can call upon the collaboration of different types of movement-linked organizations for rapidly organized issue campaigns.' Acknowledging these changes raises the prospect of a 'social movement society', in which the nationally bounded social movements of the past give way to movements without borders (Meyer and Tarrow 1997).

The World Social Forums, with their democratic principles (see 'Global society 21.2'), give us one example of this possibility, though it is important to recognize that the global networks of al-Qaeda – a social movement terrorist organization – provides another (Sutton and Vertigans 2006). There is no certainty that an emerging movement society will see the widespread adoption of the non-violence that characterized the wave of NSMs in the 1960s and 1970s in the industrialized

world. Indeed, ready access to weapons and the information needed to build them holds out the more terrifying prospect of a violent social movement society.

> See chapter 22, 'Nations, War and Terrorism', for a wider discussion of violence in human affairs.

Social movements have been radically transformed in recent years. Castells (1997) examined the cases of three social movements which, while completely dissimilar in their concerns and objectives, all attracted international attention to their cause through the effective use of information technology. The Mexican Zapatista rebels, the American 'militia' movement and the Japanese Aum Shinrikyo sect all used media skills to spread their message of opposition to the effects of globalization and to express anger at losing control over their own destinies.

Without the Internet, Zapatista rebels would have remained an isolated guerrilla movement in southern Mexico. Instead, within hours of their armed uprising in January 1994, local, national and international support groups had emerged online to promote their cause and to condemn the Mexican government's brutal repression of the rebellion. The Zapatistas used telecommunications, videos and media interviews to voice their objections to trade policies, such as the North American Free Trade Agreement (NAFTA), which further exclude impoverished Indians of the Oaxaca and Chiapas areas from the benefits of globalization. As a result, they were able to force negotiations with the Mexican government and to draw international attention to the harmful effects of free trade on indigenous populations (Castells 1997).

Conclusion

The sphere of politics has clearly undergone some major changes over recent decades. Democracy has become more widespread around the world, but, in many of the established representative democracies, many voters are less than enthusiastic participants. On the other hand, social movements are thriving, bringing new issues and campaigning methods into the mainstream. The conventional left–right political division now looks much less clear-cut. Is opposing road-building on environmental grounds a right-wing or a left-wing position? Are those who propose that animals have rights on the political left or right? These issues seem to cut across the old political divide and, particularly in the case of environmentalism, are becoming more relevant to younger generations than the older materialist politics rooted in the workplace.

The financial crisis which began in 2008 has also brought home just how tightly integrated the global economy has become. But it also showed that political coordination and global governance lag far behind reality. Even within regional groupings such as the European Union, national interests tend to take precedence in difficult times, precisely when coordinated action is required for the collective good. For example, eurozone countries were deeply divided about how best to assist heavily indebted Greece and who should pay for bailouts. The tortuous process of devising a European-wide plan, agreeing a course of action and moving towards implementation created even more uncertainty in global financial markets. The world, it seems, remains a very long way from establishing effective forms of global governance.

However, the global crisis and its aftermath may have an unintended consequence. It has demonstrated conclusively that the concept of a 'national interest' needs to be reformulated in a globalizing world. International cooperation is no longer optional or opposed to a country's national interest. Similarly, the increasing evidence of anthropogenic climate change demands global agreement if national self-interest is to be best served. Today, pursuing 'the national interest' increasingly demands that governments work together to create forms of global governance that are able to regulate their collective affairs more effectively.

Chapter review

1 What distinguishes political sociology as a specialist field of inquiry?
2 What binds citizens to nation-states? Why has the nation-state become the most common arena for government?
3 'Power is the capacity to achieve one's aims even against the resistance of others.' Whose view of power is this? Outline the additional two dimensions of power discussed by Stephen Lukes.

4 In authoritarian states, how would you characterize the relationship between the state and the people?

949

5   How do 'the people' actually 'rule' themselves under systems of representative democracy?

6   What are the main problems faced by the established democratic systems? Are these problems likely to be solved or do you see them worsening in the future?

7   Provide an outline of the problems that bureaucratic systems may present for democratic politics.

8   What is elite theory and how relevant is it for explaining contemporary societies?

9   How have class-oriented party political systems changed over the last forty years or so? Using examples from a country of your choice, what evidence is there that the link between class and party has been eroded?

10 What is meant by 'global governance' and how realistic is it? What obstacles stand in its way?

11 What are social movements? Give some old and more recent examples of how they pursue social and political change.

12 Describe movement theories of social unrest, social strain and resource mobilization. Explore one social movement using the 'toolkit' of concepts from these perspectives.

13 List the ways in which 'new social movements' differ from 'old' ones. What is meant by a 'social movement society' and how is globalization helping to bring this about?

Research in practice

In historical terms the European Union is a very recent political experiment. Now a federation of twenty-eight nation-states, the EU, in spite of its various problems, may be seen as a success story. Yet there have always been 'Eurosceptics' who object to the EU's pooling of national sovereignty, overarching legal system, open borders and ambition to become a European 'super-state'. Nowhere has this scepticism been stronger than in the UK, which has seen electoral success for the UK Independence Party (UKIP) and where a majority voted to leave the EU in 2016. Has Euroscepticism now 'come of age'?

Read Nicholas Startin's (2015) 'Have We Reached a Tipping Point?', *International Political Science Review*, 36(3): 311–23, which explores the movement over time of the UK's Eurosceptics from outsiders into the mainstream of British politics. Then address the questions below.

1   How does the author define 'Euroscepticism'?

2   How did Britain gain its reputation as the 'awkward partner' within the EU?

3   How does the paper explain the fact that EU integration was opposed primarily by the political left in the 1970s and the right in the 1980s? What is the position today?

4   What factors explain the mainstreaming of Euroscepticism in the UK?

5   The author sees certain national newspapers as playing a key role in promoting Euroscepticism. Why might this view be mistaken?

Thinking it through

The fundamental left–right political cleavage has been seen as less helpful today at a time when it is less clear where the key political issues lie on the spectrum. If I believe in anthropogenic climate change, am I on the left or the right? Where am I if I want to remain in the EU? How about if I support globalization? Which issues are touchstones for left- and right-wing attitudes today, and does it even make sense to continue to view political ideas and ideologies through the old lens of left and right?

The Political Compass has been available online since 2001, allowing individuals to take a 'test' of their political attitudes. Take the test here: www.politicalcompass.org/. The compass positions people on the left–right political scale and an authoritarian–libertarian one. Where did it place you? Do you agree with the result? To what extent do these axes encompass your political attitudes? What do tests such as these miss in terms of contemporary political views and values? How could the test be modified to make it more comprehensive?

Society in the arts

1 An old anarchist slogan says 'Don't vote, it only encourages them.' As we have seen in this chapter, there is some evidence that the gap between democratic political elites and the citizens they represent is growing. But what would happen if the mass of people really did not turn out to vote? How might those in power react?

This scenario is the premise of the Portuguese novelist Jose Saramago (2007) in *Seeing* (London: Vintage Books), in which a large majority hand in blank voting forms. The election is re-run, but the same thing happens, with an even larger number refusing to vote. Read the novel and consider whether the response of your government might be similar to that in the novel. What reforms can you suggest which might prevent such an occurrence in the future?

2 Watch the film *Too Big to Fail* (2011), directed by Curtis Hanson. This is a drama about the emerging financial crisis of 2008 and the way that the US government tried to prevent a banking collapse. 'Too big to fail' is a comment many commentators made about certain large banks which governments believed they had to intervene to save, as allowing them to fail would cause serious harm to the global economy.

Consider the relationship portrayed between government, politicians and big business. Whom does the film see as being 'in charge'? What power does the US government have over large corporations? Is there any evidence that, as Marx (1848) once said, 'The executive of the modern state is but an organising committee for managing the common affairs of the whole bourgeoisie'?

Further reading

A good introductory text which should give a feel for political sociology is Kate Nash's (2010) *Contemporary Political Sociology: Globalization, Politics and Power* (Oxford: Wiley-Blackwell). Michael Drake's (2010) *Political Sociology for a Globalizing World* (Cambridge: Polity) is particularly useful for theories.

For comprehensive coverage of political ideologies, Andrew Heywood's (2012) *Political Ideologies: An Introduction* (5th edn, Basingstoke: Palgrave Macmillan) is a tried and trusted work. And, for democratization, David Held's (2006) *Models of Democracy* (3rd edn, Cambridge: Polity) looks at the history of the concept and its real-world manifestations.

Greg Martin's (2015) *Understanding Social Movements* (London: Routledge) is a lively read with many contemporary examples of social movements which illustrate the various theories. Jeff Goodwin and James M. Jasper's (2014) *The Social Movements Reader: Cases and Concepts* (3rd edn, Oxford: Blackwell) is an edited collection, engagingly organized according to the process of a movement life cycle.

 Finally, another edited collection, by Thomas Janoski, Robert Alford, Alexander Hicks and Mildred Schwartz (2005), *The Handbook of Political Sociology: States, Civil Societies, and Globalization* (Cambridge: Cambridge University Press), is a useful resource with a broad coverage.

 For a collection of original readings on political sociology, see the accompanying *Sociology: Introductory Readings* (3rd edn, Cambridge: Polity, 2010).

Internet links

@ **Additional information and support for this book at Polity:**
www.politybooks.com/giddens

@ **ASA Section on Political Sociology – the American Sociological Association's own resources:**
http://asapoliticalsoc.org

@ **Foreign Policy – US site based in Washington, DC, with lots of political articles and comment:**
http://foreignpolicy.com

@ **openDemocracy – London, UK-based site which publishes blogs and debates how people are governed:**
www.opendemocracy.net

@ **The International Institute for Democracy and Electoral Assistance – based in Stockholm, Sweden, provides information and analysis in support of democratization:**
www.idea.int

@ ***World Politics Review* – 'a daily foreign policy, national security and international affairs Web publication':**
www.worldpoliticsreview.com

@ **Social Movement Study Network – US site with lots of resources and links:**
www.socialmovementstudy.net

CHAPTER 22

Nations, War and Terrorism

Contents

In 2015, following US airstrikes, Kurdish *peshmerga* forces drove Islamic State militants out of Sinjar in Iraq. In 2014 IS had declared a new caliphate in the region.

In June 2014 the creation of a new caliphate – a state governed by Sharia or Islamic law – was declared by the violent militant Islamist group Islamic State (IS), also known as Daesh, with its leader, Abu Bakr al-Baghdadi (an alias, not his real name) as caliph. The new state was territorially located, initially at least, in parts of Iraq and Syria (see figure 22.1), with the intention of expanding the caliphate across the Middle East and beyond to create a global Islamic community or *umma*. Despite the many terrorist actions carried out by IS activists and support for them around the world, establishing a 'lasting and expanding' Islamic state along fundamentalist lines was the main goal (Lister 2015).

The group was originally formed in Iraq following the overthrow of Saddam Hussein's regime in 2003, and in 2004 it was allied to Osama bin Laden's al-Qaeda network. At that time it was known as al-Qaeda in Iraq (AQI) and was led by Abu Musab Al-Zarqawi. When Zarqawi was killed in 2006, a new organization was formed called the Islamic State in Iraq (ISI), but its strength was eroded by opposition from Sunni Muslim tribes who objected to its violent methods. Only when Baghdadi took over as leader in 2010 did ISI begin to rebuild its forces. Baghdadi created the al-Nusra Front in neighbouring Syria and in 2013 merged operations across the two countries. Despite opposition from al-Qaeda and al-Nusra Front leaders, he renamed the group the Islamic State in Iraq and the Levant (ISIL).

By mid-2014, ISIL's ruthless attacks led to its taking territory in Iraq, including the cities of Falluja and Mosul, at which point the group was renamed again, becoming Islamic State (IS) (many Muslims see the group as neither 'Islamic' nor a 'state' and prefer to use the derogatory name Daesh). A new caliphate was declared, and Baghdadi demanded that all other militant groups and Muslims swear allegiance to him as caliph (Burke 2015). IS has used extreme violence in its military campaigns, ruthlessly killing members of the police and armed forces, religious minorities (such as the Yazidis in Iraq), gay men and so-called apostates, forcing girls and women into sex slavery, beheading Western hostages on camera, and destroying ancient buildings and sites (Byman 2015: 175–7). It makes extensive use of social media and digital technologies to recruit activists from all around the world to fight in Syria. One analyst has argued that 'Without digital technology it is highly unlikely that Islamic State would ever have come into existence, let alone been able to survive and expand. This is why I choose to describe the new entity as a "digital caliphate"' (Atwan 2015: 1). IS is also well resourced after taking over banks and oil production facilities, collecting taxes and capturing military hardware.

As a Sunni *jihadist* group, IS shares an ideological similarity with al-Qaeda, but there is a clear difference. Al-Qaeda expressly concentrated on terrorizing the 'far enemy' – the USA and Europe – while IS focused on the 'near enemy' – non-Muslims and states in the Middle East – in order to 'purify' Islam in the region from foreign influence. Since 2015, IS strategy has shifted with the group, also organizing and coordinating attacks against European targets. The group's fundamentalist approach is rooted in a Salafist interpretation of Islam, which insists that Muslims should return to the very earliest tenets and norms of Islam and countries should adopt Sharia law (*salaf* means 'predecessors' or 'ancestors'). IS has also been influenced by Saudi Wahhabism – a particular form of Islam stemming from the ideas of Muhammad ibn Abd-al-Wahhab in the eighteenth century which rejects religious pluralism and encourages coercion to enforce Sharia law. For example, in IS-controlled areas of Syria, Christians are told they must convert to Islam, pay a special tax or be killed.

By the end of 2015, the IS advance in Iraq had been halted and even reversed in some areas as US airstrikes enabled Kurdish *peshmerga* fighters on the ground to regain some territory. In Syria, a coalition of US-led forces including France, the UK, Qatar and Australia targeted IS, degrading their resources and preventing further rapid expansion. Russia also hit IS targets after the group claimed it had brought down a Russian civilian plane, though Russia's main aim was to support President Assad's government against other rebel forces in the Syrian civil war rather than removing IS. In 2015 there remained between 20,000 and 32,000 IS fighters in Iraq and Syria, up to 5,000 of whom are estimated to be from Western countries (BBC News 2015c). IS successes also inspired many attacks around the world, among them those in Tunisia, Turkey, Egypt, Paris, Yemen, Lebanon and California, which killed around 1,000 people in 2015 alone.

Despite criticisms from mainstream Islamic scholars, commentators and politicians, IS

US-led coalition strikes: **IRAQ: 10,043, SYRIA: 5,493**

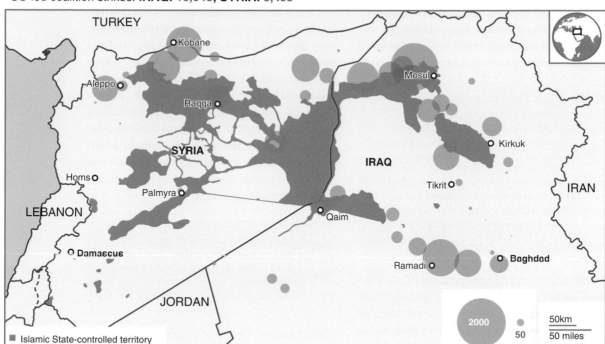

Islamic State-controlled territory

Source: IHS Conflict Monitor, 31 Oct 2016

BBC

Figure 22.1 Areas under Islamic State control in Iraq and Syria and the main location of airstrikes against IS targets

Source: BBC News (2016).

is attempting to create a new caliphate or 'Islamic state', albeit through extreme violence, human rights abuses and terrorism. It may adopt terrorist methods in the manner of al-Qaeda, but its attempt at state-building as a first stage in creating a global caliphate marks it out as different from most of the many *jihadist* groups that have emerged in the last twenty-four years or so. The group collects taxes, has its own military forces and implements a Sharia legal system in territories it takes and controls. In Alberto Melucci's (1989) terms, by implementing its own fundamentalist version of Islam and 'behaving like a state', IS practises in the present the changes it looks to bring about in the future. For Baghdadi, the 'nation of Islam' needs its own state, which IS aims to carve out in Iraq and Syria before expanding outwards.

As the activities of IS illustrate, the political map of the world is in constant flux. Today's map of nation-states looks very different from that of 1945 or even that of 1975. However solid, 'natural' or permanent the world's states may feel, in fact they are one of the more fluid aspects of human existence. Nation-states are regularly created or destroyed; civil wars divide established nations leading to their break-up, and regional blocs are formed from previously disparate nation-states. This chapter deals with the themes of nationalism, communal violence, warfare, terrorism and peace processes. These issues have exercised social scientists studying a variety of conflicts, such as that in Sudan – where South Sudan became an independent country in 2011 – and the chronic conflict between Israel and Palestine. Why is the desire for national

957

independence in the form of a nation-state so powerful? How is nationalism related to wars within and between nations? What is war anyway and are there really 'rules' of warfare that govern acceptable conduct?

The subject of revolutions is covered primarily in chapter 21, 'Politics, Government and Social Movements', though there are useful shorter discussions in chapters 1, 'What is Sociology?', 2, 'Asking and Answering Sociological Questions', 3, 'Theories and Perspectives', 4, 'Globalization and Social Change', 12, 'Stratification and Social Class', and 17, 'Religion'.

We begin with a discussion of nations and nationalism, asking how globalization might be changing people's sense of their own national identity. We then move on to look at conflict, especially war and its close relation genocide, focusing particularly on conflicts involving modern nation-states. As war logically implies its opposite, we end this section with a brief look at recent scholarship on peace processes. Next we explore a phenomenon that seems to have become ever present in the modern world – terrorism – before drawing some tentative conclusions about the future prospects for conflict, war and peace.

Nations and nationalism

Some of the most important social movements in history have been nationalist movements, but, perhaps surprisingly, the early sociologists showed little interest in nationalism. Marx and Durkheim saw nationalism as, above all, a destructive tendency. Durkheim believed that the increasing economic integration produced by modern industry would cause its rapid decline, while Marx considered that nationalism would fade away under socialism. Only Weber spent much time analysing nationalism or was prepared to declare himself a nationalist.

In the twenty-first century, nationalism is not only alive but flourishing. Although the human world has become more interdependent, especially over the past thirty or forty years, this interdependence has not meant the end of nationalism. In some respects, it has probably helped to intensify it. Recent scholarly debate has suggested contrasting ideas about why this is so. There are also disagreements about the stage of history at which nationalism, the nation and the nation-state came into being. Some say they have much earlier origins than others.

The resurgence of nationalism in the former Yugoslavia is discussed in chapter 16, 'Race, Ethnicity and Migration'.

Nationalism and modern societies

One of the leading theorists of nationalism, Ernest Gellner (1925–95), argued that nationalism, the nation and the nation-state are all products of modern development, whose origins lie in the French and Industrial revolutions of the late eighteenth century. Nationalism and the feelings or sentiments associated with it do not have deep roots in 'human nature'. Rather, they are products of the new large-scale societies which industrialism creates. According to Gellner (1983), nationalism is unknown in previous forms of society, as was the idea of 'the nation'.

There are several features of modern societies that have led to the emergence of national phenomena. First, a modern industrial society is associated with rapid economic development and a complex division of labour. Gellner points out that modern industrialism creates the need for a much more effective system of state and government than existed before. Second, in the modern state, individuals must interact all the time with strangers, since the basis of society is no longer the local village or town but a very much larger unit. Mass education, based on an 'official language' taught in the schools, is the main

Flags are a potent symbol of national communities and pride. But they are also burned in anger by opponents to symbolically attack a nation. Here, Muslims in Karachi, Pakistan, burn the Danish flag after a Danish newspaper published satirical cartoons of the Prophet Muhammad.

means whereby a large-scale society can be organized and kept unified.

Gellner's theory has been criticized in more than one respect. It is a functionalist theory, which argues that education functions to produce social unity. As with the functionalist approach more generally, this view tends to underestimate the role of education in producing conflicts and divisions. Gellner's theory does not really explain the passions that nationalism can, and often does, arouse. The power of nationalism is probably related not just to education but also to its capacity to create an identity for people – something that individuals cannot live without. In that sense, perceived threats to national interests can also be understood as threats to the integrity of people's self-identity.

The need for *identity* is certainly not born with the emergence of modern, industrialized societies. Gellner is therefore wrong to separate nationalism and the nation so strongly from pre-modern times. Nationalism is in some ways quite modern, but it also draws on sentiments and forms of symbolism that go back much further into the past. According to one of the best-known current scholars of nationalism, Anthony Smith (1986), nations tend to have direct lines of continuity with earlier ethnic communities – or what he calls ethnies. An ethnie is a group that shares ideas of common ancestry, a common cultural identity and a link with a specific homeland.

Many nations, Smith points out, do have pre-modern continuities, and at previous periods of history there have been ethnic communities that resemble nations. The Jews, for example, have formed a distinct ethnie for more than 2,000 years. At certain periods, Jews clustered in communities that had some of the characteristics of nations. In 1948, following the genocide of Jews during the Second World War, the state of Israel was founded, marking the culmination of the Zionist movement, whose aim was to create a homeland for Jews scattered around the world. The Palestinian minority in Israel traces its origins to a quite different ethnic background and claims that the creation of the Israeli state has displaced the Palestinians from their ancient homelands – hence the persistent tensions between them and the Jews in Israel and between Israel and most surrounding Arab states.

Nations have followed divergent patterns of development in relation to ethnies. In some, including most of the nations of Western Europe, a single ethnie expanded so as to push out earlier rivals. Thus in France up to the nineteenth century, several other

Classic Studies 22.1 Norbert Elias on state formation and the civilizing process

The research problem

How have some nations come to see themselves as 'civilized' and others as 'uncivilized'? How can self-styled 'civilized nations' conduct wars involving extreme violence and mass killing yet still maintain their civilized self-image? The German-born sociologist Norbert Elias (1897–1990) studied these issues in his two-volume *The Civilizing Process* (2000), first published in 1939. That year was not the time to be talking about 'civilized behaviour', as war was breaking out in Europe for the second time in just twenty-five years. Consequently, it was only when *The Civilizing Process* was published in English in 1969 that sociologists begin to take account of the book's wide-ranging significance.

Elias's explanation

Elias begins *The Civilizing Process* with an observation: the concept of civilization 'expresses the self-consciousness of the West. One could even say: the national consciousness.' He continues:

> It sums up everything in which Western society of the last two or three centuries believes itself superior to earlier societies or 'more primitive' contemporary ones. By this term, Western society seeks to describe what constitutes its special character and what it is proud of: the level of its technology, the nature of its manners, the development of its scientific knowledge or view of the world, and much more. (Elias 2000 [1939]: 5)

In short, people in modern Western nations have come to understand their societies as setting the standard for civilized conduct and, therefore, as being superior to other types of society.

Comparing and contrasting England, France and Germany, the first volume of *The Civilizing Process* looks at the development of typically modern psychic structures and codes of manners. Elias uses many historical examples from etiquette and manners books to show how standards of behaviour in relation to table manners, bodily functions (such as spitting and toileting), sexual expression and violence slowly changed. In particular, he demonstrates that the direction of change since the medieval period was towards increasing thresholds of repugnance and shame, with many behaviours previously considered 'normal' gradually coming to be seen as unacceptable. People developed stronger internalized self-restraints and exhibited a much more stable control over their emotions.

In the second volume, Elias develops a theory to explain these changes. He finds the key factors to be the process of state formation and the increasingly long and complex webs of interdependent relations in the early modern period. As courtiers vied with each other for prestige and influence in the European royal courts, new codes of conduct imposed on them a tighter and more even control of their emotions and violent outbursts. With this, a more individualized personality type developed among courtiers, making them the first 'modern people' (Korte 2001: 29). The cultivated and refined manners of courtiers set the standard for rising bourgeois classes and eventually spread to other social groups too. This more even, balanced and tightly regulated type of self-control, which became 'second-nature', can appear to others as rather detached and calculating.

The absolutist monarchies of seventeenth- and eighteenth-century Europe exemplified the increasing centralization of societies. Competition for power among rival regions, towns and social groups often led to violent conflict and the elimination of the weakest or less well-organized group. As a result, fewer but larger social units developed via the logic of what Elias calls a 'monopoly mechanism'. This mechanism led to 'a state in which all opportunities are controlled by a single authority: a system with open opportunities has become a system with closed opportunities.' Thus, Elias explains the emergence of the modern nation-state, with its monopolization of the means of physical force and taxation (cited in Van Krieken 1998: 101).

What Elias shows in *The Civilizing Process* is

that the formation of national states, alongside increasingly denser webs of social relations, is intimately tied to the emergence of the typically modern personality type. Only where the state monopolization of physical force is relatively stable and secure can individuals, from infancy onwards, become attuned to a new, higher level of self-control which then becomes 'second nature'.

Critical points

Elias's work has attained the status of a modern classic today, but it has also been criticized on several grounds. First, some have suggested that Elias overplays the differences between the modern individual and people in other societies. The German ethnologist Hans Peter Duerr argues that the notion of the civilizing process is 'a myth'. Human beings today are essentially similar to human beings of the past; there have been no 'uncivilized' or 'primitive' people. Duerr (1988) asserts, for example, that public 'nakedness' has always been a cause of shame and is not the product of 'civilization'.

Second, Elias sees social processes as essentially the unplanned outcome of many intentional actions. But critics point out that this assumption needs to be tested against the evidence in particular cases and seems to ignore 'civilizing offensives', such as those carried out by powerful social elites (Van Krieken 1998). Third, Elias's focus on civilizing processes may be criticized for neglecting or under-theorizing the 'dark side' of such processes. Western

civilization was not a painless process, and, as Foucault has shown, it can feel far from 'civilized' for many social groups. Powell (2011) argues that the 'normal' operation of Western civilization can produce genocides, as the history of twentieth-century conflicts demonstrates. Hence, civilization and barbarism are not opposites; 'civilized conduct' among insider groups may be closely linked to 'barbaric acts' against outsiders.

Contemporary significance

Elias's ideas have been influential in many fields, not least historical sociology, sociology of the body and the study of human emotions. What continues to attract scholars to his work is the way it allows macro and micro levels to be linked through a central focus on dynamic social processes. Given current concerns about levels of violence in society, terrorism and genocide, it is likely that the study of civilizing and *decivilizing* processes will be one important aspect of sociology's attempts to understand why the recourse to physical violence continues to produce so much human suffering.

THINKING CRITICALLY

What evidence is there from recent wars and conflicts that the civilizing process identified by Elias is continuing in the twenty-first century? What could be the consequences of the slow *demise* of the nation-state in the face of globalization?

---

languages were spoken to which different ethnic histories were linked. The French state forced schoolchildren to learn French – they would be punished if they spoke their home language – so that, by the early twentieth century, French became the dominant language and most of the rival languages largely disappeared.

Yet remnants of these have persisted, and many are officially encouraged again. One is the Basque language, from the area that

overlaps the French and Spanish frontiers. The Basque language is quite different from either French or Spanish, and the Basques claim a separate cultural history of their own. Some Basques want their own nation-state, completely separate from France and Spain. While there has not been the same level of violence that other areas have seen – such as in East Timor or Chechnya in southern Russia – around 800 people were killed during the forty-year-long bombing campaigns by

Graffiti on the security wall built between Israel and Palestine. The continuing conflict between Israel and the stateless Palestinian people has led to Israel building the controversial security wall. As the graffiti show, the unresolved problems of nations and states has made peace all but impossible so far.

the Basque separatist group ETA. However, in October 2011, ETA announced a 'definitive cessation' of their armed struggle, saying that they were in the transition to peaceful methods of achieving independence.

Nations without states

The persistence of well-defined ethnies within established nations leads to the phenomenon of nations without states. In these situations, many of the essential characteristics of the nation are present, but those who comprise the nation lack an independent political community. Separatist movements, such as those in Chechnya and the Basque country, as well as those in many other areas of the world – for example, in Kashmir in northern India – are driven by the desire to set up an autonomous, self-governing state.

Several different types of nations without states can be recognized, depending on the relationship between the ethnie and the larger nation-state in which it exists (Guibernau 1999). First, in some situations, a nation-state may accept the cultural differences found among its minority or minorities and allow them a certain amount of active development. Thus, in Britain, both Scotland and Wales are recognized as possessing histories and cultural features that are partly divergent from the rest of the UK and so have some of their own institutions.

Scotland, for instance, has a tradition of Presbyterianism represented in the Church of Scotland and the country has separate educational and legal systems from those of England and Wales. Scotland and Wales achieved further autonomy within the UK as a whole with the setting up of a Scottish Parliament and a Welsh Assembly in 1999. The Scottish National Party (SNP), which is committed to independence, was elected to government in 2007 and won outright in 2011. Although it lost a vote on independence from the UK in 2014, the SNP took all but three of the Scottish seats in the 2015 UK election. Similarly, the Basque country and Catalonia (the area around Barcelona in northern Spain) are both recognized as 'autonomous communities' within Spain. They possess their own parliaments, which have a certain number of rights and powers. In both Britain and Spain, however, much power still remains in the hands of the national governments and parliaments, located in London and Madrid respectively.

A second type of nations without states consists of those that have a higher degree of autonomy. In Quebec (the French-speaking province of Canada) and Flanders (the Dutch-speaking area in the north of Belgium), regional political bodies, without actually being fully independent, have the power to take major decisions. As with those nations mentioned under the first type, they contain nationalist movements agitating for complete independence.

Third, there are some nations which more or less completely lack recognition from the majority population or the state that contains them. In such cases, the larger nation-state uses force in order to deny recognition to the minority. The fate of the Palestinians is one example; others are the Tibetans in China and the Kurds, whose homeland overlaps parts of Turkey, Syria, Iran and Iraq. The Tibetans and Kurds date their cultural history back over many centuries. The Tibetan leader in exile, the Dalai Lama, is at the centre of movements outside the country which aim to achieve a separate Tibetan state through non-violent means. Among the Kurds, on the other hand, several independence movements, mostly located abroad, proclaimed violence as the means of achieving their ends, and the Kurds have a 'parliament in exile', based in Brussels. However, after the first Gulf War of 1990–1, allied forces established a 'safe haven' and a level of autonomy for Kurds in northern Iraq, which was extended and consolidated following the overthrow of Saddam Hussein's regime in 2003.

In the case of the Tibetans, there is little chance of achieving even limited autonomy unless the Chinese government decides at some point to change its existing policies. But, in other instances, it is possible that national minorities might opt for autonomy within, rather than complete independence from, the states in which they are located. In the Basque country, Catalonia and Scotland, for example, a minority of the populations currently support complete independence. In Quebec, a provincial referendum in 1995 on independence from Canada was defeated when it failed to gain the necessary popular votes.

THINKING CRITICALLY

Nations have been described as 'imagined communities' (Anderson 2006 [1983]) – as no one can know all of the people within a nation, its unity is assumed or imagined. What practical activities keep imagined communities alive over generations, even where no state exists?

In the case of national minorities in Europe, the European Union has a significant part to play. The EU was formed through allegiances created by the major nations of Western Europe. Yet a key element of the philosophy of the EU is the devolution of power to localities and regions. One of its explicit goals is to create a 'Europe of the regions'. This emphasis is strongly supported by most Basques, Scots, Catalans and other national minority groups. Their right to relate directly to EU organizations, such as the European Parliament or European courts of law, might give them sufficient autonomy to be satisfied that they are in control of their own destinies. Hence it is perhaps conceivable that national minorities may push for independence within the EU while also accepting a cooperative relationship with the larger nations of which they are a part.

The basic roles and functions of the EU are introduced in chapter 21, 'Politics, Government and Social Movements'.

Nations and nationalism in developing countries

In most of the developing world, the course followed by nationalism, the nation and the nation-state has been different to that of the industrial societies. Most developing countries were once colonized by Europeans and achieved independence at some point in the second half of the twentieth century. In many of these countries, boundaries between colonial administrations were agreed arbitrarily in Europe and did not take into account existing economic, cultural or ethnic divisions among the population. The colonial powers defeated or subjugated the kingdoms and tribal groupings existing on the African subcontinent, in India and in other parts of Asia and set up their own colonial administrations or protectorates. As a consequence, each colony was 'a collection of peoples and old states, or fragments of these, brought together within the same boundaries' (Akintoye 1976: 3). Most colonized areas contained a mosaic of ethnies and other groups.

When former colonies achieved independence, they often found it difficult to create a sense of nationhood and national belonging. Although nationalism played a great part in securing the independence of colonized areas, it was confined largely to small groups from the urban elites and intellectuals. Nevertheless, nationalist ideas did influence large numbers of people, though political differences often crystallized around ethnic differences, such as those in Rwanda or Kenya. Even today, many postcolonial states are continually threatened by internal rivalries and competing claims to political authority.

The continent that was most completely colonized was Africa. Nationalist movements promoting independence in Africa following the Second World War sought to free the colonized areas from European domination. Once this had been achieved, new leaders everywhere faced the challenge of trying to create national unity. This was not easy, as many of the leaders in the 1950s and 1960s had been educated in Europe or the USA and there was a vast gulf between them and their citizens.

Under colonialism, some ethnic groups had prospered more than others; these groups had different interests and goals and legitimately saw one another as enemies.

Sudan, Zaire and Nigeria all saw civil wars, while ethnic rivalries and antagonisms characterized many other postcolonial states, in both Africa and Asia. In the case of Sudan, about 40 per cent of the population (mostly in the north) were Muslim of Arabic ethnic origin, while in other regions of the country, particularly the south, most of the population was black and followed traditional religions (such as animism), though a minority were Christian. Once the nationalists took power, they embarked on a programme for national integration based on Arabic as the national language. The attempt was only partly successful, as many in the south saw the new government as imposing Islam and an Arabic identity.

Civil war broke out in 1955 between the south and Sudan's government in the north. A peace accord in 1972 gave new powers and some autonomy to the south, but, when the government annulled these agreements in 1983, liberation armies rose up again. The ensuing conflict lasted until 2005, when a comprehensive peace agreement was reached which gave the south its regional autonomy. In July 2011, a referendum was held that finally gave South Sudan full independence from the north (the latter is still called Sudan). However, internal conflicts and land disputes at the border continued even after independence.

Nigeria provides another example of the issues involved as African countries move on from the legacy of colonial domination. The country has a population of some 120 million people – roughly one out of every four Africans is a Nigerian. Nigeria was formerly a British colony and achieved independence on 1 October 1960. The country contains many ethnic groups but three are dominant: the Yoruba, Ibo and Hausa. Armed struggles developed in the country in 1966 between different ethnic groups, and a military government ruled until 1999 when elections were held.

Successive governments have attempted to build a clearer sense of national identity around

Global Society 22.1 Free-market democracy and ethnic hatred

Many commentators have maintained that the best way to reduce ethnic conflicts, such as those discussed above, is to establish democracy and introduce free markets. They argue that this would promote peace by allowing everyone a say in running the country and by giving them access to the prosperity that comes from trading with others. However, Amy Chua's (2003) *World on Fire: How Exporting Free Market Democracy Breeds Ethnic Hatred and Global Instability* (2003) contests this view.

Chua's starting point is that, in many developing countries, a small ethnic minority enjoys disproportionate economic power. One obvious example is the white minority that exploited the non-white ethnic groups in apartheid South Africa. Chua reasons that the massacre of Tutsis by Hutus in Rwanda in 1994 and the hatred felt by Serbs towards Croats in the former Yugoslavia were also partly related to the economic advantage enjoyed by the Tutsis and the Croats in their respective countries. Another example that Chua often uses concerns the Chinese ethnic minority in Indonesia.

The pro-market reforms of the former Indonesian dictator General Suharto benefited particularly the country's small Chinese minority. In turn, Chinese Indonesians tended to support the Suharto dictatorship. In 1998, the year that mass pro-democracy demonstrations forced Suharto out of office, Chinese Indonesians,

who made up just 3 per cent of the population, controlled 70 per cent of Indonesia's private economy. The end of Suharto's regime was accompanied by violent attacks against the Chinese minority, who were perceived as 'stealing' the country's indigenous wealth. Chua writes: 'The prevailing view among the pribumi [ethnic] majority was that it was worthwhile to lose 10 years of growth to get rid of the Chinese problem once and for all.'

As General Suharto's dictatorship collapsed, the USA and other Western countries called for the introduction of democratic elections. Yet, Chua claims that introducing democracy to countries with what she calls 'market dominant minorities', such as the Chinese in Indonesia, is not likely to bring peace. Instead, she argues that the competition for votes in a democracy is likely to lead to a backlash from the country's ethnic majority. Political leaders will emerge who seek to scapegoat the resented minority and encourage the ethnic majority to 'reclaim' the country's wealth for the 'true' owners of the nation, as the pribumi majority in Indonesia did against the Chinese minority.

Chua's account shows us that, although democracy and the market economy are seen by many as, in principle, beneficent forces, they must be grounded in an effective system of law and civil society. Where they are not, new and acute ethnic conflicts can develop.

---

the theme of 'motherland Nigeria', but creating a sense of national unity and purpose remains difficult and authoritarianism persists within the political culture. However, the 2011 presidential election was widely seen as overwhelmingly fair and free from violence, and in the 2015 election Muhammadu Buhari's victory saw the first democratic transfer of power and heightened hopes for a democratic future.

In summary, most states in the developing world came into being as a result of different processes of nation formation from those that occurred in the industrialized world. States

were imposed externally on areas that often had no prior cultural or ethnic unity, sometimes resulting in civil war after independence. Modern nations have arisen most effectively either in areas that were never fully colonized or where there was already a great deal of cultural unity – such as Japan, China, Korea or Thailand.

The nation-state, national identities and human rights

How does globalization affect nationalism and national identity? Pilkington (2002) argues that nationalism is actually quite a recent phenomenon, despite the fact that many nationalists claim their nations have histories stretching back into the mists of time. Until relatively recently in historical terms, humans survived in small settlements, largely unaware of what went on outside their own groups, and the idea of being members of a larger nation would have seemed alien. Only later, from the eighteenth century onwards, with the development of mass communications and media, did the idea of a national community develop and spread. Pilkington reckons that it was during this period that national identities were 'constructed'.

>> Social constructionism is discussed in more detail in chapter 2, 'Asking and Answering Sociological Questions', chapter 5, 'The Environment', and chapter 8, 'Social Interaction and Daily Life'.

Crucial in developing a sense of nationhood was the existence of some 'Other', against which a national identity was formed. For instance, central to the shaping of a (Protestant) British identity was the existence of (Catholic) France. Pilkington documents how a sense of Britishness spread downwards from the country's elite to the rest of society as levels of literacy spread throughout the whole population and as communications technology enabled the spread of ideas. If national identity is socially constructed, then it is possible that it will change and develop, and one of the main factors in changing national identity today is globalization.

Globalization produces conflicting pressures between centralization and decentralization and, as a result, brings about a dual threat to national identity: centralization creates pressures from above, particularly with the growing powers of the European Union, and decentralization creates pressures from below, through the strengthening of ethnic identities. Pilkington says that a parallel response is also found among some members of ethnic minority groups who, feeling excluded from British

identity, strengthen their local identities and assert their differences from other ethnic groups. A second response to globalization, which Pilkington clearly thinks is a healthier one, is to accept that there are multiple identities – to argue, for example, that it is possible to be English, British and European all at the same time. Such 'hybrid identities' are found among ethnic minority groups in the UK, such as British Asians and other 'hyphenated identities'.

> **THINKING CRITICALLY**
>
> Why might national identities actually become stronger rather than weaker in the globalized future? Are there examples of regional identifications that are growing in strength?

In some parts of Africa, nations and nation-states are not fully formed. Yet in other areas of the world some writers are already speaking of the 'end of the nation-state' in the face of globalization. According to the Japanese writer Kenichi Ohmae (1995), as a result of globalization we increasingly live in a 'borderless world' in which national identity is becoming weaker. How valid is this point of view? All states are certainly being affected by globalizing processes, but it would not be accurate to say that we are witnessing the end of the nation-state.

Today, every country in the world is, or aspires to be, a nation-state, but for much of the twentieth century colonized areas and empires existed alongside nation-states. The last empire to collapse was Soviet communism in 1991. The Soviet Union was effectively at the centre of an empire embracing its satellite states in Eastern Europe, but all of these are now independent, as are many areas inside what was formerly the Soviet Union. However, in a blow to Ukrainian independence, Russian troops effectively annexed its Crimea region, leading to the 'Republic of Crimea' joining the Russian Federation in 2014 after a hasty referendum. Some 9,000 people died in the conflict in southern and eastern regions of Ukraine,

Hybrid social identities, such as British Asian, may offer a way of constructing national identities in the multicultural societies emerging from globalization processes.

and the EU imposed economic and military sanctions on Russia for its involvement.

There are actually far more sovereign nations in the world today than there were twenty-five years ago, and nation-states have been the central actors in the most severe and devastating conflicts ever experienced. Yet the nation-state is also the political body capable of granting and protecting the rights of its own citizens and promoting the rights of the individual more generally. As we shall see in the next section, there are some important differences between the concept of national citizenship and that of human rights.

Human rights – universal and particular

It may appear obvious that the concept of individual human rights stands in opposition to organized violence such as war, genocide and terrorism, but historically this is not the case. Malešević (2015: 560) argues that the demand for the recognition of basic rights first emerged in the twelfth and thirteenth centuries in the context of intra-Christian conflicts and discrimination against Jewish people in Poland. But it was the French and American revolutions that led to the establishment of formal documents setting out human rights, in the US Declaration of Independence and Virginia Declaration of Rights (1776) and the French Declaration of the Rights of Man and the Citizen (1789).

A global concept of human rights took root in the wake of the Second World War, prompted by the massive loss of life and the deliberate targeting of civilian populations (Turner 2006). This was set out in 1948 by the UN in the Universal Declaration of Human Rights. This document ran to thirty Articles covering fundamental principles such as the right to life, liberty, privacy and security alongside specific issues such as slavery, torture, cruelty, arrest and detention, marriage and property (UN 1948). It is important to note that this modern conception of human rights applies to everyone by virtue of being human, and in that sense it has universal application. Despite this, Turner argues that the idea of human rights means little unless those rights are enforceable. The contrast between national citizenship and universal rights shows how significant this insight is.

Where nation-states grant citizenship to all of those people living within their territories, citizenship rights can be enforced by using the full panoply of the state: a police force, armed forces, and a legal system, as well as local and national government. Citizenship also involves contributions by citizens, such as the payment of taxes and obeying state laws, which entitles them to protection and state benefits. But there exists no similar global body or set of institutions that is capable of enforcing human rights around the world, and human rights are not linked to any corresponding duties or obligations on the part of individuals.

Organizations such as Amnesty International, together with governments and individuals around the world, have expressed horror at the unfathomable violence meted out by Islamic State to civilians, and the UN carried a resolution in 2015 stating that member states which have the capacity to do so should 'take all necessary measures' to remove IS from Iraq and Syria. Yet this was approved on grounds of national self-defence rather than the individual human rights of Iraqis and Syrians. As Turner (2006: 5) says, there is a clear distinction between the 'social rights of citizens and the human rights of persons', and citizenship is a more effective basis for upholding people's rights.

For some sociologists, universal rights rooted in simply 'being human' is not a good starting point. Benjamin Gregg (2011) argues that human rights are socially constructed, locally developed and achieved by communities, not imposed 'from above'. All ideas of universal human rights that are immediately applicable across culture and societies are unattainable and unrealistic. For instance,

what is the right to life? Gregg suggests this is not as clear as may at first appear: 'Does it mean a right of a human embryo to the life it has? Would "the life it has" mean a right to be free of genetic manipulation? Might it mean a right of an embryo in vitro to be implanted into a uterus ... Is it a right to a chance of life?' (2011: 3). If such a basic right as this is questionable, how much more culturally variable and contentious are other human rights?

Yet the concept of universal human rights applicable to all persons across the world continues to motivate a range of people, organizations and social groups to protect and defend those facing discrimination and persecution, wherever they may be. It seems likely that the idea of universal human rights, like other hard-to-pin-down concepts such as socialism or sustainable development, is an 'active utopia' (Bauman 1982). That is, although there may be widespread acknowledgement that achieving universality may not be possible, the process of working towards it is more important in establishing what real and practically achievable rights can be enjoyed by humans. As Frezzo (2014: xxi) points out, 'we must envisage universalism not as a *fait accompli*, but rather as a project to be pursued on an ongoing basis.'

War, genocide and peace processes

One major theoretical tradition in sociology is the conflict tradition, which includes important research by Marxists, feminists and Weberian scholars (see chapter 1). However, much of this work concentrates on chronic social conflicts *within* societies, such as those involving social classes, gender relations and ethnic conflicts, that do not break out into open violence. Even when sociologists investigate cross-national conflicts, these are seen in similar terms. For example, the 2003 invasion of Iraq has been explained by some Marxists in essentially economic terms, as an attempt to establish secure oil supplies for the USA and its allies. Such studies and explanations have much to tell us about conflict, but, as a discipline, sociology has not given the study of war and violent conflict as much prominence as it could have, preferring to leave the subject to historians and military theorists.

One important reason for this is the widely held view that war is not a 'normal' state of affairs and is not central to the development of sociological theories and explanations. After all, it does not make much sense to base general social theories on highly unusual and very specific events. But this assumption is not correct. Warfare is as old as human societies, and over the course of human history there have been more than 14,000 wars (Roxborough 2004). Estimating the number of deaths in or caused by warfare in history is fraught with difficulties. Some suggest the overall figure may be as high as 4 billion, but it is extremely challenging to come to firm conclusions given the lack of proper records for most of that time and disagreements over which conflicts count as 'wars'. Even the recent past does not yield agreement. Twentieth-century wars are said to have accounted for 'more than 110 million' deaths (Malešević 2010: 7) or, alternatively, a more definitive '231 million' deaths (Leitenberg 2006: 1). Whatever the correct figure may be, the point remains that wars are not 'unusual' events.

From a global perspective, a very good case could be made for the opposite assumption: that the existence of wars is normal in human affairs, while periods of real peace have been quite rare. In the developed countries, the period since 1945 has been just such a period, and perhaps it is this that has contributed to the idea that war is somehow abnormal (Inglehart 1977). As the figures above show, massive loss of life and human suffering demands that sociologists explore the causes and consequences of war. Additionally, Joas and Knöbl (2012: 5) rightly argue that, 'if we fail to take account of war, we can understand neither the constitution of modernity through the *nation-state* – rather than transnational processes – nor many of the social and cultural changes that have occurred in the modern age.'

Theorizing war and genocide

What is war? Martin Shaw (2003: 5) defines it as 'the clash of two organized armed forces that seek to destroy each other's power and especially their will to resist, principally by killing members of the opposing force'. This definition makes organized killing central to the actual practice of war, a fact that was borne out in the enormous loss of life in two twentieth-century world wars, in which a large number of the world's societies became involved. The definition also makes clear that the central aim of war is to 'destroy the enemy's power', thus rendering it unable to resist. As we will see in 'Classic studies 22.2', this notion was expressed in Carl von Clausewitz's (1993 [1832]) classic statement that 'war is the continuation of political intercourse by other means'.

Clausewitz argues that wars are engaged in by states and are fought because political calculations are made about the likelihood of success and decisions taken by leaders. They require economic resources to be committed, and they usually play on real, perceived or created cultural differences in order to mobilize populations emotionally. War is therefore a social phenomenon whose nature has changed over time.

Historically, those killed in war have tended to be armed combatants rather than civilians, which shows that war is not simply chaotic, random killing – hence the idea of the 'rules of war' that regulate what opposing forces can legitimately do in combat and afterwards. Nevertheless, such rules have often been broken in battle conditions, and in many conflicts of the past century there has been much deliberate targeting of civilian populations as another means of 'destroying the enemy's will to resist'. Shaw describes the deliberate extension of targets to unarmed civilians as a form of illegitimate or 'degenerate war', seen in the Japanese massacres of more than 260,000 Chinese

USING YOUR SOCIOLOGICAL IMAGINATION

22.1 Using the atomic bomb

Hiroshima bomb pilot dies aged 92

The commander of the B-29 plane that dropped the first atomic bomb, on Hiroshima in Japan, has died. Paul Warfield Tibbets Jr died at his home in Columbus, Ohio, aged 92.

The five-ton 'Little Boy' bomb was dropped on the morning of 6 August 1945, killing about 140,000 Japanese, with many more dying later. On the 60th anniversary of the bombing, the three surviving crew members of the Enola Gay – named after Tibbets's mother – said they had 'no regrets'.

'No headstone'

A friend of the retired brigadier-general told AP news agency that Paul Tibbets had died after a two-month decline in health. Gen. Tibbets had asked for no funeral or headstone as he feared opponents of the bombing may use it as a place of protest, the friend, Gerry Newhouse, said.

The bombing of Hiroshima marked the beginning of the end of the war in the Pacific. Japan surrendered shortly after a second bomb was dropped, on Nagasaki, three days later.

On the 60th anniversary of Hiroshima, the surviving members of the Enola Gay crew – Gen. Tibbets, Theodore J. 'Dutch' Van Kirk (the navigator) and Morris R. Jeppson (weapon test officer) said: 'The use of the atomic weapon was a necessary moment in history. We have no regrets.' Gen. Tibbets said then: 'Thousands of former soldiers and military family members have expressed a particularly touching and personal gratitude suggesting that they might not be alive today had it been necessary to resort to an invasion of the Japanese home islands to end the fighting.'

Source: BBC (2007d).

> **THINKING CRITICALLY**
>
> Given the justification for the use of nuclear weapons – that it brought Japanese resistance to a swifter end, which saved many lives – can any episode of 'degenerate war' be considered legitimate?

civilians in 1937, the British fire-bombing of German cities, including Hamburg in 1943 and Dresden in 1945, and the American nuclear bombing of the Japanese cities of Hiroshima and Nagasaki in 1945.

The changing nature of war

Before the twentieth century, most wars made extensive use of mercenary armies or men conscripted into armed forces. Weaponry consisted of swords and, latterly, firearms, and military transport was based on horses, horse-drawn carriages and sailing boats. Even during the First World War (1914–18), horses remained a major form of transport. By the time of the Second World War, weapons and transport had changed considerably. Machine guns, tanks, chemical weapons and aeroplanes made it much easier for armies to engage in the mass killing that characterizes war today.

A common-sense view would perhaps see wars as conflicts between nation-states for dominance, and, until quite recently, many social scientists might have agreed. However, interstate wars seem to be becoming less common. Of eighty conflicts that took place around the world between 1989 and 1992, just three were interstate wars; the remainder were communal conflicts within countries (Malcolm 1996). On the other hand, internal conflicts seem to be increasing. Of the 213 civil wars that took place in the 181 years between 1816 and 1997, 104 took place in just forty-three years, between 1944 and 1997 (Hironaka 2005). The balance between *inter*state and *intra*state wars seems to have shifted significantly.

In addition, Shaw (2005) argues that, in many contemporary wars affecting Western

Classic Studies 22.2 Carl von Clausewitz, *On War* (1832)

Carl von Clausewitz (1780–1831) is the classic modern theorist of war. A Prussian army officer who fought in the revolutionary and Napoleonic wars (1793–1815), he taught at the military academy, where he wrote the book published posthumously as *On War*. If social scientists fully recognized the centrality of war in modern society, this work of Clausewitz would figure in canons of social thought alongside those of near contemporaries such as the philosophers Immanuel Kant and Georg Wilhelm Friedrich Hegel, the sociologist Auguste Comte and the revolutionary Karl Marx.

Clausewitz's book contained a number of seminal ideas.

1   His most famous maxim is that 'war is the continuation of political intercourse [also translated as either policy or politics] by other means.' This is often interpreted as meaning that the course of war is determined by its political objectives. However, Clausewitz's real originality lay in his exploration of the 'otherness' of military means.

2   He emphasized that war is 'an act of force' designed to compel an enemy to submit, and hence has 'no logical limit'. From this he concluded that escalation is a law of war, and that there is a general tendency for war to become absolute. Restricted political objectives can limit escalation only partially, since the clash of arms is always likely to surpass preordained political limits and so is intrinsically unpredictable.

3   War was likely to be contained by *friction* – i.e., the obstacles to escalation created by inhospitable climate and terrain together with the logistical difficulties of deploying armies over long distances.

4   War can be compared as a social process to commerce. In this light, battle is the moment of realization – the end to which all activity is geared – in war in the same way as exchange in commerce.

5   War is a *trinity* of policy (the province of government), military craft (the business of generals) and raw violence (supplied by the people). Thus the involvement of the people (the nation in arms) is partly responsible for the peculiarly destructive character of modern war in comparison with those of earlier periods.

Modern war is sometimes described as 'Clausewitzian'. The main problem with this description is that industrial society gave war enormously more powerful means of destruction – not only weaponry but also military and political organization – than Clausewitz could foresee. Modern *total war* combined total social mobilization with absolute destructiveness. From the middle of the nineteenth century, this radically expanded the scope for slaughter beyond Clausewitzian conditions. The logical conclusion of this process was the truly total, simultaneous and mutual destruction threatened by nuclear war.

Source: Shaw (2003: 19–20)

THINKING CRITICALLY

How do Clausewitz's main arguments stand up today, especially in relation to the development and spread of nuclear weapons? Which aspects are undermined by the doctrine of 'mutually assured destruction' (MAD)?

states – such as those involving the USA and its allies in Iraq and Afghanistan – attempts are now made to protect the lives of Western military personnel in order to avoid potentially damaging media coverage that might lead to negative political and electoral consequences

for governments at home. This is one reason why recent Western involvement often takes the preferred forms of drone strikes and massive air strikes, which minimize the risk to armed forces. But, in effect, this amounts to the transference of the risks of warfare onto

The Hutu regime in Rwanda claimed the lives of more than 800,000 Tutsis during the genocide of 1994 (see 'Global Society 16.2', p. 687, for more details)

civilian populations below, whose deaths become 'collateral damage' or 'unavoidable accidents of war'. This new mode of 'risk transfer' war has the potential to damage the older, rule-governed type and thus opens Western states and everyone else to even more risks. When civilians are intentionally targeted, the question of whether 'genocide' has been committed is now commonly raised.

Genocide is a term that has been used with increasing regularity in the mass media and political discourse. It was used, for example, to describe the Serb regime's assault on ethnic Albanians in Kosovo and the Hutu regime's attacks on Tutsis in Rwanda. Originally employed by Raphael Lemkin in his book *Axis Rule in Occupied Europe* (1944), it was adopted in 1948 by the United Nations Convention on the Prevention and Punishment of the Crime of Genocide (Article 2), which says:

Genocide means any of the following acts committed with intent to destroy, in whole or in part, a national, ethnic, racial or religious group, as such:

(a) killing members of the group;
(b) causing serious bodily or mental harm to members of the group;
(c) deliberately inflicting on the group conditions of life calculated to bring about its physical destruction in whole or in part;
(d) imposing measures intended to prevent births within the group;
(e) forcibly transferring children of the group to another group.

This was among the first attempts to define genocide and is clearly rooted in the Nazi racial policies against many sections of the European population, including the attempt to exterminate the Jewish people, in the Second

Global Society 22.2 | Cambodia's 'Khmer Rouge' regime

The Khmer Rouge was the ruling party in Cambodia from 1975 to 1979, but during this short time it was responsible for one of the worst mass killings of the twentieth century. The brutal regime claimed the lives of more than a million people – and some estimates say up to 2.5 million perished. Under the Marxist leader Pol Pot, the Khmer Rouge . . . [forced] millions of people from the cities to work on communal farms in the countryside. But this dramatic attempt at social engineering had a terrible cost, and whole families died from execution, starvation, disease and overwork.

Communist philosophy

The Khmer Rouge had its origins in the 1960s, as the armed wing of the Communist Party of Kampuchea – the name the Communists used for Cambodia. Based in remote jungle and mountain areas in the north-east of the country, the group initially made little headway. But after a right-wing military coup toppled the head of state Prince Norodom Sihanouk in 1970, the Khmer Rouge entered into a political coalition with him and began to attract increasing support. In a civil war that continued for nearly five years, it gradually increased its control in the countryside. Khmer Rouge forces finally took over the capital, Phnom Penh, and therefore the nation as a whole in 1975.

During his time in the remote north-east, Pol Pot had been influenced by the surrounding hill tribes, who were self-sufficient in their communal living, had no use for money and were 'untainted' by Buddhism. When he came to power, he and his henchmen quickly set about transforming Cambodia – now renamed Kampuchea – into what they hoped would be an agrarian utopia. Declaring that the nation would start again at 'Year Zero', Pol Pot isolated his people from the rest of the world and set about emptying the cities, abolishing money, private property and religion, and setting up rural collectives.

Anyone thought to be an intellectual of any sort was killed. People were often condemned for wearing glasses or for knowing a foreign language. Hundreds of thousands of the educated middle classes were tortured and executed in special centres. The most notorious of these centres was the S21 jail in Phnom Penh, where more than 17,000 men, women and children were imprisoned during the regime's four years in power. . . .

Opening up

The Khmer Rouge government was finally overthrown in 1979 by invading Vietnamese troops, after a series of violent border confrontations. The higher echelons of the party retreated to remote areas of the country, where they remained active for a while but gradually became less and less powerful.

In the years that followed, as Cambodia began the process of reopening to the international community, the full horrors of the regime became apparent. Survivors told their stories to shocked audiences, and in the 1980s the Hollywood movie *The Killing Fields* brought the plight of the Khmer Rouge victims to worldwide attention.

Pol Pot was denounced by his former comrades in a show trial in July 1997, and was sentenced to house arrest in his jungle home. But less than a year later he was dead – denying the millions of people who were affected by this brutal regime the chance to bring him to justice. However, in 2011, the regime's four most senior surviving leaders (all over 80 years old) were brought for trial on charges of genocide, and a former Khmer Rouge prison chief, known as 'Duch', was found guilty of crimes against humanity and sentenced to 35 years imprisonment after an unsuccessful appeal.

Source: BBC (2007e); BBC News (2012a).

World War (1939–45). Genocide is seen here as separate from war. Whereas killing in war can be considered legitimate (if the rules of war are not broken), genocide is, by definition, always wrong. The UN definition makes intention central to genocide. A particular social group need not *actually be* exterminated for genocide to be deemed to have taken place; what matters is that the perpetrator's *intention* was to exterminate the enemy.

A problem is demonstrating intention in order to prove that genocide has taken place. Orders to kill may never be written down, evidence may be incomplete or non-existent, and many things can be achieved by acts of omission as well as acts of commission. That is, the destruction of a social group can be brought about by neglect and indifference as well as by deliberate attacks. Also, non-combatants in civil wars should not be seen merely as passive victims of large-scale political violence orchestrated by states. In many civil wars, civilians have used the context of violence to pursue their existing local and interpersonal disputes. Indeed, Kalyvas (2006) suggests that analysing the ways in which the political issues of conflicts interact with such local disputes offers a productive way of bridging the divide between macro- and micro-level studies of warfare.

Shaw (2003, 2007) rejects the separation of genocide and war. As he notes, most genocides occur within interstate or civil wars. In most historical cases of genocide, states (or power centres within states) were the perpetrators, state armies, police forces and party organizations carried them out, and they took place within the context of war. Hence, it may be more accurate to define genocide as 'a form of war in which social groups are the enemy' (Shaw 2003: 44–5). And, if genocide *is* a form of war, it raises the question of whether the dominant form of war is changing.

Old and new wars

Warfare is always based on the available resources, social organization and level of technological development of societies. Some recent theories have argued that we are witnessing a revolution in military affairs (RMA) based on the increased use of information technologies, which are moving to the centre of military strategy. For example, satellite targeting systems, drones and computers played key roles in the conflicts in Iraq (1990–1 and 2003), Afghanistan (2001–) and Libya (2011). It is clear that methods of waging war are never fixed but, rather, change over time alongside the economic, social and political development of societies.

Similarly, the industrialized, *total wars* of the early twentieth century, with their mobilization of entire national populations in the war effort, were radically different from earlier conflicts involving much smaller armies, which took place without the participation of large parts of civilian populations, many of which were unaffected by them. Some scholars of war have argued that the nature of war has changed quite dramatically again over the past thirty years or so, as a type of war has come to the fore which contrasts sharply with the nation-state wars of the twentieth century.

Whereas 'old' wars were fought by nation-states against each other, 'new' warfare threatens to undermine the nation-state as the primary 'survival unit' (Elias 1991: 205), which guarantees the safety and security of individual citizens, by challenging one of its central characteristics: the state monopoly of organized violence. The transnational connections involved in new wars challenge the state monopoly 'from above', while the 'privatization of violence' in paramilitary groups and the involvement of organized crime threatens the state monopoly 'from below'. There are several general theories of wars and warfare, including sociobiology, culturalism, economism and organizational materialism, which we cannot cover in this section. For those looking to pursue theories of war, these are discussed and usefully compared by Malešević (2010, 2011). However, we now turn to one highly influential account of the 'new wars', Mary Kaldor's (2006) *New and Old Wars*.

Kaldor argues that a new type of war began to emerge in Africa and Eastern Europe from

22.2 Modernity and the Holocaust

'The Holocaust' is a phrase used to describe a specific instance of genocide: the systematic attempt by German National Socialists, led by Adolf Hitler, to exterminate Jews in Europe during the Second World War. Jewish populations in Germany and other countries that were invaded by German troops were persecuted, crowded into ghettos and transported to extermination camps, where mass killing took place in gas chambers. Approximately 6 million Jewish people were murdered in these few short years as part of the Nazis' 'Final Solution of the Jewish Question'. Although many other social groups, such as Eastern European Roma, disabled people, gay men and communists, were also singled out for persecution, conventionally these have not been included in definitions of the Holocaust.

Zygmunt Bauman (1989) discovered that sociologists have had very little to say about the Holocaust or its consequences for social science. He suggests that part of the reason for this is that the Holocaust is seen as a specific aspect of Jewish history which holds no general lessons for other times and places. Second, there exists a widely accepted interpretation of the Holocaust, which sees it as an aberration, a dreadful and unique episode of barbarism in the otherwise peaceful flow of social life in civilized, modern societies. Bauman argues that we cannot let modern societies off the hook so lightly; the Holocaust, he says, is the ultimate *test of* modernity.

In fact, says Bauman, it was the characteristically modern elements that made the Holocaust possible. Modern technology was deployed to speed up the process of mass killing, bureaucratic systems of administration ensured the most efficient method of processing 'human bureaucratic objects', and the bureaucratic mentality dehumanized Jewish people, allowing individuals to avoid moral responsibility for their actions. Bauman also explores the role of racist ideology and the way that victims were led into acquiescence in the extermination process through rational calculation of survival chances at every stage. All of these elements – modern technology, bureaucracies, racism and rational calculation – are 'normal' or common aspects of modern societies.

In the Holocaust these elements were brought together in a unique way. Bauman theorizes that this became possible as the German state systematically set about dismantling and destroying the voluntary organizations, trade unions and other tissues that make for a strong civil society. This left the centralized nation-state, with its monopolization of the means of violence, free to pursue its social-engineering projects without any controls or countervailing powers. In short, modernity provided the *necessary* resources that made the Holocaust possible, but this was not *sufficient* without the state's emancipation from the restrictions placed on it by society at large.

For Bauman, there are two main lessons from the Holocaust. The first is 'the facility with which most people, put into a situation that does not contain a good choice, or renders such a good choice very costly, argue themselves away from the issue of moral duty (or fail to argue themselves towards it), adopting instead the precepts of rational interest and self-preservation. *In a system where rationality and ethics point in opposite directions, humanity is the main loser'* (1989: 206; emphasis in the original). But the second lesson is: '*It does not matter how many people chose moral duty over the rationality of self-preservation – what does matter is that some did. Evil is not all-powerful. It can be resisted*' (ibid.; emphasis in the original). Of course we may agree with Bauman that people's actions aimed at self-preservation were indeed a choice rather than an inevitability. But the context in which such choices were made did largely shape the overall outcome. As the historian E. H. Carr (1962: 62) once argued, 'numbers count in history'.

THINKING CRITICALLY

Does Jewish resistance in the face of overwhelmingly more powerful forces support Bauman's point about moral duty being a choice we *all* face, even in the worst of times? Why might the choice between self-preservation and moral duty to others not be quite as simple as Bauman's conclusion suggests?

There were numerous attempts at resistance by Jewish people during the Second World War, including a rebellion in 1943 at the Treblinka concentration camp and several in Jewish ghettos. During the Warsaw ghetto uprising of January 1943, several thousand Jewish people fought the Nazi SS and killed hundreds of German soldiers. They were eventually overwhelmed by the German army, and 13,000 Jewish people lost their lives.

the late twentieth century. One way of describing this has been to see it as 'low-intensity conflict', essentially similar to small-scale guerrilla warfare, or even terrorism. Low-intensity conflicts involve localized violence, and many could be called civil wars within particular nation-states. However, Kaldor rejects the 'civil war' label for such conflicts. She points out that, although they are usually localized, they also involve many transnational connections, and this makes the old distinction between external aggression and internal repression impossible to sustain. New wars also erode the boundaries between warfare among states, organized crime and violations of basic human rights as these have become linked.

For example, in the Bosnian war of 1992–5, a genocidal conflict between Serbian, Croatian and Bosnian nationalist groups resulted in at least 100,000 deaths. On all sides, human rights violations took place in attempts to create ethnically 'pure' areas. Bosnian Serbs received financial and logistical support from Serbia (which, at that time, covered much of the Federal Republic of Yugoslavia) and during the conflict embarked on a campaign of 'ethnic cleansing' (attempts to displace an ethnic group from a specific area) against non-Serbs; this involved many human rights abuses against civilians, including the systematic mass rape of women and civilian massacres.

The massacre of some 8,000 boys and men at Srebrenica in July 1995 was declared genocide by an International Criminal Tribunal at The Hague. The tribunal reported that:

> By seeking to eliminate a part of the Bosnian Muslims, the Bosnian Serb forces committed genocide. They targeted for extinction the forty thousand Bosnian Muslims living in Srebrenica, a group which was emblematic of the Bosnian Muslims in general. They stripped all the male Muslim prisoners, military and civilian, elderly and young, of their personal belongings and identification, and deliberately and methodically killed them solely on the basis of their identity. (Traynor 2004)

However, in 2007, the International Court of Justice declared that the *state* of Serbia did not directly commit the genocide (though some individuals were charged) but that it had broken international law by failing to stop it. This was the first time a state had faced genocide charges. Kaldor argues that such large-scale violations of human rights make new wars illegitimate and that ways must be found to prevent them.

Kaldor maintains that the end of the Cold War is one factor in the rise of new war. But more significant is the increasingly rapid process of globalization that began in the 1970s, carried along on the wave of new information technologies. Globalization, she says, lies at the heart of new wars:

> The global presence in these wars can include international reporters, mercenary troops and military advisers, and diaspora volunteers as well as a veritable 'army' of international agencies ranging from non-governmental organizations (NGOs) such as Oxfam, Save the Children, Médecins Sans Frontières, Human Rights Watch and the International Red Cross to international institutions such as the United Nations High Commissioner for refugees (UNHCR), the European Union (EU), the United Nations Children's Fund (UNICEF), the Organization for Security and Cooperation in Europe (OSCE), the African Union (AU) and the United Nations (UN) itself, including peacekeeping troops. Indeed, the wars epitomize a new kind of global/local divide between those members of a global class who can speak English, have access to faxes, the Internet and satellite televisions, who use dollars or euros or credit cards, and who can travel freely, and those who are excluded from global processes, who live off what they can sell or barter or what they receive in humanitarian aid, whose movement is restricted by roadblocks, visas and the cost of travel, and who are prey to sieges, forced famines, landmines, etc. (Kaldor 2006: 4–5)

Kaldor's argument seems to imply that we may be witnessing a reversal of the state-formation processes identified by Norbert Elias and Max Weber. During the emergence of the modern state, *centripetal* forces were in the ascendancy as the means of violence became more centralized. However, since the late twentieth century, *centrifugal* forces are gaining the upper hand as the means of violence become distributed more widely among populations. As the number of new wars has increased in the wake of the ending of the Cold War, it may be that the close of an old world order has created a climate in which new war has flourished. The collapse of communist regimes has left a legacy of surplus weaponry as well as a power vacuum, which local militia groups and armies can use to their advantage.

Critics of the new war thesis say that some of its key arguments are exaggerated and that nation-states are likely to remain the key actors in wars and conflicts. One group of critics claims that the apparently new elements of recent warfare can be found in previous times. For example, the historian Antony Beevor (2007) maintains that the targeting of civilian populations can be seen in many previous conflicts. In particular, during the Second World War, the targeting of civilians by all sides was a significant aspect of operations on the Eastern Front.

Paul Hirst (2001) sees the activities of armed militias in the Greek–Turkish war of 1921–2 and the Spanish Civil War of 1936–9 as essentially similar to the more recent low-intensity conflicts identified by Kaldor. Similarly, contemporary wars in the developing world can be viewed as closer to conventional warfare than to low-intensity conflict. Earlier European wars similarly involved the use of famine as part of warfare, as well as the plundering of resources and guerrilla tactics avoiding direct confrontations – all features described in the new war thesis as recent developments (Angstrom 2005).

Kaldor's reliance on the thesis of rapid globalization has also been criticized. Hirst (2001) argues that the new war thesis underplays the continuing significance of 'old' interstate wars, such as those between Iran and Iraq or the Arab–Israeli wars. For Hirst, the new war theory is far too dependent on the notion that 'globalization changes everything', when the evidence is that the nation-state is still the institution in which people invest their loyalty and on which they ultimately rely to protect their interests. This is an important point, as it undermines the importance placed by Kaldor on international institutions in resolving conflicts. International humanitarian interventions, such as the UN's role in the Bosnian war (discussed above), are just as likely to reactivate old problems as they are to produce long-lasting solutions, given the involvement of 'old' nation-states with their historical alliances and enmities.

Perhaps it is too early to be sure that new wars will become the dominant type of war in the future. But, assuming that the present trend continues, should we welcome the purported slow demise of interstate warfare? Certainly, it is unlikely that new wars will produce the sheer scale of death and destruction that interstate wars of the twentieth century did. But in their place may arise a more insidious privatization of the means of violence, which threatens to 'decivilize' societies by challenging the assumption that the state can guarantee a relatively pacified internal space for citizens (Fletcher 1997). The modern world will have to find ways of dealing with the localized, but chronically destablizing, conflicts of the future.

> ### THINKING CRITICALLY
> The conflicts in former Yugoslavia shocked 'civilized' Europeans, who had thought such genocidal violence was a thing of the past. Is there any evidence that contemporary 'nations without states' may be heading in a similar direction? What could international bodies do to prevent more 'new wars' in the future?

Peace processes

While there has always been sociological interest in social conflicts and, in recent years, more sociological research into war, genocide and terrorism has taken place, it is true to say that 'academic interest in peace studies has been rather negligible' (Chatterjee 2005: 17). This may, in part, be due to the common-sense assumption that conflict is a form of deviance that needs to be explained, while peace is somehow the 'normal' condition of social life. On the other hand, there has also been much biological and ethological speculation that aggression and violence are somehow inherent in human nature. However, sociological research sidesteps these overly philosophical issues, focusing instead on drawing some general conclusions from comparative, historical and empirical case studies (Das 2005).

Our starting point here is that both war and peace are possibilities in human relations. And, while much effort has been expended on understanding the causes of wars and communal violence, this has not been matched by studies of peace processes – all of those official and informal activities aimed at preventing future violence and ensuring fairness and equitable resource distribution in post-conflict situations. There is an important role for a sociological perspective here, as sociology offers analyses that look at peace processes as they are played out across the whole of society. This includes assessing the roles played by the many groups and organizations that make up civil society, as well as the professional negotiators, politicians and official initiatives which form the basis of most other studies.

Peace processes are linked to the type of violence that has previously occurred and have been seen as moving through four phases. The *pre-negotiation* phase often involves secret negotiations aimed at agreeing terms for cessation of the violence. This is followed in the second phase by a *formal ceasefire* and in the third stage by *negotiations*, often difficult and protracted, during which political agreement is reached between the adversaries, perhaps via a neutral mediator. In the final phase – *post-settlement peacebuilding* – combatants are reintegrated into society and victims are involved in processes of reconciliation (Darby 2001).

In the aftermath of violent conflict, some societies achieve a 'positive peace' in which fairness and an equitable distribution of resources is more or less achieved. However, others have to make do with a 'negative peace', in which physical violence is removed or controlled but underlying tensions and issues of inequality and a lack of fairness remain. Post-violence societies are those which have moved from wars or communal violence towards non-violence, as in Rwanda, South Africa, Sri Lanka and Northern Ireland. Brewer (2010: 19–27) identifies three basic types: 'conquest', 'cartography' and 'compromise'.

Conquest post-violence societies are mainly those affected by wars between nation-states, though the category also includes those where internal communal violence is ended by conquest, as in civil wars or colonial wars. The *cartography* type is where peace has been achieved mainly by physically separating the previous adversaries by changing national borders, creating new states or devolving power to new regional authorities. Finally, *compromise* post-violence refers to all of those instances where neither force nor physical separation is possible. Instead, previous combatants are forced to negotiate and reach an accord which involves both a ceasefire and agreement on what constitutes a 'fair' settlement for all parties.

Brewer also suggests that three factors are crucial in determining the shape of and prospects for post-violence peace. First is the extent to which previous adversaries share common values, norms and traditions – what he calls 'relational distance-closeness'. Where previous adversaries are 'relationally close' – as in Northern Ireland – post-violence reconstruction may be easier, as the common shared heritage forms the basis for reorienting people's perspective. Where relational distance exists – as in Sri Lanka or the Basque region of Spain – it may be necessary to maintain social divisions and to find political ways of managing these to prevent future violence.

Second is whether the previous adversaries live apart or together on common land and share nationality (a 'spatial separation–territorial integrity' axis). In some post-violence societies, especially where there is relational closeness, territorial integrity may not pose insurmountable problems and previous combatants can live side by side. But, in others, the extent of the violence may have been so damaging as to make spatial separation necessary for a lasting settlement. This has been the outcome in the former Yugoslavia and in the separation of India and Pakistan, for example.

Finally, Brewer notes a third axis of 'cultural capital or cultural annihilation' in post-violence societies. Do former adversaries, particularly those on the losing side, retain their cultural resources and historical memories or have these been effectively annihilated? In some cases, where the vanquished play key economic roles, have access to education or are simply large in number, they may retain their cultural capital, which enables the original causes of the conflict to be kept alive. For example, Palestinians have successfully retained their cultural capital in the conflict with Israel, and Africans in South Africa maintained their cultural capital in submerged forms during the period of white minority rule. Yet vanquished groups may not be able to resist – as with Australian Aboriginal peoples and North American indigenous groups – and thus face effective 'cultural annihilation'. This does not mean the complete elimination of defeated social groups, but it does point to their cultural subordination in the post-violence situation.

What Brewer's distinctly sociological approach enables is a realistic assessment of the prospects for peace in contemporary conflicts and peace processes around the world. More specifically, it provides a schema that can be used in the study of post-violence peace processes. However, approaches such as this one may also help all of those working within peace processes to understand better some of the obstacles and opportunities they face.

> **THINKING CRITICALLY**
>
> Using Brewer's framework of three types of post-violence society, explore the current situation in Northern Ireland, South Sudan and Sri Lanka. Which category do each of these countries fall into? Which of the three cases is most likely to achieve a 'positive peace' and which may have to live with a 'negative peace'?

Terrorism

The first decade of the twenty-first century will probably be remembered as the decade of global terrorism. It began at about 8.45 a.m. on 11 September 2001, when four commercial aeroplanes in the United States were hijacked by al-Qaeda terrorists claiming to be acting in defence of Muslims across the world. One plane was flown into the North Tower of the World Trade Center in New York, another into the South Tower. Within an hour, both burning buildings had collapsed, killing thousands of people at the start of their working day. An hour or so later, a third plane was flown into the Pentagon, headquarters of the US military, near Washington, DC, killing many more people, and the fourth, said to be heading for the White House, crashed into a field in rural Pennsylvania after passengers took on the hijackers. The planes (belonging to American companies) and the targets – the World Trade Center, the Pentagon and the White House – were chosen to strike symbolically at the heart of American economic, military and political power.

These attacks became known as '9/11' (the 11th day of the 9th month), and US President George W. Bush's response was to declare a 'war on terror'. A month later, the first major military response was an attack on Afghanistan by a coalition of countries. Afghanistan was ruled by the fundamentalist Islamic regime of the Taliban, which had supported al-Qaeda and its leader, Osama bin Laden, by facilitating terrorist training camps in the country.

The years following the attacks in America saw many more acts of terrorism for which al-Qaeda claimed responsibility. An attack on a nightclub on the Indonesian island of Bali in October 2002 killed more than 200 people, many of them young tourists on holiday from nearby Australia. Bombs on a rush-hour train in Madrid killed around 200 commuters in March 2004. And, in London, fifty-two people died and several hundred more were injured in a coordinated series of explosions on three underground trains and a bus in July 2005.

The global terrorism decade came to a symbolic end on 1 May 2011, when the ten-year hunt for the al-Qaeda leader finally came to an end. The new US president, Barack Obama, ordered a raid on a compound in Abbottabad, Pakistan, where intelligence sources suggested bin Laden might be hiding. US Special Forces attacked the compound and killed bin Laden, who may have been hiding there for up to five years. However, though the al-Qaeda network suffered a series of setbacks from 2001, many groups remain active in East Africa, North Africa, Afghanistan, Pakistan and Indonesia, and several bombing plots have been uncovered in Western Europe. Since its formation in 2009, al-Qaeda in the Arabian Peninsula – a merger of activists in Yemen and Saudi Arabia – has been seen as one of the most capable and active parts of the global al-Qaeda network.

Although the concept of terrorism has almost become synonymous with the organizational style and activities of al-Qaeda's global network, in fact, the latter is atypical when seen against the historical record of terrorist groups. To grasp this point we need first to try and establish exactly what is meant when we use the term 'terrorism'.

What is terrorism?

The word terrorism has its origins in the French Revolution of 1789. Thousands of people – originally aristocrats, but later many more ordinary citizens – were hunted down by the political authorities and executed by guillotine. The term 'terror' was invented not by the revolutionaries themselves but by the counter-revolutionaries: people who despised the French Revolution and what it stood for and who believed that the blood-letting which went on was a form of terrorizing the population (Laqueur 2003). 'Terror', in the sense of the use of violence to intimidate, was employed extensively in the twentieth century – for example, by the Nazis in Germany and the Russian secret police under Stalin. However, this kind of use of violence also pre-dates the origins of the term in the French Revolution.

Although 'terror' was not coined until the eighteenth century, the phenomenon of terrorizing people through violence is a very old one. In ancient civilizations, when one army invaded a city held by the enemy, it was not at all uncommon for the soldiers to raze the entire city to the ground and kill all the men, women and children. The point was not just physically to destroy the enemy but also to create terror in those living in other cities. Clearly, the phenomenon of using violence to terrify populations is older than the term 'terrorism'.

Social scientists disagree not only about the definition of terrorism but also as to whether the concept is useful at all. That is, can it ever be used in a reasonably objective and unbiased way? One issue concerns the shifting moral assessments that people make of terrorism and terrorists. It is often said that 'one person's terrorist is another person's freedom fighter'. Similarly, not all of those with radical beliefs join terror groups and by no means do all of those who join such groups hold radical beliefs (Crenshaw 2011: 6). Some join for financial gain, others for friendship or to join up with relatives. People who were once terrorists can later come to condemn terrorism just as vehemently as they practised it. It might be argued, for example, that the early history of the Zionist movement was punctuated by terrorist activity; but in the twenty-first century the Israeli leadership declares itself part of the international 'war on terror' and regards terrorists as the enemy. The former South African leader Nelson Mandela was widely reviled as a violent terrorist, but today he is one of the most revered political figures of our times.

A second issue concerns the role of the state. Can states be said to practise 'state terrorism', or is this a contradiction in terms? After all, states have been responsible for many more deaths than any other type of organization in history. States have brutally murdered civilian populations and carried out something comparable to the razing of cities that occurred in traditional civilizations. As we saw earlier, towards the end of the Second World War, systematic fire-bombing by the British RAF and the USAAF largely destroyed the German city of Dresden, where many thousands of civilians were killed. Some historians argue that this action was of no strategic advantage to the Allies and its aim was merely to create terror and fear, weakening the resolve of civilians to carry on the war. Was this an act of state terrorism?

Nonetheless, unless we restrict it to those groups and organizations that work *outside* the state, the concept of terrorism becomes too close to that of war. For our purposes in this section, a pretty good working definition is 'any action [by a non-state organization] . . . that is intended to cause death or serious bodily harm to civilians or non-combatants, when the purpose of such an act, by its nature or context, is to intimidate a population, or to compel a government or an international organization to do or to abstain from doing any act' (Panyarachun et al. 2004). In other words, terrorism is 'the targeted and intentional use of violence for political purposes' (Vertigans 2008: 3).

One final point to bear in mind is that discussing 'terrorists' as a distinct category of person is, in most cases, misleading. Vertigans (2011) argues that a more productive way forward is to recognize that, for most of those who become involved in terrorism, there is a route into terrorist activity (for example via peer groups, relatives or media messages), activity while within terrorist groups (organizing, recruiting and carrying out actions) and, very often, routes out of terrorism (such as weakening of belief, weariness with violence, forming new friendships outside or the collapse of the terror group itself). Seeing terrorist involvement in this way, as a social process characterized by a series of stages, avoids propagating media stereotypes and offers a genuinely sociological approach to the subject.

Old and new terrorism

Terrorism, as defined above, can be distinguished from the violent acts of previous historical periods, such as the ancient razing of cities. To terrorize populations on a fairly wide spectrum, information about the violence has to reach those populations affected quite quickly, and it was not until the rise of modern communications in the late nineteenth century that this was the case. With the invention of the electronic telegraph, instantaneous communication became possible, transcending time and space. Before this, information could take days or even months to spread. For example, as we saw in chapter 18 on the media, news of Abraham Lincoln's assassination took many days to reach the UK. Once instantaneous communication becomes feasible, symbolic acts of terrorist violence can be projected at distance so that it is not just the local population that knows about them (Neumann 2009).

Old terrorism

It is possible to make a distinction between an old and a new style of terrorism (Laqueur 2000). Old terrorism was dominant for most of the twentieth century and still exists today. This kind is associated mainly with the rise of nationalism and the establishment of nations as sovereign, territorially bounded entities, which occurred in Europe from the late eighteenth century onwards. All national boundaries are fixed somewhat arbitrarily, either as lines on a map, as they were by Western colonizers in Africa and Asia, or through conquest, battle and struggle. Ireland, for example, was brought into the United Kingdom in 1800, leading to independence struggles, which resulted in the partition of the country into North and South in the early 1920s. The patchwork of nations mapped out by colonial administrators, or founded by force, has led to numerous nations that do not have their own state – that is, nations with a claim to having a common cultural identity but without the territorial and state apparatus which normally belongs to a nation-state. Much old-style terrorism is linked to nations without states.

The aim of much old-style terrorism is to establish states in areas where nations do not have control of the territory's state apparatus. This was true, for example, of Irish nationalists, such as the Irish Republican Army (IRA), and Basque nationalists, such as ETA in Spain. The main issues are territorial integrity and identity in the formation of a state. Old-style terrorism is found where there are nations without states and where terrorists are prepared to use violence to achieve their ends. Older terrorism is fundamentally local because its ambitions are local. It wants to establish a state in a specific national area. Arguably, Islamic State's activism is aimed at founding a state suitable for their interpretation of the 'Muslim nation', though the group's methods comprise a mixture of the old and the very contemporary and their version of 'the nation' includes all Muslims across the world.

In recent years, old-style terrorism has often had an international component, drawing on external support and campaigning for strength. For example, Libya, Syria and some Eastern European countries, as well as groups within the United States, in varying degrees, supported the terrorist acts of the IRA in Northern Ireland and Basque separatists in Spain (Thompson 2015: 46, 395). But, although old-style terrorism might involve a wider network of supporters for its funding or in filtering arms or drugs to buy weaponry, its ambitions are decidedly local or national.

As well as being limited in its ambitions, old-style terrorism is limited in its use of violence. For example, although many people have lost their lives as the result of the conflict in Northern Ireland, the number of people killed as a result of terrorism since the 'Troubles' recommenced in the 1970s, including British soldiers, is on average smaller than those who have died in road accidents. With old-style terrorism, although the numbers of people maimed and killed are significant, the use of violence is limited, because the aims of this kind of terrorism are also relatively limited – fearsome and horrific though this violence still is.

New terrorism

A fundamental distinction can be drawn between old- and new-style terrorism (Tan and Ramakrishna 2002). New terrorism is made possible by the digital revolution that has also driven globalization. This type of terrorism has become intimately associated with the fundamentalist Islamist networks of al-Qaeda and the social media presence of Islamic State, though it is by no means limited to these groups. However, understanding the al-Qaeda network helps us pinpoint some of the main differences between old and new terrorism.

Al-Qaeda ('the base') was formed in the wake of the Soviet withdrawal from Afghanistan in 1989 with Osama bin Laden as its founder and leader. The organization was formed of Arab volunteers who had travelled to Afghanistan to oust Soviet communism from a Muslim nation. These fighters were battle-hardened and strongly committed, having won a major victory over a world superpower. Around 1996, al-Qaeda's training camps moved from Sudan to Afghanistan, where the Taliban regime provided support. But after the attacks on America in 2001, the US response overthrew the Taliban and forced al-Qaeda activists to flee. And though since 2001 bin Laden and several other al-Qaeda leaders have been tracked down and killed, the network's groups and activists continue to operate across the world.

Al-Qaeda differs from the tightly knit, militaristic groups of the past, such as the Red Brigades in Italy or the IRA in Northern Ireland. It operates as a global 'network of networks', broadly in line with Castells's ideas of an emerging network society (Sageman 2004; also see chapter 18). But, within this structure, local groups have a high degree of autonomy. For some, this very loose organizational form suggests that what

Memorials to the victims of the November 2015 terrorist attacks at the Bataclan theatre and elsewhere in Paris. These attacks followed a series of terrorist incidents in Paris throughout 2015. Do the resilient responses to such attacks reflect a growing sense that urban terrorism is now 'normal'?

Western scholars and commentators call 'al-Qaeda' is really more of a shared idea or ideology with similarly shared tactics and methods (Burke 2004). The new terrorism also differs in its organizational structures. Kaldor (2006) shows that there are similarities between the infrastructure of new terrorist groups and international non-governmental organizations (NGOs), such as Oxfam or Friends of the Earth. Both new terrorist organizations and NGOs are driven by a sense of mission and commitment that allows a fairly loose global organization to flourish (Glasius et al. 2002).

Sutton and Vertigans (2006) argue that al-Qaeda exhibits many organizational similarities with the new social movements (NSMs) of the 1970s and 1980s. In particular, its loose forms of organization and transnational networks bear comparison with those of non-violent NSMs such as environmentalism and those against globalization. The extreme violence used by al-Qaeda has often been targeted at highly symbolic sites as a way of demonstrating that the West, and the USA in particular, is weak. These attacks also encourage others to join their fight. While NSMs have made use of symbolic, non-violent direct actions, al-Qaeda has used symbolic violence to further its cause.

 See chapter 21, 'Politics, Government and Social Movements', for more on NSMs.

There are other ways in which the new terrorism differs from older forms. One of the distinguishing features of al-Qaeda is that it has a global geopolitical aim – the restructuring of world society. Parts of the leadership seek to reconstruct an Islamic society stretching from the Indian subcontinent into Europe. This would involve establishing Islamic governments throughout the Middle East as well as recapturing North Africa. Al-Qaeda activists argue that, over the last millennium, the West has expelled Islamic groups from those areas to which it has a legitimate claim, such as the Balkans and those parts of Spain previously ruled by the Moors (Muslims originally from North Africa who controlled much of Spain between the eighth and the fifteenth century). Large expanses of what we now regard as Europe were previously Muslim lands, ruled either by the Ottoman Empire or from North Africa. Al-Qaeda aims to re-establish the global role of Islam in these regions and areas.

There is a characteristic tension between modernism and anti-modernism in the worldview of al-Qaeda and similar groups. In attempting to re-establish the Islamic dominance of large parts of Europe, the Middle East and Asia, they make great use of digital media to criticize modernity and adopt violence to reverse what they see as the moral degeneracy of Western societies (Gray 2003). Some groups not only cause mass casualties but seem much more eager to do so than in the past (Crenshaw 2011). Al-Qaeda websites, for example, explicitly say that terrorist acts should be carried out which kill as many people as possible, evident in the founding statement of al-Qaeda from 1998:

> The ruling to kill the Americans and their allies – civilians and military – is an individual duty for every Muslim who can do it in any country in which it is possible to do it, in order to liberate the [Muslim holy sites of the] al-Aqsa Mosque and the Holy Mosque [Mecca] from their grip, and in order for their armies to move out of all the lands of Islam, defeated and unable to threaten any Muslim. (Cited in Halliday 2002: 219)

This is very different from the more limited use of violent means characteristic of old-style terrorism, though there are some cases where the two overlap. This can be seen in Chechnya in the former Soviet Union, for example, where a separatist struggle became a recruiting ground for newer forms of terrorist activity.

THINKING CRITICALLY

Is the emergence of Islamic State, al-Qaeda and the many *jihadist* groups evidence of an impending 'clash of civilizations' (Huntington 1996)? What counter-evidence can you point to which may undermine that thesis? Refer to chapter 17, 'Religion', for Huntington's ideas.

Conclusion

How should the United Nations group of states and international organizations respond to the threat of new-style terrorism and the localized wars? The coalition which attacked Afghanistan in 2001 did destroy some of the al-Qaeda terrorist networks. Yet, despite that success, the terrorist groups they targeted are very different from conventional enemies such as hostile nation-states. This has led some sociologists and political scientists to question the concept of a 'war on terrorism' (Rogers 2008).

The conventional military approach to the 2003 Iraq invasion successfully overthrew Saddam Hussain's regime but later faced new forms of warfare and terrorism: a protracted and bloody post-violence situation and the rise of Islamic State, which took over Falluja, Mosul and other areas and spread into Syria, where it committed terrible atrocities. Intervention (via airstrikes) by the UK in Libya's emerging civil war removed Gaddafi's regime in 2011, but since then the country has seen much factional violence, armed local militias and competing power centres – effectively a second civil war. Will the interventions in Iraq and Syria by developed states bring about a 'positive peace' or is the likelihood yet more internal chaos, division and bloodshed?

The debate about whether terrorism can be tackled through conventional warfare raises further difficult questions regarding the relationship between terrorism and nation-states, such as Afghanistan, that have supported it. In turn, this leads to questions about global governance. In a global age, what international support and proof is needed in order to act to prevent a perceived threat? And what are the best institutions to deal with a global terrorist threat?

Many scholars today argue for a 'cosmopolitan' approach to the problems associated with new wars and terrorism. Cosmopolitan thinkers, like advocates of universal human rights, believe that all individuals should ideally be treated in equal ways, regardless of where they live in the world. Of course, this was considered a utopian dream in an age of strong nation-states which enforced national boundaries against potential threats. However, as the nation-state begins to lose its central place, it becomes possible to see international institutions emerging that may, in time, be able to make the vision of a cosmopolitan democracy a reality.

We can see emerging evidence of this in the involvement of the United Nations, the African Union, the European Union and others in peacekeeping missions, in relief work and as mediators in negotiations between warring parties. Yet these efforts are still in their historically early stages and, so far, have tended to be engaged in only *after* conflicts have started or ended. Making use of such institutions to *prevent* wars and terrorism is a laudable aim, but it is a long way off and remains a project for the long term.

Chapter review

1 What is nationalism and how is it related to the nation and the state? Why is nationalism still a motivating force in the twenty-first century?

2 Provide some examples of 'nations without states' and speculate on their future. Are any of these nations likely to become states in the next thirty years or so?

3 'The idea of universal human rights is nonsense.' Why do some scholars agree with this statement? How can the idea be defended?

4 Clausewitz said that war is 'politics by other means'. Do you agree, or is war simply the outgrowth of the primal human urge to aggression? Which position best accounts for the 'total wars' of the twentieth century?

5 What are 'new wars'? What distinguishes these wars from earlier forms of conflict?

6 What is a 'peace process'? Using examples from the chapter, evaluate Brewer's key concepts for the comparative study of peace processes.

7 What does Elias mean by the 'civilizing process'? Do the 'new wars' suggest we are in a period of 'decivilization'?

8 What distinguishes genocide from war? Is genocide a recent phenomenon or has it always been a tendency in warfare?

9 Define 'terrorism'. Does the definition 'fit' both al-Qaeda's loose networks and the more organized Islamic State group?

10 In what ways does the 'new terrorism' differ from old-style terrorism in its scope, organization, structure and methods?

Research in practice

During the 2015 UK General Election campaign, one Labour Party MP resigned her position as a shadow minister after facing criticism for posting an image on her Twitter account showing a house draped in English flags, with a white van parked on the driveway. Labour faced a strong challenge from the right-wing, Eurosceptic, UK Independence Party (UKIP), and many saw the image as suggesting that working-class people who fly the English flag are more likely to support UKIP's nationalist views. But are they? A similar question was posed by researchers in Australia in relation to flag-flying on Australia Day. Read the following paper and answer the questions below: Fozdar, F., Spittles, B., and Hartley, L. K. (2015) 'Australia Day, Flags on Cars and Australian Nationalism', *Journal of Sociology*, 51(2): 317–36.

1   How was the study conducted? How would you characterize the research?
2   What do the authors mean by 'exclusionary nationalism'?
3   What relationship existed, if any, between flag-flying on cars and Australian nationalism?
4   What did the research find about people's attitudes towards minority ethnic groups and the 'White Australia' policy?
5   What does this study tell us about the flying of national flags in public places? Is this finding specific to Australia or could it be generalized to other nations?

Thinking it through

Will the twenty-first century be as bloody as the twentieth? Are wars between nation-states less likely as people and political leaders learn from the mistakes of the past? Or is this just wishful thinking? Some scholars claim to perceive a global shift in attitudes to war and conflict, which may offer the prospect of a more peaceable future.

One example of this is Ari Sitas's (2011) 'Beyond the Mandela Decade: The Ethic of Reconciliation?', *Current Sociology*, 59(5): 571–89. Read the article and note the *four sources* of an 'emerging ethic of reconciliation' recorded in this piece. Taking each in turn, what evidence is there in this chapter and chapter 21 in favour of Sitas's argument? What evidence is there to suggest that such an ethic may prove ineffectual in the face of hard-nosed national interests, ethnic hatreds and terrorism? What is your conclusion about the supposed emerging ethic of reconciliation?

Society in the arts

Representing terrorism in the arts is a difficult task. Most examples in film, plays and TV are extremely serious, focusing on the threats to security and ordinary lives posed by modern terrorism. Understandably, perhaps, they also tend to represent terrorists as either irrational and fanatical or very clever and capable people. A recent example is *Zero Dark Thirty* (2012, directed by Kathryn Bigelow), the dramatization of the US government's hunt for and eventual killing of Osama bin Laden, leader of al-Qaeda.

However, *Four Lions* (2010, directed by Christopher Morris) goes against this grain. It is a comedy about British *jihadis* whose plan to become suicide bombers turns into farce.

Watch both films and consider the following.

- How are terrorists represented – for example, as intelligent, ordinary, masterminds, psycho/sociopaths, and so on?
- Are the forces of law represented as 'normal' and 'right'?
- Do the terrorists depicted come across as 'terrorists by character' or do the films treat them as people who have become involved in terrorist acts?
- What is the main message of the film in relation to terrorism and the state's actions?
- Which of these very different film genres best 'fits' what social science has to tell us about the phenomenon of terrorism?

Further reading

An excellent entry point into debates on nations and nationalism is Anthony D. Smith's (2010) *Nationalism* (2nd edn, Cambridge: Polity), which is a comprehensive introduction. Claire Sutherland's (2011) *Nationalism in the Twenty-First Century: Challenges and Responses* (Basingstoke: Palgrave Macmillan) is a very good read, covering much ground. Theoretical approaches can then be tackled in Umut Özkirimli's (2010) *Theories of Nationalism: A Critical Introduction* (2nd edn, New York: St Martin's Press). Mark Frezzo's (2014) *The Sociology of Human Rights* (Cambridge: Polity) is one of several excellent introductions to this field.

Sociological research on war is covered in Siniša Malešević's (2010) *The Sociology of War and Violence* (Cambridge: Cambridge University Press), which covers a lot of ground and compares theories of war. Adam Jones's (2010) *Genocide: A Comprehensive Introduction* (2nd edn, London: Routledge) offers exactly what it says. Issues in peace building can then be found in John D. Brewer's (2010) *Peace Processes: A Sociological Approach* (Cambridge: Polity), which is a stimulating read.

For newcomers to sociology, it is best to begin with a general introduction to the phenomenon of terrorism, such as Charles Townshend's (2011) *Terrorism: A Very Short Introduction* (2nd edn, Oxford: Oxford University Press). Then the arguments around types of terrorism can be explored in Peter R. Neumann's (2009) *Old & New Terrorism* (Cambridge: Polity) and Stephen Vertigans's (2011) *The Sociology of Terrorism* (Abingdon: Routledge), which takes a much needed sociological approach to the subject.

For a collection of original readings on political sociology, see the accompanying *Sociology: Introductory Readings* **(3rd edn, Cambridge: Polity, 2010).**

Internet links

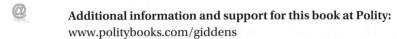

Additional information and support for this book at Polity:
www.politybooks.com/giddens

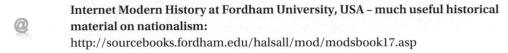

Internet Modern History at Fordham University, USA – much useful historical material on nationalism:
http://sourcebooks.fordham.edu/halsall/mod/modsbook17.asp

@ **The Nationalism Project – a clearing house for scholarly resources on nations and nationalism, including some of the key figures in the field:**
www.nationalismproject.org

@ **Centre for the History of War and Society, University of Sussex – useful materials on the impact of war on societies:**
www.sussex.ac.uk/chws

@ **The Web Genocide Documentation Centre, based at the University of the West of England – archived resources on genocide, war crimes and episodes of mass killing:**
www.phdn.org/archives/www.ess.uwe.ac.uk/genocide

@ **The Peace Research Institute, Oslo – conducts research into peaceful coexistence between states, people and groups:**
www.prio.org

@ **CSTPV – Handa Centre for the Study of Terrorism and Political Violence, University of St Andrews in Scotland – many links here to terror-related websites and its own journal:**
www.st-andrews.ac.uk/~cstpv

@ **GTReC – Global Terrorism Research Centre, based at Monash University, Australia – research studies, projects and other resources here:**
http://artsonline.monash.edu.au/gtrec

Glossary

Absent father A father who, as a result of divorce or for other reasons, has little or no contact with his children.

Absolute poverty Poverty as defined in terms of the minimum requirements necessary to sustain a healthy existence.

Achieved status Social status based on an individual's effort, rather than traits assigned by biological factors. Examples include 'veteran', 'graduate' or 'doctor'.

Affective individualism The belief in romantic attachment as a basis for contracting marriage ties.

Age-grade The system in small-scale cultures in which people belonging to a similar age group are categorized together and have similar rights and obligations.

Ageing The combination of biological, psychological and social processes that affect people as they grow older.

Ageism Discrimination or prejudice against a person on the grounds of age.

Agencies of socialization Social contexts within which processes of socialization take place. The family, peer groups, schools, the media and the workplace are key socializing agencies.

Agrarian societies Societies whose means of subsistence is based on agricultural production (crop-growing).

Alienation The feeling that we are losing control over our own abilities as human beings. Karl Marx saw alienation under capitalism as workers' loss of control over their labour tasks, the products of their labour, other workers and their essential 'species being'.

Al-Qaeda Literally, 'the base' – a global network of terrorist activists whose stated ideology is 'radical Islamist', seeking to install an Islamic caliphate and remove foreign influence from Muslim countries. Founded in Afghanistan in 1988/9, its leader until his assassination in 2011 was Osama bin Laden.

Alter-globalization movements An international or global coalition of groups and protest networks that is opposed to the dominant, neo-liberal, global economy but advocates alternative forms of cooperative globalization under the slogan 'Another world is possible'.

Alternative medicine Numerous therapies which lie outside orthodox biomedical practice and tend to adopt a holistic approach to health and illness.

Animism The belief that events in the world are mobilized by the activities of spirits.

Anomie 'Normlessness' or a lack of social norms. Used by Durkheim to describe desperate feelings of aimlessness and despair provoked by rapid social change, which loosens the hold of existing norms.

Anthropogenic climate change Any significant change in the global climate (mainly global warming) brought about wholly or in part by human activities.

Apartheid The official system of racial segregation established in South Africa between 1948 and 1994.

Applied social research Research which not only aims to understand or explain social problems but also contributes to solving them.

Ascribed status Social status based on biological factors, such as race, sex or age.

Assimilation The acceptance of a minority group by a majority population, in which the former adopts the values and norms of the dominant culture.

Assisted dying An option being sought by campaigners that would allow terminally ill people (who meet certain criteria) to take prescribed life-ending medication.

Asylum-seeker   A person who has applied for refuge in a foreign country because of fear of religious or political persecution in his or her country of origin.

Atavism   In criminology, a nineteenth-century theory that criminals display traits held over from the history of human evolution which accounts for their criminality.

Austerity politics   The framework of discussion or *discourse*, which developed after the 2008 global financial crisis, that focuses on reducing the budget deficits of governments through a mix of public spending cuts and tax increases.

Authoritarian states   Political systems in which the needs and interests of the state take priority over those of citizens and participation in politics is severely limited or denied.

Authority   Following Max Weber, the legitimate power which one person or a group holds over another. Authority depends on the acceptance by subordinates of the right of those above them to give orders or directives.

Automation   Production processes monitored and controlled by machines with only minimal supervision from people.

Back region   An area away from 'front region' performances (such as staff rest rooms in restaurants), where individuals are able to relax and behave in an informal way.

Bias   Generally a preference or an inclination, especially one that inhibits impartial judgement. In statistical sampling or testing, an error caused by systematically favouring some outcomes over others.

Big data analytics   The process of analysing very large datasets to uncover patterns, trends and correlations.

Big Society   The idea, adopted by the British prime minister David Cameron, that an expanded and strengthened civil society generates individual responsibility and community cohesion, enabling less state involvement in society.

Bilateral   'On both sides' – used to describe political negotiations between two parties.

Binuclear families   Family structure in which a child has parents living in two different homes after separating, with both still involved in the child's upbringing.

Biodiversity   The diversity of species of life forms on planet Earth.

Biographical research   Research that takes individual lives or life histories as the main focus. Oral histories, life stories, autobiographies and biographies are examples.

Biomedical model   A set of principles underpinning Western medical systems and practices. Biomedicine defines diseases objectively via the presence of recognized symptoms and treats illness according to scientific principles.

Bisexual   An orientation of sexual activities or feelings towards people of either sex.

Black feminism   A strand of feminist thought highlighting the multiple disadvantages of gender, class and race which shape the experiences of non-white women. Black feminists reject the idea of a single unified gender oppression experienced evenly by all women.

Blended family   A family in which at least one adult has children from a previous relationship. Also commonly called a 'stepfamily' or 'reconstituted family'.

Bureaucracy   Hierarchical organizational forms based on a pyramid of authority. According to Weber, modern bureaucracy is the most efficient type of large-scale human organization and thus is likely to spread.

Capital punishment   State-sanctioned execution of a person who has been convicted of a crime punishable by death; commonly known as the 'death penalty'.

Capitalism   An economic system based on profit-seeking and market exchange. 'Capital' refers to any asset, including money, property and machines, which can be used to produce commodities for sale or invested in a market with the hope of achieving a profit.

Capitalists Those who own the means of production – companies, land, stocks and shares – and use these to generate an economic return.

Caste A form of stratification in which an individual's social position is fixed at birth and cannot be changed. India's caste system has been established for the longest time.

Causal relationship A relationship in which one state of affairs – the effect – is brought about by another – the cause.

Causation The causal influence of one factor on another. Causal factors in sociology include the reasons individuals give for what they do, as well as external influences on their behaviour.

Childhood The early period of a person's life, usually divided into stages (such as infant, child, youth), leading towards adulthood. Childhood is always subject to social construction.

Church A large body of people belonging to an established religious organization. Churches normally have a formal structure with a hierarchy of religious officials.

Cisgender A term denoting people whose gender identity and/or performance corresponds with that which is assigned gender at birth or according to dominant norms of masculinity and femininity.

Citizen A member of a political community, having both rights and duties associated with that membership.

City In modern times, the largest form of human settlement. In sociological theory, 'a sociological entity that is formed spatially', characterized by loose social bonds and the rational, matter-of-fact attitudes of its inhabitants.

Civil inattention The process whereby individuals in the same physical setting demonstrate to one another that they are aware of one another's presence, without being threatening or overly friendly.

Civil partnership A legally sanctioned relationship between two people of the same sex; it gives same-sex couples legal recognition as well as some or all of the rights of married couples.

Civil society The realm of activity between the state and the market, including family, schools, community associations and non-economic institutions.

Civilizing process A theory of social change in the work of Norbert Elias, linking the formation of European nation-states with the pacification of society, changes in the internalized emotional controls of individuals and social codes of manners.

Class For Marx, a group of people standing in a common relationship to the means of production as owners or non-owners. Weber saw class as an economic category but stressed its interaction with social status and the affinities of 'party' affiliation. More recent definitions stress occupation, the ownership of property and wealth or lifestyles.

Class consciousness The process through which the working classes in capitalist societies would become aware of their subordinate and exploited class position. In Marxist theory, this is a necessary step towards revolution.

Clock time Time as measured by the clock – that is, assessed in hours, minutes and seconds – rather than as measured by the rising and setting of the sun.

Cloud computing The practice of using a service over the Internet, via remote datacentres which store, manage and process data, rather than an individual device.

Cognition Human thought processes involving perception, reasoning and remembering.

Cohabitation Two people living together in a sexual relationship of some permanence without being married to each other.

Cohort A group of people sharing common experiences within a certain period of time, usually in 'birth cohorts' – people born in the same year or few years.

Cold War The conflictual relationship between the USA and the Soviet Union, together with their allies, from the late

1940s until 1990. The period was known as the 'Cold War' because the two sides never engaged in direct military confrontation with each other.

Collective behaviour   Group activities that normally emerge spontaneously, such as crowds, riots, crazes and panics.

Collective consumption   A concept used by Manuel Castells, referring to the consumption of common goods promoted by the city, such as transport services and leisure amenities.

Collective effervescence   The sense of heightened energy created in collective gatherings and rituals, used by Durkheim to explain the religious experience as essentially social.

Colonialism   The process through which Western nations established their rule in parts of the world far away from their home territories.

Communication   The transmission of information from one individual or group to another, including face-to-face conversation, the use of language and bodily cues, and print and electronic media such as Internet chatrooms and smartphones.

Communism   Theoretically, a society characterized by communal ownership of the means of production and distribution. Usually associated with Karl Marx and used to describe the former Soviet Union and much of Eastern Europe.

Comparative questions   Questions concerned with drawing comparisons between one context in a society and another, or contrasting examples from different societies, for the purposes of sociological theory or research.

Comparative research   Research that compares a set of findings about one society with the same type of findings about other societies.

Complicit masculinity   R. W. Connell's term for a type of masculinity embodied by many men who do not live up to the ideal of 'hegemonic masculinity', yet benefit from its dominant position in the gender order.

Compulsion to proximity   A need felt by individuals to interact with others in face-to-face settings rather than at a distance.

Concrete operational stage   A stage of cognitive development in Piaget's theory, in which the child's thinking is based primarily on physical perception of the world rather than abstract concepts or hypothetical situations.

Conflict theories   Sociological theories which focus on the tensions, divisions and competing interests that are present in all human societies as groups struggle to gain access to and control scarce resources.

Confluent love   Active and contingent forms of love, as opposed to the 'forever' qualities of romantic love.

Consumer society   A type of society which promotes the consumption of mass-produced products, partly through the ideology of consumerism, which suggests that increasing mass consumption is beneficial for all.

Control theory   A theory which sees crime as the outcome of an imbalance between impulses towards criminal activity and the controls which deter it. Criminals are seen as rational beings who maximize rewards unless rendered unable to do so through social or physical controls.

Controls   A statistical or experimental means of holding some variables constant in order to examine the causal influence of other variables.

Conurbation   A clustering of towns or cities in an unbroken urban environment.

Convenience sampling   The arbitrary selection of respondents for a study, based on simple opportunity rather than a rigorous quest for representativeness; used to study hard-to-reach social groups.

Conversation analysis   The empirical study of conversations, employing techniques drawn from ethnomethodology. Conversation analysis tries to uncover the organizational principles of talk and its role in the social order.

Core countries   According to world-systems theory, the most advanced industrial countries, which take the lion's share of profits from the world economic system.

Corporate crime Offences and major harm committed by large corporations in society, including pollution, false advertising and violations of health and safety regulations.

Corporate culture A branch of management theory that seeks to increase productivity and competitiveness through the creation of a unique organizational culture involving all members of a firm.

Corporate social responsibility The responsibility of companies to engage in social and environmental practices that go beyond basic legal requirements and aim to meet the expectations of consumers and the public.

Corporation A type of organization that is a legal entity in its own right and has both rights and responsibilities. Business corporations are created by groups of shareholders who own the corporation and organize its effective management.

Correlation A regular relationship between two dimensions or variables, often expressed in statistical terms. Correlations may be positive or negative. A positive correlation exists where a high rank on one variable is regularly associated with a high rank on the other. A negative correlation exists where a high rank on one variable is regularly associated with a low rank on the other.

Correlation coefficient A measure of the degree of correlation between two variables.

Cosmopolitanism A concept describing the shift beyond nation-state-based thinking towards analysing the human world as a single community.

Created environment Those aspects of the physical world deriving from the application of technology, such as cities and towns involving roads, railways, factories, offices, private homes and other buildings.

Credit crunch A term coined in 2008 to describe the severe shortage of credit availability and money in the global economy as a result of unprecedented mortgage defaults in the USA and elsewhere.

Crime Any action that contravenes the laws established by a political authority.

Criminalization The processes through which certain individuals, groups or behaviour become categorized as criminal and therefore subject to legal sanctions.

Criminology The study of forms of behaviour that are sanctioned by criminal law and justice systems.

Crisis of masculinity The idea that traditional forms of masculinity are being undermined and that young men are unsure of themselves and their role in society.

Critical race theory (CRT) A perspective on ethnic relations which begins from the premise that racism is embedded in legal systems and other social institutions and is the normal, everyday experience of many minority ethnic groups.

Critical realism An approach to science which insists on the existence of an objective external reality that is amenable to investigation (contrast with social constructionism). Critical realists look to uncover the underlying causes of observable events, which are not usually directly observable.

Crude birth rate A basic statistical measure representing the number of births within a given population per year, normally calculated in terms of the number of births per 1,000 members.

Crude death rate A statistical measure representing the number of deaths that occur annually in a given population per year, normally calculated as the ratio of deaths per 1,000 members.

Cult A fragmentary religious grouping to which individuals are loosely affiliated but which lacks any permanent structure. Cults quite often form round an inspirational leader.

Cultural capital Types of knowledge, skills and education which confer advantages on those who acquire them. Cultural capital can be embodied (in forms of speech or bodily comportment), objectified (in cultural products such as works of art) or institutionalized (in educational qualifications).

Cultural pluralism   The coexistence of numerous cultures within a given society.

Cultural reproduction   The transmission of cultural values and norms from generation to generation. Cultural reproduction refers to the mechanisms by which continuity of cultural experience is sustained across time.

Culture   The values, norms, habits and ways of life characteristic of a coherent social group.

Culture of poverty   The thesis that poverty is not the result of individual inadequacies but the outcome of being socialized into a wider culture that transmits values, beliefs, lifestyles, habits and traditions common among people in conditions of material deprivation.

Cyberbullying   The targeting, harassment and threatening of people via digital technologies, including social media, chatrooms, email and text messaging.

Cybercrime   Criminal activities conducted through electronic networks or involving the use of new information technologies. Electronic money laundering, personal identity theft and electronic hacking are types of cybercrime.

Cyberspace   Electronic networks of interaction between individuals at different computer terminals, linking people in a dimension that crosses space and territorial boundaries.

De-bureaucratization   Decline in the predominance of Weberian-style bureaucracies as the typical organizational form within modern society.

Decommodification   In the context of welfare provision, the degree to which welfare services are free of market principles. In a commodified system, welfare services are treated as commodities to be sold on the market.

Deforestation   The destruction of forested land, often by commercial logging.

Degree of dispersal   The range or distribution of a set of figures.

Deinstitutionalization   The process by which individuals cared for in state facilities are returned to their families or to community-based residences.

Democracy   A political system providing for the participation of citizens in political decision-making, often by the election of representatives to governing bodies.

Demographic transition   An interpretation of long-term population change, which suggests a series of stages in the ratio of births to deaths, culminating in population stability once a certain level of economic prosperity has been reached.

Demography   The study of the characteristics of human populations, including their size, composition and dynamics.

Denomination   A religious sect which has lost its revivalist dynamism and has become an institutionalized body commanding the adherence of significant numbers of people.

Dependency culture   A term popularized by Charles Murray to describe the way that reliance on welfare benefits undermines individuals' capacity to forge a living through their own efforts.

Dependency ratio   The ratio of people of dependent ages (children and the elderly) to people of economically active ages.

Dependency theory   Theory of economic development, derived from Marxism, arguing that the poverty of low-income countries stems directly from their exploitation by wealthy countries and the transnational corporations that are based in the latter.

Dependent variable   A variable, or factor, causally influenced by another (the independent variable).

Desertification   Instances of intense land degradation resulting in desert-like conditions over large areas.

Deskilling   The process through which the skills of workers are downgraded or, over time, eliminated and taken over by machines and/or managers.

Developed countries Those high-income countries that have undergone a process of industrialization and have relatively high GDP per capita and high living standards.

Developing countries Those low-income countries which have relatively low GDP per capita and have not yet industrialized as fully as the developed societies.

Developmental questions Questions posed by sociologists trying to understand the origins and paths of development of social institutions from the past to the present.

Deviance Actions which do not conform to the norms or values held by most of the members of a group or society. What is regarded as 'deviant' varies widely across societies.

Deviancy amplification The consequence when an agency of control unintentionally provokes more (amplifies) deviant behaviour.

Deviant subculture A subculture whose members have values which differ substantially from those of the majority in a society.

Diaspora The dispersal of an ethnic population from an original homeland into foreign areas, often in a forced manner or under traumatic circumstances.

Differential racialization The history and experience of different ethnic groups in relation to the stereotypes and characterizations of them deployed at various times by the dominant groups in societies.

Direct action A form of political action, associated with new social movements, in which activists protest at the actual site of the issue at hand – for instance, climate change activists clamping themselves to aircraft on runways rather than lobbying MPs.

Disability studies A field of inquiry that investigates the position of disabled people in society, including their experiences, their history and campaigns, and their organizations.

Discourse analysis A general term covering several approaches to the study of the impact of language in society. Most sociological versions aim to understand language use within specific social and historical contexts.

Discourses The frameworks of thinking in a particular area of social life. For instance, the discourse of criminality refers to dominant ways of thinking about and discussing crime.

Discrimination Actions which deny to the members of a particular group the resources or rewards that are available to the majority.

Disengagement theory A functionalist theory of ageing which holds that it is functional for society to remove people from their traditional roles when they become elderly, thereby freeing up those roles for others.

Displacement The transferring of ideas or emotions from their true source to another object.

Division of labour The division of a production or economic system into specialized work tasks or occupations, creating economic interdependence.

Doubling time The time it takes for a particular level of population to double.

Dramaturgical analysis Goffman's approach to the study of social interaction, based on the use of metaphors derived from the theatre.

Dualism Literally, the condition of being divided into two parts. In sociological theorizing, dualisms include mind and body, individual and society, structure and agency, micro and macro.

Dysfunction Features of social life that challenge or create tensions in a social system.

Eco-efficiency The development of technologies that generate economic growth, but which do so at minimal cost to the natural environment.

Ecological citizenship A relatively recent extension of citizenship to include the rights and responsibilities of people towards the natural environment or 'nature'.

Ecological modernization Economic development that also incorporates environmental protection. Advocates of ecological modernization argue that economic growth and ecological protection are not incompatible.

Economic capital In Pierre Bourdieu's work, resources such as money, property or land that form part of a system of material exchange.

Economic interdependence The outcome of specialization and the division of labour, when people come to depend on one another for the things they need to sustain their lives.

Economic recession Typically, the decline of economic activity – often measured in GDP – for two or more consecutive months.

Economic sociology The study of economic phenomena, including markets, corporations, finance and work, using sociological theories and concepts.

Economy The system of production and exchange which provides for the material needs of individuals living in a given society. Economic systems differ markedly; capitalism has become the most dynamic and widely adopted system in the contemporary world.

Education A social institution which promotes and enables the transmission of knowledge and skills across generations.

Egocentric Egocentric thinking involves understanding objects and events in the environment solely in terms of a very young child's own position.

Elaborated code A form of speech, typical of the middle classes, involving the deliberate and constructed use of words to designate precise meanings, that is adaptable to various cultural settings.

Elite A small, more or less cohesive social group that rules over the majority of people in a society.

Embodiment In sociology, the notion that self-experience and identity are bounded by individual bodies which express and partly shape self-identities.

Embourgeoisement thesis The process through which middle-class aspirations

and styles of life become institutionalized within the working class.

Emigration The movement of people out of one country in order to settle in another.

Emotional intelligence The ability of individuals to use their emotions to develop qualities such as empathy, self-control, enthusiasm and persistence.

Emphasized femininity In R. W. Connell's writings, emphasized femininity is an important complement to hegemonic masculinity, because it is oriented to accommodating the interests and needs of men. Many representations of women in the media embody emphasized femininity.

Empirical investigation Factual inquiry carried out in any given area of sociological study.

Encounter A meeting between two or more individuals in a situation of face-to-face interaction. In modern societies, many encounters involve strangers rather than friends and family.

Endogamy The forbidding of marriage or sexual relations outside one's social group.

Endogenous In sociology, things which develop or originate within the society being studied rather than being introduced from outside (exogenous).

Entrepreneur Someone who starts or owns a business venture and takes personal responsibility for the risks involved and the potential rewards gained.

Environment The non-human, natural world within which human societies exist. In its broadest sense, the environment is the planet Earth.

Environmental criminology An approach to crime reduction and prevention focusing on designing crime-resistant environments rather than trying to reform criminals.

Environmental issues All of those issues in society which involve both social relations and non-human, natural phenomena – that is, they are hybrids of society and nature.

Environmental justice The idea that all people have the right to a healthy and sustainable environment. Campaigns have focused on removing the disproportionate environmental risks borne by poor communities.

Epidemic The occurrence of an infectious disease which spreads rapidly throughout a particular community.

Epidemiology The study of the distribution and incidence of disease and illness within a population.

Essentialism The assumption that human behaviour and/or social phenomena can be explained with reference to a fixed 'human nature' or some other immutable and universal biological element(s).

Estate A form of stratification involving inequalities between groups of individuals established by law.

Ethical religions Religions which depend on the ethical appeal of a 'great teacher' (such as Buddha or Confucius) rather than on a belief in supernatural beings.

Ethnic cleansing The creation of ethnically homogeneous territories through the mass expulsion of other ethnic populations.

Ethnicity A form of social identity related to 'descent and cultural differences' which become effective or active in certain social contexts.

Ethnie A term used by Anthony Smith to describe a group that shares ideas of common ancestry, a common cultural identity and a link with a specific homeland.

Ethnocentric transnational An international corporation, based in the country of origin, whose practices around the world are cultural extensions of the original company.

Ethnocentrism Understanding the ideas or practices of another culture in terms of one's own. Ethnocentrism judges other cultures negatively in comparison with the host culture.

Ethnography The study of people at first hand using participant observation or interviewing.

Ethnomethodology The study of how people make sense of what others say and do in the course of day-to-day social interaction. Ethnomethodology is concerned with the 'ethnomethods' by means of which human beings sustain meaningful interchanges with one another.

Eugenics Attempts to improve the fitness of the human race through selective reproduction methods.

Euthanasia The intentional ending of a person's life in order to relieve extreme suffering.

Evangelicalism A form of Protestantism characterized by a belief in spiritual rebirth (being 'born again').

Experiment A research method in which a hypothesis can be tested in a controlled and systematic way, either in an artificial situation constructed by the researcher or in naturally occurring settings.

Exploitation A social or institutional relationship in which one party benefits at the expense of the other through an imbalance in power.

Extended family A family group consisting of more than two generations of close relatives living in the same household or in close and continuous relationships with one another.

External risk Hazards that spring from the natural world and are unrelated to the actions of humans, such as droughts, earthquakes, famines and storms.

Factual questions Questions that raise issues concerning matters of fact rather than theoretical or moral issues.

Family A group of individuals related to one another by blood ties, marriage or adoption that form a unit, the adult members of which are responsible for the upbringing of children.

Family capitalism Capitalistic enterprise owned and administered by entrepreneurial families.

Family displays All of the ways by which people demonstrate to others that they are engaged in appropriate 'family' practices and relationships.

Family practices All of those activities engaged in by people which they perceive to be related to family life.

Fecundity A measure of the number of children that it is biologically possible for a woman to produce.

Feminist theories Those theories which emphasize the centrality of gender for any analysis of the social world. All strands of feminist theory share the desire to explain gender inequalities in society and to work to overcome them.

Fertility The average number of live-born children produced by women of child-bearing age in a particular society.

Field In Pierre Bourdieu's work, the social contexts within which people struggle for competitive advantage and dominance using various forms of capital. Each field has its own set of rules: for instance, art and art appreciation has a very different set of rules to that of business.

Figurational sociology A theoretical perspective, stemming from the work of Norbert Elias, which dispenses with philosophical forms of thinking, insisting that sociology is a distinct subject that studies people and the interdependent relations they form with one another.

Figurations In figurational sociology, the social patterns formed by the interweaving of people who are inevitably in relations of interdependence with one another.

Flexible production Process in which computers design customized products for a mass market.

Focus group A small group of people, selected from a larger sample, to take part in a discussion on topics of interest to the researcher.

Focused interaction Interaction between individuals engaged in a common activity or a direct conversation with one another.

Fordism The system of production and consumption pioneered by Henry Ford, involving the introduction of the moving assembly line, linking methods of mass production to the cultivation of a mass market for the goods produced, such as Ford's Model T car.

Formal operational stage According to Piaget, a stage of cognitive development at which the growing child becomes capable of handling abstract concepts and hypothetical situations.

Formal relations Relations which exist in groups and organizations laid down by the norms or rules of the 'official' system of authority.

Front region A setting of social activity in which individuals seek to put on a definite 'performance' for others.

Functionalism A theoretical perspective based on the idea that social institutions can best be explained in terms of the functions they perform – that is, the contributions they make to the continuity of a society.

Fundamentalism A religious belief in returning to the literal meanings of scriptural texts; also used to describe movements based on this belief.

Gender Social expectations about behaviour regarded as appropriate for the members of each sex, conventionally as masculine or feminine.

Gender inequality The differences in the status, power and prestige that women and men have in groups, collectivities and societies.

Gender order A term associated with the writings of R. W. Connell to represent the structured power relations between masculinities and femininities that exist in society.

Gender regime The configuration of gender relations within a particular setting, such as a school, a family or a neighbourhood.

Gender relations The societally patterned interactions between men and women.

Gender roles Social roles assigned to each sex and labelled as masculine or feminine.

Gender socialization The processes through which individuals develop different gender characteristics in the course of socialization.

Generalized other In the work of George Herbert Mead, when the individual takes over the general values of a given group or society during the socialization process.

Generation The whole group of individuals who are born and are living at the same time. Generations are born into and their experience is shaped by a particular society.

Genetically modified organisms Plants or crops that have been produced through manipulation of the genes that compose them.

Genocide The systematic, planned attempt to destroy a racial, political or cultural group.

Genre In media studies, a distinct type of media product or cultural item – for example, in television: soap opera, comedy, news programmes, sport and drama.

Gentrification A process of urban renewal in which older, decaying housing is refurbished by affluent people moving into the area.

Geocentric transnationals Transnational corporations characterized by an international management structure across numerous countries.

Global city A city, such as London, New York or Tokyo, which has become an organizing centre of the new global economy.

Global commodity chains A worldwide network of labour and production processes yielding a finished product.

Global economic inequality Inequalities of income and material standards of life between the nation-states of the world. Many studies of global economic inequality concentrate on the differences between the developed and the developing countries.

Global governance The framework of rules and norms governing international affairs and the diverse set of institutions needed to guarantee this framework.

Global village An idea associated with Marshall McLuhan, who saw the spread of electronic communication (such as TV and the Internet) as binding the world into a coherent single community.

Global warming The gradual increase in average temperature at the surface of the Earth. Although the 'greenhouse effect' occurs naturally, global warming implies an enhanced greenhouse effect resulting from human activity.

Globalization Growing interdependence between different peoples, regions and countries as social and economic relationships come to stretch worldwide.

Glocalization The mix of globalizing processes and local contexts which often leads to a strengthening rather than diminishing of local and regional cultures.

Government We can speak of 'government' as a process or of 'the government' to refer to political authorities overseeing the implementation of their policies by officials. In most modern societies, political authorities are elected and their officials appointed on the basis of expertise and qualifications.

Grand theories Theories which attempt to arrive at an overall explanation of social life and/or overall social development. Karl Marx's theory of class conflicts as the driving force of history is the best example.

Greenhouse effect The build-up of heat-trapping gases within the Earth's atmosphere. A 'natural' greenhouse effect keeps the Earth's temperatures at a comfortable level, but the build-up of high concentrations of greenhouse gases through human activities has been linked to rapid global warming.

Greying A term used to indicate that an increasing proportion of a society's population is becoming elderly.

Gross domestic product (GDP) All the goods and services produced by a country's economy in a particular year.

Gross national income (GNI) GDP plus net property income (interest, rent, dividends and profits) from abroad. GNI is now used in preference to GNP – gross national product – which is an older measure.

Group closure The means whereby a group establishes a clear boundary for itself and thereby separates itself from other groups.

Group production Production organized by means of small groups rather than individuals.

Habitus In Pierre Bourdieu's work, the set of dispositions (including ways of thinking and acting) which members of particular social groups and social classes acquire, largely unconsciously, by virtue of living in similar objective conditions.

Hate crimes Criminal acts (such as assaults) targeting members of a specific social group purely because of that membership. Hate crimes include attacks on members of religious or ethnic groups, gay men and lesbians, disabled people and others.

Health technologies Material (such as prosthetic limbs and ultrasound scanning) and social (such as fasting and dieting) interventions aimed at achieving a state of socially defined 'good health'.

Health transition The shift from predominantly acute, infectious diseases to chronic non-infectious diseases as the main cause of death in a society.

Hegemonic masculinity In R. W. Connell's work, the dominant form of masculinity within the gender hierarchy. In most Western societies today, hegemonic masculinity is associated with whiteness, heterosexuality, marriage, authority and physical toughness.

Heteronormativity The dominant assumption and set of attitudes in a society that there are two genders (male and female) and that heterosexuality is the 'natural' norm.

Heterosexuality An orientation in sexual activity or feelings towards people of the opposite sex.

Hidden curriculum Traits of behaviour or attitudes that are learned at school, but not through a formal curriculum. The hidden curriculum is the 'unstated agenda' conveying, for example, aspects of gender differences.

Higher education Education beyond school level, in colleges or universities.

High-trust systems Organizations or work settings in which individuals are permitted a great deal of autonomy and control over the work task.

Homeless people Those who have no permanent residence and sleep over with friends and family, are temporarily housed by the state, or sleep in free shelters or public places. A small proportion of the homeless are 'rough sleepers'.

Homophobia An irrational fear or hatred of homosexuals.

Homosexual masculinity According to Connell, forms of masculinity associated with gay men which are stigmatized and located at the bottom of the gender hierarchy for men.

Homosexuality The orientation of sexual activities or feelings towards others of the same sex.

Household All of the people occupying and residing in a housing unit, sharing common living rooms and making common provision for the essentials such as food.

Housework Unpaid work carried out, usually by women, in the home: domestic chores such as cooking, cleaning and shopping.

Human trafficking The forced movement of people across national borders or within countries for the purposes of sexual exploitation, labour, begging, adoption or delinquency. Most trafficked people are women, young adults and children.

Hunting and gathering societies Societies whose mode of subsistence is gained from hunting animals, fishing, and gathering edible plants.

Hyperreality The 'more real than real', hyperreality results from the spread of electronic communications, as there is no longer a separate 'reality' to which representations refer.

Hypothesis An idea, or an educated guess, about a given state of affairs, put forward in exact terms to provide the basis for empirical testing.

Hypothetico-deductive method   A model of scientific practice which posits that science begins with a general hypothesis or theory about the world from which specific, testable hypotheses can be deduced and tested against observable evidence.

Iatrogenesis   'Physician-caused illness'. Ivan Illich saw clinical, social and cultural forms. Clinical iatrogenesis is when people become ill as a consequence of medical treatment. Social and cultural iatrogenesis occur as medicine becomes powerful and dominant, deskilling ordinary people, who become dependent on medical professionals.

Ideal type   A 'pure type', constructed by emphasizing certain traits of a given social phenomenon into an analytical model which does not necessarily exist anywhere in reality. An example is Max Weber's model of bureaucratic organization.

Identity   The distinctive aspects of a person's character which relate to who they are and what is meaningful to them. The main sources are gender, sexual orientation, nationality or ethnicity, and social class.

Ideology   Shared ideas or beliefs which serve to justify the interests of dominant groups.

Immigration   The movement of people into one country from another for the purpose of settlement.

Impression management   People's attempt to 'manage' or control the impressions others have of them by choosing what to conceal and what to reveal.

Incest   Sexual activity between close family members.

Independent variable   A variable, or factor, that causally influences another (the dependent variable).

Individual model of disability   A model which holds that individual limitations are the main cause of the problems experienced by disabled people: bodily 'abnormality' is seen as causing some degree of 'disability' or functional limitation.

Induction   A model of scientific practice which posits that scientists gather evidence from which patterns may be observed. General theories may follow which provide explanations for the observations and patterns.

Industrial Revolution   The broad spectrum of social, economic and technological transformations that surrounded the development of modern forms of industry in the mid-eighteenth and the early twentieth century.

Industrial societies   Societies in which the vast majority of the labour force works in industrial production or associated employment sectors.

Industrialization   The replacement of human and animal labour with machines, beginning with the development of modern forms of industry in factories, machines and large-scale production processes.

Infant mortality rate   The number of infants who die during the first year of life, per 1,000 live births.

Informal economy   Economic transactions carried on outside the sphere of orthodox paid employment.

Informal relations   Relations which exist in groups and organizations on the basis of personal connections; ways of doing things that depart from formal procedures.

Informalization   The social process through which formal codes of manners and behaviour, characteristic of an earlier period, lose their hold, resulting in a wider range of acceptable behaviours.

Information poverty   The 'information poor' consist of those who have little or no access to information technology, such as computers.

Information society   A society no longer based primarily on the production of material goods but on the production of knowledge; closely bound up with the rise of information technology.

Information technology Forms of technology based on information processing and requiring microelectronic circuitry.

Institutional capitalism Capitalistic enterprise organized on the basis of institutional shareholding.

Institutional racism The collective failure of organizations to provide services to people because of their colour, culture or ethnic origin. This can involve processes, attitudes and behaviour and can intentionally or unwittingly generate prejudice, ignorance, thoughtlessness and racist stereotyping which disadvantages minority ethnic people.

Intelligence Level of intellectual ability, particularly as measured by IQ (intelligence quotient) tests.

Interactional vandalism The deliberate subversion of the tacit rules of conversation.

Intergenerational mobility Movement up or down a social stratification hierarchy from one generation to another.

International governmental organization (IGO) An international organization established by treaties between governments for the purpose of conducting business between the nations making up its membership.

International non-governmental organization (INGO) An international organization established by agreements between the individuals or private organizations making up its membership.

Internet A global system of connections between computers allowing people to communicate with one another and find information on the worldwide web by visuals, sounds and text.

Internet-based learning Educational activity connected through the medium of the Internet.

Interpretative sociology Several approaches to the study of society, including symbolic interactionism and phenomenology, which investigate the meaningful character of social life for its participants.

Intersectionality The study of multiple oppressions and their impact. For instance, where class and ethnicity or gender and class overlap, people may face deeper and more complex forms of inequality.

Interviews One-to-one conversations aimed at eliciting information about some aspect of social life. Interviews can be structured, semi-structured or open-ended depending on the kind of information being sought.

Intragenerational mobility Movement up or down a social stratification hierarchy within the course of an individual career.

IQ Short for 'intelligence quotient', a score attained on tests consisting of a mixture of conceptual and computational problems.

Iron law of oligarchy A term coined by Robert Michels, meaning that large organizations always centralize power in the hands of a small minority.

Job insecurity A sense of apprehension experienced by employees about both the stability of their work position and their role within the workplace.

Kinship Relationships which link individuals through blood ties, marriage or adoption. Kinship relations are involved in marriage and the family but extend much more broadly.

Knowledge economy A society no longer based primarily on the production of material goods but on the production of knowledge in universities and research facilities, which is applied to production.

Knowledge society Another common term for the information society – a society based on the production and consumption of knowledge and information.

Kuznets Curve A formula, advanced by the economist Simon Kuznets, showing that inequality increases during the early stages of industrial capitalism, then declines, and eventually stabilizes at a relatively low level.

Labelling theory An approach to the study of deviance which suggests that people become 'deviant' in part through the application of labels by others.

Latent functions Functional consequences that are not intended or recognized by the members of a social system in which they occur.

Lateral mobility Movement of individuals from one region of a country to another, or across countries.

Left Realism A strain of criminology, popularized in the 1980s by the work of Lea and Young, that focused on the victims of crime and called for socialist criminology to engage with issues of crime control and social policy.

Legitimacy The acceptance by those being governed that a given situation is just and valid.

Lesbianism Homosexual activities or attachment between women.

Liberal democracy A system of democracy based on parliamentary institutions, coupled to the free market system in the area of economic production.

Liberal feminism A type of feminist theory that sees gender inequality as the product of reduced access for women and girls to equal rights. Liberal feminists seek solutions through legislative change.

Life course The various transitions people experience over their lives. Such transitions vary widely across history and cultures, thus the life course is socially as well as biologically shaped (contrast with life cycle).

Life cycle The common-sense view that all human beings pass through the same biological stages from birth to death (contrast with life course).

Life expectancy The length of time, on average, that people can expect to live. Specifically, the number of years a newborn infant can be expected to live if prevailing patterns of mortality stay the same throughout life.

Life histories Studies of the overall lives of individuals, often based both on self-reporting and documents such as letters or diaries.

Life span The maximum length of life that is biologically possible for a member of a given species.

Lifelong learning The idea that learning and the acquisition of skills should occur at all stages of an individual's life, not simply in the compulsory, formal educational system. Adult continuing education programmes, mid-career training, Internet-based learning opportunities, and community-based 'learning banks' are all forms of lifelong learning.

Lifestyle choices Decisions made by individuals about their consumption of goods, services and culture; these are seen by many sociologists as important reflections of class positions.

Lifeworld The everyday world of routine, lived experience. A concept devised by Alfred Schutz, it forms the basic subject matter of phenomenological sociology.

Literacy The ability to read and write.

Logical positivism A philosophy of science which focuses on deductive reasoning and empirical verification and adopts a correspondence theory of truth which demands that scientific statements are 'true' only if they correspond exactly with real-world phenomena.

Low-trust system An organizational or work setting in which individuals are allowed little responsibility for, or control over, the work task.

Macrosociology The study of large-scale groups, organizations or social systems.

Majority/minority worlds Umbrella terms to describe collectively the societies of the global South, which constitute the majority of the world's population, and those of the global North, which form the minority; an alternative conceptualization of the commonly used 'developed' and 'developing' countries.

Male breadwinner Until recently, in many developed societies the traditional role of the man in providing for the whole family through employment outside the home. The 'male breadwinner model' has declined in significance with the steady growth in the number of women entering the labour market.

Male inexpressiveness The difficulties men have in expressing, or talking about, their feelings to others.

Malestream sociology Most of the sociological theories and research before the feminist interventions of the 1960s and later, which paid scant regard to women or issues of gender relations.

Malthusianism The idea, first advanced by Thomas Malthus in 1798, that population growth tends to outstrip the resources available to support it. Malthus argued that people must limit their frequency of sexual intercourse to avoid a future of misery and starvation.

Managerial capitalism Capitalistic enterprises administered by managerial executives rather than by owners.

Manifest functions The functions of a type of social activity that are known to and intended by the individuals involved in the activity.

Manufactured risk Dangers created by the impact of human knowledge and technology on the natural world. Examples include global warming and genetically modified foods.

Market-oriented theories Theories about economic development which assume the best possible economic consequences will result if individuals are free to make their own economic decisions, uninhibited by governmental constraint.

Marriage A socially approved sexual relationship between two individuals. Marriage has been restricted to people of opposite sexes, but in some cultures certain types of homosexual marriage are allowed. Recently, many developed societies have moved towards the acceptance of gay marriage.

Mass customization The large-scale production of items designed for particular customers through the use of new technologies.

Mass media Forms of large-scale communication, such as newspapers, magazines, radio and television, designed to reach mass audiences.

Mass production The production of long runs of goods using machine power. Mass production was one outcome of the Industrial Revolution.

Master status The status or statuses that generally take priority over other indicators of social standing and determine a person's overall position in society.

Materialist conception of history The view developed by Marx according to which 'material' or economic factors have a prime role in determining historical change.

Maternal deprivation The absence of a stable and affectionate relationship between a child and its mother early in life. John Bowlby argued that this can lead to mental illness or deviant behaviour later in life.

Matrilineal Relating to, based on, or tracing ancestral descent through the maternal line.

Matrilocal Family systems in which the husband is expected to live near the wife's parents.

Mature adulthood In modern societies, the period of individual lives between the late thirties and retirement age, typically characterized by formal employment and the formation of a family.

Mean A statistical measure of central tendency, or average, based on dividing a total by the number of individual cases.

Means of production The means whereby the production of material goods is carried on in a society, including not just technology but the social relations between producers.

Means-tested benefits Welfare services that are available only to citizens who meet certain criteria based not only on need but also on levels of income and savings.

Measures of central tendency These are ways of calculating averages, the three most common being the mean, the median and the mode.

Mechanical solidarity According to Durkheim, an early form of social solidarity characterized by similarities and the subsumption of individualism within the collectivity.

Media convergence   The increasing intertwining of previously separate and distinct forms of media.

Media imperialism   A version of imperialism enabled by communications technology, claimed by some to have produced a cultural empire in which media content originating in the industrialized countries is imposed on less developed nations which lack the resources to maintain their cultural independence.

Media regulation   The use of legal means to control media ownership and the content of media communications.

Median   The number that falls halfway in a range of numbers – a way of calculating central tendency that is sometimes more useful than calculating a mean.

Medical gaze   In modern medicine, the detached and value-free approach taken by medical specialists in viewing and treating a sick patient.

Medicalization   The process through which 'normal' behaviours, such as hyperactivity in children, come to be defined and treated as medical conditions.

Megacities   A term favoured by Manuel Castells to describe large, intensely concentrated urban spaces that serve as connection points for the global economy.

Megalopolis   A term meaning 'city of all cities', coined in ancient Greece to refer to a city-state that was planned to be the envy of all civilizations. Used in modern times to refer to very large – or overlarge – conurbations.

Melting pot   A model of migration based on the idea that ethnic differences can be combined to create new patterns with flourishing, diverse cultural sources.

Meritocracy   A system in which social positions are filled on the basis of individual merit and achievement, rather than on ascribed criteria such as inherited wealth or social background.

Meso level   A level of social reality between the micro and the macro. Often said to include families, groups and organizations.

Metanarratives   Broad, overarching theories or beliefs about the operation of society and the nature of social change.

Microsociology   The study of human behaviour in contexts of face-to-face interaction.

Middle class   A broad spectrum of people working in professional, managerial and administrative occupations with associated norms, values and lifestyles.

Minority ethnic group   A group of people who, because of their physical or cultural characteristics, find themselves in situations of discrimination or inequality. Minority ethnic groups are not necessarily in a numerical minority.

Mixed methods   The use of both quantitative and qualitative research methods as part of a single research study.

Mobilities   A sociological perspective that analyses the movement of things, people and information rather than focusing on relations between static, national societies.

Mode   The number that appears most often in a given set of data. This can sometimes be a helpful way of portraying central tendency.

Mode of production   Within Marxism, the constitutive characteristic of a society based on the socio-economic system predominant within it – for example, capitalism, feudalism or socialism.

Modern slavery   All forms of slavery-like practices that are common in the contemporary world, including sex trafficking, forced domestic labour, forced marriage and debt bondage.

Modernity   The period following the mid-eighteenth-century European Enlightenment, characterized by the combination of secularization, rationalization, democratization, individualism and the rise of scientific thinking.

Modernization theory   A version of market-oriented development theory which argues that low-income societies develop economically if they adopt modern economic institutions, technologies, and cultural values that emphasize savings and productive investment.

Monarchies   Those political systems headed by a single person whose power is passed down through their family across generations.

Monogamy   A form of marriage in which each married partner is allowed only one spouse at any given time.

Monopoly   A situation in which a single firm dominates in a given industry.

Monotheism   Belief in a single God.

Moral consensus   The shared values emphasized by functionalists which, they argue, are necessary for a well-ordered society.

Moral panic   A term popularized by Stan Cohen to describe a societal overreaction to a certain group or type of behaviour that is taken as symptomatic of general social disorder.

Mortality rate   The death rate in a society, usually expressed as number of deaths   per 1,000 head of population.

Multiculturalism   Adoption by the state of a policy encouraging and facilitating cultural pluralism, which allows all ethnic groups to share equally in economic and political life.

Multilateral   Involving many different sides or parties, normally used to describe relations and meetings involving a number of national governments.

Multimedia   The combination of what used to be different media requiring different technologies (for instance, visuals and sound) on a single medium, such as a DVD, which can be played on a computer.

Nation   A group of people bound together by a strong sense of shared values, cultural characteristics such as language and religion, and a perceived common history.

Nation-state   A particular type of state in which a government has sovereign power within a defined territorial area and the mass of the population are citizens who know themselves to be part of a single national community.

Nationalism   A set of beliefs, political ideas and movements expressing identification with a given national community and pursuing the interests of that community.

Nations without states   Instances in which the members of a nation lack political sovereignty (a state) over the area they claim as their own.

Nature   Generally taken today to be the non-human environment of animals, plants, seas and land.

Neo-liberalism   The economic belief that free market forces, achieved by minimizing government restrictions on business, provide the only route to economic growth.

Neo-local residence   Involves the creation of a new household each time a child marries or when she or he reaches adulthood and becomes economically active.

Netiquette   The emerging body of advice, rules and norms governing online communications, particularly those on email and social media sites.

Network   A set of informal and formal social ties that link people to one another.

New Age movement   The diverse spectrum of beliefs and practices oriented towards inner spirituality, including paganism, Eastern mysticism, shamanism, alternative forms of healing and astrology.

New criminology   The 'new criminologists' of the 1970s argued that crime and deviance could be understood only in the context of power and inequality within society. Crime was therefore often political in character.

New Labour   The reformed British Labour Party of the mid-1990s, which abolished Clause 4, which committed the party to socialism and the public ownership of industry.

New media   All of those media forms founded on digital technology and digitization, including mobile and smartphones, the Internet, digital TV, and radio and video games.

New migration A term referring to changes in patterns of migration in Europe in the years following the end of the Cold War and the fall of the Berlin Wall, altering the dynamic between traditional 'countries of origin' and 'countries of destination'.

New racism Racist attitudes, also referred to as cultural racism, predicated on perceived cultural or religious differences rather than biological ones.

New religious movements (NRMs) The broad range of religious and spiritual groups, cults and sects that have emerged alongside mainstream religions.

New social movements (NSMs) A group of social movements which emerged in Western societies in the 1960s and 1970s, including student movements, second-wave feminism, environmentalism, the anti-nuclear movement and 'anti-globalization' demonstrations. NSMs exhibit new social issues, loose organizational form, a new middle-class base and non-violent action repertoires.

New sociology of childhood A recent paradigm which begins from the premise that childhood is a social construction that differs across societies.

Newly industrializing countries Those developing countries, such as South Korea, Taiwan, Brazil and Singapore, which have rapidly developed a strong industrial base and economy.

Non-verbal communication Communication between individuals based on facial expression or bodily gesture rather than on the use of language.

Norms Rules of behaviour that reflect or embody a culture's values, either prescribing a given type of behaviour or forbidding it.

Nuclear family A family group consisting of mother, father (or one of these) and dependent children.

Occupation Any form of paid employment in which an individual works in a regular way.

Occupational gender segregation The way that men and women are clustered in different types of jobs, based on prevailing understandings of what is appropriate 'male' and 'female' work.

OECD Organization for Economic Cooperation and Development – an international organization formed in 1961. The OECD aims to assist its members to achieve 'sustainable economic growth' and employment.

Oligopoly The domination of a small number of firms in a given industry.

Oral history Information gathered through interviews with people about events they witnessed or experienced earlier in their lives.

Organic solidarity According to Emile Durkheim, a form of social cohesion that results from the various parts of a society functioning as an integrated whole, particularly through the extended division of labour.

Organization A large group of individuals, involving a definite set of authority relations, with a clear purpose and set of aims. There are quite close links between the development of organizations and a tendency towards bureaucracy.

Organized crime Types of activity which are similar to orthodox businesses but are illegal, including human trafficking, illegal gambling, drug trading, prostitution, large-scale theft and protection rackets.

Outsourcing The contracting out of a company's work tasks, previously carried out internally, from simple tasks, such as the production of one part of a product, to the work of whole departments.

Pandemic According to the World Health Organization, an epidemic occurring worldwide, or over a very wide area, crossing international boundaries and affecting a large number of people.

Paradigm In science, a framework of theoretical assumptions about the world within which scientific practice and the training of new scientists takes place.

Participant observation A method of research, widely used in sociology and anthropology, in which the researcher takes part in the activities of a group or community being studied.

Participatory culture   A culture with relatively low barriers to artistic expression and civic engagement which involves sharing and support for sharing and which erodes the boundary between active producers and passive consumers.

Participatory democracy   A system of democracy in which all members of a group or community participate collectively in the taking of major decisions.

Party   A group of individuals who work together because they have common backgrounds, aims or interests. According to Weber, party is one factor, alongside class and status, that shapes patterns of social stratification.

Pastoral societies   Societies whose subsistence derives from rearing domesticated animals, though there is often a need to migrate according to seasonal changes.

Pathologies   Literally, the scientific study of the nature of diseases, their causes, processes, development and consequences.

Patriarchy   A type of societal organization based around the central domestic authority of the father, involving the generalized dominance of men over women.

Patrilineal   Relating to, based on, or tracing ancestral descent through the paternal line.

Patrilocal   Family systems in which the wife is expected to live near the husband's parents.

Pauperization   Literally, to make a pauper of, or impoverish. Marx used the term to describe the process by which the working class grows increasingly impoverished.

Peace processes   All of those activities aimed at preventing violence in post-conflict situations, whether official efforts by professionals or the informal actions of groups in civil society.

Peer group   A friendship group composed of individuals of similar age and social status.

Peripheral countries   Countries that have a marginal role in the world economy and are thus dependent on the core-producing societies for their trading relationships.

Personal space   The physical space individuals maintain between themselves and others.

Personality stabilization   According to functionalists, the emotional security provided by the conventional nuclear family for the adult individuals that constitute it.

Phenomenology   A sociological perspective centred on understanding how the taken-for-granted social world is variously experienced by individuals.

Philosophy of science   A branch of philosophy concerned with the basis and practices of science as compared to other forms of knowledge.

Pilot studies   Trial runs in survey research.

Plastic sexuality   Human sexuality freed from the needs of reproduction and moulded by individual choices.

Political economy   Study of the ways in which political institutions of government and economic systems influence each other.

Political party   An organization established with the aim of achieving governmental power by electoral means and using that power to pursue a specific programme.

Politics   The means by which power is employed and contested to influence the nature and content of governmental activities. The sphere of the 'political' includes the activities of government and also those of social movements and other groups.

Polyandry   A form of marriage in which a woman may simultaneously have two or more husbands.

Polycentric transnationals   Transnational corporations whose administrative structure is global but whose corporate practices are adapted according to local circumstances.

Polygamy   A form of marriage in which a person may have two or more spouses simultaneously.

Polygyny A form of marriage in which a man may have more than one wife at the same time.

Polytheism Belief in two or more gods.

Population In the context of social research, the people who are the focus of a study or survey.

Portfolio worker A worker who possesses a diversity of skills or qualifications and is therefore able to move easily from job to job.

Positivism In sociology, the view that the study of the social world should be conducted according to the principles of natural science. A positivist approach to sociology holds that objective knowledge can be produced through careful observation, comparison and experimentation.

Postcolonial theory Social theories which seek to expose the implicit colonial legacy embedded in mainstream social theory and concepts, and to transform these in distinctively postcolonial directions by bringing in the forgotten voices and accounts of the colonized.

Post-development A critical perspective on mainstream theories of development which looks to promote alternative modes of progress in the developing countries to the dominant Western ideas of capitalism and industrialization.

Post-Fordism A general term used to describe the transition from mass industrial production, characterized by Fordist methods, to more flexible forms of production favouring innovation and aimed at meeting niche markets for customized products.

Post-industrial society Post-industrial societies are based on services and the production of information rather than material goods. Most developed societies are post-industrial in this sense.

Postmodern feminism Postmodern feminism involves, among other things, opposition to essentialism in the study of gender and a belief in plural modes of knowledge.

Postmodernism A perspective based on the idea that society is not governed by history or progress but is highly pluralistic and diverse, with no 'grand narrative' guiding its development.

Poststructuralism An approach to social science derived from the field of linguistics and popularized in sociology by the work of Michel Foucault. Poststructuralists reject the idea that absolute truths about the world can be discovered, arguing instead that plural interpretations of reality are inevitable.

Post-violence societies Those societies that have experienced war or internal communal violence and are moving towards non-violence.

Poverty line An official measure used by governments to define those living below a certain income level as living in poverty.

Power Power is a contested concept. For Weber, power is the ability of individuals or groups to achieve their aims or further their interests, even against opposition. Others see power as a pervasive aspect of all human relationships which can be productive as well as destructive (see Foucault).

Precariat An emerging social class of the twenty-first century, consisting of various social groups and individuals whose life chances are marked by insecurity, unpredictability and instability.

Precautionary principle The presumption that, where there is sufficient doubt about the possible risks, it is better to maintain existing practices than to change them.

Prejudice Holding preconceived ideas about an individual or group; ideas that are resistant to change even in the face of new information. Prejudice may be either positive or negative.

Pre-operational stage A stage of cognitive development, in Piaget's theory, in which the child has advanced sufficiently to master basic modes of logical thought.

Primary deviance An initial act of crime or deviance. According to Lemert, acts at the level of primary deviance remain marginal to an individual's self-identity.

Primary identity   Those identities formed in early life such as gender and ethnicity.

Primary socialization   The process by which children learn the cultural norms of the society into which they are born. Primary socialization occurs largely in the family.

Primary source   Any source that is originally produced in the time period which researchers are interested in studying (contrast with secondary source).

Profane   That which belongs to the mundane, everyday world.

Proletariat   For Karl Marx, the working class under capitalism.

Prophets   Religious leaders who mobilize followers through their interpretation of sacred texts.

Prostitution   The granting of sexual services or favours for monetary gain.

Psychopathic   A specific personality type. Such individuals lack the moral sense and concern for others that most normal people have.

Public sphere   An idea associated with the German sociologist Jürgen Habermas. The public sphere is the arena of public debate and discussion in modern societies.

Pure relationship   A relationship of sexual and emotional equality.

Push and pull factors   In the early study of global migration, internal and external forces believed to influence patterns of migration. 'Push factors' refer to dynamics within the country of origin, such as unemployment, war, famine or political persecution. 'Pull factors' describe features of destination countries, such as a buoyant labour market, lower population density and a high standard of living.

Qualitative research methods   Those methods which gather detailed, rich data with the aim of gaining a better understanding of the social phenomena being studied.

Quality circle (QC)   Types of industrialized group production, where workers use their expertise to participate actively in decision-making.

Quantitative research methods   Those sociological methods which allow social phenomena to be measured and analysed using mathematical models and statistical techniques.

Queer theory   Theory which does not assume that heterosexuality is the norm. Queer theory argues that non-heterosexual voices must be brought to the fore in sociology and other social sciences to remove heterosexist assumptions.

Race   A set of social relationships which allow individuals and groups to be located, and various attributes or competencies assigned, on the basis of biologically grounded features.

Racialization   The process through which an understanding of 'race' is used to classify individuals or groups of people to the advantage of some and the disadvantage of others.

Racism   The attribution of characteristics of superiority or inferiority to a population sharing certain physically inherited features, often skin colour. Racist ideas became entrenched during the period of Western colonial expansion but also rest on mechanisms of prejudice and discrimination found in many other human societies.

Radical feminism   Form of feminist theory that believes that gender inequality is the result of male domination in all aspects of social and economic life.

Random sampling   A method in which a sample is chosen so that every member of the population has the same probability of being included.

Rationalization   A concept used by Max Weber to refer to the process by which modes of precise calculation and organization, involving abstract rules and procedures, increasingly come to dominate the social world.

Recidivism   Reoffending by individuals previously found guilty of a crime.

Reconstituted family   A family in which at least one of the adults has children from a previous union, either living in the home or nearby; commonly known as a 'step-family'.

Reference group A group to which other groups or individuals compare themselves for purposes of evaluation.

Reflexivity In sociological research studies, the researchers' awareness of how their own ethnicity, class, gender or political views might impact on their practice, along with strategies to mitigate or eliminate such impacts.

Regionalization Divisions of time and space which may be used to 'zone' activities at the local, domestic level or the larger division of social and economic life into regional settings or zones at a scale either above or below that of the nation-state.

Reincarnation Rebirth of the soul in another body or form. This belief is most often associated with Hindus and Buddhists.

Relative deprivation The thesis that people's subjective feelings of deprivation are not absolute but related to their assessment of themselves in comparison with others.

Relative poverty Poverty defined by reference to the overall standard of living in any given society.

Religion A set of beliefs adhered to by the members of a community, involving symbols regarded with a sense of awe or wonder, together with ritual practices.

Religious economy A theoretical framework which argues that religions can be fruitfully understood as organizations in competition with one another for resources and followers.

Representative democracy A political system in which decisions affecting a community are taken not by its members as a whole but by people they have elected for this purpose.

Representative sample A sample from a larger population that is statistically typical of that population.

Reproductive technology Techniques of influencing the human reproductive process.

Research methods The diverse methods of investigation used to gather empirical (factual) information. Numerous research methods are used in sociology, and there is a trend towards 'mixed methods'.

Resistant femininity A term associated with R. W. Connell's writings. Women embodying resistant femininity reject the conventional norms of femininity in society ('emphasized femininity') and adopt liberated lifestyles and identities. Feminism and lesbianism, for example, are forms of resistant femininity.

Resource allocation How different social and material resources are shared out between and employed by social groups or other elements of society.

Resource mobilization theory (RMT) An American approach to social movement studies which begins from the premise that movements require resources to be successful. Studying how movements gather resources in a competitive field is the basis of the theory.

Response cries Seemingly involuntary exclamations which individuals make when, for example, being taken by surprise, dropping something inadvertently or expressing pleasure.

Restorative justice A branch of criminal justice which rejects punitive measures in favour of community-based sentences that raise awareness among offenders of the effects of their actions.

Restricted code A mode of speech that rests on strongly developed cultural understandings, so that many ideas do not need to be – and are not – put into words.

Revolution A process of political change, involving the mobilizing of a mass social movement, which successfully overthrows an existing regime. Revolutions are distinguished from coups d'état because they involve a mass movement. They can involve violence, but in recent times some have also been essentially peaceful or 'velvet revolutions'.

Right Realism In criminology, Right Realism links the perceived escalation of crime and delinquency to a decline in individual responsibility and moral degeneracy. To Right Realists, crime and deviance are an individual pathology – a set of destructive lawless behaviours actively chosen and perpetrated by individual selfishness, a lack of self-control and morality.

Risk society   A thesis associated with Ulrich Beck, who argued that advanced industrial societies have created many new hazards or manufactured risks unknown in previous ages, such as global warming.

Rituals   Formalized modes of behaviour in which the members of a group or community regularly engage. Religion represents one of the main contexts in which rituals are practised, but the scope of ritual behaviour extends into many other spheres of life.

Romantic love   Romantic love, which emerged in the eighteenth century, involves the idea that marriage is based on mutual attraction rather than economic convenience. It is a prelude to, but is also in tension with, the idea of a pure relationship.

Sacred   That which inspires attitudes of awe or reverence among believers in a given set of religious ideas.

Salafism   A school of Sunni Islam with diverse strands, all of which insist that the behaviour of Muslims should match, as far as is possible, that of the first three generations following the death of the Prophet Muhammad.

Sampling   Studying a proportion of individuals or cases from a larger population as representative of that population as a whole.

Sanction   A mode of reward or punishment that reinforces socially expected forms of behaviour.

Scapegoating   Blaming an individual or social group for perceived wrongs that generally arise from socio-economic change.

Schooling   A formal process of instruction, usually in specialized organizational settings – schools. Schooling transmits skills and knowledge via a designated curriculum.

Science   Science – and sociology as a scientific endeavour – involves the disciplined marshalling of empirical data, combined with the construction of theories which illuminate or explain those data.

Secondary deviance   An idea associated with Lemert. Secondary deviance is where a label becomes attached to the individual who carried out the act, as where the person stealing from the shop is labelled a 'shoplifter'.

Secondary identity   Those identities which are mainly learned, including roles and achieved statuses.

Secondary source   Any sources which discusses, interprets or re-presents material that originated at an earlier time (contrast with primary source).

Sect   A religious movement which breaks away from orthodoxy.

Secularization   A process of gradual decline in the influence of religion in society. Secularization can refer to levels of involvement with religious organizations, the social and material influence wielded by religious organizations, and the extent to which people hold religious beliefs.

Self-consciousness   Awareness of one's distinct social identity, as a person separate from others. Human beings are not born with self-consciousness but acquire an awareness of self as a result of early socialization.

Self-identity   The ongoing process of self-development and definition of individual identity through which people formulate a unique sense of themselves.

Semi-peripheral countries   Countries that supply sources of labour and raw materials to the core industrial countries and the world economy but are not themselves fully industrialized.

Sensorimotor stage   According to Piaget, a stage of human cognitive development in which the child's awareness of its environment is dominated by perception and touch.

Service class A term adopted by John H. Goldthorpe to describe those whose employment is based on a code of service rather than on a labour contract, and whose work therefore involves a high degree of trust and autonomy. The service class refers to professional, senior administrative and senior managerial employees.

Sex The anatomical differences which define men and women. Sociologists often contrast sex with gender, which is learned.

Sex tourism International travel oriented towards procuring prostitution and sexual services. The term usually describes the practices of men from developed countries who travel for the opportunity to engage in sexual liaisons with women and children.

Sex work All forms of labour involving the provision of sexual services in a financial exchange between consenting adults.

Sexual harassment Unwanted sexual advances, remarks or behaviour by one person towards another, persisted in even though it is made clear that such conduct is unwelcome.

Sexual orientation The direction of one's sexual or romantic attraction.

Sexuality A broad term which refers to the sexual characteristics, and sexual behaviour, of human beings.

Shaman An individual believed to have special magical powers; a sorcerer or witch doctor.

Shared understandings The common assumptions which people hold and which allow them to interact in a systematic way with one another.

Sick role A term, associated with Talcott Parsons, to describe the patterns of behaviour which a sick person adopts in order to minimize the disruptive impact of his or her illness on others.

Simulacra In the theory of hyperreality evoked by Jean Baudrillard, simulacra are copies of items for which there is no original.

Situational crime prevention An approach to crime prevention that focuses on the creation of crime-resistant environments and communities to reduce the opportunities for people to commit crimes. It is based on the principles of surveillance and target hardening.

Slavery A form of social stratification in which some individuals are literally owned by others as their property.

Snowball sampling A method of gathering a sample for research studies based on research participants recruiting acquaintances and friends for the study.

Social action Action that is subjectively meaningful and oriented towards other people.

Social age The norms, values and roles that are culturally associated with a particular chronological age.

Social capital The social knowledge and connections that enable people to accomplish their goals and extend their influence.

Social change Alteration in the basic structures of a social group or society. Social change is an ever-present phenomenon in social life but has become especially intense in the modern era.

Social constraint A term referring to the fact that the groups and societies of which we are a part exert a conditioning influence on our behaviour. Social constraint was regarded by Durkheim as a distinctive property of 'social facts'.

Social constructionism An approach to sociological research which sees social reality as the creation of the interaction of individuals and groups.

Social embeddedness A concept in economic sociology which refers to the way that apparently instrumental economic action is always embedded within dense social networks.

Social evolution A theory originally used by nineteenth-century scholars who sought to use evolutionary theory from biology to study the long-term development of societies.

Social exclusion The outcome of multiple deprivations which prevent individuals or groups from participating fully in the economic, social and political life of the society in which they are located.

Social facts   According to Emile Durkheim, the aspects of social life that shape our actions as individuals. Durkheim believed that social facts could be studied scientifically.

Social gerontology   The study of ageing and the elderly.

Social group   A collection of individuals who interact in systematic ways with one another. Groups may range from very small associations to large-scale organizations or societies. It is a defining feature of a group, whatever its size, that its members have an awareness of a common identity.

Social interaction   Any form of social encounter between individuals. Social interaction refers to both formal and informal situations in which people meet one another. An illustration of a formal situation of social interaction is a school classroom; an example of informal interaction is two people meeting in the street or at a party.

Social mobility   Movement of individuals or groups between different socio-economic positions. Vertical mobility refers to movement up or down a hierarchy in a stratification system. Lateral mobility is physical movement of individuals or groups from one region to another.

Social model of disability   A theory that locates the cause of disability within society rather than in the individual. It is not individual limitations that cause disability but the barriers that society places in the way of full participation for disabled people.

Social movement   Collective attempts to further a common interest or secure a common goal through action outside the sphere of established political institutions. Social movements seek to bring about or block social change and normally exist in relations of conflict with organizations whose objectives and outlook they frequently oppose.

Social position   The social identity an individual has within a given group or society. Social positions may be either general in nature (those associated with gender roles) or more specific (occupational positions).

Social reflexivity   The increasing and continuous reflection of people on the circumstances of their own lives and the choices they must make.

Social reproduction   The process through which a society reproduces its institutional and structural continuity over a long period of time.

Social role   The expected behaviour of an individual occupying a particular social position. In every society, individuals play a number of different social roles, according to the varying contexts of their activities.

Social self   The basis of self-consciousness in human individuals, according to the theory of G. H. Mead. The social self is the identity conferred upon an individual by the reactions of others.

Social stratification   The existence of structured inequalities between groups in society, in terms of their access to material or symbolic rewards. While all societies involve some forms of stratification, the most distinctive form of stratification in modern societies involves class divisions.

Social structure   Patterns of interaction between individuals, groups and institutions. Most of our activities are structured: they are organized in a regular and repetitive way.

Social theories   Theories of society that do not necessarily develop from within sociology and often contain normative or political critiques of the existing social order.

Social unrest   The stage of dissatisfaction with existing society which can give rise to more focused collective behaviour and social movements.

Socialist feminism   A perspective based on the idea that women are treated as second-class citizens in patriarchal capitalist societies and that both the ownership of the means of production and women's social experience need to be transformed.

Socialization The social processes through which children develop an awareness of social norms and values and achieve a distinct sense of self. Although socialization processes are particularly significant in infancy and childhood, they continue to some degree throughout life.

Socialization of nature The process by which we control phenomena regarded as 'natural', such as reproduction.

Society A system of structured social and institutional relationships within a bounded territory. Societies can be small, numbering a few dozen people, or very large, encompassing hundreds of millions.

Sociological imagination The application of imaginative thought to the asking and answering of sociological questions. The sociological imagination involves 'thinking oneself away' from the familiar routines of day-to-day life.

Sociological theories Theories of society or aspects of society which are developed from within professional sociology, using scientific methods and aiming to avoid normative bias.

Sociology The scientific study of interactions, human groups and whole societies. Sociology is one of a group of social sciences which also includes anthropology, economics, political science and human geography.

Sociology of deviance The branch of sociology concerned with the study of deviant behaviour and with understanding why some behaviour is identified as deviant.

Sociology of knowledge A branch of sociology which studies the relationship between human knowledge and the social context from which it emerges and develops.

Sociology of the body The branch of sociology that focuses on how our bodies are affected by social influences and how embodiment influences individual lives.

Soil degradation The process by which the quality of the Earth is made worse and its valuable natural elements are stripped away through overuse, drought or inadequate fertilization.

Solidarity For Durkheim, the internal social forces of cohesion which can be divided into 'mechanical' and 'organic' forms.

Source A document, a passage from a publication, or other information.

Sovereignty The title to supreme power of a monarch, leader or government over an area with a clear-cut border.

Standard deviation A way of calculating the spread of a group of figures.

State A political apparatus (government institutions, plus civil service officials) ruling over a given territory, with an authority backed by law and the ability to use force. Not all societies are characterized by the existence of a state. The emergence of the state marks a distinctive transition in human history, because the centralization of political power involved in state formation introduces new dynamics into processes of social change.

State-centred theory Development theories that argue that appropriate government policies do not interfere with economic development but, rather, can play a key role in bringing it about.

Status The social honour or prestige accorded to a person or a particular group by other members of a society. Status groups normally involve distinct styles of life – patterns of behaviour which the members of a group follow. Status privilege may be positive or negative.

Status set An individual's group of social statuses.

Stereotypes Fixed and inflexible characterizations of a group of people based on little or no evidence.

Stigma Any physical or social characteristic believed to be demeaning.

Strike A stoppage of work/withdrawal of labour by a group of workers for specific ends.

Structural functionalism A theoretical perspective rooted in the work of Talcott Parsons. Structural functionalism analyses societies as social systems in which interlinked social institutions perform specific functions, ensuring the smooth operation of the system as a whole.

Structuration The two-way process by which we shape our social world through our individual actions but are ourselves reshaped by society.

Subaltern All of those social groups who have been marginalized and silenced by the dominance of Western imperial and colonial power and its discursive constructions of 'the other' as inferior beings.

Subculture Any segment of the population which is distinguishable from the wider society by its cultural pattern.

Suburbanization The development of suburbia, areas of low-rise housing outside inner cities.

Super-diversity A concept used in studies of racial and ethnic diversity within a society to describe a level of complexity surpassing anything that has been experienced previously.

Surplus value In Marxist theory, the value of an individual's labour power which is 'left over' when an employer has repaid the cost involved in hiring a worker.

Surveillance The supervising of the activities of some individuals or groups by others in order to ensure compliant behaviour.

Surveillance society A society in which individuals are regularly watched and their activities documented. The increase in the number of video cameras on motorways, in streets and in shopping centres is one aspect of the expansion of surveillance.

Survey A method of sociological research usually involving the administration of questionnaires to a population being studied and the statistical analysis of their replies to find patterns or regularities.

Sustainable city A type of city designed to minimize the input of energy and other resources and to reduce its output of wastes, including CO_2 and pollutants.

Sustainable cities aim to reduce their ecological footprint as far as is practicable.

Sustainable development The notion that economic growth should proceed only insofar as natural resources are recycled rather than depleted, biodiversity is maintained, and clean air, water and land are protected.

Sweatshop A derogatory term for a factory or shop in which employees work long hours for low pay under poor conditions.

Symbol One item used to stand for or represent another – as in the case of a flag, which symbolizes a nation.

Symbolic capital In the work of Pierre Bourdieu, those resources that confer high status, distinction, honour and social prestige on people. For example, voluntary charity work may lead to a person being held in high esteem that would not otherwise have accrued from their formal employment or business ownership.

Symbolic interactionism A theoretical approach, developed by G. H. Mead, which emphasizes the role of symbols and language as core elements of all human interaction.

Taliban A fundamentalist Islamic militia which took control of Afghanistan in 1996 and set up an Islamic government that enforced a strict code of behaviour. The Taliban were overthrown by an American-led international coalition in 2001 after allowing the establishment of Al-Qaeda terrorist training camps.

Talk The carrying on of conversations or verbal exchanges in the course of day-to-day social life. Increasingly, this has been seen as a subject for scrutiny by sociologists, particularly ethnomethodologists.

Target hardening Crime-deterrence techniques that aim to make it more difficult for crime to take place through direct interventions into potential crime situations. Vehicle immobilizers and CCTV are examples.

Taylorism A set of ideas, also referred to as 'scientific management', developed by

Frederick Winslow Taylor, according to which productivity could be immensely increased by breaking down industrial tasks into a series of simple operations that could be precisely timed and optimally coordinated.

Technology   The application of knowledge to production from the material world. Technology involves the creation of material instruments (such as machines) used in human interaction with nature.

Telecommunications   The communication of information, sounds or images at a distance through a technological medium.

Terrorism   Usually, violent acts designed to instil fear into a population for political ends.

Thatcherism   Policy doctrines associated with former British prime minister Margaret Thatcher, including freeing up business, cutting back the reach of the state and reforming welfare.

Theism   A belief in a god or gods.

Theoretical questions   Questions posed by the sociologist when seeking to explain a particular range of observed events. The asking of theoretical questions is crucial to allowing us to generalize about the nature of social life.

Theory   An attempt to identify general properties that explain regularly observed events. While theories tend to be linked to broader theoretical approaches, they are also strongly influenced by the research results they help generate.

Theory of broken windows   The idea that there is a connection between the appearance of disorder, such as a broken window or vandalism, and actual crime levels.

Third age   The years in later life when people are free from parenting responsibilities and formal work. In developed societies, the third age is longer than ever before, allowing older people to live active and independent lives.

Third Way   A political philosophy, pioneered by New Labour and favoured by other centrist democratic leaders, committed to preserving the values of socialism while endorsing market-based policies for generating wealth and reducing inequality.

Three worlds model   An older model dividing the world into first, second and third worlds: a first world of countries with high levels of economic development, a second world of emerging economies, and a third world of poorer countries in the southern hemisphere with little or no industrial development.

Total fertility rate (TFR)   A measure used by several international agencies to predict population trends. The average number of children a woman would have over her childbearing years (15–49) if current birth rates remain constant.

Total institutions   A term popularized by Erving Goffman to refer to facilities, such as asylums, prisons and monasteries, that impose on their residents a forcibly regulated system of existence in complete isolation from the outside world.

Totemism   A system of religious belief which attributes divine properties to a particular type of animal or plant.

Transgender   A term which covers a variety of people exhibiting 'gender variance', including those whose gender identity and/or performance of gender diverges from that assigned at birth or expected according to dominant social norms of femininity and masculinity.

Transnational corporations (TNCs)   Business corporations located in two or more countries. Even when TNCs have a clear national base, they are oriented to global markets and global profits.

Triangulation   The use of multiple research methods as a way of producing more reliable empirical data than are available from any single method.

Typification   A concept used by Alfred Schutz to describe the way that people make judgements of individuals, based on prior assumptions about the typical character and behaviour of categories of people.

Underclass A class of individuals situated right at the bottom of the class system, often composed of people from ethnic minority backgrounds.

Underdevelopment A concept used in social science to describe the economic state of societies that were exploited and/or previously colonized by Western countries. Underdevelopment suggests a process through which powerful, wealthy states actively exploit the poor and less powerful.

Unemployment Refers to being out of formal, paid employment. Rates of unemployment measure the proportion of people who are 'economically active' but also available for work. A person who is 'out of work' is not necessarily unemployed. Housewives, for instance, do not receive any pay, but they usually work very hard.

Unfocused interaction Interaction occurring among people present in the same setting but where they are not engaged in direct face-to-face communication.

Unintended consequences All of those unpredicted effects that result from the intentional actions of people, organizations and governments, especially those that work against the original objectives of the actors involved.

Universal benefits Welfare benefits that are available equally to all citizens, regardless of their level of income or economic status, as opposed to being means-tested.

Upper class A social class broadly composed of the more affluent members of society, especially those who have inherited wealth, own large businesses or hold large numbers of stocks and shares.

Urban ecology An approach to the study of urban life based on an analogy with the adjustment of plants and organisms to the physical environment. According to ecological theorists, the various neighbourhoods and zones within cities are formed as a result of natural processes of adjustment on the part of urban populations as they compete for resources.

Urban recycling The refurbishing of deteriorating neighbourhoods by encouraging the renewal of old buildings and the construction of new ones on previously developed land, rather than extending out to fresh sites.

Urban renewal Reviving deteriorating neighbourhoods by such processes as recycling land and existing buildings, improving the urban environment, managing local areas better and with the participation of local citizens, and using public funds both to regenerate the area and to attract further private investment.

Urbanism A term used by Louis Wirth to denote the distinctive characteristics of urban social life, such as its impersonality.

Urbanization The development of towns and cities.

Value-added model of social movements Neil Smelser's stage model of social movement development in which each succeeding stage 'adds value' to the movement's overall development.

Values Ideas held by human individuals or groups about what is desirable, proper, good or bad. Differing values represent key aspects of variations in human culture. What individuals value is strongly influenced by the specific culture in which they happen to live.

Variable A dimension along which an object, individual or group may be categorized, such as income or height, allowing specific comparisons with others or over time.

Vertical mobility Movement up or down a hierarchy of positions in a social stratification system.

Vicarious religion The situation in which an active minority of people attend church regularly on behalf of and with the tacit approval of the non-active majority.

Victimization studies Surveys aimed at revealing the proportion of the population that has been victimized by crime over a certain period. Victim surveys attempt to compensate for the 'dark figure of unreported crime' by focusing directly on people's actual experience of crime.

Virtual community Internet-based groups, rooted in public discussions which are long-lasting and contain sufficient human feeling to constitute personal relationships in cyberspace.

War The clash of at least two organized armed forces that seek to destroy each other's power and especially their will to resist, principally by killing members of the opposing force.

Welfare capitalism Practice in which large corporations protect their employees from the vicissitudes of the market.

Welfare dependency A situation where people on welfare, such as those receiving unemployment benefit, treat this as a 'way of life' rather than attempting to secure a paid job.

Welfare state A political system that provides a wide range of welfare benefits for citizens.

White-collar crime Criminal activities carried out by those in white-collar or professional jobs.

Work The activity by which human beings produce useful things from the natural world and so ensure their survival. In modern societies there remain many types of work, including housework, which do not involve direct payment of wages or salary.

Working class A social class broadly composed of people involved in blue-collar or manual occupations.

World-accommodating movement A religious movement that emphasizes the importance of inner religious life and spiritual purity over worldly concerns.

World-affirming movement A religious movement that seeks to enhance followers' ability to succeed in the outside world by helping them to unlock their human potential.

World-rejecting movement A religious movement that is exclusive in nature, highly critical of the outside world, and demanding of its members.

World-systems theory Pioneered by Immanuel Wallerstein, this theory emphasizes the interconnections among countries based on the expansion of a capitalist world economy. The world-system is made up of core countries, semi-peripheral countries and peripheral countries.

Young adulthood A life-course stage between adolescence and mature adulthood. Young adulthood is not seen as a universal life-course stage, but the concept has some currency in the developed societies.

Youth culture The specific cultural forms associated with young people in a given period. Youth culture involves behavioural norms, dress codes, language use and other aspects, many of which tend to differ from the adult culture of the time.

Zemiology In criminology, the study of all of the various causes of social harm, rather than just those harms caused by crimes and criminal acts.

Zero tolerance policing An approach to crime prevention and control that targets petty crime and minor disturbances as a way of deterring more serious crime.

References

Abbott, D. (2001) 'The Death of Class?', *Sociology Review*, 11 (November).

Abbott, P., Wallace, C., and Tyler, M. (2005) *An Introduction to Sociology: Feminist Perspectives* (3rd edn, London: Routledge).

Abeles, R., and Riley, M. W. (1987) 'Longevity, Social Structure and Cognitive Aging', in C. Schooler and K. W. Schaie (eds), *Cognitive Functioning and Social Structure Over the Lifecourse* (Norwood, NJ: Ablex).

Abrahamson, M. (2014) *Urban Sociology: A Global Introduction* (New York: Cambridge University Press).

Acharya, A. (2014) *The End of American World Order* (Cambridge: Polity).

Acheson, D. (1998) *Independent Inquiry into Inequalities in Health* (London: HMSO).

Acker, J. (1989) 'Making Gender Visible', in R. A. Wallace (ed.), *Feminism and Sociological Theory* (London: Sage): 65–81.

Adorno, T. (1976 [1950]) *Introduction to the Sociology of Music* (New York: Seabury Press).

Agyeman, J., Bullard, R. D., and Evans, B. (2003) *Just Sustainabilities: Development in an Unequal World* (London: Earthscan).

Ahmed, A. S., and Donnan, H. (1994) 'Islam in the Age of Postmodernity', in A. S. Ahmed and D. Hastings (eds), *Islam, Globalization and Postmodernity* (London: Routledge).

Akintoye, S. (1976) *Emergent African States: Topics in Twentieth Century African History* (London: Longman).

Al Jazeera (2015) 'Libya: A Tale of Two Governments', www.aljazeera.com/news/2015/04/libya-tale-governments-150404075631141.html.

Alanen, L. (2015) 'Are We All Constructionists Now?', *Childhood*, 22(2): 149–53.

Alatas, S. F. (2006) 'Ibn Khaldun and Contemporary Sociology', *International Sociology*, 21(6): 782–95.

Albrow, M. (1997) *The Global Age: State and Society Beyond Modernity* (Stanford, CA: Stanford University Press).

Aldridge, A. (2007) *Religion in the Contemporary World: A Sociological Introduction* (2nd edn, Cambridge: Polity).

Aldridge, H., Kenway, P., and Born, T. B. (2015) *What Happened to Poverty under the Coalition?* (London: New Policy Institute); http://npi.org.uk/files/5214/3031/5186/What_happened_to_poverty_under_the_Coalition_FINAL.pdf.

Alexander, J. C. (1985) *Neofunctionalism* (London: Routledge).

Alexander, J. C. (ed.) (1997) *Neofunctionalism and After: Collected Readings* (Oxford: Blackwell).

Alexander, Z. (1999) *The Department of Health Study of Black, Asian and Ethnic Minority Issues* (London: Department of Health).

Alway, J. (1995) 'The Trouble with Gender: Tales of the Still-Missing Feminist Revolution in Sociological Theory', *Sociological Theory*, 13(3): 209–28.

Alwin, D. F., McCammon, R. J., and Hofer, S. M. (2006) 'Studying the Baby Boom Cohorts within a Demographic and Developmental Context: Conceptual and Methodological Issues', in S. K. Whitbourne and S. L. Willis (eds), *The Baby Boomers Grow Up: Contemporary Perspectives on Midlife* (Mahwah, NJ: Lawrence Erlbaum): 45–71.

American Psychological Association (2010) *Report of the APA Taskforce on the Sexualization of Girls*, www.apa.org/pi/women/programs/girls/report-full.pdf.

Amin, A. (ed.) (1994) *Post-Fordism: A Reader* (Oxford: Blackwell).

Amin, A., and Thrift, N. (2002) *Cities: Reimagining the Urban* (Cambridge: Polity).

Amsden, A. H. (1989) *Asia's Next Giant: South Korea and Late Industrialization* (New York: Oxford University Press).

Amsden, A. H., Kochanowicz, J., and Taylor, L. (1994) *The Market Meets its Match: Restructuring the Economies of Eastern Europe* (Cambridge, MA: Harvard University Press).

REFERENCES

Anable, J. (2005) 'Complacent Car Addicts or Aspiring Environmentalists? Identifying Travel Behaviour Segments Using Attitude Theory', *Transport Policy*, 12(1): 65–78.

Andersen, M. L., and Collins, P. H. (eds) (2009) *Race, Class, and Gender: An Anthology* (7th edn, Belmont, CA: Wadsworth).

Anderson, B. (2006 [1983]) *Imagined Communities: Reflections on the Origin and Spread of Nationalism* (rev. edn, London: Verso).

Anderson, E. (1990) *Streetwise: Race, Class, and Change in an Urban Community* (Chicago: University of Chicago Press).

Anderson, R. (2011) 'Masters of the Universe: Meet the World's Best-Paid Men', BBC News, 2 February, www.bbc.co.uk/news/business-11942117.

Anderson, S., and Cavanagh, J. (2000) *Top 200: The Rise of Corporate Global Power* (Washington, DC: Institute for Policy Studies); www.ips-dc.org/reports/top_200_the_rise_of_corporate_global_power.

Andreasson, K. (ed.) (2015) *Digital Divides: The New Challenges and Opportunities of e-Inclusion* (Boca Raton, FL: CRC Press).

Andrews, D., and Leigh, A. (2009) 'More Inequality, Less Social Mobility', *Applied Economics Letters*, 19: 1489–92.

Angstrom, J. (2005) 'Introduction: Debating the Nature of Modern War', in I. Duyvesteyn and J. Angstrom (eds), *Rethinking the Nature of War* (London and New York: Frank Cass).

Annandale, E. (2009) *Women's Health and Social Change* (London: Routledge).

Appadurai, A. (1986) 'Introduction: Commodities and the Politics of Value', in A. Appadurai (ed.), *The Social Life of Things* (Cambridge: Cambridge University Press).

Appelbaum, R. P., and Christerson, B. (1997) 'Cheap Labor Strategies and Export-Oriented Industrialization: Some Lessons from the East Asia/Los Angeles Apparel Connection', *International Journal of Urban and Regional Research*, 21(2): 202–17.

Appelbaum, R. P., and Henderson, J. (eds) (1992) *States and Development in the Asian Pacific Rim* (Newbury Park, CA: Sage).

Arber, S., and Ginn, J. (2004) 'Ageing and Gender: Diversity and Change', *Social Trends 34* (London: HMSO).

Arber, S., and Thomas, H. (2005) 'From Women's Health to a Gender Analysis of Health', in W. Cockerham (ed.), *The Blackwell Companion to Medical Sociology* (Oxford: Blackwell).

Archer, L., and Francis, B. (2007) *Understanding Minority Ethnic Achievement: Race, Gender, Class and 'Success'* (London: Routledge).

Archer, M. (1995) *Realist Social Theory: The Morphogenetic Approach* (Cambridge: Cambridge University Press).

Archer, M. (2003) *Structure, Agency and the Internal Conversation* (Cambridge: Cambridge University Press).

Ariès, P. (1965) *Centuries of Childhood* (New York: Random House).

Arnot, M. (2001) 'Bernstein's Sociology of Pedagogy: Female Dialogues and Feminist Elaborations', in K. Weiler (ed.), *Feminist Engagements: Reading, Resisting and Revisioning Male Theorists in Education and Cultural Studies* (New York: Routledge).

Ashton, D. N. (1986) *Unemployment under Capitalism: The Sociology of British and American Labour Markets* (London: Wheatsheaf).

Ashworth, A. E. (1980) *Trench Warfare, 1914–1918* (London: Macmillan).

Askwith, R. (2003) 'Contender', *The Observer*, 6 April.

Atchley, R. C. (2000) *Social Forces and Aging: An Introduction to Social Gerontology* (Belmont, CA: Wadsworth).

Atkinson, A. B. (2003) *Income Inequality in OECD Countries: Data and Explanations*, CESifo Working Paper no. 881 (Hamburg: Centre for Economic Studies/Institute for Economic Research).

Atlantic Cable (2010) 'Cable Signalling Speed and Traffic Capacity', www.atlantic-cable.com/Cables/speed.htm.

Attali, J. (1985) *Noise: The Political Economy of Music* (Minneapolis: University of Minnesota Press).

Atwan, A. B. (2015) *Islamic State: The Digital Caliphate* (London: Saqi Books).

Baba, H. (2013) 'Slim in Sudan: Female Fleshiness Loses its Allure', 14 May, www.bbc.co.uk/news/magazine-22455559.

Back, L. (1995) *Ethnicities, Multiple Racisms: Race and Nation in the Lives of Young People* (London: UCL Press).

Back, L., and Ware, V. (2001) O*ut of Whiteness: Color, Politics and Culture* (Chicago: University of Chicago Press).

Bäckström, A., and Davie, G. (2010) 'A Preliminary Conclusion: Gathering the Threads and Moving On', in A. Bäckström and G. Davie (eds), *Welfare and Religion in 21st Century Europe*, Vol. 1: *Configuring the Connections* (Farnham: Ashgate): 183–92.

Bagguley, P. (2002) 'Contemporary British Feminism: A Social Movement in Abeyance?', *Social Movement Studies*, 1(2): 169–85.

Bailey, R. (2011) *Letting Children Be Children: Report of an Independent Review of the Commercialisation and Sexualisation of Childhood* (London: Department for Education).

Bales, K., Trodd, Z., and Kent Williamson, A. (2009) *Modern Slavery: The Secret World of 27 Million People* (Oxford: OneWorld).

Ball, S. (2013) 'Free Schools: Our Education System has Been Dismembered in Pursuit of Choice', *The Guardian*, 23 October, www.theguardian.com/commentisfree/2013/oct/23/education-system-dismembered-choice.

Baltes, P. B., and Schaie, K. W. (1977) 'The Myth of the Twilight Years', in S. Zarit (ed.), *Readings in Aging and Death: Contemporary Perspectives* (New York: Harper & Row).

Bamforth, A. (1999) 'The Restive Season', *The Guardian*, 15 December.

Bancroft, A., Zimpfer, M. J., Murray, O., and Karels, M (2014) 'Working at Pleasure in Young Women's Alcohol Consumption: A Participatory Visual Ethnography', *Sociological Research Online*, 19(3): 20, www.socresonline.org.uk/19/3/20.html.

Banister, D. (1992) 'Energy Use, Transport and Settlement Patterns', in M. Breheny (ed.), *Sustainable Development and Urban Form* (London: Pion): 160–81.

Banks, C. (2013) *Youth, Crime and Justice* (Abingdon: Routledge).

Barash, D. (1979) *The Whisperings Within* (New York: Harper & Row).

Barker, M. (1981) *The New Racism: Conservatives and the Ideology of the Tribe* (Frederick, MD: University Publications of America).

Barker, R. (1997) *Political Ideas in Modern Britain* (London and New York: Routledge).

Barnard, A. (ed.) (2004) *Hunter-Gatherers in History, Archaeology and Anthropology* (Oxford: Berg).

Barnard, H., and Turner, C. (2011) *Poverty and Ethnicity: A Review of the Evidence* (York: Joseph Rowntree Foundation).

Barnes, C. (1991) *Disabled People in Britain and Discrimination* (London: Hurst).

Barnes, C. (2003) 'Disability Studies: What's the Point?', paper given at a conference at the University of Lancaster, 4 September, www.lancs.ac.uk/fass/events/disabilityconference_archive/2003/papers/barnes2000.pdf.

Barnett, A. (2007) 'The Three Faces of the World Social Forum', 30 January, www.opendemocracy.net/globalization-protest/wsf_faces_4297.jsp.

Barret-Ducrocq, F. (1992) *Love in the Time of Victoria: Sexuality and Desire among Working-Class Men and Women in Nineteenth-Century London* (Harmondsworth: Penguin).

Barry, J. M. (2005) *The Great Influenza: The Story of the Deadliest Pandemic in History* (New York: Penguin).

Barth, F. (1969) *Ethnic Groups and Boundaries* (London: Allen & Unwin).

Bartle, J., and Allen, N. (eds) (2010) *Britain at the Polls 2010* (London: Sage).

Basu, A. (ed.) (1995) *The Challenge of Local Feminisms: Women's Movements in Global Perspective* (Boulder, CO: Westview Press).

Bates, L. (2014) *Everyday Sexism* (London: Simon & Schuster).

Batty, E., Beatty, C., Foden, M., Lawless, P., Pearson, S., and Wilson, I. (2010) *The New Deal for Communities Experience: A Final Assessment* (London: HMSO).

Baudrillard, J. (1983) *Simulations* (New York: Semiotex(e)).

Baudrillard, J. (2004 [1991]) *The Gulf War Did Not Take Place* (Sydney: Power Publications).

Bauman, Z. (1976) *Socialism: The Active Utopia* (New York: Holmes & Meier).

Bauman, Z. (1982) *Memories of Class: The Pre-History and After-Life of Class* (London: Routledge & Kegan Paul).

Bauman, Z. (1989) *Modernity and the Holocaust* (Cambridge: Polity).

Bauman, Z. (1992) *Intimations of Postmodernity* (London: Routledge).

REFERENCES

Bauman, Z. (1997) *Postmodernity and its Discontents* (Cambridge: Polity).

Bauman, Z. (2000) *Liquid Modernity* (Cambridge: Polity).

Bauman, Z. (2003) *Liquid Love: On the Frailty of Human Bonds* (Cambridge: Polity).

Bauman, Z. (2007) *Liquid Times: Living in an Age of Uncertainty* (Cambridge: Polity).

Baym, N. K. (2015) *Personal Connections in the Digital Age* (2nd edn, Cambridge: Polity).

BBC (2001) 'Murdoch Heads Media Power List', 16 July, http://news.bbc.co.uk/1/hi/entertainment/1441094.stm.

BBC (2002) 'Falwell "Sorry" for Mohammed Remark', 13 October, http://news.bbc.co.uk/1/hi/world/americas/2323897.stm.

BBC (2003) 'Why I Want You to Look Me in the Face', 6 August, http://news.bbc.co.uk/1/hi/magazine/3128203.stm.

BBC (2004) 'Official Downloads Chart Launches', 28 June, http://news.bbc.co.uk/1/hi/entertainment/music/3846455.stm.

BBC (2007a) 'Behaviour Lessons for Teenagers', 30 April, http://news.bbc.co.uk/1/hi/education/6607333.stm.

BBC (2007b) 'Berlin Integration Plan Attacked', 12 July, http://news.bbc.co.uk/1/hi/world/europe/6294832.stm.

BBC (2007c) 'Inmate Sent Mother Suicide Note', 1 May, http://news.bbc.co.uk/1/hi/england/lancashire/6611603.stm.

BBC (2007d) 'Hiroshima Bomb Pilot Dies Aged 92', 1 November, http://news.bbc.co.uk/1/hi/world/americas/7073441.stm.

BBC (2007e) 'Cambodia's Brutal Khmer Rouge Regime', 19 September, http://news.bbc.co.uk/1/hi/world/asia-pacific/7002629.stm.

BBC (2007f) 'Offshore Boost for Finance Sector', 22 June, http://news.bbc.co.uk/1/hi/business/6229164.stm.

BBC (2008a) 'How "Gay" Became Children's Insult of Choice', 18 March, http://news.bbc.co.uk/1/hi/7289390.stm.

BBC (2008b) 'Isolated Tribe Spotted in Brazil', 30 May, http://news.bbc.co.uk/1/hi/world/americas/7426794.stm.

BBC (2010) 'Q & A: Professor Phil Jones', 13 February, http://news.bbc.co.uk/1/hi/sci/tech/8511670.stm.

BBC (2011) 'Rwanda: How the Genocide Happened', 17 May, www.bbc.co.uk/news/world-africa-13431486.

BBC News (2011) 'World's Oldest Man Walter Breuning Dies in US Aged 114', 15 April, www.bbc.co.uk/news/world-us-canada-13090291.

BBC News (2012a) 'Life Term for Cambodia Khmer Rouge Jailer Duch', 3 February, www.bbc.co.uk/news/world-asia-16865834.

BBC News (2012b) 'Teachers Warn on Rise of Academies', 7 April, www.bbc.co.uk/news/education-17637793.

BBC News (2014a) 'Ebola: How Bad Can it Get?', 6 September, www.bbc.co.uk/news/health-29060239.

BBC News (2014b) 'Ebola: Kofi Annan "Bitterly Disappointed" by Response to Ebola', 16 October, www.bbc.co.uk/news/health-29654784.

BBC News (2014c) 'Profile: Malala Yousafzai', 10 December, www.bbc.co.uk/news/world-asia-23241937.

BBC News (2014d) 'Sir Elton John and David Furnish Marry', 21 December, www.bbc.co.uk/news/entertainment-arts-30568634.

BBC News (2015a) 'EU Leaders Agree to Relocate 40,000 Migrants', 26 June, www.bbc.co.uk/news/world-europe-33276443.

BBC News (2015b) 'Myanmar's President Promises Smooth Transfer of Power', 15 November, www.bbc.co.uk/news/world-asia-34825998.

BBC News (2015c) 'What is "Islamic State"?', 2 December, www.bbc.co.uk/news/world-middle-east-29052144.

BBC News (2016) 'Islamic State and the Crisis in Iraq and Syria in Maps', 18 October, www.bbc.co.uk/news/world-middle-east-27838034.

Beall, J. (1998) 'Why Gender Matters', *Habitat Debate*, 4(4).

Beasley, C. (1999) *What Is Feminism?* (Thousand Oaks, CA, and London: Sage).

Beck, U. (1992) *Risk Society: Towards a New Modernity* (London: Sage).

Beck, U. (1999) *World Risk Society* (Cambridge: Polity).

Beck, U. (2002) *Ecological Politics in an Age of Risk* (Cambridge: Polity).

Beck, U. (2006) *Cosmopolitan Vision* (Cambridge: Polity).

Beck, U. (2009) *World at Risk* (Cambridge: Polity).

Beck, U., and Beck-Gernsheim, E. (1995) *The Normal Chaos of Love* (Cambridge: Polity).

Beck, U., and Grande, E. (2007) *Cosmopolitan Europe* (Cambridge: Polity).

Becker, H. (1950) *Through Values to Social Interpretation* (Durham, NC: Duke University Press).

Becker, H. S. (1963) *Outsiders: Studies in the Sociology of Deviance* (New York: Free Press).

Becker, H. S. (1982) *Art Worlds* (Berkeley: University of California Press).

Beckett, K., and Herbert, S. (2010) *Banished: The New Social Control in Urban America* (New York: Oxford University Press).

Beckford, J. A. (2008) *Social Theory and Religion* (Cambridge: Cambridge University Press).

Beer, D., and Burrows, R. (2007) 'Sociology and, of and in Web 2.0: Some Initial Considerations', *Sociological Research Online*, 12(5): 17, www.socresonline.org.uk/12/5/17.html.

Beer, D., and Geesin, B. (2009) 'Rockin' with the Avatars: "Live" Music and the Virtual Spaces of Second Life', in D. Heider (ed.), *Living Virtually: Researching New Worlds* (New York: Peter Lang): 111–30.

Beevor, A. (2007) *Berlin: The Downfall 1945* (London: Penguin).

Beggs, C. (2009) *Energy: Management, Supply and Conservation* (Oxford: Butterworth-Heinemann).

Begum, N. (2004) 'Characteristics of the Short-Term and Long-Term Unemployed', *Labour Market Trends*, 112: 139–44.

Bell, A., Weinberg, M., and Hammersmith, S. (1981) *Sexual Preference: Its Development in Men and Women* (Bloomington: Indiana University Press).

Bell, D. (1987) 'The World and the United States in 2013', *Daedalus*, 116(3): 1–31.

Bell, M. M. (2004) *An Invitation to Environmental Sociology* (2nd edn, Newbury Park, CA: Pine Forge Press).

Bell, M. M. (2011) *An Invitation to Environmental Sociology* (4th edn, Thousand Oaks, CA: Sage).

Bellah, R. N., Madsen, S., Sullivan, W. M., Swidler, A., and Tipton, S. M. (2008 [1985]) *Habits of the Heart: Individualism and Commitment in American Life* (Berkeley: University of California Press).

Bengtson, V. L. (2001) 'Beyond the Nuclear Family: The Increasing Importance of Multigenerational Bonds', *Journal of Marriage and Family*, 63(1): 1–16.

Benhabib, S. (2006) *Another Cosmopolitanism: Hospitality, Sovereignty and Democratic Iterations* (New York: Oxford University Press).

Benhabib, S., and Resnik, J. (eds) (2009) *Migrations and Mobilities: Citizenship, Borders and Gender* (New York and London: New York University Press).

Bennett, K., and LeCompte, M. (1990) *How Schools Work: A Sociological Analysis of Education* (New York: Longman).

Benton, T. (1994) *Natural Relations: Ecology, Animal Rights and Social Justice* (London: Verso).

Benton, T., and Craib, I. (2001) *Philosophy of Social Science: The Philosophical Foundations of Social Thought* (Basingstoke: Palgrave).

Berberoglu, B. (2005) *An Introduction to Classical and Contemporary Social Theory: A Critical Perspective* (Lanham, MD: Rowman & Littlefield).

Beresford, P., and Wallcraft, J. (1997) 'Psychiatric System Survivors and Emancipatory Research: Issues, Overlaps and Differences', in C. Barnes and G. Mercer (eds), *In Doing Disability Research* (Leeds: Disability Press).

Berger, M. T., and Guidroz, K. (eds) (2009) *The Intersectional Approach: Transforming the Academy through Race, Class, and Gender* (Chapel Hill: University of North Carolina Press).

Berger, P. L. (1963) *Invitation to Sociology* (Garden City, NY: Anchor Books).

Berger, P. L. (1986) *The Capitalist Revolution: Fifty Propositions about Prosperity, Equality, and Liberty* (New York: Basic Books).

Berger, P. L., Davie, G., and Fokas, E. (2008) *Religious America, Secular Europe? A Theme and Variations* (Aldershot: Ashgate).

Berman, M. (1983) *All That Is Solid Melts into Air: The Experience of Modernity* (London: Verso).

Bernstein, B. (1975) *Class, Codes and Control*, Vol. 3: *Towards a Theory of Educational Transmissions* (London: Routledge).

Bernstein, B. (1990) *Class, Codes and Control*, Vol. 4: *The Structuring of Pedagogic Discourse* (London: Routledge).

Bertelson, D. (1986) *Snowflakes and Snowdrifts: Individualism and Sexuality in America* (Lanham, MD: University Press of America).

Berthoud, R. (1998) *The Incomes of Ethnic Minorities*, ISER report 98-1 (Colchester: University of Essex, Institute for Social and Economic Research).

Berthoud, R. (2000) *Family Formation in Multi-Cultural Britain: Three Patterns of Diversity*, Working Paper 2000-34 (Colchester: University of Essex, Institute for Social and Economic Research).

Beynon, H., and Nichols, T. (eds) (2006) *Patterns of Work in the Post-Fordist Era: Fordism and Post-Fordism*, 2 vols (Cheltenham: Edward Elgar).

Bhambra, G. K. (2007) 'Sociology and Postcolonialism: Another "Missing" Revolution?', *Sociology*, 41(5): 871–84.

Bhattacharya, S. (2003) 'Global Warming "Kills 160,000 a Year"', *New Scientist*, 1 October; www.newscientist.com/article/dn4223-global-warming-kills-160000-a-year.html.

Biagi, S. (2011) *Media Impact: An Introduction to Mass Media* (10th edn, Boston: Wadsworth).

Birren, J. E., and Schaie, K. W. (eds) (2001) *Handbook of the Psychology of Aging* (5th edn, San Diego and London: Academic Press).

Björnberg, U. (2002) 'Ideology and Choice between Work and Care: Swedish Family Policy for Working Parents', *Critical Social Policy*, 22(1): 33–52.

Blanden, J., Goodman, A., Gregg, P., et al. (2002) *Changes in Intergenerational Mobility in Britain* (London: Centre for the Economics of Education, London School of Economics and Political Science).

Blankenhorn, D. (1995) *Fatherless America* (New York: Basic Books).

Blau, P. M. (1963) *The Dynamics of Bureaucracy* (Chicago: University of Chicago Press).

Blau, P. M., and Duncan, O. D. (1967) *The American Occupational Structure* (New York: Wiley).

Blauner, R. (1964) *Alienation and Freedom* (Chicago: University of Chicago Press).

Blaxter, M. (2010) *Health* (2nd edn, Cambridge: Polity).

Blinder, A. S. (2006) 'Fear of Offshoring', *Foreign Affairs*, 85(2).

Blofeld, J. (2003) *Independent Inquiry into the Death of David Bennett* (Cambridge: Norfolk, Suffolk and Cambridgeshire Strategic Health Authority).

Bloomberg (2011) 'Global Box Office Sales Rose 8% in 2010 to Record $31.8 Billion', 23 February, www.bloomberg.com/news/2011-02-23/global-box-office-sales-rose-8-in-2010-to-record-31-8-billion.html.

Blumer, H. (1969) *Symbolic Interactionism: Perspective and Method* (Englewood Cliffs, NJ: Prentice-Hall).

Blumer, H. (1970 [1933]) *Movies and Conduct* (New York: Arno Press).

Boatcă, M., and Costa, S. (2010) 'Postcolonial Sociology: A Research Agenda', in E. G. Rodríguez, M. Boatcă and S. Costa (eds), *Decolonizing European Sociology: Transdisciplinary Approaches* (Farnham: Ashgate): 13–32.

Bobak, L. (1996) 'India's Tiny Slaves', *Ottowa Sun*, 23 October.

Boden, D., and Molotch, H. (1994) 'The Compulsion to Proximity', in R. Friedland and D. Boden (eds), *NowHere: Space, Time, and Modernity* (Berkeley: University of California Press).

Boffey, D. (2011) 'Lord Lawson's "Misleading" Climate Claims Challenged by Scientific Adviser', *The Guardian*, 27 March; www.guardian.co.uk/environment/2011/mar/27/lord-lawson-climate-scientific-adviser.

Bonacich, E., and Appelbaum, R. P. (2000) *Behind the Label: Inequality in the Los Angeles Garment Industry* (Berkeley: University of California Press).

Bone, J. D. (2009) 'The Credit Crunch: Neo-Liberalism, Financialisation and the Gekkoisation of Society', *Sociological Research Online*, 14(2), www.socresonline.org.uk/14/2/11.html.

Bonney, N. (1992) 'Theories of Social Class and Gender', *Sociology Review*, 1(3): 2–5.

Boocock, S. (1980) *Sociology of Education: An Introduction* (2nd edn, Boston: Houghton Mifflin).

Boorstin, D. (1961) *The Image: A Guide to Pseudo-Events in America* (New York: Vintage).

Booth, A. (1977) 'Food Riots in the North-West of England, 1770–1801', *Past and Present*, 77: 84–107.

Bootle, R. (2011) *The Trouble with Markets: Saving Capitalism from Itself* (London: Nicholas Brealey).

Borger, J. (2008) 'They Think it's All Over', *The Guardian*, 6 December; www.theguardian.com/football/2008/dec/06/football-brand-globalisation-china-basketball.

Borja, J., and Castells, M. (1997) *Local and Global: The Management of Cities in the Information Age* (London: Earthscan).

Boseley, S. (2006) 'Ritalin Heart Attacks Warning Urged after 51 Deaths in US', *The Guardian*, 11 February; www.guardian.co.uk/society/2006/feb/11/health.medicineandhealth.

Boswell, J. (1995) *The Marriage of Likeness: Same-Sex Unions in Pre-Modern Europe* (London: Fontana).

Bourdieu, P. (1986) *Distinction: A Social Critique of the Judgement of Taste* (London: Routledge & Kegan Paul).

Bourdieu, P. (1988) *Language and Symbolic Power* (Cambridge: Polity).

Bourdieu, P. (1990) *The Logic of Practice* (Cambridge: Polity).

Bourdieu, P. (1992) *An Invitation to Reflexive Sociology* (Chicago: University of Chicago Press).

Bourdieu, P. (2001) *Masculine Domination* (Cambridge: Polity).

Bourdieu, P., and Passeron, J. C. (1977) *Reproduction in Education, Society and Culture* (London: Sage).

Bowles, S., and Gintis, H. (1976) *Schooling in Capitalist America: Educational Reform and Contradictions of Economic Life* (New York: Basic Books).

Box, S. (1983) *Power, Crime and Mystification* (London: Tavistock).

Boyer, R., and Drache, D. (1996) *States against Markets: The Limits of Globalization* (London: Routledge).

Braithwaite, J. (1999) *Crime, Shame and Reintegration* (Cambridge: Cambridge University Press).

Brannen, J. (2003) 'The Age of Beanpole Families', *Sociology Review*, 13(1): 6–9.

Braun, B., and Castree, N. (eds) (1998) *Remaking Reality: Nature at the Millennium* (London: Routledge).

Braverman, H. (1974) *Labor and Monopoly Capital: The Degradation of Work in the Twentieth Century* (New York: Monthly Review Press).

Breen, R., and Goldthorpe, J. H. (1999) 'Class Inequality and Meritocracy: A Critique of Saunders and an Alternative Analysis', *British Journal of Sociology*, 50: 1–27.

Brennan, T. (1988) 'Controversial Discussions and Feminist Debate', in N. Segal and E. Timms (eds), *The Origins and Evolution of Psychoanalysis* (New Haven, CT: Yale University Press).

Brewer, J. D. (2010) *Peace Processes: A Sociological Approach* (Cambridge: Polity).

Brewer, R. M. (1993) 'Theorizing Race, Class and Gender: The New Scholarship of Black Feminist Intellectuals and Black Women's Labor', in S. M. James and A. P. A. Busia (eds), *Theorizing Black Feminisms: The Visionary Pragmatism of Black Women* (New York: Routledge).

Brierley, P. (2006) *Pulling out of the Nosedive: 2005 English Church Census*, Religious Trends 6 (London: Christian Research).

Brinkley, I., and Lee, N. (2007) *The Knowledge Economy in Europe – A Report Prepared for the 2007 EU Spring Council* (London: Work Foundation).

Britton, D. (2011) *The Gender of Crime* (Lanham, MD: Rowman & Littlefield).

Brown, C., and Jasper, K. (eds) (1993) *Consuming Passions: Feminist Approaches to Eating Disorders and Weight Preoccupations* (Toronto: Second Story Press).

Brown, D. A. (2007) *Critical Race Theory: Cases, Materials and Problems* (2nd edn, Eagan, MN: Thompson West).

Brown, P., and Lauder, H. (1997) *Education: Culture, Economy, Society* (Oxford: Oxford University Press).

Browne, J., and Hood, A. (2016) *Living Standards, Poverty and Inequality in the UK: 2015–16 to 2020–21* (London: Institute for Fiscal Studies).

Browne, K. (2005) *An Introduction to Sociology* (3rd edn, Cambridge: Polity).

Brownmiller, S. (1975) *Against our Will: Men, Women and Rape* (London: Secker & Warburg).

Brubaker, R. (2005) 'The "Diaspora" Diaspora', *Ethnic and Racial Studies*, 28(1): 1–19.

Brubaker, R. (2006) *Ethnicity without Groups* (Cambridge, MA: Harvard University Press).

Bruce, S. (1990) *Pray TV: Televangelism in America* (New York: Routledge).

Bruce, S. (1996) *Religion in the Modern World: From Cathedrals to Cults* (Oxford: Oxford University Press).

Bruce, S., and Voas, D. (2010) 'Vicarious Religion: An Examination and Critique', *Journal of Contemporary Religion*, 25(2): 243–59.

Brumberg, J. J. (1997) *The Body Project* (New York: Vintage).

Bruneforth, M. (2006) 'Interpreting the Distribution of Out-of-School Children by Past and Expected Future School Enrolment', Background paper for *EFA Global Monitoring Report 2007* (Paris: UNESCO).

Bruns, A. (2009) *Blogs, Wikipedia, Second Life, and Beyond: From Production to Produsage* (New York: Peter Lang).

Bryman, A. (2015) *Social Research Methods* (4th edn, Oxford: Oxford University Press).

Bryson, V. (1993) 'Feminism', in R. Eatwell and A. Wright (eds), *Contemporary Political Ideology* (London: Pinter).

Buckingham, D. (2000) *After the Death of Childhood: Growing up in the Age of Electronic Media* (Cambridge: Polity).

Budd, J. W. (2011) *The Thought of Work* (Ithaca, NY: Cornell University Press).

Buffett, W. E. (2011) 'Stop Coddling the Super-Rich', *New York Times*, 14 August 14; www.nytimes.com/2011/08/15/opinion/stop-coddling-the-super-rich.html.

Bull, P. (1983) *Body Movement and Interpersonal Communication* (New York: Wiley).

Bullard, R. D. (ed.) (1993) *Confronting Environmental Racism: Voices from the Grassroots* (Cambridge, MA: South End Press).

Burawoy, M. (2005) 'For Public Sociology: 2004 Presidential Address', *American Sociological Review*, 70: 4–28.

Burbridge, M., and Walters, J. (1981) *Breaking the Silence: Gay Teenagers Speak for Themselves* (London: Joint Council for Gay Teenagers).

Burchell, B., et al. (1999) *Job Insecurity and Work Intensification: Flexibility and the Changing Boundaries of Work* (York: York Publishing Services).

Burgoon, J. K., Buller, D. B., and Woodall, W. G. (1996) *Nonverbal Communication: The Unspoken Dialogue* (2nd edn, New York: McGraw-Hill).

Burke, J. (2004) *Al-Qaeda: The True Story of Radical Islam* (New York: I. B. Tauris).

Burke, J. (2015) *The New Threat from Islamic Militancy* (London: Bodley Head).

Burkitt, I. (1999) *Bodies of Thought: Social Relations, Activity and Embodiment* (London: Sage).

Burkitt, I. (2008) *Social Selves: Theories of Self and Society* (2nd edn, London: Sage).

Burt, R. S. (1982) *Toward a Structural Theory of Action* (New York: Academic Press).

Business in the Community (2010) *Race into Higher Education: Today's Diverse Generation into Tomorrow's Workforce* (London: BitC).

Butler, J. (1990) *Gender Trouble: Feminism and the Subversion of Identity* (London: Routledge).

Butler, J. (1993) *Bodies that Matter: On the Discursive Limits of 'Sex'* (New York: Routledge).

Butler, J. (1997) *Excitable Speech: A Politics of the Performative* (London and New York: Routledge).

Butler, J. (2004) *Undoing Gender* (London: Routledge).

Butler, T., with Robson, G. (2003) *London Calling: The Middle Classes and the Re-Making of Inner London* (Oxford: Berg).

Butler, T., and Savage, M. (1995) *Social Change and the Middle Classes* (London: UCL Press).

Byman, D. (2015) *Al Qaeda, The Islamic State, and the Global Jihadist Movement: What Everyone Needs to Know* (Oxford: Oxford University Press).

Bynner, J., Ferri, E., and Shepherd, P. (eds) (1997) *Twenty-Something in the 1990s: Getting on, Getting by, Getting Nowhere* (Aldershot: Ashgate).

Bytheway, B. (1995) *Ageism* (Buckingham, and Bristol, PA: Open University Press).

CACE (Central Advisory Council for Education) (1959) *15 to 18* (London: HMSO) [Crowther Report]; www.educationengland.org.uk/documents/crowther/.

Cahill, S. E., Distler, W., Lachowetz, C., Meaney, A., Tarallo, R., and Willard, T. (1985) 'Meanwhile Backstage: Public Bathrooms and the Interaction Order', *Journal of Contemporary Ethnography*, 14(1): 33–58.

Calhoun, C. (1993) '"New Social Movements" of the Early Nineteenth Century', *Social Science History*, 17(3): 385–427.

Calhoun, C. (2005) 'The Promise of Public Sociology', *British Journal of Sociology*, 56(3): 355–63.

Campbell, C. (1992) *The Romantic Ethic and the Spirit of Modern Consumerism* (Oxford: Blackwell).

Cantle, T. (2001) *Independent Report of the Community Cohesion Review Team* (London: Home Office).

Capps, W. H. (1995) *The New Religious Right: Piety, Patriotism, and Politics* (rev. edn, Columbia: University of South Carolina Press).

Caraway, T. L. (2007) *Assembling Women: The Feminization of Global Manufacturing* (Ithaca, NY: Cornell University Press).

Cardoso, F. H., and Faletto, E. (1979) *Dependency and Development in Latin America* (Berkeley: University of California Press).

Carlen, P. (1983) *Women's Imprisonment: A Study in Social Control* (London and Boston: Routledge & Kegan Paul).

Carr, E. H. (1962) *What is History?* (New York: Alfred A. Knopf).

Carroll, W. K. (2004) *Corporate Power in a Globalizing World: A Study in Elite Social Organization* (Oxford: Oxford University Press).

Carsten, J. (ed.) (2000) *Cultures of Relatedness: New Approaches to the Study of Kinship* (Cambridge: Cambridge University Press).

Cashmore, E. (2006) *Celebrity Culture* (London: Routledge).

Castells, M. (1983) *The City and the Grass Roots: A Cross-Cultural Theory of Urban Social Movements* (London: Edward Arnold).

Castells, M. (1991) *The Informational City: Economic Restructuring and Urban Development* (Oxford: Blackwell).

Castells, M. (1992) 'Four Asian Tigers with a Dragon Head: A Comparative Analysis of the State, Economy, and Society in the Asian Pacific Rim', in R. P. Appelbaum and J. Henderson (eds), *States and Development in the Asian Pacific Rim* (Newbury Park, CA: Sage).

Castells, M. (1996) *The Rise of the Network Society* (Oxford: Blackwell).

Castells, M. (1997) *The Power of Identity* (Oxford: Blackwell).

Castells, M. (1998) *End of Millennium* (Oxford: Blackwell).

Castells, M. (2001) *The Internet Galaxy: Reflections on the Internet, Business, and Society* (Oxford: Oxford University Press).

Castells, M. (2006) *The Network Society: From Knowledge to Policy* (Baltimore: Johns Hopkins University Press).

Castles, S., and Miller, M. J. (1993) *The Age of Migration: International Population Movements in the Modern World* (Basingstoke: Palgrave Macmillan).

Castles, S., and Miller, M. J. (2009) *The Age of Migration: International Population Movements in the Modern World* (4th edn, Basingstoke: Palgrave Macmillan).

Cathcart, B. (2011) 'The Ordeal of Christopher Jefferies', *FT Magazine*, 8 October; www.ft.com/cms/s/2/22eac290-eee2-11e0-959a-00144feab49a.html.

Catton, W., Jr., and Dunlap, R. E. (1978) 'Environmental Sociology: A New Paradigm', *American Sociologist*, 13: 41–9.

Cavanagh, M. (2011) 'Youth Unemployment Must be Addressed', *New Statesman*, 10 August; www.newstatesman.com/blogs/the-staggers/2011/08/youth-unemployment-police-long.

Cayton, H. (2000) 'Alzheimer's: Looking Ahead in the Twenty-First Century', from personal correspondence, Buckingham Palace.

Centers for Disease Control (2014) 'Severe Acute Respiratory Syndrome', www.cdc.gov/sars/about/faq.html.

Centre for Contemporary Cultural Studies (1982) *The Empire Strikes Back: Race and Racism in 70s Britain* (London: Hutchinson).

Centre for Social Justice (2009) *Dynamic Benefits: Towards Welfare that Works*. London: CSJ.

Chamberlain, M. (1999) 'Brothers and Sisters, Uncles and Aunts: A Lateral Perspective on Caribbean Families' in E. B. Silva and C. Smart (eds). *The New Family?* (London: Sage).

Chambers, D. (2006) *New Social Ties: Contemporary Connections in a Fragmented Society* (Basingstoke: Palgrave Macmillan).

Chambers, D. (2012) *A Sociology of Family Life: Change and Diversity in Intimate Relations* (Cambridge: Polity).

Chambers, P., Allan, G., and Phillipson, C. (2009) *Family Practices in Later Life* (Bristol: Policy Press).

Chambliss, W. J. (1978) *On the Take: From Petty Crooks to Presidents* (Bloomington: Indiana University Press).

Chapkis, W. (1997) *Live Sex Acts: Women Performing Erotic Labour* (London: Routledge).

Chaplin, E. (1994) *Sociology and Visual Representation* (London: Routledge).

Charles, N., and James, E. (2003) 'The Gender Dimensions of Job Insecurity in a Local Labour Market', *Work, Employment and Society*, 17(3): 531–52.

Charlton, J. I. (1998) *Nothing about Us without Us: Disability Oppression and Empowerment* (Berkeley: University of California Press).

Charters, A. (ed.) (2001) *Beat Down to your Soul: What was the Beat Generation?* (New York: Penguin).

Chase-Dunn, C. (1989) *Global Formation: Structures of the World Economy* (Oxford: Blackwell).

Chatterjee, P., Bailey, D., and Aronoff, A. (2001) 'Adolescence and Old Age in 12 Communities', *Journal of Sociology and Social Welfare*, 28(4): 121–59.

Chatterjee, S. (2005) 'Introduction', in S. K. Das (ed.), *Peace Processes and Peace Accords* (New Delhi: Sage India): 17–19.

Chen, X. (2009) 'Introduction: A Globalizing City on the Rise: Shanghai's Transformation in Comparative Perspective', in X. Chen (ed.), *Shanghai Rising: State Power and Local Transformations in a Global Megacity* (Minneapolis: University of Minnesota Press): xv–xxxv.

Chiles, D. P. (2013) *Principles of Netiquette* (CreateSpace Independent Publishing).

Chiozza, G. (2002) 'Is there a Clash of Civilizations? Evidence from Patterns of International Conflict Involvement, 1946–97', *Journal of Peace Research*, 39(6): 711–34.

Chodorow, N. (1978) *The Reproduction of Mothering* (Berkeley: University of California Press).

Chodorow, N. (1988) *Psychoanalytic Theory and Feminism* (Cambridge: Polity).

Chomsky, N. (1991) *Media Control: The Spectacular Achievements of Propaganda* (New York: Seven Stories Press).

Chowdry, H., Crawford, C., and Goodman, A. (2010) 'Outcomes in the Secondary School Years: Evidence from the Longitudinal Study of Young People in England', in A. Goodman and P. Gregg (eds), *Poorer Children's Educational Attainment: How Important Are Attitudes and Behaviour?* (York: Joseph Rowntree Foundation): 34–43.

Chua, A. (2003) *World on Fire: How Exporting Free Market Democracy Breeds Ethnic Hatred and Global Instability* (New York: Doubleday).

CIA (2007) *The World Factbook*, www.umsl.edu/services/govdocs/wofact2007/index.html.

CIA (2012) *The World Factbook 2012*, www.cia.gov/library/publications/the-world-factbook/index.html.

Cixous, H. (1976) 'The Laugh of the Medusa', *Signs*, 1(4): 875–93.

Clark, D. (ed.) (1993) *The Sociology of Death: Theory, Culture, Practice* (Oxford: Blackwell).

Clausewitz, C. von (1993 [1832]) *On War* (London: Everyman's Library).

Clegg, M., Finney, A., and Thorpe, K. (2005) *Crime in England and Wales: Quarterly Update to December 2004* (London: Home Office).

CNN (2001) 'Falwell Apologizes to Gays, Feminists, Lesbians', 14 September, http://archives.cnn.com/2001/US/09/14/Falwell.apology/.

Cockerham, W. (2007) *Social Causes of Health and Disease* (Cambridge: Polity).

Cohen, A. (1955) *Delinquent Boys* (London: Free Press).

Cohen, R. (1997) *Global Diasporas: An Introduction* (London: UCL Press).

Cohen, S. (2003 [1972]) *Folk Devils and Moral Panics: The Creation of the Mods and Rockers* (Oxford: Martin Robertson).

Cole, T. R. (1992) *The Journey of Life: A Cultural History of Aging in America* (Cambridge: Cambridge University Press).

Collier, P. (2007) *The Bottom Billion: Why the Poorest Countries Are Failing and What Can be Done about It* (Oxford: Oxford University Press).

Collins, J. (2000) 'Quality by Other Means', Unpublished manuscript, Department of Sociology, University of Wisconsin-Madison.

Collins, P. H. (2000) *Black Feminist Thought: Knowledge, Consciousness and the Politics of Empowerment* (New York: Routledge).

Colquhoun, I. (2004) *Design out Crime: Creating Safe and Sustainable Communities* (Amsterdam: Elsevier).

Connell, R. W. (1987) *Gender and Power: Society, the Person and Sexual Politics* (Cambridge: Polity).

Connell, R. W. (2001) *The Men and the Boys* (Berkeley and Los Angeles: Allen & Unwin).

Connell, R. W. (2005) *Masculinities* (2nd edn, Cambridge: Polity).

Connell, R. W. (2011) *Confronting Equality: Gender, Knowledge and Global Change* (Cambridge: Polity).

Conrad, P. (2002) 'A Mirage of Genes', in S. Nettleton and U. Gustafsson (eds), *The Sociology of Health and Illness Reader* (Cambridge: Polity): 76–87.

Cook, K. S., Snijders, C., Buskers, V., and Cheshire, C. (eds) (2009) *eTrust: Forming Relationships in the Online World* (New York: Russell Sage Foundation).

Coontz, S. (1992) *The Way We Never Were: American Families and the Nostalgia Trap* (New York: Basic Books).

Cooper, C. (2016) 'Government Loses Major House of Lords Vote to Redefine Child Poverty', *The Independent*, 26 January; www.independent.co.uk/news/uk/politics/government-loses-vote-to-keep-child-poverty-numbers-secret-a6833156.html.

Cooper, H. (2002) 'Investigating Socio-Economic Explanations for Gender and Ethnic Inequalities in Health', *Social Science & Medicine*, 54(5): 693–706.

Corbin, J., and Strauss, A. (1985) 'Managing Chronic Illness at Home: Three Lines of Work', *Qualitative Sociology*, 8(3): 224–47.

Corrigan, P. (1997) *The Sociology of Consumption: An Introduction* (London: Sage).

Corsaro, W. (2005) *The Sociology of Childhood* (2nd edn, Thousand Oaks, CA: Pine Forge Press).

Coser, L. A. (1977) *Masters of Sociological Thought: Ideas in Historical and Social Context* (New York: Harcourt, Brace, Jovanovich).

Cotgrove, S., and Duff, A. (1980) 'Environmentalism, Middle Class Radicalism and Politics', *Sociological Review*, 28(2): 333–51.

Councell, R., and Simes, J. (2002) *Projections of Long Term Trends in the Prison Population to 2009*, Research Report 14/02 (London: Home Office).

Council of Europe (2005) *Reconciling Labour Flexibility with Social Cohesion – Facing the Challenge* (Strasbourg: Council of Europe).

Council of Europe (2006) *Campaign to Combat Violence against Women, including Domestic Violence*, Fact sheet, www.coe.int/t/dg2/equality/domesticviolencecampaign/fact_sheet_en.asp.

Coward, R. (1984) *Female Desire: Women's Sexuality Today* (London: Paladin).

Cowie, J., and Heathcott, J. (eds) (2003) *Beyond the Ruins: The Meanings of Deindustrialization* (Ithaca, NY: Cornell University Press).

Cox, O. C. (1959) *Class, Caste and Race: A Study in Social Dynamics* (New York: Monthly Review Press).

Cox, O. C. (1964) 'The Pre-Industrial City Reconsidered', *Sociological Quarterly*, 5: 133–44.

Crenshaw, K. W. (1991) 'Mapping the Margins: Intersectionality, Identity Politics and Violence against Women of Color', *Stanford Law Review*, 43(6): 1241 99.

Crenshaw, M. (2011) *Explaining Terrorism: Causes, Processes and Consequences* (Abingdon: Routledge).

Crick, B. (2004) 'Is Britain Too Diverse? The Responses', www.carnegiecouncil.org/media/replies.pdf.

Croall, H. (2001) *Understanding White Collar Crime* (Buckingham: Open University Press).

Croall, H. (2011) *Crime and Society in Britain* (2nd edn, London: Longman).

Crompton, R. (2006) *Employment and the Family: The Reconfiguration of Work and Family Life in Contemporary Societies* (Cambridge: Cambridge University Press).

Crompton, R. (2008) *Class and Stratification: An Introduction to Current Debates* (3rd edn, Cambridge: Polity).

Crompton, R., Brockmann, M., and Lyonette, C. (2005) 'Attitudes, Women's Employment and the Domestic Division of Labour: A Cross-National Analysis in Two Waves', *Work, Employment and Society*, 19(2): 213–33.

Crossley, N. (2002) *Making Sense of Social Movements* (Buckingham: Open University Press).

Crossley, N. (2003) 'Even Newer Social Movements? Anti-Corporate Protests, Capitalist Crises and the Remoralization of Society', *Organization*, 10(2): 287–305.

Crossley, R. (2014) 'Will Workplace Robots Cost More Jobs Than They Create?', www.bbc.co.uk/news/technology-27995372.

Crothers, C. (1996) *Social Structure* (London: Routledge).

Crowther, D., and Rayman-Bacchus, L. (eds) (2004) *Perspectives on Corporate Social Responsibility* (Aldershot: Ashgate).

Cumberbatch, G., and Negrine, R. (1992) *Images of Disability on Television* (London: Routledge).

Cumings, B. (1987) 'The Origins and Development of the Northeast Asian Political Economy: Industrial Sectors, Product Cycles, and Political Consequences', in F. C. Deyo (ed.), *The Political Economy of the New Asian Industrialism* (Ithaca, NY: Cornell University Press).

Cumings, B. (2005) *Korea's Place in the Sun: A Modern History* (rev. edn, New York: W. W. Norton).

Cumming, E., and Henry, W. E. (1961) *Growing Old: The Process of Disengagement* (New York: Basic Books).

Cunningham, K. (2011) *The Bubonic Plague* (Edina, MN: ABDO).

Curran, J., and Seaton, J. (2003) *Power without Responsibility: The Press, Broadcasting and New Media in Britain* (London: Routledge).

Currie, E. (1998) *Crime and Punishment in America* (New York: Metropolitan Books).

Cylke, F. K. (1993) *The Environment* (New York: HarperCollins).

Daly, G. (2013) *Homeless: Policies, Strategies and Lives on the Streets* (3rd edn, Abingdon: Routledge).

Damaske, S. (2011) *For the Family? How Class and Gender Shape Women's Work* (Oxford: Oxford University Press).

D'Anieri, P., Ernst, C., and Kier, E. (1990) 'New Social Movements in Historical Perspective', *Comparative Politics*, 22(4): 445–58.

Darby, J. (2001) *The Effects of Violence on Peace Processes* (Washington, DC: US Institute of Peace Press).

D'Arcy, C., and Kelly, G. (2015) *Analysing the National Living Wage: Impact and Implications for Britain's Low Pay Challenge* (London: Resolution Foundation).

Darwin, C. (2008 [1859]) *On the Origin of Species* (Oxford: Oxford University Press).

Das, S. K. (2005) *Peace Processes and Peace Accords* (New Delhi: Sage India).

David, M. E. (2003) *Personal and Political: Feminisms, Sociology and Family Lives* (Stoke-on-Trent: Trentham Books).

Davie, G. (1994) *Religion in Britain since 1945: Believing without Belonging* (Oxford: Blackwell).

Davie, G. (2000) *Religion in Modern Europe: A Memory Mutates* (Oxford: Oxford University Press).

Davies, B. (1991) *Frogs and Snails and Feminist Tales* (Sydney: Allen & Unwin).

Davies, J. B., Sandström, S., Shorrocks, A., and Wolff, E. N. (2007) *Estimating the Level and Distribution of Global Household Wealth*, Research Paper no. 2007/77 (Helsinki: UNU-WIDER).

Davis, H. (2004) *Understanding Stuart Hall* (London: Sage).

Davis, K. (1949) *Human Society* (New York: Macmillan).

Davis, K. (1965) 'The Urbanization of the Human Population', *Scientific American*, 213 (September): 41–53.

Davis, M. (1990) *City of Quartz: Excavating the Future in Los Angeles* (London: Vintage).

Davis, M. (2006) *City of Quartz: Excavating the Future in Los Angeles* (2nd edn, London: Verso).

Davis, S. M. (1988) *2001 Management: Managing the Future Now* (London: Simon & Schuster).

Dawkins, R. (1986) *The Blind Watchmaker* (London: Longman).

Dawkins, R. (2006) *The God Delusion* (London: Bantam Press).

Dawood, F. S., Iuliano, A. D., Reed, C., et al. (2012) 'Estimated Global Mortality Associated with the First 12 Months of 2009 Pandemic Influenza A H1N1 Virus Circulation: A Modelling Study', *The Lancet Infectious Diseases*, 12(9): 687–95.

DCMS (Department for Culture, Media and Sport) (2011) 'Tourism', www.culture.gov.uk/what_we_do/tourism/default.aspx.

De Swaan, A. (2001) *Words of the World: The Global Language System* (Cambridge: Polity).

De Vaus, D. (2008) 'Australian Families: Social and Demographic Patterns', in C. B. Hennon and S. M. Wilson (eds), *Families in a Global Context* (New York: Routledge): 379–406.

De Witt, K. (1994) 'Wave of Suburban Growth Is Being Fed by Minorities', *New York Times*, 15 August.

Deem, R. (ed.) (1980) *Schooling for Women's Work* (London: Routledge & Kegan Paul).

Defra (2016) *Digest of Waste and Resource Statistics* (London: Defra); https://www.gov.uk/government/uploads/system/uploads/attachment_data/file/508787/Digest_of_Waste_and_Resource_Statistics_rev.pdf.

Delanty, G. (1997) *Social Science: Beyond Constructivism and Realism* (Buckingham: Open University Press).

Delbès, C., Gaymu, J., and Springer, S. (2006) 'Women Grow Old Alone, but Men Grow Old with a Partner: A European Overview', *Population & Societies*, 419 (January).

Delgado, R., and Stefancic, J. (2001) *Critical Race Theory: An Introduction* (New York: New York University Press).

Della Porta, D., and Diani, M. (2006) *Social Movements: An Introduction* (Oxford: Blackwell).

Della Salla, V. (2011) 'A Less Close Union? The European Union's Search for Unity amid Crisis', in C. Calhoun and G. Derluguian (eds), *The Deepening Crisis: Governance Challenges after Neoliberalism* (New York: New York University Press): 135–56.

DeLong-Bas, N. J. (2004) *Wahhabi Islam: From Revival and Reform to Global Jihad* (New York: I. B. Tauris).

Dennis, A., Philburn, R., and Smith, G. (2013) *Sociologies of Interaction* (Cambridge: Polity).

Dennis, K., and Urry, J. (2009) *After the Car* (Cambridge: Polity).

Dennis, N., and Erdos, G. (1992) *Families without Fatherhood* (London: IEA Health and Welfare Unit).

DeNora, T. (2000) *Music in Everyday Life* (Cambridge: Cambridge University Press).

Denver, D. (2011) *The Scottish Parliament Elections of 2011: Report to the Electoral Commission*, www.electoralcommission.org.uk/__data/assets/pdf_file/0007/141379/SP-2011-electoral-data-report-WEB.pdf.

Denzin, N. K. (1970) *The Research Act in Sociology* (Chicago: Aldine).

Denzin, N. K., Lincoln, Y. S., and Tuhiwai Smith, L. (eds) (2008) *Handbook of Critical and Indigenous Methodologies* (New York: Sage).

Dermott, E., and Seymour, J. (eds) (2011) *Displaying Families: A New Concept for the Sociology of Family Life* (Basingstoke: Palgrave Macmillan).

Derrida, J. (1976) *Of Grammatology* (Baltimore: Johns Hopkins University Press).

Derrida, J. (1978) *Writing and Difference* (London: Routledge & Kegan Paul).

Derrida, J. (1981) *Positions* (London: Athlone Press).

Devall, B. (1990) *Simple in Means, Rich in Ends: Practising Deep Ecology* (London: Green Print).

Deyo, F. C. (1989) *Beneath the Miracle: Labor Subordination in the New Asian Industrialism* (Berkeley: University of California Press).

DfE (Department for Education) (2012) *A Profile of Pupil Exclusions in England* (London: DfE).

DfE (Department for Education) (2014a) *Permanent and Fixed Period Exclusions in England: 2012 to 13* (London: DfE).

DfE (Department for Education) (2014b) 'Pupil Premium: Funding for Schools and Alternative Provision', https://www.gov.uk/pupil-premium-information-for-schools-and-alternative-provision-settings.

DfE (Department for Education) (2015) 'NEET Statistics Quarterly Brief: January to March 2015', https://www.gov.uk/government/statistics/neet-statistics-quarterly-brief-january-to-march-2015.

DHSS (Department of Health and Social Security) (1980) *Inequalities in Health* (London: DHSS) [Black Report].

Dickens, P. (1996) *Reconstructing Nature: Alienation, Emancipation and the Division of Labour* (London: Routledge).

Dickens, P. (2004) *Society and Nature: Changing Nature, Changing Ourselves* (Cambridge: Polity).

Diehl, M., and Dark-Freudeman, A. (2006) 'The Analytic Template in the Psychology of Aging', in D. J. Sheets, D. B. Bradley and J. Hendricks (eds), *Enduring Questions and Changing Perspectives in Gerontology* (New York: Springer).

Dobash, R. E., and Dobash, R. P. (1992) *Women, Violence and Social Change* (London: Routledge).

Dobson, A., and Bell, D. (eds) (2006) *Environmental Citizenship* (Cambridge, MA: MIT Press).

Dodd, V. (2015) 'Stephen Lawrence: New Criminal Inquiry into Claims Police Shielded Killers', https://www.theguardian.com/uk-news/2015/oct/16/stephen-lawrence-inquiry-hunts-police-alleged-to-have-shielded-killers.

DoH (Department of Health) (2003) *Tackling Health Inequalities: A Programme for Action* (London: DoH).

DoH (Department of Health) (2006) *Smoking, Drinking and Drug Misuse among Young People in England in 2002* (London: DoH).

Doherty, P. C. (2013) *Pandemics: What Everyone Needs to Know* (Oxford: Oxford University Press).

Doig, A. (2011) *State Crime* (Abingdon: Willan).

Doogan, K. (2009) *New Capitalism? The Transformation of Work* (Cambridge: Polity).

Douglas, M. (1994) *Risk and Blame* (London: Routledge).

Dowd, J. (1986) 'The Old Person as Stranger', in V. W. Marshall (ed.), *Later Life: The Social Psychology of Ageing* (Beverly Hills, CA: Sage): 147–87.

Doyal, L. (1995) *What Makes Women Sick: Gender and the Political Economy of Health* (London: Macmillan).

Drentea, P., and Moren-Cross, J. L. (2005) 'Social Capital and Social Support on the Web: The Case of an Internet Mother Site', *Sociology of Health and Illness*, 27(7): 920–43.

Drever, F., and Whitehead, M. (1997) *Health Inequalities* (London: The Stationery Office).

DTI (Department of Trade and Industry) (2000) *Just Around the Corner* (London: DTI).

Du Gay, P. (2000) *In Praise of Bureaucracy: Weber, Organization, Ethics* (London: Sage).

Duerr, H. P. (1988) *Der Mythos vom Zivilsationsprozess*, Vol. 1: *Nacktheit und Scham* (Frankfurt am Main: Suhrkamp).

Duffett, M. (2014) 'Introduction', in M. Duffett (ed.), *Popular Music Fandom: Identities, Roles and Practices* (New York: Routledge): 1–15.

Duffy, B., and Frere-Smith, T. (2014) *Perceptions and Reality: Public Attitudes to Immigration*, https://www.ipsos-mori.com/DownloadPublication/1634_sri-perceptions-and-reality-immigration-report-2013.pdf.

Duggan, M., Ellison, N. B., Lampe, C., Lenhart, A., and Madden, M. (2015) *Social Media Update 2014*, Pew Research Center, www.pewinternet.org/2015/01/09/social-media-update-2014/.

Duneier, M. (1999) *Sidewalk* (New York: Farrar, Straus & Giroux).

Duneier, M., and Molotch, H. (1999) 'Talking City Trouble: Interactional Vandalism, Social Inequality, and the "Urban Interaction Problem"', *American Journal of Sociology*, 104(5): 1263–95.

Dunlap, R. E., Buttel, F. H., Dickens, P., and Gijswijt, A. (eds) (2002) *Sociological Theory and the Environment: Classical Foundations, Contemporary Insights* (Oxford: Rowman & Littlefield).

Durkheim, E. (1952 [1897]) *Suicide: A Study in Sociology* (London: Routledge & Kegan Paul).

Durkheim, E. (1965 [1912]) *The Elementary Forms of the Religious Life* (New York: Free Press).

Durkheim, E. (1982 [1895]) *The Rules of Sociological Method* (London: Macmillan).

Durkheim, E. (1984 [1893]) *The Division of Labour in Society* (London: Macmillan).

Durkheim, E. (2011 [1925]) *Moral Education* (New York: Dover).

Dutt, M. (1996) 'Some Reflections on US Women of Color and the United Nations Fourth World Conference on Women and NGO Forum in Beijing, China', *Feminist Studies*, 22(3).

DWP (Department for Work and Pensions) (2002) *Disabled for Life? Attitudes Towards, and Experiences of, Disability in Britain* (London: HMSO).

DWP (Department for Work and Pensions) (2005) *Family Resources Survey, 2004–5* (London: HMSO).

DWP (Department for Work and Pensions) (2007) *The Pensioners' Income Series, 2005–6* (London: HMSO).

DWP (Department for Work and Pensions) (2010) *Universal Credit: Welfare that Works* (London: HMSO).

DWP (Department for Work and Pensions) (2011) *Households below Average Income: An Analysis of the Income Distribution, 1994/5–2009/10* (London: HMSO).

DWP (Department for Work and Pensions) (2012) *Family Resources Survey: United Kingdom 2010/11* (London: DWP).

DWP (Department for Work and Pensions) (2014) 'Disability Prevalence Estimates, 2011–12', https://www.gov.uk/government/uploads/system/uploads/attachment_data/file/321594/disability-prevalence.pdf.

Dwyer, P. (2004) 'Creeping Conditionality in the UK: From Welfare Rights to Conditional Entitlements?', *Canadian Journal of Sociology*, 29(2): 265–87.

Dyck, I. (1992) *William Cobbett and Rural Popular Culture* (Cambridge: Cambridge University Press).

Easton, P. B. (2006) *Creating a Literate Environment: Hidden Dimensions and Implications for Policy* (Hamburg: UNESCO Institute for Education).

Eberstadt, N., and Satel, S. (2004) 'Health, Inequality and the Scholars', *The Public Interest*, no. 157 (Fall): 100–18.

Eckersley, R. (1989) 'Green Politics and the New Class: Selfishness or Virtue?', *Political Studies*, 37(2): 205–23.

The Economist (1995) 'Book Review of David Blankenhorn, Fatherless America', April.

The Economist (2004a) 'The Kindness of Strangers?', 26 February.

The Economist (2004b) 'More or Less Equal? Is Economic Inequality around the World Getting Better or Worse?, 11 March; www.economist.com/node/2498851?story_id=2498851.

The Economist (2005) 'Backgrounder: EU Enlargement', 23 June.

The Economist (2010) 'Europe's Irreligious', 9 August; www.economist.com/node/16767758.

Edwards, R., Gillies, V., and Ribbens McCarthy, J. (2012) 'The Politics of Concepts: Family and its (Putative) Replacements', *British Journal of Sociology*, 63(4): 730–46.

Edwards, T. (1998) 'Queer Fears: Against the Cultural Turn', *Sexualities*, 1(4): 471–84.

Efron, S. (1997) 'Eating Disorders Go Global', *Los Angeles Times*, 18 October.

EHRC (Equality and Human Rights Commission) (2010a) *How Fair is Britain? Equality, Human Rights and Good Relations in 2010: The First Triennial Review*, www.equalityhumanrights.com/uploaded_files/triennial_review/how_fair_is_britain_-_complete_report.pdf.

EHRC (Equality and Human Rights Commission) (2010b) *40 Years since the Equal Pay Act and Scotland's Women are Still Paid Less than Men*, www.equalityhumanrights.com/scotland/scottish-news/press-releases-2010/40-years-since-the-equal-pay-act-and-scotlands-women-are-still-paid-less-than-men/.

EHRC (Equality and Human Rights Commission) (2011) *Sex and Power 2011* (Manchester: EHRC).

Ehrenreich, B., and Ehrenreich, J. (1979) 'The Professional-Managerial Class', in P. Walker (ed.), *Between Labour and Capital* (Hassocks: Harvester Press).

Eibl-Eibesfeldt, I. (1973) 'The Expressive Behaviour of the Deaf-and-Blind Born', in M. von Cranach and I. Vine (eds), *Social Communication and Movement* (New York: Academic Press).

Ekman, P., and Friesen, W. V. (1978) *Facial Action Coding System* (New York: Consulting Psychologists Press).

Elder, G. H. J. (1974) *Children of the Great Depression: Social Change in Life Experience* (Chicago and London: University of Chicago Press).

Eldridge, J. (ed.) (1993) *Getting the Message: News, Truth and Power* (London: Routledge).

Elgin, D. (2010) *Voluntary Simplicity* (2nd edn, New York: HarperCollins).

Elias, N. (1978) *What is Sociology?* (New York: Columbia University Press).

Elias, N. (1985) *The Loneliness of the Dying* (London: Continuum).

Elias, N. (1987a) 'On Human Beings and their Emotions: A Process-Sociological Essay', *Theory, Culture and Society*, 4(2–3): 339–61.

Elias, N. (1987b) *Involvement and Detachment* (Oxford: Blackwell).

Elias, N. (1991) *The Society of Individuals* (New York: Continuum).

Elias, N. (2000 [1939]) *The Civilizing Process: Sociogenetic and Psychogenetic Investigations* (rev. edn, Oxford: Blackwell).

Ell, K. (1996) 'Social Networks, Social Support and Coping with Serious Illness: The Family Connection', *Social Science and Medicine*, 42(2): 173–83.

Elliott, L. (2013) 'Chinese Downturn Fuels Fears Crisis is Spreading East', *The Guardian*, 21 April; www.theguardian.com/business/2013/apr/21/chinese-downturn-fuels-fears-dangerous-crash.

Elliott, R., and Elliott, C. (2005) 'Idealized Images of the Male Body in Advertising: A Reader-Response Exploration', *Journal of Marketing Communications*, 11(1): 3–19.

Elshtain, J. B. (1987) *Women and War* (New York: Basic Books).

Emmanuel, A. (1972) *Unequal Exchange: A Study of the Imperialism of Trade* (New York: Monthly Review Press).

Engels, F. (2010 [1884]) *The Origin of the Family, Private Property and the State* (London: Penguin).

Epley, N. S., Hillis, K., and Petit, M. (eds) (2006) *Everyday eBay: Culture, Collecting and Desire* (New York: Routledge).

Epstein, D. (ed.) (1998) *Failing Boys? Issues in Gender and Achievement* (Buckingham: Open University Press).

Epstein, S. (2002) 'A Queer Encounter: Sociology and the Study of Sexuality', in C. L. Williams and A. Stein (eds), *Sexuality and Gender* (Oxford: Blackwell).

Equality Challenge Unit (2013) *Equality in Higher Education: Statistical Report 2013. Part 1, Staff* (London: ECU).

Ericson, R. (2005) 'Publicizing Sociology', *British Journal of Sociology*, 56(3): 365–72.

Escobar, A. (1995) *Encountering Development: The Making and Unmaking of the Third World* (Princeton, NJ: Princeton University Press).

Esping-Andersen, G. (1990) *The Three Worlds of Welfare Capitalism* (Cambridge: Polity).

Estes, C. L., Biggs, S., and Phillipson, C. (2003) *Social Theory, Social Policy and Ageing* (Buckingham: Open University Press).

Estes, C. L., Binney, E. A., and Culbertson, R. A. (1992) 'The Gerontological Imagination: Social Influences on the Development of Gerontology, 1945–Present', *Aging and Human Development*, 35(1): 67–82.

Esteva, G. (1992) 'Development', in W. Sachs (ed.), *The Development Dictionary: A Guide to Knowledge as Power* (Johannesburg: Witwatersrand University Press).

Ethnic Minority Employment Taskforce (2006) *Ethnic Minorities in the Labour Market* (London: HMSO).

EUFRA (European Union Fundamental Rights Agency) (2007) *Trends and Developments in Racism, Xenophobia and Anti-Semitism, 1997–2005* (Vienna: EUFRA).

Europaworld (2007) 'Global Unemployment Remains at Historic High Despite Strong Economic Growth', www.europaworld.com/pub/.

European Commission (2001) *Promoting a European Framework for Corporate Social Responsibility*, Green Paper (Brussels: European Commission).

European Commission (2006) *Eurobarometer 66: Public Opinion in the European Union* (Luxembourg: European Commission).

European Commission (2015a) 'Reducing Emissions from Transport', http://ec.europa.eu/clima/policies/transport/index_en.htm.

European Commission (2015b) 'Acceding and Candidate Countries', http://ec.europa.eu/economy_finance/international/non_eu/candidate/index_en.htm.

European Environment Agency (2013) *Managing Municipal Solid Waste: A Review of Achievements in 32 European Countries* (Copenhagen: EEA); www.eea.europa.eu/ publications/managing-municipal-solid-waste.

European Parliament (2014) *European Parliament: Facts and Figures*, www.europarl.europa.eu/EPRS/EPRS-Briefing-542150-European-Parliament-Facts-and-Figures-FINAL.pdf.

Eurostat (2010) *Europe in Figures: Eurostat Yearbook 2010* (Luxembourg: European Union).

Eurostat (2011) 'Population Structure and Ageing', http://epp.eurostat.ec.europa.eu/statistics_explained/index.php/Population_structure_and_ageing.

Eurostat (2014) 'Tertiary Education Statistics', http://ec.europa.eu/eurostat/statistics-explained/index.php/Tertiary_education_statistics#Further_Eurostat_information.

Eurostat (2015a) 'People at Risk of Poverty or Social Exclusion', http://ec.europa.eu/eurostat/statistics-explained/index.php/People_at_risk_of_poverty_or_social_exclusion#Main_tables.

Eurostat (2015b) 'Crude Marriage and Divorce Rates, EU-28, 1970–2011', http://ec.europa.eu/eurostat/statistics-explained/index.php/File:Crude_marriage_and_divorce_rates,_EU-28,_1970%E2%80%932011_(%C2%B9)_(per_1_000_inhabitants)_YB15.png.

Evans, D. J. (1992) 'Left Realism and the Spatial Study of Crime', in D. J. Evans, N. R. Fyfe and D. T. Herbert (eds), *Crime, Policing and Place: Essays in Environmental Criminology* (London: Routledge).

Evans, M. (2000) 'Poor Show', *The Guardian*, 6 March.

Evans, P. (1979) *Dependent Development* (Princeton, NJ: Princeton University Press).

Evans-Pritchard, A. (2015) 'Liquidity Evaporates in China as "Fiscal Cliff" Nears', *The Telegraph*, 4 March; www.telegraph.co.uk/finance/comment/ambroseevans_pritchard/11450691/Liquidity-evaporates-in-China-as-fiscal-cliff-nears.html.

Fainstein, S. (2001) *The City Builders: Property Development in New York and London, 1980–2000* (2nd edn, Lawrence: University Press of Kansas).

Fairclough, N. (1989) *Language and Power* (London: Longman).

Fairclough, N. (1992) *Critical Language Awareness* (London: Longman).

Fairclough, N. (2000) *New Labour, New Language?* (London: Routledge).

Fairclough, N. (2003) *Analysing Discourse: Textual Analysis for Social Research* (London: Routledge).

Faludi, S. (1991) *Backlash: The Undeclared War against Women* (London: Chatto & Windus).

FAO/IFAD/ILO (Food and Agriculture Organization/International Fund for Agricultural Development/International Labour Organization) (2010) 'Breaking the Rural Poverty Cycle: Getting Girls and Boys out of Work and into School', www.fao.org/docrep/013/i2008e/i2008e07.pdf.

Farndale, N. (2011) 'Brian Cox: I'm Not Anti-Religion, I'm Anti-Maniac', *The Telegraph*, 21 February; www.telegraph.co.uk/news/science/8330863/Brian-Cox-Im-not-anti-religion.-Im-anti-maniac.html.

Farrington, D. P. (2003) 'Advancing Knowledge about the Early Prevention of Adult Antisocial Behaviour', in D. P. Farrington and J. W. Coid (eds), *Early Prevention of Adult Antisocial Behaviour* (Cambridge: Cambridge University Press): 1–31.

Farrington, D. P., and Welsh, B. C. (2007) *Saving Children from a Life of Crime: Early Risk Factors and Effective Interventions* (Oxford: Oxford University Press).

Featherstone, M., and Hepworth, M. (1989) 'Ageing and Old Age: Reflections on the Postmodern Life Course', in B. Bytheway et al. (eds), *Becoming and Being Old* (London: Sage).

Featherstone, M., and Renwick, A. (eds) (1995) *Images of Aging: Cultural Representations of Later Life* (London and New York: Routledge).

Felson, M. (1994) *Crime and Everyday Life: Insights and Implications for Society* (Thousand Oaks, CA: Pine Forge Press).

Felstead, A., Jewson, N., and Walters, S. (2005) *Changing Places of Work* (Basingstoke: Palgrave Macmillan).

Fensom, A. (2015) 'Asia's Growth Gap: India Versus the Rest', *The Diplomat*, 15 April; http://thediplomat.com/2015/04/asias-growth-gap-india-versus-the-rest/.

Fenton, S. (2010) *Ethnicity* (2nd edn, Cambridge: Polity).

Ferrera, M. (2005) *The Boundaries of Welfare: European Integration and the New Spatial Politics of Social Protection* (Oxford: Oxford University Press).

Feuerbach, L. (1957 [1853]) *The Essence of Christianity* (New York: Harper & Row).

Feyerabend, P. (1975) *Against Method* (London: Verso).

Fihlani, P. (2011) 'Is South Africa's Aids Plan Working?', 30 November, www.bbc.co.uk/news/world-africa-15854793.

Financial Fraud Action UK (2014) *Fraud: The Facts 2014* (London: FFAUK).

Finch, J. (2007) 'Displaying Families', *Sociology*, 41(1): 65–81.

Finke, R., and Stark, R. (1988) 'Religious Economies and Sacred Canopies: Religious Mobilization in American Cities, 1906', *American Sociological Review*, 53(1): 41–9.

Finke, R., and Stark, R. (1992) *The Churching of America, 1776–1990: Winners and Losers in our Religious Economy* (New Brunswick, NJ: Rutgers University Press).

Finkelstein, V. (1980) *Attitudes and Disabled People* (New York: World Rehabilitation Fund).

Finkelstein, V. (1981) 'To Deny or Not to Deny Disability', in A. Brechin et al. (eds), *Handicap in a Social World* (Sevenoaks: Hodder & Stoughton).

Firestone, S. (1970) *The Dialectic of Sex: The Case for Feminist Revolution* (London: Jonathan Cape).

Firth, R. W. (ed.) (1956) *Two Studies of Kinship in London* (London: Athlone Press).

Fischer, C. S. (1984) *The Urban Experience* (2nd edn, New York: Harcourt).

Fisher, P., and Nandi, A. (2015) *Poverty across Ethnic Groups through Recession and Austerity* (York: Joseph Rowntree Foundation).

Fiske, J. (1989) *Reading the Popular* (London: Unwin Hyman).

Flaherty, J., Veit-Wilson, J., and Dornan, P. (2004) *Poverty: The Facts* (5th edn, London: Child Poverty Action Group).

Flatley, J., Kershaw, C., Smith, K., Chaplin, R., and Moon, D. (eds) (2010) *Crime in England and Wales, 2009/10* (London: Home Office).

Fletcher, J. (1997) *Violence and Civilization: An Introduction to the Work of Norbert Elias* (Cambridge: Polity).

Florack, F. (2014) 'Free Schools in England: The Future of British Education?', in *International Conference on 'The Future of Education'*, 4th edn, Florence, Italy, 12–13 June: 219–22.

Flouri, E. (2005) *Fathering and Child Outcomes* (Chichester: John Wiley).

Forbes (2014a) 'Forbes Billionaires: Full List of the World's 500 Richest People', www.forbes.com/sites/abrambrown/2014/03/03/forbes-billionaires-full-list-of-the-worlds-500-richest-people/.

Forbes (2014b) 'Inside the Forbes 2014 Billionaires List: Facts and Figures', www.forbes.com/sites/luisakroll/2014/03/03/inside-the-2014-forbes-billionaires-list-facts-and-figures/.

Forbes (2015) 'Mark Zuckerberg: Real Time Net Worth', www.forbes.com/profile/mark-zuckerberg/.

Ford, C. S., and Beach, F. A. (1951) *Patterns of Sexual Behaviour* (New York: Harper & Row).

Foreign Policy (2014) 'Mongolia Versus eBay', www.foreignpolicy.com/articles/2012/02/27/mongolia_vs_ebay.

Foresight (2011) *The Future of Food and Farming: Final Project Report* (London: Government Office for Science); www.bis.gov.uk/assets/foresight/docs/food-and-farming/11-546-future-of-food-and-farming-report.pdf.

Forman, L. (2008) *Assisted Suicide* (Edina, MN: ABDO).

Foucault, M. (1967) *Madness and Civilization: A History of Insanity in the Age of Reason* (London: Tavistock).

Foucault, M. (1973) *The Birth of the Clinic: An Archaeology of Medical Perception* (London: Tavistock).

Foucault, M. (1975) *Discipline and Punish* (Harmondsworth: Penguin).

Foucault, M. (1978) *The History of Sexuality* (London: Penguin).

Foucault, M. (1988) 'Technologies of the Self', in L. H. Martin, H. Gutman and P. H. Hutton (eds), *Technologies of the Self: A Seminar with Michel Foucault* (Amherst: University of Massachusetts Press).

Francis, B. (2000) *Boys, Girls and Achievement: Addressing the Classroom Issues* (London: Routledge).

Frank, A. G. (1966) 'The Development of Underdevelopment', *Monthly Review*, 18: 17–31.

Frank, A. G. (1969) *Capitalism and Underdevelopment in Latin America: Historical Studies of Chile and Brazil* (New York: Monthly Review Press).

Frank, D. J., and McEneaney, E. H. (1999) 'The Individualization of Society and the Liberalization of State Policies on Same-Sex Sexual Relations, 1984–1995', *Social Forces*, 7(3): 911–43.

Fraser, N. (1992) *Revaluing French Feminism: Critical Essays on Difference, Agency and Culture* (Indianapolis: Indiana University Press).

Fraser, S. (1995) *The Bell Curve Wars: Race, Intelligence, and the Future of America* (New York: Basic Books).

Freidson, E. (1970) *Profession of Medicine: A Study of the Sociology of Applied Knowledge* (New York: Dodd, Mead).

Fremlin, J. H. (1964) 'How Many People Can the World Support?', *New Scientist*, 29 October.

Freud, S. (1995 [1933]) *New Introductory Lectures on Psycho-analysis* (New York: W. W. Norton).

Frey, C. B., and Osborne, M. A. (2013) 'The Future of Employment: How Susceptible are Jobs to Computerization?', www.oxfordmartin.ox.ac.uk/downloads/academic/The_Future_of_Employment.pdf.

Frezzo, M. (2014) *The Sociology of Human Rights* (Cambridge: Polity).

Friedan, B. (1963) *The Feminine Mystique* (London: Victor Gollancz).

Friedlander, D., and Burtless, G. (1994) *Five Years After: The Long-Term Effects of Welfare-to-Work Programs* (New York: Russell Sage).

Fries, J. F. (1980) 'Aging, Natural Death, and the Compression of Morbidity', *New England Journal of Medicine*, 303(3): 130–5.

Frisby, D. (2002) *Georg Simmel* (rev. edn, London: Routledge).

Fukuyama, F. (1992) *The End of History and the Last Man* (Harmondsworth: Penguin).

Fuller, B. (1978) 'Accommodating Human Unsettlement', *Town Planning Review*, 49 (January): 51–60.

Gallup (2004) 'Poll Topics and Trends: Religion', 1 August.

Gallup (2014) 'In U.S., 42% Believe Creationist View of Human Origins', 2 June, www.gallup.com/poll/170822/believe-creationist-view-human-origins.aspx.

Gamble, A. (1999) *Marxism after Communism: The Interregnum: Controversies in World Politics 1989–1999* (Cambridge: Cambridge University Press).

Gammons, H. (2011) *The Art of Music Publishing* (Oxford: Elsevier).

Gamson, J. (1994) *Claims to Fame: Celebrity in Contemporary America* (Berkeley: University of California Press).

Gans, H. J. (1962) *The Urban Villagers: Group and Class in the Life of Italian-Americans* (2nd edn, New York: Free Press).

Gardner, C. B. (1995) *Passing By: Gender and Public Harassment* (Berkeley: University of California Press).

Garfinkel, H. (1963) 'A Conception of, and Experiments with, "Trust" as a Condition of Stable Concerted Actions', in O. J. Harvey (ed.), *Motivation and Social Interaction* (New York: Ronald Press).

Garrioch, D. (2004) *The Making of Revolutionary Paris* (Berkeley: University of California Press).

Gatto, J. T. (2002) *Dumbing Us Down: The Hidden Curriculum of Compulsory Schooling* (Philadelphia: New Society).

GaWC (2012) 'The World According to GaWC, 2012', www.lboro.ac.uk/gawc/world2012t.html.

Gellner, E. (1983) *Nations and Nationalism* (Oxford: Blackwell).

Gerbner, G. (1997) 'Gender and Age in Prime-Time Television', in S. Kirschner and D. A. Kirschner (eds), *Perspectives on Psychology and the Media* (Washington, DC: American Psychological Association).

Gereffi, G. (1995) 'Contending Paradigms for Cross-Regional Comparison: Development Strategies and Commodity Chains in East Asia and Latin America', in P. H. Smith (ed.), *Latin America in Comparative Perspective: New Approaches to Methods and Analysis* (Boulder, CO: Westview Press).

Gershuny, J. (1994) 'The Domestic Labour Revolution: A Process of Lagged Adaptation', in M. Anderson, F. Bechofer and J. Gershuny (eds), *The Social and Political Economy of the Household* (Oxford: Oxford University Press).

Gershuny, J. I., and Miles. I. D. (1983) *The New Service Economy: The Transformation of Employment in Industrial Societies* (London: Frances Pinter).

Gerstenfeld, P. B. (2010) *Hate Crimes: Causes, Controls and Controversies* (New York: Sage).

Gewirtz, S., Ball, S., and Bowe, R. (1995) *Markets, Choice, and Equity in Education* (Buckingham: Open University Press).

Gibbs, L. (2002) 'Citizen Activism for Environmental Health: The Growth of a Powerful New Grassroots Health Movement', *Annals of the American Academy of Political and Social Science*, 584: 97–109.

Gibson, W. (1993) 'Disneyland with the Death Penalty', *Wired*, 1 April, www.wired.com/1993/04/gibson-2/.

Giddens, A. (1984) *The Constitution of Society* (Cambridge: Polity).

Giddens, A. (1991a) *Modernity and Self-Identity: Self and Society in the Late Modern Age* (Cambridge: Polity).

Giddens, A. (1991b) *The Consequences of Modernity* (Cambridge: Polity).

Giddens, A. (1993) *The Transformation of Intimacy: Love, Sexuality and Eroticism in Modern Societies* (Cambridge: Polity).

Giddens, A. (1994) *Beyond Left and Right: The Future of Radical Politics* (Cambridge: Polity).

Giddens, A. (1998) *The Third Way: The Renewal of Social Democracy* (Cambridge: Polity).

Giddens, A. (ed.) (2001) *The Global Third Way Debate* (Cambridge: Polity).

Giddens, A. (2002) *Runaway World: How Globalisation is Reshaping our Lives* (London: Profile).

Giddens, A. (2006) 'Misunderstanding Multiculturalism', 14 October, https://www.theguardian.com/commentisfree/2006/oct/14/tonygiddens.

Giddens, A. (2009) *The Politics of Climate Change* (Cambridge: Polity).

Giddens, A. (2011) *The Politics of Climate Change* (2nd edn, Cambridge: Polity).

Gillborn, D., and Youdell, D. (2001) 'The New IQism: Intelligence, "Ability" and the Rationing of Education', in J. Demaine (ed.), *Sociology of Education Today* (London: Palgrave).

Gilleard, C., and Higgs, P. (2005) *Contexts of Ageing: Class, Cohort and Community* (Cambridge: Polity).

Gilligan, C. (1982) *In a Different Voice: Psychological Theory and Women's Development* (Cambridge, MA: Harvard University Press).

Gillis, J. (1996) *A World of Their Own Making: Myth, Ritual and the Quest for Family Values* (New York: Basic Books).

Gillis, S., Howie, G., and Munford, R. (2007) *Third Wave Feminism: A Critical Exploration* (2nd edn, Basingstoke: Palgrave Macmillan).

Gillon, S. (2004) *Boomer Nation: The Largest and Richest Generation Ever, and How it Changed America* (New York: Free Press)

Ginn, J., and Arber, S. (2000) 'Ethnic Inequality in Later Life: Variation in Financial Circumstances by Gender and Ethnic Group', *Education and Ageing*, 15(1): 65–83.

Ginzburg, C. (1980) *The Cheese and the Worms* (London: Routledge & Kegan Paul).

Giroux, H. (1983) *Theory and Resistance in Education: A Pedagogy for the Opposition* (South Hadley, MA: Bergin & Garvey).

Gittins, D. (1993) *The Family in Question: Changing Households and Familiar Ideologies* (Basingstoke: Macmillan).

Glascock, J. (2001) 'Gender Roles on Prime-Time Network Television: Demographics and Behaviors', *Journal of Broadcasting & Electronic Media*, 45(4): 656–69.

Glaser, B. G., and Strauss, A. L. (1965) *Awareness of Dying* (Chicago: Aldine).

Glasgow University Media Group (1976) *Bad News* (London: Routledge).

Glasius, M., Kaldor, M., and Anheier, H. (eds) (2002) *Global Civil Society 2002* (Oxford: Oxford University Press).

Glass, D. (1954) *Social Mobility in Britain* (London: Routledge & Kegan Paul).

Global Slavery Index (2014) '2014 Global Slavery Index', www.globalslaveryindex.org/.

Glover, I., and Hughes, M. (1996) *The Professional Managerial Class: Contemporary British Management in the Pursuer Mode* (Aldershot: Avebury).

Glover, J. (2011) 'Europeans are Liberal, Anxious and Don't Trust Politicians, Poll Reveals', *The Guardian*, 13 March; www.guardian.co.uk/world/2011/mar/13/guardian-icm-europe-poll-2011.

Goffman, E. (1963) *Stigma* (Englewood Cliffs, NJ: Prentice-Hall).

Goffman, E. (1967) *Interaction Ritual* (New York: Doubleday/Anchor).

Goffman, E. (1968 [1961]) *Asylums: Essays on the Social Situation of Mental Patients and Other Inmates* (Harmondsworth: Penguin).

Goffman, E. (1971) *Relations in Public: Microstudies of the Public Order* (London: Allen Lane).

Goffman, E. (1980 [1959]) *The Presentation of Self in Everyday Life* (London: Penguin).

Goffman, E. (1981) *Forms of Talk* (Philadelphia: University of Pennsylvania Press).

Gold, T. (1986) *State and Society in the Taiwan Miracle* (Armonk, NY: M. E. Sharpe).

Goldenberg, S., Vidal, J., Taylor, L., Vaughn, A., and Harvey, F. (2015) 'Paris Climate Deal: Nearly 200 Nations Sign in End of Fossil Fuel Era', *The Guardian*, 12 December; www.theguardian.com/environment/2015/dec/12/paris-climate-deal-200-nations-sign-finish-fossil-fuel-era.

Golding, P., and Murdock, G. (eds) (1997) *The Political Economy of the Media* (Cheltenham: Edward Elgar).

Goldscheider, F. K., and Waite, L. J. (1991) *New Families, No Families? The Transformation of the American Home* (Berkeley: University of California Press).

Goldsmith, E. (1988) *The Great U-Turn: Deindustrialising Society* (Bideford: Green Books).

Goldsmith, E., et al. (1972) *A Blueprint for Survival* (London: Penguin).

Goldthorpe, J. H. (1968–9) *The Affluent Worker in the Class Structure*, 3 vols (Cambridge: Cambridge University Press).

Goldthorpe, J. H. (1983) 'Women and Class Analysis in Defence of the Conventional View', *Sociology*, 17(4): 465–76.

Goldthorpe, J. H. (2000) *On Sociology* (Oxford: Oxford University Press).

Goldthorpe, J. H., and McKnight, A. (2004) *The Economic Basis of Social Class*, CASE Paper 80 (London: Centre for Analysis of Social Exclusion, London School of Economics).

Goldthorpe, J. H., and Payne, C. (1986) 'Trends in Intergenerational Class Mobility in England and Wales 1972–1983', *Sociology*, 20: 1–24.

Goldthorpe, J. H., Llewellyn, C., and Payne, C. (1987 [1980]) *Social Mobility and Class Structure in Modern Britain* (2nd edn, Oxford: Clarendon Press).

Goleman, D. (1996) *Emotional Intelligence: Why it Can Matter More than IQ* (London: Bloomsbury).

Golsh, K. (2003) 'Employment Flexibility in Spain and its Impact on Transitions to Adulthood', *Work, Employment and Society*, 17(4): 691–718.

Goode, W. J. (1963) *World Revolution in Family Patterns* (New York: Free Press).

Goodhart, D. (2004) 'Too Diverse? Is Britain Becoming Too Diverse to Sustain the Mutual Obligations behind a Good Society and the Welfare State?' *Prospect*, 20 February; www.prospectmagazine.co.uk/2004/02/too-diverse-david-goodhart-multiculturalism-britain-immigration-globalisation/.

Goodman, A., and Gregg, P. (eds) (2010) *Poorer Children's Educational Attainment: How Important Are Attitudes and Behaviour?* (York: Joseph Rowntree Foundation).

Goodwin, J., and Jasper, J. (eds) (2002) *The Social Movements Reader: Cases and Concepts* (Oxford: Wiley Blackwell).

Gordon, D., Levitas, R., Pantazis, C., et al. (2000) *Poverty and Social Exclusion in Britain* (York: Joseph Rowntree Foundation) [PSE survey].

Gorz, A. (1982) *Farewell to the Working Class* (London: Pluto Press).

Gorz, A. (1985) *Paths to Paradise: On the Liberation from Work* (London: Pluto Press).

Gottdiener, M., Hutchison, R., and Ryan, M. T. (2015) *The New Urban Sociology* (5th edn, Boulder, CO: Westview Press).

Gottfredson, M. R., and Hirschi, T. (1990) *A General Theory of Crime* (Stanford, CA: Stanford University Press).

Goudsblom, J. (1992) *Fire and Civilization* (London: Allen Lane).

Grabosky, P. N., and Smith, R. G. (1998) *Crime in the Digital Age: Controlling Telecommunications and Cyberspace Illegalities* (New Brunswick, NJ: Transaction Books).

Graef, R. (1989) *Talking Blues* (London: Collins).

Graef, R. (2001) *Why Restorative Justice? Repairing the Harm Caused by Crime* (London: Calouste Gulbenkian Foundation).

Graham, F. (2011) 'Is the Internet Going to be the Death of Television?', BBC News, 13 May, www.bbc.co.uk/news/business-13377164.

Graham, H. (1987) 'Women's Smoking and Family Health', *Social Science and Medicine*, 25(1): 47–56.

Graham, H. (1994) 'Gender and Class as Dimensions of Smoking Behaviour in Britain: Insights from a Survey of Mothers', *Social Science and Medicine*, 38(5): 691–8.

Graham, L. (1995) *On the Line at Subaru-Isuzu* (Ithaca, NY: Cornell University Press).

Graham, S. (2010) 'When Infrastructures Fail', in S. Graham (ed.), *Disrupted Cities: When Infrastructure Fails* (London: Routledge): 1–26.

Graham, S. (2011) *Cities under Siege: The New Military Urbanism* (London: Verso).

Graham, S., and McFarlane, C. (eds) (2015) *Infrastructural Lives: Urban Infrastructure in Context* (Abingdon: Routledge).

Graham, S., Desai, R., and McFarlane, C. (2015) 'Water Wars in Mumbai', in S. Graham and C. McFarlane (eds), *Infrastructural Lives: Urban Infrastructure in Context* (Abingdon: Routledge): 61–85.

Graham-Harrison, E. (2015) 'Hassan Rouhani: Reformist Insider Who Has Ended Iran's Isolation', *The Guardian*, 5 April; www.theguardian.com/world/2015/apr/05/profile-hassan-rouhani-iran.

Granovetter, M. (1973) 'The Strength of Weak Ties', *American Journal of Sociology*, 78(6): 1360–56.

Granovetter, M. (1985) 'Economic Action and Social Structure: The Problem of Embeddedness', *American Journal of Sociology*, 91(3): 481–510.

Gray, D., and Watt, P. (2013) *Giving Victims a Voice: Joint Report into Sexual Allegations made Against Jimmy Savile* (London: MPS/NSPCC); https://www.nspcc.org.uk/globalassets/documents/research-reports/yewtree-report-giving-victims-voice-jimmy-savile.pdf.

Gray, J. (1993) *Men are from Mars, Women are from Venus* (New York: HarperCollins).

Gray, J. (2003) *Al Qaeda and What it Means to Be Modern* (Chatham: Faber & Faber).

Gray, J., Lee Harrington, C., and Sandvoss, C. (eds) (2007) *Fandom: Identities and Communities in a Mediated World* (New York: New York University Press).

Greed, C. (1994) *Women and Planning: Creating Gendered Realities* (London: Routledge).

Green, D. G. (2000) *Institutional Racism and the Police: Fact or Fiction?* (London: CIVITAS).

Green, L. (2015) 'Age and the Life Course: Continuity, Change and the Modern Mirage of Infinite Choice', in M. Holborn (ed.), *Contemporary Sociology* (Cambridge: Polity): 96–129.

Green, L. (2016) *Understanding the Life-Course: Sociological and Psychological Perspectives* (2nd edn, Cambridge: Polity).

Greenberg, J., Schimel, J., and Mertens, A. (2004) 'Ageism: Denying the Face of the Future', in T. D. Nelson (ed.), *Ageism: Stereotyping and Discrimination against Older Persons* (Cambridge, MA: MIT Press): 27–48.

Gregg, B. (2011) *Human Rights as Social Construction* (New York: Cambridge University Press).

Gregg, M. (2011) *Work's Intimacy* (Cambridge: Polity).

Gregg, P., and Washbrook, E. (2010) 'From Birth through Primary School: Evidence from the Avon Longitudinal Study of Parents and Children', in A. Goodman and P. Gregg (eds), *Poorer Children's Educational Attainment: How Important Are Attitudes and Behaviour?* (York: Joseph Rowntree Foundation): 26–33.

Gregori Signes, C. (2000) *A Genre Based Approach to Daytime Talk on Television* (Valencia: Universitat de València).

Grey, S., and Sawyer, M. (eds) (2008) *Women's Movements: Flourishing or in Abeyance?* (London: Routledge).

Griffin, C. (1985) *'Typical Girls': Young Women from School to the Job Market* (London: Routledge & Kegan Paul).

Grint, K., and Nixon, D. (2015) *The Sociology of Work: An Introduction* (4th edn, Cambridge: Polity).

Grogan, S. (2008) *Body Image: Understanding Body Dissatisfaction in Men, Women and Children* (2nd edn, London: Routledge).

Grossman, C. L. (2010) 'Most Americans Believe in God, but Don't Know Religious Tenets', *USA Today*, 27 September; www.usatoday.com/news/religion/2010-09-28-pew28_ST_N.htm.

Grusky, D. B., and Hauser, R. M. (1984) 'Comparative Social Mobility Revisited: Models of Convergence and Divergence in 16 Countries', *American Sociological Review*, 49: 19–38.

The Guardian (2009) 'Caster Semenya Row: Who are White People to Question the Makeup of an African Girl? It is Racism', 23 August; www.theguardian.com/sport/2009/aug/23/caster-semenya-athletics-gender.

The Guardian (2011) 'How Likely are You to Live to 100?', 4 August; www.guardian.co.uk/news/datablog/2011/aug/04/live-to-100-likely.

The Guardian (2014) 'Full List of Free Schools Approved for 2014 Opening', www.theguardian.com/education/2013/may/22/free-schools-full-list-2014.

The Guardian (2015) 'Lives Transformed: Do Famous Transgender People Help the Cause?', 23 August, www.theguardian.com/society/2015/aug/23/famous-transgender-help-the-cause-caitlyn-jenner-laverne-cox-kellie-maloney.

Guibernau, M. (1999) *Nations without States: Political Communities in a Global Age* (Cambridge: Polity).

Habermas, J. (1981) 'New Social Movements', *Telos*, 49 (Fall): 33–7.

Habermas, J. (1983) 'Modernity – an Incomplete Project', in H. Foster (ed.), *The Anti-Aesthetic* (Port Townsend, WA: Bay Press).

Habermas, J. (1985) *The Philosophical Discourse of Modernity* (Cambridge: Polity).

Habermas, J. (1989 [1962]) *The Structural Transformation of the Public Sphere* (Cambridge, MA: MIT Press).

Habermas, J. (2008) 'Notes on Post-Secular Society', *New Perspectives Quarterly*, 25(4): 17–29.

Hackett, R. A., and Zhao, Y. (eds) (2005) *Democratizing Global Media: One World, Many Struggles* (Oxford: Rowman & Littlefield).

Hadaway, C. K., and Marler, P. L. (2005) 'How Many Americans Attend Worship Each Week? An Alternative Approach to Measurement', *Journal for the Scientific Study of Religion*, 44(3): 307–22.

Hadden, J. (1997) 'New Religious Movements Mission Statement', http://religiousmovements.lib.virginia.edu/welcome/welcome.htm.

Hafferty, F. W., and Castellani, B. (2011) 'Two Cultures: Two Ships: The Rise of a Professionalism Movement within Modern Medicine and Medical Sociology's Disappearance from the Professionalism Debate', in B. A. Pescosolido et al. (eds), *Handbook of the Sociology of Health, Illness and Healing: A Blueprint for the 21st Century* (New York: Springer): 201–20.

Hajer, M. A. (1996) 'Ecological Modernisation as Cultural Politics', in S. Lash, B. Szerszynski and B. Wynne (eds), *Risk, Environment and Modernity: Towards a New Ecology* (London: Sage).

Hales, J., Nevill, C., Pudney, S., and Tipping, S. (2009) *Longitudinal Analysis of the Offending, Crime and Justice Survey 2003–06*, Research Report 19 (London: Home Office).

Hall, E. T. (1969) *The Hidden Dimension* (New York: Doubleday).

Hall, E. T. (1973) *The Silent Language* (New York: Doubleday).

Hall, R., James, S., and Kertesz, J. (1984) *The Rapist who Pays the Rent* (2nd edn, Bristol: Falling Wall Press).

Hall, S. (1980) *Culture, Media, Language: Working Papers in Cultural Studies, 1972–79* (London: Hutchinson, in association with the Centre for Contemporary Cultural Studies, University of Birmingham).

Hall, S. (1991) 'Old and New Identities, Old and New Ethnicities', in A. D. King (ed.), *Culture, Globalization and the World-System: Contemporary Conditions for the Representation of Identity* (Basingstoke: Macmillan): 41–68.

Hall, S. (2006 [1989]) 'New Ethnicities', in B. Ashcroft, G. Griffiths, and H. Tiffin (eds), *The Post-Colonial Studies Reader* (2nd edn, London: Routledge): 199–202.

Hall, S., et al. (1978) *Policing the Crisis: Mugging, the State, and Law and Order* (London: Macmillan).

Halliday, F. (2002) *Two Hours that Shook the World: September 11, 2001: Causes and Consequences* (London: Saqi Books).

Halligan, J. (2012) 'Foreword', in R. M. Kowalski, S. P. Limber and P. W. Agatston, *Cyberbullying: Bullying in the Digital Age* (Chichester: John Wiley & Sons): vi–viii.

Halsey, A. H. (ed.) (1997) *Education: Culture, Economy, and Society* (Oxford: Oxford University Press).

Hamilton, M. C., Anderson, D., Broaddus, M., and Young, K. (2006) 'Gender Stereotyping and Under-Representation of Female Characters in 200 Popular Children's Picture Books: A Twenty-First Century Update', *Sex Roles*, 55(11–12): 757–65.

Handy, C. (1994) *The Empty Raincoat: Making Sense of the Future* (London: Hutchinson).

Hannigan J. A. (2006) *Environmental Sociology: A Social Constructionist Perspective* (2nd edn, London: Routledge).

Hannigan, J. A. (2014) *Environmental Sociology* (3rd edn, New York: Routledge).

Haraway, D. (1989) *Primate Visions: Gender, Race and Nature in the World of Modern Science* (New York: Routledge).

Haraway, D. (1991) *Simians, Cyborgs and Women: The Reinvention of Nature* (New York; Routledge).

Harman, S., and Williams, D. (2013) 'Introduction: Governing the World?' in S. Harman and D. Williams (eds), *Governing the World? Cases in Global Governance* (Abingdon: Routledge): 1–11.

Harman, V., and Cappellini, B. (2015) 'Mothers on Display: Lunchboxes, Social Class and Moral Accountability', *Sociology*, 49(4): 1–18.

Harper, D. (2010) *Visual Sociology: An Introduction* (London: Routledge).

Harrabin, R. (2015) 'Moroccan Solar Plant to Bring Energy to a Million People', 23 November, www.bbc.co.uk/news/science-environment-34883224.

Harrington, A. (2004) *Art and Social Theory* (Cambridge: Polity).

Harris, J. R. (1998) *The Nurture Assumption: Why Children Turn out the Way They Do* (New York: Free Press).

Harris, M. (1978) *Cannibals and Kings: The Origins of Cultures* (New York: Random House).

Harrison, M. (1985) *TV News: Whose Bias?* (Hermitage, Berks: Policy Journals).

Harrison, P. (1983) *Inside the Inner City: Life under the Cutting Edge* (Harmondsworth: Penguin).

Harvey, D. (1982) *The Limits to Capital* (Oxford: Blackwell).

Harvey, D. (1985) *Consciousness and the Urban Experience: Studies in the History and Theory of Capitalist Urbanization* (Oxford: Blackwell).

Harvey, D. (1989) *The Condition of Postmodernity* (Oxford: Blackwell).

Harvey, D. (1993) 'The Nature of Environment: The Dialectics of Social and Environmental Change', *Socialist Register*: 1–51.

Harvey, D. (2006) *Spaces of Global Capitalism: Towards a Theory of Uneven Geographical Development* (London: Verso).

Harvey, D. (2008) 'The Right to the City', *New Left Review*, 53: 23–40.

Harvey, R. (2010) 'Vietnam's Bid to Tame the Internet Boom', 18 August, www.bbc.co.uk/news/world-asia-pacific-11010924.

Hasler, F. (1993) 'Developments in the Disabled People's Movement', in J. Swain (ed.), *Disabling Barriers, Enabling Environments* (London: Sage).

Hass, J. K. (2007) *Economic Sociology: An Introduction* (London: Routledge).

Haughton, G., and Hunter, C. (2003) *Sustainable Cities* (London: Routledge).

Havel, V. (1988) 'Anti-Political Politics', in J. Keane (ed.), *Civil Society and the State: New European Perspectives* (London and New York: Verso).

Hawkins, K. (2015) 'Lizzie Velasquez: Online Bullies Called Me the World's Ugliest Woman', 14 March, www.bbc.co.uk/news/blogs-ouch-30948179.

Hawley, A. H. (1950) *Human Ecology: A Theory of Community Structure* (New York: Ronald Press).

Hawley, A. H. (1968) *Human Ecology* (Glencoe, IL: Free Press).

Health Inequalities Unit, Department of Health (2009) *Tackling Health Inequalities: 2006–08 Policy and Data Update for the 2010 National Target*, www.dh.gov.uk/prod_consum_dh/groups/dh_digitalassets/@dh/@en/@ps/@sta/@perf/documents/digitalasset/dh_109468.pdf.

Healy, M. (2001) 'Pieces of the Puzzle', *Los Angeles Times*, 21 May.

Heaphy, B. (2011) 'Critical Relational Displays', in J. Seymour and E. Dermott (eds), *Displaying Families: A New Concept for the Sociology of Family Life* (Basingstoke: Palgrave Macmillan): 19–37.

Hearn, J., and McKie, L. (2008) 'Gendered Policy and Policy on Gender: The Case of "Domestic Violence"', *Politics and Policy*, 36(1): 75–91.

Heath, A. (1981) *Social Mobility* (London: Fontana).

Heath, S., and Calvert, E. (2013) 'Gifts, Loans and Intergenerational Support for Young Adults', *Sociology*, 47(6): 1120–35.

Heath, S., and Cleaver, E. (2003) *Young, Free and Single? Twenty-Somethings and Household Change* (Basingstoke: Palgrave Macmillan).

Heath, S., McGhee, D., and Trevina, S. (2011) 'Lost in Transnationalism: Unraveling the Conceptualisation of Families and Personal Life through a Transnational Gaze', *Sociological Research Online*, 16(4): 12, www.socresonline.org.uk/16/4/12.html.

Hebdige, D. (1997) *Cut 'n' Mix: Culture, Identity, and Caribbean Music* (London: Methuen).

Heelas, P. (2002) 'The Spiritual Revolution: From "Religion" to "Spirituality"', in L. Woodhead, P. Fletcher, H. Kawanami and D. Smith (eds), *Religions in the Modern World* (London: Routledge): 357–77.

Heelas, P. (2015) 'Religion and Sources of Significance: The Dawning of a Secular Age?', in M. Holborn (ed.), *Contemporary Sociology* (Cambridge: Polity): 415–43.

Heidensohn, F. (1996) *Women and Crime* (2nd edn, Basingstoke: Palgrave Macmillan).

Heinich, N. (2010) 'About "Social Construction"', *Newsletter of the Research Committee on Sociological Theory*, www.isa-sociology.org/pdfs/rc16newsletter-spring-2010.pdf.

Held, D. (2004) *Global Covenant: The Social Democratic Alternative to the Washington Consensus* (Cambridge: Polity).

Held, D. (2006) *Models of Democracy* (3rd edn, Cambridge: Polity).

Held, D., Goldblatt, D., McGrew, A., and Perraton, J. (1999) *Global Transformations: Politics, Economics and Culture* (Cambridge: Polity).

Hemerijck, J. (2013) *Changing Welfare States* (Oxford: Oxford University Press).

Henderson, J., and Appelbaum, R. P. (1992) 'Situating the State in the Asian Development Process', in R. P. Appelbaum and J. Henderson (eds), *States and Development in the Asian Pacific Rim* (Newbury Park, CA: Sage).

Hendricks, J. (1992) 'Generation and the Generation of Theory in Social Gerontology', *Aging and Human Development*, 35(1): 31–47.

Henslin, J. M., and Biggs, M. A. (1997 [1971]) 'Behaviour in Public Places: The Sociology of the Vaginal Examination', in J. M. Henslin (ed.), *Down to Earth Sociology: Introductory Readings* (9th edn, New York: Free Press).

Hepworth, M. (2000) *Stories of Ageing* (Buckingham: Open University Press).

Heritage, J. (1984) *Garfinkel and Ethnomethodology* (Cambridge: Polity).

Herman, E. S., and McChesney, R. W. (1997) *The Global Media: The New Missionaries of Global Capitalism* (London: Cassell).

Herman, E. S., and McChesney, R. W. (2003) 'Media Globalization: The US Experience and Influence', in R. C. Allen and A. Hill (eds), *The Television Studies Reader* (London: Routledge).

Herrnstein, R. J., and Murray, C. (1994) *The Bell Curve: Intelligence and Class Structure in American Life* (New York: Free Press).

HESA (Higher Education Statistics Agency) (2010) 'Staff at Higher Education Institutions in the United Kingdom, 2008/09', www.hesa.ac.uk/index.php?option=com_content&task=view&id=1590&Itemid=161.

Hewson, C., Yule, P., Laurent, D., and Vogel C. (2002) *Internet Research Methods: A Practical Guide for the Social and Behavioural Sciences* (London: Sage).

Hexham, I., and Poewe, K. (1997) *New Religions as Global Cultures* (Boulder, CO: Westview Press).

Heywood, A. (2012) *Political Ideologies: An Introduction* (5th edn, Basingstoke: Palgrave Macmillan).

Hickson, K. (2004) 'Equality', in R. Plant, M. Beech and K. Hickson (eds), *The Struggle for Labour's Soul: Understanding Labour's Political Thought since 1945* (London: Routledge).

Higher Education Commission (2014) *Too Good to Fail: The Financial Sustainability of Higher Education in England* (London: HEC).

Hills, J., et al. (2010) *An Anatomy of Economic Inequality in the UK: Report of the National Equality Panel* (London: Government Equalities Office).

Hillyard, P., Pantazis, C., Tombs, S., and Gordon, D. (eds) (2004) *Beyond Criminology? Taking Harm Seriously* (London: Pluto Press).

Hironaka, A. (2005) *Neverending Wars: The International Community, Weak States, and the Perpetuation of Civil War* (Cambridge, MA: Harvard University Press).

Hirschi, T. (1969) *Causes of Delinquency* (Berkeley: University of California Press).

Hirst, P. (1997) 'The Global Economy: Myths and Realities', *International Affairs*, 73(3): 409–25.

Hirst, P. (2001) *War and Power in the 21st Century: The State, Military Conflict and the International System* (Cambridge: Polity).

Hirst, P., and Thompson, G. (1992) 'The Problem of "Globalization": International Economic Relations, National Economic Management, and the Formation of Trading Blocs', *Economy and Society*, 21(4): 357–96.

Hirst, P., and Thompson, G. (1999) *Globalization in Question: The International Economy and the Possibilities of Governance* (rev. edn, Cambridge: Polity).

HMIC (2014) 'Police Force Figures on Rape Made Publicly Available', 31 January, www.justice inspectorates.gov.uk/hmic/news/news-feed/police-force-figures-on-rape-made-publicly-available/.

HMRC (Her Majesty's Revenue and Customs) (2010) 'Personal Wealth', www.hmrc.gov.uk/stats/personal_wealth/13-5-table-2005.pdf.

Ho, S. Y. (1990) *Taiwan: After a Long Silence* (Hong Kong: Asia Monitor Resource Center).

Hobson, B. (ed.) (2002) *Making Men into Fathers: Men, Masculinities and the Social Politics of Fatherhood* (Cambridge: Cambridge University Press).

Hobson, D. (2002) *Soap Opera* (Cambridge: Polity).

Hochschild, A. (1983) *The Managed Heart: Commercialization of Human Feeling* (Berkeley: University of California Press).

Hochschild, A. (1989) *The Second Shift: Working Parents and the Revolution at Home* (New York: Viking).

Holmes, M. (2011) 'Emotional Reflexivity in Contemporary Friendships: Understanding it Using Elias and Facebook Etiquette', *Sociological Research Online*, 16(1): 11, www.socresonline.org.uk/16/1/11.html.

Holmwood, J. (2010) 'Three Tiers for Sociology as Funding is Slashed', *Network* [newsletter of the British Sociological Association].

Home Office, ONS and Ministry of Justice (2013) *An Overview of Hate Crime in England and Wales, December 2013*, https://www.gov.uk/government/uploads/system/uploads/attachment_data/file/266358/hate-crime-2013.pdf.

hooks, b. (1981) *Ain't I a Woman? Black Women and Feminism* (Boston: South End Press).

hooks, b. (1997) *Bone Black: Memories of Girlhood* (London: Women's Press).

Hopper, P. (2007) *Understanding Cultural Globalization* (Cambridge: Polity).

Horkheimer, M., and Adorno, T. W. (2002 [1947]) *Dialectic of Enlightenment: Philosophical Fragments* (Stanford, CA: Stanford University Press).

Horlick-Jones, T., Walls, J., Rowe, G., Pidgeon, N., Poortinga, W., Murdock, G., and O'Riordan, T. (2009) *The GM Debate: Risk, Politics and Public Engagement* (London: Routledge).

Howard, J. H., et al. (1986) 'Change in "Type A" Behaviour a Year after Retirement', *The Gerontologist*, 26(6): 643–9.

Howard, M., Garnham, A., Fimister, G., and Veit-Wilson, J. (2001) *Poverty: The Facts* (4th edn, London: Child Poverty Action Group).

Hughes, E. C. (1945) 'Dilemmas and Contradictions of Status', *American Journal of Sociology*, 50(5): 353–9.

Hughes, G. (1998) *Understanding Crime Prevention: Social Control, Risk and Late Modernity* (Buckingham: Open University Press).

Humphreys, L. (1970) *Tearoom Trade: A Study of Homosexual Encounters in Public Places* (London: Duckworth).

Hunt, P. (ed.) (1966) *Stigma: The Experience of Disability* (London: Geoffrey Chapman).

Hunt, S. (2016) *The Life-Course: A Sociological Introduction* (2nd edn, Basingstoke: Palgrave Macmillan).

Huntington, S. P. (1996) *The Clash of Civilizations and the Remaking of World Order* (New York: Simon & Schuster).

Hutchby, I. (2005) *Media Talk: Conversation Analysis and the Study of Broadcasting* (Buckingham: Open University Press).

Hutchison, E. D. (2007) *Dimensions of Human Behavior: The Changing Life Course* (3rd edn, Thousand Oaks, CA: Sage).

Hutton, W. (1995) *The State We're in* (London: Jonathan Cape).

Hylton, K. (2009) *'Race' and Sport: Critical Race Theory* (London: Routledge).

Hyman, R. (1984) *Strikes* (2nd edn, London: Fontana).

Iacovou, M., and Skew, A. (2010) *Household Structure in the EU*, ISER Working Paper no. 2010-10 (Colchester: University of Essex: Institute for Social and Economic Research).

IBRD (International Bank for Reconstruction and Development)/World Bank (2007) *Millennium Development Goals: Global Monitoring Report* (Washington DC: World Bank).

IFS (Institute for Fiscal Studies) (2011) *Poverty and Inequality in the UK: 2011* (London: IFS).

Iganski, P., and Payne, G. (1999) 'Socio-Economic Restructuring and Employment: The Case of Minority Ethnic Groups', *British Journal of Sociology*, 50(2): 195–215.

ILGA (International Lesbian, Gay, Bisexual, Trans and Intersex Association) (2015) The Lesbian, Gay and Bisexual Map of World Laws, http://old.ilga.org/Statehomophobia/ILGA_WorldMap_2015_ENG.pdf.

Illich, I. (1975) *Medical Nemesis: The Expropriation of Health* (London: Calder & Boyars).

Illich, I. D. (1971) *Deschooling Society* (Harmondsworth: Penguin).

ILO (International Labour Organization) (1999) 'C182 Worst Forms of Child Labour Convention', www.ilo.org/ilolex/cgi-lex/convde.pl?C182.

ILO (International Labour Organization) (2007a) *Global Employment Trends for Women, Brief, March 2007*, www.ilo.org/empelm/pubs/WCMS_114287/lang--es/index.htm.

ILO (International Labour Organization) (2007b) *Harvest for the Future: Agriculture without Children* (Geneva: ILO).

ILO (International Labour Organization) (2010) *Accelerating Action against Child Labour* (Geneva: ILO).

ILO (International Labour Organization) (2011a) *Global Employment Trends 2011: The Challenge of a Jobs Recovery* (Geneva: ILO).

ILO (International Labour Organization) (2011b) 'Eliminating Child Labour in Rural Areas through Decent Work', www.ilo.org/wcmsp5/groups/public/ ed_emp/documents/publication/wcms_165305.pdf.

ILO (International Labour Organization) (2012) *World of Work Report: Better Jobs for a Better Economy*, www.ilo.org/wcmsp5/groups/public/---dgreports/---dcomm/---publ/documents/publication/wcms_179453.pdf.

IMS (2013) 'Amazon Forges Another Competitive Advantage over Retailers', www.imsresultscount.com/resultscount/2013/10/amazon-forges-another-competitive-advantage-over-retailers.html.

The Independent (2007) 'Nigeria: Learning the Hard Way', 17 October; www.independent.co.uk/news/world/africa/nigeria-learning-the-hard-way-397090.html.

The Independent (2012) 'Elton John: The Historic Fight for Equality Must Go On: Let's Get on and Legalise Same-Sex Marriage', 8 October; www.independent.co.uk/voices/comment/elton-john-the-historic-fight-for-equality-must-go-on-lets-get-on-and-legalise-samesex-marriage-8202686.html.

The Independent (2013) 'Olympics Legacy: Did the Games Succeed in rejuvenating East London?' 16 July; www.independent.co.uk/sport/olympics/olympics-legacy-did-the-games-succeed-in-rejuvenating-east-london-8711691.html.

The Independent (2014) 'Sunday Times Rich List: Wealthiest Britons Own a Third of the Nation's Wealth', 18 May; www.independent.co.uk/news/people/sunday-times-rich-list-wealthiest-britons-own-a-third-of-the-nations-wealth-9391634.html.

Inglehart, R. (1977) *The Silent Revolution: Changing Values and Political Styles among Western Publics* (Princeton, NJ: Princeton University Press).

Inglehart, R. (1990) 'Values, Ideology, and Cognitive Mobilization', in R. J. Dalton and M. Kuechler (eds), *Challenging the Political Order: New Social and Political Movements in Western Democracies* (Oxford: Blackwell).

Inglehart, R. (1997) *Modernization and Postmodernization: Cultural, Economic and Political Change in 43 Societies* (Princeton, NJ: Princeton University Press).

Institute for Child and Family Policy (2004) 'Lone Parents/Lone Mother Families with Children', www.childpolicyintl.org/.

International Organization for Migration (2012) 'Facts and Figures', www.iom.int/jahia/Jahia/about-migration/facts-and-figures/lang/en.

Internet World Stats (2015) 'World Internet Penetration Rates by Geographic Regions, 2014 Q4', www.internetworldstats.com/stats.htm.

IPCC (Intergovernmental Panel on Climate Change) (2007) *Climate Change 2007: Synthesis Report*, Fourth Assessment Report, www.ipcc.ch/publications_and_data/publications_ipcc_fourth_assessment_report_synthesis_report.htm.

IPCC (Intergovernmental Panel on Climate Change) (2015) *Climate Change 2014: Synthesis Report, Contribution of Working Groups I, II and III to the Fifth Assessment Report of the Intergovernmental Panel on Climate Change* (Geneva: IPCC).

IPPR (Institute for Public Policy Research) (1999) *Unsafe Streets: Street Homelessness and Crime* (London: IPPR).

Ipsos MORI (2007) 'The Most Important Issues Facing Britain Today', www.ipsos-mori.com/research publications/researcharchive/poll.aspx?oItemID=56&view=wide#2007.

Ipsos MORI (2015) 'How Britain Voted in 2015', https://www.ipsos-mori.com/researchpublications/researcharchive/3575/How-Britain-voted-in-2015.aspx?view=wide.

Irwin, A. (2001) *Sociology and the Environment: A Critical Introduction to Society, Nature and Knowledge* (Cambridge: Polity).

ISNA (Intersex Association of North America) (2015) 'What is Intersex?', www.isna.org/faq/what_is_intersex.

ITU (International Telecommunication Union) (2014) *The World in 2014: ICT Facts and Figures* (Geneva: ITU); www.itu.int/en/ITU-D/Statistics/Documents/facts/ICTFactsFigures2014-e.pdf.

Jackson, M., and Goldthorpe, J. H. (2007) 'Intergenerational Class Mobility in Contemporary Britain: Political Concerns and Empirical Findings', *British Journal of Sociology*, 58(4): 525–46.

Jackson, S. (2001) 'Why a Materialist Feminism is (Still) Possible – and Necessary', *Women's Studies International Forum*, 24(3/4): 283–93.

Jackson, S., and Jones, J. (eds) (1998) *Contemporary Feminist Theories* (New York: New York University Press).

Jaishankar, K. (2011) 'Conclusion', in K. Jaishankar (ed.), *Cyber Criminology: Exploring Internet Crimes and Criminal Behavior* (Boca Raton, FL: CRC Press): 411–14.

James, A., Jenks, C., and Prout, A. (1998) *Theorizing Childhood* (Cambridge: Polity).

Jamieson, L. (1998) *Intimacy: Personal Relationships in Modern Societies* (Cambridge: Polity).

Jamieson, L. (2013) 'Personal Relationships, Intimacy and the Self in a Mediated and Global Digital Age', in K. Orton-Johnson and N. Prior (eds), *The Palgrave Macmillan Digital Sociology: Critical Perspectives* (Basingstoke: Palgrave Macmillan): 13–33.

Jay, A. (2014) *Independent Inquiry Into Child Sexual Exploitation in Rotherham 1997–2013*, www.rotherham.gov.uk/downloads/file/1407/independent_inquiry_cse_in_rotherham.

Jeffreys, S. (2015) *Beauty and Misogyny: Harmful Cultural Practices in the West* (2nd edn, London: Routledge).

Jencks, C. (1994) *The Homeless* (Cambridge, MA: Harvard University Press).

Jenkins, C. (1990) *The Professional Middle Class and the Origins of Progressivism: A Case Study of the New Education Fellowship 1920–1950*, CORE 14(1).

Jenkins, H. (2009) *Confronting the Challenges of Participatory Culture: Media Education for the 21st Century* (Cambridge, MA: MIT Press).

Jenkins, H., Ito, M., and boyd, d. (2016) *Participatory Culture in a Networked Era* (Cambridge: Polity).

Jenkins, P. (2001) *Paedophiles and Priests: Anatomy of a Contemporary Crisis* (Oxford: Oxford University Press).

Jenkins, R. (1996) *Social Identity* (2nd edn, London: Routledge).

Jenkins, R. (2008) *Social Identity* (3rd edn, London: Routledge).

Jenkins, S. P. (2011) *Changing Fortunes: Income Mobility and Poverty Dynamics in Britain* (Oxford: Oxford University Press).

Jenks, C. (2005) *Childhood* (2nd edn, London: Routledge).

Jenks, M., and Jones, C. (eds) (2009) *Dimensions of the Sustainable City* (New York: Springer).

Jensen, A. (1969) 'How Much Can We Boost IQ and Scholastic Achievement?', *Harvard Educational Review*, 39(1): 1–123.

Jensen, A. (1979) *Bias in Mental Testing* (New York: Free Press).

Joas, H., and Knöbl, W. (2012) *War in Social Thought: Hobbes to the Present* (Princeton, NJ: Princeton University Press).

Jobe, A. (2010) *The Causes and Consequences of Re-Trafficking: Evidence from the IOM Human Trafficking Database* (Geneva: International Organization for Migration).

Jobling, R. (1988) 'The Experience of Psoriasis under Treatment', in M. Bury and R. Anderson (eds), *Living with Chronic Illness: The Experience of Patients and their Families* (London: Unwin Hyman).

John, M. T. (1988) *Geragogy: A Theory for Teaching the Elderly* (New York: Haworth).

Johnson, B. (2007) 'Families of Abused Teenagers Sue MySpace', *The Guardian*, 19 January; www.guardian.co.uk/media/2007/jan/19/digitalmedia.usnews.

Joint Council for Qualifications (2013) 'Entry Trends, Gender and Regional Charts, GCE 2013', www.jcq.org.uk/media-centre/news-releases/entry-trends-gender-regional-charts-gce-2013.

Jones, D. E., Doty, S., Grammich, C., et al. (2002) *Religious Congregations & Membership in the United States 2000: An Enumeration by Region, State and County Based on Data Reported for 149 Religious Bodies* (Nashville, TN: Glenmary Research Centre).

Jones, T., and Newburn, T. (2007) *Policy Transfer and Criminal Justice: Exploring US Influence over British Crime Control Policy* (Maidenhead: Open University Press).

Jónsson, Ö. D. (2010) *Good Clean Fun: How the Outdoor Hot Tub Became the Most Frequented Gathering Place in Iceland*, http://skemman.is/stream/get/1946/6754/18560/1/243-249_%C3%96rn_D_Jonsson_VIDbok.pdf.

Judge, K. (1995) 'Income Distribution and Life Expectancy: A Critical Appraisal', *British Medical Journal*, 311: 1282–7.

Jung, S., and Shim, D. (2014) 'Social Distribution: K-Pop Fan Practices in Indonesia and the "Gangnam Style" Phenomenon', *International Journal of Cultural Studies*, 17(5): 485–501.

Kagan, M. (2011) '10 essential Twitter Stats', http://blog.hubspot.com/blog/tabid/6307/bid/12234/10-Essential-Twitter-Stats-Data.aspx.

Kaldor, M. (2006) *New and Old Wars: Organized Violence in a Global Era* (2nd edn, Cambridge: Polity).

Kalyvas, S. N. (2006) *The Logic of Violence in Civil War* (Cambridge: Cambridge University Press).

Kanbur, R., and Summer, A. (2011) *Poor Countries or Poor People? Development Assistance and the New Geography of Global Poverty*, Working Paper 2011-08 (Ithaca, NY: Cornell University).

Karlsen, S. (2007) *Ethnic Inequalities in Health: The Impact of Racism*, Better Health Briefing 3 (London: Race Equality Foundation).

Karpf, A. (1988) *Doctoring the Media: The Reporting of Health and Medicine* (London: Routledge).

Karyotis, G., and Gerodimos, R. (2015) 'Introduction: Dissecting the Greek Debt Crisis', in G. Karyotis and R. Gerodimos (eds), *The Politics of Extreme Austerity: Greece in the Eurozone Crisis* (Basingstoke: Palgrave Macmillan): 1–14.

Kasarda, J. D., and Janowitz, M. (1974) 'Community Attachment in Mass Society', *American Sociological Review*, 39: 328–39.

Katz, E., and Lazarsfeld, P. (1955) *Personal Influence* (New York: Free Press).

Katz, J., Rice, R. E., and Aspden, P. (2001) 'The Internet, 1995–2000: Access, Civic Involvement, and Social Interaction', *American Behavioral Scientist*, 45(3): 405–19.

Katz, S. (1996) *Disciplining Old Age: The Formation of Gerontological Knowledge* (Charlottesville and London: University Press of Virginia).

Kaufman, E. (2007) *The End of Secularization in Europe? A Demographic Perspective*, Working Paper (Birkbeck College, University of London).

Kautsky, J. (1982) *The Politics of Aristocratic Empires* (Chapel Hill: University of North Carolina Press).

Keddie, A., and Mills, M. (2007) *Teaching Boys: Classroom Practices that Work* (Crow's Nest, NSW: Allen & Unwin).

Kelly, M. P. (1992) *Colitis* (London: Tavistock).

Kendall, D. (2005) *Framing Class: Media Representations of Wealth and Poverty in America* (Lanham, MD: Rowman & Littlefield).

Kepel, G. (1994) *The Revenge of God: The Resurgence of Islam, Christianity and Judaism in the Modern World* (Cambridge: Polity).

Kiecolt, K. J., and Nelson, H. M. (1991) 'Evangelicals and Party Realignment, 1976–1988', *Social Science Quarterly*, 72: 552–69.

Kiely, R. (1999) 'The Last Refuge of the Noble Savage? A Critical Assessment of Post-Development Theory', *European Journal of Development Research*, 11(1): 30–55.

Kilminster, R. (2007) *Norbert Elias: Post-Philosophical Sociology* (London: Routledge).

Kim, C. E. (2012) 'Nonsocial Transient Behavior: Social Disengagement on the Greyhound Bus', *Symbolic Interaction* 35(3): 267–83.

King, P. (2011) *The New Politics: Liberal Conservatism or Same Old Tories?* (Bristol: Policy Press).

King, Z., Burke, S., and Pemberton, J. (2005) 'The "Bounded" Career: An Empirical Study of Human Capital, Career Mobility and Employment Outcomes in a Mediated Labour Market', *Human Relations*, 58(8): 981–1007.

Kinsey, A. C. (1948) *Sexual Behaviour in the Human Male* (Philadelphia: W. B. Saunders).

Kinsey, A. C. (1953) *Sexual Behaviour in the Human Female* (Philadelphia: W. B. Saunders).

Kirkwood, T. (2001) *Ageing Vulnerability: Causes and Interventions* (Chichester: Wiley).

Knorr-Cetina, K., and Cicourel, A. V. (1981) *Advances in Social Theory and Methodology: Towards an Interpretation of Micro- and Macro-Sociologies* (London: Routledge & Kegan Paul).

Kofman, E. (2004) 'Family-Related Migration: A Critical Review of European Studies', *Journal of Ethnic and Migration Studies*, 30(2): 243–62.

Kolakowski, L. (2005) *Main Currents of Marxism: The Founders, the Golden Age, the Breakdown* (New York: W. W. Norton).

Kolker, R. (2009) *Media Studies: An Introduction* (Chichester: Wiley-Blackwell).

Kollock, P. (1999) 'The Production of Trust in Online Markets', *Advances in Group Processes*, vol. 16, ed. S. R. Thye et al. (Stamford, CT, and London: JAI Press).

Korte, H. (2001) 'Perspectives on a Long Life: Norbert Elias and the Process of Civilization', in T. Salumets (ed.), *Norbert Elias and Human Interdependencies* (Montreal and Kingston: McGill-Queen's University Press).

Koser, K., and Lutz, H. (1998) 'The New Migration in Europe: Contexts, Constructions and Realities', in K. Koser and H. Lutz (eds), *The New Migration in Europe: Social Constructions and Social Realities* (Basingstoke: Macmillan).

Kosmin, B. A., and Keysar, A. (2009) *American Religious Identification Survey: Summary Report* (Hartford, CT: Program on Public Values).

Koss, S. E. (1973) *Fleet Street Radical: A. G. Gardiner and the Daily News* (London: Allen Lane).

Kraut, R., Brynin, M., and Kiesler, S. (eds) (2006) *Computers, Phones and the Internet: Domesticating Internet Technology* (Buckingham: Open University Press).

Kristeva, J. (1977) *Polylogue* (Paris: Seuil).

Kristeva, J. (1984) *Revolution in Poetic Language* (New York: Columbia University Press).

Krolløke, C., and Sørensen, A. S. (2006) *Gender Communication Theories and Analyses: From Silence to Performance* (London: Sage).

Krupat, E. (1985) *People in Cities: The Urban Environment and its Effects* (Cambridge: Cambridge University Press).

Kuhn, T. (1962) *The Structure of Scientific Revolutions* (Chicago: University of Chicago Press).

Kulkarni, V. G. (1993) 'The Productivity Paradox: Rising Output, Stagnant Living Standards', *Business Week*, 8 February.

Kuznets, S. (1955) 'Economic Growth and Income Inequality', *Economic Review*, 45(1): 1–28.

Lacan, J. (1995) *Lacan's Four Fundamental Concepts of Psychoanalysis* (New York: SUNY Press).

Laming, Lord (2003) *The Victoria Climbie Inquiry*, CM 5730 (London: HMSO).

Land, K. C., Deane, G., and Blau, J. R. (1991) 'Religious Pluralism and Church Membership', *American Sociological Review*, 56(2): 237–49.

Landes, D. S. (2003) *The Unbound Prometheus: Technological Change and Industrial Development in Western Europe from 1750 to the Present* (2nd edn, New York: Cambridge University Press).

Lansley, S., and Mack, J. (2015) *Breadline Britain: The Rise of Mass Poverty* (London: Oneworld).

Lappe, F. M. (1998) *World Hunger: 12 Myths* (New York: Grove Press).

Laqueur, T. (1990) *Making Sex: Body and Gender from the Greeks to Freud* (Cambridge, MA: Harvard University Press).

Laqueur, W. (2000) *The New Terrorism: Fanaticism and the Arms of Mass Destruction* (New York: Oxford University Press).

Laqueur, W. (2003) *No End to War: Terrorism in the 21st Century* (New York: Continuum).

Lareau, A. (2003) *Class, Race and Family Life* (Berkeley: University of California Press).

Larsen, J., Urry, J., and Axhausen, K. (2006) *Social Networks and Future Mobilities: Report to the UK Department for Transport* (Lancaster and Zurich: University of Lancaster and IVT, ETH Zurich).

Lask B., and Bryant-Waugh, R. (eds) (2000) *Anorexia Nervosa and Related Eating Disorders in Childhood and Adolescence* (Hove: Psychology Press).

Last J. M. (ed.) (2001) *A Dictionary of Epidemiology* (4th edn, New York: Oxford University Press).

Laumann, E. O. (1994) *The Social Organization of Sexuality: Sexual Practices in the United* States (Chicago: University of Chicago Press).

Law, I. (2009) *Racism and Ethnicity: Global Debates, Dilemmas, Directions* (Harlow: Pearson Education).

Lawson, N. (2009) *An Appeal to Reason: A Cool Look at Global Warming* (London: Duckworth Overlook).

Le Roux, B., Rouanet, H., Savage, M., and Warde, A. (2007) *Class and Cultural Division in the UK*, Working Paper no. 40 (CRESC, University of Manchester).

Lea, J., and Young, J. (1984) *What Is to Be Done about Law and Order?* (London: Penguin).

Leadbeater, C. (1999) *Living on Thin Air: The New Economy* (London: Viking).

Lee, D., and Newby, H. (1983) *The Problem of Sociology* (London: Routledge).

Lee, N. (2001) *Childhood and Society: Growing Up in an Age of Uncertainty* (Buckingham: Open University Press).

Lee, R. B., and De Vore, I. (eds) (1968) *Man the Hunter* (Chicago: Aldine).

Lee, S. (2001) 'Fat Phobia in Anorexia Nervosa: Whose Obsession Is It?', in M. Nasser, M. Katzman and R. Gordon (eds), *Eating Disorders and Cultures in Transition* (New York: Brunner-Routledge).

Lees, L., Slater, T., and Wyly, E. (eds) (2008) *Gentrification* (New York: Routledge).

Lees, S. (1993) *Sugar and Spice: Sexuality and Adolescent Girls* (London: Penguin).

Leisering, L., and Leibfried, S. (1999) *Time and Poverty in Western Welfare States* (Cambridge: Cambridge University Press).

Leitenberg, M. (2006) *Deaths in Wars and Conflicts in the 20th Century*, Occasional Paper no. 29 (3rd edn, Ithaca, NY: Cornell University).

Lelkes, O. (2007) *Poverty among Migrants in Europe* (Vienna: European Centre for Social Welfare Policy and Research).

Lemert, E. (1972) *Human Deviance, Social Problems and Social Control* (Englewood Cliffs, NJ: Prentice-Hall).

Lemkin, R. (1944) *Axis Rule in Occupied Europe: Laws of Occupation, Analysis of Government, Proposals for Redress* (New York: Carnegie Endowment for International Peace).

Lenski, G. (1963) *The Religious Factor* (New York: Doubleday).

LeVay, S. (1993) *The Sexual Brain* (Cambridge, MA: MIT Press).

Levitas, R. (2005) *The Inclusive Society: Social Exclusion and New Labour* (2nd edn, Basingstoke: Palgrave Macmillan).

Lev-On, A. (2009) 'Cooperation with and without Trust Online', in K. S. Cook, C. Snijders, V. Buskers and C. Cheshire (eds), *eTrust: Forming Relationships in the Online World* (New York: Russell Sage Foundation): 292–318.

Lewis, M. W. (1994) *Green Delusions: An Environmentalist Critique of Radical Environmentalism* (Durham, NC, and London: Duke University Press).

Lewis, P., and Newburn, T. (2012) *Reading the Riots* (London: Guardian Books).

Lewontin, R. (1995) 'Sex, Lies and Social Science', *New York Review of Books*, 42: 24–9.

Li, H., Lau, J. T. F., Holroyd, E., and Yi, H. (2010) 'Sociocultural Facilitators and Barriers to Condom Use during Anal Sex among Men who Have Sex with Men in Guangzhou, China: An Ethnographic Study', *AIDS Care: Psychological and Socio-Medical Aspects of AIDS/HIV*, 22(12): 1481–6.

Li, Y., and Heath, A. (2007) *Minority Ethnic Groups in the British labour Market (1972–2005): Exploring Patterns, Trends and Processes of Minority Ethnic Disadvantages*, https://www.research.manchester.ac.uk/portal/files/31105707/FULL_TEXT.PDF.

Liebes, T., and Katz, E. (1993) *The Export of Meaning: Cross-Cultural Readings of Dallas* (Cambridge: Polity).

Lim, L. L. (1998) *The Sex Sector: The Economic and Social Bases of Prostitution in Southeast Asia* (Geneva: International Labour Organization).

Linz, J. J. (2000) *Totalitarian and Authoritarian Regimes* (Boulder, CO: Lynne Rienner).

Lipset, S. M. (1991) 'Comments on Luckmann', in P. Bourdieu and J. S. Coleman (eds), *Social Theory for a Changing Society* (Boulder, CO: Westview Press): 185–8.

Lipset, S. M., and Bendix, R. (1959) *Social Mobility in Industrial Society* (Berkeley: University of California Press).

Lister, C. R. (2015) *The Islamic State: A Brief Introduction* (Washington, DC: Brookings Institution Press).

Lister, R. (ed.) (1996) *Charles Murray and the Underclass: The Developing Debate* (London: IEA Health and Welfare Unit, in association with the Sunday Times).

Lister R. (2004) *Poverty* (Cambridge: Polity).

Lister, R. (2011) 'The Age of Responsibility: Social Policy and Citizenship in the Early 21st Century', in C. Holden, M. Kilkey and G. Ramia (eds), *Analysis and Debate in Social Policy, 2011* (Bristol: Policy Press): 63–84.

Lister, R., et al. (2007) *Gendering Citizenship in Western Europe: New Challenges for Citizenship Research in a Cross-National Context* (Bristol: Policy Press).

Livi-Bacci, M. (2012) *A Concise History of World Population* (5th edn, Oxford: Wiley-Blackwell).

Livingstone, S. (2009) *Children and the Internet: Great Expectations, Changing Realities* (Cambridge: Polity).

Livingstone, S., and Bovill, M. (1999) *Young People, New Media* (London: London School of Economics).

Livingstone, S., and Lunt, P. (1993) *Talk on Television: Audience Participation and Public Debate* (London: Routledge).

Locke, J., and Pascoe, E. (2000) 'Can a Sense of Community Flourish in Cyberspace?', *The Guardian*, 11 March; www.guardian.co.uk/theguardian/2000/mar/11/debate.

Lomborg, B. (2001) *The Skeptical Environmentalist: Measuring the Real State of the World* (Cambridge: Cambridge University Press).

Longworth, N. (2003) *Lifelong Learning in Action: Transforming Education in the 21st Century* (London: Kogan Page).

Lorber, J. (1994) *Paradoxes of Gender* (New Haven, CT: Yale University Press).

Louie, M. C. Y. (2001) *Sweatshop Warriors: Immigrant Women Workers Take on the Global Factory* (Boston: South End Press).

Loungani, P. (2003) 'Inequality: Now You See it, Now You Don't', in *Finance and Development* (Washington, DC: International Monetary Fund).

Low Pay Commission (2009) *National Minimum Wage: Low Pay Commission Report 2009* (Norwich: The Stationery Office).

Lucas, K., Blumenberg, E., and Weinberger, R. (eds) (2011) *Auto Motives: Understanding Car Use Behaviours* (Bingley: Emerald Group).

Lukes, S. (1974) *Power: A Radical View* (London: Macmillan).

Lukes, S. (2004) *Power: A Radical View* (2nd edn, Basingstoke: Macmillan).

Lull, J. (1990) *Inside Family Viewing: Ethnographic Research on Television's Audiences* (London: Routledge).

Lull, J. (1997) 'China Turned on (Revisited): Television, Reform and Resistance', in A. Sreberny-Mohammadi et al. (eds), *Media in Global Context: A Reader* (London: Edward Arnold).

Lune, H. (2010) *Understanding Organizations* (Cambridge: Polity).

Lupton, D. (ed.) (1999) *Risk and Sociocultural Theory: New Directions and Perspectives* (Cambridge: Cambridge University Press).

Lykke, N. (2011) 'Intersectional Invisibility: Inquiries into a Concept of Intersectionality Studies', in H. Lutz, M. T. H. Vivar and L. Supik (eds), *Framing Intersectionality: Debates on a Multi-Faceted Concept in Gender Studies* (Farnham: Ashgate): 207–20.

Lynch, M. (2006) *Voices of the New Arab Public: Iraq, Al-Jazeera, and Middle East Politics Today* (New York: Columbia University Press).

Lyon, C., and de Cruz, P. (1993) *Child Abuse* (London: Family Law).

Lyotard, J.-F. (1984) *The Postmodern Condition* (Minneapolis: University of Minnesota Press).

Mac an Ghaill, M. (1994) *The Making of Men: Masculinities, Sexualities and Schooling* (Buckingham: Open University Press).

Mac an Ghaill, M. (1996) 'Introduction', in M. Mac an Ghaill (ed.), *Understanding Masculinities* (Buckingham: Open University Press): 1–15.

McAuley, R. (2006) *Out of Sight: Crime Youth and Exclusion in Modern Britain* (Cullompton, Devon: Willan).

McCoombs, M. (2014) *Setting the Agenda: Mass Media and Public Opinion* (2nd edn, Cambridge: Polity).

McDowell, L. (2004) 'Thinking through Work: Gender, Power and Space', in T. Barnes et al., *Reading Economic Geography* (Oxford: Blackwell): 315–28.

McFadden, D., and Champlin, C. A. (2000) 'Comparison of Auditory Evoked Potentials in Heterosexual, Homosexual, and Bisexual Males and Females', *Journal of the Association for Research in Otolaryngology*, 1(1): 89–99.

MacFarlane, A. (1990) 'Official Statistics and Women's Health and Illness', in H. Roberts (ed), *Womens' Health Counts* (London: Routledge): 18–62.

MacGregor, S. (2003) 'Social Exclusion', in N. Ellison and C. Pierson (eds), *Developments in British Social Policy 2* (Basingstoke: Palgrave Macmillan).

MacGregor, S., and Pimlott, B. (1991) 'Action and Inaction in the Cities', in *Tackling the Inner Cities: The 1980s Reviewed, Prospects for the 1990s* (Oxford: Clarendon Press).

McGuinness, F. (2015) *Unemployment by Ethnic Background*, Briefing Paper 6385 (London: House of Commons Library); www.parliament.uk/briefing-papers/SN06385.pdf.

MacInnes, T., Aldridge, H., Bushe, S., Tinson, A., and Born, T. B. (2014) *Monitoring Poverty and Social Exclusion 2014* (York: Joseph Rowntree Foundation).

MacInnes, T., Tinson, A., Hughes, C., Born, T. B., and Aldridge, H. (2015) *Monitoring Poverty and Social Exclusion 2015* (York: Joseph Rowntree Foundation).

McIntosh, M. (1968) 'The Homosexual Role', *Social Problems*, 16(2): 182–92.

Mack, J., and Lansley, S. (1985) *Poor Britain* (London: Allen & Unwin).

Mack, J., and Lansley, S. (1992) *Breadline Britain 1990s: The Findings of the Television Series* (London: London Weekend Television).

McKenna, H., et al. (2001) 'Qualified Nurses' Smoking Prevalence: Their Reasons for Smoking and Desire to Quit', *Journal of Advanced Nursing*, 35(5): 769–75.

McKeown, T. (1979) *The Role of Medicine: Dream, Mirage or Nemesis?* (Oxford: Blackwell).

McKnight, A. (2000) *Earnings Inequality and Earnings Mobility, 1977–1997: The Impact of Mobility on Long Term Inequality*, Employment Relations Research Series no. 8 (London: Department of Trade and Industry).

Maclean, M., Harvey, C., and Press, J. (2006) *Business Elites and Corporate Governance in France and the UK* (Basingstoke: Palgrave Macmillan).

McLennan, G. (2010) 'Eurocentrism, Sociology, Secularity', in E. G. Rodríguez, M. Boatcă and S. Costa (eds), *Decolonizing European Sociology: Transdisciplinary Approaches* (Farnham: Ashgate): 119–34.

McLeod, J., and Yates, L. (2008) 'Class and the Middle: Schooling, Subjectivity, and Social Formation', in L. Weis (ed.), *The Way Class Works: Readings on School, Family, and the Economy* (New York: Routledge): 347–62.

McLuhan, M. (1964) *Understanding Media* (London: Routledge & Kegan Paul).

McMichael, P. (1996) *Development and Social Change: A Global Perspective* (Thousand Oaks, CA: Pine Forge Press).

Macnaghten, P., and Urry, J. (1998) *Contested Natures* (London: Sage).

McNamara, K. R. (2010) 'The Eurocrisis and the Uncertain Future of European Integration', in S. Patrick (ed.), *Crisis in the Eurozone: Transatlantic Perspectives* (New York: Council on Foreign Relations): 22–4.

Macnicol, J. (2010) *Ageing and Discrimination: Some Analytical Issues* (London: ILC-UK).

Macpherson, S. W. (1999) *The Stephen Lawrence Inquiry*, Cm 4262-I (London: HMSO); www.archive.official-documents.co.uk/document/cm42/4262/4262.htm [Macpherson Report].

McQuail, D. (2000) *McQuail's Mass Communication Theory* (London: Sage).

Macrae, S., Maguire, M., and Milbourne, M. (2003) 'Social Exclusion: Exclusion from School', *International Journal of Inclusive Education*, 7(2): 89–101.

McRobbie, A. (1991) *Feminism and Youth Culture: From Jackie to Just Seventeen* (Cambridge, MA: Unwin Hyman).

McRobbie, A., and Garber, J. (1975) 'Girls and Subcultures', in S. Hall and T. Jefferson (eds), *Resistance through Rituals: Youth Subcultures in Post-War Britain* (London: Hutchinson).

McVeigh, T. (2010) 'Women Told to Forget about Babies if They Want to Scale Career Heights', *The Observer*, 15 August; www.guardian.co.uk/lifeandstyle/2010/aug/15/women-children-career-top-jobs.

Maffesoli, M. (1995) *The Time of the Tribes: The Decline of Individualism in Mass Society* (London: Sage).

Maguire, J. (1999) *Global Sport: Identities, Societies, Civilizations* (Cambridge: Polity).

Maguire, M. B. (2008) *Lived Religion: Faith and Practice in Everyday Life* (Oxford: Oxford University Press).

Mahalingam, R., and McCarthy, C. (eds) (2000) *Multicultural Curriculum: New Directions for Social Theory, Practice and Social Policy* (London: Routledge).

Maier, E. (2011) 'Implicit Human–Computer Interaction by Posture Recognition', in V. G. Duffy (ed.), *Digital Human Modelling* (Heidelberg: Springer): 143–50.

Makino, M., Tsuboi, K., and Dennerstein, L. (2004) 'Prevalence of Eating Disorders: A Comparison of Western and Non-Western Countries', *Medscape General Medicine*, 6(3): 49.

Malakooti, A., and Davin, E. (2015) *Migration Trends across the Mediterranean: Connecting the Dots*, www.altaiconsulting.com/docs/migration/Altai_Migration_trends_accross_the_Mediterranean_v3.pdf.

Malcolm, N. (1996) *Bosnia: A Short History* (New York: New York University Press).

Malešević, S. (2010) *The Sociology of War and Violence* (Cambridge: Cambridge University Press).

Malešević, S. (2011) *Sociological Theory and Warfare* (Stockholm: Forsvarshogskolan).

Malešević, S. (2015) 'Violence, Coercion and Human Rights: Understanding Organized Brutality', in M. Holborn (ed.), *Contemporary Sociology* (Cambridge: Polity): 534–65.

Mallin, C. A. (ed.) (2009) *Corporate Social Responsibility: A Case Study Approach* (Cheltenham: Edward Elgar).

Maloney, K. (2015) *Frankly Kellie: Becoming a Woman in a Man's World* (London: Blink).

Malthus, T. (1976 [1798]) *Essay on the Principle of Population* (New York: W. W. Norton).

Mannheim, K. (1972 [1928]) 'The Problem of Generations', in P. Kecskemeti (ed.), *Essays on the Sociology of Knowledge* (London: Routledge & Kegan Paul).

Marcus, A. D. (2014) 'Gene-Therapy Trial for "Bubble-Boy Syndrome" Shows Promise', *Wall Street Journal*, 8 October; www.wsj.com/articles/gene-therapy-trial-for-bubble-boy-syndrome-shows-promise-1412802002.

Marcuse, H. (1964) *One-Dimensional Man: Studies in the Ideology of Advanced Industrial Society* (London: Routledge & Kegan Paul).

Marcuse, H., and van Kempen, R. (eds) (2000) *Globalizing Cities: A New Spatial Order?* (Oxford: Blackwell).

Marin, L., Zia, H., and Soler, E. (1998) *Ending Domestic Violence: Report from the Global Frontlines* (San Francisco: Family Violence Prevention Fund).

Marmot, M. (2010) *Fair Society, Healthy Lives: Executive Summary* (London: The Marmot Review); www.instituteofhealthequity.org/projects/fair-society-healthy-lives-the-marmot-review.

Marsh, I., and Melville, G. (2011) 'Moral Panics and the British Media: A Look at Some Contemporary "Folk Devils"', *Internet Journal of Criminology*, www.internetjournalofcriminology.com/Marsh_Melville_Moral_Panics_and_the_British_Media_March_2011.pdf.

Marshall, A. J. (2007) *Vilfredo Pareto's Sociology: A Framework for Political Psychology* (Aldershot: Ashgate).

Marshall, G., and Firth, D. (1999) 'Social Mobility and Personal Satisfaction: Evidence from Ten Countries', *British Journal of Sociology*, 50(1): 28–48.

Marshall, G., et al. (1988) *Social Class in Modern Britain* (London: Hutchinson).

Marshall, L. (2015) 'Copyright', in J. Shepherd and K. Devine (eds), *The Routledge Reader on the Sociology of Music* (New York: Routledge): 287–98.

Marshall, T. H. (1973) *Class, Citizenship and Social Development* (Westport, CT: Greenwood Press).

Martell, L. (1994) *Ecology and Society: An Introduction* (Cambridge: Polity).

Martell, L. (2006) *The Sociology of Globalization* (2nd edn, Cambridge: Polity).

Martin, D. (1990) *Tongues of Fire: The Explosion of Protestantism in Latin America* (Oxford: Blackwell).

Martineau, H. (1962 [1837]) *Society in America* (New York: Doubleday).

Martocci, L. (2015) *Bullying: The Social Destruction of Self* (Philadelphia: Temple University Press).

Marx, K. (1938 [1875]) *Critique of the Gotha Programme* (New York: International).

Marx, K. (1970 [1859]) *A Contribution to the Critique of Political Economy* (Moscow: Progress).

Marx, K., and Engels, F. (1970 [1846]) *The German Ideology* (New York: International).

Marx, K., and Engels, F. (2008 [1848]) *The Communist Manifesto* (Rockville, MD: Wildside Press).

Mason, A., and Palmer, A. (1996) *Queer Bashing: A National Survey of Hate Crimes against Lesbians and Gay Men* (London: Stonewall).

Mason, D. (1995) *Race and Ethnicity in Modern Britain* (Oxford: Oxford University Press).

Mason, D. (2000) *Race and Ethnicity in Modern Britain* (2nd edn, Oxford: Oxford University Press).

Massey, D. (2007) *World City* (Cambridge: Polity).

Matsuura, J. H. (2004) 'Anticipating the Public Backlash: Public Relations Lessons for Nanotechnology from the Biotechnology Experience', *Nanotech*, 3: 491–3; www.nsti.org/publications/Nanotech/2004/pdf/B3-129.pdf.

Matthews, R., and Young, J. (1986) *Confronting Crime* (London: Sage).

Mattioli, G. (2014) 'Where Sustainable Transport and Social Exclusion Meet: Households without Cars and Car Dependence in Great Britain', *Journal of Environmental Policy and Planning*, 16: 1–22.

Maugh, T. H., and Zamichow, N. (1991) 'Medicine: San Diego's Researcher's Findings Offer First Evidence of a Biological Cause for Homosexuality', *Los Angeles Times*, 30 August.

Mauss, M. (1973) 'Techniques of the Body', *Economy and Society*, 2: 70–88.

Mauthner, M. L. (2005) *Sistering: Power and Change in Female Relationships* (Basingstoke: Palgrave Macmillan).

May, S., and Sleeter, C. E. (eds) (2010) *Critical Multiculturalism: Theory and Praxis* (London: Routledge).

May, V. (2015) 'Families and Personal Life: All Change?, in M. Holborn (ed.), *Contemporary Sociology* (Cambridge: Polity): 472–98.

May-Chahal, C., and Herczog, M. (2003) *Child Sexual Abuse in Europe* (Strasbourg: Council of Europe).

Mead, G. H. (1934) *Mind, Self and Society from the Standpoint of a Social Behaviorist* (Chicago: University of Chicago Press).

Mead, M. (1978) *Culture and Commitment: A Study of the Generation Gap* (Garden City, NY: Natural History Press).

Meadows, D. H., et al. (1972) *The Limits to Growth* (New York: Universe Books).

Meadows, D. H., Meadows, D. L., and Randers, J. (1992) *Beyond the Limits: Global Collapse or a Sustainable Future?* (London: Earthscan).

Meadows, D. H., Meadows, D. L., and Randers, J. (2004) *Limits to Growth: The 30-Year Update* (White River Junction, VT: Chelsea Green).

Meadows, P. (1996) *The Future of Work: Contributions to the Debate* (York: Joseph Rowntree Foundation).

Mega, V. (2010) *Sustainable Development, Energy and the City: A Civilization of Concepts and Actions* (New York: Springer).

Meijer, R. (2009) 'Introduction', in R. Meijer (ed.), *Global Salafism: Islam's New Religious Movement* (New York: Columbia University Press):1–32.

Melucci, A. (1985) 'The Symbolic Challenge of Contemporary Movements', *Social Research*, 52(4): 781–816.

Melucci, A. (1989) *Nomads of the Present: Social Movements and Individual Needs in Contemporary Society* (London: Hutchinson Radius).

Mennell, S. (1996) 'Civilizing and Decivilizing Processes', in J. Goudsblom, E. Jones and S. Mennell, *The Course of Human History: Economic Growth, Social Process, and Civilization* (London: M. E. Sharpe): 101–16.

Mennell, S. (1998) *Norbert Elias: An Introduction* (Oxford: Blackwell).

Menzel, P. [photographs], and D'Alusio, F. [text] (2005) *Hungry Planet: What the World Eats* (Berkeley, CA: Ten Speed Press)

Merton, R. K. (1957) *Social Theory and Social Structure* (rev. edn, Glencoe, IL: Free Press).

Meyer, D. S., and Tarrow, S. (eds) (1997) *The Social Movement Society: Contentious Politics for a New Century* (Lanham, MD: Rowman & Littlefield).

Meyer, J. W., and Rowan, B. (1977) 'Institutionalized Organizations: Formal Structure as Myth and Ceremony', *American Journal of Sociology*, 83: 340–63.

Meyer, S. C. (2013) *Darwin's Doubt: The Explosive Origin of Animal Life and the Case for Intelligent Design* (New York: HarperCollins).

Meyers, M. (1999) *Mediated Women: Representations in Popular Culture* (Cresskill, NJ: Hampton Press).

Michels, R. (1967 [1911]) *Political Parties* (New York: Free Press).

Michie, R. (2012) 'The Stock Market and the Corporate Economy: A Historical Overview', in G. Poitras (ed.), *Handbook of Research on Stock Market Globalization* (Cheltenham: Edward Elgar): 28–67.

Miles, H. (2005) *Al Jazeera: The Inside Story of the Arab News Channel that is Challenging the West* (New York: Grove Press).

Miles, R. (1993) *Racism after 'Race Relations'* (London: Routledge).

Miles, S. (2000) *Youth Lifestyles in a Changing World* (Buckingham: Open University Press).

Mill, J. S. (1869) *The Subjection of Women* (New York: D. Appleton).

Miller, T. (2011) 'Falling Back into Gender? Men's Narratives and Practices around First-Time Fatherhood', *Sociology*, 45(6): 1094–109.

Mills, C. Wright (1956) *The Power Elite* (New York: Oxford University Press).

Mills, C. Wright (1970) *The Sociological Imagination* (Harmondsworth: Penguin).

Mills, M. P., and Huber, P. W. (2002) 'How Technology will Defeat Terrorism', *City Journal*, 12(1): 24–34.

Ministry of Justice (2011) 'Prison Population and Accommodation Briefing for 14th January 2011', www.justice.gov.uk/downloads/statistics/hmps/10004C3414012011_web_report.doc.

Ministry of Justice (2013) 'An Overview of Sexual Offending in England and Wales', 10 January, https://www.gov.uk/government/uploads/system/uploads/attachment_data/file/214970/sexual-offending-overview-jan-2013.pdf.

Ministry of Justice (2014) 'Population and Capacity Briefing for Friday 28 November 2014', https://www.gov.uk/government/statistics/prison-population-figures-2014.

Ministry of Justice (2015) 'Prison Population Figures 2015', https://www.gov.uk/government/statistics/prison-population-figures-2015.

Minkler, M., and Estes, C. L. (eds) (1991) *Critical Perspectives on Aging: The Political and Moral Economy of Growing Old* (Amityville, NY: Baywood).

Mirza, H. (1986) *Multinationals and the Growth of the Singapore Economy* (New York: St Martin's Press).

Mitchell, J. (1966) *Women: The Longest Revolution: Essays in Feminism and Psychoanalysis* (London: Virago).

Mitchell, J. (1971) *Women's Estate* (London: Penguin).

Mitchell, J. (1975) *Psychoanalysis and Feminism* (New York: Random House).

Mithen, S. (2003) *After the Ice: A Global Human History 20,000–5,000 BC* (London: Orion Books).

Moberg, M., Granholm, K., and Nynäs, P. (2014) 'Trajectories of Post-Secular Complexity: An Introduction', in P. Nynäs, M. Lassander and T. Utriainen (eds), *Post-Secular Society* (New Brunswick, NJ: Transaction).

Modood, T. (1994) 'Political Blackness and British Asians', *Sociology*, 28(4): 859–76.

Modood, T., Berthoud, R., Lakey, J., Nazroo, J., Smith, P., Virdee, S., and Beishon, S. (1997) *Ethnic Minorities in Britain: Diversity and Disadvantage* (London: Policy Studies Institute) [Fourth PSI Survey].

Mohammadi, A. (ed.) (2002) *Islam Encountering Globalization* (London: Routledge).

Mol, A. P. J. (2001) *Globalization and Environmental Reform: The Ecological Modernization of the Global Economy* (Cambridge, MA: MIT Press).

Mol, A. P. J., and Sonnenfeld, D. A. (2000) 'Ecological Modernisation around the World: An Introduction', *Environmental Politics*, 9(1): 3–16.

Moore, B. (1966) *Social Origins of Dictatorship and Democracy: Lord and Peasant in the Making of the Modern World* (Boston: Beacon Press).

Moore, K. (2015) 'Where Do the Wealthiest 1% Live?', 25 January, www.bbc.co.uk/news/magazine-30949796.

Moore, L. R. (1994) *Selling God: American Religion in the Marketplace of Culture* (New York: Oxford University Press).

Moore, R. (1995) *Ethnic Statistics and the 1991 Census* (London: Runnymede Trust).

Morais, A., Neves, I., Davies, B., and Daniels, H. (eds) (2001) *Towards a Sociology of Pedagogy* (New York: Peter Lang).

Moran, J. (2005) *Reading the Everyday* (London: Routledge).

Moran, L. J., and Skeggs, B., with Tyrer, P., and Corteen, K. (2004) *Sexuality and the Politics of Violence and Safety* (London: Routledge).

Morgan, D. H. J. (1996) *Family Connections: An Introduction to Family Studies* (Cambridge: Polity).

Morgan, D. H. J. (1999) 'Risk and Family Practices: Accounting for Change and Fluidity in Family Life', in E. Silva and C. Smart (eds), *The New Family* (London: Sage).

Morgan, D. H. J. (2011) *Rethinking Family Practices* (Basingstoke: Palgrave Macmillan).

Morgan, P. (1999) *Family Policy, Family Changes* (London: CIVITAS).

Morris, L. (1993) *Dangerous Classes: The Underclass and Social Citizenship* (London: Routledge).

Morris, L. (1995) *Social Divisions: Economic Decline and Social Structural Change* (London: Routledge).

Mort, M., May, C. R., and Williams, T. (2003) 'Remote Doctors and Absent Patients: Acting at a Distance in Telemedicine?', *Science, Technology and Human Values*, 28(2): 274–95.

Mosca, G. (1939 [1896]) *The Ruling Class* (New York: McGraw-Hill).

Mouzelis, N. P. (1995) *Sociological Theory: What Went Wrong? Diagnosis and Remedies* (London: Routledge).

Moynihan, D. P. (1993) 'Defining Deviancy Down', *American Scholar*, 62(1): 17–30.

Mueller, M. L. (2011) *Networks and States: The Global Politics of Internet Governance* (Cambridge, MA: MIT Press).

Mullan, P. (2002) *The Imaginary Time Bomb: Why an Ageing Population Is Not a Social Problem* (London: I. B. Tauris).

Muncie, J. (2009) *Youth and Crime* (3rd edn, London: Sage).

Muncie, J. (2015) *Youth and Crime* (4th edn, London: Sage).

Murdock, G. P. (1949) *Social Structure* (New York: Macmillan).

Murphy, J. (2011) 'Indian Call Centre Workers: Vanguard of a Global Middle Class?', *Work, Employment and Society*, 25(3): 417–33.

Murphy, R. (1997) *Sociology and Nature: Social Action in Context* (Boulder, CO: Westview Press).

Murray, C. A. (1984) *Losing Ground: American Social Policy 1950–1980* (New York: Basic Books).

Murray, C. A. (1990) *The Emerging British Underclass* (London: Institute of Economic Affairs).

Najam, A., Huq, S., and Sokona, Y. (2003) 'Climate Negotiations beyond Kyoto: Developing Countries Concerns and Interests', *Climate Policy*, 3: 221–31; http://climate-talks.net/2006-ENVRE130/PDF/Najam-CliPol%20Climate%20and%20SD.pdf.

Nanda, M. (2004) *Prophets Facing Backward: Postmodern Critiques of Science and Hindu Nationalism in India* (New Brunswick, NJ: Rutgers University Press).

Nasser, M. (2006) 'Eating Disorders across Cultures', *Psychiatry*, 5(11): 392–5.

National Committee of Inquiry into Higher Education (1997) *Report* (London: Department for Education and Employment) [Dearing Report].

National Equality Panel (2010) *An Anatomy of Economic Inequality in the UK: Report of the National Equality Panel* (London: Government Equalities Office).

Nederveen Pieterse, J. (2004) *Globalization or Empire?* (London and New York: Routledge).

Negroponte, N. (1995) *Being Digital* (London: Hodder & Stoughton).

Negus, K. (1999) *Music Genres and Corporate Cultures* (London: Routledge).

Neslen, A. (2015) 'Morocco Poised to Become a Solar Superpower with Launch of Desert Mega-Project', *The Guardian*, 26 October, https://www.theguardian.com/environment/2015/oct/26/morocco-poised-to-become-a-solar-superpower-with-launch-of-desert-mega-project.

Nettleton, S. (2013) *The Sociology of Health and Illness* (3rd edn, Cambridge: Polity).

Neumann, P. R. (2009) *Old & New Terrorism* (Cambridge: Polity).

New Scientist (2015) 'Nitrogen Oxides in Car Exhaust Kill Tens of Thousands in UK', 28 September; https://www.newscientist.com/article/dn28245-nitrogen-oxide-is-not-so-harmless-and-could-damage-human-health/.

Newman, K. S. (2000) *No Shame in my Game: The Working Poor in the Inner City* (New York: Vintage).

Newman, K. S. (2012) *The Accordion Family: Boomerang Kids, Anxious Parents, and the Private Toll of Global Competition* (Boston: Beacon Press).

Nicholas, S., Kershaw, C., and Walker, A. (2007) *Crime in England and Wales 2006/07*, Statistical Bulletin 11/07 (London: Home Office).

Niebuhr, H. R. (1929) *The Social Sources of Denominationalism* (New York: Henry Holt).

Nielsen, F. (1994) 'Income Inequality and Industrial Development: Dualism Revisited', *American Sociological Review*, 59(5): 654–77.

Nobelprize.org (2012) 'Democracies in the World', 23 February, www.nobelprize.org/educational/peace/democracy_map/.

Norwood, G. (2016) 'The Impact of Buy-to-Leave on Prime London's Housing Market', *Financial Times*, 12 February, www.ft.com/cms/s/0/6954f798-cb2c-11e5-a8ef-ea66e967dd44.html.

NPI (New Policy Institute) (2010) *Monitoring Poverty and Social Exclusion 2010* (York: Joseph Rowntree Foundation).

The Numbers (2015) 'Highest Grossing Films of All Time by Worldwide Box Office Sales, at 9 August 2015', www.the-numbers.com/movie/records/All-Time-Worldwide-Box-Office.

Nursing Times (2009) 'NHS Hospital Patient Deaths Due to Errors up 60% in England', 7 January; www.nursingtimes.net/whats-new-in-nursing/nhs-hospital-patient-deaths-due-to-errors-up-60-in-england/1960339.article.

Oakley, A. (1974a) *Housewife* (London: Allen Lane).

Oakley, A. (1974b) *The Sociology of Housework* (Oxford: Martin Robertson).

Oakley, A. (1984) *The Captured Womb: A History of the Medical Care of Pregnant Women* (Oxford: Blackwell).

Oakley, A., et al. (1994) 'Life Stress, Support and Class Inequality: Explaining the Health of Women and Children', *European Journal of Public Health*, 4: 81–91.

Oberschall, A. (1973) *Social Conflict and Social Movements* (Englewood Cliffs, NJ: Prentice-Hall).

O'Brien, M., Alldred, P., and Jones, D. (1996) 'Children's Constructions of Family and Kinship', in J. Brannen and M. O'Brien (eds), *Children in Families: Research and Policy* (London: Falmer Press): 84–100.

Ó Dochartaigh, N. (2009) *Internet Research Skills: How to Do your Literature Search and Find Research Information Online* (2nd edn, London: Sage).

Odum, E. P. (1989) *Ecology and our Endangered Life-Support Systems* (Sunderland, MA: Sinauer Associates).

OECD (2005) *OECD Factbook 2005: Economic, Environmental and Social Statistics*, www.oecd-ilibrary.org/economics/oecd-factbook-2005_factbook-2005-en.

OECD (2006) *Environment at a Glance: Environmental Indicators 2006* (Paris: OECD).

Ofcom (2010) *Communications Market Report: UK, 2010*, http://stakeholders.ofcom.org.uk/binaries/research/cmr/753567/CMR_2010_FINAL.pdf.

Ofcom (2011) *Communications Market Report: UK, 2011*, http://stakeholders.ofcom.org.uk/binaries/research/cmr/cmr11/UK_CMR_2011_FINAL.pdf.

Ofcom (2015) *Adults' Media Use and Attitudes Report 2015*, http://stakeholders.ofcom.org.uk/binaries/research/media-literacy/media-lit-10years/2015_Adults_media_use_and_attitudes_report.pdf.

Ohmae, K. (1990) *The Borderless World: Power and Strategy in the Industrial Economy* (London: Collins).

Ohmae, K. (1995) *The End of the Nation State: The Rise of Regional Economies* (London: Free Press).

Oliver, M. (1983) *Social Work with Disabled People* (Basingstoke: Macmillan).

Oliver, M. (1990) *The Politics of Disablement* (Basingstoke: Macmillan).

Oliver, M. (1996) *Understanding Disability: From Theory to Practice* (Basingstoke: Macmillan).

Oliver, M., and Zarb, G. (1989) 'The Politics of Disability: A New Approach', *Disability, Handicap & Society*, 4(3): 221–40.

Olshansky, S., Passaro, D., Hershow, R., et al. (2005) 'A Potential Decline in Life Expectancy in the United States in the 21st Century', *New England Journal of Medicine* 352(11): 1138–45.

Olson, M. (1965) *The Logic of Collective Action* (Cambridge, MA: Harvard University Press).

Omi, M., and Winant, H. (1994) *Racial Formation in the United States from the 1960s to the 1990s* (2nd edn, New York: Routledge).

O'Neill, J. (2013) *The Growth Map: Economic Opportunity in the BRICs and Beyond* (London: Portfolio Penguin).

O'Neill, M. (2000) *Prostitution and Feminism: Towards a Politics of Feeling* (Cambridge: Polity).

O'Neill, O. (2002) *The Reith Lectures: A Question of Trust*, www.bbc.co.uk/radio4/reith2002/.

O'Neill, R. (2002) *Experiments in Living: The Fatherless Family* (London: CIVITAS).

ONS (Office for National Statistics) (2000) *Social Trends 30* (London: HMSO).

ONS (Office for National Statistics) (2002a) *Labour Force Survey*, Spring (London: ONS).

ONS (Office for National Statistics) (2002b) *Focus on Ethnicity and Identity* (London: ONS).

ONS (Office for National Statistics) (2003) *A Century of Labour Market Change* (London: ONS).

ONS (Office for National Statistics) (2004a) *Focus on the Labour Market 2002* (London: ONS).

ONS (Office for National Statistics) (2004b) *Social Trends 34* (London: HMSO).

ONS (Office for National Statistics) (2005) *Social Trends 35* (London: HMSO).

ONS (Office for National Statistics) (2007) *Social Trends 37* (London: HMSO).

ONS (Office for National Statistics) (2010a) *Social Trends 40* (Basingstoke: Palgrave Macmillan).

ONS (Office for National Statistics) (2010b) *Divorces in England and Wales 2008, revised bulletin* (London: ONS).

ONS (Office for National Statistics) (2010c) *National Population Projections, 2008-Based* (London: ONS).

ONS (Office for National Statistics) (2011a) 'Internet Access', www.statistics.gov.uk/cci/nugget.asp?id=8.

ONS (Office for National Statistics) (2011b) 'Nearly Half of Those Who Have Never Been Online are Disabled', News Release, 18 May (Newport: ONS).

ONS (Office for National Statistics) (2011c) *Population Estimates by Ethnic Group 2002–2009* (Newport: ONS).

ONS (Office for National Statistics) (2011d) 'Labour Market Statistics: September 2011', www.ons.gov.uk/ons/dcp171778_232238.pdf.

ONS (Office for National Statistics) (2011e) *Trends in Life Expectancy by the National Statistics Socio-economic Classification 1982-2006* (Newport: ONS).

ONS (Office for National Statistics) (2011f) *Crime and Justice, Social Trends 41* (Newport: ONS).

ONS (Office for National Statistics) (2012a) *Religion in England and Wales 2011*, www.ons.gov.uk/ons/dcp171776_290510.pdf.

ONS (Office for National Statistics) (2012b) *Ethnicity and National Identity in England and Wales 2011*, www.ons.gov.uk/ons/dcp171776_290558.pdf.

ONS (Office for National Statistics) (2013a) *The Health Gap in England and Wales, 2011 Census*, www.ons.gov.uk/ons/rel/census/2011-census-analysis/health-gaps-by-socio-economic-position-of-occupations-in-england--wales--english-regions-and-local-authorities--2011/info-health-gap.html.

ONS (Office for National Statistics) (2013b) *Full Report – Women in the Labour Market*, www.ons.gov.uk/ons/dcp171776_328352.pdf.

ONS (Office for National Statistics) (2013c) 'Chapter 3 – Households, Familes and People (General Lifestyle Survey Overview – A Report on the 2011 General Lifestyle Survey)', http://webarchive.nationalarchives.gov.uk/20160105160709/http://www.ons.gov.uk/ons/dcp171776_302210.pdf.

ONS (Office for National Statistics) (2014a) *Crime in England and Wales, Year Ending March 2014*, www.ons.gov.uk/ons/dcp171778_371127.pdf.

ONS (Office for National Statistics) (2014b) *Crime in England and Wales, Year Ending June 2014*, www.ons.gov.uk/ons/dcp171778_380538.pdf.

ONS (Office for National Statistics) (2014c) *Crime Survey for England and Wales, 2012–13*, www.ons.gov.uk/ons/dcp171776_352362.pdf.

ONS (Office for National Statistics) (2014d) *Crime in England and Wales, Year Ending March 2014*, www.ons.gov.uk/ons/dcp171778_371127.pdf.

ONS (Office for National Statistics) (2014e) *UK Labour Market, December 2014*, www.ons.gov.uk/ons/dcp171778_385648.pdf.

ONS (Office for National Statistics) (2014f) *Annual Survey of Hours and Earnings 2014, Provisional Results*, www.ons.gov.uk/ons/dcp171778_385428.pdf.

ONS (Office for National Statistics) (2014g) *Divorces in England and Wales 2012*, www.ons.gov.uk/ons/dcp171778_351693.pdf.

ONS (Office for National Statistics) (2014h) '8 Facts about Young People', www.ons.gov.uk/ons/rel/uncategorised/summary/facts-about-young-people/sty-facts-about-young-people.html.

ONS (Office for National Statistics) (2015a) *Poverty and Employment Transitions in the UK and EU, 2008–2012*, www.ons.gov.uk/ons/dcp171776_395768.pdf.

ONS (Office for National Statistics) (2015b) *Migration Statistics Quarterly Report, May 2015*, www.ons.gov.uk/ons/dcp171778_404613.pdf.

ONS (Office for National Statistics) (2015c) *Families and Households 2014*, www.ons.gov.uk/ons/dcp171778_393133.pdf.

ONS (Office for National Statistics) (2015d) *Chapter 1: Violent Crime and Sexual Offences – Overview*, www.ons.gov.uk/ons/dcp171776_394474.pdf.

ONS (Office for National Statistics) (2015e) *Civil Partnerships in England and Wales 2014*, www.ons.gov.uk/peoplepopulationandcommunity/birthsdeathsandmarriages/marriagecohabitationandcivilpartnerships/bulletins/civilpartnershipsinenglandandwales/2015-10-20#civil-partnerships-by-sex.

Open Society Institute (2010) *Muslims in Europe: A Report on 11 EU Cities* (London: Open Society Institute), https://www.opensocietyfoundations.org/reports/muslims-europe-report-11-eu-cities.

Osalor, P. (2011) 'The Informal Economy and Entrepreneurial development', 23 January, www.vanguardngr.com/2011/01/the-informal-economy-and-entrepreneurial-development.

Osborne, J. W. (2007) 'Linking Stereotype Threat and Anxiety', *Educational Psychology*, 27(1): 135–54.

Oxfam (2014) *Even it Up: Time to End Extreme Inequality* (Oxford: Oxfam GB).

Oxfam (2015) *Wealth: Having it All and Wanting More* (Oxford: Oxfam GB).

Paehlke, R. (1989) *Environmentalism and the Future of Progressive Politics* (New Haven, CT, and London: Yale University Press).

Pahl, J. (1989) *Money and Marriage* (Basingstoke: Macmillan).

Pakulski, J., and Waters, M. (1996) *The Death of Class* (London: Sage).

Palmer, G., MacInnes, T., and Kenway, P. (2006) *Monitoring Poverty and Social Exclusion 2006* (York: Joseph Rowntree Foundation).

Palmer, G., MacInnes, T., and Kenway, P. (2007) *Monitoring Poverty and Social Exclusion 2007* (York: Joseph Rowntree Foundation).

Palmer, M. A. (2010) 'Water Resources: Beyond Infrastructure', *Nature*, 467, 30 September: 534–5.

Palmore, E. B. (1985) *Retirement: Causes and Consequences* (New York: Springer).

Panyarachun, A., et al. (2004) *A More Secure World: Our Shared Responsibility: Report of the High-Level Panel on Threats, Challenges and Change* (New York: United Nations).

Papadakis, E. (1988) 'Social Movements, Self-Limiting Radicalism and the Green Party in West Germany', *Sociology*, 22(3): 171–92.

Papworth Trust (2013) *Disability in the United Kingdom 2013: Facts and Figures* (Cambridge: Papworth Trust).

Parekh, B. (2000) *Rethinking Multiculturalism: Cultural Diversity and Political Theory* (Basingstoke: Palgrave Macmillan).

Parekh, B. (2004) 'Is Britain Too Diverse? The Responses', www.carnegiecouncil.org/media/replies.pdf.

Pareto, V. (1935 [1916]) *The Mind and Society: A Treatise on General Sociology*, 2 vols (New York: Harcourt Brace).

Park, A., Bryson, C., Clery, E., Curtice, J., and Phillips, M. (eds) (2013) *British Social Attitudes: the 30th Report* (London: NatCen Social Research).

Park, R. E. (1952) *Human Communities: The City and Human Ecology* (New York: Free Press).

Parke, R. D., and Clarke-Stewart, A. (2010) *Social Development* (Hoboken, NJ: John Wiley).

Parker, S. (2003) *Urban Theory and the Urban Experience: Encountering the City* (London: Routledge).

Parr, C. (2014) 'Women and Ethnic Minorities Still Marginalised at Top of Universities', *Times Higher Education*, 18 November; www.timeshighereducation.co.uk/news/women-and-ethnic-minorities-still-marginalised-at-top-of-universities/2017026.article.

Parsons, T. (1937) *The Structure of Social Action* (New York: McGraw-Hill).

Parsons, T. (1952) *The Social System* (London: Tavistock).

Parsons, T., and Bales, R. F. (1956) *Family Socialization and Interaction Process* (London: Routledge & Kegan Paul).

Parsons, T., and Smelser, N. J. (1956) *Economy and Society* (London: Routledge & Kegan Paul).

Pawson, R. (2013) *The Science of Evaluation: A Realist Manifesto* (London: Sage).

Pearce, F. (1976) *Crimes of the Powerful: Marxism, Crime and Deviance* (London: Pluto Press).

Pearson, L. J., Newton, P. W., and Roberts, P. (eds) (2014) *Resilient Sustainable Cities: A Future* (New York: Routledge).

Peet, R., and Hartwick, E. (2009) *Theories of Development: Conditions, Arguments, Alternatives* (2nd edn, London: Guilford Press).

Peng, W. (2011) 'GM Crop Cultivation Surges, but Novel Traits Languish', *Nature Biotechnology*, 29: 302.

Pensions and Investments (2010) 'Largest Hedge Fund Managers', 8 March, www.pionline.com/article/20100308/CHART2/100309910.

Pérez-Agote, A. (2014) 'The Notion of Secularization: Drawing the Boundaries of its Contemporary Scientific Validity', *Current Sociology*, 62(6): 886–904.

Perlmutter, H. V. (1972) 'Towards Research on and Development of Nations, Unions, and Firms as World-wide Institutions', in H. Gunter (ed.), *Transnational Industrial Relations* (New York: St Martin's Press).

Perry, E., and Francis, B. (2010) *The Social Class Gap for Educational Achievement: A Review of the Literature* (London: RSA).

Petersen, A., and Lupton, D. (2000) *The New Public Health: Health and Self in the Age of Risk* (London: Sage).

Peterson, K. (2014) 'As Sales Plunge, Can Barbie Stay Relevant?', CBS News, 3 February, www.cbsnews.com/news/as-sales-plunge-can-barbie-stay-relevant/.

Peterson, P. G. (1999) *Gray Dawn: How the Coming Age Wave will Transform America – and the World* (New York: Random House).

Peterson, R. A. (ed.) (1976) *The Production of Culture* (London: Sage).

Peterson, R. A., and Berger, D. G. (1975) 'Cycles in Symbol Production: The Case of Popular Music', *American Sociological Review*, 40(2): 158–73.

Petre, J. (2006) 'Migrants Fill Empty Pews as Britons Lose Faith', *Daily Telegraph*, 18 September; www.telegraph.co.uk/news/uknews/1529106/Migrants-fill-empty-pews-as-Britons-lose-faith.html.

Pew Forum on Religion and Public Life (2010) *Religion among the Millennials: Less Religiously Active than Older Americans, but Fairly Traditional in Other Ways*, 17 February, www.pewforum.org/Age/Religion-Among-the-Millennials.aspx.

Pew Research Center (2005) *Pew Global Attitudes Project: 2005 Datasets*, www.pewglobal.org/category/datasets/2005/.

Pew Research Center (2015) *Gay Marriage Around the World*, www.pewforum.org/2015/06/26/gay-marriage-around-the-world-2013/.

Philo, G., and Berry, M. (2004) *Bad News from Israel* (London: Pluto Press).

Piachaud, D. (1987) 'Problems in the Definition and Measurement of Poverty', *Journal of Social Policy*, 16(2): 147–64.

Piaget, J. (1951) *Play, Dreams and Imitation in Childhood* (London: Heinemann).

Piaget, J. (1957) *Construction of Reality in the Child* (London: Routledge & Kegan Paul).

Pierson, C. (1994) *Dismantling the Welfare State? Reagan, Thatcher and the Politics of Retrenchment* (Cambridge: Cambridge University Press).

Pierson, J. (2010) *Tackling Social Exclusion* (2nd edn, London: Routledge).

Pierson, P. (2011) 'The Welfare State over the Very Long Run', http://econpapers.repec.org/paper/zbwzeswps/022011.htm.

Piketty, T. (2014) *Capital in the Twenty-First Century* (Cambridge, MA, and London: Harvard University Press).

Pilcher, R., Williams, J., and Pole, C. (2003) 'Rethinking Adulthood: Families, Transitions and Social Change', *Sociological Research Online*, 8(4), www.socresonline.org.uk/8/4/pilcher.html.

Pilkington, A. (2002) 'Cultural Representations and Changing Ethnic Identities in a Global Age', in M. Holborn (ed.), *Developments in Sociology* (Ormskirk: Causeway Press).

Pilkington, A. (2015) 'Race, Ethnicity and Nationality: The Future of Multiculturalism in a Global Age', in M. Holborn (ed.) *Contemporary Sociology* (Cambridge: Polity): 65–95.

Pintor, R. L., and Gratschew, M. (2002) *Voter Turnout since 1945: A Global Report* (Stockholm: International Institute for Democracy and Electoral Assistance); www.idea.int/publications/vt/upload/VT_screenopt_2002.pdf.

Piore, M., and Sabel, C. F. (1984) *The Second Industrial Divide: Possibilities for Prosperity* (New York: Basic Books).

Piven, F. F., and Cloward, R. A. (1977) *Poor People's Movements: Why They Succeed, How They Fail* (New York: Pantheon Books).

Platt, L. (2013) 'Poverty', in G. Payne (ed.), *Social Divisions* (3rd edn, Basingstoke: Palgrave Macmillan): 305–31.

Player, E. (1989) 'Women and Crime in the City', in D. Downes (ed.), *Crime in the City* (Basingstoke: Macmillan): 122–5.

Plummer, K. (1975) *Sexual Stigma: An Interactionist Account* (London: Routledge & Kegan Paul).

Plummer, M. L., et al. (2004) '"A Bit More Truthful": The Validity of Adolescent Sexual Behaviour Data Collected in Rural Northern Tanzania Using Five Methods', *Sexually Transmitted Infections*, 80: 49–56.

Plummer, R. (2015) 'Greece Debt Crisis: What's the Deal?', 13 July, www.bbc.co.uk/news/business-33505555.

Pollak, O. (1950) *The Criminality of Women* (Philadelphia: University of Pennsylvania Press).

Pollert, A. (1988) 'Dismantling Flexibility', *Capital and Class*, 34: 42–75.

Portes, A. (2007) *Economic Sociology: A Systematic Inquiry* (Princeton, NJ: Princeton University Press).

Postman, N. (1986) *Amusing Ourselves to Death: Public Discourse in the Age of Show Business* (London: Heinemann).

Postman, N. (1995) *The Disappearance of Childhood* (New York: Vintage Books).

Potter, G. W., and Miller, K. S. (2002) 'Thinking about White-Collar Crime', in G. W. Potter (ed.), *Controversies in White-Collar Crime* (Abingdon: Routledge): 1–32.

Povey, D., Coleman, K., Kaiza, P., and Roe, S. (2009) *Homicides, Firearms Offences and Intimate Violence 2007/08 (Supplementary Volume 2 to Crime in England and Wales, 2007/08)*, Statistical Bulletin 02/09 (London: Home Office); http://webarchive.nationalarchives.gov.uk/20110218135832/rds.homeoffice.gov.uk/rds/pdfs09/hosb0209.pdf.

Powell, C. (2011) *Barbaric Civilization: A Critical Sociology of Genocides* (Montreal: McGill-Queen's University Press).

Price, M. (2010) 'Mexico's Struggle to Win "War" on Drugs', 9 June, www.bbc.co.uk/news/10275565.

Procter, J. (2004) *Stuart Hall* (London: Routledge).

Prout, A. (2005) *The Future of Childhood: Towards the Interdisciplinary Study of Childhood* (London: Routledge).

Prout, A., and James, A. (eds) (1990) *Constructing and Reconstructing Childhood* (London: Falmer Press).

Puddington, A. (2011) 'Freedom in the World 2011: The Authoritarian Challenge to Democracy', www.freedomhouse.org/report/freedom-world-2011/essay-freedom-world-2011-authoritarian-challenge-democracy.

Putnam, R. (1995) 'Bowling Alone: America's Declining Social Capital', *Journal of Democracy*, 6(1): 65–78.

Putnam, R. (2000) *Bowling Alone: The Collapse and Revival of American Community* (New York: Simon & Schuster).

Quah, D. (1999) *The Weightless Economy in Economic Development* (London: Centre for Economic Performance).

Rabinow, P. (1999) *French DNA: Trouble in Purgatory* (Chicago: University of Chicago Press).

Race, R. (2010) *Multiculturalism and Education* (London: Continuum).

Radway, J. A. (1984) *Reading the Romance* (Chapel Hill: University of North Carolina Press).

Ragnedda, M., and Muschert, G. W. (2013) *The Digital Divide: The Internet and Social Inequality in International Perspective* (Abingdon: Routledge).

Rahman, M., and Jackson, S. (2010) *Gender and Sexuality: Sociological Approaches* (Cambridge: Polity).

Rahnema, M. (1997) 'Towards Post-Development: Searching for Signposts, a New Language and a Paradigm', in M. Rahnema and V. Bawtree (eds), *The Post-Development Reader* (London: Zed Books): 277–404.

Rake, K. (ed.) (2000) *Women's Incomes over the Lifetime* (London: HMSO).

Rallings, C., and Thrasher, M. (2015) *The 2015 General Election: Aspects of Participation and Administration*, www.electoralcommission.org.uk/__data/assets/pdf_file/0008/191861/Plymouth-UKPGE-electoral-data-report-final-WEB.pdf.

Ranis, G. (1996) *Will Latin America Now Put a Stop to 'Stop-and-Go?'* (New Haven, CT: Yale University, Economic Growth Center).

Rapoport, R. N., Fogarty, M. P., and Rapoport, R. (eds) (1982) *Families in Britain* (London: Routledge & Kegan Paul).

Rattansi, A. (1992) 'Changing the Subject? Racism, Culture and Education', in J. Donald and A. Rattansi (eds), *'Race', Culture and Difference* (London: Sage).

Rattansi, A. (2011) *Multiculturalism: A Very Short Introduction* (Oxford: Oxford University Press).

Rawsthorne, S. (2002) 'England and Wales', in R. W. Summers and A. M. Hoffman (eds), *Domestic Violence: A Global View* (Westport, CT: Greenwood Press).

Redman, P. (1996) 'Empowering Men to Disempower Themselves: Heterosexual Masculinities, HIV and the Contradictions of Anti-Oppressive Education', in M. Mac an Ghaill (ed.), *Understanding Masculinities* (Buckingham: Open University Press).

Reich, R. (1991) *The Work of Nations: Preparing Ourselves for 21st-Century Capitalism* (New York: Knopf).

Reskin, B., and Roos, P. A. (1990) *Job Queues, Gender Queues: Explaining Women's Inroads into Male Occupations* (Philadelphia: Temple University Press).

Resnick, P., Zeckhauser, R., Swanson, J., and Lockwood, K. (2006) 'The Value of Reputation on eBay: A Controlled Experiment', *Experimental Economics*, 9(2): 79–101.

Reuters (2007) 'Young Keep it Simple in High-Tech World: Survey', 24 July, www.reuters.com/article/2007/07/24/us-technology-teens-idUSL236796320070724.

Reuters (2015) 'Global Life Expectancy Rises, but People Live Sicker for Longer', www.reuters.com/article/2015/08/27/us-health-longevity-idUSKCN0QV2JL20150827#WeOJqbi9YD5V633K.97.

Revill, J. (2008) 'Forced Marriage in UK "a Widespread Problem"', *The Observer*, 9 March; www.guardian.co.uk/world/2008/mar/09/gender.communities.

Rheingold, H. (2000) *The Virtual Community* (Cambridge, MA: MIT Press).

Rich, A. (1980) *Compulsory Heterosexuality and Lesbian Existence* (London: Onlywomen Press).

Richardson, D., and May, H. (1999) 'Deserving Victims? Sexual Status and the Social Construction of Violence', *Sociological Review*, 47(2): 308–31.

Riesman, D., with Glazer, N., and Denney, R. (1961) *The Lonely Crowd: A Study of the Changing American Character* (New Haven, CT: Yale University Press).

Riley, M. W., Foner, A., and Waring, J. (1988) 'Sociology of Age', in N. J. Smelser (ed.), *Handbook of Sociology* (Newbury Park, CA: Sage).

Riley, M. W., Kahn, R. L., and Foner, A. (1994) *Age and Structural Lag: Changes in Work, Family, and Retirement* (Chichester: Wiley).

Riots (Communites and Victims) Panel (2011) *5 Days in August: An Interim Report on the 2011 English Riots* (London: Riots Panel).

Ritzer, G. (1983) 'The McDonaldization of Society', *Journal of American Culture*, 6(1): 100–7.

Ritzer, G. (1993) *The McDonaldization of Society* (Newbury Park, CA: Pine Forge Press).

Ritzer, G. (1998) *The McDonaldization Thesis: Explorations and Extensions* (London: Sage).

Ritzer, G. (2009) *Globalization: A Basic Text* (Oxford: Wiley-Blackwell).

Ritzer, G. (2011) *Globalization: The Essentials* (Chichester: Wiley-Blackwell).

Rix, S. (2008) 'Age and Work in the United States of America', in P. Taylor (ed.), *Ageing Labour Forces: Promises and Prospects* (Cheltenham: Edward Elgar).

Robertson, R. (1970) *The Sociological Interpretation of Religion* (Oxford: Blackwell).

Robertson, R. (1992) *Globalization: Social Theory and Global Culture* (London: Sage).

Robertson, R. (1995) 'Glocalization: Time–Space and Homogeneity–Heterogeneity', in M. Featherstone, S. Lash and R. Robertson (eds), *Global Modernities* (London: Sage).

Roe, S. (2010) 'Intimate Violence: 2008/09 British Crime Survey', in K. Smith and J. Flatley (eds), *Homicides, Firearms Offences and Intimate Violence 2008/09 (Supplementary Volume 2 to Crime in England and Wales 2008/09)*, Statistical Bulletin 01/10 (London: Home Office): 57–82.

Rogers, P. (2008) *Why We're Losing the War on Terror* (Cambridge: Polity).

Rojek, C. (2003) *Stuart Hall* (Cambridge: Polity).

'Rona' (2000) 'Why We Need a Union', *Respect!: Journal of the International Union of Sex Workers*, no. 1.

Roof, W. C. (1993) *A Generation of Seekers: The Spiritual Journeys of the Baby Boom Generation* (San Francisco: Harper).

Roof, W. C., and McKinney, W. (1990) *American Mainline Religion: Its Changing Shape and Future Prospects* (New Brunswick, NJ: Rutgers University Press).

Rootes, C. (2005) 'A Limited Transnationalization? The British Environmental Movement', in D. Della Porta and S. Tarrow (eds), *Transnational Protest and Global Activism* (Lanham, MD: Rowman & Littlefield).

Rose, S., Kamin, L., and Lewontin, R. C. (1984) *Not in our Genes: Biology, Ideology and Human Nature* (Harmondsworth: Penguin).

Rosenau, J. N. (1997) *Along the Domestic–Foreign Frontier: Exploring Governance in a Turbulent World* (Cambridge: Cambridge University Press).

Ross, J. I. (ed.) (2000) *Controlling State Crime* (2nd edn, New Brunswick, NJ: Transaction).

Rossi, A. (1973) 'The First Woman Sociologist: Harriet Martineau', in *The Feminist Papers: From Adams to De Beauvoir* (New York: Columbia University Press).

Rossner, M. (2013) *Just Emotions: Rituals of Restorative Justice* (Oxford: Oxford University Press).

Rostow, W. W. (1961) *The Stages of Economic Growth* (Cambridge: Cambridge University Press).

Rothenberg, C. E. (2010) 'Re-architected Cloud Data Centre Networks and their Impact on the Future Internet', in T. Tronco (ed.), *New Network Architectures: The Path to the Future of the Internet* (Heidelberg: Springer): 179–88.

Rothman, R. A. (2005) *Inequality and Stratification: Class, Race and Gender* (5th edn, Upper Saddle River, NJ: Prentice-Hall).

Roxborough, I. (2004) 'Thinking about War', *Sociological Forum*, 19(3): 505–28 [book reviews].

Rubin, L. B. (1990) *The Erotic Wars: What Happened to the Sexual Revolution?* (New York: Farrar).

Rubin, L. B. (1994) *Families on the Fault Line* (New York: HarperCollins).

Rudé, G. (1964) *The Crowd in History: A Study of Popular Disturbances in France and England, 1730–1848* (New York: Wiley).

Ruspini, E. (2000) 'Longitudinal Research in the Social Sciences', *Social Research Update*, no. 20; http://sru.soc.surrey.ac.uk/SRU28.html.

Russell, M. (2010) *The Independent Climate Change E-mails Review* (Norwich: University of East Anglia).

Russett, B. M., Oneal, J. R., and Cox, M. (2000) 'Clash of Civilizations or Realism and Liberalism Déjà Vu? Some Evidence', *Journal of Peace Research*, 37(5): 583–608.

Rusting, R. L. (1992) 'Why Do We Age?', *Scientific American*, 267 (December): 131–41.

Sachs, J. (2000) 'A New Map of the World', *The Economist*, 22 June.

Sachs, W. (1992) *The Development Dictionary: A Guide to Knowledge as Power* (London: Zed Books).

Sadovnik, A. R. (ed.) (1995) *Knowledge and Pedagogy: The Sociology of Basil Bernstein* (Norwood, NJ: Ablex).

Sage, G. (2002) 'Global Sport and Global Mass Media', in A. Laker (ed.), *The Sociology of Sport and Physical Education: An Introductory Reader* (London: Routledge): 211–33.

Sageman, M. (2004) *Understanding Terror Networks* (Philadelphia: Pennsylvania University Press).

Said, E. (1978) *Orientalism: Western Conceptions of the Orient* (London: Routledge & Kegan Paul).

Saks, M. (1992) *Alternative Medicine in Britain* (Oxford: Clarendon Press).

Salway, S., Platt, S., Chowbey, P., Harriss, K., and Bayliss, E. (2007) *Long-Term Ill Health, Poverty and Ethnicity* (York: Joseph Rowntree Foundation).

Sanders, T. (2008) *Paying for Pleasure: Men Who Buy Sex* (Cullompton, Devon: Willan).

Sanders, T., and Hardy, K. (2011) *The Regulatory Dance: Investigating the Structural Integration of Sexual Consumption in the Night Time Economy* (Swindon: Economic and Social Research Council); www.esrc.ac.uk/my-esrc/grants/RES-000-22-3163/outputs/read/effe5312-8101-49ae-b35e-aff8c0cba43f.

Sandilands, C. (1999) *The Good-Natured Feminist: Ecofeminism and the Quest for Democracy* (Minneapolis: University of Minnesota Press).

Sassen, S. (1991) *The Global City: New York, London, Tokyo* (Princeton, NJ: Princeton University Press).

Sassen, S. (1998) *Globalization and its Discontents: Essays on the Mobility of People and Money* (New York: New Press).

Sassen, S. (2001) *The Global City: New York, London, Tokyo* (2nd edn, Princeton, NJ: Princeton University Press).

Sassen, S. (2004) 'Is Britain Too Diverse? The Responses', 23 November, www.carnegiecouncil.org/media/replies.pdf.

Saunders, P. (1990) *Social Class and Stratification* (London: Routledge).

Saunders, P. (1996) *Unequal but Fair? A Study of Class Barriers in Britain* (London: IEA Health and Welfare Unit).

Saunders, P. (2010) *Social Mobility Myths* (London: CIVITAS).

Savage, J. (2007) *Teenage: The Creation of Youth Culture* (New York: Viking).

Savage, M., et al. (1992) *Property, Bureaucracy, and Culture: Middle-Class Formation in Contemporary Britain* (London: Routledge).

Savage, M., et al. (2013) 'A New Model of Social Class? Findings from the BBC's Great British Class Survey Experiment', *Sociology*, 47(2): 219–50.

Sayers, J. (1986) *Sexual Contradiction: Psychology, Psychoanalysis and Feminism* (London: Tavistock).

Scarman, L. G. (1982) *The Scarman Report: The Brixton Disorders, 10–12 April 1981* (Harmondsworth: Penguin).

Schaie, K. W. (1979) 'The Primary Mental Abilities in Adulthood: An Exploration in the Development of Psychometric Intelligence', in P. B. Baltes and O. G. Brim (eds), *Lifespan Development and Behavior*, Vol. 2 (New York: Academic Press).

Schaie, K. W. (1996) 'Intellectual Development in Adulthood', in J. E. Birren and K. W. Schaie (eds), *Handbook of the Psychology of Aging* (4th edn, San Diego: Academic Press): 266–86.

Schmiedek, F., Lövdén, M., and Lindenberger, U. (2013) 'Keeping it Steady: Older Adults Perform More Consistently on Cognitive Tasks than Younger Adults', *Psychological Science*, 24(9): 1747–54.

Schnaiberg, A. (1980) *The Environment: From Surplus to Scarcity* (New York: Oxford University Press).

Schwartz, M. S. (2011) *Corporate Social Responsibility: An Ethical Approach* (New York: Broadview Press).

Schwarz, J., and Volgy, T. (1992) *The Forgotten Americans* (New York: W. W. Norton).

Scott, A. (2000) 'Risk Society or Angst Society? Two Views of Risk, Consciousness and Community', in B. Adam, U. Beck and J. van Loon (eds), *The Risk Society and Beyond: Critical Issues for Social Theory* (London: Sage).

Scott, J. (1991) *Who Rules Britain?* (Cambridge: Polity).

Scott, S. (2009) 'Re-clothing the Emperor: The Swimming Pool as a Negotiated Order', *Symbolic Interaction*, 32(2): 123–45.

Scott, S. (2010) 'How to Look Good (Nearly) Naked: The Performative Regulation of the Swimmer's Body', *Body and Society*, 16(2): 143–68.

Scott, S., and Morgan, D. (1993) 'Bodies in a Social Landscape', in S. Scott and D. Morgan (eds), *Body Matters: Essays on the Sociology of the Body* (London: Falmer Press).

Segura, D. A., and Pierce, J. L. (1993) 'Chicana/o Family Structure and Gender Personality: Chodorow, Familism, and Psychoanalytic Sociology Revisited', *Signs*, 19: 62–91.

Seidman, S. (1997) *Difference Troubles: Queering Social Theory and Sexual Politics* (Cambridge: Cambridge University Press).

Sen, A. (1999) *Development as Freedom* (Oxford: Oxford University Press).

Sen, A. (2001) *Development as Freedom* (Oxford: Oxford University Press).

Sen, A. (2007) *Identity and Violence: The Illusion of Destiny* (London: Penguin).

Sen, S., and Nair, P. M. (2004) *A Report on Trafficking in Women and Children in India, 2002–2003*, Vol.1 (New Delhi: Institute of Social Sciences/National Human Rights Commission/UNIFEM); http://nhrc. nic.in/Documents/ReportonTrafficking.pdf.

Sennett, R. (1993) *The Conscience of the Eye: The Design and Social Life of Cities* (London: Faber & Faber).

Sennett, R. (1998) *The Corrosion of Character: The Personal Consequences of Work in the New Capitalism* (London: W. W. Norton).

Sennett, R. (2003 [1977]) *The Fall of Public Man* (Cambridge: Cambridge University Press).

Seung Lam, M., and Pollard, A. (2006) 'A Conceptual Framework for Understanding Children as Agents in the Transition from Home to Kindergarten', *Early Years*, 26(2): 123–41.

Shaheen, J. (1984) *The TV Arab* (Bowling Green, OH: Bowling Green State University Press).

Shaheen, J. (2001) *Reel Bad Arabs: How Hollywood Vilifies a People* (New York: Olive Branch Press).

Shakespeare, T., and Watson, N. (2002) 'The Social Model of Disability: An Outdated Ideology?', *Research in Social Science and Disability*, 2: 9–28.

Sharkansky, I. (2000) 'A State Action May be Nasty but is Not Likely to be a Crime', in J. I. Ross (ed.), *Controlling State Crime* (2nd edn, New Brunswick, NJ: Transaction): 35–52.

Sharkey, H. J. (2004) 'Globalization, Migration and Identity: Sudan 1800–2000', in B. Schaebler and L. Stenberg (eds), *Globalization and the Muslim World: Culture, Religion and Modernity* (Syracuse, NY: Syracuse University Press).

Sharma, U. (1992) *Complementary Medicine Today: Practitioners and Patients* (London: Routledge).

Sharma, U. (1999) *Caste* (Buckingham: Open University Press).

Sharpe, S. (1994) *Just Like a Girl: How Girls Learn to be Women: From the Seventies to the Nineties* (London: Penguin).

Shaw, M. (2003) *War and Genocide: Organized Killing in Modern Society* (Cambridge: Polity).

Shaw, M. (2005) *The New Western Way of War: Risk-Transfer and its Crisis in Iraq* (Cambridge: Polity).

Shaw, M. (2007) *What is Genocide? A New Social Theory* (Cambridge: Polity).

Sheldon, W. A. (1949) *Varieties of Delinquent Youth* (New York: Harper).

Sheller, M., and Urry, J. (2004) *Tourism Mobilities: Places to Stay, Places in Play* (London: Routledge).

Shelton, B. A. (1992) *Women, Men, and Time: Gender Differences in Paid Work, Housework, and Leisure* (Westport, CT: Greenwood Press).

Shiva, V. (1993) *Ecofeminism* (London: Zed Books).

Silverman, B. (2014) 'Modern Slavery: an Application of Multiple Systems Estimation', https://www. gov.uk/government/uploads/system/uploads/attachment_data/file/386841/Modern_Slavery_an_ application of MSE revised.pdf.

Silverstone R. (1994) *Television and Everyday Life* (London: Routledge).

Simmel, G. (1950 [1903]) 'The Metropolis and Mental Life', in K. H. Wolff (ed.), *The Sociology of Georg Simmel* (New York: Free Press).

Simmons, J., and Dodds, T. (2003) *Crime in England and Wales 2002/03* (London: Home Office).

Simpson, J. H. (1985) 'Socio-Moral Issues and Recent Presidential Elections', *Review of Religious Research*, 27(2): 115–23.

Sinclair, P. (1987) *Unemployment: Economic Theory and Evidence* (Oxford: Blackwell).

Sinclair, T. J. (2012) *Global Governance* (Cambridge: Polity).

Sjoberg, G. (1960) *The Pre-Industrial City: Past and Present* (New York: Free Press).

Sjoberg, G. (1963) 'The Rise and Fall of Cities: A Theoretical Perspective', *International Journal of Comparative Sociology*, 4: 107–20.

Skeggs, B. (1997) *Formations of Class and Gender: Becoming Respectable* (London: Sage).

Skeie, G. (2009) 'Introduction', in G. Skeie (ed.), *Religious Diversity and Education: Nordic Perspectives* (Munster: Waxmann): 7–11.

Skinner, Q. (ed.) (1990) *The Return of Grand Theory in the Human Sciences* (Cambridge: Cambridge University Press).

Skocpol, T. (1979) *States and Social Revolutions: A Comparative Analysis of France, Russia and China* (Cambridge: Cambridge University Press).

Slapper, G., and Tombs, S. (1999) *Corporate Crime* (Harlow: Longman).

Slattery, M. (2003) *Key Ideas in Sociology* (Cheltenham: Nelson Thornes).

Smart, C. (2007) *Personal Life: New Directions in Sociological Thinking* (Cambridge: Polity).

Smart, C., and Neale, B. (1999) *Family Fragments?* (Cambridge: Polity).

Smart, C., Neale, B., and Wade, A. (2001) *The Changing Experience of Childhood: Families and Divorce* (Cambridge: Polity).

Smelser, N. J. (1962) *Theory of Collective Behavior* (London: Routledge & Kegan Paul).

Smelser, N. J., and Swedberg, R. (eds) (2005) *The Handbook of Economic Sociology* (Princeton, NJ: Princeton University Press).

Smith, A. (1991 [1776]) *The Wealth of Nations* (London: Everyman's Library).

Smith, A. D. (1986) *The Ethnic Origins of Nations* (Oxford: Blackwell).

Smith, A. D. (1998) *Nationalism and Modernity: A Critical Survey of Recent Theories of Nations and Nationalism* (New York: Routledge).

Smith, C. S. (2007) 'In Poland, a Jewish Revival Thrives – Minus Jews', *New York Times*, 12 July; www.nytimes.com/2007/07/12/world/europe/12krakow.html?pagewanted=all.

Smith, D. (1990) *Stepmothering* (London: Harvester Press).

Smith, M. J. (1998) *Ecologism: Towards Ecological Citizenship* (Buckingham: Open University Press).

Smith, M. J., and Pangsapa, P. (2008) *Environment and Citizenship: Integrating Justice, Responsibility and Civic Engagement* (London: Zed Books).

Smith, P., and Prior, G. (1997) *The Fourth National Survey of Ethnic Minorities: Technical Report* (London: National Centre for Social Research).

Smith, P. K., Mahdavi, J., Carvalho, M., Fisher, S., Russell, S., and Tippett, N. (2008) 'Cyberbullying: Its Nature and Impact in Secondary School Pupils', *Journal of Child Psychology and Psychiatry*, 49(4): 376–85.

Smith, S. L., and Cook, C. A. (2008) *Gender Stereotypes: An Analysis of Popular Films and TV* (Los Angeles: Geena Davis Institute for Gender and Media).

Smooth, W. G. (2010) 'Intersectionalities of Race and Gender and Leadership', in K. O'Connor (ed.), *Gender and Women's Leadership: A Reference Handbook*, Vol. 1 (London: Sage): 31–40.

Snowdon, C. (2010) *The Spirit Level Delusion: Fact-Checking the Left's New Theory of Everything* (Ripon: Little Dice).

Social Mobility and Child Poverty Commission (2014) *Elitist Britain?* (London: SMCPC).

Solomos, J., and Back, L. (1996) *Racism and Society* (Basingstoke: Macmillan).

Soothill, K., and Walby, S. (1991) *Sex Crime in the News* (London: Routledge).

Sosinsky, B. (2011) *Cloud Computing Bible* (Indianapolis: Wiley).

Southall, R. (2004) 'The ANC and Black Capitalism in South Africa', *Review of African Political Economy*, 100: 313–28.

Soyka, P. A. (2012) *Creating a Sustainable Organization: Approaches for Enhancing Corporate Value through Sustainability* (Upper Saddle River, NJ: FT Press).

Spencer, S. (2014) *Race and Ethnicity: Culture, Identity and Representation* (Abingdon: Routledge).

Spender, D. (1982) *Invisible Women: The Schooling Scandal* (London: Writers and Readers Publishing Cooperative Society).

Spivak, G. (1987) *In Other Worlds: Essays in Cultural Politics* (London: Routledge).

Sreberny-Mohammadi, A., Winseck, D., McKenna, J., and Boyd-Barrett, O. (eds) (1997) *Media in Global Context: A Reader* (London: Hodder Arnold).

Standing, G. (2011) *The Precariat: The New Dangerous Class* (London: Bloomsbury).

Stanley, L., and Wise, S. (1993) *Breaking Out Again: Feminist Ontology and Epistemology* (new edn, London: Routledge).

Stanley, L., and Wise, S. (2002) 'What's Wrong with Socialization?', in S. Jackson and S. Scott (eds), *Gender: A Sociological Reader* (London: Routledge): 273–9.

Stanworth, M. (1983) *Gender and Schooling* (London: Hutchinson).

Stanworth, M. (1984) 'Women and Class Analysis: A Reply to John Goldthorpe', *Sociology*, 18(2): 159–70.

Stark, R., and Bainbridge, W. S. (1980) 'Towards a Theory of Religious Commitment', *Journal for the Scientific Study of Religion*, 19: 114–28.

Stark, R., and Bainbridge, W. S. (1985) *The Future of Religion: Secularism, Revival, and Cult Formation* (Berkeley: University of California Press).

Stark, R., and Bainbridge, W. S. (1987) *A Theory of Religion* (New Brunswick, NJ: Rutgers University Press).

Statham, J. (1986) *Daughters and Sons: Experiences of Non-Sexist Childraising* (Oxford: Blackwell).

Steele, C. M. (1997) 'A Threat in the Air: How Stereotypes Shape Intellectual Identity and Performance', *American Psychologist*, 52: 613–29.

Steele, C. M., and Aronson, J. (1995) 'Stereotype Threat and the Intellectual Test Performance of African Americans', *Journal of Personality and Social Psychology*, 69(5): 797–811.

Steinberg, R. (1990) 'Social Construction of Skill: Gender, Power and Comparable Worth', *Work and Occupations*, 17(4): 449–82.

Stephens, P. (2014) 'Gene Therapy Effective to Treat "Bubble-Boy" Syndrome', 9 October, www.bbc.co.uk/news/health-29534859.

Stephen-Smith, S. (2008) *Routes In, Routes Out: Quantifying the Gendered Experience of Trafficking to the UK* (London: Poppy Project).

Stern, V. (1989) *Bricks of Shame: Britain's Prisons* (London: Penguin).

Stewart, H. (2015) 'Has George Osborne Really Introduced a Living Wage?', *The Guardian*, 8 July; www.theguardian.com/society/reality-check/2015/jul/08/george-osborne-budget-national-living-wage.

Stewart, S. (2010) *Culture and the Middle Classes* (Farnham: Ashgate).

Stillwaggon, E. (2000) 'HIV Transmission in Latin America: Comparisons with Africa and Policy Implications', *South African Journal of Economics*, 68(5): 985–1011.

Stoll, C. (1995) *Silicon Snake Oil: Second Thoughts on the Information Highway* (New York: Anchor Books).

Stone, L. (1980) *The Family, Sex, and Marriage in England, 1500–1800* (New York: Harper & Row).

Stonewall (2003) *Profiles of Prejudice: The Nature of Prejudice in England* (London: Stonewall).

Storr, M. (2002) 'Sociology and Social Movements: Theories, Analyses and Ethical Dilemmas', in P. Hamilton and K. Thompson (eds), *Sociology and Society*: Vol. 4: *The Uses of Sociology* (Buckingham: Open University Press).

Strand, G. (2008) 'Keyword: Evil: Google's Addiction to Cheap Electricity', *Harper's Magazine*, March.

Strand, S. (2011) 'The Limits of Social Class in Explaining Ethnic Gaps in Educational Attainment', *British Journal of Educational Research*, 37(2): 197–229.

Strang, H., and Braithwaite, J. (eds) (2001) *Restorative Justice and Civil Society* (Cambridge: Cambridge University Press).

Strangleman, T. (2015) 'Work: Experience, Identities and Meanings', in M. Holborn (ed.), *Contemporary Sociology* (Cambridge: Polity): 134–64.

Strategy Unit (2003) *Ethnic Minorities and the Labour Market* (London: HMSO).

Straus, M. A., and Gelles, R. J. (1986) 'Societal Change and Change in Family Violence from 1975 to 1985 as Revealed by Two National Surveys', *Journal of Marriage and the Family*, 48(3): 465–79.

Strawbridge, M. (2006) *Netiquette: Internet Etiquette in the Age of the Blog* (Ely, Cambridgeshire: Software Reference).

Sullivan, O. (1997) 'Time Waits for No (Wo)man: An Investigation of the Gendered Experience of Domestic Time', *Sociology*, 31(2): 221–39.

Sullivan, O. (2000) 'The Domestic Division of Labour: Twenty Years of Change', *Sociology*, 34(3): 437–56.

Sumner, A. (2010) *Global Poverty and the New Bottom Billion*, IDS Working Paper (Sussex: Institute of Development Studies).

Sunday Times (2007) 'Rich List 2007', 29 April.

Sunday Times (2010) 'The Sunday Times Rich List: Fortunes of Super-Rich Soar by a Third', 25 April.

Surtees, R. (2005) *Second Annual Report on Victims of Trafficking in South-Eastern Europe* (Geneva: International Organization for Migration).

Sutton, P. W. (2000) *Explaining Environmentalism: In Search of a New Social Movement* (Aldershot: Ashgate).

Sutton, P. W. (2007) *The Environment: A Sociological Introduction* (Cambridge: Polity).

Sutton, P. W., and Vertigans, S. (2005) *Resurgent Islam: A Sociological Approach* (Cambridge: Polity).

Sutton, P. W., and Vertigans, S. (2006) 'Islamic New Social Movements? Al-Qa'ida, Radical Islam, and Social Movement Theory', *Mobilization: An International Journal of Social Movement Research*, 11(1): 101–16.

Svensson, N. L. (2006) 'Extraterritorial Accountability: An Assessment of the Effectiveness of Child Sex Tourism Laws', *Loyola of Los Angeles International and Comparative Law Review*, 28: 641–64; http://digitalcommons.lmu.edu/ilr/vol28/iss3/6.

Swann Committee (1985) *Education for All: Report of the Committee into the Education of Ethnic Minority Children* (London: HMSO).

Swingewood, A. (1977) *The Myth of Mass Culture* (London: Macmillan).

Syn, J. (2014) 'The Social Licence: Empowering Communities and a Better Way Forward', *Social Epistemology*, 28(3–4): 318–39.

Szasz, A. (1994) *EcoPopulism: Toxic Waste and the Movement for Environmental Justice* (Minneapolis: University of Minnesota Press).

Der Tagesspiegel (2008) 'Wenn Sie das trinken, gibt es kein Zurück', 29 March; www.tagesspiegel.de/weltspiegel/wenn-sie-das-trinken-gibt-es-kein-zurueck/1198414.html [interview with Ludwig Minelli of Dignitas].

Tan, A., and Ramakrishna, K. (eds) (2002) *The New Terrorism* (Singapore: Eastern Universities Press).

Tarrow, S. (1998) *Power in Movement: Social Movements, Collective Action and Politics* (Cambridge: Cambridge University Press).

Tasker, Y., and Negra, D. (eds) (2007) *Interrogating Postfeminism: Gender and the Politics of Popular Culture* (Durham, NC: Duke University Press).

Tatchell, P. (2000) '30 Years of Gay Liberation', www.petertatchell.net/lgbt_rights/history/30years.htm.

Tawney, R. H. (1964 [1931]) *Equality* (London: Unwin).

Taylor, C. (1992) *Sources of the Self: The Making of the Modern Identity* (Cambridge: Cambridge University Press).

Taylor, C. (2007) *A Secular Age* (Cambridge, MA: Harvard University Press).

Taylor, I., Evans, K., and Fraser, P. (1996) *A Tale of Two Cities: Global Change, Local Feeling and Everyday Life in the North of England: A Study in Manchester and Sheffield* (London: Routledge).

Taylor, I., Walton, P., and Young, J. (1973) *The New Criminology: For a Social Theory of Deviance* (London: Routledge & Kegan Paul).

Taylor, M. W. (1992) *Men versus the State: Herbert Spencer and Late Victorian Individualism* (Oxford: Clarendon Press).

Taylor, Y., and Hines, S. (2012) *Sexualities: Past Reflections, Future Directions* (Basingstoke: Palgrave Macmillan).

Taylor-Gooby, P. (2013) *The Double Crisis of the Welfare State and What We Can Do about It* (Basingstoke: Palgrave Macmillan).

Taylor-Gooby, P., and Stoker, G. (2011) 'The Coalition Programme: A New Vision for Britain or Politics as Usual?', *Political Quarterly*, 82(1): 4–15.

The Telegraph (2011) 'Child Brain Scans to Pick out Future Criminals', 22 February; www.telegraph.co.uk/news/science/8339772/Child-brain-scans-to-pick-out-future-criminals.html.

Tempest, R. (1996) 'Barbie and the World Economy', *Los Angeles Times*, 22 September.

Therborn, G. (2004) *Between Sex and Power: Family in the World, 1900–2000* (London: Routledge).

Therborn, G. (2011) *The World: A Beginner's Guide* (Cambridge: Polity).

Thomas, C. (1999) *Female Forms: Experiencing and Understanding Disability* (Buckingham: Open University Press).

Thomas, C. (2002) 'Disability Theory: Key Ideas, Issues and Thinkers', in C. Barnes, L. Barton and M. Oliver (eds), *Disability Studies Today* (Cambridge: Polity).

Thomas, K. (1984) *Man and the Natural World: Changing Attitudes in England 1500–1800* (London: Penguin).

Thomas, N. (2009) 'Sociology of Childhood', in T. Maynard and N. Thomas (eds), *An Introduction to Early Childhood Studies* (2nd edn, London: Sage): 33–46.

Thomas, W. I. (with Thomas, D. S.) (1928) *The Child in America: Behavior Problems and Programs* (New York: Knopf).

Thomas, W. I., and Znaniecki, F. (1966 [1918–20]) *The Polish Peasant in Europe and America: Monograph of Our Immigrant Group*, 5 vols (New York: Dover).

Thompson, J. B. (1990) *Ideology and Modern Culture* (Cambridge: Polity).

Thompson, J. B. (1995) *The Media and Modernity: A Social Theory of the Media* (Cambridge: Polity).

Thompson, W. C. (2015) *Western Europe: The World Today Series, 2015–2016* (34th edn, Lanham, MD: Rowman & Littlefield).

Thompson, W. S. (1929) 'Population', *American Journal of Sociology*, 34: 959–75.

Thorne, B. (1993) *Gender Play: Girls and Boys in School* (New Brunswick, NJ: Rutgers University Press).

Tilly, C. (1978) *From Mobilization to Revolution* (London: Longman).

Tilly, C. (1995) 'Globalization Threatens Labor's Rights', *International Labor and Working-Class History*, 47: 1–23.

Tipple, G., and Speak, S. (2009) *The Hidden Millions: Homelessness in Developing Countries* (Abingdon: Routledge).

Tizard, B., and Hughes, M. (1984) *Young Children Learning, Talking and Thinking at Home and at School* (London: Fontana).

Toke, D. (2004) *The Politics of GM Food: A Comparative Study of the UK, USA, and EU* (New York: Routledge).

Tolson, A. (2005) *Media Talk: Spoken Discourse on TV and Radio* (Edinburgh: Edinburgh University Press).

Tomlinson, J. (1991) *Cultural Imperialism: A Critical Introduction* (London: Pinter).

Tonkiss, F. (2006) *Contemporary Economic Sociology: Globalisation, Production, Inequality* (London: Routledge).

Tönnies, F. (2001 [1887]) *Community and Civil Society*, trans. J. Harris and M. Hollis (Cambridge and New York: Cambridge University Press).

Tough, J. (1976) *Listening to Children Talking* (London: Ward Lock).

Touraine, A. (1971) *The Post-Industrial Society: Tomorrow's Social History: Classes, Conflict and Culture in the Programmed Society* (New York: Random House).

Touraine, A. (1981) *The Voice and the Eye: An Analysis of Social Movements* (Cambridge: Cambridge University Press).

Townsend, P. (1979) *Poverty in the United Kingdom* (Harmondsworth: Penguin).

Travis, A. (2011) 'Young Black Men Make up Four In Ten of Youth Jail Population', *The Guardian*, 26 October; www.guardian.co.uk/society/2011/oct/26/young-black-men-youth-jails.

Traynor, I. (2004) 'Hague Rules Srebrenica Was Act of Genocide', *The Guardian*, 20 April; www.guardian.co.uk/world/2004/apr/20/warcrimes.

Treas, J. (1995) 'Older Americans in the 1990s and Beyond', *Population Bulletin*, 50(2): 1–48.

Troeltsch, E. (1981 [1931]) *The Social Teaching of the Christian Churches*, 2 vols (Chicago: University of Chicago Press).

Tuchman, G. (1978) 'Introduction: The Symbolic Annihilation of Women by the Mass Media', in G. Tuchman, A. K. Daniels and J. Benét, *Hearth and Home: Images of Women in the Mass Media* (New York: Oxford University Press).

Tunstall, J. (1977) *The Media Are American: Anglo-American Media in the World* (London: Constable).

Tunstall, J. (2007) *The Media Were American: US Mass Media in Decline* (New York: Oxford University Press).

Tunstall, R., Bevan, M., Bradshaw, J., et al. (2013) *The Links Between Housing and Poverty: An Evidence Review* (York: Joseph Rowntree Foundation).

Turner, B. S. (1974) *Weber and Islam: A Critical Study* (London: Routledge).

Turner, B. S. (1990) 'Outline of a Theory of Citizenship', *Sociology*, 24(2): 189–217.

Turner, B. S. (1993) *Max Weber: From History to Modernity* (London: Routledge).

Turner, B. S. (1995) *Medical Power and Social Knowledge* (London: Sage).

Turner, B. S. (2006) *Vulnerability and Human Rights* (University Park: Pennsylvania State University Press).

Turner, G. (2004) *Understanding Celebrity* (London: Sage).

Tyler, T. R. (2006) *Why People Obey the Law* (Princeton, NJ: Princeton University Press).

UK Political Info (2015) 'General Election Turnout 1945-2015', available at: http://www.ukpolitical.info/Turnout45.htm.

UN (1948) *The Universal Declaration of Human Rights*, www.un.org/en/universal-declaration-human-rights/.

UN (2006) *World Population Prospects: The 2006 Revision* (New York: UN Department of Economic and Social Affairs).

UN (2009) 'President's Summary of the Thematic Debate on Drugs and Crime as a Threat to Development', www.un.org/en/ga/president/66/Issues/drugs/pga_summary_debate.pdf.

UN (2010) *World Urbanization Prospects: The 2009 Revision* (New York: UN Department of Economic and Social Affairs, Population Division).

UN (2011) 'Press Release: World Population to Reach 10 Billion by 2100 if Fertility in All Countries Converges to Replacement Level', Department of Economic and Social Affairs, 3 May; http://esa.un.org/wpp/Other-Information/Press_Release_WPP2010.pdf.

UN Commission on Global Governance (2005 [1995]) 'A New World', in R. Wilkinson (ed.) *The Global Governance Reader* (London: Routledge): 26–44.

UN Convention on the Rights of Persons with Disabilities (2006), preamble, www.un.org/disabilities/convention/facts.shtml.

UN ESA (2014) *World Urbanization Prospects: The 2014 Revision, Highlights*, http://esa.un.org/unpd/wup/Highlights/WUP2014-Highlights.pdf.

UN Millennium Ecosystem Assessment Board (2005) *Living Beyond our Means: Natural Assets and Human Well-Being* (Washington, DC: Island Press).

UNAIDS (2008) *Report on the Global AIDS Epidemic 2008: Executive Summary* (Geneva: UNAIDS).

UNAIDS (2014) *The Gap Report* (Geneva: UNAIDS).

UNCTAD (2007) *The Universe of the Largest Transnational Corporations* (New York and Geneva: United Nations).

UNDP (1998) *Human Development Report* (New York: UN Development Programme).

UNDP (2003) *Human Development Report* (New York: UN Development Programme).

UNDP (2004) *Human Development Report: Cultural Liberty in Today's Diverse World* (New York: UN Development Programme).

UNDP (2007a) *Human Development Report 2007/2008* (New York: UN Development Programme).

UNDP (2007b) *United Nations Development Programme, Annual Report 2007* (New York: UN Development Programme).

UNDP (2010) *Human Development Report 2010: The Real Wealth of Nations: Pathways to Human Development* (Basingstoke: Palgrave Macmillan).

UNDP (2014) *Human Development Report 2014: Sustaining Human Progress: Reducing Vulnerabilities and Building Resilience* (New York: UNDP).

UNDP (2015) *Human Development Report 2015: Work for Human Development* (New York: UNDP).

UNESCO (1982) *Declaration on Race and Racial Prejudice*, www.unesco.org/education/information/nfsunesco/pdf/RACE_E.PDF.

UNESCO (2008) *EFA Global Monitoring Report: Strong Foundations, Early Childhood Care and Education* (Paris: UNESCO); www.efareport.unesco.org.

UNESCO (2009a) *Water in a Changing World: UN World Water Development Report 3* (London: Earthscan).

UNESCO (2009b) 'Nollywood Rivals Bollywood in Film/Video Production', www.unesco.org/en/creativity/dynamic-content-single-view-copy-1/news/nollywood_rivals_bollywood_in_filmvideo_production/back/19123/cHash/f8233ace54/.

UNESCO (2010) *EFA Global Monitoring Report: Reaching the Marginalised: Summary* (Paris: UNESCO); www.efareport.unesco.org.

UNESCO (2014a) *Teaching and Learning: Achieving Equality for All* (Paris: UNESCO).

UNESCO (2014b) International Literacy Data, 2014, www.uis.unesco.org/literacy/Pages/literacy-data-release-2014.aspx.

UNFAO (2015) *The State of Food Insecurity in the World 2015*, www.fao.org/hunger/en/.

UNFPA (2011) *State of the World Population 2011* (New York: UNFPA); http://foweb.unfpa.org/SWP2011/reports/EN-SWOP2011-FINAL.pdf.

UNICEF (2000a) *The State of the World's Children, 2000* (New York: UN Children's Fund).

UNICEF (2000b) *Domestic Violence against Women and Girls* (Florence: UN Children's Fund).

UNICEF (2012) *Global Initiative on Out-of-School Children: Nigeria Country Study* (Abuja: UNICEF).

UNICEF/WHO (2015) *Progress on Sanitation and Drinking Water: 2015 Update and MDG Assessment* (Geneva: WHO).

Universities UK (2010) *Higher Education in Facts and Figures* (London: Universities UK).

UNODC (2010) *The Globalization of Crime: A Transnational Organized Crime Threat Assessment*, www.unodc.org/documents/data-and-analysis/tocta/TOCTA_Report_2010_low_res.pdf.

UNSDSN (2012) 'Global Profile of Extreme Poverty', http://unsdsn.org/wp-content/uploads/2014/02/121015-Profile-of-Extreme-Poverty.pdf.

UNWFP (2001) 'News Release: WFP Head Releases World Hunger Map and Warns of Hunger "Hot Spots" in 2001', 9 January, http://reliefweb.int/node/74045.

UPIAS (1976) *Fundamental Principles of Disability* (London: Union of Physically Impaired Against Segregation).

Urban Task Force (1999) *Towards a Strong Urban Renaissance: Final Report of the Urban Task Force*, chaired by Lord Rogers of Riverside (London: Department of the Environment, Transport and the Regions); www.urbantaskforce.org/UTF_final_report.pdf.

Urry, J. (2000) *Sociology beyond Societies: Mobilities for the Twenty-First Century* (London: Routledge).

Urry, J. (2002) *The Tourist Gaze: Leisure and Travel in Contemporary Societies* (2nd edn, London: Sage).

Urry, J. (2003) 'Social Networks, Travel and Talk', *British Journal of Sociology*, 54(2): 155–75.

Urry, J. (2007) *Mobilities* (Cambridge: Polity).

Urry, J. (2011) *Climate Change and Society* (Cambridge: Polity).

Urry, J., and Larsen, J. (2011) *The Tourist Gaze 3.0* (3rd edn, London: Sage).

US Census Bureau (2011) *Statistical Abstract of the United States: 2011* (130th edn, Washington, DC: Census Bureau).

Valk, A. M. (2008) *Radical Sisters: Second-Wave Feminism and Black Liberation in Washington, DC* (Urbana: University of Illinois Press).

Vallas, S. P., and Beck, J. P. (1996) 'The Transformation of Work Revisited: The Limits of Flexibility in American Manufacturing', *Social Problems*, 43(3): 339–61.

Van der Veer, P. (1994) *Religious Nationalism: Hindus and Muslims in India* (Berkeley: University of California Press).

Van Dijk, T. A. (1997) *Discourse Studies: A Multidisciplinary Introduction*, 2 vols (London: Sage).

Van Krieken, R. (1998) *Norbert Elias* (London: Routledge).

Vaswani, K. (2007) 'Can India Close the Wealth Gap?', 14 August, http://news.bbc.co.uk/1/hi/business/6940966.stm.

Vatican (2004) 'Letter to the Bishops of the Catholic Church on the Collaboration of Men and Women in the Church and in the World', 31 May, www.vatican.va/roman_curia/congregations/cfaith/documents/rc_con_cfaith_doc_20040731_collaboration_en.html.

Vaughan, D. (1990) *Uncoupling: Turning Points in Intimate Relationships* (New York: Vintage).

Veit-Wilson, J. (1998) *Setting Adequate Standards* (Bristol: Policy Press).

Vertigans, S. (2008) *Terrorism and Societies* (Aldershot: Ashgate).

Vertigans, S. (2011) *The Sociology of Terrorism: People, Places and Processes* (Abingdon: Routledge).

Vertovec, S. (2006) *The Emergence of Super-Diversity in Britain*, Centre on Migration, Policy and Society, Working Paper no.25, University of Oxford.

Vertovec, S. (2007) 'Super-Diversity and its Implications', *Ethnic and Racial Studies*, 30(6): 1024–54.

Vertovec, S., and Cohen, R. (eds) (2002) *Conceiving Cosmopolitanism: Theory, Context and Practice* (Oxford: Oxford University Press).

Victor, C. (2005) *The Social Context of Ageing: A Textbook of Gerontology* (London: Routledge).

Vidal, J. (2011) 'Climate Sceptic Willie Soon Received $1m from Oil Companies, Papers Show', *The Guardian*, 28 June; www.guardian.co.uk/environment/2011/jun/28/climate-change-sceptic-willie-soon.

Vincent, J. (1999) *Politics, Power, and Old Age* (Buckingham: Open University Press).

Vincent, J. (2003) *Old Age* (London: Routledge).

Visgilio, G. R., and Whitelaw, D. M. (eds) (2003) *Our Backyard: A Quest for Environmental Justice* (Lanham, MD, and Oxford: Rowman & Littlefield).

Voas, D. (2009) 'The Rise and Fall of Fuzzy Fidelity in Europe', *European Sociological Review*, 25(2): 155–68.

Voas, D., and Crockett, A. (2005) 'Religion in Britain: Neither Believing Nor Belonging', *Sociology*, 39(1): 11–28.

Vogel, P. (2015) *Generation Jobless? Turning the Youth Unemployment Crisis into Opportunity* (Basingstoke: Palgrave Macmillan).

Vogler, C., and Pahl, J. (1994) 'Money, Power and Inequality in Marriage', *Sociological Review*, 42(2): 263–88.

Voicu, B., Voicu, M., and Strapkova, K. (2007) *Engendered Housework: A Cross-European Analysis*, IRISS Working Paper (Luxembourg: Centre d'Etudes de Populations, de Pauvreté et de Politiques Socio-economiques); www.ceps.lu/pdf/11/art1234.pdf.

Vörösmarty, C. J., et al. (2010) 'Global Threats to Human Water Security and River Biodiversity', *Nature*, 467 (September): 555–61.

Vygotsky, L. (1986 [1934]) *Thought and Language* (Cambridge, MA: MIT Press).

Wachman, R. (2007) 'Water Becomes the New Oil as World Runs Dry', *The Observer*, 9 December.

Wacquant, L. (2010) *Deadly Symbiosis: Race and the Rise of the Penal State* (Cambridge: Polity).

Waddington, D., Critcher, C., Dicks, B., and Parry, D. (2001) *Out of the Ashes? The Social Impact of Industrial Contraction and Regeneration on Britain's Mining Communities* (London: Routledge).

Wagar, W. (1992) *A Short History of the Future* (Chicago: University of Chicago Press).

Walby, S. (1986) 'Gender, Class and Stratification: Towards a New Approach', in R. Crompton and M. Mann (eds), *Gender and Stratification* (Cambridge: Polity).

Walby, S. (1990) *Theorizing Patriarchy* (Oxford: Blackwell).

Walby, S. (2011) *The Future of Feminism* (Cambridge: Polity).

Walby, S., and Allen, J. (2004) *Domestic Violence, Sexual Assault and Stalking: Findings from the British Crime Survey*, Research Study 276 (London: Home Office).

Wales Online (2014) 'North Wales Child Abuse Inquiry: Two More Men Charged by Police', www.walesonline.co.uk/news/wales-news/north-wales-child-abuse-inquiry-7659247.

Walker, C. (1994) 'Managing Poverty', *Sociology Review* (April).

Wall, D. (2007) *Cybercrimes: The Transformation of Crime in the Information Age* (Cambridge: Polity).

Wall, M. (2014) 'Ebola: Can Big Data Analytics Help Contain its Spread?', 15 October, www.bbc.co.uk/news/business-29617831.

Wallerstein, I. (1974) *The Modern World-System*, Vol. 1: *Capitalist Agriculture and the Origins of the European World-Economy in the Sixteenth Century* (New York: Academic Press).

Wallerstein, I. (1980) *The Modern World-System*, Vol. 2: *Mercantilism and the Consolidation of the European World-Economy, 1600–1750* (New York: Academic Press).

Wallerstein, I. (1989) *The Modern World-System*, Vol. 3: *The Second Era of Great Expansion of the Capitalist World-Economy, 1730–1840s* (New York: Academic Press).

Wallis, R. (1984) *The Elementary Forms of New Religious Life* (London: Routledge & Kegan Paul).

Walmsley, R. (2013) *World Prison Population List* (10th edn, London: International Centre for Prison Studies).

Walsh, D., and Poole, A. (eds) (1983) *A Dictionary of Criminology* (London: Routledge & Kegan Paul).

Walter, A. (1994) *The Revival of Death* (London and New York: Routledge).

Walter, A. (1999) *On Bereavement: The Culture of Grief* (Buckingham: Open University Press).

Walton, P., and Young, J. (eds) (1998) *The New Criminology Revisited* (London: Macmillan).

Warner, S. (1993) 'Work in Progress toward a New Paradigm for the Sociological Study of Religion in the United States', *American Journal of Sociology*, 98: 1044–93.

Warren, B. (1980) *Imperialism: Pioneer of Capitalism* (London, Verso).

Wasserstein, B. (1996) *Vanishing Diaspora: The Jews in Europe since 1945* (London: Hamish Hamilton).

Waters, M. (2001) *Globalization* (2nd edn, London: Routledge).

Watson, T. J. (2008) *Sociology, Work and Industry* (5th edn, London: Routledge).

Watts, M. (1997) 'Black Gold, White Heat: State Violence, Local Resistance and the National Question in Nigeria', in S. Pile and M. Keith (eds), *Geographies of Resistance* (New York: Routledge).

WCED (World Commission on Environment and Development) (1987) *Our Common Future* (Oxford: Oxford University Press) [Brundtland Report].

Weaver, M. (2001) 'Urban Regeneration – the Issue Explained', *The Guardian*, 19 March.

Weber, M. (1948) *From Max Weber: Essays in Sociology*, ed. H. H. Gerth and C. W. Mills (London: Routledge & Kegan Paul).

Weber, M. (1951) *The Religion of China* (New York: Free Press).

Weber, M. (1952) *Ancient Judaism* (New York: Free Press).

Weber, M. (1958) *The Religion of India* (New York: Free Press).

Weber, M. (1963) *The Sociology of Religion* (Boston: Beacon Press).

Weber, M. (1979 [1925]) *Economy and Society: An Outline of Interpretive Sociology* (Berkeley: University of California Press).

Weber, M. (1992 [1904–5]) *The Protestant Ethic and the Spirit of Capitalism* (London: Allen & Unwin).

Weeks, J. (1986) *Sexuality* (London: Methuen).

Weeks, J. (1999) *Making Sexual History* (Cambridge: Polity).

Weeks, J., Heaphy, B., and Donovan, C. (2004) 'The Lesbian and Gay Family', in J. Scott, J. Treas and M. Richards (eds), *The Blackwell Companion to the Sociology of Families* (Oxford: Blackwell).

Weinberg, S. (1998) 'The Revolution that Didn't Happen', *New York Review of Books*, 45(15): 48–52.

Weinberg, T. (2008) *The Ultimate Social Media Etiquette Handbook*, www.techipedia.com/2008/social-media-etiquette-handbook/.

Weiss, T. G. (2013) *Global Governance: Why? What? Whither?* (Cambridge: Polity).

Weiss, T. G., and Thakur, R. (2010) *Global Governance and the UN: An Unfinished Journey* (Bloomington: Indiana University Press).

Weitzer, R. (2000) *Sex for Sale: Prostitution, Pornography, and the Sex Industry* (New York: Routledge).

Weitzman, L., Eifler, D., Hokada, E., and Ross, C. (1972) 'Sex-Role Socialization in Picture Books for Preschool Children', *American Journal of Sociology*, 77(6): 1125–50.

Wessendorf, S. (2014) *Commonplace Diversity: Social Relations in a Super-Diverse Context* (Basingstoke: Palgrave Macmillan).

Westergaard, J. (1995) *Who Gets What? The Hardening of Class Inequality in the Late Twentieth Century* (Cambridge: Polity).

Western, B. (1997) *Between Class and Market: Postwar Unionization in the Capitalist Democracies* (Princeton, NJ: Princeton University Press).

Wetherell, M., and Edley, N. (1999) 'Negotiating Hegemonic Masculinity: Imaginary Positions and Psycho-Discursive Practices', *Feminism & Psychology*, 9(3): 335–56.

Wharton, A. S. (2012) *The Sociology of Gender: An Introduction to Theory and Research* (2nd edn, Chichester: John Wiley).

Wheatley, P. (1971) *Pivot of the Four Quarters: A Preliminary Enquiry into the Origins and Character of the Ancient Chinese City* (Edinburgh: Edinburgh University Press).

Wheeler, D. L. (2006) *The Internet in the Middle East: Global Expectations and Local Imaginations in Kuwait* (Albany: State University of New York Press).

Whelehan, I. (1999) *Modern Feminist Thought: From the Second Wave to 'Post-Feminism'* (Edinburgh: Edinburgh University Press)

White C., van Galen, F., and Huang Chow, Y. (2003) 'Trends in Social Class Differences in Mortality by Cause, 1986 to 2000', *Health Statistics Quarterly*, 20(4): 25–37.

White, H. C. (1981) 'Where do Markets Come From?', *American Journal of Sociology*, 87(3): 517–47.

WHO (World Health Organization) (2005) *Multi-Country Study on Women's Health and Domestic Violence against Women: Initial Results on Prevalence, Health Outcomes and Women's Responses* (Geneva: WHO).

WHO (World Health Organization) (2006a) *Preventing Child Maltreatment: A Guide to Taking Action and Generating Evidence* (Geneva: WHO).

WHO (World Health Organization) (2006b) *Constitution of the World Health Organization* (45th edn, Supplement), www.who.int/governance/eb/who_constitution_en.pdf.

WHO (2011) *World Report on Disability: Summary*, http://apps.who.int/iris/bitstream/10665/70670/1/WHO_NMH_VIP_11.01_eng.pdf.

WHO (World Health Organization) (2014a) 'WHO: Ebola Response Roadmap Update, 10 October', http://apps.who.int/iris/bitstream/10665/136161/1/roadmapupdate10Oct14_eng.pdf?ua=1.

WHO (World Health Organization) (2014b) 'Suicide Prevention', www.who.int/mental_health/prevention/suicide/suicideprevent/en/.

WHO (World Health Organization) (2016a) 'World: Life Expectancy at Birth, Both Sexes', http://gamapserver.who.int/mapLibrary/Files/Maps/Global_LifeExpectancy_bothsexes_2015.png.

WHO (World Health Organization) (2016b) 'World: Adult HIV Prevalence (15–49 Years) by WHO Region, 2014', http://gamapserver.who.int/mapLibrary/Files/Maps/HIV_adult_prevalence_2014.png.

Wicks, R. (2004) 'Labour's Unfinished Business', in *Overcoming Disadvantage: An Agenda for the Next 20 Years* (York: Joseph Rowntree Foundation); www.jrf.org.uk/system/files/1859351433.pdf.

Wikström, P. (2009) *The Music Industry: Music in the Cloud* (Cambridge: Polity).

Wiktorowicz, Q. (2006) 'Anatomy of the Salafi Movement', *Studies in Conflict and Terrorism*, 29(3): 207–39.

Wilkins, L. T. (1964) *Social Deviance: Social Policy Action and Research* (London: Tavistock).

Wilkinson, H. (1994) *No Turning Back* (London: Demos).

Wilkinson, H., and Mulgan, G. (1995) *Freedom's Children: Work, Relationships and Politics for 18–34 Year Olds in Britain Today* (London: Demos).

Wilkinson, R. (1996) *Unhealthy Societies: The Afflictions of Inequality* (London: Routledge).

Wilkinson, R., and Pickett, K. (2010) *The Spirit Level: Why Equality is Better for Everyone* (London: Penguin).

Will, C. M., Armstrong, D., and Marteau, T. M. (2010) 'Genetic Unexceptionalism: Clinician Accounts of Genetic Testing for Familial Hypercholesterolaemia', *Social Science and Medicine*, 71(5): 910–17.

Williams, C. D. (2003) *Tales from Sacred Wind: Coming of Age in Appalachia* (Jefferson, NC: McFarland).

Williams, R. (1987) *Keywords: A Vocabulary of Culture and Society* (London: Fontana).

Williams, S. J. (1993) *Chronic Respiratory Illness* (London: Routledge).

Williams, S. J. (2010) 'New Developments in Neuroscience and Medical Sociology', in W. C. Cockerham (ed.), *The New Blackwell Companion to Medical Sociology* (Chichester: Wiley-Blackwell): 530–51.

Willis, P. (1977) *Learning to Labour: How Working-Class Kids Get Working-Class Jobs* (London: Saxon House).

Wilson, B. (1982) *Religion in Sociological Perspective* (Oxford: Clarendon Press).

Wilson, E. (2002) 'The Sphinx in the City: Urban Life, the Control of Disorder, and Women', in G. Bridge and S. Watson (eds), *The Blackwell City Reader* (Oxford: Blackwell).

Wilson, J. Q., and Kelling, G. L. (1982) 'Broken Windows: The Police and Neighbourhood Safety', *Atlantic Monthly*, March.

Wilson, W. J. (1978) *The Declining Significance of Race: Blacks and Changing American Institutions* (Chicago: University of Chicago Press).

Wilson, W. J. (1999) *The Bridge over the Racial Divide: Rising Inequality and Coalition Politics* (Berkeley: University of California Press).

WIN-Gallup International (2012) 'Global Index of Religion and Atheism: Press Release', http://redcresearch. ie/wp-content/uploads/2012/08/RED-C-press-release-Religion-and-Atheism-25-7-12.pdf.

Wingfield-Hayes, R. (2015) 'The Beauty Contest Winner Making Japan Look at Itself', 4 June, www.bbc. co.uk/news/world-asia-32957610.

Wirth, L. (1938) 'Urbanism as a Way of Life', *American Journal of Sociology*, 44(1): 1–24.

Wolfe, N. (2011) *The Viral Storm: The Dawn of a New Pandemic Age* (London: Allen Lane).

Wolitzky-Taylor, K. B., Resnick, H. S., McCauley, J. L., Amstadter, A. B., Kilpatrick, D. G., and Ruggerio, K. J. (2010) 'Is Reporting of Rape on the Rise? A Comparison of Women with Reported versus Unreported Rape Experiences in the National Women's Study-Replication', *Journal of Interpersonal Violence*, 26(4): 807–32.

Women and Equality Unit (2004) *Women and Men in the Workplace* (London: Department of Trade and Industry).

Wood, J. (1984) 'Groping towards Sexism: Boys' Sex Talk', in A. McRobbie and M. Nava (eds), *Gender and Generation* (London: Macmillan).

Wood, M., Hales, J., Purdon, S., Sejersen, T., and Hayllar, O. (2009) *A Test of Racial Discrimination in Recruitment Practice in British Cities* (Norwich: The Stationery Office).

Wood, S. (1989) *The Transformation of Work? Skills, Flexibility and the Labour Process* (London: Unwin Hyman).

Woodrum, E. (1988) 'Moral Conservatism and the 1984 Presidential Election', *Journal for the Scientific Study of Religion*, 27(2): 192–210.

Woodward, K. (2015) 'Sex, Gender and Sexuality: The Case for Critical Analysis', in M. Holborn (ed.), *Contemporary Sociology* (Cambridge: Polity): 35–64.

World Atlas (2016) 'Populations of 150 Largest Cities of the World', www.worldatlas.com/citypops.htm.

World Bank (1995) *Workers in an Integrating World* (New York: Oxford University Press).

World Bank (1997) *World Development Report 1997: The State in a Changing World* (New York: Oxford University Press).

World Bank (2000) *Attacking Poverty: World Development Report 2000/1* (New York: Oxford University Press).

World Bank (2001) *Povertynet: Topics Relevant to Social Capital* (New York: Oxford University Press).

World Bank (2004) *World Development Report: Making Services Work for Poor People* (New York: Oxford University Press).

World Bank (2007) *World Development Indicators* (New York: Oxford University Press).

World Bank (2011a) *World Development Indicators 2011* (Washington, DC: World Bank).

World Bank (2011b) 'World Bank Report Reviews Early Insights from the Sino-Singapore Tianjin Eco-City Project', 19 January, www.worldbank.org/en/news/2011/01/19/world-bank-report-reviews-early-insights-sino-singapore-tianjin-eco-city-project.

World Bank (2013) 'Education Expenditures: A Global Report', http://datatopics.worldbank.org/education/wStateEdu/StateEducation.aspx.

World Bank (2015) 'Morocco to Make History with First-of-its-Kind Solar Plant', www.worldbank.org/en/news/feature/2015/11/20/morocco-to-make-history-with-first-of-its-kind-solar-plant.

World Economic Forum (2007) *The Global Gender Gap Report 2007* (Geneva: World Economic Forum).

World Population Review (2015) 'Shanghai Population', http://worldpopulationreview.com/world-cities/shanghai-population/.

Worrall, A. (1990) *Offending Women: Female Law-Breakers and the Criminal Justice System* (London: Routledge).

Wouters, C. (2002) 'The Quest for New Rituals in Dying and Mourning: Changes in the We–I Balance', *Body and Society*, 8(1): 1–27.

Wouters, C. (2004) *Sex and Manners: Female Emancipation in the West 1890–2000* (London and New York: Sage).

Wright, C. (1992) *Race Relations in the Primary School* (London: David Fulton).

Wright, E. O. (1978) *Class, Crisis and the State* (London: New Left Books).

Wright, E. O. (1985) *Classes* (London: Verso).

Wright, E. O. (1997) *Class Counts: Comparative Studies in Class Analysis* (Cambridge: Cambridge University Press).

Wrigley, E. A. (1968) *Population and History* (New York: McGraw-Hill).

Wuthnow, R. (1988) 'Sociology of Religion', in N. J. Smelser (ed.), *Handbook of Sociology* (Newbury Park, CA: Sage).

Wykes, M., and Gunter, B. (2005) *The Media and Body Image* (London: Sage).

Yinger, J. M. (1970) *The Scientific Study of Religion* (London: Routledge).

Young, I. M. (1980) 'Throwing Like a Girl: A Phenomenology of Feminine Body Comportment, Motility and Spatiality', *Human Studies*, 3: 137–56.

Young, I. M. (1990) *Throwing Like a Girl and Other Essays in Feminist Philosophy and Social Theory* (Bloomington: Indiana University Press).

Young, I. M. (2005) *On Female Body Experience: Throwing Like a Girl and Other Essays* (New York: Oxford University Press).

Young, J. (1998) 'Breaking Windows: Situating the New Criminology', in P. Walton and J. Young (eds), *The New Criminology Revisited* (London: Macmillan).

Young, J. (1999) *The Exclusive Society: Social Exclusion, Crime and Difference in Late Modernity* (London: Sage).

Young, M. D., and Willmott, P. (1957) *Family and Kinship in East London* (London: Routledge & Kegan Paul).

Young, M. D., and Willmott, P. (1973) *The Symmetrical Family: A Study of Work and Leisure in the London Region* (London: Routledge & Kegan Paul).

Yousafzai, M., with Lamb, C. (2013) *I am Malala: The Girl Who Stood up for Education and Was Shot by the Taliban* (London: Weidenfeld & Nicolson).

Zald, M., and McCarthy, J. (1987) *Social Movements in an Organizational Society: Collected Essays* (New Brunswick, NJ: Transaction).

Zammuner, V. L. (1986) 'Children's Sex-Role Stereotypes: A Cross-Cultural Analysis', in P. Shaver and C. Hendrick (eds), *Sex and Gender* (Beverly Hills, CA: Sage).

Zamudio, M. M., Russell, C., Rios, F. A., and Bridgeman, J. L. (eds) (2011) *Critical Race Theory Matters: Education and Ideology* (New York: Routledge).

Zayani, M. (ed.) (2005) *The Al Jazeera Phenomenon: Critical Perspectives on New Arab Media* (New York: Paradigm).

Ziai, A. (ed.) (2007) *Exploring Post-Development: Theory and Practice, Problems and Perspectives* (London: Routledge).

Zimbardo, P. G. (1969) 'The Human Choice: Individuation, Reason, and Order versus Deindividuation, Impulse, and Chaos', in W. J. Arnold and D. Levine (eds), *Nebraska Symposium on Motivation* (Lincoln: University of Nebraska Press).

Zippel, K. S. (2006) *The Politics of Sexual Harassment: A Comparative Study of the United States, the European Union and Germany* (Cambridge: Cambridge University Press).

Žižek, S. (2011) *Living in the End Times* (rev. edn, London: Verso).

Žižek, S. (2012) *Less than Nothing: Hegel and the Shadow of Dialectical Materialism* (London: Verso).

Zolfagharifard, E. (2014) 'Meet Bob, Britain's First ROBOTIC Security Guard: Droid Roams Offices Looking for Suspicious Behaviour – and Calls for Backup', www.dailymail.co.uk/sciencetech/article-2659036/Meet-Bob-Britains-ROBOTIC-security-guard-Droid-roams-offices-looking-suspicious-behaviour-calls-backup.html.

Zubaida, S. (1996) 'How Successful is the Islamic Republic in Islamizing Iran?', in J. Beinen and J. Stork (eds), *Political Islam: Essays from Middle East Report* (Berkeley: University of California Press).

Zuboff, S. (1988) *In the Age of the Smart Machine: The Future of Work and Power* (New York: Basic Books).

Picture acknowledgements

Chapter 1
3 © Aluxum/iStock.
6 © Rosemarie Gearhart/ iStock.
7 © UK Dept for International Development/Flickr.
10 © Google Art Project/ Wikimedia Commons.
16 © Neil Cummings/ Wikimedia Commons.
18 © KPA/Zuma/Rex Features.
21 © R Neil Marshman/ Wikimedia Commons.
23 © Denis Closon/Rex Features.

Chapter 2
33 © Fredrik Rubusson/Flickr.
37 © Bill Ross/Corbis.
39 © joyt/iStock.
41 © The New Yorker Collection 1986 J. B. Handelsman from Cartoonbank.com. All rights reserved.
47 © Doonesbury © 1985 & 1980 G. B. Trudeau. Reprinted with permission of Universal Press Syndicate. All rights reserved.
48 © Peanuts 1993 © UPS.
49 © Andrew Fox/Corbis.
51 © Mackerl.
52 © Bob Sacha/Corbis.
56 © Philip Zimbardo/ Stanford University.
59 © Michael Stillwell/Flickr.

Chapter 3
69 © Piblet/Flickr.
75 © Mary Evans Picture Library.
77 © Bettmann/Corbis.
81 © Nic Bothma/epa/Corbis.
84 © Sean Locke/iStock.

88 © Chensiyuan/Wikimedia Commons.
90 © Intel Free Press/Flickr.
96 © Nabita Mujusson. Courtesy of Southall Black Sisters.
100 © Britta Pedersen/dpa/ Corbis.
103 © IAEA Imagebank, Greg Webb/Flickr.

Chapter 4
110 © Jamie McDonald/ GettyImages.
113 © Woodhouse/Flickr.
116 © Mlenny/Flickr.
118 © Gleisen Miranda, FUNAI, Survival International.
125 © Wikimedia Commons.
130 © Ho/Reuters/Corbis.
134 © Emma Longstaff.
136 © RomitaGirl67/Flickr.
142 © Barbaragin/Flickr.

Chapter 5
154 © Bloomberg/GettyImages.
156 © Alfredo Dagli Orti/The Art Archive/Corbis.
160 © Alan Levine/Flickr.
163 © Chad Ehlers/Stock connection/Rex Features.
167 © Moodboard/Corbis.
177 [l] © G.M.B. Akash/Panos Pictures.
177 [r] © Jamie Jones/Rex Features.
184 © Ralf Hettler/iStock.
191 © Fadel Senna/ GettyImages.
192 © Tedder/Wikimedia Commons.

Chapter 6
202 Raguenet 'A View of Paris from the Pont Neuf' Wikimedia Commons.

204 © Paul Bica/Flickr.
209 © Werner Bayer/Flickr.
213 © Andrew Fox/Corbis.
217 © Adalberto Rios Szalay/ Sexto Sol/Getty Images.
224 © Adrian Beesley/iStock.
226 © Hilary h/Flickr.
230 © Viviane Moos/Corbis.
238 © SludgeG/Flickr.
240 © Nikada/iStock.

Chapter 7
246 © George Baboukos/ Athena Pix/Rex/ Shutterstock.
252 © Emma Longstaff.
254 © Bettmann/Corbis.
257 © Sion Touhig/Corbis.
260 © Betty Press/Panos.
271 © Studio-Annika/iStock.
273 © Dean Mitchell/iStock.
278 © Jagadeesh/Reuters/ Corbis.
284 © Charles O'Rear/Corbis.

Chapter 8
296 © Daniel Zucknik/ GettyImages.
300 © Paul Ekman.
302 © Peter Stokes/Wikimedia.
304 © Mike Stokoe/www. cartoonstock.com.
307 © David Hoffman.
310 © Getty Images.
311 © Jacques Langevin/ Sygma/Corbis.
317 © Mike Kemp/Rubberball/ Corbis.
322 © Pearleye/iStock.
325 © Dax Dover/Flickr.

Chapter 9
332 © ArtMarie/iStock.
335 © Sandra Ramirez / STOCK4B.
338 © Peter Dench/In Pictures/ Corbis.

PICTURE ACKNOWLEDGEMENTS

344 © Henry Diltz/Corbis.
348 © Christian Stewart/ iStock.
352 © Rex Features.
358 © Lisa Wollett/ Photofusion Picture Library.
367 © Gary Sludden/iStock.
370 © Advertising Archives.

Chapter 10
378 © Sipa/Rex/Shutterstock.
382 © Monkeybusiness images/iStock.
388 © PeopleImages/iStock.
391 © Marcel Pelletier/ iStock.
400 © Jonathan Banks/Rex Features.
409 © Gisele/iStock.
410 © www.cartoonstock. com.
413 © Eric Audras/Onoky/ Corbis.
419 © Kevin Chodzinski/ Flickr.

Chapter 11
429[l] ©Albanpix/Rex/ Shutterstock.
429[r] © AFP/Getty Images.
430 'The Toilet of Venus' c 1613 Rubens. Private Collection, © Giraudon/ Bridgeman Art Library.
434 © Intel Free Press/ Wikimedia Commons.
438 © Burger/Phanie/Rex Features.
440 © Cora Reed/iStock.
445 © UNMEER/Flickr.
451 © David White/Rex Features.
453 © New Yorker Collection 2001/David Sipress from Cartoonbank.com.
464 © US Army/Flickr.
467 © Vicky Lucas.

Chapter 12
477 © Alessio Jacona/Flickr.
478 Courtesy of Lord Noon.
481 © 38 Degrees/Flickr.
483 © Thomas Schoch/ Wikimedia Commons.

489 © Chris Schmidt/iStock.
493 © Geoffrey Robinson/Rex Features.
495 © Alisdair McDonald/Rex Features.
500 © Startraks Photo/Rex/ Shutterstock.
504 © Peter Dench/In Pictures/Corbis.
510 © Radius Images/Corbis.

Chapter 13
523 © Northern Ireland Executive/Flickr.
528 © Frans Lanting/Corbis.
529 © Photofusion Library/ Alamy.
537 © Commission for Racial Equality (now incorporated into the Equality and Human Rights Commission).
540 © Martin Jenkinson/ Alamy.
546 © Daniel Ross/iStock.
548 © iStock.
552 © Ken Pyne.
557 © Rozenn Leboucher/Rex Features.

Chapter 14
565 © Ahn Young-joon/AP Photos.
567 © AP Photos/Press Assocation.
571 © Dean Conger/Corbis.
579 © Finbarr O'Reilly/ Reuters/Corbis.
582 © Peter Menzel/Science Photo Library.
583 © Peter Menzel/Science Photo Library.
585 © David Rose/Panos Pictures.
593 © Emmanuel Dyan/Flickr.
597 © Toru Hanai/Reuters/ Corbis.
603 © Danny Lehman/Corbis.
607 © Reuters/Corbis.

Chapter 15
615 © Andrew Fox/Rex/ Shutterstock.
616 © Global Panorama/ Flickr.

620 © Polity.
623 © Jrmodugno/Wikimedia Commons.
627 © Alfa Lifestyle Productions.
629 © Martin/Flickr.
633 © Tiziana and Gianni Baldizzone/Corbis.
637 © Paul Kooi/iStock.
643 © Charles Sykes/Rex/Rex Features.
647 © Kieran Meehan/ Cartoonstock.com.
653 © AFP/Getty Images.

Chapter 16
661 © Kyodo/AP Images.
664 © FIFA/Getty Images.
669 © PA Photos.
685 © Peter Lawson/Rex Features.
690 © Popperfoto/Getty Images.
694 © Louise George/MOD/ Rex/Shutterstock.
698 © Lorraine Boogich/ iStock.

Chapter 17
706 © Zuma/Rex/ Shutterstock.
710 © John Peters/ GettyImages.
714 © Pascal Deloche/Getty Images.
721 © Mike Longhurst/Rex Features.
731 © Ted Spiegel/Corbis.
734 © Brian Harris/Rex Features.
737 © Kippa Ltd/Rex/ Shutterstock.
739 © PA Photos.
742 © Burak Kara/Getty Images.

Chapter 18
751 © Yanis Vanoufakis/ Twitter.
753 © DDP USA/Rex/ Shutterstock.
759 © Sherwin Crasto/ Reuters/Corbis.
766 © Phil Boorman/cultura/ Corbis.

769 © Paul Piebinga/iStock.
776 © Lehtikuva Oy/Rex Features.
782 © Peter Turnley/Corbis.
784 © Dem10/iStock.
790 © Somrerk Kosolwitthayant/ Shutterstock.
794 © PA Photos.

Chapter 19
802 © UK DIFD/Flickr.
803 © Action Press/Rex/ Shutterstock.
806 © Duncan Hill/Flickr.
812 © AFP/GettyImages.
817 © Homer Sykes/Alamy.
825 © DavidF/iStock.
832 © Janine Weidel Photo Library/Alamy.
841 © Sturti/iStock.

Chapter 20
855 © Wellcome Images Library.

858 © Action Press/Rex Features.
860 © Morton Beebe/Corbis.
863 [l] © VisualCommunica tions/iStock.
863 [r] © Sarah/Flickr.
867 © Sipa Press/Rex Features.
871 © Gilles Paire/iStock.
872 © New Yorker Collection 1997 Michael Mastin/ Cartoonbank.com.
887 © Eddie Mulholland/Rex Features.
892 © Topfoto.
895 © AFP/Getty Images.

Chapter 21
906 © Associated Press.
912 © Xinhua News Agency/ Rex/Shutterstock.
915 © WPA Pool/GettyImages.
918 © bkang83/Flickr.
925 © Sipa Press/Rex Features.

928 © Robert Perry/Rex/ Shutterstock.
932 © Royston Robertson/ Cartoonstock.com.
934 © Geoff Robinson/Rex Features.
940 © Sutton-Hibbert/Rex Features.
945 © PA Photos.

Chapter 22
955 © John Moore/ GettyImages.
959 © Ilyas J Dean/Rex Features.
962 © Neil Ward/Flickr.
967 © Ken Straiton/Corbis.
972 © Sven Torfinn/Panos Pictures.
976 © Bettmann/Corbis.
984 © Takver/Flickr.

Index